NINTH EDITION
POLITICS IN AMERICA

Thomas R. Dye
Emeritus McKenzie
Professor of Government
Florida State University

Longman
Boston   Columbus   Indianapolis   New York   San Francisco   Upper Saddle River
Amsterdam   Cape Town   Dubai   London   Madrid   Milan   Munich   Paris   Montreal   Toronto
Delhi   Mexico City   Sao Paulo   Sydney   Hong Kong   Seoul   Singapore   Taipei   Tokyo

To my students over the years,
who taught me more than I taught them.

Executive Editor: Reid Hester
Director of Development: Meg Botteon
Development Editors: Leslie Kauffman, Jean Findley
Editorial Assistant: Elizabeth Alimena
Senior Marketing Manager: Lindsey Prudhomme
Supplements Editor: Donna Garnier
Senior Media Producer: Regina Vertiz
Production Manager: Stacey Kulig
Project Coordination, Text Design, and Electronic Page Makeup: Nesbitt Graphics, Inc.
Senior Cover Design Manager/Cover Designer: Nancy Danahy
Cover Image: © Alamy Photos
Photo Researcher: Connie Gardner
Senior Manufacturing Buyer: Dennis J. Para
Printer and Binder: Quad/Graphics
Cover Printer: Coral Graphics Services, Inc.

For permission to use copyrighted material, grateful acknowledgment is made to the copyright holders on pp. PC1–PC2, which are hereby made part of this copyright page.

Library of Congress Cataloging-in-Publication Data

Dye, Thomas R.
  Politics in America / Thomas R. Dye — 9th ed.
     p. cm.
  ISBN 978-0-205-82609-4
  1. United States—Politics and government—Textbooks. I. Title.
JK276.D926 2011b
320.473—dc22

                        2010046767

1 2 3 4 5 6 7 8 9 10—QGD—13 12 11 10

Longman
is an imprint of

www.pearsonhighered.com

ISBN-13: 978-0-205-82609-4
ISBN-10:   0-205-82609-1

BRIEF CONTENTS

CONTENTS

PART THREE Participants

People strive for power—to get the most of what there is to get.

Harold Lasswell

PART FOUR Institutions

Authority is the expected and legitimate possession
of power.

Harold Lasswell

PART FIVE Outcomes

That political science concentrates upon the influential does not imply the neglect of the total distribution of values throughout the community. . . . The emphasis upon the probability that the few (elite) will get the most does not imply that the many (mass) do not profit from some political changes.

Harold Lasswell

14 POLITICS AND PERSONAL LIBERTY   494

15 POLITICS AND CIVIL RIGHTS   540

16 POLITICS AND THE ECONOMY   584

PREFACE

Politics is an activity by which people try to get more of whatever there is to get. It is about the struggle over the allocation of values and resources in a society. Simply put, it is about "who gets what, when, and how."

By using Harold Lasswell's classic definition of politics as its unifying framework, *Politics in America, Ninth Edition,* strives to present a clear, concise, and stimulating introduction to the American political system. Politics consists of all the activities—reasonable discussion, impassioned oratory, campaigning, balloting, fund-raising, advertising, lobbying, demonstrating, rioting, street fighting, and waging war—by which conflict is carried on. By examining the struggle for power—the participants, the stakes, the processes, and the institutional arenas—*Politics in America* introduces students to the political struggles that drive democracy.

What's New in the Ninth Edition?

In the early Obama years, the struggle for power was as intense as ever in American politics. The Wall Street bailout, the massive "stimulus" package, new financial regulations, proposals for "cap and trade" legislation, and the transformation of the nation's health care system are described in the context of the government's growing role in society. The Republican resurgence in the 2010 midterm congressional elections is described and analyzed.

Among the new topics introduced in the *Ninth Edition*:

- Republicans rebound in 2010
- ObamaCare and its challenge to federalism
- Can Arizona pass its own immigration law?
- Social mobility: getting ahead in America
- The tea party protests
- California to bypass parties
- How Obama changed campaign fund-raising through the Internet
- The argument over corporate campaign contributions
- Are federal employees paid too much?
- Service Employees International Union
- Politics and sexual orientation

- Health care transformation
- Rahm Emanuel, exercising power behind the scenes
- Sonia Sotomayor, a Latina for the Supreme Court
- Cesar Chavez, mobilizing Latino workers
- Scott Brown, revolt in Massachusetts
- Is government growing too big?
- How Washington dealt with financial crisis
- Is big government the "change" that Americans wanted?
- The war in Afghanistan
- Additionally, descriptions of proportional representation and the parliamentary system have been added to the *Compared to What?* features.

The Appendix contains Federalist No. 10 and No. 51, both newly annotated by the author. Students are encouraged to read and understand these vital documents themselves.

Longman has added learning objectives and assessments to each chapter. Professor John Robey of the University of Texas-Brownsville assisted in the development of these teaching and learning tools.

Why *Politics in America*?

Politics in America was written with the principal objective of interesting students in politics and public affairs. Politics is not a dull topic and textbooks should not make it so. This book is designed to challenge students to think about and talk about controversial issues. We would rather have students leave the course saying that it was one of the most interesting courses they have ever taken than to have them leave reciting "how a bill becomes a law." We strive to inspire a continuing interest in politics and public affairs. This does not mean that we overlook the basics of American government. But the focus of this text is on conflict and controversy—the struggle for power.

Politics in America is *not* politically correct. It presents balanced arguments on highly sensitive issues, including abortion, gun control, same-sex marriage, marijuana for medical use, affirmative action, and immigration reform. An underlying question throughout the text is whether or not American government is growing too powerful.

Each chapter contains a variety of special features designed to inspire discussion and controversy in the classroom:

What Do You Think? features in each chapter ask students to take sides on controversial questions; for example: Can you trust the government? Does immigration help or hurt America? Are the media biased? Should we scrap the electoral college? How would you rate the presidents? How much money does the government waste? Are persons captured on the battlefields of Afghanistan and Iraq entitled to constitutional protections? Do you favor affirmative action? When should the United States use military force?

Controversy features present students with some of the more vexing questions currently confronting American politics; for example: Is the government growing too big? Are we one nation "under God"? Marijuana for medical use? Should violence against women be a federal crime? Did the media favor Obama? And they present the issues of Abortion: the "hot-button" issue; Political correctness versus free speech on campus; and the tea party protests.

A Conflicting View features challenge students to rethink conventional wisdom in American politics, for example: sometimes it's right to disobey the law; anti-Federalist objections to the Constitution; the dark side of federalism; easy voting encourages fraud; Fox News "fair and balanced"?; eliminate campaign-finance limits; terrorism requires restrictions on civil liberties; we should enact a flat tax; and is big government the "change" Americans voted for?

People in Politics features focus on the early education and entrance into politics of key figures—from historical figures such as George Washington, Thomas Jefferson, James Madison, Martin Luther King, Jr., and Cesar Chavez; to contemporary figures such as Barack Obama, Hillary Clinton, John McCain, Nancy Pelosi, Scott Brown, Rahm Emanuel, and Bill O'Reilly.

Politics Up Close features provide students with engaging examples of political issues, organizations, and events; for example: dirty politics, Hillary versus Barack, Obama versus McCain, the Christian Coalition, the American Civil Liberties Union, EMILY's List, how Obama changed campaign funding using the Internet, *Bush v. Gore* in the Supreme Court, and how to run for office (brief guidelines for students interested in running for office themselves).

Compared to What? features provide students with a comparative perspective on many key elements of the American political system, including: freedom and democracy around the world, income and inequality, the European Union and federalism, world opinion about the U.S., voter turnout, proportional representation, parliamentary government, and the size of government.

WHO GETS WHAT

This balanced and highly readable text uses Harold Lasswell's classic definition of politics—**"who gets what, when and how"**—as a framework for presenting a clear, concise, and stimulating introduction to the American political system. The absorbing narrative examines this struggle for power—the participants, the stakes, the processes, and the institutions—**in a way that provokes thinking and discussion**.

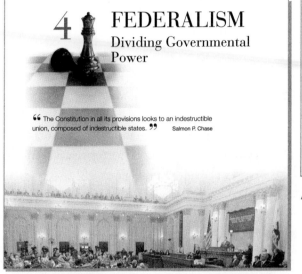

4 FEDERALISM
Dividing Governmental Power

❝ The Constitution in all its provisions looks to an indestructible union, composed of indestructible states. ❞ Salmon P. Chase

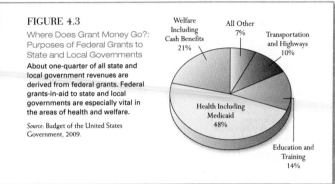

FIGURE 4.3
Where Does Grant Money Go?: Purposes of Federal Grants to State and Local Governments

About one-quarter of all state and local government revenues are derived from federal grants. Federal grants-in-aid to state and local governments are especially vital in the areas of health and welfare.

Source: Budget of the United States Government, 2009.

Welfare Including Cash Benefits 21%
All Other 7%
Transportation and Highways 10%
Health Including Medicaid 48%
Education and Training 14%

▲ The theme of a competition for resources runs throughout *Politics in America*, from the chapter opening pages to the features and figures, to the chapter ending summaries.

▲ Each chapter begins with a quote that **provides a tangible link between the topic of each chapter and the theme of a competition for resources.**

A PROVOCATIVE THEME

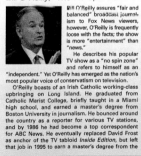

44 CHAPTER 2 • Political Culture: Ideas in Conflict

PEOPLE IN POLITICS

Bill O'Reilly, "The No Spin Zone"?

Bill O'Reilly assures "fair and balanced" broadcast journalism to Fox News viewers, however, O'Reilly is frequently loose with the facts; the show is more "entertainment" than "news."

He describes his popular TV show as a "no spin zone" and refers to himself as an "independent." Yet O'Reilly has emerged as the nation's most popular voice of conservatism on television.

O'Reilly boasts of an Irish Catholic working-class upbringing on Long Island. He graduated from Catholic Marist College, briefly taught in a Miami high school, and earned a master's degree from Boston University in journalism. He bounced around the country as a reporter for various TV stations, and by 1986 he had become a top correspondent for ABC News. He eventually replaced David Frost as anchor of the TV tabloid *Inside Edition*, but left that job in 1995 to earn a master's degree from the

John F. Kennedy School of Government at Harvard University.

The Fox News network recruited O'Reilly to create a new evening talk show, *The O'Reilly Factor*. The show quickly grew into the most watched program on cable news, outdistancing even *Larry King Live*. And O'Reilly gave up his popular talk radio show in order to concentrate on television.

O'Reilly mixes humor with bombast. He constantly interrupts guests, both conservatives and liberals, to broadcast his own views. He is convinced that liberal "secularists" are waging war against religion, Christmas, and traditional moral values. Liberal critic and now U.S. Senator Al Franken wrote a satirical mockery of the Fox network and O'Reilly himself, entitled *Lies and the Lying Liars Who Tell Them: A Fair and Balanced Look at the Right.* O'Reilly prompted Fox News to sue, but the suit was thrown out of federal court. O'Reilly's favorite targets include Hollywood liberals, Jesse Jackson, and the American Civil Liberties Union. The occasional twinkle in his Irish eyes tempers his often venomous commentary.

▲ The **People in Politics** features personalize politics and illustrate that **the participants in the struggle for power are real people.** Students are introduced to some of the key players who have helped shape American politics, as well as their backgrounds and careers.

40 CHAPTER 2 • Political Culture: Ideas in Conflict

POLITICS UP CLOSE

Could You Pass the Citizenship Test?

To ensure that new citizens "understand" the history, principles, and form of government of the United States, the CIS administers a citizenship test. Below is a sample of questions from the American government section of the test. Can you answer these questions?

1. What is the supreme law of the land?
2. The idea of self-government is in the first three words of the Constitution. What are these words?
3. What do we call the first 10 amendments to the Constitution?
4. How many amendments does the Constitution have?
5. Who is in charge of the executive branch?
6. Who makes federal laws?
7. What are the two parts of the U.S. Congress?
8. How many U.S. Senators are there?
9. We elect a U.S. Senator for how many years?
10. The House of Representatives has how many voting members?
11. We elect a U.S. Representative for how many years?
12. We elect a President for how many years?
13. In what month do we vote for President?
14. If the President can no longer serve, who becomes President?
15. If both the President and the Vice President can no longer serve, who becomes President?

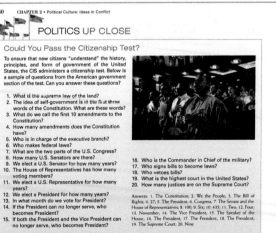

16. Who is the Commander in Chief of the military?
17. Who signs bills to become laws?
18. Who vetoes bills?
19. What is the highest court in the United States?
20. How many justices are on the Supreme Court?

Answers: 1. The Constitution, 2. We the People, 3. The Bill of Rights, 4. 27, 5. The President, 6. Congress, 7. The Senate and the House of Representatives, 8. 100, 9. Six, 10. 435, 11. Two, 12. Four, 13. November, 14. The Vice President, 15. The Speaker of the House, 16. The President, 17. The President, 18. The President, 19. The Supreme Court, 20. Nine

Source: Bureau of Citizenship and Immigration Services.

▲ **Politics Up Close** illustrates specific **struggles over who gets what** and covers a wide variety of current political conflicts.

THINK ABOUT POLITICS

Marginal learning aids **encourage critical thinking and dispel conventional notions of American politics** by allowing students to compare their initial responses to critical issues in American politics with the responses they have later, as they work through the chapter.

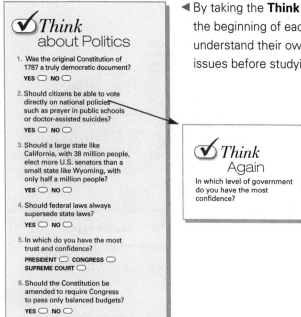

◀ By taking the **Think About Politics** poll at the beginning of each chapter, students understand their own beliefs on these issues before studying the chapter content.

✓ Think about Politics

1. Was the original Constitution of 1787 a truly democratic document?
   YES ◯ NO ◯

2. Should citizens be able to vote directly on national policies such as prayer in public schools or doctor-assisted suicides?
   YES ◯ NO ◯

3. Should a large state like California, with 38 million people, elect more U.S. senators than a small state like Wyoming, with only half a million people?
   YES ◯ NO ◯

4. Should federal laws always supersede state laws?
   YES ◯ NO ◯

5. In which do you have the most trust and confidence?
   PRESIDENT ◯ CONGRESS ◯
   SUPREME COURT ◯

6. Should the Constitution be amended to require Congress to pass only balanced budgets?
   YES ◯ NO ◯

✓ Think Again

In which level of government do you have the most confidence?

◀ The **Think Again** marginal questions in the chapter help students revisit their thinking on issues as they move through the chapter discussion.

WHAT DO YOU THINK?

Should Government Leaders Pay More Attention to Public Opinion?

In 1774 the British parliamentarian Edmund Burke told his Bristol constituents: "Your representative owes you, not his industry only, but his judgment; and he betrays, instead of serving you, if he sacrifices it to your opinion." Since then, "Burkean representation" has come to refer to political delegates using their own judgment in decision making, without paying much or any attention to public opinion polls. Indeed, many politicians boast of their own courage and independence and of their willingness to ignore public opinion polls on major issues. And political experts in higher education and the media repeatedly point out that the American public is woefully ill informed about political facts—whether about American government or the world at large—that the public is unstable and vacillating in its opinions and priorities, and that Americans are often highly emotional in their responses to difficult and complex issues. Shaping policy to public opinion would be irresponsible and possibly downright dangerous.

But other experts believe that the country would be much better off if politicians paid more attention to public opinion. A number of political scientists point out that public opinion is much more stable and much more reasonable than policy makers and the media would have us believe. There is evidence in polling data over a 30-year period that shows the wisdom and steadfastness of the American public with respect to important issues in U.S. foreign policy—one of the chief areas in which policy makers are wary of the public's judgment.[a] Despite the fact that Americans have limited political knowledge and pay only scant and often fleeting attention to politics, they take reasonable positions: they seek international justice and domestic prosperity and not just security from attack, and they seek to pursue such goals in cooperation with other countries—multilaterally, that is—rather than on their own.

Polls show that the American public certainly believes that the country would be much better off if politicians paid more attention to public opinion.

Q. If the leaders of the nation followed the views of the public more closely, do you think that the nation would be better off or worse off than it is today?

Better — 81%
Worse — 10%

Indeed, most Americans believe that members of Congress should "read up on the polls" in order to "get a sense of the public's views."

Q. Please tell me which statement you agree with most: (A) When members of Congress are thinking about how to vote on an issue, they should read up on the polls, because this can help them get a sense of the public's views on the issue. (B) When members of Congress are thinking about how to vote on an issue, they should not read the polls, because this will distract them from thinking about what is right.

Should read polls — 67%
Should not read polls — 26%

But other evidence shows that most members of Congress do not put much stake in public opinion. When members of Congress were asked, "Do you think the American public knows enough about the issues you face to form wise opinions about what should be done about these issues, or not," fewer than one-third (31 percent) said "Yes," whereas almost half (47 percent) said "No" (17 percent answered "Maybe").

Political scientists Lawrence R. Jacobs and Robert Y. Shapiro found that members of Congress did not so much use information on public opinion to guide their decisions, but rather used it for their own tactical reasons; they ignored public opinion polls when public opinion conflicted with their decisions, and they publicized their agreement with public opinion when poll results meshed with their own judgments.[b]

[a] Benjamin I. Page with Marshall M. Bouton, *The Foreign Policy Disconnect: What Americans Want from Our Leaders but Don't Get.* Chicago: University of Chicago Press, 2006.
[b] Lawrence R. Jacobs and Robert Y. Shapiro, *Politicians Don't Pander: Political Manipulation and the Loss of Democratic Responsiveness.* Chicago: University of Chicago Press, 2000.

▲ **What Do You Think?** features present students with a controversial issue and ask them to take a stance.

A CONFLICTING VIEW

Easy Voting Encourages Fraud

Since the civil rights battles of the 1960s, the nation has been primarily concerned with expanding voter participation—to bring more people, especially minorities, into the political process. These efforts have led to an easing of the burdens of registration—registration by mail, mass registration drives, registration on the same day as voting, and so forth—as well as an easing of the burdens of voting itself—absentee voting, voting by mail, voting over an extended period, and so forth. Voting via the Internet is also being advocated in many jurisdictions. Yet there is no strong evidence to suggest that these innovations lead to higher voter turnouts.

There are nearly 200,000 voting precincts in the United States. Usually representatives of both the Democratic and Republican parties are present at each precinct to ensure the honesty of the vote. Voters who have previously registered show their voter cards or present other identification and then sign their names on the voter registration lists. This ensures that the voters are who they say they are, and that they do not vote more than once.

But registration by mail and absentee voting are rising over time. Voter registration cards are widely distributed, to be filled out by persons eligible to vote, and then collected and sent to the county election office. As the election nears, registered voters may request an absentee ballot, to be filled out and mailed to the county election office.

Increasingly, party operatives as well as independent "get-out-the-vote" organizations are going to nursing homes, assisted-living facilities, and other institutions housing the elderly, as well as large condominium projects, filling out registration forms for the residents as well as absentee ballot requests, and then "helping out" in marking the ballots, collecting them, and mailing them en masse to voting offices. It has been charged that some groups collecting registration forms and absentee ballots conveniently discard those that do not match the group's preferences.[*]

Few states have the resources, and many politicians lack the will, to investigate and prosecute voter fraud. Finding the right balance between promoting greater participation and maintaining the integrity of the electoral system is creating political conflict in many states and cities today.

[*]See Larry J. Sabato and Glenn R. Simpson, *Dirty Little Secrets: The Persistence of Corruption in American Politics.* New York: Random House, 1996.

▲ **A Conflicting View** features challenge students to rethink conventional wisdom in American politics by presenting them **with views on important topics that clash with popular opinion.**

THINKING CRITICALLY

The Constitution of the United States

More than two centuries after its ratification, our Constitution remains the operating charter of our republic. It is neither self-explanatory nor a comprehensive description of our constitutional rules. Still, it remains the starting point. Many Americans who swear by the Constitution have never read it seriously, although copies can be found in most American government and American history textbooks.

Justice Hugo Black, who served on the Supreme Court for 34 years, kept a copy of the Constitution with him at all times. He read it often. Reading the Constitution would be a good way for you to begin (and then reread again to end) your study of the government of the United States. We have therefore included a copy of it at this point in the book. Please read it carefully.

THE PREAMBLE

We the People of the United States, in Order to form a more perfect Union, establish Justice, insure domestic Tranquility, provide for the common defense, promote the general Welfare, and secure the Blessings of Liberty to ourselves and our Posterity, do ordain and establish this Constitution for the United States of America.

"We, the people." Three simple words, yet of profound importance and contentious origin. Every government in the world at the time of the Constitutional Convention was some type of monarchy wherein sovereign power flowed from the top. The Founders of our new country rejected monarchy as a form of government and proposed instead a republic, which would draw its sovereignty from the people.

The Articles of Confederation that governed the United States from 1776 until 1789 started with: "We the under signed Delegates of the States." Early drafts of the new constitution started with: "We, the states . . ." But again, the Founders were not interested in another union of states but rather the creation of a new national government. Therefore, "We, the states" was changed to "We, the people."

The remainder of the preamble describes the generic functions of government.

One of these generic functions of government is to provide for the general welfare. For a good discussion of a right versus entitlement to welfare, see the Constitutional Note at the end of Chapter 17, page 000.

ARTICLE I—THE LEGISLATIVE ARTICLE

Legislative Power

The very first article in the Constitution established the legislative branch of the new national government. Why did the framers start with the legislative power instead of the executive branch?

Under the Articles of Confederation, the legislature was the only functional instrument of government. Therefore, the framers truly believed it was the most important component of the new government.

Section 1 All legislative Powers herein granted shall be vested in a Congress of the United States, which shall consist of a Senate and House of Representatives.

Section 1 established a bicameral (two-chamber) legislature of an upper (Senate) and lower (House of Representatives) organization of the legislative branch.

House of Representatives: Composition; Qualifications; Apportionment; Impeachment Power

Section 2 Clause 1. The House of Representatives shall be composed of Members chosen every second Year by the People of the several States, and the Electors in each State shall have the Qualifications requisite for Electors of the most numerous Branch of the State Legislature.

This section sets the term of office for House members (2 years) and indicates that those voting for Congress will have the same qualifications as those voting for the state legislatures. Originally, states limited voters to white property owners. Some states even had religious disqualifications, such as Catholic or Jewish. Most property and religious qualifications for voting were removed by the 1840s, but race and gender restrictions remained, until the 15th and 19th amendments were passed.

Clause 2. No Person shall be a Representative who shall not have attained to the Age of twenty five Years, and been seven Years a Citizen of the United States, and who shall not, when elected, be an inhabitant of that State in which he shall be chosen.

This section sets forth the basic qualifications of a representative: at least 25 years of age, a U.S. citizen for at least 7 years, and a resident of a state. Note that the Constitution does not require a person to be a resident of the district he or she represents. At the time the Constitution was written, life expectancy was about 43 years of age. So a

A CONSTITUTIONAL NOTE

How Is National and State Power Divided?

The Constitution gives to Congress—that is, to the national government—seventeen specific grants of power, the so-called "enumerated powers." These are followed by an eighteenth "necessary and proper" power—"to make all laws which shall be necessary and proper for carrying into Execution the foregoing powers, and all other Powers vested by this Constitution in the Government of the United States . . ." (Article I, Section 8). It is this last "implied powers" or "elastic" clause that has been used extensively by the national government to greatly expand its power.

But what of the states? The Founders believed that the Constitution left all other governmental powers to the states. The 10th Amendment solidified that idea: "The powers not delegated to the United States by the Constitution, nor prohibited by it to the States, are reserved to the States respectively, or to the people." The "reserved powers" of the states are limited only by a few paragraphs in the text of the Constitution, notably Article I, Section 10, which, among other things, prohibits the states from entering into treaties with other nations, or coining money, or passing laws impairing the obligation of contracts, or granting any title of nobility, or placing taxes or duties on imports or exports, or engaging in war with a foreign power "unless actually invaded."

In brief, the original Constitution envisioned the states as having the principal responsibility for the health, safety, education, welfare, law enforcement, and protection of their people. This constitutional "division of power" remains in the Constitution, despite great shifts in power to the national government. Subsequent amendments prohibited slavery in the states (13th Amendment); prohibited states from abridging the privileges or immunities of citizens of the United States, or depriving any person of life, liberty, or property without due process of law, or denying any person within this jurisdiction equal protection of the laws (14th Amendment); or prohibiting citizens the right to vote because of race, color, or previous condition of servitude (15th Amendment); or denying the right to vote for failure to pay any poll tax or other tax (24th Amendment); or denying anyone 18 years of age or older the right to vote on account of age (26th Amendment).

So anyone reading the Constitution, without knowledge of the history of constitutional change in the United States, would not really understand the nature of American federalism.

▲ **A Constitutional Note** in each chapter expands and integrates topic coverage in the context of the Constitution.

◀ An **Annotated Constitution** is included after Chapter 3, providing **extended commentary on key sections and clauses** to give students a deeper insight into the intentions behind this important document.

◀ Global context is essential to the study of American politics today. **Compared to What?** provides comparisons of the United States with other nations, **challenging students to think differently about such topics as the size of government, tax burdens, voter turnout, and health care.**

COMPARED TO WHAT?

Income and Inequality

Capitalism has proven successful in creating wealth. The free market system has provided Americans with more purchasing power than any other people. ("Purchasing power parity" is a statistic used by international economists to adjust for the cost of living differences in measuring how much it costs to purchase a standard "basket" of goods and services.) However, relatively high incomes of average Americans exist side by side with relatively high inequality among Americans. The United States ranks well below many European countries in measures of income inequality. (The "Gini index" is a statistic used by economists to measure income equality/inequality.) But poverty and inequality exist side by side in most of the world's less-developed countries (not ranked below).

Rank by Purchasing Power per Capita		Rank by Equality (Gini Index)	
1. UNITED STATES	16. Greece	1. Sweden	16. Bulgaria
2. Switzerland	17. Czech Republic	2. Denmark	17. Ireland
3. Hong Kong	18. South Korea	3. Slovenia	18. Spain
4. Netherlands	19. Portugal	4. Iceland	19. Canada
5. Belgium	20. Hungary	5. Austria	20. Greece
6. Canada	21. Saudi Arabia	6. Czech Republic	21. Italy
7. United Kingdom	22. Argentina	7. Finland	22. Switzerland
8. Japan	23. Poland	8. Luxembourg	23. United Kingdom
9. Sweden	24. South Africa	9. Slovakia	24. Australia
10. Australia	25. Chile	10. Belgium	25. Poland
11. Germany	26. Russia	11. France	26. Portugal
12. France	27. Mexico	12. Germany	27. Japan
13. Singapore	28. Romania	13. Hungary	28. Israel
14. Italy	29. Bulgaria	14. Netherlands	29. Russia
15. Spain	30. Turkey	15. South Korea	30. UNITED STATES

Sources: Rank by purchasing power, World Bank, *World Development Indicators*, 2005; rank by Gini index, Central Intelligence Agency, *The World Factbook*, 2005. Both sources rank many more nations.

RESOURCES IN PRINT AND ONLINE

Name of Supplement	Print	Online	Available to	Description
MyClassPrep		✓	Instructor	This new resource provides a rich database of figures, photos, videos, simulations, activities, and much more that instructors can use to create their own lecture presentation. For more information visit **www.mypoliscilab.com.**
Instructor's Manual 0205057225		✓	Instructor	Offers chapter overviews, lecture outlines, teaching ideas, discussion topics, and research activities. All resources hyperlinked for ease of navigation.
Test Bank 0205043348		✓	Instructor	Contains over 100 questions per chapter in multiple-choice, true-false, short answer, and essay format. Questions are tied to text Learning Objectives and have been reviewed for accuracy and effectiveness.
MyTest 0205031544		✓	Instructor	All questions from the Test Bank can be accessed in this flexible, online test generating software.
PowerPoint 0205056954		✓	Instructor	Slides include a lecture outline of the text, graphics from the book, and quick check questions for immediate feedback on student comprehension.
Transparencies 0205059392		✓	Instructor	These slides contain all maps, figures, and tables found in the text.
Pearson Political Science Video Program	✓		Instructor	Qualified adopters can peruse our list of videos for the American government classroom. Contact your local Pearson representative for more details.
Classroom Response System (CRS) 0205082289		✓	Instructor	A set of lecture questions, organized by American government topics, for use with "clickers" to garner student opinion and assess comprehension.
American Government Study Site		✓	Instructor/Student	Online package of practice tests, flashcards and more organized by major course topics. Visit **www.pearsonamericangovernment.com.**
You Decide! Current Debates in American Politics, 2011 Edition 020511489X	✓		Student	This debate-style reader by John Rourke of the University of Connecticut examines provocative issues in American politics today by presenting contrasting views of key political topics.
Voices of Dissent: Critical Readings in American Politics, Eighth Edition 0205697976	✓		Student	This collection of critical essays assembled by William Grover of St. Michael's College and Joseph Peschek of Hamline University goes beyond the debate between mainstream liberalism and conservatism to fundamentally challenge the status quo.
Diversity in Contemporary American Politics and Government 0205550363	✓		Student	Edited by David Dulio of Oakland University, Erin E. O'Brien of Kent State University, and John Klemanski of Oakland University, this reader examines the significant role that demographic diversity plays in our political outcomes and policy processes, using both academic and popular sources.
Writing in Political Science, Fourth Edition 0205617360	✓		Student	This guide, written by Diane Schmidt of California State University—Chico, takes students through all aspects of writing in political science step-by-step.
Choices: An American Government Database Reader		✓	Student	This customizable reader allows instructors to choose from a database of over 300 readings to create a reader that exactly matches their course needs. For more information go to **www.pearsoncustom.com/database/choices.html.**
Ten Things That Every American Government Student Should Read 020528969X	✓		Student	Edited by Karen O'Connor of American University. We asked American government instructors across the country to vote for the ten things beyond the text that they believe every student should read and put them in this brief and useful reader. Available at no additional charge when packaged with the text.
American Government: Readings and Cases, Eighteenth Edition 0205697984	✓		Student	Edited by Peter Woll of Brandeis University, this longtime best-selling reader provides a strong, balanced blend of classic readings and cases that illustrate and amplify important concepts in American government, alongside extremely current selections drawn from today's issues and literature. Available at a discount when ordered packaged with this text.
Penguin-Longman Value Bundles	✓		Student	Longman offers 25 Penguin Putnam titles at more than a 60 percent discount when packaged with any Longman text. Go to **www.pearsonhighered.com/penguin** for more information.
Longman State Politics Series	✓		Student	These primers on state and local government and political issues are available at no extra cost when shrink-wrapped with the text. Available for Texas, California, and Georgia.

* Visit the Instructor Resource Center to download supplements at **www.pearsonhighered.com/educator.**

Save Time and Improve Results with

The most popular online teaching/learning solution for American government, MyPoliSciLab moves students from studying and applying concepts to participating in politics. Completely redesigned and now organized by the book's chapters and learning objectives, the new MyPoliSciLab is easier to integrate into any course.

✔ STUDY A flexible learning path in every chapter.

Pre-Tests. See the relevance of politics with these diagnostic assessments and get personalized study plans driven by learning objectives.

Pearson eText. Navigate by learning objective, take notes, print key passages, and more. From page numbers to photos, the eText is identical to the print book.

Flashcards. Learn key terms by word, definition, or learning objective.

Post-Tests. Featuring over 50% new questions, the pre-tests produce updated study plans with follow-up reading, video, and multimedia

Chapter Exams. Also featuring over 50% new questions, test mastery of each chapter using the chapter exams.

✔ APPLY Over 150 videos and multimedia activities.

Video. Analyze current events by watching streaming video from the AP and ABC News.

Simulations. Engage the political process by experiencing how political actors make decisions.

Comparative Exercises. Think critically about how American politics compares with the politics of other countries.

Timelines. Get historical context by following issues that have influenced the evolution of American democracy.

Visual Literacy Exercises. Learn how to interpret political data in figures and tables.

MyPoliSciLibrary. Read full-text primary source documents from the nation's founding to the present.

✔ PARTICIPATE Join the political conversation.

PoliSci News Review. Read analysis of—and comment on—major new stories.

AP Newsfeeds. Follow political news in the United States and around the world.

Weekly Quiz. Master the headlines in this review of current events.

Weekly Poll. Take the poll and see how your politics compare.

Voter Registration. Voting is a right—and a responsibility.

Citizenship Test. See what it takes to become an American citizen.

✔ MANAGE Designed for online or traditional courses.

Grade Tracker. Assign and assess nearly everything in MyPoliSciLab.

Instructor Resources. Download supplements at the Instructor Resource Center.

Sample Syllabus. Get ideas for assigning the book and MyPoliSciLab.

MyClassPrep. Download many of the resources in MyPoliSciLab for lectures.

✔ 📖 👁 ✳ **The icons in the book and eText point to resources in MyPoliSciLab.**

With proven book-specific and course-specific content, MyPoliSciLab is part of a better teaching/learning system only available from Pearson Longman.

✔ To see demos, read case studies, and learn about training, visit www.mypoliscilab.com.

✔ To order this book with MyPoliSciLab at no extra charge, use ISBN 0-205-07768-4.

✔ Questions? Contact a local Pearson Longman representative: www.pearsonhighered.com/replocator.

🐦 Follow MyPoliSciLab on Twitter.

ACKNOWLEDGMENTS

We would like to thank James Corey of High Point University for preparing the annotated Constitution. We are also indebted to the many reviewers who evaluated the text and contributed invaluable advice.

Danny Adkinson, Oklahoma State University

Weton Agor, University of Texas at El Paso

Lee Almaguer, Midland College

John Bertalan, Hillsborough Community College

Angela Burger, UWC–Marathon Company

Stefanie Chambers, Trinity College

Charles W. Chapman, University of Texas at Brownsville

Frank Colon, Lehigh University

James Corey, High Point University

Irasema Coronado, University of Texas at El Paso

Sara Crook, Peru State College

Paul B. Davis, Truckee Meadows Community College

Roy Dawes, University of Southwestern Louisiana

Brian Dille, Odessa College

Nelson Dometrius, Texas Tech University

Kevin R. den Dulk, Grand Valley State University

John Ellis, San Antonio College

Larry Elowitz, University of Southwestern Louisiana

Traci Fatimi, Irvine Valley College

Robert Glen Findley, Odessa College

Edward Fox, Eastern Washington University

Marilyn A. W. Garr, Johnson County Community College

Dana K. Glencross, Oklahoma City Community College

Henry Glick, Florida State University

John Green, University of Akron

Dale Herspring, Kansas State University

John C. Hughes, Sr., Oklahoma City Community College

Elizabeth Hull, Rutgers University

Aleisha Karjala, University of Science and Arts of Oklahoma

Fred Kramer, University of Massachusetts at Amherst

Dale Krane, University of Nebraska at Omaha

James W. Lamare, Florida Atlantic University

Jonathan Lair, South Plains College

John Linantud, University of Houston—Downtown

Fred Lokken, Truckee Meadows Community College

Christopher C. Lovett, Emporia State University

Roger Marietta, Darton College

Nancy McGlen, Niagara University

John McGlennon, College of William and Mary

James Meader, Augustana College

Katarina Moyon, Winthrop University

Jo Anne Myers, Marist College

Max Neiman, University of California–Riverside

Paul Peretz, California State University, Fullerton

John Pratt, Cedar Valley College

Wayne Pryor, Brazosport College

Laurie Robertstad, Navarro College

John Robey, University of Texas—Brownsville

Andre Robinson, Pulaski Technical College

Martin Rochester, University of Missouri—St. Louis

Bruce Rogers, American River College

Bill Rutherford, Odessa College

Earl T. Sheridan, University of North Carolina

Mark W. Shomaker, Blinn College, Bryan Campus

Robert Small, Massosoit County College

Henry Steck, SUNY–Cortland

Dean Stone, Clinton Community College

Gerald Strom, University of Illinois at Chicago

Jon Taylor, University of St. Thomas

Albert Waite, Central Texas College

Morris M. Wilhelm, Indiana University Southeast

Thomas R. Dye

ABOUT THE AUTHOR

Thomas R. Dye, Emeritus McKenzie Professor of Government at Florida State University, regularly taught large introductory classes in American politics. He received his B.A. and M.A. degrees from Pennsylvania State University and his Ph.D. degree from the University of Pennsylvania. He is the author of numerous books and articles on American government and public policy, including *The Irony of Democracy; Politics in States and Communities; Understanding Public Policy; Who's Running America?; American Politics in the Media Age; Power in Society; Politics, Economics, and the Public;* and *American Federalism: Competition Among Governments.* His books have been translated into many languages, including Russian and Chinese, and published abroad. Dye has served as president of the Southern Political Science Association, president of the Policy Studies Organization, and secretary of the American Political Science Association. He has taught at the University of Pennsylvania, the University of Wisconsin, and the University of Georgia, and served as a visiting scholar at Bar-Ilan University, Israel; the Brookings Institution in Washington, D.C.; and elsewhere. He is a member of Phi Beta Kappa, Omicron Delta Kappa, and Phi Kappa Phi and is listed in most major biographical directories. Additional information is available at www.thomasrdye.com.

1 POLITICS
Who Gets What, When, and How

66 The study of politics is the study of influence and the influential. . . . The influential are those who get the most of what there is to get. Those who get the most are elite; the rest are mass. 99

Harold Lasswell

Chapter Outline and Learning Objectives

Politics and Political Science
▶ 1.1 *Distinguish between politics and political science.*

Politics and Government
▶ 1.2 *Compare and contrast governmental politics with politics in other societal organizations.*

The Purposes of Government
▶ 1.3 *Identify the purposes for which government is established.*

The Meaning of Democracy
▶ 1.4 *Outline the major principles of democracy.*

The Paradox of Democracy
▶ 1.5 *Analyze the inherent conflict between majority rule and individual freedom.*

Direct Versus Representative Democracy
▶ 1.6 *Compare and contrast representational government and direct government.*

Who Really Governs?
▶ 1.7 *Show how elitism and pluralism reach different conclusions about who governs in America.*

Democracy in America
▶ 1.8 *Evaluate the implications of the elitist and pluralist views for the realization of American democratic ideals.*

✔ *Think* about Politics

1. Should any group other than the government have the right to use force?
   YES ◯ NO ◯

2. Is it ever right to disobey the law?
   YES ◯ NO ◯

3. Can you trust the government to do what is right most of the time?
   YES ◯ NO ◯

4. Should important decisions in a democracy be submitted to voters rather than decided by Congress?
   YES ◯ NO ◯

5. In a democracy should "majority rule" be able to limit the rights of members of an unpopular or dangerous minority?
   YES ◯ NO ◯

6. Is government trying to do too many things that should be left to individuals?
   YES ◯ NO ◯

7. Is the government run by a few big interests looking out for themselves?
   YES ◯ NO ◯

Who has power and how they use it are the basis of all these questions. Issues of power underlie everything we call politics and the study of political science.

Politics and Political Science

▶ 1.1 *Distinguish between politics and political science.*

Politics is deciding "who gets what, when, and how."[1] It is an activity by which people try to get more of whatever there is to get—money, prestige, jobs, respect, sex, even power itself. Politics occurs in many different settings. We talk about office politics, student politics, union politics, church politics, and so forth. But political science usually limits its attention to *politics in government.*

Political science is the study of politics, or the study of who gets what, when, and how.[2] The *who* are the participants in politics—voters, special-interest groups, political parties, television and the press, corporations and labor unions, lawyers and lobbyists, foundations and think tanks, and both elected and appointed government officials, including members of Congress, the president and vice president, judges, prosecutors, and bureaucrats. The *what* of politics are public policies—the decisions that governments make concerning social welfare, health care, education, national defense, law enforcement, the environment, taxation, and thousands of other issues that come before governments. The *when* and *how* are the political process—campaigns and elections, political reporting in the news media, television debates, fund-raising, lobbying, decision making in the White House and executive agencies, and decision making in the courts.

Political science is generally concerned with three questions: *Who governs? For what ends? By what means?* Throughout this book, we are concerned with who participates in politics, how government decisions are made, who benefits most from those decisions, and who bears their greatest costs (see Figure 1.1).

politics
Deciding who gets what, when, and how.

political science
The study of politics: who governs, for what ends, and by what means.

3

FIGURE 1.1

Who Gets What, When, and How

Political science is the study of politics. The distinguished political scientist Harold Lasswell entitled his most popular book *Politics: Who Gets What, When, and How*. The first topic of politics is "Who?" (that is, who are the participants in politics, both within and outside of government?), "When and how are political decisions made?" (that is, how do the institutions and processes of politics function?), and "What outcomes are produced?" (that is, what public policies are adopted?). Shown here are some of the topics of concern to political science.

Who Governs: Participants

Governmental

President and White House staff
Executive Office of the President, including Office of Management and Budget
Cabinet officers and executive agency heads
Bureaucrats

Congress members
Congressional staff

Supreme Court justices
Federal appellate and district judges

Nongovernmental

Voters
Campaign contributors
Interest-group leaders and members
Party leaders and party identifiers in the electorate
Corporate and union leaders
Media leaders, including press and television anchors and reporters
Lawyers and lobbyists
Think tanks and foundation personnel

When and How: Institutions and Processes

Institutions

Constitution
  Separation of powers
  Checks and balances
  Federalism
  Judicial review
  Amendment procedures
  Electoral system

Presidency
Congress
  Senate
  House of Representatives

Courts
  Supreme Court
  Appellate courts
  District courts

Parties
  National committees
  Conventions
  State and local organizations

Media
  Television
  Press
  Internet

Processes

Socialization and learning
Opinion formation
Party identification
Voting
Contributing
Joining organizations
Talking politics

Running for office
Campaigning
Polling
Fund-raising
Parading and demonstrating
Nonviolent direct action
Violence

Lobbying
Logrolling
Deciding
Budgeting
Implementing and evaluating
Adjudicating

Agenda setting
News making
Interpreting
Persuading

What Outcomes: Public Policies

Civil liberties
Civil rights
Equality
Criminal justice
Welfare
Social Security
Health
Education
Energy

Environmental protection
Economic development
Economic stability
Taxation
Government spending and deficits
National defense
Foreign affairs
Homeland Security

Politics would be simple if everyone agreed on who should govern, who should get what, who should pay for it, and how and when it should be done. But conflict arises from disagreements over these questions, and sometimes the question of confidence in the government itself underlies the conflict (see *What Do You Think?*: "Can You Trust the Government?").

Conflict All Around
Conflict exists in all activities as participants struggle over who gets what, when, and how. From the streets to the Congress to the campaign trail, participants in the political process compete to further their goals and ambitions.

Politics and Government

▶ 1.2 *Compare and contrast governmental politics with politics in other societal organizations.*

What distinguishes governmental politics from politics in other institutions in society? After all, parents, teachers, unions, banks, corporations, and many other organizations make decisions about who gets what in society. The answer is that only **government** decisions can *extend to the whole society*, and only government can *legitimately use force*. Other institutions encompass only a part of society: for example, students and faculty in a college, members of a church or union, employees or customers of a corporation. And individuals have a legal right to voluntarily withdraw from *non*governmental organizations. But governments make decisions affecting everyone, and no one can voluntarily withdraw from government's authority (without leaving the country, and thus becoming subject to some other government's authority). Some individuals and organizations—muggers, gangs, crime families—occasionally use physical force to get what they want. But only governments can use force legitimately—that is, people generally believe it is acceptable for the government to use force if necessary to uphold its laws, but they do not extend this right to other institutions or individuals.

Most people would say that they obey the law in order to avoid fines and stay out of prison. But if large numbers of people all decided to disobey the law at the same time, the government would not have enough police or jails to hold them all.

government
Organization extending to the whole society that can legitimately use force to carry out its decisions.

✓ *Think*
Again

Should any group other than the government have the right to use force?

WHAT DO YOU THINK?

Can You Trust the Government?

Americans are suspicious of big government. Many do not trust the government in Washington to "do what is right." Trust in government has varied over the years, as measured by polls asking, "How much of the time do you think you can trust the government in Washington to do what is right? Just about always? Most of the time? Some of the time? None of the time?" Low levels of trust and confidence in government may represent a profound disaffection with the political system, or a more superficial dissatisfaction with current politicians and political leaders or with policies.[a] Americans' trust in the national government used to be higher. In the 1950s and through the early 1960s, during the Eisenhower, Kennedy, and first years of the Johnson administrations, the public overwhelmingly had confidence in the government. But in the late '60s through the '70s, with the defeat in Vietnam, the Watergate scandal and the forced resignation of President Richard Nixon—the first resignation of a president in U.S. history—public confidence fell, and kept falling.[b]

Throughout this period of decline, television broadcasted many negative images of government and government policy. Television producers want news of scandal, violence, corruption, and incompetence; they want what is simple and sensational, not good news or much in-depth reporting of complicated news (see Chapter 6, "Mass Media: Setting the Agenda").

Economic recessions erode public confidence in government. People expect the president and Congress to lead them out of "hard times." So while President George H. W. Bush raised public confidence in the early 1990s with the military success of Desert Storm in Iraq, his administration's perceived failure to act decisively to take the United States out of the economic recession of the early 1990s helped to send public confidence in government back down. But then sustained economic growth in the 1990s under President Clinton improved public trust in government.

But public confidence in government can be revived, as it was during the Reagan presidency. President Reagan's popularity may have contributed to the restoration of the public's confidence in government.[c] Americans' trust in government also revived after the terrorist attacks of September 11, 2001. Public trust in government doubled immediately after September 11, as America rallied behind the government. American flags and images of Old Glory sprouted from homes and businesses, and on vehicles. Trust in government "to do what is right" leaped to levels not seen since the early 1970s. But the public trust gradually eroded as the war in Iraq dragged on. The election of Barack Obama inspired a modest upswing of trust corresponding to the "honeymoon" period that newly elected presidents enjoy. But as Obama's approval ratings declined, so did trust in government (see "Political Resources of the President" in Chapter 11).

The government can rely on force only against relatively small numbers of offenders. Most of us, most of the time, obey laws out of habit—the habit of compliance. We have been taught to believe that law and order are necessary and that government is right to punish those who disobey its laws.

Government thus enjoys **legitimacy**, or rightfulness, in its use of force.[3] A democratic government has a special claim to legitimacy because it is based on the consent of its people, who participate in the selection of its leaders and the making of its laws. Those who disagree with a law have the option of working for its change by speaking out, petitioning, demonstrating, forming interest groups or parties, voting against unpopular leaders, or running for office themselves. Since people living in a democracy can effect change by "working within the system," they have a greater moral obligation to obey the law than people living under regimes in which they have no voice. However, there may be some occasions when "civil disobedience" even in a democracy may be morally justified (see *A Conflicting View*: "Sometimes It's Right to Disobey the Law").

legitimacy
Widespread acceptance of something as necessary, rightful, and legally binding.

Think Again

Is it ever right to disobey the law?

The Purposes of Government

▶ 1.3 *Identify the purposes for which government is established.*

All governments tax, penalize, punish, restrict, and regulate their people. Governments in the United States—the federal government in Washington, the 50 state governments, and the more than 87,000 local governments—take

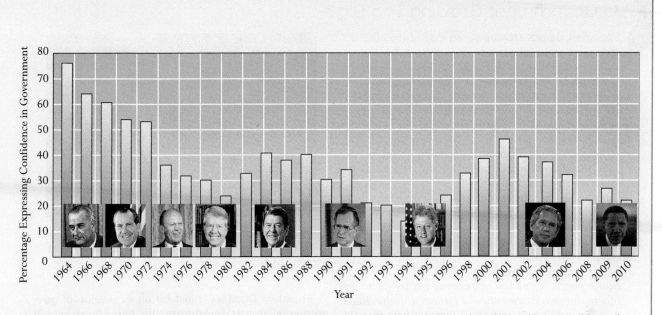

Public Confidence, That the Federal Government Can Be Trusted to "Do What Is Right Just About Always or Most of the Time"

How much of the time do you think you can trust government in Washington to do what is right—just about always, most of the time, or only some of the time?

[a]Timothy E. Cook and Paul Gronke, "The Skeptical American," *Journal of Politics* 67 (Aug. 2005): 784–803

[b]Marc J. Hetherington, *Why Trust Matters*. Princeton, N.J.: Princeton University Press, 2005.

[c]Arthur H. Miller, "Confidence in Government During the 1980s," *American Politics Quarterly* 19 (April 1991): 147–73.

Source: Data from Gallup Opinion Polls (http://www.gallup.com/poll/topics/trust_gov.asd).

nearly 40 cents out of every dollar Americans earn. Each year, the Congress enacts about 500 laws; federal bureaucracies publish about 20,000 rules and regulations, the state legislatures enact about 25,000 laws; and cities, counties, school districts, and other local governments enact countless local ordinances. Each of these laws restricts our freedom in some way.

Why do people put up with governments? An answer to this question can be found in the words of the Preamble to the Constitution of the United States:

> We the people of the United States, in Order to form a more perfect Union, establish Justice, insure domestic Tranquility, provide for the common defense, promote the general Welfare, and secure the Blessings of Liberty to ourselves and our Posterity, do ordain and establish this Constitution for the United States of America.

To Establish Justice and Insure Domestic Tranquility

Government manages conflict and maintains order. We might think of government as a **social contract** among people who agree to allow themselves to be regulated and taxed in exchange for protection of their lives and property. No society can allow individuals or groups to settle their conflicts by street fighting, murder, kidnapping, rioting, bombing, or terrorism. Whenever government fails to control such violence, we describe it as "a breakdown in law and order." Without the protection of government, human lives and property are endangered, and only those skilled with fists and weapons have much of a chance of survival. The

social contract
Idea that government originates as an implied contract among individuals who agree to obey laws in exchange for protection of their rights.

CONTROVERSY

Is Government Growing Too Big?

President Barack Obama came into office with an extensive political agenda, including a bailout of the nation's financial institutions, a government stimulus package for the economy, a transformation of the nation's health care system, a new "cap and trade" initiative for dealing with climate change, and comprehensive immigration reform. Together, these policy initiatives envision a vast enlargement of the federal government, huge increases in federal spending, and the resulting skyrocketing of federal deficit levels. Is government growing too big?

Over half of a national sample of adult Americans polled say that the government is trying to do too many things (57%), with others thinking that the government should do more (38%), or others expressing mixed feelings (4%).

President Barack Obama's policy agenda envisions a vast expansion of government power. Is government trying to do too much?

Some people think the government is trying to do too many things that should be left to individuals and businesses. Others think that the government should do more to solve our country's problems. Which comes closer to your own view?

Government doing too much	57%
Government should do more	38%
Mixed/depends (volunteered)	4%
No opinion	1%

President Obama's quest for an expansion of governmental power to address the nation's economic problems is generally approved (53%), but most of those who approve would like to see the government's role reduced once the crisis is over.

Thinking about the way the federal government has responded to the financial crisis in recent months, generally speaking, do you approve or

seventeenth-century English political philosopher Thomas Hobbes described life without government as "a war where every man is enemy to every man," where people live in "continual fear and danger of violent death."[4]

To Provide for the Common Defense   Many anthropologists link the origins of government to warfare—to the need of early communities to protect themselves from raids by outsiders and to organize raids against others. Since the Revolutionary War, the U.S. government has been responsible for the country's defense. During the long Cold War, when America confronted a nuclear-armed, expansionist-minded, communist-governed Soviet Union, the United States spent nearly half of the federal budget on national defense. With the end of the Cold War, defense spending fell to about 15 percent of the federal budget, but defense spending has begun to creep upward again as the nation confronts the new war on terrorism. National defense will always remain a primary responsibility of United States government.

public goods
Goods and services that cannot readily be provided by markets, either because they are too expensive for a single individual to buy or because if one person bought them, everyone else would use them without paying.

To Promote the General Welfare   Government promotes the general welfare in a number of ways. It provides **public goods**—goods and services that private markets cannot readily furnish either because they are too expensive for individuals to buy for themselves (for example, a national park, a highway, or a sewage disposal plant) or because if one person bought them, everyone else would "free-ride," or use them without paying (for example, clean air, police protection, or national defense).

disapprove of the expansion of the government's role in the economy?

Approve of expanded role	53%
Disapprove of expanded role	44%
No opinion	2%

Overall, Obama's proposals are not perceived to be too big an expansion of governmental power.

Do you think President Obama's proposals to address the economic problems of the country call for too big an expansion of government power, the right amount, or not a big enough expansion of government power?

Too big an expansion	40%
Right amount	46%
Not big enough	10%
No opinion	4%

Many Americans are wary of the federal government's power, but at the same time they want the government to have enough power to deal with the nation's problems.

[a]*Time*, June 15, 2009: 26.

Source: Gallup Opinion Poll, 2009, as reported in The Polling Report, www.pollingreport.com.

Do you think the federal government today has too much power, has about the right amount of power, or has too little power?

Too much	50%
About the right amount	42%
Too little	7%
No opinion	2%

Traditionally, Americans seem to turn to the government in Washington during hard economic times, such as during the New Deal expansion of government under President Franklin D. Roosevelt in the Great Depression of the 1930s. Today's "Great Recession" encourages President Barack Obama to offer a wide variety of new policy initiatives. White House Chief of Staff Rahm Emanuel is quoted as saying: "Never allow a crisis to go to waste. Crises are opportunities to do big things."[a] But it is not clear that the American people are as trustful of big government as they once might have been.

Nevertheless, Americans acquire most of their goods and services on the **free market**, through voluntary exchange among individuals, firms, and corporations. The **gross domestic product (GDP)**—the dollar sum of all the goods and services produced in the United States in a year—amounts to more than $15 trillion. Government spending in the United States—federal, state, and local governments combined—now amounts to about $5 trillion, or an amount equivalent to one-third of the gross domestic product. (See *Controversy*: "Is Government Growing Too Big?")

Governments also regulate society. Free markets cannot function effectively if individuals and firms engage in fraud, deception, or unfair competition, or if contracts cannot be enforced. Moreover, many economic activities impose costs on persons who are not direct participants in these activities. Economists refer to such costs as **externalities**. A factory that produces air pollution or wastewater imposes external costs on community residents who would otherwise enjoy cleaner air or water. A junkyard that creates an eyesore makes life less pleasant for neighbors and passersby. Many government regulations are designed to reduce these external costs.

To promote general welfare, governments also use **income transfers** from taxpayers to people who are regarded as deserving. Government agencies and programs provide support and care for individuals who cannot supply these things for themselves through the private job market, for example, ill, elderly, and disabled people, and dependent children who cannot usually be expected to find productive employment. The largest income transfer programs are Social Security and Medicare, which are paid to the elderly regardless of their personal wealth. Other

free market
Free competition for voluntary exchange among individuals, firms, and corporations.

gross domestic product (GDP)
Measure of economic performance in terms of the nation's total production of goods and services for a single year, valued in terms of market prices.

externalities
Costs imposed on people who are not direct participants in an activity.

income transfers
Government transfers of income from taxpayers to persons regarded as deserving.

equality of opportunity refers to the ability to make of oneself what one can, to develop one's talents and abilities, and to be rewarded for one's work, initiative, and achievement. Equality of opportunity means that everyone comes to the same starting line in life, with the same chance of success, and that whatever differences develop over time do so as a result of abilities, talents, initiative, hard work, and perhaps good luck.

Americans do not generally resent the fact that physicians, engineers, airline pilots, and others who have spent time and energy acquiring particular skills make more money than those whose jobs require fewer skills and less training. Neither do most Americans resent the fact that people who risk their own time and money to build a business, bring new or better products to market, and create jobs for others make more money than their employees. Nor do many Americans begrudge multimillion-dollar incomes to sports figures, rock stars, and movie stars whose talents entertain the public. And few Americans object when someone wins a million-dollar lottery, as long as everyone who entered the lottery had an equal chance at winning. Americans are generally willing to have government act to ensure equality of opportunity—to ensure that everyone has an equal chance at getting an education, landing a job, and buying a home, and that no barriers of race, sex, religion, or ethnicity bar individual advancement.

Equality of Results Equality of results refers to the equal sharing of income and material rewards. Equality of results means that everyone starts *and finishes* the race together, regardless of ability, talent, initiative, or work. Those who argue on behalf of this notion of equality say that if individuals are truly equal, then everyone should enjoy generally equal conditions in life. According to this belief, we should appreciate an individual's contributions to society without creating inequalities of wealth and income. Government should act to *transfer* wealth and income from the rich to the poor to increase the total happiness of all members of society.

equality of results
Equal sharing of income and material goods.

Equality of results, or absolute equality, was referred to as "leveling" by Thomas Jefferson and was denounced by the nation's Founders:

> To take from one, because it is thought his own industry and that of his fathers has acquired too much, in order to spare to others who have not exercised equal industry and skill, is to violate arbitrarily . . . the guarantee to everyone the free exercise of his industry and the fruits acquired by it.[6]

The taking of private property from those who acquired it legitimately, for no other reason than to equalize wealth or income, was once widely viewed as morally wrong. Moreover, many people believed that society generally would suffer if incomes were equalized. Absolute equality, in this view, would remove incentives for people to work, save, or produce. Everyone would slack off, production would decline, goods would be in short supply, and everyone would end up poorer than ever.

But support for equality of results appears to be growing in recent years. President Barack Obama proposed tax legislation that would increase income taxes on wealthy families and provide tax payments to middle- and lower-income families (see Chapter 16). This combination of tax changes will make the federal Tax Code much more progressive—redistributing after-tax income from rich to poor. Critics charge that redistributing income in this fashion is "socialism," and that it penalizes work, initiative, and talent. Americans generally believe in tax progressivity—higher income people can afford to be taxed at higher rates than lower income people. But deliberate attempts by the government to use the Tax Code to equalize incomes represents a new direction in tax policy.[7]

Fairness Americans value "fairness" even though they do not always agree on what is fair. Most Americans support a "floor" on income and material well-being—a level that no one, regardless of his or her condition, should be permitted to fall below—even though they differ over how high that floor should be. Indeed, the belief in a floor is consistent with the belief in equality of opportunity; extreme poverty would deny people, especially children, the opportunity to compete in life.[8] But few Americans want to place a "ceiling" on income or wealth. Generally, Americans want people who cannot provide for themselves to be well cared for, especially children, the elderly, the ill, and the disabled. They are often willing to "soak the rich" when searching for new tax sources, believing that the rich can easily afford to bear the burdens of government. But, unlike citizens in other Western democracies, Americans generally do *not* believe that government should equalize incomes.

Inequality of Income and Wealth

▶ 2.4 *Characterize American values related to wealth and income, the current distribution of wealth and income, and trends affecting this distribution.*

Conflict in society is generated more often by inequalities among people than by hardship or deprivation. Material well-being and standards of living are usually expressed in aggregate measures for a whole society—for example, gross domestic product per capita, income per capita, average life expectancy, infant mortality rate. These measures of societal well-being are vitally important to a nation and its people, but *political* conflict is more likely to occur over the *distribution* of well-being *within* a society. Unequal distributions can generate conflict even in a very affluent society with high levels of income and a high standard of living (see *Compared to What?:* "Income and Inequality").

Think
Again

Are income differences in America widening?

How Much Inequality? Let us examine inequality of income in the United States systematically. Figure 2.1 divides all American households into two groups—the lowest one-fifth in income and the highest one-fifth—and shows the shares (percentage) of total household income received by each of these groups over the years. (If perfect income equality existed, each fifth of American households would receive 20 percent of all personal income.) The poorest one-fifth received only 4.5 percent of all household income in 1929; today, this group does a little worse, at 3.4 percent of household income. The highest one-fifth received 54.0 percent of all household income in 1929; today, its percentage stands at 50.0.

Inequality has actually *increased* in recent decades. The income of the poorest households declined from 4.1 to 3.4 percent of total income between 1970 and 2008; the income of the highest quintile rose from 43.3 to 50.0 percent of total income. This reversal of trends has generated both political rhetoric and serious scholarly inquiry about both its causes and consequences.[9]

Explaining Increases in Inequality Increases in income inequality in the United States are a product of several social and economic trends: (1) the decline of the manufacturing sector of the economy (and the loss of many relatively high-paying blue-collar jobs) and the ascendancy of the communications, information, and service sectors of the economy (with a combination of high-paying and low-paying jobs); (2) the rise in the number of two-wage families, making single-wage, female-headed households relatively less affluent; (3) demographic trends, which include larger proportions of aged and larger proportions of female-headed

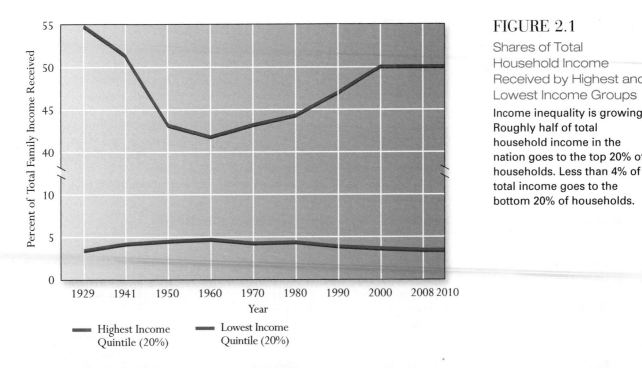

FIGURE 2.1

Shares of Total Household Income Received by Highest and Lowest Income Groups

Income inequality is growing. Roughly half of total household income in the nation goes to the top 20% of households. Less than 4% of total income goes to the bottom 20% of households.

families; and (4) global competition, which restrains wages in unskilled and semiskilled jobs while rewarding people in high-technology, high-productivity occupations.

Social Mobility

▶ 2.5 *Analyze the relationships among social mobility, inequality, and class conflict.*

Political conflict over inequality might be greater in the United States if it were not for the prospect of **social mobility**. All societies are stratified, or layered, but societies differ greatly in the extent to which people move upward or downward in income and status over a lifetime or over generations. When there is social mobility, people have a good opportunity to get ahead if they study or work long and hard, save and invest wisely, or display initiative and enterprise in business affairs. Fairly steep inequalities may be tolerated politically if people have a reasonable expectation of moving up over time, or at least of seeing their children do so.

social mobility
Extent to which people move upward or downward in income and status over a lifetime or over generations.

How Much Mobility?   The United States describes itself as the land of opportunity. The really important political question may be how much real opportunity exists for individual Americans to improve their conditions in life relative to others. The impression given by Figure 2.1 is one of a static distribution system, with families permanently placed in upper or lower fifths of income earners. But there is considerable evidence of both upward and downward movement by people among income groupings.[10] Almost half of the families in the poorest one-fifth will move upward within a decade, and about half of families in the richest one-fifth will fall out of this top category (see *Politics Up Close:* "Getting Ahead in America").

Mobility, Class Conflict, and Class Consciousness   Social mobility and the expectation of mobility, over a lifetime or over generations, may be the key to understanding why **class conflict**—conflict over wealth and power among social classes—is not as widespread or as intense in America as it is in many other nations. The *belief* in social mobility reduces the potential for class conflict

class conflict
Conflict between upper and lower social classes over wealth and power.

COMPARED TO WHAT?

Income and Inequality

Capitalism has proven successful in creating wealth. The free market system has provided Americans with more purchasing power than any other people. ("Purchasing power parity" is a statistic used by international economists to adjust for the cost of living differences in measuring how much it costs to purchase a standard "basket" of goods and services.) However, relatively high incomes of average Americans exist side by side with relatively high inequality among Americans. The United States ranks well below many European countries in measures of income inequality. (The "Gini index" is a statistic used by economists to measure income equality/inequality.) But poverty and inequality exist side by side in most of the world's less-developed countries (not ranked below).

Rank by Purchasing Power per Capita

1. UNITED STATES	16. Greece
2. Switzerland	17. Czech Republic
3. Hong Kong	18. South Korea
4. Netherlands	19. Portugal
5. Belgium	20. Hungary
6. Canada	21. Saudi Arabia
7. United Kingdom	22. Argentina
8. Japan	23. Poland
9. Sweden	24. South Africa
10. Australia	25. Chile
11. Germany	26. Russia
12. France	27. Mexico
13. Singapore	28. Romania
14. Italy	29. Bulgaria
15. Spain	30. Turkey

Rank by Equality (Gini Index)

1. Sweden	16. Bulgaria
2. Denmark	17. Ireland
3. Slovenia	18. Spain
4. Iceland	19. Canada
5. Austria	20. Greece
6. Czech Republic	21. Italy
7. Finland	22. Switzerland
8. Luxembourg	23. United Kingdom
9. Slovakia	24. Australia
10. Belgium	25. Poland
11. France	26. Portugal
12. Germany	27. Japan
13. Hungary	28. Israel
14. Netherlands	29. Russia
15. South Korea	30. UNITED STATES

Sources: Rank by purchasing power, World Bank, *Word Development Indicators*, 2005; rank by Gini index, Central Intelligence Agency, *The World Factbook*, 2005. Both sources rank many more nations.

class consciousness
Awareness of one's class position and a feeling of political solidarity with others within the same class in opposition to other classes.

because it diminishes **class consciousness**, the awareness of one's class position and the feeling of political solidarity with others in the same class in opposition to other classes. If class lines were impermeable and no one had any reasonable expectation of moving up or seeing his or her children move up, then class consciousness would rise and political conflict among classes would intensify.

Two Americas

Income inequality in America has increased in recent decades.

POLITICS UP CLOSE

Getting Ahead in America

America is a land of opportunity. But how much of a chance do Americans *really* have of moving up the income ladder over time?

To measure mobility we must observe the ups and downs of families *over time*. This calls for longitudinal studies—studies of the same families over a period of time, how many move up or down the income ladder. The University of Michigan's Panel Study of Income Dynamics (PSID) has been tracing the income, health, and poverty status of the same American families since 1968. Using the PSID, researchers have produced the following data about income mobility of American families.

Researchers began by ranking families in 1968–70 by income quintiles (20% intervals) from lowest to highest income. Then the same families were observed 20 years later, 1989–91, and again ranked into income quintiles. The table shows the percentage of each of the families from the early 1968–70 income quintiles that fell into the various income quintiles in 1989–91.

The table is interpreted in the following way: The number 53.8 in the upper left-hand cell shows that 53.8 percent of families that started in the poorest quintile in 1968–70 remained in the poorest quintile in 1989–91. The remaining families in the lowest quintile moved up, most to the second and third quintiles. Very few, 0.9 percent, made it all the way from the poorest to the richest quintile.

The table also shows that 46.1 percent of the families that were in the richest quintile in 1968–70 remained in the richest quintile in 1989–91. Many of them fell to the third and fourth quintile, but an unlucky few, 7.0 percent, fell all the way to the poorest quintile.

What does this table tell us about mobility? Almost half of the poorest American families will move up the income ladder over a twenty year period. Over half of America's richest families can be expected to fall out of the top category over the same period. America is certainly not a caste society; if it were, then 100 percent of the lowest quintile would remain there over time, and 100 percent of the highest income quintile would remain at the top. So America experiences considerable mobility. But it is not perfectly mobile either. While some families started poor and ended up rich and vice versa, poor families were more likely to stay poor and rich families were more likely to stay rich.

Mobility Among American Families over Two Decades

Income Quintile in 1968–70	Income Quintile in 1989–91				
	Lowest	Second	Third	Fourth	Highest
Lowest	53.8	21.8	18.8	4.8	0.9
Second	22.7	25.4	18.5	25.8	7.7
Third	11.1	21.4	24.4	27.8	15.4
Fourth	5.3	22.6	23.0	19.3	29.8
Highest	7.0	8.6	16.2	22.2	46.1

Source: University of Michigan, Institute for Social Research, Panel Study of Income Dynamics.

Sources: Robert S. Rycroft, *The Economics of Inequality, Discrimination, Poverty, and Mobility.* Armonk, N.Y.: M. E. Sharpe, 2009; Samuel Bowles, ed., *Unequal Chances: Family Background and Economic Success,* New York: Princeton University Press, 2005.

Most Americans describe themselves as "middle class" rather than "rich" or "poor" or "lower class" or "upper class." There are no widely accepted income definitions of "middle class." The federal government officially defines a "poverty level" each year based on the annual cash income required to maintain a decent standard of living (approximately $22,000 in 2010). Roughly 12 to 13 percent of the U.S. population lives with annual cash incomes below this poverty line. This is the only income group in which a majority of people describe themselves as poor. Large majorities in every other income group identify themselves as middle class. So it is no surprise that presidents, politicians, and political parties regularly claim to be defenders of America's "middle class"!

✓ *Think*
Again

Is American culture racist and sexist?

Race, Ethnicity, and Immigration

▶ 2.6 *Describe the current immigration trends and ethnic composition of the United States.*

America has always been an ethnically and racially pluralist society. All groups were expected to adopt the American political culture—including individual liberty, economic freedom, political equality, and equality of opportunity—and to learn American history and the English language. The nation's motto "E Pluribus Unum" (from many, one) is inscribed on its coins. Yet each of America's racial and ethnic groups brings its own traditions and values to the American political culture.

African Americans   Historically African Americans constituted the nation's largest minority. Blacks composed about 20 percent of the population at the time the U.S. Constitution was written in 1787 (although as we shall see in Chapter 3 an enslaved African American was to be counted as only three-fifths of a person in the original Constitution). Heavy European immigration in the late nineteenth century diluted the black population to roughly 12 percent of the nation's total. As late as 1900, most African Americans (90 percent) were still concentrated in the southern states. But World Wars I and II provided job opportunities in large cities of the Northeast and Midwest. Blacks could not cast ballots in most southern counties, but they could "vote with their feet." The migration of African Americans from the rural South to the urban North was one of the largest internal migrations in our history. Today only about half of the nation's African Americans live in the South— still more than in any other region but less of a concentration than earlier in American history. Today the nation's 40 million African Americans comprise about 13 percent of the total population of the United States (see Figure 2.2). "African American Politics in Historical Perspective" is discussed in Chapter 15, as well as the long struggle against slavery, segregation, and discrimination. This struggle has given African Americans a somewhat different perspective on American politics (see "Race and Opinion" in Chapter 5).

Hispanic Americans   Hispanics are now the nation's largest minority. The term *Hispanic* generally refers to persons of Spanish-speaking ancestry and culture; it includes Mexican Americans, Cuban Americans, and Puerto Ricans. Today there are an estimated 50 million Hispanics in the United States, or about 16 percent of the total population. The largest subgroup is Mexican Americans, some of whom are descendants of citizens living in Mexican territory that was annexed to the United States in 1848, but most of whom have come to the United States in accelerating numbers in recent years. The largest Mexican American populations are found in Texas, Arizona, New Mexico, and California (see Figure 2.3).

Controversy over Immigration

Many Hispanic Americans have protested against bills targeting illegal immigrants. Many white Americans resent the presence of illegal immigrants.

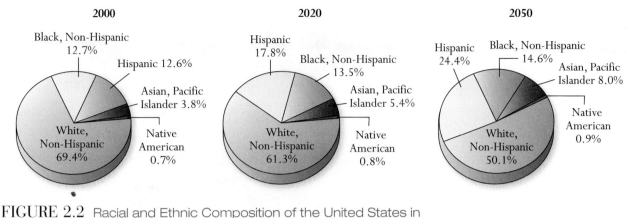

| 2000 | 2020 | 2050 |

Black, Non-Hispanic
12.7%

Hispanic 12.6%

Asian, Pacific
Islander 3.8%

White,
Non-Hispanic
69.4%

Native
American
0.7%

Hispanic
17.8%

Black, Non-Hispanic
13.5%

Asian, Pacific
Islander 5.4%

White,
Non-Hispanic
61.3%

Native
American
0.8%

Hispanic
24.4%

Black, Non-Hispanic
14.6%

Asian, Pacific
Islander 8.0%

Native
American
0.9%

White,
Non-Hispanic
50.1%

FIGURE 2.2 Racial and Ethnic Composition of the United States in 2000, 2020, 2050

Current trends in population growth and change suggests that America will become more ethnically and racially diverse over time.

Source: U.S. Bureau of the Census (Middle Series). Two or more races not shown. www.census.gov

The second-largest subgroup is Puerto Ricans, many of whom move back and forth from the island to the mainland, especially New York City. The third-largest subgroup is Cubans, many of whom fled from Castro's Cuba. They live mainly in the Miami metropolitan area. The politics of each of these Hispanic groups differs somewhat (see "Hispanic Politics" in Chapter 15).

A Nation of Immigrants The United States is a nation of immigrants, from the first "boat people" (Pilgrims) to the later Haitian refugees and Cuban *balseros* ("rafters"). Historically, most of the people who came to settle in this country did so because they believed their lives would be better here, and American political culture today has been greatly affected by the beliefs and values they brought with them. Americans are proud of their immigrant heritage and the freedom and opportunity the nation has extended to generations of "huddled masses yearning

An Education in Diversity

Immigration places responsibility on public schools to provide for the needs of children from different cultures. Here, first grade Latino children use audio equipment to help with reading in a bilingual Spanish-English class in San Rafael, California.

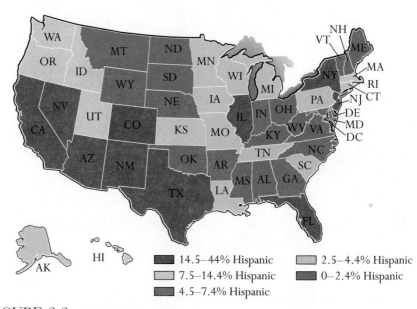

FIGURE 2.3   Hispanic Populations

The Hispanic population in the United States in heavily concentrated in a few states—California, Colorado, Arizona, New Mexico, Texas, and Florida. Even within these states Latinos are concentrated in particular counties, especially counties along the southern border as well as Miami-Dade County in Florida (Cubans) and New York City (Puerto Ricans). This concentration facilitates the continuing use of the Spanish language—in newspapers, television (Univision, TeleMundo), business, and commercial establishments. It often inspires bilingual education in public schools, colleges, and universities.

Source: Map data from the Pew Hispanic Center, 2005.

to breathe free"—words emblazoned on the Statue of Liberty in New York's harbor. Today about 12 percent of the U.S. population is foreign-born.

immigration policy
Regulating the entry of non-citizens into the country.

Immigration policy is a responsibility of the national government. It was not until 1882 that Congress passed the first legislation restricting entry into the United States of persons alleged to be "undesirable" and virtually all Asians. After World War I, Congress passed the comprehensive Immigration Act of 1921, which established maximum numbers of new immigrants each year and set a quota for immigrants for each foreign country at 3 percent of the number of that nation's foreign-born who were living in the United States in 1910, later reduced

Rights of Passage
The U.S. Coast Guard may intercept boats at sea and return their occupants to their country of origin. But once immigrants reach the U.S. shore, they are entitled to a hearing in any deportation proceedings.

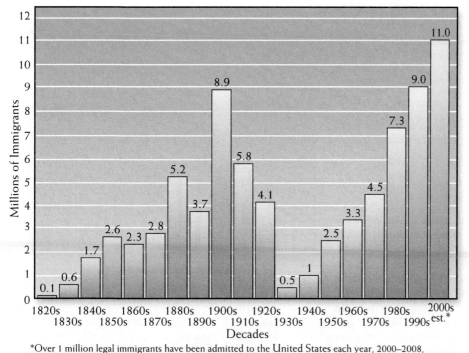

FIGURE 2.4

Legal Immigration to the United States by Decades

Currently about one million legal immigrants are admitted into the United States each year. Today the nation is experiencing its second great wave of immigration, following the great wave of the early 1900s.

*Over 1 million legal immigrants have been admitted to the United States each year, 2000–2008, leading to an estimate of 11 million for the current decade.

Source: Statistical Abstract of the United States, 2009, p. 9.

to 2 percent of the number living here in 1890. These restrictions reflected anti-immigration feelings that were generally directed at the large wave of Southern and Eastern European Catholic and Jewish immigrants (from Poland, Russia, Hungary, Italy, and Greece) entering the United States prior to World War I (see Figure 2.4). It was not until the Immigration and Naturalization Act of 1965 that national origin quotas were abolished, replaced by preference categories for close relatives of U.S. citizens, professionals, and skilled workers.

Immigration "reform" was the announced goal of Congress in the Immigration Reform and Control Act of 1986, also known as the Simpson-Mazzoli Act. It sought to control immigration by placing principal responsibility on employers; it set fines for knowingly hiring illegal **aliens**. However, it allowed employers to accept many different forms of easily forged documentation and at the same time subjected them to penalties for discriminating against legal foreign-born residents. To win political support, the act granted **amnesty** to illegal aliens who had lived in the United States since 1982. But the act failed to reduce the flow of either legal or illegal immigrants.

Today, more than a million people per year are admitted *legally* to the United States as "lawful permanent residents" (persons who have needed job skills or who have relatives who are U.S. citizens) or as "political refugees" (persons with "a well-founded fear of persecution" in their country of origin). In addition, each year more than 33 million people are awarded temporary visas to enter the United States for study, business, or tourism (see *What Do You Think?*: "Does Immigration Help or Hurt America?").

Illegal Immigration   The United States is a free and prosperous society with more than 5,000 miles of borders (2,000 with Mexico) and hundreds of international air- and seaports. In theory, a sovereign nation should be able to maintain secure borders, but in practice the United States has been unwilling and unable to do so. Estimates of illegal immigration vary widely, from the official U.S. Bureau of Immigration and Citizenship Services estimate of 400,000 per year (about 45 percent of

aliens
Persons residing in a nation who are not citizens.

amnesty
Government forgiveness of a crime, usually granted to a group of people.

WHAT DO YOU THINK?

Does Immigration Help or Hurt America?

Most Americans think that immigration in general is a good thing:

Q. On the whole, do you think immigration is a good thing or a bad thing for this country today?

Good thing	61%
Bad thing	34%
Mixed or no opinion	5%

AMERICA'S MIXED MESSAGE...

But Americans are divided as to the *effects* of immigration—whether immigrants make the United States a better place or make it worse off. On the one hand, immigrants do work that others would not do. As the National Restaurant Association's legislative affairs director says, "Restaurants, hotels, nursing homes, agriculture—a very broad group of industries—are looking for a supply of workers to remain productive." He adds that in many parts of the country, workers are not available for such jobs at any price. On the other hand, the strong demand for cheap labor is just that: the demand by employers not to have to pay as much as they would to native-born Americans.

Q. Do you think immigrants mostly help the economy by providing low-cost labor, or mostly hurt the economy by driving wages down for many Americans?

Mostly hurt	48%
Mostly help	42%
Neither	3%
Both	1%
Don't know	5%

Americans are more of one mind, though, when it comes to *illegal* immigration in particular—the 10 to 12 million persons in the United States who entered the country illegally.

A large majority of Americans agree that the U.S. government should take a tough stand on illegal immigration.

Q. When people are caught trying to enter the United States illegally, which do you think should be government policy?

Immediately send them back to their home country	61%

Allow them to appeal their case using legal representation and a court hearing	35%
Neither, don't know	4%

Q. Do you favor or oppose stricter penalties on illegal immigrants?

Favor	77%
Oppose	18%
Don't know	5%

Yet Americans are more tolerant of illegal immigrants if they meet various requirements, such as establishing how long they have lived in the United States, paying fees for residing in the U.S. illegally, and speaking the English language, among others.

Q. Which comes closer to your view about what government policy should be toward illegal immigrants currently living in the U.S. Should the government deport all illegal immigrants back to their home country, allow illegal immigrants to remain in the U.S. in order to work but for only a limited amount of time, or allow illegal immigrants to remain in the U.S. and become U.S. citizens only if they meet certain requirements over a period of time?

Deport all	24%
Remain in the U.S. in order to work	15%
Remain in the U.S. and become citizens	59%

Source: Various recent national polls reported in Public Agenda, www.publicagenda.com, and in iPoll at the Roper Center.

the legal immigration) to unofficial estimates ranging up to 3 million per year. The government estimates that about 4 million illegal immigrants currently reside in the United States; unofficial estimates range up to 15 million or more. Many illegal immigrants slip across U.S. borders or enter ports with false documentation; many more overstay tourist, worker, or student visas. The responsibility for the enforcement of immigration laws rests with Immigration and Customs Enforcement, ICE (formerly the Immigration and Naturalization Service [INS]).

As a free society, the United States is not prepared to undertake massive roundups and summary deportations of millions of illegal residents. The Fifth and Fourteenth Amendments to the U.S. Constitution require that every *person* (not just citizen) be afforded "due process of law." The government may turn back persons at the border or even hold them in detention camps. The Coast Guard may intercept boats at sea and return persons to their country of origin.[11] Aliens have no constitutional right to come to the United States. However, once in the United States, whether legally or illegally, every person is entitled to due process of law and equal protection of the laws. People are thus entitled to a fair hearing prior to any government attempt to deport them. Aliens are entitled to apply for asylum and present evidence at a hearing of their "well-founded fear of prosecution" if returned to their country. Experience has shown that the only way to reduce the flow of **illegal immigration** is to control it at the border, an expensive and difficult, but not impossible, task. Localized experiments in border enforcement have indicated that, with significant increases in personnel and technology, illegal immigration can be reduced by half or more.

illegal immigration
The unlawful entry of a person into a nation.

Immigration Reform   Comprehensive immigration reform has been the subject of intense political conflict in Washington over the past two decades. Among the conflicting interests: employers seeking to keep immigration as open as possible in order to lower their labor costs; millions of currently illegal immigrants seeking a lawful path to citizenship; and residents seeking border security and opposing amnesty for illegal immigrants. "Comprehensive" reform implies compromise among these interests. In 2007, Congress considered a comprehensive bill co-sponsored by Senators Edward M. Kennedy and John McCain that included the following major provisions: strengthening border enforcement, including funding of 700 miles of fencing along the Mexican border; granting legal status to millions of undocumented immigrants currently living in the country; providing a path to citizenship that includes criminal background checks, payment of fees, and acquiring English proficiency; establishing a temporary (two-year) guest worker program; shifting the criteria for legal immigration from family-based preferences to a greater emphasis on skills and education. But opponents of one or another of these various provisions, both Democrats and Republicans, united to defeat the bill. Nonetheless, the major provisions of this effort at comprehensive reform are now a part of the Obama administration's own immigration reform efforts.

Citizenship   Persons born in the United States are U.S. citizens. People who have been lawfully admitted into the United States and granted permanent residence, and who have resided in the United States for at least five years and in their home state for the last six months, are eligible for naturalization as U.S. citizens. Federal district courts as well as offices of the Citizenship and Immigration Services (CIS) may grant applications for citizenship. By law, the applicant must be over age eighteen, be able to read, write, and speak English, possess good moral character, and understand and demonstrate an attachment to the history, principles, and form of government of the United States (see *Politics Up Close:* "Could You Pass the Citizenship Test?").

Citizens of the United States are entitled to a **passport**, issued by the U.S. State Department upon presentation of a photo plus evidence of citizenship—a birth certificate or naturalization papers. A passport enables U.S. citizens to reenter the country after travel abroad. When traveling abroad, your U.S. passport may be

passport
Evidence of U.S. citizenship, allowing people to travel abroad and reenter the United States.

POLITICS UP CLOSE

Could You Pass the Citizenship Test?

To ensure that new citizens "understand" the history, principles, and form of government of the United States, the CIS administers a citizenship test. Below is a sample of questions from the American government section of the test. Can you answer these questions?

1. What is the supreme law of the land?
2. The idea of self-government is in the first three words of the Constitution. What are these words?
3. What do we call the first 10 amendments to the Constitution?
4. How many amendments does the Constitution have?
5. Who is in charge of the executive branch?
6. Who makes federal laws?
7. What are the two parts of the U.S. Congress?
8. How many U.S. Senators are there?
9. We elect a U.S. Senator for how many years?
10. The House of Representatives has how many voting members?
11. We elect a U.S. Representative for how many years?
12. We elect a President for how many years?
13. In what month do we vote for President?
14. If the President can no longer serve, who becomes President?
15. If both the President and the Vice President can no longer serve, who becomes President?

16. Who is the Commander in Chief of the military?
17. Who signs bills to become laws?
18. Who vetoes bills?
19. What is the highest court in the United States?
20. How many justices are on the Supreme Court?

Answers: 1. The Constitution; 2. We the People; 3. The Bill of Rights; 4. 27; 5. The President; 6. Congress; 7. The Senate and the House of Representatives; 8. 100; 9. Six; 10. 435; 11. Two; 12. Four; 13. November; 14. The Vice President; 15. The Speaker of the House; 16. The President; 17. The President; 18. The President; 19. The Supreme Court; 20. Nine

Source: Bureau of Citizenship and Immigration Services.

---

visa
A document or stamp on a passport allowing a person to visit a foreign country.

your most valuable possession. A **visa** is a document or stamp on a passport, issued by a foreign country, that allows a citizen of one nation to visit another.

Religion and Secularism in Politics

▶ 2.7 *Assess the roles of religion and secularism in U.S. politics.*

The United States is one of the most religious societies in the world. Over 90 percent of Americans report in polls that they believe in God. Over 80 percent say that prayer is part of their daily lives, and 60 percent say that they attend church at least once a month. Over 80 percent claim some religious affiliation. Evangelical Protestants are the largest single group and the fastest-growing (see Figure 2.5).

At the same time, however, most Americans are concerned about religious leaders exercising influence in political life. Most respondents say it is "not appropriate for religious leaders to talk about their political beliefs as part of their religious activities" (61 percent), "religious leaders should not try to influence how people vote in elections" (64 percent), and "religious groups should not advance their beliefs by being involved in politics and working to affect policy" (54 percent).[12]

American's religious commitments and their belief in the separation of religion from politics sometimes clash.

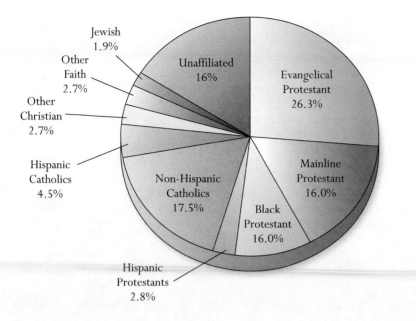

FIGURE 2.5

Religious Affiliations of Americans

Americans are a religious people. Over 80 percent claim some religious affiliation. Evangelical Protestants are the largest and fastest-growing religious group in the country.

Source: From Pew Forum on Religion & Public Life Survey of 4,000 U.S. adults in March–May 2004. Copyright © 2004 by The Pew Research Center. Reprinted by Permission.

Challenging Religion in Public Life

There is a growing divide in America between religious faith and **secular** politics on a number of key public issues. The most religious among us, as determined by frequency of church attendance and belief in the literal interpretation of the Bible, generally support limitations on abortion, including parental notification when minors seek abortions, and would prohibit "partial-birth abortions" (intact dilation and extraction). They also support abstinence in sex education; oppose same-sex marriage, support the phrase "under God" in the Pledge of Allegiance; support the display of religious symbols in public places; and generally believe that religion should play an important role in addressing "all or most of today's problems."

In contrast, challenges to religion in public life are increasingly being raised in American politics, especially in the courts. Organizations such as the American Civil Liberties Union (see *Politics Up Close*: "The American Civil Liberties Union" in Chapter 14) and Americans United for the Separation of Church and State are challenging many traditional religious practices and symbols in public life. Most of these challenges are based upon the First Amendment's "no establishment of religion" clause (see "Freedom of Religion" in Chapter 14). Among these challenges: removing "under God" from the Pledge of Allegiance and eliminating the national motto "In God We Trust" from our coins; removing religious symbols—Christmas displays, the Ten Commandments, and so on—from public places; supporting the teaching of evolution and opposing the teaching of "creationism" in the schools; opposing the use of public school vouchers to pay for students attending religious schools; supporting gay rights, including same-sex marriages; and threatening to remove tax exemptions from churches whose religious leaders endorse candidates or involve themselves in politics.

Religious/Political Alignments

Interestingly, the religious-versus-secular division on these issues does *not* depend upon *which* religion (for example, Protestants, Catholic, Jewish) that Americans identify themselves. Rather, this division appears to be more closely aligned with the *intensity* of people's religious commitments; in polls, for example, their self-identification as "born-again" or "evangelical"; their frequency of church attendance; and their agreement with statements such as "prayer is an important part of my daily life." An overwhelming majority of Americans (80 percent) say they have "old-fashioned values about family and marriage."

secular

In politics, a reference to opposition to religious practices and symbols in public life.

Christ Fellowship, an evangelical church in Palm Beach Gardens, Florida, uses multimedia and other nontraditional approaches to spread the gospel to all age groups.

Increasingly, this division between religious and secular viewpoints is coming to correspond with the division between liberals and conservatives in American politics. Religious traditionalists are more likely to describe themselves as conservatives or moderates, while secularists are more likely to describe themselves as liberal in politics.[13]

Ideologies: Liberalism and Conservatism

▶ 2.8 *Compare and contrast the main principles of conservatism and liberalism.*

An **ideology** is a consistent and integrated system of ideas, values, and beliefs. A political ideology tells us who *should* get what, when, and how; that is, it tells us who *ought* to govern and what goals they *ought* to pursue. When we use ideological terms such as *conservatism* and *liberalism*, we imply reasonably integrated sets of values and beliefs. And when we pin ideological labels on people, we imply that those people are fairly consistent in the application of these values and beliefs in public affairs. In reality, neither political leaders nor citizens always display integrated or consistent opinions; many hold conservative views on some issues and liberal views on others. Many Americans avoid ideological labeling, either by describing themselves as "moderate" or "middle-of-the-road" or by simply declining to place themselves on an ideological scale. But as Figure 2.6 shows, among those who choose an ideological label to describe their politics, conservatives consistently outnumber liberals.

Despite inconsistencies in opinion and avoidance of labeling, ideology plays an important role in American politics. Political *elites*—elected and appointed officeholders; journalists, editors, and commentators; party officials and interest-group leaders; and others active in politics—are generally more consistent in their political views than nonelites and are more likely to use ideological terms in describing politics.[14]

Modern Conservatism: Individualism plus Traditional Values   Modern **conservatism** combines a belief in free markets, limited government, and individual self-reliance in economic affairs with a belief in the value of tradition, law, and morality in social affairs. Conservatives wish to retain our historical commitments to

---

ideology
Consistent and integrated system of ideas, values, and beliefs.

Think Again

Do you consider yourself politically conservative, moderate, or liberal?

conservatism
Belief in the value of free markets, limited government, and individual self-reliance in economic affairs, combined with a belief in the value of tradition, law, and morality in social affairs.

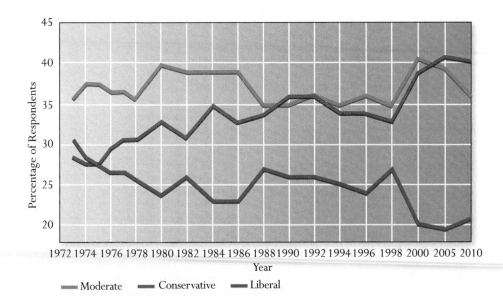

FIGURE 2.6

Americans: Liberal,
Moderate, Conservative

Americans are more likely to describe themselves as moderates or conservatives than as liberals.

Source: General Social Surveys, National Opinion Research Center, University of Chicago; updated from Gallup polls to 2010.

individual freedom from governmental controls; reliance on individual initiative and effort for self-development; a free-enterprise economy with a minimum of governmental intervention; and rewards for initiative, skill, risk, and hard work. These views are consistent with the early classical liberalism of Locke, Jefferson, and the nation's Founders, discussed at the beginning of this chapter. The result is a confusion of ideological labels: modern conservatives claim to be the true inheritors of the (classical) liberal tradition.

Conservatism is less optimistic about human nature. Traditionally, conservatives have recognized that human nature includes elements of irrationality, ignorance, hatred, and violence. Thus they have been more likely to place their faith in *law* and *traditional values* than in popular fads, trends, or emotions. To conservatives, the absence of law does not mean freedom but, rather, exposure to the tyranny of terrorism and violence. They believe that without the guidance of traditional values, people would soon come to grief through the unruliness of their passions, destroying both themselves and others. Conservatives argue that strong institutions—family, church, and community—are needed to control individuals' selfish and immoral impulses and to foster civilized ways of life.

It is important to note that conservatism in America incorporates different views of the role of government in economic versus social affairs. Conservatives generally prefer *limited noninterventionist government in economic affairs*—a government that relies on free markets to provide and distribute goods and services; minimizes its regulatory activity; limits social welfare programs to the "truly needy"; keeps taxes low; and rejects schemes to equalize income or wealth. On the other hand, conservatives would *strengthen government's power to regulate social conduct*. They support restrictions on abortion; endorse school prayer; favor a war on drugs and pornography; oppose the legitimizing of homosexuality; support the death penalty; and advocate tougher criminal penalties.

Modern Liberalism: Governmental Power to "Do Good"

Modern **liberalism** combines a belief in a strong government to provide economic security and protection for civil rights with a belief in freedom from government intervention in social conduct. Modern liberalism retains the classical liberalism commitment to individual dignity, but it emphasizes the importance of social and economic security for the whole population. In contrast to classical liberalism,

liberalism
Belief in the value of strong government to provide economic security and protection for civil rights, combined with a belief in personal freedom from government intervention in social conduct.

PEOPLE IN POLITICS

Bill O'Reilly, "The No Spin Zone"?

Bill O'Reilly assures "fair and balanced" broadcast journalism to Fox News viewers, however, O'Reilly is frequently loose with the facts; the show is more "entertainment" than "news."

He describes his popular TV show as a "no spin zone" and refers to himself as an "independent." Yet O'Reilly has emerged as the nation's most popular voice of conservatism on television.

O'Reilly boasts of an Irish Catholic working-class upbringing on Long Island. He graduated from Catholic Marist College, briefly taught in a Miami high school, and earned a master's degree from Boston University in journalism. He bounced around the country as a reporter for various TV stations, and by 1986 he had become a top correspondent for ABC News. He eventually replaced David Frost as anchor of the TV tabloid *Inside Edition*, but left that job in 1995 to earn a master's degree from the John F. Kennedy School of Government at Harvard University.

The Fox News network recruited O'Reilly to create a new evening talk show, *The O'Reilly Factor*. The show quickly grew into the most watched program on cable news, outdistancing even *Larry King Live*. And O'Reilly gave up his popular talk radio show in order to concentrate on television.

O'Reilly mixes humor with bombast. He constantly interrupts guests, both conservatives and liberals, to broadcast his own views. He is convinced that liberal "secularists" are waging war against religion, Christmas, and traditional moral values. Liberal critic and now U.S. Senator Al Franken wrote a satirical mockery of the Fox network and O'Reilly himself, entitled *Lies and the Lying Liars Who Tell Them: A Fair and Balanced Look at the Right*. O'Reilly prompted Fox News to sue, but the suit was thrown out of federal court. O'Reilly's favorite targets include Hollywood liberals, Jesse Jackson, and the American Civil Liberties Union. The occasional twinkle in his Irish eyes tempers his often venomous commentary.

which looked at governmental power as a potential threat to personal freedom, modern liberalism looks on the power of government as a positive force for eliminating social and economic conditions that adversely affect people's lives and impede their self-development. The modern liberal approves of the use of governmental power to correct the perceived ills of society (see *People in Politics*: "Barbara Boxer, Defending Liberalism in Congress"). The prevailing impulse is to "do good," to perform public services, and to assist the least fortunate in society, particularly the poor and minorities. Modern liberalism is impatient with what it sees as the slow progress of individual initiative and private enterprise toward solving socioeconomic problems, so it seeks to use the power of the national government to find solutions to society's troubles.

Modern liberalism contends that individual dignity and equality of opportunity depend in some measure on *reduction of absolute inequality* in society. Modern liberals believe that true equality of opportunity cannot be achieved where significant numbers of people are suffering from hopelessness, hunger, treatable illness, or poverty. Thus modern liberalism supports government efforts to reduce inequalities in society.

Liberals also have different views of the role of government in economic versus social affairs. Liberals generally prefer an *active, powerful government in economic affairs*— a government that provides a broad range of public services; regulates business; protects civil rights; protects consumers and the environment; provides generous unemployment, welfare, and Social Security benefits; and reduces economic inequality. But many of these same liberals would *limit the government's power to regulate social conduct.* They oppose restrictions on abortion; oppose school prayer; favor "decriminalizing" marijuana use and "victimless" offenses like public intoxication and vagrancy; support gay rights and tolerance toward alternative lifestyles; oppose government restrictions on speech, press, and protest; oppose the death

PEOPLE IN POLITICS

Barbara Boxer, Defending Liberalism in Congress

Perhaps no one has been more successful in defending liberal causes in Congress than California's outspoken U.S. senator Barbara Boxer. Her political résumé boasts awards and honors from such organizations as Planned Parenthood (family planning, reproductive health, and abortion rights), the Sierra Club (environmental causes), Mobilization against AIDS, Anti-Defamation League (civil rights), and Public Citizen (consumer affairs).

A graduate of Brooklyn College with a B.A. in economics, Boxer worked briefly as a stockbroker before moving to San Francisco, where she became a journalist and later a campaign aide to a local congressional representative. Her political career is based in Marin County, a trendy, upper-class, liberal community north of San Francisco, where she first won elected office as a member of the County Board of Supervisors. She was elected to the U.S. House of Representatives from her Marin County district in 1982 and quickly won a reputation as one of the most liberal members of the House.

When her state's liberal Democratic senator, Alan Cranston, announced he would not seek reelection to the Senate in the wake of his censure in the Keating Five affair, Boxer sought the open seat. Her opponent, conservative Republican radio and TV commentator Bruce Herschensohn, hammered at Boxer's frequent absenteeism, and her extensive use of congressional perks. But with the help of Clinton's 1992 landslide (47 to 32 percent) victory over George H. W. Bush in California, Boxer eked out a 48 to 46 percent victory over Herschensohn. Her victory, together with that of Dianne Feinstein, gave California a historical first—two women U.S. senators.

Boxer quickly emerged as a powerful force in the U.S. Senate on behalf of abortion rights. She led the Senate fight for a federal law protecting abortion clinics from obstruction by demonstrators. On the Environmental and Public Works Committee she helped block efforts to relax federal environmental regulations. She helped lead the fight for the Family Medical Leave Act, passed in the early days of the Clinton administration. She voted against the ban on partial birth abortions passed by Congress. She voted against Senate confirmation of Chief Justice John Roberts and Associate Justice Samuel Alito. She has been a strong voice in support of gay and lesbian causes; she opposed the Defense of Marriage Act and supports partnerships for same-sex couples.

Following the Democratic victory in the 2006 congressional midterm elections, Boxer assumed the Chair of the Senate Environment and Public Works Committee. She has led the battle to block oil drilling in the Arctic National Wildlife Refuge. She has led in fights to cut further emissions from power plants, to reduce energy consumption, and to curb global warming.

Boxer won a fourth term in 2010, holding off a strong challenge from Carly Fiorina, a former CEO of Hewlett-Packard. Boxer defended her liberal record and her support of the Obama agenda, while attacking her opponent's corporate record, including large-scale employee layoffs.

penalty; and strive to protect the rights of criminal defendants. Liberalism is the prevailing ideology among college professors (see Figure 2.7).

The Ideological Battlefield If Americans aligned themselves along a single liberal-conservative dimension, politics in the United States would be easier to describe, but far less interesting. We have already defined liberals as supporting a

Political Ideology of Professors

	Liberal	Middle of the Road	Conservative
All	51%	17%	28%
Humanities	76%	9%	15%
Social Sciences	72%	14%	14%
Biological Sciences	61%	17%	23%
Physical Sciences	54%	19%	26%
Engineering	40%	22%	38%
Law	36%	22%	42%
Business	31%	17%	52%

■ Liberal ■ Middle of the Road ■ Conservative

FIGURE 2.7

Ideology Among Professors

Most professors describe their politics as "liberal," especially professors in the humanities and social sciences.

Source: American Enterprise, vol. 2, July/August 1991, http:/www.TAEmag .com. Published by the American Enterprise Institute for Public Policy Research, Washington, D.C.

FIGURE 2.8

Mapping the Ideological
Battlefield

We can classify people's
views on whether they prefer
more or less government
intervention, first in economic
affairs (the vertical axis), and,
second, in social affairs (the
horizontal axis). The result is a
fourfold classification scheme
distinguishing types
(economic and social) of
liberals and conservatives.

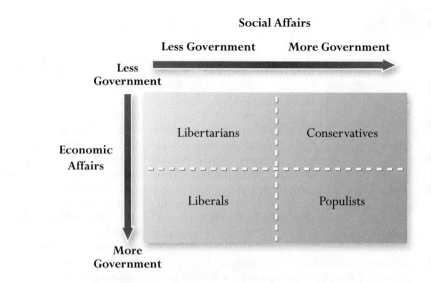

strong government in economic affairs and civil rights, but opposing government intervention in social affairs. And we have described conservatives as supporting a limited government in economic affairs and civil rights, but favoring government regulation of social conduct. Thus neither liberals nor conservatives are really consistent in their view of the role of government in society, each differentiating between economic and social affairs.

Yet some people consistently support strong government to regulate business and provide economic security, and also to closely regulate social conduct. While few people use the term *populist* to describe themselves, these people may actually make up a fairly large proportion of the electorate. Liberal politicians can appeal for their votes by stressing government intervention to provide economic security, while conservative politicians can appeal to them by stressing the maintenance of traditional social values.

libertarian
Opposing government
intervention in both economic
and social affairs, and favoring
minimal government in all
sectors of society.

And some people, often referred to as **libertarians**, oppose government intervention in *both* economic affairs and in the private lives of citizens. They are against most environmental regulations, consumer protection laws, antidrug laws, defense spending, foreign aid, and government restrictions on abortion. In other words, they favor minimal government intervention in all sectors of society.

The result may be a two-dimensional ideological battlefield—identifying more or less government intervention and separating economic from social affairs—resulting in four separate groups—liberals, conservatives, populists, and libertarians (see Figure 2.8). (See also *Controversy*: "The Libertarian Party: A Dissenting Voice," in Chapter 7).

Youth and Ideology   Young people are more likely to hold liberal views than their elders. Especially on social issues, young people age 18–24 are more likely to describe themselves as liberals (see Table 2.1). Older adults are more likely to describe themselves as conservatives on social as well as economic issues.

left
A reference to the liberal,
progressive, and/or socialist
side of the political spectrum.

Dissent in the United States

▶ 2.9 *Differentiate various political ideologies that depart from conservatism and liberalism.*

right
A reference to the
conservative, traditional,
anticommunist side of the
political spectrum.

Dissent from the principal elements of American political culture—individualism, free enterprise, democracy, and equality of opportunity—has arisen over the years from both the *left* and the *right*. The **left** generally refers to socialists and communists, but it is sometimes used to brand liberals. The **right** generally refers to fascists and extreme nationalists, although it is sometimes used to stamp conservatives.

TABLE 2.1 Ideology and Age

Younger people are more likely to describe their views as "liberal" than older people. More people describe their views as "conservative" on economic issues than on social issues.

Thinking about social issues, would you say your views on social issues are conservative, moderate, or liberal?

Age	Conservative	Moderate	Liberal
18–24	27%	36%	36%
25–38	33	34	31
39 plus	40	38	19

Thinking about economic issues, would you say your views on economic issues are conservative, moderate, or liberal?

Age	Conservative	Moderate	Liberal
18–24	33%	40%	26%
25–38	39	39	20
39 plus	47	38	12

Source: Gallup Poll reported May 20, 2003. Copyright © 2003 by The Gallup Organization.

Antidemocratic ideas have historical roots in movements that originated primarily outside America's borders. These movements have spanned the political spectrum from the far right to the far left.

Fascism   At the far-right end of this spectrum lies **fascism**, an ideology that asserts the supremacy of the state or race over individuals. The goal of fascism is unity of people, nation, and leadership—in the words of Adolf Hitler: *"Ein Volk, Ein Reich, Ein Führer"* ("One People, One Nation, One Leader"). Every individual, every interest, and every class are to be submerged for the good of the nation. Against the rights of liberty or equality, fascism asserts the duties of service, devotion, and discipline. Its goal is to develop a superior type of human being, with qualities of bravery, courage, genius, and strength. The World War II defeat of the two leading fascist regimes in history—Adolf Hitler's Nazi Germany and Benito Mussolini's fascist Italy—did not extinguish fascist ideas. Elements of fascist thought are found today in extremist movements in both the United States and Europe.

fascism
Political ideology in which the state and/or race is assumed to be supreme over individuals.

Marxism   **Marxism** arose out of the turmoil of the Industrial Revolution as a protest against social evils and economic inequalities. Karl Marx (1818–83), its founder, was not an impoverished worker but rather an upper-middle-class intellectual unable to find an academic position. Benefiting from the financial support of his wealthy colleague Friedrich Engels (1820–95), Marx spent years writing *Das Kapital* (1867), a lengthy work describing the evils of capitalism, especially the oppression of factory workers (the proletariat) and the inevitability of revolution. The two men collaborated on a popular pamphlet entitled *The Communist Manifesto* (1848), which called for a workers' revolution: "Workers of the world, unite. You have nothing to lose but your chains."

It fell to Vladimir Lenin (1870–1924) to implement Marx and Engels's revolutionary ideology in the Russian Revolution in 1917. According to **Leninism**, the key to a successful revolution is the organization of small, disciplined, hard-core groups of professional revolutionaries into a centralized totalitarian party. To explain why Marx's predictions about the ever-worsening conditions of the

Marxism
The theories of Karl Marx, among them that capitalists oppress workers and that worldwide revolution and the emergence of a classless society are inevitable.

Leninism
The theories of Vladimir Lenin, among them being that advanced capitalist countries turned toward war and colonialism to make their own workers relatively prosperous.

CONTROVERSY

Are You a Conservative or a Liberal?

Not everyone consistently takes a conservative or a liberal position on every issue. But if you find that you agree with more positions under one of the following "conservative" or "liberal" lists, you are probably ready to label yourself ideologically.

	You Are *Conservative* If You Agree That . . .	You are *Liberal* If You Agree That . . .
Economic policy	Free-market competition is better at protecting the public than government regulation.	Government should regulate business to protect the public interest.
	Taxes should be kept as low as possible.	The rich should pay higher taxes to support public services for all.
	Government welfare programs destroy incentives to work.	Government spending for social welfare is a good investment in people.
Crime	Government should place primary emphasis on providing more police and prisons and stop courts from coddling criminals.	Government should place primary emphasis on alleviating the social conditions (such as poverty and joblessness) that cause crime.
Social policy	Government should restrict abortion and not use taxpayer money for abortions.	Government should protect the right of women to choose abortion and fund abortions for poor women.
	Government should not grant preferences to anyone based on race or sex.	Government should pursue affirmative action programs on behalf of minorities and women in employment, education, and so on.
	Government should allow prayers and religious observances in schools and public places.	Government should keep religious prayers and ceremonies out of schools and public places.
National security policy	Government should pursue the "national interest" of the United States.	Government should support "human rights" throughout the world.
	Military spending must reflect a variety of new dangers in this post–Cold War period.	Military spending should be reduced now that the Cold War is over.

masses under capitalism proved untrue (workers' standards of living in Western democracies rose rapidly in the twentieth century), Lenin devised the theory of imperialism: advanced capitalist countries turned to war and colonialism, exploiting the Third World, in order to make their own workers relatively prosperous.

communism
System of government in which a single totalitarian party controls all means of production and distribution of goods and services.

Communism

Communism is the outgrowth of Marxist-Leninist ideas about the necessity of class warfare, the inevitability of a worldwide proletarian revolution, and the concentration of all power in the "vanguard of the proletariat"—the Communist Party. Communism justifies violence as a means to attain power by arguing that the bourgeoisie (the capitalistic middle class) will never voluntarily give up its control over "the means of production" (the economy). Democracy is only "window dressing" to disguise capitalist exploitation. The Communist Party justifies authoritarian single-party rule as the "dictatorship of the proletariat." In theory, after a period of rule by the Communist Party, all property will be owned by the government, and a "classless" society of true communism will emerge.

socialism
System of government involving collective or government ownership of economic enterprise, with the goal being equality of results, not merely equality of opportunity.

Socialism

Socialism shares with communism a condemnation of capitalist profit making as exploitative of the working classes. Communists and socialists agree on the "evils" of industrial capitalism: the concentration of wealth, the insensitivity of the profit motive to human needs, the insecurities and suffering brought on by the

Ideologies in Action

Liberals' concern about efforts to curtail social welfare programs reflects their support of strong government, whereas conservatives' demands for tax cuts reflect their preference for government that encourages self-reliance and individual initiative.

business cycle, the conflict of class interests, and the tendency of capitalist nations to involve themselves in imperialist wars. However, socialists are committed to the democratic process as a means of replacing capitalism with collective ownership of economic enterprise. Socialists generally reject the notion of violent revolution as a way to replace capitalism and instead advocate peaceful, constitutional roads to bring about change. Moreover, many socialists are prepared to govern in a free society under democratic principles, including freedom of speech and press and the right to organize political parties and oppose government policy. Socialism is egalitarian, seeking to reduce or eliminate inequalities in the distribution of wealth. It attempts to achieve equality of results, rather than mere equality of opportunity.

The End of History?   Much of the history of the twentieth century was the struggle between democratic capitalism and totalitarian communism. Thus the collapse of communism in Eastern Europe and the Soviet Union, symbolized by the tearing down of the Berlin Wall in 1989 as well as the worldwide movement toward free markets and democracy at the end of the twentieth century, has been labeled the **end of history**.[15] Democratic revolutions were largely inspired by the realization that free-market capitalism provided much higher standards of living than communism. The economies of Eastern Europe were falling further and further behind the economies of the capitalist nations of the West. Similar comparative observations of the successful economies of the Asian capitalist "Four Tigers"— South Korea, Taiwan, Singapore, and Hong Kong—even inspired China's communist leadership to undertake market reforms. Communism destroyed the individual's incentive to work, produce, innovate, save, and invest in the future. Under communism, production for government goals (principally a strong military) came first; production for individual needs came last. The result was long lines at stores, shoddy products, and frequent bribery of bureaucrats to obtain necessary consumer items. More important, the concentration of both economic and political power in the hands of a central bureaucracy proved to be incompatible with democracy. Communism relies on central direction, force, and repression. Communist systems curtail individual freedom and prohibit the development of separate parties and interest groups outside of government.

Capitalism does not *ensure* democracy; some capitalist nations are authoritarian. But economic freedom inspires demands for political freedom. Thus market

end of history
The collapse of communism and the worldwide movement toward free markets and political democracy.

Extremism, Left and Right

Political extremists on the left and right often have more in common than they would like to admit. Although decidedly different in their political philosophies, both members of radical left wing groups and members of white supremacist groups typically reject democratic politics and assert the supremacy of the "people" over laws, institutions, and individual rights. Gregory Johnson (left) was the catalyst for the flag-burning controversy that still rages from time to time, and the young men on the right are members of a U.S. neo-Nazi group.

reforms, initiated by communist leaders to increase productivity, led to democracy movements, and those movements eventually dismantled the communist system in Eastern Europe and the old Soviet Union.

The worldwide ideological battles of the twentieth century—notably the struggles between democracy, fascism, and communism—may no longer drive world politics. But this is not the end of history or the end of global political conflict. The principal sources of conflict in the twenty-first century are likely to be cultural and religious—a clash of civilizations.[16] Western civilization—modern, secular, and democratic—now faces challenge from the Muslim world—traditional, religious, and authoritarian. Nation states may increasingly find themselves aligned along Western versus non-Western civilizations.

Academic Radicalism   Marxism survives on campuses today largely as an academic critique of the functioning of capitalism. Contemporary Marxists argue that the institutions of capitalism have conditioned people to be materialistic, competitive, and even violent. The individual has been transformed into a one-dimensional person in whom genuine humanistic values are repressed.[17] Profitability, rather than humanistic values, remains the primary criterion for decision making in the capitalist economy, and thus profitability is the reason for poverty and misery despite material abundance. Without capitalist institutions, life would be giving, cooperative, and compassionate. Only a *radical restructuring* of social and economic institutions will succeed in liberating people from these institutions to lead humanistic, cooperative lives.

A CONSTITUTIONAL NOTE

Natural Born Versus Naturalized Citizenship

The 14th Amendment to the Constitution requires the states, and by implication the national government, to treat natural born and naturalized citizens the same: "all persons born or naturalized in the United States, and subject to the jurisdiction thereof, are citizens of the United States. . . . No State shall make or enforce any law which shall abridge the privileges or immunities of citizens of the United States. . . ." But there is one key difference between natural born and naturalized citizens written into the original Constitution of 1787: "No Person except a natural born Citizen, or a Citizen of the United States, at the time of the Adoption of this Constitution, shall be eligible to the Office of President. . . ."

Requiring that the President be born in the United States is the only constitutional difference between born and naturalized citizens. Perhaps this difference made more sense in 1787 when many aspiring politicians had only recently moved into the country. But is it relevant today? Does it deny some very qualified people the opportunity to run for the nation's highest office?

To American radicals, the problem of social change is truly monumental, because capitalist values and institutions are deeply rooted in this country. Since most people are not aware that they are oppressed and victimized, the first step toward social change is consciousness raising—that is, making people aware of their misery.

The agenda of academic radicalism has been labeled **politically correct (PC)** thinking. Politically correct thinking views American society as racist, sexist, and homophobic. Overt bigotry is not the real issue, but rather Western institutions, language, and culture, which systematically oppress and victimize women, people of color, homosexuals, and others.

Academic radicalism "includes the assumption that Western values are inherently oppressive, that the chief purpose of education is political transformation, and that all standards are arbitrary.[18] In PC thinking, "everything is political." Therefore curriculum, courses, and lectures—even language and demeanor—are judged according to whether they are politically correct or not. Universities have always been centers for the critical examination of institutions, values, and culture, but PC thinking does not really tolerate open discussion or debate. Opposition is denounced as "insensitive," racist, sexist, or worse, and intimidation is not infrequent (see *Controversy*: "Political Correctness Versus Free Speech on Campus" in Chapter 14).

politically correct (PC)
Repression of attitudes, speech, and writings that are deemed racist, sexist, homophobic (anti-homosexual), or otherwise "insensitive."

Summary

► 2.1 *Define the concept of political culture.*

The American political culture is a set of widely shared values and beliefs about who should govern, for what ends, and by what means.

Americans share many common ways of thinking about politics. Nevertheless, there are often contradictions between professed values and actual conditions, problems in applying abstract beliefs to concrete situations, and even occasional conflict over fundamental values.

► 2.2 *Outline the main principles of classic liberalism.*

Individual liberty is a fundamental value in American life. The classic liberal tradition that inspired the nation's Founders included both political liberties and economic freedoms.

► 2.3 *Differentiate among the various kinds of equality.*

Equality is another fundamental American value. The nation's Founders believed in equality before the law; yet political equality, in the form of universal voting rights, required nearly two centuries to bring about.

► 2.4 *Characterize American values related to wealth and income, the current distribution of wealth and income, and trends affecting this distribution.*

Equality of opportunity is a widely shared value; most Americans are opposed to artificial barriers of race, sex, religion, or ethnicity barring individual advancement. But equality of results is not a widely shared value; most Americans support a "floor" on income and well-being for their fellow citizens but oppose placing a "ceiling" on income or wealth.

▶ **2.5** *Analyze the relationships among social mobility, inequality, and class conflict.*

Income inequality has increased in recent years primarily as a result of economic and demographic changes. Most Americans believe that opportunities for individual advancement are still available, and this belief diminishes the potential for class conflict.

▶ **2.6** *Describe the current immigration trends and ethnic composition of the United States.*

The United States is a nation of immigrants. For many years, favoritism was granted to European immigrants, but in 1965 the national origins quota system was abolished. Today, preferences are granted to professionals, relatives of U.S. citizens, and skilled workers. About one million legal immigrants enter the country each year. Our immigration policies have resulted in a society where Latinos now outnumber African Americans and they have become the largest minority in the United States. Illegal immigration continues but it is affected by the state of the economy and the potential for finding employment.

▶ **2.7** *Assess the roles of religion and secularism in U.S. politics.*

A great majority of Americans claim religious affiliation. But there is a growing divide between religious and secular viewpoints on the role of religion in public life. Secularists have challenged many traditional religious practices and symbols, such as the words *under God* in the Pledge of Allegiance.

▶ **2.8** *Compare and contrast the main principles of conservatism and liberalism.*

Conservative and liberal ideologies in American politics present somewhat different sets of values and beliefs, even though they share a common commitment to individual dignity and private property. Generally, conservatives favor minimal government intervention in economic affairs and civil rights but support many government restrictions on social conduct. Generally, liberals favor an active, powerful government to provide economic security and protection for civil rights but oppose government restrictions on social conduct.

▶ **2.9** *Differentiate various political ideologies that depart from conservatism and liberalism.*

Many Americans who identify themselves as conservatives or liberals are not always consistent in applying their professed views. Populists are liberals on economic issues but conservative in their views on social issues. Libertarians are conservative on economic issues but liberal in their social views.

The collapse of communism in Eastern Europe and the former Soviet Union and the worldwide movement toward free markets and democracy have undermined support for socialism throughout the world. Yet Marxism survives in academic circles as a critique of the functioning of capitalism.

Chapter Test

▶ **2.1** *Define the concept of political culture.*

1. Political culture refers to
   a. the division of values and beliefs
   b. shared ideas about what is good
   c. the various subcultures in society
   d. widely shared ideas as to who should govern for what ends, and by what means

2. Variations of the prevailing values and beliefs in a society would be a good definition of
   a. political culture
   b. the liberal–conservative spectrum of opinion
   c. subcultures
   d. political philosophy

▶ **2.2** *Outline the main principles of classic liberalism.*

3. Classical liberalism includes a belief in which of the following?
   a. natural law
   b. limited government
   c. the social contract
   d. all of the above

4. The idea that a person has the right to own property and buy, sell, trade, or rent that property is associated with
   a. democratic socialism
   b. capitalism

   c. economic determinism
   d. Marxism

▶ **2.3** *Differentiate among the various kinds of equality.*

5. Those that would like to see everyone enjoying equal conditions in life regardless of talent or work would most likely support the principles of
   a. political equality
   b. equality of opportunity
   c. equality of results
   d. elitism

6. The belief that the law should apply equally to all persons is most closely associated with
   a. political equality
   b. economic equality
   c. legal equality
   d. equality of opportunity

7. The famous French observer of the early American scene, Alexis de Tocqueville, thought that the distinguishing characteristic of American political values was the belief in
   a. a mixed slave and free market economy
   b. liberty
   c. equality
   d. the pursuit of individual happiness

▶ 2.4 *Characterize American values related to wealth and income, the current distribution of wealth and income, and trends affecting this distribution.*

8. Recent rises in measurements of income inequality may be explained by
   a. the decline in the manufacturing sector
   b. demographic trends
   c. global competition
   d. all of the above

▶ 2.5 *Analyze the relationships among social mobility, inequality, and class conflict.*

9. Social mobility refers to
   a. pedestrian rights in central cities
   b. moving up the social strata of society
   c. moving down the social strata of society
   d. b and c

▶ 2.6 *Describe the current immigration trends and ethnic composition of the United States.*

10. It would be accurate to say that
    a. Hispanics are the largest minority group in America
    b. Puerto Ricans are the largest subgroup of Hispanics in the United States.
    c. most illegal immigrants are coming from Asia
    d. most illegal immigrants come from Haiti and the Caribbean

11. The principle responsibility for enforcing the immigration laws belongs with
    a. the F.B.I.
    b. the military
    c. the Immigration and Citizenship Services
    d. the U.S. Border and Frontier Control Force

▶ 2.7 *Assess the roles of religion and secularism in U.S. politics.*

12. The United States is
    a. a secular nation with a population that is largely non-religious

    b. primarily a nation founded on Catholic religious ideals
    c. a secular nation but the people are largely religious
    d. a country that does not put limitations on freedom of religion

13. Protestant religious fundamentalists would most likely be
    a. conservative Democrats
    b. conservative Republicans
    c. liberal Democrats
    d. liberal Republicans

▶ 2.8 *Compare and contrast the main principles of conservatism and liberalism.*

14. The belief in the value of free markets, limited government, and self-reliance in economic affairs would most likely be associated with
    a. conservatism
    b. liberalism
    c. socialism
    d. the works of Karl Marx

15. The belief that the government should not intervene in economic or social affairs would be consistent with
    a. liberalism
    b. libertarianism
    c. Marxism
    d. "compassionate conservatism"

▶ 2.9 *Differentiate various political ideologies that depart from conservatism and liberalism.*

16. The belief in a system of government involving the collective ownership of society's economic output is most closely associated with the values of
    a. capitalism   b. fascism
    c. socialism   d. libertarianism

17. The *End of History* refers to
    a. the rejection of communism in favor of free markets
    b. tearing down the Berlin Wall
    c. a surge toward democratic values
    d. all of the above

---

mypoliscilab EXERCISES

Apply what you learned in this chapter on MyPoliSciLab.

Read on mypoliscilab.com
eText: Chapter 2

Study and Review on mypoliscilab.com
Pre-Test
Post-Test
Chapter Exam
Flashcards

Watch on mypoliscilab.com
Video: The President Addresses School Children
Video: Facebook Privacy Concerns
Video: Who is in the Middle Class?

Explore on mypoliscilab.com
Simulation: What Are American Civic Values?
Comparative: Comparing Political Landscapes
Timeline: Major Technological Innovations that Have Changed the Political Landscape
Visual Literacy: Using the Census to Understand Who Americans Are
Visual Literacy: Who Are Liberals and Conservatives? What's the Difference?

Key Terms

political culture 25	equality of opportunity 28	illegal immigration 39	right 46
values 25	equality of results 29	passport 40	fascism 47
beliefs 25	social mobility 31	visa 40	Marxism 47
subcultures 25	class conflict 31	secular 41	Leninism 47
classical liberalism 26	class consciousness 32	ideology 42	communism 48
natural law 26	immigration policy 36	conservatism 42	socialism 48
capitalism 27	aliens 37	liberalism 43	end of history 49
legal equality 28	amnesty 37	libertarian 46	politically correct (PC) 51
political equality 28		left 46	

Suggested Readings

Ball, Terrance, and Richard Dagger. *Political Ideologies and the Democratic Ideal.* New York: Longman, 2009. An overview of the major political ideologies, their origins, and development.

Baradat, Leon P. *Political Ideologies: Their Origin and Impact.* 10th ed. New York: Longman, 2009. Text coverage of evolution of political ideologies over the past three centuries.

de Tocqueville, Alexis. *Democracy in America* (1835). Chicago: University of Chicago Press, 2000. Classic early assessment of American political culture by a French traveler.

Dolbeare, Kenneth M., and Michael S. Cummings. *American Political Thought.* 6th ed. Washington, D.C.: CQ Press, 2009. A compilation of key writings and speeches from Franklin, Madison, Adams, and Paine, to Bill Clinton, Ronald Reagan, Pat Buchanan, Al Gore and Barack Obama.

Garcia, Chris, F., and Gabriel Sanchez. *Hispanics and the U.S. Political System: Moving into the Mainstream.* New York: Longman, 2008. Historic, contemporary, and future role of Hispanics in American politics.

Herrnstein, Richard J., and Charles Murray. *The Bell Curve: Intelligence and Class Structure in American Life.* New York: Free Press, 1994. A controversial argument that success in life is mainly a result of inherited intelligence and that a very bright "cognitive elite" will continue to distance themselves from the duller masses.

Huntington, Samuel P. *The Clash of Civilizations and the Remaking of World Order.* New York: Simon & Schuster, 1996. The nation's leading political scientist assesses the state of world politics after the fall of communism. He explains how conflict between "civilizations," for example, Western versus Islamic, have replaced nations and ideologies as the driving force in global politics today.

Huntington, Samuel P. *Who We Are? The Challenges to America's National Identity.* New York: Simon & Schuster, 2004. A controversial argument that our national identity, including the English language, individualism, and respect for law, is being eroded by the problems of assimilating massive numbers of immigrants. The author argues the need to reassert the core values that make us Americans.

Jacobs, Lawrence R., and Theda Skocpol, eds. *Inequality and American Democracy.* New York: Russell Sage Foundation, 2005. A series of essays on the political consequences of growing income inequality in America.

Love, Nancy S. *Understanding Dogmas and Dreams.* 2nd ed. Washington, D.C.: CQ Press, 2006. An introduction to liberalism, conservatism, socialism, anarchism, fascism, feminism, environmentalism, and globalism.

Rycroft, Robert. *The Economics of Inequality, Discrimination, Poverty, and Mobility.* Armonk, N.Y.: M. E. Sharpe, 2009. Text survey of the economics of growing inequality as well as mobility among income classes.

Wolff, Edward N. *Top Heavy.* 2nd ed. New York: News Press, 2002. A fact-filled report on the increasing inequality of wealth in America, together with a proposal to tax wealth as well as income.

Suggested Web Sites

Americans United for Separation of Church and State www.au.org

An interest group formed to keep religion out of public places, especially schools.

American Conservative Union www.conservative.org

Conservative news and views and rankings of Congress members on conservative index.

Americans for Democratic Action www.adaction.org
> The ADA is the nation's oldest liberal political action organization.

Bill O'Reilly www.billoreilly.com
> Popular Web site for conservative views as well as promotion of O'Reilly programs, books, editorials, etc.

Bureau of Citizenship and Immigration Services (CIS)
www.immigration.gov
> Official site with information on immigration laws, citizenship requirements, etc.

Center for Equal Opportunity www.ceousa.org
> Think tank advocating equality of opportunity over equality of results.

Center for Immigration Studies www.cis.org
> Advocacy organization for strengthening enforcement of immigration law.

Family Religious Council www.frc.org
> An interest group championing religion, family, and marriage, and government support of these values.

Global Policy Forum www.globalpolicy.org
> Information on many global issues. Click to "social and economic policy" and then to "inequality of wealth and income" for cross national data.

Heritage Foundation www.heritage.org
> This think tank site includes a ranking of over 150 nations on an "Index of Economic Freedom." The U.S. ranks sixth; Hong Kong ranks first.

Immigration and Customs Enforcement (ICE) www.ice.gov
> Agency responsible for enforcement of immigration and customs laws.

Monticello www.monticello.org
> Biography, letters, and a "Day in the Life" of Thomas Jefferson.

National Association of Scholars www.nas.org
> Association of college and university professors opposed to PC restrictions on campus.

People for the American Way www.pfaw.org
> An influential interest group on the Left which, among other issues, strongly opposes religious symbols in public.

Philosophy Pages www.philosophypages.com
> History of Western philosophy and discussion of major democratic philosophers, including John Locke, Jean Jacques Rousseau, and Thomas Hobbes, among others.

Socialist Party USA http://sp-usa.org
> News and views from America's Socialist party.

U.S. Senator Barbara Boxer www.senate.gov/~boxer/
> The official Web site of U.S. Senator Barbara Boxer of California contains biographical material, information about Boxer's committee assignments, and her stands on various political issues.

Young Americans for Freedom www.yaf.com
> The "YAF" archives site contains background on the conservative organization and conservative views on key issues of the day.

Chapter Test Answer Key

1. D	4. B	7. C	10. A	13. B	16. C
2. C	5. C	8. D	11. C	14. A	17. D
3. D	6. C	9. D	12. C	15. B	

3 THE CONSTITUTION
Limiting Governmental Power

> " Ambition must be made to counteract ambition. "
>
> James Madison

Chapter Outline and Learning Objectives

Constitutional Government

▶ 3.1 *Identify the major principles of constitutionalism.*

The Constitutional Tradition

▶ 3.2 *Trace the evolution of constitutionalism in the United States.*

Troubles Confronting a New Nation

▶ 3.3 *Assess the obstacles to nationhood.*

Consensus in Philadelphia

▶ 3.4 *Outline the principles on which the Founders were in agreement.*

Conflict in Philadelphia

▶ 3.5 *Characterize areas of conflict among the Founders.*

Resolving the Economic Issues

▶ 3.6 *Analyze the economic issues that the Founders faced and the solutions they reached.*

Protecting National Security

▶ 3.7 *Trace the evolution of early American military and foreign policy.*

The Structure of the Government

▶ 3.8 *Explain how the Constitution structured the new government.*

Separation of Powers and Checks and Balances

▶ 3.9 *Analyze the separation of powers and the checks and balances established by the Constitution.*

Conflict over Ratification

▶ 3.10 *Outline the arguments made for and against ratification of the Constitution.*

A Bill of Rights

▶ 3.11 *Assess the protections provided by the Bill of Rights.*

Constitutional Change

▶ 3.12 *Determine various means through which the Constitution may be changed.*

Think about Politics

1. Was the original Constitution of 1787 a truly democratic document?
   YES ○ NO ○

2. Should citizens be able to vote directly on national policies such as prayer in public schools or doctor-assisted suicides?
   YES ○ NO ○

3. Should a large state like California, with 38 million people, elect more U.S. senators than a small state like Wyoming, with only half a million people?
   YES ○ NO ○

4. Should federal laws always supersede state laws?
   YES ○ NO ○

5. In which do you have the most trust and confidence?
   PRESIDENT ○ CONGRESS ○
   SUPREME COURT ○

6. Should the Constitution be amended to require Congress to pass only balanced budgets?
   YES ○ NO ○

7. Should the Constitution be amended to guarantee that equal rights shall not be denied based on sex?
   YES ○ NO ○

In a democracy "of the people, by the people, and for the people," who really has the power to govern? Are strong national government and personal liberty compatible? Can majorities limit individual rights? America's Founders struggled with such questions, and in resolving them established the oldest existing constitutional government.

constitutionalism
A government of laws, not people, operating on the principle that governmental power must be limited and government officials should be restrained in their exercise of power over individuals.

Constitutional Government

▶ 3.1 *Identify the major principles of constitutionalism.*

Constitutions govern government. **Constitutionalism**—a government of laws, not of people—means that those who exercise governmental power are restricted in their use of it by a higher law. If individual freedoms are to be placed beyond the reach of government and beyond the reach of majorities, then a constitution must truly limit the exercise of authority by government. It does so by setting forth individual liberties that the government—even with majority support—cannot violate.

A **constitution** legally establishes government authority. It sets up governmental bodies (such as the House of Representatives, the Senate, the presidency, and the Supreme Court in the United States). It grants them powers. It determines how their members are to be chosen. And it prescribes the rules by which they make decisions.

Constitutional decision making is deciding how to decide; that is, it is deciding on the rules for policy making. It is not policy making itself. Policies will be decided later, according to the rules set forth in the constitution.

constitution
The legal structure of a political system, establishing governmental bodies, granting their powers, determining how their members are selected, and prescribing the rules by which they make their decisions. Considered basic or fundamental, a constitution cannot be changed by ordinary acts of governmental bodies.

A constitution cannot be changed by the ordinary acts of governmental bodies; change can come only through a process of general popular consent.[1] The U.S. Constitution, then, is superior to ordinary laws of Congress, orders of the president, decisions of the courts, acts of the state legislatures, and regulations of the bureaucracies. Indeed, the Constitution is "the supreme law of the land."

The Constitutional Tradition

▶ 3.2 *Trace the evolution of constitutionalism in the United States.*

Americans are strongly committed to the idea of a written constitution to establish government and limit its powers. In fact, the Constitutional Convention of 1787 had many important antecedents.

The Magna Carta, 1215 English lords, traditionally required to finance the king's wars, forced King John to sign the Magna Carta, a document guaranteeing their feudal rights and setting the precedent of a limited government and monarchy.

Mayflower Compact
Agreement among Pilgrim colonists to establish a government, setting the precedent of government by contract among the governed.

The Mayflower Compact, 1620 Pilgrim colonists, while still aboard the *Mayflower*, signed a compact, among themselves and other passengers, establishing a "civil body politic . . . to enact just and equal laws . . . for the general good of the colony, unto which we promise all due submission and obedience." After the Pilgrims landed at Plymouth, in what is today Massachusetts, they formed a colony based on the **Mayflower Compact**, thus setting a precedent of a government established by contract among the governed.

colonial charters
Documents granted by the English Monarch to individuals, companies, and groups of settlers in the new American colonies, authorizing a degree of self-government, setting the precedent of written contracts defining governmental power.

The Colonial Charters, 1624–1732 The **colonial charters** that authorized settlement of the colonies in America were granted by royal action. For some of the colonies, the British king granted official proprietary rights to an individual, as in Maryland (granted to Lord Baltimore), Pennsylvania (to William Penn), and Delaware (also to Penn). For other colonies, the king granted royal commissions to companies to establish governments, as in Virginia, Massachusetts, New Hampshire, New York, New Jersey, Georgia, and North and South Carolina. Royal charters were granted directly to the colonists themselves only in Connecticut and Rhode Island. These colonists drew up their charters and presented them to the king, setting a precedent in America for written contracts defining governmental power.

The "Charter Oak Affair" of 1685–88 began when King James II became displeased with his Connecticut subjects and issued an order for the repeal of the Connecticut Charter. In 1687 Sir Edmund Andros went to Hartford, dissolved the colonial government, and demanded that the charter be returned. But Captain John Wadsworth hid it in an oak tree. After the so-called Glorious Revolution in England in 1688, the charter was taken out and used again as the fundamental law of the colony. Subsequent British monarchs silently acquiesced in this restoration of rights, and the affair strengthened the notion of loyalty to the constitution rather than to the king.

The Declaration of Independence, 1776 The First Continental Congress, a convention of delegates from twelve of the thirteen original colonies, came together in 1774 to protest British interference in American affairs. But the Revolutionary War did not begin until April 19, 1775. The evening before, British regular troops marched out from Boston to seize arms stored by citizens in

PEOPLE IN POLITICS

Thomas Jefferson and the Declaration of Independence

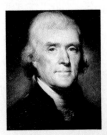

Thomas Jefferson's opening words of the Declaration of Independence provide the most succinct summary of the role of government in a free society:

We hold these truths to be self evident, that all men are created equal, that they are endowed by their Creator with certain unalienable Rights, that among these are Life, Liberty and the pursuit of Happiness. That to secure these rights Governments are instituted among Men, deriving their just powers from the consent of the governed. That whenever any Form of Government becomes destructive of these ends, it is the Right of the People to alter or abolish it, and to institute new Government. . . .

In this single paragraph, Jefferson asserts natural law and the natural rights derived from it, the social contract as the origin of government, government by the consent of the governed, and the right of revolution.

Jefferson was born into wealth and privilege in Virginia in 1743. He mastered Latin, Greek, and French and at age 14 inherited 5,000 acres of land and dozens of slaves on the plantation that eventually became known as Monticello. He graduated in 2 years from the College of William and Mary in Williamsburg with highest honors. He practiced law and served in the Virginia House of Burgesses and was sent by Virginia to the Continental Congress. There he was delegated the task of writing the Declaration of Independence, which was formally adopted July 4, 1776. He later served as governor of Virginia and as the American Minister to France, America's most important ally at the time. He did not attend the Constitutional Convention and gave only lukewarm support to the new Constitution, believing that it was flawed for lack of a Bill of Rights. After returning from France, he served as the nation's first Secretary of State under President George Washington.

Jefferson can be credited with founding the American party system. In Washington's cabinet he argued against the policies of Secretary of the Treasury Alexander Hamilton—policies that would strengthen the role of the federal government in business, banking, and commerce. He resigned from the cabinet and became the principal spokesperson for the emerging Anti-Federalists. He lost the presidency in 1796 to the Federalist candidate John Adams, but won enough electoral votes to become vice president. Prior to the election of 1800, Jefferson worked closely with Aaron Burr of New York to organize the Democratic-Republican party that would eventually become the Democratic Party. When all his party's electors cast their two votes for Jefferson and Burr, intending that Jefferson should be president and Burr vice president, the two men actually tied for the presidency. The Federalist-controlled House, after thirty-six ballots, and on the advice of Alexander Hamilton, finally elected Jefferson as president and Burr as vice president. Later Burr would kill Hamilton in a duel.

Jefferson's presidency was highlighted by the Louisiana Purchase, which doubled the size of the United States. He hoped that this purchase would provide the American people with farmland "to the hundredth and thousandth generation." When he spoke warmly of the wisdom of "the people," he was actually referring to those who owned and managed their own farms and estates. He believed that only those who owned land could make good citizens. He disliked aristocracy, but he also held the urban masses in contempt. He wanted to see the United States become a nation of free, educated, land-owning farmers. After leaving the presidency, Jefferson plunged into the planning and designing of the University of Virginia. His dream was realized with the opening of the university in 1825.

President John F. Kennedy welcomed forty-nine Nobel Prize winners to the White House in 1962, with his now famous tribute to Jefferson: "I think this is the most extraordinary collection of talent and of human knowledge that has ever been gathered together at the White House—with the possible exception of when Thomas Jefferson dined alone."

Lexington and Concord, Massachusetts. At dawn the next morning, the Minutemen—armed citizens organized for the protection of their towns—engaged the British regulars in brief battles, then harassed them all the way back to Boston. In June of that year, the Second Continental Congress appointed George Washington Commander-in-Chief of American forces and sent him to Boston to take command of the American militia surrounding the city. Still, popular support for the Revolution remained limited, and even many members of the Continental Congress hoped only to force the king and his government to make changes—not to split off from Britain.

©1989 SEATTLE POST-INTELLIGENCER
NORTH AMERICA SYNDICATE

Declaration of Independence
The resolution adopted by the Second Continental Congress on July 4, 1776, that the American colonies are to be "free and Independent states." Drafted by Thomas Jefferson, it asserts natural law, inalienable rights, government by contract, and the right of revolution. John Hancock is said to have signed first in large letters so King George III could read it without his glasses.

As this hope died, however, members of the Continental Congress came to view a formal **Declaration of Independence** as necessary to give legitimacy to their cause and establish the basis for a new nation. Accordingly, on July 2, 1776, the Continental Congress "Resolved, that these United Colonies are, and, of right, ought to be free and independent States." Thomas Jefferson had been commissioned to write a justification for the action, which he presented to the Congress on July 4, 1776. (See *People in Politics*: "Thomas Jefferson and the Declaration of Independence.") In writing the Declaration of Independence, Jefferson lifted several phrases directly from the English political philosopher John Locke asserting the rights of individuals, the contract theory of government, and the right of revolution. The declaration was signed first by the president of the Continental Congress, John Hancock. (See Declaration of Independence in the Appendix.)

The Revolutionary War effectively ended when British General Charles Cornwallis surrendered at Yorktown, Virginia, in October 1781. But even as the war was being waged, the new nation was creating the framework of its government.

Articles of Confederation
The original framework for the government of the United States, adopted in 1781 and superseded by the U.S. Constitution in 1789. It established a "firm league of friendship" among the states, rather than a government "of the people."

The Articles of Confederation, 1781–1789

Although Richard Henry Lee, a Virginia delegate to the Continental Congress, first proposed that the newly independent states form a confederation on July 6, 1776, the Continental Congress did not approve the **Articles of Confederation** until November 15, 1777, and the last state to sign them, Maryland, did not do so until March 1, 1781. Under the Articles, Congress was a single house in which each state had two to seven members but only one vote. Congress itself created and appointed executives, judges, and military officers. It also had the power to make war and peace, conduct foreign affairs, and borrow and print money. But Congress could *not* collect taxes or enforce laws directly; it had to rely on the states to provide money and enforce its laws. The United States under the Articles was really a confederation of nations. Within this "firm league of friendship" (Article III of the Articles of Confederation), the national government was thought of as an alliance of independent states, not as a government "of the people."

Troubles Confronting a New Nation

▶ 3.3 *Assess the obstacles to nationhood.*

Over two centuries ago the United States was struggling to achieve nationhood. The new U.S. government achieved enormous successes under the Articles of Confederation: it won independence from Great Britain, the world's most powerful colonial nation at the time; it defeated vastly superior forces in a prolonged war for independence; it established a viable peace and won powerful allies (notably, France) in the international community; it created an effective army and navy, established a postal system, and laid the foundations for national unity. But despite these successes in war and diplomacy, the political arrangements under the Articles were unsatisfactory to many influential groups—notably, bankers and investors who held U.S. government bonds, plantation owners, real estate developers, and merchants and shippers.

Financial Difficulties   Under the Articles of Confederation, Congress had no power to tax the people directly. Instead, Congress had to ask the states for money to pay its expenses, particularly the expenses of fighting the long and costly War of Independence with Great Britain. There was no way to force the states to make their payments to the national government. In fact, about 90 percent of the funds requisitioned by Congress from the states were never paid, so Congress had to borrow money from wealthy patriot investors to fight the war. Without the power to tax, however, Congress could not pay off these debts. Indeed, the value of U.S. governmental bonds fell to about 10 cents for every dollar's worth because few people believed the bonds would ever be paid off. Congress even stopped making interest payments on these bonds.

Commercial Obstacles   Under the Articles of Confederation, states were free to tax the goods of other states. Without the power to regulate interstate commerce, the national government was unable to protect merchants from heavy tariffs imposed on shipments from state to state. Southern planters could not ship their agricultural products to northern cities without paying state-imposed tariffs, and northern merchants could not ship manufactured products from state to state without interference. Merchants, manufacturers, shippers, and planters all wanted to develop national markets and prevent the states from imposing tariffs or restrictions on interstate trade.

Currency Problems   Under the Articles, the states themselves had the power to issue their own currency, regulate its value, and require that it be accepted in payment of debts. States had their own "legal tender" laws, which required creditors to accept state money if "tendered" in payment of debt. As a result, many forms of money were circulating: Virginia dollars, Rhode Island dollars, Pennsylvania dollars, and so on. Some states (Rhode Island, for example) printed a great deal of money, creating inflation in their currency and alienating banks and investors whose loans were being paid off in this cheap currency. If creditors refused payment in a particular state's currency, the debt could be abolished in that state. So finances throughout the states were very unstable, and banks and creditors were threatened by cheap paper money.

Western Lands   Men of property in early America actively speculated in western land. But the Confederation's military weakness along its frontiers kept the value of western lands low. A strong central government with enough military power to oust the British from the Northwest and to protect western settlers against Indian attacks could open the way for the development of the American West. The

A Weakness Exposed

In an attempt to prevent the foreclosure of farms by creditors, Revolutionary War veteran Daniel Shays led an armed mass of citizens in a march on a western Massachusetts courthouse. This uprising, which came to be known as Shays's Rebellion, exposed the Confederation's military weakness and increased support for a strong central government.

protection and settlement of western land would cause land values to skyrocket and make land speculators rich. Moreover, under the Articles of Confederation each state lay claim to western lands. Indeed, Maryland's ratification of the Articles was withheld until the states with claims to lands west of the Appalachians were ceded to Congress in 1781 for "the good of the whole."

Shays's Rebellion
An armed revolt in 1786, led by a Revolutionary War Officer Daniel Shays, protesting the discontent of small farmers over debts and taxes, and raising concerns about the ability of the U.S. government under the Articles of Confederation to maintain internal order.

Annapolis Convention
A 1786 meeting at Annapolis, Maryland, to discuss interstate commerce, which recommended a larger convention—the Constitutional Convention of 1787.

Civil Disorder   In several states, debtors openly revolted against tax collectors and sheriffs attempting to repossess farms on behalf of creditors who held unpaid mortgages. The most serious rebellion broke out in the summer of 1786 in western Massachusetts, where a band of 2,000 insurgent farmers captured the courthouses in several counties and briefly held the city of Springfield. Led by Daniel Shays, a veteran of the Revolutionary War battle at Bunker Hill, the insurgent army posed a direct threat to investors, bankers, creditors, and tax collectors by burning deeds, mortgages, and tax records to wipe out proof of the farmers' debts. Shays's Rebellion, as it was called, was finally put down by a small mercenary army, paid for by well-to-do citizens of Boston.

Reports of **Shays's Rebellion** filled the newspapers of the large Eastern cities. George Washington, Alexander Hamilton, James Madison, and many other prominent Americans wrote their friends about it. The event galvanized property owners to support the creation of a strong central government capable of dealing with "radicalism." Only a strong central government, they wrote one another, could "insure domestic tranquility," guarantee "a republican form of government," and protect property "against domestic violence." It is no accident that all of these phrases appear in the Constitution of 1787.

The Road to the Constitutional Convention

In the spring of 1785, some wealthy merchants from Virginia and Maryland met at Alexandria, Virginia, to try to resolve a conflict between the two states over commerce and navigation on the Potomac River and Chesapeake Bay. George Washington, the new nation's most prominent citizen, took a personal interest in the meeting. As a wealthy plantation owner and a land speculator who owned more than 30,000 acres of land upstream on the Potomac, Washington was keenly interested in commercial problems under the Articles of Confederation. He lent his great prestige to the Alexandria meeting by inviting the participants to his house at Mount Vernon. Out of this conference came the idea for a general economic conference for all of the states, to be held in Annapolis, Maryland, in September 1786.

The **Annapolis Convention** turned out to be a key stepping-stone to the Constitutional Convention of 1787. Instead of concentrating on commerce and navigation between the states, the delegates at Annapolis, including Alexander Hamilton and James Madison, called for a general constitutional convention to suggest remedies to what they saw as defects in the Articles of Confederation.

On February 21, 1787, the Congress called for a convention to meet in Philadelphia for the "sole and express purpose" of *revising* the Articles of Confederation and reporting to the Congress and the state legislatures "such alterations and provisions therein as shall, when agreed to in Congress and confirmed by the states, render the federal Constitution adequate to the exigencies of government and the preservation of the union." Notice that Congress

Independence Hall in Philadelphia
The meeting place of the second Continental Congress in 1776 and later the Constitutional Convention in 1787. Now a major tourist attraction in Philadelphia.

did not authorize the convention to write a new constitution or to call constitutional conventions in the states to ratify a new constitution. State legislatures sent delegates to Philadelphia expecting that their task would be limited to revising the Articles and that revisions would be sent back to Congress and state legislatures for their approval. But that is not what happened.

The Nation's Founders   The fifty-five delegates to the Constitutional Convention, which met in Philadelphia in the summer of 1787, quickly discarded the congressional mandate to merely "revise" the Articles of Confederation. The Virginia delegation, led by James Madison, arrived before a quorum of seven states had assembled and used the time to draw up an entirely new constitutional document. After the first formal session opened on May 25 and George Washington was elected president of the convention, the Virginia Plan became the basis of discussion. Thus, at the very beginning of the convention, the decision was made to scrap the Articles of Confederation altogether, write a new constitution, and form a new national government.[2]

The Founders were very confident of their powers and abilities. They had been selected by their state legislatures (only Rhode Island, dominated by small farmers, refused to send a delegation). When Thomas Jefferson, then serving in the critical post of ambassador to France (the nation's military ally in the Revolutionary War), first saw the list of delegates, he exclaimed, "It is really an assembly of demigods." Indeed, among the nation's notables, only Jefferson and John Adams (then serving as ambassador to England) were absent. The eventual success of the convention, and the ratification of the new Constitution, resulted in part from the enormous prestige, experience, and achievements of the delegates themselves.

Above all, the delegates at Philadelphia were cosmopolitan. They approached political, economic, and military issues from a "continental" point of view. Unlike most Americans in 1787, their loyalties extended beyond their states. They were truly nationalists.[3]

Consensus in Philadelphia

▶ 3.4 *Outline the principles on which the Founders were in agreement.*

The Founders shared many ideas about government, based on **the Enlightenment**. We often focus our attention on *conflict* in the Convention of 1787 and the compromises reached by the participants, but the really important story of the Constitution is the *consensus* that was shared by these men of influence.

Natural Rights to Liberty and Property   The Founders had read John Locke and absorbed his idea that the purpose of government is to protect individual liberty and property. (See *People in Politics*: "John Locke, Guiding the Founders.") They believed in a **natural law**, superior to any human-made laws, that endowed each person with certain **inalienable rights**—the rights to life, liberty, and property. They believed that all people were equally entitled to these rights. Most of them, including slave owners George Washington and Thomas Jefferson, understood that the belief in personal liberty conflicted with the practice of slavery and found the inconsistency troubling.

Social Contract   The Founders believed that government originated in an implied contract among people. People agreed to establish government, obey laws, and pay taxes in exchange for protection of their natural rights. This **social contract** gave government its legitimacy—a legitimacy that rested on the consent of the governed, not with gods or kings or force. If a government violated individual liberty, it broke the social contract and thus lost its legitimacy.

the Enlightenment
Also known as the Age of Reason, a philosophical movement in eighteenth-century Western thought based on a belief in reason and the capacities of individuals, a faith in a scientific approach to knowledge, and a confidence in human progress.

✔ *Think* Again

Was the original Constitution of 1787 a truly democratic document?

natural law
The law that would govern humans in a state of nature before governments existed.

inalienable rights
The rights of all people derived from natural law and not bestowed by governments, including the rights to life, liberty, and property.

social contract
The idea the government originates from an implied contract among people who agree to obey laws in exchange for the protection of their natural rights.

PEOPLE IN POLITICS

John Locke, Guiding the Founders

The English political philosopher John Locke had a profound influence on America's founders. Indeed, the Declaration of Independence may be thought of as a restatement of Locke's basic ideas. Writing in 1690, Locke rejected the notion of the divine right of kings to rule and asserted the rights of human beings who are "by nature free, equal, and independent" to establish their own government by "social contract" to gain security from an unstable "state of nature." In other words, people consent to be governed to protect themselves and their property. But if the government they create becomes arbitrary, enslaves its people, or takes away their property, then the people have the "right of revolution" against such a government. Locke had been read by most of the Founders, who accepted his ideas of a "social contract" as the origin of government, and even a "right of revolution" as a last resort to a despotic government.

Representative Government   Although most of the world's governments in 1787 were hereditary monarchies, the Founders believed the people should have a voice in choosing their own representatives in government. They opposed hereditary aristocracy and titled nobility. Instead, they sought to forge a republic. **Republicanism** meant government by representatives of the people. The Founders expected the masses to consent to be governed by their leaders—men of principle and property with ability, education, and a stake in the preservation of liberty. The Founders believed the people should have only a limited role in directly selecting their representatives: they should vote for members of the House of Representatives, but senators, the president, and members of the Supreme Court should be selected by others more qualified to judge their ability.

republicanism
Government by representatives of the people rather than directly by the people themselves.

Limited Government   The Founders believed unlimited power was corrupting and a concentration of power was dangerous. They believed in a written constitution that limited the scope of governmental power. They also believed in dividing power within government by creating separate bodies able to check and balance one another's powers.

Nationalism   Most important, the Founders shared a belief in **nationalism**—a strong and independent national (federal) government with power to govern directly, rather than through state governments. They sought to establish a government that would be recognized around the world as representing "We the people of the United States." Not everyone in America shared this enthusiasm for a strong federal government; indeed, opposition forces, calling themselves Anti-Federalists, almost succeeded in defeating the new Constitution. But the leaders meeting in Philadelphia in the summer of 1787 were convinced of the need for a strong central government that would share power with the states.

nationalism
Belief that shared cultural, historical, linguistic, and social characteristics of a people justify the creation of a government encompassing all of them and that the resulting nation-state should be independent and legally equal to all other nation-states.

Conflict in Philadelphia

▶ 3.5 *Characterize areas of conflict among the Founders.*

Consensus on basic principles of government was essential to the success of the Philadelphia convention. But conflict over the implementation of these principles not only tied up the convention for an entire summer but also later threatened to prevent the states from ratifying, or voting to approve, the document the convention produced.

Representation   Representation was the most controversial issue in Philadelphia. Following the election of George Washington as president of the convention,

TABLE 3.1 Constitutional Compromise

A Senate with equal representation according to each state and a House with representation based on population, and a requirement that both bodies must approve legislation before it is enacted into law, was a political compromise between large and small states reached at the Constitutional Convention of 1787.

The Virginia Plan	The New Jersey Plan	The Connecticut Compromise / The Constitution of 1787
Two-house legislature, with the lower house directly elected based on state population and the upper house elected by the lower.	One-house legislature, with equal state representation, regardless of population.	Two-house legislature, with the House directly elected based on state population and the Senate selected by the state legislatures; two senators per state, regardless of population.
Legislature with broad power, laws including veto power over passed by the state legislatures.	Legislature with the same power as under the Articles of Confederation, plus the power to levy some taxes and to regulate commerce.	Legislature with broad power, including the power to tax and to regulate commerce.
President and cabinet elected by the legislature.	Separate multiperson executive, elected by the legislature, removable by petition from a majority of the state governors.	President chosen by an Electoral College.
National judiciary elected by the legislature.	National judiciary appointed by the executive.	National judiciary appointed by the president and confirmed by the Senate.
"Council of Revision" with the power to veto laws of the legislature.	National Supremacy Clause similar to that found in Article VI of the 1787 Constitution.	National Supremacy Clause: the Constitution is "the supreme Law of the Land."

Governor Edmund Randolph of Virginia rose to present a draft of a new constitution. This Virginia Plan called for a legislature with two houses: a lower house chosen by the people of the states, with representation according to population and an upper house to be chosen by the lower house (see Table 3.1). Congress was to have the broad power to "legislate in all cases to which the separate States are incompetent, or in which the harmony of the United States may be interrupted." Congress was to have the power to nullify state laws that it believed violated the Constitution, thus ensuring the national government's supremacy over the states. The Virginia Plan also proposed a form of **parliamentary government**, in which the legislature (Congress) chose the principal executive officers of the government as well as federal judges. Finally, the Virginia Plan included a curious "council of revision," with the power to veto acts of Congress.

Delegates from New Jersey and Delaware objected strongly to the great power given to the national government in the Virginia Plan, the larger representation it proposed for the more populous states, and the plan's failure to recognize the role of the states in the composition of the new government. After several weeks of debate, William Paterson of New Jersey submitted a counterproposal.[4] The New Jersey Plan called for a single-chamber Congress in which each state, regardless of its population, had one vote, just as under the Articles of Confederation. But unlike the Articles, the New Jersey Plan proposed separate executive and judicial branches of government and the expansion of the powers of Congress to include levying taxes and regulating commerce. Moreover, the New Jersey Plan included a National Supremacy Clause, declaring that the Constitution and federal laws would supersede state constitutions and laws.

Debate over representation in Congress raged into July 1787. At one point, the convention actually voted for the Virginia Plan, 7 votes to 3, but without New York, New Jersey, and Delaware, the new nation would not have been viable.

parliamentary government
A government in which power is concentrated in the legislature, which chooses from among its members a prime minister and cabinet.

PEOPLE IN POLITICS

George Washington, Founder of a Nation

From the time he took command of the American Revolutionary forces in 1775 until he gave his Farewell Address to the nation in 1796 and returned to his Mount Vernon plantation, George Washington (1732–99) was, indeed, "First in war, first in peace, first in the hearts of his countrymen." His military success, combined with his diplomacy and practical political acumen, gave him overwhelming moral authority, which he used to inspire the Constitutional Convention, to secure the ratification of the Constitution, and then to guide the new nation through its first years.

Washington was raised on a Virginia plantation and inherited substantial landholdings, including his Mount Vernon plantation on the Potomac River. He began his career as a surveyor. His work took him deep into the wilderness of America's frontier. This experience later served him well when, at age 21, he was appointed to be an officer in the Virginia militia. In 1754 he led a small force toward the French Fort Duquesne, but after a brief battle at makeshift "Fort

Necessity" he was obliged to retreat. In 1755 British Major General Edward Braddock asked the young militia officer to accompany his heavy regiments on a campaign to dislodge the French from Fort Duquesne. Braddock disregarded Washington's warnings about concealed ways of fighting in the New World; Braddock's parading redcoat forces were ambushed by the French and Indians near Pittsburgh, and the general was killed. Washington rallied what remained of the British forces and led them in a successful retreat back to Virginia.

Washington was viewed by Virginians as a hero, and at age 22 he was appointed by the Virginia Assembly "Colonel of the Virginia Regiment and Commander in Chief of all Virginia Forces." But regular British officers ridiculed the militia forces and asserted their authority over Washington. British General John Forbes occupied Fort Duquesne, renamed it Fort Pitt, and gave Washington's men the task of garrisoning it.

In 1759, having completed his service in the French and Indian Wars, Washington left his military post and returned to plantation life. He married a wealthy widow, Martha Custis, expanded his plantation holdings, and prospered in western land speculation.

Connecticut Compromise
A constitutional plan that merged elements of a Virginia plan and a New Jersey plan into the present arrangement of the U.S. Congress: one house in which each state has an equal number of votes (the Senate) and one house in which states' votes are based on population (the House of Representatives).

Eventually, Roger Sherman of Connecticut came forward with a compromise. This **Connecticut Compromise**—sometimes called the Great Compromise—established two houses of Congress: in the upper house, the Senate, each state would have two members regardless of its size; in the lower body, the House of Representatives, each state would be represented according to population. Members of the House would be directly elected by the people; members of the Senate would be selected by their state legislatures. Legislation would have to pass both houses to be enacted. This compromise was approved by the convention on July 16.

Slavery   Another conflict absorbing the attention of the delegates was slavery. In 1787 slavery was legal everywhere except in Massachusetts. Nevertheless, the delegates were too embarrassed to use the word *slave* or *slavery* in their debates or in the Constitution itself. Instead, they referred to "other persons" and "persons held to service or labour."

Delegates from the Southern states, where slaves were a large proportion of the population, believed slaves should be counted in representation afforded the states, but not counted if taxes were to be levied on a population basis. Delegates from the Northern states, with small slave populations, believed that "the people" counted for representation purposes should include only free persons. The Connecticut Plan included the now-infamous **Three-Fifths Compromise**: three-fifths of the slaves of each state would be counted for purposes both of representation in the House of Representatives and for apportionment for direct taxes.

Three-Fifths Compromise
A compromise in the Constitutional Convention of 1787 between pre- and slave states in which slaves would be counted as three-fifths of a person for both taxation and representation.

Slave owners also sought protection for their human "property" in the Constitution itself. They were particularly concerned about slaves running away to other states and claiming their freedom. So they succeeded in writing into the Constitution (Article IV, Section 2) a specific guarantee: "No person held to Service or Labour in one State . . .

The Virginia legislature elected Washington to attend the First Continental Congress in September 1774. Washington was the most celebrated veteran of the French and Indian Wars who was still young enough (42) to lead military forces in a new struggle. John Adams of Massachusetts was anxious to unite the continent in the coming contest, and he persuaded the Second Continental Congress to give the Virginian command of the American Revolutionary forces surrounding the British Army in Boston in 1775.

Throughout the Revolutionary War Washington persevered by employing many of the tactics later defined as the principles of guerrilla warfare. By retreating deep into Pennsylvania's Valley Forge, Washington avoided defeat and saved his army. His bold Christmas night attack against Hessian troops at Trenton, New Jersey, encouraged French intervention on America's behalf. Slowly, Washington was able to wear down the British resolve to fight. In the end, he succeeded in trapping the British at Yorktown, Virginia. Assisted by a French naval blockade, he accepted the surrender of Lord Cornwallis and 8,000 of his men on October 19, 1781.

Perhaps Washington's greatest contribution to democratic government occurred in 1783 in Newburgh, New York, near West Point, where the veterans of his Continental Army were encamped. Despite their hardships and ultimate victory in the Revolutionary War, these soldiers remained unpaid by Congress. Indeed, Congress ignored a series of letters, known as the Newburgh Addresses, that threatened military force if Congress continued to deny benefits to the veterans. Washington was invited to Newburgh by officers who hoped he would agree to lead a military coup against the Congress. But when Washington mounted the platform he denounced the use of force and the "infamous propositions" contained in their earlier addresses to Congress. There is little doubt that he could have chosen to march on the Congress with his veteran army and install himself as military dictator. World history is filled with revolutionary army leaders who did so. But Washington chose to preserve representative government.

One of the few noncontroversial decisions of the Constitutional Convention in 1787 was the selection of George Washington to preside over the meetings. He took little part in the debates; however, his enormous prestige helped to hold the convention together and later to win support for the new Constitution.

escaping into another, shall . . . be discharged from such Service or Labour, but shall be delivered up on Claim of the Party to whom such Service or Labour may be due."

Yet another compromise dealt with the slave trade. The capture, transportation, and "breaking in" of African slaves was considered a nasty business, even by Southern planters. Many wealthy Maryland and Virginia plantations were already well supplied with slaves and thus could afford the luxury of conscience to call for an end to slave importation. But other planters from the less-developed Southern states, particularly South Carolina and Georgia, wanted additional slave labor. The final compromise prohibited the slave trade—but not before the year 1808, thereby giving the planters twenty years to import all the slaves they needed before the slave trade ended.

Voter Qualifications   Another important conflict centered on qualifications for voting and holding office in the new government. Most of the delegates believed that voters as well as officeholders should be men of property. (Only Benjamin Franklin went so far as to propose universal *male* suffrage.) But delegates argued over the specific wording of property qualifications, their views on the subject reflecting the source of their own wealth. Merchants, bankers, and manufacturers objected to making the ownership of a certain amount of land a qualification for officeholding. James Madison, a plantation owner himself, was forced to admit that "landed possessions were no certain evidence of real wealth. Many enjoyed them who were more in debt than they were worth."

After much debate, the convention approved a constitution without any expressed property qualifications for voting or holding office, except those that the states might impose themselves: "The Electors in each State shall have the Qualifications requisite for Electors of the most numerous Branch of the State Legislature." At the time, every state had property qualifications for voting, and

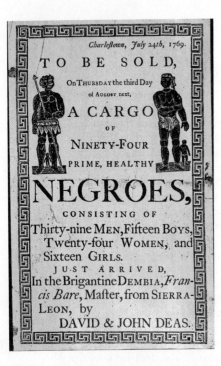

Slavery in the Constitution

Slavery was protected in the Constitution as written in 1787. The buying and selling of slaves was common at the time in the Southern states. The slave trade from Africa to America was given protection for 20 years, until 1808.

taxes
Compulsory payments to the government.

tariff
Tax imposed on imported products (also called a customs duty).

women were not permitted to vote or hold office. (The New Jersey Constitution of 1776 enfranchised women as well as men who owned property, but in 1787 a new state law limited the vote to "free white male citizens.")

Resolving the Economic Issues

▶ **3.6** *Analyze the economic issues that the Founders faced and the solutions they reached.*

The Founders were just as concerned with "who gets what, when, and how" as today's politicians are. Important economic interests were at stake in the Constitution. Historian Charles A. Beard pointed out that the delegates to the Constitutional Convention were men of wealth: planters, slaveholders, merchants, manufacturers, shippers, bankers and investors, and land speculators. Moreover, most of the delegates owned Revolutionary War bonds that were now worthless and would remain so unless the national government could obtain the tax revenues to pay them off[5] (see *A Conflicting View*: "An Economic Interpretation of the Constitution"). But it is certainly not true that the Founders acted only out of personal interest. Wealthy delegates were found on both sides of constitutional debates, arguing principles as well as economic interests.[6]

Levying Taxes   A central purpose of the Constitution was to enable the national government to levy its own **taxes**, so that it could end its dependence on state contributions and achieve financial credibility. The very first power given to Congress in Article I, Section 8, is the power to tax: "The Congress shall have Power to lay and collect Taxes, Duties, Imposts and Excises, to pay the Debts and provide for the common Defence and general Welfare."

The financial credit of the United States and the interests of Revolutionary War bondholders were guaranteed by Article VI in the Constitution, which specifically declared that the new government would be obligated to pay the debts of the old government. Indeed, the nation's first secretary of the treasury, Alexander Hamilton, made repayment of the national debt the first priority of the Washington administration.

The original Constitution placed most of the tax burden on consumers in the form of **tariffs** on goods imported into the United States. For more than a century, these tariffs provided the national government with its principal source of revenue. Tariffs were generally favored by American manufacturers, who wished to raise the price paid for foreign goods to make their home-produced goods more competitive. No taxes were permitted on *exports*, a protection for southern planters, who exported most of their tobacco and, later, cotton. Direct taxes on individuals were prohibited (Article I, Section 2) except in proportion to *population*. This provision prevented the national government from levying direct taxes in proportion to income until the 16th Amendment (income tax) was ratified in 1913.

The power to tax and spend was given to Congress, not to the president or executive agencies. Instead, the Constitution was very specific: "No Money shall

The Value of a Dollar

Under the Articles of Confederation, each state issued its own currency. Differences in currency regulation from state to state led to financial uncertainty and inflation. By creating a national currency and putting the national government in charge of the money supply, the Founders hoped to restore stability and control inflation.

be drawn from the Treasury, but in Consequence of Appropriations made by Law." This is the constitutional basis of Congress's "power of the purse."

Regulating Commerce   The new Constitution gave Congress the power to "regulate Commerce with foreign Nations, and among the several States" (Article I, Section 8), and it prohibited the states from imposing tariffs on goods shipped across state lines (Article I, Section 10). This power created what we call today a **common market**; it protected merchants against state-imposed tariffs and stimulated trade among the states. States were also prohibited from "impairing the Obligation of Contracts"—that is, passing any laws that would allow debtors to avoid their obligations to banks and other lenders.

common market
Unified trade area in which all goods and services can be sold or exchanged free from customs or tariffs.

Protecting Money   The Constitution also ensured that the new national government would control the money supply. Congress was given the power to coin money and regulate its value. More important, the states were prohibited from issuing their own paper money, thus protecting bankers and creditors from the repayment of debts in cheap state currencies. (No one wanted to be paid for goods or labor in Rhode Island's inflated dollars.) If only the national government could issue money, the Founders hoped, inflation could be minimized.

Protecting National Security

▶ 3.7 *Trace the evolution of early American military and foreign policy.*

At the start of the Revolutionary War, the Continental Congress had given George Washington command of a small regular army—"Continentals"—paid for by Congress, and also had authorized him to take command of state militia units. During the entire war, most of Washington's troops had been state militia. (The "militia" in those days was composed of every free adult male; each was expected to bring his own gun.) Washington himself had frequently decried the militia units as undisciplined, untrained, and unwilling to follow his orders. He wanted the new United States to have a *regular* army and navy, paid for by the Congress with its new taxing power, to back up the state militia units.

War and the Military Forces   Congress was authorized to "declare War," to raise and support a regular army and navy, and to make rules regulating these forces. It was also authorized to call up the militia, as it had done in the Revolution, in order to "execute the Laws of the Union, suppress Insurrections and repel Invasions." When the militia are called into national service, they come under the rule of Congress and the command of the president.

The United States relied primarily on militia—citizen-soldiers organized in state units—until World War I. The regular U.S. Army, stationed in coastal and frontier forts, directed most of its actions against Native Americans. The major actions in America's nineteenth-century wars—the War of 1812 against the British, the Mexican War of 1846–48, the Civil War in 1861–65, and the Spanish-American War in 1898—were fought largely by citizen-soldiers from these state units.

Commander-in-Chief   Following the precedent set in the Revolutionary War, the new president, whom everyone expected to be George Washington, was made "Commander-in-Chief of the Army and Navy of the United States, and of the Militia of the several States, when called into the actual Service of the United States." Clearly, there is some overlap in responsibility for national defense: Congress has the power to declare war, but the president is Commander-in-Chief. During the next two centuries, the president would order U.S. forces into 200 or more military actions, but Congress would pass an official Declaration of War only five times. Conflict

A CONFLICTING VIEW

An Economic Interpretation of the Constitution

Charles Beard, historian and political scientist, provided the most controversial historical interpretation of the origin of American national government in his landmark book, *An Economic Interpretation of the Constitution of the United States* (1913). Not all historians agree with Beard's economic interpretation, but all concede that it is a milestone in understanding the U.S. Constitution. Beard closely studied unpublished financial records of the U.S. Treasury Department and the personal letters and financial accounts of the fifty-five delegates to the Philadelphia convention. He concluded that they represented the following five economic interest groups, each of which benefited from specific provisions of the Constitution:

- **Public security interests** (persons holding U.S. bonds from the Revolutionary War; thirty-seven of the fifty-five delegates). The taxing power was of great benefit to the holders of public securities, particularly when it was combined with the provision in Article VI that "all Debts contracted and Engagements entered into, before the Adoption of this Constitution, shall be as valid against the United States under this Constitution, as under the Confederation." That is, the national government would be obliged to pay off all those investors who held U.S. bonds, and the taxing power would give the national government the ability to do so on its own.

- **Merchants and manufacturers** (persons engaged in shipping and trade; eleven of the fifty-five delegates). The Interstate Commerce Clause, which eliminated state control over commerce, and the provision in Article I, Section 9, which prohibited the states from taxing exports, created a free-trade area, or "common market," among the thirteen states.

- **Bankers and investors** (twenty-four of fifty-five delegates). Congress was given the power to make bankruptcy laws, to coin money and regulate its value, to fix standards of weights and measures, to punish counterfeiting, to establish post offices and post roads, to pass copyright and patent laws to protect authors and inventors, and

to punish piracies and felonies committed on the high seas. Each of these powers is a specific asset to bankers and investors as well as merchants, authors, inventors, and shippers.

- **Western land speculators** (persons who purchased large tracts of land west of the Appalachian Mountains; fourteen of the fifty-five delegates). If western settlers were to be protected from the Indians, and if the British were to be persuaded to give up their forts in Ohio and open the way to American westward expansion, the national government could not rely on state militias but must have an army of its own. Western land speculators welcomed the creation of a national army that would be employed primarily as an Indian-fighting force over the next century.

- **Slave owners** (fifteen of the fifty-five delegates). Protection against domestic insurrection also appealed to the Southern slaveholders' deep-seated fear of a slave revolt. The Constitution permitted Congress to outlaw the *import of slaves* after the year 1808. But most Southern planters were more interested in protecting their existing property and slaves than they were in extending the slave trade, and the Constitution provided an explicit advantage to slaveholders in Article IV, Section 2 (later revoked by the 13th Amendment, which abolished slavery), by specifically requiring the forced return of slaves who might escape to free states.

Beard argued that the members of the Philadelphia convention who drafted the Constitution were, with a few exceptions, immediately, directly, and personally interested in, and derived economic advantages from, the establishment of the new system. But many historians disagree with Beard's emphasis on the economic motives of the Founders. The Constitution, they point out, was adopted in a society that was fundamentally democratic, and it was adopted by people who were primarily middle-class property owners, especially farmers, rather than owners of businesses. The Constitution was not just an economic document, although economic factors were certainly important.

---

between the president and Congress over war-making powers continues to this day (see the section "Commander-in-Chief" in Chapter 11).

Foreign Affairs   The national government also assumed full power over foreign affairs and prohibited the states from entering into any "Treaty, Alliance, or Confederation." The Constitution gave the president, not Congress, the power to "make Treaties" and "appoint Ambassadors." However, the Constitution stipulated that the president could do these things only "by and with the Advice and Consent of the Senate," indicating an unwillingness to allow the president to act autonomously in these matters. The Senate's power to "advise and consent" to

The president's role as Commander-in-Chief was written into the Constitution with George Washington in mind. Pictured here are wartime presidents Franklin D. Roosevelt (WWII), Lyndon B. Johnson (Vietnam), and Barack Obama (greeting troops in Baghdad, Iraq, 2009).

treaties and appointments, together with the congressional power over appropriations, gives the Congress important influence in foreign affairs. Nevertheless, the president remains the dominant figure in this arena.

The Structure of the Government

▶ 3.8 *Explain how the Constitution structured the new government.*

The Constitution that emerged from the Philadelphia convention on September 17, 1787, founded a new government with a unique structure. That structure was designed to implement the Founders' beliefs in nationalism, limited government, republicanism, the social contract, and the protection of liberty and property. The Founders were realists; they did not have any romantic notions about the wisdom and virtue of "the people." James Madison wrote, "A dependence on the people is, no doubt, the primary control on the government, but experience has taught mankind the necessity of auxiliary precautions." The key structural arrangements in the Constitution—national supremacy, federalism, republicanism, separation of powers, checks and balances, and judicial review—all reflect the Founders' desire to create a strong national government while at the same time ensuring that it would not become a threat to liberty or property.

Think
Again

Should a large state like California, with 38 million people, elect more U.S. senators than a small state like Wyoming, with only half a million people?

National Supremacy Clause
The clause in Article VI of the U.S. Constitution declaring the Constitution and federal laws "the supreme Law of the Land" superior to state laws and constitutions and requiring state judges to be bound thereby.

✓ *Think*
Again

Should federal laws always supercede state laws?

National Supremacy

The heart of the Constitution is the **National Supremacy Clause** of Article VI:

> This Constitution, and the Laws of the United States which shall be made in Pursuance thereof, and all Treaties made, or which shall be made, under the Authority of the United States, shall be the supreme Law of the Land, and the Judges in every State shall be bound thereby, any Thing in the Constitution or Laws of any State to the Contrary notwithstanding.

This sentence ensures that the Constitution itself is the supreme law of the land and that laws passed by Congress supersede state laws. This National Supremacy Clause establishes the authority of the Constitution and the U.S. government. (See *Controversy:* "The Supremacy Clause at Work: Marijuana for Medical Use?")

Federalism

The Constitution *divides power* between the nation and the states (see Chapter 4). It recognizes that both the national government and the state governments have independent legal authority over their own citizens: both can pass their own laws, levy their own taxes, and maintain their own courts. The states have an important role in the selection of national officeholders—in the apportionment of congressional seats and in the allocation of electoral votes for president. Most important, perhaps, both the Congress and three-quarters of the states must consent to changes in the Constitution itself.

Republicanism

To the Founders, a *republican* government meant the delegation of powers by the people to a small number of gifted individuals "whose wisdom may best discern the true interest of their country, and whose patriotism and love of justice, will be least likely to sacrifice it to temporary or partial considerations."[7] The Founders believed that enlightened leaders of principle and property with ability, education, and a stake in the preservation of liberty could govern the people better than the people could govern themselves. So they gave the voters only a limited voice in the selection of government leaders.

TABLE 3.2 Decision-Making Bodies in the Constitution of 1787

The Constitution of 1787 established four decision-making bodies, only one of which—the House of Representatives—was to be directly elected by the people.

House of Representatives	Senate	President	Supreme Court
Members alloted to each state "according to their respective numbers," but each state guaranteed at least one member.	"Two senators from each state" (regardless of the size of the state).	Single executive.	No size specified in the Constitution, but by tradition nine.
Two-year term. No limits on number of terms that can be served.	Six-year term. No limits on number of terms that can be served.	Four-year term (later limited to two terms by the 22nd Amendment in 1951).	Life term or until retirement
Directly elected by "the People of the several States."	Selected by the state legislatures (later changed to direct election by the 17th Amendment in 1913).	Selected by "Electors," appointed in each state "In such Manner as the Legislature thereof may direct" and equal to the total number of U.S. senators and House members to which the state is entitled in Congress.	Appointed by the president, "by and with the Advice and Consent of the Senate."

CONTROVERSY

The Supremacy Clause at Work: Marijuana for Medical Use?

Many doctors, patients, and organizations contend that marijuana, medically known as cannabis, is valuable in the treatment of glaucoma, HIV-AIDS, nausea, and pain relief, especially in cancer patients. As of 2010, several states—including Alaska, California, Colorado, Hawaii, Maine, Maryland, Michigan, Montana, Nevada, New Mexico, Oregon, Rhode Island, Vermont, and Washington—have enacted medical marijuana laws reversing state-level penalties for possession and cultivation when patients possess written documentation from physicians stating that they benefit from its medical use.[a] Wherever the issue has appeared on state referenda, it has passed by large margins. National polls regularly report that 75 percent of the American public support making marijuana legally available to seriously ill patients.

Congress, however, has never exempted the medical use of marijuana from its Controlled Substance Act, which makes it a federal crime "to manufacture, distribute, or dispense, or possess . . . a controlled substance." Various petitions to the federal Drug Enforcement Agency to declassify marijuana as a controlled substance and allow physicians to legally prescribe its use have been rejected.

Clearly, federal law is in direct conflict with the laws of many states on this issue. But the Supremacy Clause of the Constitution clearly requires that federal law prevail over state law in cases of conflict.

The issue reached the U.S. Supreme Court in 2001. The Court recognized that whether or not the activities of individuals or organizations regarding marijuana were legal under California law, they nonetheless violated federal law, notably the Controlled Substance Act. The Court further held that "medical necessity" does not allow anyone to violate the Controlled Substance Act; Congress made no exemption in this act

The Supremacy Clause of the Constitution dictates that the laws of Congress prevail over those of the states. Some states have legalized the use of marijuana for medical purposes. But the laws of Congress have not made an exception for such use. However, the Obama administration announced that it would not prosecute marijuana users who are in compliance with state laws.

for medical necessity. The Supreme Court recognized that the states have concurrent powers with the federal government in regulating drugs and medications. However, "Under the Supremacy Clause, any state law, however clearly within a state's acknowledged power, which interferes with or is contrary to federal laws must yield."[b]

Politically, however, prosecuting seriously ill patients or their doctors for using marijuana medically is very unpopular. Under President Obama the U.S. Department of Justice announced that it would not "focus federal resources" on marijuana users who were in compliance with state laws.

[a]National Association for the Reform of Marijuana Laws. www.norml.org.
[b]*United States v. Oakland Cannabis Buyers Cooperatives* 523 U.S. 483 (2001).

The Constitution of 1787 created *four* decision-making bodies, each with separate numbers of members, terms of office, and selection processes (see Table 3.2). Note that in the *original* Constitution only one of these four bodies—the House of Representatives—was to be directly elected by the people. The other three were removed from direct popular control: state legislatures selected U.S. senators; "electors" (chosen at the discretion of the state legislatures) selected the president; the president appointed Supreme Court and other federal judges.

Democracy? The Founders believed that government rests ultimately on "the consent of the governed." But their notion of republicanism envisioned decision making by *representatives* of the people, not the people themselves (see *A Conflicting View*: "Let the People Vote on National Issues"). The U.S. Constitution does not provide for *direct* voting by the people on national questions; that is, unlike many

✔ *Think*
Again

Was the original Constitution of 1787 a truly democratic document?

WHAT DO YOU THINK?

Should We Call a New Constitutional Convention?

Does the United States need a new, more democratic, more perfect Constitution? The U.S. Constitution was drafted more than 220 years ago for a small newly independent federation with about three million persons in 13 member states. Does it work today for the world's most powerful nation with over 300 million persons, 50 states, 5 territories, and global interests? Thomas Jefferson once wrote that "no society can make a perpetual constitution, or even a perpetual law. The earth belongs always to the living generation. . . . Every Constitution then, and every law, naturally expires at the end of 19 years. If it be enforced longer, it is an act of force and not of right." Should we take Jefferson's position to heart? Should we call a new Constitutional Convention?

What are the problems that exist with the present-day U.S. Constitution? Prominent political scientists have pondered this question and voiced the following concerns:

- The current Constitution gives small population states the same influence in the U.S. Senate as it gives large states. The current constitution severely dilutes the voice of citizens in large population states such as California, Texas, and New York, and greatly amplifies the voice of citizens in small states, such as Wyoming, Alaska, and Vermont.

- Not only is the Senate a seriously undemocratic body, but the Electoral College (with the number of each state delegation equal to the number of its congressional delegation of members of the House and Senate) also distorts the voice of the American people in presidential elections. George W. Bush was elected president in 2000 despite losing the national popular vote.

- Members of the U.S. House face very few competitive elections, depriving voters of effective choices for their congressional representatives, largely be-

cause members of Congress work with state parties in redistricting to design electoral districts to maximize "safe" seats.

- Presidents can go to war and send U.S. troops into combat around the world contrary to the wishes of Congress and the American people.

What should be done? Among the recommendations:

- Grant states up to four senators based on population size.

- Mandate nonpartisan redistricting for House elections.

- Establish term limits for representatives and senators, thus restoring the founders' principle of frequent rotation in office.

- Add a Balance Budget Amendment, with appropriate escape clauses, in order to encourage fiscal fairness to future generations.

- Limit presidential war-making powers and expand Congress's oversight of war-making by incorporating into the Constitution a requirement for congressional assent to ongoing wars at regular intervals.

But would a Constitutional Convention create more heat than light, more conflict than consensus, more threats than guarantees to individual liberty? Conflicts over the current hot-button social and cultural issues—immigration, abortion, prayer in schools, gay rights, the death penalty, the rights of criminal defendants, gun control, and the like—may poison debate and make compromise on these topics unlikely. "Any attempt to place constitutional provisions on either side of these cultural grenades would probably explode the process." Efforts to reform the structure of American government and politics would most likely give way to attempts to "strengthen" or "weaken" the Bill of Rights.

Sources: Sanford Levinson, *Our Undemocratic Constitution: Where the Constitution Goes Wrong (and How the People Can Correct It).* New York: Oxford University Press, 2006. Larry J. Sabato, *A More Perfect Constitution: 25 Proposals, to Revitalize Our Constitution and Make America a Fairer Country.* New York: Walker & Company, 2007.

referenda
Proposed laws or constitutional amendments submitted to the voters for their direct approval or rejection, found in state constitutions, but not in the U.S. Constitution.

state constitutions today, it does *not* provide for national **referenda**. Moreover, as noted earlier, only the House of Representatives (sometimes referred to even today as "the people's house") was to be elected directly by voters in the states.

These republican arrangements may appear "undemocratic" from our perspective today, but in 1787 the U.S. Constitution was more democratic than any other governing system in the world. Although other nations were governed by monarchs, emperors, chieftains, and hereditary aristocracies, the Founders recognized that government depended on the *consent of the governed*. Later democratic impulses in America greatly altered the original Constitution (see "Constitutional Change" later in this chapter) and reshaped it into a much more democratic document. (See also *What Do You Think?*: "Should We Call a New Constitutional Convention?")

Separation of Powers and Checks and Balances

▶ 3.9 *Analyze the separation of powers and the checks and balances established by the Constitution.*

The Founders believed that unlimited power was corrupting and that the concentration of power was dangerous. James Madison wrote, "Ambition must be made to counteract ambition." The **separation of powers** within the national government—the creation of separate legislative, executive, and judicial branches in Articles I, II, and III of the Constitution—was designed to place internal controls on governmental power. Power is not only apportioned among three branches of government, but, perhaps more important, each branch is given important **checks and balances** over the actions of the others (see Figure 3.1). According to Madison, "The constant aim is to divide and arrange the several offices in such a manner as

separation of powers
Constitutional division of powers among the three branches of the national government—legislative, executive, and judicial.

checks and balances
Constitutional provisions giving each branch of the national government certain checks over the actions of other branches.

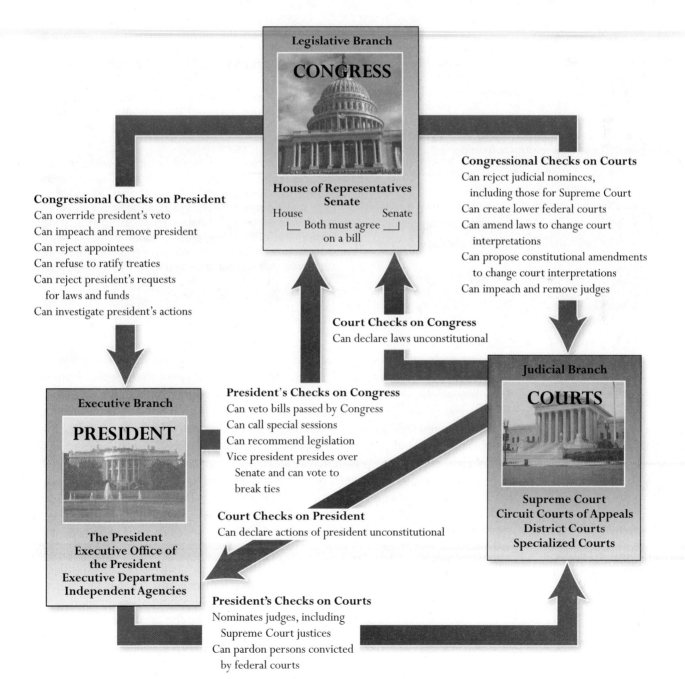

Legislative Branch

CONGRESS

House of Representatives
Senate

House   Senate
⎿ Both must agree ⏌
on a bill

Congressional Checks on President
Can override president's veto
Can impeach and remove president
Can reject appointees
Can refuse to ratify treaties
Can reject president's requests
    for laws and funds
Can investigate president's actions

Congressional Checks on Courts
Can reject judicial nominees,
    including those for Supreme Court
Can create lower federal courts
Can amend laws to change court
    interpretations
Can propose constitutional amendments
    to change court interpretations
Can impeach and remove judges

Court Checks on Congress
Can declare laws unconstitutional

President's Checks on Congress
Can veto bills passed by Congress
Can call special sessions
Can recommend legislation
Vice president presides over
    Senate and can vote to
    break ties

Executive Branch

PRESIDENT

The President
Executive Office of
the President
Executive Departments
Independent Agencies

Court Checks on President
Can declare actions of president unconstitutional

Judicial Branch

COURTS

Supreme Court
Circuit Courts of Appeals
District Courts
Specialized Courts

President's Checks on Courts
Nominates judges, including
    Supreme Court justices
Can pardon persons convicted
    by federal courts

FIGURE 3.1 Checks and Balances

A CONFLICTING VIEW

Let the People Vote on National Issues

"Direct democracy" means that the people themselves can initiate and decide policy questions by popular vote. The Founders were profoundly skeptical of this form of democracy. They had read about direct democracy in the ancient Greek city-state of Athens, and they believed the "follies" of direct democracy far outweighed any virtues it might possess. It was not until more than 100 years after the U.S. Constitution was written that widespread support developed in the American states for direct voter participation in policy making. Direct democracy developed in states and communities, and it is to be found today *only* in state and local government.

Why not extend our notion of democracy to include nationwide referenda voting on key public issues? Perhaps Congress should be authorized to place particularly controversial issues on a national ballot. Perhaps a petition signed by at least 1 million voters should also result in a question being placed on a national ballot.

Proponents of direct voting on national issues argue that national referenda would

- Enhance government responsiveness and accountability to the people.
- Stimulate national debate over policy questions.
- Increase voter interest and turnout on election day.
- Increase trust in government and diminish feelings of alienation from Washington.
- Give voters a direct role in policy making.

Opponents of direct democracy, from our nation's Founders to the present, argue that national referenda voting would

- Encourage majorities to sacrifice the rights of individuals and minorities.
- Lead to the adoption of unwise and unsound policies because voters are not sufficiently informed to cast intelligent ballots on many complex issues.
- Prevent consideration of alternative policies or modifications or amendments to the proposition set forth on the ballot. (In contrast, legislators devote a great deal of attention to writing, rewriting, and amending bills, as well as seeking out compromises among interests.)
- Enable special interests to mount expensive referendum campaigns; the outcomes of referenda would be heavily influenced by paid television advertising.

How would voters' decisions in national referenda differ from current government policies? National polls suggest that voters would approve of many policy initiatives that Congress has rejected, including a constitutional requirement to balance the budget; making English the official language; a constitutional amendment to limit the terms of Congress members; and a constitutional amendment to allow prayer in public schools.[a]

[a]Gallup. www.gallup.com.

Think Again

In which do you have the most trust and confidence? President, Congress, Supreme Court

that each may be a check on the other."[8] No bill can become a law without the approval of both the House and the Senate. The president shares legislative power through the power to sign or to veto laws of Congress, although Congress may override a presidential veto with a two-thirds vote in each house. The president may also suggest legislation, "give to the Congress Information of the State of the Union, and recommend to their Consideration such Measures as he shall judge necessary and expedient." The president may also convene special sessions of Congress.

However, the president's power of appointment is shared by the Senate, which confirms cabinet and ambassadorial appointments. The president must also secure the advice and consent of the Senate for any treaty. The president must execute the laws, but it is Congress that provides the money to do so. The president and the rest of the executive branch may not spend money that has not been appropriated by Congress. Congress must also authorize the creation of executive departments and agencies. Finally, Congress may impeach and remove the president from office for "Treason, Bribery, or other High Crimes and Misdemeanors."

Members of the Supreme Court are appointed by the president and confirmed by the Senate. Traditionally, this court has nine members, but Congress may determine the number of justices. More important, Congress must create lower federal district courts as well as courts of appeal. Congress must also determine the

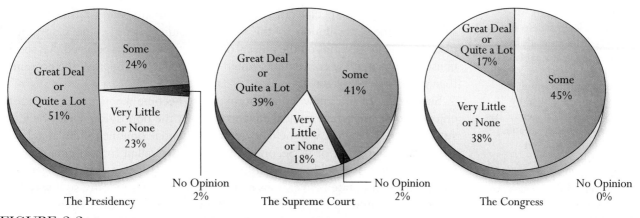

FIGURE 3.2 Confidence in the Three Branches of Government

"Now I am going to read you a list of institutions in American society. Please tell me how much confidence you, yourself, have in each one—a great deal or quite a lot, some, or very little or none?"

Source: Derived from Gallup, June 2009.

number of these judgeships and determine the jurisdiction of federal courts. But the most important check of all is the Supreme Court's power of judicial review.

Judicial review, which is not specifically mentioned in the Constitution itself, is the power of the judiciary to overturn laws of Congress and the states and actions of the president that the courts believe violate the Constitution (see "Judicial Power" in Chapter 13). Judicial review, in short, ensures compliance with the Constitution.

Many Federalists, including Alexander Hamilton, believed the Constitution of 1787 clearly implied that the Supreme Court could invalidate any laws of Congress or presidential actions it believed to be unconstitutional. Hamilton wrote in 1787, "[Limited government] . . . can be preserved in no other way than through the medium of courts of justice, whose duty it is to declare all acts contrary to the manifest tenor of the Constitution void."[9] But it was not until *Marbury v. Madison* in 1803 that Chief Justice John Marshall asserted in a Supreme Court ruling that the Supreme Court possessed the power of judicial review over laws of Congress. (See *People in Politics*: "John Marshall and Early Supreme Court Politics" in Chapter 13.) Today the American people express more trust and confidence in the Supreme Court than in either the president or the Congress (see Figure 3.2).

judicial review
Power of the U.S. Supreme Court and federal judiciary to declare laws of Congress and the states and actions of the president unconstitutional and therefore legally invalid.

Conflict over Ratification

▶ 3.10 *Outline the arguments made for and against ratification of the Constitution.*

Today the U.S. Constitution is a revered document, but in the winter of 1787–88, the Founders had real doubts about whether they could get it accepted as "the supreme Law of the Land." Indeed, the Constitution was ratified by only the narrowest of margins in the key states of Massachusetts, Virginia, and New York.

The Founders adopted a **ratification** procedure that was designed to enhance chances for acceptance of the Constitution. The ratification procedure written into the new Constitution was a complete departure from what was then supposed to be the law of the land, the Articles of Confederation, in two major ways. First, the Articles of Confederation required that amendments be approved by *all* of the states. But since Rhode Island was firmly in the hands of small farmers, the Founders knew that unanimous approval was unlikely. So they simply wrote into their new Constitution that approval required only nine of the states. Second, the

ratification
Power of a legislature to approve or reject decisions made by other bodies. State legislators or state conventions must have the power to ratify constitutional amendments submitted by Congress. The U.S. Senate has the power to ratify treaties made by the president.

Federalists
Supporters of the ratification of the Constitution, who later coalesced into a political party supporting John Adams for president in 1800.

Anti-Federalists
Opponents of the ratification of the Constitution, who later coalesced into a political party supporting Thomas Jefferson for president in 1800.

Founders called for special ratifying conventions in the states rather than risk submitting the Constitution to the state legislatures. Because the Constitution placed many prohibitions on the powers of states, the Founders believed that special constitutional ratifying conventions would be more likely to approve the document than would state legislatures.

Supporters of the new constitution, who become known as **Federalists**, enjoyed some important tactical advantages over the opposition. First, the Constitutional Convention was held in secret; potential opponents did not know what was coming out of it. Second, the Federalists called for ratifying conventions to be held as quickly as possible so that the opposition could not get itself organized. Many state conventions met during the winter months, so it was difficult for some rural opponents of the Constitution to get to their county seats in order to vote (see Figure 3.3 below).

The Federalists also waged a very professional (for 1787–88) media campaign in support of the Constitution. James Madison, Alexander Hamilton, and John Jay issued a series of eighty-five press releases, signed simply "Publius," on behalf of the Constitution. Major newspapers ran these essays, which were later collected and published as *The Federalist Papers*. The essays provide an excellent description and explanation of the Constitution by three of its writers and even today serve as a principal reference for political scientists and judges faced with constitutional ambiguities (see *People in Politics*: "James Madison and the Control of 'Faction'"). Two of the most important *Federalist Papers* are reprinted and annotated in the Appendix to this textbook.

Nevertheless, opponents of the Constitution—the **Anti-Federalists**—almost succeeded in defeating the document in New York and Virginia. They charged that

FIGURE 3.3

The Fight over Ratification

The vote for ratification of the Constitution of 1787 reflects divisions in the country, with support linked to a commercial economy and disapproval to more agricultural sectors.

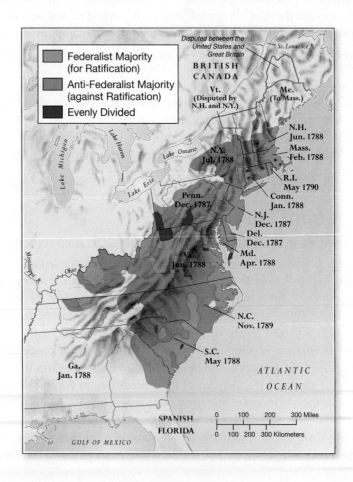

PEOPLE IN POLITICS

James Madison and the Control of "Faction"

The most important contributions to American democracy by James Madison (1751–1836) were his work in helping to write the Constitution and his insightful and scholarly defense of it during the ratification struggle. Indeed, Madison is more highly regarded by political scientists and historians as a *political theorist* than as the fourth president of the United States.

Madison's family owned a large plantation in Virginia. He graduated from the College of New Jersey (now Princeton University) at 18 and assumed a number of elected and appointed positions in Virginia's colonial government. In 1776 Madison drafted a new Virginia Constitution. While serving in Virginia's Revolutionary assembly, he met Thomas Jefferson; the two became lifetime political allies and friends. In 1787 Madison represented Virginia at the Constitutional Convention and took a leading role in its debates over the form of a new federal government.

Madison's political insights are revealed in *The Federalist Papers*, a series of eighty-five essays published in major newspapers in 1787–88, all signed simply "Publius." Alexander Hamilton and John Jay contributed some of them, but Madison wrote the two most important essays: Number 10, which explains the nature of political conflict (faction) and how it can be "controlled," and Number 51, which explains the system of separation of powers and checks and balances

(both reprinted and annotated in the Appendix to this textbook). According to Madison, "controlling faction" was the principal task of government.

What creates faction? Madison believed that conflict is part of human nature. In all societies, we find "a zeal for different opinions concerning religion, concerning government, and many other points," as well as "an attachment to different leaders ambitiously contending for preeminence and power." Even when there are no serious differences among people, these "frivolous and fanciful distinctions" will inspire "unfriendly passions" and "violent conflicts."

Clearly, Madison believed conflict could arise over just about any matter. Yet "the most common and durable source of factions, has been the various and unequal distribution of property." That is, economic conflicts between rich and poor and between people with different kinds of wealth and sources of income are the most serious conflicts confronting society.

Madison argued that factions could best be controlled in a republican government extending over a large society with a "variety of parties and interests." He defended republicanism (representative democracy) over "pure democracy," which he believed "incompatible with personal security, or the rights of property." And he argued that protection against "factious combinations" can be achieved by including a great variety of competing interests in the political system so that no one interest will be able to "outnumber and oppress the rest." Modern pluralist political theory (see Chapter 1) claims Madison as a forerunner.

the new Constitution would create an "aristocratic tyranny" and pose a threat to the "spirit of republicanism." They argued that the new Senate would be an aristocratic upper house and the new president a ruling monarch. They complained that neither the Senate nor the president was directly elected by the people. They also argued that the new national government would trample state governments and deny the people of the states the opportunity to handle their own political and economic affairs. Virginia patriot Patrick Henry urged the defeat of the Constitution "to preserve the poor Commonwealth of Virginia." Finally, their most effective argument was that the new Constitution lacked a bill of rights to protect individual liberty from government abuse (see *A Conflicting View*: "An Anti-Federalist's Objections to the Constitution").

A Bill of Rights

▶ 3.11 *Assess the protections provided by the Bill of Rights.*

It may be hard to imagine today, but the original Constitution had no **Bill of Rights**. This was a particularly glaring deficiency because many of the new state constitutions proudly displayed these written guarantees of individual liberty.

Bill of Rights
Written guarantees of basic individual liberties; the first ten amendments to the U.S. Constitution.

The Founders certainly believed in limited government and individual liberty, and they did write a few liberties into the body of the Constitution, including protection against ex post facto laws, a limited definition of treason, a guarantee of the writ of habeas corpus, and a guarantee of trial by jury (see Chapter 14).

The Federalists argued that there was really no need for a bill of rights because (1) the national government was one of **enumerated powers** only, meaning it could not exercise any power not expressly enumerated, or granted, in the Constitution; (2) the power to limit free speech or press, establish a religion, or otherwise restrain individual liberty was not among the enumerated powers; (3) therefore it was not necessary to specifically deny these powers to the new government. But the Anti-Federalists were unwilling to rest fundamental freedoms on a thin thread of logical inference from the notion of enumerated powers. They wanted specific written guarantees that the new national government would not interfere with the rights of individuals or the powers of the states. So Federalists at the New York, Massachusetts, and Virginia ratifying conventions promised to support the addition of a bill of rights to the Constitution in the very first Congress.

A young member of the new House of Representatives, James Madison, rose in 1789 and presented a bill of rights that he had drawn up after reviewing more than 200 recommendations sent from the states. Interestingly, the new Congress was so busy debating new tax laws that Madison had a difficult time attracting attention to his bill. Eventually, in September 1789, Congress approved a Bill of Rights as ten **amendments**, or formal changes, to the Constitution and sent them to the states. (Congress actually passed twelve amendments. One was never ratified; another, dealing with pay raises for Congress, was not ratified by the necessary three-quarters of the states until 1992.) The states promptly ratified the first ten amendments to the Constitution (see Table 3.3), and these changes took effect in 1791.

The Bill of Rights was originally designed to limit the powers of the new *national* government. The Bill of Rights begins with the command "Congress shall make no law. . . ." It was not until after the Civil War that the Constitution was amended to also prohibit states from violating individual liberties. The 14th Amendment, ratified in 1868, includes the command "No State shall. . . ." It prohibits the states from depriving any person of "life, liberty or property, without due process of law," or abridging "the privileges or immunities of citizens of the United States," or denying any person "equal protection of the laws." Today virtually all of the liberties guaranteed in the Constitution protect individuals not only from the national government but also from state governments and their subdivisions, including cities, counties, and school districts.

enumerated powers
Powers specifically mentioned in the Constitution as belonging to the national government.

amendments
Formal changes in a bill, law, or constitution.

Think Again

Should the Constitution be amended to guarantee that equal rights shall not be denied based on sex?

Constitutional Change

▶ 3.12 *Determine various means through which the Constitution may be changed.*

The purpose of a constitution is to govern government—to place limits on governmental power. Thus government itself must not be able to alter or amend a constitution easily. Yet the U.S. Constitution has changed over time, sometimes by formal amendment and other times by judicial interpretation, presidential and congressional action, and general custom and practice.

Amendments   A constitutional amendment must first be proposed, and then it must be ratified. The Constitution allows two methods of *proposing* a constitutional amendment: (1) by passage in the House and the Senate with a two-thirds

TABLE 3.3 The Bill of Rights

Thomas Jefferson, in a letter to James Madison in 1787, wrote: "A bill of rights is what the people are entitled to against every government on earth. . . ." This table summarizes and groups rights by their major purpose.

Guaranteeing Freedom of Expression

First Amendment prohibits the government from abridging freedoms of speech, press, assembly, and petition.

Guaranteeing Religious Freedom

First Amendment prohibits the government from establishing a religion or interfering with the free exercise of religion.

Affirming the Right to Bear Arms and Protecting Citizens from Quartering Troops

Second Amendment guarantees the right to bear arms.

Third Amendment prohibits troops from occupying citizens' homes in peacetime.

Protecting the Rights of Accused Persons

Fourth Amendment protects against unreasonable searches and seizures.

Fifth Amendment requires an indictment by a grand jury for serious crimes; prohibits the government from trying a person twice for the same crime; prohibits the government from taking life, liberty, or property without due process of law; and prohibits the government from taking private property for public use without fair compensation to the owner.

Sixth Amendment guarantees a speedy and public jury trial, the right to confront witnesses in court, and the right to legal counsel for defense.

Seventh Amendment guarantees the right to a jury trial in civil cases.

Eighth Amendment prohibits the government from setting excessive bail or fines or inflicting cruel and unusual punishment.

Protecting the Rights of People and States

Ninth Amendment protects all other unspecified rights of the people.

Tenth Amendment reserves to the states or to the people those powers neither granted to the federal government nor prohibited to the states in the Constitution.

vote, or (2) by passage in a national convention called by Congress in response to petitions by two-thirds of the state legislatures. Congress then chooses the method of *ratification*, which can be either (1) by vote in the legislatures of three-fourths of the states, or (2) by vote in conventions called for that purpose in three-fourths of the states (see Figure 3.4).

Of the four possible combinations of proposal and ratification, the method involving proposal by a two-thirds vote of Congress and ratification by three-quarters of the legislatures has been used for all the amendments except one. Only for the 21st Amendment's repeal of Prohibition did Congress call for state ratifying conventions (principally because Congress feared that southern Bible Belt state legislatures would vote against repeal). The method of proposal by national convention has never been used.

In addition to the Bill of Rights, most of the constitutional amendments ratified over the nation's 200 years have expanded our notion of democracy. Today the Constitution includes 27 amendments, which means that only 17 (out of more than 10,000) proposed amendments have been ratified since the passage of the Bill of Rights. It is possible to classify the amendments that have been ratified

FIGURE 3.4

Constitutional
Amendment Process

The Constitution set up
two alternative routes for
proposing amendments
and two for ratifying them.
One of the four possible
combinations has actually
been used for all except one
(the 21st) amendment.
However, in our time there
have been persistent calls for
a constitutional convention to
propose new amendments
permitting school prayer,
making abortion illegal, and
requiring a balanced national
budget.

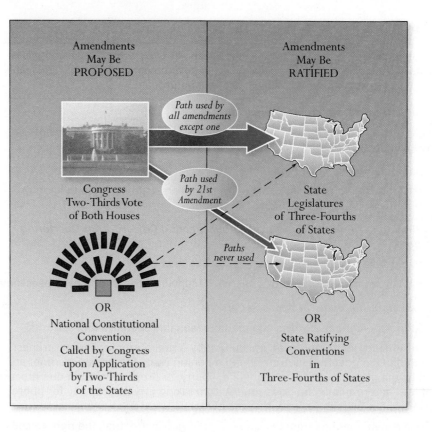

**Equal Rights
Amendment (ERA)**
Proposed amendment to the
Constitution guaranteeing
that equal rights under the
law shall not be denied or
abridged on account of sex.
Passed by Congress in 1972,
the amendment failed to win
ratification by three of the
necessary three-fourths of
the states.

into the broad categories of constitutional processes, Prohibition, income tax,
individual liberty, and voting rights (see Table 3.4).

Amending the U.S. Constitution requires not only a two-thirds vote in both houses
of Congress, reflecting *national* support, but also ratification by three-fourths of the
states, reflecting widespread support within the states. The fate of the **Equal Rights
Amendment**, popularly known as the ERA, illustrates the need for nationwide consensus in order to amend the Constitution. The Equal Rights Amendment is a simple
statement to which the vast majority of Americans agree, according to public opinion
polls: "Equality of rights under the law shall not be denied or abridged by the United
States or any state on account of sex." Congress passed the ERA in 1972 with far more
than the necessary two-thirds vote; both Republicans and Democrats supported the
ERA, and it was endorsed by Presidents Nixon, Ford, and Carter as well as most other
national political leaders and organizations. By 1978, thirty-five state legislatures
had ratified the amendment—three states short of the necessary thirty-eight (three-
quarters). (Five states subsequently voted to rescind, or cancel, their earlier ratification.
However, because there is no language in the Constitution regarding rescission, there
is some disagreement about the constitutionality of this action.) Promising that the
"ERA won't go away," proponents of the amendment have continued to press their
case. But to date Congress has not acted to resubmit the ERA to the states.

Judicial Interpretations   Some of the greatest changes in the Constitution
have come about not by formal amendment but by interpretations of the document by federal courts, notably the U.S. Supreme Court.

Indeed, through judicial review, the U.S. Supreme Court has come to play the
central role in giving meaning to the Constitution. Judicial review is the power of
federal courts, and ultimately the Supreme Court, to declare laws of Congress
and actions of the president unconstitutional and therefore invalid. This power
was first asserted by Chief Justice John Marshall in the case of *Marbury v. Madison*

TABLE 3.4 Amendments to the Constitution Since the Bill of Rights

The Constitution has been amended a total of 27 times, including the first 10 amendments of the Bill of Rights. This table summarizes and groups subsequent amendments by their major purpose.

Perfecting Constitutional Processes

Eleventh Amendment (1798) forbids federal lawsuits against a state by citizens of another state or nation.

Twelfth Amendment (1804) provides separate ballots for president and vice president in the Electoral College to prevent confusion.

Twentieth Amendment (1933) determines the dates for the beginning of the terms of Congress (January 3) and the president (January 20).

Twenty-second Amendment (1951) limits the president to two terms.

Twenty-fifth Amendment (1967) provides for presidential disability.

Twenty-seventh Amendment (1992) prevents Congress from raising its own pay in a single session.

The Experiment with Prohibition

Eighteenth Amendment (1919) prohibits the manufacture, sale, or transportation of intoxicating liquors.

Twenty-first Amendment (1933) repeals the Eighteenth Amendment.

The Income Tax

Sixteenth Amendment (1913) allows Congress to tax incomes.

Expanding Liberty

Thirteenth Amendment (1865) abolishes slavery.

Fourteenth Amendment (1868) protects life, liberty, and property and the privileges and immunities of citizenship and provides equal protection of the law.

Expanding Voting Rights

Fifteenth Amendment (1870) guarantees that the right to vote shall not be denied because of race.

Seventeenth Amendment (1913) provides for the election of senators by the people of each state.

Nineteenth Amendment (1920) guarantees that the right to vote shall not be denied because of sex.

Twenty-third Amendment (1961) gives the District of Columbia electoral votes for presidential elections.

Twenty-fourth Amendment (1964) guarantees that the right to vote shall not be denied because of failure to pay a poll tax or other tax.

Twenty-sixth Amendment (1971) guarantees that the right to vote shall not be denied to persons 18 years of age or older.

in 1803 (see *People in Politics*: "John Marshall and Early Supreme Court Politics" in Chapter 13). It is now an important part of the system of checks and balances (see Figure 3.1). This power is itself an interpretation of the Constitution, because it is not specifically mentioned in the document.

Supreme Court interpretations of the Constitution have given specific meaning to many of our most important constitutional phrases. Among the most important examples of constitutional change through judicial interpretation are the meanings given to the 14th Amendment, particularly its provisions that "No State shall . . .

A CONFLICTING VIEW

An Anti-Federalist's Objections to the Constitution

Virginia's George Mason was a delegate to the Constitutional Convention of 1787, but he refused to sign the final document and became a leading opponent of the new Constitution. Mason was a wealthy plantation owner and a heavy speculator in western (Ohio) lands. He was a friend of George Washington, but he considered most other political figures of his day to be "babblers" and he generally avoided public office. However, in 1776 he authored Virginia's Declaration of Rights, which was widely copied in other state constitutions and later became the basis for the Bill of Rights. Although an ardent supporter of states' rights, he attended the Constitutional Convention of 1787 and, according to James Madison's notes on the proceedings, was an influential force in shaping the new national government. His refusal to sign the Constitution and his subsequent leadership of the opposition to its ratification made him the recognized early leader of the Anti-Federalists.

Mason's first objection to the Constitution was that it included no Bill of Rights. But he also objected to the powers given to the Senate, which was not directly elected by the people in the original document; to the federal courts; and to the president. He was wary of the Necessary and Proper Clause, which granted Congress the power to "make all laws which shall be necessary and proper" for carrying out the enumerated powers—those specifically mentioned in the Constitution. Mason correctly predicted that this clause would be used to preempt the powers of the states.

In his "Objections to the Constitution" Mason wrote,

There is no declaration of rights; and the laws of the general government being paramount to the laws and constitutions of the several States, the declaration of rights in the separate States are no security.

Senators are not the representatives of the people, or amenable to them.

The judiciary of the United States is so constructed and extended as to absorb and destroy the judiciaries of the several States; thereby rendering law as tedious, intricate and expensive . . .

Under their own construction of the general clause at the end of the enumerated powers, the Congress may . . . extend their power as far as they shall think proper; so that the State Legislatures have no security for the powers now presumed to remain to them; or the people for their rights.

Note that virtually all of Mason's objections to the original Constitution had to be remedied at a later date. The Bill of Rights was added as the first ten amendments. Eventually (1913) the 17th Amendment, for the direct election of U.S. senators, was passed. And Mason correctly predicted that the federal judiciary would eventually render the law "tedious, intricate, and expensive" and that the Necessary and Proper Clause, which he refers to as "the general clause at the end of the enumerated powers," would be used to expand national powers at the expense of the states.

deprive any person of life, liberty, or property, without due process of law; nor deny to any person within its jurisdiction the equal protection of the laws":

- Deciding that "equal protection of the laws" requires an end to segregation of the races (*Brown v. Board of Education of Topeka,* 1954, and subsequent decisions).

- Deciding that "liberty" includes a woman's right to choose an abortion, and that the term *person* does not include the unborn fetus (*Roe v. Wade,* 1973, and subsequent decisions).

- Deciding that "equal protection of the laws" requires that every person's vote should be weighed equally in apportionment and districting plans for the House of Representatives, state legislatures, city councils, and so on (*Baker v. Carr,* 1964, and subsequent decisions).

Presidential and Congressional Action Congress and the president have also undertaken to interpret the Constitution. Nearly every president, for example, has argued that the phrase "executive Power" in Article II includes more than the specific powers mentioned afterward. Thomas Jefferson purchased the

A CONSTITUTIONAL NOTE

How Democratic Was the Constitution of 1787?

The Constitution established *four* decision-making bodies—the House and the Senate in the legislative branch (Article I); the president in the executive branch (Article II); and the Supreme Court and "such inferior Courts as the Congress may from time to time ordain and establish" in the judicial branch (Article III). But in 1787 only one of these bodies was to be elected by the people—the House of Representatives. The other three bodies were removed from direct popular control: State legislatures selected U.S. Senators; "electors," chosen in a fashion decided by state legislatures, chose the president; and the president appointed the Supreme Court and other federal judges "with the Advice and Consent of the [then unelected] Senate." Of course, over time state legislatures provided for the direct election of presidential electors and the 17th Amendment provided for the direct election of U.S. Senators.

The Constitution of 1787 also recognized slavery—"persons held to Service or Labor" (Article IV, Section 2)—and even protected it, by requiring states that capture runaway slaves to "deliver up," that is, to return them to their owners. In terms of representation, the Constitution of 1787 distinguishes between "free persons" and three-fifths of "all other Persons" (Article I, Section 2), that is, slaves. And Congress could not prohibit the importation of slaves until after 1808 (Article I, Section 9).

Louisiana Territory from France in 1803 even though there is no constitutional authorization for the president, or even the national government, to acquire new territory. Presidents from George Washington to Richard Nixon have argued that Congress cannot force the executive branch to turn over documents it does not wish to disclose (see Chapter 11).

Congress by law has tried to restrict the president's power as Commander-in-Chief of the Armed Forces by requiring the president to notify Congress when U.S. troops are sent to "situations where imminent involvement in hostilities is clearly indicated" and limiting their stay to sixty days unless Congress authorizes an extension. This War Powers Resolution (1973), passed by Congress over President Richard Nixon's veto in the immediate aftermath of the Vietnam War, has been ignored by every president to date (see Chapter 11). Yet it indicates that Congress has its own ideas about interpreting the Constitution.

Custom and Practice   Finally, the Constitution changes over time as a result of generally accepted customs and practice. It is interesting to note, for example, that the Constitution never mentions political parties. (Many of the Founders disapproved of parties because they caused "faction" among the people.) But soon after Thomas Jefferson resigned as President Washington's first secretary of state (in part because he resented the influence of Secretary of the Treasury Alexander Hamilton), the Virginian attracted the support of Anti-Federalists, who believed the national government was too strong. When Washington retired from office, most Federalists supported John Adams as his successor. But many Anti-Federalists ran for posts as presidential electors, promising to be "Jefferson's men." Adams won the presidential election of 1796, but the Anti-Federalists organized themselves into a political party, the Democratic-Republicans, to oppose Adams in the election of 1800. The party secured pledges from candidates for presidential elector to cast their electoral vote for Jefferson if they won their post, and then the party helped win support for its slate of electors. In this way the Electoral College was transformed from a deliberative body where leading citizens from each state came together to decide for themselves who should be president into a ceremonial body where pledged electors simply cast their presidential vote for the candidate who had carried their state in the presidential election. (For a full discussion of the current operation of the Electoral College, see *What Do You Think?*: "Should We Scrap the Electoral College?" in Chapter 8.)

Summary

▶ **3.1** *Identify the major principles of constitutionalism.*

Constitutionalism includes the principles of a government of law which is limited in power and where liberties may not be infringed upon even by the majority. Constitutions govern government and establish the legal authority for government.

▶ **3.2** *Trace the evolution of constitutionalism in the United States.*

The American tradition of written constitutions extends back through the Articles of Confederation, the colonial charters, and the Mayflower Compact to the thirteenth-century English Magna Carta. The Second Continental Congress in 1776 adopted a written Declaration of Independence to justify the colonies' separation from Great Britain. All of these documents strengthened the idea of a written contract defining governmental power.

▶ **3.3** *Assess the obstacles to nationhood.*

The movement for a Constitutional Convention in 1787 was inspired by the new government's inability to levy taxes under the Articles of Confederation, its inability to fund the Revolutionary War debt, obstacles to interstate commerce, monetary problems, and civil disorders, including Shays's Rebellion.

▶ **3.4** *Outline the principles on which the Founders were in agreement.*

The nation's Founders—fifty-five delegates to the Constitutional Convention in Philadelphia in 1787—shared a broad consensus on liberty and property, the social contract, republicanism, limited government, and the need for a national government.

▶ **3.5** *Characterize areas of conflict among the Founders.*

The Founders compromised their differences over representation by creating two co-equal houses in the Congress: the House of Representatives, with members apportioned to the states on the basis of population and directly elected by the people for two-year terms, and the Senate, with two members allotted for each state regardless of its population, and originally selected by state legislatures for six-year terms.

▶ **3.6** *Analyze the economic issues that the Founders faced and the solutions they reached.*

The founders were confronted with many economic problems including conflicts over levying taxes, regulating commerce, tariffs, establishing a uniform currency and a common market, and resolving the questions over the national debt.

▶ **3.7** *Trace the evolution of early American military and foreign policy.*

The national government assumed power over the new country's foreign and military affairs, at first relying on state militias comprised for citizen soldiers and later developing a professional army. The new Constitution gave the federal government authority to negotiate treaties with foreign nations and established the president as the Commander-in-Chief.

▶ **3.8** *Explain how the Constitution structured the new government.*

The structure of the national government reflects the Founders' beliefs in national supremacy, federalism, republicanism, separation of powers, checks and balances, and judicial review.

▶ **3.9** *Analyze the separation of powers and the checks and balances established by the Constitution.*

The separation of powers and checks and balances written into the Constitution were designed, in Madison's words, "to divide and arrange the several offices in such a manner as that each may be a check on the other." Judicial review was not specifically described in the original Constitution, but the Supreme Court soon asserted its power to overturn laws of Congress and the states, as well as presidential actions, that the Court determined to be in conflict with the Constitution.

▶ **3.10** *Outline the arguments made for and against ratification of the Constitution.*

Opposition to the new Constitution was strong. Anti-Federalists argued that it created a national government that was aristocratic, undemocratic, and a threat to the rights of the states and the people. Their concerns resulted in the Bill of Rights: ten amendments added to the original Constitution, all designed to limit the power of the national government, and protect the rights of individuals and states.

▶ **3.11** *Assess the protections provided by the Bill of Rights.*

The Bill of Rights provides for the protection of many liberties including freedom of speech, press, religion, privacy, and the rights of criminal defendants. It intended to limit the power of the national government and protect the people's individual freedoms.

▶ **3.12** *Determine various means through which the Constitution may be changed.*

Over time, constitutional changes have come about as a result of formal amendments, judicial interpretations, presidential and congressional actions, and changes in custom and practice. The most common method of constitutional amendment has been proposal by two-thirds vote of both houses of Congress followed by ratification by three-fourths of the state legislatures.

Chapter Test

▶ **3.1** *Identify the major principles of constitutionalism.*

1. The Constitution established a government
   a. of limited power
   b. based on law
   c. with three branches at the federal level
   d. all of the above

2. The Constitution
   a. established the charters that gave the colonies legal authority
   b. provided for the Commander-in-Chief to consolidate all governmental power in emergencies
   c. established the legal structure of the federal government
   d. determined how the states were to select the members of the state legislatures

▶ **3.2** *Trace the evolution of constitutionalism in the United States.*

3. Which of the following had the *least* impact on American constitutionalism?
   a. The Magna Carta
   b. The Mayflower Compact
   c. The French Revolution
   d. The Charter Oak Affair

4. The Articles of Confederation
   a. established a strong national government for protection from the British
   b. really established a league of friendship between sovereign states
   c. provided for a bicameral (two chambers) national legislature
   d. provided for equal representation for each state in Congress

▶ **3.3** *Assess the obstacles to nationhood.*

5. Congress under the Articles of Confederation relied on _____ as a major source of funding.
   a. the new income tax
   b. loans from wealthy patriots
   c. the sales tax
   d. taxes on interstate commerce

▶ **3.4** *Outline the principles on which the Founders were in agreement.*

6. Which of the following was not a principle that the Founders agreed to easily?
   a. natural rights
   b. limited government
   c. representation in Congress
   d. republicanism

7. Republicanism
   a. guarantees direct democracy
   b. provides for stability through the continuity that comes with a monarchy
   c. guarantees both direct democracy and the social contract
   d. provides for a government of representatives

▶ **3.5** *Characterize areas of conflict among the Founders.*

8. Which of the following was a principle that Founders had trouble reconciling?
   a. the social contract
   b. natural right to property
   c. representation in Congress
   d. natural right to liberty

9. Which of the following was resolved by the Connecticut Compromise?
   a. the border dispute between Massachusetts and Rhode Island
   b. the problem of how the states were to be represented in Congress
   c. the conflict over the respresentation of slaves
   d. the conflict over taxation of interstate commerce

▶ **3.6** *Analyze the economic issues that the Founders faced and the solutions they reached.*

10. Which of the following was *not* an economic issue that confronted the Founders?
    a. raising monies and levy taxes
    b. establishing a common market
    c. controlling the money supply
    d. establishing the federal reserve

11. Which of the following economic groups played little role in the development of the Constitution?
    a. slave owners
    b. land speculators
    c. the government bureaucracy
    d. bankers and investors

▶ **3.7** *Trace the evolution of early American military and foreign policy.*

12. It is true that in the area of foreign affairs
    a. the national and state government share power over foreign policy
    b. the national government has almost total control over foreign policy
    c. the state governments cannot get involved in military affairs but they can make peace treaties with other nations
    d. Congress is the dominant controlling force in determining foreign policy

▶ **3.8** *Explain how the Constitution structured the new government.*

13. The provision in the Constitution that makes state law inferior to federal law is
    a. the full faith and credit clause
    b. the interstate commerce clause
    c. state inferiority clause
    d. the national supremacy clause

14. The Constitution provided for
    a. a federal system of government
    b. a unified one house Congress
    c. a federal judiciary which had little power
    d. a unitary government

▶ **3.9** *Analyze the separation of powers and the checks and balances established by the Constitution.*

15. It would be accurate to say that the power of judicial review provides that
    a. Congress may review the financial affairs of the federal courts
    b. the Supreme Court may declare an act of Congress unconstitutional
    c. the executive has the authority to review the judiciary for impropriety
    d. each state supreme court may review the constitutionality of federal statutes

16. Congress can exercise a check upon the president by
    a. refusing to allocate funding for his programs
    b. refusing to confirm his appointments
    c. refuse to give advice and consent to treaties
    d. all of the above

▶ **3.10** *Outline the arguments made for and against ratification of the Constitution.*

▶ **3.11** *Assess the protections provided by the Bill of Rights.*

17. The Bill of Rights were included into the new Constitution in order to
    a. provide protection from ex post facto laws
    b. outline the basic structure of the judiciary
    c. provide safeguards and protections for individual liberties
    d. provide for writs of habeus corpus

▶ **3.12** *Determine various means through which the Constitution may be changed.*

18. The Constitution is an evolving document, which has been changed by which of the following?
    a. custom and practices
    b. judicial interpretation
    c. presidential actions
    d. all of the above

---

myp⦿liscilab EXERCISES

Apply what you learned in this chapter on MyPoliSciLab.

📖 **Read** on mypoliscilab.com

   eText: Chapter 3

✔ **Study** and **Review** on mypoliscilab.com

   Pre-Test

   Post-Test

   Chapter Exam

   Flashcards

👁 **Watch** on mypoliscilab.com

   Video: Animal Sacrifice and Free Exercise

   Video: Polygamy and the U.S. Constitution

✳ **Explore** on mypoliscilab.com

   Simulation: You Are James Madison

   Simulation: You Are Proposing a Constitutional Amendment

   Comparative: Comparing Constitutions

   Timeline: The History of Constitutional Amendments

   Visual Literacy: The American System of Checks and Balances

---

Key Terms

Suggested Readings

Beard, Charles. *An Economic Interpretation of the Constitution.* New York: Macmillan, 1913. A classic work setting forth the argument that economic self-interest inspired the Founders in writing the Constitution.

Dahl, Robert A. *How Democratic is the American Constitution?* 2nd ed. New Haven, Conn.: Yale University Press, 2003.

A discussion of the undemocratic features of the Constitution.

Epstein, Lee, and Thomas G. Walker. *Constitutional Law for a Changing America: Institutional Powers and Constraints.* 6th ed. Washington, D.C.: CQ Press, 2007. Supreme Court cases and explanatory narrative regarding the separation of power, federalism, national and state powers, national security, and so on.

Finkelman, Paul. *Slavery and the Founders*. 2nd ed. Armonk, N.Y.: M. E. Sharpe, 2000. A critical account of the Founders' attitudes toward slavery and the resulting three-fifths' compromise.

Frohren, Bruce, ed. *The American Republic: Primary Sources*. Indianapolis: Liberty Fund Inc., 2002. Excellent collection of earliest American documents, from the Mayflower Compact to the Declaration of Independence.

Levin, Mark. *Liberty and Tyranny*. New York: Simon & Schuster, 2009. An argument that modern conservatism embodies the principles of the Founders—principles that can preserve liberty and defeat liberal tyranny.

Madison, James, Alexander Hamilton, and John Jay. *The Federalist Papers*. New York: Modern Library, 1937. These eighty-five collected essays, written in 1787–88 in support of ratification of the Constitution, remain the most important commentary on that document. Numbers 10 and 51 (reprinted in the Appendix) ought to be required reading for all students of American government.

Mason, Alpheus Thomas, and Donald Grier Stephenson, Jr. *American Constitutional Law*. 14th ed. Upper Saddle River, N.J.: Prentice Hall, 2005. The now classic introduction to the Constitution and the Supreme Court through essays and case excerpts.

McDonald, Forrest B. *Novus Ordo Seculorum*. Lawrence: University Press of Kansas, 1986. A description of the intellectual origins of the Constitution and the "new secular order" that it represented.

Peltason, J. W., and Sue Davis. *Understanding the Constitution*. 16th ed. New York: Harcourt Brace, 2004. Of the many books that explain the Constitution, this is one of the best. It contains explanations of the Declaration of Independence, the Articles of Confederation, and the Constitution. The book is written clearly and well suited for undergraduates.

Rossiter, Clinton L. *1787, The Grand Convention*. New York: Macmillan, 1960. A very readable account of the people and events surrounding the Constitutional Convention in 1787, with many insights into the conflicts and compromises that took place there.

Sabato, Larry J. *A More Perfect Constitution*. New York: Walker, 2007. Proposals for a new Constitutional Convention to consider.

Storing, Herbert J. *What the Anti-Federalists Were For*. Chicago: University of Chicago Press, 1981. An examination of the arguments of the Anti-Federalists in opposition to the ratification of the Constitution.

Suggested Web Sites

The Anti-Federalist Papers
www.thisnation.com/library/antifederalist
Essays by Anti-Federalists opposed to the ratification of the Constitution.

Constitution Society www.constitution.org
Web site includes comprehensive list of founding documents, essays, and commentaries on the Constitution.

Constitutional Law
www.law.cornell.edu/topics/constitutional
Cornell University Law School overview of the Constitution.

The Electoral College Official FEC site
www.fec.gov/pages/ecmenu
Provides brief history of the Electoral College and a description of how it works.

George Washington Papers http://gwpapers.virginia.edu
The life of George Washington with images, maps, documents, and papers.

The Great Compromise www.jmu.edu/madison
James Madison University Web site on Madison with information on constitutional compromises, including the slavery compromise.

James Madison www.jmu.edu/madison
The legacy of Madison organized by topic.

National Constitution Center www.constitutioncenter.org
Located in Philadelphia's Independence Mall, this museum is devoted to explaining the U.S. Constitution.

Our Documents www.ourdocuments.gov
National Archives Web site with access to 100 "milestone documents" in American history.

U.S. History www.ushistory.org
The Independence Hall Association Web site with "Documents of Freedom" including Mayflower Compact, Declaration of Independence, Articles of Confederation, etc.

Chapter Test Answer Key

1. D	4. B	7. D	10. D	13. D	16. D
2. C	5. B	8. C	11. C	14. A	17. C
3. C	6. C	9. B	12. B	15. B	18. D

The Constitution of the United States

More than two centuries after its ratification, our Constitution remains the operating charter of our republic. It is neither self-explanatory nor a comprehensive description of our constitutional rules. Still, it remains the starting point. Many Americans who swear by the Constitution have never read it seriously, although copies can be found in most American government and American history textbooks.

Justice Hugo Black, who served on the Supreme Court for 34 years, kept a copy of the Constitution with him at all times. He read it often. Reading the Constitution would be a good way for you to begin (and then reread again to end) your study of the government of the United States. We have therefore included a copy of it at this point in the book. Please read it carefully.

THE PREAMBLE

We the People of the United States, in Order to form a more perfect Union, establish Justice, insure domestic Tranquility, provide for the common defense, promote the general Welfare, and secure the Blessings of Liberty to ourselves and our Posterity, do ordain and establish this Constitution for the United States of America.

"We, the people." Three simple words, yet of profound importance and contentious origin. Every government in the world at the time of the Constitutional Convention was some type of monarchy wherein sovereign power flowed from the top. The Founders of our new country rejected monarchy as a form of government and proposed instead a republic, which would draw its sovereignty from the people.

The Articles of Confederation that governed the United States from 1776 until 1789 started with: "We the under signed Delegates of the States." Early drafts of the new constitution started with: "We, the states . . ." But again, the Founders were not interested in another union of states but rather the creation of a new national government. Therefore, "We, the states" was changed to "We, the people."

The remainder of the preamble describes the generic functions of government.

One of these generic functions of government is to provide for the general welfare. For a good discussion of a right versus entitlement to welfare, see the Constitutional Note at the end of Chapter 17, page 626.

ARTICLE I—THE LEGISLATIVE ARTICLE

Legislative Power

The very first article in the Constitution established the legislative branch of the new national government. Why did the framers start with the legislative power instead of the executive branch?

Under the Articles of Confederation, the legislature was the only functional instrument of government. Therefore, the framers truly believed it was the most important component of the new government.

Section 1 All legislative Powers herein granted shall be vested in a Congress of the United States, which shall consist of a Senate and House of Representatives.

Section 1 established a bicameral (two-chamber) legislature of an upper (Senate) and lower (House of Representatives) organization of the legislative branch.

House of Representatives: Composition; Qualifications; Apportionment; Impeachment Power

Section 2 Clause 1. The House of Representatives shall be composed of Members chosen every second Year by the People of the several States, and the Electors in each State shall have the Qualifications requisite for Electors of the most numerous Branch of the State Legislature.

This section sets the term of office for House members (2 years) and indicates that those voting for Congress will have the same qualifications as those voting for the state legislatures. Originally, states limited voters to white property owners. Some states even had religious disqualifications, such as Catholic or Jewish. Most property and religious qualifications for voting were removed by the 1840s, but race and gender restrictions remained, until the 15th and 19th amendments were passed.

Clause 2. No Person shall be a Representative who shall not have attained to the Age of twenty five Years, and been seven Years a Citizen of the United States, and who shall not, when elected, be an inhabitant of that State in which he shall be chosen.

This section sets forth the basic qualifications of a representative: at least 25 years of age, a U.S. citizen for at least 7 years, and a resident of a state. Note that the Constitution does not require a person to be a resident of the district he or she represents. At the time the Constitution was written, life expectancy was about 43 years of age. So a

person 25 years old was middle aged. Considering today's life expectancy of about 78 years, the equivalent age of 25 would be about 45. The average age of a current representative is 53.

Clause 2 does not specify how many terms a representative can serve in Congress. Calls for Congress members to be term limited have never been enacted. Some states passed legislation to limit the terms of their U.S. representatives. Because of the specificity of the qualifications for office, the USSC ruled in *U.S. Term Limits, Inc. v. Thomton*, 514 U.S. 779 (1995) that term limits for U.S. legislators could not be imposed by any state but would require a constitutional amendment.

Clause 3. Representatives and direct Taxes[1] shall be apportioned among the several States which may be included within this Union, according to their respective Numbers, which shall be determined by adding to the whole Number of free Persons, including those bound to Service for a Term of Years, and excluding Indians not taxed, three fifths of all other Persons.[2] The actual Enumeration shall be made within three Years after the first Meeting of the Congress of the United States, and within every subsequent Term of ten Years in such Manner as they shall by Law direct. The Number of Representatives shall not exceed one for every thirty Thousand, but each State shall have at Least one Representative, and until such enumeration shall be made, the State of New Hampshire shall be entitled to chuse three, Massachusetts eight, Rhode Island and Providence Plantations one, Connecticut five, New York six, New Jersey four, Pennsylvania eight, Delaware one, Maryland six, Virginia ten, North Carolina five, South Carolina five, and Georgia three.

This clause contains the Three-Fifths Compromise wherein American Indians and African American slaves were only counted as 3/5 of a person for congressional representation purposes. This clause also addresses the question of congressional reapportionment every 10 years, which requires a census. Since the 1911 Reapportionment Act, the size of the House of Representatives has been set at 435. This is the designated size that is reapportioned every 10 years. Based on changes of population, some states gain and some states lose representatives. This clause also provides that every state, regardless of population, will have at least one (1) representative. Currently, seven states have only one representative.

States are required to draw new congressional district boundaries after each reapportionment if the state gains or loses congressional seat(s). The USSC has ruled that legislative districts must contain an approximate equal number of voters. They have also ruled that minority voters must be protected by the creation of majority-minority districts where minority voters can be concentrated. Redrawing of district lines to promote party interests is not prohibited.

Clause 4. When vacancies happen in the Representation from any State, the Executive Authority thereof shall issue Writs of Election to fill such Vacancies.

This clause provides a procedure for replacing a U.S. representative in the case of death, resignation, or expulsion from the House. Generally, if less than half a term is left, the governor will appoint a successor. If more than half a term is remaining, most states require a special election to fill the vacancy.

Clause 5. The House of Representatives shall chuse their Speaker and other Officers, and shall have the sole Power of Impeachment.

Only one officer of the House is specified—the Speaker. All other officers are decided by the House. This clause also gives the House authority for impeachments (accusations) against officials of the executive and judicial branches.

Senate Composition: Qualifications, Impeachment Trials

Section 3 Clause 1. The Senate of the United States shall be composed of two Senators from each State, chosen by the Legislature thereof,[3] for six Years and each Senator shall have one Vote.

This clause treats each state equally—all have two senators each. Originally, senators were chosen by state legislators, but since passage and ratification of the 17th Amendment, they are now elected by popular vote. This clause also establishes the term of a senator—6 years—three times that of a House member.

Clause 2. Immediately after they shall be assembled in Consequence of the first Election, they shall be divided as equally as may be into three Classes. The Seats of the Senators of the first Class shall be vacated at the Expiration of the second Year, of the second Class at the Expiration of the fourth Year, and of the third Class at the Expiration of the sixth Year, so that one third may be chosen every second Year, and if Vacancies happen by Resignation, or otherwise, during the Recess of the Legislature of any State, the Executive thereof may make temporary Appointments until the next Meeting of the Legislature which shall then fill such Vacancies.[4]

To prevent a wholesale election of senators every six years, this clause provides that one-third of the Senate will be elected every two years. Senate vacancies are filled similar to the House—either appointment by the governor or a special election.

Clause 3. No person shall be a Senator who shall not have attained to the Age of thirty Years, and been nine Years a Citizen of the United States, and who shall not, when elected, be an Inhabitant of that State for which he shall be chosen.

This clause sets forth the qualifications for U.S. senator: at least 30 years old, a U.S. citizen for at least 9 years, and a citizen of a state. The average age of a U.S. senator at present is 58 years.

Clause 4. The Vice President of the United States shall be President of the Senate but shall have no Vote, unless they be equally divided.

---

[1]Modified by the 16th Amendment
[2]Replaced by Section 2, 14th Amendment

[3]Repealed by the 17th Amendment
[4]Modified by the 17th Amendment

The only constitutional duty of the vice president is specified in this clause—presiding officer of the Senate. The vice president only has a vote if there is a tie vote in the Senate; then the vice president's vote breaks the tie.

Clause 5. The Senate shall chuse their other Officers, and also a President pro tempore, in the Absence of the Vice President, or when he shall exercise the Office of President of the United States.

One official office in the U.S. Senate is specified— temporary president, who fills in during the vice president's absence (which is normally the case). All other Senate officers are designated and selected by the Senate.

Clause 6. The Senate shall have the sole Power to try all Impeachments. When sitting for that Purpose, they shall be on Oath or Affirmation. When the President of the United States is tried, the Chief Justice shall preside. And no Person shall be convicted without the Concurrence of two thirds of the Members present.

Judgment in Cases of impeachment shall not extend further than to removal from Office, and disqualification to hold and enjoy any Office of honor, Trust or Profit under the United States, but the Party convicted shall nevertheless be liable and subject to Indictment, Trial, Judgment and Punishment according to Law.

The Senate acts as a trial court for impeached federal officials. If the accused is the president, the Chief Justice of the U.S. Supreme Court presides. Otherwise, the vice president normally presides. Conviction of the charges requires a 2/3 majority vote of those senators present at the time of the vote. Conviction results in the federal official's removal from office and disqualification to hold any other federal appointed office. Removal from office does not bar further prosecution under applicable criminal or civil laws, nor does it apparently bar one from elected office. A current representative, Alcee L. Hastings, was impeached and removed as a federal district judge. He subsequently ran for Congress and represents Florida's 23rd Congressional District.

Congressional Elections: Times, Places, Manner

Section 4 The Times, Places and Manner of holding Elections for Senators and Representatives, shall be prescribed in each State by the Legislature thereof, but the Congress may at any time by Law make or alter such Regulations, except as to the Places of chusing Senators.

The Congress shall assemble at least once in every Year, and such Meeting shall be on the first Monday in December, unless they shall by Law appoint a different Day.[5]

The states determine the place and manner of electing representatives and senators, but Congress has the right to make or change these laws or regulations, except for the election sites. Congress is required to meet annually, and now, by law, annual meetings begin in January.

Powers and Duties of the Houses

Section 5 Clause 1. Each House shall be the Judge of the Elections, Returns and Qualifications of its own Members, and a Majority of each shall constitute a Quorum to do Business, but a smaller Number may adjourn from day to day, and may be authorized to compel the Attendance of absent Members, in such Manner, and under the Penalties as each House may provide.

This clause enables each legislative branch to essentially make its own rules. Normally, to take a vote, a quorum is necessary. But if no votes are scheduled, fewer than a quorum can convene a session.

Clause 2. Each House may determine the Rules of its Proceedings, punish its Members for disorderly Behaviour, and with the Concurrence of two thirds, expel a Member.

Essentially, each branch promulgates its own rules and punishes its own members. The ultimate punishment is expulsion of the member, which requires a 2/3 vote. Expulsion does not prevent the member from running again.

Clause 3. Each House shall keep a Journal of its Proceedings, and from time to time publish the same, excepting such Parts as may in their Judgment require Secrecy, and the Yeas and Nays of the Members of either House on any question shall, at the Desire of one fifth of those Present, be entered on the Journal.

An official record called the Congressional Record, House Journal, etc., is kept for all sessions. It is a daily account of House and Senate floor debates, votes, and members' remarks. However, a record is not printed if a proceeding is closed to the public for security reasons. Many votes are by voice vote, and if at least 1/5 of the members request, a recorded vote of Yeas and Nays will be conducted and recorded. This procedure permits analysis of congressional roll-call votes.

Clause 4. Neither House, during the Session of Congress shall, without the Consent of the other, adjourn for more than three days, nor to any other Place than that in which the two Houses shall be sitting.

This clause prevents one branch from adjourning for a long period or to some other location without the consent of the other branch.

Rights of Members

Section 6 Clause 1. The Senators and Representatives shall receive a Compensation for their Services, to be ascertained by Law, and paid out of the Treasury of the United States. They shall in all Cases, except Treason, Felony and Breach of the Peace, be privileged from Arrest during their Attendance at the Session of their respective Houses, and in going to and returning from the same, and for any Speech or Debate in either House, they shall not be questioned in any other Place.

This section ensures that senators and congressional representatives will be paid a salary from the U.S. Treasury. This salary is determined by no

---

[5]Changed by the 20th Amendment

other than the legislature. The current salary for members of Congress is $174,000. A small number of leadership positions, like Speaker of the House, receive a somewhat higher salary. In addition, members of Congress receive many other benefits: free health care, fully funded retirement system, free gyms, free round trips to their home state or district, etc. This section also provides immunity from arrest or prosecution for congressional actions on the floor or in travel to and from the Congress. For example, few members of Congress have ever been charged with drunk driving.

Clause 2. No Senator or Representative, shall, during the Time for which he was elected, be appointed to any civil Office under the Authority of the United States, which shall have been created, or the Emoluments whereof shall have been encreased during such time; and no Person holding any Office under the United States, shall be a Member of either House during his Continuance in Office.

This section prevents the United States from adopting a parliamentary democracy, since congressional members cannot hold executive offices and members of the executive branch cannot be members of Congress.

Legislative Powers: Bills and Resolutions

Section 7 Clause 1. All Bills for raising Revenue shall originate in the House of Representatives; but the Senate may propose or concur with Amendments as on other Bills.

This clause specifies one of the few powers specific to the U.S. House—revenue bills.

Clause 2. Every Bill which shall have passed the House of Representatives and the Senate, shall, before it becomes a Law, be presented to the President of the United States; If he approve he shall sign it, but if not he shall return it, with his Objections to that House in which it shall have originated, who shall enter the Objections at large on their Journal, and proceed to reconsider it. If after such Reconsideration two thirds of that House shall agree to pass the Bill, it shall be sent, together with the Objections, to the other House, by which it shall likewise be reconsidered, and if approved by two thirds of that House, it shall become a Law. But in all such Cases the Votes of both Houses shall be determined by Yeas and Nays, and the Names of the Persons voting for and against the Bill shall be entered on the Journal of each House respectively. If any Bill shall not be returned by the President within ten Days (Sundays excepted) after it shall have been presented to him, the Same shall be a Law, in like Manner as if he had signed it, unless the Congress by their Adjournment prevent its Return, in which Case it shall not be a Law.

The heart of the checks and balances system is contained in this clause. Both the House and Senate must pass a bill and present it to the president. If the president fails to act on the bill within 10 days (not including Sundays), the bill will automatically become law. If the president signs the bill, it becomes law. If the president vetoes the bill and sends it back to Congress, this body may override the veto by a 2/3 vote in each house. This vote must be a recorded vote.

Clause 3. Every Order, Resolution, or Vote to which the Concurrence of the Senate and House of Representatives may be necessary (except on a question of Adjournment) shall be presented to the President of the United States; and before the Same shall take Effect, shall be approved by him, or being disapproved by him, shall be repassed by two thirds of the Senate and House of Representatives, according to the Rules and Limitations prescribed in the Case of a Bill.

This clause covers every other type of legislative action other than a bill. Essentially, the same procedures apply in most cases. There are a few exceptions. For example, a joint resolution proposing a new congressional amendment is not subject to presidential veto.

Powers of Congress

Section 8 Clause 1. The Congress shall have Power to lay and collect Taxes, Duties, Imposts and Excises, to pay the Debts and provide for the common Defence and general Welfare of the United States, but all Duties, Imposts and Excises shall be uniform throughout the United States.

To borrow Money on the credit of the United States;

To regulate Commerce with foreign Nations, and among the several States, and with the Indian Tribes;

To establish an uniform Rule of Naturalization, and uniform Laws on the subject of Bankruptcies throughout the United States;

To coin Money, regulate the Value thereof, and of foreign Coin, and fix the Standard of Weights and Measures;

To provide for the Punishment of counterfeiting the Securities and current Coin of the United States;

To establish Post Offices and post Roads;

To promote the Progress of Science and useful Arts, by securing for limited Times to Authors and Inventors the exclusive Right to their respective Writings and Discoveries;

To constitute Tribunals inferior to the supreme Court;

To define and punish Piracies and Felonies committed on the high Seas, and Offences against the Law of Nations;

To declare War, grant Letters of Marque and Reprisal, and make Rules concerning Captures on Land and Water;

To raise and support Armies, but no Appropriation of Money to that Use shall be for a longer Term than two Years;

To provide and maintain a Navy;

To make Rules for the Government and Regulation of the land and naval Forces;

To provide for calling for the Militia to execute the Laws of the Union, suppress Insurrections and repel Invasions;

To provide for organizing, arming, and disciplining, the Militia, and for governing such Part of them as may be employed in the Service of the United States, reserving to the States respectively, the Appointment of the Officers, and the Authority of training the Militia according to the discipline prescribed by Congress;

This *extensive* clause establishes what are known as "enumerated," or "expressed" or "specified" powers of Congress. In theory, this serves as a limit or brake on congressional power.

Clause 2. To exercise exclusive Legislation in all Cases whatsoever, over such District (not exceeding ten Miles square) as may, by Cession of particular States, and the Acceptance of Congress, become the Seat of the Government of the United States, and to exercise like Authority over all Places purchased by the Consent of the Legislature of the State in which the Same shall be, for the Erection of Forts, Magazines, Arsenals, dock Yards, and other needful Buildings—And

This clause establishes the seat of the federal government, which was first located in New York but eventually was moved to Washington, D.C., when both Maryland and Virginia ceded land to the new national government, which then established the District of Columbia.

Clause 3. To make all Laws which shall be necessary and proper for carrying into Execution the foregoing Powers, and all other Powers vested by this Constitution in the Government of the United States, or in any Department or Officer thereof.

This clause, known as the "Elastic Clause," provides the basis for the doctrine of "implied" congressional powers, which was first introduced in the U.S. Supreme Court case of *McCulloch v. Maryland*, 1819. This doctrine tremendously expanded the power of Congress to pass legislation and make regulations.

Powers Denied to Congress

Section 9 Clause 1. The Migration or Importation of such Persons as any of the States now existing shall think proper to admit, shall not be prohibited by the Congress prior to the Year one thousand eight hundred and eight, but a Tax or duty may be imposed on such Importation, not exceeding ten dollars for each Person.

This clause was part of the Three-Fifths Compromise. Essentially, the new Congress was prohibited from stopping the importation of slaves until 1808, but it could impose a head tax, not to exceed ten dollars for each slave.

Clause 2. The Privilege of the Writ of Habeas Corpus shall not be suspended, unless when in Cases of Rebellion or Invasion the public Safety may require it.

Congress cannot suspend the writ of habeas corpus except in cases of rebellion or invasion. The writ of habeas corpus permits a judge to inquire about the legality of detention or deprivation of liberty of any citizen.

Clause 3. No Bill of Attainder or ex post facto Law shall be passed.

This provision prohibits Congress from passing either a bill of attainder (forfeiture of property in capital cases) or ex post facto laws (retroactive crimes after passage of legislation). Similar restrictions were enshrined in many state constitutions.

Clause 4. No Capitation, or other direct Tax shall be laid, unless in Proportion to the Census or Enumeration herein before directed to be taken.[6]

This clause prevented Congress from passing an income tax. Only with passage of the 16th Amendment in 1913 did Congress gain this power.

Clause 5. No Tax or Duty shall be laid on Articles exported from any State.

This section establishes free trade within the United States. The federal government cannot tax state exports.

[6]Modified by the 16th Amendment

Clause 6. No Preference shall be given by any Regulation of Commerce or Revenue to the Ports of one State over those of another; nor shall Vessels bound to, or from one State, be obliged to enter, clear, or pay Duties in another.

This clause also applies to free trade within the United States. The national government cannot show any preference to any state or maritime movements among the states.

Clause 7. No Money shall be drawn from the Treasury, but in Consequence of Appropriations made by Law, and a regular Statement and Account of the Receipts and Expenditures of all public Money shall be published from time to time.

This provision of the Constitution prevents any expenditure unless it has been specifically provided for in an appropriations bill. At the beginning of most fiscal years, Congress has not completed its work on the budget. Technically, the government cannot spend any money according to this provision and would have to shut down. So Congress normally passes a Continuing Resolution providing temporary authority to continue to spend money until the final budget is approved and signed into law.

Clause 8. No Title of Nobility shall be granted by the United States. And no Person holding any Office of Profit or Trust under them, shall, without the Consent of Congress, accept of any present, Emolument, Office, or Title, of any kind whatever, from any King, Prince, or foreign State.

Feudalism would not be established in the new country. We would have no nobles. No federal official can even accept a title of nobility (even honorary) without permission of Congress.

Powers Denied to the States

This section sets out the prohibitions on state actions.

Section 10 Clause 1. No State shall enter into any Treaty, Alliance, or Confederation, grant Letters of Marque and Reprisal, coin Money, emit Bills of Credit, make any Thing but gold and silver Coin a Tender in Payment of Debts, pass any Bill of Attainder, ex post facto Law, or Law impairing the Obligation of Contracts of grant any Title of Nobility.

This particular clause presents a list of denied powers. Note that these restrictions cannot even be waived by Congress. States are not to engage in foreign relations, nor acts of war. A letter of Marque and Reprisal was used during the Revolutionary War to provide legal cover for privateers. The federal government's currency monopoly is established. The sanctity of contracts is specified. And similar state prohibitions are specified for bills of attainder, ex post facto, etc.

Clause 2. No State shall, without the Consent of the Congress, lay any Imposts or Duties on Imports or Exports, except what may be absolutely necessary for executing its inspection Laws: and the net Produce of all Duties and Imposts, laid by any State on Imports or Exports, shall be for the Use of the Treasury of the United States, and all such Laws shall be subject to the Revision and Controul of the Congress.

This section establishes the monopoly control of the national government in matters of both national and international trade. The only concession to states is health and safety inspections.

Clause 3. No State shall, without the Consent of Congress, lay any Duty of Tonnage, keep Troops, or Ships of War in time of Peace, enter into any Agreement or Compact with another State, or with a foreign Power, or engage in War, unless actually invaded, or in such imminent Danger as will not admit of delay.

This final section of the Legislative article establishes the war monopoly power of the national government. The only exception to state action is actual invasion or threat of imminent danger.

ARTICLE II—THE EXECUTIVE ARTICLE

This article establishes an entirely new concept in government—an elected executive power.

Nature and Scope of Presidential Power

Section 1 Clause 1. The executive Power shall be vested in a President of the United States of America. He shall hold his Office during the Term of four Years and, together with the Vice President, chosen for the same Term, be elected, as follows.

This clause establishes the executive power in the office of the president of the United States of America. It also establishes a second office—vice president. A 4-year term was established, but no limit on the number of terms. A limit was later established by the 22nd Amendment.

Clause 2. Each State shall appoint, in such Manner as the Legislature thereof may direct, a Number of Electors, equal to the whole Number of Senators and Representatives to which the State may be entitled in the Congress: but no Senator or Representative, or Person holding an Office of Trust or Profit under the United States, shall be appointed an Elector.

This paragraph essentially establishes the Electoral College to choose the president and vice president.

Clause 3. The Electors shall meet in their respective States, and vote by Ballot for two Persons, of whom one at least shall not be an Inhabitant of the same State with themselves. And they shall make a List of all the Persons voted for, and of the Number of Votes for each; which List they shall sign and certify, and transmit sealed to the Seat of the Government of the United States, directed to the President of the Senate. The President of the Senate shall, in the Presence of the Senate and House of Representatives, open all the Certificates, and the Votes shall then be counted. The Person having the greatest Number of Votes shall be the President, if such Number be a Majority of the whole Number of Electors appointed; and if there be more than one who have such Majority and have an equal Number of Votes, then the House of Representatives shall immediately chuse by Ballot one of them for President; and if no Person have a Majority, then from the five highest on the List the said House shall in like Manner chuse the President. But in chusing the President, the Votes shall be taken by States, the Representation from each State having one Vote; a quorum for this Purpose shall consist of a Member or Members from two thirds of the States, and a Majority of all the States shall be necessary to a

Choice. In every Case, after the Choice of the President, the Person having the greatest Number of Votes of the Electors shall be the Vice President. But if there should remain two or more who have equal Votes, the Senate shall chuse from them by Ballot the Vice President.[7]

This paragraph has been superseded by the 12th Amendment. The original language did not require a separate vote for president and vice president. This resulted in a tied vote in the Electoral College in 1800 when both Thomas Jefferson and Aaron Burr received 73 electoral votes. The 12th Amendment requires a separate vote for each. Only one of the two can be from the state of the elector. This means that it is highly unlikely that the presidential and vice presidential candidates would be from the same state. This question arose in the 2000 election when Dick Cheney, who lived and worked in Texas, had to reestablish his residence in Wyoming, so that he would have a different state residence than Texan George W. Bush.

The original language provided for a House election in the case of no majority vote or a tie vote among the top five candidates. The amendment lowered the number of candidates to the top three. The Senate is to select the vice president if a candidate does not have an electoral majority or in the case of a tie vote. The Senate considers only the top two candidates. The amendment also clarifies that the qualifications of the vice president are the same as those for president.

In the 2008 presidential campaign, some promoted the Hispanic Senator from Florida, Mel Martinez, as a possible running mate for John McCain to help win the Hispanic vote. There was, however, a big problem. Mel Martinez was born in Cuba and thus would not meet the qualification to become president of the United States. Once this was realized, all talk about Martinez disappeared.

Clause 4. The Congress may determine the Time of chusing the Electors, and the Day on which they shall give their Votes; which Day shall be the same throughout the United States.

Congress is given the power to establish a uniform day and time for the state selection of electors.

Clause 5. No Person except a natural born Citizen, or a Citizen of the United States, at the time of the Adoption of this Constitution, shall be eligible to the Office of President; neither shall any Person be eligible to that Office who shall not have attained to the Age of thirty five Years, and been fourteen Years a Resident within the United States.

The qualifications for the offices of president and vice president are specified here—at least 35 years old, 14 years' resident in the United States, and a natural-born citizen or citizen of the United States. The requirement that the president be born in the United States may bar the candidacy of otherwise qualified persons, for example Arnold Schwarzenegger, Governor of California in 2010.

---

[7]Changed by the 12th and 20th Amendments

See further discussion of this issue in the Constitutional Note at the end of Chapter 2, page 51.

Clause 6. In Case of the Removal of the President from Office, or of his Death, Resignation, or Inability to discharge the Powers and Duties of the said Office, the Same shall devolve on the Vice President, and the Congress may by Law provide for the Case of Removal, Death, Resignation, or Inability, both of the President and Vice President, declaring what Officer shall then act as president, and such Officer shall act accordingly, until the Disability be removed, or a President shall be elected.[8]

This clause has been modified by the 25th Amendment. Upon the death, resignation, or impeachment and conviction of the president, the vice president becomes president. The new president nominates a new vice president, who assumes the office, if approved by a majority vote in both congressional branches. The president is also now able to notify the Congress of his inability to perform his office.

This clause was tested when Richard Nixon resigned as president and Gerald Ford, who was vice president, moved up to become president. President Ford nominated Nelson Rockefeller to become the new vice president, who was approved by a majority vote of the House and Senate. However, Ford assumed the vice presidency because Spiro Agnew, who was elected with Richard Nixon in 1968, also resigned office in 1973. This was an extreme test of the 25th Amendment.

Clause 7. The President shall, at stated Times, receive for his Services, a Compensation which shall neither be encreased nor diminished during the Period of which he shall have been elected, and he shall not receive within that Period any other Emolument from the United States, or any of them.

This section covers the compensation of the president, which cannot be increased or decreased during his office. The current salary is $400,000/year.

Clause 8. Before he enter on the Execution of his Office, he shall take the following Oath or Affirmation—"I do solemnly swear (or affirm) that I will faithfully execute the Office of President of the United States, and will to the best of my Ability, preserve, protect and defend the Constitution of the United States."

This final clause in Section 1 is the oath of office administered to the new president. The Chief Justice of the United States customarily swears in the president on Inauguration Day. But Chief Justice John Roberts botched the language of the oath when swearing in President Barack Obama, causing the new president to be sworn in a second time the next day.

Powers and Duties of the President

Section 2 Clause 1. The President shall be the Commander in Chief of the Army and Navy of the United States, and of the Militia of the several States; when called into the actual Service of the United States, he may require the Opinion, in writing, of the principal Officer in each of the executive Departments, upon any Subject relating to the Duties of their respective Offices, and he shall

have the Power to grant Reprieves and Pardons for Offences against the United States, except in Cases of Impeachment.

This clause establishes the president as Commander-in-Chief of the U.S. armed forces. George Washington actually led U.S. armed forces during the Whiskey Rebellion. The second provision provides the basis for cabinet meetings that are used to acquire the opinions of executive department heads. The last provision provides an absolute pardon or reprieve power from the president. The provision was controversial, but legal, when President Gerald Ford pardoned Richard Nixon following the Watergate scandal.

Clause 2. He shall have Power, by and with the Advice and Consent of the Senate to make Treaties, provided two thirds of the Senators present concur, and he shall nominate, and by and with the Advice and Consent of the Senate, shall appoint Ambassadors, other public Ministers and Consuls, Judges of the supreme Court, and all other Officers of the United States, whose Appointments are not herein otherwise provided for, and which shall be established by Law but the Congress may by Law vest the Appointment of such inferior Officers, as they think proper in the President alone, in the Courts of Law, or in the Heads of Departments.

This clause covers two important presidential powers, treaty making and appointments. The president (via the State Department) can negotiate treaties with other nations, but these do not become official until ratified by a 2/3 vote of the U.S. Senate. The president is empowered to appoint judges, ambassadors, and other U.S. officials (cabinet officers, military officers, agency heads, etc.) subject to Senate approval. The Congress can and does delegate this approval to the president in the case of inferior officers. For example, junior military officer promotions are not submitted to the Senate, but senior officer promotions are.

Clause 3. The President shall have Power to fill up all Vacancies that may happen during the Recess of the Senate, by granting Commissions which shall expire at the End of their next Session.

This provision allows recess appointments of the officials listed in Clause 2 above. These commissions automatically expire unless approved by the Senate by the end of the next session. Presidents have used this provision to fill jobs when the nomination process is stalled.

Section 3 He shall from time to time give to the Congress Information of the State of the Union, and recommend to their Consideration such Measures as he shall judge necessary and expedient, he may, on extraordinary Occasions convene both Houses, or either of them and in Case of Disagreement between them, with Respect to the Time of Adjournment, he may adjourn them to such Time as he shall think proper, he shall receive Ambassadors and other public Ministers, he shall take Care that the Laws be faithfully executed, and shall Commission all the Officers of the United States.

This section provides for the annual State of the Union address to a joint session of Congress and the American people. The president is also authorized

---

[8]Modified by the 25th Amendment

to call special meetings of either the House or Senate. If there is disagreement between the House and Senate regarding adjournment, the president is empowered to adjourn them. This would be extremely rare. The president formally receives other nations' ambassadors; this power of diplomatic recognition can be used to accept or reject governments around the world. The next to last provision to faithfully execute laws provides the basis for the whole administrative apparatus of the presidency. All officers of the United States receive a formal commission from the president (most of these are signed with a signature machine).

Section 4 The President, Vice President and all civil Officers of the United States, shall be removed from Office on Impeachment for, and Conviction of, Treason, Bribery, or other high Crimes and Misdemeanors.

This section provides the constitutional authority for the impeachment and trial of the president, vice president, and all civil officers of the United States for treason, bribery, or other high crimes and misdemeanors (the exact meaning of this phrase is unclear and is often more political than judicial).

ARTICLE III—THE JUDICIAL ARTICLE

Judicial Power, Courts, Judges

Section 1 The judicial Power of the United States, shall be vested in one supreme Court, and in such inferior Courts as the Congress may from time to time ordain and establish. The Judges, both of the supreme and inferior Courts, shall hold their Offices during good Behaviour, and shall, at stated Times, receive for their Services, a Compensation, which shall not be diminished during their Continuance in Office.

This section establishes the judicial branch in very general terms. It specifically provides only for the Supreme Court. Congress is given the responsibility to flesh out the court system. It initially did so in the Judiciary Act of 1789, when it established 13 district courts (one for each state) and 3 appellate courts. All federal judges hold their offices for life and can only be removed for breaches of good behavior—a very nebulous term. Federal judges have been removed for drunkenness, accepting bribes, and other misdemeanors. To date, no justice of the U.S. Supreme Court has ever been removed.

The salary of federal judges is set by congressional act, but can never be reduced. Although the American Bar Association and the Federal Bar Association consider federal judges' salaries inadequate, most Americans would probably disagree. Federal district judges earn $169,300/year, appellate judges $179,500, and Supreme Court justices $208,100. The Chief Justice is paid $212,100. These are lifetime salaries, even upon retirement.

Jurisdiction

Section 2 The judicial Power shall extend to all Cases, in Law and Equity, arising under this Constitution, the Laws of the United States, and Treaties made, or which shall be made, under their Authority,—to all Cases affecting Ambassadors, other public Ministers and Consuls;—to all Cases of admiralty and maritime Jurisdiction;—to Controversies to which the United States shall be a Party;—to Controversies between two or more States; between a State and Citizens of another State;[9]—between Citizens of different States;—between Citizens of the same State claiming Lands under Grants of different States, and between a State, or the Citizens thereof, and foreign States, Citizens, or Subjects.

In all Cases affecting Ambassadors, other public Ministers and Consuls, and those in which a State shall be Party, the supreme Court shall have original Jurisdiction. In all the other Cases before mentioned, the supreme Court shall have appellate Jurisdiction, both as to Law and Fact, with such Exceptions, and under such Regulations as Congress shall make.

The Trial of all Crimes, except in Cases of Impeachment, shall be by Jury; and such Trial shall be held in the State where the said Crimes shall have been committed; but when not committed within any State, the Trial shall be at such Place or Places as the Congress may by Law have directed.

This section establishes the original and appellate jurisdiction of the U.S. Supreme Court. With the Congress of Vienna's 1815 establishment of "diplomatic immunity," the U.S. Supreme Court no longer hears cases involving ambassadors. Since 1925, the Supreme Court no longer hears every case on appeal but can select which cases it will accept, which is now only about 100–150 cases per year. This section also establishes the right of trial by jury for federal crimes.

Treason

Section 3 Treason against the United States, shall consist only in levying War against them, or in adhering to their Enemies, giving them Aid and Comfort. No Person shall be convicted of Treason unless on the Testimony of two Witnesses to the same overt Act, or on Confession in open Court.

The Congress shall have Power to declare the Punishment of Treason, but no Attainder of Treason shall work Corruption of Blood, or Forfeiture except during the Life of the Person attainted.

Treason is the only crime defined in the U.S. Constitution. Congress established the penalty of death for treason convictions. Note that two witnesses are required to convict anyone of treason. Even in cases of treasonable conduct, seizure of estates is prohibited.

ARTICLE IV—INTERSTATE RELATIONS

Full Faith and Credit Clause

Section 1 Full Faith and Credit shall be given in each State to the public Acts, Records, and judicial Proceedings of every other State. And the Congress may by general Laws prescribe the Manner in which such Acts, Records and Proceedings shall be proved, and the Effect thereof.

This section provides that the official acts and records of one state will be recognized and given credence by other states, e.g., marriages and divorces.

---

[9]Modified by the 11th Amendment

Privileges and Immunities, Interstate Extradition

Section 2 Clause 1. The Citizens of each State shall be entitled to all Privileges and Immunities of Citizens in the several States.

This clause requires states to treat citizens of other states equally. For example, when driving in another state, one's driver's license is recognized. One area not so clear is that of charging higher tuitions at state educational institutions for out-of-state students.

Clause 2. A person charged in any State with Treason, Felony or other Crime, who shall flee from Justice, and be found in another State, shall on Demand of the executive Authority of the State from which he fled, be delivered up, to be removed to the State having Jurisdiction of the Crime.

Extradition is the name of this clause. A criminal fleeing to another state, if captured, can be returned to the state where the crime was committed. But this is not an absolute. A state's governor can refuse, for good reason, to extradite someone to another state.

Clause 3. No person held to Service or Labour in one State, under the Laws thereof, escaping into another, shall, in Consequence of any Law or Regulation therein, be discharged from such Service or Labour, but shall be delivered up on Claim of the Party to whom such Service or Labour may be due.[10]

This clause was included to cover runaway slaves. It has been made inoperable by the 13th Amendment, which abolished slavery.

Admission of States

Section 3 New States may be admitted by the Congress into this Union but no new State shall be formed or erected within the Jurisdiction of any other State, nor any State to be formed by the Junction of two or more States, or Parts of States, without the Consent of the Legislatures of the States concerned as well as of the Congress.

The Congress shall have Power to dispose of and make all needful Rules and Regulations respecting the Territory or other Property belonging to the United States, and nothing in this Constitution shall be so construed as to Prejudice any Claims of the United States, or of any particular State.

This section concerns the admission of new states to the Union. In theory, no state can be created from part of another state without permission of the state legislature. But West Virginia was formed from Virginia during the Civil War without the permission of Virginia, which was part of the Confederacy. With fifty states now part of the Union, this section has not been used for many decades. The only future use may be in the case of Puerto Rico or perhaps Washington, D.C.

Republican Form of Government

Section 4 The United States shall guarantee to every State in this Union a Republican Form of Government, and shall protect each of them against Invasion, and on Application of the Legislature, or of the Executive (when the Legislature cannot be convened) against domestic Violence.

This section commits the federal government to guarantee a republican form of government to each state and protect the state against foreign invasion or domestic insurrection.

See discussion in the Constitutional Note at the end of Chapter 1, Page 20.

ARTICLE V—THE AMENDING POWER

The Congress, whenever two thirds of both Houses shall deem it necessary, shall propose Amendments to this Constitution, or, on the Application of the Legislatures of two thirds of the several States, shall call a Convention for proposing Amendments, which, in either Case, shall be valid to all Intents and Purposes, as Part of this Constitution, when ratified by the Legislatures of three fourths of the several States, or by Conventions in three fourths thereof, as the one or the other Mode of Ratification may be proposed by the Congress; Provided that no Amendment which may be made prior to the Year One thousand eight hundred and eight shall in any Manner affect the first and fourth Clauses in the Ninth Section of the first Article; and that no State, without its Consent, shall be deprived of its equal Suffrage in the Senate.

Amendment to the U.S. Constitution can be originated by a 2/3 vote in both the U.S. House and Senate or by 2/3 of the state legislatures asking for a convention to propose amendments. Proposed amendments, by either route, must be approved by 3/4 of state legislatures or by 3/4 of conventions convened in the states for purposes of ratification. Only one amendment has been ratified by the convention method—Amendment 21 to repeal the 18th Amendment establishing Prohibition.

Thousands of amendments have been proposed; few have been passed by 2/3 vote in each branch of Congress. The Equal Rights Amendment was one such case, but it was not ratified by 3/4 of state legislatures. There have only been 27 successful amendments to the U.S. Constitution.

ARTICLE VI—THE SUPREMACY CLAUSE

Clause 1. All Debts contracted and Engagements entered into, before the Adoption of this Constitution, shall be as valid against the United States under the Constitution, as under the Confederation.

This clause made the new national government responsible for all debts incurred during the Revolutionary War. This was very important to banking and commercial interests.

Clause 2. This Constitution, and the Laws of the United States which shall be made in Pursuance thereof, and all Treaties made, or which shall be made, under the Authority of the United States, shall be the supreme Law of the Land, and the Judges in every State shall be bound thereby any Thing in the Constitution or Laws of any State to the Contrary notwithstanding.

This is the Supremacy Clause, the heart of the Constitution. It provides the basis for the supremacy of the Constitution itself, as well as federal laws "made in pursuance thereof," over the constitutions and laws of the states.

---

[10]Repealed by the 13th Amendment

Clause 3. The Senators and Representatives before mentioned, and the Members of the several State Legislatures, and all executive and judicial Officers, both of the United States and of the several States, shall be bound by Oath or Affirmation, to support this Constitution, but no religious Test shall ever be required as a Qualification to any Office or public Trust under the United States.

This clause requires essentially all federal and state officials to swear or affirm their allegiance to and support of the U.S. Constitution. Note that a religious test was prohibited for federal office. However, some states used religious tests for voting and office qualification until the 1830s.

ARTICLE VII—RATIFICATION

The Ratification of the Conventions of nine States, shall be sufficient for the Establishment of this Constitution between the States so ratifying the Same.

Done in Convention by the Unanimous Consent of the States present the Seventeenth Day of September in the Year of our Lord one thousand seven hundred and Eighty seven and of the Independence of the United States of America the Twelfth. *In Witness whereof We have hereunto subscribed our Names.*

Realizing the unanimous ratification of the thirteen states of the new Constitution might never have occurred, the framers wisely specified that only nine states would be needed for ratification. Even this proved to be a test of wills between Federalists and Anti-Federalists, leading to publication of the great political work *The Federalist*.

AMENDMENTS THE BILL OF RIGHTS

[The first ten amendments were ratified on December 15, 1791, and form what is known as the "Bill of Rights."]

The Bill of Rights applied initially only to the federal government and not to state or local governments. Beginning in 1925 in the case of *Gitlow v. New York*, the U.S. Supreme Court began to selectively incorporate the Bill of Rights, making its provisions applicable to state and local governments.

AMENDMENT 1—RELIGION, SPEECH, ASSEMBLY, AND POLITICS

Congress shall make no law respecting an establishment of religion, or prohibiting the free exercise thereof; or abridging the freedom of speech, or of the press; or the right of the people peaceably to assemble, and to petition the Government for a redress of grievances.

This is the godfather of all amendments in that it protects five fundamental freedoms: religion, speech, press, assembly, and petition. Note that the press is the only business that is specifically protected by the U.S. Constitution. Freedom of religion and speech are two of the most contentious issues and generate a multitude of Supreme Court cases.

AMENDMENT 2—MILITIA AND THE RIGHT TO BEAR ARMS

A well-regulated Militia, being necessary to the security of a free State, the right of the people to keep and bear Arms, shall not be infringed.

For many years controversy surrounded this amendment. Did it apply only to state militia (National Guard) units? Or did it protect the right of individual citizens to possess guns? The U.S. Supreme Court finally decided in 2008 that "the Second Amendment protects an individual right to possess a firearm unconnected with service in a militia."

AMENDMENT 3—QUARTERING OF SOLDIERS

No Soldier shall, in time of peace be quartered in any house, without the consent of the Owner, nor in time of war, but in manner to be prescribed by law.

It was the practice of the British government to insist that colonists provide room and board to British troops. This amendment was designed to prohibit this practice. Today, military and naval bases provide the necessary quarters.

AMENDMENT 4—SEARCHES AND SEIZURES

The right of the people to be secure in their persons, houses, papers, and effects, against unreasonable searches and seizures, shall not be violated, and no Warrants shall issue, but upon probable cause, supported by Oath or affirmation, and particularly describing the place to be searched, and the persons or things to be seized.

This is an extremely important amendment to prevent the abuse of state police powers. Essentially, searches or seizures of homes, persons, or property cannot be undertaken without probable cause or a warrant that specifically describes the place to be searched, the person involved, and suspicious things to be seized. However, there are a number of exceptions, including searches accompanying a valid arrest.

AMENDMENT 5—GRAND JURIES, SELF-INCRIMINATION, DOUBLE JEOPARDY, DUE PROCESS, AND EMINENT DOMAIN

No person shall be held to answer for a capital, or otherwise infamous crime, unless on a presentment or indictment of a Grand jury, except in cases arising in the land or naval forces, or in the Militia, when in actual service in time of War or public danger; nor shall any person be subject for the same offence to be twice put in jeopardy of life or limb, nor shall be compelled in any criminal case to be a witness against himself, nor be deprived of life, liberty, or property, without due process of law; nor shall private property be taken for public use, without just compensation.

Only a grand jury can indict a person for a federal crime. This provision does not apply to state/local governments. This amendment also covers double jeopardy, or being tried twice for the same crime

in the same jurisdiction. Note that since the federal government and state governments are different jurisdictions, one could be tried in each jurisdiction for essentially the same crime. For example, it is a federal crime to kill a congressperson. It is also a state crime to murder anyone. Further, this amendment also covers the prohibition of self-incrimination. Pleading the 5th Amendment is common among defendants. The deprivation of life, liberty, or property by any level of government is prohibited unless due process of law is applied. Finally, private property may not be taken under the doctrine of "eminent domain" unless the government provides just compensation and the taking is for public purposes.

AMENDMENT 6—CRIMINAL COURT PROCEDURES

In all criminal prosecutions, the accused shall enjoy the right to a speedy and public trial, by an impartial jury of the State and district wherein the crime shall have been committed, which district shall have been previously ascertained by law, and to be informed of the nature and cause of the accusation, to be confronted with the witnesses against him, to have compulsory process for obtaining witnesses in his favor, and to have the Assistance of Counsel for his defence.

This amendment requires public trials by jury for criminal prosecutions. Anyone accused of a crime is guaranteed the right to be informed of the charges; confront witnesses; to subpoena witnesses for his or her defense; and to have a lawyer for his or her defense. The government must provide a lawyer for a defendant unable to afford one.

AMENDMENT 7—TRIAL BY JURY IN COMMON LAW CASES

In Suits at common law, where the value in controversy shall exceed twenty dollars, the right of trial by jury shall be preserved, and no fact tried by a jury shall be otherwise re-examined in any Court of the United States, than according to the rules of the common law.

This amendment is practically without meaning in modern times. Statutory law has largely superseded common law. Federal civil law suits with a guaranteed jury are now restricted to cases that exceed $50,000. The Bill of Rights, which includes the right to trial by jury, applied originally only to the national government. Beginning in 1925, the Supreme Court began a selective process of incorporating provisions of the Bill of Rights, applicable to state/local governments as well. There are just a few provisions that have not been thus incorporated. Trial by jury is one. Some state/local governments have trials by judges, not by juries.

AMENDMENT 8—BAIL, CRUEL AND UNUSUAL PUNISHMENT

Excessive bail shall not be required, nor excessive fines imposed, nor cruel and unusual punishments inflicted.

Capital punishment is covered by this amendment, which also prohibits excessive bail. But this is relative. Million-dollar bails are not uncommon in some cases. One federal judge offered voluntary castration for sex offenders in lieu of jail time. Higher courts held this to be a cruel or unusual punishment. But it is the death penalty that generates the most heated controversy. Court cases challenging the constitutionality of capital punishment cite this amendment's language prohibiting cruel and unusual punishment. For a period of 4 years, the Supreme Court banned capital punishment. When states modified their statutes to provide a two-part judicial process of guilt determination and punishment, the Supreme Court allowed the reinstitution of capital punishment by the states.

The enumeration in the Constitution of certain rights, shall not be construed to deny or disparage others retained by the people.

This amendment implies that there may be other rights of the people not specified by the previous amendments. Indeed, the Supreme Court has established a right to privacy even though it is not mentioned in the Constitution.

AMENDMENT 10—RESERVED POWERS OF THE STATES

The powers not delegated to the United States by the Constitution, nor prohibited by it to the States, are reserved to the States respectively, or to the people.

The 10th Amendment was seen as the reservoir of reserved powers for state governments. If the national government had been limited only to expressed powers in Article 1, Section 8, of the Constitution, this would have been the case. But the doctrine of implied national government powers, which was established by the U.S. Supreme Court in *McCulloch v. Maryland* in 1819, made the intent of this amendment almost meaningless. What reserved powers that were retained by the states were virtually removed by the U.S. Supreme Court's decision in the *Garcia v. San Antonio Metropolitan Transit Authority* case in 1985, which basically told state/local governments not to look to the courts to protect their residual rights but rather to their political representatives. In subsequent cases, however, the Supreme Court has retreated somewhat from this position when the court found the federal government encroaching in traditional state jurisdictional areas.

AMENDMENT 11—SUITS AGAINST THE STATES

[Ratified February 7, 1795]

The Judicial power of the United States shall not be construed to extend to any suit in law or equity, commenced or prosecuted against one of the United States by Citizens of another State, or by Citizens or Subjects of any Foreign State.

Article 3 of the U.S. Constitution originally allowed federal jurisdiction in cases of one state citizen against another state citizen or state. This amendment removes federal jurisdiction in this area. In essence, states may not be sued in federal court by citizens of another state or country.

AMENDMENT 12—ELECTION OF THE PRESIDENT

[Ratified June 15, 1804]

The Electors shall meet in their respective states, and vote by ballot for President and Vice-President, one of whom, at least, shall not be an inhabitant of the same state with themselves; they shall name in their ballots the person voted for as President, and in distinct ballots the person voted for as Vice-President, and they shall make distinct lists of all persons voted for as President, and of all persons voted for as Vice-President, and of the number of votes for each, which lists they shall sign and certify, and transmit sealed to the seat of the government of the United States, directed to the President of the Senate;—The President of the Senate shall, in presence of the Senate and House of Representatives, open all the certificates and the votes shall then be counted;—The person having the greatest number of votes for President, shall be the President, if such number be a majority of the whole number of Electors appointed; and if no person have such majority, then from the persons having the highest numbers not exceeding three on the list of those voted for as President, the House of Representatives shall choose immediately, by ballot, the President. But in choosing the President, the votes shall be taken by states, the representation from each state having one vote; a quorum for this purpose shall consist of a member or members from two-thirds of the states, and a majority of all states shall be necessary to a choice. And if the House of Representatives shall not choose a President whenever the right of choice shall devolve upon them, before the fourth day of March next following, then the Vice-President shall act as President, as in the case of the death or other constitutional disability of the President.[11] The person having the greatest number of votes as Vice-President, shall be the Vice-President, if such a number be a majority of the whole numbers of Electors appointed, and if no person have a majority, then from the two highest numbers on the list, the Senate shall choose the Vice-President, a quorum for the purpose shall consist of two-thirds of the whole number of Senators, and a majority of the whole number shall be necessary to a choice. But no person constitutionally ineligible to the office of President shall be eligible to that of Vice-President of the United States.

This was a necessary amendment to correct a flaw in the Constitution covering operations of the Electoral College. In the election of 1800, both Thomas Jefferson and Aaron Burr, of the same Democratic-Republican Party, received the same number of electoral votes, 73, for president. Article II of the original Constitution specified that each elector would cast two ballots. It did not specify for whom. This amendment clarifies that the electoral vote must be specific for president and vice president. The original Constitution provided that if no candidate received a majority of electoral votes, the House would decide from the candidates with the top five vote totals. This amendment reduces the candidate field to the top three vote totals. If the House delays in this selection past the fourth day of March, the elected vice president will act as president until the House selects the president. The original Constitution provided that the

candidate with the second highest number of electoral votes would become vice president.

This amendment, which requires a separate vote tally for vice president, provides for selection by the U.S. Senate if no vice presidential candidate receives an electoral vote majority.

AMENDMENT 13—PROHIBITION OF SLAVERY

[Ratified December 6, 1865]

Section 1 Neither slavery nor involuntary servitude, except as a punishment for crime whereof the party shall have been duly convicted, shall exist within the United States, or any place subject to their jurisdiction.

Section 2 Congress shall have power to enforce this article by appropriate legislation.

This is the first of the three Civil War amendments. Slavery is prohibited under all circumstances. Involuntary servitude is also prohibited unless it is a punishment for a convicted crime.

AMENDMENT 14—CITIZENSHIP, DUE PROCESS, AND EQUAL PROTECTION OF THE LAWS

[Ratified July 9, 1868]

Section 1 All persons born or naturalized in the United States, and subject to the jurisdiction thereof, are citizens of the United States and of the State wherein they reside. No State shall make or enforce any law which shall abridge the privileges or immunities of citizens of the United States; nor shall any State deprive any person of life, liberty, or property, without due process of law; nor deny to any person within its jurisdiction the equal protection of the laws.

This section defines the meaning of U.S. citizenship and protection of these citizenship rights. It also establishes the Equal Protection Clause that each state must guarantee to its citizens. It extended the provisions of the 5th Amendment of due process and protection of life, liberty, and property and made these applicable to the states.

Section 2 Representatives shall be apportioned among the several States according to their respective numbers, counting the whole number of persons in each State, excluding Indians not taxed. But when the right to vote at any election for the choice of electors for President and Vice President of the United States, Representatives in Congress, the Executive and Judicial officers of a State, or the members of the Legislature thereof, is denied to any of the male inhabitants of such State, being twenty-one[12] years of age, and citizens of the United States, or in any way abridged, except for participation in rebellion, or other crime, the basis of representation therein shall be reduced in the proportion which the number of such male citizens shall bear to the whole number of male citizens twenty-one years of age in such State.

This section changes the Three-Fifths Clause of the original Constitution. If a state denies the right to vote to any male 21 or older, the number of denied

---

[11]Changed by the 20th Amendment

[12]Changed by the 26th Amendment

citizens will be deducted from the over-all state total to determine representation.

Section 3 No person shall be a Senator or Representative in Congress, or elector of President and Vice President, or hold any office, civil or military under the United States, or under any State, who, having previously taken an oath, as a member of Congress, or as an officer of the United States, or as a member of any State legislature, or as an executive or judicial officer of any State, to support the Constitution of the United States, shall have engaged in insurrection or rebellion against the same, or given aid or comfort to the enemies thereof. But Congress may by a vote of two-thirds of each House, remove such disability.

This section disqualifies from federal office or elector for president or vice president anyone who rebelled or participated in an insurrection against the Constitution. This was specifically directed against citizens of Southern states. Congress by a 2/3 vote could override this provision.

Section 4 The validity of the public debt of the United States, authorized by law, including debts incurred for payment of pensions and bounties for services in suppressing insurrection or rebellion, shall not be questioned. But neither the United States nor any State shall assume or pay any debt or obligation incurred in aid of insurrection or rebellion against the United States or any claim for the loss or emancipation of any slave, but all such debts, obligations and claims shall be held illegal and void.

Section 5 The Congress shall have power to enforce, by appropriate legislation, the provisions of this article.

These sections guarantee payment of Civil War debts incurred by the U.S. government but declare void any debts incurred by the Confederacy.

AMENDMENT 15—THE RIGHT TO VOTE

[Ratified February 3, 1870]

Section 1 The right of citizens of the United States to vote shall not be denied or abridged by the United States or by any State on account of race, color, or previous condition of servitude.

Section 2 The Congress shall have power to enforce this article by appropriate legislation.

This final Civil War amendment guarantees that voting rights cannot be denied by any states on account of race, color, or previous servitude. Unfortunately, it did not mention sex or gender.

AMENDMENT 16—INCOME TAXES

[Ratified February 3, 1913]

The Congress shall have power to lay and collect taxes on incomes, from whatever source derived, without apportionment among the several States, and without regard to any census or enumeration.

Article 1, Section 9, of the original Constitution prohibited Congress from enacting a direct tax (head tax) unless in proportion to a census. Congress in 1894 passed an income tax law, levying a 2 percent tax on incomes over $4,000. In 1895, the U.S. Supreme Court in a split decision (5–4) found

that the income tax was a direct tax not apportioned among the states and was therefore unconstitutional. Thus Congress proposed an amendment allowing it to enact an income tax. Once this amendment was ratified, the flow of tax money to Washington increased tremendously.

AMENDMENT 17—DIRECT ELECTION OF SENATORS

[Ratified April 8, 1913]

The Senate of the United States shall be composed of two Senators from each State, elected by the people thereof, for six years and each Senator shall have one vote. The electors in each State shall have the qualifications requisite for electors of the most numerous branch of the State legislatures.

When vacancies happen in the representation of any State in the Senate, the executive authority of such State shall issue writs of election to fill such vacancies: Provided, That the legislature of any State may empower the executive thereof to make temporary appointment until the people fill the vacancies by election as the legislature may direct.

This amendment shall not be so construed as to affect the election or term of any Senator chosen before it becomes valid as part of the Constitution.

Prior to this amendment, U.S. senators were selected by state legislatures. Now U.S. senators would be selected by popular vote in each state. Further, the governor of each state may fill vacancies, subject to state laws.

AMENDMENT 18—PROHIBITION

[Ratified January 16, 1919, Repealed December 5, 1933, by Amendment 21]

Section 1 After one year from the ratification of this article the manufacture, sale, or transportation of intoxicating liquors within, the importation thereof into, or the exportation thereof from the United States and all territory subject to the jurisdiction thereof for beverage purposes is hereby prohibited.

Section 2 The Congress and the several States shall have concurrent power to enforce this article by appropriate legislation.

Section 3 This article shall be inoperative unless it shall have been ratified as an amendment to the Constitution by the legislatures of the several States, as provided in the Constitution, within seven years from the date of the submission hereof to the States by the Congress.[13]

This amendment was largely the work of the Women's Christian Temperance Union and essentially banned the manufacture, sale, or transportation of alcoholic beverages. Unintended consequences of this attempt to legislate morality were the brewing of "bathtub gin" and moonshine liquor, and the involvement of the mob in importing liquor from Canada. This ill-fated social experiment was corrected by the 21st Amendment. This is also the first amendment for which Congress fixed a period for ratification—7 years.

---

[13]Repealed by the 21st Amendment

AMENDMENT 19—WOMEN'S SUFFRAGE

[Ratified August 18, 1920]

The right of the citizens of the United States to vote shall not be denied or abridged by the United States or by any State on account of sex.

Congress shall have power to enforce this article by appropriate legislation.

At long last, women achieved voting parity with men.

AMENDMENT 20—THE LAME DUCK AMENDMENT

[Ratified January 23, 1933]

Section 1 The terms of the President and Vice President shall end at noon on the 20th day of January, and the terms of the Senators and Representatives at noon on the 3d day of January, of the years in which such terms would have ended if this article had not been ratified, and the terms of their successors shall then begin.

Section 2 The Congress shall assemble at least once in every year, and such meeting shall begin at noon on the 3d day of January, unless they shall by law appoint a different day.

Section 3 If, at the time fixed for the beginning of the term of the President, the President elect shall have died, the Vice President elect shall become President. If a President shall not have been chosen before the time fixed for the beginning of his term, or if the President elect shall have failed to qualify, then the Vice President elect shall act as President until a President shall have qualified, and the Congress may by law provide for the case wherein neither a President elect nor a Vice President elect shall have qualified, declaring who shall then act as President, or the manner in which one who is to act shall be selected, and such person shall act accordingly until a President or Vice President shall have qualified.

Section 4 The Congress may by law provide for the case of the death of any of the persons from whom the House of Representatives may choose a President whenever the right of choice shall have devolved upon them, and for the case of the death of any of the persons from whom the Senate may choose a Vice President whenever the right of choice shall have devolved upon them.

Section 5 Sections 1 and 2 shall take effect on the 15th day of October following the ratification of this article.

Section 6 This article shall be inoperative unless it shall have been ratified as an amendment to the Constitution by the legislatures of three-fourths of the several States within seven years from the date of its submission.

Called the Lame Duck amendment, this amendment fixes the dates for the end of presidential and legislative terms. A new president is elected in November, but the current president remains in office until January 20 of the following year. Thus the term "lame duck." Legislative terms begin earlier, on January 3.

AMENDMENT 21—REPEAL OF PROHIBITION

[Ratified December 5, 1933]

Section 1 The eighteenth article of amendment to the Constitution of the United States is hereby repealed.

Section 2 The transportation or importation into any State, Territory, or possession of the United States for delivery or use therein of intoxicating liquors, in violation of the laws thereof, is hereby prohibited.

Section 3 This article shall be inoperative unless it shall have been ratified as an amendment to the Constitution by conventions in the several States, as provided in the Constitution, within seven years from the date of the submission hereof to the States by the Congress.

This unusual amendment nullified the 18th Amendment. It ended federal Prohibition; now only state laws regulate liquors.

AMENDMENT 22—NUMBER OF PRESIDENTIAL TERMS

[Ratified February 27, 1951]

Section 1 No person shall be elected to the office of the President more than twice, and no person who has held the office of President, or acted as President, for more than two years of a term to which some other person was elected President shall be elected to the office of the President more than once. But this article shall not apply to any person holding the office of President when this article was proposed by the Congress, and shall not prevent any person who may be holding the office of President, or acting as President, during the term within which this article becomes operative from holding the office of President or acting as President during the remainder of such term.

Section 2 This article shall be inoperative unless it shall have been ratified as an amendment to the Constitution by the legislatures of three-fourths of the several states within seven years from the date of its submission to the states by the Congress.

This amendment could be called the Franklin D. Roosevelt amendment. It was FDR who broke the previous unwritten custom of no more than two-term presidents. Democrat Roosevelt won an unprecedented four terms as president. When the Republicans took control of the Congress in 1948, they pushed through the 22nd Amendment, limiting the U.S. president to a lifetime of two full four-year terms of office.

AMENDMENT 23—PRESIDENTIAL ELECTORS FOR THE DISTRICT OF COLUMBIA

[Ratified March 29, 1961]

Section 1 The District constituting the seat of government of the United States shall appoint in such manner as the Congress may direct:

A number of electors of President and Vice President equal to the whole number of Senators and Representatives in Congress to which the District would be entitled if it were a state, but in no event more than the least populous state, they shall be in addition to those appointed by the states, but they shall be considered for the purposes of the election of President and Vice President, to be electors appointed by a state, and they shall meet in the District and perform such duties as provided by the twelfth article of amendment.

Section 2 The Congress shall have power to enforce this article by appropriate legislation.

This amendment gave electoral votes to the citizens of Washington, D.C., which is not a state and thus not included in the original scheme of

state electoral votes. Currently, Washington, D.C., has 3 electoral votes, bringing the total of presidential electoral votes to 538. Puerto Ricans and the residents of Guam, U.S. Virgin Islands, and the Northern Marianas are citizens of the U.S. but have no electoral votes.

AMENDMENT 24—THE ANTI-POLL TAX AMENDMENT

[Ratified January 23, 1964]

Section 1 The right of citizens of the United States to vote in any primary or other election for President or Vice President, for electors for President or Vice President or for Senator or Representative in Congress, shall not be denied or abridged by the United States or any state by reason of failure to pay any poll tax or other tax.

Section 2 The Congress shall have power to enforce this article by appropriate legislation.

The poll tax was a procedure used mostly in Southern states to discourage poor white and African-American voters from registering to vote. Essentially, one would have to pay a tax to register to vote. As part of the assault against disenfranchisement of voters, the poll tax was abolished. Literacy tests, another device to disqualify voters, were abolished by the Voting Rights Act of 1965.

AMENDMENT 25—PRESIDENTIAL DISABILITY, VICE PRESIDENTIAL VACANCIES

[Ratified February 10, 1967]

Section 1 In case of the removal of the President from office or his death or resignation, the Vice President shall become President.

Section 2 Whenever there is a vacancy in the office of the Vice President, the President shall nominate a Vice President who shall take the office upon confirmation by a majority vote of both Houses of Congress.

Section 3 Whenever the President transmits to the President pro tempore of the Senate and the Speaker of the House of Representatives his written declaration that he is unable to discharge the powers and duties of his office, and until he transmits to them a written declaration to the contrary, such powers and duties shall be discharged by the Vice President as Acting President.

Section 4 Whenever the Vice President and a majority of either the principal officers of the executive departments or of such other body as Congress may by law provide, transmit to the President pro tempore of the Senate and the Speaker of the House of Representatives their written declaration that the President is unable to discharge the powers and duties of his office, the Vice President shall immediately assume the powers and duties of the office as Acting President.

Thereafter, when the President transmits to the President pro tempore of the Senate and the Speaker of the House of Representatives his written declaration that no inability exists, he shall resume the powers and duties of his office unless the Vice President and a majority of either the principal officers of the executive departments, or of such other body as Congress may by law provide, transmit within four days to the President pro tempore of the Senate and the Speaker of the House of Representatives their written declaration that the President is unable to discharge the powers and duties of his office. Thereupon Congress shall

decide the issue, assembling within forty-eight hours for that purpose if not in session. If the Congress, within twenty-one days after receipt of the latter written declaration, or, if Congress is not in session, within twenty-one days after Congress is required to assemble, determines by two-thirds vote of both Houses that the President is unable to discharge the powers and duties of his office, the Vice President shall continue to discharge the same as Acting President; otherwise the President shall resume the powers and duties of his office.

During the administration of President Woodrow Wilson, his final year in office, in 1919, was marked by serious illness. It is rumored that his wife acted as president. There was no constitutional provision to cover an incapacitating illness of a president. So this amendment provides a procedure for this eventuality. The president can inform congressional leaders of his incapacitation and the vice president takes over. When he recovers, the president can so inform congressional leaders and he resumes office.

But the amendment also recognizes that the president may not be able or wish to indicate this debilitation; so the vice president and a majority of cabinet members can inform congressional leaders and the vice president takes over. When the president informs congressional leadership that he is back in form, he resumes the presidency unless the vice president and a majority of the cabinet disagree. Then Congress must decide. The likelihood that this procedure will ever be used is very small.

The most immediate importance of this amendment concerns the office of vice president. The original Constitution did not address the issue of a vacancy in this office. So the 25th Amendment established the procedure, just in time! This amendment was ratified in 1967. In 1973, the sitting vice president, Spiro Agnew, resigned his office. Under the provisions of this amendment, President Nixon nominated Gerald Ford as vice president. A former member of the House, the Congress quickly approved him. But a year later, President Nixon also resigned. Now Vice President Ford became President Ford, and he in turn appointed Nelson Rockefeller as the new vice president. For the first time in our history, we had both a president and vice president, neither of whom was elected by the Electoral College.

AMENDMENT 26—EIGHTEEN-YEAR-OLD VOTE

[Ratified July 1, 1971]

Section 1 The right of citizens of the United States, who are 18 years of age or older, to vote, shall not be denied or abridged by the United States or by any state on account of age.

Section 2 The Congress shall have power to enforce this article by appropriate legislation.

During the Vietnam War, 18-year-olds were being drafted and sent out to possibly die in the service of their country. Yet they did not even have the right to vote. This incongruity led to the 26th

Amendment, which lowered the legal voting age from 21 to 18.

AMENDMENT 27—CONGRESSIONAL SALARIES

[Ratified May 7, 1992]

No law varying the compensation for the services of the Senators and Representatives shall take effect until an election of Representatives shall be intervened.

This is a "sleeper" amendment that was part of 12 amendments originally submitted by the first Congress to the states for ratification. The states only ratified 10 of the 12, which collectively became known as the Bill of Rights. But since Congress did not set a time limit for ratification, the other 2 amendments remained on the table. Much to the shock of the body politic, in 1992, 3/4 of the states ratified original amendment 12 of 12. This reflected the disgust of seeing Congress continuing to increase its salary and benefits. The amendment delays any increase of compensation for at least one election cycle.*

_____

*Annotations by James Corey

4 FEDERALISM
Dividing Governmental Power

66 The Constitution in all its provisions looks to an indestructible union, composed of indestructible states. 99   Salmon P. Chase

Chapter Outline and Learning Objectives

Indestructible Union, Indestructible States

▶ 4.1 *Distinguish the federal form of government from confederal and unitary forms.*

Why Federalism? The Argument for a "Compound Republic"

▶ 4.2 *Evaluate the arguments in favor of federalism.*

The Original Design of Federalism

▶ 4.3 *Distinguish the delegated, reserved, concurrent, and denied powers granted to the state and federal governments.*

The Evolution of American Federalism

▶ 4.4 *Trace the evolution of American federalism.*

Federalism Revived?

▶ 4.5 *Assess how Court decisions in recent decades have impacted federalism.*

Federalism and Direct Democracy?

▶ 4.6 *Explain how federal grants impact the distribution of power between the federal and state governments.*

Money and Power Flow to Washington

▶ 4.7 *Assess the impact of coercive federalism on state-national relations.*

Coercive Federalism: Preemptions and Mandates

▶ 4.8 *Describe coercive federalism and explain how it has altered state–national relations.*

Think about Politics

1. Which level of government deals best with the problems it faces?
   FEDERAL ⬭ **STATE** ⬭ **LOCAL** ⬭

2. In which level of government do you have the most confidence?
   FEDERAL ⬭ **STATE** ⬭ **LOCAL** ⬭

3. Should the national government be able to prosecute a high school student for bringing a gun to school?
   YES ⬭ **NO** ⬭

4. Should welfare benefits be the same in all states?
   YES ⬭ **NO** ⬭

5. Should each state determine its own minimum age for drinking alcohol?
   YES ⬭ **NO** ⬭

6. Should each state determine its own maximum highway speed limit?
   YES ⬭ **NO** ⬭

7. When the federal government requires states to provide safe drinking water, clean air, or access for the handicapped, should it provide funds to carry out these mandates?
   YES ⬭ **NO** ⬭

8. Should violence against women be a federal crime?
   YES ⬭ **NO** ⬭

What should be the relationship between the national government and the states? Questions like these lie at the heart of the issue of who gets what, when, and how. They affect employment, transportation, health, education, the very air we breathe. And when there has been disagreement, the nation has been plunged into conflict at best and the bloodiest war in its history at worst.

Indestructible Union, Indestructible States

▶ 4.1 *Distinguish the federal form of government from confederal and unitary forms.*

In December 1860 South Carolina seceded from the Union and in April 1861 authorized its state militia to expel U.S. troops from Fort Sumter in Charleston harbor. Although there is no provision in the Constitution for states leaving the Union, eleven Southern states—South Carolina, Mississippi, Florida, Alabama, Georgia, Louisiana, Texas, Virginia, Arkansas, Tennessee, and North Carolina, in that order—argued that the Union was a voluntary association and they were entitled to withdraw.[1] President Abraham Lincoln declared these states to be in armed rebellion and sent federal troops to crush the "rebels." The result was the nation's bloodiest war: more than 250,000 battle deaths and another 250,000 deaths from disease and privation, out of a total population of less than 30 million.

Following the Civil War, Chief Justice Salmon P. Chase confirmed what had been decided on the battlefield: "The Constitution in all its provisions looks to an indestructible union, composed of indestructible states."[2]

Federalism divides power between two separate authorities—the nation and the states—each of which enforces its own laws directly on its citizens. Both the nation and the states pass laws, impose taxes, spend money, and maintain their own courts. Neither the nation nor the states can dissolve the Union or amend the Constitution without the consent of the other. The Constitution itself is the only legal source of authority

FIGURE 4.1

Federal, Confederation, and Unitary Systems of Government

In theory, power in a federal system is divided between a national government and the states; power in a confederation remains with the member states; power in a unitary system is concentrated in the national government. The United States, the European Union, and Great Britain resemble federal, confederation, and unitary systems; but no government completely conforms to these designs.

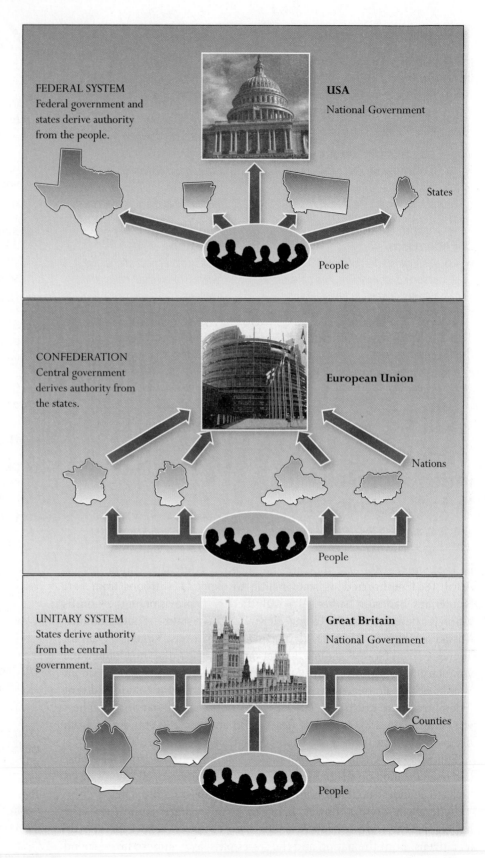

FEDERAL SYSTEM
Federal government and states derive authority from the people.

USA
National Government

States

People

CONFEDERATION
Central government derives authority from the states.

European Union

Nations

People

UNITARY SYSTEM
States derive authority from the central government.

Great Britain
National Government

Counties

People

TABLE 4.1 How Many American Governments?

Over 89,000 governments function in the United States. The U.S. Constitution recognizes only the national government and the states. Local governments are created and empowered by state laws and constitutions.	
U.S. government	1
States	50
Counties	3,033
Municipalities	19,492
Townships	16,519
Special districts	37,381
School districts	13,051
All governments	*89,527*

Source: Census of Governments, 2007.

federalism
A constitutional arrangement whereby power is divided between national and subnational governments, each of which enforces its own laws directly on its citizens and neither of which can alter the arrangement without the consent of the other.

for both the states and the nation, the states do not get their power from the national government, and the national government does not get its power from the states. Both national and state governments derive their power directly from the people.

American federalism differs from a **unitary system** of government, in which formal authority rests with the national government, and whatever powers are exercised by states, provinces, or subdivisions are given to those governments by the national government. Most of the world's governments—including France and Great Britain—are unitary. Federalism also differs from a **confederation** of states, in which the national government relies on the states for its authority, not the people (see Figure 4.1). Under the Articles of Confederation of 1781, the United States was a confederation. The national government could not even levy taxes; it had to ask the states for revenue. Like the United States, a number of other countries were confederations before establishing federal systems, and today new types of confederations with limited functions are being formed (see *Compared to What?*: "The European Union").

People in the United States often think of the *federal government* when the word *government* comes up. In fact, today there are more than 89,000 American governments. These state and local governments are important in American life, for they provide such essential day-to-day services as schools, water, and police and fire departments (see Table 4.1). However, the U.S. Constitution, the supreme Law of the Land, recognizes the existence of only the national government and the states. Local governments have no guarantees of power—or even existence—under the U.S. Constitution. Whatever powers they have are given to them by their state governments. States can create or abolish local governments, grant or withhold their powers, or change their boundaries without their consent. Some local governments have powers guaranteed in *state* constitutions, and some are even given **home rule**—the power to pass laws affecting local affairs, so long as those laws do not conflict with state or federal laws. About 60,000 of these 89,000 governments have the power to levy taxes to support activities authorized by state law.

In short, the American federal system is large and complex, with three levels of government—national, state, and local—sharing power. Indeed, the numbers and complexity of governments in the United States make **intergovernmental relations**—all of the interactions among these governments and their officials—a major concern of political scientists and policy makers.

unitary system
Constitutional arrangement whereby authority rests with the national government; subnational governments have only those powers given to them by the national government.

confederation
Constitutional arrangement whereby the national government is created by and relies on subnational governments for its authority.

home rule
Power of local government to pass laws affecting local affairs, so long as those laws do not conflict with state or federal laws.

intergovernmental relations
Network of political, financial, and administrative relationships between units of the federal government and those of state and local governments.

COMPARED TO WHAT?

The European Union

The European Union (EU) incorporates features of both federalism and confederation. The EU now includes twenty-seven member nations and embraces more than 455 million people. It grew slowly from a European Economic Community established in 1957 (designed to reduce and eventually abolish all tariffs among member nations), through a European Community established in 1965 (designed to create a single market free of all barriers to the movement of goods, services, capital, and labor), to its much more unified European Union established in 1991. The Treaty of Lisbon, ratified in 2009, further strengthens the Union.

European Parliament Deputies of the European Parliament are directly elected every five years by the EU's 455 million citizens. The major political parties operating in each of the member nations nominate candidates. The Parliament oversees the EU budget and passes on proposals to the Council of Ministers and the Commission. The Parliament also passes on new applicants to the EU.

Council of the EU The Council is the EU's principal decision-making body. It is composed of the foreign ministers of the member nations. Each country takes the presidency for six months; the Council votes by majority, although each country's vote is weighted differently.

The Commission The Commission of the EU supervises the implementation of EU treaties, implements EU policies, and manages EU funds. It is composed of twenty commissioners appointed by member governments. The five largest countries—France, Germany, Italy, Spain, and the United Kingdom—appoint two commissioners each; the remaining countries appoint one commissioner each.

The Court of Justice A Court of Justice hears complaints about member governments' treaty violations and interprets EU treaties and legislation. Its fifteen justices are appointed by the member governments and serve six-year terms.

The "Euro" Perhaps the most far-reaching accomplishment of the EU was the introduction of the "euro"—a single European currency for use in all member states. The euro was first introduced January 1, 1999, and officially replaced old national currencies—such as francs, marks, pesetas, and lira—on January 1, 2002. However, the United Kingdom, Sweden, and Denmark have refused to substitute the euro for their own currency.

The Treaty of Lisbon The Treaty of Lisbon, ratified by all twenty-seven member nations, moves the European Union closer to a federal union. It establishes an elected

Distribution of Seats in the European Parliament

Austria	18	Latvia	9
Belgium	24	Lithuania	13
Bulgaria	18	Luxembourg	6
Cyprus	6	Malta	5
Czech Republic	24	Netherlands	27
Denmark	14	Poland	54
Estonia	6	Portugal	24
Finland	14	Romania	35
France	78	Slovakia	14
Germany	99	Slovenia	7
Greece	24	Spain	54
Hungary	24	Sweden	19
Ireland	13	United Kingdom	78
Italy	78		

Think Again

Which level of government deals best with the problems it faces?

Why Federalism? The Argument for a "Compound Republic"

▶ 4.2 *Evaluate the arguments in favor of federalism.*

The nation's Founders believed that "republican principles" would help make government responsible to the people, but they also argued that "auxiliary precautions" were necessary to protect the liberties of minorities and individuals. They believed that majority rule in a democratic government made it particularly important to devise ways to protect minorities and individuals from "unjust" and "interested" *majorities*. They believed that federalism would better protect liberty, disperse power, and manage "faction" (conflict).

president and adds to the powers of the directly elected European Parliament. (Ireland and the Czech Republic were the last to ratify the Treaty in 2009.) During the ratification process, many of the questions addressed by Europeans were the same as those discussed in the American Constitutional Convention of 1787.

This map, produced by the EU, uses the languages of the nations portrayed. Test yourself by translating these names into English, for example Osterreich = Austria.

Source: Reprinted from www.europa.eu.int/abc/maps/index_en.htm Copyright © European Communities, 1995–2006.

Protecting Liberty   Constitutional guarantees of individual liberty do not enforce themselves. The Founders argued that to guarantee liberty, government should be structured to encourage "opposite and rival" centers of power *within* and *among* governments. So they settled on both *federalism*—dividing powers between the national and state governments—and *separation of powers*—the dispersal of power among branches within the national government.

In the compound republic of America, the power surrendered by the people is first divided between two distinct governments, and then the portion allotted to each is subdivided among distinct and separate departments. Hence a double security arises to the rights of the people. The different governments will control each other, at the same time that each will be controlled by itself.[3]

POLITICS UP CLOSE

Federalism Is the Enemy of Uniformity

Should taxes and services be uniform throughout the United States? Or should federalism allow variations among the states in tax burdens as well as the services provided?

Federalism allows citizens in each state to decide levels of public services (schools, transportation, police and fire protection, and other state and local functions), as well as how much they pay in state and local taxes. If some state voters want more public services and are willing to pay higher taxes for them, and voters in other states want fewer public services and enjoy lower taxes, then federalism allows for a better match between citizen preferences and public policy. Of course, the result is a lack of uniformity across the states.

Consider, for example, differences in per capita state and local taxes paid by residents of different states.

Ten High-Tax States		Ten Low-Tax States	
New York	$6,900	Oklahoma	$3,308
Wyoming	6,203	Missouri	3,248
Connecticut	6,047	Arkansas	3,230
New Jersey	5,955	Kentucky	3,220
Hawaii	5,141	Idaho	3,177
Massachusetts	4,942	South Carolina	3,120
Maryland	4,804	South Dakota	3,001
California	4,774	Mississippi	2,989
Vermont	4,725	Tennessee	2,975
Minnesota	4,559	Alabama	2,902

States Without Income Taxes

Alaska	New Hampshire[a]	Texas
Florida	South Dakota	Washington
Nevada	Tennessee[a]	Wyoming

States Taxing Individual Income (rate ranges in parentheses)

Alabama (2.0–5.0)	Kentucky (2.0–6.0)	North Carolina (6.0–7.7)
Arizona (2.6–4.5)	Louisiana (2.0–6.0)	North Dakota (1.8–4.9)
Arkansas (1.0–7.0)	Maine (2.0–8.5)	Ohio (0.6–6.2)
California (1.0–10.5)	Maryland (2.0–6.2)	Oklahoma (0.5–5.5)
Colorado (4.6)	Massachusetts (5.3)	Oregon (5.0–11.0)
Connecticut (3.0–6.5)	Michigan (4.4)	Pennsylvania (3.0)
Delaware (2.2–6.9)	Minnesota (5.3–7.8)	Rhode Island (3.8–9.9)
Georgia (1.0–6.0)	Mississippi (3.0–5.0)	South Carolina (2.5–7.0)
Hawaii (1.4–11.0)	Missouri (1.5–6.0)	Utah (5.0)
Idaho (1.6–7.8)	Montana (1.0–6.9)	Vermont (3.6–9.0)
Illinois (3.0)	Nebraska (2.5–6.8)	Virginia (2.0–5.75)
Indiana (3.4)	New Jersey (1.4–10.8)	West Virginia (3.0–6.5)
Iowa (0.4–9.0)	New Mexico (1.7–4.9)	Wisconsin (4.6–7.7)
Kansas (3.5–6.5)	New York (4.0–9.0)	

[a]State income tax is limited to dividends and interest only, and excludes wage income.

Source: Data from www.taxadmin.org (2009).

Thus the Founders deliberately tried to create competition within and among governmental units as a means of protecting liberty. Rather than rely on the "better motives" of leaders, the Founders sought to construct a system in which governments and government officials would be constrained by competition with other governments and other government officials: "Ambition must be made to counteract ambition."[4]

Dispersing Power   Federalism distributes power widely among different sets of leaders, national as well as state and local officeholders. The Founders believed that multiple leadership groups offered more protection against tyranny than a single set of all-powerful leaders. State and local government offices also provide a political base for the opposition party when it has lost a national election. In this way, state and local governments contribute to party competition in the United States by helping to tide over the losing party after electoral defeat at the national level so that it can remain strong enough to challenge incumbents at the next election. And finally, state and local governments often provide a training ground for national political leaders. National leaders can be drawn from a pool of leaders experienced in state and local government.

Increasing Participation   Federalism allows more people to participate in the political system. With more than 89,000 governments in the United States— state, county, municipality, township, special district, and school district—nearly a million people hold some kind of public office.

Improving Efficiency   Federalism also makes government more manageable and efficient. Imagine the bureaucracy, red tape, and confusion if every governmental activity—police, schools, roads, fire fighting, garbage collection, sewage disposal, and so forth—in every local community in the nation were controlled by a centralized administration in Washington. Government can become arbitrary when a bureaucracy far from the scene directs local officials. Thus decentralization often softens the rigidity of law.

Ensuring Policy Responsiveness   Federalism encourages policy responsiveness. The existence of multiple governments offering different packages of benefits and costs allows a better match between citizen preferences and public policy. Americans are very mobile. People and businesses can "vote with their feet" by relocating to those states and communities that most closely conform to their own policy preferences. This mobility not only facilitates a better match between citizen preferences and public policy but also encourages competition between states and communities to offer improved services at lower costs.[5]

Encouraging Policy Innovation   The Founders hoped that federalism would encourage policy experimentation and innovation. Today federalism may seem like a "conservative" idea, but it was once the instrument of liberal reformers. Federal programs as diverse as the income tax, unemployment compensation, Social Security, wage and hour legislation, bank deposit insurance, and food stamps were all state programs before becoming national undertakings. Today much of the current "liberal" policy agenda— mandatory health insurance for workers, child-care programs, notification of plant closings, government support of indus-

President Barack Obama listens to Vermont Governor James H. Douglas, chairman of the National Governors Association, during a White House meeting in 2010.

trial research and development—has been embraced by various states. The phrase **laboratories of democracy** is generally attributed to the great progressive jurist Supreme Court Justice Louis D. Brandeis, who used it in defense of state experimentation with new solutions to social and economic problems.[6]

laboratories of democracy
A reference to the ability of states to experiment and innovate in public policy.

Some Important Reservations   Despite the strengths of federalism, it has its problems. First of all, federalism can obstruct action on national issues. Although decentralization may reduce conflict at the national level, it may do so at the price

**delegated, or enumerated,
powers**
Powers specifically mentioned
in the Constitution as
belonging to the national
government.

**Necessary and Proper
Clause**
Clause in Article I, Section 8, of
the U.S. Constitution granting
Congress the power to enact all
laws that are "necessary and
proper" for carrying out those
responsibilities specifically
delegated to it. Also referred to
as the Implied Powers Clause.

implied powers
Powers not mentioned
specifically in the Constitution
as belonging to Congress but
inferred as necessary and
proper for carrying out the
enumerated powers.

National Supremacy Clause
Clause in Article VI of the
U.S. Constitution declaring
the constitution and laws of
the national government "the
supreme law of the land"
superior to the constitutions
and laws of the states.

concurrent powers
Powers exercised by both the
national government and state
governments in the American
federal system.

of "sweeping under the rug" very serious national injustices (see *A Conflicting View*: "The Dark Side of Federalism"). Federalism also permits local leaders and citizens to frustrate national policy, to sacrifice national interest to local interests. Decentralized government provides an opportunity for local NIMBYs (people who subscribe to the motto "Not in My Back Yard") to obstruct airports, highways, waste disposal plants, public housing, drug rehabilitation centers, and many other projects that would be in the national interest.

The Original Design of Federalism

▶ 4.3 *Distinguish the delegated, reserved, concurrent, and denied powers granted to the state and federal governments.*

The U.S. Constitution *originally* defined American federalism in terms of (1) the powers expressly delegated to the national government plus the powers implied by those that are specifically granted, (2) the concurrent powers exercised by both states and the national government, (3) the powers reserved to the states, (4) the powers denied by the Constitution to both the national government and the states, and (5) the constitutional provisions giving the states a role in the composition of the national government (see Figure 4.2).

Delegated Powers   The U.S. Constitution lists seventeen specific grants of power to Congress, in Article I, Section 8. These are usually referred to as the **delegated, or enumerated, powers**. They include authority over war and foreign affairs, authority over the economy ("interstate commerce"), control over the money supply, and the power to tax and spend "to pay the Debts and provide for the common Defence and general Welfare." After these specific grants of power comes the power "to make all laws which shall be necessary and proper for carrying into execution the foregoing powers, and all other powers vested by this Constitution in the government of the United States or in any department or officer thereof." This statement is generally known as the **Necessary and Proper Clause**, and it is the principal source of the national government's **implied powers**—powers not specifically listed in the Constitution but inferred from those that are.

National Supremacy   The delegated and implied powers, when coupled with the assertion of "national supremacy" (in Article VI), ensure a powerful national government. The **National Supremacy Clause** is very specific in asserting the supremacy of federal laws over state and local laws.

> This Constitution, and the laws of the United States which shall be made in pursuance thereof, and all treaties made, or which shall be made, under the authority of the United States, shall be the supreme law of the land, and the Judges in every state shall be bound thereby, any thing in the constitution or laws of any state to the contrary notwithstanding.

Concurrent and Reserved Powers   Despite broad grants of power to the national government, the states retain considerable governing power. **Concurrent powers** are those recognized in the Constitution as belonging to *both* the national and state governments, including the power to tax and spend, make and enforce laws, and establish courts of justice. The 10th Amendment reassured the states that "the powers not delegated to the United States . . . are reserved to the States respectively, or to the people." Through these

POWERS GRANTED BY THE CONSTITUTION

NATIONAL GOVERNMENT	NATIONAL AND STATE GOVERNMENTS	STATE GOVERNMENTS
Delegated Powers	**Concurrent Powers**	**Reserved to the States**

Military Affairs and Defense
- Provide for the common defense (I-8).
- Declare war (I-8).
- Raise and support armies (I-8).
- Provide and maintain a navy (I-8).
- Define and punish piracies (I-8).
- Define and punish offenses against the law of nations (I-8).
- Provide for calling forth the militia to execute laws, suppress insurrections, and repel invasions (I-8).
- Provide for organizing, arming, and disciplining the militia (I-8).
- Declare the punishment of treason (III-3).

Economic Affairs
- Regulate commerce with foreign nations, among the several states, and with Indian tribes (I-8).
- Establish uniform laws on bankruptcy (I-8).
- Coin money and regulate its value (I-8).
- Fix standards of weights and measures (I-8).
- Provide for patents and copyrights (I-8).
- Establish post offices and post roads (I-8).

Governmental Organization
- Constitute tribunals inferior to the Supreme Court (I-8, III-1).
- Exercise exclusive legislative power over the seat of government and over certain military installations (I-8).
- Admit new states (IV-3).
- Dispose of and regulate territory or property of the United States (IV-3).

"Implied" Powers
- Make laws necessary and proper for carrying the expressed powers into execution (I-8).

Concurrent Powers:
- Levy taxes (I-8).
- Borrow money (I-8).
- Contract and pay debts (I-8).
- Charter banks and corporations (I-8).
- Make and enforce laws (I-8).
- Establish courts (I-8).
- Provide for the general welfare (I-8).

Reserved to the States:
- Regulate intrastate commerce.
- Conduct elections.
- Provide for public health, safety, and morals.
- Establish local government.
- Maintain the militia (National Guard).
- Ratify amendments to the federal Constitution (V).
- Determine voter qualifications (I-2).

"Reserved" Powers
- Powers not delegated to national government nor denied to the States by the Constitution (X).

POWERS DENIED BY THE CONSTITUTION

NATIONAL GOVERNMENT	NATIONAL AND STATE GOVERNMENTS	STATE GOVERNMENTS

National Government:
- Give preference to the ports of any state (I-9).
- Impose a tax or duty on articles exported from any state (I-9).
- Directly tax except by apportionment among the states on a population basis (I-9), now superseded as to income tax (Amendment XVI).
- Draw money from the Treasury except by appropriation (I-9).

National and State Governments:
- Grant titles of nobility (I-9).
- Limit the suspension of habeas corpus (I-9).
- Issue bills of attainder (I-10).
- Make ex post facto laws (I-10).
- Establish a religion or prohibit the free exercise of religion (Amendment I).
- Abridge freedom of speech, press, assembly, or right of petition (Amendment I).
- Deny the right to bear arms (Amendment II).
- Quarter soldiers in private homes (Amendment III).
- Conduct unreasonable searches or seizures. (Amendment IV).
- Deny guarantees of fair trials (Amendment V, Amendment VI, and Amendment VII).
- Impose excessive bail or unusual punishments (Amendment VII).
- Take life, liberty, or property without due process (Amendment V).
- Permit slavery (Amendment XIII).
- Deny life, liberty, or property without due process of law (Amendment XIV).
- Deny voting because of race, color, previous servitude (Amendment XV), sex (Amendment XIX), or age if 18 or over (Amendment XXVI).
- Deny voting because of nonpayment of any tax (Amendment XXIV).

State Governments:

Economic Affairs
- Use legal tender other than gold or silver coin (I-10).
- Issue separate state coinage (I-10).
- Impair the obligation of contracts (I-10).
- Emit bills of credit (I-10).
- Levy import or export duties, except reasonable inspection fees, without the consent of Congress (I-10).
- Abridge the privileges and immunities of national citizenship (Amendment XIV)
- Make any law that violates federal law (Amendment VI).
- Pay for rebellion against the United States or for emancipated slaves (Amendment XIV).

Foreign Affairs
- Enter into treaties, alliances, or confederations (I-10).
- Make compact with a foreign state, except by congressional consent (I-10).

Military Affairs
- Issue letters of marque and reprisal (I-10).
- Maintain standing military forces in peace without congressional consent (I-10).
- Engage in war, without congressional consent, except in imminent danger or when invaded (I-10).

FIGURE 4.2 Who Gets What?: The Original Constitutional Distribution of Powers

Under the Constitution of 1787, certain powers were delegated to the national government, other powers were shared by the national and state governments, and still other powers were denied by the Constitution to the national government, other powers were denied to both the national and state governments, and still other powers were denied only to state governments. Later amendments especially protected individual liberties.

A CONFLICTING VIEW

The Dark Side of Federalism

Segregationists once regularly used the argument of "states' rights" to deny equal protection of the law to African Americans. Indeed, *states' rights* became a code word for opposition to federal civil rights laws. In 1963 Governor George Wallace invoked the states' rights argument when he stood in a doorway at the University of Alabama to prevent the execution of a federal court order that the university admit two African American students and thus integrate. Federal marshals were on hand to enforce the order, and Wallace only temporarily delayed them. Shortly after his dramatic stand in front of the television cameras, he retreated to his office. Later in his career, Wallace sought African American votes, declaring, "I was wrong. Those days are over."

Federalism in America remains tainted by its historical association with slavery, segregation, and discrimination. In the Virginia and Kentucky Resolutions of 1798, Thomas Jefferson and James Madison asserted the doctrine of "nullification," claiming that states could nullify unconstitutional laws of Congress. Although the original intent of this doctrine was to counter congressional attacks on a free press under the Alien and Sedition Acts of 1798, it was later revived to defend slavery. John C. Calhoun of South Carolina argued forcefully in the years before the Civil War that slavery was an issue for the states to decide and the Constitution gave Congress no power to interfere with slavery in the southern states or in the new western territories.

In the years immediately following the Civil War, the issues of slavery, racial inequality, and African American voting rights were *nationalized*. Nationalizing these issues meant removing them from the jurisdiction of the states and placing them in the hands of the national government. The 13th, 14th, and 15th Amendments to the Constitution were enforced by federal troops in the southern states during the post–Civil War Reconstruction era. But after the Compromise of 1876 led to the withdrawal of federal troops from the southern states, legal and social segregation of African Americans became a "way of life" in the region. Segregation was *denationalized*, which reduced national conflict over race but exacted a high price from the nation's African American population. Not until the 1950s and 1960s were questions of segregation and equality again made into national issues. The civil rights movement asserted the supremacy of national law and in 1954 won a landmark decision in the case of *Brown v. Board of Education of Topeka*, when the U.S. Supreme Court ruled that segregation enforced by state (or local) officials violated the 14th Amendment's guarantee that no state could deny any person the equal protection of the law. Later the *national* Civil Rights Act of 1964 outlawed discrimination in private employment and businesses serving the public.

Only after national constitutional and legal guarantees of equal protection of the law were in place was it possible to reassess the true worth of federalism.

In an attempt to block the admission of two African American students to the University of Alabama in 1963, Governor George Wallace barred the doors with his body in the face of U.S. federal marshals. The tactic did not succeed and the two students were admitted.

---

reserved powers
Powers not granted to the national government or specifically denied to the states in the Constitution that are recognized by the 10th Amendment as belonging to the state governments. This guarantee, known as the Reserved Powers Clause, embodies the principle of American federalism.

reserved powers, the states generally retain control over property and contract law, criminal law, marriage and divorce, and the provision of education, highways, and social welfare activities. The states control the organization and powers of their own local governments. Finally, the states, like the federal government, retain the power to tax and spend for the general welfare.

Powers Denied to the States
The Constitution denies the states some powers in order to safeguard national unity. States are specifically denied the power to coin money, enter into treaties with foreign nations, interfere with the "obligation of contracts," levy taxes on imports or exports, or engage in war.

Powers Denied to the Nation and the States   The Constitution denies some powers to both national and state government—namely, the powers to abridge individual rights. The Bill of Rights originally applied only to the national government, but the 14th Amendment, passed by Congress in 1866 and ratified by 1868, provided that the states must also adhere to fundamental guarantees of individual liberty.

State Role in National Government   The states are basic units in the organizational scheme of the national government. The House of Representatives apportions members to the states by population, and state legislatures draw up the districts that elect representatives. Every state has at least one member in the House of Representatives, regardless of its population. Each state elects two U.S. senators, regardless of its population. The president is chosen by the electoral votes of the states, with each state having as many electoral votes as it has senators and representatives combined. Finally, three-fourths of the states must ratify amendments to the U.S. Constitution.

State Obligations to Each Other   To promote national unity, the Constitution requires the states to recognize actions and decisions taken by other states. Article IV requires the states to give "Full Faith and Credit . . . to the public Acts, Records, and judiciary Proceedings of every other State." This provision ensures that contracts, property ownership, insurance, civil judgments, marriages and divorces, among other things, made in one state are recognized in all states.

"Look, the American people don't want to be bossed around by federal bureaucrats. They want to be bossed around by state bureaucrats."

Source: © 2002 Robert Mankoff from cartoonbank.com. All Rights Reserved.

The Evolution of American Federalism

▶ 4.4 *Trace the evolution of American federalism.*

American federalism has evolved over 200 years from a state-centered division of power to a national-centered system of government. Although the original constitutional wordings have remained in place, *power has flowed toward the national government since the earliest days of the Republic.* American federalism has been forged in the fires of political conflicts between states and nation, conflicts that have usually been resolved in favor of the national government. (See *Politics Up Close:* "Historic Landmarks in the Development of American Federalism.") Generalizing about the evolution of American federalism is no easy task. But let us try to describe broadly some major periods in the evolution of federalism and then look at five specific historical developments that had far-reaching impact on that evolution.

State-Centered Federalism, 1787–1868   From the adoption of the Constitution of 1787 to the end of the Civil War, the states were the most important units in the American federal system. It is true that during this period the legal foundation for the expansion of national power was being laid, but people looked to the states for resolving most policy questions and providing most public services. Even the issue of slavery was decided by state governments. The supremacy of the national government was frequently questioned, first by the Anti-Federalists (including Thomas Jefferson) and later by John C. Calhoun and other defenders of slavery.

Dual Federalism, 1868–1913   The supremacy of the national government was decided on the battlefields of the Civil War. Yet for nearly a half-century

A State Issue?

Marriage and adoption have traditionally been state issues. But federal courts may rule that the Equal Protection Clause of the 14th Amendment requires states to recognize same-sex marriage and adoption. The photo depicts same-sex partners in Pennsylvania who are seeking to adopt the child.

dual federalism
Early concept of federalism in which national and state powers were clearly distinguished and functionally separate.

after that conflict, the national government narrowly interpreted its delegated powers, and the states continued to decide most domestic policy issues. The resulting pattern has been described as **dual federalism**. Under this pattern, the states and the nation divided most governmental functions. The national government concentrated its attention on the "delegated" powers—national defense, foreign affairs, tariffs, interstate commerce, the coinage of money, standard weights and measures, post office and post roads, and the admission of new states. State governments decided the important domestic policy issues—education, welfare, health, and criminal justice. The separation of policy responsibilities was once compared to a layer cake, with local governments at the base, state governments in the middle, and the national government at the top.[7]

Cooperative Federalism, 1913–64   The distinction between national and state responsibilities gradually eroded in the first half of the twentieth century. American federalism was transformed by the Industrial Revolution and the development of a national economy, by the federal income tax in 1913, which shifted financial resources to the national government, and by the challenges of two world wars and the Great Depression. In response to the Great Depression of the 1930s, state governors welcomed massive federal public works projects under President Franklin D. Roosevelt's New Deal program. In addition, the federal government intervened directly in economic affairs, labor relations, business practices, and agriculture. Through its grants of money, the national government cooperated with the states in public assistance, employment services, child welfare, public housing, urban renewal, highway building, and vocational education.

cooperative federalism
Model of federalism in which national, state, and local governments work together exercising common policy responsibilities.

This new pattern of federal-state relations was labeled **cooperative federalism**. Both the nation and the states exercised responsibilities for welfare, health, highways, education, and criminal justice. This merging of policy responsibilities was compared to a marble cake: "As the colors are mixed in a marble cake, so functions are mixed in the American federal system."[8] Yet even in this period of shared national-state responsibility, the national government emphasized cooperation in achieving common national and state goals. Congress generally acknowledged that it had no direct constitutional authority to regulate public health, safety, or welfare. Instead, it relied primarily on its powers to tax and spend for the general welfare, providing financial assistance to state and local governments to achieve shared goals. Congress did not usually legislate directly on local matters.

Centralized Federalism, 1964–80   Over the years, it became increasingly difficult to maintain the fiction that the national government was merely assisting the states to perform their domestic responsibilities. By the time President Lyndon B. Johnson launched the Great Society program in 1964, the federal government clearly had its own *national* goals. Virtually all problems confronting American society—from solid-waste disposal and water and air pollution to consumer safety, home insulation, noise abatement, and even "highway beautification"—were declared to be national problems. Congress legislated directly on any matter it chose, without regard to its *enumerated powers* and without pretending to render only financial assistance. The Supreme Court no longer concerned itself with the reserved powers of the states, and the 10th Amendment lost most of its meaning. The pattern of national-state relations became **centralized federalism**. As for the cake analogies, one commentator observed, "The frosting had moved to the top, something like a pineapple upside-down cake."[9]

New Federalism, 1980–85   **New federalism** was a phrase frequently applied to efforts to reverse the flow of power to Washington and to return responsibilities to states and communities. (The phrase originated in the administration of Richard M. Nixon, 1969–74, who used it to describe general revenue sharing—making federal grants to state and local governments with few strings attached.) New Federalism was popular early in the administration of President Ronald Reagan, who tried to reduce federal involvement in domestic programs and encourage states and cities to undertake greater policy responsibilities themselves. The result was that state and local governments were forced to rely more on their own sources of revenue and less on federal money. Still, centralizing tendencies in the American federal system continued. While the general public usually gave better marks to state and local governments than to the federal government, paradoxically that same public also favored greater federal involvement in policy areas traditionally thought to be state or local responsibilities. (See *What Do You Think?*: "Which Level of Government Does the Best Job?")

Representational Federalism, 1985–95   Despite centralizing tendencies, it was still widely assumed prior to 1985 that the Congress could not directly legislate how state and local governments should go about performing their traditional functions. However, in its 1985 *Garcia v. San Antonio Metropolitan Transit Authority* decision, the U.S. Supreme Court appeared to remove all barriers to direct congressional legislation in matters traditionally reserved to the states. The case arose after Congress directly ordered state and local governments to pay minimum wages to their employees. The Court dismissed arguments that the nature of American federalism and the Reserved Powers Clause of the 10th Amendment prevented Congress from directly legislating in state affairs. It said that the only protection for state powers was to be found in the states' role in electing U.S. senators, members of the U.S. House of Representatives, and the president. The Court's ruling asserts a concept known as **representational federalism**: federalism is defined by the role of the states in electing members of Congress and the president, not by any constitutional division of powers. The United States is said to retain a federal system because its national officials are selected from subunits of government—the president through the allocation of

centralized federalism
Model of federalism in which the national government assumes primary responsibility for determining national goals in all major policy areas and directs state and local government activity through conditions attached to money grants.

new federalism
Attempts to return power and responsibility to the states and reduce the role of the national government in domestic affairs.

representational federalism
Assertion that no constitutional division of powers exists between the nation and the states but the states retain their constitutional role merely by selecting the president and members of Congress.

POLITICS UP CLOSE

Historic Landmarks in the Development of American Federalism

The American federal system is a product of more than its formal constitutional provisions. It has also been shaped by interpretations by the courts of constitutional principles as well as the history of disputes that have occurred over state and national authority.

Marbury v. Madison (1803): Expanding Federal Court Authority

Chief Justice John Marshall, who presided over the Supreme Court from 1801 to 1835, became a major architect of American federalism. Under John Marshall, the Supreme Court assumed the role of arbiter in disputes between state and national authority. It was under John Marshall that the Supreme Court in *Marbury v. Madison* assumed the power to interpret the U.S. Constitution authoritatively.[a] The fact that the referee of disputes between state and national authority has been the *national* Supreme Court has had a profound influence on the development of American federalism. Since the Supreme Court is a *national* institution, one might say that in disputes between nation and states, one of the members of the two contending teams is also serving as umpire. Constitutionally speaking, then, there is really *no* limitation on national as against state authority if all three branches of the national government—the Congress, the president, and the Court—act together to override state authority.

McCulloch v. Maryland (1819): Expanding Implied Powers of the National Government

In the case of *McCulloch v. Maryland*, Chief Justice John Marshall provided a broad interpretation of the Necessary and Proper Clause:

> Let the end be legitimate, let it be within the scope of the Constitution, and all means which are appropriate, which are plainly adopted to the end, which are not prohibited but consistent with the letter and the spirit of the Constitution, are constitutional.[b]

The *McCulloch* case firmly established the principle that the Necessary and Proper Clause gives Congress the right to choose its means for carrying out the enumerated powers of the national government. Today, Congress can devise programs, create agencies,

Dead Soldiers, Civil War, 1865

and establish national laws on the basis of long chains of reasoning from the most meager phrases of the constitutional text because of the broad interpretation of the Necessary and Proper Clause.

Secession and the Civil War (1861–65): Maintaining the "Indestructible Union"

The Civil War was, of course, the greatest crisis of the American federal system. Did a state have the right to oppose national law to the point of secession? In the years preceding the Civil War, John C. Calhoun argued that the Constitution was a compact made by the *states* in a sovereign capacity rather than by the *people* in their national capacity. Calhoun contended that the federal government was an agent of the states, that the states retained their sovereignty in this compact, and that the federal government must not violate the compact, under the penalty of state nullification or even secession from the Union.

The issue was decided in the nation's bloodiest war. What was decided on the battlefield between 1861 and 1865 was confirmed by the Supreme Court in 1869: "Ours is an indestructible union, composed of indestructible states."[c] Yet the states' rights doctrines, and political disputes over the character of American federalism, did not disappear with Lee's surrender at Appomattox. The 13th, 14th, and 15th Amendments, passed by the Reconstruction Congress, were clearly aimed at limiting state power in the interests of individual freedom. The 13th Amendment eliminated slavery in the states; the 15th Amendment prevented states from discriminating against blacks in the right to vote; and the

[a]*Marbury v. Madison*, 1 Cranch 137 (1803).
[b]*McCulloch v. Maryland*, 4 Wheaton 316 (1819).
[c]*Texas v. White*, 7 Wallace 700 (1869).

14th Amendment declared that "No State shall make or enforce any law which shall abridge the privileges or immunities of citizens of the United States; nor shall any state deprive any person of life, liberty, or property without due process of law; nor deny to any person within its jurisdiction the equal protection of the laws." These amendments delegated to Congress the power to secure their enforcement. Yet for several generations these amendments were narrowly construed and added little, if anything, to national power.

The Income Tax and Federal Grants (1913)

With the money provided to Washington by the passage of the 16th (income tax) Amendment in 1913, Congress embarked on cash grants to the states. Among the earliest cash grant programs were the Federal Highway Act of 1916 and the Smith-Hughes Act of 1917 (vocational education). With federal money came federal direction. For example, states that wanted federal money for highways after 1916 had to accept uniform standards of construction and even a uniform road-numbering system (U.S. 1, U.S. 30, and so on). Shortly after these programs began, the U.S. Supreme Court considered the claim that these federal grants were unconstitutional intrusions into areas "reserved" for the states. But the Court upheld grants as a legitimate exercise of Congress's power to tax and spend for the general welfare.[d]

National Labor Relations Board v. Jones and Laughlin Steel Corp. (1937): Expanding Interstate Commerce

The Industrial Revolution in America created a *national* economy with a nationwide network of transportation and communication and the potential for national economic depressions. Yet for a time, the Supreme Court placed obstacles in the way of national authority over the economy, and by so doing the Court created a "crisis" in American federalism. For many years, the Court narrowly construed interstate commerce to mean only the movement of goods and services across state lines, insisting that agriculture, mining, manufacturing, and labor relations were

outside the reach of the delegated powers of the national government. However, when confronted with the Great Depression of the 1930s and President Franklin D. Roosevelt's threat to "pack" the Court with additional members to secure approval of his New Deal measures, the Court yielded. In *National Labor Relations Board v. Jones and Laughlin Steel Corp.* in 1937, the Court recognized the principle that production and distribution of goods and services for a national market could be regulated by Congress under the Interstate Commerce Clause.[e] The effect was to give the national government effective control over the national economy.

Brown v. Board of Education (1954): Guaranteeing Civil Rights

After World War I, the Supreme Court began to build a national system of civil rights that was based on the 14th Amendment. In early cases, the Court held that the 14th Amendment prevented states from interfering with free speech, free press, or religious practices. Not until 1954, in the Supreme Court's landmark desegregation decision in *Brown v. Board of Education* in Topeka, Kansas, did the Court begin to call for the full assertion of national authority on behalf of civil rights.[f] The Supreme Court's use of the 14th Amendment to ensure a national system of civil rights supported by the power of the federal government was an important step in the evolution of the American federal system.

Voting Rights Act (1965) and Bush v. Gore (2000): Federal Oversight of Elections

The Voting Rights Act of 1965 plunged the federal government into direct oversight of state and local as well as federal elections in an effort to end discriminatory practices. The act and subsequent amendments to it require the Justice Department to approve any election law changes in states and communities covered by the act. It provides that intent to discriminate need not be proven if the results demonstrate a discriminatory impact on minorities.

In the contested presidential election of 2000, the U.S. Supreme Court confirmed national oversight of Electoral College voting and vote counting in *Bush v. Gore*.[g] In this landmark case the Court reversed a Florida Supreme Court interpretation of that state's election laws and ruled that voting and vote counting are entitled to Equal Protection and Due Process under the 14th Amendment.

[d]*Massachusetts v. Wellon*, 262 vs. 447 (1923).

[e]*National Labor Relations Board v. Jones and Laughlin Steel Corp.*, 301 vs. 1 (1937).

[f]*Brown v. Board of Education of Topeka, Kansas*, 347 U.S. 483 (1954).

[g]*Bush v. Gore*, 531 U.S. 98 (2000).

Hand in Hand

During the Great Depression of the 1930s, President Franklin D. Roosevelt and the Democratic-controlled U.S. Congress sponsored extended public works within the states. This image of WPA workers bagging a street in anticipation of spring flood is an example of cooperative federalism.

 *Think* Again

Should the national government be able to prosecute a high school student for bringing a gun to school?

Electoral College votes to the states and the Congress through the allocation of two Senate seats per state and the apportionment of representatives based on state population. Whatever protection exists for state power and independence must be found in the national political process, in the influence of state and district voters on their senators and representatives. In a strongly worded dissenting opinion in *Garcia*, Justice Lewis Powell argued that if federalism is to be retained, the Constitution—not Congress—should divide powers. "The states' role in our system of government is a matter of constitutional law, not legislative grace. . . . [This decision] today rejects almost 200 years of the understanding of the constitutional status of federalism."[10]

These two persons are standing outside the U.S. Supreme Court as the court heard arguments in the *District of Columbia v. Heller* case on March 18, 2008, regarding Washington, D.C.'s ban on handguns. The Court, in a 5–4 decision, ruled that the city's law, as it was written, was in violation of the Constitution and the 2nd Amendment's protection to bear arms.

WHAT DO YOU THINK?

Which Level of Government Does the Best Job?

Americans appear to be ambivalent about federalism. On the one hand, most surveys show that Americans have greater confidence in their state and local governments than in the federal government. In general, they would prefer that power be concentrated at the state rather than the federal level.

Yet at the same time most Americans want the federal government, rather than state or local governments, to run programs in many specific policy areas, like health care, the environment, and the economy.

Trust and Confidence

Generally speaking, which of the following cares more about the important problems that affect you personally?

The governor, my state legislature	52
The president and Congress	36
Neither	10
Don't know/refused	2

For each issue, tell me whether the state government or the federal government should take the lead

Issue	Federal	State	DK/Ref.
Education	24	75	1
Highways and roads	27	73	0
Health care	72	27	1
Crime	27	72	1
Environment	72	28	1
Jobs and the economy	56	43	1

Source: "Immigration, Federalism," Andres McKenna Research. January 15–25, 2004.

Federalism Revived?

▶ **4.5** *Assess how Court decisions in recent decades have impacted federalism.*

The U.S. Supreme Court today appears to be somewhat more respectful of the powers of states and somewhat less willing to see these powers trampled upon by the national government.[11]

In 1995 the U.S. Supreme Court issued its first opinion in more than 60 years that recognized a limit on Congress's power over interstate commerce and reaffirmed the Founders' notion of a national government with only the powers enumerated in the Constitution.[12] The Court found that the federal Gun-Free School Zones Act was unconstitutional because it exceeded Congress's powers under the Interstate Commerce Clause. When a student, Alfonso Lopez, was apprehended at his Texas high school carrying a .38 caliber handgun, federal agents charged him with violating the *federal* Gun-Free School Zones Act of 1990.

The U.S. government argued that the act was a constitutional exercise of its interstate commerce power, because "violent crime reduces the willingness of individuals to travel to areas within the country that are perceived to be unsafe." But after reviewing virtually all of the key commerce clause cases in its history, the Court determined that an activity must *substantially affect* interstate commerce in order to be regulated by Congress. Chief Justice William H. Rehnquist, writing for the majority in a 5–4 decision in *U.S. v. Lopez*, even cited James Madison with approval: "The powers delegated by the proposed Constitution to the federal government are few and defined. Those which are to remain in the state governments are numerous and indefinite" (*Federalist*, No. 45).

Brady's Appeal for a Federal Law

Former presidential press secretary James Brady was permanently disabled in the assassination attempt on President Reagan in 1981. Brady and his wife led the effort to pass the Brady Act, which, among other things, ordered state and local officials to conduct background checks on gun purchasers. The Supreme Court held that portion of the act to be an unconstitutional violation of the principle of federalism.

In another victory for federalism, the U.S. Supreme Court ruled in 1996 in *Seminole Tribe v. Florida* that the 11th Amendment shields states from lawsuits by private parties that seek to force states to comply with federal laws enacted under the commerce power.[13] And in 1999 in *Alden v. Maine*, the Supreme Court held that states were also shielded in their own courts from lawsuits in which private parties seek to enforce federal mandates. In an opinion that surveyed the history of American federalism, Justice Kennedy wrote: "Congress has vast power but not all power. . . . When Congress legislates in matters affecting the states it may not treat these sovereign entities as mere prefectures or corporations."[14]

In defense of federalism, the Supreme Court invalidated a provision of a very popular law of Congress—the Brady Handgun Violence Protection Act. The Court decided in 1997 that the law's command to local law enforcement officers to conduct background checks on gun purchasers violated "the very principle of separate state sovereignty." The Court affirmed that the federal government "may neither issue directives requiring the states to address particular problems, nor command the states' officers, or those of their political subdivisions, to administer or enforce the federal regulatory program."[15] And the Court held that in the Violence Against Women Act, Congress also invaded the reserved police power of the states[16] (see *Controversy*: "Should Violence Against Women Be a Federal Crime?").

Will the Supreme Court continue its revival of federalism? Historically, the Court has interpreted the Constitution's Interstate Commerce Clause in a broad fashion, giving Congress extensive powers not originally envisioned by the Founders. The recent cases described above represent a modest change in the direction of recognizing the reserved powers of the states. No doubt the Supreme Court will continue to be called upon to consider the constitutionality of expanding federal powers (see *Controversy*: "ObamaCare and Federalism").

CONTROVERSY

Should Violence Against Women Be a Federal Crime?

When a student at VPI (Virginia Polytechnic Institute) was raped, she argued that the attack violated the federal Violence Against Women Act of 1994, a popular bill that passed overwhelmingly in Congress and was signed by President Bill Clinton. The act allowed victims of "gender-motivated violence," including rape, to sue their attackers for monetary damages in *federal* court. The U.S. government defended its constitutional authority to involve itself in crimes against women by citing the Interstate Commerce Clause, arguing that crimes against women interfered with interstate commerce, the power over which is given to the national government in Article I of the Constitution.

But in 2000 the U.S. Supreme Court said, "If accepted, this reasoning would allow Congress to regulate any crime whose nationwide, aggregated impact has substantial effects on employment, production, transit, or consumption. Moreover, such reasoning will not limit Congress to regulating violence, but may be applied equally as well to family law and other areas of state regulation since the aggregate effect of marriage, divorce, and childrearing on the national economy is undoubtedly significant." The Court reasoned that "the Constitution requires a distinction between what is truly national and what is truly local, and there is no better example of the police power, which the Founders undeniably left reposed in the States and denied the central government." In Justice Scalia's opinion, allowing Congress to claim that violence against women interfered with interstate commerce would open the door to federalizing all crime because all crime affects interstate commerce.

Source: U.S. v. Morrison, 259 U.S. 598 (2000).

Federalism and Direct Democracy

▶ 4.6 *Explain how federal grants impact the distribution of power between the federal and state governments.*

Direct democracy means that the people themselves can initiate and decide policy questions by popular vote. The nation's Founders were profoundly skeptical of this form of democracy; they believed that the "follies" of direct democracy far outweighed any virtues it might possess. The U.S. Constitution has no provision for direct voting by the people on national policy questions. It was not until over 100 years after the Constitution was written that widespread support developed in the American states for direct voter participation in policy making. Direct democracy developed in states and communities and can be found today only in state and local governments.

direct democracy
Decisions are made directly by the people, usually by popular initiative and referenda voting, as opposed to decisions made by elected representatives.

Origins of Direct Democracy in the States At the beginning of the twentieth century, a strong populist movement in the Midwestern and Western states attacked railroads, banks, corporations, and the politicians that were said to be under their control. The populists were later joined by progressive reformers who attacked "bosses," "machines," and parties as corrupt. The populists believed that their elected representatives were ignoring the needs of farmers, debtors, and laborers. They wanted to bypass governors and legislatures and directly enact popular legislation.

The populists and progressives were responsible for the widespread adoption of three forms of direct democracy: the initiative, referendum, and recall.

Initiative The **initiative** is a device whereby a specific number or percent of voters, through the use of a petition, may have a proposed state constitutional amendment or a state law placed on the ballot for adoption or rejection by the electorate of a state. This process bypasses the legislature and allows citizens to both propose and adopt laws and constitutional amendments. Table 4.2 lists the states that allow popular initiatives for constitutional amendments.

initiative
Allows a specified number or percentage of voters by use of a petition to place a state constitutional amendment or a state law on the ballot for adoption or rejection by the state electorate.

CONTROVERSY

ObamaCare and Federalism

Does ObamaCare pose a challenge to federalism? In the health care reform act—officially the Patient Protection and Affordable Care Act of 2010—there is a provision requiring every individual in the country to purchase government approved health insurance. Failure to comply will be punished by an annual tax penalty of $750 or 2.5 percent of income, whichever is higher.

Never before has the federal government required people to purchase a private product. But supporters of the Act claim that this "individual mandate" is a constitutional exercise of Congress's power over inter-state commerce. The Commerce Clause has histori-cally been given broad interpretation by the Supreme Court. Congress can regulate any economic activity that "taken in the aggregate substantially affects inter-state commerce."[a] But the Supreme Court has also held that the Commerce Clause cannot justify any fed-eral regulation whatsoever. The Court has ruled that carrying a gun near a school does not significantly affect interstate commerce,[b] and the Court overturned a law making violence against women a federal crime on the same grounds.[c] Yet arguably, mandating health insurance purchases is more closely related to inter-state commerce than gun carrying or violence against women.

Several state Attorneys General have undertaken legal action challenging the Act as an unconstitutional expansion of federal power over the citizens of their states. The 10th Amendment to the Constitution states plainly, "The powers not delegated to the United States by this Constitution, nor prohibited by it to the States, are reserved to the States respectively, or to the people." Does the 10th Amendment carry any meaning in the twenty-first century? If Congress can force Americans to buy a product, what remains of the notion of a national government of limited and enu-merated powers? Can Congress require Americans to buy GM cars or require obese Americans to eat their vegetables or pay a fat tax penalty?

Arguments over the Act are highly partisan. It was passed in Congress without a single Republican vote. Democrats claim that the mandate is justified under the Commerce Clause, because health care and health insurance are a form of interstate commerce. They also claim that the mandate is constitutional because it is structured as a tax, which is constitu-tional under the 16th Amendment. (The Internal Rev-enue Service is charged with the responsibility of ensuring that everyone purchases health insurance or pays the tax penalty.)

Nevertheless, ObamaCare breaks new constitu-tional ground in its direct mandate that everyone buy health insurance. The Attorneys General have an obli-gation to test the Act against the Founders' federalist framework of federalism.

[a]*Gonzales v. Raich* 545 U.S. I (2005).
[b]*U.S. v. Lopez* 514 U.S. 549 (1995).
[c]*U.S. v. Morrison* 529 U.S. 598 (2000).

referenda
Proposed laws or constitutional amendments submitted to the voters for their direct approval or rejection; found in some state constitutions but not in the U.S. Constitution.

recall
An election to allow voters to decide whether or not to remove an elected official before his or her term expires.

Referendum   The referendum is a device by which the electorate must approve decisions of the legislature before these become law or become part of the state constitution. As we noted earlier, most states require a favorable referen-dum vote for a state constitutional amendment. **Referenda** on state laws may be submitted by the legislature (when legislators want to shift decision-making responsibility to the people), or referenda may be demanded by popular petition (when the people wish to change laws passed by the legislature).

Recall   **Recall** elections allow voters to remove an elected official before his or her term expires. Usually a recall election is initiated by a petition. The number of signatures required is usually expressed as a percentage of votes cast in the last election for the official being recalled (frequently 25 percent). Currently sixteen states provide for recall election for some or all of their elected officials (see Table 4.2). Although officials are often publicly threatened with recall, rarely is anyone ever removed from office through this device. A recall of a state elected official requires an expensive petition drive as well as a campaign against the incumbent. The "granddaddy of all recalls" removed California Governor Gray Davis from office in 2003. The *Terminator* movie star Arnold Schwarzenegger was voted in as his replacement.

TABLE 4.2 Initiative and Recall in the States

Currently eighteen states allow voters by petition to place state constitutional amendments on the ballot. And eighteen states allow voters' petitions to force a recall vote.

Initiative for Constitutional Amendments (Signatures Required to Get on Ballot)[a]	Recall (Signatures Required to Force a Recall Election)[b]
Arizona (15%)	Alaska (25%)
Arkansas (10%)	Arizona (25%)
California (8%)	California (12%)
Colorado (5%)	Colorado (25%)
Florida (8%)	Georgia (15%)
Illinois (8%)	Idaho (20%)
Massachusetts (3%)	Kansas (40%)
Michigan (10%)	Louisiana (33%)
Mississippi (12%)	Michigan (25%)
Missouri (8%)	Minnesota (25%)
Montana (10%)	Montana (10%)
Nebraska (10%)	Nevada (25%)
Nevada (10%)	New Jersey (25%)
North Dakota (4% of state population)	North Dakota (25%)
Ohio (10%)	Oregon (15%)
Oklahoma (15%)	Rhode Island (15%)
Oregon (8%)	Washington (25%)
South Dakota (10%)	Wisconsin (25%)

[a]Figures expressed as percentage of vote in last governor's election unless otherwise specified; some states also require distribution of votes across counties and districts.
[b]Figures are percentages of voters in last general elections of the official sought to be recalled.

Source: Derived from Council of State Governments, *The Book of the States, 2009 Edition.*

Politics of State Initiatives   State initiatives often reflect popular attitudes rather than the opinions of leaders in business and government. Among the more popular initiatives in recent years: limiting terms for public officials, limiting taxes of various kinds, making English the official language, prohibiting same-sex marriages, allowing gambling, allowing marijuana for medical purposes, and allowing physician-assisted suicide. Of course, citizen initiatives are often backed by "special interests"—specific businesses or industries, religious organizations, the gambling industry, and so on. Often a great deal of money is spent for paid workers to gather the necessary signatures and then later to promote the initiative in the media.

Money and Power Flow to Washington

▶ 4.7 *Assess the impact of coercive federalism on state-national relations.*

Over the years, power in the federal system has flowed to Washington because tax money has flowed to Washington. With its financial resources, the federal government has been able to offer assistance to state and local governments and thereby involve itself in just about every governmental function performed by these governments. Today the federal government is no longer one of *enumerated* or *delegated* powers. No activities are really *reserved* to the states. Through its power to tax and spend for the *general welfare*, the national government is now deeply

Think Again

When the federal government requires states to provide safe drinking water, clean air, or access for the handicapped, should it provide funds to carry out these mandates?

involved in welfare, education, transportation, police protection, housing, hospitals, urban development, and other activities that were once the exclusive domain of state and local government (see *Politics Up Close*: "How Congress Set a National Drinking Age").

Grants-in-Aid

grant-in-aid
Payment of funds from the national government to state or local governments or from a state government to local governments for a specified purpose.

Today grant-in-aid programs are the single most important source of federal influence over state and local activity. A **grant-in-aid** is defined as "payment of funds by one level of government (national or state) to be expended by another level (state or local) for a specified purpose, usually on a matching-funds basis (the federal government puts up only as much as the state or locality) and in accordance with prescribed standards of requirements."[17] No state or local government is *required* to accept grants-in-aid. Participation in grant-in-aid programs is voluntary. So in theory, if conditions attached to the grant money are too oppressive, state and local governments can simply decline to participate and pass up these funds.

About one-quarter of all state and local government revenues currently come from federal grants. Federal grants are available in nearly every major category of state and local government activity. Over 500 separate grant programs are administered by various federal agencies. So numerous and diverse are these grants that state and local officials often lack information about their availability, purpose, and requirements. "Grantsmanship"—knowing where and how to obtain federal grants—is highly valued in state and local governments. Federal grants can be obtained to preserve historic buildings, develop minority-owned businesses, aid foreign refugees, drain abandoned mines, subsidize school milk programs, and so on. However, welfare (including cash benefits and food stamps) and health (including Medicaid for the poor) account for two-thirds of federal aid money (see Figure 4.3).

Thus many of the special projects and ongoing programs carried out today by state and local governments are funded by grants from the federal government. These funds have generally been dispersed as either categorical grants or block grants.

categorical grants
Federal grants to a state or local government for specific purposes or projects; may be allocated by formulas or by projects.

• *Categorical Grant:* A grant for a specific purpose or project. The project must be approved by a federal administrative agency. Most federal aid money is distributed in the form of categorical grants. **Categorical grants** can be distributed on a project basis or a formula basis. Grants made on a project basis are distributed by federal administrative agencies to state or local governments that compete for project funds

FIGURE 4.3

Where Does Grant Money Go?: Purposes of Federal Grants to State and Local Governments

About one-quarter of all state and local government revenues are derived from federal grants. Federal grants-in-aid to state and local governments are especially vital in the areas of health and welfare.

Source: Budget of the United States Government, 2009.

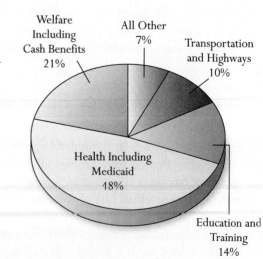

Welfare Including Cash Benefits 21%

All Other 7%

Transportation and Highways 10%

Health Including Medicaid 18%

Education and Training 14%

POLITICS UP CLOSE

How Congress Set a National Drinking Age

Traditionally, the *reserved* powers of the states included protection of the health, safety, and well-being of their citizens. The *enumerated* powers of Congress in the Constitution did not include regulating the sale and consumption of alcoholic beverages. Every state determined its own minimum age for drinking.

But the minimum drinking age became a national issue as a result of emotional appeals by groups such as Mothers Against Drunk Driving (MADD). Tragic stories told at televised committee hearings by grieving relatives of dead teenagers swept away federalism arguments. A few Congress members tried to argue that a national drinking age infringed on state power in a matter traditionally under state control. However, the new law, enacted in 1984, did not directly mandate a national drinking age. Instead, it ordered the withholding of 10 percent of all federal highway funds from any state that failed to raise its minimum drinking age to 21. States retained the rights to ignore the national minimum and give up a portion of their highway funds. (Congress used this same approach in 1974 in establishing a national 55-mile-per-hour speed limit.) Opponents of this device labeled it federal blackmail and a federal intrusion into state responsibilities. For some state officials, then, the issue was not teen drinking but rather the preemption of state authority.

From a purely constitutional perspective, Congress simply exercised its power to spend money for the general welfare; it did not *directly* legislate in an area *reserved* to the states. Technically, states remain free to set their own minimum drinking age. Despite heated arguments in many state legislatures, all of the states adopted the 21-year-old minimum national drinking age by 1990.

Appeals by groups such as Mothers Against Drunk Driving (MADD) helped overcome concerns that legislation effectively setting a national drinking age would infringe on state authority.

in their applications. Federal agencies have a great deal of discretion in selecting specific projects for support, and they can exercise direct control over the projects. Most categorical grants are distributed to state or local governments according to a fixed formula set by Congress. Medicaid and Food Stamps (see Chapter 17) are the largest categorical grant programs.

- *Block Grant*: A grant for a general governmental function, such as health, social services, law enforcement, education, or community development. State and local governments have fairly wide discretion in deciding how to spend federal block grant money within a functional area. For example, cities receiving "community development" block grants can decide for themselves about specific neighborhood development projects, housing projects, community facilities, and so on. All **block grants** are distributed on a formula basis set by Congress. Federal administrative agencies may require reports and adherence to rules and guidelines, but they do not choose which specific projects to fund.

block grants
Federal grants to state or local governments for general government functions allowing greater flexibility in the use of money.

State–Local Dependency on Federal Grants   Prior to 1980, state and
local governments throughout the United States were becoming increasingly dependent upon federal grant money. From 1960 to 1980 federal grants as a percent of state–local spending rose from 14.8 percent to 27.4 percent. President

FIGURE 4.4

State and Local
Government
Dependency on Federal
Grants

State and local governments
depend on federal grants for
about one-quarter of their
revenues. This dependency
declined somewhat during
the Reagan administration in
the 1980s but has since
returned to previous levels.

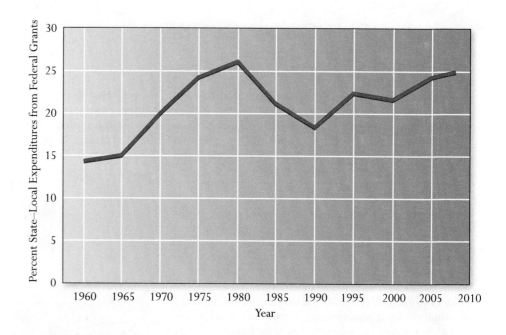

Ronald Reagan made significant cutbacks in the flow of federal funds to state and local governments, and by 1990 federal grants constituted only 18.9 percent of state–local spending (see Figure 4.4). Reagan achieved most of this reduction by transforming categorical grants into block grants and then reducing the size of the block grants below the sum of the categorical grants. But following Reagan's efforts, federal grants again began to creep up under Presidents Bill Clinton and George W. Bush, and today federal grants again account for about one-quarter of all state and local government spending.

devolution
Passing down of responsibilities
from the national government
to the states.

"Devolution"   Controversy over federalism—what level of government should do what and who should pay for it—is as old as the nation itself (see *Controversy*: "Liberals, Conservatives, and Federalism"). Beginning in 1995, with a Republican majority in both houses of Congress and Republicans holding a majority of state governorships, debates over federalism were renewed. The new phrase was **devolution**—the passing down of responsibilities from the national government to the states.

Welfare reform turned out to be the key to devolution. Bill Clinton once promised "to end welfare as we know it," but it was a Republican Congress in 1996 that did so. After President Clinton had twice vetoed welfare reform bills, he and Congress finally agreed to merge welfare reform with devolution. A new Temporary Assistance to Needy Families program (see Chapter 17) replaced direct federal cash aid welfare "entitlements." The program:

• Establishes block grants with lump-sum allocations to the states for cash welfare payments.

• Grants the states broad flexibility in determining eligibility and benefit levels for persons receiving such aid.

• Limits the use of federally aided cash grants for most recipients to two continuing years and five years over their lifetime.

• Allows states to deny additional cash payments for children born to women already receiving welfare assistance and allowing states to deny cash payments to parents under eighteen who do not live with an adult and attend school.

Since Franklin D. Roosevelt's New Deal, with its federal guarantee of cash Aid to Families with Dependent Children (AFDC), low-income mothers and children had

CONTROVERSY

Liberals, Conservatives, and Federalism

From the earliest days of the Republic, American leaders and scholars have argued over federalism. Political interests that constitute a majority at the national level and control the national government generally praise the virtue of national supremacy. Political interests that do not control the national government but exercise controlling influence in one or more states generally see great merit in preserving the powers of the states.

In recent years, political conflict over federalism—over the division between national versus state and local responsibilities and finances—has tended to follow traditional "liberal" and "conservative" political cleavages. Generally, liberals seek to enhance the power of the *national* government because they believe people's lives can be changed—and bettered—by the exercise of national governmental power. The government in Washington has more power and resources than do state and local governments, which many liberals regard as too slow, cumbersome, weak, and unresponsive. Thus liberalism and centralization are closely related in American politics.

In contrast, conservatives generally seek to return power to *state and local* governments. Conservatives are skeptical about the "good" that government can do and believe that adding to the power of the national government is not an effective way of resolving society's problems. On the contrary, they argue that "government is the problem, not the solution." Excessive government regulation, burdensome taxation, and inflationary government spending combine to restrict individual freedom, penalize work and savings, and destroy incentives for economic growth. Government should be kept small, controllable, and close to the people.

There is no way to settle the argument over federalism once and for all. Debates about federalism are part of the fabric of American politics.

---

enjoyed a federal "entitlement" to welfare payments. But welfare reform, with its devolution of responsibility to the states, ended this 60-year-old federal entitlement. Note, however, that Congress continues to place "strings" on the use of federal welfare funds, including a 2-year limit on continuing payments to beneficiaries and a 5-year lifetime limit.

Political Obstacles to Devolution and Federalism   Politicians in Washington are fond of the rhetoric of federalism. They know that Americans generally prefer governments closer to home. Yet at the same time they confront strong political pressures to "DO SOMETHING!" about virtually every problem that confronts individuals, families, or communities, whether or not doing so may overstep the enumerated powers of the national government. Politicians gain very little by telling their constituents that a particular problem—violence in the schools, domestic abuse, physician-assisted suicide, and so on—is not a federal responsibility and should be dealt with at the state or local level of government. So both federal and state politicians compete to address well-publicized problems.[18]

Moreover, neither presidents nor members of Congress are inclined to restrain their own power. Both liberals and conservatives in Washington are motivated to tie their own strings to federal grant-in-aid money, issue their own federal mandates, and otherwise "correct" what they perceive to be errors or inadequacies of state policies.

Coercive Federalism: Preemptions and Mandates

▶ *4.8 Describe coercive federalism and explain how it has altered state–national relations.*

Traditionally, Congress avoided issuing direct orders to state and local governments. Instead, it sought to influence them by offering grants of money with federal rules, regulations, or "guidelines" attached. In theory at least, states and communities were free to forgo the money and ignore the strings attached to it. But increasingly Congress has been guilty of **coercive federalism**, undertaking direct regulation of

coercive federalism
A term referring to direct federal orders (mandates) to state and local governments to perform a service or conform to federal law in the performance of a function.

CONTROVERSY

Can Arizona Pass Its Own Immigration Law?

Frustrated by the failure of the federal government to enforce existing federal immigration laws, Arizona passed its own illegal-immigration law in 2010. The Arizona law mirrors federal law dealing with aliens, requiring them to carry valid immigration documents. It makes it a *state* crime to be in the country illegally. Police are given broad powers to detain anyone suspected of being an illegal alien.

The key provision of the Arizona law states that: "For any lawful contact made by a law enforcement officer . . . where reasonable suspicion exists that a person is an alien who is unlawfully present in the United States, a reasonable attempt shall be made when practicable to determine the immigration status of the person. . . ." A "lawful contact" presumably means that a police officer has stopped an individual for violating another law, most likely a traffic stop. "Reasonable suspicion" may involve a combination of circumstances, but the law specifically prohibits officers from using race or ethnicity as factors in determining reasonable suspicion. The law also states that if a person produces a state drivers' licence or other state-issued identification, he or she is presumed to be here legally. Once identified as illegal immigrants, persons can be taken into custody, prosecuted for violating Arizona law, or turned over to federal Immigration and Customs Enforcement (ICE) for deportation.

The U.S. Justice Department filed suit against the Arizona law arguing that it violates the Supremacy Clause of the Constitution: "A state may not establish its own immigration policy or enforce state laws in a manner that interferes with federal immigration laws. The Constitution and federal immigration laws do not permit the development of a patchwork of state and local immigration policy throughout the country." Although the Arizona law was written to ensure it was not in conflict with federal laws, federal courts must answer the question, "Do federal laws preempt state laws on immigration?"

Another constitutional question is whether the Arizona law poses a threat to the 14th Amendment's Equal Protection Clause by encouraging racial profiling in its enforcement. Federal courts may find that the Arizona law is an invitation to harassment and discrimination against Hispanics. Despite the wording of the law prohibiting racial profiling, racial discrimination may be found to be inherent in its enforcement.

---

preemption
Total or partial federal assumption of power in a particular field, restricting the authority of the states.

total preemption
Federal government's assumption of all regulatory powers in a particular field.

partial preemption
Federal government's assumption of some regulatory powers in a particular field, with the stipulation that a state law on the same subject as a federal law is valid if it does not conflict with the federal law in the same area.

standard partial preemption
Form of partial preemption in which the states are permitted to regulate activities already regulated by the federal government if the state regulatory standards are at least as stringent as the federal government's.

areas traditionally reserved to the states and restricting state authority to regulate these areas. And it has issued direct orders to state and local governments to perform various services and comply with federal law in the performance of these services.

Federal Preemptions   The supremacy of federal laws over those of the states, spelled out in the National Supremacy Clause of the Constitution, permits Congress to decide whether or not there is **preemption** of state laws in a particular field by federal law. In **total preemption**, the federal government assumes all regulatory powers in a particular field—for example, copyrights, bankruptcy, railroads, and airlines. No state regulations in a totally preempted field are permitted. **Partial preemption** stipulates that a state law on the same subject is valid as long as it does not conflict with the federal law in the same area. For example, the Occupational Safety and Health Act of 1970 specifically permits state regulation of any occupational safety or health issue on which the federal Occupational Safety and Health Administration (OSHA) has *not* developed a standard; but once OSHA enacts a standard, all state standards are nullified. A specific form of partial preemption called **standard partial preemption** permits states to regulate activities in a field already regulated by the federal government, as long as state regulatory standards are at least as stringent as those of the federal government. Usually states must submit their regulations to the responsible federal agency for approval; the federal agency may revoke a state's regulating power if that state fails to enforce the approved standards. For example, the federal Environmental Protection Agency (EPA) permits state environmental regulations that meet or exceed EPA standards. (See *Controversy*: "Can Arizona Pass Its Own Immigration Law?")

Federal Mandates   Federal **mandates** are direct orders to state and local governments to perform a particular activity or service or to comply with federal laws

A CONSTITUTIONAL NOTE

How Is National and State Power Divided?

The Constitution gives to Congress—that is, to the national government—seventeen specific grants of power, the so-called "enumerated powers." These are followed by an eighteenth "necessary and proper" power—"to make all laws which shall be necessary and proper for carrying into Execution the foregoing powers, and all other Powers vested by this Constitution in the Government of the United States . . ."(Article I, Section 8). It is this last "implied powers" or "elastic" clause that has been used extensively by the national government to greatly expand its power.

But what of the states? The Founders believed that the Constitution left all other governmental powers to the states. The 10th Amendment solidified that idea: "The powers not delegated to the United States by the Constitution, nor prohibited by it to the States, are reserved to the States respectively, or to the people." The "reserved powers" of the states are limited only by a few paragraphs in the text of the Constitution, notably Article I, Section 10, which, among other things, prohibits the states from entering into treaties with other nations, or coining money, or passing laws impairing the obligation of contracts, or granting any title of nobility, or placing taxes or duties on imports

or exports, or engaging in war with a foreign power "unless actually invaded."

In brief, the original Constitution envisioned the states as having the principal responsibility for the health, safety, education, welfare, law enforcement, and protection of their people. This constitutional "division of power" remains in the Constitution, despite great shifts in power to the national government. Subsequent amendments prohibited slavery in the states (13th Amendment); prohibited states from abridging the privileges or immunities of citizens of the United States, or depriving any person of life, liberty, or property without due process of law, or denying any person within this jurisdiction equal protection of the laws (14th Amendment); or prohibiting citizens the right to vote because of race, color, or previous condition of servitude (15th Amendment); or denying the right to vote for failure to pay any poll tax or other tax (24th Amendment); or denying anyone 18 years of age or older the right to vote on account of age (26th Amendment).

So anyone reading the Constitution, without knowledge of the history of constitutional change in the United States, would not really understand the nature of American federalism.

---

in the performance of their functions. Federal mandates occur in a wide variety of areas, from civil rights to minimum-wage regulations. Their range is reflected in some recent examples of federal mandates to state and local governments:

- *Age Discrimination Act, 1986*: Outlaws mandatory retirement ages for public as well as private employees, including police, firefighters, and state college and university faculty.

- *Asbestos Hazard Emergency Act, 1986*: Orders school districts to inspect for asbestos hazards and remove asbestos from school buildings when necessary.

- *Safe Drinking Water Act, 1986*: Establishes national requirements for municipal water supplies; regulates municipal waste treatment plants.

- *Clean Air Act, 1990*: Bans municipal incinerators and requires auto emission inspections in certain urban areas.

- *Americans with Disabilities Act, 1990*: Requires all state and local government buildings to promote handicapped access.

- *National Voter Registration Act, 1993*: Requires states to register voters at driver's license, welfare, and unemployment compensation offices.

- *No Child Left Behind Act, 2001*: Requires states and their school districts to test public school pupils.

- *Help America Vote Act, 2003*: Requires states to modernize registration and voting procedures and technologies.

mandates
Perceptions of popular support for a program or policy based on the margin of electoral victory won by a candidate who proposed it during a campaign; direct federal orders to state and local governments requiring them to perform a service or to obey federal laws in the performance of their functions.

- *Homeland Security Act*, 2002: Requires states and communities as "first responders" to train, equip, and prepare for terrorist attacks.

- *Real ID Act*, 2005: Requires states to issue secure driver's licenses as defined by the Department of Homeland Security.

unfunded mandates

Mandates that impose costs on state and local governments (and private industry) without reimbursement from the federal government.

"Unfunded" Mandates   Federal mandates often impose heavy costs on states and communities. When no federal monies are provided to cover these costs, the mandates are said to be **unfunded mandates**. Governors, mayors, and other state and local officials have often urged Congress to stop imposing unfunded mandates on states and communities. Private industries have long voiced the same complaint. Regulations and mandates allow Congress to address problems while pushing the costs of doing so onto others.

Summary

▶ **4.1** *Distinguish the federal form of government from confederal and unitary forms.*

Federalism is the division of power between two separate authorities, the nation and the state, each of which enforces its own laws directly on its citizens and neither of which can change the division of power without the consent of the other.

▶ **4.2** *Evaluate the arguments in favor of federalism.*

Federalism has also been defended as a means of increasing opportunities to hold public office, improving governmental efficiency, ensuring policy responsiveness, encouraging policy innovation, and managing conflict.

▶ **4.3** *Distinguish the delegated, reserved, concurrent, and denied powers granted to the state and federal governments.*

The U.S. Constitution originally defined American federalism in terms of the powers (delegated, implied, reserved, and shared) that belong—or are denied—to the national and state governments. The Founders placed a larger emphasis on the powers of state and local governments to make public policy than is placed on them today.

▶ **4.4** *Trace the evolution of American federalism.*

Power has flowed to the national government over time, as the original state-centered division of power has evolved into a national-centered system of government. Among the most important historical influences on this shift in power toward Washington have been the Supreme Court's broad interpretation of national power, the national government's victory over the secessionist states in the Civil War, the establishment of a national system of civil rights based on the 14th Amendment, the growth of a national economy

governed by Congress under its interstate commerce power, and the national government's accumulation of power through its greater financial resources.

▶ **4.5** *Assess how Court decisions in recent decades have impacted federalism.*

The Supreme Court in its *Garcia* decision in 1985 removed all constitutional barriers to direct congressional legislation in matters traditionally reserved to the states. Establishing the principle of representational federalism, the Court said that states could defend their own interests through their representation in the national government.

▶ **4.6** *Explain how federal grants impact the distribution of power between the federal and state governments.*

Direct democracy means that people can initiate and decide policy questions without the intervention of elected officials. It was started by the Progressives and Populists and has been used in California most notably. Variations of direct democracy include initiatives, recall elections, and referenda.

▶ **4.7** *Assess the impact of coercive federalism on state-national relations.*

Federal grants to state and local governments have greatly expanded the national government's powers in areas previously regarded as *reserved* to the states.

▶ **4.8** *Describe coercive federalism and explain how it has altered state–national relations.*

Although Congress has generally refrained from directly legislating in areas traditionally *reserved* to the states, federal power in local affairs has grown as a result of federal rules, regulations, and guidelines established as conditions for the receipt of federal funds.

Chapter Test

▶ 4.1 *Distinguish the federal form of government from confederal and unitary forms.*

1. It would be accurate to say that under a Unitary form of government
   a. the central government derives its authority from the states
   b. the state governments derive their authority from the people
   c. the states derive their authority from the central government
   d. the central authority shares power with the states

2. Although the federal system of government provides for national supremacy, states still have
   a. very significant powers
   b. some power, but it is very limited power
   c. the ability to nullify laws they consider unconstitutional
   d. the authority to tax interstate commerce

▶ 4.2 *Evaluate the arguments in favor of federalism.*

3. The advantages of federalism include that it
   a. centralizes power
   b. leads to less governmental efficiency
   c. prohibits local leaders from frustrating national policy
   d. encourages policy innovation

4. One of the disadvantages of federalism is that it
   a. does not allow for much policy innovation
   b. allows local, state, and community leaders to frustrate national policy
   c. encourages uniformity
   d. decreases political participation

▶ 4.3 *Distinguish the delegated, reserved, concurrent, and denied powers granted to the state and federal governments.*

5. The National Supremacy Clause provides for
   a. a constitutional justification for a "my country right or wrong" mindset
   b. a constitutional justification for judicial review of state laws
   c. those powers not delegated to the states to be reserved to the national government
   d. the constitution and national law to be the supreme law of the country

6. Powers that are specifically mentioned in the Constitution as belonging to the national government are
   a. referred to as "federal concurrent" powers
   b. referred to as "delegated" or "enumerated" powers
   c. referred to as "federal reserve" powers
   d. the "necessary and proper" powers

▶ 4.4 *Trace the evolution of American federalism.*

7. The case that did more than any other to expand national judicial power by giving the Supreme Court the power to interpret the Constitution was
   a. *Marbury v. Madison*
   b. *McCulloch v. Maryland*
   c. *National Labor Relations Board v. Jones and Laughlin Steel Corporation*
   d. *Brown v. Board of Education*

8. The type of federalism that attempted to reverse the flow of power to Washington in the 1980s and return more responsibilities to the states was
   a. Cooperative federalism
   b. Representational federalism
   c. New federalism
   d. Competitive federalism

9. A current controversy involving the "full faith and credit clause" of the constitution revolves around whether or not that clause may be used to force states to
   a. "harmonize" speed limits
   b. recognize the legality of same-sex marriages
   c. decriminalize marijuana
   d. recognize the legality of pari-mutuel gambling

▶ 4.5 *Assess how Court decisions in recent decades have impacted federalism.*

10. The Supreme Court ruled that the federal "Violence Against Women Act"
    a. exceeded Congress's authority to control the police power of the states
    b. was constitutional
    c. should be sent back to the state court for review
    d. exceeded Congress's authority to control interstate commerce

11. Recent decisions of the Supreme Court to take a more restrictive look at what type of federal regulations will be allowed under the interstate commerce clause involved
    a. gun control and crimes against women
    b. marijuana legalization and taxation
    c. gun control and taxation
    d. crimes against women and legalization of marijuana

▶ 4.6 *Explain how federal grants impact the distribution of power between the federal and state governments.*

12. Which of the following is *not* a form of direct democracy?
    a. initiatives
    b. elected officials making decisions
    c. referenda
    d. recall elections

13. The recall process has been used most recently (2003) by _____ to remove the state's governor.
    a. Florida
    b. California
    c. Texas
    d. Iowa

▶ 4.7 *Assess the impact of coercive federalism on state-national relations.*

14. The federal government is now deeply involved in many activities that previously were the domain of the state and local governments because of
    a. the 10th amendment, which gives many powers to the national government
    b. the federal power to ensure domestic tranquility
    c. the power to tax and spend for the general welfare
    d. the nationalist interpretation of the full faith and credit clause

15. The passing down of responsibilities from the national to the state governments is known as
    a. federal preemption
    b. reverse federalism
    c. coercive state rights
    d. devolution

▶ 4.8 *Describe coercive federalism and explain how it has altered state–national relations.*

16. A direct order (mandate) from the federal government to the state and local governments to perform a service and/or conform to federal law is known as
    a. partial preemption
    b. coercive federalism
    c. voluntary mandates
    d. total preemption

17. Unfunded mandates
    a. are usually not supported by state and local governments
    b. impose extra financial costs on the federal government
    c. are legislative priorities for which funding is not yet available
    d. impose less financial costs on the state and local governments

18. The use of "mandates" has allowed the federal government to
    a. achieve more policy diversity at more economical costs
    b. address public problems at more economical costs
    c. achieve more policy experimentation and push the costs onto others
    d. address public problems and the push the costs onto other governments

mypoliscilab EXERCISES

Apply what you learned in this chapter on MyPoliSciLab.

📖 **Read** on **mypoliscilab.com**

eText: Chapter 4

✔ **Study** and **Review** on **mypoliscilab.com**

Pre-Test

Post-Test

Chapter Exam

Flashcards

👁 **Watch** on **mypoliscilab.com**

Video: Proposition 8

Video: The Real ID

Video: Water Wars

✳ **Explore** on **mypoliscilab.com**

Simulation: You Are a Federal Judge

Simulation: You Are a Restaurant Owner

Comparative: Comparing Federal and Unitary Systems

Timeline: Federalism and the Supreme Court

Visual Literacy: Federalism and Regulations

Key Terms

federalism 107
unitary system 109
confederation 109
home rule 109
intergovernmental relations 109
laboratories of democracy 113
delegated, or enumerated, powers 114

Necessary and Proper Clause 114
implied powers 114
National Supremacy Clause 114
concurrent powers 114
reserved powers 116
dual federalism 118
cooperative federalism 118

centralized federalism 119
new federalism 119
representational federalism 119
direct democracy 125
initiative 125
referenda 126
recall 126
grant-in-aid 128
categorical grants 128

block grants 129
devolution 130
coercive federalism 131
preemption 132
total preemption 132
partial preemption 132
standard partial preemption 132
mandates 132
unfunded mandates 134

Suggested Readings

Dye, Thomas R. *American Federalism: Competition Among Governments.* Lexington, Mass.: Lexington Books, 1990. A theory of "competitive federalism" arguing that rivalries among governments improve public services while lowering taxes, restrain the growth of government, promote innovation and experimentation in public policies, inspire greater responsiveness to the preferences of citizen-taxpayers, and encourage economic growth.

Dye, Thomas R., and Susan A. MacManus. *Politics in States and Communities.* 13th ed. Upper Saddle River, N.J.: Prentice Hall, 2009. A general introduction to state and local government and politics, with an extended discussion of the politics of federalism.

Elazar, Daniel J. *The American Partnership.* Chicago: University of Chicago Press, 1962. Classic study of the historical evolution of federalism, stressing the nation-state sharing of policy concerns and financing, from the early days of the Republic, and the politics behind the gradual growth of national power.

Gerston, Larry M. *American Federalism.* New York: M. E. Sharpe, 2007. A brief introduction to federalism, including "change events" that shaped American federal principles over time.

Nagel, Robert F. *The Implosion of Federalism.* New York: Oxford University Press, 2001. America's political institutions are collapsing into the center, reducing the opportunity for competition and participation.

Ostrum, Vincent. *The Meaning of American Federalism.* San Francisco: ICS Press, 1991. A theoretical examination of federalism, setting forth the conditions for a self-governing society and arguing that multiple, overlapping units of government, with various checks on one another's power, provide a viable democratic system of conflict resolution.

O'Toole, Laurence J., ed. *American Intergovernmental Relations.* 4th ed. Washington, D.C.: CQ Press, 2006. A collection of readings, both classic and contemporary, describing the theory, history, and current problems of intergovernmental relations in America.

Peterson, Paul E. *The Price of Federalism.* Washington, D.C.: Brookings Institution, 1995. Historical, theoretical, and empirical perspectives merged into a model of federalism that would allocate social welfare functions to the national government and education and economic development to states and communities.

Riker, William H. *Federalism: Origin, Operation, Significance.* Boston: Little, Brown and Co. 1964. A classic account of federalism that considers the history of federalism, compares federalism as applied in different countries, and describes and analyses its operational principles.

Van Horn, Carl E. *The State of the States.* 4th ed. Washington, D.C.: CQ Press, 2005. An assessment of the challenges facing state governments as a result of the devolution revolution.

Suggested Web Sites

The Close Up Foundation www.closeup.org
A nonprofit, nonpartisan citizenship education organization with excellent historical materials about federalism's evolution and information about federalism issues. A related link on the Close Up site contains the complete text of the pro-states' rights 1798 Kentucky and Virginia Resolutions (authored by Jefferson and Madison).

Council of State Governments www.csg.org
Official organization of U.S. states, providing information on their governmental structures, officials, and current issues.

European Union Online Official Site www.europa.eu.int
Describes the structure of the organization, its membership, current issues, and so forth.

National Conference of State Legislatures www.ncsl.org
This conference site provides information on 50 state legislatures and the issues they confront.

Urban Institute www.urban.org
Washington think tank offers viewpoints on federalism and issues confronting state/local government.

Chapter Test Answer Key

1. C	4. B	7. A	10. A	13. B	16. B
2. A	5. D	8. C	11. A	14. C	17. A
3. D	6. B	9. B	12. B	15. D	18. D

5 OPINION AND PARTICIPATION

Thinking and Acting in Politics

66 Rulers and ruling classes are under a necessity of considering the interests of those who have the suffrage **99**   John Stuart Mill

Chapter Outline and Learning Objectives

Politics and Public Opinion

▶ 5.1 *Analyze the relationships between politics, public opinion, and policy changes.*

Socialization: The Origins of Political Opinions

▶ 5.2 *Explain how the agents of socialization influence the development of political opinions.*

Ideology and Opinion

▶ 5.3 *Determine the role of ideology in shaping opinion.*

Gender and Opinion

▶ 5.4 *Describe the relationship between gender and opinion.*

Race and Opinion

▶ 5.5 *Describe the relationship between race and opinion.*

Hispanic Opinion

▶ 5.6 *Describe the reasons for the growing importance of Hispanics in the American political process.*

Policy and Opinion

▶ 5.7 *Assess how and to what extent public opinion influences public policy making.*

Individual Participation in Politics

▶ 5.8 *Identify the various ways in which a citizen may participate in politics.*

Securing the Right to Vote

▶ 5.9 *Trace the expansion of the right to vote.*

Why Vote?

▶ 5.10 *Analyze the factors that influence the decision of whether to vote.*

The Politics of Voter Turnout

▶ 5.11 *Analyze the political factors that influence voter turnout.*

Voters and Nonvoters

▶ 5.12 *Identify demographic factors that correlate with higher and lower turnout rates.*

Nonvoting: What Difference Does It Make?

▶ 5.13 *Assess the consequences of nonvoting.*

Protest as Political Participation

▶ 5.14 *Characterize protest as a form of political participation.*

Think about Politics

1. Should political leaders pay attention to public opinion polls when making decisions for the country?
   YES ◯ NO ◯

2. Do you believe that your representative in Congress cares about your personal opinion on important issues?
   YES ◯ NO ◯

3. Can you name the two U.S. senators from your state?
   YES ◯ NO ◯

4. Is our government really legitimate when only about half the people vote in presidential elections?
   YES ◯ NO ◯

5. Do you identify yourself with the same political party as your family?
   YES ◯ NO ◯

6. Is it appropriate for religious leaders to try to influence how people vote?
   YES ◯ NO ◯

7. Have you ever personally called or written to your representative in Congress?
   YES ◯ NO ◯

8. Do you think you will ever run for public office yourself?
   YES ◯ NO ◯

By thinking about politics and acting on your political opinions—voting, talking to friends, writing letters, joining organizations, attending meetings and rallies, contributing money, marching in demonstrations, or running for office yourself—you are participating in politics.

Politics and Public Opinion

▶ 5.1 *Analyze the relationships between politics, public opinion, and policy changes.*

For most Americans, politics is not as interesting as football or basketball, or the sex lives of celebrities, or prime-time television entertainment. Although politicians, pollsters, and commentators frequently assume that Americans have formed opinions on major public issues, in fact, most have not given them very much thought. Nevertheless, **public opinion** commands the attention of politicians, the news media, and political scientists.

Public opinion is considered important in democracies because democratic governments rest on the consent of the governed. Major shifts in public opinion in the United States generally translate into policy change. Both the president and Congress appear to respond over time to *general* public preferences for "more" or "less" government regulation, "more" or "less" government spending, "getting tough on crime," "reforming welfare," and so on.[1] But public opinion is often weak, unstable, ill informed, or nonexistent on *specific* policy issues. Consequently, elected officials have greater flexibility in dealing with these issues—and, at the same time, there is an increase in the influence of lobbyists, interest groups, reporters, commentators, and

public opinion
Aggregate of preferences and opinions of individuals on significant issues.

139

POLITICS UP CLOSE

Can We Believe the Polls?

Survey research is a flourishing political enterprise. The national news media—notably CBS, NBC, ABC, FOX, and CNN television networks, the *New York Times* and the *Washington Post*, and *Time* and *Newsweek* magazines—regularly sponsor independent national surveys, especially during election campaigns. Major survey organizations—the American Institute of Public Opinion (Gallup), Louis Harris and Associates, National Opinion Research Center (NORC), the Roper Organization, National Election Studies (University of Michigan)—have been in business for a long time and have files of survey results going back many years. Political candidates also contract with private marketing and opinion research firms to conduct surveys in conjunction with their campaigns.

Public opinion surveys depend on the selection of a *random sample* of persons chosen in a way which ensures that every person in the *universe* of people about whom information is desired has an equal chance of being selected for interviewing. National samples, representative of all adults or all voters, usually include only about 1,000 persons. First, geographical areas (for example, counties or telephone area codes) that are representative of all such areas in the nation are chosen. Then residential telephone numbers are randomly selected within these areas. Once the numbers have been selected at random, the poll taker does not make substitutions but calls back several times if necessary to make contact so as not to bias the sample toward people who stay at home.

Even when random-selection procedures are closely followed, the sample may not be truly representative of the universe. But survey researchers can estimate the *sampling error* through the mathematics of probability. The sampling error is usually expressed as a percentage range—for example, plus or minus 3 percent—above and below the sample response within which there is a 95 percent likelihood that the same response would be found if the entire universe were questioned. For example, if 65 percent of the survey respondents favor the death penalty and the sampling error is calculated at plus or minus 3 percent, then we can say there is a 95 percent probability that a survey of the whole population (the universe) would produce a response of between 62 and 68 percent in favor of the death penalty.

"Loaded" or "leading" questions are often used by unprofessional pollsters simply to produce results favorable to their side of an argument. An even worse abuse in telephone polling is the "push poll"—questions asked by political campaign workers posing as independent pollsters, deliberately worded to create an opinion—for example, "If you knew that Congressman Smith would soon be indicted for child molestation, would you vote for him?"

Professional pollsters strive for questions that are clear and precise, easily understood by the respondents, and as neutral and unbiased as possible. Nevertheless, because all questions have a potential bias, it is often better to examine *changes over time* in response to identically worded questions. Perhaps the best-known continuing question in public opinion polling is the presidential approval rating: "Do you approve or disapprove of the way___is handling his job as president?" Changes over time in public response to this question alert scholars, commentators, and presidents themselves to their public standing (see Chapter 11).

A survey can only measure opinions *at the time* it is taken. A few days later public opinion may change, especially if major events that receive heavy television coverage intervene. Some political pollsters conduct continuous "tracking" surveys until election night in order to catch last-minute opinion changes.

An altogether different type of poll is the *exit poll*, during which election day voters are personally interviewed as they leave the voting booth. Exit polls are used by the media to "call" winners early on election night even before all votes are counted. Television networks now jointly contract with an independent company, VNS, to select voting precincts at random, interview voters, and fast-forward the results to the networks. The networks analyze the results and make their own "calls." In response to criticism that early calls reduce voter turnout, the networks have agreed not to call a state result until the polls close in that state.

others who have direct access to policy makers. Moreover, the absence of well-formed public opinion on an issue provides interest groups and the media with the opportunity to influence policy indirectly by shaping popular opinion.

Politicians read the opinion polls. And even though many elected representatives claim that they exercise independent judgment about what is best for the nation in their decision making, we can be reasonably sure their "independent judgment" is influenced at least in part by what they think their constituents want. The cynical stereotype of the politician who reads the opinion polls before taking stands on the issues is often embarrassingly accurate.

All this attention to public opinion has created a thriving industry in public opinion polling and **survey research**. Polls have become a fixture of American political life (see *Politics Up Close*: "Can We Believe the Polls?"). But how much do Americans really think about politics? How informed, stable, and consistent is public opinion?

Knowledge Levels

Most Americans do *not* follow politics closely enough to develop well-informed opinions on many public issues (see Figure 5.1). Low levels of knowledge about government and public affairs make it difficult for people to form opinions on specific issues or policy proposals. Many opinion surveys ask questions about topics that people had not considered before being interviewed. Few respondents are willing to admit that they know nothing about the topic or have "no opinion." Respondents believe they should provide some sort of answer, even if their opinion was nonexistent before the question was asked. The result is that the polls themselves "create" opinions.[2]

The "Halo Effect"

Many respondents give "good citizen" or socially respectable answers, whether they are truthful or not, even to an anonymous interviewer. This **halo effect** leads to an *underestimation* of the true extent of prejudice, hatred, and bigotry. Another common example of the halo effect is the fact that people do not like to admit that they do not vote. Surveys regularly report higher percentages of people *saying* they voted in an election than the actual number of ballots cast. Moreover, postelection surveys almost always produce higher percentages of people who say they voted for the winner than the actual vote tally for the winner. Apparently poll respondents do not like to admit that they backed the loser.

Inconsistencies

Because so many people hold no real opinion on political issues, the wording of a question frequently determines their response. People respond

survey research
Gathering of information about public opinion by questioning a representative sample of the population.

halo effect
Tendency of survey respondents to provide socially acceptable answers to questions.

✔ *Think* Again

Should political leaders pay attention to public opinion polls when making decisions for the country?

FIGURE 5.1

Cause for Concern?: What Americans [Don't] Know About Politics

Politics is not the major interest of most Americans, and as a result knowledge about the political system is limited. Less than one-third of the general public knows the names of their representatives in Congress or their U.S. senators, and knowledge of specific foreign and domestic matters is even more limited.

Source: Data from Robert S. Erikson and Kent L. Tedin, *American Public Opinion*, 7th ed. (New York: Pearson Longman, 2007), p. 62 citing various polls.

	Percent
Know the president's term is 4 years	96%
Can name the governor of home state	74%
Can name vice president	78%
Know which party has U.S. House majority	69%
Know there are two U.S. senators per state	52%
Can name their House member	40%
Aware Bill of Rights is first ten amendments to U.S. Constitution	39%
Can name both of their U.S. senators	39%
Can name current U.S. secretary of state	34%
Know term of U.S. House member is 2 years	30%
Can name Chief Justice of United States	8%

CONTROVERSY

Abortion: The "Hot-Button" Issue

Although public opinion may be weak or nonexistent on many policy questions, there are a few "hot-button" issues in politics—issues on which virtually everyone has an opinion and many people feel very intensely about.

Abortion is one such highly sensitive issue. Both *pro-choice* proponents of legalized abortion and *pro-life* opponents claim to have public opinion on their side. *Interpretation* of the poll results becomes

a political activity itself. Consider, for example, responses to the general question posed in the graph pictured here.

Pro-choice forces interpret these results as overwhelming support for legalized abortion; pro-life commentators interpret these results as majority support for restricting abortion. Indeed, public opinion appears to support *specific restrictions* on abortion but oppose a constitutional ban on abortions.

Question: *Do you think abortions should be legal under any circumstances, legal only under certain circumstances, or illegal in all circumstances?*

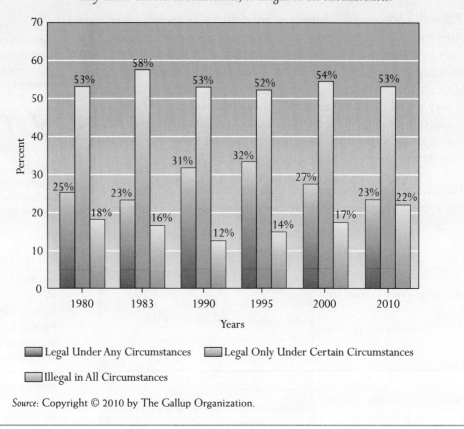

Source: Copyright © 2010 by The Gallup Organization.

positively to positive phrases (for example, "helping poor people," "improving education," "cleaning up the environment") and negatively to negative phrases (for example, "raising taxes," "expanding governmental power," "restricting choice").

The wording of questions, combined with weak or nonexistent opinion, often produces inconsistent responses. For example, when asked whether they agreed or disagreed with the statement that "people should have the right to purchase a sexually explicit book, magazine, or movie, if that's what they want to do," an overwhelming 80 percent endorsed the statement. However, when the same respondents were also asked whether they agreed with the opposite statement that "community authorities should be able to prohibit the selling of magazines or movies they consider to be pornographic," 65 percent approved of this view as well.[3]

Salience People are likely to think more about issues that receive a great deal of attention in the mass media—television, newspapers, magazines. **Salient issues** are those that people think about most—issues on which they hold stronger and more consistent opinions. These are issues that people feel relate directly to their own lives, such as abortion (see *Controversy*: "Abortion: The 'Hot-Button' Issue"). Salient issues are, therefore, more important in politics.

Salient issues change over time. In general, during recessions the most salient issue is "Jobs, Jobs, Jobs!"—that is, unemployment and the economy. During inflationary periods, the issue is "the high cost of living." During wartime, the war itself becomes the public's principal concern. A gasoline shortage can turn public concern toward energy issues. These salient issues drive the political debate of the times.

Socialization: The Origins of Political Opinions

▶ 5.2 *Explain how the agents of socialization influence the development of political opinions.*

Where do people acquire their political opinions? Political **socialization** is the learning of political values, beliefs, and opinions. It begins early in life when a child acquires images and attitudes toward public authority. Preschool children see "police officer" and "president" as powerful yet benevolent "helpers." These figures—police officer and president—are usually the first recognized sources of authority above the parents who must be obeyed. They are usually positive images of authority at these early ages:

> Q: What does the policeman do?
> A: He catches bad people.[4]

Even the American flag is recognized by most U.S. preschoolers, who pick it out when asked, "Which flag is your favorite?" These early positive perceptions about political figures and symbols may later provide **diffuse support** for the political system—a reservoir of goodwill toward governmental authority that lends legitimacy to the political order.

Family The family is the first agent of socialization. Children in the early school grades (3 to 5) begin to identify themselves as Republicans or Democrats. These childhood party identifications are almost always the same as those of the parents. Indeed, parent–child correspondence in party identification may last a lifetime. The children who abandon the party of their parents tend to become independents rather than identify with the opposition party. However, party identification appears to be more easily passed on from parent to child than specific opinions on policy questions. Perhaps the reason is that parental party identifications are known to children, but few families conduct specific discussions of policy questions.[5]

Recent research linking genetics to political behavior suggests that family may influence political behavior and attitudes through genetic inheritance as well as through environmental socialization. Identical twins are more likely to hold similar political attitudes than nonidentical twins. (Both types of twins share the same home environment, but identical twins also share the same genetic makeup.) The genetic influence appears to extend to the likelihood of voting, contributing to campaigns, running for office, and joining political organizations; as well as to specific political opinions, including the death penalty, abortion, gay rights, and school prayer.[6]

salient issues
Issues about which most people have an opinion.

socialization
The learning of a culture and its values.

diffuse support (for the political system)
goodwill toward governmental authority learned early in life.

School   Political revolutionaries once believed that the school was the key to molding political values and beliefs. After the communist revolutions in Russia in 1917 and China in 1949, the schools became the focus of political indoctrination of the population. Today political battles rage in America over textbooks, teaching methods, prayer in schools, and other manifestations of politics in the classroom. But no strong evidence indicates a causal relationship between what is taught in the schools and the political attitudes of students.

Certainly the schools provide the factual basis for understanding government—how the president is chosen, the three branches of government, how a law is passed. But even this elemental knowledge is likely to fade if not reinforced by additional education or exposure to the news media or discussion with family or peers.

The schools *try* to inculcate "good citizenship" values, including support for democratic rules, tolerance toward others, the importance of voting, and the legitimacy (rightfulness) of government authority. Patriotic symbols and rituals abound in the classroom—the flag, the Pledge of Allegiance—and students are taught to respect the institutions of government. Generally the younger the student, the more positive the attitudes expressed toward political authority.[7] Yet despite the efforts of the schools to inspire support for the political system, distrust and cynicism creep in during the high school years. Although American youth retain a generally positive view of the political system, they share with adults increasing skepticism toward specific institutions and practices. During high school, students acquire some ability to think along liberal-conservative dimensions. The college experience appears to produce a "liberalizing" effect: college seniors tend to be more liberal than entering freshmen (see also *Controversy*: "College Students' Opinions"). But over the years following graduation, liberal views tend to moderate.

Although no direct evidence indicates that the schools can inculcate democratic values, people with more education tend to be more tolerant than those with less education and to be generally more supportive of the political system (see Table 5.1). Higher education is also associated with greater political participation, including voting. But it is not clear whether education itself is a cause of political participation, or whether people who choose a college experience are predisposed to participate in civic affairs.[8]

TABLE 5.1   Education and Tolerance: A Strong Correlation

Tolerance generally increases with educational level.					
Percentage Responding "Yes" (by highest degree completed)					
Less than High School	**High School**	**Junior College**	**Bachelor**	**Graduate**	**Total**
If such a person wanted to make a speech in your community, should he be allowed to speak? (Yes)					
Atheist 48%	73%	83%	88%	91%	71%
Racist 50	56	81	72	71	59
Homosexual 54	77	86	91	94	75
Should such a person be allowed to teach in a college or university? (Yes)					
Atheist 31%	52%	65%	73%	80%	52%
Racist 36	43	51	57	64	45
Homosexual 43	68	80	85	89	67

Source: General Social Survey, Cumulative Index, 1972–2008 (Chicago: National Opinion Research Center). Tabulations by Professor Terri Towner, Oakland University.

democratic government depends heavily on "that thin stratum of persons referred to variously as the political elite, the political activists, the leadership echelons, or the influentials."[15] Thus political *participation* appears to be the essential link between opinion and policy.

Individual Participation in Politics

▶ 5.8 *Identify the various ways in which a citizen may participate in politics.*

Democracies provide a variety of ways for individuals to participate in politics. People may run for, and win, public office; take part in marches, demonstrations, and protests; make financial contributions to political candidates or causes; attend political meetings, speeches, and rallies; write letters to public officials or to newspapers; wear a political button or place a bumper sticker on their car; belong to organizations that support or oppose particular candidates or take stands on public issues; attempt to influence friends while discussing candidates or issues; and vote in elections. Individuals may also participate in politics passively, by simply following political issues and campaigns in the media, acquiring knowledge, forming opinions about public affairs, and expressing their views to others. These forms of political participation can be ranked according to their order of frequency (see Figure 5.4). Only a little more than half of the voting-age population vote in presidential elections, and far fewer vote in congressional and state and local elections.

Securing the Right to Vote

▶ 5.9 *Trace the expansion of the right to vote.*

Popular participation in government is part of the very definition of democracy. The long history of struggle to secure the right to vote—**suffrage**—reflects the democratizing of the American political system.

The Elimination of Property Qualifications, 1800–40 The Constitution of 1787 left it to the states to determine voter qualifications. The Founders generally

✔ *Think* Again

Do you think you will ever run for public office yourself?

suffrage
Legal right to vote.

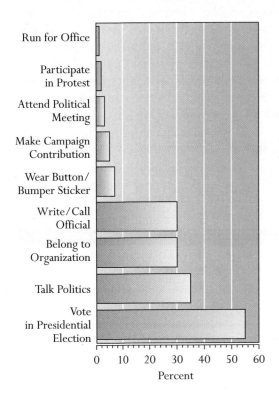

FIGURE 5.4

Political Participation: How—and How Many—People Get Involved

Only a small percentage of the American people are actively engaged in the political process, yet they receive most of the media attention. Less than 1 percent of the population runs for office at any level of government, and only about half of all voting-age Americans bother to go to the polls even in a presidential election.

Source: National Election Studies Cumulative File.

property qualifications
Early American state requirement of property ownership in order to vote.

believed that only men of property had a sufficient "stake in society" to exercise their vote in a "responsible" fashion. However, the Founders could not agree on the wording of **property qualifications** for insertion into the Constitution, so they left the issue to the states, feeling safe in the knowledge that at the time every state had property qualifications for voting. Yet over time, Jeffersonian and Jacksonian principles of democracy, including confidence in the judgment of ordinary citizens, spread rapidly in the new Republic. The states themselves eliminated most property qualifications by 1840. Thus before the Civil War (1861–65), the vote had been extended to virtually all *white males* over 21 years of age.

The 15th Amendment, 1870

The first important limitation on state powers over voting came with the ratification of the 15th Amendment: "The right of citizens of the United States to vote shall not be denied or abridged by the United States or by any state on account of race, color, or previous condition of servitude." The object of this amendment, passed by the Reconstruction Congress after the Civil War and ratified in 1870, was to extend the vote to former African American slaves and prohibit voter discrimination on the basis of race. The 15th Amendment also gave Congress the power to enforce African American voting rights "by appropriate legislation." The states retain their right to determine voter qualifications, *as long as they do not practice racial discrimination*, and Congress has the power to pass legislation ensuring African American voting rights.

Continued Denial of Voting Rights, 1870–1964

For almost 100 years after the adoption of the 15th Amendment, white politicians in the southern states were able to defeat its purposes. Social and economic pressures and threats of violence were used to intimidate many thousands of would be African American voters.

There were also many "legal" methods of disenfranchisement, including a technique known as the **white primary**. So strong was the Democratic Party throughout the south that the Democratic nomination for public office was tantamount to election. Thus *primary elections* to choose the Democratic nominee were the only elections in which real choices were made. If African Americans were prevented from voting in Democratic primaries, they could be effectively disenfranchised. Therefore, southern state legislatures resorted to the simple device of declaring the Democratic Party in southern states a private club and ruling that only white people could participate in its elections—that is, in primary elections. Blacks were free to vote in "official" general elections, but all whites tacitly agreed to support the Democratic, or "white man's," Party in general elections, regardless of their differences in the primary. Not until 1944, in *Smith v. Allwright*, did the Supreme Court declare the white primary unconstitutional and bring primary elections under the purview of the 15th Amendment.[16]

Despite the 15th Amendment, many local registrars in the south succeeded in barring African American registration by an endless variety of obstacles, delays, and frustrations. Application forms for registration were lengthy and complicated; even a minor error, such as underlining rather than circling in the "Mr.—Mrs.—Miss" set of choices, as instructed, would lead to rejection. Literacy tests were the most common form of disenfranchisement. Many a African American college graduate failed to interpret "properly" the complex legal documents that were part of the test. White applicants for voter registration were seldom asked to go through these lengthy procedures.

white primary
Democratic Party primary elections in many southern counties in the early part of the twentieth century that excluded black people from voting.

The Civil Rights Act, the 24th Amendment, and the Voting Rights Act, 1964–65

The Civil Rights Act of 1964 made it unlawful for registrars to apply unequal standards in registration procedures or to reject applications because of immaterial errors. It required that literacy tests be in writing and made a sixth-grade education a presumption of literacy. In 1970 Congress outlawed literacy tests altogether.

The 24th Amendment to the Constitution, ratified in 1964, made **poll taxes**—taxes required of all voters—unconstitutional as a requirement for voting in national elections. In 1966 the Supreme Court declared poll taxes unconstitutional in state and local elections as well.[17]

In early 1965 civil rights organizations led by Martin Luther King, Jr., effectively demonstrated against local registrars in Selma, Alabama, who were still keeping large numbers of African Americans off the voting rolls. Registrars there closed their offices for all but a few hours every month, placed limits on the number of applications processed, went out to lunch when black applicants appeared, delayed months before processing African American applications, and used a variety of other methods to keep African Americans disenfranchised. In response to the Selma march, Congress enacted the strong Voting Rights Act in 1965. The U.S. attorney general, upon evidence of voter discrimination, was empowered to replace local registrars with federal registrars, abolish the **literacy test**, and register voters under simplified federal procedures. Southern counties that had previously discriminated in voting registration hurried to sign up African American voters just to avoid the imposition of federal registrars. The Voting Rights Act of 1965 proved to be very effective, and Congress has voted to extend it over the years.

The 19th Amendment, 1920

Following the Civil War, many of the women who had been active in the abolitionist movement to end slavery turned their attention to the condition of women in the United States. As abolitionists, they had learned to organize, conduct petition campaigns, and parade and demonstrate. Now they sought to improve the legal and political rights of women. In 1869 the Wyoming territory adopted women's suffrage; later, several other western states followed suit. But it was not until the **19th Amendment** was added to the U.S. Constitution in 1920 that women's right to vote in all elections was constitutionally guaranteed.

The 26th Amendment, 1971

The movement for 18-year-old voting received its original impetus during World War II. It was argued successfully in Georgia in 1944 that because 18-year-olds were being called upon to fight and die for their

poll taxes
Taxes imposed as a prerequisite to voting; prohibited by the 24th Amendment.

literacy test
Examination of a person's ability to read and write as a prerequisite to voter registration, outlawed by Voting Rights Act (1965) as discriminatory.

19th Amendment
The 1920 constitutional amendment guaranteeing women the right to vote.

Opening the Voting Booth

Passage of the Voting Rights Act of 1965 opened the voting booth to millions of African American voters formerly kept from the polls by a variety of discriminatory regulations in the south. Here African Americans in rural Alabama in 1966 line up at a local store to cast their votes in a primary that focused on an issue central to their existence— segregation.

Just Cause

The turn of the century saw the acceleration of the women's suffrage movement. Although Woodrow Wilson expressed support for granting the vote to women even before he took office in 1912, it took the activities of women "manning the homefront" during World War I to persuade the male electorate to pass the 19th Amendment and give women access to the ballot box throughout the nation.

26th Amendment
The 1971 constitutional amendment guaranteeing 18-year-olds the right to vote.

"Motor Voter Act"
Federal mandate that states offer voter registration at driver's licensing and welfare offices.

turnout
Number of voters who actually cast ballots in an election, as a percentage of people eligible to register and vote.

country, they deserved to have a voice in the conduct of government. However, this argument failed to convince adult voters in other states; qualifications for military service were not regarded as the same as qualifications for rational decision making in elections. In state after state, voters rejected state constitutional amendments designed to extend the vote to 18-year-olds.

Congress intervened on behalf of 18-year-old voting with the passage of the **26th Amendment** to the Constitution. The states quickly ratified this amendment in 1971 during a period of national turbulence over the Vietnam War. Many supporters of the amendment believed that protests on the campuses and streets would be reduced if youthful protesters were given the vote.

The National Voter Registration Act, 1993   The National Voter Registration Act of 1993, popularly known as the "Motor Voter Act," mandates that the states offer people the opportunity to register to vote when they apply for driver's licenses or apply for welfare services. States must also offer registration by mail, and they must accept a simplified registration form prepared by the Federal Election Commission. Finally, it bars states from removing the names of people from registration lists for failure to vote. Did the "**Motor Voter Act**" work? Careful research indicates that it succeeded in increasing voter registration, but its effects on actual turnout at the polls were very limited.[18] Apparently, easy registration does not automatically increase voter turnout.

Why Vote?

▶ 5.10 *Analyze the factors that influence the decision of whether to vote.*

Deciding whether to cast a vote in an election is just as important as deciding which candidate to vote for. *About 40 percent of the voting-age population in the United States typically fails to vote, even in presidential elections.* Voter **turnout**—the number of actual voters in relation to the number of people eligible to register and vote—is even lower in off-year congressional and state elections, when presidential elections are not held. Turnout in local elections (for example, city, county, school board) is even lower when these elections are held separately from national elections. Voter turnout in presidential elections steadily declined for several decades (see Figure 5.5). The three-way presidential race in 1992 temporarily reversed the downward trend.

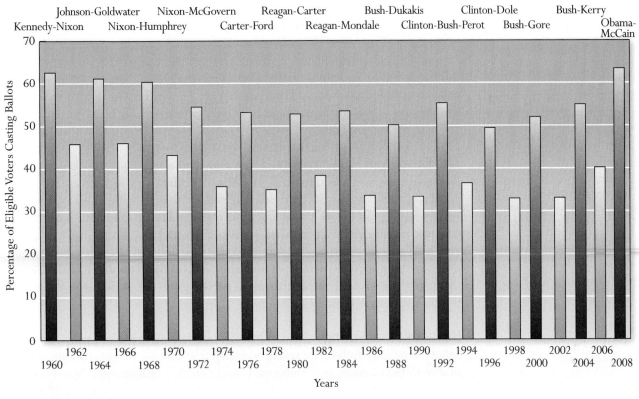

FIGURE 5.5 Trending Upward: Voter Turnout in Presidential and Congressional Elections

Voter turnout is always higher in years with a presidential election. However, voter turnout has generally declined since 1960, even in presidential election years. The exception came in 1992, when intense interest in the contest between George H. W. Bush and Bill Clinton—spiced by the entry of independent Ross Perot—led to a higher-than-normal turnout. In 1996 fewer than half of voting-age Americans bothered to cast ballots. However, in 2004 and 2008 voter turnout rose to levels not seen since the 1960s.

In 2004 and 2008 voter turnout surged to levels not seen since the 1960s. Various explanations have been offered: the expected closeness of these elections in key states, the experience of 2000 when only a few votes in Florida decided the outcome, the war in Iraq, the financial crises in 2008, and the historic opportunity in that year to elect an African American president.

Why vote? Usually, this question is asked in the negative: Why do so many people fail to register and vote? But greater insight into the question of voter participation can be obtained if we try to understand what motivates the people who do go to the polls.

The Rational Voter From a purely "rational" perspective, an individual should vote only if the costs of voting (time spent in registering, informing oneself about the candidates, and going to the polls) are *less* than the expected value of having the preferred candidate win (the personal benefits gained from having one's candidate win), multiplied by the probability that one's own vote will be the deciding vote. Why vote when registering, following the political news, and getting to the polls take away time from work, family, or leisure activity? Why vote when the winner will not really change one's life for the better, or even do things much differently from what the loser would have done? Most important, why vote when the chance that one individual vote will determine who wins is very small? Thought of in this fashion, the wonder is that millions of Americans continue to vote.

The "rational" model can explain voter turnout only by adding "the intrinsic rewards of voting" to the equation. These rewards include the ethic of voting, patriotism, a sense of duty, and allegiance to democracy. People exercise their right to vote out of respect for that right rather than for any personal tangible benefit they expect to receive. They can look at the voting returns on television later in the evening, knowing they were part of an important national event. These psychological rewards do not depend on whether a single vote determines the outcome. Millions of people vote out of a sense of duty and commitment to democracy.

registration
Requirement that prospective voters establish their identity and place of residence prior to an election in order to be eligible to vote.

The Burden of Registration

Voter **registration** remains an obstacle to voting, despite the easing of requirements for registration by many states. Not only must citizens care enough to go to the polls on election day; they must also expend time and energy, weeks before the election, to register. This may involve a trip to the county courthouse and a procedure more complicated than voting itself. Approximately 85 percent of *registered voters* turn out for a presidential election, but this figure represents only about 50 percent of the *voting-age population*. This discrepancy suggests that registration is a significant barrier to participation (see *A Conflicting View*: "Easy Voting Encourages Fraud").

Burdensome Voting

Deciding upon voting times, places, equipment, and ballots is the responsibility of state governments, most of which pass on this responsibility to their county governments. County elected or appointed "supervisors of elections" function throughout the nation preparing ballots and handling the streams of voters on election day. Nationwide, over 1 million "poll workers," usually volunteers from the local Democratic and Republican party organizations, assist in the voting process and later the counting of votes.

The contested 2000 presidential election spotlighted many of the flaws of ballots and vote counting throughout the nation. That election revealed the variety of voting methods used among the states and even within the same state.[19] Some states and counties use traditional paper or mark-sense ballots, others older lever machines and punch-card ballots, while still others are progressing toward touch screen and other electronic voting equipment. Paper and punch-card ballots regularly produce "overvotes" (where voters mark or punch votes for more than one candidate for the same office) or "undervotes" (where voters fail to make a selection for a particular office), or otherwise spoil their ballot. These ballots are "uncounted"; nationwide, they usually amount to about 2 percent of all ballots cast. Many state laws are fuzzy regarding when and how to conduct "recounts"— requiring election officials to undertake a second or third counting of the ballots. Reformers generally recommend touch-screen voting machines, carefully designed ballot layouts, better training of poll workers, uniform rules for recounts, and better voter education programs, including sample ballots distributed well before election day. However, even electronic voting is subject to error. Opponents of "black box" voting argue that every vote on a single machine may be lost to computer error or malfunction. They urged the use of ballots that leave a "paper trail."[20]

Some states now require photo identification at the polling place in order to ensure that voters are who they say they are. But opponents of photo ID argue that it has a disparate impact on poor and minority voters. The U.S. Supreme Court upheld the photo ID requirement in 2008.[21]

Help America Vote Act

Congress passed a Help America Vote Act in 2002 in reaction to the controversy surrounding the 2000 presidential election (see *Politics Up Close*: "*Bush v. Gore* in the U.S. Supreme Court" in Chapter 13). The act authorizes

A CONFLICTING VIEW

Easy Voting Encourages Fraud

Since the civil rights battles of the 1960s, the nation has been primarily concerned with expanding voter participation—to bring more people, especially minorities, into the political process. These efforts have led to an easing of the burdens of registration—registration by mail, mass registration drives, registration on the same day as voting, and so forth—as well as an easing of the burdens of voting itself—absentee voting, voting by mail, voting over an extended period, and so forth. Voting via the Internet is also being advocated in many jurisdictions. Yet there is no strong evidence to suggest that these innovations lead to higher voter turnouts.

There are nearly 200,000 voting precincts in the United States. Usually representatives of both the Democratic and Republican parties are present at each precinct to ensure the honesty of the vote. Voters who have previously registered show their voter cards or present other identification and then sign their names on the voter registration lists. This ensures that the voters are who they say they are, and that they do not vote more than once.

But registration by mail and absentee voting are rising over time. Voter registration cards are widely distributed, to be filled out by persons eligible to vote, and then collected and sent to the county election office. As the election nears, registered voters may request an absentee ballot, to be filled out and mailed to the county election office.

Increasingly, party operatives as well as independent "get-out-the-vote" organizations are going to nursing homes, assisted-living facilities, and other institutions housing the elderly, as well as large condominium projects, filling out registration forms for the residents as well as absentee ballot requests, and then "helping out" in marking the ballots, collecting them, and mailing them en masse to voting offices. It has been charged that some groups collecting registration forms and absentee ballots conveniently discard those that do not match the group's preferences.[a]

Few states have the resources, and many politicians lack the will, to investigate and prosecute voter fraud. Finding the right balance between promoting greater participation and maintaining the integrity of the electoral system is creating political conflict in many states and cities today.

[a]See Larry J. Sabato and Glenn R. Simpson, *Dirty Little Secrets: The Persistence of Corruption in American Politics.* New York: Random House, 1996.

federal aid to the states to help replace punch cards and lever voting machines and establishes minimum election administration standards throughout the country. States devise their own plans for upgrading voting practices, so considerable variations remain among the states. The act also mandates that each polling place have at least one voting system for individuals with disabilities, including the blind and visually impaired. It requires states to develop and maintain statewide voter

Charges of Voter Fraud

Originally an association of community-based organizations advocating better housing for low income families, ACORN employees were charged with widespread voter registration fraud in the 2008 presidential election. Scandals resulted in a loss of funding and ACORN closed its national offices in 2010. The photo shows executive director Steve Kest defending ACORN in 2008.

registration lists. It requires that individuals who are determined at a polling place to be ineligible to vote be allowed to cast a provisional ballot, to be counted later if the voter is subsequently found to be eligible. It also requires that voting systems provide the opportunity for voters to change or correct any errors in their ballot before it is cast and counted.

The Politics of Voter Turnout

▶ 5.11 *Analyze the political factors that influence voter turnout.*

Politics drives the debate over easing voter registration requirements. Democrats generally favor minimal requirements—for example, same-day registration, registration by mail, and registration at welfare and motor vehicle licensing offices. They know that nonvoters are heavily drawn from groups that typically support the Democratic Party, including the less-educated, lower-income, and minority groups. Republicans are often less enthusiastic about easing voting requirements, but it is politically embarrassing to appear to oppose increased participation. It is not surprising that the Motor Voter Act of 1993 was a product of a Democratic Congress and a Democratic president, Bill Clinton.

The Stimulus of Competition   The more lively the competition between parties or between candidates, the greater the interest of citizens and the larger the voter turnout. When parties and candidates compete vigorously, they make news and are given large play by the mass media. Consequently, a setting of competitive politics generates more political stimuli than does a setting with weak competition. People are also more likely to perceive that their votes count in a close contest, and thus they are more likely to cast them. Moreover, when parties or candidates are fighting in a close contest, their supporters tend to spend more time and energy campaigning and getting out the vote.

political alienation
Belief that politics is irrelevant to one's life and that one cannot personally affect public affairs.

Political Alienation   People who feel politics is irrelevant to their lives—or who feel they cannot personally affect public affairs—are less likely to vote than people who feel they themselves can affect political outcomes and that these outcomes affect their lives. Given the level of **political alienation** (two-thirds of respondents agree with the statement, "Most public officials are not really interested in the problems of people like me"),[22] it is surprising that so many people vote. Alienation is high among voters, and it is even higher among nonvoters.

Intensity   Finally, as we might expect, people who feel strongly about politics and who hold strong opinions about political issues are more likely to vote than people who do not. For example, people who describe themselves as *extreme* liberals or *extreme* conservatives are more likely to vote than people who describe themselves as moderates.

Age and Turnout   Young people do not vote in the same proportions as older people (see Figure 5.6). After the electorate was expanded by the 26th Amendment to include persons 18 years of age and over, voter turnout actually dropped, from 60.9 percent in the 1968 presidential election to 55.2 percent in the 1972 presidential election, the largest turnout decline in successive presidential elections.

Party Organization   Strong party organizations can help increase turnout. But strong party organizations, or machines, that canvassed neighborhoods, took citizens to the courthouse to register them, contacted them personally during

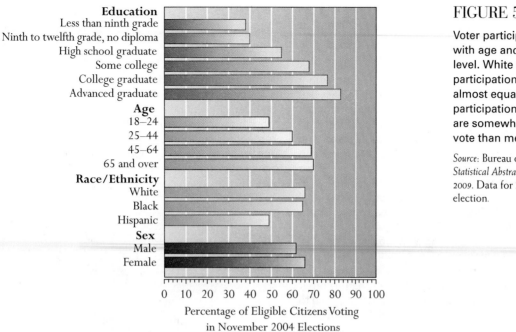

FIGURE 5.6 Who Votes

Voter participation increases with age and educational level. White and black participation levels are almost equal, but Hispanic participation lags. Women are somewhat more likely to vote than men.

Source: Bureau of the Census, *Statistical Abstract of the United States,* 2009. Data for 2004 presidential election.

campaigns, and saw to it that they got to the polls on election day have largely disappeared (see Chapter 7).

Regardless of the explanations offered, it is interesting to note that most European democracies report higher voter turnout rates than the United States (see *Compared to What?:* "Voter Turnout in Western Democracies").

Voters and Nonvoters

▶ 5.12 *Identify demographic factors that correlate with higher and lower turnout rates.*

Who votes and who doesn't? The perceived benefits and costs of voting apparently do not fall evenly across all social groups. Nonvoting would generate less concern if voters were a representative cross section of nonvoters. But voters differ from nonvoters in politically important ways.

Voters are better educated than nonvoters. Education appears to be the most important determinant of voter turnout (see Figure 5.5). It may be that schooling promotes an interest in politics, instills the ethic of citizen participation, or gives people a better awareness of public affairs and an understanding of the role of elections in a democracy. Education is associated with a sense of confidence and political *efficacy,* the feeling that one can indeed have a personal impact on public affairs.

Age is another factor affecting voter participation. Perhaps because young people have more distractions, more demands on their time in school, work, or new family responsibilities, nonvoting is greatest among 18- to 24-year-olds. In contrast, older Americans are politically influential in part because candidates know they turn out at the polls.

High-income people are more likely to vote than are low-income people. Most of this difference stems from the fact that high-income people are more likely to be well educated and older. But poor people may also feel alienated from the political system—they may lack a sense of political efficacy; they may feel they have little control over their own lives, let alone over public affairs. Or poor people may simply be so absorbed in the problems of life that they have little time or energy to spend on registering and voting.

COMPARED TO WHAT?

Voter Turnout in Western Democracies

Other Western democracies regularly report higher voter turnout rates than the United States (see figure). Yet in an apparent paradox, Americans seem to be more supportive of their political institutions, less alienated from their political system, and even more patriotic than citizens of Western European nations. Why, then, are voter turnouts in the United States so much lower than in these other democracies?

The answer to this question lies primarily in the legal and institutional differences between the United States and the other democracies. First of all, in Austria, Australia, Belgium, and Italy, voting is *mandatory*. Penalties and the level of enforcement vary within and across these countries. Moreover, registration laws in the United States make voting more difficult than in other countries. In Western Europe, all citizens are required to register with the government and obtain identification cards. These cards are then used for admission to the polls. In contrast, voter registration is entirely voluntary in the United States, and voters must reregister if they change residences. Nearly 50 percent of the U.S. population changes residence at least once in a 5-year period, thus necessitating reregistration.

Parties in the United States are more loosely organized, less disciplined, and less able to mobilize voters than are European parties. Moreover, many elections in the United States, notably elections for Congress, are not very competitive. The United States organizes congressional elections by district with winner-take-all rules, whereas many European parliaments are selected by proportional representation, with seats allocated to parties based on national vote totals. Proportional representation means every vote counts toward seats in the legislative body. Thus greater competition and proportional representation may encourage higher voter turnout in European democracies.

But cultural differences may also contribute to differences in turnout. The American political culture,

with its tradition of individualism and self-reliance and its reluctance to empower government (see Chapter 2), encourages Americans to resolve their problems through their own efforts rather than looking to government for solutions. Government is not as central to Americans as it is to Europeans, and therefore getting to the polls on election day is not seen as so important.

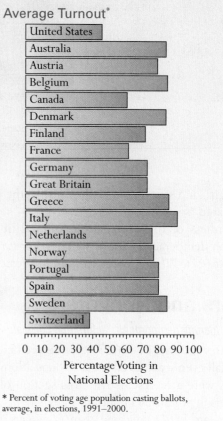

Average Turnout*

United States
Australia
Austria
Belgium
Canada
Denmark
Finland
France
Germany
Great Britain
Greece
Italy
Netherlands
Norway
Portugal
Spain
Sweden
Switzerland

0 10 20 30 40 50 60 70 80 90 100

Percentage Voting in
National Elections

* Percent of voting age population casting ballots, average, in elections, 1991–2000.

Source: Center for Voting and Democracy, 2008. www.fairvote.org. Reprinted by permission.

Income and education differences between participants and nonparticipants are even greater when other forms of political participation are considered. Higher-income, better-educated people are much more likely to be among those who make campaign contributions, who write or call their elected representatives, and who join and work in active political organizations.[23]

Historically, race was a major determinant of nonvoting. Black voter turnout, especially in the South, was markedly lower than white voter turnout. African Americans continue today to have a slightly lower overall voter turnout than whites, but most of the remaining difference is attributable to differences between blacks and whites in educational and income levels. Blacks and whites at the same educational and income levels register and vote with the same frequency.

The greatest disparity in voter turnout is between Hispanics and others. Low voter participation by Hispanics may be a product of language differences,

POLITICS UP CLOSE

The Changing American Voter

The nation's voters in the 2008 presidential election were the most racially and ethnically diverse in American history. Nearly one in four votes were cast by nonwhites. The nation's three largest minority groups—African Americans, Hispanics, and Asians—each accounted for unprecedented shares of the presidential vote.

Overall, whites made up 76.3% of the record 131 million people who voted in 2008, while blacks made up 12.1%, Hispanics 7.4%, and Asians 2.5%. The white share of the electorate is the lowest ever, yet it is still higher than the 65.8% white share of the total U.S. population. The increasing diversity of the electorate was driven by increases both in number and in the turnout rates of minority voters. Levels of participation by blacks, Hispanics, and Asians all increased in 2008, reducing the voter participation gap between minorities and white eligible voters. Voter turnout among blacks increased substantially to a point where it nearly matches the voter turnout of white voters. Hispanic participation levels also increased but they remain lower than blacks or whites.

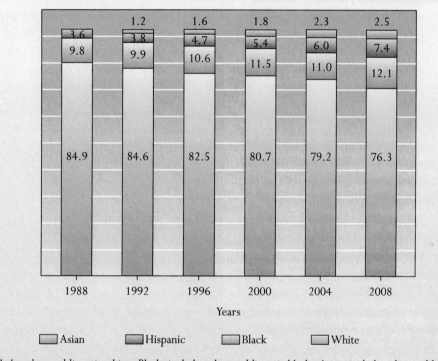

Note: Whites include only non-Hispanic whites. Blacks include only non-Hispanic blacks. Asians include only non-Hispanic Asians. Native Americans and mixed-race groups not shown. Asian share not available prior to 1990.

Source: Pew Research Center tabulations from the Current Population Survey, November Supplements data. Reprinted with permission from Pew Hispanic Center. "Dissecting the 2008 Electorate: Most Diverse in U.S. History." http://pewhispanic.org/reports/report.php?ReportID=108.

lack of cultural assimilation, or noncitizenship status (see also *Politics Up Close:* "The Changing American Voter").

Nonvoting: What Difference Does It Make?

▶ 5.13 *Assess the consequences of nonvoting.*

How concerned should we be about low levels of participation in American politics? Certainly the democratic ideal envisions an active, participating citizenry. Democratic government, asserts the Declaration of Independence, derives its "just powers from the consent of the governed." The legitimacy of democratic government can be more easily questioned when half of the people fail to vote. That is, it is easier to

✔ *Think* Again

Is our government really legitimate when only about half the people vote in presidential elections?

question whether the government truly represents "the people" when only half of the people vote even in a presidential election. Voting is an expression of good citizenship, and it reinforces attachment to the nation and to democratic government. Nonvoting suggests alienation from the political system.

However, the *right* to vote is more important to democratic government than voter turnout. The nineteenth-century English political philosopher John Stuart Mill wrote, "Men, as well as women, do not need political rights in order that they may govern, but in order that they may not be misgoverned."[24] As long as all adult Americans possess the right to vote, politicians must consider their interests. "Rulers and ruling classes are under a necessity of considering the interests of those who have the suffrage."[25] Democratic governments cannot really ignore the interests of anyone who can vote. People who have the right to vote, but who have voluntarily chosen not to exercise it in the past, can always change their minds, go to the polls, and "throw the rascals out."

Voluntary nonvoting is not the same as being denied the suffrage. Politicians can indeed ignore the interests of people denied the vote by restrictive laws or practices or by intimidation or force. But when people choose not to exercise their right to vote, they may be saying that they do not believe their interests are really affected by government. The late Senator Sam Ervin is widely quoted on the topic of nonvoters:

> I'm not going to shed any crocodile tears if people don't care enough to vote. I don't believe in making it easy for apathetic, lazy people. I'd be extremely happy if nobody in the United States voted except for the people who thought about the issues and made up their own minds and wanted to vote.[26]

Protest as Political Participation

▶ 5.14 *Characterize protest as a form of political participation.*

Protests, marches, and demonstrations are important forms of political participation. Indeed, the 1st Amendment guarantees the right "peaceably to assemble, and to petition the government for a redress of grievances." A march to the steps of Congress, a mass assembly of people on the Washington Mall with speakers, sign waving, and songs, and the presentation of petitions to government officials are all forms of participation protected by the 1st Amendment.

protests
Public marches or demonstrations designed to call attention to an issue and motivate others to apply pressure on public officials.

Protests Protests are generally designed to call attention to an issue and to motivate others to apply pressure on public officials. In fact, protests are usually directed at the news media rather than at public officials themselves. If protesters could persuade public officials directly in the fashion of lobbyists and interest groups, they would not need to protest. Protests are intended to generate attention and support among previously uncommitted people—enough so the ultimate targets of the protest, public officials, will be pressured to act to redress grievances.

Coverage by the news media, especially television, is vital to the success of protest activity. The media not only carry the protesters' message to the mass public but also inform public officials about what is taking place. Protests provide the media with "good visuals"—pictorial dramatizations of political issues. The media welcome opportunities to present political issues in a confrontational fashion because confrontation helps capture larger audiences. Thus protesters and the media use each other to advance their separate goals.

Protests are most commonly employed by groups that have little influence in electoral politics. They were a key device of the civil rights movement at a time

A CONSTITUTIONAL NOTE

Who Can Vote?

The Founders generally believed that only property-owning free white males, 21 or older, should be entitled to vote. But they failed to include these qualifications in the original Constitution of 1787. Instead, they left it up to the states to decide who should vote: ". . . the Electors in each State shall have the Qualifications requisite for Electors of the most numerous Branch of the State Legislature" (Article I, Section 2). Why leave it up to the states to decide the voter qualifications for national elections? In committee and in floor discussions the delegates could not agree on what kind of property should qualify a person to vote. Plantation owners argued for qualifications to be expressed in land acreage; bankers wanted them expressed in the size of one's bank account; shippers and businessmen, in the value of their inventories or ships; and so on. In frustration, the delegates dropped the issue into the laps of the states secure in the knowledge that in 1787 all the states had some form of property qualifications and no state permitted women, slaves, or persons under 21 to vote. But this opening in the Constitution began a long journey toward full voting rights in the United States. Jacksonian democracy swept the nation in the 1840s and property qualifications were dropped by the states themselves. Not until after the Civil War was the Constitution amended to prevent the states from denying the right to vote on account of race (15th Amendment, 1870). The long fight for women's suffrage finally resulted in a constitutional guarantee of women's right to vote (19th Amendment, 1920); poll taxes were constitutionally banned (24th Amendment, 1964); and 18-year-olds secured the constitutional right to vote (26th Amendment, 1971).

when many African Americans were barred from voting. In the absence of protest, the majority white population—and the public officials they elected—were at best unconcerned with the plight of black people in a segregated society. Protests, including a dramatic march on Washington in 1963 at which Martin Luther King, Jr., delivered his inspirational "I Have a Dream" speech, called attention to the injustices of segregation and placed civil rights on the agenda of decision makers.

Protests can be effectively employed by groups that are relatively small in number but whose members feel very intensely about the issue. Often the protest is a means by which these groups can obtain bargaining power with decision makers. Protests may threaten to tarnish the reputations of government officials or private corporations, or may threaten to disrupt their daily activities or reduce their business through boycotts or pressure on customers. If the protest is successful, protest leaders can then offer to end the protest in exchange for concessions from their targets.

Civil Disobedience Civil disobedience is a form of protest that involves breaking what are perceived as "unjust" laws. The purpose is to call attention to the existence of injustice. In the words of Martin Luther King, Jr., civil disobedience "seeks so to dramatize the issue that it can no longer be ignored"[27] (see *A Conflicting View*: "Sometimes It's Right to Disobey the Law" in Chapter 1). Those truly engaging in civil disobedience do not attempt to evade punishment for breaking the law but instead willingly accept the penalty. By doing so, they demonstrate not only their sincerity and commitment but also the injustice of the law. Cruelty or violence directed at the protesters by police or others contributes further to the drama of injustice. Like other protest activity, the success of civil disobedience depends on the willingness of the mass media to carry the message to both the general public and the political leadership.

civil disobedience
Form of public protest involving the breaking of laws believed to be unjust.

Violence Violence can also be a form of political participation. Indeed, political violence—for example, assassinations, rioting, burning, looting—has been uncomfortably frequent in American politics over the years. It is important to distinguish

POLITICS UP CLOSE

How to Run for Office

Many rewards come with elected office—the opportunity to help shape public policy, public attention and name recognition, and many business, professional, and social contacts. But there are many drawbacks as well—the absence of privacy; a microscopic review of one's past; constant calls, meetings, interviews, and handshaking; and, perhaps most onerous of all, the continual need to solicit campaign funds.

Before You Run—Getting Involved

Get involved in various organizations in your community:

- Neighborhood associations.
- Chambers of commerce, business associations.
- Churches and synagogues (become an usher, if possible, for visibility).
- Political groups (Democratic or Republican clubs, League of Women Voters, and so on).
- Parent-Teacher Associations (PTAs).
- Service clubs (Rotary, Kiwanis, Civitan, Toastmasters).
- Recreation organizations (Little League, flag football, soccer leagues, running and walking clubs, for example, as participant, coach, or umpire).

Deciding to Run—Know What You're Doing

In deciding to run, and choosing the office for which you wish to run, you should become thoroughly familiar with the issues, duties, and responsibilities.

- Attend council or commission meetings, state legislative sessions, and/or committee hearings.
- Become familiar with current issues and officeholders, and obtain a copy of and read the budget.
- Learn the demographics of your district (racial, ethnic, and age composition; occupational mix; average income; neighborhood differences). If you do not fit the prevailing racial, ethnic, or age composition, think about moving to another district.
- Memorize a brief (preferably less than seven seconds) answer to the question, "Why are you running?"

Getting in the Race

Contact your county elections department to obtain the following:

- Qualifying forms and information.
- Campaign financing forms and regulations.
- District and street maps for your district.
- Recent election results in your district.
- Election-law book or pamphlet.

- Voter registration lists (usually sold as lists, or labels, or tapes).
- Contact your party's county chairperson for advice; convince the party's leaders that you can win. Ask for a list of their regular campaign contributors.

Raising Money

The easiest way to finance a campaign is to be rich enough to provide your own funds. Failing that, you must:

- Establish a campaign fund, according to the laws of your state.
- Find a treasurer/campaign-finance chairperson who knows many wealthy, politically involved people.
- Invite wealthy, politically involved people to small coffees, cocktail parties, dinners; give a brief campaign speech and then have your finance chairperson solicit contributions.
- Follow up fund-raising events and meetings with personal phone calls.
- Be prepared to continue fund-raising activities throughout your campaign; file accurate financial disclosure statements as required by state law.

Getting Organized

Professional campaign managers and management firms almost always outperform volunteers. If you cannot afford professional management, you must rely on yourself or trusted friends to perform the following:

- Draw up a budget based on reasonable expectations of campaign funding.
- Interview and select a professional campaign-management firm, or appoint a trusted campaign manager.
- Ask trusted friends from various clubs, activities, neighborhoods, churches, and so on, to meet and serve as a campaign committee. If your district is racially or ethnically diverse, make sure all groups are represented on your committee.
- Decide on a campaign theme; research issues important to your community; develop brief, well-articulated positions on these issues.
- Open a campaign headquarters with desks and telephones. Buy a cell phone; use call forwarding; stay in contact. Use your garage if you can't afford an office.
- Arrange to meet with newspaper editors, editorial boards, TV station executives, and political reporters. Be prepared for tough questions.

violence from protest. Peaceful protest is constitutionally protected. Often, organized protest activity harnesses frustrations and hostilities, directs them into constitutionally acceptable activities, and thus avoids violence. Likewise,

- Hire a media consultant or advertising agency, or appoint a volunteer media director who knows television, radio, and newspaper advertising.
- Arrange a press conference to announce your candidacy. Notify all media well in advance. Arrange for overflow crowd of supporters to cheer and applaud.
- Produce eyecatching, inspirational 15- or 30-second television and radio ads that present a favorable image of you and stress your campaign theme.
- Prepare and print attractive campaign brochures, signs, and bumper stickers.
- Hire a local survey-research firm to conduct telephone surveys of voters in your district, asking what they think are the most important issues, how they stand on them, whether they recognize your name and your theme, and how they plan to vote. Be prepared to change your theme and your position on issues if surveys show strong opposition to your views.

On the Campaign Trail

Campaigns themselves may be primarily media centered or primarily *door-to-door* ("retail") or some combination of both.

- Buy media time as early as possible from television and radio stations; insist on prime-time slots before, during, and after popular shows.
- Buy newspaper ads; insist on their placement in popular, well-read sections of the paper.
- Attend every community gathering possible, just to be seen, even if you do not give a speech. Keep all speeches short. Focus on one or two issues that your polls show are important to voters.
- Recruit paid or unpaid volunteers to hand out literature door-to-door. Record names and addresses of voters who say they support you.
- Canvass door-to-door with a brief (seven-second) self-introduction and statement of your reasons for running. Use registration lists to identify members of your own party, and try to address them by name. Also canvass offices, factories, coffee shops, shopping malls—anywhere you find a crowd.
- Organize a phone bank, either professional or volunteer. Prepare *brief* introduction and phone statements. Record names of people who say they support you.
- Know your opponent: Research his or her past affiliations, indiscretions if any, previous voting record, and public positions on issues.

- Be prepared to "define" your opponent in negative terms. Negative advertising works. But be fair: base your comments on your opponent's public record. Emphasize his or her positions that clearly deviate from your district voters' known preferences.

Primary Versus General Elections

Remember that you will usually have to campaign in two elections—your party's primary and the general election.

- Before the primary, identify potential opposition in your own party, try to dissuade them from running.
- Allocate your budget first to win the primary election. If you lose the primary, you won't need any funds for the general election.
- In general elections, you must broaden your appeal without distancing your own party supporters. Deemphasize your party affiliation unless your district regularly elects members of your party; in a close district or a district that regularly votes for the opposition party, stress your independence and your commitment to the *district's* interests.

On Election Day

Turning out your voters is the key to success. Election day is the busiest day of the campaign for you and your staff.

- Use your phone bank to place as many calls as possible to party members in your district (especially those who have indicated in previous calls and visits that they support you). Remind them to vote; make sure your phone workers can tell each voter where to go to cast his or her vote.
- Solicit volunteers to drive people to the polls.
- Assign workers to as many polling places as possible. Most state laws require that they stay a specified distance from the voting booths. But they should be in evidence with your signs and literature to buttonhole voters before they go into the booths.
- Show up at city or county election office on election night with prepared victory statement thanking supporters and pledging your service to the district. (Also draft a courteous concession statement pledging your support to the winner, in case you lose.)
- Attend victory party with your supporters; meet many "new" friends.

civil disobedience should be distinguished from violence. Civil disobedience breaks only "unjust" laws, without violence, and willingly accepts punishment without trying to escape.

Civil Disobedience,
Uncivil Rest

Cruelty or violence directed at peaceful protesters further dramatizes their cause. In Jackson, Mississippi, in 1963, segregationists poured mustard, ketchup, and sugar over lunch counter sit-in protesters. But far more serious violence, including murder, was perpetrated against civil rights protesters in the 1960s.

Effectiveness How effective are protests? Protests can be effective in achieving some goals under some conditions. But protests are useless or even counter-productive in pursuit of other goals under other conditions. Here are some generalizations about the effectiveness of protests:

- Protests are more likely to be effective when directed at specific problems or laws rather than at general conditions that cannot readily be remedied by governmental action.

- Protests are more likely to be effective when targeted toward public officials who are capable of granting the desired concession or resolving the specific problem. Protests with no specific targets and protests directed at officials who have no power to change things are generally unproductive.

- Protests are more likely to succeed when the goal is limited to gaining access or representation in decision making or to placing an issue on the agenda of decision makers.

- Protests are not always effective in actually getting laws changed and are even less effective in ensuring that the impact of the changes will really improve the conditions that led to the protest.

Public officials can defuse protest activity in a variety of ways. They may greet protesters with smiles and reassurances that they agree with their goals. They may dispense symbolic satisfaction without any tangible results. They may grant token concessions with great publicity, perhaps remedying a specific case of injustice while doing little to affect general conditions. Or public officials may claim to be constrained either legally or financially from doing anything—the "I-would-like-to-help-you-but-I-can't" strategy. Or public officials can directly confront the protesters by charging that they are unrepresentative of the groups they are trying to help.

Perhaps the most challenging and sometimes most effective kind of "protest" is to run for public office (see *Politics Up Close:* "How to Run for Office" on pages 168–69). Whether at the local level, such as the school board, or at the state or national level, the participation of one individual as a candidate—even when not elected—can make a difference in public affairs.

Summary

▶ **5.1** *Analyze the relationships between politics, public opinion, and policy changes.*

Public opinion is the combined preferences and opinions of individuals on significant issues. Major shifts in public opinion usually translate into policy changes, although there is little agreement on whether public opinion should or should not direct government policy.

▶ **5.2** *Explain how the agents of socialization influence the development of political opinions.*

Political socialization—the learning of political values, beliefs, and opinions—starts at an early age. It is influenced by family, school, church, peer group, and the media.

▶ **5.3** *Determine the role of ideology in shaping opinion.*

Ideology also shapes opinion, especially among politically interested and active people who employ fairly consistent liberal or conservative ideas in forming their opinions on specific issues.

▶ **5.4** *Describe the relationship between gender and opinion.*

On "women's issues" (e.g., abortion or the role of women in business and politics) there is no big difference between men's and women's opinions. The most important political difference between men and women is that more women identify with the Democratic Party than do men and that women tend to vote slightly more than men do.

▶ **5.5** *Describe the relationship between race and opinion.*

Political opinion continues to show a divide between whites and African Americans over the extent of discrimination that exists in the U.S. African Americans tend to have a more positive view of the need for a more active government but they are less sanguine about the American criminal justice system.

▶ **5.6** *Describe the reasons for the growing importance of Hispanics in the American political process.*

Hispanics are the fastest growing minority group in the United States and they now are the largest minority group surpassing African Americans in total numbers. Hispanics are generally in favor of an activist government and strong welfare programs but at the same time they have strong family values and are conservative on many foreign policy, social, and religious issues.

▶ **5.7** *Assess how and to what extent public opinion influences public policy making.*

Political leaders, elites, and other decision makers are relatively unconstrained by mass opinion because it is unstable, ill informed, and inconsistent. The essential link between opinion and policy is political participation

▶ **5.8** *Identify the various ways in which a citizen may participate in politics.*

Individuals can exercise power in a democratic political system in a variety of ways. They can run for public office, take part in demonstrations and protests, make financial contributions to candidates, attend political events, write letters to newspapers or public officials, belong to political organizations, vote in elections, or simply hold and express opinions on public issues.

▶ **5.9** *Trace the expansion of the right to vote.*

Securing the right to vote for all Americans required nearly 200 years of political struggle. Key victories included the elimination of property qualifications by 1840, the 15th Amendment in 1870 (eliminating restrictions based on race), the 19th Amendment in 1920 (eliminating restrictions based on gender), the Civil Rights Act of 1964 and Voting Rights Act of 1965 (eliminating racial obstacles), the 24th Amendment in 1964 (eliminating poll taxes), and the 26th Amendment in 1971 (extending the right to vote to 18-year-olds).

▶ **5.10** *Analyze the factors that influence the decision of whether to vote.*

Many people do not vote due to feelings of political alienation and distrust of government.

▶ **5.11** *Analyze the political factors that influence voter turnout.*

About half of the voting-age population fails to vote even in presidential elections. Voter turnout has steadily declined in recent decades. Voter registration is a major obstacle to voting. Young people have the poorest record of voter turnout of any age group.

▶ 5.12 *Identify demographic factors that correlate with higher and lower turnout rates.*

Some of the primary factors that influence whether or not someone is a voter include education level, age, and income. Historically, race has also been a factor. Currently, the greatest disparity in voters is between Hispanics and others. This lack of voters may be due to language differences, lack of cultural assimilation, or noncitizenship status.

▶ 5.13 *Assess the consequences of nonvoting.*

Voluntary nonvoting is not as serious a threat to democracy as denial of the right to vote. Nevertheless, the class bias in voting may tilt the political system toward the interests of higher income, better-educated, older whites at the expense of lower-income, less-educated, younger minorities.

▶ 5.14 *Characterize protest as a form of political participation.*

Protest is an important form of participation in politics. Protests are more commonly employed by groups with little direct influence over public officials. The object is to generate attention and support from previously uncommitted people in order to bring new pressure on public officials to redress grievances. Media coverage is vital to the success of protests.

Chapter Test

▶ 5.1 *Analyze the relationships between politics, public opinion, and policy changes.*

1. It would be accurate to say that public opinion on specific policy issues is often
   a. ill informed
   b. unstable
   c. poorly organized
   d. all of the above

2. The tendency of some respondents to give socially respectable responses whether or not they are true is known as the
   a. false transference problem
   b. halo effect
   c. rainbow effect
   d. the politically correct survey research problem

3. A poll that attempts to interview respondents after they have voted is referred to as a
   a. "tracking" poll.
   b. push poll.
   c. random sample.
   d. exit poll.

▶ 5.2 *Explain how the agents of socialization influence the development of political opinions.*

4. Which of the following has the most influential impact on the development of political values and opinions?
   a. the Church
   b. the schools
   c. peer group values
   d. the family

5. The real power of television on public opinion is it's power to
   a. persuade people to take one side or another on political issues
   b. decide what will be decided or added to the political agenda
   c. slant the news
   d. to raise money and present public service announcements

▶ 5.3 *Determine the role of ideology in shaping opinion.*

6. A fairly consistent and integrated set of principles might be a good definition of
   a. liberalism
   b. conservatism
   c. ideology
   d. opinion

▶ 5.4 *Describe the relationship between gender and opinion.*

7. It would be accurate to say that men's and women's opinions do not differ much on the issue of
   a. abortion
   b. the role of women in business
   c. supporting a qualified woman for the presidency
   d. all of the above

8. The most important political difference among men and women is
   a. over the issue of abortion
   b. the propensity of women to identify more with the Republicans than the Democrats
   c. the propensity of men to identify more with the Republicans than the Democrats
   d. over the use of medical marijuana

▶ 5.5 *Describe the relationship between race and opinion.*

9. Since many African Americans are supporters of _____, it is not surprising that they describe themselves as _____.
   a. a small, less active government/conservatives
   b. a large, more active government/liberals
   c. a small, less active government/liberals
   d. a large, more active government/conservatives

▶ 5.6 *Describe the reasons for the growing importance of Hispanics in the American political process.*

10. In general, Hispanics believe that _____ the U.S. economy.
    a. immigration helps
    b. immigration hurts
    c. immigration has little or no impact on
    d. unemployment is high enough and it is time to curtail immigration before it hurts

...tent public opinion
...ing.

...d opinions among the

...ways in which a citizen may
...n politics.

...cal participation in democracies occurs most frequently
by citizens
a. voting
b. joining political organizations
c. writing or calling public officials
d. wearing buttons, placing signs and bumper stickers

▶ 5.9 *Trace the expansion of the right to vote.*

13. In the effort to expand the right to vote, the first voter qualification barrier to fall were those regarding
   a. race
   b. gender
   c. property
   d. literacy

▶ 5.10 *Analyze the factors that influence the decision of whether to vote.*

14. The idea that a person should vote only if the costs of voting are less than the expected value of having the preferred candidate win would be most closely associated with
   a. pluralism
   b. the "rational" voter
   c. the elite model
   d. the minimax voter

▶ 5.11 *Analyze the political factors that influence voter turnout.*

15. Political alienation involves the idea that
   a. the socialization process was a failure
   b. aliens cannot be socialized in American values
   c. political competition can compensate for political isolation
   d. politics is not relevant to one's life

▶ 5.12 *Identify demographic factors that correlate with higher and lower turnout rates.*

16. It would be accurate to say that
   a. the young vote more often than the middle-aged
   b. women are more likely to vote than men
   c. young women vote more than elderly women
   d. Hispanics are more likely to vote than are African Americans

▶ 5.13 *Assess the consequences of nonvoting.*

17. Nonvoting is often associated with
   a. getting on in years
   b. political socialization
   c. political alienation
   d. being middle class

▶ 5.14 *Characterize protest as a form of political participation.*

18. The right to peacefully protest an action of government is guaranteed in
   a. the Declaration of Independence
   b. the Articles of Confederation
   c. the Bill of Rights
   d. the Emancipation Proclamation

---

mypoliscilab EXERCISES

Apply what you learned in this chapter on MyPoliSciLab.

Read on **mypoliscilab.com**

   eText: Chapter 5

Study and **Review** on **mypoliscilab.com**

   Pre-Test

   Post-Test

   Chapter Exam

   Flashcards

Watch on **mypoliscilab.com**

   Video: Chicago Gun Laws

   Video: Opinion Poll on the U.S. Economy

   Video: Obama Approval Rating

   Video: Teen Sues for Equal Protection

   Video: Candidates Court College Students

   Video: L.A. Riots: 15 Years Later

Explore on **mypoliscilab.com**

   Simulation: You Are a Polling Consultant

   Simulation: You Are an Informed Voter Helping Your Classmates

   Simulation: You Are the Leader of Concerned Citizens for World Justice

   Comparative: Comparing Governments and Public Opinion

   Timeline: War, Peace and Public Opinion

   Visual Literacy: Voting Turnout: Who Votes in the United States?

Key Terms

public opinion 139	generation gap 145	poll taxes 157	registration 160
survey research 141	gender gap 148	literacy test 157	political alienation
halo effect 141	suffrage 155	19th Amendment 157	162
salient issues 143	property qualifications	26th Amendment 158	protests 166
socialization 143	156	"Motor Voter Act" 158	civil disobedience
diffuse support 143	white primary 156	turnout 158	167

Suggested Readings

Asher, Herbert. *Polling and the Public: What Every Citizen Should Know.* 7th ed. Washington, D.C.: CQ Press, 2007. Explains methods of polling and how results can be influenced by wording, sampling, and interviewing techniques; also covers how polls are used by the media and in campaigns.

Conway, M. Margaret, Gertrude A. Stevernagel, and David Ahern. *Women and Political Participation.* 2nd ed. Washington, D.C.: CQ Press, 2004. An examination of cultural change and women's participation in politics, including treatment of the gender gap in political attitudes and the impact of women's membership in the political elite.

Drexler, Kateri M., and Gwen Garcelon. *Strategies for Active Citizenship.* Upper Saddle River, N.J.: Prentice Hall, 2005. A handbook for becoming active in politics.

Erikson, Robert S., and Kent L. Tedin. *American Public Opinion,* 7th ed. New York: Longman, 2007. A comprehensive review of the forces influencing public opinion and an assessment of the influence of public opinion in American politics.

Graham, Bob. *America, The Owner's Manual: Making Government work for you.* Washington, D.C.: CQ press, 2009. Student-oriented instructions on how to advance a political issue by a former U.S. senator.

Greenstein, Fred I. *Children and Politics.* New Haven, Conn.: Yale University Press, 1985. Early research on what children know about politics and how they learned it.

Jacobs, Lawrence R., and Robert Y. Shapiro. *Politicians Don't Pander: Political Manipulation and the Loss of Democratic Responsiveness.* Chicago: University of Chicago Press, 2000. A study of how politicians use public opinion to suit their own purposes.

Page, Benjamin I., and Robert Y. Shapiro. *The Rational Public.* Chicago: University of Chicago Press, 1992. An examination of 50 years of public opinion polls convinces these authors that American government is generally responsive to the views of the majority.

Stimson, James A. *Tides of Consent: How Public Opinion Shapes American Politics.* New York: Cambridge University Press, 2004. The movement of public opinion over time moves public policy.

Walton, Hanes, and Robert C. Smith. *American Politics and the African American Quest for Universal Freedom.* New York: Pearson Longman, 2010. A comprehensive American government textbook emphasizing the diversity of African American opinions and behavior.

Zaller, John R. *The Nature and Origins of Mass Opinion.* New York: Cambridge University Press, 1992. An effort to develop and test a conceptual model of how people form political preferences, how political views and arguments diffuse through the population, and how people evaluate this information and convert their reactions into public opinion.

Suggested Websites

Americans United for Separation of Church and State
www.au.org
Advocacy organization opposed to religious influence in government.

Center for Voting and Democracy **www.fairvote.org**
Reform organization devoted to expanding voter participation; Web site includes data on voter turnout nationally and by state.

Center for Women in Politics
www.rci.rutgers.edu/~cawp
Extensive information on women officeholders, as well as gender gap data on voting and attitudes on public policy.

Christian Coalition **www.cc.org**
Organization advocating greater Christian involvement in politics and government.

Gallup www.gallup.com
Oldest public opinion organization, with latest polls and large archive.

National Urban League www.nul.org
Organization devoted to advancing the economic well-being of African Americans, often reflecting opinions of the growing black middle class. Publishes annual *State of Black America*.

The Polling Report www.pollingreport.com
Recent public opinion polls on policy issues, political actors, government institutions, and so on.

The Pollster www.pollster.com
A Web site summarizing recent polls with links to blogs about polls and polling results.

Protest Net www.protest.net
Radical organization provides calendar of protests against military actions, world trade, animal experiments, and so forth.

Public Agenda Online www.publicagenda.org
Recent opinion polls on a variety of policy issues.

State of the Vote www.stateofthevote.org
Official Web site of the National Association of Secretaries of State (state voting officials) urging young people to register and vote.

Chapter Test Answer Key

1. D	4. D	7. D	10. A	13. C	16. B
2. B	5. B	8. C	11. D	14. B	17. C
3. D	6. C	9. B	12. A	15. E	18. C

6 MASS MEDIA
Setting the Political Agenda

66 The mass media may not be successful in telling people what to think, but the media are stunningly successful in telling their audience what to think about. **99**

Bernard Cohen

Chapter Outline and Learning Objectives

The Power of the Media
▶ 6.1 *Identify functions and components of the media.*

Sources of Media Power
▶ 6.2 *Explain the sources of the media's power.*

The Business of the Media
▶ 6.3 *Describe the business of the media.*

The Politics of the News
▶ 6.4 *Assess how the politics of the media are shaped by their economic interests, environment, and ideological leanings.*

Polarization of the Media
▶ 6.5 *Characterize the political polarization of media audiences.*

Mediated Elections
▶ 6.6 *Analyze the role of the media in shaping campaigns and elections.*

Freedom Versus Fairness
▶ 6.7 *Distinguish between freedom of the press and fairness of the press.*

Libel and Slander
▶ 6.8 *Describe the law regarding libel and slander.*

Politics and the Internet
▶ 6.9 *Evaluate the effects of the Internet on politics.*

Media Effects: Shaping Political Life
▶ 6.10 *Assess the effects that the media have on public opinion and political behavior.*

✓ *Think* about Politics

1. Are media professionals—news reporters, editors, anchors—the true voice of the people in public affairs?

   YES ◯   NO ◯

2. Do the media mirror what is really news, rather than deciding themselves what's important and then making it news?

   YES ◯   NO ◯

3. Is television your most important source of news?

   YES ◯   NO ◯

4. Should the media report on all aspects of the private lives of public officials?

   YES ◯   NO ◯

5. Do the media report equally fairly on Democratic and Republican candidates for office?

   YES ◯   NO ◯

6. Should the media be legally required to be fair and accurate in reporting political news?

   YES ◯   NO ◯

7. Are you more alienated than attracted by the media's coverage of politics?

   YES ◯   NO ◯

8. Is your choice of candidates in elections affected by their advertising?

   YES ◯   NO ◯

Ask yourself how much of your knowledge about politics in America comes from television and newspapers and the radio. What you know about politics and how you participate are, in fact, largely determined by the power of the media to decide what they want you to know.

The Power of the Media

▶ 6.1 *Identify functions and components of the media.*

Politics—the struggle over who gets what, when, and how—is largely carried out in the **mass media**. The arenas of political conflict are the various media of mass communication—television, newspapers, magazines, radio, books, recordings, motion pictures, and the Internet. What we know about politics comes to us largely through these media. Unless we ourselves are admitted to the White House Oval Office or the committee rooms of Congress or dinner parties at foreign embassies, or unless we ourselves attend political rallies and demonstrations or travel to distant battlefields, we must rely on the mass media to tell us about politics. Furthermore, few of us ever have the opportunity to personally evaluate the character of presidential candidates or cabinet members or members of Congress, or to learn their views on public issues by talking with them face to face. Instead, we must learn about people as well as events from the mass media.

Great power derives from the control of information. *Who knows what* helps to determine *who gets what*. The media not only provide an arena for politics; they are also themselves players in that arena. The media not only report on the struggles for power in society; they are also themselves participants in those struggles. The media have long been referred to as America's "fourth branch" of government—and for good reason.[1]

The Power of Television   Television is the most powerful medium of communication. It is a true *mass* communication medium. Virtually every home in the United States has a television set, and the average home has the set turned on for about 7 hours a day. Television is regularly chosen over other news media by Americans as the most common news source.

FIGURE 6.1

Check Your Sources: Where Americans Get Their News

Local TV news has long been America's favorite news source. Nightly network news is losing ground to cable news and the Internet. Newspaper readership is declining but remains a major source of news.

Note: More than one answer accepted in survey, so the sum adds up to well over 100 percent.

Source: Adapted from the Pew Research Center for the People and the Press, "Source of News for Americans," Jan. 2, 2007. www.people-press.org.

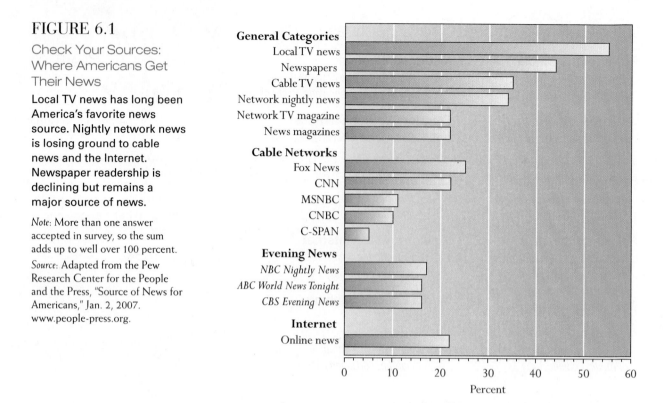

mass media
All means of communication with the general public, including television, newspapers, magazines, radio, books, recordings, motion pictures, and the Internet.

Americans turn to *local* TV news broadcasts as their most regular source of news. Daily newspapers are read by less than half of the adult public (see Figure 6.1). The national network evening news shows (*NBC Nightly News, ABC World News Tonight, CBS Evening News*) have lost viewership in recent years. But viewership of CNN, and Fox News has risen. Television weekly news magazines, notably CBS's *60 Minutes*, have also become major sources of news for many Americans.

A growing number of Americans, especially young people, are turning to online news sources (see *Politics Up Close*: "The Generation Gap in News").

During a national crisis—for example, the terrorist attack of 9/11—Americans become even more dependent on television for their news. When asked "Where would you go first?" for information during a crisis, 66 percent of Americans said they would turn on their TV sets. CNN was mentioned most often.[2]

Accuracy and Fairness   But Americans are losing confidence in the accuracy and fairness of the media. Just 29 percent say that news organizations generally "get their facts straight," the lowest level in more than two decades (see Figure 6.2). And fewer Americans believe that the media "deal fairly with all sides" in news reporting. Republicans and conservatives are more critical of the media than Democrats and liberals.

Newspapers and Magazines   Less than one-half of the adult population reads one of the nation's 1,400 daily newspapers. But the nation's prestige newspapers—the *New York Times, Washington Post*, and *Wall Street Journal*—are regularly read by government officials, corporate chiefs, interest-group leaders, and other media people. Stories appearing in these newspapers are generally picked up by daily papers around the country, and these stories almost always appear on national network television.

The leading weekly newsmagazines—*Time, Newsweek*, and *U.S. News & World Report*—reach a smaller but more politically attentive audience than do newspapers. Magazines of political commentary—for example, the *Nation* (liberal), *New Republic*

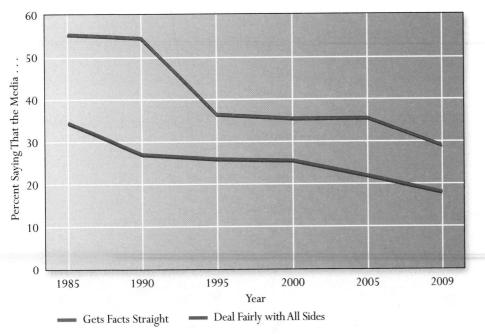

FIGURE 6.2
Accuracy and Fairness in the Media
Americans are losing confidence in the accuracy and fairness of the media.

Source: Adapted from the Pew Research Center for the People and the Press (2009). www.people-press.org.

(liberal), *National Review* (conservative), *American Spectator* (conservative), *Weekly Standard* (conservative), *Public Interest* (neo-conservative), and *Washington Monthly* (neo-liberal)—reach very small but politically active audiences.

Television's Emotional Communication   The power of television derives not only from its large audiences, but also from its ability to communicate emotions as well as information. Television's power is found in its visuals—angry faces in a rioting mob, police beating an African American motorist, wounded soldiers being unloaded from a helicopter—scenes that convey an emotional message. Gripping pictures can inflame public opinion, inspire a clamor for action, and even pressure the government into hasty action—the "CNN effect."

Moreover, television focuses on the faces of individuals as well as on their words, portraying honesty or deception, humility or arrogance, compassion or indifference, humor or meanness, and a host of other personal characteristics. Skillful politicians understand that *what* one says may not be as important as *how* one says it. Image triumphs over substance on television.[3]

Influence on Decision Makers   The media's impact on political decision makers is vastly more significant than their impact on ordinary viewers. Media stories often relate more directly to the immediate concerns of politicians and government officials. They are more attentive to these stories; they are often asked to respond or comment upon news stories. They correctly perceive that media coverage of particular events and issues sets the agenda for public discussion. Even media stories that have relatively little widespread public interest can create a buzz "inside the Beltway," that is, within Washington circles.

The Myth of the Mirror   Media people themselves often deny that they exercise great power. They sometimes claim that they only "mirror" reality. They like to think of themselves as unbiased reporters who simply narrate happenings and transmit videotaped portrayals of people and events as they really are. But whether or not the editors, reporters, producers, or anchors acknowledge their own power, it is clear that they do more than passively mirror reality.

POLITICS UP CLOSE

The Generation Gap in News

Young people are far less likely to spend time watching the news than older people. Indeed, people 65 and older are nearly twice as likely as those under 30 to watch television news. And older people are more than twice as likely to read a newspaper.

However, young people are more likely than older people to hear radio news, perhaps because radio news periodically interrupts music programming. And young people are the principal consumers of online news. Yet overall, young people are exposed to far less news than seniors.

The News Generation Gap

	18–29	30–49	50–64	65+
Watch TV news	40%	52%	62%	73%
Local TV	28	41	49	52
Network evening news	17	25	38	46
Cable TV news	16	23	30	35
Morning TV news	11	16	21	27
Read newspaper	26	37	52	59
Listen to radio news	34	49	42	29
News magazines	12	13	15	13
Online news	31	30	24	7
No news (yesterday)	33	19	15	12

Source: Pew Research Center for the People and the Press. www.people-press.org. Reprinted by permission of Pew Research Center for the People and the Press.

Sources of Media Power

▶ 6.2 *Explain the sources of the media's power.*

Government and the media are natural adversaries. (Thomas Jefferson once wrote that he would prefer newspapers without government to a government without newspapers. But after serving as president, he wrote that people who never read newspapers are better informed than those who do, because ignorance is closer to the truth than the falsehoods spread by newspapers.) Public officials have long been frustrated by the media. But the U.S. Constitution's 1st Amendment guarantee of a free press anticipates this conflict between government and the media. It prohibits government from resolving this conflict by silencing its critics.

Media professionals—television and newspaper reporters, editors, anchors, and producers—are not neutral observers of American politics but rather are active participants. They not only report events but also discover events to report, assign them political meaning, and predict their consequences. They seek to challenge government officials, debate political candidates, and define the problems of society. They see their profession as a "sacred trust" and themselves as the true voice of the people in public affairs.

Think Again

Do the media mirror what is really news, rather than deciding themselves what's important and then making it news?

newsmaking
Deciding what events, topics, presentations, and issues will be given coverage in the news.

Newsmaking   Deciding what is "news" and who is "newsworthy"—**newsmaking**—is the most important source of media power. It is only through the media that the general public comes to know about events, personalities, and issues. Media attention makes topics public, creates issues, and elevates personalities from obscurity to celebrity. Each day, editors, producers, and reporters must select

Facing the Media
Democratic presidential candidate U.S. Senator Barack Obama speaks to the traveling media on the tarmac at the airport in Eau Claire, Wisconsin, August 24, 2008.

from millions of events, topics, and people those that will be videotaped, written about, and talked about. The media can never be a "picture of the world" because the whole world cannot be squeezed into the picture. The media must decide what is and is not "news."

Politicians have a love-hate relationship with the media. They need media attention to promote themselves, their message, and their programs. They crave the exposure, the name recognition, and the celebrity status that the media can confer. At the same time, they fear attack by the media. They know the media are active players in the political game, not just passive spectators. The media seek sensational stories of sin, sexuality, corruption, and scandal in government to attract viewers and readers, and thus the media pose a constant danger to politicians. Politicians understand the power of the media to make or break their careers.

Agenda Setting
Agenda setting is the power to decide what will be decided. It is the power to define society's "problems," to create political issues, and to set forth alternative solutions. Deciding which issues will be addressed by government may be even more important than deciding how the issues will be resolved. The distinguished political scientist E. E. Schattschneider once wrote, "He who determines what politics is about runs the country."[4]

The real power of the media lies in their ability to set the political agenda for the nation. This power grows out of their ability to decide what is news. Media coverage determines what both citizens and public officials regard as "crises" or "problems" or "issues" to be resolved. Conditions ignored by the media seldom get on the agenda of political leaders. Media attention forces public officials to speak on the topic, take positions, and respond to questions. Media inattention allows problems to be ignored by government. "TV is the Great Legitimator. TV confers reality. Nothing happens in America, practically everyone seems to agree, until it happens on television."[5]

Political issues do not just "happen." The media are crucial to their development. Organized interest groups, professional public relations firms, government bureaucracies, political candidates, and elected officials all try to solicit the assistance of the media in shaping the political agenda. Creating an issue, publicizing

agenda setting
Deciding what will be decided, defining the problems and issues to be addressed by decision makers.

Made for TV

Janice Dickinson and the
Dickinson Models march on
Hollywood Blvd. for the People
for the Ethical Treatment of
Animal's (PETA's) "We'd Rather
Go Naked Than Wear Fur"
campaign on August 20, 2007,
in Hollywood, California.

socialization
The learning of a culture and
its values.

it, dramatizing it, turning it into a "crisis," getting people to talk about it, and ultimately forcing government to do something about it are the tactics of agenda setting. The participation of the mass media is vital to their success.[6]

Interpreting   The media not only decide what will be news; they also interpret the news for us. Editors, reporters, and anchors provide each story with an *angle*, an interpretation that places the story in a context and speculates about its meaning and consequences. The interpretation tells us what to think about the news.

News is presented in "stories." Reporters do not report facts; they tell stories. The story structure gives meaning to various pieces of information. Some common angles or themes of news stories are these:

- *Good guys versus bad guys*: for example, corrupt officials, foreign dictators, corporate polluters, and other assorted villains versus honest citizens, exploited workers, endangered children, or other innocents.

- *Little guys versus big guys*: for example, big corporations, the military, or insensitive bureaucracies versus consumers, taxpayers, poor people, or the elderly.

- *Appearance versus reality*: for example, the public statements of government officials or corporate executives versus whatever contradicting facts hardworking investigative reporters can find.

News is also "pictures." A story without visuals is not likely to be selected as television news in the first place. The use of visuals reinforces the angle. A close-up shot can reveal hostility, insincerity, or anxiety on the face of villains or can show fear, concern, sincerity, or compassion on the face of innocents. To emphasize elements of a story, an editor can stop the action, use slow motion, zoom the lens, add graphics, cut back and forth between antagonists, cut away for audience reaction, and so on. Videotaped interviews can be spliced to make the interviewees appear knowledgeable, informed, and sincere or, alternatively, ignorant, insensitive, and mean-spirited. The media jealously guard the right to edit interviews themselves, rejecting virtually all attempts by interviewees to review and edit their own interviews.

Socializing   The media have power to socialize audiences to the political culture. News, entertainment, and advertising all contribute to **socialization**—to the learning of political values. Socialization through television and motion pictures begins in early childhood and continues throughout life. Most of the political information people learn comes to them through television—specific facts as well as general values. Election coverage, for example, shows "how democracy works," encourages political participation, and legitimizes the winner's control of government. Advertising shows Americans desirable middle-class standards of living even while it encourages people to buy automobiles, detergent, and beer, and entertainment programming socializes them to "acceptable" ways of life. Political values such as racial tolerance, sexual equality, and support for law enforcement are reinforced in movies, situation comedies, and police shows.

Persuading   The media, in both paid advertising and news and entertainment programming, engage in direct efforts to change our attitudes, opinions, and behavior. Newspaper editorials have traditionally been employed for direct persuasion. A great deal of the political commentary on television news and interview programs is aimed at persuading people to adopt the views of the commentators. Even many entertainment programs and movies are intended to promote specific political viewpoints. But most direct persuasion efforts come to us through paid advertising.

Political campaigning is now largely a media battle, with paid political advertisements as the weapons. Candidates rely on professional campaign-management firms, with their pollsters, public relations specialists, advertising-production people, and media consultants, to carry on the fight (see Chapter 8).

Governments and political leaders must rely on persuasion through the mass media to carry out their programs. Presidents can take their message directly to people in televised speeches, news conferences, and the yearly State of the Union message. Presidents by custom are accorded television time whenever they request it. In this way, they can go over the heads of Congress and even the media executives and reporters themselves to communicate directly with the people.

In short, persuasion is central to politics, and the media are the key to persuasion.

The Business of the Media

▶ 6.3 *Describe the business of the media.*

The business of the media is to gather mass audiences to sell to advertisers. Economic interest drives all media to try to attract and hold the largest numbers of readers and viewers in order to sell time and space to advertisers. Over one-quarter of all prime-time television (8–11 P.M.) is devoted to commercial advertising. Americans get more than 1 minute of commercials for every 3 minutes of news and entertainment. Television networks and commercial stations charge advertisers on the basis of audience estimates made by rating services. One rating service, A. C. Nielsen, places electronic boxes in a national sample of television homes and calculates the proportion of these homes that watch a program (the rating), as well as the proportion of homes with their television sets turned on that watch a particular program (the share). Newspapers' and magazines' advertising revenue is based primarily on circulation figures.

Soft Fluff Versus Hard Programming   Lightweight entertainment—"soft fluff"—prevails over serious programming in virtually all media, but particularly on television. Critics of the "boob tube" abound in intellectual circles, but the mass public clearly prefers fluffy entertainment programming. Political scientist Doris Graber writes:

> Although "lightweight" programming draws the wrath of many people, particularly intellectual elites, one can argue that their disdain constitutes intellectual snobbery. Who is to say that the mass public's tastes are inferior to those of elites? . . . Proof is plentiful that the mass public does indeed prefer light entertainment to more serious programs.[7]

And it is the mass public that advertisers want to reach. Channels devoted to highbrow culture, including public television stations, languish with low ratings.

Public Television and Radio   The Corporation for Public Broadcasting (CPB) was created by Congress in 1967 to provide "noncommercial high quality programs . . . to inform, enlighten and enrich the public." As a nonprofit government corporation CPB relies on taxpayer funding in annual appropriations from Congress. In turn, it provides the funding for Public Broadcasting Service (PBS) and National Educational Television (NET). PBS had some early successes in programming—*Masterpiece Theatre, Sesame Street*—but in more recent years commercial broadcasting has exceeded PBS in both quality and viewership. Commercial channels—History Channel, Discovery Channel, National Geographic Channel, and others—regularly broadcast high-quality programs to much larger audiences and do not rely on taxpayer funding. Opponents of continued government funding of PBS complain of left-leaning bias in its news and commentary.

POLITICS UP CLOSE

60 Minutes, News as Entertainment

Television's longest-running prime-time program is *60 Minutes*. For over 40 years this news/entertainment show has been ranked at or near the top of all prime-time television shows, including dramas, comedies, sports, and other news shows. It was created in 1968 by the late Don Hewitt, its legendary producer. He devised reporter-centered, hard-hitting, investigative features centering on scandal and corruption in corporations and governments. The focus is usually on individual wrongdoers who are sometimes the object of confrontational interviews, and at other times ambushed by a reporter and shown mumbling denials or fleeing the camera. The regular cast of *60 Minutes* includes Morley Safer, Steve Croft, Lesley Stahl, Bob Simon, and Scott Pelley. It ends with occasionally humorous comments by its resident curmudgeon, Andy Rooney.

Features stories on nightly news broadcasts seldom exceed two minutes of air time. But features on

60 Minutes run 12 to 15 minutes; each show usually includes three feature stories. The features are designed to entertain, dramatize, and otherwise capture audience attention. The show often includes interviews with celebrities and even with important political figures, for example, Mike Wallace's interviews with the drug dealing Panamanian dictator Manuel Noriega, Russian President Vladimir Putin, and Iran's current leader Mahmoud Ahmadinejad.

60 Minutes demonstrates that news can be presented as entertainment and can capture large audiences. The show has many imitators, including some successful ones—*20/20, Dateline NBC,* and *48 Hours.*

Source: www.cbsnews.com.

News as TV Entertainment   Increasingly news is being presented as television entertainment. In recent years there has been a dramatic increase in the number of entertainment-oriented, quasi-news programming, sometimes referred to as the "soft news media."[8] **Soft news** comes in various formats: talk shows, both daytime and nighttime; and tabloid news programs (such as *60 Minutes, 20/20, Dateline NBC, 48 Hours*). Even late-night entertainment hosts and programs—Jay Leno, David Letterman, *Politically Incorrect, The Colbert Report, The Daily Show with John Stewart*—include comedy monologues that often refer to political events or issues.

Soft news
News featured in talk shows, late-night comedy, and TV news magazines—reaches more people than regular news broadcasts.

Soft news is a major source of information for people who are not interested in politics or public affairs. It is true, of course, that most soft news programming favors celebrity gossip, murder trials, sex scandals, disasters, and other human interest stories. But on some high-profile news issues these programs provide an otherwise inattentive public with what little information it absorbs. For example,

Bad News Bias
The media favor bad news over good news. Wars, fires and natural disasters, and crime are all well reported. But good news about things going well, such as improved health, higher standards of living, or new construction going as planned, get far less attention.

Oprah attracts more viewers than any of the nightly network newscasts; *60 Minutes* attracts more viewers than any other soft news program (see *Politics Up Close:* "*60 Minutes*, News as Entertainment").

Politicians themselves have come to understand the importance of soft news programming in reaching segments of the public that seldom watch news programs, speeches or debates, or campaign advertising. Presidential candidates welcome invitations to appear with Oprah, or Leno, or Letterman, and try to reformulate their messages in a light, comedic style that fits the program.

The Politics of the News

▶ 6.4 *Assess how the politics of the media are shaped by their economic interests, environment, and ideological leanings.*

The politics of the news media are shaped by (1) their *economic interest*, (2) their *professional environment*, and (3) their *ideological leanings*.

Sensationalism   The economic interest of the media—the need to capture and hold audience attention—creates a bias toward "hype" in the selection of news, its presentation, and its interpretation. To attract viewers and readers, the media bias the news toward violence, conflict, scandal, corruption, sex, scares of various sorts, and the personal lives of politicians and celebrities. News is selected primarily for its emotional impact on audiences; its social, economic, or political significance is secondary to the need to capture attention.

News must "touch" audiences personally, arouse emotions, and hold the interest of people with short attention spans. Scare stories—street crime, drug use, AIDS, nuclear power plant accidents, global warming, and a host of health alarms—make "good" news, for they cause viewers to fear for their personal safety. The sex lives of politicians, once by custom off-limits to the press, are now public "affairs." Scandal and corruption among politicians, as well as selfishness and greed among business executives, are regular media themes.[9]

Negativism   The media are biased toward bad news. Bad news attracts larger audiences than good news. Television news displays a pervasive bias toward the negative in American life—in government, business, the military, politics, education, and everywhere else. Bad-news stories on television vastly outnumber good-news stories.

Good news gets little attention. For example, television news watchers are not likely to know that illegal drug use is declining in the United States, that both the air and water are measurably cleaner today than in past decades, that the nuclear power industry has the best safety record of any major industry in the United States, and that the aged in America are wealthier and enjoy higher incomes than the nonaged. The violent crime rate is down 50 percent since 1990. Teenage pregnancies and abortion rates are both down significantly. Television has generally failed to report these stories or, even worse, has implied that the opposite is true. Good news—stories about improved health statistics, longer life spans, better safety records, higher educational levels, for example—seldom provides the dramatic element needed to capture audience attention. The result is an overwhelming bad-news bias, especially on television.[10]

muckraking
Journalistic exposés of corruption, wrongdoing, or mismanagement in government, business, and other institutions of society.

Muckraking   The professional environment of reporters and editors predisposes them toward an activist style of journalism once dubbed **muckraking**. Reporters today view themselves as "watchdogs" of the public trust. They see themselves in noble terms—enemies of corruption, crusaders for justice, defenders of the disadvantaged. "The watchdog function, once considered remedial and subsidiary . . . [is now] paramount: the primary duty of the journalists is to focus attention on problems and deficits, failures and threats."[11] Their professional models are the crusading "investigative reporters" who expose wrongdoing in government, business, the military, and every other institution in society—except the media.

"feeding frenzy"
Intense media coverage of a scandal or event that blocks out most other news.

The "Feeding Frenzy"

Occasionally, muckraking episodes grow into "**feeding frenzies**"—intense coverage of a scandal or event that blocks out most other news. Political scientist Larry Sabato describes the feeding frenzy: "In such situations a development is almost inevitably magnified and overscrutinized, the crush of cameras, microphones, and people, combined with the pressure of instant deadlines and live broadcasts, hype events and make it difficult to keep them in perspective. When a frenzy begins to gather, the intensity grows exponentially . . . Television news time is virtually turned over to the subject of the frenzy."[12] Increasingly stiff competition among the media for attention and the need for round-the-clock cable news to fill long hours contribute to feeding frenzies.

Liberalism in the Newsroom

The activist role that the media have taken upon themselves means that the personal values of reporters, editors, producers, and anchors are a very important element of American politics. The political values of the media are decidedly liberal and reformist. Political scientist Doris A. Graber writes about the politics of the media: "Economic and social liberalism prevails, especially in the most prominent media organizations. So does a preference for an internationalist foreign policy, caution about military intervention, and some suspicion about the ethics of established large institutions, particularly big business and big government."[13] Most Americans agree that media news coverage is biased and the bias is in a liberal direction (see *What Do You Think?*: "Are the Media Biased?").

Liberalism in Hollywood

With a few exceptions, Hollywood producers, directors, writers, studio executives, and actors are decidedly liberal in their political views, especially when compared with the general public. Of the Hollywood elite, more than 60 percent describe themselves as liberal and only 14 percent as conservative,[14] whereas in the general public, self-described conservatives outnumber liberals by a significant margin. Hollywood leaders are five times more likely to be Democrats than Republicans, and Hollywood is a major source of Democratic Party campaign funds. On both economic and social issues, the Hollywood elite is significantly more liberal than the nation's general public or college-educated public.[15] (However, see *A Conflicting View*: "Fox News: 'Fair and Balanced'?").

Conservatism on Talk Radio

Talk radio is the one medium where conservatism prevails. The single most listened-to talk radio show is the *Rush Limbaugh Show*, whose host regularly bashes "limousine liberals," "femi-Nazis," "environmental wackos," and "croissant people."[16] Talk radio might be portrayed as "call-in democracy." Callers respond almost immediately to reported news events. Call-in shows are the first to sense the public mood. Callers are not necessarily representative of the general public. Rather they are usually the most intense and outraged of citizens. But their complaints are early warning signs for wary politicians.

WHAT DO YOU THINK?

Are the Media Biased?

Are the media biased, and if so, in what direction—liberal or conservative? Arguments over media bias have grown in intensity as the media have come to play a central role in American politics.

The American public is more likely to say that the news media are "too liberal" rather than "too conservative" or "about right." Political partisanship helps to shape Americans' feelings toward bias in the news. Republicans and conservatives are much more likely to say that the media are "too liberal" than Democrats and liberals who are more inclined to say that the media is "just about right."

Q. In general do you think the news media is—too liberal, just about right, or too conservative?[a]

	Too Liberal	Just About Right	Too Conservative
All	44%	33%	19%
Democrats	20	53	23
Independents	40	37	19
Republicans	77	17	5
Liberals	16	45	37
Moderates	39	42	15
Conservatives	68	24	6

Most journalists are personally liberal and vote Democratic, and the media's coverage of issues such as gun control, affirmative action, abortion, gay rights, and religion in America reveals a leftward slant.[b] Fox News, and the *Wall Street Journal* (now owned by the same News Corp.) are exceptions to the rest of the mainstream media. The elite newspapers (the *New York Times* and the *Washington Post*), the television networks (ABC, CBS, NBC, CNN), and the newsweeklies (*Time* and *Newsweek*) are liberal in tone and content. However, more than one in five Americans say that they get their news from talk radio—the programming of which is reported to be 90 percent conservative.[c]

Yet at the same time, Americans have high expectations of the role of the media in society: they expect the media to protect them from "abuse of power" by government, to hold public officials accountable, and to identify and help solve the problems of society.

[a]Gallup News Service, October 8, 2007.
[b]Bernard Goldberg, *Arrogance: Rescuing America from the Media Elite*. New York: Warner Books, 2003.
[c]Robert F. Kennedy, Jr., *Crimes Against Nature*. New York: Harper Collins, 2005.

Televised Incivility and Political Trust   Does watching political shows on television, in which hosts, guests, pundits, and others hurl insults at each other, interrupt and shout over each other, and use especially contentious and uncivil language, reduce levels of trust in politicians and government? One experiment, with some viewers watching friendly, polite, and simple political discussions, and other viewers watching rude, emotional, quarrelsome political confrontations, concluded that incivility has a detrimental effect on trust in government and attitudes toward political leaders.[17] Yet it is not likely that televised politics will ever become more civil. Politics for most people cannot compete with entertainment shows for TV audiences, so increasingly political shows are creating dramatic tension and uncivil conflict to gain viewers.

News Versus Entertainment   Cable television and the Internet have produced dramatic increases in available political information. Yet overall political knowledge and turnout have not changed noticeably. The key to understanding this apparent paradox is the vast expansion in choices now available to viewers.[18]

A CONFLICTING VIEW

Fox News: "Fair and Balanced"?

For many years conservatives complained about the liberal tilt of television news. But despite their ample financial resources, conservative investors failed to create their own network or purchase an existing one. It was an Australian billionaire, Rupert Murdoch, who eventually came to the rescue of American conservatives.

Murdoch's global media empire, News Corp, includes Fox Network, Fox News Cable, 20th Century Fox, Fox Movie Channel, MySpace, the *New York Post*, the *Times* and the *Sun* of London, HarperCollins Publishing, the *Weekly Standard*, and thirty-five local TV stations. He began his career by injecting glitz and vulgarity into previously dull Australian newspapers he inherited. The formula worked worldwide: The *New York Post* became a noisy tabloid after Murdoch took over (most memorable headline: "HEADLESS BODY FOUND IN TOPLESS BAR"), and Fox TV entertainment airs even more vulgar shows than the mainstream networks.

Murdoch himself is not particularly conservative in his politics. (He has held fundraising events for Hillary Clinton.) But he recognized an unfilled market for conservative views on American television. In 1996 he founded Fox News and hired Roger Ailes (former TV ad producer for Richard Nixon, Ronald Reagan, and George H. W. Bush) to head up the new network. Ailes quickly signed Bill O'Reilly (see *People in Politics* in Chapter 2) for an hour-long nightly conservative talk show. Brit Hume, one of the few prominent TV reporters considered to be a conservative, was made managing editor.

Fox proclaims "fair and balanced" news—"We report, you decide." The implication is that mainstream media has a liberal bias and that Fox is rectifying it with its own fair and balanced reporting. According to Fox, if its reporting appears conservative, it is only because the country has become so accustomed to left-leaning media that a truly balanced network just seems conservative.

Regular news reporting on Fox is not much different than other networks, except that Fox may cover some stories ignored by the mainstream media, for example, political correctness running amok on college campuses, ridiculous environmental regulations, hypocrisy among Hollywood liberals, and so on. But it is the talk and commentary shows that outrage liberals and warm the hearts of conservatives. Liberals bold enough to appear on Fox are badgered mercilessly, while conservative guests are tossed softball questions. The bottom line, financially as well as politically, is that Fox News is now the most watched cable news network, even surpassing CNN. Whatever its flaws, Fox News has added diversity of views to American television.

In 2007, Murdoch invaded the financial world with his purchase of Dow Jones & Co., publishers of the *Wall Street Journal*. Traditionalists worry that Murdoch will popularize the *Journal* and perhaps detract from its prestige and influence in the financial world. But others believe that changes in the *Journal* will be modest and that Murdoch will use it to further expand his media empire.

People can now choose from numerous cable channels and Web sites. Increasingly there is a division between people who prefer entertainment programming and those who prefer news shows. There is some evidence that people who prefer news shows acquire greater political knowledge and go to the polls more often than those who mainly watch entertainment shows. Greater media choice, then, appears to widen the "knowledge gap." Because people who like news and take advantage of additional information in the media gain political knowledge, while people who prefer entertainment programming learn less about politics, the mean levels of political knowledge in the population have essentially remained constant.

Polarization of the Media

▶ 6.5 *Characterize the political polarization of media audiences.*

Increasingly, media audiences are becoming politically polarized, with Republicans and conservatives, and Democrats and liberals, choosing to listen to and view separate media outlets. Listeners and viewers are choosing sides in their sources of news (see Table 6.1).

News audiences in the aggregate are somewhat more conservative than the general public. The Pew Research Center reports that of those who regularly watch, read, or listen to the news, conservatives comprise 36 percent, moderates

TABLE 6.1 Ideology and News Sources: What Does Your News Say about You?

Liberals and conservatives differ in their sources of news and commentary.				
Of those who regularly watch, read or listen to . . .	**Conservative**	**Moderate**	**Liberal**	**Don't Know**
Rush Limbaugh Show	77%	16%	7%	0%
O'Reilly Factor	72	23	4	1
Religious radio	53	26	12	9
Fox News	52	30	13	5
Business magazines	49	35	14	2
Call-in radio shows	45	33	18	4
Local news	38	41	15	6
Morning news	38	39	17	6
Newspaper	37	41	17	5
Network News Magazines	37	40	17	6
Political magazines	37	29	29	5
CNN	36	39	20	5
Larry King Live	35	41	16	8
CNBC	35	40	18	7
Letterman/Leno	34	41	21	4
MSNBC	33	41	22	4
Nightly Network news	33	41	18	8
NPR	31	33	30	6
Literary magazines	19	38	36	7

Source: Pew Research Center for the People and the Press, June 8, 2004, www.people-press.org. Reprinted by permission of Pew Research Center for the People and the Press.

38 percent, and liberals 18 percent. The favorites of conservatives are the *Rush Limbaugh Show* on radio and the *O'Reilly Factor* on Fox television, followed by religious radio, Fox News, business magazines, and call-in radio shows. Moderates and liberals turn to *Larry King Live*, the nightly ABC, CBS, and NBC news, National Public Radio, and literary magazines.[19]

Mediated Elections

▶ 6.6 *Analyze the role of the media in shaping campaigns and elections.*

Political campaigning is largely a media activity, and the media, especially television, shape the nation's electoral politics.

The Media and Candidate-Voter Linkage   The media are the principal link between candidates and the voters. At one time, political party organizations performed this function, with city, ward, and precinct workers knocking on doors, distributing campaign literature, organizing rallies and candidate appearances, and getting out the vote on election day. But television has largely replaced party organizations and personal contact as the means by which candidates communicate with voters. Candidates come directly into the living room via television—on the nightly news, in broadcast debates and interviews, and in paid advertising (see Table 6.2).

Media campaigning requires candidates to possess great skill in communications. Candidates must be able to project a favorable media *image*. The image is a composite of the candidate's words, mannerisms, appearance, personality, warmth,

TABLE 6.2 When It Counts: Where the Public Learns about Presidential Campaigns

Over time, newspapers and the nightly network news (ABC, CBS, NBC) have been declining as sources of presidential campaign news. In contrast, the Internet has risen rapidly as a source of campaign information.

	2000	**2004**	**2008**
Local TV news	48%	42%	40%
Cable news networks	34	38	38
Nightly network news	45	35	32
Daily newspaper	40	31	31
Internet	9	13	24
TV news magazines	29	25	22
Morning TV shows	18	20	22
National Public Radio	12	14	18
Talk radio	15	17	16
Cable political talk	14	14	15
Late-night talk shows	9	9	9
Religious radio	7	5	9
C-SPAN	9	8	8
Comedy TV shows	6	8	8

Source: Adapted from Pew Research Center for the People and the Press (2009). www.people-press.org.

friendliness, humor, and ease in front of a camera. Policy positions have less to do with image than the candidate's ability to project personal qualities—leadership, compassion, strength, and character.

The Media and Candidate Selection   The media strongly influence the early selection of candidates. Media coverage creates **name recognition**, an essential quality for any candidate. Early media "mentions" of senators, governors, and other political figures as possible presidential contenders help to sort out the field even before the election year begins. Conversely, media inattention can condemn aspiring politicians to obscurity.

Serious presidential campaigns now begin at least 6 months to a year before the New Hampshire primary (or almost 2 years before the November presidential election). This early time period, "the invisible primary," is increasingly critical for campaigns.[20] Candidates must position themselves relative to competitors in their own party—build their name recognition, raise poll numbers, and build a campaign war chest. Inasmuch as campaign contributions are just beginning to come in, candidates have relatively little money to spend on paid advertising. They are forced to focus their efforts on attracting media attention by staging media events and issuing press releases. But from the media's perspective, campaign news is neither timely nor immediately relevant. Candidates must try to win media coverage by catering to the conflict and horse race stories preferred by the media. Press releases and speeches focused on issues are most likely to be ignored.[21]

The media sort out the serious candidates early in a race. They even assign front-runner status, which may be either a blessing or a curse, depending on subsequent media coverage. In presidential primaries, the media play the *expectations game*, setting vote margins that the front-runner must meet in order to maintain *momentum*. If the front-runner does not win by a large enough margin, the media may declare the runner-up the "real" winner. This sorting out of candidates by the media influences not

name recognition
Public awareness of a candidate—whether they even know his or her name.

only voters, but—more important—financial contributors. The media-designated favorite is more likely to receive campaign contributions; financial backers do not like to waste money on losers. And as contributions roll in, the favorite can buy more television advertising, adding momentum to the campaign.[22]

The Media as Kingmakers

In the early months of a campaign, media coverage of candidates and their standing in public opinion polls tend to move together. Candidates who receive heavy media coverage usually do well in the polls. Good poll ratings create more media coverage. Good poll ratings and increased media coverage inspire campaign contributions, which then allow candidates to buy television advertising to further increase their poll numbers. Media-sponsored public opinion polls play an important role in kingmaking. The CBS/*New York Times* poll, the NBC/Associated Press poll, the ABC/*Washington Post* poll, and the CNN/*USA Today* poll are widely reported; they become the benchmarks for voters, telling them who the winners and losers are.

The name of the game for candidates early in the race is *exposure*. Even appearances on entertainment shows, once considered "unpresidential," are now highly valued by political candidates. They vie to appear on *Larry King Live* and on late-night comedy talk shows.

Media Effects on the Campaign

Political candidates are aware of the importance of the media to their success. Their campaign managers must be "media-savvy" and they must hire media consultants early in the campaign. Candidates are advised to arrange daily newsworthy events to keep their name and image in the news. Television producers, reporters, and editors do not like to receive position papers on substantive issues or to present "talking heads"—shots only of the faces of speakers. Rather they prefer attention-getting, action-oriented, emotion-laden videotape. Candidates and their managers know this and so, to attract media attention, they often resort to **media events**—staged activities designed to polish the image of the candidate. Candidates arrange to appear at police conventions, at schools, at hazardous waste sites, on aircraft carriers, at flag factories, and so on in order to project an image on television of their concern for crime, education, the environment, national defense, patriotism, and the like. (See also "Campaign Strategies" in Chapter 8.)

Popular Voices
Conservative talk-show host Rush Limbaugh has become a symbol of the talk-radio phenomenon.

media events
Staged activities designed to attract media attention.

Win or Lose
An unhappy Hillary Clinton faces the media following a disappointing third-place finish in the Iowa caucus in January 2008.

Good Media Relations
Barack Obama enjoyed positive media coverage throughout the primary and general presidential elections in 2008.

horse-race coverage
Media coverage of electoral campaigns that concentrates on who is ahead and who is behind, and neglects the issues at stake.

The Media and the Horse Race The media give election campaigns **horse-race coverage**: reporting on who is ahead or behind, what the candidates' strategies are, how much money they are spending, and, above all, what their current standing in the polls is. Such stories account for more than half of all television news coverage of an election. Additional stories are centered on *campaign* issues—controversies that arise on the campaign trail itself, including verbal blunders by the candidate—and *character* issues, such as the sex life of the candidate. In contrast, *policy* issues typically account for only about one-third of the television news stories in a presidential election campaign.

The Bad News Bias The media's bad-news bias is evident in election campaigns as well as in general news reporting. Negative stories about all presidential candidates usually outnumber positive stories. The media generally see their function in political campaigns as reporting on the weaknesses, blunders, and vulnerabilities of the candidates. It might be argued that exposing the flaws of the candidates is an important function in a democracy. But the media's negative reporting about candidates and generally skeptical attitude toward their campaign speeches, promises, and advertisements may contribute to political alienation and cynicism among voters.

The media focus intense scrutiny on the personal lives of candidates—their marriages, sex lives, drug or alcohol use, personal finances, past friendships, military service, club memberships, and other potential sources of embarrassment. Virtually any past error in judgment or behavior by a candidate is given heavy coverage. But the media defend their attention to personal scandal on the ground that they are reporting on the "character issue." They argue that voters must have information on candidates' character as well as on their policy positions.

The Shrinking Sound Bite Reporters and newsroom anchors dominate television broadcasting. They report roughly three-quarters of all campaign news themselves. The candidates are allocated less than 15 percent of the time devoted to campaign news stories. (Other sources—pundits, commentators, voters, and so forth—account for the remaining airtime.) The candidates themselves have very little direct contact with audiences in network news. The average **sound bite**—time allowed the candidates to speak on their own behalf—has shrunk to less than 8 seconds!

sound bite
Concise and catchy phrase that attracts media coverage.

Paid Campaign Ads Candidates cannot allow the news media to define them or their messages. Rather, they must endeavor to do so themselves, and of course they must try to define their opponents in negative terms. Television ads account for the largest portion of campaign spending. Nearly one million political commercials will be aired during a primary and general election cycle, for president, Congress, governorships, and state legislatures. Heavy costs are incurred in the production of ads as well as the purchase of broadcast time. Networks may charge $1 million or more for 30 seconds of nationwide prime-time advertising on a popular show.

Television advertising is most effective in motivating supporters to vote. Advertising can do so by creating a favorable image of the candidate, or more likely by creating a negative image of the opponent. But television ads run the risk of creating boredom and frustration among viewers who grow tired of the constant barrage of political ads. To counter these effects, advertising executives and their political consultants must develop interesting and captivating ads, and they must regularly develop new ads in the course of the campaign. Ads may change themes in response to polls or focus groups that indicate new or developing concerns among the electorate. And ads can also be changed to counter attacks from the opposition.

CONTROVERSY

Media Favors Obama, 2008

Media coverage of "Election '08" was especially heavy. The Center for Media and Public Affairs recorded more stories about the presidential campaign in 2008 than in any other election with the exception of the disputed election of 2000. The Center counted the number and types of stories dealing with the presidential campaign that appeared on national network evening news broadcasts of CBS, NBC, ABC, and Fox. Relatively few stories dealt with the candidates' records or positions on policy issues. Far more stories dealt with the "horserace"—the candidates' standing in the race and their strategies and tactics for winning.[a]

During the long primary season Barack Obama received more media attention and more positive coverage than any other candidate. Hillary Clinton received more negative than positive coverage on all four television networks. John McCain was the early media favorite among Republican candidates, but his coverage turned sour as soon as he wrapped up the nomination. Among the networks, only Fox news delivered relatively balanced stories among the candidates; ABC, CBS, and especially NBC heavily favored Obama.

The presidential campaign accounted for about 50 percent of all news broadcast time during the fall. The nation's financial crisis was the second-leading topic of news stories, receiving about 25 percent of broadcast time.

Obama continued to be the media favorite during the general election campaign. Obama received 65 percent positive coverage on the broadcast networks, while McCain's coverage was only 31 percent positive. Only

Out of Favor
Republican candidate John McCain received very little positive media coverage during the 2008 presidential campaign.

Fox News gave Obama mostly negative coverage; Fox also gave McCain mostly negative coverage.[a]

Democrats and Republicans disagreed over the quality of media coverage in the presidential campaign. Most Republicans believe that media coverage was "poor" and tilted toward Obama. In contrast, most Democrats believe that media coverage was "good."[b]

Quality of Media Coverage

	Good	Poor	Don't Know
Republicans	38%	61%	1%
Democrats	70	28	2
Independents	47	53	—

In addition, late-night talk shows joked about McCain far more often than about Obama. McCain's age was a frequent target: "McCain was asked how he's going to conserve energy. He said by taking three naps a day."
—Jay Leno

Favorable Network News Stories

	ABC	CBS	NBC	Fox	Total
Obama	57%	73%	56%	28%	65%
McCain	42	31	16	39	31

Source: Center for Media and Public Affairs, August 23–October 24, N = 979.

[a]Center for Media and Public Affairs. www.cmpa.com.
[b]Pew Research Center for the People and the Press. www.people-press.org.

As election day approaches, ads are more likely to "go negative," that is, to attack the opponent. The ad battle is the most visible element of an election campaign. (See "Campaign Strategies" in Chapter 8.)

Freedom Versus Fairness

▶ 6.7 *Distinguish between freedom of the press and fairness of the press.*

Complaints about the fairness of media are as old as the printing press. Most early newspapers in the United States were allied with political parties; they were not expected to be fair in their coverage. It was only in the early 1900s that many large newspapers broke their ties with parties and proclaimed themselves

Think Again

Should the media be legally required to be fair and accurate in reporting political news?

independent. And it was not until the 1920s and 1930s that the norms of journalistic professionalism and accuracy gained widespread acceptance.

The Constitution protects the *freedom* of the press; it was not intended to guarantee *fairness*. The 1st Amendment's guarantee of freedom of the press was originally designed to protect the press from government attempts to silence criticism. Over the years, the U.S. Supreme Court has greatly expanded the meaning of the free-press guarantee.

prior restraint
Government actions to restrict publication of a magazine, newspaper, or books on grounds of libel, obscenity, or other legal violations prior to actual publication of the work.

No Prior Restraint
The Supreme Court has interpreted freedom of the press to mean that government may place no **prior restraint** on speech or publication (that is, before it is said or published). Originally, this doctrine was designed to prevent the government from closing down or seizing newspapers. Today, the doctrine prevents the government from censoring any news items. In the famous case of the Pentagon Papers, the *New York Times* and *Washington Post* undertook to publish secret information stolen from the files of the State Department and Defense Department regarding U.S. policy in Vietnam while the war was still going on. No one disputed the fact that stealing the secret material was illegal. What was at issue was the ability of the government to prevent the publication of stolen documents in order to protect national security. The Supreme Court rejected the national security argument and reaffirmed that the government may place no prior restraint on publication.[23] If the government wishes to keep military secrets, it must not let them fall into the hands of the American press.

Press Versus Electronic Media
In the early days of radio, broadcast channels were limited, and anyone with a radio transmitter could broadcast on any frequency. As a result, interference was a common frustration of early broadcasters. The industry petitioned the federal government to regulate and license the assignment and use of broadcast frequencies.

The Federal Communications Commission (FCC) was established in 1934 to allocate broadcast frequencies and to license stations for "the public interest, convenience and necessity." The act clearly instructed the FCC: "Nothing in this Act shall be understood or construed to give the Commission the power of censorship." However, the FCC views a broadcast license and exclusive right to use a particular frequency as a *public trust*. Thus broadcasters, unlike newspapers and magazines, are licensed by a government agency and supposed to operate in the *public interest*.

Decency
From time to time, the FCC has cracked down on "indecency" on radio and television, presumably doing so in the "public interest." CBS was fined for the Super Bowl halftime "wardrobe malfunction" by singer Janet Jackson. "Shock-jock" Howard Stern incurred millions of dollars in fines for himself and his stations before giving up regular programming and moving to unregulated satellite radio. Government suppression of "indecency" is constitutionally permitted over broadcast waves on the theory that these channels are limited, they belong to the public, and government licenses broadcasters. Otherwise, mere "indecency" that does not constitute "obscenity" is constitutionally protected by the 1st Amendment (see Chapter 14).

equal-time rule
Federal Communications Commission (FCC) requirement that broadcasters who sell time to any political candidate must make equal time available to opposing candidates at the same price.

The Equal-Time Requirement
The FCC requires radio and television stations that provide airtime to a political candidate to offer competing candidates the same amount of airtime at the same price. Stations are not required to give free time to candidates, but if stations choose to give free time to one candidate, they must do so for the candidate's opponents. But this **equal-time rule** does *not* apply to

newscasts, news specials, or even long documentaries, nor does it apply to talk shows like *Larry King Live*. Nor does it apply to presidential press conferences or presidential addresses to the nation, although the networks now generally offer free time for a "Democratic response" to a Republican president, and vice versa. A biased news presentation does not require the network or station to grant equal time to opponents of its views. And it is important to note that newspapers, unlike radio and television, have never been required to provide equal time to opposing views.

Libel and Slander

▶ 6.8 *Describe the law regarding libel and slander.*

Communications that wrongly damage an individual are known in law as **libel** (when written) and **slander** (when spoken). The injured party must prove in court that the communication caused actual damage and was either false or defamatory. A damaging falsehood or words or phrases that are defamatory (such as "Joe Jones is a rotten son of a bitch") are libelous and are not protected by the 1st Amendment from lawsuits seeking compensation.

Public Officials   Over the years, the media have sought to narrow the protection afforded public officials against libel and slander. In 1964 the U.S. Supreme Court ruled in the case of *New York Times v. Sullivan* that public officials did not have a right to recover damages for false statements unless they are made with "malicious intent."[24] The **Sullivan rule** requires public officials not only to show that the media published or broadcast false and damaging statements but also to prove they did so knowing that their statements were false and damaging or that they did so with "reckless disregard" for the truth or falsehood of their statements. The effect of the Sullivan rule is to free the media to say virtually anything about public officials. Indeed, the media have sought to expand the definition of "public officials" to "public figures"—that is, to include anyone they choose as the subject of a story.

libel
Writings that are false and malicious and intended to damage an individual.

slander
Oral statements that are false and malicious and intended to damage an individual.

Sullivan rule
Court guideline that false and malicious statements regarding public officials are protected by the 1st Amendment unless it can be proven they were known to be false at the time they were made or were made with "reckless disregard" for their truth or falsehood.

"INTERESTING.....IT'S LIKE A PORTABLE 500K FILE and YOU DON'T HAVE TO WAIT FOR IT TO DOWNLOAD.... AND YOU SAY IT'S CALLED A NEWSPAPER?"

©1997 Jim Borgman, Cincinnati Enquirer. Reprinted with permission of King Features Syndicate.

Think
Again

Should the media report on all aspects of the private lives of public officials?

"Absence of Malice"   The 1st Amendment protects the right of the media to be biased, unfair, negative, sensational, and even offensive. Indeed, even *damaging falsehoods* may be printed or broadcast as long as the media can show that the story was not deliberately fabricated by them with malicious intent, that is, if the media can show an "absence of malice."

Shielding Sources   The media argue that the 1st Amendment allows them to refuse to reveal the names of their sources, even when this information is required in criminal investigations and trials. Thus far, the U.S. Supreme Court has not given blanket protection to reporters to withhold information from court proceedings. However, a number of states have passed *shield laws* protecting reporters from being forced to reveal their sources.

Politics and the Internet

▶ 6.9 *Evaluate the effects of the Internet on politics.*

The development of any new medium of communications invariably affects political life. Just as, first, radio and, later, television reshaped politics in America, today the Internet is having its own unique impact on public affairs. The Internet provides a channel for *interactive mass participation* in politics. It is unruly and chaotic by design. It offers the promise of abundant and diverse information and the opportunity for increased political participation. It empowers everyone who can design a Web site to spread their views, whether their views are profound and public-spirited or hateful and obscene.

Chaotic by Design   During the Cold War, the RAND Corporation, a technological research think tank, proposed the Internet as a communications network that might survive a nuclear attack. It was deliberately designed to operate without any central authority or organization. Should any part of the system be destroyed, messages would still find their way to their destinations. The later development of the World Wide Web language allowed any connected computer in the world to communicate with any other connected computer. And introduction of the World Wide Web in 1992 also meant that users no longer needed computer expertise to communicate. By 1995, Americans were buying more computers than television sets and sending more e-mail than "snail mail." Since then, Internet usage has continued to mushroom (see Figure 6.3).

Political Web Sites Abound   The Internet is awash in political Web sites. The simple query "politics" on a standard search program can return well over a million matches. Almost all federal agencies, including the White House, Congress, the federal judiciary, and executive departments and agencies, maintain Web sites. Individual elected officeholders, including all members of Congress, maintain sites that include personal biographies, committee assignments, legislative accomplishments, issue statements, and press releases. The home pages of the Democratic and Republican parties offer political news, issue positions, opportunities to become active in party affairs, and invitations to send them money. No serious candidate for major public office lacks a Web site; these campaign sites usually include flattering biographies, press releases, and, of course, invitations to contribute financially to the candidates' campaigns. All major interest groups maintain Web sites—business, trade, and professional groups; labor unions; ideological and issue groups; women's, religious, environmental, and civil rights groups. Indeed, this virtual tidal wave of politics on the Internet may turn out to offer too much information in too fragmented a fashion, thereby simply adding to apathy and indifference.[25]

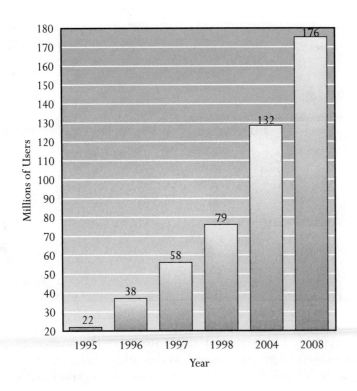

FIGURE 6.3

Online America: Growth of Internet Users

Internet use has mushroomed over the last decade.

Source: Statistical Abstract of the United States, 2009, p. 710.

Internet Fund-Raising   All political candidate Web sites solicit credit card campaign contributions. These sites are particularly effective in getting large numbers of small contributions—$10, $25, $50. In 2008, Democratic candidate Barack Obama was very effective in Internet fund-raising, surpassing Hillary Clinton and John McCain in dollar amounts and number of contributors.

People who access a candidate's Web site, and especially people who make contributions on it, can be tracked during the campaign to solicit more contributions, and, as election day nears, to urge them to go to the polls. The value of a Web site, then, is primarily in motivating supporters to contribute money and later to cast votes on election day. Web sites, however well designed, seldom turn opponents into supporters.

Internet Uncensored   The Internet allows unrestricted freedom of expression, from scientific discourses on particle physics and information on the latest developments in medical science, to invitations to join in paramilitary "militia" and offers to exchange pornographic photos and messages. Commercial sex sites outnumber any other category on the Web.

Congress unsuccessfully attempted to outlaw "indecent" and "patently offensive" material on the Internet with its Communications Decency Act of 1996. But the U.S. Supreme Court gave 1st Amendment protection to the Internet in 1997 in *Reno v. American Civil Liberties Union.*[26] The Court recognized the Internet as an important form of popular expression protected by the Constitution. Congress had sought to make it a federal crime to send or display "indecent" material to persons under 18 years of age (material describing or displaying sexual activities or organs in "patently offensive" fashion). But the Supreme Court reiterated its view that government may not limit the adult population to "only what is fit for children." The Court decision places the burden of filtering Internet messages on parents. Filtering software can be installed on home computers, but a 1st Amendment issue arises when it is installed on computers in public libraries.

The Bloggers   The Internet has spawned a myriad of individual Web sites, commonly known as "blogs," that frequently criticize the professional media.

Campaigning on the Internet

Barack Obama's campaign Web site was the most popular site during the 2008 presidential race. More important, it raised record amounts of campaign contributions.

The more reputable blog sites fact-check stories in the mainstream media, or publish stories ignored by them, as well as toss in their own opinions. They have been labeled the media's "back-seat" drivers. (One of the earliest and most quoted bloggers is the "Drudge Report," posted by maverick journalist Matt Drudge.) While many bloggers offer little more than their own often-heated opinions, bloggers have forced the mainstream media to cover stories they may not otherwise have covered, as well as forcing some professional journalists to check the accuracy of their stories before publication.

Think Again

Is your choice of candidates in elections affected by their advertising?

Media Effects: Shaping Political Life

▶ 6.10 *Assess the effects that the media have on public opinion and political behavior.*

What effects do the media have on public opinion and political behavior? Let us consider media effects on (1) information and agenda setting, (2) values and opinions, and (3) behavior. These categories of effects are ranked by the degree of influence the media are likely to have over us. The strongest effects of the media are on our information levels and societal concerns. The media also influence values and opinions, but the strength of media effects in these areas is diluted by many other influences. Finally, it is most difficult to establish the independent effect of the media on behavior.

Information and Agenda-Setting Effects
The media strongly influence what we know about our world and how we think and talk about it. Years ago, foreign-policy expert Bernard Cohen, in the first book to assess the effects of the media on foreign policy, put it this way: "The mass media may not be successful in telling people what to think, but the media are stunningly successful in telling their audience what to think about."[27]

information overload
Situation in which individuals are subjected to so many communications that they cannot make sense of them.

However, **information overload** diminishes the influence of the media in determining what we think about. So many communications are directed at us that we cannot possibly process them all. A person's ability to recall a media report depends on repeated exposure to it and reinforcement through personal experience. For example, an individual who has a brother in a trouble spot in the Middle East is more likely to be aware of reports from that area of the world. But too many voices with too many messages cause most viewers to block out a great deal of information.

Information overload may be especially heavy in political news. Television tells most viewers more about politics than they really want to know. Political scientist Austin Ranney writes, "The fact is that for most Americans politics is still far from being the most interesting and important thing in life. To them, politics is usually confusing, boring, repetitious, and above all irrelevant to the things that really matter in their lives."[28]

Effects on Values and Opinions   The media often tell us how we *should* feel about news events or issues, especially those about which we have no prior feelings or experiences. The media can reinforce values and attitudes we already hold. However, the media seldom *change* our preexisting values or opinions. Media influence over values and opinions is reduced by **selective perception**, mentally screening out information or opinions we disagree with. People tend to see and hear only what they want to see and hear. For example, television news concentration on scandal, abuse, and corruption in government has not always produced the liberal, reformist values among viewers that media people expected. On the contrary, the focus of network executives on governmental scandals— Watergate, the Iran-Contra scandal, the sexual antics of politicians, and so on—has produced feelings of general political distrust and cynicism toward government and the political system. These feelings have been labeled **television malaise**, a combination of social distrust, political cynicism, feelings of powerlessness, and disaffection from parties and politics that seems to stem from television's emphasis on the negative aspects of American life.

The media do not *intend* to create television malaise; they are performing their self-declared watchdog role. They expect their stories to encourage liberal reform of our political institutions. But the result is often alienation rather than reform.

selective perception
Mentally screening out information or opinions with which one disagrees.

television malaise
Generalized feelings of distrust, cynicism, and powerlessness stemming from television's emphasis on the negative aspects of American life.

Direct Effects on Public Opinion   Can the media change public opinion, and if so, how? For many years, political scientists claimed that the media had only minimal effects on public opinions and behavior. This early view was based

largely on the fact that newspaper editorial endorsements seldom affected people's votes. But serious research on the effects of television tells a different story.

In an extensive study of 80 policy issues over 15 years, political scientists examined public opinion polls on various policy issues at a first point in time, then media content over a following interval of time, and finally public opinion on these same issues at the end of the interval. The purpose was to learn if media content— messages scored by their relevance to the issue, their salience in the broadcast, their pro/con direction, the credibility of the news source, and quality of the reporting—changed public opinion. Most people's opinions remained constant over time (opinion at the first point in time is the best predictor of opinion at the second point in time). However, when opinion did change, it changed in the direction supported by the media. "News variables alone account for nearly half the variance in opinion change." Other findings include the following:

* Anchors, reporters, and commentators have the greatest impact on opinion change. Television newscasters have high credibility and trust with the general public. Their opinions are crucial in shaping mass opinion.

* Independent experts interviewed by the media have a substantial impact on opinion, but not as great as newscasters themselves.

* A popular president can also shift public opinion somewhat. Unpopular presidents do not have much success as opinion movers, however.

* Interest groups on the whole have a slightly negative effect on public opinion. "In many instances they seem actually to have antagonized the public and created a genuine adverse effect"; such cases include war protesters, animal rights advocates, and other demonstrators and protesters, even peaceful ones.[29]

Effects on Behavior   Many studies have focused on the effects of the media on behavior: studies of the effects of TV violence, studies of the effects of television on children, and studies of the effects of obscenity and pornography.[30] Although it is difficult to generalize from these studies, television appears more likely to reinforce behavioral tendencies than to change them. For example, televised violence may trigger violent behavior in children who are already predisposed

The first televised presidential election debates were in 1960 between Senator John F. Kennedy and Vice President Richard Nixon. Nixon came armed with statistics, but his dour demeanor, "five o'clock shadow," and stiff presentation fared poorly in contrast to Kennedy's open, relaxed, confident air.

A CONSTITUTIONAL NOTE

Can the Federal Communications Commission Ban Profanity from Radio and Television?

When the Bill of Rights was passed by the nation's first Congress, the 1st Amendment's reference to freedom of the press could hardly have envisioned radio, television, or the Internet. When radio broadcasting began in the 1920s, there was a scarcity of broadcast frequencies. Stations fought over frequencies and even jammed each other's programming. The industry welcomed the Federal Communications Act of 1934 which created the Federal Communications Commission (FCC) to license stations for the exclusive use of radio frequencies. The law stated that the use of a frequency was a "public trust" and that the FCC should ensure that it was used in "the public interest." Although technology has vastly multiplied radio and television channels, the FCC has continued to fine broadcasters for indecency or profanity. The Supreme Court has continued to uphold the powers of the FCC. "Shock-jock"

radio personality Howard Stern has been fined almost $2 million. Janet Jackson's "wardrobe malfunction" during the 2004 Super Bowl half-time performance also cost her network a large fine. In short, the FCC has retained its power over radio and television despite the fact that its original rationale, the scarcity of broadcast frequencies, has disappeared. We can contrast the control that the Supreme Court allows the government to exercise over radio and television with the freedom the same Court grants to users of the Internet. The Supreme Court held that the Communications Decency Act of 1996, making it a federal crime to send or display "indecent" material to persons under 18 years of age over the Internet, was unconstitutional. The Supreme Court held that the government may not limit the adult population to "only what is fit for children."[a] Commercial sex sites deluge the Internet.

[a]*Reno v. American Civil Liberties Union*, 521 U.S. 471 (1997).

to such behavior, but televised violence has little behavioral effect on average children.[31] Nevertheless, we know that television advertising sells products. And we know that political candidates spend millions to persuade audiences to go out and vote for them on election day. Both manufacturers and politicians create name recognition, employ product differentiation, try to associate with audiences, and use repetition to communicate their messages. These tactics are designed to affect our behavior both in the marketplace and in the election booth.

Political ads are more successful in motivating a candidate's supporters to go to the polls than they are in changing opponents into supporters. It is unlikely that voters who dislike a candidate will be persuaded by political advertising to change their votes. But many potential voters are undecided, and the support of many others is dubbed "soft." Going to the polls on election day requires effort—people have errands to do, it may be raining, they may be tired. Television advertising is more effective with the marginal voters.

Summary

▶ 6.1 *Identify functions and components of the media.*

It is only through the media that the general public comes to know about political events, personalities, and issues. Newsmaking—deciding what is or is not "news"—is a major source of media power. Media coverage not only influences popular discussion but also forces public officials to respond.

▶ 6.2 *Explain the sources of the media's power.*

Media power also derives from the media's ability to set the agenda for public decision making—to determine what citizens and public officials will regard as "crises," "problems," or "issues" to be resolved by government.

▶ *6.3 Describe the business of the media.*

The business of the media is to sell mass audiences to advertisers in order to make a profit for the owners.

▶ *6.4 Assess how the politics of the media are shaped by their economic interests, environment, and ideological leanings.*

The politics of the media are shaped by their economic interests in attracting readers and viewers. This interest largely accounts for the sensational and negative aspects of news reporting.

▶ *6.5 Characterize the political polarization of media audiences.*

The professional environment of newspeople encourages an activist, watchdog role in politics. The politics of most newspeople are liberal and Democratic.

▶ *6.6 Analyze the role of the media in shaping campaigns and elections.*

Political campaigning is largely a media activity. The media have replaced the parties as the principal linkage between candidates and voters. But the media tend to report the campaign as a horse race, at the expense of issue coverage, and to focus more on candidates' character than on their voting record.

▶ *6.7 Distinguish between freedom of the press and fairness of the press.*

The 1st Amendment guarantee of freedom of the press protects the media from government efforts to silence or censor them and allows the media to be "unfair" when they choose to be. The Federal Communications Commission exercises some modest controls over the electronic media, since the right to exclusive use of broadcast frequencies is a public trust.

▶ *6.8 Describe the law regarding libel and slander.*

Public officials are provided very little protection by libel and slander laws. The Supreme Court's Sullivan rule allows even damaging falsehoods to be written and broadcast as long as newspeople themselves do not deliberately fabricate lies with "malicious intent" or "reckless disregard."

▶ *6.9 Evaluate the effects of the Internet on politics.*

The development of the Internet has provided for interactive mass participation in politics, blogging, political Web sites, and new sources of fund-raising opportunities.

▶ *6.10 Assess the effects that the media have on public opinion and political behavior.*

Media effects on political life can be observed in (1) information and agenda setting, (2) values and opinions, and (3) behavior—in that order of influence. The media strongly influence what we know about politics and what we talk about. The media are less effective in changing existing opinions, values, and beliefs than they are at creating new ones. Nevertheless, the media can change many people's opinions, based on the credibility of news anchors and reporters. Direct media effects on behavior are limited. Political ads are more important in motivating supporters to go to the polls, and in swinging undecided or "soft" voters, than in changing the minds of committed voters.

Chapter Test

▶ *6.1 Identify functions and components of the media.*

1. The print news that is *least* believable probably would come from
   a. the *New York Times*
   b. *USA Today*
   c. the *National Enquirer*
   d. *Time* magazine

2. The most common source for news in the United States is
   a. the Internet
   b. local TV news
   c. the national evening news
   d. newspapers and magazines

▶ *6.2 Explain the sources of the media's power.*

3. It is true that the media
   a. is a natural adversary of government
   b. mirrors reality
   c. does not try to persuade but merely presents facts
   d. none of the above

▶ *6.3 Describe the business of the media.*

4. The primary motivating force behind the media's endeavors is to
   a. present the truth to its audiences
   b. persuade people to buy advertised products
   c. provide a public service
   d. provide amusement to the masses

▶ *6.4 Assess how the politics of the media are shaped by their economic interests, environment, and ideological leanings.*

5. It would be accurate to say that the media
   a. tries to reach the emotions of its audience
   b. is biased in favor of "hyping" the news to pump up ratings
   c. likes bad news more than good news
   d. all of the above

6. Which of the following statements is true?
   a. Talk radio has a liberal bias
   b. Hollywood has a libertarian bias

c. The media is perceived as having a liberal bias

d. Fox News is perceived as having a liberal bias

▶ 6.5 *Characterize the political polarization of media audiences.*

7. It would be accurate to say that a favorite source of news for conservatives is
   a. the *Rush Limbaugh Show*
   b. MSNBC
   c. CNN
   d. National Public Radio (NPR)

8. It is accurate to say that
   a. Republicans are becoming more associated with liberal ideologies
   b. Democrats are becoming more aligned with modern conservative ideas
   c. media audiences are becoming increasingly polarized
   d. news audiences in the aggregate are somewhat more liberal than the general public

▶ 6.6 *Analyze the role of the media in shaping campaigns and elections.*

9. A staged event designed to improve the image of a political candidate is known as
   a. a choreographed activity
   b. a media event
   c. a "framed" event
   d. an image enhancement moment

10. The most common link between the candidates and the voters is
    a. the political party
    b. the Internet and U.S. Postal Service
    c. television
    d. personal contact

▶ 6.7 *Distinguish between freedom of the press and fairness of the press.*

11. "No prior restraint" refers to
    a. giving the benefit of the doubt to someone who has never had to be legally restrained before
    b. the early restraint placed upon radio broadcasts
    c. the prohibition upon the government from restraining publications and speech
    d. the early restraints placed upon TV broadcasters

▶ 6.8 *Describe the law regarding libel and slander.*

12. The 1st Amendment protects the right of the media to be
    a. biased
    b. unfair

c. offensive

d. all of the above

13. "Shield laws" protect
    a. people from slander
    b. people from libel
    c. the press from revealing the identity of their sources
    d. diplomats

14. The "Sullivan rule"
    a. held that speech that was disloyal was not covered by the 1st Amendment
    b. expanded the right of the press to publish materials about public officials
    c. limited the right of the press to make damaging statements
    d. upheld the right of the government to suppress obscene publications

▶ 6.9 *Evaluate the effects of the Internet on politics.*

15. The Internet has
    a. not really impacted political fund-raising
    b. often been able to persuade political opponents to become political supporters
    c. allowed unrestricted freedom of political expression
    d. stopped the spread of untruthful bloggers

16. The Internet was designed to
    a. allow any connected computer in the world to communicate with any other connected computer in the world
    b. be chaotic
    c. provide abundant and diverse sources of information
    d. all of the above

▶ 6.10 *Assess the effects that the media have on public opinion and political behavior.*

17. The media is effective in
    a. the transmission of political values
    b. providing political information
    c. creating political values
    d. stimulating political behavior

18. The media are
    a. very effective at changing political values
    b. very effective at "agenda setting"
    c. very effective at changing behavior
    d. not very effective at any of the above

mypoliscilab EXERCISES

Apply what you learned in this chapter on MyPoliSciLab.

📖┤**Read** on **mypoliscilab.com**

    eText: Chapter 6

✔┤**Study** and **Review** on **mypoliscilab.com**

    Pre-Test

    Post-Test

    Chapter Exam

    Flashcards

👁┤**Watch** on **mypoliscilab.com**

    Video: YouTube Politics

    Video: The Pentagon's Media Message

✳┤**Explore** on **mypoliscilab.com**

    Simulation: You Are the News Editor

    Comparative: Comparing News Media

    Timeline: Three Hundred Years of American Mass Media

    Visual Literacy: Use of the Media by the American Public

Key Terms

mass media   177
newsmaking   180
agenda setting   181
socialization   182
soft news   184

muckraking   185
"feeding frenzy"   186
name recognition   190
media events   191
horse-race coverage   192

sound bite   192
prior restraint   194
equal-time rule   194
libel   195
slander   195

Sullivan rule   195
information overload   198
selective perception   199
television malaise   199

Suggested Readings

Alterman, Eric. *What Liberal Media?* New York: Simon & Schuster, 2003. A contrarian argument that the media does *not* have a liberal bias but rather bends over backward to include conservative views.

Bennett, Lance W. *News: The Politics of Illusion.* New York: Longman, 2007. How presidents, Congress members, interest groups, and political activists try to get their messages into the news.

Fallows, James. *Breaking the News: How the Media Undermine American Democracy.* New York: Pantheon, 1996. An argument that today's arrogant, cynical, and scandal-minded news reporting is turning readers and viewers away and undermining support for democracy.

Goldberg, Bernard. *Bias: A CBS Insider Exposes How the Media Distort the News.* New York: Perennial, 2003. The title says it all.

Graber, Doris A. *Mass Media and American Politics.* 8th ed. Washington, D.C.: CQ Press, 2009. A wide-ranging description of media effects on campaigns, parties, and elections, as well as on social values and public policies.

Patterson, Thomas E. *Out of Order.* New York: Random House, 1994. The antipolitical bias of the media poisons national election campaigns; policy questions are ignored in favor of the personal characteristics of candidates, their campaign strategies, and their standing in the horse race.

Prindle, David F. *Risky Business.* Boulder, Colo.: Westview Press, 1993. An examination of the politics of Hollywood, its liberalism, activism, self-indulgence, and celebrity egotism.

Sabato, Larry J. *Feeding Frenzy: How Attack Journalism Has Transformed American Politics.* New York: Free Press, 1991. A strong argument that the media prefer "to employ titillation rather than scrutiny" and as a result produce "trivialization rather than enlightenment."

West, Darrell M. *Air Wars: Television Advertising in Election Campaigns.* 5th ed. Washington, D.C.: CQ Press, 2009. The evolution of campaign advertising from 1952 to 2008 and how voters are influenced by television ads.

Suggested Web Sites

Accuracy in Media www.aim.org
A self-described watchdog organization critical of liberal bias in the media.

American Journalism Review www.ajr.org
Features articles on current topics in print and television reporting, together with links to newspapers, television networks and stations, radio stations, media companies, and so forth.

Annenberg Public Policy Center www.appcpenn.org
The Annenberg Center of the University of Pennsylvania conducts research on political use of the media, including the Internet.

Center for Media and Public Affairs www.cmpa.com
Studies of news and entertainment media, including election coverage.

Drudge Report www.drudgereport.com
Controversial site that links to stories not always carried by mainstream media. Links to all major media outlets.

Federal Communication Commission www.fcc.gov
The FCC's official Web site with announcements and consumer information.

National Association of Broadcasters www.nab.org
News and views of the media industry from their trade association.

Network Television www.cbsnews.com
www.abcnews.com   www.cnn.com   www.msnbc.com
www.foxnews.com
All major networks now maintain news sites on the Web.

Newspaper Web Sites www.usatoday.com
www.nytimes.com   www.washingtonpost.com
www.wallstreetjournal.com
Virtually all major daily newspapers have Web sites that summarize each day's stories. For national news the most frequently consulted sites are *USA Today, Wall Street Journal, New York Times, Washington Post.*

People for the American Way www.pfaw.org
Web site founded by Hollywood "liberals" to combat "right-wing" influence.

Pew Research Center for People and the Press
www.people-press.org
Information, including opinion polls, on the media.

Politico www.politico.com
Favorite blog of political junkies, with links to multiple news articles and political commentaries.

Chapter Test Answer Key

1. C	4. B	7. A	10. C	13. C	16. D
2. B	5. D	8. C	11. C	14. B	17. B
3. A	6. C	9. B	12. D	15. C	18. B

7 POLITICAL PARTIES
Organizing Politics

66 Political parties created democracy, and modern democracy is unthinkable save in terms of the parties. 99

E. E. Schattschneider

Chapter Outline and Learning Objectives

The Power of Organization
▶ 7.1 *Show how the relationship between organization and political power explains political parties and interest groups.*

American Parties: A Historical Perspective
▶ 7.2 *Trace changes in political parties over the course of American history.*

Political Parties and Democratic Government
▶ 7.3 *Outline functions of political parties as "responsible" organizations and perceptions of the two major American political parties.*

Party Finances
▶ 7.4 *Explain how the two major American political parties are financed.*

Parties as Organizers of Elections
▶ 7.5 *Assess the changing role of the political parties in the electoral process.*

Where's the Party?
▶ 7.6 *Differentiate the three political arenas in which the parties battle.*

National Party Conventions
▶ 7.7 *Describe changes in the function of the national party conventions.*

Party Voters
▶ 7.8 *Assess the trends regarding party identification and loyalty of voters.*

Third Parties in the U.S. System
▶ 7.9 *Evaluate the role of third parties within the U.S. electoral system.*

Why the Two-Party System Persists
▶ 7.10 *Determine why the American two-party system has persisted.*

Think about Politics

1. Generally speaking, how would you identify yourself: as a Republican, Democrat, Independent, or something else?
   REPUBLICAN ⬭ DEMOCRAT ⬭
   INDEPENDENT ⬭ OTHER ⬭

2. Which major political party better represents the interests of people like yourself?
   REPUBLICAN ⬭ DEMOCRAT ⬭

3. Does the Republican Party favor the rich more than the middle class or poor?
   YES ⬭ NO ⬭

4. Does the Democratic Party favor the poor more than the middle class or rich?
   YES ⬭ NO ⬭

5. Which major party does a better job of protecting the Social Security system?
   REPUBLICAN ⬭ DEMOCRAT ⬭

6. Which major party does a better job of handling foreign affairs?
   REPUBLICAN ⬭ DEMOCRAT ⬭

7. Should elected officials be bound by their party's platform?
   YES ⬭ NO ⬭

8. Do we need a third party to challenge the Republican and Democratic parties?
   YES ⬭ NO ⬭

How much power do political parties really have to determine who gets what in America? We hear the terms Republican and Democratic linked to people and to policies, but do these parties have real power beyond that of organizing for elections?

political organizations
Parties and interest groups that function as intermediaries between individuals and government.

The Power of Organization

▶ 7.1 *Show how the relationship between organization and political power explains political parties and interest groups.*

In the struggle for power, organization grants advantage. Italian political scientist Gaetano Mosca once put it succinctly: "A hundred men acting uniformly in concert, with a common understanding, will triumph over a thousand men who are not in accord and can therefore be dealt with one by one."[1] Thus politics centers on organization—on organizing people to win office and to influence public policy.

Political organizations—parties and interest groups—function as intermediaries between individuals and government. They organize individuals to give them power in selecting government officials—who govern—and in determining public policy—for what ends. Generally, **political parties** are more concerned with winning public office in elections than with influencing policy, whereas *interest groups* are more directly concerned with public policy and involve themselves with elections only to advance their policy interests (see Figure 7.1). In other words, parties and interest groups have an informal division of functions, with parties focusing on personnel and interest groups focusing on policy. Yet both organize individuals for more effective political action.

FIGURE 7.1

Political Democracy: Organizations as Intermediaries

All political organizations function as intermediaries between individuals and government. Parties are concerned primarily with winning elected office; interest groups are concerned with influencing policy.

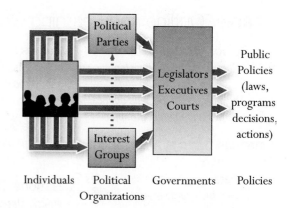

Individuals   Political   Governments   Policies

Organizations

American Parties: A Historical Perspective

▶ 7.2 *Trace changes in political parties over the course of American history.*

Parties are *not* mentioned in the Constitution. Indeed, the nation's Founders regarded both parties and interest groups as "factions," citizens united by "some common impulse of passion, or of interest, adverse to the rights of other citizens, or to the permanent and aggregate interests of the community." The Founders viewed factions as "mischievous" and "dangerous."[2] Yet the emergence of parties was inevitable as people sought to organize themselves to exercise power over who governs (see Figure 7.2).

The Emergence of Parties: Federalists and Democratic-Republicans

In his Farewell Address, George Washington warned the nation about political parties: "Let me . . . warn you in the most solemn manner against the baneful effects of the spirit of party generally."[3] As president, Washington stood above the factions that were coalescing around his secretary of the treasury, Alexander Hamilton, and around his former secretary of state, Thomas Jefferson. Jefferson had resigned from Washington's cabinet in 1793 to protest the fiscal policies of Hamilton, notably his creation of a national bank and repayment of the states' Revolutionary War debts with federal funds. Washington had endorsed Hamilton's policies, but so great was the first president's prestige that Jefferson and his followers directed their fire not against Washington but against Hamilton, John Adams, and their supporters, who called themselves **Federalists** after their leaders' outspoken defense of the Constitution during the ratification process. By the 1790s, Jefferson and Madison, as well as many **Anti-Federalists** who had initially opposed the ratification of the Constitution, began calling themselves *Republicans* or *Democratic-Republicans*, terms that had become popular after the French Revolution in 1789.

Adams narrowly defeated Jefferson in the presidential election of 1796. This election was an important milestone in the development of the parties and the presidential election system. For the first time, two candidates campaigned as members of opposing parties, and candidates for presidential elector in each state pledged themselves as "Adams's men" or "Jefferson's men." By committing themselves in advance of the actual presidential vote, these pledged electors enabled voters in each state to determine the outcome of the presidential election.

Jefferson's Democratic-Republicans

Party activity intensified in anticipation of the election of 1800. Jefferson's Democratic-Republican Party first saw the importance of organizing voters, circulating literature, and rallying the

---

political parties
Organizations that seek to achieve power by winning public office.

Federalists
Those who supported the U.S. Constitution during the ratification process and who later formed a political party in support of John Adams's presidential candidacy.

Anti-Federalists
Those who opposed the ratification of the U.S. Constitution and the creation of a strong national government.

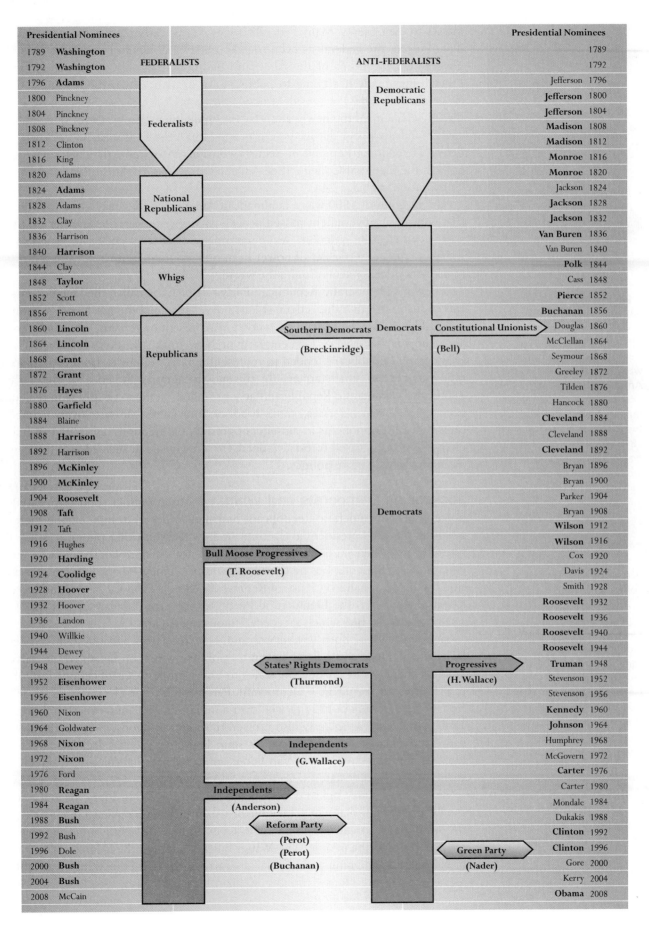

FIGURE 7.2 Change and Continuity: The American Party System, 1789–2008

Opening the Party System

A picture of Andrew Jackson late in his life. Andrew Jackson is widely viewed as the founder of the Democratic Party. Jackson was born in Tennessee, the American frontier at the time, and was also a celebrated military leader who defeated the British in New Orleans in 1815 (after the War of 1812 was officially over), and had led numerous campaigns against the Indians.

majority
Election by more than 50 percent of all votes cast in the contest.

plurality
Election by at least one vote more than any other candidate in the race.

Democratic Party
One of the main parties in American politics; it traces its origins to Thomas Jefferson's Democratic-Republican Party, acquiring its current name under Andrew Jackson in 1828.

Whig Party
Formed in 1836 to oppose Andrew Jackson's policies; it elected presidents Harrison in 1840 and Tyler in 1848 but soon disintegrated over the issue of slavery.

masses to their causes. Many Federalists viewed this early party activity with disdain. Indeed, the Federalists even tried to outlaw public criticism of the federal government by means of the Alien and Sedition Acts of 1798, which among other things made it a crime to publish false or malicious writings against the (Federalist) Congress or president or to "stir up hatred" against them. These acts directly challenged the newly adopted 1st Amendment guarantees of freedom of speech and the press. But in the election of 1800, the Federalists went down to defeat. Democratic-Republican electors won a **majority** (more than half the votes cast) in the Electoral College. (See *A Constitutional Note*: "Political Parties and the Constitution" on page 244).

The election of 1800 was a landmark in American democracy—the first time that control of government passed peacefully from one party to another on the basis of an election outcome. As commonplace as that may seem to Americans today, the peaceful transfer of power from one group to another remains a rarity in many political systems around the world.

Jefferson's Democratic-Republican Party—later to be called the Democrats—was so successful that the Federalist Party never regained the presidency or control of Congress. The Federalists tended to represent merchants, manufacturers, and shippers, who were concentrated in New York and New England. The Democratic-Republicans tended to represent agrarian interests, from large plantation owners to small farmers. In the mostly agrarian America of the early 1800s, the Democratic-Republican Party prevailed.[4] Jefferson easily won reelection in 1804, and his allies, James Madison and James Monroe, overwhelmed their Federalist opponents in subsequent presidential elections. By 1820, the Federalist Party had ceased to exist. Indeed, for a few years, it seemed as if the new nation had ended party politics.

Jacksonian Democrats and Whigs Partisan politics soon reappeared, however. The Democratic-Republicans had already begun to fight among themselves by the 1824 presidential election. Andrew Jackson won a **plurality** (at least one more vote than anyone else in the race) but not a majority of the popular and Electoral College vote, but he then lost to John Quincy Adams in a close decision by the factionalized House of Representatives. Jackson led his supporters to found a new party, the **Democratic Party**, to organize popular support for his 1828 presidential bid, which succeeded in ousting Adams.

Jacksonian ideas both *democratized* and *nationalized* the party system. Under Jackson, the Democratic Party began to mobilize voters on behalf of the party and its candidates. It pressed the states to lower property qualifications for voting in order to recruit new Democratic Party voters. The electorate expanded from 365,000 voters in 1824 to well over a million in 1828 and over 2 million in 1840. The Democratic Party also pressed the states to choose presidential electors by popular vote rather than by state legislatures. Thus Jackson and his Democratic successor, Martin Van Buren, ran truly national campaigns directed at the voters in every state.

At the same time, Jackson's opponents formed the **Whig Party**, named after the British party of that name. Like the British Whigs, who opposed the power of the king, the American Whigs charged "King Andrew" with usurping the powers of Congress and the people. The Whigs quickly adopted the Democrats' tactics of national campaigning and popular organizing. By 1840, the Whigs were able to gain the White House, running William Henry Harrison—nicknamed "Old Tippecanoe" from his victory at Tippecanoe over Native Americans in 1811—and John Tyler and featuring the slogan "Tippecanoe and Tyler too."

POLITICS UP CLOSE

The Donkey and the Elephant

The popular nineteenth-century cartoonist Thomas Nast is generally credited with giving the Democratic and Republican parties their current symbols: the donkey and the elephant. In *Harper's Weekly*'s 1870s cartoons, Nast critically portrayed the Democratic Party as a stubborn mule "without pride of ancestry nor hope of posterity." During this period of Republican Party dominance, Nast portrayed the Republican Party as an elephant, the biggest beast in the political jungle. Now both party symbols are used with pride.

"A LIVE JACKASS KICKING A DEAD LION."
And such a Lion! and such a Jackass!

In the 1870 cartoon on the left, published following the death of Lincoln's Secretary of War E. M. Stanton, Nast shows a donkey (labeled "Copperheads," a disparaging term for the mostly Democratic Northerners who were sympathetic to the South during the Civil War) kicking the dead Stanton, who is portrayed as a lion. The 1874 cartoon on the right features the elephant as The Republican Vote and the donkey masquerading as a lion.

Post–Civil War Republican Dominance   Whigs and Democrats continued to share national power until the slavery conflict that ignited the Civil War destroyed the old party system. The Republican Party had formed in 1854 to oppose the spread of slavery to the western territories. By the election of 1860, the slavery issue so divided the nation that four parties offered presidential candidates: Lincoln, the Republican; Stephen A. Douglas, the northern Democrat; John C. Breckinridge, the southern Democrat; and John Bell, the Constitutional Union Party candidate. No party came close to winning a majority of the popular vote, but Lincoln won in the Electoral College.

The new party system that emerged from the Civil War featured a victorious **Republican Party** that generally represented the northern industrial economy and a struggling Democratic Party that generally represented a southern agricultural economy. The Republican Party won every presidential election from 1860 to 1912 except for two victories by Democratic reformer and New York governor Grover Cleveland (see *Politics Up Close*: "The Donkey and the Elephant").

Yet the Democratic Party offered a serious challenge in the election of 1896 and realigned the party affiliations of the nation's voters. The Democratic Party nominated William Jennings Bryan, a talented orator and a religious fundamentalist. Bryan sought to rally the nation's white "have-nots" to the Democratic Party banner, particularly the debt-ridden farmers of the South and West. His plan was to stimulate inflation (and thus enable debtors to pay their debts with "cheaper," less valuable dollars) through using plentiful, western-mined "free silver," rather

Republican Party
One of the two main parties in American politics, it traces its origins to the anti-slavery and nationalist forces that united in the 1850s and nominated Abraham Lincoln for president in 1860.

On the Attack

Negative advertising has a long history in American politics. In the election of 1896, Republican presidential candidate William McKinley portrayed his Democratic opponent William Jennings Bryan as an unpatriotic destroyer of America's interests, represented by the flag.

GOP

"Grand Old Party"—popular label for the Republican Party.

New Deal

Policies of President Franklin D. Roosevelt during the Depression of the 1930s that helped form a Democratic Party coalition of urban working-class, ethnic, Catholic, Jewish, poor, and southern voters.

than gold, as the monetary standard. He defeated Cleveland's faction and the "Gold Democrats" in the 1896 Democratic Party convention with his famous Cross of Gold speech: "You shall not crucify mankind upon a cross of gold."

But the Republican Party rallied its forces in perhaps the most bitter presidential battle in history. It sought to convince the nation that high tariffs, protection for manufacturers, and a solid monetary standard would lead to prosperity for industrial workers as well as the new tycoons. The campaign, directed by Marcus Alonzo Hanna, attorney for John D. Rockefeller's Standard Oil Company, spent an unprecedented $16 million (an amount in inflation-adjusted dollars that has never been equaled) to elect Republican William McKinley, advertised as the candidate who would bring a "full dinner pail" to all. The battle also produced one of the largest voter turnouts in history. McKinley won in a landslide. Bryan ran twice again but lost by even larger margins. The Republican Party solidified the loyalty of industrial workers, small-business owners, bankers, and large manufacturers, as well as black voters, who respected "the party of Lincoln" and despised the segregationist practices of the southern Democratic Party.

Republican Split, Democratic Win So great was the Republican Party's dominance in national elections that only a split among Republicans enabled the Democrat Woodrow Wilson to capture the presidency in 1912. Republican Theodore Roosevelt (who became president following McKinley's assassination and had won reelection in 1904) sought to recapture the presidency from his former protégé, Republican William Howard Taft. At the **GOP** ("Grand Old Party," as the Republicans began labeling themselves) convention, party regulars rejected the unpredictable Roosevelt in favor of Taft, even though Roosevelt had won the few primary elections that had recently been initiated. An irate Teddy Roosevelt launched a third, progressive party, the "Bull Moose," which actually outpolled the Republican Party in the 1912 election—the only time a third party has surpassed one of the two major parties in U.S. history. But the result was a victory for the Democratic candidate, former Princeton political science professor Woodrow Wilson. Following Wilson's two terms, Republicans again reasserted their political dominance with victories by Warren G. Harding, Calvin Coolidge, and Herbert Hoover.

The New Deal Democratic Party The promise of prosperity that empowered the Republican Party to hold its membership together faded in the light of the Great Depression. The U.S. stock market crashed in 1929, and by the early 1930s, one-quarter of the labor force was unemployed. Having lost confidence in the nation's business and political leadership, in 1932 American voters turned out incumbent Republican President Herbert Hoover in favor of Democrat Franklin D. Roosevelt, who promised the country a **New Deal**.

More than just bringing the Democrats to the White House, the Great Depression marked another party realignment. This time, traditionally Republican voting groups changed their affiliation and enabled the Democratic Party to dominate national politics for a generation. This realignment actually began in 1928, when Democratic presidential candidate Al Smith, a Catholic, won many northern, urban, ethnic voters away from the Republican Party. By 1932, a majority New Deal Democratic coalition had been formed in American politics. It consisted of the following groups:

• Working classes and union members, especially in large cities.

• White ethnic groups who had previously aligned themselves with Republican machines.

ELECTORAL COLLEGE VOTES IN THE 2008 ELECTION

THE UNITED STATES
A political map showing the number of electoral votes per state

A political map with states drawn in proportion to the number of electoral votes

- Catholics and Jews.

- African Americans, who ended their historic affiliation with the party of Lincoln to pursue new economic and social goals.

- Poor people, who associated the New Deal with expanded welfare and Social Security programs.

- Southern whites, who had provided the most loyal block of Democratic voters since the Civil War.

To be sure, this majority coalition had many internal factions: southern "Dixiecrats" walked out of the Democratic Party convention in 1948 to protest a party platform that called for an end to racial discrimination in employment. But the promise of a New Deal—with its vast array of government supports for workers, elderly and disabled people, widows and children, and farmers—held this coalition together reasonably well. President Harry Truman's **Fair Deal** proved that the coalition could survive its founder, Franklin D. Roosevelt. Republican Dwight D. Eisenhower made inroads into this coalition by virtue of his personal popularity and the Republican Party's acceptance of most New Deal programs. But John F. Kennedy's "New Frontier" demonstrated the continuing appeal of the Democratic Party tradition. Lyndon Johnson's **Great Society** went further than the programs of any of his predecessors in government intervention in the economic and social life of the nation. Indeed, it might be argued that the Great Society laid the foundation for a political reaction that eventually destroyed the old Democratic coalition and led to yet another new party alignment.

Party Turmoil   The American political system underwent massive convulsions in the late 1960s as a result of both the civil rights revolution at home and an unpopular war in Vietnam. Strains were felt in all of the nation's political institutions, from the courts to the Congress to the presidency. And when Lyndon Johnson announced his decision not to run for reelection in 1968, the Democratic Party erupted in a battle that ultimately destroyed its majority support among presidential voters.

✔ *Think* Again

Does the Democratic Party favor the poor more than the middle class or rich?

Fair Deal
Policies of President Harry Truman extending Roosevelt's New Deal and maintaining the Democratic Party's voter coalition.

Great Society
Policies of President Lyndon Johnson that promised to solve the nation's social and economic problems through government intervention.

Think Again

Does the Republican Party favor the rich more than the middle class or poor?

At the 1968 Democratic Party convention in Chicago, Vice President Hubert Humphrey controlled a majority of the delegates inside the convention hall, but anti-war protesters dominated media coverage outside the hall. When Chicago police attacked unruly demonstrators with batons, the media broadcast to the world an image of the nation's turmoil. In the presidential campaign that followed, both candidates—Democrat Hubert Humphrey and Republican Richard Nixon—presented nearly identical positions supporting the U.S. military commitment in Vietnam while endorsing a negotiated, "honorable" settlement of the war. But the image of the Democratic Party became associated with the street protesters. Inside the convention hall, pressure from women and minorities led party leaders to adopt changes in the party's delegate-selection process for future conventions to assure better representation of these groups—at the expense of Democratic office-holders (see "Making Party Rules" later in this chapter for more details).

In 1972 the Democratic Party convention strongly reflected the views of anti-war protesters, civil rights advocates, feminist organizations, and liberal activists generally. The visibility of these activists, who appeared to be well to the left of both Democratic Party voters and the electorate in general, allowed the Republican Party to portray the Democratic presidential nominee, George McGovern, as an unpatriotic liberal, willing to "crawl to Hanoi" and to sacrifice the nation's honor for peace. It also allowed the Republicans to characterize the new Democratic Party as soft on crime, tolerant of disorder, and committed to racial and sexual quotas in American life. Richard Nixon, never very popular personally, was able to win in a landslide in 1972. The Watergate scandal and Nixon's forced resignation only temporarily stemmed the tide of "the new Republican majority." Democrat Jimmy Carter's narrow victory over Republican Gerald R. Ford in 1976 owed much to the latter's pardon of Nixon.

The Reagan Coalition   Under the leadership of Ronald Reagan, the Republican Party was able to assemble a majority coalition that dominated presidential elections in the 1980s, giving Reagan landslide victories in 1980 and 1984 and George H. W. Bush a convincing win in 1988. The **Reagan Coalition** consisted of the following groups:

Reagan Coalition
Combination of economic and social conservatives, religious fundamentalists, and defense-minded anti-communists who rallied behind Republican President Ronald Reagan.

- Economic conservatives concerned about high taxes and excessive government regulation, including business and professional voters who had traditionally supported the Republican Party.

- Social conservatives concerned about crime, drugs, and racial conflict, including many white ethnic voters and union members who had traditionally voted Democratic.

- Religious fundamentalists concerned about such issues as abortion and prayer in schools.

- Southern whites concerned about racial issues, including affirmative action programs.

- Internationalists and anti-communists who wanted the United States to maintain a strong military force and to confront Soviet-backed Marxist regimes around the world.

Reagan held this coalition together in large part through his personal popularity and his infectious optimism about the United States and its future. Although sometimes at odds with one another, economic conservatives, religious fundamentalists, and internationalists could unite behind the "Great Communicator." Reagan's presidential victory in 1980 helped to elect a Republican majority to the U.S. Senate

REAGAN IS PRO-LIFE

The Power of Unity
President Ronald Reagan created a Republican majority coalition in the 1980s by uniting Republican factions—economic conservatives, social conservatives, religious fundamentalists, and anti-communists—and adding many southern white Democrats.

and encouraged Democratic conservatives in the Democrat-controlled House of Representatives to frequently vote with Republicans. As a result, Reagan got most of what he asked of Congress in his first term: cuts in personal income taxes, increased spending for national defense, and slower growth of federal regulatory activity. With the assistance of the Federal Reserve Board, inflation was brought under control. But Reagan largely failed to cut government spending as he had promised, and the result was a series of huge federal deficits. Reagan appointed conservatives to the Supreme Court and the federal judiciary (see Chapter 13), but no major decisions were reversed (including the *Roe v. Wade* decision, protecting abortion); social conservatives had to be content with the president's symbolic support.

During these years, the national Democratic Party was saddled with an unpopular image as the party of special-interest groups. As more middle-class and working-class voters deserted to the GOP, the key remaining loyal Democratic constituencies were African Americans and other minorities, government employees, union leaders, liberal intellectuals in the media and universities, feminist organizations, and environmentalists. Democratic presidential candidates Walter Mondale in 1984 and Michael Dukakis in 1988 were obliged to take liberal positions to win the support of these groups in the primary elections. Later, both candidates sought to move toward the center of the ideological battleground in the general election. But Republican Party strategists were able to "define" Mondale and Dukakis through negative campaign advertising (see Chapter 8) as liberal defenders of special-interest groups. The general conservative tilt of public opinion in the 1980s added to the effectiveness of the GOP strategy of branding Democratic presidential candidates with the "L word" (*liberal*).

Clinton and the "New" Democrats

Yet even while Democratic candidates fared poorly in presidential elections, Democrats continued to maintain control of the House of Representatives, to win back control of the U.S. Senate in 1986, and to hold more state governorships and state legislative seats than the Republicans. Thus the Democratic Party retained a strong leadership base on which to rebuild itself.

During the 1980s, Democratic leaders among governors and senators came together in the Democratic Leadership Council to create a "new" Democratic Party closer to the center of the political spectrum. The chair of the Democratic

Presidential Gathering

Five presidents assemble for a historic photo, from left to right George H. W. Bush, Barack Obama, George W. Bush, Bill Clinton, and Jimmy Carter. Despite party and policy differences, they share the same experience in the Oval Office.

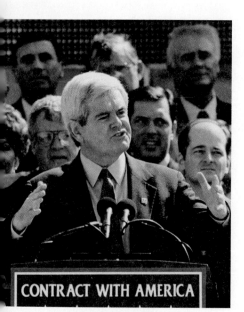

Leading a GOP Resurgence

Newt Gingrich addresses a rally on Capitol Hill on April 7, 1995. Gingrich, from Georgia, led the Republican resurgence of 1994. He served in the U.S. House of Representatives from 1979 to 1999, was coauthor of the 1994 Contract with America, and was House Speaker from 1995 to 1999.

Leadership Council was the young, energetic, and successful governor of Arkansas, Bill Clinton. The concern of the council was that the Democratic Party's traditional support for social justice and social welfare programs was overshadowing its commitment to economic prosperity. Many council members argued that a healthy economy was a prerequisite to progress in social welfare. Not all Democrats agreed with the council agenda. African American leaders (including the Reverend Jesse Jackson), as well as liberal and environmental groups, feared that the priorities of the council would result in the sacrifice of traditional Democratic Party commitments to minorities, poor people, and the environment.

In the 1992 presidential election, Bill Clinton was in a strong position to take advantage of the faltering economy under George H. W. Bush, to stress the "new" Democratic Party's commitment to the middle class, and to avoid being labeled as a liberal defender of special interests. At the same time, he managed to rally the party's core activist groups—liberals, intellectuals, African Americans, feminists, and environmentalists. Many liberals in the party deliberately soft-pedaled their views during the 1992 election in order not to offend voters, hoping to win with Clinton and then fight for liberal programs later. Clinton won with 43 percent of the vote, to Bush's 38 percent. Independent Ross Perot captured a surprising 19 percent of the popular vote, including many voters who were alienated from both the Democratic and Republican parties. Once in office, Clinton appeared to revert to liberal policy directions rather than to pursue the more moderate line he had espoused as a "new" Democrat. As Clinton's ratings sagged, the opportunity arose for a Republican resurgence.

Republican Resurgence A political earthquake shook Washington in the 1994 congressional elections, when the Republicans for the first time in 40 years captured the House of Representatives, regained control of the Senate, and captured a majority of the nation's governorships. For the first time in history Republicans won more seats in the South than the Democrats. This southern swing to the Republicans in congressional elections seemed to confirm the realignment of southern voters that had begun earlier in presidential elections. Just 2 years after a Democratic president had been elected, the GOP won its biggest nationwide victory since the Great Depression.[5]

Clinton Holds On   Following the Republican victory, the Democratic Party appeared to be in temporary disarray. The new Republican House Speaker, Newt Gingrich, tried to seize national policy leadership; Clinton was widely viewed as a failed president. But the Republicans quickly squandered their political opportunity. They had made many promises in a well-publicized "Contract with America"— a balanced federal budget, congressional term limits, tax cuts, welfare reform, and more—but they delivered little. Majority Leader Bob Dole failed by one vote to pass the Balanced Budget Amendment in the Senate. President Clinton took an unexpectedly hard line toward GOP spending cuts and vetoed several budget bills. When the federal government officially "closed down" for lack of appropriated funds, the public appeared to blame Republicans. Polls showed a dramatic recovery in the president's approval ratings. Clinton skillfully portrayed GOP leaders, especially Newt Gingrich, as "extremists" and himself as a responsible moderate prepared to trim the budget, reduce the deficit, and reform welfare, "while still protecting Medicare, Medicaid, education, and the environment." By early 1996, Clinton had set the stage for his reelection campaign.

Bill Clinton was the first Democratic president to be reelected since Franklin D. Roosevelt. Clinton rode to victory on a robust economy. Voters put aside doubts about Clinton's character, and they ignored Republican Bob Dole's call for tax reductions. Clinton won with 49 percent of the popular vote to Dole's 41 percent and Perot's 8 percent. But Clinton's victory failed to rejuvenate the Democratic Party's fortunes across the country. The GOP retained its majorities in both houses of Congress.

Bill Clinton, 42nd President of the United States (1993–2001), delivers his State of the Union address in 1999.

2000—A Nation Divided   The nation was more evenly divided in 2000 between the Democratic and Republican parties than perhaps at any other time in history. Democrat Al Gore won a narrow victory in the popular vote for president. But after a month-long battle for Florida's electoral vote, Republican George W. Bush, former Texas governor and son of the former President Bush, emerged as the winner of the Electoral College vote, 271 to 267 (see *Politics Up Close: "Bush v. Gore* in the U.S. Supreme Court" in Chapter 13). Not only was the presidential vote almost tied, but also both houses of Congress were split almost evenly between Democrats and Republicans. The Republican Party lost seats in the House of Representatives in 1998 and again in 2000. Yet the GOP still retained a razor-thin margin of control of that body. In the Senate, the 2000 election created a historic 50–50 tie between Democrats and Republicans. The vote of the Senate's presiding officer, Republican Vice President Dick Cheney, would have given the GOP the narrowest of control of that body. But in 2001, Vermont's Republican Senator Jim Jeffords decided to switch his support to the Democratic Party, swinging control of the Senate to the Democrats.

The Republican Party defied tradition in 2002 by gaining seats in the Senate and expanding its majority in the House. Historically, the party in control of the White House *lost* seats in midterm elections. But in an era in which presidents are not supposed to have coattails, especially in midterm congressional elections, President George W. Bush campaigned energetically across the country for GOP candidates, focusing attention on the war on terrorism. Democratic complaints about the weak economy were muted. Bush's intense efforts appeared to motivate Republican voters; a higher-than-usual midterm voter turnout resulted in Republican victories in hotly contested Senate and House races across the country.

Republicans Take Control   In 2004, the GOP further consolidated its control over the White House, Senate, and House of Representatives. Throughout the

Republicans Rebound—2010

Haley Barber (R-MS), Chairman of the Republican Governors Conference, Mitch McConnell (R-KY), Senate Republican Leader, and John Boehner (R-OH), House Republican Leader, celebrate Republican gains in the midterm congressional elections in November, 2010.

2004 election campaign, polls showed the nation evenly split, with Republican President Bush and Democratic Senator Kerry running neck and neck. There was considerable fear of another contested presidential election and concern that the popular vote winner might again lose in the Electoral College. But Republicans showed unexpected strength, with Bush winning both the popular vote and the Electoral College vote. Turnout was high. (Republican turnout may have been helped by referenda banning same-sex marriage that appeared on the ballot in eleven states; polls consistently show regular churchgoers tending to vote Republican.) Republicans added to their controlling margins in both the House and the Senate.

Democrats Recover—2006 The war in Iraq undermined the Republican Party's hold on congressional voters in 2006. For the first time in 12 years, the GOP lost control of the House of Representatives. They also gave up control of the Senate; Democrats won just enough seats to give them a 51 to 49 margin in that body. Polls suggested that voters had lost confidence in President Bush; his approval ratings remained below 40 percent throughout the election year. Midterm elections are seldom a referendum on national policy, but just enough voters in close House and Senate races decided in favor of "change," bringing back Democratic majorities in both houses of Congress.

Democrats Sweep—2008 Economic instability traditionally has helped Democratic candidates. And not since the Great Depression of the 1930s have Americans experienced so much economic anxiety as they did in 2008. A plunge in housing values, a sharp decline in the stock market, emergency government takeovers of leading banks and investment houses, and Washington's $700 billion bailout of Wall Street all contributed to voter concern over the economy. Republican President George W. Bush suffered the lowest approval ratings of any president since Richard Nixon. The stage was set for sweeping Democratic victories in the Senate, House of Representatives, and the White House.

Barack Obama led his party to a decisive sweep, putting Democrats in control of the House, Senate, and White House, creating unified Democratic Party control of the federal government for the first time since 1994. (See *Politics Up Close:* "Campaign '08—Obama Versus McCain" in Chapter 8.)

Republicans Recover—2010 Continuing high unemployment and a perceived failure of the Democrats in power to deal effectively with the sagging economy brought the GOP roaring back in the midterm congressional election. Republicans recaptured control of the House of Representatives and improved their numbers in the Senate. But polls showed that both parties were viewed unfavorably by a majority of voters. Republican successes were attributed in part to dissatisfaction with the Obama administration's policies, including massive government spending and huge budget deficits. (See *Politics Up Close:* "Republicans Rebound— The 2010 Congressional Elections" in Chapter 10.)

PEOPLE IN POLITICS

Hillary Clinton, Leading the Way for Women

Secretary of State Hillary Rodham Clinton came very close to becoming the first woman President of the United States (see *Politics Up Close*: "Hillary Versus Barack, 2008"). She is the first First Lady ever elected to Congress and the first woman senator from New York.

Hillary Rodham grew up in suburban Chicago, the daughter of wealthy parents who sent her to the private, prestigious Wellesley College. A 1969 honors graduate with a counterculture image—horn-rimmed glasses, long, straggling hair, no makeup—she was chosen by her classmates to give a commencement speech—a rambling statement about "more immediate, ecstatic, and penetrating modes of living."

At Yale Law School Hillary met a long-haired, bearded Rhodes scholar from Arkansas, Bill Clinton, who was just as politically ambitious as she was. Both Hillary and Bill received their law degrees in 1973. Bill returned to Arkansas to build a career in state politics, and Hillary went to Washington as an attorney—first for a liberal lobbying group, the Children's Defense Fund, and later on the staff of the House Judiciary Committee seeking to impeach President Richard Nixon. But Rodham and other Yale grads traveled to Arkansas to help Clinton run, unsuccessfully, for Congress in 1974. Hillary decided to stay with Bill in Little Rock: they married before his next campaign, a successful run for state attorney general in 1976. Hillary remained Hillary Rodham, even as her husband went on to the governorship in 1978.

Her husband's 1980 defeat for reelection as governor was blamed on his liberal leanings; therefore, in his 1982 comeback Bill repackaged himself as a moderate and centrist. Hillary cooperated by becoming Mrs. Bill Clinton, shedding her horn-rims for contacts, blonding her hair, and echoing her husband's more moderate line. These tactics helped propel them back into the governor's mansion. Hillary soon became a full partner in Little Rock's Rose law firm regularly earning more than $200,000 a year (while Bill earned only $35,000 as Arkansas governor). She won national recognition as one of the "100 most influential lawyers in the United States," according to the *American National Law Journal*. She chaired the American Bar Association's Commission on Women and the Profession.

Hillary's steadfast support of Bill during the White House sex scandals and subsequent impeachment by the House of Representatives in all likelihood saved his presidency. Her approval ratings in public opinion polls skyrocketed during the affair. Whatever she thought in private, she never chastised her husband in public and blamed much of the scandal on "a vast right-wing conspiracy."

Her Senate race attracted national media attention as well as campaign contributions from supporters throughout the nation. When New York City's Mayor Rudolph Giuliani announced that he would *not* run for the Senate, Hillary was relieved to confront a little-known opponent, Congressman Rick Lazio. New York voters were unimpressed with charges that Hillary was not a true New Yorker. She studied New York problems diligently, and overwhelmed Lazio in the campaign. Over $85 million was spent by the candidates, making the campaign the most expensive congressional campaign in history.

Senator Clinton developed a reputation as an advocate for children and families. Her early work with the Children's Defense Fund and Marian Wright Edelman (see *People in Politics*: "Marian Wright Edelman, Lobbying for the Poor" in Chapter 9) was carried forward in her book *It Takes a Village* in 1997. She was prominently mentioned in all of the early 2004 presidential polls, but she declined to run. She crushed her Republican opponent in her 2006 reelection to the Senate, setting the stage for her presidential campaign in 2008.

President Barack Obama convinced Hillary to leave the Senate in early 2009 and to serve as Secretary of State in his administration. She promised world leaders that U.S. foreign policy would change direction, that America would act in concert with other nations rather than go it alone in world affairs.

Political Parties and Democratic Government

▶ 7.3 *Outline functions of political parties as "responsible" organizations and perceptions of the two major American political parties.*

"Political parties created democracy, and modern democracy is unthinkable save in terms of the parties."[6] Traditionally, political scientists have praised parties as indispensable to democratic government. They have argued that parties are essential for organizing popular majorities to exercise control over government. The development of political parties in all the democracies of the world testifies to the underlying importance of parties to democratic government. But political parties in the United States have lost their preeminent position as instruments of democracy. Other structures and organizations in society—interest groups, the mass media, independent campaign organizations, primary elections, social welfare agencies—now perform many of the functions traditionally regarded as prerogatives of political parties. Nevertheless, the Democratic and Republican parties remain important organizing structures for politics in the United States.

"Responsible" Parties in Theory   In theory, political parties function in a democracy to organize majorities around broad principles of government in order to win public office and enact these principles into law. A "responsible" party should:

Think Again

Should elected officials be bound by their party's platform?

- Adopt a platform setting forth its principles and policy positions.

- Recruit candidates for public office who agree with the party's platform.

- Inform and educate the public about the platform.

- Organize and direct campaigns based on platform principles.

- Organize the legislature to ensure party control in policy making.

- Hold its elected officials responsible for enacting the party's platform.

If responsible, disciplined, policy-oriented parties competed for majority support, *if* they offered clear policy alternatives to the voters, and *if* the voters cast their ballots on the basis of these policy options, *then* the winning party would have a "policy mandate" from the people to guide the course of government. In that way, the democratic ideal of government by majority rule would be implemented.

responsible party model
System in which competitive parties adopt a platform of principles, recruiting candidates and directing campaigns based on that platform, and holding their elected officials responsible for enacting it.

But Winning Wins over Principle   However, the **responsible party model** never accurately described the American party system. The major American parties have been loose coalitions of individuals and groups seeking to attract sufficient votes to gain control of government. *Winning has generally been more important than any principles or policies.* America's major parties must appeal to tens of millions of voters in every section of the nation and from all walks of life. If a major party is to acquire a majority capable of controlling the U.S. government, it cannot limit its appeal by relying on a single unifying principle. Instead, it must form coalitions of voters from as many sectors of the population as it can. Major American parties therefore usually do not emphasize particular principles or ideologies so much as try to find a common ground of agreement among many different people. This emphasis does not mean no policy differences exist between the American parties. On the contrary, each party tends to appeal to a distinctive coalition of interests, and therefore each party expresses somewhat distinctive policy views (see *Controversy:* "Which Party Does a Better Job?").

In their efforts to win, major American political parties strive to attract the support of the large numbers of people near the center of public opinion. Generally more votes are at the center of the ideological spectrum—the middle-of-the-road—than on the extreme liberal or conservative ends. Thus *no real incentive exists for vote-maximizing parties to take strong policy positions in opposition to each other* (see Figure 7.3).

Party and Ideology   Despite incentives for the parties to move to the center of the political spectrum, the Republican and Democratic parties are perceived by the public as ideologically separate. The electorate tends to perceive the Republican Party as conservative and the Democratic Party as liberal.

Indeed, polls suggest that Republican voters described themselves as conservatives far more often than as liberals. And Democratic voters are more likely to

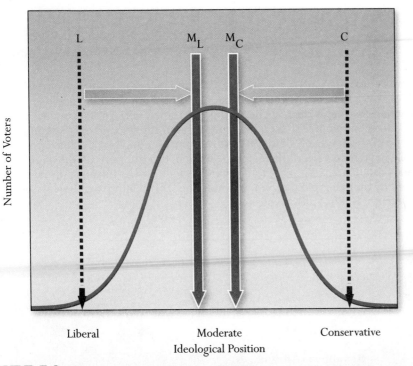

Number of Voters

L   M\ :sub:`L`   M\ :sub:`C`   C

Liberal   Moderate   Conservative
Ideological Position

FIGURE 7.3 Why Parties Drift to the Center

Why don't we have a party system based on principles, with a liberal party and a conservative party, each offering the voters a real ideological choice? Let's assume that voters generally choose the party closest to their own ideological position. If the liberal party (L) took a strong ideological position to the left of most voters, the conservative party (C) would move toward the center, winning more moderate votes, even while retaining its conservative supporters, who would still prefer it to the more liberal opposition party. Likewise, if the conservative party took a strong ideological position to the right of most voters, the liberal party would move to the center and win. So both parties must abandon strong ideological positions and move to the center, becoming moderate in the fight for support of moderate voters.

identify themselves as liberals than as conservatives, although many like to think of themselves as moderates (see Table 7.1).

This relationship between ideological self-identification and party self-identification is relatively stable over time. It suggests that the parties are not altogether empty jars. Later we will observe that Democratic and Republican party activists (notably, delegates to the party conventions) are even more ideologically separate than Democratic and Republican party voters.

TABLE 7.1 Who Votes for the Parties? Party and Ideology Among Voters

	Democratic Voters	Republican Voters	Independent Voters	Total
Self-identified liberals tend to vote Democratic, while conservatives tend to vote Republican.				
Liberals	54%	4%	25%	28%
Moderates	29	13	42	28
Conservatives	17	82	32	43

Source: Data from the 2008 National Election Study. University of Michigan. Tabulations by Professor Terri Towner, Oakland University.

CONTROVERSY

Which Party Does a Better Job?

What do Americans think of the Democratic and Republican parties? Generally speaking, the Democratic Party has been able to maintain an image of "the party of the common people," and the Republican Party has long been saddled with an image of "favoring the rich." And more people have reported a "favorable" image of the Democratic Party.

But the Republican Party is trusted by more people to "do a better job" in handling foreign affairs and maintaining a strong national defense. It also enjoys a reputation of being better at "holding down taxes."

The Democratic Party enjoys its greatest advantage on "compassion issues" such as helping poor, elderly, and homeless people. And the Democrats have long enjoyed the support of the high-voter-turnout over-65 age group because it is trusted to do a better job "protecting the Social Security system."

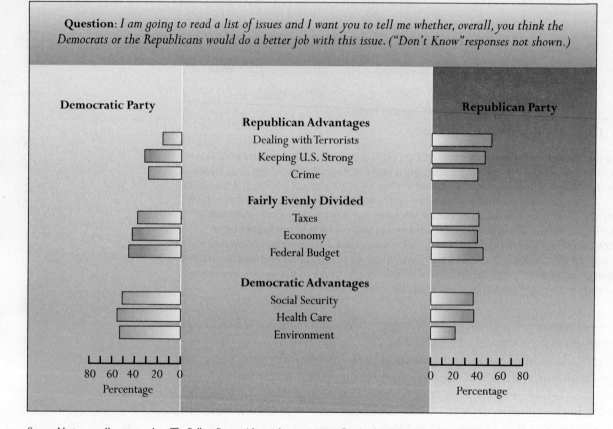

Question: *I am going to read a list of issues and I want you to tell me whether, overall, you think the Democrats or the Republicans would do a better job with this issue. ("Don't Know" responses not shown.)*

Source: Various polls reported in *The Polling Report,* November 22, 1999. September 10, 2001, January 28, 2002, August 11, 2003, September 18, 2007, September 2, 2009. Percentages vary over time; relative advantages remain stable.

party polarization
The tendency of the Democratic Party to take more liberal positions and the Republican Party to take more conservative positions on key issues.

Democratic and Republican party activists have become more ideologically separate in recent years. And voters have become increasingly aware of this **party polarization**. Indeed many voters are now prepared to say that the Democratic Party is more liberal and the Republican Party is more conservative on a variety of high-profile issues, including government services and spending, government provision of health insurance, and government help to African Americans.[7]

The Republican Party tends to include defenders of the free enterprise system and opponents of government regulation, together with strongly religious people who hold traditional views on moral issues. The Republican Party also appeals to people strongly supportive of the military and an assertive foreign policy. The

Democratic Party includes liberals with strong views on social issues such as homosexuality, abortion, and environmental protection, as well as reluctance to the use of military force. Yet another part of the Democratic coalition includes the people supportive of the role of government in providing a social safety net—efforts to provide jobs, help to the needy, and economic opportunity for all.

The Erosion of Traditional Party Functions

Parties play only a limited role in campaign organization and finance. *Campaigns are generally directed by professional campaign management firms or by the candidates' personal organizations, not by parties.* Party organizations have largely been displaced in campaign activity by advertising firms, media consultants, pollsters, and others hired by the candidates themselves (see Chapter 8).

Most political candidates today are self-recruited. American political parties also play only a limited role in recruiting candidates for elected office. People initiate their own candidacies, first contacting friends and financial supporters. Often in state and local races, candidates contact party officials only as a courtesy, if at all.

The major American political parties cannot really control who their **nominee**—*the party's entry in a general election race—will be.* Rather, party **nominations** for most elected offices are won in **primary elections**. In a primary election, registered voters select who will be their party's nominee in the general election. Party leaders may endorse a candidate in a primary election and may even work to try to ensure the victory of their favorite, but the voters in that party's primary select the nominee.

Candidates usually communicate directly with voters through the mass media. Television has replaced the party organization as the principal medium of communication between candidates and voters. Candidates no longer rely much on party workers to carry their message from door to door. Instead, candidates can come directly into the voters' living rooms via television.

Even if the American parties wanted to take stronger policy positions and to enact them into law, they would not have the means to do so. *American political parties have no way to bind their elected officials to the party platform or even to their campaign promises.* Parties have no strong disciplinary sanctions to use against members of Congress who vote against the party's policy position. The parties cannot deny them renomination. At most, the party's leadership in Congress can threaten the status, privileges, and pet bills of disloyal members (see Chapter 10). Party cohesion, where it exists, is more a product of like-mindedness than of party discipline.

American political parties no longer perform social welfare functions—trading off social services, patronage jobs, or petty favors in exchange for votes. Traditional party organizations, or **machines**, especially in large cities, once helped immigrants get settled in, found **patronage** jobs in government for party workers, and occasionally provided aid to impoverished but loyal party voters. But government bureaucracies have replaced the political parties as providers of social services. Government employment agencies, welfare agencies, civil service systems, and other bureaucracies now provide the social services once undertaken by political machines in search of votes.

Divided Party Government

Finally, to further confound the responsible party model, Americans seem to prefer **divided party government**—where one party controls the executive branch while the other party controls one or both houses of the legislative branch. Over the last 40 years, American presidents have been more likely to face a Congress in which the opposition party controls one or both houses than to enjoy their own party's full control of Congress. (Divided party government in the states—where one party controls the

---

nominee
Political party's entry in a general election race.

nominations
Political party's selections of its candidates for public office.

primary elections
Elections to choose party nominees for public office; may be open or closed.

machines
Tightly disciplined party organizations, headed by a boss, that rely on material rewards—including patronage jobs—to control politics.

patronage
Appointment to public office based on party loyalty.

divided party government
One party controls the presidency while the other party controls one or both houses of Congress.

POLITICS UP CLOSE

The Appeal of the Republican and Democratic Parties

What explains partisanship among voters? What is it about the Republican and Democratic parties that appeals to voters? A Gallup survey asked Americans—after they identified themselves as Republicans or Democrats (or Independents who said they lean toward either party)—to explain in their own words just what it is about their chosen party that appeals to them most.

Republicans justify their allegiance to the GOP most often with a reference to the party's conservatism or conservative positions on moral issues. Beyond that, Republicans mention the party's conservative economic positions and its preference for smaller government.

In contrast to Republicans who mention conservatism as their rationale for identifying with the GOP, the proportion of Democrats who mention liberalism is comparatively small. Democrats are more likely to say that the Democratic Party appeals to them because it is for the working class, the middle class, or the "common man."

Q. What is it about the Republican Party that appeals to you most? (Asked of Republicans)

Conservative/more conservative (nonspecific)	26%
Conservative family/moral values	15
Overall platform/philosophy/policies (nonspecific)	12%
Conservative on fiscal/economic issues	10
Favors smaller government	8
Favors individual responsibility/self-reliance	5
Always been a Republican	4
For the people/working people	3
Low taxes	3
Favor strong military	3
Pro-life on abortion	2

Q. What is it about the Democratic Party that appeals to you most? (Asked of Democrats)

For the middle class/working class/common man	25%
Social/moral issue positions	18
Overall platform/philosophy/policies (nonspecific)	14
Liberal/more liberal (nonspecific)	11
Help the poor	7
Always been a Democrat	5
Antiwar	3
Health-care reform	2
Pro-environment/conservation	1

Note: "Other" and "no opinion" percentages not shown.

Source: Gallup Poll, November 13, 2007. www.gallup.com.

governorship and the opposition party controls one or both houses of the state legislature—is also increasing over time.)[8] Divided party control of government makes it difficult for either party to fully enact its platform. It is noteworthy that American public opinion seems to prefer divided party government over unified party control.

Getting Out the Vote
Political campaigns are designed not only to win over supporters, but also to inspire supporters to turn out and cast ballots on election day.

TABLE 7.2 Where's the Money?: Party Finances (in millions)

Parties as well as candidates solicit campaign contributions. At the national level, contributions go to the Democratic and Republican National Committees and to the Democratic and Republican House and Senate Campaign Committees.

	2000	2004	2008
Totals			
Democratic Party	$520	$731	$961
Republican Party	715	993	920
National Committees			
Dem. National Com.	260	311	260
Rep. National Com.	379	392	428
House Party Committees			
Dem. Cong. Camp. Com.	105	92	176
Nat'l Rep. Cong. Com.	145	186	118
Senate Party Committees			
Dem. Senatorial Camp. Com.	104	89	163
Nat'l Rep. Senatorial Camp. Com.	96	79	94

Source: Center for Responsive Politics, www.opensecrets.org, 2008 data released July 17, 2009.

Party Finances

▶ 7.4 *Explain how the two major American political parties are financed.*

Parties as well as candidates raise hundreds of millions of dollars in every election year. (Later, in Chapter 8, we will examine campaign financing by candidates themselves.) At the national level, contributions to the parties go to the Democratic and Republican National Committees, and to the Democratic and Republican House and Senatorial Committees (see Table 7.2).

The Partisan Tilt of Campaign Contributions   Traditionally, the Republican Party was able to raise and spend more money in each election cycle than the Democratic Party. But the dollar differences have narrowed over the years. Perhaps more interesting are the differences in sources of support for each party. Broken down by sector (as in Table 7.3), the Democratic Party relies more heavily on lawyers and law firms, on the TV, movie and music industry (Hollywood), teachers and public sector employee unions, and industrial and building trade unions. Business interests divide their contributions, but they tilt toward the Republican Party, notably the health care industry, insurance, manufacturing, oil and gas, automotive, and general and special contractors.

Parties as Organizers of Elections

▶ 7.5 *Assess the changing role of the political parties in the electoral process.*

Despite the erosion of many of their functions, America's political parties survive as the principal institutions for organizing elections.[9] Party nominations organize electoral choice by narrowing the field of aspiring office seekers to the Democratic and Republican candidates. Very few independents or third-party candidates are elected to high political office in the United States. **Nonpartisan elections**— elections in which there are no party nominations and all candidates run without an official party label—are common only in local elections, for city council, county commission, school board, judgeships, and so on. Only Nebraska has nonpartisan elections for its unicameral (one-house) state legislature. Party conventions are still

nonpartisan elections
Elections in which candidates do not officially indicate their party affiliation; often used for city, county, school board, and judicial elections.

TABLE 7.3 Who Finances the Parties?: Contributors to the Republican and Democratic Parties by Sector

The Democratic Party relies more heavily on contributions from lawyers and law firms, TV, the movie and music industry, teacher and public employee unions, and industrial and building trade unions. The Republican Party relies more heavily on contributions from various business sectors.

Democratic Party	Republican Party
1. Lawyers/law firms	1. Securities/investment
2. Securities/investment	2. Real estate
3. Real estate	3. Health professionals
4. TV/movies/music	4. Lawyers/law firms
5. Business services	5. Oil and gas
6. Education	6. Business services
7. Health professionals	7. Manufacturing/distributing
8. Computers/Internet	8. Insurance
9. Lobbyists	9. General contractors
10. Public sector unions	10. Commercial banks
11. Industrial unions	11. Computers/Internet
12. Building trade unions	12. Automotive

Source: Center for Responsive Politics. Candidate committees, miscellaneous, and "retired" excluded from this table. Data from 2008 presidential election.

held in many states in every presidential year, but these conventions seldom have the power to determine the parties' nominees for public office.

Early Party Conventions Historically, party nominations were made by caucus or convention. The **caucus** was the earliest nominating process; party leaders (party chairs, elected officials, and "bosses") would simply meet several months before the election and decide on the party's nominee themselves. The early presidents—Thomas Jefferson, James Madison, James Monroe, and John Quincy Adams—were nominated by caucuses of Congress members. Complaints about the exclusion of the people from this process led to nominations by convention—large meetings of delegates sent by local party organizations—starting in 1832. Andrew Jackson was the first president to be nominated by convention. The convention was considered more democratic than the caucus.

For nearly a century, party conventions were held at all levels of government—local, state, and national. City or county conventions included delegates from local **wards** and **precincts**, who nominated candidates for city or county office, for the state legislature, or even for the House of Representatives when a congressional district fell within the city or county. State conventions included delegates from counties, and they nominated governors, U.S. senators, and other statewide officers. State parties chose delegates to the Republican and Democratic national conventions every 4 years to nominate a president.

Party Primaries Today, primary elections have largely replaced conventions as the means of selecting the Democratic and Republican nominees for public office.[10] (See *Politics Up Close:* "Hillary Versus Barack, 2008.") Primary elections, introduced as part of the progressive reform movement of the early twentieth century, allow the party's *voters* to choose the party's nominee directly. The primary election was designed to bypass the power of party organizations and party leaders and to further democratize the nomination process. It generally succeeded in

caucus
Nominating process in which party members or leaders meet to nominate candidates or select delegates to conventions.

wards
Divisions of a city for electoral or administrative purposes or as units for organizing political parties.

precincts
Subdivisions of a city, county, or ward for election purposes.

The Driving Force

Parties provide the organizational structure for political campaigns. Top left: The Executive Committee of the Republican National Convention in Chicago in 1880. Conventions emerged as the main way for parties to select candidates in the nineteenth century. Top right: Democratic presidential hopeful Senator John Edwards (D-NC) campaigning in Iowa in 2007. Bottom left: Republican presidential candidate John McCain greeting party workers. Bottom right: Campaign signs lining the street.

doing so, but it also had the effect of seriously weakening political parties, since candidates seeking a party nomination need only appeal to party *voters*—not *leaders*—for support in the primary election.[11]

Types of Primaries

There are some differences among the American states in how they conduct their primary elections. **Closed primaries** allow only voters who have previously registered as Democrats or Republicans (or in some states voters who choose to register as Democrats or Republicans on primary election day) to cast a ballot in their chosen party's primary. Closed primaries tend to discourage people from officially registering as Independents, even if they think of themselves as Independent, because persons registered as Independents cannot cast a ballot in either party's primary.

Open primaries allow voters to choose on election day which party primary they wish to participate in. Anyone, regardless of prior party affiliation, may choose to vote in either party's primary election. Voters simply request the ballot of one party or the other.[12] Open primaries provide opportunities for voters to cross over party lines and vote in the primary of the party they usually do not support. Opponents of open primaries have argued that these types of primary elections allow for **raiding**— organized efforts by one party to get its members to cross over to the opposition

closed primaries
Primary elections in which voters must declare (or have previously declared) their party affiliation and can cast a ballot only in their own party's primary election.

open primaries
Primary elections in which a voter may cast a ballot in either party's primary election.

raiding
Organized efforts by one party to get its members to cross over in a primary and defeat an attractive candidate in the opposition party's primary.

POLITICS UP CLOSE

Hillary Versus Barack, 2008

The historic clash between Barack Obama and Hillary Clinton brought passion, intensity, and a record voter turnout to the Democratic presidential primaries in 2008. At the beginning of the year, Hillary Clinton was far ahead in the polls and seen as the "inevitable" Democratic nominee. But the excitement began with the very first contest, the Iowa caucuses, where Obama's surprise victory demonstrated his appeal across racial lines. Hillary struck back a week later winning the New Hampshire primary and demonstrating that organization was still an essential component of a presidential primary campaign. She went on to win the Florida and Michigan primaries, but these were hollow victories. The Democratic National Committee had ruled that if Florida and Michigan held their primaries too early, their delegates would not be seated and their votes not counted at the Democratic convention.

Super Tuesday

Most observers thought that "Super Tuesday," February 5, with its front-loaded 21 state primaries would determine the party's nominee. But instead

the outcome reflected the bitter division that was to characterize the race. Clinton won the big states—California, New York, New Jersey, and even Massachusetts (despite Ted Kennedy's endorsement of Obama). But Obama won more states by wider margins and picked up more pledged convention delegates. South Carolina Senator John Edwards, the Democratic vice presidential nominee in 2004, dropped out of the race after finishing a poor third on Super Tuesday.

Barack Moves Ahead

The trend lines began to point in Obama's favor; national polls showed him creeping up in the support of likely Democratic Party voters. The Illinois senator projected a "rock star" image—a young, fresh, handsome, new presence on the national scene. He added young people and Independents to his base of African American voters. The enthusiasm he engendered among his followers inspired them to attend drawn-out party meetings, giving him an advantage in caucus states. Following Super Tuesday, Obama went on to win a string of state primaries and caucuses. Indeed, by "Super Tuesday II," March 4, Hillary appeared on the brink of defeat.

Hillary's Comeback

Hillary clung tenaciously to traditional Democratic voters, appealing especially to white women, lower-income blue-collar workers, and Latinos. Her hopes rested on the Super Tuesday II primaries in Ohio and

party's primary and defeat an attractive candidate and thereby improve the raiding party's chances of winning the general election. But there is little evidence to show that large numbers of voters connive in such a fashion.

Louisiana is unique in its nonpartisan primary elections. All candidates, regardless of their party affiliation, run in the same primary election. If a candidate gets over 50 percent of the vote, he or she wins the office, without appearing on the general election ballot. If no one receives over 50 percent of the primary election votes, then the top two vote-getters, regardless of party, face each other in the general election.[13]

Some states hold a **runoff primary** when no candidate receives a majority or a designated percentage of the vote in the party's first primary election. A runoff primary is limited to the two highest vote-getters in the first primary. Runoff

runoff primary
Additional primary held between the top two vote-getters in a primary where no candidate has received a majority of the vote.

Texas. She touted her experience, her ability to get things done, and the relative prosperity of the 1990s during her husband's presidency. She won the popular vote in these pivotal states and gave notice that the race for the Democratic nomination was not over.

Obama's Pastor Problem

Even before clips from the sermons of the Reverend Jeremiah Wright were broadcast on cable news channels, Barack Obama knew he had a preacher problem. Wright had been Obama's pastor, friend, and spiritual adviser for over 20 years at the Trinity United Church of Christ in Chicago. Wright had officiated at Obama's wedding and baptized both his children. Obama knew of his incendiary racist and anti-American comments and had withdrawn an invitation to Wright to deliver the invocation at his presidential candidacy announce-ment speech in early 2007. But efforts to keep Wright under wraps were destroyed in March 2008 when video clips emerged of Wright shouting "God damn America."

Obama responded with a carefully crafted address to the nation in which he disavowed the specific comments of his pastor but asked voters to understand the racial contex of Wright's anger. Obama would not "disown" Wright, or the Trinity Church, or black liberation theology. He asked Americans to come to grips with racial divisions and to transcend them; white middle-class Americans may have heard divisive, racist, and unpatriotic pronouncements, but blacks, on the other hand, heard righteous anger about racial injustice. Later, following a National Press Club diatribe by Wright, Obama finally rejected his former pastor. And near the end of the primary contests, Obama left the Trinity Church.

Hillary's Sniper Problem

Just when Hillary appeared to be gaining momentum she sabotaged her own campaign by fibbing about coming under sniper fire in Bosnia in 1996. Videotape of her deplaning revealed that rather than running to avoid sniper fire as she claimed, she calmly attended a ceremony on the open tarmac with a young child presenting her with flowers. Her fib and the conflicting video were widely shown on TV networks.

The Delegate Count

As the primary season wound down in May, Hillary claimed that she was ahead in the popular vote count and that she had won in states that would be crucial for the Democratic nominee in the November general election. But Obama was ahead in pledged delegates, won in primaries and caucuses, and he had won twice as many states as Clinton. The DNC rules committee voted to reinstate the Michigan and Florida delegations but to limit them to one half of their allotted votes. The decision angered Hillary's supporters. Hillary could only win the nomination by convincing uncommitted superdelegates that she would be a better candidate against Republican nominee John McCain. She argued that her late wins in West Virginia, Kentucky, South Dakota, and Puerto Rico demonstrated Obama's weakness especially among white blue-collar workers and Latinos. But Obama's late victories in Oregon and Montana again demonstrated his appeal across racial lines. Moreover, the superdelegates were wary of appearing to overturn Obama's legitimate lead in pledged delegates; to do so might split the Democratic Party along racial lines.

On June 3, the end of the primary season, Barack Obama proclaimed himself the Democratic nominee. He had won over enough superdelegates that combined with the pledged delegates he had won in primaries and caucuses put him over the top. Four days later, Hillary conceded and urged her supporters to back Barack Obama. The longest and most heated primary contest in modern political history came to a close.

elections are more common in the southern United States. In most states, only a plurality of votes is needed to win a primary election.

Party Caucuses   Some state parties select their candidates, as well as their delegates to the national party conventions, in caucuses rather than primary elections. A caucus is a meeting of party members, usually to select delegates to state or national party conventions. The Iowa presidential caucuses are well publicized as the first presidential contests in the nation. Rather than going to the polls as in primary elections, caucusgoers in each party gather at set times and set locations in schools, churches, libraries, and recreation centers in their neighborhoods. They discuss party platforms, select county committee members, and, most important, in presidential years they indicate their choice for their party's presidential nomination. Because attending a caucus takes more time and effort than voting in a primary election, caucuses tend to be dominated by people with stronger partisan or ideological biases. Caucuses tend to be of advantage to the best-organized candidates—candidates who can persuade and assist supporters in making the extra effort to attend a caucus. Attending a caucus also requires a participant to declare their party affiliation and to openly indicate their support for the candidate of their choice.

General Elections Following the parties' selections of their nominees, the **general election** (held in November, on the first Tuesday after the first Monday for presidential and most state elections) determines who will occupy elective office. Winners of the Democratic and Republican primary elections must face each other—and any Independent or third-party candidates—in the general election. Voters in the general election may choose any candidate, regardless of how they voted earlier in their party's primary or whether they voted in the primary at all.

Independent and minor-party candidates can get on the general election ballot, although the process is usually very difficult. Most states require independent candidates to file a petition with the signatures of several thousand registered voters. The number of signatures varies from state to state and office to office, but it may range up to 5 or 10 percent of *all* registered voters, a very large number that, in a big state especially, presents a difficult obstacle. The same petition requirements usually apply to minor parties, although some states automatically carry a minor party's nominee on the general election ballot if that party's candidate or candidates received a certain percentage (for example, 10 percent) of the vote in the previous general election.

Where's the Party?

▶ 7.6 *Differentiate the three political arenas in which the parties battle.*

The Democratic and Republican parties are found in different political arenas (see Figure 7.4). There is, first of all, the **party-in-the-electorate**—the voters

general election
Election to choose among candidates nominated by parties and/or Independent candidates who gained access to the ballot by petition.

party-in-the-electorate
Voters who identify themselves with a party.

FIGURE 7.4

Where's the Party?

Even among Americans who strongly identify with a major party, there are differences among those who are strictly members of the party-in-the-electorate (voters), those who are members of the party-in-the-government (elected officials), and those who are members of the party organization (national and state party committee members).

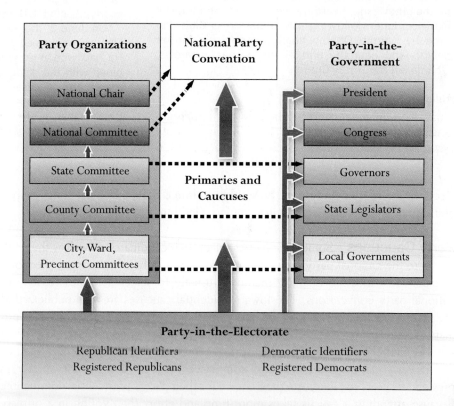

who identify themselves as Democrats or Republicans and who tend to vote for the candidates of their party. The party-in-the-electorate appears to be in decline today. Party loyalties among voters are weakening. More people identify themselves as Independents, and more **ticket splitters** divide their votes between candidates of different parties for different offices in the same general election.

The second locus of party activity is the **party-in-the-government**—officials who received their party's nomination and won the general election. The party-in-the-government includes members of Congress, state legislators and local government officials, and elected members of the executive branch, including the president and governors.

Party identification and loyalty among elected officeholders (the party-in-the-government) are generally stronger than party identification and loyalty among the party-in-the-electorate. Nevertheless, party loyalties among elected officials have also weakened over time. (We examine the role of parties in Congress in Chapter 9 and the president's party role in Chapter 10.)

Finally, there is the **party organization**—national and state party officials and workers, committee members, convention delegates, and others active in the party. The Democratic and Republican party organizations formally resemble the American federal system, with national committees, officers and staffs, and national conventions, 50 state committees, and more than 3,000 county committees with city, ward, and precinct levels under their supervision. State committees are not very responsive to the direction of the national committee; and in most states, city and county party organizations operate quite independently of the state committees. In other words, no real hierarchy of authority exists in American parties.

National Party Structure   The Democratic and Republican national party conventions possess *formal* authority over the parties. They meet every 4 years not only to nominate candidates for president and vice president but also to adopt a party platform, choose party officers, and adopt rules for the party's operation. Because the convention is a large body that meets for only 3 or 4 days, however, its real function is to ratify decisions made by national party leaders, as well as to formally nominate presidential and vice-presidential candidates.

The Democratic and Republican national committees, made up of delegates from each state and territory, are supposed to govern party affairs *between* conventions. But the *real* work of the national party organizations is undertaken by the national party chairs and staff. The national chair is officially chosen by the national committee. If the party wins the presidency, the national chair usually serves as a liaison with the president for party affairs. If the party loses, the chair may be replaced before the next national convention. The national chair is supposed to be neutral in the party's primary battles, but when an incumbent president is seeking reelection, the national chair and staff lean very heavily in the president's favor.

State Party Organizations   State party organizations consist of a state committee, a state chair who heads the committee, and a staff working at the state capital. Democratic and Republican state committees vary from state to state in composition, organization, and function. The state party chair is generally selected by the state committee, but this selection is often dictated by the

The Path to Student Power

Danielle Wipperfurth (left), of Minneapolis, Minn., gets help from Mary Jo Clark (right), as she registers to vote at Davidson College in Davidson, N.C., Thursday, April 10, 2008.

ticket splitters
Persons who vote for candidates of different parties for different offices in a general election.

party-in-the-government
Public officials who were nominated by their party and who identify themselves in office with their party.

party organization
National and state party officials and workers, committee members, convention delegates, and others active in the party.

CONTROVERSY

California to Bypass Parties

In a change that is likely to have a far-reaching effect upon the state's political parties. California voters approved a state constitutional amendment in 2010 known as Proposition 14, the Top Two Primaries Act. From now on, California primary elections will be open to all candidates and all voters, regardless of party affiliation. All candidates for major state and federal offices, including the U.S. Senate and House of Representatives, governor, and state legislature, will appear on the same primary ballot. Candidates may or may not choose to have a party affiliation next to their name on the ballot. The two candidates receiving the most votes in the primary will appear on the November general election ballot, regardless of their party affiliation, if any.

This "top two" primary system strips the parties of their central function—selecting candidates for the general election. Supporters believe that it is a cure for "partisanship," and that it reduces the power of the most loyal, interested, and active party members in the selection of candidates. No longer will Democratic candidates be obliged to espouse "liberal" positions to attract the votes of ideologically motivated activists in the Democratic primary and then shift their positions to the center for the general election. Similarly, Republican candidates will no longer have

to take "conservative" positions to appeal to GOP activists in the party's primary, only to shift to the center in the general election. All candidates will be encouraged to become "centrists" to appeal to all voters in both the primary and general elections.

The Top Two Primaries Act was placed on the ballot by a Democratic-controlled state legislature, it was supported by Republican Governor Arnold Schwarzenegger, and it was approved by a vote of 54 to 46 percent. The proposition does not apply to presidential elections. Third parties, such as the Green Party and the Libertarian Party, will not be able to access the general election ballot, unless their candidate wins one of the top two spots in the open primary.

Opponents argued unsuccessfully that Proposition 14 only "masquerades as reform," that it reinforces incumbent advantage, and that it squeezes out third parties. It limits voter choice by minimizing policy differences between candidates so that personality trumps substance. Louisiana and Washington have experimented with similar primary systems, but few believe that these states were successful in electing more moderates to office. The Top Two system may increase overall costs of running for office by requiring candidates to spend money to appeal to the full electorate in two separate elections.

party's candidate for governor. Membership on the state committee may range from about a dozen up to several hundred. The members may be chosen through party primaries or by state party conventions. Generally, representation on state committees is allocated by counties, but occasionally other units of government are recognized in state party organizations.

Most state party organizations maintain full-time staffs, including an executive director and public relations, fund-raising, and research people. These organizations help to raise campaign funds for their candidates, conduct registration drives, provide advice and services to their nominees, and even recruit candidates to run in election districts and for offices where the party would otherwise have no names on the ballot. Services to candidates may include advertising and media consulting, advice on election-law compliance, polling, research (including research on opponents), registration and voter identification, mailing lists, and even seminars on campaign techniques.

Legislative Party Structures   The parties organize the U.S. Senate and House of Representatives, and they organize most state legislatures as well. The majority party in the House meets in caucus to select the Speaker of the House as well as the House majority leader and whip (see "Organizing Congress: Party and Leadership" in Chapter 10). The minority party elects its own minority leader and whip. The majority party in the Senate elects the president pro tempore, who presides during the (frequent) absences of the vice president, as well as the Senate majority leader and whip. The minority party in the Senate elects its own minority leader and whip. Committee assignments in both the House and the Senate are allocated on a party basis; committee chairs are always majority-party members.

County Committees   The nation's 3,000 Republican and 3,000 Democratic county chairs probably constitute the most important building blocks in party organization in the nation. City and county party officers and committees are chosen in local primary elections; they cannot be removed by state or national party authorities.

National Party Conventions

▶ 7.7 *Describe changes in the function of the national party conventions.*

The Democratic and Republican parties are showcased every 4 years at the national party **convention**. The official purpose of these 4-day fun-filled events is the nomination of the presidential candidates and their vice-presidential running mates. Yet the presidential choices have usually already been made in the parties' **presidential primaries** and caucuses earlier in the year. By midsummer, delegates pledged to cast their convention vote for one or another of the presidential candidates have already been selected. Not since 1952, when the Democrats took three convention ballots to select Adlai Stevenson as their presidential candidate, has convention voting gone beyond the first ballot.[14] The possibility exists that in some future presidential race no candidate will win a majority of delegates in the primaries and caucuses, and the result will be a *brokered* convention in which delegates will exercise independent power to select the party nominee. But this event is unlikely.

The Democratic and Republican national conventions are really televised party rallies, designed to showcase the presidential nominee, confirm the nominee's choice for a running mate, and inspire television viewers to support the party and its candidates in the forthcoming general election. Indeed, the national party conventions are largely media events, carefully staged to present an attractive image of the party and its nominees. Party luminaries jockey for key time slots at the podium, and the party prepares slick videotaped commercials touting its nominee for prime-time presentation.

Convention Delegates   Convention **delegates** are generally party activists, ideologically motivated and strongly committed to their presidential candidates. Democratic delegates are much more *liberal* than Democratic voters, and Republican delegates are more *conservative* than Republican voters (see Figure 7.5). There is a slight tendency for Democratic and Republican delegates to differ in social backgrounds; usually more African Americans, women, public employees, and union members are found among Democratic delegates than among Republican delegates.

Making Party Rules   National party conventions make rules for the party, including rules governing the selection of delegates at the next party convention. Democrats are especially likely to focus on delegate selection rules. In 1972 the Democratic Party responded to charges that African Americans, women, and other minorities were underrepresented among the delegates by appointing a special commission chaired by Senator George McGovern to "reform" the party. The McGovern Commission took "affirmative steps" to ensure that the next convention would include "goals" for the representation of African Americans, women, and other minorities among the delegates in proportion to their presence

convention
Nominating process in which delegates from local party organizations select the party's nominees.

presidential primaries
Primary elections in the states in which voters in each party can choose a presidential candidate for their party's nomination. Outcomes help determine the distribution of pledged delegates to each party's national nominating convention.

delegates
Accredited voting members of a party's national presidential nominating convention.

Convention Hoopla

Flag-waving delegates from each of the states listen on the floor of the Democratic Convention in the Moscone Center, San Francisco.

in the Democratic electorate. The effect of these reforms was to reduce the influence of Democratic officeholders (members of Congress, governors, state legislators, and mayors) at the convention and to increase the influence of ideologically motivated activists. Later rule changes eliminated the *unit vote*, in which all delegates from a state were required to vote with the majority of the state's delegation and which required that all delegates who were pledged to a candidate vote for that candidate unless *released* by the candidate.

Then, in the 1980s, the Democratic Leadership Council pressed the party to reserve some convention delegate seats for **superdelegates**—elected officials and party leaders not bound to one candidate—with the expectation that these delegates would be more moderate than the liberal party activists. The notion was that the superdelegates would inject more balanced, less ideological political judgments into convention deliberations, thus improving the party's chances of victory in the general elections. As a result, many Democratic senators, governors, and members of Congress now attend the convention as superdelegates. If presidential candidates fail to win a majority of delegates in the primaries and caucus, these superdelegates may control a nomination.

superdelegates
Delegates to the Democratic Party national convention selected because of their position in the government or the party and not pledged to any candidate.

platform
Statement of principles adopted by a political party at its national convention (specific portions of the platform are known as planks); a platform is not binding on the party's candidates.

Party Platforms   National conventions also write party platforms, setting out the party's goals and policy positions. Because a party's **platform** is not binding on its nominees, platform *planks* are largely symbolic, although they often

FIGURE 7.5

Ideologies of Party Activists Compared to Voters

Democratic and Republican party activists (convention delegates in 2000) are far more likely to hold divergent liberal and conservative views than voters generally.

Source: As reported in the *New York Times*, August 14, 2000.

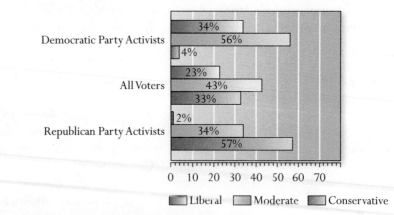

provide heated arguments and provide distinct differences between the parties to present to voters (see *Politics Up Close*: "Democratic and Republican Platforms").

Selecting a Running Mate
Perhaps the only suspense remaining in national party conventions centers on the presidential nominee's choice of a vice-presidential running mate. Even a presidential candidate who has decided on a running mate well in advance of the convention may choose to wait until the convention to announce the choice, otherwise there would be little real "news value" to the convention, and the television networks would give less coverage to it. By encouraging speculation about who the running mate will be, the candidate and the convention manager can sustain media interest. (For a discussion of various strategies in selecting a running mate, see "The Vice-Presidential Waiting Game" in Chapter 11.)

The convention *always* accepts the presidential candidate's recommendation for a running mate. No formal rules require the convention to do so, but it would be politically unacceptable for the convention to override the first important decision of the party's presidential nominee. Convention delegates set aside any personal reservations they may have and unanimously endorse the presidential nominee's choice.

Campaign Kickoff
The final evening of the national conventions is really the kickoff for the general election campaign. The presidential nominee's acceptance speech tries to set the tone for the fall campaign. Party celebrities, including defeated presidential candidates, join hands at the podium as a symbol of party unity. Presidential and vice-presidential candidates, spouses, and families assemble under balloons and streamers, amid the happy noise and hoopla, to signal the start of the general election campaign. TV coverage helps provide the parties with small postconvention "bumps" in the polls.[15]

Party Voters

▶ 7.8 *Assess the trends regarding party identification and loyalty of voters.*

Traditionally, the Democratic Party has been able to claim to be the majority party in the United States (see Figure 7.6). In opinion polls, those who "identify" with the Democratic Party generally outnumber those who "identify" with the

Barack Obama, 2008 Democratic presidential nominee. The smiling candidate accepts the Democratic Party nomination following the longest primary battle in modern history. His opponent, Hillary Clinton, would later accept appointment as Secretary of State.

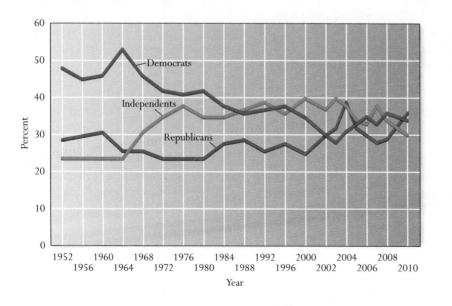

FIGURE 7.6
Party Identification in the Electorate

For many years, the Democratic Party enjoyed a substantial lead in party identification among voters. This Democratic lead eroded in the late 1960s as more people began to identify themselves as Independents. The electorate turned substantially more Republican in the 2010 congressional elections.

Source: Data from *National Election Studies*, University of Michigan, updated from Gallup Polls.

POLITICS UP CLOSE

Democratic and Republican Platforms: Can You Tell the Difference?

Iraq

A. "To renew American leadership in the world, we would first bring the Iraq war to a responsible end."

B. "The outcome is too critical to our own national security to be jeopardized by artificial or politically inspired timetables that neither reflect conditions on the ground nor respect the essential advice of our military commanders."

Taxes

A. "For families making more than $250,000 we will ask them to give back a portion of the Bush tax cuts to invest in health care and other key priorities."

B. "Along with making the 2001 and 2003 tax cuts permanent so American families will not face a large tax hike, we will advance tax policies to support American families."

Abortion

A. "We strongly and unequivocally support *Roe v. Wade* and a woman's right to choose a safe and legal abortion regardless of ability to pay."

B. "We assert the inherent dignity and sanctity of all human life and affirm that the unborn child has a fundamental right to life which cannot be infringed."

Energy

A. "We know we can't drill our way to energy independence."

B. "We support accelerated exploration, drilling and development of the nation's coasts and onshore fields."

Immigration

A. "Allow immigrants who pay taxes and don't have trouble with the law a path to earn the opportunities and responsibilities of citizenship."

B. "We oppose amnesty. The rule of law suffers if government policies encourage or reward illegal activity."

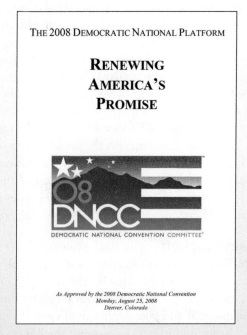

THE 2008 DEMOCRATIC NATIONAL PLATFORM

RENEWING AMERICA'S PROMISE

08 DNCC
DEMOCRATIC NATIONAL CONVENTION COMMITTEE®

*As Approved by the 2008 Democratic National Convention
Monday, August 25, 2008
Denver, Colorado*

Other

A. "We support equal rights to democratic self-government and congressional representation for the citizens of our nation's capital."

B. "Judicial activism is a grave threat to the rule of law because unaccountable federal judges are usurping democracy, ignoring the Constitution and its separation of powers, and imposing their personal opinions upon the public."

A. "The key is to make tough choices, in particular, pay-as-you-go budgetary rules."

B. "We favor adoption of the Balanced Budget Amendment [to the Constitution] to require a balanced budget except in time of war."

Source: Excerpts from Democratic [A] and Republican [B] party platforms, 2008.

---

party identification
Self-described identification with a political party, usually in response to the question, "Generally speaking, how would you identify yourself: as a Republican, Democrat, Independent, or something else?"

Republican Party. (**Party identification** is determined by response to the question, "Generally speaking, how would you identify yourself: as a Republican, Democrat, Independent, or something else?") But the Democratic Party advantage among the voters eroded over time, partly as a result of a gradual increase in the number of people who call themselves Independents.

Dealignment   Dealignment describes the decline in attractiveness of the political parties to the voters, the growing reluctance of people to identify themselves with either party, and a decrease in reliance on a candidate's party affiliation in voter choice. Dealignment is evident not only in the growing numbers of self-described Independents, but also in the declining numbers of those who identify themselves as "strong" Democrats or Republicans. In short, the electorate is less partisan than it once was.

Party Loyalty in Voting   Despite the decline in partisan identification in the electorate, it is important to note that *party identification is a strong influence in voter choice in elections*. Most voters cast their ballot for the candidate of their party. This is true in presidential elections (see Figure 7.7) and even more true in congressional and state elections. Republican Ronald Reagan was able to win more

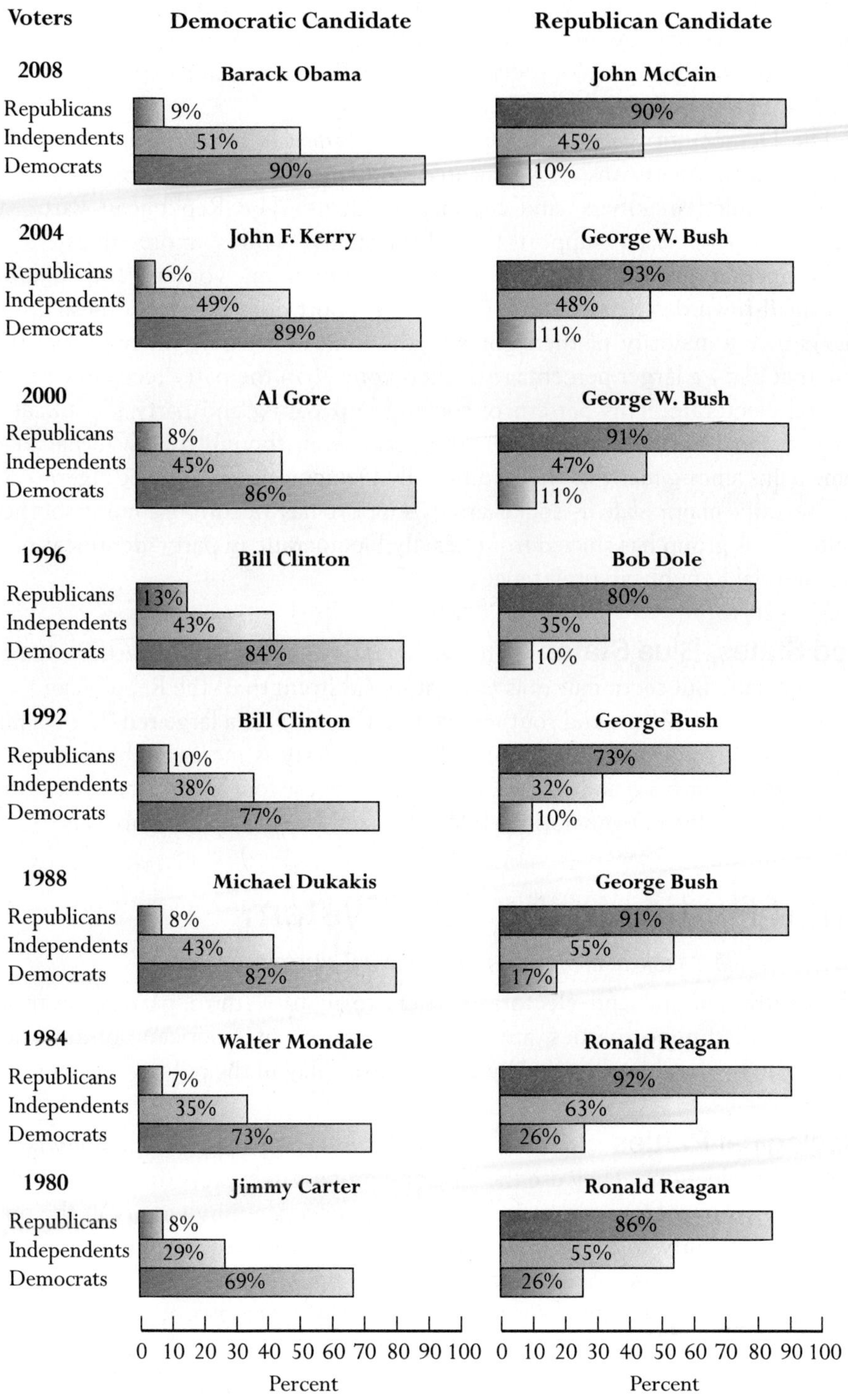

dealignment
Declining attractiveness of the parties to the voters, a reluctance to identify strongly with a party, and a decrease in reliance on party affiliation in voter choice.

FIGURE 7.7

Who Voted How?: Republican, Democratic, and Independent Voters in Presidential Elections

As the percentages here indicate, in recent years registered Democrats have been more likely to "cross over" and vote for a Republican candidate for president than registered Republicans have been to vote for the Democratic presidential candidate.

Source: New York Times.

than one-quarter of self-identified Democrats in 1980 and 1984, earning these crossover voters the label "Reagan Democrats."[16]

Realignment?

Realignment?   Although Democratic Party loyalty has eroded over the last 30 years, it is not clear whether or not this erosion is a classic party **realignment**.[17] Most scholars agree that party realignments occurred in the presidential elections of 1824 (Jackson, Democrats), 1860 (Lincoln, Republicans), 1896 (Bryan, Democrats), and 1932 (Roosevelt, Democrats). This historical sequence gave rise to a theory that realigning elections occur every 36 years. According to this theory, the election of 1968 should have been a realigning one. It is true that Richard Nixon's 1968 victory marked the beginning of a 24-year Republican era in presidential election victories that was broken only by Jimmy Carter in 1976. But there was relatively little shifting of the party loyalties of major social groups, and the Democratic Party remained the dominant party in the electorate and in Congress.

The Democratic Party still receives *disproportionate* support from Catholics, Jews, African Americans, less-educated and lower-income groups, blue-collar workers, union members, and big-city residents. The Republican Party still receives *disproportionate* support from Protestants, whites, more-educated and higher-income groups, white-collar workers, nonunion workers, and suburban and small-town dwellers. Disproportionate support does not mean these groups *always* give a majority of their votes to the indicated party, but only that they give that party a larger percentage of their votes than the party receives from the general electorate. This pattern of social-group voting and party identification has remained relatively stable over the years, even though the GOP has made some gains among many of the traditionally Democratic groups (see Figure 7.8).

The only major *shift* in social-group support has occurred among southern whites. This group has shifted from heavily Democratic in party identification to a substantial Republican preference.

Red States, Blue States

Red States, Blue States   The Democratic and Republican parties compete in every state. But sectionalism is evident in the strength of the Republican Party in the mountain, plains, and southern states. The result is a large red "L" on a map of the states (see Figure 7.9). The Democratic Party is increasingly bicoastal—strong in the Northeast and on the Pacific Coast. Of the four largest states, California and New York lean Democratic, while Texas and Florida lean Republican.

Third Parties in the U.S. System

▶ *7.9 Evaluate the role of third parties within the U.S. electoral system.*

Despite the cultural and electoral barriers to victory, **third parties**, more accurately called minor parties, are a common feature of American politics. These parties can be roughly classified by the role they play in the political system.

Ideological Parties

Ideological Parties   **Ideological parties** exist to promote an ideology rather than to win elections. They use the electoral process to express their views and to rally activists to their cause, and they measure success not by victory at the polls but by their ability to bring their names and their views to the attention of the American public. The socialist parties, which have run candidates in virtually every presidential election in this century, are prime examples of ideological parties in the United States.

---

realignment
Long-term shift in social-group support for various political parties that creates new coalitions in each party.

Think Again

Do we need a third party to challenge the Republican and Democratic parties?

third parties
Political parties that challenge the two major parties in an election.

ideological parties
Third parties that exist to promote an ideology rather than to win elections.

Family Income

Family Income	Democrat	Republican
Under $10,000	42%	9%
$10–19,000	51%	17%
$20–29,000	38%	16%
$30–49,000	41%	26%
$50,000 and over	29%	38%

Religion

Religion	Democrat	Republican
Protestant	30%	42%
Catholic	38%	27%
Jewish	66%	19%
Other	43%	21%

Race

Race	Democrat	Republican
White	29%	34%
Black	72%	3%
Other	46%	14%

Education

Education	Democrat	Republican
Grade 8 or less	59%	22%
Some high school	41%	15%
High school graduate	37%	24%
Some college	33%	27%
College graduate	32%	39%
Advanced degree	39%	34%

☐ Democrat   ■ Republican

FIGURE 7.8

Who Backs Whom?: Social-Group Support for the Democratic and Republican Parties

The Democratic Party draws disproportionate support from low-income, less-educated, Catholic, Jewish, and African American voters. The Republican Party relies more heavily on support from high-income, college-educated, white Protestant voters.

Note: Independents not shown.

Source: Data from the 2008 National Election Studies, University of Michigan. Compiled by Professor Terri Towner, Oakland University.

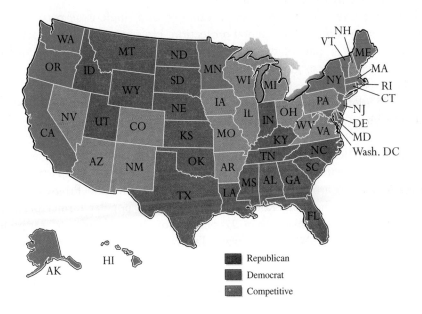

FIGURE 7.9

Red States, Blue States

Republican leaning states are traditionally shown in red, while Demoractic leaning states are shown in blue. The Democratic Party is strongest in the Northeast and West Coast. The GOP fares better in the Southern and Midwestern states.

■ Republican
■ Democrat
▨ Competitive

protest parties
Third parties that arise in response to issues of popular concern which have not been addressed by the major parties.

Protest Parties

Protest parties arise around popular issues or concerns that the major parties have failed to address. An important historical example of a protest party is the Populist Party of the late 1800s. It arose as a protest by Midwestern farmers against eastern railroads, "trusts" and monopolies, and the gold standard. The Populists threatened to capture the wave of popular support for railroad regulation, cheap money, and anti-monopoly legislation, and thus they endangered the established Democratic and Republican parties. But when the Democratic Party nominated William Jennings Bryan in 1896, the Populist Party officially endorsed Bryan and temporarily disappeared as a significant independent political organization. Populist ideas were set forth again in a new Progressive Party, which nominated Robert M. La Follette for president in 1924; the Democratic and Republican parties both nominated conservative candidates that year, helping La Follette to win almost 17 percent of the popular vote.

Not all major protest movements have been accompanied by the formation of third parties. Indeed, protest leaders have often argued that a third-party effort distracts the movement from a more effective strategy of capturing control of one or both of the major parties. The labor-union-organizing movement of the 1930s and the civil rights and anti-war movements of the 1960s did not spark a separate third party but instead worked largely *within* the Democratic Party to advance their goals. Recent "Tea Party" protesters work largely in the Republican Party (see *Controversy:* "The Tea Party Protests").

single-issue parties
Third parties formed around one particular cause.

Single-Issue Parties

Single-issue parties have frequently formed around a particular cause. Single-issue parties are much like protest parties, although somewhat narrower in their policy focus. The Greenback Party of the late 1800s shared with the Populists a desire for cheap inflated currency in order to ease the burden of debt and mortgage payments by farmers. But the Greenback Party focused on a single remedy: an end to the gold standard and the issuance of cheap currency—"greenbacks."

Perhaps the most persistent of minor parties over the years has been the Prohibition Party. It achieved temporary success with the passage of the 18th Amendment to the U.S. Constitution in 1919, which prohibited the manufacture, sale, or transportation of "intoxicating liquors," only to see its "noble experiment" fail and be repealed by the 21st Amendment.

Today the Green Party provides an example of a single-issue party, with its primary emphasis on environmental protection. However, the Green Party itself contends that it is "part of the worldwide movement that promotes ecological wisdom, social justice, grassroots democracy and non-violence." Ralph Nader was the Green Party presidential candidate in 2000; he won about 2 percent of the vote. Nader's critics claimed that he helped Republican George W. Bush win that election by siphoning off votes from Democrat Al Gore.

splinter parties
Third parties formed by a dissatisfied faction of a major party.

Splinter Parties

Finally, many third parties in American politics are really **splinter parties**, parties formed by a dissatisfied faction of a major party. Splinter parties may form around a particular individual, as did the Progressive (Bull Moose) Party of Theodore Roosevelt in 1912. As a popular former president, Teddy Roosevelt won more than 27 percent of the popular vote, outpolling Republican candidate William Howard Taft but allowing Democrat Woodrow Wilson to win the presidency.

Splinter parties also may emerge from an intense intraparty policy dispute. For example, in 1948 the States' Rights (Dixiecrat) Party formed in protest to the civil rights (fair employment practices) plank in the Democratic Party platform of that year and nominated Strom Thurmond for president. In 1968 George Wallace's

CONTROVERSY

The Tea Party Protests

The "Tea Party" protest movement seeks to evoke the image of the 1773 Boston Tea Party of the American Revolution and the early patriots' opposition to excessive taxation and repressive government. Tea Party protests first appeared as grassroots outcries against President Barack Obama's massive health care plan. Over time they attracted a wide variety of people opposed to big government, Wall Street bailouts, stimulus spending, exploding deficits, and tax increases. (The letters T E A reportedly stand for Taxed Enough Already.) Tea Party protests have often been held on key dates, including the Fourth of July and Tax Day, April 15.

There is no officially recognized Tea Party. It does not nominate candidates and does not appear on the ballot in any state. Supporters claim that it is a grassroots protest movement, originating out of popular frustration with government in Washington. Critics note that Fox News regularly features Tea Party protests and demonstrations and that these activities appear to be coordinated throughout the nation. Several national organizations (Tea Party Nation, Tea Party Express, Tea Party Patriots) have attempted to co-opt the Tea Party banner.

Tea Party protesters frequently express their contempt for all incumbent politicians, both Democrats and Republicans. But most of the Tea Party protesters' political activity has focused on the Republican Party, including support for GOP candidates espousing protest themes. Tea partiers are ideologically hostile to liberal Democrats.

Protesting Big Government

Tea Party protesters express their opposition to big government, corporate bailouts, stimulus spending, exploding deficits, and tax increases. Most are active within the Republican Party.

American Independent Party won nearly 14 percent of the popular vote. Wallace attacked school desegregation and busing to achieve racial balance in schools, as well as crime in the streets, welfare "cheats," and meddling federal judges and bureaucrats. He abandoned his third-party organization in 1972 to run in the Democratic presidential primary elections. Following some Democratic primary victories, he was shot and disabled for life.

An Anti-Party Party   Many Americans feel disgusted with "politics as usual." They view both the Democratic and Republican parties as ineffective, unprincipled, and even corrupt. They represent a dealignment from the current party system; that is, they have no party loyalty and they usually describe themselves as "Independents." In 1992 Texas billionaire Ross Perot was able to mobilize many of these Independents into a third-party challenge to the two-party system. He spent nearly $100 million of his own money to build a nationwide organization, the Reform Party (originally called United We Stand) and to place his name on the ballot of all fifty states. Early in the campaign his poll numbers mushroomed to 35 percent, higher than any other independent candidate's support in the history of modem polling. His political support came mostly from the center of the political spectrum—people who identified themselves as Independents. Perot participated in the first three-way presidential television debates and won 19 percent of the popular vote in the general election, the highest percentage won by a third-party

A Dissenting Voice
Ralph Nader, the nation's most visible interest-group entrepreneur, continues his fight against auto companies, speaking here to Toledo residents unhappy with tax breaks given to Daimler-Chrysler to keep its plant in the city. In the 2000 presidential election, Nader was the Green Party's nominee. In 2004 and again in 2008, he ran as an Independent.

candidate since Teddy Roosevelt in 1912. But he failed to win a single electoral vote. Perot ran again in 1996, but when his early poll numbers languished, he was excluded from the presidential debates. On Election Day he won fewer than half of the votes (9 percent) that he had garnered 4 years earlier, and again failed to win any state's electoral votes. In 2000 the Reform Party imploded in a raucous convention, with rival factions almost coming to blows over control of the microphone. The party officially nominated conservative firebrand Pat Buchanan, but Buchanan's right-wing rhetoric attracted less than 1 percent of the voters. By 2004 many states had dropped the Reform Party from their ballots.

Third-Party Prospects   In recent years, polls have reported that a majority of Americans favor the idea of a third party. But support for the *general* idea of a third party has never been matched by voter support for *specific* third-party or Independent presidential candidates (see Table 7.4).[18] Moreover, it is very difficult for a third party or Independent candidate to win electoral votes. Only Theodore

TABLE 7.4 Opposing the Two-Party System: Twentieth-Century Third-Party Presidential Votes

Independent and third-party presidential candidates have failed to win any electoral votes over the last 40 years.

Third-Party Presidential Candidates	Popular Vote (percentage)	Electoral Votes (number)
Theodore Roosevelt (1912), Progressive (Bull Moose) Party	27.4%	88
Robert M. La Follette (1924), Progressive Party	16.6	13
George C. Wallace (1968), American Independent Party	13.5	46
John Anderson (1980), Independent	6.6	0
Ross Perot (1992), Independent	18.9	0
Ross Perot (1996), Reform Party	8.5	0
Ralph Nader (2000), Green Party	2.7	0
Ralph Nader (2004), Independent	0.4	0
Ralph Nader (2008), Independent	0.4	0

COMPARED TO WHAT?

Proportional Representation

A proportional representation electoral system differs significantly from the single-member, winner-take-all system used in United States. Proportional representation (PR) grants seats in a governing body to political parties in proportion to the number of votes they receive in elections. This ensures that minority voices will be given some influence in the legislature.

In most PR countries, political parties draw up lists of their candidates for the legislature prior to the election. Voters then cast their ballots for the party list of their choice. The voting district may be the nation as a whole, or individual states or provinces. When all the votes are counted, each party is allocated seats in the legislature in proportion to the votes received. For example, if Party A received 55 percent of the total votes, then Party A would be allocated 55 percent of the seats in the legislature. Party A's seats would be filled from the top of the party list down; the listing of names is determined by the party itself, with the party leadership usually at the top of the list. If Party B received 45 percent of the vote, it would be allowed to fill only 45 percent of the seats from its party list.

Proportional representation encourages multiple minor parties to enter the electoral fray. A party that can claim the support of 10 percent of the voters can win 10 percent of the legislative seats. The multiplication of parties in a PR election often results in no party receiving a majority of the vote and therefore no party winning a majority of the legislative body. In such cases, a coalition of parties must be formed in order to gain a majority in the legislature. This is particularly troublesome in a parliamentary system where a majority is required to select the prime minister and cabinet (see *Compared to What?:* "The Parliamentary System" in Chapter 10).

Roosevelt, Robert M. La Follette, and George C. Wallace managed to win any electoral votes in the past century. The Reform Party, founded by billionaire Ross Perot in 1992, was the latest serious yet unsuccessful attempt to create a nationwide third party.

Why the Two-Party System Persists

▶ **7.10** *Determine why the American two-party system has persisted.*

The two-party system is deeply ingrained in American politics. Although third parties have often made appearances in presidential elections, no third-party candidate has ever won the Oval Office. (Lincoln's new Republican Party in 1860 might be counted as an exception, but it quickly became a major party.) Very few third-party candidates have won seats in Congress. Many other democracies have multiple-party systems, so the question arises as to why the United States has had a two-party system throughout its history.[19]

Cultural Consensus   One explanation of the nation's continuing two-party system focuses on the broad consensus supporting the American political culture (see Chapter 2). The values of democracy, capitalism, free enterprise, individual liberty, religious freedom, and equality of opportunity are so widely shared that no party challenging these values has ever won much of a following. There is little support in the American political culture for avowedly fascist, communist, authoritarian, or other anti-democratic parties. Moreover, the American political culture includes a strong belief in the separation of church and state. Political parties with religious affiliations, common in European democracies, are absent from American politics. Socialist parties have frequently appeared on the scene under various labels—the Socialist Party, the Socialist Labor Party, and the Socialist Workers Party. But the largest popular vote ever garnered by a socialist candidate in a presidential election was the 6 percent won by Eugene V. Debs in 1912. In contrast, socialist parties have frequently won control of European governments.

A CONSTITUTIONAL NOTE

Political Parties and the Constitution

Political parties had not yet formed in 1787 when the Founders met in Philadelphia to draft the Constitution. Indeed, George Washington and other Founders believed that the new nation might be destroyed by the "baneful effects of the spirit of party." Nowhere in the Constitution do we find any reference to "parties." Indeed, the original Constitution called for presidential electors to cast two votes for president, with the candidate receiving the highest number becoming president and the candidate with the second-highest becoming vice president. But by 1800 parties had formed: the Federalists rallied around John Adams, the second president; and the Democratic-Republicans (often called Republicans, but not to be confused with today's Republican Party) supported Thomas Jefferson. Candi-

dates for the Electoral College ran under these labels (or sometimes as just Adams's men or Jefferson's men). In the 1800 presidential election the Democratic-Republican party won a majority of electors. But all of them had cast their votes for both Jefferson and his intended vice president Aaron Burr. Thus Jefferson and Burr ended up with the same number of electoral votes, 73, for president. For a while, Burr considered challenging Jefferson for president, but in the end conceded the office. The incident illustrated the failure of the Founders to envision parties as central to the electoral process. Congress and the states were obliged to add the 12th Amendment to the Constitution by 1804 in order to separate "in distinct ballots" the persons voted for as president and vice president.

On broad policy issues, most Americans cluster near the center. This general consensus tends to discourage multiple parties. There does not appear to be sufficient room for them to stake out a position on the ideological spectrum that would detach voters from the two major parties.

This cultural explanation blends with the influence of historical precedents. The American two-party system has gained acceptance through custom. The nation's first party system developed from two coalitions, Federalists and Anti-Federalists, and this dual pattern has been reinforced over two centuries.

Winner-Takes-All Electoral System   Yet another explanation of the American two-party system focuses on the electoral system itself. Winners in presidential and congressional elections, as well as in state gubernatorial and legislative elections, are usually determined by a plurality, winner-takes-all vote. Even in elections that require a majority of more than 50 percent to win—which may involve a runoff election—only one party's candidate wins in the end. Because of the winner-takes-all nature of U.S. elections, parties and candidates have an overriding incentive to broaden their appeal to a plurality or majority of voters. Losers come away empty-handed. There is not much incentive in such a system for a party to form to represent the views of 5 or 10 percent of the electorate.

Americans are so accustomed to winner-takes-all elections that they seldom consider alternatives. In some countries, legislative bodies are elected by **proportional representation**, whereby all voters cast a single ballot for the party of their choice and legislative seats are then apportioned to the parties in proportion to their total vote in the electorate (see also *Compared to What?*: "Proportional Representation"). Minority parties are assured of legislative seats, perhaps with as little as 10 or 15 percent of the vote. If no party wins 50 percent of the votes and seats, the parties try to form a coalition of parties to establish control of the government. In these nations, party coalition building to form a governing majority occurs *after* the election rather than *before* the election, as it does in winner-takes-all election systems.

proportional representation
Electoral system that allocates seats in a legislature based on the proportion of votes each party receives in a national election.

Legal Access to the Ballot   Another factor in the American two-party system may be electoral system barriers to third parties. The Democratic and

Republican nominees are automatically included on all general election ballots, but third-party and Independent candidates face difficult obstacles in getting their names listed. In presidential elections, a third-party candidate must meet the varied requirements of fifty separate states to appear on their ballots along with the Democratic and Republican nominees. These requirements often include filing petitions signed by up to 5 or 10 percent of registered voters. In addition, states require third parties to win 5 or 10 percent of the vote in the last election in order to retain their position on the ballot in subsequent elections. In 1980 Independent John Anderson gained access to the ballot in all fifty states, as did Independent Ross Perot in 1992. But just doing so required a considerable expenditure of effort and money that the major parties were able to avoid.

Summary

▶ **7.1** *Show how the relationship between organization and political power explains political parties and interest groups.*

In the political arena organization grants advantage. Political parties organize people in order to give them power in selecting government officials. Interest groups and political parties act as intermediaries between individuals and the government. Political parties compete for office and interest groups attempt to influence the making of public policy.

▶ **7.2** *Trace changes in political parties over the course of American history.*

Political parties are not mentioned in the U.S. Constitution, yet they have played a central role in American political history. Major party realignments have occurred at critical points in American history, as major social groups shifted their political loyalties.

▶ **7.3** *Outline functions of political parties as "responsible" organizations and perceptions of the two major American political parties.*

In theory, political parties are "responsible" organizations that adopt a principled platform, recruit candidates who support the platform, educate the public about it, direct an issue-oriented campaign, and then legislate and ensure that their candidates enact the party's platform.

▶ **7.4** *Explain how the two major American political parties are financed.*

Political parties and candidates raise hundreds of millions of dollars each election year. Traditionally, the Republicans were able to raise more money than the Democrats but the gap between the two parties has narrowed in recent years. The Republicans usually have the support of the health care, insurance, manufacturing, and oil and gas interests, while the Democrats enjoy the support of teachers, union members, and the TV, movie, and music industries.

▶ **7.5** *Assess the changing role of the political parties in the electoral process.*

American parties have lost many of their traditional functions over time. Party nominations are won by individual candidates in primary elections rather than through selection by party leaders. Most political candidates are self-selected; they organize their own campaigns. Television has replaced the party as the principal means of educating the public. And governmental bureaucracies, not party machines, provide social services.

Party nominations are won in primary elections as earlier caucus and convention methods of nomination have largely disappeared. Party primary elections in the various states may be open or closed and may or may not require runoff primaries. The nominees selected in each party's primary election then battle each other in the general election.

▶ **7.6** *Differentiate the three political arenas in which the parties battle.*

The parties battle in three major arenas. The *party-in-the-electorate* refers to party identification among voters. The *party-in-government* refers to party identification and organization among elected officials. The *party organization* refers to party offices at the local, state, and national levels.

▶ **7.7** *Describe changes in the function of the national party conventions.*

Since presidential nominations are now generally decided in primary elections—with pledged delegates selected before the opening of the national conventions and with party platforms largely symbolic and wholly unenforceable on the candidates—the conventions have become largely media events designed to kick off the general election.

▶ **7.8** *Assess the trends regarding party identification and loyalty of voters.*

Dealignment refers to a decline in the attractiveness of the parties to voters, a growing reluctance of people to identify strongly with either party, and greater voter willingness to cross party lines. Despite dealignment, party identification remains a strong influence in voter choice.

▶ **7.9** *Evaluate the role of third parties within the U.S. electoral system.*

Opinion polls indicate that most Americans support the general idea of a third party, but throughout the twentieth century no third-party candidate won very many votes.

▶ **7.10** *Determine why the American two-party system has persisted.*

In the United States, many aspects of the political system—including cultural consensus, the winner-take-all electoral system, and legal restriction to ballot access—place major obstacles in the way of success for third parties and Independent candidates. Although never successful at gaining federal office in significant numbers, ideological, protest, single-issue, and splinter third parties have often been effective at getting popular issues on the federal agenda.

Chapter Test

▶ **7.1** *Show how the relationship between organization and political power explains political parties and interest groups.*

1. Both political parties and interest groups
   a. are interested in winning political office
   b. are focused on ideology and policy
   c. function as intermediaries between individuals and government
   d. are bound by very formal divisions of functions

▶ **7.2** *Trace changes in political parties over the course of American history.*

2. Many of the people who were opposed to ratifying the new Constitution were called
   a. Republicans
   b. Federalists
   c. Whigs
   d. Anti-Federalists

3. The present-day Democratic Party grew out of the
   a. Federalists
   b. Democratic-Republicans
   c. Whigs
   d. Anti-Whigs

4. The New Deal Democratic Party was a coalition of all *but* which of the following groups?
   a. southern whites
   b. the wealthy
   c. union members
   d. African Americans

▶ **7.3** *Outline functions of political parties as "responsible" organizations and perceptions of the two major American political parties.*

5. A "responsible party" is expected to do all *but* which of the following functions?
   a. Recruit candidates who agree with the party platform
   b. Hold elected officials accountable
   c. Adopt a platform stating the party principles
   d. Win office by compromising principles.

6. It would be accurate to say that Republicans are perceived as
   a. liberals who want less government
   b. conservatives who want less government
   c. liberals who want more government
   d. conservatives who want more government

▶ **7.4** *Explain how the two major American political parties are financed.*

7. A large source of financial contributions for *both* political parties would be all of the following groups *except*
   a. law firms
   b. public sector unions
   c. local governments
   d. securities and investment firms

8. It would be accurate to say that Democrats can usually rely on _____ for financial support.
   a. insurance companies
   b. the oil and gas industry
   c. general contractors
   d. teachers unions

▶ **7.5** *Assess the changing role of the political parties in the electoral process.*

9. A nominating process in which the party members select delegates to conventions is called a
   a. nonpartisan election
   b. caucus
   c. closed primary
   d. open primary

10. Today the _____ have largely replaced conventions as the means of selecting nominees for public office.
    a. nonpartisan elections
    b. caucuses
    c. primary elections
    d. general elections

11. The principal institution that takes responsibility for organizing elections is/are the
    a. Congress
    b. Federal Elections Administration Authority
    c. political parties
    d. National Election Commission

▶ 7.6 *Differentiate the three political arenas in which the parties battle.*

12. The "real work" of the national party organization is undertaken by the
    a. president of each party
    b. governors of each state
    c. Congress's Political Parties Committee
    d. National Party Chairs and staff

▶ 7.7 *Describe changes in the function of the national party conventions.*

13. It would be correct to contend that
    a. party convention delegates are not ideologically motivated
    b. union members are more likely to be Democratic delegates rather than Republican delegates
    c. Republican delegates tend to be more liberal than Republican voters
    d. Democratic delegates tend to be more conservative than Democratic voters

14. "Superdelegates" are
    a. from one of the big population (e.g., California, Texas, and New York) states
    b. the Democratic delegates from the big population states
    c. delegates that are chosen because of their positions in the party and/or the government
    d. the "fat cats" who deliver large contributions to the party

▶ 7.8 *Assess the trends regarding party identification and loyalty of voters.*

15. It would be accurate to state that
    a. John McCain got about 90 percent of the Republican vote in 2008

    b. about 50 percent of African Americans identify with the Republican Party
    c. more Independents voted for John McCain than Barack Obama
    d. all of the above

16. It would be accurate to say that
    a. Texas leans Republican
    b. California leans Democratic
    c. New York leans Democratic
    d. all of the above

▶ 7.9 *Evaluate the role of third parties within the U.S. electoral system.*

17. Minority parties have a better chance of gaining some legislative seats in a
    a. single-party system
    b. proportional representation system
    c. two-party system
    d. super primary state

▶ 7.10 *Determine why the American two-party system has persisted.*

18. An electoral system that allocates seats on the basis of the percentage of votes received is referred to as
    a. single-member representation
    b. a republic
    c. a winner-takes-all system
    d. proportional representation

---

mypoliscilab EXERCISES

Apply what you learned in this chapter on MyPoliSciLab.

📖 **Read** on **mypoliscilab.com**
   eText: Chapter 7

✔ **Study** and **Review** on **mypoliscilab.com**
   Pre-Test
   Post-Test
   Chapter Exam
   Flashcards

👁 **Watch** on **mypoliscilab.com**
   Video: Republicans and Democrats Divide on Tax Cut
   Video: Senator Specter Switches Parties
   Video: Green Party Candidates Stay on Ballot

Video: New Ballots Bring New Complications in New York
Video: Tea Party Victories Concern for GOP

✳ **Explore** on **mypoliscilab.com**
   Simulation: You Are a Campaign Manager: Help McCain Win Swing States and Swing Voters
   Comparative: Comparing Political Parties
   Timeline: The Evolution of Political Parties in the United States
   Timeline: Third Parties in American History
   Visual Literacy: State Control and National Platforms

Key Terms

Suggested Readings

Hershey, Marjorie. *Party Politics in America*. 13th ed. New York: Longman, 2008. An authoritative text on the American party system—party organizations, the parties-in-government, and the parties-in-the-electorate.

Downs, Anthony. *An Economic Theory of Democracy*. New York: Harper & Row, 1957. The classic work describing rational choice winning strategies for political parties and explaining why there is no incentive for vote-maximizing parties in a two-party system to adopt widely separate policy positions.

Hetherington, Marc J., and Bruce A. Larson. *Parties, Politics, and Public Policy in America*. 11th ed. Washington, D.C.: CQ Press, 2009. A comprehensive survey of American political parties, from the nominating process to campaign finance and the changing affiliations of voters.

Lowi, Theodore E., and Joseph Romange. *Debating the Two Party System*. Boulder, Colo.: Rowman & Littlefield, 1997. Lowi argues that the two-party system is no longer adequate to represent the people of a diverse nation; Romange counters that two parties help unify the country and instruct Americans about the value of compromise.

Wattenberg, Martin P. *The Decline of American Political Parties, 1952–1992*. Cambridge, Mass.: Harvard University Press, 1994. An authoritative discussion of increasing negative attitudes toward the parties and the growing dealignment in the electorate.

White, John Kenneth, and Daniel M. Shen. *New Party Politics*. 2nd ed. Belmont, Calif.: Wadsworth, 2004. Historical approach to evolution of the American party system.

Suggested Web Sites

Center for Responsive Politics www.opensecrets.org
  Source of information on campaign finances—contributors, recipients, PACs, lobbyists, and so forth.

Democratic Leadership Council/New Democrats Online www.ndol.org
  Moderate Democrats in the House and Senate set forth their views.

Democratic Party Web Site of the Democratic National Committee (DNC) www.democrats.org
  With news, press releases, policy positions, and so forth.

Franklin D. Roosevelt (FDR) Heritage Center www.fdrheritage.org
  Biography on F.D.R. and information on the New Deal.

Libertarian Party www.lp.org
  This Web site reflects the Libertarian Party's strong ideological commitments to individual liberty, free markets, and nonintervention in world affairs.

MoveOn www.moveon.org
  Web site of the liberal political action committee.

The Polling Report www.pollingreport.com
Up-to-date polling information from a variety of polls on Democratic and Republican party preferences.

Reagan Information Page www.presidentreagan.info
Web site celebrating Reagan's presidential achievements.

Reform Party www.reformparty.org
The Reform Party site provides information about founder Ross Perot and the principles of and news about the party.

Republican Party Web Site of the Republican National Committee (RNC) www.rnc.org
With GOP news, press releases, policy positions, and so forth.

Chapter Test Answer Key

1. C	4. B	7. B	10. C	13. B	16. D
2. D	5. D	8. D	11. C	14. C	17. B
3. B	6. B	9. C	12. D	15. A	18. D

8 CAMPAIGNS AND ELECTIONS
Deciding Who Governs

66 Any elite which fails to coincide with prosperity and victory may be rejected by the masses. 99

Harold Lasswell

Chapter Outline and Learning Objectives

Elections in a Democracy
▶ 8.1 *Evaluate the role of elections in American democracy.*

Power and Ambition
▶ 8.2 *Characterize the various factors that motivate people to pursue a political career.*

The Advantages of Incumbency
▶ 8.3 *Explain the advantages of incumbency.*

Campaign Strategies
▶ 8.4 *Identify the main components of campaign strategies.*

How Much Does It Cost to Get Elected?
▶ 8.5 *Analyze the role of money in campaigns.*

Raising Campaign Cash
▶ 8.6 *Identify the major sources of funding for political campaigns.*

What Do Contributors "Buy"?
▶ 8.7 *Assess the motivations of contributors to political campaigns.*

Regulating Campaign Finance
▶ 8.8 *Evaluate efforts to regulate campaigns finances.*

The Presidential Campaign: The Primary Race
▶ 8.9 *Outline candidates' strategies for primary races.*

The Presidential Campaign: The General Election Battle
▶ 8.10 *Outline candidates' strategies for the general election.*

The Voter Decides
▶ 8.11 *Assess influences on voters' choices.*

Elections in a Democracy

▶ 8.1 *Evaluate the role of elections in American democracy.*

Democratic government is government by "the consent of the governed." Elections give practical meaning to this notion of "consent." Elections allow people to choose among competing candidates and parties and to decide who will occupy public office. Elections give people the opportunity to pass judgment on current officeholders, either by reelecting them (granting continued consent) or by throwing them out of office (withdrawing consent).

In a representative democracy, elections function primarily to choose personnel to occupy public office—to decide "who governs." But elections also have an indirect influence on public policy, allowing voters to influence policy directions by choosing between candidates or parties with different policy priorities. Thus elections indirectly influence "who gets what"—that is, the outcomes of the political process.

Elections as Mandates? However, it is difficult to argue that elections serve as "policy mandates"—that is, that elections allow voters to direct the course of public policy. Frequently, election winners claim a **mandate**—overwhelming support from the people—for their policies

mandate
Perception of popular support for a program or policy based on the margin of electoral victory won by a candidate who proposed it during a campaign.

and programs. But for elections to serve as policy mandates, four conditions have to be met:

1. Competing candidates have to offer clear policy alternatives.

2. The voters have to cast their ballots on the basis of these policy alternatives alone.

3. The election results have to clearly indicate the voters' policy preferences.

4. Elected officials have to be bound by their campaign promises.[1]

As we shall see, *none* of these conditions is fully met in American elections. Often candidates do not differ much on policy questions, or they deliberately obscure their policy positions to avoid offending groups of voters. Voters themselves frequently pay little attention to policy issues in elections but rather vote along traditional party lines or group affiliations, or on the basis of the candidate's character, personality, or media image.

Moreover, even in elections in which issues seem to dominate the campaign, the outcome may not clearly reflect policy preferences. Candidates take stands on a variety of issues. It is never certain on which issues the voters agreed with the winner and on which issues they disagreed yet voted for the candidate anyway.

Finally, candidates often fail to abide by their campaign promises once they are elected. Some simply ignore their promises, assuming voters have forgotten about the campaign. Others point to changes in circumstances or conditions as a justification for abandoning a campaign pledge.

retrospective voting
Voting for or against a candidate or party on the basis of past performance in office.

Retrospective Voting   Voters can influence future policy directions through **retrospective voting**—votes cast on the basis of the performance of incumbents, by either reelecting them or throwing them out of office.[2] Voters may not know what politicians will do in the future, but they can evaluate how well politicians performed in the past. When incumbent officeholders are defeated, it is reasonable to assume that voters did not like their performance and that newly elected officials should change policy course if they do not want to meet a similar fate in the next election. But it is not always clear what the defeated incumbents did in office that led to their ouster by the voters. Nor, indeed, can incumbents who won reelection assume that all of their policies are approved of by a majority of voters. Nevertheless, retrospective voting provides an overall judgment of how voters evaluate performance in office.

✔ *Think* Again

Should elected officials be bound by their campaign promises?

Protection of Rights   Elections also provide protection against official abuse. The long struggle for African American voting rights in the United States was premised on the belief that once black people acquired the right to vote, government would become more responsive to their concerns. In signing the Voting Rights Act of 1965, President Lyndon Johnson expressed this view: "The vote is the most powerful instrument ever devised by man for breaking down injustice and destroying the terrible walls which imprison men because they are different from other men."[3]

✔ *Think* Again

Do you think that personal ambition, rather than civic duty, motivates most politicians?

Power and Ambition

▶ 8.2 *Characterize the various factors that motivate people to pursue a political career.*

Personal ambition is a driving force in politics. Politics attracts people for whom *power*—the drive to shape the world according to one's own beliefs and values—and *celebrity*—the public attention, deference, name recognition, and social status that accompany public office—are more rewarding than money, leisure, or privacy. "Political office today flows to those who want it enough to spend the time and energy mastering its pursuit. It flows in the direction of ambition—and talent."[4]

Communication Skills   Another important personal qualification is the ability to communicate with others. Politicians must know how to talk, and talk, and talk—to large audiences, in press conferences and interviews, on television, to reporters, to small groups of financial contributors, on the phone, at airports and commencements, to their staffs, on the floor of Congress or the state legislature. It matters less what politicians say than how they look and sound saying it. They must communicate sincerity, compassion, confidence, and good humor, as well as ideas.

Professionalism   Politics is increasingly characterized by **professionalism.** "Citizen officeholders"—people with business or professional careers who get into politics part time or for short periods of time—are being driven out of political life by career politicians—people who enter politics early in life as a full-time occupation and expect to make it their career. Politics increasingly demands all of a politician's time and energy. At all levels of government, from city council to state legislatures to the U.S. Congress, political work is becoming full-time and year-round.

professionalism
In politics, a reference to the increasing number of officeholders for whom politics is a full-time occupation.

Careerism   Professional political careers begin at a relatively early age. **Careerism** in politics begins when ambitious young people seek out internships and staff positions with members of Congress, with congressional committees, in state legislators' or governors' offices, in mayors' offices, or in council chambers. Others volunteer to work in political campaigns. Many find political mentors from whom they learn how to organize campaigns, contact financial contributors, and deal with the media. Soon they are ready to run for local office or the state legislature. Rather than challenge a strong incumbent, they may wait for an open seat to be created by retirement, by reapportionment, or by its holder seeking another office. Over time, running for and holding elective office become their career.

careerism
In politics, a reference to people who started young working in politics, running for and holding public office, and who made politics their career.

Lawyers in Politics   The prevalence of lawyers in politics is an American tradition. Among the fifty-five delegates to the Constitutional Convention in 1787, some twenty-five were lawyers. The political dominance of lawyers continues today, with lawyers filling about half of U.S. Senate seats and nearly half of the seats in the U.S. House of Representatives.

It is sometimes argued that lawyers dominate in politics because of the parallel skills required in law and politics. Lawyers represent clients, so they can apply their professional experience to represent constituents in Congress. Lawyers are trained to deal with statutory law, so they are assumed to be reasonably familiar with the United States Code (the codified laws of the U.S. government) when they arrive in Congress to make or amend these statutes.

But it is more likely that people attracted to politics decide to go to law school fully aware of the tradition of lawyers in American politics. Moreover, political officeholding at the state and local level as well as in the national government can help a struggling lawyer's private practice through free public advertising and opportunities to make contacts with potential clients. Finally, there are many special opportunities for lawyers to acquire public office in "lawyers only" posts as judges and prosecuting attorneys in federal, state, and local governments. Law school graduates who accept modest salaries as U.S. attorneys in the Justice Department or in state or county prosecuting offices can gain valuable experience for later use in either private law practice or politics.

Most of the lawyers in the Congress, however, have become professional politicians over time. They have left their legal practices behind.

The Advantages of Incumbency

▶ 8.3 *Explain the advantages of incumbency.*

In theory, elections offer voters the opportunity to "throw the rascals out." But in practice, voters seldom do so. **Incumbents**, people already holding public office, have a strong advantage when they seek reelection. The **reelection rates** of incumbents for *all* elective offices—city council, mayor, state legislature, governor, and especially Congress—are very high. Since 1950, more than 90 percent of all members of the House of Representatives who have sought reelection have been successful. The success rate of U.S. Senate incumbents is not as great, but it is still impressive; since 1950, more than 70 percent of senators seeking reelection have been successful.[5]

Why do incumbents win so often? This is a particularly vexing question, inasmuch as so many people are distrustful of government and hold politicians in low esteem. Congress itself is the focal point of public disapproval and even ridicule. Yet people seem to distinguish between Congress as an institution—which they distrust—and their own members of Congress—whom they reelect. The result is something of a contradiction: popular members of Congress serving in an unpopular Congress (see *What Do You Think?*: "Why Do Voters Reelect Members of an Unpopular Congress?" in Chapter 10). Three major advantages tend to enhance incumbents' chances of winning: name recognition, campaign contributions, and the resources of office.

Name Recognition   One reason for incumbents' success is that they begin the campaign with greater **name recognition** than their challengers, simply because they are the incumbent and their name has become familiar to their constituents over the previous years. Much of the daily work of all elected officials, especially members of Congress, is really public relations. Name recognition is a strategic advantage at the ballot box, especially if voters have little knowledge of policy positions or voting records. Voters tend to cast ballots for recognizable names over unknowns. Cynics have concluded that there is no such thing as bad publicity, only publicity. Even in cases of well-publicized scandals, incumbent members of Congress have won reelection; presumably voters preferred "the devil they knew" to the one they did not.

The somewhat lower rate of reelection of Senate versus House members may be a result of the fact that Senate challengers are more likely to have held high-visibility offices—for example, governor or member of Congress—before running for the Senate. Thus Senate challengers often enjoy some name recognition even before the campaign begins. Greater media attention to a statewide Senate race also helps to move the challenger closer to the incumbent in public recognition. In contrast, House challengers are likely to have held less visible local or state legislative offices or to be political novices, and House races attract considerably less media attention than Senate races do.

Campaign Contributions   Incumbents have a strong advantage in raising campaign funds, simply because individuals and groups seeking access to those already in office are inspired to make contributions (see Table 8.1). **Challengers**

---

incumbents
Candidates currently in office seeking reelection.

reelection rates
Percentages of incumbents running for reelection who are successful.

name recognition
Public awareness of a political candidate—whether they are familiar with his or her name.

challengers
In politics, a reference to people running against incumbent officeholders.

have no immediate favors to offer; they must convince a potential contributor that they will win office and also that they are devoted to the interests of their financial backers.[6]

Contributing individuals and interest groups show a strong preference for incumbents over challengers. They do not wish to offend incumbent officeholders by contributing to their challengers; doing so risks both immediate retribution and future "freezing out" in the likely event of the challengers' defeat. Thus only when an incumbent has been especially hostile to an organization's interest, or in rare cases where an incumbent seems especially vulnerable, will an interest group support a challenger. Yet challengers need even larger campaign war chests than incumbents to be successful. Challengers must overcome the greater name recognition of incumbents, their many office resources, and their records of constituency service. Thus even if incumbents and challengers had equal campaign treasuries, incumbents would enjoy the advantage.

Resources of Office
Successful politicians use their offices to keep their names and faces before the public in various ways—public appearances, interviews, speeches, and press releases. Congressional incumbents make full use of the **franking privilege** (free use of the U.S. mails) to send self-promotional newsletters to tens of thousands of households in their district at taxpayers' expense. They travel on weekends to their district virtually year-round, using tax-funded travel allowances, to make local appearances, speeches, and contacts.

Members of Congress have large staffs working every day over many years with the principal objective of ensuring the reelection of their members. Indeed, Congress is structured as an "incumbent-protection society" organized and staffed to help guarantee the reelection of its members (see "Home Style" in Chapter 10). Service to constituents occupies the energies of congressional office staffs both in Washington and in local district offices established for this purpose. Casework wins voters one at a time: tracing lost Social Security checks, ferreting out which federal loans voters qualify for and helping them with their applications, and performing countless other personal favors. These individual "retail-level" favors are supplemented by larger-scale projects that experienced members of Congress can bring to their district or state (roads, dams, post offices, buildings, schools, grants, contracts), as well as undesirable projects (landfills, waste disposal sites, halfway houses) that they can keep out of their district. The longer incumbents have occupied the office, the more favors they have performed and the larger their networks of grateful voters.

Lose the Primary, Win the General Election
Senator Joe Lieberman (D-CT) lost in his Democratic Party primary for reelection to the U.S. Senate—a rare occurrence for an incumbent. Lieberman was the Democratic vice-presidential candidate on the ticket with Al Gore in 2000. Liberal activists led the way to his defeat, attacking his support of the invasion of Iraq. Lieberman subsequently was reelected as an Independent candidate in the general election.

franking privilege
Free use of the U.S. mails granted to members of Congress to promote communication with constituents.

TABLE 8.1   In the Money: Incumbent Advantage in Fund-Raising

Incumbent House and Senate members seeking reelection are able to raise much more than their challengers in campaign contributors.				
	2004	**2006**	**2008**	**2010**
Senate				
Average Incumbent Raised	$7,212,068	$11,317,025	8,740,153	10,782,810
Average Challenger Raised	869,688	1,814,844	1,152,182	850,110
House				
Average Incumbent Raised	982,941	1,270,855	1,356,481	1,364,380
Average Challenger Raised	171,551	283,075	335,638	231,899

Source: Center for Responsive Politics; figures for 2004, 2006, 2008, and 2010 congressional elections.

Campaign Strategies

▶ 8.4 *Identify the main components of campaign strategies.*

Campaigning is largely a media activity, especially in presidential and congressional campaigns. Media campaigns are highly professionalized, relying on public relations and advertising specialists, professional fund-raisers, media consultants, and pollsters. Campaign management involves techniques that strongly resemble those employed in marketing commercial products. Professional media campaign management includes developing a **campaign strategy**: compiling computerized mailing lists and invitations for fund-raising events; selecting a campaign theme and coming up with a desirable candidate image; monitoring the progress of the campaign with continual polling of the voters; producing television tapes for commercials, newspaper advertisements, signs, bumper stickers, and radio spots; selecting clothing and hairstyles for the candidate; writing speeches and scheduling appearances; and even planning the victory party.

campaign strategy
Plan for a political campaign, usually including a theme, an attempt to define the opponent or the issues, and an effort to coordinate images and messages in news broadcasts and paid advertising.

negative campaigning
Speeches, commercials, or advertising attacking a political opponent during a campaign.

Selecting a Theme   Finding the right theme or "message" for a campaign is essential; this effort is not greatly different from that of launching an advertising campaign for a new detergent. A successful theme or "message" is one that characterizes the candidate or the electoral choice confronting the voters. A campaign theme need not be controversial; indeed, it need not even focus on a specific issue. It might be as simple as "Change we can believe in"—an attempt to "package" the candidate as fresh, new, and believable.

Most media campaigns focus on candidates' personal qualities rather than on their stands on policy issues. Professional campaigns are based on the assumption that a candidate's "image" is the most important factor affecting voter choice. This image is largely devoid of issues, except in very general terms: for example, "stands up to the special interests," "fights for the taxpayer," or "cares about you."

Ambiguity in a theme or message may be a winning strategy.[7] Voters tend to interpret ambiguous statements as agreement with their own views. In contrast, contradictory statements, even those made to different audiences, may hurt candidates, especially when contradictions are videotaped and shown side by side.

Negative Campaigning: "Defining" the Opponent   A media campaign also seeks to "define" the opponent in negative terms. The original negative TV ad is generally identified as the 1964 "Daisy Girl" commercial, aired by the Lyndon B. Johnson presidential campaign (see *Politics Up Close*: "Dirty Politics"). Negative ads can serve a purpose in exposing the record of an opponent. But **negative campaigning** risks an opponent's counterattack charges of "mudslinging," "dirty tricks," and "sleaze."

Research into the opponent's public and personal background ("oppo research") provides the data for negative campaigning. Previous speeches and writings can be mined for embarrassing or mean-spirited statements. The voting record of the opponent can be scrutinized for unpopular policy positions. Any evils that occurred during an opponent's term of office can be attributed to him or her, either directly ("She knew and conspired in it") or indirectly ("He should have known and done something about it"). Personal scandals or embarrassments can be developed as evidence of "character." If campaign managers fear that highly personal attacks on an opponent will backfire, they may choose to leak the information to reporters and try to avoid attribution of the story to themselves or their candidate.

A Winning Theme
Illinois Senator Barack Obama chose the popular campaign theme of "change" and used the Internet and his campaign Web site, as this sign shows, to his advantage.

POLITICS UP CLOSE

Dirty Politics

Political campaigning frequently turns ugly with negative advertising that is vicious and personal. It is widely believed that television's focus on personal character and private lives—rather than on policy positions and governmental experience—encourages negative campaigning. But vicious personal attacks in political campaigns began long before television. They are nearly as old as the nation itself.

"If Jefferson is elected," proclaimed Yale's president in 1800, "the Bible will be burned and we will see our wives and daughters the victims of legal prostitution." In 1864 *Harper's Weekly* decried the "mudslinging" of the day, lamenting that President Abraham Lincoln was regularly referred to by his opponent as a "filthy storyteller, despot, liar, thief, braggart, buffoon, monster, Ignoramus Abe, robber, swindler, tyrant, fiend, butcher, and pirate."

Television's first memorable attack advertisement was the "Daisy Girl" commercial broadcast by Lyndon Johnson's presidential campaign in 1964 against his Republican opponent, Barry Goldwater. Although never mentioning Goldwater by name, the purpose of the ad was to "define" him as a warmonger who would plunge the world into a nuclear holocaust. The ad opens with a small, innocent girl standing in an open field plucking petals from a daisy and counting, "1, 2, 3 . . ." When she reaches 9, an ominous adult male voice begins a countdown: "10, 9, 8 . . ." as the camera closes in on the child's face. At "zero," a mushroom cloud appears, reflected in her eyes, and envelops the screen. Lyndon Johnson's voice is heard: "These are the stakes."

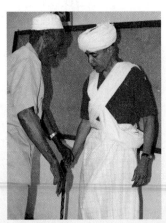

Senator Obama is dressed as a Somali Elder by Sheikh Mahmed Hassan (left), during his visit to Wajir in northeastern Kenya, near the Somali and Ethiopian borders, on August 27, 2006. Obama's deceased father, from whom he was estranged, was Kenyan.

"Attack ads" have multiplied in recent elections at all levels of government. John Kerry had volunteered for Vietnam following his graduation from Yale. In 4 months as commander of a small "swift boat" he won a Silver Star, a Bronze Star, and three Purple Hearts. But an independent group, Swift Boat Veterans for the Truth, challenged the legitimacy of Kerry's medals in a series of TV ads. Later, the Swift Boat group redirected their attacks toward Kerry's post-Vietnam behavior as a leader in the Vietnam Veterans against the War. These ads showed a young Kerry at a congressional hearing accusing his fellow veterans of terrible atrocities, "murdering civilians, cutting off heads, and burning villages." These ads corresponded to a slight drop in Kerry's poll numbers.

The Internet further facilitates dirty politics. The anonymity of the Net often inspires false and misleading postings. Perhaps the most offensive in 2008 was the recurring assertion that Barack Obama was a Muslim. These postings frequently referred to his middle name, Hussein, and later included a photo of him in African costume (from a 2006 trip to Kenya).

What are the effects of negative advertising? First of all, it works more often than not. Controlled experiments indicate that targets of attack ads are rated less positively by people who have watched these ads. But another effect of negative advertising is to make voters more cynical about politics and government in general. There is conflicting evidence about whether or not negative campaigning by opposing candidates reduces voter turnout.

What, if anything, can be done? Government regulation of political speech directly contravenes the 1st Amendment. American democracy has survived negative campaigning for a long time.

Frames from Lyndon Johnson's 1964 "Daisy Girl" commercial.

VOTE FOR PRESIDENT JOHNSON ON NOVEMBER 3.

Sources: Kathleen Hall Jamieson, *Dirty Politics: Deception, Distraction, and Democracy* (New York: Oxford University Press, 1992); also Stephen Ansolabehere et al., "Does Attack Advertising Demobilize the Electorate?" *American Political Science Review* 88 (December 1994): 829–38; Kim Fridkin Kahn and Patrick J. Kenney, "Do Negative Campaigns Mobilize or Suppress Turnout?" *American Political Science Review* 93 (December, 1999): 877–89.

Focus Group in Action

A woman records a focus group in action at a California advertisement agency. Because of the one-way mirror, the video operator can see the focus group at work, but the persons in the room only see their own reflections.

Negative advertising is often blamed on television's dominant role in political campaigns. "The high cost of television means now that you have to go for the jugular."[8] A political consultant summarized the current rules of political engagement as follows:

1. Advertise early if you have the money.

2. Go negative early, often, and right through Election Day, if necessary.

3. Appeal to the heart and gut, rather than to the head.

4. Define your opponent to the voters before he or she can define him/herself or you.

5. If attacked, hit back even harder.

6. It's easier to give voters a negative impression of your opponent than it is to improve their image of you.[9]

focus group
In a political context, a small number of people brought together in a comfortable setting to discuss and respond to themes and issues, allowing campaign managers to develop and analyze strategies.

Using Focus Groups and Polling Focus group techniques can help in selecting campaign themes and identifying negative characteristics in opponents. A **focus group** is a small group of people brought together to view videotapes, listen to specific campaign appeals, and respond to particular topics and issues. Media professionals then develop a campaign strategy around "hot-button" issues—issues that generate strong responses by focus groups—and avoid themes or issues that fail to elicit much interest.

The results of focus group work can then be tested in wider polling. Polling is a central feature of professional campaigning. Serious candidates for national and statewide offices almost always employ their own private polling firms, distinct from the national survey organizations that supply the media with survey data. Initial polling is generally designed to determine candidates' name recognition—the extent to which the voters recognize the candidates—and whatever positive and negative images are already associated with their names.

Campaign polling is highly professionalized, with telephone banks, trained interviewers, and computer-assisted-telephone-interviewing (CATI) software that records and tabulates responses instantly and sends the results to campaign managers. In well-financed campaigns, polling is continual throughout the campaign, so that managers can assess progress on a daily basis. Polls chart the candidate's progress and, perhaps more important, help assess the effectiveness of specific campaign themes. If the candidate appears to be gaining support, the campaign stays on course. But if the candidate appears to be falling in the polls, the campaign manager comes under intense pressure to change themes and strategies. As election day nears, the pressure increases on the trailing candidate to "go negative"—to launch even more scathing attacks on the opponent.

Think
Again

Would you vote for a candidate who used negative ads to discredit an opponent?

Incumbent Versus Challenger Strategies Campaign strategies vary by the offices being sought, the nature of the times, and the imagination and inventiveness of the candidates' managers. But incumbency is perhaps the most important factor affecting the choice of a strategy. The challenger must attack the record of the incumbent, deplore current conditions in the city, state, or nation; and stress the need for change. Challengers are usually freer to take the offensive; incumbents must defend their record in office and either boast of accomplishments during their term or blame the opposition for blocking them. Challengers frequently opt for the "outsider" strategy, capitalizing on distrust and cynicism toward government.

News Management   News management is the key to the media campaign. News coverage of the candidates is more credible in the eyes of viewers than paid advertisements. The campaign is planned to get the maximum favorable "free" exposure on the evening news. Each day a candidate must do something interesting and "newsworthy," that is, likely to be reported as news. Pictures are as important as words. Candidates must provide good **photo ops** for the media—opportunities where they can be photographed in settings or backgrounds that emphasize their themes. For example, if the theme is patriotism, then the candidate appears with war veterans, at a military base, or at a flag factory. If the theme is education, the candidate appears at a school; if crime control, then with police officers; if environmentalism, then in a wilderness area; if the economy, then at a closed factory or unemployment line or soup kitchen for the homeless.

Themes must be stated in concise and catchy **sound bites** that will register in the viewers' minds. Candidates now understand that the news media will select only a few seconds of an entire day of speech making for broadcast. The average length of a network news sound bite has shrunk from 45 to 7 seconds over the last 30 years. Thus extended or serious discussion of issues during a campaign is sacrificed to the need for one-liners on the nightly news. Indeed, if a campaign theme cannot fit on a bumper sticker, it is too complex.

Paid Advertising   Television "spot" ads must be prepared prior to and during the campaign. They involve employing expensive television advertising and production firms well in advance of the campaign and keeping them busy revising and producing new ads throughout the campaign to respond to changing issues or opponents' attacks. Commercial advertising is the most expensive aspect of the campaign. Heavy costs are incurred in the production of the ads and in the purchase of broadcast time. The Federal Communications Commission (FCC) does not permit television networks or stations to charge more than standard commercial rates for political ads, but these rates are already high. Networks and stations are required to offer the same rates and times to all candidates, but if one candidate's campaign treasury is weak or exhausted, an opponent can saturate broadcast airtime.

Paid spot ads on television are usually only 15 or 30 seconds long, owing to the expense of television time. The result is that these ads pay relatively little attention to issues but rather try to appeal to the viewers' emotions. There is some evidence that simply showing enthusiasm for the candidate motivates participation and activates existing supporters to

News Management

Presidential candidate Barack Obama keeps up with the *New York Times* while traveling to a campaign stop in April, 2008. Managing the news is the key to a modern media campaign.

photo ops
Staged opportunities for the media to photograph the candidate in a favorable setting.

sound bites
Concise and catchy phrases that attract media coverage.

Photo Ops

Staged opportunities for the media to photograph a candidate or politician in a favorable setting, such as this picture of Senator McCain visiting the popular Shorja market in central Baghdad, Iraq, on April 1, 2007.

Affordable Choices

Paid Media

Candidates buy advertising in the media, carefully targeted to particular demographics, so as to reach and persuade viewers of their qualities for office. The picture shows a frame from Senator Hillary Rodham Clinton's television ad for her health care plan.

mobilize
In politics, to activate supporters to work for candidates and turn out on Election Day.

✔ *Think*
Again

Are high campaign costs discouraging good people from becoming candidates?

get out and vote, whereas appealing to fear is somewhat more effective in changing behavior, including swinging the votes of undecideds. However, advertising campaigns, whether they are directed at inspiring enthusiasm for the candidate or fear of a candidate's opponent, must be kept going over time. Bursts of emotion are likely to fade if the ad campaign does not keep the drumbeat going.[10] An accumulation of short spot ads, all aimed at the same theme, can have a meaningful impact on the course of an election.

Television ads are much maligned by scholars and commentators. And it is easy to identify particular ads that are silly, offensive, uninformative, and even misleading. Nevertheless, there is increasing evidence that paid political advertising does create a somewhat more attentive, more informed, and more-likely-to-vote citizenry. Moreover, paid ads appear to affect people with less political information and less interest in politics more than the better informed and more active citizens. Thus campaign ads are often petty, sometimes offensive, and seldom uplifting. But they do serve an important political function.[11]

Free Airtime   All candidates seek free airtime on news and talk shows, but the need to gain free exposure is much greater for underfunded candidates. They must go to extremes in devising media events, and they must encourage and participate in free televised debates. The debate format is particularly well suited for candidates who cannot match their opponents in paid commercial advertising. Thus well-funded and poorly funded candidates may jockey over the number and times of public debates.

The Effects of Campaigning   Campaigns serve primarily to activate a candidate's supporters—to ensure that they go to the polls on Election Day. They serve secondarily to try to persuade undecideds to become supporters. Campaigns are designed to **mobilize** core supporters more than to persuade undecideds or opponents to vote for candidates. Undecideds must be both persuaded *and* mobilized to vote—a more difficult task than simply activating core supporters. Observers may wonder why candidates appear before partisan crowds, visit with supporters, and advertise in areas that appear to support them anyway. "Core party voters are more likely to receive and respond to campaign information, implying that successful campaigns are those that mobilize their supporters enough to translate their natural predispositions into actual votes."[12]

How Much Does It Cost to Get Elected?

▶ 8.5 *Analyze the role of money in campaigns.*

Getting elected to public office has never been more expensive. The professionalization of campaigning and the heavy costs of television advertising drive up the costs of running for office (see Figure 8.1). The Presidential race in 2008 saw total campaign costs rise to almost $2 billion!

Congressional Costs   The typical winning campaign for a seat in the House of Representatives costs over $1.4 million. House members seeking to retain their seats must raise this amount *every 2 years*. The typical winning campaign for a U.S. Senate seat costs over $7 million. But Senate campaign costs vary a great deal from state to state; Senate seats in the larger states may cost $25 million to $50 million or more. For example, multimillionaire Democrat Jon Corzine spent about $60 million of his *own* money in his successful bid for a U.S. Senate seat from New Jersey in 2002. The all-time record for personal contributions to one's

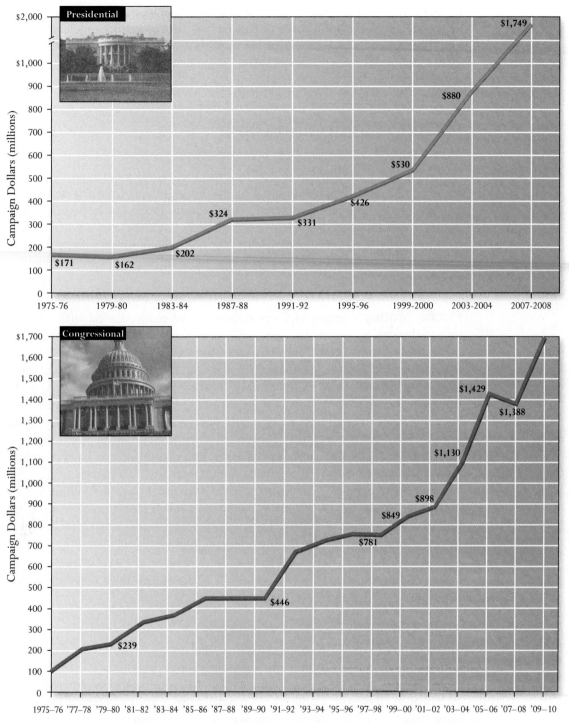

Note: Figures include campaign and party expenditures in primary and general elections, but exclude expenditures by independent groups.

FIGURE 8.1 Sparing No Expense: The Growing Costs of Campaigns

The costs of presidential and congressional campaigns now exceeds $1.7 billion, and this figure does not include expenditures by independent groups.

Source: Data from Center for Responsive Politics, www.opensecrets.org.

own campaign is held by Michael Bloomberg who reportedly spent $100 million in his 2009 race for Mayor of New York City.

Spending for House seats also varies a great deal from one race to another. In nearly two-thirds of all House districts, one candidate (almost always the incumbent) outspends his or her opponent by a factor of ten to one or more. Only about 16 percent of House campaigns are financially competitive; that is, neither candidate spends more than twice as much as his or her opponent. In the remaining 84 percent of House campaigns, one candidate spends more than twice as much as his or her opponent.[13]

Raising Campaign Cash

▶ 8.6 *Identify the major sources of funding for political campaigns.*

Fund-raising to meet the high costs of campaigning is the most important hurdle for any candidate for public office. Campaign funds come from a wide range of sources—small donors, big donors, interest group PACs of every stripe, labor unions, even taxpayers. In some cases, candidates pay their own way (or most of it). More typically, however, candidates for high public office—particularly incumbents—have become adept at running their campaigns using other people's money, not their own.

Public Money   Presidential campaigns can be partly funded with taxpayer money through an income tax checkoff system. Each year taxpayers are urged to check the box on their tax forms that authorizes $3 of their tax payment to go to the Federal Elections Commission for distribution to presidential candidates' campaigns as well as to political party conventions. However, taxpayers are becoming less and less willing to allow their tax monies to go into political campaigning (even though the $3 checkoff does not add to the taxpayers' total taxes). Only about 11 percent of taxpayers currently check the box. The Presidential Election Campaign Fund has been in jeopardy of not having enough money to make its promised payments to the candidates and parties.

Presidential candidates may opt out of taxpayer-financed funding if they choose to do so. This allows them to spend as much money as they wish, but they receive no public money. (Democrat Barack Obama was so successful in raising cash in 2008 that he declined federal funding. Republican John McCain faced a cash shortage and was obliged to accept federal money.) Nonetheless, all presidential candidates, and all candidates for Congress, must abide by federal campaign finance laws (see below).

Small Donations   Millions of Americans participate in campaign financing, either by giving directly to candidates or the parties or by giving to political action committees, which then distribute their funds to candidates (see *Politics Up Close*: "How Obama Changed Campaign Fund-Raising Using the Internet"). For members of Congress, small donors typically make up less than 20 percent of their campaign funds. The proportion is higher for presidential candidates. For donations under $200, contributors' names and addresses are recorded only by the candidates and parties, not passed along to the Federal Election Commission as part of the public record.

Large Individual Donors   "Fat cats" are the preferred donors. These are the donors whose names are on the candidates' Rolodexes. They are the ones in attendance when the president, the Speaker of the House, or other top political dignitaries travel around the country doing fund-raisers. They are also the ones who are wined, dined, prodded, and cajoled in a seemingly ceaseless effort by the parties and the candidates to raise funds for the next election.

POLITICS UP CLOSE

How Obama Changed Campaign Fund-Raising Using the Internet

Barack Obama raised more money for his presidential campaign in 2008 than any other candidate in history. He heavily outspent his opponents—Hillary Clinton in the Democratic primaries and John McCain in the general election. He declined public funding for his campaign and thereby avoided Federal Elections Commission spending limits. He raised more money through small contributions than any previous presidential contender. How did he do it?

Obama's extraordinary success in raising funds through the Internet is likely to change campaign fund-raising in future years. Obama reportedly raised $500 million from more than 3 million donors over the Internet.[a] About one-third of these donations came in amounts of less than $200. No previous presidential contender had ever raised so much money through such small donations.

Asking for money via the Internet can be much more timely and immediate than raising money through the mail or through events like dinners or concerts. Internet fund-raising is cheap; it does not entail significant costs. Internet solicitation is continuous; it does not require the candidate to spend time in personal appearances. Because it is so inexpensive, even small donations of $5 or $10 can be profitably solicited. And people making donations over the Internet can be tracked and solicited again and again throughout the campaign. New e-mail messages can be sent out as events occur that may inspire supporters to make repeat donations.

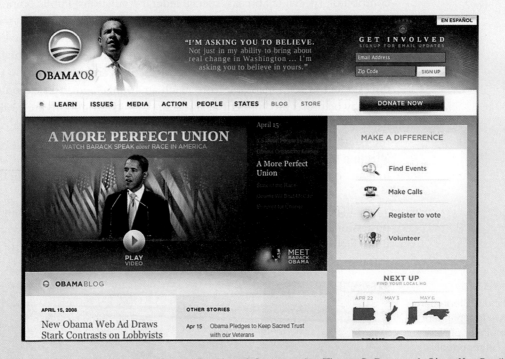

[a]See David B. Magleby, "How Barack Obama Changed Presidential Campaigns," in Thomas R. Dye, et. al. *Obama Year One* (New York: Longman, 2010).

In its 2002 campaign finance reform legislation, Congress raised the maximum individual contribution to federal candidates to $2,000 (up from $1,000 in the 2000 election). The maximum contribution is indexed to inflation; in 2008 it was $2,300. Fat cats are expected to give the maximum, and indeed even more. They can do so by giving their maximum $2,300 once in the primary election and a second time in the general election. And their spouses can do the same. And, of course, they can also give to the parties and to independent political organizations committed to helping their preferred candidates.

Candidate Self-Financing Candidates for federal office also pump millions into their own campaigns. There are no federal restrictions on the amount of money individuals can spend on their own campaign.[14] Senate and House candidates frequently put $50,000 to $100,000 or more of their own money into their campaigns, through outright gifts or personal loans. (Candidates who loan themselves the money to run are able to pay themselves back later from outside contributions.)

Issue Ads   Issue ads advocate policy positions rather than explicitly advising voters to cast their ballots for or against particular candidates. But most of these ads leave little doubt about which candidate is being supported or targeted. There are no dollar limits on the size of contributions to sponsoring groups (often referred to as 527s from the section of the Internal Revenue code under which they operate).

What Do Contributors "Buy"?

▶ 8.7 *Assess the motivations of contributors to political campaigns.*

What does money buy in politics? A cynic might say that money can buy anything—for example, special appropriations for public works directly benefiting the contributor, special tax breaks, special federal regulations. Public opinion views big-money contributions as a major problem in the American political system. Scandals involving the direct (quid pro quo) purchase of special favors, privileges, exemptions, and treatments have been common enough in the past, and they are likely to continue in the future. But campaign contributions are rarely made in the form of a direct trade-off for a favorable vote. Such an arrangement risks exposure as bribery and may be prosecuted under the law. Campaign contributions are more likely to be made without any *explicit* quid pro quo but rather with a general understanding that the contributor has confidence in the candidate's good judgment on issues directly affecting the contributor. The contributor expects the candidate to be smart enough to figure out how to vote in order to keep the contributions coming in the future.

The Big-Money Contributors   Big-money contributors—businesses, unions, professional associations—pump millions into presidential and congressional elections. Figure 8.2 lists the top fifty contributors to candidates and parties from 1989 through 2010. Note that union contributions are heavily weighted toward

issue ads
Ads that advocate policy positions rather than explicitly supporting or opposing particular candidates.

Think Again

Do political campaign contributions have too much influence on elections and government policy?

The Billionaire Mayor
Billionaire Michael Bloomberg funded his own independent campaign for Mayor of New York in 2009. He reportedly spent $100 million of his own money, a record for a self-financed campaign.

Rank	Contributor	Total Contributions (millions)	% Dem.	% Rep.	Rank	Contributor	Total Contributions (millions)	% Dem.	% Rep.
1.	AT&T Inc.	$43.5	44%	55%	25.	National Beer Wholesalers Assn.	$20.5	31%	68%
2.	American Fedn. of State, County & Municipal Employees	$41.4	98	1	26.	Microsoft Corp.	$19.8	53	46
					27.	Time Warner	$19.7	71	28
3.	National Assn. of Realtors	$35.2	48	51	28.	JP Morgan Chase & Co.	$19.4	51	48
					29.	National Assn. of Letter Carriers	$19.3	88	11
4.	Goldman Sachs	$31.2	64	35	30.	Morgan Stanley	$18.2	45	53
5.	American Assn. for Justice (trial lawyers)	$31.0	90	9	31.	AFL-CIO	$18.1	95	4
6.	Intl. Brotherhood of Electrical Workers	$30.9	97	2	32.	Lockheed Martin	$17.9	42	57
					33.	Verizon Communications	$17.8	39	59
7.	National Education Assn.	$29.9	92	6	34.	FedEx Corp.	$17.7	40	58
8.	Laborers Union	$28.4	92	7	35.	General Electric	$17.4	50	49
9.	Service Employees International Union	$27.7	95	3	36.	National Rifle Assn.	$17.2	17	82
10.	Carpenters & Joiners Union	$27.6	89	10	37.	Sheet Metal Workers Union	$17.0	97	2
11.	Teamsters Union	$27.4	92	6	38.	Credit Union National Assn.	$16.9	47	51
12.	Communications Workers of America	$26.7	99	0	39.	Ernst & Young	$16.8	44	55
13.	Citigroup Inc.	$26.6	50	49	40.	Bank of America	$16.6	47	52
14.	American Medical Assn.	$26.2	39	60	41.	Operating Engineers Union	$16.3	85	14
15.	American Federation of Teachers	$26.0	98	0	42.	American Dental Assn.	$16.1	46	53
16.	United Auto Workers	$25.8	98	0	43.	American Hospital Assn.	$16.1	52	46
17.	Machinists & Aerospace Workers Union	$24.8	98	0	44.	Plumbers & Pipefitters Union	$15.9	94	5
18.	National Auto Dealers Assn.	$24.0	31	68	45.	Blue Cross/Blue Shield	$15.8	39	60
19.	Altria Group	$23.9	28	71	46.	International Assn. of Fire Fighters	$15.5	82	17
20.	United Food & Commercial Workers Union	$23.9	98	1	47.	Air Line Pilots Assn.	$15.5	84	15
					48.	Deloitte Touche Tohmatsu	$15.4	34	65
21.	United Parcel Service	$23.6	36	63	49.	Pricewaterhouse-Coopers	$15.1	36	63
22.	American Bankers Assn.	$21.9	41	58					
23.	National Assn. of Home Builders	$21.6	36	63	50.	National Assn./ Insurance & Financial Advisors	$14.9	42	56
24.	EMILY's List	$21.0	99	0					

FIGURE 8.2 Who Gives What?: Fifty Big-Money Contributors, 1989–2010

Source: Data from Center for Responsive Politics, www.opensecrets.org.

Democrats, as are the contributions of the trial lawyers. Businesses and business associations tend to split their contributions between the parties, but Republicans usually get the largest share.

Buying Access to Policymakers
Large contributors expect to be able to call or visit and present their views directly to "their" officeholders. At the presidential level, major contributors who cannot get a meeting with the president expect to meet at least with high-level White House staff or cabinet officials. At the congressional level, major contributors usually expect to meet or speak directly with their representative or senator. Members of Congress boast of responding to letters, calls, or visits by any constituent, but contributors can expect a more immediate and direct response than noncontributors can. Lobbyists for contributing organizations routinely expect and receive a hearing from members of Congress.

political action committees (PACs)
Organizations that solicit and receive campaign contributions from corporations, unions, trade associations, and ideological and issue-oriented groups, and their members, then distribute these funds to political candidates.

Political Action Committees   Political action committees (PACs) are the most reliable source of money for reelection campaigns in Congress. Corporations and unions form PACs to seek contributions from managers and stockholders and their families, or union workers and their families. PACs are organized not only by corporations and unions but also by trade and professional associations, environmental groups, and liberal and conservative ideological groups. The wealthiest PACs are based in Washington, D.C. (see "PAC Power" in Chapter 9). PACs are very cautious; their job is to get a maximum return on their contributions, winning influence and goodwill with as many lawmakers as possible in Washington. There's no return on their investment if their recipients lose at the polls; therefore most PACs—particularly business PACs—give most of their dollars to incumbents seeking reelection.

Individual Contributors   Most individual contributors are ideologically motivated. They make their contributions based on their perception of the ideological position of the candidate (or perhaps their perception of the candidate's opponent). They may make contributions to congressional candidates across the country who share their policy views. Liberal and conservative networks of contributors can be contacted through specialized mailing lists. Feminists have been effective in soliciting individual contributions across the country and funneling them very early in a campaign to women candidates through EMILY's List. Ideological contributors may only get the satisfaction of knowing that they are financially backing their cause in the political process. Some contributors simply enjoy the opportunity to be near and to be seen with high-ranking politicians. Politicians pose for photos with contributors, who later frame the photos and hang them in their office to impress their friends, associates, and customers. Contributors are disproportionately high-income, older people with strong partisan views (see Figure 8.3).

Buying Government Assistance   Many large contributors do business with government agencies. They expect any representative or senator they have supported to intervene on their behalf with these agencies, sometimes acting to cut red tape, ensure fairness, and expedite their cases, and other times pressuring the agencies for a favorable decision. Officials in the White House or the cabinet may also be expected to intervene on behalf of major contributors. There is little question raised when the intervention merely expedites consideration of a contributor's case, but pressure to bend rules or regulations to get favorable decisions raises ethical problems for officeholders (see "Congressional Ethics" in Chapter 10). Corporations that do business with government agencies, and those that are heavily regulated by government agencies, may make contributions simply to "flex their muscles"—to signal bureaucrats that if they wished to do so, they could fight any agency's specific decisions.[15]

Celebrities Help Raise Funds

Senator Hillary Rodham Clinton receives a kiss and a hug from British musician Elton John at an April 9, 2008, fund-raising concert for her campaign in New York.

Fund-Raising Chores   Fund-raising occupies more of a candidate's time than any other campaign activity. Candidates must personally contact as many individual contributors as possible. They work late into the evening on the telephone with potential contributors. Fund-raising dinners, cocktail parties, barbecues, fish frys, and so on, are scheduled nearly every day of a campaign. The candidate is expected to appear personally to "press the flesh" of big contributors. Movie and rock stars and other assorted celebrities may also be asked to appear at fund-raising affairs to generate attendance. Dinners may run to $2,300 a plate in presidential affairs, although often less in Senate or House campaigns. Tickets may be "bundled" to well-heeled individual contributors or sold in blocks to organizations.

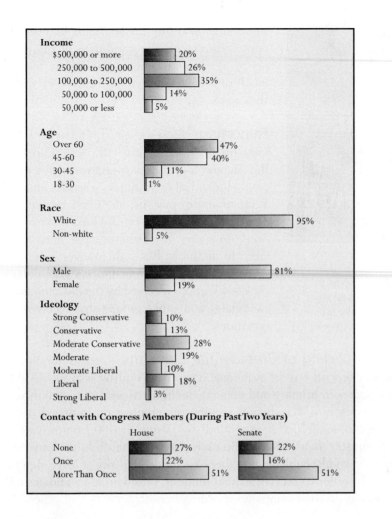

FIGURE 8.3

Who's Giving?: Characteristics of Individual Political Contributors

Contributors to political campaigns generally are older and have higher incomes than most Americans. Whites and males contribute more than blacks and females, and conservatives contribute more than liberals.

Source: John Green, Paul Herrnson, Lynda Powell, and Clyde Wilcox, "Individual Congressional Campaign Contributors," press release, June 9, 1998, Center for Responsive Politics, www.opensecrets.org. Reprinted by permission.

Regulating Campaign Finance

▶ 8.8 *Evaluate efforts to regulate campaigns finances.*

The **Federal Election Commission (FEC)**, created in 1974, is responsible for enforcing limits on individual and organizational contributions to all federal elections, administering the public funding of presidential campaigns, and requiring full disclosure of all campaign financial activity in presidential and congressional elections. Enforcement of these federal election and campaign finance laws lies in the hands of the 6-member FEC. Appointed by the president to serve staggered 6-year terms, commission members are traditionally split 3 to 3 between Republicans and Democrats.

Federal Election Commission (FEC)
Agency charged with enforcing federal election laws and disbursing public presidential campaign funds.

Limits on Contributions
The FEC now limits direct individual contributions to a candidate's campaign to $2,300 per election (in 2008) and organizational contributions to $5,000 per election. But there are many ways in which individuals and organizations can legally surmount these limits. Contributors may give a candidate $2,300 for each member of their family in a primary election and then another $2,300 per member in the general election. Organizations may generate much more than the $5,000 limit by bundling (combining) contributions from individual members.

Independent Organization Spending
Independent organizations can spend whatever they wish in order to promote their political views, so long as

The Oprah Embrace

Candidates often seek the support of celebrities so as to appeal to the public and raise campaign money. Oprah Winfrey embraces Senator Barack Obama at a rally on December 8, 2007, in Des Moines, Iowa. Michelle Obama, the candidate's wife, looks on.

soft money
Previously unregulated contributions to the parties, now prohibited; contributions to parties now limited.

these organizations do so "without cooperation or consultation with the candidate of his or her campaign." Finally, as noted, individuals may spend as much of their own money on their own campaigns as they wish.

Reporting By law, every candidate for federal office must file periodic reports with the FEC detailing both the income and the expenditures of his or her campaign. Individual contributors who give an aggregate of $200 or more must be identified by name, address, occupation, and employer. All PAC and party contributions, no matter how large or small, must also be itemized. In addition, PACs themselves must file reports with the FEC at least four times a year, detailing both the contributions received by the PAC and the names of candidates and other groups that received the PAC's donations.

Federal Funding of Presidential Elections Federal funding, financed by the $3 checkoff box on individual income tax returns, is available to presidential candidates in primary and general elections, as well as to major-party nominating conventions. Candidates seeking the nomination in presidential primary elections can qualify for federal funds by raising $5,000 from private contributions no greater than $250 each in each of twenty states. In the general election, Democratic and Republican nominees are funded equally at levels determined by the FEC. In order to receive federal funding, presidential candidates must agree to FEC limits on their campaign spending in both primary and general elections.

Campaign Finance Reform In the 2000 Republican presidential primaries, U.S. Senator John McCain made campaign finance reform his principal issue. He surprised the Republican Party leaders by defeating George W. Bush in the New Hampshire primary that year. Bush and both Democratic and Republican leaders decided to jump on the campaign finance reform bandwagon, although with little real enthusiasm. In 2002, a somewhat reluctant Congress finally passed the Bipartisan Campaign Finance Reform Act.

Among other things, this act eliminated **soft-money** contributions to the parties; increased the individual contribution limit to candidates' campaigns from $1,000 to $2,000 (now $2,300); prohibited independent groups from coordinating their campaign spending with candidates or parties; and did not allow independent groups to mention the name of a candidate in their issue ads. (See *A Conflicting View*: "Eliminate Campaign Spending Limits").

But contributions to nonprofit independent groups remain unregulated. Big money contributors who can no longer provide large amounts of cash to candidates or to parties *can* establish nonprofit independent groups (known as "527s," referring to their Internal Revenue Service code) to accept big contributions to enable them to produce and broadcast campaign advertisements (see *Controversy*: "527s: Evading Campaign Finance Reform").

The Supreme Court and Campaign Finance The U.S. Supreme Court has recognized that limitations on campaign *contributions* help further a compelling government interest—"preventing corruption and the appearance of corruption"

A CONFLICTING VIEW

Eliminate Campaign Spending Limits

Political speech is the heart of the 1st Amendment. Expenditures for political speech must be constitutionally protected. Spending money to broadcast one's political views, regarding candidates, issues, and public affairs generally, is an integral part of political speech. Speech must be heard by others to be effective, and in today's society this means spending money to again access to the mass media. Limitations on political spending in effect limit political speech and therefore violate the 1st Amendment's guarantee of freedom of speech. Any "undue influence" of money in politics is outweighed by the loss for democracy resulting from restrictions on free speech.

The Supreme Court was correct in its 2010 holding that corporations and unions could not be prohibited from engaging in political speech. The Court said, "Because speech is an essential mechanism for democracy—it is the means to hold officials out of both to the people—political speech must prevail against laws that would suppress it by design or inadvertence." The same reasoning applies to dollar limits placed upon individual and group contributions to federal candidates for public office. Individuals and groups should be permitted to contribute as much as they wish to their favored candidates.

It is true that individuals and organizations usually find ways to get around campaign finance laws in any case. The Supreme Court itself noted that "Political speech is so ingrained in this country's culture that speakers find ways around campaign finance laws." But there is no reason to evade these laws; they ought to be judged unconstitutional. "Restrictions on the amount of money a person or group can spend on political communication during a campaign . . . necessarily reduces the quantity of expression by restricting the number of issues discussed, the depth of their exploration, and the size of the audience reached."

The public's interest in combating corruption in politics can be satisfied by open disclosure laws—requiring candidates to disclose during the campaign the names of organizations and individuals that are contributing to their campaigns and the amounts of these contributions. Let the voters decide whether or not a candidate is supported by the "wrong" individuals or organizations, or whether or not a candidate is too heavily indebted to a particular contributor.

Source: Quotations from *Citizens United v. FEC*, January 21, 2010.

in election campaigns. But the Court has been reluctant to allow governments to limit campaign *expenditures*, because paying to express political views is necessary in the exercise of free speech. In an important early case, *Buckley v. Valeo* (1976), the Court held that limiting a candidate's campaign expenditures that are made from his own personal funds violated the 1st Amendment's guarantee of free speech.[16]

Later, when called upon to consider the constitutionality of the Bipartisan Campaign Reform Act (BCRA), the Court upheld limitations on contributions directly to federal candidates and to national parties. It also upheld limits on "soft-money" contributions to state and local parties, recognizing that these provisions were designed to prevent circumventions of valid prohibitions on campaign contributions.[17]

But still later, the Supreme Court reconsidered the BCRA's provisions limiting individual and organization electioneering communications. The Court distinguished between "express advocacy" on behalf of a candidate or party and "issue ads" that are *not* the functional equivalent of express advocacy. (In other words, ads that do not urge viewers or listeners to vote for or against a particular candidate or party.) "When it comes to defining what speech qualifies as the functional equivalent of express advocacy, the Court should give the benefit of the doubt to speech, not censorship."[18] The effect of the decision is to permit political contributors to support organizations unaffiliated with a candidate or party, including nonprofit "527" organizations, that air television ads not expressly endorsing a candidate right up to election day.

CONTROVERSY

527s: Evading Campaign Finance Reform

The Bipartisan Campaign Reform Act was supposed to eliminate big money contributions from national elections. After years of struggle, reformers thought they had eliminated loopholes that allow individuals, corporations, and labor unions to pump millions of dollars into presidential and congressional campaigns.

But campaign cash is like the Pillsbury doughboy: Push it in one place and it pops out in another. The act banned big soft-money contributions to the parties. But Congress did not block individuals or nonprofit independent groups from spending as much as they want to broadcast their own views. So early in the 2004 election campaign, big-money contributors and politically savvy consultants, especially in the Democratic Party, began to build a network of nonprofit organizations—organizations into which they could funnel millions of dollars and expect to see them broadcast issue ads in favor of their candidates during the campaign. These organizations became popularly known as "527s," in reference to the section in the U.S. Tax Code authorizing them.

George Soros, one of the world's richest men, has given away billions to promote democracy in former Soviet bloc nations, including his birthplace, Hungary. In addition, Soros funds a wide variety of liberal causes through his Open Society Institute. He has given millions to a series of liberal organizations. Among the recipients of his political generosity:

- MoveOn, an organization originally formed by Silicon Valley entrepreneurs to defend President Bill Clinton against impeachment. It now boasts having over 3 million members and claims to be "one of the largest Political Action Committees in the country."

- Americans Coming Together (ACT), an organization formed by officers of the AFL-CIO, the Sierra Club, and the Service Employees International Union "to mobilize voters and elect progressive candidates across all America."

- America Votes, created by former Texas Gov. Ann Richards and her daughter to coordinate get-out-the-vote of anti-George Bush groups. Now a "grassroots voter mobilization effort" for liberal Democratic candidates.

- Partnership for America's Families, another group formed by the Service Employees International Union to get "progressive" voters to the polls in big cities.

In 2008, "527s" were broadcasting TV ads favoring both presidential candidates. Yet these ads did not mention the names of candidates in order to avoid campaign contribution limits.

Corporations and Unions   In 2010 the Supreme Court struck down a long-standing prohibition on political expenditures from corporate and union treasuries. Previously, corporations and unions were obliged to create separate political action committees—PACs—to solicit separate funds from managers and stockholders and union members for political activity. But the Supreme Court held in a 5–4 decision that corporations and unions could spend money directly "for express advocacy or electioneering communications purposes." "Political speech cannot be banned based on the speaker's corporate identity."[19] Corporations and unions are still prohibited from contributing directly to federal political candidates or directly to political parties ("soft money"). But "Political speech is indispensable to democracy, and this is no less true because the speech comes from a corporation." The case started as an appeal by a conservative nonprofit corporation, Citizens United, of a ruling by the FEC preventing it from airing an anti–Hillary Clinton movie.

Critics of the decision complained that it will increase the influence of special-interest money in politics. President Barack Obama said, "It is a major victory for big oil, Wall Street banks, health insurance companies and the other powerful interests that marshal their power every day in Washington to drown out the voices of everyday Americans." It is not clear which party will benefit most from the Supreme Court's decision, although the decision generally drew praise from Republicans and criticism from Democrats.

The Presidential Campaign: The Primary Race

▶ 8.9 *Outline candidates' strategies for primary races.*

The phrase *presidential fever* refers to the burning political ambition required to seek the presidency. The grueling presidential campaign is a test of strength, character, endurance, and determination. It is physically exhausting and mentally and emotionally draining. Every aspect of the candidates' lives—and the lives of their families—is subject to microscopic inspection by the news media. Most of this coverage is critical, and much of it is unfair. Yet candidates are expected to handle it all with grace and humor, from the earliest testing of the waters through a full-fledged campaign.

Media Mentions   Politicians with presidential ambitions may begin by promoting presidential *mentions* by media columnists and commentators. The media help to identify "presidential timber" years in advance of a presidential race simply by drawing up lists of potential candidates, commenting on their qualifications, and speculating about their intentions. Mentions are likely to come to prominent governors or senators who start making speeches outside their states, who grab the media spotlight on a national issue, or who simply let it be known to the media "off the record" that they are considering a presidential race. Visiting New Hampshire and Iowa and giving speeches there is viewed as "testing the waters" and a signal of presidential ambitions.

Presidential Credentials   Political experience as vice president, governor, U.S. senator, or member of Congress not only inspires presidential ambition but also provides vital experience in political campaigning. However, virtually all presidential candidates testify that the presidential arena is far more challenging than politics at any other level. The experience of running for and holding high public office appears to be a political requirement for the presidency. Some presidential aspirants have tried to make a virtue of their lack of previous political office holding, no doubt hoping to attract support from the many Americans who disdain "politics as usual." But for over a century no major party nominee for president has not previously held office as vice president, governor, U.S. senator, or member of Congress except World War II hero General Dwight D. Eisenhower.

The Decision to Run   The decision to run for president involves complex personal and political calculations. Ambition to occupy the world's most powerful office must be weighed against the staggering costs—emotional as well as financial—of a presidential campaign.

Serious planning, organizing, and fund raising must begin at least 2 years before the general election. A staff must be assembled—campaign managers and strategists, fund-raisers, media experts, pollsters, issues advisers and speechwriters, lawyers and accountants—and supporters must be identified in key states throughout the nation. Paid and volunteer workers must be assembled (see Figure 8.4). Leaders among important interest groups must be contacted. A general campaign strategy must be developed, an organization put in place, and several millions of dollars in campaign contributions pledged in advance of the race. Often the decision to run hinges on whether initial pledges of campaign contributions appear adequate. The serious presidential candidate must be able to anticipate contributions of $100 million or more for primary elections. Most of this work must be accomplished in the preprimary season—the months after Labor Day of the year preceding the election, and before the first primary election.

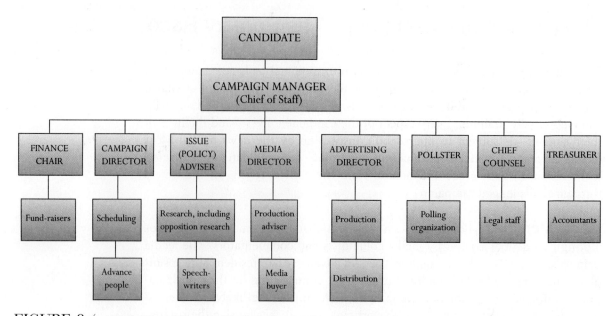

FIGURE 8.4 Who Does What?: Typical Campaign Organization

Campaign organizations vary, but most assign someone to perform these tasks: funding, scheduling appearances, speechwriting, media production and buying, polling, advertising, legal compliance, and checkwriting, even if, in local campaigns, all these tasks must be performed by the candidate or her or his family members.

A Strategy for the Primaries   The road to the White House consists of two separate races: the primary elections and caucuses leading to the Democratic and Republican party nominations, and the general election. Each of these races requires a separate strategy. The primary race requires an appeal to party activists and the more ideologically motivated primary voters in key states. The general election requires an appeal to the less partisan, less attentive, more ideologically moderate general election voters. Thus the campaign strategy developed to win the nomination must give way after the national conventions to a strategy to win the November general election.

Primary Campaigns   Primary campaigns come in different varieties. An incumbent president with no serious competition from within his own party can safely glide through his party's primaries, saving campaign money for the general election. In contrast, the party out of the White House typically goes through a rough-and-tumble primary (and preprimary) season, with multiple presidential aspirants. And when no incumbent president is running for reelection, both parties experience heavy party infighting among multiple presidential hopefuls. (See *Politics Up Close:* "Hillary Versus Barack, 2008" in Chapter 7.)

Candidates strive during the preprimary season to win media attention, to climb the poll ratings, and raise campaign funds. Early front-runners must beware of stumbles and gaffes; they must be prepared for close scrutiny by the media; and they must expect to be the targets of their competitors. Not infrequently, early front-runners lose their momentum even before the first primary elections.

Primary voters are heavily weighted toward party activists, who are more ideologically motivated than the more moderate voters in general elections. Democratic primary voters are more liberal, and Republican primary voters are more conservative, than the voters in the November general election. Democratic primary voters include large numbers of the party's core constituents—union members, public employees, minorities, environmentalists, and feminists.

Presidential candidates must try to appeal not only to the ideological predispositions of their party's primary voters but also convince them of their

The Democratic presidential hopefuls appear at the CNN debate on July 23, 2007, in Charleston, South Carolina. From left to right: Senator Mike Gravel (D-AK); Senator Christopher Dodd (D-CT); former Senator John Edwards (D-NC); Senator Hillary Rodham Clinton (D-NY); Senator Barack Obama (D-IL); New Mexico Gov. Bill Richardson; Senator Joseph Biden (D-DE); and Rep. Dennis Kucinich (D-OH).

The ten Republican presidential hopefuls pose before the start of a nationally televised political debate in Columbia, South Carolina. From left to right: Senator John McCain (R-AZ); former New York City Mayor Rudolph W. Giuliani; former Arkansas governor Mike Huckabee; Rep. Duncan Hunter (R-CA); Senator Sam Brownback (R-KS); former Secretary of Health and Human Services and former Wisconsin governor Tommy G. Thompson; former Massachusetts governor Mitt Romney; former Virginia governor Jim Gilmore; Rep. Tom Tancredo (R-CO); and Rep. Ron Paul (R-TX).

"electability"—the likelihood that they can win the party's nomination and more important go on to win the presidential election. Often primary voters are torn between voting for their favorite candidate based on his or her ideological and issue positions, or voting for the most electable candidate.

The Iowa Caucuses   Iowa has traditionally held party caucuses even before the New Hampshire primary. Rather than going to the polls and casting ballots as in a primary election, Iowans gather at set times and at set locations in each of 1,700 precincts. At the Republican caucuses, a straw vote is taken indicating the voters' choice for presidential nominee. At Democratic caucuses participants divide into groups supporting their preferred presidential nominee. A "viability threshold" eliminates groups with too few members; these members are urged to realign in support of more viable candidates. Finally, a head count is taken which apportions delegates to the county convention and later district conventions. Delegates pledged to a presidential candidate seldom abandon their chosen candidate. The Iowa caucuses, like the New Hampshire primary, inspire retail politics, with presidential candidates shaking hands through small Midwestern towns. The Iowa parties have pledged to keep the Iowa caucuses at least one week ahead of the New Hampshire primary.

The New Hampshire Primary

The New Hampshire Primary   The primary season begins in the winter snows of New Hampshire, traditionally the first state to hold a presidential primary election. New Hampshire is far more important *strategically* to a presidential campaign than it is in delegate strength. As a small state, New Hampshire supplies fewer than 1 percent of the delegates at the Democratic and Republican conventions. But the New Hampshire primary looms very large in media coverage and hence in overall campaign strategy. Although the popular Democratic Iowa party caucuses are held even earlier, New Hampshire is the nation's first primary, and the media begin speculating about its outcome and reporting early state-poll results months in advance.

The New Hampshire primary inspires **retail politics**—direct candidate contact with the voters. Presidential aspirants begin visiting New Hampshire in the year preceding the primary elections, speaking at town hall meetings, visiting with small groups, standing outside of supermarkets, walking through restaurants, greeting workers at factories and offices, and so on. These personal contacts bypass the media's filtering and interpreting of the candidate's personality and message. Retail politics is largely confined to New Hampshire, a small state and a year of preprimary time to reach voters personally. And there is some evidence that voters who actually meet candidates come away with a more favorable view of them.[20]

The "expectations" game is played with a vengeance in the early primaries. Media polls and commentators set the candidates' expected vote percentages, and the candidates and their spokespersons try to deflate these expectations. On election night, the candidates' **spin doctors** sally forth among the crowds of television and newspaper reporters to give a favorable interpretation of the outcome. The candidates themselves appear at campaign headquarters (and, they hope, on national television) to give the same favorable spin to the election results. But the media itself—particularly the television network anchors and reporters and commentators—interpret the results for the American people, determining the early favorites in the presidential horse race.

Iowa and New Hampshire provide the initial *momentum* for the presidential candidates. "Momentum" is more than just a media catchword. The Democratic and Republican winners in these states have demonstrated their voter appeal, their "electability." Favorable results inspire more financial contributions and thus the resources needed to carry the fight into the next group of primary elections. Unfavorable results tend to dry up contributions; weaker candidates may be forced into an early withdrawal.

The Front-End Strategy

The Front-End Strategy   A **front-end strategy** places heavy emphasis on the results from Iowa and New Hampshire and other early primary states. This strategy involves spending all or most of the candidate's available resources—time, energy, and money—in these early states, in the hopes that early victories will provide the momentum, in media attention and financial contributions, to continue the race.

Front Loading Primaries, 2008

Front Loading Primaries, 2008   Traditionally, both the Democratic and Republican parties allowed Iowa and New Hampshire to be the first states in the nation to express their presidential preferences. Yet, over time, resentment grew among other states regarding the influence exercised by these two small states in selecting the early leaders in the presidential race. Governors and state legislatures across the nation began to reschedule their 2008 presidential primaries, pushing

---

retail politics
Direct candidate contact with individual voters.

spin doctors
Practitioners of the art of spin control, or manipulation of media reporting to favor their own candidate.

front-end strategy
Presidential political campaign strategy in which a candidate focuses on winning early primaries to build momentum.

front loading
The scheduling of presidential primary elections early in the year.

New York Senator Hillary Clinton is surrounded by local homeowners and the media as she campaigns in New Hampshire. After finishing third in Iowa, Senator Clinton won New Hampshire.

their dates earlier into January and February. The Democratic and Republican National Committees sought to prevent a mad scramble among the states to be first in the nation in selecting convention delegates pledged to respective candidates. Both national party committees recognized the traditional first-in-the-nation positions of Iowa and New Hampshire and they also approved of early selections by Nevada and South Carolina. But they sought to restrain all other states from making their selections earlier than the first Tuesday in February. A total of twenty-four states chose to comply and to hold their presidential caucuses and primaries on February 5, "Super Tuesday," including California and New York. But Florida and Michigan chose to jump the gun and hold primary elections in late January. The Democratic National Committee at first voted to deny admission to the national convention to delegates from these states, as a penalty for violating national party rules. Later, the DNC rules committee voted to compromise the issue: the Michigan and Florida delegates would be seated at the convention but they could cast only one-half of their elected votes. Finally, after Barack Obama had claimed a majority of delegates, the Democratic convention recognized both state delegations.

Big-State Strategy   Presidential aspirants who begin the race with widespread support among party activists, heavy financial backing, and strong endorsements from the major interest groups can focus their attention on the big-state primaries. A **big-state strategy** generally requires more money, more workers, and better organization than a front-end strategy. But the big states—California, New York, Texas, Florida, Pennsylvania, Ohio, and Michigan—have the most delegates.

big-state strategy
Presidential political campaign strategy in which a candidate focuses on winning primaries in large states because of their high delegate counts.

The Presidential Campaign: The General Election Battle

▶ 8.10 *Outline candidates' strategies for the general election.*

Buoyed by the conventions—and often by postconvention bounces in the polls—the new nominees must now face the general electorate.

POLITICS UP CLOSE

Campaign '08—Obama Versus McCain

A prolonged war, a troubled economy, and an unpopular Republican president all combined to make 2008 a Democratic year. Barack Obama's theme of "change" resonated well with a disillusioned public. And Obama successfully "defined" his opponent, John McCain, as "four more years of the failed policies of George Bush." McCain sought to distance himself from Bush; he adopted the image of a "reformer" and "maverick" who had challenged the president and his party in the past. He sought to "define" Obama as an inexperienced liberal, beholden to the unpopular Democratic leadership in Congress. But his claims were drowned in a sea of voter anxiety over the economy.

John McCain was running behind in the polls when he stunned political observers with his vice-presidential choice, Governor Sarah Palin of Alaska. He hoped to change the dynamics of the race by selecting the first woman to run on a national Republican ticket. (Democrat Geraldine Ferraro was the first woman to run on either party ticket when she ran with Walter Mondale in 1984.) Palin electrified Republican convention goers with her life story as a small town "hockey mom" and a mother of five including a baby with Down syndrome. The youthful, attractive, and socially conservative newcomer described how she first joined the PTA, became a city councilwoman and mayor of Wasilla, Alaska, then fought the Republican establishment of that state to win the GOP gubernatorial nomination, and then went on to become an extremely popular governor. The Palin choice temporarily propelled McCain out of the polling doldrums and into a tie with Obama.

Obama's selection of Delaware Senator Joe Biden provided balance to the Democratic ticket, both in Washington experience and foreign-policy expertise. Biden had served 35 years in Congress and was chairman of the Senate Foreign Relations Committee. Palin captivated Republicans with her folksy charm, but Biden appeared more prepared to assume the presidency.

Obama had already recovered the lead in the polls when the financial crises hit Wall Street and threatened the nation's economic well-being. The economy quickly became the central issue in the campaign. Voters concerned with economic security traditionally turn to Democratic candidates. McCain temporarily "suspended" his campaign to work on the federal bailout of Wall Street. Both candidates supported the bailout, but the polls began to tilt heavily toward Obama.

Economic questions dominated the televised presidential debates. Obama blamed the financial crises on Republican reluctance to regulate the financial industry. He promised to raise taxes on the rich while cutting taxes on the "middle class." He reminded viewers of his early opposition to the war in Iraq and promised to end the war "responsibly." He emphasized diplomacy in dealing with international threats. John McCain blamed the crisis on Democratic support for the failed federal mortgage insurance corporations Fannie Mae and Freddie Mac. He opposed any tax increases, especially during a recession. He called for "victory" in Iraq and took hawkish stands on Iran and Russia. He attacked Obama for his willingness to sit down with dictators "without preconditions."

The Obama campaign shattered all fund-raising records. Obama was the first major party candidate to turn down public financing of his campaign, reversing his earlier stated intention to accept it. By doing so, he was able to accept private contributions that totaled well in excess of the limits that would have prevailed if he accepted federal funds. In contrast, McCain was obliged to accept federal funds and the spending limits that came with them. McCain was outspent by more than two to one.

McCain failed to embrace a single compelling theme comparable to Obama's "Change We Can Believe In." Toward the end of the campaign, McCain adopted "Joe the plumber" as a symbol of working-class Americans who questioned Obama's tax policies. Sarah Palin accused Obama of "palling around with terrorists," a reference to his association with the unrepentant radical William Ayers, a founder of the violent, 60s-era Weather Underground. But most Americans were unmoved. Instead, the looming recession, punctuated by the Wall Street financial scare, occupied their thoughts.

The Obama campaign focused heavily on expanding the electorate, especially adding African American and younger voters. Obama attracted huge and enthusiastic crowds at campaign stops. His Internet site registered millions of e-mail addresses and, perhaps more important, generated millions of dollars in small contributions. On election day Obama was able to field hundreds of thousands of workers in a stunningly successful get-out-the-vote effort. The result was a massive voter turnout not seen since the 1960s.

"Campaign '08" ended very close to where it had begun: Obama won by seven percentage points, 53 to 46. The campaign swept away the last racial barrier in American politics, as the country chose Barack Obama as its first African American president.

VP Candidates Debate
Vice presidential candidates, Democrat Joe Biden and Republican Sarah Palin, square off in a nationally televised debate, October 2, 2008. Palin was folksy and charming but Biden appeared more experienced and "presidential."

General Election Strategies

Strategies in the general election are as varied as the imaginations of campaign advisers, media consultants, pollsters, and the candidates themselves. As noted earlier, campaign strategies are affected by the nature of the times and the state of the economy; by the incumbent or challenger status of the candidate; by the issues, conditions, scandals, or events currently being spotlighted by the media; and by the dynamics of the campaign itself as the candidates attack and defend themselves (see *Politics Up Close*: "Campaign '08—Obama Versus McCain").

Presidential election campaigns must focus on the **Electoral College**. The president is not elected by the national popular vote total but rather by a majority of the *electoral* votes of the states. Electoral votes are won by plurality, winner-take-all popular voting in most of the states. (Exceptions are Nebraska and Maine.) Thus a narrow plurality win in a state delivers *all* of that state's electoral votes. Big-state victories, even by very narrow margins, can deliver big electoral prizes. With a total of 538 electoral votes at stake, *the winner must garner victories in states that total a minimum of 270 electoral votes.* (See *What Do You Think?*: "Should We Scrap the Electoral College?"on page 284.)

Electoral College
The 538 presidential electors apportioned among the states according to their congressional representation (plus three for the District of Columbia) whose votes officially elect the president and vice president of the United States.

Targeting the Swing States

In focusing on the most populous states, with their large electoral votes, candidates must decide which of these states are "winnable," then direct their time, energy, and money to these **swing states**. Candidates cannot afford to spend too much effort in states that already seem to be solidly in their column, although they must avoid the perception that they are ignoring these strong bases of support. Neither can candidates waste much effort on states that already appear to be solidly in their opponent's column. So the swing states receive most of the candidates' time, attention, and television advertising money.

swing states
States that are not considered to be firmly in the Democratic or Republican column.

The Presidential Debates

The nationally televised presidential debates are the central feature of the general election campaign. These debates attract more viewers than any other campaign event. Moreover, they enable a candidate to reach undecided voters and the opponent's supporters, as well as the candidate's own partisans. Even people who usually pay little attention to politics may be drawn in by the drama of the confrontation (see *Politics Up Close*: "The Presidential Debates").

The debates allow viewers an opportunity to see and hear candidates together and to compare their responses to questions as they stand side by side. The

POLITICS UP CLOSE

The Presidential Debates

Presidential debates attract more viewers than any other campaign activity. Most campaign activities—speeches, rallies, motorcades—reach only supporters. Such activities may inspire supporters to go to the polls, contribute money, and even work to get others to vote their way. But televised debates reach undecided voters as well as supporters, and they allow candidates to be seen by supporters of their opponent. Even if issues are not really discussed in depth, people see how presidential candidates react as human beings under pressure.

Kennedy–Nixon

Televised presidential debates began in 1960 when John F. Kennedy and Richard M. Nixon confronted each other on a bare stage before an America watching on black-and-white TV sets. Nixon was the vice president in the popular presidential administration of Dwight Eisenhower; he was also an accomplished college debate-team member. He prepared for the debates as if they were college debates, memorizing facts and arguments. But he failed to realize that image triumphs over substance on television. By contrast, Kennedy was handsome, cool, confident; whatever doubts the American people may have had regarding his youth and inexperience were dispelled by his polished manner. Radio listeners tended to think that Nixon won, and debate coaches scored him the winner. But television viewers preferred the glamorous young Kennedy. The polls shifted in Kennedy's direction after the debate, and he won in a very close general election.

Carter–Ford

President Lyndon Johnson avoided debating in 1964, and Nixon, having learned his lesson, declined to debate in 1968 and 1972. Thus televised presidential debates did not resume until 1976, when incumbent president Gerald Ford, perceiving he was behind in the polls, agreed to debate challenger Jimmy Carter. Ford made a series of verbal slips. Carter was widely perceived as having won the debate, and he went on to victory in the general election.

Reagan–Carter and Reagan–Mondale

It was Ronald Reagan who demonstrated the true power of television. Reagan had lived his life in front of a camera. It was the principal tool of both of his trades—actor and politician. In 1980 incumbent president Jimmy Carter talked rapidly and seriously about programs, figures, and budgets. But Reagan was master of the stage; he was relaxed, confident, joking. He appeared to treat the president of the United States as an overly aggressive, impulsive younger man, regrettably given to exaggeration. When it was all over, it was clear to most viewers that Carter had been bested by a true professional in media skills.

However, in the first of two televised debates with Walter Mondale in 1984, Reagan's skills of a lifetime seemed to desert him. He stumbled over statistics and groped for words. Reagan's poor performance raised the only issue that might conceivably defeat him—his age. The president looked and sounded old. But in the second debate, Reagan laid the perfect trap for his questioners. When asked about his age and capacity to lead the nation, he responded with a serious deadpan expression to a hushed audience and waiting America: "I want you to know that I will not make age an issue in this campaign. I am not going to exploit for political purposes [pause] my opponent's youth and inexperience." The studio audience broke into uncontrolled laughter. Even Mondale had to laugh. With a classic one-liner, Reagan buried the age issue and won not only the debate but also the election.

Bush–Dukakis

In 1988 Michael Dukakis ensured his defeat with a cold, detached performance in the presidential debates, beginning with the very first question. When CNN anchor Bernard Shaw asked, "Governor, if Kitty Dukakis were raped and murdered, would you favor an irrevocable death penalty for the killer?" The question demanded an emotional reply. Instead, Dukakis responded with an impersonal recitation of his stock position on law enforcement. Bush seized the opportunity to establish a more personal relationship with the viewers: Voters responded to Bush, electing him.

Clinton–Bush–Perot

The three-way presidential debates of 1992 drew the largest television audiences in the history of presidential debates. In the first debate, Ross Perot's Texas twang and down-home folksy style stole the show. Chided by his opponents for having no governmental experience, he shot back, "Well, they have a point. I don't have any experience in running up a $4 trillion dollar debt." But it was Bill Clinton's smooth performance in the second debate, with its talk-show format, that seemed to wrap up the election. Ahead in the polls, Clinton appeared at ease walking about the stage and responding to audience questions with sympathy and sincerity. By contrast, George Bush appeared stiff and formal, and somewhat ill-at-ease with the "unpresidential" format.

Clinton–Dole

A desperate Bob Dole, running 20 points behind, faced a newly "presidential" Bill Clinton in their two 1996 debates. (Perot's poor standing in the polls led to his exclusion.) Dole tried to counter his image as a grumpy old man in the first encounter; his humor actually won more laughs from the audience than Clinton's. Dole injected more barbs in the second debate, complaining of "ethical problems in the White House." But Clinton remained cool and comfortable, ignoring the challenger and focusing on the nation's economic health. Viewers, most of whom were already in Clinton's court, judged him the winner of both debates.

Bush–Gore

Separate formats were agreed upon for three debates—the traditional podium, a conference table, and a town hall setting. Gore was assertive, almost to the point of rudeness, but both candidates focused on policy differences rather than on personal attacks. Viewers gave Gore the edge in these debates but they found Bush more likable. Bush appeared to benefit more in the post-debate polls.

Bush–Kerry

Kerry prepared well for the three debates. He appeared tall, earnest, confident, well-informed, and "presidential." He spoke forcefully, avoiding the qualifying clauses and lengthy sentences that had plagued his speeches in the past. Bush appeared uncomfortable, scowling at Kerry's answers, often repeating himself, and failing to "connect" with his audiences. Polls showed Kerry winning each debate.

Obama–McCain

The debates magnified the contrasts: tall, young, and black versus short, old, and white. Obama, leading in the polls, had only to tie McCain, but he edged the aging Senator in style and presence. McCain accused Obama of compiling "the most liberal voting record in the Senate." Obama shot back: "Mostly that's just me opposing George Bush's wrongheaded policies."

Hitting the Talk Shows

Senator Barack Obama, Democratic presidential hopeful, dances with Ellen DeGeneres to the song "Crazy In Love" before taping *The Ellen DeGeneres Show* on October 17, 2007.

debates give audiences a better view of the candidates than they can get from 30-second commercial ads or 7-second news sound bites. Viewers can at least judge how the candidates react under pressure.

However, the debates emphasize candidate image over substantive policy issues. Candidates must appear presidential. They must appear confident, compassionate, concerned, and good humored. They must not appear uncertain or unsure of themselves, or aloof or out of touch with viewers, or easily upset by hostile questions. They must avoid verbal slips or gaffes or even unpolished or awkward gestures. They must remember that the debates are not really debates so much as joint press conferences in which the candidates respond to questions with rehearsed minispeeches and practiced sound bites.

Hitting the Talk Shows   Candidates know that more people watch entertainment talk shows than news shows (see Chapter 6). Oprah Winfrey, Larry King, David Letterman, and Jay Leno all have larger audiences than *Meet the Press, Hardball, Hannity, The O'Reilly Factor*, and others. Moreover, entertainment hosts rarely ask policy questions but rather toss "softball" queries about family, feelings, and personal qualities. Responding to these questions "humanizes" the candidate. And these entertainment shows reach audiences that have relatively little political knowledge or awareness. This provides an opportunity for a candidate to actually win over undecideds and persuadable opposition voters with a likable personality, good humor, and a good rapport with the host.[21] Presidential candidates expend considerable effort to get themselves on as many entertainment talk shows as possible.

The Electoral College Vote   In recent presidential elections, the Democratic candidates (Clinton in 1992 and 1996, Gore in 2000, and Kerry in 2004) have won the Northeastern states, including New York; the upper Midwestern states, including Michigan and Illinois; and, perhaps most important, the West Coast, including California (see Figure 8.5). Republican presidential candidates (Bush in 1992; Dole in 1996; Bush in 2000 and 2004; and McCain in 2008) have shown greater strength in the Great Plains and Rocky Mountain states and in the Southeastern states (forming a Republican "L" on the Electoral College map). If these patterns continue in presidential elections, Democrats can depend on two of the four largest Electoral College vote states, California (55) and New York (31). Republicans must win in the other two, Texas (34) and Florida (27). The Electoral College battleground may be states such as Ohio, Pennsylvania, and Missouri—"swing states" that have cast their votes alternatively for Democratic and Republican candidates in recent presidential elections.

The Voter Decides

▶ 8.11 *Assess influences on voters' choices.*

Understanding the reasons behind the voters' choice at the ballot box is a central concern of candidates, campaign strategists, commentators, and political scientists. Perhaps no other area of politics has been investigated as thoroughly as voting

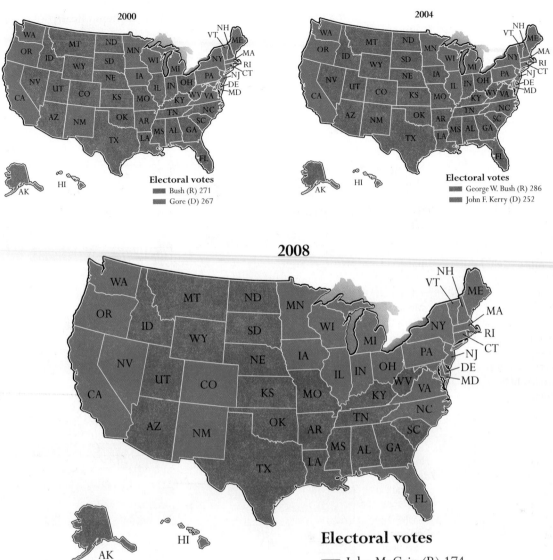

FIGURE 8.5 Red States, Blue States
Electoral College votes by state in the past three presidential elections.

behavior. Survey data on voter choice have been collected for presidential elections for the past half century.[22] We know that voters cast ballots for and against candidates for a variety of reasons—party affiliation, group interests, characteristics and images of the candidates themselves, the economy, and policy issues.[23] But forecasting election outcomes remains a risky business.

Party Affiliation Although many people claim to vote for "the person, not the party," party identification remains a powerful influence in voter choice. Party ties among voters have weakened over time, with increasing proportions of voters labeling themselves as Independents or only weak Democrats or Republicans, and more voters opting to split their tickets or cross party lines than did so a generation ago (see Chapter 7). Nevertheless, party identification remains one of the most important influences on voter choice. Party affiliation is more important in congressional than in presidential elections, but even in presidential

FIGURE 8.6

How We Vote: Party, Ideology, and Nature of the Times in Presidential Voting

Those who identify themselves as members of a major political party are highly likely to vote for the presidential candidates of their party. Likewise, those who identify themselves as liberals are more likely than average to vote for Democrats, and those who identify themselves as conservatives are more likely to vote for Republicans in presidential elections. In addition, voters who see the economic picture as better are more likely to vote for the incumbent, those who are concerned about the nation's economy are more likely to vote against the incumbent.

Source: Election exit polls, Voter News Service.

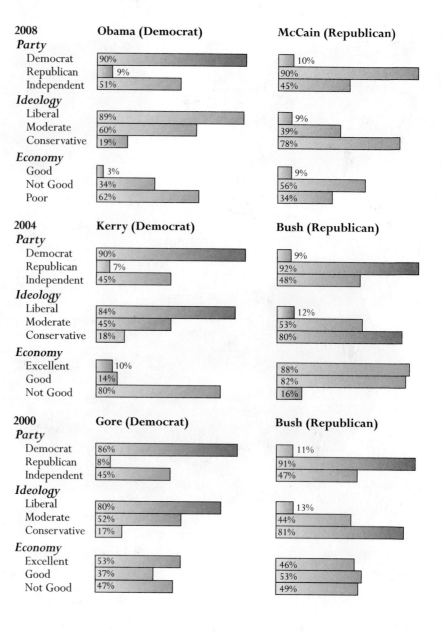

elections the tendency to see the candidate of one's own party as "the best person" is very strong.

Consider the three presidential elections (see Figure 8.6). Self-identified Republicans voted overwhelmingly for George W. Bush in 2000 and 2004, and for McCain in 2008. Self-identified Democrats voted overwhelmingly for Gore in 2000, for Kerry in 2004, and for Obama in 2008.

Because Republican identifiers are outnumbered in the electorate by Democratic identifiers, Republican presidential candidates, and many Republican congressional candidates as well, *must* appeal to Independent and Democratic crossover voters.

Group Voting We already know that various social and economic groups give disproportionate support to the Democratic and Republican parties (see Chapter 7). So it comes as no surprise that recent Democratic presidential candidates have received disproportionate support from African Americans, Catholics, Jews, the less-educated, and union workers; Republican presidential candidates have fared better among whites, Protestants, and better-educated voters (see Figure 8.7).

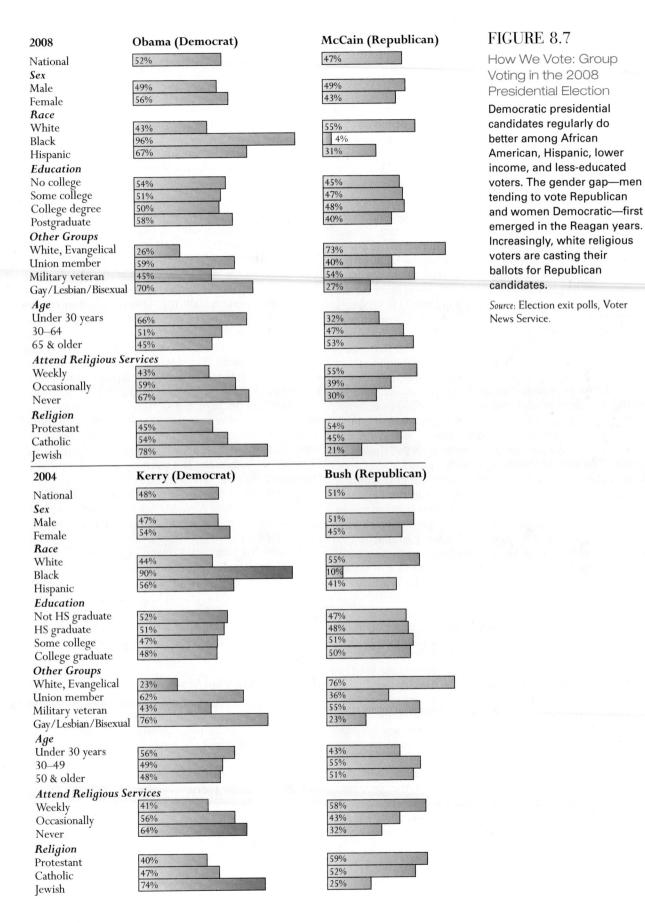

FIGURE 8.7

How We Vote: Group Voting in the 2008 Presidential Election

Democratic presidential candidates regularly do better among African American, Hispanic, lower income, and less-educated voters. The gender gap—men tending to vote Republican and women Democratic—first emerged in the Reagan years. Increasingly, white religious voters are casting their ballots for Republican candidates.

Source: Election exit polls, Voter News Service.

2008 — Obama (Democrat) / McCain (Republican)

Group	Obama (Democrat)	McCain (Republican)
National	52%	47%
Sex		
Male	49%	49%
Female	56%	43%
Race		
White	43%	55%
Black	96%	4%
Hispanic	67%	31%
Education		
No college	54%	45%
Some college	51%	47%
College degree	50%	48%
Postgraduate	58%	40%
Other Groups		
White, Evangelical	26%	73%
Union member	59%	40%
Military veteran	45%	54%
Gay/Lesbian/Bisexual	70%	27%
Age		
Under 30 years	66%	32%
30–64	51%	47%
65 & older	45%	53%
Attend Religious Services		
Weekly	43%	55%
Occasionally	59%	39%
Never	67%	30%
Religion		
Protestant	45%	54%
Catholic	54%	45%
Jewish	78%	21%

2004 — Kerry (Democrat) / Bush (Republican)

Group	Kerry (Democrat)	Bush (Republican)
National	48%	51%
Sex		
Male	47%	51%
Female	54%	45%
Race		
White	44%	55%
Black	90%	10%
Hispanic	56%	41%
Education		
Not HS graduate	52%	47%
HS graduate	51%	48%
Some college	47%	51%
College graduate	48%	50%
Other Groups		
White, Evangelical	23%	76%
Union member	62%	36%
Military veteran	43%	55%
Gay/Lesbian/Bisexual	76%	23%
Age		
Under 30 years	56%	43%
30–49	49%	55%
50 & older	48%	51%
Attend Religious Services		
Weekly	41%	58%
Occasionally	56%	43%
Never	64%	32%
Religion		
Protestant	40%	59%
Catholic	47%	52%
Jewish	74%	25%

WHAT DO YOU THINK?

Should We Scrap the Electoral College?

Americans were given a dramatic reminder in 2000 that the president of the United States is *not* elected by nationwide *popular* vote, but rather by a majority of the *electoral votes* of the states.

How the Electoral College Works

The Constitution grants each state a number of electors equal to the number of its congressional representatives and senators combined (see map). Because representatives are apportioned to the states on the basis of population, the electoral vote of the states is subject to change after each 10-year census. No state has fewer than 3 electoral votes, because the Constitution guarantees every state two U.S. senators and at least one representative. The 23rd Amendment granted 3 electoral votes to the District of Columbia even though it has no voting members of Congress. So winning the presidency requires winning in states with at least 270 of the 538 total electoral votes.

Voters in presidential elections are actually choosing a slate of presidential electors pledged to vote for their party's presidential and vice-presidential candidates. The names of electors seldom appear on the ballot, only the names of the candidates and their parties. The slate that wins a *plurality* of the popular vote in a state (more than any other slate, not necessarily a majority) casts *all* of the state's vote in the Electoral College. (This "winner-take-all" system in the states is not mandated by the Constitution; a state legislature could allocate a state's electoral votes in proportion to the split in the popular vote, as happens in Nebraska and Maine. The winner-take-all system in the states helps ensure that the Electoral College produces a majority for one candidate.)

The Electoral College never meets at a single location; rather, electors meet at their respective state capitals to cast their ballots around December 15, following the general election on the first Tuesday after the first Monday of November. The results are sent to the presiding officer of the Senate, the vice president, who in January presides over their count in the presence of both houses of Congress and formally announces the results. These procedures are usually considered a formality, but the U.S. Constitution does not *require* that electors cast their vote for the winning presidential candidate in their state, and occasionally "faithless electors" disrupt the process, although none has ever changed the outcome.

If no candidate wins a majority of electoral votes, the House of Representatives chooses the president from among the three candidates with the largest number of electoral votes, with each state casting *one* vote. The Constitution does not specify how House delegations should determine their vote, but by House rules, the state's vote goes to the candidate receiving a majority vote in the delegation.

The Historical Record

Only two presidential elections have ever been decided formally by the House of Representatives. In 1800 Thomas Jefferson and Aaron Burr tied in the Electoral College because the 12th Amendment had not yet been adopted to separate presidential from vice-presidential voting; all the Democratic-Republican electors voted for both Jefferson and Burr, creating a tie. In 1824 Andrew Jackson won the popular vote and more electoral votes than anyone else but failed to get a majority. The House chose John Quincy Adams over Jackson, causing a popular uproar and ensuring Jackson's election in 1828.

In addition, in 1876, the Congress was called on to decide which electoral results from the Southern states to validate; a Republican Congress chose to validate enough Republican electoral votes to allow Republican Rutherford B. Hayes to win, even though Democrat Samuel Tilden had won more popular votes. Hayes promised the Democratic Southern states that in return for their acknowledgment of his presidential claim, he would end the military occupation of the South.

In 1888, the Electoral College vote failed to reflect the popular vote. Benjamin Harrison received 233 electoral votes to incumbent president Grover Cleveland's 168, even though Cleveland won about 90,000 more popular votes than Harrison. Harrison served a single lackluster term; Cleveland was elected for a second time in 1892, the only president to serve two nonconsecutive terms.

2000—Gore Wins but Loses

Al Gore won the nationwide popular vote, receiving about 500,000 more votes (out of the more than 100 million ballots cast) than George W. Bush. But the vote in several states was extremely close. On election night, Gore was reported to have won 262 electoral votes to Bush's 246—that is, neither candidate had the necessary 270. The key turned out to be Florida's 25 electoral votes. (New Mexico's 5 votes eventually went to Gore.) The Florida secretary of state declared Bush the winner by a few hundred

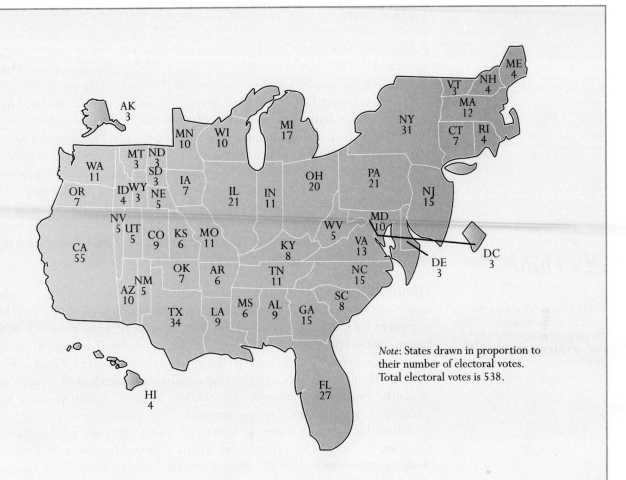

Note: States drawn in proportion to their number of electoral votes. Total electoral votes is 538.

votes out of 6 million cast in that state. The Gore campaign demanded *hand* recounts, especially in heavily Democratic counties in south Florida (including Palm Beach County, where the ballot was said to be confusing to voters). The Bush campaign responded that hand counts are subjective, unreliable, and open to partisan bias. For over a month neither Bush nor Gore would concede the election. Suits were initiated by both candidates in both federal and Florida state courts. Finally, the U.S. Supreme Court rejected Gore's appeal; Florida's votes went to Bush and he was declared the winner.

What Would Replace the Electoral College?

Constitutional proposals to reform the Electoral College have circulated for nearly two hundred years, but none has won widespread support. These reform proposals have included (1) election of the president by direct national popular vote; (2) allocation of each state's electoral vote in proportion to the popular vote each candidate received in the state; (3) allocation of electoral votes to winners of each congressional district and two to the statewide winners.

But most reform proposals create as many problems as they resolve. If the president is to be elected by direct nationwide popular vote, should a plurality vote be sufficient to win? Or should a national runoff be held in the event that no one receives a majority in the first election? Would proportional allocation of electoral votes encourage third-party candidates to enter the race in order to deny the leading candidate a majority?

That is, these groups have given a larger percentage of their vote to the Democratic or Republican candidates than the candidate received from the total electorate.

Race and Gender Gaps

Among the more interesting group voting patterns is the serious *gender gap* affecting recent Republican candidates. Although Reagan won the women's vote in both 1980 and 1984, his vote percentages among men were considerably higher than among women. George H. W. Bush lost the women's vote in both 1988 and 1992. In 1996 the gender gap widened, with 54 percent of women voting for Clinton as opposed to only 38 percent for Dole, and continued in 2000 with women giving Gore 54 percent of the vote as opposed to Bush's 43 percent. Again in 2004 women gave Democrat John F. Kerry 54 percent of their vote, and in 2008 they gave Obama 55 percent of their vote. African Americans have long constituted the most loyal group of Democratic voters, regularly giving the Democratic presidential nominee up to 90 percent or more of their vote. The overall Hispanic vote is Democratic, although a significant portion of Hispanics, notably Cuban Americans in Florida, vote Republican.

Candidate Image

In an age of direct communication between candidates and voters via television, the image of candidates and their ability to relate to audiences have emerged as important determinants of voter choice. Candidate image is most important in presidential contests, inasmuch as presidential candidates are personally more visible to the voter than candidates for lesser offices.[24]

It is difficult to identify exactly what personal qualities appeal most to voters. Warmth, compassion, strength, confidence, honesty, sincerity, good humor, appearance, and "likability" seem important.

"Character" is often a central feature of media coverage of candidates (see Chapter 6). Reports of extramarital affairs, experimentation with drugs, draft dodging, cheating in college, shady financial dealings, conflicts of interest, or lying or misrepresenting facts receive heavy media coverage because they attract large audiences. But it is difficult to estimate how many voters are swayed by so-called character issues.

Attractive personal qualities can win support from opposition-party identifiers and people who disagree on the issues. John F. Kennedy's handsome and youthful appearance, charm, self-confidence, and disarming good humor defeated the heavy-jowled, shifty-eyed, defensive, and ill-humored Richard Nixon. Ronald Reagan's folksy mannerisms, warm humor, and comfortable rapport with television audiences justly earned him the title "The Great Communicator." Reagan disarmed his critics by laughing at his own personal flubs—falling asleep at meetings, forgetting names—and by telling his own age jokes. His personal appeal won more Democratic voters than any other Republican candidate has won in modern history, and he won the votes of many people who disagreed with him on the issues.

Barack Obama's image as a fresh, young, handsome African American fit comfortably with his theme of "change" (see Table 8.2). His personal charm and eloquence served to overcome whatever lack of experience he brought to the race. Over his years in Congress, John McCain had established his "maverick" image and it fit well with his call for "reform." But his age was visible and it was difficult to shed the image of "too old."

The Economy

Fairly accurate predictions of voting outcomes in presidential elections can be made from models of the American economy. Economic

✔ *Think* Again

Should people vote on the basis of a candidate's personal character rather than on his or her policy positions?

TABLE 8.2   Public Perception: Obama and McCain Images of 2008

Considering the following qualities and characteristics, please state whether you think each one better describes Obama or McCain.			
	Most Important Quality	**Who They Voted For**	
Percentage who said:		**Obama**	**McCain**
35%	Can bring needed change	89%	9%
20	Has right experience	6	93
12	Cares about people like me	74	24

Source: Election exit polls, Voter News Service.

conditions at election time—recent growth or decline in personal income, the unemployment rate, consumer confidence, and so on—are related to the vote given the incumbent versus the challenger. Ever since the once-popular Republican incumbent Herbert Hoover was trounced by Franklin Roosevelt as the Great Depression of the 1930s deepened, politicians have understood that voters hold the incumbent party responsible for hard economic times.

Perhaps no other lesson has been as well learned by politicians: Hard economic times hurt incumbents and favor challengers. The economy may not be the only important factor in presidential voting, but it is certainly a factor of great importance.[25] Some evidence indicates that it is not voters' *own* personal economic well-being that affects their vote but rather voter perception of *general* economic conditions. People who perceive the economy as getting worse are likely to vote against the incumbent party, whereas people who think the economy is getting better support the incumbent.[26]

The economy dominated the 2008 presidential race. Nearly two-thirds of voters cited it as the "most important" issue in the election (see Table 8.3), and virtually all of these voters thought the economy was getting worse. These voters broke for Obama over McCain 53 percent to 45 percent. The war in Iraq was cited as most important by only about 10 percent of voters; these voters also tended to support Obama. Voters who thought that terrorism was the most important issue voted heavily for McCain. Voters concerned with health care voted heavily for Obama.

TABLE 8.3   What Mattered Most?: Issues the Voters Cared about in 2008

Relatively few voters cast their ballots strictly on the issue positions of the candidates. But voters cited these as the "most important" issues in 2008.				
	Most Important Issue		**Who They Voted For**	
Rank	**Percentage who said:**		**Obama**	**McCain**
1	63%	Economy	53%	45%
2	10	War in Iraq	59	39
3	9	Terrorism	13	86
4	9	Health care	72	26
5	7	Energy policy	50	47

Source: Election exit polls, Voter News Service.

PEOPLE IN POLITICS

John McCain, Republican Presidential Nominee

John McCain is a genuine American war hero. Early in the Vietnam War, October 1967, his Navy A-4 Skyhawk fighter-bomber was shot down over Hanoi. He fractured both arms and a leg parachuting into a lake. He was beaten and bayoneted by a mob before being taken to Hanoi's infamous prison, dubbed "the Hanoi Hilton." He was denied medical aid; his beatings and interrogations continued; his captors expected him to die. Only when they learned that his father was a top U.S. Navy Admiral did they give him any medical care. After 2 years in solitary confinement he was offered an opportunity to return home as a propaganda ploy by his Vietnam captors. McCain refused the offer and his torture began in earnest. Ropes bound him into painful positions and he was beaten every 2 hours for 4 days, breaking teeth and bones. He finally signed an anti-American propaganda statement, later acknowledging that "Every man has a breaking point. I had reached mine."[a] In March 1973, following the Paris Peace Agreement ending U.S. involvement in the Vietnam War, he was released from captivity. He had been a prisoner for over 5 years.

McCain's father and grandfather had both achieved four-star admiral rank in the U.S. Navy. Young John was frequently uprooted as his family followed his father to various naval stations. (McCain was born in the Panama Canal Zone.) Following family tradition, he attended the U.S. Naval Academy at Annapolis, but his undergraduate career was unimpressive. He received frequent disciplinary demerits and fared poorly in the classroom. He graduated fifth from the bottom of his class in 1958. Yet he redeemed himself by graduating from Navy flight school in 1960. While still uncomfortable with Navy regulations, he became an accomplished pilot and flight instructor.

McCain flew 22 combat missions from U.S. aircraft carriers *Forrestal* and *Oriskany* before being shot down. The Vietnam War, notably its political management, frustrated many who fought there. In McCain's book *Faith of My Fathers*, he wrote, "In all candor, we thought our civilian commanders were complete idiots."[b] Upon his return to the United States he was photographed shaking hands with President Richard Nixon. After additional medical treatment and extensive rehabilitation, McCain again qualified himself to fly carrier jets. He was given command of a training squadron at the Naval Air Station in Jacksonville, Florida. He would later serve as a Navy liaison officer to the U.S. Senate, an assignment that introduced him to Washington politics. In 1980 he divorced and remarried; his second wife was the daughter of a wealthy beer distributor in Phoenix, Arizona. In 1981 McCain retired from the Navy as a Captain, having received a Silver Star, Bronze Star, Legion of Merit, Distinguished Flying Cross, and Purple Heart.

When the long-time Arizona Republican Congressman John Rhodes announced his retirement in 1982, McCain decided to run for the open seat. With the support of the Phoenix business community, McCain edged out two experienced state legislators in the Republican primary and then went on to a lopsided victory in the heavily Republican district. McCain won two terms in the House. When Arizona's conservative icon Barry Goldwater retired from the U.S. Senate, McCain easily won the open seat in 1986 with 60 percent of the vote. He would later win reelection in 1998 with 69 percent of the vote, and in 2004 with an astonishing 77 percent.

McCain's "Straight Talk" campaign for the Republican presidential nomination in 2000 clashed with the ambitions of Texas Governor George W. Bush and the Bush family. McCain's surprise win in the early New Hampshire Republican primary inspired the GOP establishment to turn up the heat on the maverick senator. Bush went on to win the Republican nomination. Relations between McCain and the president remained cool throughout Bush's years in the White House.

Early in 2007 McCain announced on the *Late Show with David Letterman* that he would seek the Republican presidential nomination in 2008. While he described his health as "excellent," he acknowledged that at 72 he would be the oldest person in history to assume the presidency. (Ronald Reagan was 69 years old at his inauguration following the 1980 election.) Opponents as well as supporters were obliged to recognize his status as a national hero, his patriotism and his personal courage.

[a]*U.S. News and World Report*, May 14, 1973.

[b]John McCain, *Faith of My Fathers*. New York: Random House, 1999, p. 185.

A CONSTITUTIONAL NOTE

Campaign Finance and Free Speech

Both the Congress and the Supreme Court have confronted the issue of whether or not limiting campaign spending has the effect of limiting free speech. In 1976 in *Buckley v. Valeo,* the Supreme Court struck down Congress's limit on what an individual candidate or independent organization could spend to promote its own views in a campaign. "The First Amendment denies government the power to determine that spending to promote one's political views is . . . excessive. In the free society ordained by our Constitution, it is not the government but the people who must retain control over the quantity and range of debate in a political campaign."[a] This decision means that wealthy individuals can spend unlimited amounts on their own campaigns, and independent organizations can spend unlimited amounts as long as their spending is independent of a candidate's campaign. However, the Supreme Court approved limits on *contributions* by individuals and organizations—distinguishing between contributions and expenditures.

It approved the Federal Election Commission limits on individual and organizational contributions to political campaigns. Congress sought to remedy the many holes in the original Federal Election Campaign Act of 1974 in its Bipartisan Campaign Reform Act of 2002. It placed limits on "soft-money" contributions to political parties, most of which found its way into candidate campaigns. However, Congress did not challenge the Court's *Buckley* decision by trying to prevent individuals or nonprofit organizations from spending money to broadcast their views. Limiting spending for political broadcasting would "place substantial and direct restrictions on the ability of candidates, citizens, and associations to engage in protected political speech."[b] The result was the emergence of independent organizations, known as "527s," in subsequent elections. In 2010 the Supreme Court held that corporations and unions could not be prohibited from spending money "for express advocacy or electioneering purposes."[c]

[a]*Buckley v. Valeo,* 424 U.S. 1 (1976).
[b]*McConnell v. Federal Election Commission,* 590 U.S. 93 (2003).
[c]*Citizens United v. F.E.C.,* January 21, 2010.

Issue Voting   Casting one's vote exclusively on the basis of the policy positions of the candidates is rare. Most voters are unaware of the specific positions taken by candidates on the issues. Indeed, voters often believe that their preferred candidate agrees with them on the issues, even when this is not the case. In other words, voters project their own policy views onto their favorite candidate more often than they decide to vote for a candidate because of his or her position on the issues.

Nonetheless, campaigns often try to exploit "wedge issues" that may entice citizens to cross party lines and vote for the opposition candidate. A wedge issue is usually a hot-button issue, one that generates intense feelings (see *Controversy:* "Abortion: The Hot-Button Issue" in Chapter 5). Many voters hold policy positions that conflict with their own party's candidate. Campaigns may try to win over some of these "persuadable" voters by appealing intensely to their held policy positions.[27]

Summary

▶ **8.1** *Evaluate the role of elections in American democracy.*

Although winning candidates often claim a mandate for their policy proposals, in reality few campaigns present clear policy alternatives to the voters, few voters cast their ballots on the basis of policy considerations, and the policy preferences of the electorate can seldom be determined from election outcomes.

▶ **8.2** *Characterize the various factors that motivate people to pursue a political career.*

Personal ambition for power and celebrity drives the decision to seek public office. Political entrepreneurship, professionalism, and careerism have come to dominate political recruitment; lawyers have traditionally dominated American politics.

▶ **8.3** *Explain the advantages of incumbency.*

Incumbents begin campaigns with many advantages: name recognition, financial support, goodwill from services they perform for constituents, large-scale public projects they bring to their districts, and other resources of office.

▶ **8.4** *Identify the main components of campaign strategies.*

Campaigning for office is largely a media activity, dominated by professional advertising specialists, fund-raisers, media consultants, and pollsters.

▶ **8.5** *Analyze the role of money in campaigns.*

The professionalization of campaigning and the heavy costs of a media campaign drive up the costs of running for office. These huge costs make candidates heavily dependent on financial support from individuals and organizations. Fund-raising occupies more of a candidate's time than any other campaign activity.

▶ **8.6** *Identify the major sources of funding for political campaigns.*

Campaign contributions are made by politically active individuals and organizations, including political action committees.

▶ **8.7** *Assess the motivations of contributors to political campaigns.*

Many contributions are made in order to gain access to policymakers and assistance with government business. Some contributors are ideologically motivated; others merely seek to rub shoulders with powerful people.

▶ **8.8** *Evaluate efforts to regulate campaigns finances.*

The agency that is responsible for enforcing the limits on campaign contributions to federal elections is the six-member Federal Election Commission. The members are traditionally appointed in staggered terms by the president with three seats for Democrats and three seats for the Republicans.

▶ **8.9** *Outline candidates' strategies for primary races.*

Presidential primary strategies emphasize appeals to party activists and core supporters, including the more ideologically motivated primary voters.

▶ **8.10** *Outline candidates' strategies for the general election.*

In a general election campaign, presidential candidates usually seek to broaden their appeal to moderate, centrist voters while holding on to their core supporters. Campaigns must focus on states where the candidate has the best chance for gaining the 270 electoral votes needed to win.

▶ **8.11** *Assess influences on voters' choices.*

Voter choice is influenced by party identification, group membership, perceived image of the candidates, and to a lesser extent, ideology and issue preferences.

Chapter Test

▶ **8.1** *Evaluate the role of elections in American democracy.*

1. Which of the following is *not* a condition for an election to serve as a policy mandate?
   a. Competing candidates have to offer clear policy alternatives
   b. Voting must be based on policy alternatives
   c. The vote must be at least 80 percent or better in favor of the policy alternative
   d. Elected officials have to be bound by their campaign promises

2. Voting for or against someone or a party on the basis of past performance is known as
   a. payback voting
   b. *ex post facto* voting
   c. retrospective voting
   d. performance voting

▶ **8.2** *Characterize the various factors that motivate people to pursue a political career.*

3. Those seeking political office may desire all of the following *except*
   a. power
   b. celebrity
   c. privacy
   d. social status

4. The most overrepresented profession in politics is
   a. journalists
   b. academics
   c. political scientists
   d. attorneys

▶ **8.3** *Explain the advantages of incumbency.*

5. Political incumbents enjoy advantages over challengers such as
   a. greater name recognition
   b. the ability to raise money more easily
   c. office resources
   d. all of the above

▶ **8.4** *Identify the main components of campaign strategies.*

6. Most campaign strategies provide for all of the following *except*
   a. selecting a theme
   b. defining the opponent
   c. holding post-election evaluation sessions
   d. coordinating advertising messages

▶ **8.5** *Analyze the role of money in campaigns.*

7. In a large state it could easily cost in excess of _____ to run a winning campaign for the U.S. Senate.
   a. $10 million
   b. $15 million
   c. $20 million
   d. $25 million

▶ **8.6** *Identify the major sources of funding for political campaigns.*

8. Probably the most important hurdle to any candidate for office is
   a. image control
   b. fund-raising
   c. selecting the right message
   d. media access

9. The largest expenditures for campaigns are for
   a. television advertising
   b. fund-raising
   c. staff salaries
   d. polling

▶ **8.7** *Assess the motivations of contributors to political campaigns.*

10. Which of the following is not a characteristic that is commonly associated with individual contributors to political campaigns?
    a. male
    b. middle-aged
    c. white
    d. all of the above

11. Which of the following groups would be most likely to contribute to the Republican Party?
    a. Emily's List
    b. the Service Employees International Union
    c. the American Federation of Teachers
    d. the National Rifle Association

▶ **8.8** *Evaluate efforts to regulate campaigns finances.*

12. The agency (or agencies) that has the main responsibility for enforcing the laws limiting campaign contributions is the
    a. FBI, or Federal Bureau of Investigations
    b. FEC, or Federal Election Commission
    c. fifty state governments that administer the elections
    d. Congressional Election Oversight Committee

▶ **8.9** *Outline candidates' strategies for primary races.*

13. The first state to have a presidential primary election is usually
    a. New Hampshire
    b. Iowa
    c. Vermont
    d. Hawaii

14. The "front-end" strategy refers to
    a. spin control
    b. using overwhelming assets to assure victory
    c. winning the early elections to build momentum
    d. framing the story from the beginning

15. Iowa is an important state during primary season because it
    a. "mirrors" middle America
    b. has its party caucus even before the first primary election
    c. has the first primary election
    d. almost invariably foreshadows how the country will go in the general election

▶ **8.10** *Outline candidates' strategies for the general election.*

16. If a candidate is primarily interested in increasing her or his name recognition, it would be best to *miss* which of the following shows?
    a. *Oprah*
    b. *Meet the Press*
    c. *The Tonight Show with Jay Leno*
    d. *Larry King Live*

17. "Swing states" refer to those states that
    a. display tolerance for social issues like immigration
    b. are the conservative states that have swung away from social liberalism
    c. are moderate and may vote Democratic or Republican
    d. are firmly "Red" rather than "Blue"

▶ **8.11** *Assess influences on voters' choices.*

18. It would be accurate to say that Hispanics generally support the Democrats *except* for
    a. Puerto Ricans in New York
    b. Mexicans in California
    c. Mexicans in the Rio Grande Valley
    d. Cubans in Florida

myp**⊙**liscilab EXERCISES

Apply what you learned in this chapter on MyPoliSciLab.

📖—[•—Read on **mypoliscilab.com**

eText: Chapter 8

✔—[•—**Study** and **Review** on **mypoliscilab.com**

Pre-Test

Post-Test

Chapter Exam

Flashcards

👁—[•—**Watch** on **mypoliscilab.com**

Video: Money in the 2008 Presidential Race

Video: Oprah Fires Up Obama Campaign

Video: Dissecting Party Primaries

Video: State Primary Race

Video: Who Are the Superdelegates?

✳—[•—**Explore** on **mypoliscilab.com**

Simulation: You Are a Campaign Manager: McCain Navigates Campaign Financing

Simulation: You Are a Campaign Manager: Countdown to 270!

Simulation: You Are a Campaign Manager: Lead Obama to Battleground State Victory

Simulation: You Are a Media Consultant to a Political Candidate

Comparative: Comparing Voting and Elections

Comparative: Comparing Political Campaigns

Timeline: Nominating Process

Timeline: Close Calls in Presidential Elections

Timeline: Television and Presidential Campaigns

Visual Literacy: Iowa Caucuses

Visual Literacy: The Electoral College: Campaign Consequences and Mapping the Results

Key Terms

mandate   251
retrospective voting   252
professionalism   253
careerism   253
incumbents   254
reelection rates   254
name recognition   254

challengers   254
franking privilege   255
campaign strategy   256
negative campaigning   256
focus group   258
photo ops   259
sound bites   259

mobilize   260
issue ads   264
political action committees (PACs)   266
Federal Election Commission (FEC)   267
soft money   268

retail politics   274
spin doctors   274
front-end strategy   274
front loading   274
big-state strategy   275
Electoral College   277
swing states   277

Suggested Readings

Abramson, Paul R., John H. Aldrich, and David W. Rohde. *Change and Continuity in the 2008 Elections.* Washington, D.C.: CQ Press, 2009. An in-depth analysis of the 2008 presidential and congressional elections assessing the impact of party loyalties, presidential performance, group memberships, and policy preferences on voter choice.

Ferrar-Myers, Victoria, and Diana Dwyre. *Limits and Loopholes: The Quest for Money, Free Speech and Fair Elections.* Washington, D.C.: CQ Press, 2007. A description of the passage of campaign finance legislation and subsequent court cases.

Fiorina, Morris P. *Retrospective Voting in American National Elections*. New Haven, Conn.: Yale University Press, 1981. Argues that retrospective judgments guide voter choice in presidential elections.

Flanigan, William H., and Nancy H. Zingale. *Political Behavior of the American Electorate*. 12th ed. Washington, D.C.: CQ Press, 2009. A comprehensive summary of the extensive research literature on the effects of party identification, opinion, ideology, the media, and candidate image on voter choice and election outcomes.

Iyengar, Shanto, and Stephen Ansolabehere. *Going Negative: How Political Advertisements Shrink and Polarize the Electorate*. New York: Free Press, 1996. The real problem with negative political ads is not that they sway voters to support one candidate over another, but that they reinforce the belief that all are dishonest and cynical.

Lewis-Beck, Michael S. *The American Voter Revisited*. An updated replication of the original *American Voter* (1960) confirming the influences of party, ideology, nature of the times, and issues on voter choice.

Rosenstone, Steven. *Forecasting Presidential Elections*. New Haven, Conn.: Yale University Press, 1985. A discussion of the models employed to forecast presidential election outcomes based on unemployment, inflation, and personal income statistics.

Sabato, Larry J., and Glenn R. Simpson. *Dirty Little Secrets: The Persistence of Corruption in American Politics*. New York: Random House Times Books, 1996. A political scientist and a journalist combine to produce a lurid report on unethical and corrupt practices in campaigns and elections.

Suggested Web Sites

Campaigns and Elections www.campaignline.com
The Web site for *Campaigns and Elections*, a magazine directed toward candidates, campaign managers, political TV advertisers, political consultants, and lobbyists.

Center for Responsive Politics www.opensecrets.org
The site of an organization devoted to the study of campaign finance laws, the role of money in elections, PACs, "soft money," and special-interest groups.

The Center for Voting and Democracy www.fairvote.org
A site with material on possible changes in the Electoral College.

Federal Election Commission www.fec.gov
The FEC Web site contains ample information on the important regulations and statutes relating to campaign finance.

Chapter Test Answer Key

1. C	4. D	7. D	10. D	13. A	16. B
2. C	5. D	8. B	11. D	14. C	17. C
3. C	6. C	9. A	12. B	15. B	18. D

9 INTEREST GROUPS
Getting Their Share and More

" Functional interests in the United States are quite directly expressed through the hundreds of special agencies which maintain headquarters in Washington and direct lobbying activities toward officials and propaganda activities toward the electorate. "

Harold Lasswell

Chapter Outline and Learning Objectives

Interest-Group Power
▶ *9.1 Explain the origins, functions, strengths, and weaknesses of the interest-group system in America.*

Origins of Interest Groups
▶ *9.2 Trace the origins and growth of the American interest-group system.*

The Organized Interests in Washington
▶ *9.3 Characterize the interests represented by organized interest groups lobbying in Washington.*

Leaders and Followers
▶ *9.4 Explain how interest-group leaders create and build organizations.*

The Washington Lobbyists
▶ *9.5 Describe the overall environment of lobbying in Washington.*

The Fine Art of Lobbying
▶ *9.6 Identify the main activities of lobbyists.*

PAC Power
▶ *9.7 Outline the development, role, and structure of political action committees.*

Lobbying the Bureaucracy
▶ *9.8 Assess the relationships between interest groups and bureaucratic agencies.*

Lobbying the Courts
▶ *9.9 Identify ways in which interest groups seek to influence the federal court system.*

Politics as Interest-Group Conflict
▶ *9.10 Evaluate different positions on the consequences of interest groups for American democracy.*

Think about Politics

1. Do special-interest groups in America obstruct the majority of citizens' wishes on public policy?
   YES ◯ NO ◯

2. Should people join an interest group such as the American Association of Retired Persons for its discounts, magazines, and travel guides even if they disagree with its policy goals?
   YES ◯ NO ◯

3. Should state and local governments use taxpayers' money to lobby Congress to get federal funds?
   YES ◯ NO ◯

4. Should former government officials be allowed to lobby their former colleagues?
   YES ◯ NO ◯

5. Should interest groups be prohibited from making large campaign contributions in their effort to influence public policy?
   YES ◯ NO ◯

6. If a lobbyist makes a campaign contribution to a Congress member, hoping to gain support for a bill, is this a form of bribery?
   YES ◯ NO ◯

7. Is organized interest-group activity a cause of government gridlock?
   YES ◯ NO ◯

What role do interest groups play in politics? Their organization, their money, and their influence in Washington raise the possibility that interest groups, rather than individuals, may in fact hold the real power in politics. They may be the "who" that determines the "what" that the rest of us get.

interest groups
Organizations seeking to directly influence government policy.

Interest-Group Power

▶ *9.1 Explain the origins, functions, strengths, and weaknesses of the interest-group system in America.*

Organization is a means to power—to determining who gets what in society. Interest groups are organizations that seek to influence government policy. The 1st Amendment to the Constitution recognizes "the right of the people peaceably to assemble and to petition the government for a redress of grievances." Americans enjoy a fundamental right to organize themselves to influence government.

Electoral Versus Interest-Group Systems
The *electoral system* is organized to represent geographically defined constituencies—states and congressional districts in Congress. The *interest-group system* is organized to represent economic, professional, ideological, religious, racial, gender, and issue constituencies. In other words, the interest-group system supplements the electoral system by providing people with another avenue of participation. Individuals may participate in politics by supporting candidates and parties in elections, and also by joining **interest groups**, organizations that pressure government to advance their interests.[1]

Interest-group activity provides more *direct* representation of policy preferences than electoral politics. At best, individual voters can influence government policy only indirectly through elections (see Chapter 8). Elected politicians try to represent many different—and even occasionally conflicting—interests. But interest groups provide concentrated and direct representation of policy views in government.

majoritarianism
Tendency of democratic governments to allow the faint preferences of the majority to prevail over the intense feelings of minorities.

organizational sclerosis
Society encrusted with so many special benefits to interest groups that everyone's standard of living is lowered.

Think
Again

Do special-interest groups in America obstruct the majority of citizens' wishes on public policy?

Checking Majoritarianism   The interest-group system gives voice to special interests, whereas parties and the electoral system cater to the majority interest. Indeed, interest groups are often defended as a check on **majoritarianism**, the tendency of democratic governments to allow the faint preferences of a majority to prevail over the intense feelings of minorities. However, the interest-group system is frequently attacked because it obstructs the majority from implementing its preferences in public policy.

Concentrating Benefits while Dispersing Costs   Interest groups seek special benefits, subsidies, privileges, and protections from the government. The costs of these *concentrated* benefits are usually *dispersed* to all taxpayers, none of whom individually bears enough added cost to merit spending time, energy, or money to organize a group to oppose the benefit. Thus the interest-group system concentrates benefits to the few and disperses costs to the many. The system favors small, well-organized, homogeneous interests that seek the expansion of government activity at the expense of larger but less well-organized citizen-taxpayers. Over long periods of time, the cumulative activities of many special-interest groups, each seeking concentrated benefits to themselves and dispersed costs to others, result in what has been termed **organizational sclerosis**, a society so encrusted with subsidies, benefits, regulations, protections, and special treatments for organized groups that work, productivity, and investment are discouraged and everyone's standard of living is lowered.

Origins of Interest Groups

▶ 9.2 *Trace the origins and growth of the American interest-group system.*

James Madison viewed interest groups—which he called "factions"—as a necessary evil in politics. He defined a faction as "a number of citizens, whether amounting to a majority or a minority of the whole, who are united and actuated by some common impulse of passion, or of interest, adverse to the rights of other citizens, or to the permanent and aggregate interests of the community." He believed that interest groups not only conflict with each other but, more important, also conflict with the common good. Nevertheless, Madison believed that the origin of interest groups was to be found in human nature—"a zeal for different opinions concerning religion, concerning government, and many other points"—and therefore impossible to eliminate from politics.[2]

Organized Protest
The NAACP, one of the nation's oldest civil rights organizations, protests a Michigan voter referendum to end racial preferences in state affirmative action programs. The referendum passed in November, 2006, by a 58% to 42% margin.

POLITICS UP CLOSE

Super Lobby: The Business Roundtable

The Business Roundtable was established in 1972 "in the belief that business executives should take an increased role in the continuing debates about public policy."[a] The organization is composed of the chief executive officers of the largest corporations in America. It is financed through corporate membership fees. It boasts that its member corporations employ more than 12 million people and pay more than 60 percent of all corporate income taxes.

The Roundtable organizes itself into five policy areas called "initiatives." Within each initiative members direct research, supervise preparation of position papers, recommend policy, and lobby Congress and the administration. These five initiatives are: Consumer Health and Retirement (active in the health care issue, opposed to the "public option," favoring the reform of medical liability laws); Corporate Leadership (active and financial services regulatory reform); Education

and Innovation and Workforce (supporting "world-class education" and especially vocational technical schools); International Engagement (supporting free trade); Sustainable Growth (recognizing that global warming is "a real problem" but asserting that "we have an obligation to keep the lights on").

The power of the Business Roundtable stems in part from its "firm rule" that a corporate chief executive officer (CEO) cannot send a substitute to its meetings. Moreover, corporate CEOs lobby Congress in person rather than sending paid lobbyists. One congressional staff member explained, "If a corporation sends its Washington representative to our office, he's probably going to be shunted over to a legislative assistant. But the chairman of the board is going to get to see the senator. . . . Very few members of Congress would not meet with the president of a Business Roundtable Corporation."[b]

[a]See the Business Roundtable, "The History of the Business Roundtable," 1998.
[b]Quotations from *Time*, April 13, 1981, pp. 76–77.

Protecting Economic Interests   Madison believed that "the most common and durable source of factions, has been the various and unequal distribution of property." With genuine insight, he identified *economic interests* as the most prevalent in politics: "a landed interest, a manufacturing interest, a mercantile interest, a moneyed interest, with many lesser interests." From Madison's era to the present, businesspeople and professionals, bankers and insurers, farmers and factory workers, merchants and shippers have organized themselves to press their demands on government (see *Politics Up Close:* "Super Lobby: The Business Roundtable").

Advancing Social Movements   Major social movements in American history have spawned many interest groups. Abolitionist groups were formed before the Civil War to fight slavery. The National Association for the Advancement of Colored People (NAACP) emerged in 1909 to fight segregation laws and to rally public support against lynching and other violence against African Americans. Farm organizations emerged from the populist movement of the late nineteenth century to press demands for railroad rate regulation and easier credit terms. The small trade unions that workers formed in the nineteenth century to improve their pay and working conditions gave way to large national unions in the 1930s as workers sought protection for the rights to organize, bargain collectively, and strike. The success of the women's suffrage movement led to the formation of the League of Women Voters in the early twentieth century, and a generation later the feminist movement inspired the National Organization for Women (NOW).

Seeking Government Benefits   As government expands its activities, it creates more interest groups. Wars create veterans' organizations. The first large veterans' group—the Grand Army of the Republic—formed after the Civil War and successfully lobbied for bonus payments to veterans over the years. Today the American Legion, the Veterans of Foreign Wars, and the Vietnam Veterans of America engage

(a)

(b)

(c)

(d)

A History of Protests

From the Whiskey Rebellion of 1794 (a), to the women's suffrage movement of the early twentieth century (b), to the civil rights marches of the 1960s (c), to the gay rights marches of the 1990s (d), protest has a long history as an interest group activity in the United

in lobbying the Congress and monitor the activities of the Department of Veterans Affairs. As the welfare state grew, so did organizations seeking to obtain benefits for their members, including the nation's largest interest group, the American Association of Retired Persons (AARP). Over time, organizations seeking to protect and expand welfare benefits for the poor also emerged. Federal grant-in-aid programs to state and local governments inspired the development of governmental interest groups—the Council of State Governments, the National League of Cities, the National Governors Association, the U.S. Conference of Mayors, and so on—so that it is not uncommon today to see state and local governments lobby the national government (cities, towns, and even counties lobby their state governments). Expanded government support for education led to political activity by the National Education Association, the American Federation of Teachers, the American Association of Land Grant Colleges and Universities, and other educational groups.

Responding to Government Regulation

As more businesses and professions came under government regulation in the twentieth century, more organizations formed to protect and further their interests, including such large and powerful groups as the American Medical Association (doctors), the American Bar Association (lawyers), and the National Association of Broadcasters (broadcasters). Indeed, the issue of regulation—whether of public utilities, interstate transportation, mine safety, medicines, or children's pajamas—always causes the formation of interest groups. Some form to demand regulation; others form to protect their members from regulatory burdens.

The Organized Interests in Washington

▶ 9.3 *Characterize the interests represented by organized interest groups lobbying in Washington.*

There are more than 1 million nonprofit organizations in the United States, several thousand of which are officially registered in Washington as lobbyists.[3] Trade and professional associations and corporations are the most common lobbies in Washington, but unions, public-interest groups, farm groups, environmental groups, ideological groups, religious and civil rights organizations, women's groups, veterans and defense-related groups, groups organized around a single issue (for example, Mothers Against Drunk Driving), and even organizations representing state and local governments also recognize that they need to be "where the action is." Among this huge assortment of organizations, many of which are very influential in their highly specialized field, there are a number of well-known organized interests. Even a partial list of organized interest groups (see Table 9.1) demonstrates the breadth and complexities of interest-group life in American politics.

Business and Trade Organizations
Traditionally, economic organizations have dominated interest-group politics in Washington. There is ample evidence that economic interests continue to play a major role in national policy making, despite the rapid growth over the last several decades of consumer and environmental organizations. Certainly in terms of the sheer number of organizations with offices and representatives in Washington, business and professional groups and occupational and trade associations predominate. More than half of the organizations with offices in Washington are business or trade associations, and all together these organizations account for about 75 percent of all of the reported lobbying expenditures.[4]

Business interests are represented, first of all, by large inclusive organizations, such as the U.S. Chamber of Commerce, representing thousands of local chambers of commerce across the nation; the National Association of Manufacturers; the Business Roundtable, representing the nation's largest corporations; and the National Federation of Independent Businesses, representing small business. Specific business interests are also represented by thousands of **trade associations**. These associations can closely monitor the interests of their specialized memberships. Among the most powerful of these associations are the American Bankers Association, the American Gas Association, the American Iron and Steel Institute, the National Association of Real Estate Boards, the American Petroleum Institute, and the National Association of Broadcasters. In addition, many individual corporations and firms achieve representation in Washington by opening their own lobbying offices or by hiring experienced professional lobbying, public relations, or law firms.

trade associations
Interest groups composed of businesses in specific industries.

Professional Associations
Professional associations rival business and trade organizations in lobbying influence. The American Bar Association (ABA), the American Medical Association (AMA), and the National Education Association (NEA) are three of the most influential groups in Washington. For example, the ABA, which includes virtually all of the nation's practicing attorneys, and its more specialized offspring, the American Association for Justice (trial lawyers), have successfully resisted efforts to reform the nation's tort laws (see *A Conflicting View*: "America Is Drowning in a Sea of Lawsuits," Chapter 13).

TABLE 9.1   Major Organized Interest Groups, by Type

Business
Business Roundtable
National Association of Manufacturers
National Federation of Independent Businesses
National Small Business Association
U.S. Chamber of Commerce

Trade
American Bankers Association
American Gas Association
American Hospital Association
American Iron and Steel Institute
American Petroleum Institute
American Truckers Association
Automobile Dealers Association
Edison Electric Institute
Home Builders Association
Motion Picture Association of America
National Association of Broadcasters
National Association of Realtors
Pharmaceutical Mfrs. of America

Professional
American Bar Association
American Medical Association
American Association for Justice (trial lawyers)
National Education Association

Union
AFL-CIO
American Federation of State, County, and Municipal Employees
American Federation of Teachers
International Brotherhood of Teamsters
International Ladies' Garment Workers Union
National Association of Letter Carriers
United Auto Workers
United Postal Workers
United Steel Workers

Agricultural
American Farm Bureau Federation
National Cattlemen's Association
National Farmers Union
National Grange
National Milk Producers Federation
Tobacco Institute

Women
League of Women Voters
National Organization for Women

Public Interest
Common Cause
Consumer Federation of America
Public Citizen
Public Interest Research Groups

Ideological
American Conservative Union
Americans for Constitutional Action (conservative)
Americans for Democratic Action (liberal)
Federalist Society (conservative)
People for the American Way (liberal)
MoveOn (liberal)

Single Issue
Mothers Against Drunk Driving
NARAL Pro-Choice America
National Rifle Association
National Right to Life Committee
PETA
Planned Parenthood Federation of America
National Taxpayers Union

Environmental
Environmental Defense Fund
Friends of the Earth
Greenpeace
National Wildlife Federation
National Resources Defense Council
Nature Conservancy
Sierra Club
Union of Concerned Scientists

Wilderness Society
Zero Population Growth

Religious
American Israel Public Affairs Committee
Anti-Defamation League of B'nai B'rith
Christian Coalition
National Council of Churches
U.S. Catholic Conference

Civil Rights
American Civil Liberties Union
American Indian Movement
Gay Lesbian Alliance Against Discrimination
Mexican-American Legal Defense and Education Fund
National Association for the Advancement of Colored People
National Urban League
Southern Christian Leadership Conference

Age Related
American Association of Retired Persons
National Committee to Preserve Social Security
Children's Defense Fund

Veterans
American Legion
Veterans of Foreign Wars
Vietnam Veterans of America

Defense
Air Force Association
American Security Council
Army Association
Navy Association

Government
National Association of Counties
National Conference of State Legislators
National Governors Association
National League of Cities
U.S. Conference of Mayors

Organized Labor   Labor organizations have declined in membership over the last several decades. The percentage of the private workforce belonging to unions has declined from about 37 percent in the 1950s to about 8 percent today (see Figure 9.1). The major industrial unions—for example, the United Steelworkers of America, United Automobile Workers, United Mine Workers—have shrunk in membership. Only the unions of government employees—for example, the American Federation of State, County, and Municipal Employees, the National Education Association—and some transportation and service workers unions—for

WHAT DO YOU THINK?

Which Groups Deserve Washington's Attention?

Americans distinguish between groups that they believe merit the attention of Washington policymakers and those that do not. The majority of people polled believe that big corporations, Hollywood movie executives, and trial lawyers receive "too much" attention in Washington. In contrast, majorities believe that senior citizens, the poor, small business owners, and veterans receive "too little" attention in the nation's capitol.

Q. Do you think the political leaders in Washington pay too much attention, about the right amount, or too little attention to the needs of each of the following groups?

	Too Much	About Right	Too Little
Big corporations	76%	16%	6%
Hollywood movie executives	74	19	4
Trial lawyers	55	31	10
Defense contractors	53	27	16
Religious conservatives	48	33	17
Gays and lesbians	46	27	24
Labor unions	34	38	26
Hispanics	25	40	32
Doctors	22	49	26
Blacks	16	48	34
Senior citizens	5	28	66
The poor	5	18	77
Small-business owners	3	28	68
Military veterans	2	16	81

Source: Gallup Poll, March, 2007.

example, the Teamsters Union, Service Employees International, International Brotherhood of Electrical Workers—have gained members in recent years.

Nevertheless, labor unions remain a major political influence in Congress and the Democratic Party. The AFL-CIO is a federation of sixty-eight separate

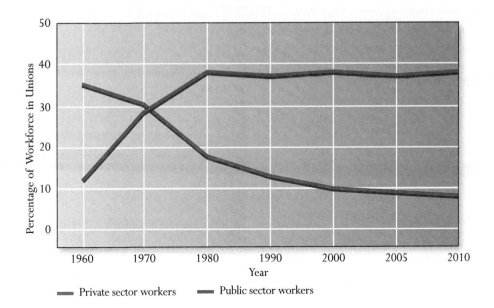

FIGURE 9.1

Going Public: Unions and the American Workforce

Public employee unions, including teachers' unions, have remained strong over recent decades, while union membership in the private sector has declined.

Source: Statistical Abstract of the United States, 2010.

Private sector workers — Public sector workers

POLITICS UP CLOSE

Service Employees International Union

The 2.1 million member Service Employees International Union (SEIU) is the nation's fastest-growing labor union. It focuses on organizing workers in the health care field, including employees of hospitals and nursing homes. It is also the largest property services union, including employees in building cleaning (janitors) and security. It competes with the American Federation of State, County, and Municipal Employees (AFSCME) in recruiting government employees.

SEIU boasts that it supports "progressive" causes and candidates. It disaffiliated itself from the AFL-CIO presumably because that union federation was not aggressive enough in organizing low-paid workers or in the pursuit of a progressive policy agenda. Rather, the SEIU sees the Teamsters, Laborers Union, and United Farm Workers as its natural "change to win" allies.

The SEIU has been particularly active in the debate over health care reform. It would have preferred a Canadian-style single-payer government health system, but supported the "public option" as a politically viable alternative. It supports immigration reform, including legalization for taxpaying immigrants. The SEIU contributes heavily to the political campaigns of liberal Democrats, both directly through its PAC and indirectly through several "527" organizations (including Move On). Its purple-shirted members fueled many Barack Obama audiences during the 2008 presidential campaign.

unions with more than 13 million members. The AFL-CIO has long maintained a large and capable lobbying staff in Washington, and it provides both financial contributions and campaign services (registration, get-out-the-vote, information, endorsements) for members of Congress it favors. Many of the larger individual unions also maintain offices in Washington and offer campaign contributions and services.

Today union influence is greatest among government employees, including teachers. About 38 percent of all public sector employees are unionized. The Service Employees International Union (SEIU), American Federation of State, County, and Municipal Employees (AFSCME), the National Education Association (NEA), the American Federation of Teachers (AFT), and the Teamsters Union (which recruits public employees in sanitation and transportation) are among the few unions growing in membership (see also *Politics Up Close*: "Service Employees International Union").

Labor union political campaign contributions (see "PAC Power" on page 315) remain a major source of union influence in Washington. The SEIU, AFSCME, NEA, Teamsters, United Auto Workers, United Steel Workers, Electrical Workers, Machinists, and Letter Carriers, as well as the AFL-CIO itself, are regularly ranked among the top contributors in congressional elections. Almost all union campaign contributions go to Democratic candidates.

Farm Organizations   Even though the farm population of the United States has declined from about 25 percent of the total population in the 1930s to less than 3 percent today, farmers—especially large agricultural producers and corporate food processors—remain a very potent political force in Washington. Agricultural interests are organized both into large inclusive groups, such as the American Farm

Bureau Federation and the National Grange, and into very effective specialized groups, such as the National Milk Producers and the National Cattlemen's Association. Small- and low-income farmers are represented by the National Farmers Union.

Women's Organizations

Women's organizations date back to the anti-slavery societies in pre–Civil War America. The first generation of feminists—Lucretia Mott, Elizabeth Cady Stanton, Lucy Stone, and Susan B. Anthony—learned to organize, hold public meetings, and conduct petition campaigns as abolitionists. After the Civil War, women were successful in changing many state laws that abridged the rights of married women and otherwise treated them as "chattel" (property) of their husbands. Women were also prominent in the Anti-Saloon League, which succeeded in outlawing prostitution and gambling in every state except Nevada and provided a major source of support for the 18th Amendment (Prohibition). In the early twentieth century, the feminist movement concentrated on obtaining the vote (suffrage) for women. Today the League of Women Voters—a broad-based organization that provides information to voters—backs registration and get-out-the-vote drives and generally supports measures seeking to ensure honesty and integrity in government.

"A <u>very</u> special interest to see you, Senator."

Interest in feminist politics revived in the wake of the civil rights movement of the 1960s. New organizations sprang up to compete with the conventional activities of the League of Women Voters by taking a more activist stance toward women's issues. The largest of these organizations is the National Organization for Women (NOW), founded in 1966.

Religious Groups

Churches and religious groups have a long history of involvement in American politics—from the pre–Civil War anti-slavery crusades, to the prohibition effort in the early twentieth century, to the civil rights movement of the 1960s. The leadership for the historic Civil Rights Act of 1964 came from the Reverend Martin Luther King, Jr., and his Southern Christian Leadership Conference. Today religious groups span the political spectrum, from liberal organizations such as the National Council of Churches and Anti-Defamation League of B'nai B'rith, to conservative and fundamentalist organizations, such as the Christian Coalition, often referred to as the "religious right" (see *Politics Up Close*: "The Christian Coalition: Organizing the Faithful").

Public-Interest Groups

Public-interest groups claim to represent broad classes of people—consumers, voters, reformers, or the public as a whole. Groups with lofty-sounding names, such as Common Cause, Public Citizen, and the Consumer Federation of America, perceive themselves as balancing the narrow, "selfish" interests of business organizations, trade associations, unions, and other "special" interests. Public-interest groups generally lobby for greater government regulation of consumer products, public safety, campaign finance, and so on. Their reform agenda, as well as their call for a larger regulatory role for government, makes them frequent allies of liberal ideological groups, civil rights organizations, and environmental groups.[5]

public-interest groups
Interest groups that claim to represent broad classes of people or the public as a whole.

Many public-interest groups were initially formed in the 1970s by "entrepreneurs" who saw an untapped "market" for the representation of these interests. Among the most influential public-interest groups are Common Cause, a self-styled "citizens' lobby," and the sprawling network of organizations created by consumer advocate Ralph Nader. Common Cause tends to focus on election-law reform, public financing of elections, and limitations on political contributions. The Nader network began as a consumer protection group focusing on auto safety but soon

POLITICS UP CLOSE

The Christian Coalition: Organizing the Faithful

Christian fundamentalists, whose religious beliefs are based on a literal reading of the Bible, have become a significant political force in the United States through effective organization. Perhaps the most influential Christian fundamentalist organization today is the Christian Coalition, with nearly 2 million active members throughout the country.

Fundamentalist Christians are opposed to abortion, pornography, and homosexuality; they favor the recognition of religion in public life, including prayer in schools; and they despair at the decline of traditional family values in American culture, including motion pictures and television broadcasting. Historically, fundamentalist Protestant churches avoided politics as profane and concentrated evangelical efforts on saving individual souls. Their few ventures into worldly politics—notably the prohibition movement in the early twentieth century—ended in defeat. Their strength tended to be in the southern, rural, and poorer regions of the country. They were widely ridiculed in the national media.

In the 1960s, television evangelism emerged as a religious force in the United States. The Reverend Pat Robertson founded the Christian Broadcasting Network (CBN) and later purchased the Family Channel. But efforts by social conservatives to build a "moral majority" for political action largely failed, as did Robertson's presidential candidacy in 1988. Televangelists, including Jerry Falwell and Tammy Faye Bakker, suffered popular disdain following some well-publicized scandals.

Although officially nonpartisan, the Coalition became an important force in Republican politics; religious fundamentalists may constitute as much as one-third of the party's voter support. The Christian Coalition does not officially endorse candidates, but its voter guides (at right) clearly indicate which candidates reflect the coalition's position on major issues. The political influence of the Christian Coalition in Republican politics, and the "religious right" generally, ensures that most GOP candidates for public office publicly express support for a "profamily" agenda. This agenda includes a constitutional amendment allowing prayer in public schools; vouchers for parents to send their children to private, religious schools; banning late-term abortions as well as banning the use of taxpayer funds to pay for abortions; restrictions on pornography on cable television and the Internet; and opposition to human embryo research and human cloning.

Photo courtesy: Christian Coalition of America

---

spread to encompass a wide variety of causes. Prominent among the Nader organizations are the campus-based Public Interest Research Groups (PIRGs).

single-issue groups
Organizations formed to support or oppose government action on a specific issue.

Single-Issue Groups
Like public-interest groups, **single-issue groups** appeal to principle and belief. But as their name implies, single-issue groups concentrate their attention on a single cause. They attract the support of individuals with a strong commitment to that cause. Single-issue groups have little incentive to compromise their position. They exist for a single cause; no other issues really matter to them. They are by nature passionate and often shrill. Their attraction to members is the intensity of their beliefs.

Among the most vocal single-issue groups in recent years have been the organizations on both sides of the abortion issue. NARAL Pro-Choice America describes itself as "pro-choice" and opposes any restrictions on a woman's right to obtain an abortion. The National Right-to-Life Committee describes itself as "pro-life" and opposes abortion for any reason other than to preserve the life of the mother. Other prominent single-issue groups include the National Rifle Association (opposed to gun control) and Mothers Against Drunk Driving (MADD).

Ideological Groups

Ideological organizations pursue liberal or conservative agendas, often with great passion and considerable financial resources derived from true-believing contributors. The ideological groups rely heavily on computerized mailings to solicit funds from persons identified as holding liberal or conservative views. The oldest of the established ideological groups is the liberal Americans for Democratic Action (ADA), well known for its annual liberalism ratings of members of the Congress according to their support for or rejection of programs of concern. The American Conservative Union (ACU) also rates members of Congress each year. Overall, Democrats do better on the liberal list and Republicans on the conservative list, although both parties include some Congress members who occasionally vote on the opposite side of the fence from the majority of their fellow party members (see Table 9.2). Other interest groups, such as the AFL-CIO, the National Taxpayers Union, and NARAL Pro-Choice America also rate members of Congress, but these groups have a narrower focus than the ADA and ACU. Yet another prominent ideological group, People for the American Way, was formed by television producer Norman Lear to coordinate the efforts of liberals in the entertainment industry as well as the general public, but it issues no ratings.

ideological organizations
Interest groups that pursue ideologically based (liberal or conservative) agendas.

Government Lobbies

The federal government's grant-in-aid programs to state and local governments (see Chapter 4) have spawned a host of lobbying efforts by these governments in Washington, D.C. Thus state- and local-government taxpayers foot the bill to lobby Washington to transfer federal taxpayers' revenues to states and communities. The National Governors Association occupies a beautiful marble building, the Hall of the States, in Washington, along with representatives of the separate states and many major cities. The National League of Cities and the National Association of Counties also maintain large Washington offices, as does the U.S. Conference of Mayors. The National Conference of State Legislators sends its lobbyists to Washington from its Denver headquarters. These groups pursue a wide policy agenda and often confront internal disputes. But they are united in their support for increased federal transfers of tax revenues to states and cities.

Leaders and Followers

▶ 9.4 *Explain how interest-group leaders create and build organizations.*

Organizations require leadership. And over time leaders develop a perspective somewhat different from that of their organizations' membership. A key question in interest-group politics is how well organization leaders represent the views of their members.

Interest-Group Entrepreneurs

People who create organizations and build membership in those organizations—**interest-group entrepreneurs**—have played a major role in strengthening the interest-group system in recent decades. These entrepreneurs help overcome a major obstacle to the formation of strong interest groups—the *free-rider* problem.

interest-group entrepreneurs
Leaders who create organizations and market memberships.

TABLE 9.2   Under the Influence?: Ideological Interest-Group Ratings for U.S. Senators*

Ideological interest groups rate Congress members according to their votes on issues deemed important to liberals and conservatives.

ADA Americans for Democratic Action (liberal)		ACU American Conservative Union (conservative)	
"Senate Heroes"		**"The Conservatives"**	
95–100% Voting with ADA		**80–100% Voting with ACU**	
Akaka	D-HI	DeMint	R-SC
Bingaman	D-NM	Allard	R-CO
Cantwell	D-WA	Bunning	R-KY
Cardin	D-MD	Coburn	R-OK
Dodd	D-CT	Corker	R-TN
Durbin	D-IL	Crapo	R-ID
Feingold	D-WI	Ensign	R-NV
Feinstein	D-CA	Enzi	R-WY
Klobuchar	D-MN	Graham	R-SC
Lautenberg	D-NJ	Gregg	R-NH
Leahy	D-VT	Hatch	R-UT
Levin	D-MI	Inhofe	R-OK
Menendez	D-NJ	Kyl	R-AZ
Sanders	I-VT	McConnell	R-KY
Schumer	D-NY	Sessions	R-AL
Stabenow	D-MI	Shelby	R-AL
"Senate Losers"		Thune	R-SD
0–10% Voting with ADA		Vitter	R-LA
Kyl	R-AZ	Wicker	R-MS
McCain	R-AZ	**"The True Liberals"**	
Allard	R-CO	**0% Voting with ACU**	
Bunning	R-KY	Akaka	D-HI
Vitter	R-LA	Biden	D-DE
Wicker	R-MS	Bingaman	D-NM
Hagel	R-NE	Byrd	D-WV
Ensign	R-NV	Conrad	D-ND
Burr	R-NC	Inouye	D-HI
Coburn	R-OK	Kennedy	D-MA
Inhofe	R-OK	Levin	D-MI
DeMint	R-SC	Mikulski	D-MD
Thune	R-SD	Murray	D-WA
Hatch	R-UT	Rockefeller	D-WV
Barrasso	R-WY		
Enzi	R-WY		

* Voting in 2008.

Sources: Americans for Democratic Action, www.adaction.org; American Conservative Union, www.conservative.org.

free-riders
People who do not belong to an organization or pay dues, yet nevertheless benefit from its activities.

Free-riders are people who benefit from the efforts of others but do not contribute to the costs of those efforts. Not everyone feels an obligation to support organizations that represent their interests or views. Some people feel that their own small contribution will not make a difference in the success or failure of the organization's goals and, moreover, that they will benefit from any successes even if they are not members. Indeed, most organizations enroll only a tiny fraction of the people they claim to represent. The task of the interest-group entrepreneur is to convince people to join the organization, either by appealing to their sense of obligation or by attracting them through tangible benefits.

Marketing Membership   Interest-group entrepreneurs make different appeals for membership depending on the nature of the organization. Some appeal to passion or purpose, as, for example, those who seek to create ideological (liberal or conservative) organizations, public-interest organizations committed to environmental or consumer protection or governmental reform, and single-issue organizations devoted to the support or opposition of a single policy issue (gun control, abortion, and so on). Entrepreneurs of these organizations appeal to people's sense of duty and commitment to the cause rather than to material rewards of membership. By using sophisticated computerized mailing lists, they can solicit support from sympathetic people.

Business, trade, and professional organizations usually offer their members many tangible benefits in addition to lobbying on behalf of their economic interests. These benefits may include magazines, journals, and newsletters that provide access to business, trade, and professional information as well as national conventions and meetings that serve as social settings for the development of contacts, friendships, and business and professional relationships. Some organizations also offer discount travel and insurance, credit cards, and the like, that go only to dues-paying members.

It is generally easier to organize smaller, specialized economic interests than larger, general, noneconomic interests. People more easily recognize that their own membership is important to the success of a small organization, and economic interests are more readily calculated in dollar terms.

Large organizations with broad goals—such as advancing the interests of all veterans or all retired people or all automobile drivers—must rely even more heavily on tangible benefits to solicit members. Indeed, some organizations have succeeded in recruiting millions of members (for example, the AARP with 39 million members, the American Automobile Association with 28 million members), most of whom have very little knowledge about the policy positions or lobbying activities of the organization. These members joined to receive specific benefits—magazines, insurance, travel tips, discounts. Leaders of these organizations may claim to speak for millions of members, but it is unlikely that these millions all share the policy views expressed by the leaders.

Organizational Democracy and Leader/Member Agreement   Most organized interest groups are run by a small group of leaders and activists. Few interest groups are governed democratically; members may drop out if they do not like the direction their organization is taking but rarely do they have the opportunity to directly challenge or replace the organization's leadership. Relatively few members attend national meetings, vote in organizational elections, or try to exercise influence within their organization. Thus the leadership may not always reflect the views of the membership, especially in large organizations that rely heavily on tangible benefits to recruit members. Leaders of these organizations enjoy considerable freedom in adopting policy positions and negotiating, bargaining, and compromising in the political arena.

The exception to this rule is the single-issue group. Because the strength of these groups is in the intensity of their members' beliefs, the leaders of such groups are closely tied to their members' views. They cannot bargain or compromise these views or adopt policy positions at variance with those of their members.

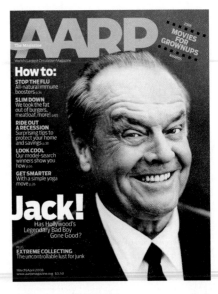

AARP—Marketing Membership

Jack Nicholson on the cover of the March–April 2008 issue of *AARP* magazine, produced by the American Association of Retired Persons.

Class Bias in Membership   Americans are joiners. A majority of the population belong to at least one organization, most often a church. Yet membership in organized interest groups is clearly linked to socioeconomic status. Membership is greatest among professional and managerial, college-educated, and high-income persons.[6]

The Washington Lobbyists

▶ **9.5** *Describe the overall environment of lobbying in Washington.*

Washington is a labyrinth of interest representatives—lawyers and law firms; independent consultants; public and governmental relations firms; business, professional, and trade associations; and advocates of special causes. It is estimated that more than 15,000 people in Washington fit the definition of **lobbyist**, a person working to influence government policies and actions. This figure suggests at least twenty-eight lobbyists for every member of Congress. Roughly $1.5 *billion* is spent on direct lobbying activities *each year*;[7] this figure does *not* include political campaign contributions. The top spenders for direct lobbying are listed in Table 9.3.

lobbyist
Person working to influence government policies and actions.

Who Are the Lobbyists?   Lobbyists in Washington share a common goal—to influence the making and enforcing of laws—and common tactics to achieve this goal. Many lobbyists are the employees of interest-group organizations who devote all of their efforts to their sponsors.

Other lobbyists are located in independent law, consulting, or public relations firms that take on clients for fees. Independent lobbyists, especially law firms, are often secretive about whom they represent, especially when they represent foreign governments. Lobbyists frequently prefer to label their activities as "government

TABLE 9.3   Money Talks: Top Lobbying Spenders, 1998–2009

Direct spending on lobbying (not including campaign contributions) amounts to over $1 billion each year.		
Rank	**Organization**	**Total Spending**
1	US Chamber of Commerce	$527,473,180
2	American Medical Assn.	212,602,500
3	General Electric	191,270,000
4	AARP	169,752,064
5	American Hospital Assn.	168,880,431
6	Pharmaceutical Rsrch. & Mfrs. of America	161,638,400
7	AT&T Inc.	151,040,816
8	Northrop Grumman	144,414,935
9	National Assn. of Realtors	132,797,380
10	Exxon Mobil	131,786,942
11	Edison Electric Institute	131,305,999
12	Business Roundtable	129,870,000
13	Blue Cross/Blue Shield	128,818,703
14	Verizon Communications	128,444,841
15	Lockheed Martin	118,735,633
16	Boeing Co.	115,398,310
17	General Motors	106,261,483
18	Southern Co.	100,970,694
19	Freddie Mac	96,194,048
20	Securities Industry & Financial Mkt. Assn.	95,353,143

Source: Center for Responsive Politics, www.opensecrets.org.

relations," "public affairs," "regulatory liaison," "legislative counseling," or merely "representation."

In reality, many independent lawyers and lobbyists in Washington are "fixers" who offer to influence government policies for a price. Many are former government officials—former Congress members, cabinet secretaries, White House aides, and the like—who "know their way around." Their personal connections help to "open doors" to allow their paying clients to "just get a chance to talk" with top officials. (Many lobbyists maintain offices on K Street in downtown Washington, D.C.; occasionally, "K Street" is used as a term to describe the Washington lobbying community.)

"Trust me Mort—no electronic-communications superhighway, no matter how vast and sophisticated, will ever replace the art of the schmooze."

Some lobbying organizations rely heavily on their campaign contributions to achieve lobbying power; others rely on large memberships, and still others on politically active members who concentrate their attention on a narrow range of issues.

Washington's army of lobbyists includes many former members of Congress. Lobbying is a favorite occupation of former members; they can command much higher salaries as lobbyists than they did as Congress members. Lobbying firms are pleased to have people who know the lawmaking process from the inside and who can easily "schmooze" with their former colleagues.

The Think Tanks   Think tanks are nonprofit tax-free policy planning organizations that concentrate on policy development, rather than direct lobbying. Nonetheless, their reports, conferences, publications, and legislative testimony are central to the policy-making process in Washington. Certain think tanks— for example, the Council on Foreign Relations, the Brookings Institution, the American Enterprise Institute, the Center for American Progress, and the Heritage Foundation—are influential in a wide range of key policy areas.*

- **Council on Foreign Relations**. The CFR is the most influential foreign-policy organization in America. It denies that it exercises any control over U.S. foreign policy. Indeed, its bylaws declare "the Council shall not take any position on questions of foreign policy and no person is authorized to speak or purport to speak for the Council on such matters." But policy initiation and consensus building does not require the CFR to officially adopt the policy positions. Most major foreign-policy decisions are first aired in the CFR's prestigious publication *Foreign Affairs*.

- **The Brookings Institution**. The Brookings Institution has long been the dominant policy-planning group for American domestic policy, despite the growing number and influence of competing think tanks in recent years. The *New York Times* columnist and Harvard historian writing team, Leonard Silk and Mark Silk, described Brookings as the central locus of the Washington "policy network" where it does "it's communicating: over lunch, whether informally

---

*Serious students of public policy are advised to read the books and journals published by these leading policy-planning organizations, especially *The Brookings Review* (published quarterly by the Brookings Institution, 1775 Massachusetts Avenue NW, Washington, D.C. 20036); *The American Enterprise* (published bimonthly by the American Enterprise Institute, 1150 17th Street NW, Washington, D.C. 20036); *Policy Review* (published quarterly by the Heritage Foundation, 214 Massachusetts Avenue NE, Washington, D.C. 20002); *Foreign Affairs* (published five times annually by the Council on Foreign Relations, 58 East 68th Street, New York, NY 10021).

in the Brookings cafeteria or at the regular Friday lunch around a great oval table . . . ; through consulting, paid or unpaid, for government or business at conferences, in the advanced studies program; and, over time, by means of the revolving door of government employment."[8] Brookings has inspired policy goals from the introduction of the first Budget of the United States Government in 1922, through the New Deal of the 1930s, and the Great Society of the 1960s, to the Clinton administration in the 1990s. It has been particularly influential in liberal Democratic administrations.

- **The American Enterprise Institute.** For many years Republicans dreamed of a "Brookings Institution for Republicans." In the late 1970s that role was assumed by the American Enterprise Institute. But AEI tries to appeal to both Democrats and Republicans, who have doubts about big government. In confronting societal problems, the AEI gravitates toward market solutions, while Brookings tends to look for government solutions.

- **The Heritage Foundation.** Conservative ideologues have never been particularly welcome in the Washington establishment. Yet influential conservative business persons gradually came to understand that without an institutional base in Washington they could never establish a strong and continuing influence in the policy network. The result of their efforts was the Heritage Foundation, which was particularly influential during the Reagan administration.

- **The Center for American Progress.** On the left of the political spectrum is the newly influential Center for American Progress (CAP), the intellectual source of policy "change" in the Obama administration.[9] CAP is funded largely by George Soros, the billionaire sponsor of other flourishing left-liberal organizations. It was founded in 2003 by John Podesta, former chief of staff to President Clinton. It is designed to give the "progressive" movement the same ideological influence in the Obama administration as the Heritage Foundation exercised in the Reagan administration. CAP promises to engage in "a war of ideas with conservatives," and to be more active on behalf of progressive policies than the more scholarly Brookings Institution.

Regulation of Lobbies The Constitution's 1st Amendment guarantee of the right "to petition the government for a redress of grievances" protects lobbying. But the government can and does regulate lobbying activities, primarily through disclosure laws. The Regulation of Lobbying Act requires lobbyists to register and to report how much they spend, but definitions of *lobbying* are unclear and enforcement is weak. Many large lobbying groups have never registered as lobbyists. These organizations claim that because lobbying is not their principal activity, they need not register under the law. In addition, financial reports of lobbyists grossly underestimate the extent of lobbying in Congress because the law requires reports of only money spent for *direct* lobbying before Congress, not money spent for public relations or grass-roots mobilization of members to pressure Congress. Another weakness in the law is that it applies only to attempts to influence Congress; it does not regulate lobbying activities in administrative agencies or litigation in the courts.

Tax laws require nonprofit organizations to refrain from direct lobbying in order to retain their tax-free status. Under current tax law, individual contributions to nonprofit charitable and educational organizations are tax deductible, and the income of these organizations is tax free. But these organizations risk losing these tax preferences if a "substantial part" of their activities is "attempting to influence legislation." Thus, for example, Washington think tanks such as the

Brookings Institution, the American Enterprise Institute, and the Heritage Foundation refrain from direct lobbying even though they make policy recommendations. But the line between public affairs "education" and "lobbying" is very fuzzy.

Tightening Lobby Regulations Recent scandals involving lobbyists (see "Lobbying Ethics" later in this chapter) have led to proposals to curtail gifts by lobbyists to Congress members, including paid vacations, dinners, flights, and so forth. Another reform proposal has been to eliminate "earmarking" of appropriations for specific projects that have been heavily lobbied. As a partial step toward reform, Congress now requires members who sponsor earmarks to be identified.

The Fine Art of Lobbying

▶ 9.6 *Identify the main activities of lobbyists.*

Any activity directed at a government decision maker with the hope of influencing decisions is a form of **lobbying**. (The term arose from the practice of waiting in the lobbies of legislative chambers to meet and persuade legislators.) For organized interests, lobbying is continuous—in congressional committees, in congressional staff offices, at the White House, at executive agencies, at Washington cocktail parties. If a group loses a round in Congress, it continues the fight in the agency in charge of executing the policy, or it challenges the policy in the courts. The following year it resumes the struggle in Congress: it fights to repeal the offending legislation, to weaken amendments, or to reduce the agency's budget enough to cripple enforcement efforts.

Lobbying techniques are as varied as the imagination of interest-group leaders, but such activities generally fall into seven categories: (1) public relations; (2) access; (3) information; (4) grass-roots mobilization; (5) protests and demonstrations; (6) coalition building; and (7) campaign support. In the real world of Washington power struggles, all these techniques may be applied simultaneously or innovative techniques may be discovered and applied at any time (see Figure 9.2).

lobbying
Activities directed at government officials with the hope of influencing their decisions.

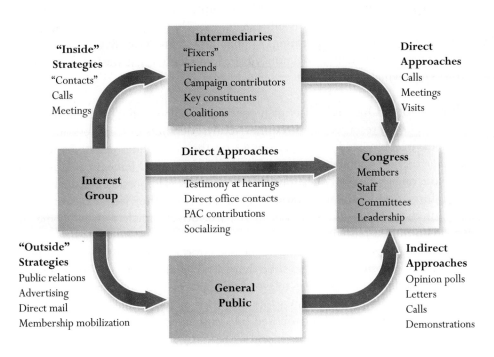

FIGURE 9.2

A Guide to the Fine Art of Lobbying

Interest groups seek to influence public policy both directly through lobbying and campaign contributions (inside strategy) and indirectly through public relations efforts to mold public opinion (outside strategy).

public relations
Building and maintaining goodwill with the general public.

Public Relations

Many interest groups actually spend more of their time, energy, and resources on **public relations**—developing and maintaining a favorable climate of opinion in the nation—than on direct lobbying of Congress. The mass media—television, magazines, newspapers—are saturated with expensive ads by oil companies, auto companies, chemical manufacturers, trade associations, teachers' unions, and many other groups, all seeking to create a favorable image for themselves with the general public. These ads are designed to go well beyond promoting the sale of particular products; they portray these organizations as patriotic citizens, protectors of the environment, providers of jobs, defenders of family values, and supporters of the American way of life. Generally, business interests have an advantage in the area of public relations because public relations and sales and marketing activities are synonymous. But paid advertising is less credible than news stories and media commentary. Hence interest groups generate a daily flood of press releases, media events, interviews, reports, and studies for the media. Media news stories appear to favor liberal public-interest groups.[10]

access
Meeting and talking with decision makers, a prerequisite to direct persuasion.

Access

"Opening doors" is a major business in Washington. To influence decision makers, organized interests must first acquire **access** to them. Individuals who have personal contacts in Congress, the White House, or the bureaucracy (or who say they do) sell their services at high prices. Washington law firms, public relations agencies, and consultants—often former insiders—all offer their connections, along with their advice, to their clients. The personal prestige of the lobbyist, together with the group's perceived political influence, helps open doors in Washington.

Washington socializing is often an exercise in access—rubbing elbows with powerful people. Well-heeled lobbyists regularly pay hundreds, even thousands, of dollars per plate at fund-raising dinners for members of Congress. Lobbyists regularly provide dinners, drinks, travel, vacations, and other amenities to members of Congress, their families, and congressional staff, as well as to White House and other executive officials. These favors are rarely provided on a direct quid pro quo basis in exchange for votes. Rather, they are designed to gain access—"just a chance to talk."

"Schmoozing," building personal relationships, consumes much of a lobbyist's time and the client's money. It is difficult to know how much this contributes to actual success in passing, defeating, or amending legislation. But, to quote one client: "I figured that half of the money I spend on lobbying is wasted. Trouble is, I don't know which half."[11]

Information

Once lobbyists gain access, their knowledge and information become valuable resources to those they lobby. Members of Congress and their staff look to lobbyists for *technical expertise* on the issue under debate as well as *political information* about the group's position on the issue. Members of Congress must vote on hundreds of questions each year, and it is impossible for them to be fully informed about the wide variety of bills and issues they face. Consequently, many of them (and administrators in the executive branch as well) come to depend on trusted lobbyists.

Lobbyists also spend considerable time and effort keeping informed about bills affecting their interests. They must be thoroughly familiar with the "ins and outs" of the legislative process—the relevant committees and subcommittees, their schedules of meetings and hearings, their key staff members, the best moments to act, the precise language for proposed bills and amendments, the witnesses for hearings, and the political strengths and weaknesses of the legislators themselves.

POLITICS UP CLOSE

AARP: The Nation's Most Powerful Interest Group

The American Association of Retired Persons (AARP) is the nation's largest and most powerful interest group, with more than 39 million members. The AARP's principal interests are the Social Security and Medicare system programs, the nation's largest and most expensive entitlements.

Like many other interest groups, the AARP has grown in membership not only by appealing to the political interests of retired people but also by offering a wide array of material benefits. For a small annual fee, members are offered a variety of services, including discounted rates on home, auto, life and health insurance; discounted mail-order drugs, tax advisory services; discounted rates on hotels, rental cars, and so on; a newsletter, *The AARP Bulletin*; a semi-monthly magazine, *AAPP, The Magazine*; *VIVA*, for Hispanic members; and for baby boomers now reaching their 50s, *My Generation*.

The political power of senior citizens is so great that prospects for limiting current or even future increases in government benefits for the elderly are slim. President G. W. Bush's proposal to allow workers to invest part of their Social Security taxes in private accounts was defeated largely by the work of the AARP. Social Security is said to be the "third rail of American politics—touch it and you're dead."

Critics of the AARP argue that its lobbyists in Washington do not fairly represent the views of the nation's senior citizens, that few of its members know what its lobbying arm does at the nation's capital. AARP keeps its dues low, and consequently its membership high, through its business ties with insurance companies, its magazine advertising revenue, and commercial royalties revenues for endorsing products and services.

Source: Reprinted, with permission, from the April 1997 issue of Reason Magazine, Copyright 2000 by the Reason Foundation, 4315 S. Sepulveda Blvd., Suite 400, Los Angeles, CA 90034, www.reason.com.

In their campaign to win congressional and bureaucratic support for their programs, lobbyists engage in many different types of activities. Nearly all testify at congressional hearings and make direct contact with government officials on issues that affect them. In addition, lobbyists provide the technical reports and analyses used by congressional staffs in their legislative research. Engaging in protest demonstrations is a less common activity, in part because it involves a high risk of alienating some members of Congress.

Experienced lobbyists develop a reputation for accurate information. Most successful lobbyists do not supply faulty information; their success depends on maintaining the trust and confidence of decision makers. A reputation for honesty is as important as a reputation for influence.

Grass-Roots Mobilization Many organized interests lobby Congress from both the *outside* and the *inside*. From the outside, organizations seek to mobilize **grass-roots lobbying** of members of Congress by their constituents. Lobbyists frequently encourage letters and calls from "the folks back home." Larger organized interests often have local chapters throughout the nation and can mobilize these local affiliates to apply pressure when necessary. Lobbyists encourage influential local people to visit the office of a member of Congress personally or to make a personal phone call on behalf of the group's position. And, naturally, members are urged to vote for or against certain candidates, based

grass-roots lobbying
Attempts to influence government decision making by inspiring constituents to contact their representatives.

Getting Out the Message

Mike Tidwell of the U.S. Climate Emergency Council and the Chesapeake Climate Action Network speaks about the impact of coal on global warming on Capitol Hill in Washington on June 14, 2007. Protesters brought buckets of coal to protest legislation calling for the liquefaction of coal as a means of reducing American dependency on oil.

on their policy stances (see *Politics Up Close:* "AARP: The Nation's Most Powerful Interest Group").

Experienced lawmakers recognize attempts by lobby groups to orchestrate "spontaneous" grass-roots outpourings of cards and letters. Pressure mail is often identical in wording and content. Nevertheless, members of Congress dare not ignore a flood of letters and telegrams from home, for the mail shows that constituents are aware of the issue and care enough to sign their names.

Protests and Demonstrations   Interest groups occasionally employ protests and demonstrations to attract media attention to their concerns and thereby apply pressure on officials to take action. For these actions to succeed in getting issues on the agenda of decision makers in Congress, in the White House, and in executive agencies, participation by the media, especially television, is essential. The media carry the message of the protest or demonstration both to the general public and directly to government officials (see as "Protest as Political Participation" in Chapter 5).

Organized interest groups most often resort to protests and demonstrations when (1) they are frustrated in more traditional "inside" lobbying efforts; and/or (2) they wish to intensify pressure on officials at a specific point in time. Demonstrations typically attract media attention for a short time only. But media coverage of specific events can carry a clear message—for example, farmers driving tractors through Washington to protest farm conditions; motorcyclists conducting a giant "bike-in" to protest laws requiring helmets; cattle raisers driving steers down the Washington Mall to protest beef prices. The potential drawbacks to such activities are that the attention is short-lived and the group's reputation may be tarnished if the protest turns nasty or violent.

coalitions
A joining together of interest groups (or individuals) to achieve common goals.

Coalition Building   Interest groups frequently seek to build **coalitions** with other groups in order to increase their power. Coalitions tend to form among groups with parallel interests: for example, the National Organization for Women, the League of Women Voters, and NARAL Pro-Choice America on women's issues. Coalitions usually form temporarily around a single piece of legislation in a major effort to secure or prevent its passage.

Campaign Support   Perhaps the real key to success in lobbying is the campaign contribution. Interest-group contributions not only help lobbyists gain access and a favorable hearing but also help elect people friendly to the group's goals. As the costs of campaigning increase, legislators must depend more heavily on the contributions of organized interests.

Most experienced lobbyists avoid making electoral threats. Amateur lobbyists sometimes threaten legislators by vowing to defeat them at the next election, but this tactic usually produces a hostile reaction among members of Congress. Legislators are likely to respond to crude pressures by demonstrating their independence and voting against the threatening lobbyist. Moreover, experienced members of Congress know that such threats are empty; lobbyists can seldom deliver enough votes to influence the outcome of an election.

Lobbying Ethics Experienced lobbyists also avoid offering a campaign contribution in exchange for a specific vote.[12] Crude "vote buying" (bribery) is illegal and risks repulsing politicians who refuse bribes. **Bribery**, when it occurs, is probably limited to very narrow and specific actions—payments to intervene in a particular case before an administrative agency; payments to insert a very specific break in a tax bill or a specific exemption in a trade bill; payments to obtain a specific contract with the government. Bribery on major issues is very unlikely; there is too much publicity and too many participants for bribery to be effective.

To the skeptical, "lobbying ethics" may seem to be an oxymoron. Lobbyists regularly send Congress members and even their staffs on expensive junkets around the world and entertain them back in Washington with golf outings, free meals at expensive restaurants, luxury skybox seats at sporting events, and a host of other perks. And, of course, they direct their clients' campaign contributions to Congress members who support their cause. Prudent lobbyists report these contributions and avoid any direct communications that would suggest that the contributions were made in exchange for a particular official action.

bribery
Giving or offering anything of value in an effort to influence government officials in the performance of their duties.

PAC Power

▶ *9.7 Outline the development, role, and structure of political action committees.*

Organized interest groups channel their campaign contributions through **political action committees (PACs)**. PACs are organized by corporations, labor unions, trade associations, ideological and issue-oriented groups, and cooperatives and nonprofit corporations to solicit campaign contributions and distribute them to political candidates.

political action committees (PACs)
Organizations that solicit and receive campaign contributions from corporations, unions, trade associations, and ideological and issue-oriented groups, and their members, and then distribute these funds to political candidates.

Distributing PAC Money Because PAC contributions are in larger lumps than individual contributions, PAC contributions often attract more attention from members of Congress. The PACs listed in Table 9.4 gave millions of dollars to finance the campaigns of their potential allies in 2008.

Most PACs use their campaign contributions to acquire access and influence with decision makers. Corporate, trade, and professional PAC contributions go overwhelmingly to incumbents, regardless of party. Leaders of these PACs know that incumbents are rarely defeated, and they do not wish to antagonize even unsympathetic members of Congress by backing challengers. However, ideological and issue-oriented PACs are more likely to allocate funds according to the candidates' policy positions and voting records. Labor PACs give almost all of their contributions to Democrats. Ideological and issue-oriented PACs give money to challengers as well as incumbents; in recent years, these groups collectively favored Democrats as women's, environmental, abortion rights, and elderly groups proliferated. (See *Politics Up Close*: "EMILY's List.") Business, trade, and professional PACs usually split their contributions in order to ensure access to both Democrats and Republicans.

PAC money is less important in the Senate than in the House. PAC contributions account for about 35 percent of House campaign contributions; they account for only about 20 percent of Senate campaign contributions. Actually, PACs contribute more *dollars* to the average senator than to the average House member. But because Senate campaigns cost so much more than House campaigns, PAC contributions are *proportionally* less. Senators must rely more on individual contributions than House members do.

TABLE 9.4 Deep Pockets: The Big Money PACs in 2007–2008

Interest-group PAC contributions account for about 35 percent of House campaign contributions and 20 percent of contributions to Senate campaigns.

Rank	Organization	Total Amount	Dem. Pct.	Repub. Pct.
1	National Assn. of Realtors	$4,020,900	58%	42%
2	Intl. Brotherhood of Electrical Workers	3,344,650	98	2
3	AT&T Inc.	3,108,200	47	52
4	American Bankers Assn.	2,918,143	43	57
5	National Beer Wholesalers Assn.	2,869,000	53	47
6	National Auto Dealers Assn.	2,860,000	34	66
7	International Assn. of Fire Fighters	2,734,900	77	22
8	Operating Engineers Union	2,704,067	87	13
9	American Assn. for Justice (trial lawyers)	2,700,500	95	4
10	Laborers Union	2,555,350	92	8
11	Honeywell International	2,515,616	52	48
12	National Assn. of Home Builders	2,480,000	46	54
13	Air Line Pilots Assn.	2,422,000	85	15
14	Credit Union National Assn.	2,331,549	54	46
15	Machinists/Aerospace Workers Union	2,321,842	97	3
16	Plumbers/Pipefitters Union	2,316,559	95	5
17	Service Employees International Union	2,285,850	94	6
18	American Federation of Teachers	2,283,250	99	1
19	Teamsters Union	2,248,950	97	3
20	National Air Traffic Controllers Assn.	2,210,475	80	20

Source: Center for Responsive Politics, www.opensecrets.org.

Payback Representatives of organized interest groups say that their PAC contributions are designed to buy access—"a chance to talk"—with members of Congress, their staffs, and executives in the administration (see "What Do Contributors 'Buy'?" in Chapter 8). Both interest groups and government officials usually deny that campaign contributions can "buy" support.

Nevertheless, the pattern of campaign contributions by major industries corresponds closely with the pattern of congressional voting on many key issues. Congress members who receive the largest PAC contributions from an industry group tend to vote in favor of that group's position. Congress members who oppose the industry's position generally receive far less.

Lobbying the Bureaucracy

▶ 9.8 *Assess the relationships between interest groups and bureaucratic agencies.*

Lobbying does not cease after a law is passed. Rather, interest groups try to influence the implementation of the law. Interest groups know that bureaucrats exercise considerable discretion in policy implementation (see "Bureaucratic Power" in Chapter 12). Thus many interests spend as much as or more time and energy trying to influence executive agencies as they do Congress.

Lobbying the bureaucracy involves various types of activities, including monitoring regulatory agencies for notices of new rules and regulatory changes; providing reports, testimony, and evidence in administrative hearings; submitting contract and grant applications and lobbying for their acceptance; and monitoring the performance of executive agencies on behalf of group members.

POLITICS UP CLOSE

EMILY's List

Fund-raising is the greatest obstacle to mounting a successful campaign against an incumbent. And the most difficult problem facing challengers is raising money *early* in the campaign, when they have little name recognition and little or no standing in the polls.

EMILY's List is a politically adroit and effective effort to support liberal Democratic women candidates by infusing *early money* into their campaigns. EMILY stands for Early Money Is Like Yeast, because "it makes the dough rise." Early contributions provide the initial credibility that a candidate, especially a challenger, needs in order to solicit additional funds from individuals and organizations. EMILY is a fund-raising network of thousands of contributors, each of whom pays $100 to join and pledges to give at least $100 to two women from a list of candidates prepared by EMILY's leaders. Most of the contributors are professional women who appreciate EMILY's screening of pro-choice, liberal women candidates around the country.

EMILY's List was begun in 1985 by a wealthy heir to a founder of IBM, Ellen Malcolm. Women challengers for congressional races traditionally faced frustration in fund-raising. Incumbent male officeholders enjoyed a huge fund-raising advantage because contributors expected them to win and therefore opened their wallets to gain access and goodwill. EMILY's List has helped to overcome defeatism among both women candidates and contributors.

Senator Barbara Milkulski, Democrat of Maryland and an early beneficiary of EMILY's List, at a news conference.

EMILY's List supports *only* Democratic women candidates who are strong supporters of abortion rights. When the list was founded, there were no women in the Senate and only a very few in the House. In 2008 there were thirteen women in the Senate (eleven supported by EMILY's List) and forty-nine in the House (forty-three supported by EMILY's list). EMILY's List currently boasts of more than 100,000 members. EMILY's List was an early supporter of Hillary Clinton in the 2008 Democratic presidential primary races.

Groups may try to influence the creation of a new agency to carry out the law or influence the assignment of implementation to an existing "friendly" agency. They may try to influence the selection of personnel to head the implementing agency. They may lobby the agency to devote more money and personnel to enforcement of the law (or less, depending on a group's preference). They may argue for strict rules and regulations—or loose interpretations of the law—by the implementing agencies. Lobbyists frequently appear at administrative hearings to offer information. They often undertake to sponsor test cases of administrative regulations on behalf of affected members. In short, lobbying extends throughout the government.

Iron Triangles In general, interest groups strive to maintain close working relationships with the departments and agencies that serve their members or regulate their industries. Conversely, bureaucracies seek to nourish relationships with powerful "client" groups that are capable of pressuring Congress to expand their authority and increase their budgets. Both bureaucracies and interest groups seek close working relationships with the congressional committees that exercise jurisdiction over their policy function. Finally, members of Congress seek the political and financial support of powerful interest groups, and members also seek to influence bureaucrats to favor supportive interest groups.

FIGURE 9.3

It's All Connected: An
Example of an Iron Triangle

The iron triangle approach
provides a convenient way to
look at the interrelationship
among interest groups, executive
agencies, and congressional
committees. As this example
shows, veterans' interest groups
work closely with both the
Department of Veterans Affairs
(executive agency) and the
House Veterans Affairs
Committee.

Department of
Veterans Affairs

House Veterans
Affairs Committee

American Legion
Veterans of Foreign Wars

iron triangles
Mutually supportive
relationships among interest
groups, government agencies,
and legislative committees
with jurisdiction over a
specific policy area.

The mutual interests of congressional committee members, organized groups, and bureaucratic agencies come together to form what have been labeled the "iron triangles" of American government. **Iron triangles** refer to stable relationships among interest groups, congressional committees, and administrative agencies functioning in the same policy area. Each of the three sides of these triangles depends on the support of the other two; their cooperation serves their own interests (see Figure 9.3).

In an iron triangle, bureaucracies, interest groups, and congressional committees "scratch each other's backs." Bureaucrats get political support from interest groups in their requests for expanded power and authority and increased budgetary allocations. Interest groups get favorable treatment of their members by the bureaucracy. Congressional committee members get political and financial support from interest groups, as well as favorable treatment for their constituents and contributors who are served or regulated by the bureaucracy.

Iron triangles are more likely to develop in specialized policy areas over which there is relatively little internal conflict. However, conflict, rather than cooperation, is more likely to characterize bureaucratic, congressional, interest-group relationships when powerful, diverse interests are at stake. For example, the Occupational Safety and Health Administration is caught between the demands of labor unions and industry groups. The U.S. Forest Service is caught between the demands of environmental groups and the lumber industry. The Environmental Protection Agency is pressured by environmental groups as well as by industry and agriculture. These kinds of conflicts break open the iron triangles or prevent them from forming in the first place.

Revolving Doors   It is not uncommon in Washington for people in a particular policy field to switch jobs, moving from a post in the government to a job in the private sector, or vice versa, or moving to different posts within the government. In one example, an individual might move from a job in a corporation (Pillsbury or General Mills) to the staff of an interest group (American Farm Bureau Federation), and then to the executive agency charged with implementing policy in the field (U.S. Department of Agriculture) or to the staff of a House or Senate committee with jurisdiction over the field (House Agricultural Committee or Senate Agriculture, Nutrition, and Forestry Committee). The common currency of moves within a network is both policy expertise and contacts within the field.

The term **revolving doors** is often used to criticize people who move from a government post (where they acquired experience, knowledge, and personal contacts) to a job in the private sector as a consultant, lobbyist, or salesperson. Defense contractors may recruit high-ranking military officers or Defense Department officials to help sell weapons to their former employers. Trade associations may recruit congressional staffers, White House staffers, or high-ranking agency heads as lobbyists, or these people may leave government service to start their own lobbying firms. Attorneys from the Justice Department, the Internal Revenue Service, and federal regulatory agencies may be recruited by Washington law firms to represent clients in dealings with their former employers.

Former members of Congress are considered the most viable commodity a lobby firm can offer their clients. The Center for Responsive Politics reports that 125 to 150 former Congress members are lobbyists, many of them among the highest paid in the profession. When asked, lobbyists themselves, especially former members of Congress, acknowledge that their success depends mostly on "schmoozing" with their former colleagues.[13]

Concern about revolving doors centers not only on individuals cashing in on their knowledge, experience, and contacts obtained through government employment, but also on the possibility that some government officials will be tempted to tilt their decisions in favor of corporations, law firms, or interest groups that promise these officials well-paid jobs after they leave government employment.

The Ethics in Government Act limits postgovernment employment in an effort to reduce the potential for corruption. Former members of Congress are not permitted to lobby Congress for 1 year after leaving that body. Former employees of executive agencies are not permitted to lobby their agency for 1 year after leaving government service, and they are not permitted to lobby their agency for 2 years on any matter over which they had any responsibility while employed by the government.

Lobbying the Courts

▶ 9.9 *Identify ways in which interest groups seek to influence the federal court system.*

Interest groups play an important role in influencing federal courts. Many of the key cases brought to the federal courts are initiated by interest groups. Indeed, **litigation** is becoming a favored instrument of interest-group politics. Groups that oppose a new law or an agency's action often challenge it in court as unconstitutional or as violating the law. Interest groups bring issues to the courts by (1) supplying the attorneys for individuals who are parties to a case; (2) bringing suits to the courts on behalf of classes of citizens; or (3) filing companion **amicus curiae** (literally "friend of the court") arguments in cases in which they are interested.

The nation's most powerful interest groups all have legal divisions specializing in these techniques. The American Civil Liberties Union is one of the most active federal court litigants on behalf of criminal defendants (see *Politics Up Close:* "Lobbying the Courts: The American Civil Liberties Union"). The early civil rights strategy of the National Association for the Advancement of Colored People (NAACP) was directed by its Legal Defense and Education Fund under the leadership of Thurgood Marshall. The NAACP chose to sponsor a suit by Linda Brown against the Board of Education in her hometown—Topeka, Kansas—in order to win the historic 1954 desegregation decision.[14] NARAL Pro-Choice America is active in sponsoring legal challenges to abortion restrictions. The Environmental Defense Fund and the Natural Resources Defense Council specialize in environmental litigation.

revolving doors
The movement of individuals from government positions to jobs in the private sector, using the experience, knowledge, and contacts they acquired in government employment.

litigation
Legal dispute brought before a court.

amicus curiae
Person or group other than the defendant or the plaintiff or the prosecution that submits an argument in a case for the court's consideration.

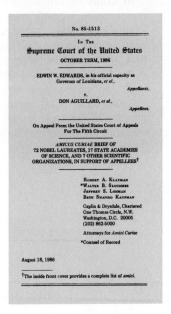

Friend of the Court
An amicus curiae brief filed by American scientists in opposition to a Louisiana state law mandating the teaching of creation science, "Creationism," in public schools whenever evolution is being taught. The Supreme Court ruled that the Louisiana law was an unconstitutional infringement of the Establishment Clause.

POLITICS UP CLOSE

Lobbying the Courts: The American Civil Liberties Union

The American Civil Liberties Union (ACLU) is one of the largest and most active interest groups devoted to litigation. Its Washington offices employ a staff of several hundred people; it counts on some five thousand volunteer lawyers across the country; and it has affiliates in every state and most large cities. The ACLU claims that its sole purpose is defense of civil liberty, that it has no other political agenda, that it defends the Communist Party and the Ku Klux Klan alike—not because it endorses their beliefs but because "the Bill of Rights is the ACLU's only client." And indeed on occasion it has defended the liberties of Nazis, Klansmen, and other right-wing extremists to express their unpopular views. But most ACLU work has involved litigation on behalf of liberal causes, such as abortion rights, resistance to military service, support for affirmative action, and opposition to the death penalty.

The ACLU was founded in 1920 by Roger Baldwin, a wealthy radical activist who opposed both capitalism and war. Baldwin graduated from Harvard University and briefly taught sociology at Washington University in St. Louis. He refused to be drafted during World War I and served a year's imprisonment for draft violation. In prison, Baldwin joined the Industrial Workers of the World (IWW, or the "Wobblies"), a radical labor union that advocated violence to achieve its goals. In the early 1920s, the ACLU defended socialists, "Bolsheviks," labor organizers, and World War I pacifists.

Later, the ACLU concentrated its efforts on the defense of 1st Amendment freedoms of speech, press, religion, and assembly. In the famous "Monkey Trial" of 1925, the ACLU helped defend schoolteacher John Scopes for having taught the theory of evolution in violation of Tennessee state law. In 1942, the ACLU stood alone in denouncing the round-up and internment of Japanese Americans. Later, it played a supporting role in the litigation efforts of the National Association for the Advancement of Colored People in the elimination of segregation; it defended Vietnam War protesters; it brought cases to court to ban prayer and religious exercise in public schools; it has opposed the death penalty and fought for abortion rights; and it defended the rights of people to burn the American flag as a form of symbolic speech.

Currently, the ACLU has a full agenda of cases and arguments. It is active in support of the detainees at the U.S. prison at Guantánamo Bay, Cuba, arguing that they should be given full constitutional rights (see *What Do You Think?*: "Are Persons Captured on the Battlefields of Iraq and Afghanistan Entitled to the Protections of the U.S. Constitution" in Chapter 14). It continues its long opposition to capital punishment and defends many death row inmates. It is suing the state of Florida over racial differences in dropout rates. It supports affirmative action on university campuses across the country. It supports full recognition of same-sex marriages. It opposes the major provisions of the PATRIOT Act, including federal tracking of Internet communications, credit card transactions, bank records, and other personal information of suspected terrorists (see *A Conflicting View*: "Terrorism Requires Restrictions on Civil Liberties" in Chapter 14).

The special rules of judicial decision making preclude direct lobbying of judges by interest groups (see "The Special Rules of Judicial Decision Making" in Chapter 13). Directly contacting federal judges about a case, letter writing, telephoning, and demonstrating outside of federal courtrooms are all considered inappropriate conduct. They inspire more resentment than support among federal judges. However, interest groups have been very active in direct lobbying of Congress over judicial appointments. Key interest groups supporting abortion rights—NARAL Pro-Choice America, People for the American Way, the National Organization for Women, and so on—have played a central role in confirmation battles (see *Controversy*: "The Confirmation of Clarence Thomas" in Chapter 13).

Politics as Interest-Group Conflict

▶ 9.10 *Evaluate different positions on the consequences of interest groups for American democracy.*

Politics can be viewed as a struggle among interest groups over government policy. Interest groups, rather than individual citizens, can be viewed as the principal participants in American politics.

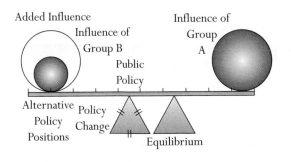

FIGURE 9.4

Balancing Act: Understanding the Interest-Group Model

According to pluralist theorists, policy in a democracy is the result of various special-interest groups "reaching equilibrium"—arriving at a compromise position that requires all parties to give up something but gives all parties something they wanted.

Pluralism as Democratic Politics   Pluralism (see Chapter 1) is the idea that democracy can be preserved in a large, complex society through individual membership in interest groups that compete, bargain, and compromise over government policy. Individuals are influential in politics only when they act as part of, or on behalf of, groups. (Only leaders of organizations participate directly in policy making.) The group becomes the essential bridge between the individual and the government. Pluralists argue that interest-group politics is a natural extension of the democratic ideals of popular participation in government, freedom of association, and competition over public policy.

Pluralism portrays public policy at any given time as the equilibrium reached in the struggle among interest groups to influence policy (see Figure 9.4). This equilibrium is determined by the relative influence of interest groups. Changes in the relative influence of any interest group can be expected to result in changes in public policy; policy will move in the direction desired by the groups gaining in influence and away from the desires of groups losing influence.

According to this view of political life, government plays a passive role, merely "refereeing" group struggles. Public policy at any given moment represents the "equilibrium" point of the group pressures—the balance of competing interests. The job of politicians is to function as brokers of group interests, arranging compromises and balancing interests.

Balancing Group Power   Pluralism assumes that compromises *can* be arranged and that interests *can* be balanced in relatively stable fashion. It assumes that no single interest will ever become so dominant that it can reject compromise and proceed to impose its will on the nation without regard for the interests of other people. This assumption is based on several beliefs. The first is that interest groups act as a check on each other and that a system of *countervailing power* will protect the interests of all. For example, the power of big business will be checked by the countervailing power of big labor and big government.

A second belief is that *overlapping group membership* will tend to moderate the demands of particular groups and lead to compromise. Because no group can command the undivided loyalty of all its members, its demands will be less drastic and its leaders more amenable to compromise. If the leaders of any group go too far with their demands, those of its members who also belong to other groups endangered by these immoderate demands will balk.

A third belief is that radical programs and doctrinaire demands will be checked by the large, unorganized, but potentially significant *latent interest group* that is composed of Americans who oppose extremist politics.

Interest-Group Politics: How Democratic?   There are several problems with accepting pluralism as the legitimate heir to classic democratic theory.

A CONFLICTING VIEW

Interest-Group Politics Create Gridlock and Paralysis

Even if the pluralists are correct that the public interest is only the equilibrium of special-interest claims, some consensus among major interest groups is required if government is to function at all. Democracies require a sense of community and common purpose among the people. If the demands of special interests displace the public interest, government cannot function effectively. Uncompromising claims by conflicting special interests create policy *gridlock*. Yet if politicians try to placate every special interest, the result is confusing, contradictory, and muddled policy—or worse, no policy at all.

Interest-group paralysis and the resulting inability of government to act decisively to resolve national problems weaken popular confidence in government. (see table below). Political scientist Samuel P. Huntington writes, "The function of government is to govern. A weak government, a government which lacks authority, fails to perform its function, is immoral in the same sense in which a corrupt judge, a cowardly soldier, or an ignorant teacher, is immoral."[a]

Over time, the continued buildup of special protections, privileges, and treatments in society results in "institutional sclerosis." Economist Mancur Olson argues that the accumulation of special-interest subsidies, quotas, and protections leads to economic stagnation. Interest groups focus on gaining distributive advantages—a larger share of the pie for themselves—rather than on growth of the whole economy—a larger pie.[b] Major interest groups are more interested in winning income transfers to themselves through government action than in promoting the growth of national income. The more entrenched the interest-group system becomes, the slower the growth of the national economy.

Too Much Power?: Public Views of Interest Groups

The American public believes that "special-interest groups" are the most responsible for "what is wrong with government today."

Among the following, which one or two would you say are most responsible for what is wrong with government today?

Special-interest groups	38%
The media	29
Elected officials	24
Political parties	24
The public	14
Government employees	6
Other	8
Not sure	2

Source: As reported in *The Polling Report*, November 11, 2003.

[a]Samuel P. Huntington, *Political Order in Changing Societies* (New Haven, Conn.: Yale University Press, 1965), p. 28.
[b]Mancur Olson, *The Rise and Decline of Nations* (New Haven, Conn.: Yale University Press, 1982).

Democratic theory envisions public policy as the rational choice of *individuals* with equal influence who evaluate their needs and reach a majority decision with due regard for the rights of others. This traditional theory does not view public policy as a product of interest-group pressures. In fact, classic democratic theorists viewed interest groups and even political parties as intruders into an individualistic brand of citizenship and politics. Today, critics of pluralism charge that interest groups dominate the political arena, monopolize access to governmental power, and thereby restrict individual participation rather than enhance it.

Another assumption of pluralism is that group membership enhances the individual's influence on policy. But only rarely are interest groups democratically governed. Individuals may provide the numerical strength for organizations, but interest groups are usually run by a small elite of officers and activists. Leaders of

A CONSTITUTIONAL NOTE

Controlling the Effects of Interest Groups

The Constitution's 1st Amendment includes a guarantee of "the right of the people to assemble and petition their government for redress of grievances." The Constitution, then, protects the formation of groups and their right to lobby in Washington on behalf of their own interests. Yet the Founders worried about "the mischiefs of faction," and James Madison, in *Federalist* No. 10, defined a faction as "a number of citizens, whether amounting to a majority or minority of the whole, who are united and actuated by some common impulse of passion, or interests, adverse to the rights of other citizens, or the permanent and aggregate interests of the community." But Madison also understood that "the latent causes of faction are thus sown in the nature of man." A faction could only be destroyed by destroying liberty itself, "by giving to every citizen the same opinions." According to Madison, a wiser and more practical approach would be to control the effects of faction by "first, the delegation of the government [in a republic] to a small number of citizens elected by the rest; secondly, the greater number of citizens and greater sphere of country over which [a republic] may be extended. The influence of factious leaders may kindle a flame within their particular States but will be unable to spread a general conflagration throughout the other States." Today, however, with national means of communication, interest groups are capable of doing exactly what Madison feared. They can mobilize mass opinion, intimidate elected representatives, and dominate the national political arena.

corporations, banks, labor unions, medical associations, and bar associations—whose views and agendas often differ from those of their memberships—remain in control year after year. Very few people attend meetings, vote in organizational elections, or make their influence felt within their organizations. (See *A Conflicting View*: "Interest-Group Politics Create Gridlock and Paralysis.")

Finally, pluralists hope that the power of diverse institutions and organizations in society will roughly balance out and prevent the emergence of a power monopoly. Yet inequality of power among organizations is commonplace. Examples abound of narrow, organized interests achieving their goals at the expense of the broader, unorganized public. Furthermore, producer interests, bound together by economic ties, usually dominate less well-organized consumer groups and groups based on noneconomic interests. Special interests seeking governmental subsidies, payments, and "entitlements" regularly prevail over the broader yet unorganized interests of taxpayers.

✓ *Think* Again

Is organized interest-group activity a cause of government gridlock?

Summary

▶ **9.1** *Explain the origins, functions, strengths, and weaknesses of the interest-group system in America.*

The interest-group system supplements the electoral system as a form of representation. The electoral system is designed to respond to broad majority preferences in geographically defined constituencies. The interest-group system represents narrower minority interests in economic, professional, ideological, religious, racial, gender, and issue constituencies.

▶ **9.2** *Trace the origins and growth of the American interest-group system.*

Interest groups originated to protect economic interests, to advance social movements, to seek government benefits, and to respond to government activity. As government has expanded into more sectors of American life, more interest groups have formed to influence government policy.

▶ **9.3** *Characterize the interests represented by organized interest groups lobbying in Washington.*

Washington lobbying groups represent a wide array of organized interests. But business, trade, and professional associations outnumber labor union, women's, public-interest, single-issue, and ideological groups.

▶ **9.4** *Explain how interest-group leaders create and build organizations.*

Interest-group formation has been aided in recent decades by entrepreneurs who create and build group memberships. They urge people to join organizations either by appealing to their sense of obligation or by providing an array of direct tangible benefits.

▶ **9.5** *Describe the overall environment of lobbying in Washington.*

Most organized groups are dominated by small groups of leaders and activists. Few groups are governed democratically; members who oppose the direction of the organization usually drop out rather than challenge the leadership. Group membership and especially group leadership over-represent educated, upper-middle-class segments of the population.

▶ **9.6** *Identify the main activities of lobbyists.*

Lobbying activities include advertising and public relations, obtaining access to government officials, providing them with technical and political information, mobilizing constituents, building coalitions, organizing demonstrations, and providing campaign support. Bribery is illegal, and most lobbyists avoid exacting specific vote promises in exchange for campaign contributions.

▶ **9.7** *Outline the development, role, and structure of political action committees.*

Organized political action committees (PACs) proliferated following the 1974 "reform" of campaign finance laws. Most PAC money goes to incumbents; interest-group leaders know that incumbents are rarely defeated.

▶ **9.8** *Assess the relationships between interest groups and bureaucratic agencies.*

The mutual interests of organized groups, congressional committees, and bureaucratic agencies sometimes come together to form "iron triangles" of mutual support and cooperation in specific policy areas. In many policy areas, loose "policy networks" emerge among people who share an interest and expertise—although not necessarily opinions—about a policy and are in regular contact with each other.

The "revolving door" problem emerges when individuals use the knowledge, experience, and contacts obtained through government employment to secure high-paying jobs with corporations, law firms, lobbying and consulting firms, and interest groups doing business with their old agencies.

▶ **9.9** *Identify ways in which interest groups seek to influence the federal court system.*

Interest groups influence the nation's courts not only by providing financial and legal support for issues of concern to them but also lobbying Congress over judicial appointments.

▶ **9.10** *Evaluate different positions on the consequences of interest groups for American democracy.*

Pluralism views interest-group activities as a form of democratic representation. According to the pluralists, public policy reflects the equilibrium of group influence and a reasonable approximation of society's preferences. Competition among groups, overlapping group memberships, and latent interest groups all combine to ensure that no single group dominates the system.

Critics of pluralism warn that interest groups may monopolize power and restrict individual participation in politics rather than enhance it. They note that interest groups are not usually democratically governed, nor are their leaders or members representative of the general population. They warn that accommodation rather than competition may characterize group interaction and that narrow producer interests tend to achieve their goals at the expense of broader consumer (taxpayer) interests.

The growing power of special interests, when combined with the declining power of parties and the fragmentation of government, may lead to gridlock and paralysis in policy making. The general public interest may be lost in the conflicting claims of special interests.

Chapter Test

▶ **9.1** *Explain the origins, functions, strengths, and weaknesses of the interest-group system in America.*

1. It would be accurate to maintain that
   a. interest groups represent geographically defined constituencies and provide more direct representation of policy preferences than do political parties
   b. parties represent geographically defined constituencies and provide more direct representation of policy preferences than do interest groups
   c. interest groups represent various economic, ideological, and political constituencies and provide more direct

   representation of policy preferences than do political parties
   d. parties represent various economic, ideological, and political constituencies and provide more direct representation of policy preferences than do interest groups

2. When a society becomes so burdened with benefits for special interest groups that the general standard of living starts to decline it is said to be because of
   a. mission creep
   b. the "not in my backyard" mindset
   c. economic recession
   d. organizational sclerosis

▶ 9.2 *Trace the origins and growth of the American interest-group system.*

3. James Madison
   a. called interest groups "factions"
   b. believed economic interests to be the most prevalent in politics
   c. thought that interest groups grew out of human nature and a zeal for differing opinions
   d. all of the above

4. Generally speaking, interest groups do *not* seek
   a. political office
   b. to protect economic interests
   c. to advance social movements
   d. government benefits

▶ 9.3 *Characterize the interests represented by organized interest groups lobbying in Washington.*

5. Traditionally the _____ have dominated interest-group politics in America.
   a. unions
   b. business and trade organizations
   c. ideologically oriented groups
   d. single-issue groups

6. A Christian fundamentalist would probably feel most at home with which of the following groups?
   a. American Civil Liberties Union
   b. Anti-Defamation League
   c. Christian Coalition
   d. Planned Parenthood Association

▶ 9.4 *Explain how interest-group leaders create and build organizations.*

7. An individual who creates an organization and works to build up the membership of the group is said to be
   a. a "free rider"
   b. a special-interest magnate
   c. an administrator of the interest-group incubator
   d. an interest-group entrepreneur

8. In general, it is easier to organize interest groups that are _____ and wish to pursue _____.
   a. smaller; broad goals
   b. larger; broad goals
   c. smaller; narrowly focused goals
   d. larger; narrowly focused goals

▶ 9.5 *Describe the overall environment of lobbying in Washington.*

9. The most influential foreign policy organization in America is the
   a. Heritage Foundation
   b. Council on Foreign Relations
   c. Brookings Institution
   d. American Enterprise Institute

10. *Fortune* magazine has ranked which of the following as the most powerful lobbying group in America?
    a. American Association of Retired Persons
    b. American Israel Public Affairs Committee
    c. American Bankers Association
    d. AFL-CIO

▶ 9.6 *Identify the main activities of lobbyists.*

11. In order to influence public policy, interest groups engage in
    a. presenting information to decision makers
    b. mobilizing the "grass roots"
    c. engaging in protests
    d. all of the above

▶ 9.7 *Outline the development, role, and structure of political action committees.*

12. Political action committees are primarily interested in
    a. organizing the electoral process
    b. providing information to the candidates
    c. soliciting and distributing campaign contributions
    d. organizing protests and marches

▶ 9.8 *Assess the relationships between interest groups and bureaucratic agencies.*

13. An "iron triangle" is
    a. slang for the relationship between the Supreme Court, Congress, and Executive branches of government
    b. a mutually beneficial relationship between the legislative committees, interest groups, and government agencies
    c. nomenclature for the pattern of amending, reconciling, and passing legislation
    d. a situation where the local, state, and national governments all have concurrent jurisdiction

14. The movement of individuals from positions in the government to jobs in the private sector where they use knowledge and contacts they acquired while in governmental service is referred to as
    a. the "more of the same" system
    b. revolving doors
    c. old wine in a new bottle
    d. the "up the down stairs" syndrome

▶ 9.9 *Identify ways in which interest groups seek to influence the federal court system.*

15. Interest groups most typically attempt to influence judicial decision making by
    a. engaging in direct lobbying
    b. initiating litigation
    c. letter writing
    d. telephoning

16. It would be accurate to say that the ACLU
    a. defends capital punishment
    b. defends the sanctity of the traditional marriage of man and woman
    c. opposes major provisions of the PATRIOT Act
    d. believes that the color-blind standard is preferable to affirmative action

▶ 9.10 *Evaluate different positions on the consequences of interest groups for American democracy.*

17. Adherents of pluralism believe that public policy making is primarily achieved
    a. by a very small ruling elite at the top of society
    b. through conflict between competing interest groups
    c. by lobbying the bureaucracy
    d. through the application of the principles of direct democracy

18. Critics of pluralism maintain that it cannot be the heir to classic democratic theory because
    a. public policy making is not the product of rational choice by *individuals*
    b. interest groups are only rarely governed democratically
    c. very few people attend interest-group meetings
    d. all of the above

Key Terms

interest groups   295
majoritarianism   296
organizational sclerosis   296
trade associations   299
public-interest groups   303
single-issue groups   304

ideological
   organizations   305
interest-group
   entrepreneurs   305
free-riders   306
lobbyist   308

lobbying   311
public relations   312
access   312
grass-roots lobbying   313
coalitions   314
bribery   315

political action committees
   (PACs)   315
iron triangles   318
revolving doors   319
litigation   319
amicus curiae   319

Suggested Readings

Berry, Jeffrey M. *The New Liberalism: The Rising Power of Citizen Groups*. Washington, D.C.: Brookings Institution Press, 1999. A description of the increasing number and activities of liberal interest groups in Washington and their success in defeating both business and conservative groups.

Berry, Jeffrey M., and Clyde Wilcox. *The Interest Group Society*. 5th ed. New York: Longman, 2009. Text coverage of organized interests, their relations with parties, PACs, "527s," and more.

Cigler, Allan J., and Burdett A. Loomis, eds. *Interest Group Politics*. 7th ed. Washington, D.C.: CQ Press, 2006. A collection of essays examining interest-group politics.

Goldstein, Kenneth M. *Interest Groups, Lobbying and Participation in America*. New York: Cambridge University Press, 2003. When and why people join interest groups, how they are recruited, and how groups try to influence legislation.

Hernson, Paul S., Ronald G. Shaiko, and Clyde Wilcox. The *Interest Group Connection: Electioneering, Lobbying and Policy-making*. 2nd ed. Washington, D.C.: CQ Press, 2004. Interest group activities in the electoral, legislative, judicial, and policy-making processes.

Lowi, Theodore J. *The End of Liberalism*. New York: Norton, 1969. The classic critique of "interest-group liberalism," describing how special interests contribute to the growth of government and the development of "clientism."

Olson, Mancur. *The Logic of Collective Action*. Cambridge, Mass.: Harvard University Press, 1965. A highly theoretical inquiry into the benefits and costs to individuals of joining groups and the obstacles (including the free-rider problem) to forming organized interest groups.

Olson, Mancur. *The Rise and Decline of Nations*. New Haven, Conn.: Yale University Press, 1982. Argues that, over time, the development of powerful special-interest lobbies has led to institutional sclerosis, inefficiency, and slowed economic growth.

Rozell, Mark J., Clyde Wilcox, and David Madland. *Interest Groups in American Campaigns*. Washington, D.C.: CQ Press, 2005. The role of interest groups in campaigns, including their adjustments to the Bipartisan Campaigns Reform Act of 2002 and the creation of "527s" to circumvent the act.

Suggested Web Sites

AARP www.aarp.org
The AARP site covers issues and provides information relevant to the concerns of citizens who are 50 years of age or older.

AFL-CIO www.alfcio.org
Homepage of labor confederation; includes information on wages, unemployment, strikes, as well as news and press releases on union affairs.

American Farm Bureau www.fb.com
The American Farm Bureau site reveals that the largest farm organization in America represents more than 5 million families in the fifty states and Puerto Rico.

American League of Lobbyists www.alldc.org
Lobbyists have their own Web site, one devoted to "ethical conduct" in the lobbying process and the "advancement of the lobbying profession."

American Medical Association www.ama-assn.org
Professional organization of doctors that both lobbies and publishes medical research in the prestigious Journal of the American Medical Association (JAMA).

Business Roundtable www.businessroundtable.org
Organization representing the largest U.S. corporations.

Children's Defense Fund www.childrendefense.org
Advocacy organization for welfare programs; "the voice of children in America."

Christian Coalition www.cc.org
Organization "defending our godly heritage" by giving "people of faith a voice in government."

EMILY's List www.emilyslist.org
Political network for pro-choice Democratic women that raises early money for women candidates.

NAACP www.naacp.org
Oldest civil rights organization, working on behalf of African Americans.

National Organization for Women www.now.org
An organization of "feminist activists" concerned with abortion rights, lesbian rights, sexual harassment, affirmative action, and electing feminists.

National Rifle Association www.nra.org
The National Rifle Association site is devoted to opposing gun control legislation as well as employing the 2nd Amendment in its anti-gun control argument.

Public Citizen www.publiccitizen.com
Organization founded by Ralph Nader; devotes its site to "protecting health, safety and democracy" as well as lobbying for "strong citizen and consumer protection laws."

U.S. Chamber of Commerce www.uschamber.com
Representing business, "3 million companies of all sizes."

Chapter Test Answer Key

1. C	4. A	7. D	10. A	13. B	16. C
2. D	5. B	8. C	11. D	14. B	17. B
3. D	6. C	9. B	12. C	15. B	18. D

10 CONGRESS
Politics on Capitol Hill

" The local legislator often devotes himself to the advancement of neighborhood projects by striking bargains on national issues. **"**

Harold Lasswell

Chapter Outline and Learning Objectives

The Powers of Congress
▶ 10.1 *Explain the sources of Congress's power.*

Congressional Apportionment and Redistricting
▶ 10.2 *Explain the processes of congressional apportionment and redistricting, and assess how representative Congress is of the general population.*

Getting to Capitol Hill
▶ 10.3 *Describe congressional elections and the hurdles that challengers face.*

Party Fortunes in Congress
▶ 10.4 *Evaluate the successes and failures of the two parties in Congress.*

Life in Congress
▶ 10.5 *Characterize the working life of member of Congress.*

Home Style
▶ 10.6 *Identify the techniques used by representatives to enhance their image among constituents.*

Organizing Congress: Party and Leadership
▶ 10.7 *Analyze the roles of parties and leadership in organizing Congress.*

In Committee
▶ 10.8 *Characterize the legislative work of committees and assess the repercussions of committees for distribution of power in Congress.*

On the Floor
▶ 10.9 *Outline the process for a bill that has reached the floor and identify obstacles to passage.*

Decision Making in Congress
▶ 10.10 *Assess the influences on congressional decision making.*

Customs and Norms
▶ 10.11 *Outline the customs and norms of Congress, their function, and recent changes.*

Congressional Ethics
▶ 10.12 *Evaluate the mechanisms for ensuring ethical behavior in Congress.*

✓ *Think about Politics*

1. Should members of Congress be limited in the number of terms they can serve?
   YES ⬭ NO ⬭

2. Should congressional districts be drawn to ensure that minorities win seats in Congress in rough proportion to their populations in the states?
   YES ⬭ NO ⬭

3. Do Congress members spend too much time in their home districts seeking reelection?
   YES ⬭ NO ⬭

4. Is the nation better served when the president and the majority in Congress are from the same party?
   YES ⬭ NO ⬭

5. Is it ethical for Congress members to pay special attention to requests for assistance by people who make large campaign contributions?
   YES ⬭ NO ⬭

6. Are there too many lawyers in Congress?
   YES ⬭ NO ⬭

7. Are members of Congress obliged to vote the way their constituents wish, even if they personally disagree?
   YES ⬭ NO ⬭

Who are the members of Congress? How did they get there, and how do they manage to stay there? How did Congress—the official institution for deciding who gets what in America—get its powers, and how does it use them?

The Powers of Congress

▶ 10.1 *Explain the sources of Congress's power.*

The Constitution gives very broad powers to Congress. "All legislative Powers herein granted shall be vested in a Congress of the United States, which shall consist of a Senate and House of Representatives." *The nation's Founders envisioned Congress as the first and most powerful branch of government.* They equated national powers with the powers of Congress and gave Congress the most clearly specified role in national government.

Institutional Conflict Yet over two centuries, the three separate branches of the national government—the Congress, the presidency and the executive branch, and the Supreme Court and federal judiciary— have struggled for power and preeminence in governing. This struggle for power among the separate institutions is precisely what the Founders envisioned. In writing the Constitution, they sought to create "opposite and rival interests" among the separate branches of the national government. "The constant aim," explained Madison, "is to divide and arrange the several offices in such a manner as that each may be a check on the other"[1] (see Appendix, *The Federalist*, No. 51). From time to time, first

Congress in Joint Session

President Barack Obama addresses a joint session of the Congress (House and Senate). Vice president Joe Biden and Speaker of the House Nancy Pelosi preside. Joint sessions are held in the House chamber; special guests are seated in the balconies.

the Congress, then the presidency, and occasionally the Supreme Court have appeared to become the most powerful branch of government.

"The President Initiates, Congress Deliberates"

Throughout much of the twentieth century, Congress ceded leadership in national policy making to the president and the executive branch. Congress largely responded to the policy initiatives and spending requests originating from the president, executive agencies, and interest groups. Congress did not merely ratify or "rubber-stamp" these initiatives and requests; it played an independent role in the policy-making process. But this role was essentially a deliberative one, in which Congress accepted, modified, amended, or rejected the policies and budget requests initiated by the president and the executive branch.

It is easier for the Congress to obstruct the policy initiatives of the president than it is to assume policy leadership itself. Congress can defeat presidential policy proposals, deny presidential budget requests, delay or reject presidential appointments, investigate executive agencies, hold committee hearings to spotlight improprieties, and generally immobilize the executive branch. It can investigate and question nominees for the Supreme Court and the federal judiciary; it can legislate changes in the jurisdiction of the federal courts; and it can try to reverse court decisions by amending laws or the Constitution itself. The Congress can even threaten to impeach the president or federal judges. But these are largely reactive, obstructionist actions, usually accompanied by a great deal of oratory.

Dividing Congressional Power: House and Senate   Congress must not only share national power with the executive and judicial branches of government; it must also share power within itself. The framers of the Constitution took the advice of the nation's eldest diplomat, Benjamin Franklin: "It is not enough that your legislature should be numerous; it should also be divided. . . . One division should watch over and control the other, supply its wants, correct its blunders, and cross its designs, should they be criminal or erroneous."[2] Accordingly, the U.S. Congress is **bicameral**—composed of two houses (see Figure 10.1).

No law can be passed and no money can be spent unless both the House of Representatives and the Senate pass identical laws. Yet the House and the Senate have very different constituencies and terms. The House consists of 435 voting members, elected from districts within each state apportioned on the basis of equal population. (The average congressional district since the 2000 census has a population of about 650,000; the House also includes nonvoting delegates from Puerto Rico, the District of Columbia, Guam, the Virgin Islands, and American Samoa.) All House members face election every 2 years. The Senate consists of 100 members serving 6-year terms, elected by statewide constituencies. Senate terms are staggered so that one-third of senators are elected every 2 years (see Table 10.1).

The House of Representatives, with its 2-year terms, was designed to be more responsive to the American people. Representatives are fond of referring to their chamber as "the people's House," and the Constitution requires that all revenue-raising bills originate in the House. The Senate was designed to be a smaller, more deliberative body, with its members serving 6-year terms. Indeed, the Senate is the more prestigious body. House members frequently give up their seats to run for the Senate; the reverse has seldom occurred. Moreover, the Senate exercises certain powers not given to the House: the power to ratify treaties and

bicameral
Any legislative body that consists of two separate chambers or houses; in the United States, the Senate represents 50 statewide voter constituencies, and the House of Representatives represents voters in 435 separate districts.

HOUSE OF REPRESENTATIVES   SENATE

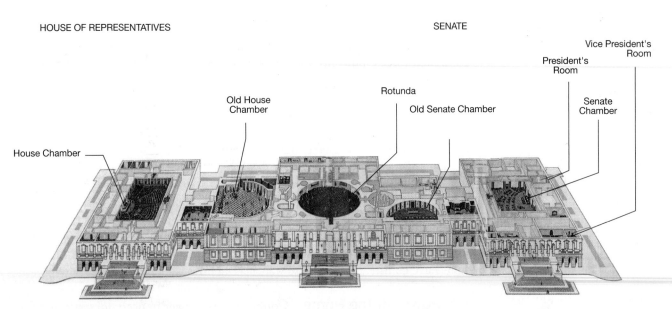

FIGURE 10.1 Corridors of Power: Congress

The architecture and floor plan of the Capitol Building in Washington reflect the bicameral division of Congress, with one wing for the House of Representatives and one for the Senate.

the power to confirm federal judges, ambassadors, cabinet members, and other high executive officials.

Domestic Versus Foreign and Defense Policy
Congress is more powerful in domestic than in foreign and military affairs. It is freer to reject presidential initiatives in domestic policy areas such as welfare, health, education, the environment, and taxation. But Congress usually follows presidential leadership

TABLE 10.1 Comparing the House and Senate

	House of Representatives	**Senate**
Terms	2 years	6 years
Members	435	100
Elections	All every 2 years	One-third every 2 years
Constituencies	Congressional districts	States
Unique powers	Originate tax bills Bring impeachment charges	Advise and consent to (ratify) treaties by two-thirds vote Confirm appointments Try impeachment charges
Debate on bills	Limited by Rules Committee	Unlimited, except by unanimous consent or vote to close debate (three-fifths)
Member prestige	Modest; smaller personal staffs, fewer committee assignments	High: larger personal staffs, more committee assignments, always addressed as "Senator"
Leadership	Hierarchical, with speaker, majority and minority leaders and whips and committees, especially Rules, concentrating power	Less hierarchical, with each senator exercising more influence on leadership, committees, and floor votes
Committees	Twenty standing and select committees Each member on about five committees Difficult to bypass	Twenty standing and select committees Each member on about seven committees Easier to bypass

in foreign and defense policy even though constitutionally the president and Congress share power in these arenas. The president is "Commander-in-Chief" of the armed forces, but only Congress can "declare war." The president appoints and receives ambassadors and "makes treaties," but the Senate must confirm appointments and provide "advice and consent" to treaties. Historically presidents have led the nation in matters of war and peace.

The Vietnam experience inspired Congress to try to reassert its powers over war and peace. Military embarrassment, prolonged and indecisive fighting, and accumulating casualties—all vividly displayed on national television—encouraged Congress to challenge presidential war-making power. The War Powers Resolution of 1973, passed over the veto of President Richard Nixon, who was weakened by the Watergate scandal, sought to curtail the president's power to commit U.S. military forces to combat (see "Commander-in-Chief" in Chapter 11). But this legislation has not proven effective, and both Republican and Democratic presidents have continued to exercise war-making powers.

power of the purse
Congress's exclusive constitutional power to authorize expenditures by all agencies of the federal government.

The Power of the Purse   Congress's real power in both domestic and foreign (defense) policy centers on its **power of the purse**—its power over federal taxing and spending. Only Congress can "lay and collect Taxes, Duties, Imposts and Excises" (Article I, Section 8), and only Congress can authorize spending: "No Money shall be drawn from the Treasury, but in Consequence of Appropriations made by Law" (Article I, Section 9).

Congress jealously guards these powers. Presidents initiate taxing and spending policies by sending their budgets to the Congress each year (see "The Budgetary Process" in Chapter 12 for details). But Congress has the last word on taxing and spending. The most important bills that Congress considers each year are usually the budget resolutions setting ceilings on various categories of expenditures and the later appropriations bills authorizing specific expenditures. It is often in these appropriations bills that Congress exercises its greatest influence over national policy. Thus, for example, the Congress's involvement in foreign affairs centers on its annual consideration of appropriations for foreign aid, its involvement in military affairs centers on its annual deliberations over the defense appropriations bill, and so on.

oversight
Congressional monitoring of the activities of executive branch agencies to determine if the laws are being faithfully executed.

Oversight of the Bureaucracy   Congressional **oversight** of the federal bureaucracy is a continuing process by which Congress reviews the activities of the executive branch. The *formal* rationale of oversight is to determine whether the purposes of laws passed by Congress are being achieved by executive agencies and whether appropriations established by Congress are being spent as intended. Often the *real* purpose is to influence executive branch decisions, secure favorable treatment for friends and constituents, embarrass presidential appointees, undercut political support for particular programs or agencies, lay the political groundwork for budgetary increases or decreases for an agency, or simply enhance the power of congressional committees and subcommittees and those who chair them.

Oversight is carried out primarily through congressional committees and subcommittees. Individual senators and representatives can engage in a form of oversight simply by writing or calling executive agencies, but committees and their staffs carry on the bulk of oversight activity. Because committees and subcommittees specialize in particular areas of policy making, each tends to focus its oversight activities on particular executive departments and agencies. Oversight is particularly intense during budget hearings. Subcommittees of both the House and the Senate Appropriations Committees are especially interested in how money is being spent by the agencies they oversee.

Senate Advice and Consent and Confirmation of Presidential Appointments

The Constitution provides that the president must obtain the **advice and consent** of the Senate for treaties "provided that two-thirds of the Senators present concur." In fact, the Senate has seldom provided "advice" to the president regarding treaties prior to their submission to the Senate for "consent." The president enjoys a high degree of autonomy over U.S. foreign policy (see "Global Leader" in Chapter 11). The process of treaty ratification begins when a president submits an already negotiated treaty to the Senate. Once submitted, treaties are referred to the Senate Foreign Relations Committee. That Committee cannot make changes in the treaty itself; it can either reject the treaty or forward it to the full Senate. The Senate itself cannot make changes in the formal treaty but must accept or reject it. Ratification requires a two-thirds vote. The Senate can, however, express its reservations to a treaty and/or instruct the president in how the treaty is to be interpreted.[3]

The Senate also exercises a special power over the president and the executive branch of government through its constitutional responsibility for approving presidential appointments of key executive officers, including Cabinet members, ambassadors, and other high officials (see "Congressional Constraints on the Bureaucracy" in Chapter 12). And the Senate exercises a special power over the judicial branch through its constitutional responsibility for the **confirmation** of presidential appointments to the federal judiciary including the Supreme Court (see "The Politics of Selecting Judges" in Chapter 13).

Agenda Setting and Media Attention

Congressional hearings and investigations often involve agenda setting—bringing issues to the public's attention and placing them on the national agenda. For agenda-setting purposes, congressional committees or subcommittees need the assistance of the media. Televised hearings and investigations are perhaps the most effective means by which Congress can attract attention to issues as well as to itself and its members.

Hearings and investigations are similar in some ways, but hearings are usually held on a specific bill in order to build a record of both technical information (what is the problem and how legislation might be crafted to resolve it) and political information (who favors and who opposes various legislative options). In contrast, investigations are held on alleged misdeeds or scandals. Although the U.S. Supreme Court has held that there must be some "legislative purpose" behind a **congressional investigation**, that phrase has been interpreted very broadly indeed.[4]

The constitutional rationale for congressional investigations is that Congress is seeking information to assist in its lawmaking function. But from the earliest Congress to the present, the investigating powers of Congress have often been used for political purposes: to rally popular support for policies or programs favored by Congress; to attack the president, other high officials in the administration, or presidential policies or programs; to focus media attention and public debate on particular issues; or simply to win media coverage and popular recognition for members of Congress.

Congressional investigators have the legal power to **subpoena** witnesses (force them to appear), administer oaths, compel testimony, and initiate criminal charges for **contempt** (refusing to cooperate) and **perjury** (lying). These powers can be exercised by Congress's regular committees and subcommittees and by committees appointed especially to conduct a particular investigation.

Congress cannot impose criminal punishments as a result of its investigations. But the information uncovered in a congressional investigation can be turned over

advice and consent
The constitutional power of the U.S. Senate to reject or ratify (by a two-thirds vote) treaties made by the president.

confirmation
The constitutionally required consent of the Senate to appointments of high-level executive officials by the president and appointments of federal judges.

congressional hearings
Congressional committee sessions in which members listen to witnesses who provide information and opinions on matters of interest to the committee, including pending legislation.

congressional investigation
Congressional committee hearings on alleged misdeeds or scandals.

subpoena
A written command to appear before a court or a congressional committee.

contempt
Willfull disobedience to, or open disrespect of, a court or congressional body.

perjury
Lying while under oath after swearing to tell the truth.

Ticket of admission to the U.S. Senate galleries for the impeachment trial of President Andrew Johnson in 1868.

impeachment
Formal changes of wrongdoing brought against a government official, resulting in a trial and upon conviction removal from office.

to the U.S. Department of Justice, which may proceed with its own criminal investigation and perhaps indictment and trial of alleged wrongdoers in federal courts.

Congressional investigations have long been used as an opportunity for Congress to expose wrongdoing on the part of executive branch officials. The first congressional investigation (1792) examined why General Arthur St. Clair had been defeated by the Indians in Ohio; the Crédit Mobilier investigations (1872–73) revealed scandals in the Grant administration; the Select Committee on Campaign Practices, known universally as the "Watergate Committee," exposed the activities of President Richard Nixon's inner circle that led to impeachment charges and Nixon's forced resignation; a House and Senate Joint Select Committee conducted the Iran-Contra investigation in the Reagan administration; the Senate Special Whitewater Committee investigated matters related to Bill and Hillary Clinton's real estate investments in Arkansas.

Impeachment and Removal Potentially, Congress's most formidable power is that of impeaching and removing from office the president, other officers of the United States, and federal judges, including Supreme Court justices. Congress can do so only for "Treason, Bribery or other High Crimes and Misdemeanors." The House of Representatives has the sole authority to bring charges of **impeachment**, by a simple majority vote. Impeachment is analogous to a criminal indictment; it does not remove an officer but merely subjects him or her to trial by the Senate. Only the Senate, following a trial, can remove the federal official from office, and then only by a two-thirds vote.

Bill Clinton was the second president in the nation's history to be impeached by the U.S. House of Representatives. (Andrew Johnson was the first in 1867; after a one-month trial in the Senate, the "guilty" vote fell one short of two-thirds needed for Johnson's removal. President Richard Nixon resigned just prior to an impending impeachment vote in 1974.) The 1998 House impeachment vote split along partisan lines, with Republicans voting "yes" and Democrats voting "no." Two Articles of Impeachment were passed, one for perjury before a grand jury and one for obstruction of justice. In the subsequent Senate trial, only 45 senators (less than a majority and far less than the needed two-thirds) voted to convict President Clinton on the first charge, and only 50 voted to convict on the second (see *Politics Up Close*: "Sex, Lies, and Impeachment" in Chapter 11).

Congressional Apportionment and Redistricting

▶ 10.2 *Explain the processes of congressional apportionment and redistricting, and assess how representative Congress is of the general population.*

The Constitution states that "Representatives . . . shall be apportioned among the several states . . . according to their respective Numbers." It orders an "actual enumeration" (census) every 10 years. And it provides that every state shall have at least one representative, in addition to two senators, regardless of population. But the Constitution is silent on the size of the House of Representatives. Congress itself determines its own size; for more than a century, it allowed itself to grow to accommodate new states and population growth. In 1910 it fixed the membership of the House at 435.

The effect of doing so has been to expand the population of House districts over the years. Following the 2010 census, House districts have populations of

Think
Again

Should congressional districts be drawn to ensure that minorities win seats in Congress in rough proportion to their populations in the states?

about 715,000. It is sometimes argued that such large House constituencies prevent meaningful communication between citizens and their representatives. (The Framers originally envisioned House districts of no more than 30,000 people.) But expanding the size of the House would complicate its work, reduce the influence of individual members, require more procedural controls, and probably strengthen the power of party leaders.

Apportionment

Apportionment refers to the allocation of House seats to the states after each 10-year census. The Constitution does not specify a mathematical method of apportionment; Congress adopted a complex "method of equal proportion" in 1929, which so far has withstood court challenges.

Malapportionment

Historically, state legislatures were notorious for their **malapportionment**—congressional (and state legislative) districts with grossly unequal numbers of people. Some congressional districts had twice the average number of people per district, and others had only half as many. In a district twice the size of the average district, the value of an individual's vote was heavily diluted. In a district half the size of the average, the value of an individual's vote was greatly magnified.

Enter the Supreme Court

Prior to 1962, the Supreme Court refused to intervene in apportionment, holding that this question belonged to the state legislatures and that the federal courts should avoid this "political thicket." So the Supreme Court's decision in the landmark case *Baker v. Carr* (1962) came as a surprise. The Court ruled that inequalities in voters' influence resulting from different-size districts violated the Equal Protection Clause of the 14th Amendment. The case dealt with a complaint about Tennessee's state legislative districts, but the Court soon extended its holding to congressional districts as well.[5] "The conception of political equality from the Declaration of Independence to Lincoln's Gettysburg Address, to the 14th, 15th, 17th, and 19th Amendments, can mean only one thing—one person, one vote."[6]

The shift in the Supreme Court's policy raised a new question: How equal must districts be in order to guarantee voters "equal protection of the law"? The courts have ruled that only official U.S. Bureau of the Census figures may be

apportionment
The allocation of legislative seats to jurisdictions based on population. Seats in the U.S. House of Representatives are apportioned to the states on the basis of their population after every 10-year census.

malapportionment
Unequal numbers of people in legislative districts resulting in inequality of voter representation.

Counting the Votes

On the back wall is the electronic tally board in the U.S. House of Representatives chamber in the Capitol. The board is used to count the votes of the members on the bills up for consideration before the House.

Drawing the Lines: The Original Gerrymander

The term *gerrymander* immortalizes Governor Elbridge Gerry (1744–1814) of Massachusetts, who in 1811 redistricted the state legislature to favor Democrats over Federalists. A district north of Boston was designed to concentrate, and thus "waste," Federalist votes. This political cartoon from the *Boston Gazette*, March 26, 1812, depicted the new district lines as a salamander, dubbing the process the "gerrymander."

redistricting
Drawing of legislative district boundary lines following each 10-year census.

gerrymandering
Drawing district boundary lines for political advantage.

used: estimated changes since the last census may *not* be used. In recent years, the courts have insisted on nearly exact mathematical equality in populations in congressional districts in a state.

"Actual Enumeration" The U.S. Constitution is very specific in its wording: It calls for an "actual Enumeration" (Article I, Section 2) of the population in each 10-year census. However, the U.S. Bureau of the Census has considered the use of samples and estimates to correct what it perceives to be "undercounts." Undercounting is said to occur when certain populations are difficult to identify and count on an individual basis, populations such as recent non-English-speaking immigrants or residents of neighborhoods likely to mistake government census takers for law enforcement officers or other unwelcome government officials. Political leaders (usually Democrats) of states and cities with large immigrant and minority populations have favored the substitution of samples and estimates for actual head counts. However, the U.S. Supreme Court held in 1999 that the Census Act of 1976 prohibits sampling for purposes of apportioning House members among the states.[7] Congress may use sampling for determining the allocation of grant-in-aid funds if it wishes.

Redistricting Redistricting refers to the drawing of boundary lines of congressional districts following the census. After each census, some states gain and others lose seats, depending on whether their populations have grown faster or slower than the nation's population. In addition, population shifts within a state may force districting changes. Congressional district boundaries are drawn by state legislatures in each state; a state's redistricting act must pass both houses of the state legislature and win the governor's signature (or be passed over a gubernatorial veto). The U.S. Justice Department and the federal judiciary are also deeply involved in redistricting issues, particularly questions of whether or not redistricting disadvantages African Americans or other minorities.

Gerrymandering Gerrymandering is the drawing of district lines for political advantage (see Figure 10.2). The population of districts may be equal, yet the district boundaries are drawn in such a fashion as to grant advantage or disadvantage to parties and candidates. Gerrymandering has long been used by parties in control of the state legislatures to maximize their seats in Congress and state legislatures.

Gerrymandering, with the aid of sophisticated computer-mapping programs and data on past voting records of precincts, is a highly technical task. But consider a simple example where a city is entitled to three representatives and the eastern third of the city is Republican but the western two-thirds is Democratic (see Figure 10.2). If the Republicans could draw the district lines, they might draw them along a north–south direction to allow their party to win in one of the

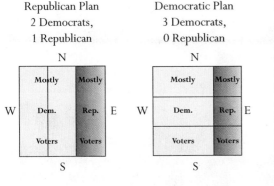

Republican Plan
2 Democrats,
1 Republican

Democratic Plan
3 Democrats,
0 Republican

FIGURE 10.2

Gerrymandering in Action

Depending on how an area is divided into districts, the result may benefit one party or the other. In this example, dividing the area so one district has virtually all the Republicans gives that party a victory in that district while ceding the other two districts to the Democrats. In contrast, Democrats benefit when Republican voters are divided among the three districts so that their votes are splintered.

three districts. In contrast, if Democrats could draw the district lines, they might draw them along an east–west direction to allow their party to win all three districts by diluting the Republican vote. Such dividing up and diluting of a strong minority to deny it the power to elect a representative is called **splintering**. Often gerrymandering is not as neat as our example; district lines may twist and turn, creating grotesque patterns in order to achieve the desired effects. Another gerrymandering strategy—**packing**—is the heavy concentration of one party's voters in a single district in order to "waste" their votes and allow modest majorities of the party doing the redistricting to win in other districts.

splintering
Redistricting in which a strong minority is divided up and diluted to prevent it from electing a representative.

packing
Redistricting in which partisan voters are concentrated in a single district, "wasting" their majority vote and allowing the opposition to win by modest majorities in other districts.

Partisan Gerrymandering   Partisan gerrymandering does not violate federal court standards for "equal protection" under the 14th Amendment. There is no constitutional obligation to allocate seats "to the contending parties in proportion to what their anticipated statewide vote will be."[8] For several years the Supreme Court threatened to intervene to correct partisan gerrymandering,[9] but in 2004 it finally decided that the issue was "nonjusticiable"—there were no "judicially manageable standards for adjudicating [party] claims." The Court decided that "'Fairness' is not a judicially manageable standard."[10] Parties are free to try to advantage themselves in redistricting.

Reredistricting   The redrawing of congressional districts usually occurs after each 10-year census. However, several states have been embroiled in a second round of redistricting, notably Texas. (If one party dominated a state legislature during the first redistricting after the census and drew district lines in a partisan fashion, there is then a strong temptation for the opposition party to undertake a second round of partisan redistricting if it subsequently wins control of the state legislature.) It is theoretically possible that redistricting could be undertaken every time a state legislature changes party control.

In a controversial case, the Supreme Court upheld the practice of reredistricting. After a protracted partisan struggle in 2003, a new Republican majority in the Texas Legislature redrew congressional boundaries that had been drawn by a Democratic-controlled legislature after the 2000 census. The result was a significant increase in Republican congressional seats and a corresponding decrease in Democratic seats in that state. But the Supreme Court declined to intervene: "Neither the Constitution nor Congress has stated any explicit prohibition on mid-decade redistricting to change districts drawn earlier in conformance with a decennial census."[11] And the Court approved a mid-decade redistricting when racial or ethnic groups appeared to have been disadvantaged by earlier redistricting.

The Freshman Class
New members of the 111th Congress (elected in November, 2008) pose in front of the U.S. Capitol. The group photo is a tradition for freshmen members.

incumbent gerrymandering
Drawing legislative district boundaries to advantage incumbent legislators.

Incumbent Gerrymandering
Yet another problem confronting state legislatures in redistricting is the preservation of incumbent Congress members, that is, **incumbent gerrymandering**. Incumbents generally have sufficient political clout with their state parties to inspire efforts in the legislature to protect their districts.

Incumbent gerrymandering means drawing district lines in such a way as to ensure that districts of incumbents include enough supporters of their party to provide a high probability of their reelection. But often ensuring incumbents' security and maximizing the party's total number of seats are conflicting goals. It is not always possible to redraw district lines in such a way as to protect incumbents and at the same time ensure the largest number of party seats in a state. Incumbents themselves want the largest number of their party's voters packed in their district. But this tactic may result in losses for their party in other districts that have been robbed of party voters. Redistricting almost always confronts incumbents with new voters—voters who were previously in a different incumbent's district. As a result, incumbents usually have a somewhat more difficult reelection campaign following redistricting than in other elections.[12]

Racial Gerrymandering
Racial gerrymandering to disadvantage African Americans and other minorities violates both the Equal Protection Clause of the 14th Amendment and the Voting Rights Act of 1965. The Voting Rights Act specifies that redistricting in states with a history of voter discrimination or low voter participation must be "cleared" in advance with the U.S. Justice Department. The act extends special protection not only to African American voters but also to Hispanic, Native American, Alaska Native, and Asian voters.

In 1982 Congress strengthened the Voting Rights Act by outlawing any electoral arrangement that has the effect of weakening minority voting power. This *effects test* replaced the earlier *intent test*, under which redistricting was outlawed only if boundaries were intentionally drawn to dilute minority political influence. In *Thornburg v. Gingles* (1986), the Supreme Court interpreted the effects test to require state legislatures to redistrict their states in a way that maximizes minority representation in Congress and the state legislatures.[13] The effect of this ruling was to require **affirmative racial gerrymandering**—the creation of predominantly African American and minority districts (labeled "majority-minority" districts) whenever possible. Following the 1990 census, redistricting in legislatures in states with large minority populations was closely scrutinized by the U.S. Justice Department and the federal courts. The result was a dramatic increase in African American and Hispanic representation in Congress (see Figure 10.6 later in this chapter).

However, the Supreme Court later expressed constitutional doubts about bizarre-shaped districts based *solely* on racial composition. In a controversial 5 to 4 decision in *Shaw v. Reno* (1993), Justice Sandra Day O'Connor wrote, "Racial gerrymandering, even for remedial purposes, may balkanize us into competing racial factions. . . . A reapportionment plan that includes in one district individuals who have little in common with one another but the color of their skin bears an uncomfortable resemblance to political apartheid"[14] (see Figure 10.3). Later, the Court held that the use of race as the "predominant factor" in drawing district lines is unconstitutional: "When the state assigns voters on the basis of race, it engages in the offensive and demeaning assumption that voters of a particular race, because of their race, think alike, share the same political interests and will prefer the same candidates at the polls."[15] But the Court has stopped short of saying that *all* race-conscious districting is unconstitutional.

Partisanship Interacts with Race

Racial gerrymandering appears to help Republican congressional candidates. If African American voters are concentrated in heavily black districts, the effect is to "bleach" surrounding districts of Democratic-leaning black voters and thus improve the chances for Republican victories. Republican Party congressional gains in the South during the 1990s may be partly attributed to racial gerrymandering.[16] In what has been described as a "paradox of representation," the creation of majority-minority districts brought more minority members to Congress, but it also led to a more conservative House of Representatives, as Republicans gained seats previously held by white liberal Democrats.[17]

Republican-led efforts to "pack" black (Democratic) voters into relatively few districts suffered a setback in 2003 when the U.S. Supreme Court recognized

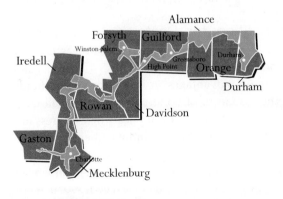

affirmative racial gerrymandering
Drawing district boundary lines to maximize minority representation.

FIGURE 10.3

Affirmative Racial Gerrymandering

North Carolina's Twelfth Congressional District was drawn up to be a "majority-minority" district by combining African American communities over a wide region of the state. The U.S. Supreme Court in *Shaw v. Reno* (1993) ordered a court review of this district to determine whether it incorporated any common interest other than race. The North Carolina legislature redrew the district in 1997, lowering its black population from 57 to 46 percent, yet keeping its lengthy connection of black voters from Charlotte to Greensboro.

that doing so might diminish the power of African American voters overall. The Court approved of a plan that "unpacked" some heavily concentrated majority-minority districts in Georgia. The Court reasoned that the result would be to create additional black "influence" districts where African American voters would not be in a majority but would be a large influential voting bloc.[18]

Getting to Capitol Hill

▶ **10.3** *Describe congressional elections and the hurdles that challengers face.*

Members of Congress are independent political entrepreneurs—selling themselves, their services, and their personal policy views to the voters in 435 House districts and fifty states across the country. They initiate their own candidacies, raise most of their campaign funds from individual contributors, put together personal campaign organizations, and get themselves elected with relatively little help from their party. Their reelection campaigns depend on their ability to raise funds from individuals and interest groups and on the services and other benefits they provide to their constituents.

Think Again

Are there too many lawyers in Congress?

open seat
Seat in a legislature for which no incumbent is running for reelection.

Who Runs for Congress? Members of Congress come from a wide variety of backgrounds, ranging from acting and professional sports to medicine and the ministry. However, exceptionally high percentages of senators and representatives have prior experience in at least one of three fields—law, business, or public service. Members of Congress are increasingly career politicians, people who decided early in life to devote themselves to running for and occupying public office.[19] The many lawyers, by and large, are *not* practicing attorneys. Rather, the typical lawyer-legislator is a political activist with a law degree. These are people who graduated from law school and immediately sought public jobs—as federal or state prosecuting attorneys, as attorneys for federal or state agencies, or as staff assistants in congressional, state, or city offices. They used their early job experiences to make political contacts and learn how to organize a political campaign, find financial contributors, and deal with the media. Another group of Congress members are former business-people—not employees of large corporations, but people whose personal or family businesses brought them into close contact with government and their local community, in real estate, insurance, franchise dealerships, community banks, and so forth.

Debating Health Care

Rep. Paul Ryan (R-WS) debates health care reform at a meeting of the House Rules Committee, with Chair Rep. Louise Slaughter (D-NY) March 20, 2010.

Competition for Seats Careerism in Congress is aided by the electoral advantages enjoyed by incumbents over challengers. Greater name recognition, advantages in raising campaign funds, and the resources of congressional offices all combine to limit competition for seats in Congress and to reelect the vast majority of incumbents (see "The Advantages of Incumbency" in Chapter 8). The result is an incumbent reelection percentage for House members that usually exceeds 90 percent. The average reelection rate for U.S. senators is more than 80 percent (see Figure 10.4).

Aspirants for congressional careers are well advised to wait for an **open seat**. Open seats in the House of Representatives are created when incumbents retire, die, or vacate the seat to run for higher office (see *People in Politics*: "Scott Brown—Revolt in

PEOPLE IN POLITICS

Scott Brown—Revolt in Massachusetts

Brown campaigning in his pick-up truck.

Republican Scott Brown, previously a little-known Massachusetts state legislator, shocked the political world in 2010 by winning the U.S. Senate seat vacated by the death of long-term liberal lion, Democrat Ted Kennedy. Brown's election produced national repercussions. His victory in the Democratic bastion of Massachusetts warned the Obama administration that their progressive policy agenda might be in danger. Brown had campaigned against the Democrats' massive health care plan, Wall Street bailouts, federal stimulus spending, and trillion dollar federal budget deficits. And his election took away the Senate Democrats' 60th vote, rendering Obama's policy initiatives vulnerable to Republican filibusters.

Brown grew up in Wakefield, Massachusetts, majored in history at Tufts University, and went on to Boston College Law School. While still a law student, he posed nude for *Cosmopolitan* magazine; he also worked briefly as an actor. He joined the Massachusetts National Guard, and eventually rose through the Judge Advocates General Corp to the rank of Lt. Col. He chose to practice real estate law. He won his first elected office in 1992 as property assessor for Wrentham, Massachusetts. Later, he would win election to that city's Board of Selectmen (city council). In 1998, he ran successfully for the Massachusetts House of Representatives and then moved on to the State Senate in 2004. Brown was one of the very few Republicans to serve in the Massachusetts state legislature.

Brown was given very little chance of success when he announced in 2009 that he would seek election in the special election to fill Ted Kennedy's seat. The favorite, Democratic Attorney General Martha Coakley, enjoyed name recognition, fund-raising advantage, and an early 30-point lead in the polls. But Brown campaigned hard, driving his GMC pickup truck around the state and performing well in televised debates with Coakley. As his poll numbers improved, he attracted campaign contributions from conservatives around the country. He even picked up support from Tea Party opponents of big government. Brown describes himself as an independent. His 52 to 47 percent victory in the liberal Democratic state stunned political observers.

House		Senate
95%	2008	80%
97%	2006	85%
98%	2004	97%
99%	2002	88%
97%	2000	83%
98%	1998	91%
94%	1996	95%
92%	1994	83%
93%	1992	86%
96%	1990	96%
98%	1988	85%
98%	1986	75%
96%	1984	90%
92%	1982	93%
91%	1980	55%

100 80 60 40 20 0
Percent

0 20 40 60 80 100
Percent

FIGURE 10.4

Familiar Faces: Incumbent Advantage in Congressional Elections

Despite periodic movements to "throw the bums out," voters in most districts and states routinely reelect their members of Congress. In recent years, more than 90 percent of representatives and 80 percent of senators who have sought reelection have been returned to Congress by votes in their districts or states.

Massachusetts"). These opportunities occur on average in about 10 percent of House seats in each election. But every 10 years reapportionment creates many new opportunities to win election to Congress. Reapportionment creates new seats in states gaining population, just as it forces out some incumbents in states losing population. Redistricting also threatens incumbents with new constituencies, where they have less name recognition, no history of casework, and perhaps no common racial or ethnic identification. Thus forced retirements and electoral defeats are more common in the first election following each 10-year reapportionment and redistricting of Congress.

Winning Big

Winning Big   Not only do incumbent Congress members usually win, they usually also win big. Over 70 percent of House members win by margins of 60 percent or more or run unopposed. (In recent years, 10 to 18 percent of House members have had *no* opposition in the general election.) Senate races are somewhat more competitive. Senate challengers are usually people who have political experience and name recognition as members of the House, governors, or other high state officials. Even so, most Senate incumbents seeking reelection are victorious over their challengers. Most members of Congress, then, sit comfortably in **safe seats**—that is, they regularly win reelection by a large margin of the vote.

safe seats
Legislative districts in which the incumbent regularly wins by a large margin of the vote.

Turnover   Despite a high rate of reelection of incumbents in Congress, about 15 percent of members arrive new to their jobs each session. **Turnover** occurs more frequently as a result of retirement, resignation (sometimes to run for higher office), or reapportionment (and the loss of an incumbent's seat) than it does as a result of an incumbent's defeat in a bid for reelection. Roughly 10 percent of Congress members voluntarily leave office when their term expires.[20]

turnover
Replacement of members of Congress by retirement or resignation, by reapportionment, or (more rarely) by electoral defeat.

Congressional Term Limits?   Public distrust of government helped to fuel a movement in the states to limit congressional terms. Several states attempted to limit their state's House members to four 2-year terms and their senators to two 6-year terms. Proponents of congressional **term limits** argued that career politicians become isolated from the lives and concerns of average citizens, that they acquire an "inside the Beltway" (the circle of highways that surround Washington) mentality. They also argued that term limits would increase competition, creating "open-seat" races on a regular basis and encouraging more people to seek public office.

term limits
Limitations on the number of terms that an elected official can serve in office. The Constitution (Amendment XXII) limits the president to two terms. There are no limits on the terms of senators or representatives.

Opponents of congressional term limits argued that they infringe on the voters' freedom of choice. If voters are upset with the performance of their Congress members, they can limit their terms by not reelecting them. But if voters wish to keep popular and experienced legislators in office, they should be permitted to do so. Opponents also argued that inexperienced Congress members would be forced to rely more on the policy information supplied them by bureaucrats, lobbyists, and staff people—thus weakening the institution of Congress.

But the U.S. Supreme Court ruled in 1995 that the states themselves cannot limit the terms of their members of Congress. "If the qualifications set forth in the text of the Constitution are to be changed, that text must be amended."[21] In a controversial 5 to 4 decision, the Court held that the Founders intended age, citizenship, and residency to be the *only* qualifications for members of Congress.

✓ Think
Again

Should members of Congress be limited in the number of terms they can serve?

It is not likely that the necessary two-thirds of both houses of Congress will ever vote for a constitutional amendment to limit their own stay in office. Thus the Supreme Court's decision effectively killed the movement for congressional term limits.

Republicans in Opposition

House Republican leader John Boehner speaks out against President Obama's health care reform bill at a news conference in October, 2009. Republicans unanimously opposed the bill, but it became law in 2010.

The Congressional Electorate Congressional elections generally fail to arouse much interest among voters.[22] Indeed, only about 60 percent of the general public can name one U.S. senator from their state, and only about 40 percent can name both of their U.S. senators. Members of the House of Representatives fare no better: less than half of the general public can name their representative. But even constituents who know the names of their congressional delegation seldom know anything about the policy positions of these elected officials or about their votes on specific issues. Turnout in congressional *general elections* averages only about 35 percent in off-year (nonpresidential) elections. Turnout in congressional *primary elections* seldom exceeds 15 to 20 percent of persons eligible to vote. This lack of public attentiveness to congressional elections gives a great advantage to candidates with high name recognition, generally the incumbents (see *What Do You Think?*: "Why Do Voters Reelect Members of an Unpopular Congress?").

Congressional Campaign Financing Raising the $1 million it can take to win a House seat or the $5 to $10 million or more for a successful Senate campaign is a major job in and of itself (see "How Much Does It Cost to Get Elected?" in Chapter 8). Even incumbents who face little or no competition still work hard at fund-raising, "banking" contributions against some future challenger. Large campaign chests, assembled well in advance of an election, can also be used to frighten off would-be challengers. Campaign funds can be used to build a strong personal organization back home, finance picnics and other festivities for constituents, expand the margin of victory, and develop a reputation for invincibility that may someday protect against an unknown challenger.[23]

Does money buy elections? In about 90 percent of all congressional races, the candidate who spends the most money wins. However, because most winning candidates are incumbents, the money probably reflects the expected political outcome rather than shaping it. But even in open-seat races, the candidate who spends the most money usually wins.

Party Fortunes in Congress

▶ 10.4 *Evaluate the successes and failures of the two parties in Congress.*

For 40 years (1954–1994) Democrats enjoyed an advantage in congressional races; in fact, the Democratic Party was said to have a "permanent majority" in the House of Representatives (see Figure 10.5). The Republican victory in the congressional election of 1994 was widely described as a political "earthquake." It gave the GOP control of the House for the first time in four decades, as well as control of the Senate. Republicans remained in control of the House and the Senate (except for a brief period in 2001–2002) until the 2006 elections. Democrats strengthened their control in both houses in the 2008 elections. But in 2010 Republicans came roaring back, capturing control of the House and improving their numbers in the Senate.

WHAT DO YOU THINK?

Why Do Voters Reelect Members of an Unpopular Congress?

Congress is the least popular branch of government. Public approval of Congress is well below that of the presidency and the Supreme Court. What accounts for this lack of popularity? The belief that members of Congress "spend more time thinking about their own political futures than they do in passing legislation" may contribute to this sentiment.

But public disapproval of Congress may also arise from a misunderstanding of democratic government. "People do not wish to see uncertainty, conflicting options, long debate, competing interests, confusion and compromised imperfect solutions. . . . They often see a patently unrealistic form of democracy."[a]

But in an apparent paradox, most voters *approve of their own* representative (see figure below), even while Congress itself is the object of popular distrust and ridicule. A majority of voters believe that their own representatives "deserve reelection."

This apparent contradiction is explained in part by differing expectations: Americans expect Congress to deal with national issues, but they expect their own representatives to deal with local concerns and even personal problems. Members of Congress understand this concern and consequently devote a great deal of their time to constituent service. Indeed, many members of Congress try to dissociate themselves from Congress, attacking Congress in their own campaigns and contributing to negative images of the institution. Finally, the national news media are highly critical of Congress, but local news media frequently portray local members of Congress in a more favorable light.

Q. Do you approve of the way the U.S. Congress is handling its job?

Q. Do you approve or disapprove of the way the representative from your own congressional district is handling his or her job?

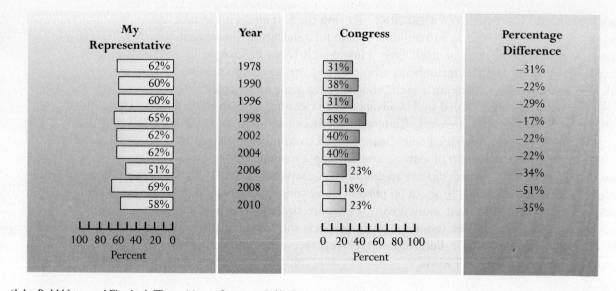

My Representative	Year	Congress	Percentage Difference
62%	1978	31%	−31%
60%	1990	38%	−22%
60%	1996	31%	−29%
65%	1998	48%	−17%
62%	2002	40%	−22%
62%	2004	40%	−22%
51%	2006	23%	−34%
69%	2008	18%	−51%
58%	2010	23%	−35%

100 80 60 40 20 0
Percent

0 20 40 60 80 100
Percent

[a]John R. Hibbing and Elizabeth Theiss-Morse, *Congress as Public Enemy.* Cambridge, Eng.: Cambridge University Press, 1995, p. 147. Also cited by Roger H. Davidson and Walter J. Oleszak, *Congress and Its Members.* 9th ed. Washington, D.C.: CQ Press, 2004, p. 487. Updated from Gallup.com.

The Historic Democratic Party Dominance of Congress The historic Democratic dominance of Congress was attributed to several factors. First, over those four decades more voters identified themselves with the Democratic Party than with the Republican Party (see Chapter 7). Party identification plays a significant role in congressional voting; it is estimated that 75 percent of those who identify themselves with a party cast their vote for the congressional candidate of their party.[24] Second, the Democratic advantage was buttressed by the fact that many voters considered local rather than national conditions when casting

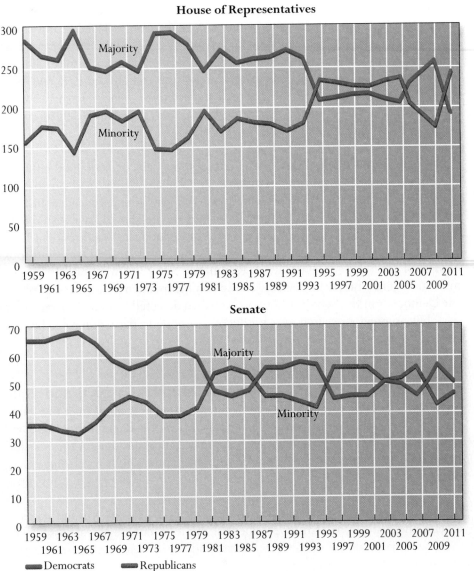

House of Representatives

Senate

Democrats Republicans

FIGURE 10.5

Parties on Capitol Hill,
Party Control of the
House and Senate

Except for two very brief
periods, Democrats
continuously controlled both
the House of Representatives
and the Senate for more than
40 years. The Democratic
Party's "permanent" control
of Congress was ended in
1994, when Republicans won
majorities in both houses.
Republicans remained in
control of the House for
12 years; Democrats won
control in 2006 when
frustrations over the war in
Iraq hurt Republican
candidates. Democrats
strengthened their hold on
both houses in 2008 when
Barack Obama won the White
House. But in 2010
Republicans won back
control of the House and
increased their numbers in
the Senate.

congressional votes. Voters may have wanted to curtail *overall* federal spending in Washington (a traditional Republican promise), but they wanted a member of Congress who would "bring home the bacon." Although both Republican and Democratic congressional candidates usually promised to bring money and jobs to their districts, Democratic candidates appeared more creditable on such promises because their party generally supported large domestic-spending programs. Finally, Democratic congressional candidates over those years enjoyed the many advantages of incumbency. It was thought that only death or retirement would dislodge many of them from their seats.

The Republican "Revolution" of 1994

The sweeping Republican victory in 1994 surprised many analysts.[25] The GOP's capture of control of both houses of Congress for the first time in 40 years raised conservatives' hopes of a "revolution" in public policy. The new Republican House Speaker, Newt Gingrich, was the acknowledged leader of the revolution, with Republican Senate Majority Leader Bob Dole in tow. But soon the revolution began to fizzle out. Two key Republican campaign promises failed to pass the Congress: the House

Newt Raising Funds for
Conservatives

Former House Speaker Newt
Gingrich led the Republican
victory in 1994, capturing
control of the House for the
first time in 40 years.

failed to muster the necessary two-thirds majority for a constitutional amendment to impose congressional term limits, and the Senate failed to do so on behalf of a balanced budget amendment.

Republicans succeeded in maintaining their control of Congress despite Clinton's reelection in 1996. But Democrats gained House seats in both the 1996 and 1998 congressional elections. Republicans had expected to benefit from Clinton's acknowledged sexual misconduct and the House impeachment investigation. But voters generally sided with Clinton.

Congress Divided in 2000
The congressional elections of 2000 reflected the close partisan division of the nation. Republicans barely held on to their majority in the House of Representatives. The election produced a historic 50–50 tie in the Senate. Formal control of the Senate should have rested with Republicans, owing to the tie-breaking vote of Republican Vice President Dick Cheney. But in a precedent-shattering midsession shift of power, Democrats took control of the Senate in 2001, when Republican Senator Jim Jeffords from Vermont abandoned his party, declared himself an Independent, but gave his vote to the Democrats in the Senate. Other senators had defected from their party in the past, but no previous switch ever produced a change in party control. The new 51–49 Democratic majority took control of all Senate committees as well as the floor of that body.

Bush Leads GOP to Congressional Victories in 2002 and 2004
In 2002, President George W. Bush designated himself as "Campaigner-in-Chief," traveling about the country raising campaign money for Republican House and Senate candidates. His continuing high approval rating throughout the year following the "9/11" terrorist attack on America made him a highly welcomed campaigner in districts and states across the nation. In his campaign stops, Bush talked about the war on terrorism and his need for "allies" in the Congress. President Bush appeared to influence just enough voters in key districts and states to reverse the historic pattern of presidential midterm congressional losses. The GOP won back control of the U.S. Senate and strengthened its majority in the House of Representatives.

Again in 2004 President Bush appeared to help GOP congressional candidates across the country. Republicans increased their control of the Senate from 51 to 55. They picked up several seats of retiring older-generation Southern Democrats. And they even succeeded in defeating the Democratic Senate Leader, Tom Daschle of South Dakota. The 2004 election also made the Senate slightly more "diverse": African American Barack Obama was elected from Illinois, and Hispanic Mel Martinez was elected from Florida. In the House, Republicans also increased their margin of control. President Bush was quick to claim that winning the White House, the Senate, and the House of Representatives meant that the American People supported his "agenda."

Democratic Revival in 2006
However, the war in Iraq seriously eroded President George Bush's popularity and led to the election of a Democratic-controlled House and Senate in the 2006 midterm congressional elections. Republican congressional control had lasted 12 years, and Democrats were anxious to bring their agenda to the Capitol. But Democrats failed to bring an end to the war in Iraq. Because the president is the Commander-in-Chief, there was little Congress could do by itself to compel changes in strategy in Iraq. In theory, Congress could have cut off funds for the war, but it proved to be too politically risky to deny funds for

American troops in the field. Efforts to place time limits on troop deployments in Iraq also failed. Congress and President Bush did agree on a $700 billion "bailout" of Wall Street in the final days of the Bush presidency.

Congress United for "Change" in 2008

Democrats not only won the White House in 2008 but also strengthened their control of both the Senate and the House of Representatives. Republicans had warned voters that this outcome would give unchecked power to Democrats "Obama, Pelosi, and Ried"—referring to the new president, the Speaker of the House, and the Senate Majority Leader. But united party government does not always ensure complete cooperation between the House, Senate, and White House.

President Obama presented Congress with a very lengthy legislative agenda, including a massive economic "stimulus" package, huge budget increases and increases in deficit spending, a comprehensive transformation of the nation's health care system, new regulations governing the nation's financial institutions, and a broad new "cap and trade" program in which the federal

Obama Traces His Roots

Senator Barack Obama (D-IL) clasps hands with his grandmother, who lives in Kenya. Obama visited Kenya following his election to the U.S. Senate in 2004.

government would set overall national ceilings on carbon emissions. Overall, the president succeeded in getting most but not all of his proposals enacted into law (see *Controversy*: "Obama Faces Congress" later in this chapter). Democratic control of Congress and the White House seemed to inspire unity and discipline among Republicans. On many key votes the GOP was united in opposition to Obama-backed proposals. Republicans complained bitterly that important legislation had been "rammed through" by the Democratic leadership (See *Politics Up Close*: "Republicans Rebound—The 2010 Congressional Elections").

Life in Congress

▶ 10.5 *Characterize the working life of member of Congress.*

"All politics is local," declared former House Speaker Thomas P. "Tip" O'Neill, himself once the master of both Boston ward politics and the U.S. House of Representatives. Attention to the local constituency is the key to survival and success in congressional politics. If Congress often fails to deal responsibly with national problems, the explanation lies in part with the design of the institution. House members must devote primary attention to their districts and Senate members to their states. Only *after* their constituencies are served can they turn their attention to national policy making.

The "Representativeness" of Congress   The Constitution requires only that members of the House of Representatives be (1) residents of the state they represent (they need not live in their congressional district, although virtually all do so); (2) U.S. citizens for at least 7 years; and (3) at least 25 years old. Senators must also be residents of the state they represent, but they must be at least 30 years old and U.S. citizens for at least 9 years.

- *African Americans*   African Americans were first elected to Congress following the Civil War—seven black representatives and one black senator served in 1875. But with the end of Reconstruction, black membership in Congress fell

POLITICS UP CLOSE

Republicans Rebound—The 2010 Congressional Elections

Voters were frustrated in 2010. Recession and continuing high unemployment, massive federal spending and record deficits, and a president seemingly out of touch with moderate to conservative voters, all combined to inspire opposition to incumbent Democrats. Many voters said their vote was a message against President Obama's programs, but *not* an endorsement of the Republicans. Indeed, both parties were viewed unfavorably by a majority of voters. But Democrats bore the brunt of the voters' anger.

Historically, the president's party has lost seats in the midterm congressional elections. But the size of the

Florida Republican Marco Rubio celebrates his 2010 election to the U.S. Senate. The son of Cuban exiles hopes to improve Republican fortunes among Hispanic voters.

Republican victory in the House of Representatives—over 60 seats switching from Democratic to Republican and the resulting loss of Democratic control of that body—promised to bring a halt to many of the policy initiatives of the Obama administration. Republicans also gained six seats in the Senate, bringing their total to 47. But Democrats retained the majority in the Senate with several key victories, including that of Majority Leader Harry Reid in Nevada.

Early in the campaign the GOP appeared to be energized by the tea party movement. Tea party–endorsed candidates won several important Republican Senate primary races, including Marco Rubio in Florida and Rand Paul in Kentucky, both of whom went on to win Senate seats. But in the general election campaign some tea party candidates, including Sharon Angle in Nevada and Christine O'Donnell in Delaware, appeared inexperienced and gaffe prone. Their losses helped Democrats retain control of the Senate. Republican Lisa Merkowski won the Alaska Senate seat as a write-in candidate against the tea party–endorsed Republican primary winner Joe Miller. Overall, the tea party seemed to be a mixed blessing for the GOP.

Polling revealed that the voters in the 2010 election were older and more conservative than in previous elections. Both groups favored Republican candidates. Obama's job performance was disapproved of by a majority of voters, and these voters also favored GOP candidates. Both the Democratic and Republican parties were viewed negatively, but incumbent Democrats suffered from the voters' anxiety over the economy and their belief that the country was "on the wrong track."

to a single seat in the House from 1891 to 1955. Following the Civil Rights Act of 1964 and the Voting Rights Act of 1965, black membership in Congress rose steadily. Redistricting following the 1990 Census resulted in many new "majority-minority" congressional districts. After the 1992 elections, black membership in the House rose dramatically (see Figure 10.6), with most elected from predominantly African American districts.[26] As a result, although African Americans today make up a little more than 12 percent of the U.S. population, they make up about 9 percent of the House membership.

• *Hispanics*   Hispanics now comprise the nation's largest minority, with about 15 percent of the U.S. population. But Hispanic representation in the Congress lags considerably behind their population growth. Currently only about 5 percent of House members are Hispanic, and three Hispanics serve in the U.S. Senate. The Voting Rights Act of 1965 protects "language minorities" as well as racial and ethnic minorities. Prior to the 1990 census and the creation

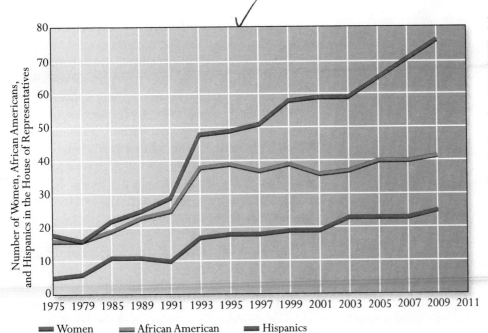

FIGURE 10.6

Minority Voices: Women, African Americans, and Hispanics in the House of Representatives

Although the House of Representatives is still far short of "looking like America," in recent years the number of African American, Hispanic, and female members has risen noticeably. Particularly impressive advances were made in the 1992 elections, following court-ordered creation of "majority-minority" districts.

of many court-ordered "majority-minority" congressional districts, very few Hispanics served in the Congress. But with the creation of new Hispanic majority districts, Hispanic representation began to increase in the House of Representatives. Most Hispanic House members come from California, Florida, and Texas.

- *Women* Women have made impressive gains in both the House and the Senate in recent years. The "year of the woman" election in 1992 brought a significant increase in the number of women in the House of Representatives. Since then, women's representation in the House continued upward; seventy-seven women served in the House in the 111th Congress (2009–2011), divided between sixty Democrats and seventeen Republicans. In the Senate, seventeen women served. California was represented by two Democratic women, Dianne Feinstein and Barbara Boxer. They were joined by nine other Democratic women senators, and five Republican women senators. Although this is the largest delegation of women ever to serve together in the U.S. Senate, it is still only 17 percent of that body. The number of women in Congress has grown as a result of many factors, including strides that women have made in the workplace and other societal institutions. Yet stereotypes about women as politicians remain. Generally, voters view women as better able to handle "feminine" issues, such as health care, child care and education, but less able to handle "masculine" issues, including the economy and war. In the past, some women candidates tried to counter these stereotypes by emphasizing their toughness, especially on crime. But evidence suggests that women candidates can use female stereotypes to their advantage by focusing the campaign on gender-owned issues—health, welfare, education, and other compassion issues.[27]

Congressional Staff Congress is composed of a great deal more than 535 elected senators and representatives. Congressional staff and other support personnel now total some 25,000 people. Each representative has a staff of twenty or

Congressional Staffers at Work

Congressional staff work on details of legislation for the House Judiciary Committee. Staffers regularly exercise influence over legislation.

more people, usually headed by a chief of staff or administrative assistant and including legislative assistants, communications specialists, constituent-service personnel, office managers, secretaries, and aides of various sorts. Senators frequently have staffs of thirty to fifty or more people. All representatives and senators are provided with offices both in Washington and in their home districts and states. In addition, representatives receive more than $500,000 apiece for office expenses, travel, and staff; and senators receive $2 million or more, depending on the size of their state's population. Overall, Congress spends more than $2 *billion* on itself each year.

Congressional staff people exercise great influence over legislation. Many experienced "Hill rats" have worked for the same member of Congress for many years. They become very familiar with "their" member's political strengths and vulnerabilities and handle much of the member's contacts with interest groups and constituents. Staff people, more than members themselves, move the legislative process—scheduling committee hearings, writing bills and amendments, and tracking the progress of such proposals through committees and floor proceedings. By working with the staff of other members of Congress or the staff of committees and negotiating with interest-group representatives, congressional staff are often able to work out policy compromises, determine the wording of legislation, or even outline "deals" for their member's vote (all subject to later approval by their member). With multiple demands on their time, members of Congress come to depend on their staff not only for information about the content of legislation but also for political recommendations about what position to take regarding it.

Support Agencies   In addition to the thousands of personal and committee staff who are supposed to assist members of Congress in research and analysis, four congressional support agencies provide Congress with information:

- The Library of Congress and its Congressional Research Service (CRS) are the oldest congressional support agencies. Members of Congress can turn to the Library of Congress for references and information. The CRS responds to direct requests of members for factual information on virtually any topic. It tracks major bills in Congress and produces summaries of each bill introduced. This information is available on computer terminals in members' offices.

Government Accountability Office

An arm of Congress that undertakes oversight of the operations and finances of executive agencies, as well as performing policy research and evaluation.

- The **Government Accountability Office** (GAO) has broad authority to oversee the operations and finances of executive agencies, to evaluate their programs, and to report its findings to Congress. Established as an arm of Congress in 1921, the GAO largely confined itself to financial auditing and management studies in its early years, but it has now expanded to more than five thousand employees and undertakes a broad agenda of policy research and evaluation. Most GAO studies and reports are requested by members of Congress and congressional committees, but the GAO also undertakes some studies on its own initiative.

- The Congressional Budget Office (CBO) was created by the Congressional Budget and Impoundment Act of 1974 to strengthen Congress's role in the budgeting process. It was designed as a congressional counterweight to the president's Office of Management and Budget (see Chapter 14). The CBO supplies the House and Senate budget committees with its own budgetary analyses and economic forecasts, sometimes challenging those found in the president's annual budget.

- The Government Printing Office (GPO), created in 1860 as the publisher of the *Congressional Record*, now distributes over 20,000 different government publications in U.S. government bookstores throughout the nation.

Power Player

Democratic House Member John Lewis is congratulated for success in passing a Voting Rights Act reauthorization bill. Lewis regularly wins his Atlanta congressional seat by large margins.

Workload Members of Congress claim to work 12- to 15-hour days: 2 to 3 hours in committee and subcommittee meetings; 2 to 3 hours on the floor of the chamber; 3 to 4 hours meeting with constituents, interest groups, other members, and staff in their offices; and 2 to 3 hours attending conferences, events, and meetings in Washington.[28] Members of Congress may introduce anywhere from ten to fifty bills in a single session of Congress. Most bills are introduced merely to exhibit the member's commitment to a particular group or issue. Cosigning a popular bill is a common practice; particularly popular bills may have 100 or 200 cosigners in the House of Representatives. Although thousands of bills are introduced, only 400 to 800 are passed in a session.[29]

Pay and Perks Taxpayers can relate directly to what members of Congress spend on themselves, even while millions—and even billions—of dollars spent on government programs remain relatively incomprehensible. Taxpayers thus were enraged when Congress, in a late-night session in 1991, gave itself a hefty pay raise. Congress claimed the pay raise was a "reform," since it was coupled with a stipulation that members of Congress would no longer be allowed to accept honoraria from interest groups for their speeches and appearances, thus supposedly reducing members' dependence on outside income. Many angry taxpayers saw only a 44 percent pay raise, in the midst of a national recession, for a Congress that was doing little to remedy the nation's problems. By 2010, automatic cost-of-living increases, also enacted by Congress, had raised members' pay to $174,000. House and Senate members receive the same pay. (Leaders of the House and Senate are paid a slightly higher salary than rank-and-file members.) Benefits, including retirement pay, are very generous.

27th Amendment As the pay-raise debate raged in Washington, several states resurrected a constitutional amendment originally proposed by James Madison. Although passed by the Congress in 1789, it had never been ratified by the necessary three-quarters of the states. The 203-year-old amendment, requiring a House election to intervene before a congressional pay raise can take effect, was added as the 27th Amendment when ratified by four states (for a total of thirty-nine) in 1992.

Think Again

Do Congress members spend too much time in their home districts seeking reelection?

home style
Activities of Congress members specifically directed at their home constituencies.

casework
Services performed by legislators or their staff on behalf of individual constituents.

pork barreling
Legislation designed to make government benefits, including jobs and projects used as political patronage, flow to a particular district or state.

earmarks
Provisions in appropriation bills specifying particular projects for which federal money is to be spent.

franking privilege
Free mail service afforded members of Congress.

Home Style

▶ 10.6 *Identify the techniques used by representatives to enhance their image among constituents.*

Members of Congress spend as much time politically cultivating their districts and states as they do legislating. **Home style** refers to the activities of senators and representatives in promoting their images among constituents and personally attending to constituents' problems and interests.[30] These activities include members' allocations of their personnel and staff resources to constituent services; members' personal appearances in the home district or state to demonstrate personal attention; and members' efforts to explain their Washington activities to the voters back home.

Casework   Casework is really a form of "retail" politics. Members of Congress can win votes one at a time by helping constituents on a personal level. Casework can involve everything from tracing lost Social Security checks and Medicare claims to providing information about federal programs, solving problems with the Internal Revenue Service, and assisting with federal job applications. Over time, grateful voters accumulate, giving incumbents an advantage at election time. Congressional staff do much of the actual casework, but letters go out over the signature of the member of Congress. Senators and representatives blame the growth of government for increasing casework, but it is also clear that members solicit casework, frequently reminding constituents to bring their problems to their member of Congress.[31]

Pork Barrel and Earmarks   Pork barreling describes the efforts of senators and representatives to "bring home the bacon"—to bring federally funded projects, grants, and contracts that primarily benefit a single district or state to their home constituencies. Opportunities for pork barreling have never been greater: roads, dams, parks, and post offices are now overshadowed by redevelopment grants to city governments, research grants to universities, weapons contracts to local plants, "demonstration" projects of all kinds, and myriad other "goodies" tucked inside each year's annual appropriations bills.

Earmarks in these appropriations bills specify the particular project for which federal money is to be spent. Members of Congress understand the importance of supporting each other's earmarks, cooperating in the "incumbent-protection society." Even though earmarking and pork barreling add to the public's negative image of Congress as an institution, individual members gain local popularity for the benefits they bring to home districts and states. Reformers have long complained about earmarks; in 2009, they succeeded in obtaining a rule that earmarks must identify the Congress members who sponsor them.

Pressing the Flesh   Senators and representatives spend a great deal of time in their home states and districts. Although congressional sessions last virtually all year, members of Congress find ways to spend more than a hundred days per year at home.[32] It is important to be seen at home—giving speeches and attending dinners, fund-raising events, civic occasions, and so on. To accommodate this aspect of home style, Congress usually follows a Tuesday-to-Thursday schedule of legislative business, allowing members to spend longer weekends in their home districts. Congress also enjoys long recesses during the late summer and over holidays.

Puffing Images   To promote their images back home, members make generous use of their **franking privilege** (free mailing) to send their constituents newsletters, questionnaires, biographical material, and information about federal programs. Newsletters "puff" the accomplishments of the members; questionnaires are designed more to flatter voters than to assess opinions; and informational brochures tout federal services members claim credit for providing and defending. Congress's penchant for self-promotion has also kept pace with the media and electronic ages. Congress now provides its members with television studios and support for making videotapes to send to local stations in home districts, and all members maintain Web sites on the Internet designed to puff their images.

Hill Styles and Home Styles   Members of Congress spend their lives "moving between two contexts, Washington and home, and between two activities, governing and campaigning."[33] They must regularly ask themselves how much time they should spend at home with their constituents versus how much time they should spend on lawmaking assignments in Washington. It is no surprise that freshman legislators spend more time in their districts; indeed, very few first-termers move their families to Washington. Long-term incumbents spend more time in Washington, but all Congress members spend more time at home in an election year.

Much of the time spent at home—with small groups of constituents, among contributors, in public speeches, and appearances on radio and television—is devoted to explaining issues and justifying the member's vote on them. "Often members defend their own voting record by belittling Congress—portraying themselves as knights errant battling sinister forces and feckless colleagues."[34]

Organizing Congress: Party and Leadership

▶ 10.7 *Analyze the roles of parties and leadership in organizing Congress.*

Congress is composed of people who think of themselves as leaders, not followers. They got elected without much help from their party. Yet they realize that their chances of attaining their personal goals—getting reelected and influencing policy—are enhanced if they cooperate with each other.

Party Organizations in Congress   The Democratic and Republican party organizations within the House of Representatives and the Senate are the principal bases for organizing Congress (see Figure 10.7). The leadership of each house of Congress, although nominally elected by the entire chamber, is actually chosen by secret ballot of the members of each party at a "conference" or caucus (see Table 10.2).

The parties and their leaders do not choose congressional candidates, nor can they deny them renomination; all members of Congress are responsible for their own primary and general election success. But party leadership in each chamber can help incumbents achieve their reelection goals. Each party in the House and Senate sponsors a campaign committee that channels some campaign funding to party members seeking reelection.

Majority status confers great power on the party that controls the House and the Senate. The majority party chooses the leadership in each body, selects the chairs of every committee, and ensures that every committee has a majority of members from the majority party. In other words, if Democrats are in the majority in either the House or the Senate or both, Democrats will occupy all leadership positions, chair every committee, and constitute a majority of the members of every committee; and, of course, the Republicans enjoy the same advantages

SENATE

HOUSE OF REPRESENTATIVES

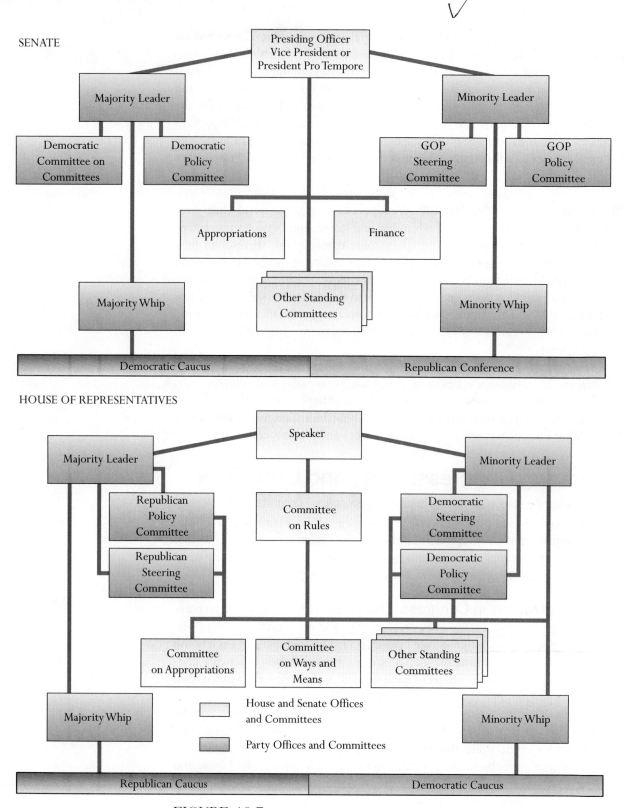

FIGURE 10.7 How It Works: Organizing the Congress

Aside from naming the Speaker of the House as head of that body's operations and the vice president as overseer of Senate deliberations, the Constitution is silent on the organization of Congress. Political parties have filled this gap: both majority and minority parties have their own leadership, which governs the appointment of members to the various committees, where much of the work of Congress actually takes place.

TABLE 10.2 Who Oversees What?: Committees in Congress

Senate	
Agriculture, Nutrition, and Forestry	Homeland Security and Environmental Affairs
Appropriations	Judiciary
Armed Services	Rules and Administration
Banking, Housing, and Urban Affairs	Small Business and Entrepreneurship
Budget	Select Aging
Commerce, Science, and Transportation	Select Ethics
Energy and Natural Resources	Select Indian Affairs
Environment and Public Works	Select Intelligence
Finance	Veterans Affairs
Foreign Relations	
Health, Education, Labor and Pensions	

House	
Agriculture	Judiciary
Appropriations	Resources
Armed Forces	Rules
Budget	Science
Energy and Commerce	Small Business
Education and the Workforce	Standards of Official Conduct
Financial Services	Transportation and Infrastructure
Government Reform	Veterans Affairs
Homeland Security	Ways and Means
House Administration	Select Intelligence
International Relations	

Joint Committees
Joint Economic Committee
Joint Taxation
Joint Committee on Printing
Joint Committee on the Library

when they capture a majority of either body. Majority-party members in each house even take in more campaign contributions than minority members.[35]

In the House: "Mr. Speaker"

In the House of Representatives, the key leadership figure is the **Speaker of the House**, who serves as both presiding officer of the chamber and leader of the majority party. In the House, the Speaker has many powers. The Speaker decides who shall be recognized to speak on the floor and rules on points of order (with advice from the parliamentarian), including whether a motion or amendment is germane (relevant) to the business at hand. The Speaker decides to which committees new bills will be assigned and can schedule or delay votes on a bill. The Speaker appoints members of select, special, and conference committees and names majority-party members to the Rules Committee. And the Speaker controls both patronage jobs and office space in the Capitol. Although the norm of fairness requires the Speaker to apply the rules of the House consistently, the Speaker is elected by the majority party and is expected to favor that party. (See *People in Politics*: "Nancy Pelosi, 'Madam Speaker.'")

Speaker of the House
Presiding officer of the House of Representatives.

majority leader
In the House, the majority-party leader and second in command to the Speaker, in the Senate, the leader of the majority party.

minority leader
In both the House and Senate, the leader of the opposition party.

whips
In both the House and Senate, the principal assistants to the party leaders and next in command to those leaders.

House Leaders and Whips   The Speaker's principal assistant is the **majority leader**. The majority leader formulates the party's legislative program in consultation with other party leaders and steers the program through the House. The majority leader also must persuade committee leaders to support the aims of party leaders in acting on legislation before their committees. Finally, the majority leader arranges the legislative schedule with the cooperation of key party members.

The minority party in the House selects a **minority leader** whose duties correspond to those of the majority leader, except that the minority leader has no authority over the scheduling of legislation. The minority leader's principal duty has been to organize the forces of the minority party to counter the legislative program of the majority and to pass the minority party's bills. It is also the minority leader's duty to consult ranking minority members of House committees and to encourage them to adopt party positions and to follow the lead of the president if the minority party controls the White House.

In both parties, **whips** assist leaders in keeping track of the whereabouts of party members and in pressuring them to vote the party line. Whips are also responsible for ensuring the attendance of party members at important roll calls and for canvassing their colleagues on their likely support for or opposition to party-formulated legislation. Finally, whips are involved regularly in the formation of party policy and the scheduling of legislation.

In the Senate: "Mr. President"   The Constitution declares the vice president of the United States to be the presiding officer of the Senate. But vice presidents seldom exercise this senatorial responsibility, largely because the presiding officer of the Senate has very little power. Having only 100 members, the Senate usually does not restrict debate and has fewer scheduling constraints than the House. The only significant power of the vice president is the right to cast a deciding vote in the event of a tie on a Senate roll call. In the usual absence of the vice president, the Senate is presided over by a *president pro tempore*. This honorific position is traditionally granted by the majority party to one of its senior stalwarts. The job of presiding over the Senate is so boring that neither the vice president nor the president pro tempore is found very often in the chamber. Junior senators are often asked to assume the chore. Nevertheless, speeches on the Senate floor begin with the salutation "Mr. President," referring to the president of the Senate, *not* the president of the United States.

Senate Majority and Minority Leaders   Senate leadership is actually in the hands of the Senate majority leader, but the Senate majority leader is not as powerful in that body as the Speaker is in the House. With fewer members, all of whom perceive themselves as powerful leaders, the Senate is less hierarchically organized than the House. The Senate majority leader's principal power is scheduling the business of the Senate and recognizing the first speaker in floor debate. To be effective in policy making, the majority leader must be skilled in interpersonal persuasion and communication. Moreover, in the media age, the Senate majority leader must also be a national spokesperson for the party, along with the Speaker of the House. The minority-party leader in the Senate represents the opposition in negotiations with the majority leader over Senate business.

Career Paths within Congress   Movement up the party hierarchy in each house is the most common way of achieving a leadership position.[36] The traditional succession pattern in the House is from whip to majority leader to Speaker. In the Senate, Republicans and Democrats frequently resort to election

PEOPLE IN POLITICS

Nancy Pelosi, "Madam Speaker"

Nancy Pelosi was the first woman in the history of the U.S. Congress to serve as Speaker of the House. Following the Democratic victory in the 2006 congressional elections, her Democratic colleagues in the House promoted her from Minority Leader, a post she had held since 2001, to Speaker. Pelosi has represented her San Francisco district since her first election to the Congress in 1987.

Pelosi comes from a highly political family. Her father, Thomas D'Alesandro, served five terms in Congress and later 12 years as mayor of Baltimore. Pelosi's brother also served as mayor of Baltimore. Young Nancy grew up in Washington and graduated from that city's Trinity College in 1962. She served as a congressional intern to her Maryland senator. She married Paul Pelosi, moved to his hometown of San Francisco, and raised five children. Prior to her election to Congress, she served on the National Democratic Committee.

In her years in Congress, Pelosi built a solid liberal reputation, serving on the powerful Appropriations Committee. But Pelosi's real strength within the Democratic Party has long been her fund-raising ability. Her San Francisco district is the home of some of the party's wealthiest individual donors, and Democrats across the nation rely heavily upon money from California. Pelosi created her own leadership PAC and has handed out millions to her Democratic colleagues. She spends relatively little on her own reelection races in her heavily Democratic district. She is regularly reelected with an astonishing 80 percent of the vote.

Pelosi's reign as Speaker was described as especially hard driving. She was quoted as saying: "Tell them what you're going to do. Do it. And then tell them what you did." She had the responsibility for guiding the Obama agenda through the House. Republicans accused her of sidetracking their amendments and "ramming down the throat" of House members thousands of unread pages of legislation. The Republican capture of control of the House in the congressional elections of 2010 brought an end to her rule as Speaker.

---

contests in choosing their party leaders, yet both parties have increasingly adopted a two-step succession route from whip to leader.[37]

Leadership PACs   House and Senate leaders, and members who aspire to become leaders, often ingratiate themselves to their colleagues by distributing campaign funds to them. In recent years, *leadership PACs* have proliferated on Capitol Hill.

In Committee

▶ 10.8 *Characterize the legislative work of committees and assess the repercussions of committees for distribution of power in Congress.*

Much of the real work of Congress is done in committee. The floor of Congress is often deserted; C-SPAN focuses on the podium, not the empty chamber. Members dash to the floor when the bell rings throughout the Capitol signaling a roll-call vote. Otherwise they are found in their offices or in the committee rooms, where the real work of Congress is done.

Standing Committees   The committee system provides for a division of labor in the Congress, assigning responsibility for work and allowing members to develop some expertise (see Table 10.2). The committee system is as old as the Congress itself: the very first Congress regularly assigned the task of wording bills to selected members who were believed to have a particular expertise. Soon

standing committee
Permanent committee of the House or Senate that deals with matters within a specified subject area.

ranking minority member
The minority-party committee member with the most seniority.

a system of **standing committees**—permanent committees that specialize in a particular area of legislation—emerged. House committees have forty to sixty or more members and Senate committees fifteen to twenty-five members each. The proportions of Democrats and Republicans on each committee reflect the proportions of Democrats and Republicans in the House and Senate as a whole. Thus the majority party has a majority of members on every committee; and every committee is chaired by a member of the majority party. The minority membership on each committee is led by the **ranking minority member**, the minority-party committee member with the most seniority.

The principal function of standing committees is the screening and drafting of legislation. With 8,000 to 10,000 or more bills introduced each session, the screening function is essential. The standing committees are the gatekeepers of Congress; less than 10 percent of the legislation introduced will pass the Congress. With rare exceptions, bills are not submitted to a vote by the full membership of the House or Senate without prior approval by the majority of a standing committee. Moreover, committees do not merely sort through bills assigned to them to find what they like. Rather, committees—or more often their subcommittees—draft (write) legislation themselves. Committees may amend, rewrite, or write their own bills. Committees are "little legislatures" within their own policy jurisdictions. Each committee guards its own policy jurisdiction jealously; jurisdictional squabbles between committees are common.

The Pecking Order of Committees

The most powerful standing committees, and, therefore, the most sought-after committee assignments, are the Appropriations Committees in the House and the Senate. These committees hold the federal purse strings, arguably Congress's most important power. These committees are closely followed in influence and desirability by the Ways and Means Committee in the House and the Senate Finance Committee; these committees must pass on all tax matters, as well as Social Security and Medicare financing. In the House, the Rules Committee is especially powerful, owing to its control over floor consideration of every bill submitted to the full House. The Senate Judiciary Committee is especially powerful because of its influence over all presidential nominees to the federal judiciary, including Supreme Court justices. The Senate Foreign Relations Committee is also a highly valued assignment. Perhaps the *least* desirable committee assignments are those on the Senate Ethics Committee and the House Standards of Official Conduct Committee; members of these ethics panels are obliged to sit in judgment of their own colleagues.

subcommittees
Specialized committees within standing committees; subcommittee recommendations must be approved by the full standing committee before submission to the floor.

Decentralization and Subcommittees

Congressional **subcommittees** within each standing committee further decentralize the legislative process. At present, the House has about 90 subcommittees and the Senate about 70 subcommittees, each of which functions independently of its full committee (see Table 10.2). Subcommittees have fixed jurisdictions (for example, the House International Relations Committee has subcommittees on Africa, Asia and the Pacific, International Economic Policy, International Operations and Human Rights, and the Western Hemisphere); they meet and schedule their own hearings; and they have their own staffs and budgets. However, bills recommended by a subcommittee still require full standing-committee endorsement before being reported to the floor of the House or Senate. Full committees usually, but not always, ratify the decisions of their subcommittees.

Chairing a committee or subcommittee gives members of Congress the opportunity to exercise power, attract media attention, and thus improve their chances

Actress Nicole Kidman testifies before the House International Organizations, Human Rights, and Oversight Subcommittee hearing on violence against women, October 21, 2009.

of reelection. Often committees have become "fiefdoms" over which their chairs exercise complete control and jealously guard their power. This situation allows a very small number of House and Senate members to block legislation. Many decisions are not really made by the whole Congress. Rather, they are made by subcommittee members with a special interest in the policy under consideration. Although the committee system may satisfy the desire of members to gain power, prestige, and reelection opportunities, it weakens responsible government in the Congress as a whole.

Committee Membership   Given the power of the committee system, it is not surprising that members of Congress have a very keen interest in their committee assignments. Members strive for assignments that will give them influence in Congress, allow them to exercise power in Washington, and ultimately improve their chances for reelection. For example, a member from a big city may seek a seat on Banking, Housing, and Urban Affairs, a member from a farm district may seek a seat on Agriculture, and a member from a district with a large military base may seek a seat on National Security or Veterans Affairs. Everyone seeks a seat on Appropriations, because both the House and the Senate Appropriations committees have subcommittees in each area of federal spending.[38]

Party leadership in both the House and the Senate largely determines committee assignments. These assignments are given to new Democratic House members by the Democratic Steering and Policy Committee; new Democratic senators receive their assignments from the Senate Democratic Steering Committee. New Republican members receive their committee assignments from the Republican Committee on Committees in both houses. The leadership

Chairman of the Joint Chiefs, Admiral Michael Mullen, testifies before the Senate Armed Forces Committee, December 9, 2009, as Secretary of State Hillary Clinton and Secretary of Defense Robert Gates listen.

generally tries to honor new members' requests and improve their chances for reelection, but because incumbent members of committees are seldom removed, openings on powerful committees are infrequent.

seniority system
Custom whereby the member of Congress who has served the longest on the majority side of a committee becomes its chair and the member who has served the longest on the minority side becomes its ranking member.

Seniority   Committee chairs are elected in the majority-party caucus. But the **seniority system** governs most movement into committee leadership positions. The seniority system ranks all committee members in each party according to the length of time they have served on the committee. If the majority-party chair exits the Congress or leaves the committee, that position is filled by the next *ranking majority-party member*. New members of a committee are initially added to the bottom of the ranking of their party; they climb the seniority ranking by remaining on the committee and accruing years of seniority. Members who stay in Congress but "hop" committees are usually placed at the bottom of their new committee's list.

The seniority system has a long tradition in the Congress. The advantage is that it tends to reduce conflict among members, who otherwise would be constantly engaged in running for committee posts. It also increases the stability of policy direction in committees over time. Critics of the system note, though, that the seniority system grants greater power to members from "safe" districts—districts that offer little electoral challenge to the incumbent. (Historically in the Democratic Party, these districts were in the conservative South, and opposition to the seniority system developed among liberal northern Democrats. But in recent decades, many liberal Democrats gained seniority and the seniority system again became entrenched.) The seniority rule for selecting committee chairs has been violated on only a few notable occasions.

drafting a bill
Actual writing of a bill in legal language.

markup
Line-by-line revision of a bill in committee by editing each phrase and word.

Committee Hearings   The decision of a congressional committee to hold public hearings on a bill or topic is an important one. It signals congressional interest in a particular policy matter and sets the agenda for congressional policy making. Ignoring an issue by refusing to hold hearings on it usually condemns it to oblivion. Public hearings allow interest groups and government bureaucrats to present formal arguments to Congress. Testimony comes mostly from government officials, lobbyists, and occasional experts recommended by interest groups or committee staff members. Hearings are usually organized by the staff under the direction of the chair. Staff members contact favored lobbyists and bureaucrats and schedule their appearances. Committee hearings are regularly listed in the *Washington Post* and are open to the public. Indeed, the purpose of many hearings is not really to inform members of Congress but instead to gain publicity and rally public support behind an issue or a bill. The media are the real target audience of many public hearings, with committee members jockeying in front of the cameras for a "sound bite" on the evening news.

Foreign Relations Committee Hearing
Senate Foreign Relations Committee Chairman John Kerry (D-MA), and ranking minority member Richard Lugar (R-IN), listen to testimony at a committee hearing, 2010.

Markup   Once hearings are completed the committee's staff is usually assigned the task of writing a report and **drafting a bill**. The staff's bill generally reflects the chair's policy views. But the staff draft is subject to committee **markup**, a line-by-line consideration of the wording of the bill. Markup sessions are frequently closed to the public in order to expedite work. Lobbyists are forced to stand in the hallways, buttonholing members as they go into and out of committee rooms.

It is in markup that the detailed work of lawmaking takes place. Markup sessions require patience and skill in negotiation. Committee or subcommittee chairs may try to develop consensus on various parts of the bill, either within the whole committee or within the committee's majority. In marking up a bill, members of a subcommittee must always remember that the bill must pass both in the full committee and on the floor of the chamber. Although they have considerable freedom in writing their own policy preferences into law, especially on the details of the legislation, they must give some consideration to the views of these larger bodies. Consultations with party leadership are not infrequent.

Most bills die in committee. Some are voted down, but most are simply ignored. Bills introduced simply to reassure constituents or interest groups that a representative is committed to "doing something" for them generally die quietly. But House members who really want action on a bill can be frustrated by committee inaction. The only way to force a floor vote on a bill opposed by a committee is to get a majority (218) of House members to sign a **discharge petition**. Out of hundreds of discharge petition efforts, only a few dozen have succeeded.[39] The Senate also can forcibly "discharge" a bill from committee by simple majority vote; but because senators can attach any amendment to any bill they wish, there is generally no need to go this route.

On the Floor

▶ 10.9 *Outline the process for a bill that has reached the floor and identify obstacles to passage.*

A favorable "report" by a standing committee of the House or Senate places a bill on the "calendar." The word *calendar* is misleading, because bills on the calendar are not considered in chronological order and many die on the calendar without ever reaching the floor.

House Rules Committee   Even after a bill has been approved by a standing committee, getting it to the floor of the House of Representatives for a vote by the full membership requires favorable action by the Rules Committee. The Rules Committee acts as a powerful "traffic cop" for the House. In order to reach the floor, a bill must receive a rule from the Rules Committee. The Rules Committee can kill a bill simply by refusing to give it a rule. A **rule** determines when the bill will be considered by the House and how long the debate on the bill will last. More important, a rule determines whether amendments from the floor will be permitted and, if so, how many. A **closed rule** forbids House members from offering any amendments and speeds up consideration of the bill in the form submitted by the standing committee. A **restricted rule** allows certain specified amendments to be considered. An **open rule** permits unlimited amendments. Most key bills are brought to the floor of the House with fairly restrictive rules. In recent sessions, about three-quarters of all bills reaching the floor were restricted, and an additional 10 to 15 percent were fully closed. Only a few bills were open.[40]

Senate Floor Traditions   The Senate has no rules committee but relies instead on a **unanimous consent agreement** negotiated between the majority and minority leader to govern consideration of a bill. The unanimous consent agreement generally specifies when the bill will be debated, what amendments will be considered, and when the final vote will be taken. But as the name implies, a single

discharge petition
Petition signed by at least 218 House members to force a vote on a bill within a committee that opposes it.

rule
Stipulation attached to a bill in the House of Representatives that governs its consideration on the floor, including when and for how long it can be debated and how many (if any) amendments may be appended to it.

closed rule
Rule that forbids adding any amendments to a bill under consideration by the House.

restricted rule
Rule that allows only specified amendments to be added to a bill under consideration by the House.

Every Vote Counts
Sen. Robert Byrd (D-WV) was brought to the Senate floor for a crucial vote on health care reform just weeks before his death, June 28, 2010, at age 92.

open rule
Rule that permits unlimited amendments to a bill under consideration by the House.

unanimous consent agreement
Negotiated by the majority and minority leaders of the Senate, it specifies when a bill will be taken up on the floor, what amendments will be considered, and when a vote will be taken.

filibuster
Delaying tactic by a senator or group of senators, using the Senate's unlimited debate rule to prevent a vote on a bill.

cloture
Vote to end debate—that is, to end a filibuster—which requires a three-fifths vote of the entire membership of the Senate.

rider
Amendment to a bill that is not germane to the bill's purposes.

roll-call vote
Vote of the full House or Senate at which all members' individual votes are recorded and made public.

conference committees
Meetings between representatives of the House and Senate to reconcile differences over provisions of a bill passed by both houses.

senator can object to a unanimous consent agreement and thus hold up Senate consideration of a bill. Senators do not usually do so, because they know that a reputation for obstructionism will imperil their own favorite bills at a later date. Once accepted, a unanimous consent agreement is binding on the Senate and cannot be changed without another unanimous consent agreement. To get unanimous consent, Senate leaders must consult with all interested senators. Unanimous consent agreements have become more common in recent years as they have become more specific in their provisions.

The Senate cherishes its tradition of unrestricted floor debate. Senators may speak as long as they wish or even try to **filibuster** a bill to death by talking nonstop and tying up the Senate for so long that the leadership is forced to drop the bill in order to go on to other work. Senate rules also allow senators to place a "hold" on a bill, indicating their unwillingness to grant unanimous consent to its consideration. Debate may be ended only if *sixty* or more senators vote for **cloture,** a process of petition and voting that limits the debate. A cloture vote requires a petition signed by sixteen senators; two days must elapse between the petition's introduction and the cloture vote. If cloture passes, then each senator is limited to 1 hour of debate on the bill. But getting the necessary sixty votes for cloture is often difficult (see *Controversy:* "Should Senate Actions Be Thwarted by Filibusters?").

Senate floor procedures also permit unlimited amendments to be offered, even those that are not germane to the bill. A **rider** is an amendment to a bill that is not germane to the bill's purposes.

These Senate traditions of unlimited debate and unrestricted floor amendments give individual senators considerably more power over legislation than individual representatives enjoy.

Floor Voting   The key floor votes are usually on *amendments* to bills rather than on their final passage. Indeed, "killer amendments" are deliberately designed to defeat the original purpose of the bill. Other amendments may water down the bill so much that it will have little policy impact. Thus the true policy preferences of senators or representatives may be reflected more in their votes on amendments than their vote on final passage. Members may later claim to have supported legislation on the basis of their vote on final passage, even though they earlier voted for amendments designed to defeat the bill's purposes.

Members may also obscure their voting records by calling for a voice vote—simply shouting "aye" or "nay"—and avoiding recording of their individual votes. In contrast, a **roll-call vote** involves the casting of individual votes, which are reported in the *Congressional Record* and are available to the media and the general public. Electronic voting machines in the House allow members to insert their cards and record their votes automatically. The Senate, truer to tradition, uses no electronic counters.

Conference Committees   The Constitution requires that both houses of Congress pass a bill with identical wording. However, many major bills pass each house in different forms, not only with different wording but sometimes with wholly different provisions. Occasionally the House or the Senate will resolve these differences by reconsidering the matter and passing the other chamber's version of the bill. But about 15 percent of the time, serious differences arise and bills are assigned to **conference committees** to reach agreement on a single version for resubmission to both houses. Conference committees are temporary, with members appointed by the leadership in each house, usually from among the senior members of the committees that approved the bills.

CONTROVERSY

Should Senate Actions Be Thwarted by Filibusters?

From the earliest days of the Senate the idea of "unlimited debate" was enshrined in its rules and customs. For over a century, the "filibuster" was honored as "insurance against the will of a majority of states being imposed over the wishes of a minority of states." Over the years, liberals and progressives in the Senate came to loathe the filibuster rule. President Woodrow Wilson (formerly a political science professor at Princeton University and author of a book on Congress) persuaded the Senate to adopt a "cloture rule" (see previous page) which called for cutting off debate with a two-thirds vote of senators present and voting. For decades afterward, liberals sought to completely eliminate the filibuster, as it became an important tool of opponents of civil rights legislation. (The Civil Rights Act of 1964 was passed only after a successful cloture vote ended a Southern filibuster.) In 1975 the Senate lowered the vote requirement for cloture to sixty, that is, three-fifths rather than two-thirds.

In recent years, filibusters have become more common as partisanship in the Senate has risen. Democrats and Republicans both regularly threaten filibusters to stop legislation they oppose. This means that controversial bills cannot get through the Senate without sixty votes, rather than a simple majority of fifty-one.

Senate Democrats used the filibuster to thwart judicial nominees submitted by Republican President George W. Bush. Republicans argued that such a use violated the Constitution, which requires only a majority vote for judicial confirmations. In 2005, they threatened "the nuclear option"—having the presiding officer of the Senate, then Republican Vice President Richard Cheney, declare the filibuster rule for judicial nominations to be unconstitutional. This ruling would then be upheld by a simple majority vote of the Senate. But a temporary truce was fashioned in which several Bush judicial appointments were confirmed and the filibuster rule was undisturbed.

Republicans resorted to the filibuster in 2009 to try to halt the passage of the massive health care reform bill. The bill had passed the House (which does not permit filibusters) and was strongly supported by President Obama. Democrats had sixty members in the Senate, barely enough to halt a filibuster; special deals were required to hold on to each Democratic member. A heavily amended health care bill finally passed with sixty votes; all forty Republican senators voted "No." But the Senate bill differed from the House bill. Ordinarily this would require a conference

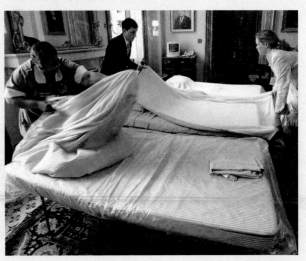

Senate filibusters can be ended only by persuasion or by a three-fifths vote (60 members). Inasmuch as at least 1 filibustering member must remain continuously on the floor of the Senate, beds are often prepared in Senate offices for periodic alternating-member breaks.

committee compromise and eventually a Senate vote on that compromise. However, Republican Scott Brown captured the Massachusetts Senate seat long held by Ted Kennedy in a special election following Kennedy's death. This changed the Senate calculus—with only fifty-nine votes Democrats could not overcome a united Republican filibuster. So rather than convene a conference committee, the Democratic-controlled House accepted the Senate bill. Later, over Republican objections, both bodies passed by majority votes a "reconciliation" bill that aligned House and Senate versions of Obamacare.

Generally, Americans support the filibuster rule:

Q. As you may know, the filibuster is a Senate procedure which has been used to prevent the Senate from passing controversial legislation or confirming controversial appointments by the president, even if a majority of senators support that action. A vote of at least sixty senators out of one hundred is needed to end a filibuster. Do you favor or oppose the use of the filibuster in the U.S. Senate?

Favor	Oppose	Unsure
56%	39%	5%

Source: The Polling Report (2009) at www.pollingreport.com.

Conference committees can be very powerful. Their final bill is usually (although not always) passed in both houses and sent to the president for approval. In resolving differences between the House and the Senate versions, the conference committee makes many final policy decisions. Although conference committees have considerable leeway in striking compromises, they focus on points of disagreement and usually do not change provisions already approved by both houses. Figure 10.8 summarizes the lawmaking process.

Decision Making in Congress

▶ **10.10** *Assess the influences on congressional decision making.*

How do senators and representatives decide how they will vote on legislation? From an almost limitless number of considerations that go into congressional decision making, a few factors recur across a range of voting decisions: party loyalty, presidential support or opposition, constituency concerns, interest-group pressures, and the personal values and ideologies of members themselves.

party votes
Majority of Democrats voting in opposition to a majority of Republicans.

Party Voting   Party appears to be the most significant influence on congressional voting. **Party votes** are roll-call votes on which a majority of voting Democrats oppose a majority of voting Republicans. Traditionally, party votes occurred on roughly *half* of all roll-call votes in Congress. Partisanship in Congress, as reflected in the percentage of party votes, rose during the 1990s but may be moderating somewhat today.

party unity
Percentage of Democrats and Republicans who stick with their party on party votes.

Party unity is measured by the percentage of Democrats and Republicans who stick by their party on party votes. Both Democratic and Republican Party unity have remained at fairly constant levels (85–95 percent) in both the House and the Senate over the past 10 years. This is higher than in previous decades when party unity was regularly 50–60 percent in both the House and Senate. Greater party unity suggests increased partisan polarization in Congress.

Sources of Partisanship   Why do Democrats and Republicans in Congress vote along party lines? First of all, the Democratic Party has become more liberal and the Republican Party has become more conservative over the years. Conservative Democrats, once very common in southern politics, are rapidly disappearing. At the same time, the ranks of liberal Republicans, mostly from the Northeast, have thinned. Second, the decline in voter turnout, especially in primary elections, has added to the importance of well-organized and ideologically motivated groups. In primary elections Republicans must be more concerned with pleasing conservative activists (e.g., the Christian Coalition, National Right-to-Life Committee, National Rifle Association, and so on), and Democrats must be more concerned with pleasing liberal groups (National Education Association, American Federation of State, County, and Municipal Employees, Sierra Club, and so on). And third, the rising costs of campaigning make members ever more dependent upon the financial support of these interests.

bipartisanship
Agreement by members of both the Democratic and the Republican parties.

Conflict between the parties occurs frequently on domestic social and economic issues—welfare, housing and urban affairs, health, business regulation, taxing, and spending. Traditionally, **bipartisanship** was the goal of both presidents and congressional leaders on foreign and defense policy issues. Since the Vietnam War, however, Democrats in the Congress have been more critical of U.S. military involvements (and defense spending in general) than have Republicans.

Presidential Support or Opposition   Presidential influence in congressional voting is closely tied to party lines. Presidents almost always receive their

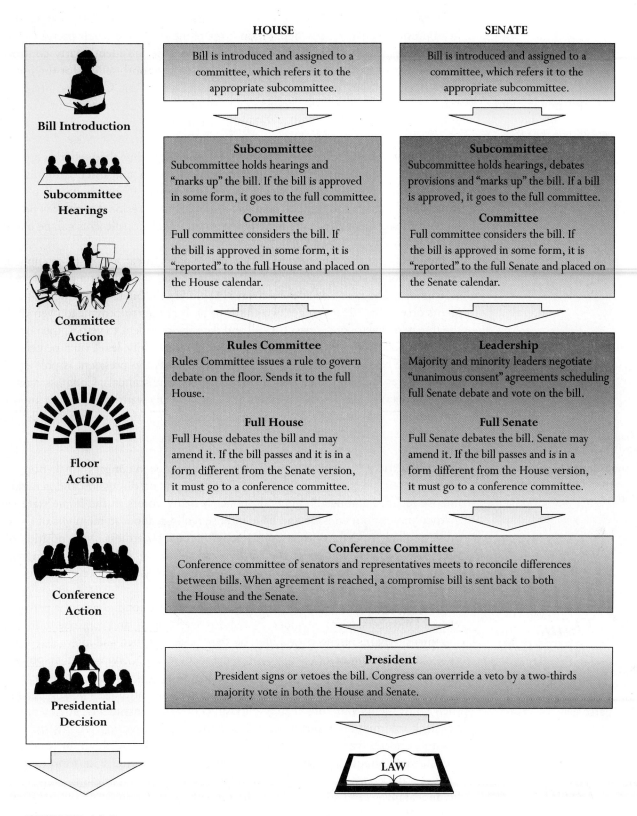

FIGURE 10.8   Running the Gauntlet: How a Bill Becomes a Law

This diagram depicts the major hurdles a successful bill must overcome in order to be enacted into law. Few bills introduced travel this full path; less than 10 percent of bills introduced are passed by Congress and sent to the president for approval or veto. Bills fail at every step along the path, but most die in committees and subcommittees, usually from inaction rather than from being voted down.

divided party government
One party controls the presidency while the other party controls one or both houses of Congress.

greatest support from members of their own party. Both Democratic and Republican presidents can usually depend on 80 percent or more of their party's members in Congress to support their position. When the president's party controls both houses of Congress, the result should be fairly smooth sailing for the president's agenda. (See *Controversy:* "Obama Faces a Democratic Congress.") In contrast, policy gridlock is often associated with **divided party government**—either a Democratic president and a Republican-controlled House or Senate, or a Republican president and a Democratic-controlled House or Senate.

Presidents often "go over the heads" of Congress, using the media to appeal directly to the people to support presidential programs and force Congress to act. The president has better access to the media than Congress has. But such threats and appeals can only be effective when (1) the president himself is popular with the public; and (2) the issue is one about which constituents can be made to feel intensely.

Presidents can also threaten to veto legislation. This threat, expressed or implied, confronts congressional leaders, committee chairs, and sponsors of a bill with several options. They must decide whether to (1) modify the bill to overcome the president's objections; (2) try to get two-thirds of both houses to commit to overriding the threatened veto; or (3) pass the bill and dare the president to veto it, then make a political issue out of the president's opposition. Historically, less than 5 percent of vetoes have been overridden by the Congress. Unless the president is politically very weak (as Richard Nixon was during the Watergate scandal), Congress cannot count on overriding a veto. If members of Congress truly want to address an important problem and not just define a political issue, they must negotiate with the White House to write a bill the president will sign.

constituency
The votes in a legislator's home district.

Constituency Influence
Constituency influence in congressional voting is most apparent on issues that attract media attention and discussion and generate intense feelings among the general public. If many voters in the home state or district know about an issue and have intense feelings about it, members of Congress are likely to defer to their constituents' feeling, regardless of the position of their party's leadership or even their own personal feelings. Members of Congress from *safe seats* seem to be just as attuned to the interests of their constituents as members from competitive seats.

Constituencies may also exercise a subtle influence by conditioning the personal views of members. Many members were born, were raised, and continue to live in the towns they represent; over a lifetime they have absorbed and internalized the views of their communities. Moreover, some members of Congress feel an obligation to represent their constituents' opinions even when they personally disagree.

However, members of Congress have considerable latitude in voting against their constituents' opinions if they choose to do so. Constituents, as noted earlier, lack information about most policy issues and the voting records of their senators and representatives. Even when constituents know about an issue and feel strongly about it, members can afford to cast a "wrong" vote from time to time. A long record of home style politics—casework, pork barreling, visits, public appearances, and so on—can isolate members of Congress from the wrath generated by their voting records. Only a long string of "wrong" votes on issues important to constituents is likely to jeopardize an incumbent.

Interest-Group Influence
Inside the Washington Beltway, the influence of interest groups, lobbyists, and fund-raisers on members of Congress is well understood. This influence is seldom talked about back home or on the

Think Again

Are members of Congress obliged to vote the way their constituents wish, even if they personally disagree?

Think Again

Is it ethical for Congress members to pay special attention to requests for assistance by people who make large campaign contributions?

CONTROVERSY

Obama Faces Congress

President Obama enjoyed the support of a Democratic-controlled Congress in the first two years of his administration. He presented the Congress with an especially full legislative agenda, and he was very successful in getting the bulk of it passed over Republican opposition. But Republican victories in the midterm congressional elections of 2010 promised to block further Obama legislative initiatives.

A massive economic "stimulus" bill—officially the American Recovery and Reinvestment Act—was the centerpiece of the president's economic program. Its combination of spending increases and tax cuts totaled $787 billion—the largest single fiscal policy measure in American history. Written in record time by the Democratic Congress, House Republicans were unanimous in opposition and only three Republican senators supported the bill. The stimulus package, together with the president's budget, created the largest year-to-year increase in federal spending in history as well as the largest federal deficit in history.

President Obama was also successful in bringing about a massive overhaul of the nation's health care system. The House promptly passed all of the key elements of the president's recommended program, including a government-run "public option" health insurance exchange, but the Senate passed a bill without this public option. The health care debate lasted over a year and consumed most of the energies of the Congress. Republicans in both the House and Senate were unified in their opposition to the bill; the election of Republican Scott Brown to the Senate from Massachusetts gave the GOP its 41st vote, just enough to filibuster successfully against any conference committee compromise bill. So Speaker Nancy Pelosi convinced the Democratic House to pass the Senate bill, thus avoiding the expected filibuster in the Senate. Opinion polls showed most Americans opposing the bill, and every Republican in the

White House Signing Ceremony
President Obama signs the comprehensive healthcare bill in a ceremony at the White House, March 23, 2010.

House and Senate voted "No." But the bill reached the president's desk for his signature as the comprehensive Patient Redaction and Affordable Care Act of 2010.

Republicans pledged to repeal "ObamaCare" following their capture of control of the House of Representatives in 2010. But Democrats continued to control the Senate and the likelihood of a presidential veto appeared to doom any attempt at repeal. Republicans promised to curtail funding for controversial parts of the health care bill. Obama's other legislative initiatives, including a broad new carbon ceiling and trading program, known as "cap and trade," appeared permanently stalled in the Congress. Immigration reform remained on the back burner. Divided government promised legislative gridlock for the second two years of Obama's presidency.

campaign trail, except perhaps by challengers. Lobbyists have their greatest effects on the *details* of public policy. Congressional decisions made in committee rooms, at markup sessions, and around conference tables can mean billions of dollars to industries and tens of millions to individual companies. Pressures from competing interest groups can be intense as lobbyists buttonhole lawmakers and try to win legislative amendments that can make or break business fortunes. One of the most potent tools in the lobbyist's arsenal is money. The prohibitive cost of modern campaigning has dictated that dollars are crucial to electoral victory, and virtually all members of Congress spend more time than they would like courting it, raising it, and stockpiling it for the next election.

Voters may be wrong when they think that all members of Congress are crooks, but they are not far off the mark when they worry that their own representatives may be listening to two competing sets of constituents—the real constituents back home in the district and the "cash constituents" who come calling in Washington.[41]

trustees
Legislators who feel obligated to use their own best judgment in decision making.

delegates
Legislators who feel obligated to present the views of their home constituents.

Personal Values It was the eighteenth-century English political philosopher Edmund Burke, himself a member of Parliament, who told his constituents; "You choose a member indeed; but when you have chosen him, he is not a member of Bristol, but he is a member of *Parliament*." Burke defended the classic notion of representatives as **trustees** who feel obligated to use their own best judgment about what is good for the nation as a whole. In this theory, representatives are not obligated to vote the views of their constituents. This notion contrasts with the idea of representatives as **delegates** who feel obligated to vote according to the views of "the folks back home" regardless of their own personal viewpoint. Most legislators *claim* to be trustees, perhaps because of the halo effect generated by the independence implied in the term.

Democratic political philosophers have pondered the merits of trustee versus delegate representation over the centuries, but the question only rarely arises in actual congressional deliberations. In many cases, members' own personal views and those of their constituents are virtually identical. Even when legislators perceive conflicts between their own views and those of their constituents, most attempt to find a compromise between these competing demands rather than choose one role or another exclusively.[42] The political independence of members of Congress—their independence from party, combined with the ignorance of their constituents about most policy issues—allows members to give great weight to their own personal ideologies in voting.

Customs and Norms

▶ 10.11 *Outline the customs and norms of Congress, their function, and recent changes.*

Over time, institutions develop customs and norms of behavior to assist in their functioning. These are not merely quaint and curious folkways; they promote the purposes of the institution. Congressional customs and norms are designed to help members work together, to reduce interpersonal conflict, to facilitate bargaining and promote compromise.

Civility Traditionally, members of Congress understood that uncivil behavior—expressions of anger, personal attacks on character, ugly confrontations, flaming rhetoric—undermined the lawmaking function. Indeed, civility was encouraged by the longstanding custom of members of Congress referring to each other in elaborately courteous terms: "my distinguished colleague from Ohio," "the honorable representative from Pennsylvania," and the like. By custom, even bitter partisan enemies in Congress were expected to avoid harsh personal attacks on each other. The purpose of this custom was to try to maintain an atmosphere in which people who hold very different opinions can nevertheless function with some degree of decorum. Unfortunately, many of these customs and norms of behavior are breaking down. Individual ambition and the drive for power and celebrity have led to a decline in courtesy, cooperation, and respect for traditional norms. One result is that it has become increasingly difficult for Congress to reach agreement on policy issues. Another result is that life in Congress is increasingly tedious, conflict-filled, and unpleasant (see *A Conflicting View*: "Congress Can Act Responsibly on Occasion").

Conference Committee Work Requires Compromises

Senate Agriculture Chairman Tom Harkin (D-IA), seated, and Senator Kent Conrad, (D-ND) and others, meet on May 1, 2008, at the start of a House-Senate conference on the farm bill.

A CONFLICTING VIEW

Congress Can Act Responsibly on Occasion

Congress is not always mired in partisanship, squabbling, and gridlock. On occasion it acts responsibly in the national interest. Indeed, consider the following congressional landmarks in U.S. history:

Louisiana Purchase (1803)

President Thomas Jefferson offered to purchase from France nearly 830,000 square miles between the Mississippi and the Rockies for $15 million—about three cents an acre. There is no constitutional provision authorizing the federal government to buy foreign territory, but the Senate, accepting Jefferson's broad interpretation of the Constitution, approved the purchase. The House appropriated the money to consummate the deal. On December 29, 1803, the United States took possession of North America's heartland, doubling the nation's size with territory that would eventually comprise thirteen states.

Homestead Act (1862)

This Civil War–era legislation allowed any family head or adult male to claim 160 acres of government land for a $10 registration fee and a promise to live there continuously for 5 years. It opened up the midwestern United States for immediate settlement. The act drew thousands of English, Irish, Germans, Swedes, Danes, Norwegians, and Czechs to the United States, pushing settlement farther west.

Social Security Act (1935)

The act was designed to secure "the men, women, and children of the nation against certain hazards and vicissitudes of life," explained President Franklin Roosevelt. The act's best-known measure is the social insurance system that provides monthly checks to the elderly.

National Labor Relations Act (1935)

By declaring workers had a right to join unions and bargain collectively with employers for pay raises and improved working conditions, the act spurred the growth of the nation's major industrial unions. Labor's Magna Carta also provided workers with the legal weapons to improve plant conditions and protect themselves from employer harassment.

G.I. Bill of Rights (1944)

The G.I. Bill of Rights, known officially as the Serviceman's Readjustment Act of 1944, offered to pay tuition for college or trade education to ex–World War II servicemen. It also mandated that they receive up to $500 a year for tuition, books, and supplies. Nearly 8 million veterans took advantage of this first G.I. Bill

and American higher education expanded rapidly as a result. Veterans also made use of the bill's guaranteed mortgages and low interest rates to buy new homes in the suburbs, inspiring a housing boom.

Truman Doctrine (1947) and NATO (1949)

The Truman Doctrine initiated U.S. resistance to expansion of the Soviet Union into Western Europe following World War II, and the NATO treaty has provided the framework for European security for half a century. Truman declared to a joint session of Congress, "I believe that it must be the policy of the United States to support free people who are resisting attempted subjugation by armed minorities or by outside pressures."

Federal Highway Act (1956)

President Dwight D. Eisenhower was right when he said, "More than any single action by the government since the end of the war, this one would change the face of America." The most expensive public-works project in U.S. history, the highway act built the 41,000-mile nationwide interstate highway system.

Civil Rights Act of 1964

Only Congress could end racial segregation in privately owned businesses and facilities. It did so by an overwhelming vote of both houses in the Civil Rights Act of 1964. Injustices endure, but the end of segregated restaurants, theaters, and drinking fountains provided new opportunities for African Americans and helped change white attitudes. In addition, Title VII of the act prohibits gender discrimination and serves as the legal bulwark for women's rights.

Voting Rights Act of 1965

President Lyndon B. Johnson signed this act in the same room in the Capitol where Abraham Lincoln had penned the Emancipation Proclamation. This legislation guaranteed all Americans the most fundamental of all rights—the right to vote. Between the 1964 and 1968 presidential elections, black voter registration increased 50 percent across the nation, even in the reluctant Southern states, giving African Americans newfound political clout.

Medicare and Medicaid (1965)

Congress amended the Social Security Act of 1935 to provide for national health insurance for the aged (Medicare) and for the poor (Medicaid). In 2003 (28 years later) Congress added prescription drug coverage to Medicare.

The Demise of the Apprenticeship Norm   Years ago, "the first rule"[43] of congressional behavior was that new members were expected to be seen but not heard on the floor, to be studious in their committee work, and to be cooperative with party leaders. But the institutional norm of apprenticeship has been swept aside as increasingly ambitious and independent senators and representatives arrive on Capitol Hill. Today new members of Congress feel free to grab the spotlight on the floor, in committee, and in front of television cameras. "The evidence is clear, unequivocal, and overwhelming: the [apprenticeship] norm is simply gone."[44] Nevertheless, experienced members are more active and influential in shaping legislation than are new members.[45]

Specialization and Deference   The committee system encourages members of Congress to specialize in particular policy areas. Even the most independent and ambitious members can perceive the advantage of developing power and expertise in an area especially relevant to their constituents. Traditionally, members who developed a special expertise and accumulated years of service on a standing committee were deferred to in floor proceedings. These specialists were "cue givers" for party members when bills or amendments were being voted on. Members are still likely to defer to specialized committee members when the issues are technical or complicated, or when the issue is outside of their own area of policy specialization, but deference is increasingly rare on major public issues.

Bargaining   Bargaining is central to the legislative process. Little could be achieved if individual members were unwilling to bargain with each other for votes both in committees and on the floor. A willingness to bargain is a long-standing functional norm of Congress.

Members of Congress are not expected to violate their consciences in the bargaining process. On the contrary, members respect one another's issues of conscience and receive respect in return. On most issues, however, members can and do bargain their support. "Horse trading" is very common in committee work. Members may bargain in their own personal interest, in the interests of constituents or groups, or even in the interests of their committee with members of other committees. Because most bargaining occurs in a committee setting, it is seldom a matter of public record. The success and reputation of committee chairs largely depend on their ability to work out bargains and compromises.

Bargaining can assume different forms. Explicit trade-offs such as "If you vote for my bill, I'll vote for yours" are the simplest form of bargaining, but implicit understandings may be more common. Members may help other members in anticipation of receiving reciprocal help at some future unspecified time. Moreover, representatives who refuse to cooperate

Women Senators Meet
Seventeen women served in the 111th Congress (2009–2011), eleven Democrats and five Republicans.

on a regular basis may find little support for their own bills. Mutual "back scratching" allows members to develop a reservoir of IOUs for the future. Building credit is good business for most members; one can never tell when one will need help in the future.

Bargaining requires a certain kind of integrity. Members of Congress must stick to their agreements. They must not consistently ask too high a price for their cooperation. They must recognize and return favors. They must not renege on promises. They must be trustworthy.

Conference-committee bargaining is essential if legislation acceptable to both houses is to be written. Indeed, it is expected that conferees from each house will bargain and compromise their differences. "Every House-Senate conference is expected to proceed via the methods of 'give and take,' 'trading back and forth,' 'pulling and hauling,' 'horse-trading and compromise,' 'splitting the difference,' etc."[46]

Logrolling   Logrolling is mutual agreement to support projects that primarily benefit individual members of Congress and their constituencies. Logrolling is closely associated with pork-barrel legislation. Yet it can occur in virtually any kind of legislation. Even interest-group lobbyists may logroll with each other, promising to support each other's legislative agendas.

logrolling
Bargaining for agreement among legislators to support each other's favorite bills, especially projects that primarily benefit individual members and their constituents.

Leader-Follower Relations   Because leaders have few means of disciplining members, they must rely heavily on their bargaining skills to solicit cooperation and get the work of Congress accomplished. Party leaders can appeal to members' concerns for their party image among the voters. Individual majority members want to keep their party in the majority—if for no other reason than to retain their committee and subcommittee chairs. Individual minority members would like their party to win control of their house in order to assume the power and privileges of committee and subcommittee chairs. Party leaders must appeal to more than partisanship to win cooperation, however.

To secure cooperation, leaders can grant—or withhold—some tangible benefits. A member of the House needs the Speaker's support to get recognition, to have a bill called up, to get a bill scheduled, to see to it that a bill gets assigned to a preferred committee, to get a good committee assignment, and to help a bill get out of the Rules Committee, for example.

Party leaders may also seek to gain support from their followers by doing favors that ease their lives in Washington, advance their legislative careers, and help them with their reelection. Favors from party leaders oblige members to respond to leaders' requests at a later time. Members themselves like to build up a reservoir of good feeling and friendship with the leadership, knowing that eventually they will need some favors from the leadership.

Gridlock   Congress is often criticized for legislative **gridlock**—the failure to enact laws, including appropriations acts, that are widely perceived to have merit. Indeed, much of the popular frustration with Congress relates to gridlock arising from policy and budgetary stalemates. Research has suggested that the following factors contribute to congressional gridlock:[47]

gridlock
Political stalemate between the executive and legislative branches arising when one branch is controlled by one major political party and the other branch by the other party.

- Divided party control of the presidency and Congress
- Divided party control of the House and Senate
- Greater ideological polarization (liberal versus conservative) of the parties

COMPARED TO WHAT?

The Parliamentary System

The parliamentary system of government evolved over centuries in Great Britain, and many countries have emulated the British model. Indeed, most of the democracies in the world today are parliamentary systems.

In a parliamentary system, power is concentrated in the legislature. The executive heads—cabinet ministers—are members of the parliament (MPs) and chosen by the majority party in that body. (If no party wins a majority in the parliament, then a coalition of parties must agree on who will serve as prime minister and who will serve in the cabinet.) The head of the majority party is the nation's prime minister; the prime minister serves as both chief executive and chief legislator. The prime minister (PM) and the cabinet are referred to as "the government." Most parliamentary systems have a head of state, often a figurehead, either a president elected by the parliament or a hereditary monarchy as in Great Britain.

There is no real separation of powers in a parliamentary system. The government remains in power as long as it commands a majority in the parliament. Only a parliamentary vote of no-confidence can oust a government from power, an unlikely event inasmuch as the government is composed of the majority party members of the parliament. The government can call new elections for parliament whenever it wishes; but by constitutional tradition in Great Britain elections must be held at least every 5 years.

What are the advantages of a parliamentary system? It is easier to pass legislation. The party in power controls both the government and the parliament itself.

Any legislation that is introduced by the government must pass the parliament; a defeat would constitute a vote of no-confidence. There is no real possibility of legislative-executive gridlock. Another advantage is that an unpopular government can be ousted at any time. There is no need to wait up to 4 years to rid the nation of an unpopular chief executive. The majority party itself can replace the prime minister, or members of the majority can desert their party, forcing a new election. Finally, parliaments tend to have a more adversarial style of debate in open sessions of the parliament. Parliamentary debates are more fun than sessions of the U.S. House of Representatives or Senate.

Among the disadvantages of a parliamentary system is that the head of the government is not directly elected by the people as in the U.S. presidential system. Rather, the prime minister is designated by the majority party in the parliament. The voters may know in advance of an election who heads the contending parties and vote for the party with the preferred leader, but voters do not directly elect the prime minister.

From the American perspective, perhaps the most serious criticism is that a parliamentary system offers no real checks and balances. Legislative and executive powers are concentrated in the majority party in the parliament. The fact that Great Britain has an unwritten constitution, a constitution that can be changed by the parliament itself, further concentrates power in a single body. (Great Britain has a largely ceremonial House of Lords, but parliamentary powers are concentrated in the House of Commons.)

• In the Senate, the willingness of members to filibuster against a bill, requiring 60 votes to overcome the opposition

In contrast, the factors that appear to lessen gridlock and encourage significant legislative accomplishment include

• Unified party control of the presidency, House, and Senate

• Larger numbers of moderates among Democrats and Republicans in Congress (as opposed to larger numbers of strong liberals and strong conservatives)

• Overwhelming public support for new legislation

Note that the constitutional structure of American government—separation of powers and checks and balances, as well as bicameralism—plays a major role in gridlock, as does the American two-party system (see *Compared to What?* "The Parliamentary System"). Overcoming gridlock requires a willingness of members of both parties in both houses of Congress, as well as the White House, to bargain and compromise over legislation. And it requires strong public opinion in support of congressional action.

Congressional Ethics

▶ 10.12 *Evaluate the mechanisms for ensuring ethical behavior in Congress.*

Although critics might consider the phrase *congressional ethics* to be an oxymoron, the moral climate of Congress today is probably better than in earlier eras of American history. Nevertheless, Congress as an institution has suffered from well-publicized scandals that continue to prompt calls for reform.

Ethics Rules   Congress has an interest in maintaining the integrity of the institution itself and the trust of the people. Thus Congress has established its own rules of ethics. These rules include the following:

- *Financial disclosure*: All members must file personal financial statements each year.

- *Honoraria*: Members cannot accept fees for speeches or personal appearances.

- *Campaign funds*: Surplus campaign funds cannot be put to personal use.

- *Gifts*: Members may not accept gifts worth more than $50 (with annual increases in these amounts for inflation).

- *Free travel*: Members may not accept free travel from private corporations or individuals for more than 4 days of domestic travel and 7 days of international travel per year. (Taxpayer-paid "junkets" to investigate problems at home or abroad or attend international meetings are not prohibited.)

- *Lobbying*: Former members may not lobby Congress for at least 1 year after retirement.

But these limited rules have not gone very far in restoring popular trust in Congress.

Gray Areas: Services and Contributions   Congress members are expected to perform services for their political contributors. However, a direct *quid pro quo*—receiving a financial contribution specifically for the performance of official duty—is illegal. Few Congress members would be so foolish as to openly state a price to a potential contributor for a specific service, and most contributors know not to state a dollar amount that would be forthcoming if the member

Ethics Problem

Idaho Senator Larry Craig, with his wife Suzanne beside him, announces his resignation from the Senate during a morning news conference on September 1, 2007, in Boise, Idaho. Behind Craig to the left is Idaho Gov. C. L. "Buth" Otter and his wife, Lori. Craig resigned after his arrest on June 11, 2007, for lewd conduct at the Minneapolis–St. Paul Airport. Craig pleaded guilty to the lesser charge of disorderly conduct.

A CONSTITUTIONAL NOTE

Congress as the First Branch

The Founders believed that the Congress would be the first and most powerful branch of government. Thus Article I establishes the Congress, describes its structure, and sets forth its powers. Note that its powers *are* the enumerated powers of the national government. Following the English precedent of two houses of the legislature, a House of Commons and a House of Lords, the Founders created two separate houses, a House of Representatives and a Senate. They did so in part as a result of the Connecticut Compromise, which balanced large population states in the House with the small population states' demands for equality in the Senate. But the Founders also wanted a Senate elected by state legislatures, not the people, "as a defense to the people against their own temporary errors and delusions." The Founders believed that the Senate would balance the interests and numerical superiority of common citizens with the property interests of the less numerous landowners, bankers, and merchants, who they expected to be sent to the Senate by the state legislatures. This defense against "temporary errors and delusions" of the people was strengthened by different lengths of tenure for the House and Senate. All House members were elected every 2 years, but Senate members were elected for 6-year terms, one-third of the Senate elected every 2 years. The longer terms of the Senate were designed to protect senators from temporary popular movements. Not until the 17th Amendment was ratified in 1913, over a century later, were senators directly elected by the people. In short, the original Constitution of 1787 was careful to limit the role of the people in lawmaking.

performed a particular service for them. But what if the contribution and the service occur close together? A Senate Ethics Committee once found that a close relationship between a service and a contribution to be an "impermissible pattern of conduct [that] violated established norms of behavior in the Senate . . . [and] was improper and repugnant."[48] But the Ethics Committee offered little in the way of a future guidance in handling services for campaign contributors.

Expulsion   The Constitution gives Congress the power to discipline its own members. "Each House may . . . punish its Members for disorderly Behaviour, and, with the Concurrence of two thirds, expel a Member." But the Constitution fails to define *disorderly behavior*. It seems reasonable to believe that criminal conduct falls within the constitutional definition of disorderly behavior. Bribery is a criminal act: it is illegal to solicit or receive anything of value in return for the performance of a government duty.

But no U.S. Senator has been expelled from Congress since the Civil War. Bob Packwood (R-OR) resigned his Senate seat in 1995 after the Ethics Committee recommended his expulsion for sexual harassment of congressional staff. Several House members have been expelled. Representative Michael Myers (D-PA) was expelled for taking bribes in an FBI sting operation in 1980. (The sting also resulted in two other House members and a senator resigning rather than face expulsion; three other representatives were defeated for reelection.) Representative James A. Traficant (D-OH) was expelled in 2002 following his conviction on ten federal corruption charges. Several House members have resigned rather than face expulsion: Representative Mel Reynolds (D-IL) resigned in 1995 following his criminal conviction on charges of sexual misconduct. (A special election to fill his vacated seat was won by Jesse Jackson, Jr., son of the popular preacher and former Democratic presidential contender.) Representative Randy Cunningham (R-CA) resigned in 2005 after pleading guilty to charges of accepting $2.4 million in bribes from lobbyists; and Representative Tom Foley (R-FL) resigned his seat in 2006 after sexually explicit messages to teenage congressional pages came to light.

Censure   A lesser punishment in the Congress than expulsion is official censure. Censured members are obliged to "stand in the well" and listen to the charges read against them. It is supposed to be a humiliating experience and fatal to one's political career. In 1983 two members of Congress, Barney Frank (D-MA) and Gerry Studds (D-MA), were censured for sexual misconduct with teenage congressional pages. Both were obliged to "stand in the well."

Lesser forms of censure include a public reprimand or admonition by the Ethics Committee expressing disapproval of the Congress member's behavior. And the Ethics Committee may also order a member to repay funds improperly received.

censure
Public reprimand for wrongdoing, given to a member standing in the chamber before Congress.

Scandal and Reelection Defeat   Many, but not all, Congress members censured or reprimanded lose their seats in subsequent elections. One reason given for the Republican loss of control of the Congress in 2006 was scandal. Six incumbent Republican representatives were variously linked to scandals, and they all went down to defeat. Six-term congress member J. D. Hayworth lost in his solidly Republican district in Arizona because he received money from the indicted lobbyist Jack Abramoff. Representative William Jefferson (D-LA) lost his solidly Democratic New Orleans seat in 2008 following a federal bribery conviction featuring $90,000 in cash hidden in his refrigerator.

Summary

▶ 10.1 *Explain the sources of Congress's power.*
The Congress represents local and state interests in policy making. The Senate's constituencies are the 50 states, and the House's constituencies are 435 separate districts. Both houses of Congress, but especially the House of Representatives, wield power in domestic and foreign affairs primarily through the "power of the purse."

Congressional powers include oversight and investigation. These powers are exercised primarily through committees. Although Congress claims these powers are a necessary part of lawmaking, their real purpose is usually to influence agency decision making, to build political support for increases or decreases in agency funding, to lay the political foundation for new programs and policies, and to capture media attention and enhance the power of members of Congress.

▶ 10.2 *Explain the processes of congressional apportionment and redistricting, and assess how representative Congress is of the general population.*
Congress is gradually becoming more "representative" of the general population in terms of race and gender. Redistricting, under federal court interpretations of the Voting Rights Act, has increased African American and Hispanic representation in Congress. And women have significantly increased their presence in Congress in recent years. Nevertheless, women and minorities do not occupy seats in Congress proportional to their share of the general population.

▶ 10.3 *Describe congressional elections and the hurdles that challengers face.*
Members of Congress are independent political entrepreneurs. They initiate their own candidacies, raise their own campaign funds, and get themselves elected with very little help from their party. Members of Congress are largely career politicians who skillfully use the advantages of incumbency to stay in office. Incumbents outspend challengers by large margins. Interest-group political action committees and individual contributors strongly favor incumbents. Congressional elections are seldom focused on great national issues but rather on local issues and personalities and the ability of candidates to "bring home the bacon" from Washington and serve their constituents.

▶ 10.4 *Evaluate the successes and failures of the two parties in Congress.*
Congress as an institution is not very popular with the American people. Scandals, pay raises, perks, and privileges reported in the media have hurt the image of the institution. Nevertheless, individual members of Congress remain popular with their districts' voters.

▶ 10.5 *Characterize the working life of member of Congress.*
If Congress fails to pay attention to national and international issues, it is in part due to their focus on issues of importance to the local constituency. Slowly, the institution is becoming more representative of minorities and women. Once elected to

Congress, members are provided with an office, a staff, and the assistance of many support agencies like the Congressional Budget Office, Government Accounting Office, Government Printing Office, and the Library of Congress. Benefits include free mailing privileges, a generous retirement plan, and excellent medical insurance.

▶ 10.6 *Identify the techniques used by representatives to enhance their image among constituents.*

Members of Congress spend as much time on "home style" activities—promoting their images back home and attending to constituents' problems—as they do legislating. Casework wins votes one at a time, gradually accumulating political support back home, and members often support each other's "pork-barrel" products.

▶ 10.7 *Analyze the roles of parties and leadership in organizing Congress.*

Despite the independence of members, the Democratic and Republican Party structures in the House and Senate remain the principal bases for organizing Congress. Party leaders in the House and Senate generally control the flow of business in each house, assigning bills to committees, scheduling or delaying votes, and appointing members to committees. But leaders must bargain for votes; they have few formal disciplinary powers. They cannot deny renomination to recalcitrant members.

▶ 10.8 *Characterize the legislative work of committees and assess the repercussions of committees for distribution of power in Congress.*

The real legislative work of Congress is done in committee. Standing committees screen and draft legislation; with rare exceptions, bills do not reach the floor without approval by a majority of a standing committee. The committee and subcommittee system decentralizes power in Congress. The system satisfies the desires of members to gain power, prestige, and electoral advantage, but it weakens responsible government in the Congress as a whole. All congressional committees are chaired by members of the majority party. Seniority is still the major determinant of power in Congress.

▶ 10.9 *Outline the process for a bill that has reached the floor and identify obstacles to passage.*

In order to become a law, a bill must win committee approval and withstand debate in both houses of Congress. The rules attached to a bill's passage in the House can significantly help or hurt its chances. Bills passed with differences in the two houses must be reworked in a conference committee composed of members of both houses and then passed in identical form in both.

▶ 10.10 *Assess the influences on congressional decision making.*

In deciding how to vote on legislation, Congress members are influenced by party loyalty, presidential support or opposition, constituency concerns, interest-group pressures, and their own personal values and ideology. Party majorities oppose each other on roughly half of all roll-call votes in Congress. Presidents receive the greatest support in Congress from members of their own party.

▶ 10.11 *Outline the customs and norms of Congress, their function, and recent changes.*

The customs and norms of Congress help reduce interpersonal conflict, facilitate bargaining and compromise, and make life more pleasant on Capitol Hill. They include the recognition of special competencies of members, a willingness to bargain and compromise, mutual "back scratching" and logrolling, reciprocity, and deference toward the leadership. But traditional customs and norms have weakened over time as more members have pursued independent political agendas. And partisanship and incivility in Congress have risen in recent years.

▶ 10.12 *Evaluate the mechanisms for ensuring ethical behavior in Congress.*

Congress establishes its own rules of ethics. The Constitution empowers each house to expel its own members for "disorderly conduct" by a two-thirds vote, but expulsion has seldom occurred. Some members have resigned to avoid expulsion; others have been officially censured yet remained in Congress.

Chapter Test

▶ 10.1 *Explain the sources of Congress's power.*

1. The most important source of Congress's power stems from its authority to
   a. ratify treaties
   b. confirm presidential appointments
   c. declare war
   d. authorize the expenditure of federal funds

2. It would be accurate to say that
   a. the House of Representatives calls itself the "People's Chamber"
   b. treaties must be ratified by a two-thirds vote of the House of Representatives

   c. all appropriation bills must first originate in the U.S. Senate
   d. the Founders envisioned that Congress would be less important than the Executive Branch

▶ 10.2 *Explain the processes of congressional apportionment and redistricting, and assess how representative Congress is of the general population.*

3. When redistricting results in partisan voters being so concentrated that much of their vote is wasted, it is called
   a. packing
   c. chubbing
   b. splintering
   d. ticket splitting

4. The Supreme Court held that inequalities in voters' influence resulting from malapportioned legislative districts
   a. violated the national supremacy clause in *Baker v. Carr*
   b. violated the due process clause in *Reynolds v. Sims*
   c. violated the equal protection clause in *Baker v. Carr*
   d. was a matter that should be left to the states as it is protected by the 10th Amendment

▶ **10.3** *Describe congressional elections and the hurdles that challengers face.*

5. The largest source of candidates for political office comes from which of the following occupations?
   a. agriculture and real estate
   b. medicine, journalism, and public relations
   c. public service and law
   d. business

6. Voters reelect incumbents even when they are members of an unpopular Congress because
   a. of name recognition
   b. most voters approve of their own representative
   c. seniority adds to their representative's power
   d. all of the above

▶ **10.4** *Evaluate the successes and failures of the two parties in Congress.*

7. After the 2010 elections
   a. the Republicans became the majority party in the House of Representatives
   b. the Democrats retained control of the House of Representatives
   c. the Republicans gained control of the Senate
   d. the Republicans became the majority party in both the Senate and the House of Representatives

▶ **10.5** *Characterize the working life of member of Congress.*

8. The Hispanic populations in _____ elect the majority of the Latino representatives that go to Washington, D.C.
   a. Texas, Louisiana, and Mississippi
   b. California, Nevada, and Oregon
   c. Texas, California, and Florida
   d. Florida, Georgia, and Alabama

9. The congressional agency that serves as a counterweight to the president's Office of Management and Budget is the
   a. GAO, General Accountability Office
   b. CRS, Congressional Research Service
   c. CBO, Congressional Budget Office
   d. OCS, Office of Congressional Support

▶ **10.6** *Identify the techniques used by representatives to enhance their image among constituents.*

10. Members of Congress use all *but* which of the following to cultivate their image at home?
    a. case work
    b. attending "junkets" overseas in order to educate themselves on policy issues
    c. making personal appearances back home
    d. earmarking projects for the home district

11. Efforts by senators and representatives to "bring home the bacon" are referred to as
    a. pork barreling and set-asides
    b. demonstration projects
    c. earmarking and pork barreling
    d. demonstration projects and set-asides

▶ **10.7** *Analyze the roles of parties and leadership in organizing Congress.*

12. The principal bases for organizing Congress come from
    a. Constitutional provisions
    b. the Democratic and Republican Party organizations in the House and the Senate
    c. the President's recommendations
    d. the House Rules Committee

13. The key leader of the House of Representatives is the
    a. Chairman of the House
    b. president pro tempore
    c. Speaker of the House
    d. House Whip

▶ **10.8** *Characterize the legislative work of committees and assess the repercussions of committees for distribution of power in Congress.*

14. The most powerful committee in the House is generally believed to be
    a. Rules Committee
    b. Appropriations Committee
    c. Armed Services Committee
    d. Judiciary Committee

▶ **10.9** *Outline the process for a bill that has reached the floor and identify obstacles to passage.*

15. A determination by the Rules Committee that forbids amending a bill under consideration by the House is a
    a. unanimous consent agreement b. limited rule
    c. open rule d. closed rule

16. A bill that has passed but has different wording in the House and Senate versions is sent to
    a. a conference committee
    b. the House Rules Committee
    c. both the House and Senate Reconciliation Committee
    d. the Senate Reconciliation Committee

▶ **10.10** *Assess the influences on congressional decision making.*

17. Constituencies have more influence on pending legislation that is
    a. a high-profile issue
    b. technical in nature
    c. in agreement with the party leaders' opinions
    d. applicable to a small number of people

▶ **10.11** *Outline the customs and norms of Congress, their function, and recent changes.*

18. Gridlock in Congress is in part a result of
    a. unified party control of the presidency and Congress
    b. greater ideological polarization of the parties
    c. unified party control of the House and Senate
    d. the willingness of House members to filibuster

▶ **10.12** *Evaluate the mechanisms for ensuring ethical behavior in Congress.*

19. The Constitution gives _____ the power to discipline members of Congress.
    a. the Supreme Court c. Congress
    b. the president d. the Department of Justice

20. Members of Congress may be punished for misbehavior by
    a. expulsion c. public reprimand
    b. censure d. all of the above

mypoliscilab EXERCISES

Apply what you learned in this chapter on MyPoliSciLab.

Read on mypoliscilab.com

eText: Chapter 10

Study and Review on mypoliscilab.com

Pre-Test

Post-Test

Chapter Exam

Flashcards

Watch on mypoliscilab.com

Video: Kagan Hearing

Video: Unknown Wins South Carolina Senate Primary

Explore on mypoliscilab.com

Simulation: You Are Redrawing the Districts in Your State

Simulation: How a Bill Becomes a Law

Simulation: You Are a Member of Congress

Comparative: Comparing Legislatures

Timeline: The Power of the Speaker of the House

Visual Literacy: Congressional Redistricting

Visual Literacy: Why is it So Hard to Defeat an Incumbent?

Key Terms

bicameral 330
power of the purse 332
oversight 332
advice and consent 333
confirmation 333
congressional hearings 333
congressional investigation 333
subpoena 333
contempt 333
perjury 333
impeachment 334
apportionment 335
malapportionment 335
redistricting 336
gerrymandering 336
splintering 337
packing 337

incumbent gerrymandering 338
affirmative racial gerrymandering 339
open seat 340
safe seats 342
turnover 342
term limits 342
Government Accountability Office 350
home style 352
casework 352
pork barreling 352
earmarks 352
franking privilege 352
Speaker of the House 355
majority leader 356

minority leader 356
whips 356
standing committee 358
ranking minority member 358
subcommittees 358
seniority system 360
drafting a bill 360
markup 360
discharge petition 361
rule 361
closed rule 361
restricted rule 361
open rule 361
unanimous consent agreement 362
filibuster 362
cloture 362

rider 362
roll-call vote 362
conference committees 362
party votes 364
party unity 364
bipartisanship 364
divided party government 366
constituency 366
trustees 368
delegates 368
logrolling 371
gridlock 371
censure 375

Suggested Readings

Davidson, Robert H., Walter J. Oleszek, and Frances E. Lee. *Congress and Its Members.* 11th ed. Washington, D.C.: CQ Press, 2007. Authoritative text on Congress covering the recruitment of members, elections, Home styles and Hill styles, leadership, decision making, and relations with

interest groups, presidency, and courts. Emphasizes tension between lawmaking responsibilities and desire to be reelected.

Fenno, Richard F. *Home Style.* Boston: Little, Brown, 1978. The classic description of how attention to constituency by members of Congress enhances their reelection prospects. Home style activities, including casework, pork barreling, travel and appearances back home, newsletters, and surveys, are described in detail.

Herrnson, Paul S. *Congressional Elections: Campaigning at Home and in Washington.* 5th ed. Washington, D.C.: CQ Press, 2007. Interviews with candidates, campaign aides, and political consultants to paint a comprehensive portrait of congressional campaigns.

Jacobson, Gary C. *The Politics of Congressional Elections.* 7th ed. New York: Longman, 2009. Coverage of congressional campaigns and elections with reference to questions of responsibility and representation.

Jones, Charles O. *Separate but Equal Branches: Congress and the Presidency.* 2nd ed. Washington, D.C.: CQ Press, 1999. Presidential–congressional relations under Johnson; Nixon; Ford; Carter; Reagan; Bush, Sr., and Clinton.

Oleszek, Walter J. *Congressional Procedures and Policy Processes.* 7th ed. Washington, D.C.: CQ Press, 2007. The definitive work on congressional rules, procedures and traditions and their effect on the course and content of legislation.

Ornstein, Norman J., Thomas E. Mann, and Michael J. Malbin. *Vital Statistics on Congress.* Washington, D.C.: CQ Press, 2008. Published biennially. Excellent source of data on members of Congress, congressional elections, campaign finance, committees and staff, workload, and voting alignments.

Sinclair, Barbara. *Unorthodox Lawmaking.* 3rd ed. Washington, D.C.: CQ Press, 2007. A description of the various detours and shortcuts a major bill is likely to take in Congress, including case studies.

Stathis, Stephen W. *Landmark Legislation 1774–2002.* Washington, D.C.: CQ Press, 2003. A summary of major congressional legislation over 225 years, in a single volume.

Suggested Web Sites

Congressional Budget Office www.cbo.gov
The Web site of the CBO is an excellent source of data on federal finances, economic projections, and the budgetary process.

Congressional Quarterly (CQ) www.cq.com
The *Congressional Quarterly Weekly Report* provides the most comprehensive coverage of events in Congress, including key issues, House and Senate roll-call votes, backgrounds of members, and political and election information. The CQ Press is a major publisher of books on politics and government.

Government Accountability Office www.gao.gov
The GAO Web site provides the latest reports evaluating government programs and spending.

Library of Congress http://thomas.loc.gov
The Thomas system allows the tracing of bills from their introduction, through the committee system, floor schedule vote, and so on.

Roll Call www.rollcall.com
This online magazine covers a variety of current topics about Congress but is especially strong on stories dealing with running for Congress and/or campaign financing.

U.S. House of Representatives www.house.gov
Official Web site of the House, with schedule of floor and committee actions, legislative information, and links to every Representative's Web site and every committee Web site.

U.S. Senate www.senate.gov
Official Senate Web site, with floor and committee schedules, Senate news, and links to each senator's Web site.

Chapter Test Answer Key

1. D
2. A
3. A
4. C
5. C
6. D
7. B
8. C
9. C
10. B
11. C
12. B
13. C
14. A
15. D
16. A
17. A
18. B
19. C
20. D

11 THE PRESIDENT

White House Politics

> " The buck stops here. "
>
> Harry Truman

Chapter Outline and Learning Objectives

Presidential Power
▶ 11.1 *Identify the powers and responsibilities of the president.*

Constitutional Powers of the President
▶ 11.2 *Identify the powers granted to the president by the Constitution.*

Political Resources of the President
▶ 11.3 *Assess the sources of the president's political power.*

Personality Versus Policy
▶ 11.4 *Analyze how presidents' personality and policy positions impact their approval ratings.*

Chief Executive
▶ 11.5 *Outline the responsibilities and powers of the president as the nation's chief executive.*

Chief Legislator and Lobbyist
▶ 11.6 *Analyze the factors affecting the success of the president as the chief legislator and lobbyist.*

Global Leader
▶ 11.7 *Assess the role of the president as a global leader.*

Commander-in-Chief
▶ 11.8 *Trace the expansion of presidential powers as Commander-in-Chief.*

The Vice-Presidential Waiting Game
▶ 11.9 *Characterize the roles and responsibilities of the vice president.*

Think about Politics

1. Do you approve of the way the president is handling his job?
   YES ⬭ NO ⬭

2. Should presidents have the power to take actions not specifically authorized by law or the Constitution that they believe necessary for the nation's well-being?
   YES ⬭ NO ⬭

3. Should the American people consider private moral conduct in evaluating presidential performance?
   YES ⬭ NO ⬭

4. Should Congress have the authority to call home U.S. troops sent by the president to engage in military actions overseas?
   YES ⬭ NO ⬭

5. Should the president be held responsible for economic recessions?
   YES ⬭ NO ⬭

6. Should Congress impeach and remove a president whose policy decisions it believes damage the nation?
   YES ⬭ NO ⬭

7. Is presidential performance more related to character and personality than to policy positions?
   YES ⬭ NO ⬭

How much power does the president of the United States really have—over policies, over legislation, over the budget, over how this country is viewed by other nations, even over how it views itself?

Presidential Power

▶ 11.1 *Identify the powers and responsibilities of the president.*

Americans look to their president for "Greatness." The presidency embodies the popular "great man" view of history and public affairs—attributing progress in the world to the actions of particular individuals. Great presidents are those associated with great events: George Washington with the founding of the nation, Abraham Lincoln with the preservation of the Union, Franklin D. Roosevelt with the nation's emergence from economic depression and victory in World War II (see *What Do You Think?*: "How Would You Rate the Presidents?"). People tend to believe that the president is responsible for "peace and prosperity" as well as for "change." They expect their president to present a "vision" of America's future and to symbolize the nation.

The Symbolic President The president personifies American government for most people. People expect the president to act decisively and effectively to deal with national problems. They expect the president to be "compassionate"—to show concern for problems confronting individual citizens. The president, while playing these roles, is the focus of public attention and the nation's leading celebrity. Presidents receive more media coverage than any other person in the nation, for everything from their policy statements to their favorite foods to their dogs and cats.

Managing Crises In times of crisis, the American people look to their president to take action, to provide reassurance, and to protect the nation and its people. It is the president, not the Congress or the courts, who is expected to speak on behalf of the American people in times of national

WHAT DO YOU THINK?

How Would You Rate the Presidents?

From time to time, historians have been polled to rate U.S. presidents (see table). The survey ratings given the presidents have been remarkably consistent. Abraham Lincoln, George Washington, and Franklin Roosevelt are universally recognized as the greatest American presidents. It is more difficult for historians to rate recent presidents; the views of historians are influenced by their own (generally liberal and reformist) political views. Richard Nixon once commented, "History will treat me fairly. Historians probably won't."

Historians may tend to rank activist presidents who led the nation through war or economic crisis higher than passive presidents who guided the nation in peace and prosperity. Initially, Dwight Eisenhower, who presided in the relatively calm 1950s, was ranked low by historians. But later, after comparing his performance with those who came after him, his steadiness and avoidance of war raised his ranking dramatically.

Arthur M. Schlesinger, Jr. (1962)

Great
1. Lincoln
2. Washington
3. F. Roosevelt
4. Wilson
5. Jefferson

Near Great
6. Jackson
7. T. Roosevelt
8. Polk
9. Truman (tie)
10. J. Adams
11. Cleveland

Average
12. Madison
13. J. Q. Adams
14. Hayes
15. McKinley
16. Taft
17. Van Buren
18. Monroe
19. Hoover
20. B. Harrison
21. Arthur
21. Eisenhower (tie)
23. A. Johnson

Below Average
24. Taylor
25. Tyler
26. Fillmore
27. Coolidge
28. Pierce
29. Buchanan

Failure
30. Grant
31. Harding

Robert Murray (1982)

Presidential Rank
1. Lincoln
2. F. Roosevelt
3. Washington
4. Jefferson
5. T. Roosevelt
6. Wilson
7. Jackson
8. Truman
9. J. Adams
10. L. Johnson
11. Eisenhower
12. Polk
13. Kennedy
14. Madison
15. Monroe
16. J. Q. Adams
17. Cleveland
18. McKinley
19. Taft
20. Van Buren
21. Hoover
22. Hayes
23. Arthur
24. Ford
25. Carter
26. B. Harrison
27. Taylor
28. Tyler
29. Fillmore
30. Coolidge
31. Pierce
32. A. Johnson
33. Buchanan
34. Nixon
35. Grant
36. Harding

Arthur M. Schlesinger, Jr. (1996)

Great
1. Lincoln
2. Washington
3. F. Roosevelt

Near Great
4. Jefferson
5. Jackson
6. T. Roosevelt
7. Wilson
8. Truman
9. Polk

High Average
10. Eisenhower
11. J. Adams
12. Kennedy
13. Cleveland
14. L. Johnson
15. Monroe
16. McKinley

Average
17. Madison
18. J. Q. Adams
19. B. Harrison
20. Clinton
21. Van Buren
22. Taft
23. Hayes
24. G.H.W. Bush
25. Reagan
26. Arthur
27. Carter
28. Ford

Below Average
29. Taylor
30. Coolidge
31. Fillmore
32. Tyler

Failure
33. Pierce
34. Grant
35. Hoover
36. Nixon
37. A. Johnson
38. Buchanan
39. Harding

Federalist Society (2000)

Great
1. Washington
2. Lincoln
3. F. Roosevelt

Near Great
4. Jefferson
5. T. Roosevelt
6. Jackson
7. Truman
8. Reagan
9. Eisenhower
10. Polk
11. Wilson

Above Average
12. Cleveland
13. Adams
14. McKinley
15. Madison
16. Monroe
17. L. Johnson
18. Kennedy

Average
19. Taft
20. J. Q. Adams
21. G.H.W. Bush
22. Hayes
23. Van Buren
24. Clinton
25. Coolidge
26. Arthur

Below Average
27. B. Harrison
28. Ford
29. Hoover
30. Carter
31. Taylor
32. Grant
33. Nixon
34. Tyler
35. Fillmore

Failure
36. A. Johnson
37. Pierce
38. Harding
39. Buchanan

CSPAN (2009)

1. Lincoln
2. Washington
3. F. Roosevelt
4. T. Roosevelt
5. Truman
6. Kennedy
7. Jefferson
8. Eisenhower
9. Wilson
10. Reagan
11. L. Johnson
12. Polk
13. Jackson
14. Monroe
15. Clinton
16. W. McKinley
17. J. Adams
18. G.H.W. Bush
19. J. Q. Adams
20. Madison
21. Cleveland
22. Ford
23. Grant
24. Taft
25. Carter
26. Coolidge
27. Nixon
28. Garfield
29. Taylor
30. B. Harrison
31. Van Buren
32. Arthur
33. Hayes
34. Hoover
35. Tyler
36. G. W. Bush
37. Fillmore
38. Harding
39. W. Harrison
40. Pierce
41. A. Johnson
42. Buchanan

Note: These ratings result from surveys of scholars ranging in number from 55 to 950.

Sources: Arthur Murphy, "Evaluating the Presidents of the United States," *Presidential Studies Quarterly* 14 (1984): 117–26; Arthur M. Schlesinger, Jr, "Rating the Presidents: Washington to Clinton," *Political Science Quarterly* 112 (1997): 179–90; CSPAN Historians Presidential Leadership Survey (2009), www.c-span.org/presidentialsurvey; "Federalist Society—*The Wall Street Journal* Survey on Presidents (2000)," www.opinionjournal.com/hail/rankings.html

triumph and tragedy. The president gives expression to the nation's pride in victory. The nation's heroes are welcomed, its scientists, writers, and poets are recognized, and its championship sports teams are feted in the White House Rose Garden.

The president also gives expression to the nation's sadness in tragedy and strives to help the nation go forward. How presidents respond to crises often defines their place in history. Franklin D. Roosevelt raised public morale during the Great Depression of the 1930s by reassuring Americans that "the only thing we have to fear is fear itself." Later he led the nation into war following the Japanese attack on Pearl Harbor, December 7, 1941, "a day which will live in infamy." When the *Challenger* spaceship disintegrated before the eyes of millions of television viewers in 1986, Ronald Reagan gave voice to the nation's feelings about the disaster: "I want to say something to the schoolchildren of America who were watching the live coverage of the shuttle's takeoff. I know it is hard to understand, but sometimes painful things like this happen. The future doesn't belong to the faint-hearted. It belongs to the brave."

Showing Concern in a Crisis

Crisis management is a key presidential responsibility. People look to the president for reassurance in times of national tragedy. Here President Obama meets with families of the victims of 9/11 on the eighth anniversary of the tragedy.

Providing Policy Leadership

The president is expected to set policy priorities for the nation. Most policy initiatives originate in the White House and various departments and agencies of the executive branch and then are forwarded to Congress with the president's approval. Presidential programs are submitted to Congress in the form of messages, including the president's annual State of the Union Address, and in the Budget of the United States Government, which the president presents each year to Congress.

As a political leader, the president is expected to mobilize political support for policy proposals. It is not enough for the president to send policy proposals to Congress. The president must rally public opinion, lobby members of Congress, and win legislative battles. To avoid being perceived as weak or ineffective, presidents must get as much of their legislative programs through Congress as possible. The president is responsible for "getting things done" in the policy arena.

Managing the Economy

The American people hold the president responsible for maintaining a healthy economy. Presidents are blamed for economic downturns, whether or not governmental policies had anything to do with market conditions. The president is expected to "Do Something!" in the face of high unemployment, declining personal income, high mortgage rates, rising inflation, high gasoline prices, or a stock market crash. Herbert Hoover in 1932, Gerald Ford in 1976, Jimmy Carter in 1980, and George H. W. Bush in 1992—all incumbent presidents defeated for reelection during recessions—learned the hard way that the general public holds the president responsible for hard economic times. Indeed, even candidates of the *party* of an incumbent president burdened with a recession face the voters' judgment, as Republican John McCain learned in 2008. Presidents must have an economic "game plan" to stimulate the economy—tax incentives to spur investments, spending proposals to create jobs, plans to lower interest rates.

Managing the Government

As the chief executive of a mammoth federal bureaucracy with 2.8 million civilian employees, the president is responsible for

PEOPLE IN POLITICS

George W. Bush: A Turbulent Presidency

George W. Bush suffered an especially turbulent presidency. From the disputed election of 2000, to the terrorist attack on America of September 11, 2001, to the war against Al Qaeda and the Taliban in Afghanistan, to the prolonged, unpopular war in Iraq, Bush experienced the highs and lows of his office. In domestic affairs Bush achieved success in bringing about tax reductions and educational reform, but he failed in trying to reform Social Security and immigration. His approval ratings skyrocketed after "9/11" but plunged to record lows as casualties mounted in the Iraq War.

Prepping for President

George W. Bush was born into his family's tradition of wealth, privilege, and public service. Bush's grandfather, investment banker Prescott Bush, was a U.S. senator from Connecticut and chairman of the Yale Corporation. Bush's father, the forty-first president, had established himself in the oil business before going into politics—first as a Houston congressman, then as Republican National Chairman, director of the CIA, Ambassador to China, and vice president under President Ronald Reagan. George "Dubya" followed in his father's footsteps to Yale University, but he was not the scholar-athlete that his father had been. Rather, he was a friendly, likable, heavy-drinking fraternity president. Upon graduation in 1968, he joined the Texas Air National Guard, completed flight school, but never faced combat in Vietnam. He earned an MBA degree from Harvard Business School and returned to Texas to enter the oil business himself. Later, he would purchase a major interest in the Texas Rangers baseball team.

Bush had never held public office before running for governor of Texas in 1994. But he had gained valuable political experience serving as an unofficial adviser to his father during his presidential campaigns. And he learned how to tap into Republican big-money campaign contributors. He heavily outspent the incumbent governor, Democrat Ann Richards, winning the governorship with 54 percent of the vote. Dubya's governing style fit comfortably with the Texas "good old boys" in both parties. Although the Texas legislature was controlled by Democrats, Bush won most of his legislative battles. He easily won reelection as governor in 1998.

"9/11"

The terrorist attack on America, September 11, 2001, became the defining moment in the presidency of

George Bush leaves the White House with a near-record low approval rating.

George W. Bush. He promptly declared a "War on Terrorism" against both the terrorist organizations and the nations that harbor and support them. Military action in Afghanistan followed quickly. Bush showed no hesitation, no indecision, no willingness to negotiate with terrorists. His approval ratings skyrocketed: 90 percent of Americans approved of the way he was handling his job. The rapid collapse of the Taliban regime in Afghanistan seemed to confirm the wisdom of Bush's actions.

Bush Policy Initiatives

During his first term, Bush enjoyed the support of a Republican-controlled Congress. He was able to set forth an ambitious policy agenda.

• *Tax reductions*. The centerpiece of Bush's domestic policy were tax cuts in 2001 and 2003 that reduced the top marginal rate from 39.6 percent to 35 percent and gave preferential treatment to capital gains and corporate dividends.

• *Education reform*. The No Child Left Behind Act redefined the federal government's role in education by setting standards of performance, requiring measures of achievement based on testing, and by threatening sanctions, including the transfer of pupils out of failing schools.

• *Health care*. The addition of prescription drug coverage to Medicare for seniors in 2003 was the

implementing policy, that is, for achieving policy goals. Policy making does not end when a law is passed. Policy implementation involves issuing orders, creating organizations, recruiting and assigning personnel, disbursing funds, overseeing work, and evaluating results. It is true that the president cannot perform all of these tasks personally. But the ultimate responsibility for implementation—in the

largest expansion of federal entitlements since the creation of Medicare in 1965.

- *Homeland security.* The Patriot Act was rushed through Congress just six weeks after the "9/11" terrorist attack. It gave the federal government broad new powers for wiretapping, surveillance, investigation, and the arrest of terrorist suspects. In 2002 Bush asked Congress to create a new Department of Homeland Security and undertake a major reorganization of the federal bureaucracy.

National Security Policy

Bush believed that the "War on Terrorism" required dramatic changes in national security policy. Bush's national security strategy refocused U.S. efforts from deterrence and containment of aggression to the pre-emption of potential threats. As his National Security Adviser put it, "We can't wait for the smoking gun to become a mushroom cloud." In addition, the Bush doctrine emphasized unilateral action in national security policy, "going it alone," rather than the traditional American emphasis on international alliances and UN support.

The War in Iraq

"Operation Iraqi Freedom" enjoyed widespread public support at its beginning in March 2003. Saddam Hussein's regime in Baghdad had violated at least a dozen UN resolutions regarding inspections for weapons of mass destruction. Bush stated that the purpose of military action in Iraq was elimination of weapons of mass destruction and a "regime change" to ensure that Saddam would not aid and assist terrorists around the world. Congress voted overwhelmingly to support military action. The U.S. military captured Baghdad in just 21 days. British forces captured the port city of Basra. Bush landed on an aircraft carrier to declare "Mission accomplished!" But the real war was just beginning.

Over time, as U.S. fatalities mounted into the thousands, Americans became disenchanted with the president's handling of affairs (see Figure 11.1 on p. 15). Critics at home, including many in Congress, complained bitterly that Bush had misled them regarding the existence of weapons of mass destruction in Iraq. Intensive searches of the country produced no evidence that Saddam had such weapons at the time of the invasion.

Years after the capture of Baghdad, Iraq remained in chaos. Civil war engulfed the country: both Sunnis and Shiites fought Americans even as they began to fight among themselves. Violence continued unabated. No real "exit strategy" emerged from the White House or the Pentagon. Yet Bush argued forcefully that an abrupt withdrawal ("cut and run") would encourage radical Islamic terrorists around the world.

The election of a Democratic-controlled Congress in 2006 appeared as a popular rejection of Bush's war policies. Yet the president successfully fought off efforts by the Democrats to cut off funds for the war, or to set a fixed date for the withdrawal of American troops from Iraq. And Bush ignored the recommendations of the prestigious Iraq Study Group to negotiate with Syria and Iran and to begin a phased withdrawal from Iraq (see "The War in Iraq" in Chapter 18). Instead he ordered a "surge" in U.S. troop levels and appointed a new commander of U.S. forces in Iraq, General David Petraeus. Critics charged that Bush was stubbornly oblivious to the "facts on the ground"; supporters praised his steadfast commitment to victory.

Fiscal Crisis

But a troubled economy eventually replaced the war in Iraq as a chief concern of Americans. The nation worried as banks faltered, investment firms teetered on bankruptcy, the stock market plunged, and unemployment rose. Bush responded with a proposal for a $700 billion bailout of the failed Wall Street banks and investment firms—an attempt to stabilize the financial sector of the economy and by so doing avoid a deep recession. Congress bickered over the details of the Bush administration plan but eventually approved the major parts of it. But the bailout itself was not popular with the general public and Bush was widely blamed for the crisis.

Last Days in Office

Bush never regained his early popularity. In his final year in office his approval rating plunged below 30 percent. The 2008 presidential election campaign overshadowed the lame-duck president. Democratic candidate Barack Obama sought to tie Republican candidate John McCain to the "failed policies of George Bush," while McCain sought to "distance" himself from Bush. Obama's victory and the Democratic sweep in Congress was in large measure a rejection of George Bush and his administration.

words of the Constitution, "to take Care that the Laws be faithfully executed"—rests with the president.

The Global President   Nations strive to speak with a single voice in international affairs; for the United States, the global voice is that of the president.

As Commander-in-Chief of the armed forces of the United States, the president is a powerful voice in foreign affairs. Efforts by Congress to speak on behalf of the nation in foreign affairs and to limit the war-making power of the president have been generally unsuccessful. It is the president who orders American troops into combat (see *People in Politics*: "George W. Bush: A Turbulent Presidency").

Constitutional Powers of the President

▶ 11.2 *Identify the powers granted to the president by the Constitution.*

Popular expectations of presidential leadership far exceed the formal constitutional powers granted to the president. Compared with the Congress, the president has only modest constitutional powers (see Table 11.1).

TABLE 11.1 Modest Formal Powers: The Constitutional Powers of the President

The formal constitutional powers of the president are very modest, especially compared to popular expectations of presidential leadership.

Chief Executive

Implement policy: "take Care that the Laws be faithfully executed" (Article II, Section 3)

Supervise executive branch of government

Appoint and remove executive officials (Article II, Section 2)

Prepare executive budget for submission to Congress (by law of Congress)

Chief Legislator

Initiate policy: "give to the Congress Information of the State of the Union, and recommend to their Consideration such Measures as he shall judge necessary and expedient" (Article II, Section 3)

Veto legislation passed by Congress, subject to override by a two-thirds vote in both houses

Convene special session of Congress "on extraordinary Occasions" (Article II, Section 3)

Chief Diplomat

Make treaties "with the Advice and Consent of the Senate" (Article II, Section 2)

Exercise the power of diplomatic recognition: "receive Ambassadors" (Article II, Section 3)

Make executive agreements (by custom and international law)

Commander-in-Chief

Command U.S. armed forces: "The president shall be Commander-in-Chief of the Army and Navy" (Article II, Section 2)

Appoint military officers

Chief of State

"The executive Power shall be vested in a President" (Article II, Section 1)

Grant reprieves and pardons (Article II, Section 2)

Represent the nation as chief of state

Appoint federal court and Supreme Court judges (Article II, Section 2)

Who May Be President?   To become president, the Constitution specifies that a person must be a natural-born citizen at least 35 years of age and a resident of the United States for 14 years.

Initially, the Constitution put no limit on how many terms a president could serve. George Washington set a precedent for a two-term maximum that endured until Franklin Roosevelt's decision to run for a third term in 1940 (and a fourth term in 1944). In reaction to Roosevelt's lengthy tenure, Congress proposed the 22nd Amendment, ratified in 1951, which officially restricts the president to two terms (or one full term if a vice president must complete more than 2 years of the previous president's term).

Presidential Succession   Until the adoption of the 25th Amendment in 1967, the Constitution had said little about presidential succession, other than designating the vice president as successor to the president "in Case of the Removal, . . . Death, Resignation, or Inability" and giving Congress the power to decide "what Officer shall then act as President" if both the president and vice president are removed. The Constitution was silent on how to cope with serious presidential illnesses. It contained no provision for replacing a vice president. The incapacitation issue was more than theoretical: James A. Garfield lingered months after being shot in 1881; Woodrow Wilson was an invalid during his last years in office (1919–20); Dwight Eisenhower suffered major heart attacks in office; and Ronald Reagan was in serious condition following an assassination attempt in 1981.

The 25th Amendment stipulates that when the vice president and a majority of the cabinet notify the Speaker of the House and the president pro tempore of the Senate in writing that the president "is unable to discharge the powers and duties of his office," then the vice president becomes *acting* president. To resume the powers of office, the president must then notify Congress in writing that "no inability exists." If the vice president and a majority of cabinet officers do not agree that the president is capable of resuming office, then the Congress "shall decide the issue" within 21 days. A two-thirds vote of both houses is required to replace the president with the vice president.

The disability provisions of the amendment have never been used, but the succession provisions have been. The 25th Amendment provides for the selection of a new vice president by presidential nomination and confirmation by a majority vote of both houses of Congress. When Vice President Spiro Agnew resigned in the face of bribery charges in 1973, President Richard Nixon nominated the Republican leader of the House, Gerald Ford, as vice president; and when Nixon resigned in 1974, Ford assumed the presidency and made Nelson Rockefeller, governor of New York, his vice president. Thus Gerald Ford's 2-year tenure in the White House marked the only time in history when the man serving as president had not been elected to either the presidency or the vice presidency. (If the offices of president and vice president are both vacated, then Congress by law has specified the next in line for the presidency as the Speaker of the House of Representatives, followed by the president pro tempore of the Senate, then the cabinet officers, beginning with the secretary of state.)

Impeachment   The Constitution grants Congress the power of **impeachment** over the president, vice president, and "all civil Officers of the United States" (Article II, Section 4). Technically, impeachment is a charge similar to a criminal indictment brought against an official. The power to bring charges of impeachment is given to the House of Representatives. The power to try all impeachments

impeachment
Equivalent of a criminal charge against an elected official; removal of the impeached official from office depends on the outcome of a trial.

388 CHAPTER 11 • The President: White House Politics

is given to the Senate, and "no Person shall be convicted without the Concurrence of two thirds of the Members present" (Article I, Section 3). Impeachment by the House and conviction by the Senate only remove an official from office; a subsequent criminal trial is required to inflict any other punishment.

The Constitution specifies that impeachment and conviction can only be for "Treason, Bribery, or other High Crimes and Misdemeanors." These words indicate that Congress is not to impeach presidents, federal judges, or any other officials simply because Congress disagrees with their decisions or policies. Indeed, the phrase implies that only serious criminal offenses, not political conflicts, can result in impeachment. Nevertheless, politics was at the root of the impeachment of President Andrew Johnson in 1867. Johnson was a Southern Democrat who had remained loyal to the Union. Lincoln had chosen him as vice president in 1864 as a gesture of national unity. A Republican House impeached him on a party-line vote, but after a month-long trial in the Senate, the "guilty" vote fell one short of the two-thirds needed for removal.[1] And partisan politics played a key role in the House impeachment and later Senate trial of Bill Clinton (see *Politics Up Close*: "Sex, Lies, and Impeachment").

Presidential Pardons

The Constitution grants the president the power to "grant Reprieves and Pardons." This power derives from the ancient right to appeal to the king to reverse errors of law or justice committed by the court system. It is absolute: the president may grant pardons to anyone convicted of a *federal* crime for any reason. The most celebrated use of the presidential pardon was President Ford's blanket pardon of former President Nixon "for all offenses against the United States which he, Richard Nixon, has committed or may have committed or taken part in." Ford defended the pardon as necessary to end "the bitter controversy and divisive national debate," but his actions may have helped cause his defeat in the 1976 election.

Executive Power

The Constitution declares that the "executive Power" shall be vested in the president, but it is unclear whether this statement grants the president any powers that are not specified later in the Constitution or given to the president by acts of Congress. In other words, does the grant of "executive Power" give presidents constitutional authority to act as they deem necessary *beyond* the actions specified elsewhere in the Constitution or specified in laws passed by Congress?

Contrasting views on this question have been offered over two centuries. President William Howard Taft provided the classic narrow interpretation of executive power: "The president can exercise no power which cannot be fairly and reasonably traced to some specific grant of power or justly implied and included within such express grant as proper and necessary to its exercise."[2] Theodore Roosevelt, Taft's bitter opponent in a three-way race for the presidency in 1912, expressed the opposite view: "My belief was that it was not only his right but his duty to do anything that the needs of the nation demanded, unless such action was forbidden by the Constitution or by the laws."[3] Although the constitutional question has never been fully resolved, history has generally sided with those presidents who have taken an expansive view of their powers.

Some Historical Examples

U.S. history is filled with examples of presidents acting independently, beyond specific constitutional powers or laws of Congress. Among the most notable:

- George Washington issued a Proclamation of Neutrality during the war between France and Britain following the French Revolution, thereby establishing the president's power to make foreign policy.

Think Again

Should presidents have the power to take actions not specifically authorized by law or the Constitution that they believe necessary for the nation's well-being?

POLITICS UP CLOSE

Sex, Lies, and Impeachment

Bill Clinton is the second president in the nation's history (following Andrew Johnson in 1867) to be impeached by the U.S. House of Representatives. (President Richard Nixon resigned just prior to an impeachment vote in 1974.)

Clinton's impeachment followed a report to the House by Independent Counsel Kenneth Starr in 1998 that accused the president of perjury, obstruction of justice, witness tampering, and "abuse of power." The Starr Report describes in graphic and lurid detail Clinton's sexual relationship with young White House intern Monica Lewinsky.

Does engaging in extramarital sex and lying about it meet the Constitution's standard for impeachment—"Treason, Bribery, or other High Crimes and Misdemeanors"? Perjury—knowingly giving false testimony in a sworn legal proceeding—is a criminal offense. But does the Constitution envision more serious misconduct?

How are such questions decided? Despite pious rhetoric in Congress about the "search for truth," "impartial investigation," and "unbiased constitutional judgment," the impeachment process, whatever the merits of the charges against a president, is *political*, not judicial.

The House vote to impeach Clinton on December 19, 1998 (228 to 205), was largely along partisan lines, with all but five Republicans voting "yes" and all but five Democrats voting "no." And the vote in Clinton's Senate "trial" on February 12, 1999, was equally partisan. Even on the strongest charge—that Clinton had tried to obstruct justice—the Senate failed to find the president guilty. Removing Clinton failed to win even a majority of Senate votes, far less than the required two-thirds. All forty-five Democrats were joined by five Republicans to create a 50–50 tie vote that left Clinton tarnished but still in office.

Most Americans believed the president had a sexual affair in the White House and subsequently lied about it; however, they also *approved* of the way Clinton was performing his job as president. Indeed, the public appeared to rally around the president following the allegations of sexual misconduct.

Various explanations have been offered for this apparent paradox—a public that believed the president

President Clinton greets well-wishers, including Monica Lewinsky, at a Democratic Party event in January 1996. Clinton's acknowledged "inappropriate behavior," and his efforts to conceal his relationship with Lewinsky were the subjects of the impeachment investigation opened against him by the House in 1998.

had an affair in the White House and lied about it, yet gave the president the highest approval ratings of his career. Many Americans believe that private sexual conduct is irrelevant to the performance of public duties. Haven't we had adulterous presidents before, from Thomas Jefferson to John F. Kennedy, presidents who are ranked highly in history?

Others argue, however, that private character counts in presidential performance, indeed, that it is a prerequisite for public trust. The president, in this view, performs a symbolic role that requires dignity, honesty, and respect. The acceptance of a president's adulterous behavior, according to one commentator, lowers society's standards of behavior. "The president's legacy . . . will be a further vulgarization and demoralization of society."[a]

[a]Gertrude Himmelfarb, "Private Lives, Public Morality," *New York Times*, February 9, 1998.

- Thomas Jefferson, who prior to becoming president argued for a narrow interpretation of presidential powers, purchased the Louisiana Territory despite the fact that the Constitution contains no provision for the acquisition of territory, let alone authorizing presidential action to do so.

- Andrew Jackson ordered the removal of federal funds from the national bank and removed his secretary of the treasury from office, establishing the president's power to *remove* executive officials, a power not specifically mentioned in the Constitution.

- Abraham Lincoln, asking, "Was it possible to lose the nation yet preserve the Constitution?" established the precedent of vigorous presidential action in national emergencies: he blockaded southern ports, declared martial law in parts of the country, and issued the Emancipation Proclamation—all without constitutional or congressional authority.

- Franklin D. Roosevelt, battling the Great Depression during the 1930s, ordered the nation's banks to close temporarily. Following the Japanese attack on Pearl Harbor in 1941, he ordered the incarceration without trial of many thousands of Americans of Japanese ancestry living on the West Coast.

Think Again

Should Congress have the authority to call home U.S. troops sent by the president to engage in military actions overseas?

Watergate
The scandal that led to the forced resignation of President Richard M. Nixon. Adding "-gate" as a suffix to any alleged corruption in government suggests an analogy to the Watergate scandal.

executive privilege
Right of a president to withhold from other branches of government confidential communications within the executive branch; although posited by presidents, it has been upheld by the Supreme Court only in limited situations.

Checking Presidential Power   President Harry Truman believed that "the president has the right to keep the country from going to hell," and he was willing to use means beyond those specified in the Constitution or authorized by Congress. In 1952, while U.S. troops were fighting in Korea, steelworkers at home were threatening to strike. Rather than cross organized labor by forbidding the strike under the terms of the Taft-Hartley Act of 1947 (which he had opposed), Truman chose to seize the steel mills by executive order and continue their operations under U.S. government control. The U.S. Supreme Court ordered the steel mills returned to their owners, however, acknowledging that the president may have inherent powers to act in a national emergency but arguing that Congress had provided a legal remedy, however distasteful to the president. Thus the president can indeed act to keep the country from "going to hell," but if Congress has already acted to do so, the president must abide by the law.[4]

The most dramatic illustration of the checking of presidential power was the forced resignation of Richard M. Nixon in 1974 (for details, see *Politics Up Close*: "Watergate and the Limits of Presidential Power"). Nixon's conduct inspired the intense hostility of the nation's media, particularly the prestigious *Washington Post*. His high public approval ratings following the Vietnam peace agreement plummeted. A Democratic-controlled Senate created a special committee to investigate **Watergate** that produced damaging revelations almost daily. Congressional Republicans began to desert the embattled president. The Supreme Court ordered him to turn over White House audiotapes to a special investigator, tapes that implicated Nixon in cash payments to the men who had burglarized the Democratic National Committee offices during his 1972 reelection campaign. Facing the enmity of the media, the loss of public approval, opposition from his own party in the Congress, and the failure of his constitutional claim of "executive privilege" in the Supreme Court, Nixon became the only president of the United States ever to resign that office.

Executive Privilege   Over the years, presidents and scholars have argued that the Constitution's establishment of a separate executive branch of government entitles the president to **executive privilege**—the right to keep confidential communications from other branches of government. Public exposure of internal executive communications would inhibit the president's ability to obtain candid advice from subordinates and would obstruct the president's ability to conduct negotiations with foreign governments or to command military operations.

But Congress has never recognized executive privilege. It has frequently tried to compel the testimony of executive officials at congressional hearings. Presidents

POLITICS UP CLOSE

Watergate and the Limits of Presidential Power

Richard Nixon is the only president ever to resign the office. He did so to escape certain impeachment by the House of Representatives and a certain guilty verdict in trial by the Senate. Yet Nixon's first term as president included a number of historic successes. He negotiated the first ever strategic nuclear arms limitation treaty, SALT I, with the Soviet Union. He changed the global balance of power in favor of the Western democracies by opening relations with the People's Republic of China and dividing the communist world. In his second term, he withdrew U.S. troops from Vietnam, negotiated a peace agreement, and ended one of America's longest and bloodiest wars. But his remarkable record is forever tarnished by his failure to understand the limits of presidential power.

Richard Nixon is the only president ever to resign the office. He did so in 1974 to avoid impeachment following the Watergate scandal. He is shown here leaving the White House for the last time.

On the night of June 17, 1972, five men with burglary tools and wiretapping devices were arrested in the offices of the Democratic National Committee in the Watergate Building in Washington. Also arrested were E. Howard Hunt, Jr., G. Gordon Liddy, and James W. McCord, Jr., all employed by the Committee to Reelect the President (CREEP). All pleaded guilty and were convicted, but U.S. District Court Judge John J. Sirica believed that the defendants were shielding whoever had ordered and paid for the operation.

Although there is no evidence that Nixon himself ordered or had prior knowledge of the break-in, he discussed with his chief of staff, H. R. Haldeman, and White House advisers John Ehrlichman and John Dean the advisability of payoffs to buy the defendants' silence. Nixon hoped his landslide electoral victory in November 1972 would put the matter to rest.

But a series of sensational revelations in the *Washington Post* kept the story alive. Using an inside source known only as Deep Throat, Bob Woodward and Carl Bernstein, investigative reporters for the *Post*, alleged that key members of Nixon's reelection committee, including its chairman, former Attorney General John Mitchell, and White House staff were actively involved in the break-in and, more important, in the subsequent attempts at a cover-up.

In February 1973, the U.S. Senate formed a Special Select Committee on Campaign Activities—the "Water-gate Committee"—to delve into Watergate and related activities. The committee's nationally televised hearings enthralled millions of viewers with lurid stories of "the White House horrors." John Dean broke with the White House and testified before the committee that he had earlier warned Nixon the cover-up was "a cancer growing on the presidency." Then, in a dramatic revelation, the committee—and the nation—learned that President Nixon maintained a secret tape-recording system in the Oval Office. Hoping that the tapes would prove or disprove charges of Nixon's involvement in the cover-up, the committee issued a subpoena to the White House. Nixon refused to comply, arguing that the constitutional separation of powers gave the president an "executive privilege" to withhold his private conversations from Congress. However, the U.S. Supreme Court, voting 8 to 0 in *United States v. Richard M. Nixon*, ordered Nixon to turn over the tapes.

Despite the rambling nature of the tapes, committee members interpreted them as confirming Nixon's involvement in the payoffs and cover-up. Informed by congressional leaders of his own party that impeachment by a majority of the House and removal from office by two-thirds of the Senate were assured, on August 9, 1974, Richard Nixon resigned his office.

On September 8, 1974, new President Gerald R. Ford pardoned former President Nixon "for all offenses against the United States which he, Richard Nixon, has committed or may have committed or taken part in" during his presidency. Upon his death in 1994, Nixon was eulogized for his foreign policy successes.

have regularly refused to appear themselves at congressional hearings and have frequently refused to allow other executive officials to appear or divulge specific information, citing executive privilege. The federal courts have generally refrained from intervening in this dispute between the executive and legislative branches. However, the Supreme Court has ruled that the president is not immune from court orders when illegal acts are under investigation. In *United States v. Nixon* (1974), the U.S. Supreme Court acknowledged that although the president might legitimately claim executive privilege where military or diplomatic matters are involved, such a privilege cannot be invoked in a criminal investigation. The Court ordered President Nixon to surrender tape recordings of White House conversations between the president and his advisers during the Watergate scandal.[5]

Presidential Impoundment   The Constitution states that "no Money shall be drawn from the Treasury, but in Consequence of appropriations made by Law" (Article I, Section 9). Clearly the president cannot spend money *not* appropriated by Congress. But the Constitution is silent on whether the president *must* spend all of the money appropriated by Congress for various purposes. Presidents from Thomas Jefferson onward frequently refused to spend money appropriated by Congress, an action referred to as **impoundment**. But taking advantage of a presidency weakened by the Watergate scandal, the Congress in 1974 passed the Budget and Impoundment Control Act, which requires the president to spend all appropriated funds. The act does provide, however, that presidents may send Congress a list of specific **deferrals**—items on which they wish to postpone spending—and **rescissions**—items they wish to cancel altogether. Congress by *resolution* (which cannot be vetoed by the president) may restore the deferrals and force the president to spend the money. Both houses of Congress must approve a rescission; otherwise the government must spend the money.

Responsibility to the Courts   The president is not "above the law"; that is, his conduct is not immune from judicial scrutiny. The president's official conduct must be lawful; federal courts may reverse presidential actions found to be unconstitutional or violative of laws of Congress. And presidents are not immune from criminal prosecution; they cannot ignore demands to provide information in criminal cases. However, the Supreme Court has held that the president has "absolute immunity" from civil suits "arising out of the execution of official duties."[6] In other words, the president cannot be sued for damages caused by actions or decisions that are within his constitutional or legal authority.

But can the president be sued for *private* conduct beyond the scope of his official duties? In 1997 the U.S. Supreme Court rejected the notion of presidential immunity from civil claims arising from actions outside of the president's official duties.[7]

Political Resources of the President

▶ 11.3 *Assess the sources of the president's political power.*

The real sources of presidential power are not found in the Constitution. The president's power is the *power to persuade*. As Harry Truman put it, "I sit here all day trying to persuade people to do things they ought to have sense enough to do without my persuading them. . . . That's all the powers of the president amount to."[8]

The president's political resources are potentially very great. The nation looks to the president for leadership, for direction, for reassurance. The president is

impoundment
Refusal by a president to spend monies appropriated by Congress; outlawed except with congressional consent by the Budget and Impoundment Control Act of 1974.

deferrals
Items on which a president wishes to postpone spending.

rescissions
Items on which a president wishes to cancel spending.

the focus of public and media attention. The president has the capacity to mobilize public opinion, to communicate directly with the American people, and to employ the symbols of office to advance policy initiatives in both foreign and domestic affairs.

The Reputation for Power   A reputation for power is itself a source of power. Presidents must strive to maintain the image of power in order to be effective. A president perceived as powerful, especially by the national media, can exercise great influence abroad with foreign governments and at home with the Congress, interest groups, and the executive bureaucracy. A president perceived as weak, unsteady, bumbling, or error prone will soon become unpopular and ineffective.

Presidential Popularity   Presidential popularity with the American people is a political resource. Popular presidents cannot always transfer their popularity into foreign policy successes or legislative victories, but popular presidents usually have more success than unpopular presidents.

Presidential popularity is regularly tracked in national opinion polls. For more than 40 years, national surveys have asked the American public: "Do you approve or disapprove of the way _____ is handling his job as president?" (see Figures 11.1 and 11.2). Analyses of variations over time in these poll results suggest some generalizations about presidential popularity (see Figure 11.1).

✔ *Think*
Again

Is presidential performance more related to character and personality than to policy positions?

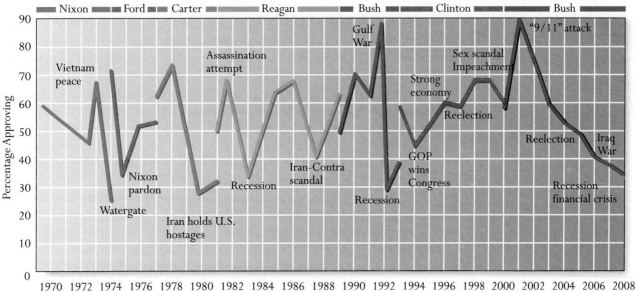

FIGURE 11.1 The Battle for Public Approval: Presidential Popularity over Time

Americans expect a great deal from their presidents and are quick to give these leaders the credit—and the blame—for major events in the nation's life. In general, public approval (as measured by response to the question "Do you approve or disapprove of the way _____ is handling the job of president?") is highest at the beginning of a new president's term in office and declines from that point. Major military conflicts generally raise presidential ratings initially but can cause dramatic decline if the conflict drags on. In addition, public approval of the president is closely linked to the nation's economic health. When the economy is in recession, Americans tend to take a negative view of the president.

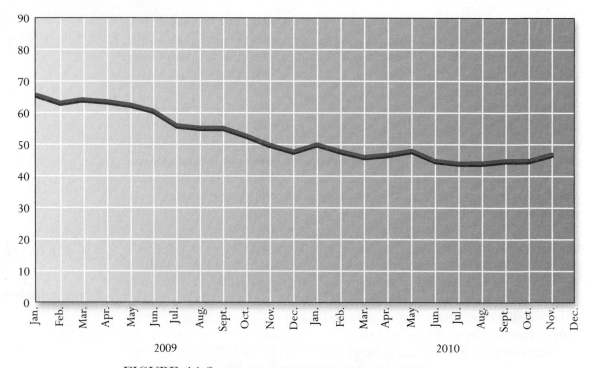

FIGURE 11.2 Barack Obama's Approval Ratings

President Obama began his term in office with high approval ratings, but over time his approval rating dropped to under 50 percent.

Source: Various polls reported in *The Polling Report, www.pollingreport.com*

Presidential popularity is usually high at the beginning of a president's term of office, but this "honeymoon" period can be very brief. The American public's high expectations for a new president can turn sour within a few months. A president's popularity will vary a great deal during a term in office, with sharp peaks and steep valleys in the ratings. But the general trend is downward.[9] Presidents usually recover some popularity at the end of their first term as they campaign for reelection.

Presidential popularity rises during crises. People "rally 'round the president" when the nation is confronted with an international threat or the president initiates a military action.[10] President George H. W. Bush, for example, registered nearly 90 percent approval during the Persian Gulf War. And the "9/11" terrorist attack on America rallied the American people behind George W. Bush (see Figure 11.1). But prolonged warfare and stalemate erode popular support. In both the Korean and the Vietnam wars, initial public approval of the president and support for the war eroded over time as military operations stalemated and casualties mounted.[11] And President George W. Bush suffered a prolonged erosion of approval as the Iraq War continued.

Major scandals *may* also hurt presidential popularity and effectiveness. The Watergate scandal produced a low of 22 percent approval for Nixon just prior to his resignation. Reagan's generally high approval ratings were blemished by the Iran-Contra scandal hearings in 1987, although he ultimately left office with a high approval rate. But highly publicized allegations of sexual improprieties against President Clinton in early 1998 appeared to have the opposite effect; Clinton's approval ratings went *up*. Perhaps the public differentiates between private sexual conduct and performance in office.

Finally, economic recessions erode presidential popularity. Every president in office during a recession has suffered loss of popular approval, including President Reagan during the 1982 recession. But no president suffered a more precipitous decline in approval ratings than George H. W. Bush, whose popularity plummeted from its Gulf War high of 89 percent in 1991 to a low of 37 percent in only a year, largely as a result of recession. His son's approval rating sank below 30 percent during the recession and financial crisis that engulfed the nation in 2008.

Access to the Media   The president dominates the news more than any other single person. All major television networks, newspapers, and news-magazines have reporters (usually their most experienced and skilled people) covering the "White House beat." The presidential press secretary briefs these reporters daily, but the president also may appear in person in the White House press room at any time. Presidents regularly use this media access to advance their programs and priorities.[12]

The **White House press corps** is an elite group of reporters assigned to cover the president. It includes the prestige press—the *New York Times, Washington Post, Wall Street Journal, Time, Newsweek, U.S. News & World Report,* as well as the television networks—ABC, CBS, NBC, CNN, FOX, and even the foreign press. Indeed, more than 1,800 journalists have White House press credentials. Fortunately, however, not all show up at once (there are only 48 seats in the White House briefing room, and attendance at press conferences is usually about 300). The great majority of daily newspapers have no Washington correspondents, but instead rely on national news services such as the Associated Press.

White House press corps
Reporters from both print and broadcast media assigned to regularly cover the president.

Formal press conferences are a double-edged sword for the president. They *can* help mobilize popular support for presidential programs. Presidents often try to focus attention on particular issues, and they generally open press conferences with a policy statement on these issues. But reporters' questions and subsequent report-ing often refocus the press conference in other directions. Often the lead media story emerging from a press conference has nothing to do with the president's purpose in holding the conference. The president cannot control questions or limit the subject matter of press conferences.

Presidents may also use direct television addresses from the White House. (President Reagan made heavy use of national prime-time television appeals to mobilize support for his programs; he was exceptionally successful in generating telephone calls, wires, and letters to Congress in support of his programs.) However, there is some evidence that with the multiplication of channels available to the public, presidential addresses may have less impact today on public opinion than in previous years. Television ratings for presidential addresses have been declining, and in reaction some broadcast networks have declined to cover presidential addresses.[13] Even the State of the Union Address attracts fewer viewers than in the past. Nonetheless, presidents continue to receive more television and press cover-age than any other political figure. And a combination of national speeches, press conferences, speeches to various groups around the country, and media interviews, together with public appearances by members of their administrations, can move public opinion in the president's direction.[14]

Personality Versus Policy

▶ 11.4 *Analyze how presidents' own personality and the policy positions impact their approval ratings.*

A president with an engaging personality—warmth, charm, and good humor—can add to his political power. And, of course, a president who seems distant, uncaring, or humorless can erode his political resources. (Richard Nixon's seeming mean-spiritedness contributed to the collapse of his approval ratings during the Watergate

PEOPLE IN POLITICS

Barack Obama, A Call for Change

Barack Obama, handsome, youthful, and charismatic, swept to the White House on the simple promise of "change," his African American heritage itself symbolizing change.

Early Life

Obama's father was born in Nyanza, Kenya, and came to the University of Hawaii as a foreign student. He met and married a fellow student, Ann Durham of Wichita, Kansas. Barack was 2 years old before they separated and divorced. Barack's inheritance from his father includes his middle name, Hussein. His mother remarried an Indonesian foreign student and the family moved to Jakarta where Barack attended elementary school. At age 10 he returned to Honolulu to live with his maternal grandparents. In his memoir, *Dreams from My Father*, Obama describes his experiences growing up in a white, upper-middle-class American family. He reflects on his struggles to reconcile the social perceptions of others of his multiracial background. He writes that he used alcohol, marijuana, and cocaine as a teenager "to push questions of who I was out of my mind."

Education

Obama attended Occidental College in Los Angeles for 2 years before transferring to Columbia University where he majored in political science and international relations. Upon graduation in 1983 he went to Chicago to work as a community organizer in a low-income public housing development. In 1988, he was admitted to Harvard Law school where he compiled an enviable record. He was elected president of the *Harvard Law Review,* the first African American to ever receive such an honor. Upon graduation in 1991, he returned to Chicago where he provided legal representation to community organizations and civil rights groups.

Audacity of Hope

Obama married Harvard Law School graduate Michelle Robinson in 1992; they have two daughters. He writes that he was detached from religion until his community work awakened him to "the power of the African American religious traditions to spawn social change." Obama and his wife joined the Trinity United Church of Christ on Chicago's South Side. At Trinity he was mentored by the charismatic and flamboyant pastor, Reverend Jeremiah Wright. He quickly mastered the cadence and phrasing of Wright's sermons, even using the title of a sermon, *The Audacity of Hope*, as the title of his autobiography. (Later, Wright's incendiary sermons would become a political burden and Obama would be obliged to "disown" his pastor and leave the church.) Through his community organizing and church affiliation, Obama gradually assembled a political base in Chicago politics.

scandal; Jimmy Carter's often cold and distant appearance failed to inspire much popular support for his programs; and George H. W. Bush appeared to be uncaring about the economic circumstances of ordinary Americans.) The public evaluates presidents as much on style as on policy substance.[15] (Perhaps no other president in recent times enjoyed so much personal popularity as Ronald Reagan.) If the public thinks the president understands and cares about their problems, they may be willing to continue to approve of the job he is doing despite policy setbacks. In other words, the public evaluates the president by how much they like him as a person. (President Bill Clinton's likability kept his public approval ratings high during the sex scandal and impeachment effort.) Yet, as we have seen, public approval ratings of presidents

Political Career

Obama was elected to the Illinois State Senate in 1996, representing Chicago's South-side neighborhood of Hyde Park. Obama's only political failure came in 2000 when he challenged a Chicago veteran politician, Bobby Rush, for his seat representing Illinois' predominantly black First Congressional District. The Chicago machine and Mayor Richard Daley supported Rush; Obama was soundly defeated. But the defeat taught Obama to work with the machine rather than against it. He made peace with Mayor Richard Daley. He sought the financial backing of white liberals including the Pritzker's, owners of Hyatt hotels. He lined up the support of powerful Illinois unions with mostly black membership—teachers, government employees, and service workers. By 2004, Obama was ready to reach for higher office.

In March 2004, Obama won the Democratic primary for an open U.S. Senate seat, winning 53 percent of the vote in a three-way race. He attracted national attention when he delivered the keynote address at the 2004 Democratic National Convention in Boston. His compelling call for unity gained him instant national celebrity: "We are one people, all of us pledging allegiance to the stars and stripes, all of us defending the United States of America." He went on to score a lopsided victory in the November general election of the U.S. Senate, winning 70 percent of the Illinois vote.

Obama was an early opponent of the war in Iraq, even before he was elected to the U.S. Senate. Indeed, in his primary battles against Senator Hillary Clinton, he criticized the New York senator for having initially supported military action in Iraq. Obama was a strong supporter of unsuccessful bills to cap troop levels in Iraq and to set deadlines for the withdrawal of U.S. forces.

Presidential Campaign

Obama demonstrated his appeal to white voters early in the primary campaign against New York senator Hillary Clinton. He skillfully steered his campaign around the rocks of racial division, distancing himself from the incendiary sermons of his Chicago pastor. And race never really emerged as a central issue in his election.

Obama chose "Change you can believe in" as his campaign theme. He stayed "on message" throughout the long primary battle with New York Senator Hillary Clinton (see *Politics Up Close*: "Hillary Versus Barack" in Chapter 7). Democratic primary voters and caucus goers had a historic choice of either the first woman presidential nominee of a major party or the first African American. Clinton claimed that she won more primary votes than Obama, but the Obama campaign wisely focused on gathering convention delegates. In the end, the unelected superdelegates chose to support the candidate with the most elected delegates, Barack Obama.

Obama carried his message of "change" into the general election campaign. As a young (47-year-old), handsome, athletic African American, he personified change. His image contrasted starkly with the aging (72-year-old) John McCain. Obama led McCain in the polls from the very beginning of the race. Only once, after the Republican convention and McCain's selection of Sarah Palin as his running mate, was McCain temporarily tied with Obama in the polls (see *Politics Up Close*: "Campaign '08—Obama Versus McCain" in Chapter 8). McCain's slim chances for victory evaporated with the financial meltdown in September. Obama won 53 percent of the popular vote.

Presidential Challenges

Perhaps Barack Obama's greatest challenge as president is to live up to the high expectations engendered by his election. President Obama inherited two wars, in Iraq and Afghanistan, as well as a recession-racked economy. He blamed much of the nation's problems on his predecessor, George W. Bush. But as time went on, Obama himself would be burdened with the problems of the nation. His promise of "change" would be set forth in a specific policy agenda, and Americans would decide whether this was the change that they wanted. (See *A Conflicting View:* "Is Big Government the 'Change' Americans Wanted" on page 399.)

can rise or fall based on wars and crises, scandals, and economic prosperity or recession, even while their personal style remains unaltered.

Party Leadership   Presidents are leaders of their party, but this role is hardly a source of great strength. It is true that presidents select the national party chair, control the national committee and its Washington staff, and largely direct the national party convention. Incumbent presidents can use this power to help defeat challengers *within* their own parties. President Ford used this power to help defeat challenger Ronald Reagan in 1976; President Carter used it to help defeat challenger Ted Kennedy in 1980; and President George H. W. Bush used it

A Media Forum

President Obama has held relatively few White House press conferences, preferring instead to travel to town halls outside of Washington, where questions are easier to handle than those coming from knowledgeable reporters.

against challenger Pat Buchanan in 1992. But the role of party leader is of limited value to a president in relations with Congress because the parties have few direct controls over their members (see Chapter 7).

Nevertheless, presidents enjoy much stronger support in Congress from members of their own party than from members of the opposition party. Some of the president's party support in Congress is a product of shared ideological values and policy positions. But Republican Congress members do have some stake in the success of a Republican president, as do Democratic members in the success of a Democratic president. Popular presidents may produce those few extra votes that make the difference for party candidates in close congressional districts.

Policy Leadership   Presidents feel an obligation to exercise policy leadership—develop a policy agenda, present it to the Congress, sell it to the American people, and lobby it through to success. Presidents are less likely than most politicians to pander to public opinion. Rather, they expect to be able to shape public opinion themselves.[16] (See *A Conflicting View*: "Is Big Government the 'Change' Americans Wanted?")

Nevertheless, there are times when presidents prudently decide to follow public opinion, rather than try to change it. First of all, presidents who are approaching a reelection contest become more responsive to public opinion. They are less likely to go off into new policy directions or to support unpopular policies. Generally, presidents present their policy initiatives at the beginning of their terms. This period usually corresponds to a president's high public approval rating. Indeed, throughout a presidential term, the higher their approval rating, the more likely they are to present new policy directions and even to take unpopular policy positions. In contrast, presidents experiencing low approval ratings are much less likely to present new policy initiatives or to pursue unpopular policies.[17]

A CONFLICTING VIEW

Is Big Government the "Change" Americans Wanted?

President Barack Obama's policy initiatives envision a vast expansion of the size and power of government, huge spending increases, and a massive federal debt. Is this the "change" Americans expected of their new president?

Wall Street Bailout   The Emergency Economic Stabilization Act of 2008 was supported by then president George W. Bush, the Democratic leadership in Congress, and both presidential candidates—Barack Obama and John McCain. But opinion polls showed that most Americans opposed a "Wall Street bailout." The Act gave the Treasury Department unprecedented power to bail out the nation's financial institutions. The Troubled Asset Relief Program (TARP) allocated over $700 billion to aid banks, insurance companies, and investment firms that held mortgage-backed "toxic assets." General Motors was added to the list of corporations receiving government assistance. Government loans were secured by preferred stock shares. Critics of the program noted that by accepting ownership shares in banks and corporations, the government was tilting toward "socialism."

The "Stimulus" Package   A massive economic "stimulus" plan was President Obama's principal response to the recession. Its combination of spending increases and tax cuts totaled $787 billion—the largest single fiscal policy measure in American history. It was financed by an unprecedented increase in the nation's deficit. Republicans complained that much of the spending had little to do with creating jobs, but instead only increased government involvement in domestic policy areas favored by liberals and Democrats.

Health Care Reform   President Obama's comprehensive health care reform program promises to transform one-sixth of the nation's economy. At the center of the reform is an individual mandate—a requirement that all Americans acquire basic health insurance. Federally supervised Health Insurance Exchanges are to be created in the states to negotiate with insurance companies to provide individuals and small businesses with affordable insurance. Private insurers will no longer be permitted to deny insurance for pre-existing conditions, or to drop coverage when patients get sick. The president failed in his efforts to get a government-run insurance program, a "public option," included in the legislation. The Congressional Budget Office estimated the cost of Obama's health care reform at nearly $1 trillion.

Greater Financial Regulation   New regulation and oversight of the nation's financial institutions is designed to avoid future financial crises. A new agency has been created to protect consumers from predatory and deceptive credit card and mortgage loan practices. New authority is granted to the Federal Reserve to intervene when banks, insurance companies, and investment firms considered "too big to fail" face financial difficulties. Critics charged that the government was being authorized to "take over" the nation's financial system.

Cap and Trade   President Obama proposed a new carbon emission ceiling and trading program known as "cap and trade." The federal government would set a total amount of emission allowances, that is, a national "cap" (or ceiling) on carbon emissions. The government would then allocate or auction off to polluting industries and firms tradable emissions allowances. In effect, industries would be given or sold allowances to pollute; these allowances could then be bought and sold among firms. The system is said to encourage innovation by individual firms; if they are successful in reducing their emissions, they can sell their allowances to other firms. The cost of the program will be borne by all energy users, passed on by industries in the form of price increases. A large government bureaucracy will be needed to monitor and enforce emission allowances.

Redistributing Wealth Via the Tax Code   Barack Obama campaigned on a promise to lower taxes on the middle class, which he defined as 95 percent of taxpayers. He also pledged to raise taxes on upper-income Americans, which he defined as families earning $250,000 a year or more. The Bush tax cuts expired at the end of 2010, resulting in an increase in the top marginal tax rate from 35 to 39.6 percent. The economic "stimulus" package included "Making Work Pay" payments of $400 to individuals with incomes under $75,000 and payments of $800 to couples with incomes under $150,000. This combination of changes in the Tax Code—tax payments to lower- and middle-income families and an increase in the top marginal tax rate—has the effect of redistributing after-tax income among Americans.

As government expands across a broad range of policy areas, it grows in size and complexity. As government spending increases, the nation goes deeper into debt. Americans increasingly are looking to government, however, rather than to themselves to resolve their problems. In an earlier era, President Ronald Reagan set the tone of American politics: "Government is not the solution. Government is the problem." But clearly under President Obama's vision of "change," government becomes the solution.

Chief Executive

▶ 11.5 *Outline the responsibilities of the president as the nation's chief executive.*

The president is the chief executive of the nation's largest bureaucracy: 2.8 million civilian employees, 60 independent agencies, 15 departments, and the large Executive Office of the President. The formal organizational chart of the federal government places the president at the head of this giant structure (see Figure 12.1, "The Federal Bureaucracy," in Chapter 12). But the president cannot command this bureaucracy in the fashion of a military officer or a corporation president. When Harry Truman was preparing to turn over the White House to Dwight Eisenhower, he predicted that the general of the army would not understand the presidency: "He'll sit here and say 'Do this! Do that!' and nothing will happen. Poor Ike—it won't be a bit like the army. He'll find it very frustrating." Truman vastly underestimated the political skills of the former general, but the crusty Missourian clearly understood the frustrations confronting the nation's chief executive. The president does not command the executive branch of government but rather stands at its center—persuading, bargaining, negotiating, and compromising to achieve goals.

The Constitutional Executive   The Constitution is vague about the president's authority over the executive branch. It vests executive power in the presidency and grants the president authority to appoint principal officers of the government "by and with the Advice and Consent of the Senate." Under the Constitution, the president may also "require the Opinion, in writing, of the principal Officer in each of the executive Departments, upon any Subject relating to the Duties of their respective Offices." This awkward phrase presumably gives the president the power to oversee operations of the executive departments. Finally, and perhaps most important, the president is instructed to "take Care that the Laws be faithfully executed."

At the same time, Congress has substantial authority over the executive branch. Through its lawmaking abilities, Congress can establish or abolish executive departments and regulate their operations. Congress's "power of the purse" allows it to determine the budget of each department each year and thus to limit or broaden or even "micromanage" the activities of these departments. Moreover, Congress can pressure executive agencies by conducting investigations, calling administrators to task in public hearings, and directly contacting agencies with members' own complaints or those of their constituents.

executive orders
Formal regulations governing executive branch operations issued by the president.

Executive Orders   Presidents frequently use **executive orders** to implement their policies. Executive orders may direct specific federal agencies to carry out the president's wishes, or they may direct all federal agencies to pursue the president's preferred course of action. In any case, they must be based on either a president's constitutional powers or on powers delegated to the president by laws of Congress. Presidents regularly issue 50 to 100 executive orders each year, but some stand out. In 1942, President Franklin D. Roosevelt issued Executive Order 9066 for the internment of Japanese Americans during World War II. In 1948, President Harry Truman issued Executive Order 9981 to desegregate the U.S. armed forces. In 1965 President Lyndon Johnson issued Executive Order 11246 to require that private firms with federal contracts institute affirmative action programs. A president can even declare a national emergency by executive order, a step that authorizes a broad range of unilateral actions.

Executive orders have legal force when they are based on the president's constitutional or statutory authority. And presidents typically take an expansive view of their own authority. (President George Washington issued an executive order declaring American neutrality in the war between France and England in 1793. While the Constitution gave the power to "declare war" to Congress, Washington assumed the authority to declare neutrality.) Federal courts have generally upheld presidential executive orders. However, the Supreme Court overturned an order by President Harry Truman in 1951 during the Korean War seizing the nation's steel mills.[18] Research on the frequency of executive orders suggests that: Democratic presidents issue more orders than Republican presidents; presidents may issue executive orders to circumvent Congress but only when they believe that Congress will not overturn their orders; and presidents issue more executive orders when they are running for reelection.[19]

Appointments   Presidential power over the executive branch derives in part from the president's authority to appoint and remove top officials. Presidents can shape policy by careful attention to top appointments—cabinet secretaries, assistant secretaries, agency heads, and White House staff. The key is to select people who share the president's policy views and who have the personal qualifications to do an effective job. However, in cabinet appointments political considerations weigh heavily: unifying various elements of the party; appealing for interest-group support; rewarding political loyalty; providing a temporary haven for unsuccessful party candidates; achieving a balance of racial, ethnic, and gender representation.[20] The appointment power gives the president only limited control over the executive branch of government. Of the executive branch's 2.8 million civilian employees, the president actually appoints only about 3,000. The vast majority of federal executive branch employees are civil servants—recruited, paid, and protected under civil service laws—and are not easily removed or punished by the president. Cabinet secretaries and heads of independent regulatory agencies require congressional confirmation, but presidents can choose their own White House staff without the approval of Congress.

Presidents have only limited power to remove the heads of independent regulatory agencies. By law, Congress sets the terms of these officials. Federal Communications Commission members are appointed for 5 years; Securities and Exchange Commission members for 5 years; and Federal Reserve Board members, responsible for the nation's money supply, enjoy the longest term of any executive officials—14 years. Congress's responsibility for term length for regulatory agencies is supposed to insulate those agencies, in particular their quasi-judicial responsibilities, from "political" influence.

Budget   Presidential authority also derives from the president's role in the budgetary process. The Constitution makes no mention of the president with regard to expenditures; rather, it grants the power of the purse to Congress. Indeed, for nearly 150 years, executive departments submitted their budget requests directly to the Congress without first submitting them to the president. But with the passage of the Budget and Accounting Act in 1921, Congress established the Office of Management and Budget (OMB) (originally named the Bureau of the Budget) to assist the president in preparing an annual Budget of the United States Government for presentation to the Congress. The president's budget is simply a set of recommendations to the Congress. Congress must pass appropriations acts before the president or any executive department or agency

Burdens of the Oval Office
The American people hold the president responsible for just about everything that happens in the country, whether or not he has the power to do anything about it.

TABLE 11.2 The Cabinet Departments

By custom, the fifteen executive departments are ranked by their dates of creation.	
Department	**Created**
State	1789
Treasury	1789
Defense*	1947
Justice	1789
Interior	1849
Agriculture†	1889
Commerce	1913
Labor	1913
Health and Human Services‡	1953
Housing and Urban Development	1965
Transportation	1966
Energy	1977
Education	1979
Veterans' Affairs	1989
Homeland Security	2002

*Formerly the War and Navy Departments, created in 1789 and 1798, respectively.

†Agriculture Department created in 1862, made part of cabinet in 1889.

‡Originally Health, Education, and Welfare; reorganized in 1979, with the creation of a separate Department of Education.

may spend money. Congress can and frequently does alter the president's budget recommendations (see "The Politics of Budgeting" in Chapter 12).

cabinet
The heads (secretaries) of the executive departments together with other top officials accorded cabinet rank by the president; only occasionally does it meet as a body to advise and support the president.

The Cabinet The **cabinet** is not mentioned in the U.S. Constitution; it has no formal powers. It consists of the secretaries of the fifteen executive departments and others the president may designate, including the vice president, the Administrator of the Environmental Protection Agency, the Director of the Office of Management and Budget, the Director of National Drug Control Policy, and the Special Trade Representative. According to custom, cabinet officials are ranked by the date their departments were created (see Table 11.2). Thus the secretary of

Obama with Cabinet
President Obama meeting with his cabinet. The president calls his cabinet together to explain and promote his views, not to decide issues.

PEOPLE IN POLITICS

Rahm Emanuel—Exercising Power Behind the Scenes

Barack Obama and Rahm Emanuel in the Oval Office

Prior to running for Mayor of Chicago, Rahm Emanuel was White House Chief of Staff. He was responsible for orchestrating President Obama's extensive policy agenda. According to Emanuel, "Never allow a crisis to go to waste. Crises are opportunities to do big things." Emanuel's "big things" included bailing out the nation's financial institutions, stimulating the nation's economy, increasing federal spending and deficit levels, making the tax structure more progressive, transforming the nation's health-care system, bringing about a new "cap and trade" energy initiative, and reforming immigration, among other things.

Emanuel's first name, Rahm, means "high" or "lofty" in Hebrew. Emanuel was born and raised in Chicago; he and his brothers went to summer camp in Israel. He attended the Evanston School of Ballet and later graduated from Sarah Lawrence College in 1981. He received a master's degree in speech and communication from Northwestern University in 1985. During the first Gulf War he served with the Israel Defense Forces as a civilian volunteer. He began his political career as a public

interest and consumer rights organizer for Illinois Public Action. But his real strength was in political fund-raising: he served as chief fund-raiser for Chicago Mayor Richard M. Daley and later as chairman of Bill Clinton's campaign finance committee in the presidential election of 1992. Following the campaign, Emanuel became a senior adviser in the Clinton White House; but he was unsuccessful in getting Hillary's health care plan through Congress. In 1998, Emanuel left the Clinton White House to become an investment banker in Chicago. He became a Director of the Federal Home Loan Mortgage Corp. (Freddie Mac), a position that would later hurt his reputation when Freddie Mac collapsed in 2008.

Emanuel resigned his investment banker post to run for the U.S. House of Representatives in 2002, for the seat vacated by Rod Blagojevich (who had just won the Illinois governorship). Emanuel defeated seven other candidates in the Democratic primary and went on to easily win the general election. Upon entering Congress he was appointed to the House Financial Services Committee, which oversees Freddie Mac. The Democratic leadership in the House recognized Emanuel's fund-raising skills and named him chair of the Democratic Congressional Campaign Committee in 2006. He proved successful in eliciting campaign contributions from the securities and investment industry. The Democratic sweep of Congress that year added to Emanuel's reputation as a political strategist. He also gained a reputation in the Congress as a highly partisan, Chicago-style, combative liberal.

Upon taking office Barack Obama recognized that he needed a well-connected powerbroker to oversee his vast policy agenda. Emanuel resigned his seat in the House and took over the White House on Inauguration Day. But after two years of exercising power behind the scenes, Emanuel left the White House to run for Mayor of Chicago.

state is the senior cabinet officer, followed by the secretary of the treasury. They sit next to the president at cabinet meetings; heads of the newest departments sit at the far ends of the table.

The cabinet rarely functions as a decision-making body. Cabinet officers in the United States are powerful because they head giant administrative organizations. The secretary of state, the secretary of defense, the secretary of the treasury, the attorney general, and, to a lesser extent, the other departmental secretaries are all people of power and prestige. But seldom does a strong president hold a cabinet meeting to decide important policy questions. More frequently, presidents know what they want and hold cabinet meetings only to help promote their views.

The Constitution requires that "Officers of the United States" be confirmed by the Senate. In the past, the Senate rarely rejected a presidential cabinet nomination; the traditional view was that presidents were entitled to pick their own people and even make their own mistakes. In recent years, however, the confirmation process has become more partisan and divisive, with the Senate conducting lengthy investigations and holding public hearings on presidential cabinet nominees. The intense public scrutiny and potential for partisan attacks, together with financial disclosure and conflict-of-interest laws, may be discouraging some well-qualified people from accepting cabinet posts.

The National Security Council   The **National Security Council** (NSC) is really an "inner cabinet" created by law in 1947 to advise the president and coordinate foreign, defense, and intelligence activities. The president is chair, and the vice president, secretary of state, secretary of defense and secretary of the treasury are participating members. The chair of the Joint Chiefs of Staff and the director of central intelligence serve as advisers to the NSC. The president's national security adviser also sits on the NSC and heads its staff. The purposes of the council are to advise and coordinate policy; but in the Iran-Contra scandal in 1987, a staff member of the NSC, Lt. Col. Oliver North, undertook to *implement* security policy by directly channeling funds and arms to Nicaraguan "contras" fighting a communist-dominated government. Various investigative committees strongly recommended that the NSC staff confine itself to an advisory role.

White House Staff   Today, presidents exercise their powers chiefly through the White House staff. This staff includes the president's closest aides and advisers. Over the years, the White House staff has grown from Roosevelt's small "brain trust" of a dozen advisers to several hundred people.

Senior White House staff members are trusted political advisers, often personal friends or long-time associates of the president (see *People in Politics*: "Rahm Emanuel—Exercising Power Behind the Scenes"). Some enjoy office space in the White House itself and daily contact with the president (see Figure 11.3). Appointed without Senate confirmation, they are loyal to the president alone, not to departments, agencies, or interest groups. Their many tasks include the following:

- Providing the president with sound advice on everything from national security to congressional affairs, policy development, and electoral politics.

- Monitoring the operations of executive departments and agencies and evaluating the performance of key executive officials.

- Setting the president's schedule, determining whom the president will see and call, where and when the president will travel, and where and to whom the president will make personal appearances and speeches.

- Above all, protecting their boss and steering the president away from scandal, political blunders, and errors of judgment.

The senior White House staff normally includes a chief of staff, the national security adviser, a press secretary, the counsel to the president (an attorney), a director of personnel (patronage appointments), and assistants for political affairs, legislative liaison, and domestic policy. Staff organization depends on each president's personal taste. Some presidents have organized their staffs hierarchically, concentrating power in the chief of staff. Others have maintained direct contact with several staff members.

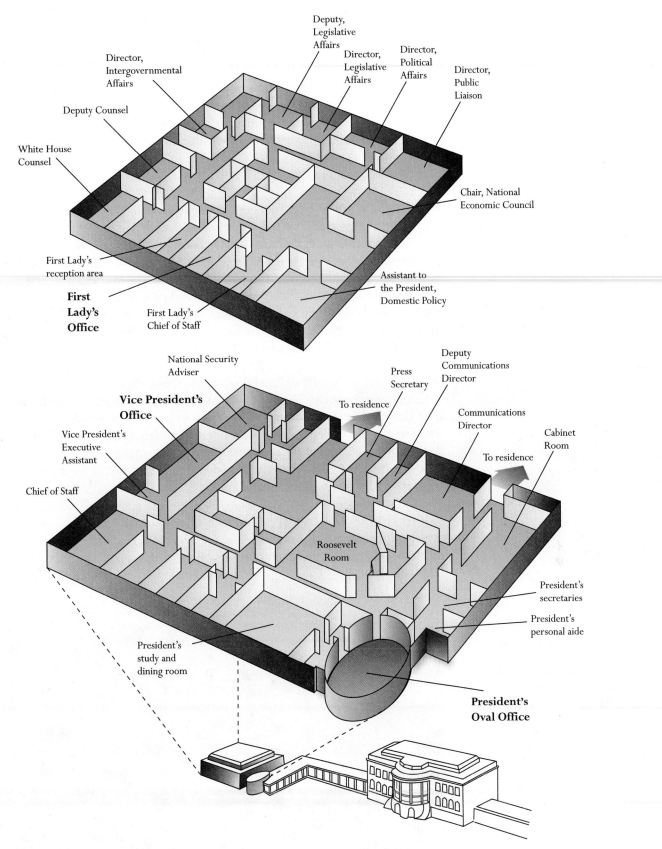

FIGURE 11.3 Corridors of Power: The White House West Wing

Presidents allocate office space in the White House according to their own desires. An office located close to the president's is considered an indication of the power of the occupant. This diagram shows the office assignments during the Clinton administration.

Chief Legislator and Lobbyist

▶ 11.6 *Analyze the factors affecting the success of the president as the chief legislator and lobbyist.*

The president has the principal responsibility for the initiation of national policy. Indeed, about 80 percent of the bills considered by Congress originate in the executive branch. Presidents have a strong incentive to fulfill this responsibility: the American people hold them responsible for anything that happens in the nation during their term of office, whether or not they have the authority or capacity to do anything about it.

Policy Initiation The Founders understood that the president would be involved in policy initiation. The Constitution requires the president to "give to the Congress Information of the State of the Union," to "recommend to their Consideration such Measures as he shall judge necessary and expedient" (Article II, Section 3). "On extraordinary Occasions" the president may call a recessed Congress into special session. Each year the principal policy statement of the president comes in the State of the Union message to Congress. It is followed by the president's Budget of the United States Government, which sets forth the president's programs with price tags attached. Many other policy proposals are developed by executive departments and agencies, transmitted to the White House for the president's approval or "clearance," and then sent to Congress.

Congress may not accept all or even most of the president's proposals. Indeed, from time to time it may even try to develop its own legislative agenda in competition with the president's. But the president's legislative initiatives usually set the agenda of congressional decision making. As one experienced Washington lobbyist put it, "Obviously when the president sends up a bill, it takes first place in the queue. All other bills take second place."[21]

White House Lobbying Presidents do not simply send their bills to Congress and then await the outcome. The president is also expected to be the chief lobbyist on behalf of the administration's bills as they make their way through the legislative labyrinth. The White House staff includes "legislative liaison" people—

Working with Congress

Presidents are expected to provide policy leadership and to work for congressional passage of their policy proposals. Here President Obama meets with the House leadership, including speaker Nancy Pelosi and Republican minority leader John Boehner.

lobbyists for the president's programs. They organize the president's legislative proposals, track them through committee and floor proceedings, arrange committee appearances by executive department and agency representatives, count votes, and advise the president on when and how to "cut deals" and "twist arms."

Presidents are not without resources in lobbying Congress. They may exchange many favors, large and small, for the support of individual members. They can help direct "pork" to a member's district, promise White House support for a member's pet project, and assist in resolving a member's problems with the bureaucracy. Presidents also may issue or withhold invitations to the White House for prestigious ceremonies, dinners with visiting heads of state, and other glittering social occasions—an effective resource because most members of Congress value the prestige associated with close White House "connections."[22]

The president may choose to "twist arms" individually—by telephoning and meeting with wavering members of Congress. Arm twisting is generally reserved for the president's most important legislative battles. There is seldom time for a president to contact individual members of Congress personally about many bills in various stages of the legislative process—in subcommittee, full committee, floor consideration, conference committee, and final passage—in both the House and the Senate. Instead, the president must rely on White House staff for most legislative contacts and use personal appeals sparingly.

President Barack Obama has relied more on an "outside strategy" for lobbying Congress, rather than direct efforts at "twisting arms" or "cutting deals" with individual members. Obama has boosted his legislative proposals in speeches and town meetings across the country in attempts to rally the grassroots. Even some of his supporters have complained that he leaves to Congress many of the details of bills, as well as the negotiations and compromises needed to pass legislation. The result is the empowerment of congressional committee chairs and Senate Majority Leader Harry Reid and the Speaker of the House Nancy Pelosi.

The Honeymoon

The **honeymoon period** at the very start of a president's term offers the best opportunity to get the new administration's legislative proposals enacted into law. Presidential influence in Congress is generally highest at this time both because the president's personal popularity is typically at its height and because the president can claim the recent election results as a popular mandate for key programs. Sophisticated members of Congress know that votes cast for a presidential candidate are not necessarily votes cast for that candidate's policy positions (see "The Voter Decides" in Chapter 8). But election results signal members of Congress, in a language they understand well, that the president is politically popular and that they must give the administration's programs careful consideration. President Lyndon Johnson succeeded in getting the bulk of his Great Society program enacted in the year following his landslide victory in 1964. Ronald Reagan pushed through the largest tax cut in American history in the year following his convincing electoral victory over incumbent president Jimmy Carter in 1980. Bill Clinton was most successful with the Congress during his first year in office, in 1993, even winning approval for a major tax increase as part of a deficit-reduction package. And George W. Bush succeeded in getting a tax cut through Congress in his first six months in office. Both Democrat Clinton and Republican Bush benefited from having their party control the Congress during their first months in office.

Democrat Barack Obama enjoyed Democratic control of the House and Senate in his first years in office. His overall success rate in Congress exceeded any previous president.

honeymoon period
Early months of a president's term in which his popularity with the public and influence with the Congress are generally high.

Presidential "Box Scores" How successful are presidents in getting their legislation through Congress? *Congressional Quarterly* regularly compiles "box scores" of presidential success in Congress—percentages of presidential victories on congressional votes on which the president took a clear-cut position. The measure does not distinguish between bills that were important to the president and bills that may have been less significant. But viewed over time (see Figure 11.4), the presidential box scores provide interesting insights into the factors affecting the president's legislative success.

The most important determinant of presidential success in Congress is party control. Presidents are far more successful when they face a Congress controlled by their own party. Democratic presidents John F. Kennedy and Lyndon Johnson enjoyed the support of Democratic-controlled Congresses and posted average success scores over 80 percent. Jimmy Carter was hardly a popular president, but he enjoyed the support of a Democratic Congress and an average of 76.8 percent presidential support. Republican presidents Richard Nixon and Gerald Ford fared poorly with Democratic-controlled Congresses. Republican president Ronald Reagan was very successful in his first term when he faced a Democratic House and a Republican Senate, but after Democrats took over both houses of Congress, Reagan's success rate plummeted. During the Reagan and Bush presidencies, divided party control of government (Republicans in the White House

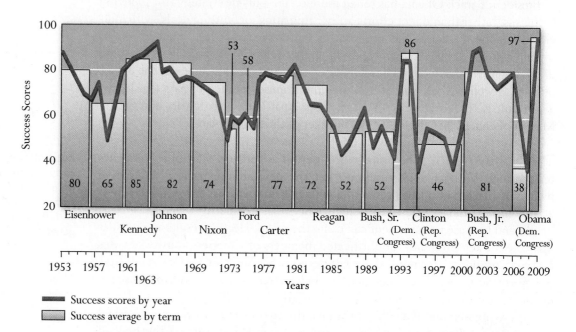

FIGURE 11.4 Box Scores: Presidential Success in Congress

Presidential "box scores"—the percentage of times that a bill endorsed by the president is enacted by Congress—are closely linked to the strength of the president's party in Congress. For example, both Dwight D. Eisenhower and Ronald Reagan benefited from having a Republican majority in the Senate in their first terms and suffered when Democrats gained control of the Senate in their second terms. Democratic control of both houses of Congress resulted in high box scores for Democratic presidents John Kennedy, Lyndon Johnson, and Jimmy Carter. Clinton was very successful in his first 2 years, when the Democrats controlled Congress, but when the Republicans won control following the 1994 midterm election, Clinton's box score plummeted. When George W. Bush enjoyed a Republican Congress, he succeeded in passing over 80 percent of his bills; but his success fell dramatically with the election of a Democratic Congress. Presidents succeed most often in their first year in office—the "honeymoon" period. Barack Obama enjoyed a record success rate in his first year.

The president is recognized throughout the world as the American "head of state"; this power aids him in dominating American foreign and defense policy making. Here President Obama meets with Chinese President Hu Jintao.

powers in foreign affairs are relatively modest. Presidents have the power to make treaties with foreign nations "with the Advice and Consent of the Senate." Presidents may negotiate with nations separately or through international organizations such as the North Atlantic Treaty Organization (NATO) or the United Nations, where the president determines the U.S. position in that body's deliberations. The Constitution also empowers the president to "appoint Ambassadors, other public Ministers, and Consuls" and to "receive Ambassadors." This power of **diplomatic recognition** permits a president to grant legitimacy to or withhold it from ruling groups around the world (to declare or refuse to declare them "rightful"). Despite controversy, President Franklin Roosevelt officially recognized the communist regime in Russia in 1933, Richard Nixon recognized the communist government of the People's Republic of China in 1972, and Carter recognized the communist Sandinistas' regime in Nicaragua in 1979. To date, all presidents have withheld diplomatic recognition of the Castro government in Cuba.

diplomatic recognition
Power of the president to grant "legitimacy" to or withhold it from a government of another nation (to declare or refuse to declare it "rightful").

Presidents have expanded on these modest constitutional powers to dominate American foreign policy making. In part, they have done so as a product of their role as Commander-in-Chief. Military force is the ultimate diplomatic language. During wartime, or when war is threatened, military and foreign policy become inseparable. The president must decide on the use of force and, equally important, when and under what conditions to order a cease-fire or an end to hostilities.

Presidents have also come to dominate foreign policy as a product of the customary international recognition of the head of state as the legitimate voice of a government. Although nations may also watch the words and actions of the American Congress, the president's statements are generally taken to represent the official position of the U.S. government.

Treaties Treaties the president makes "by and with the Advice and Consent of the Senate" are legally binding upon the United States. The Constitution specifies that "all Treaties made . . . under the Authority of the United States, shall be the supreme Law of the Land, and the Judges in every State shall be bound thereby" (Article VI). Thus **treaty** provisions are directly enforceable in federal courts.

treaty
A formal agreement with another nation (bilateral) or nations (multilateral) signed by the president and consented to by the Senate by a two-thirds vote.

Although presidents may or may not listen to "advice" from the Senate on foreign policy, no formal treaty is valid unless "two-thirds of the Senators present concur" to its ratification. Although the Senate has ratified the vast majority of treaties, presidents must be sensitive to Senate concerns. The Senate defeat of the Versailles Treaty in 1920, which formally ended World War I and established the League of Nations, prompted Presidents Roosevelt and Truman to include prominent Democratic and Republican members of the Senate Foreign Relations Committee in the delegations that drafted the United Nations Charter in 1945 and the NATO Treaty in 1949.

Executive Agreements   Over the years, presidents have come to rely heavily on **executive agreements** with other governments rather than formal treaties. An executive agreement signed by the president of the United States has much the same effect in international relations as a treaty. However, an executive agreement does not require Senate ratification. Presidents have asserted that their constitutional power to execute the laws, command the armed services, and determine foreign policy gives them the authority to make agreements with other nations and heads of state *without* obtaining approval of the U.S. Senate. However, unlike treaties, executive agreements do not supersede laws of the United States or of the states with which they conflict, but they are otherwise binding on the United States.

> **executive agreements**
> Agreements with other nations signed by the president of the United States but less formal (and hence potentially less binding) than a treaty because it does not require Senate confirmation.

The use of executive agreements in important foreign policy matters was developed by President Franklin Roosevelt. Prior to his administration, executive agreements had been limited to minor matters. But in 1940, Roosevelt agreed to trade fifty American destroyers to England in exchange for the use of naval bases in Newfoundland and the Caribbean. Roosevelt was intent on helping the British in their struggle against Nazi Germany, but before the Japanese attack on Pearl Harbor in 1941, isolationist sentiment in the Senate was too strong to win a two-thirds ratifying vote for such an agreement. Toward the end of World War II, Roosevelt at the Yalta Conference and Truman at the Potsdam Conference negotiated secret executive agreements dividing the occupation of Germany between the Western Allies and the Soviet Union.

Congress has sometimes objected to executive agreements as usurping its own powers. In the Case Act of 1972, Congress required the president to inform Congress of all executive agreements within 60 days, but the act does not limit the president's power to make agreements. It is easier for Congress to renege on executive agreements than on treaties that the Senate has ratified. In 1973 President Nixon signed an executive agreement with South Vietnamese President Nguyen Van Thieu pledging that the United States would "respond with full force" if North Vietnam violated the Paris Peace Agreement that ended American participation in the Vietnam War. But when North Vietnam reinvaded the south in 1975, Congress rejected President Gerald Ford's pleas for renewed military aid to the South Vietnamese government, and Ford knew that it had become politically impossible for the United States to respond with force.

Intelligence   The president is responsible for the intelligence activities of the United States. Presidents have undertaken intelligence activities since the founding of the nation. During the Revolutionary War, General George Washington nurtured small groups of patriots living behind British lines who supplied him with information on Redcoat troop movements.[26] Today, the Director of National Intelligence (DNI) is appointed by the president (subject to Senate confirmation) and reports directly to the president.

The DNI coordinates the activities of the "intelligence community." Some elements of the intelligence community—the Central Intelligence Agency, the Defense Intelligence Agency, the National Security Agency, the National Recon-

Secret Agreements

The "Big Three," comprised of Prime Minister Winston Churchill of Great Britain (right), Marshal Josef Stalin of the Soviet Union (left), and a gravely ill President Franklin Roosevelt (middle), traveled to Yalta, a port on Russia's Crimean peninsula, and negotiated secret executive agreements dividing Germany among the Allies in 1945. Germany remained divided until 1989, when protesters tore down the Berlin Wall and the Soviet Union under Mikhail Gorbachev acquiesced in the unification of Germany under a democratic government.

naissance Office, and the National Geo-Spacial Agency—deal exclusively with intelligence collection, analysis and distribution. Other elements of the intelligence community are located in the Department of Defense, Department of Homeland Security, Federal Bureau of Investigation, Department of State, Department of Energy, and Department of the Treasury. Indeed, the fragmentation of the intelligence community may be its principal weakness.[27]

The Central Intelligence Agency

The CIA provides intelligence on national security to the president, the DNI, the National Security Council, and other top Washington decision makers. The CIA is responsible for (1) assembly, analysis, and dissemination of intelligence information from all agencies in the intelligence community; (2) collection of human intelligence from abroad; (3) with specific "presidential findings," the conduct of **covert actions**, including paramilitary special operations.

Covert actions refer to activities in support of the national interest of the United States that would be ineffective if their sponsorship were made public. For example, one of the largest covert actions ever undertaken by the United States was the support, for nearly 10 years, of the Afghan rebels fighting Soviet occupation of their country during the Afghanistan War (1978–88). Public acknowledgment of such aid would have assisted the Soviet-backed regime in Afghanistan to claim that the rebels were not true patriots but rather "puppets" of the United States. The rebels themselves did not wish to acknowledge U.S. aid publicly, even though they knew it was essential to the success of their cause. Hence Presidents Carter and Reagan aided the Afghan rebels through covert action.

Covert action is, by definition, secret. And secrecy spawns elaborate conspiracy theories and flamboyant tales of intrigue and deception. In fact, most covert actions consist of routine transfers of economic aid and military equipment to pro-U.S. forces that do not wish to acknowledge such aid publicly. Although most covert actions would have widespread support among the American public

covert actions
Secret intelligence activities outside U.S. borders undertaken with specific authorization by the president; acknowledgment of U.S. sponsorship would defeat or compromise their purpose.

if they were done openly, secrecy opens the possibility that a president will undertake to do by covert action what would be opposed by Congress and the American people if they knew about it.

In the atmosphere of suspicion and distrust engendered by the Watergate scandal, Congress passed intelligence oversight legislation in 1974 requiring a written "presidential finding" for any covert action and requiring that members of the House and Senate Intelligence Committees be informed of all covert actions. The president does not have to obtain congressional approval for covert actions; but Congress can halt such actions if it chooses to do so.

Commander-in-Chief

▶ 11.8 *Trace the expansion of presidential powers as Commander-in-Chief.*

Global power derives primarily from the president's role as Commander-in-Chief of the armed forces of the United States. Presidential command over the armed forces is not merely symbolic; presidents may issue direct military orders to troops in the field. As president, Washington personally led troops to end the Whiskey Rebellion in 1794; Abraham Lincoln issued direct orders to his generals in the Civil War; Lyndon Johnson personally chose bombing targets in Vietnam; and George H. W. Bush personally ordered the 1991 Gulf War cease-fire after 100 hours of ground fighting. All presidents, whether they are experienced in world affairs or not, soon learn after taking office that their influence throughout the world is heavily dependent upon the command of capable military forces.

War-Making Power   Constitutionally, war-making power is divided between the Congress and the president. Congress has the power "to declare war," but the president is the "Commander-in-Chief of the Army and Navy of the United States."

In reality, however, presidents have exercised their powers as Commander-in-Chief to order U.S. forces into military action overseas on many occasions—from John Adams's ordering of U.S. naval forces to attack French ships (1798–99), to Harry Truman's decision to intervene in the Korean War (1951–53), to Lyndon Johnson's and Richard Nixon's conduct of the Vietnam War (1965–73), to George H. W. Bush's Operation Desert Storm (1991), to Bill Clinton's interventions in Bosnia and Kosovo (1998–99), to George W. Bush's military actions in Afghanistan (2001) and Iraq (2003). President Barack Obama's reduction of U.S. military forces in Iraq, and his troop increase in Afghanistan, were both made under his power as Commander-in-Chief. The Supreme Court has consistently refused to hear cases involving the war powers of the president and Congress.[28]

Thus, although Congress retains the formal power to "declare war," in modern times wars are seldom "declared." Instead, they begin with direct military actions, and the president, as Commander-in-Chief of the armed forces, determines what those actions will be. Historically, Congress accepted the fact that only the president has the information-gathering facilities and the ability to act with the speed and secrecy required for military decisions during periods of crisis. Not until the Vietnam War was there serious congressional debate over whether the president has the power to commit the nation to war.

War Powers Resolution   In the early days of the Vietnam War, the liberal leadership of the nation strongly supported Democratic President Lyndon Johnson's power to commit the nation to war. By 1969, however, many congressional leaders had withdrawn their support of the war. With a new Republican president,

Obama Increases U.S. Troop Levels in Afghanistan

Soldiers from Bravo Company, Special Troops Battalion, 82nd Airborne Division, Task Force Gladius wait for a CH-47 Chinook helicopter at the landing zone at Forward Operating Base Morales-Frasier in Afghanistan on January 20, 2008.

Richard Nixon, and a Democratic Congress, congressional attacks on presidential policy became much more partisan.

Antiwar members of Congress made several attempts to end the war by cutting off money for U.S. military activity in Southeast Asia. Such legislation only passed after President Nixon announced a peace agreement in 1973, however. It is important to note that Congress has *never* voted to cut off funds to support American armies while they were in the field.

Congress also passed the **War Powers Resolution**, designed to restrict presidential war-making powers, in 1973. (President Nixon vetoed the bill, but the Watergate affair undermined his support in Congress, which overrode his veto.) The act has four major provisions:

1. In the absence of a congressional declaration of war, the president can commit armed forces to hostilities or to "situations where imminent involvement in hostilities is clearly indicated by the circumstances" only:

 • To repel an armed attack on the United States or to forestall the "direct and imminent threat of such an attack."
 • To repel an armed attack against U.S. armed forces outside the United States or to forestall the threat of such attack.
 • To protect and evacuate U.S. citizens and nationals in another country if their lives are threatened.

2. The president must report promptly to Congress the commitment of forces for such purposes.

3. Involvement of U.S. forces must be no longer than 60 days unless Congress authorizes their continued use by specific legislation.

4. Congress can end a presidential commitment by resolution, an action that does not require the president's signature.

Presidential Noncompliance
The War Powers Resolution raises constitutional questions. A Commander-in-Chief clearly can order U.S. forces to go

War Powers Resolution
Bill passed in 1973 to limit presidential war-making powers; it restricts when, why, and for how long a president can commit U.S. forces and requires notification of and, in many cases, approval by Congress.

✓ *Think* Again

Should Congress have the authority to call home U.S. troops sent by the president to engage in military actions overseas?

anywhere. Presumably, Congress cannot constitutionally command troops, yet that is what the act attempts to do by specifying that troops must come home if Congress orders them to do so or if Congress simply fails to endorse the president's decision to commit them. No president—Democrat or Republican—can allow Congress to usurp this presidential authority. Thus, since the passage of the War Powers Resolution, presidents have continued to undertake military actions on their own initiative (see Table 18.1 in Chapter 18).

Politically, it is often important for the president to show the world, and especially enemies of the United States, that he has congressional support for going to war. For this reason, presidents have asked Congress for resolutions in support of using military means to achieve specific goals. President George H. W. Bush asked for and received (by a close vote) a resolution of support to use military force to oust Iraqi forces from Kuwait in 1991. President George W. Bush won strong support for a congressional resolution in 2002 to allow him to use military force to make Saddam Hussein comply with U.N. resolutions. Both presidents claimed that they had the constitutional authority as Commander-in-Chief to use military force even *without* such resolutions. But politically such resolutions strengthen the president when he chooses to use military force. (See "Political Support for War in Iraq" in Chapter 18.)

Presidential Use of Military Force in Domestic Affairs

Democracies are generally reluctant to use military force in domestic affairs. Yet the president has the constitutional authority to "take Care that the Laws be faithfully executed" and, as Commander-in-Chief of the armed forces, can send them across the nation as well as across the globe. The Constitution appears to limit presidential use of military forces in domestic affairs to protecting states "against domestic Violence" and only "on Application of the [state] Legislature or the [state] Executive (when the Legislature cannot be convened)" (Article IV, Section 4). Although this provision would seem to require states themselves to request federal troops before they can be sent to quell domestic violence, historically presidents have not waited for state requests to send troops when federal laws, federal court orders, or federal constitutional guarantees are being violated.

U.S. Troops Have Been Used to Enforce Federal Law

U.S. soldiers watch as African-American children go to school on October 3, 1957, in Little Rock, Arkansas.

Relying on their constitutional duty to "faithfully execute" federal laws and their command over the nation's armed forces, presidents have used military force in domestic disputes since the earliest days of the Republic. Perhaps the most significant example of a president's use of military force in domestic affairs was Dwight Eisenhower's 1957 dispatch of U.S. troops to Little Rock, Arkansas, to enforce a federal court's desegregation order. In this case, the president acted directly *against* the expressed wishes of the state's governor, Orval Faubus, who had posted state units of the National Guard at the entrance of Central High School to prevent the admission of black students, which had been ordered by the federal court. Eisenhower officially called Arkansas' National Guard units into federal service, took personal command of them, and then ordered them to leave the high school. He then replaced the Guard units with U.S. federal troops under orders to enforce desegregation. Eisenhower's action marked a turning point in the struggle over school desegregation. The Supreme Court's historic desegregation decision in *Brown v. Board of Education of Topeka* might have been rendered meaningless had not the president chosen to use military force to secure compliance.

The Vice-Presidential Waiting Game

▶ 11.9 *Characterize the roles and responsibilities of the vice president.*

Historically, the principal responsibility of the vice president is to be prepared to assume the responsibilities of the president. Eight vice presidents have become president following the death of their predecessor. But vice presidents have not always been well prepared: Harry Truman, who succeeded Franklin Roosevelt while World War II still raged, had never even been informed about the secret atomic bomb project.

Political Selection Process   The political process surrounding the initial choice of vice-presidential candidates does not necessarily produce the persons best qualified to occupy the White House. It is, indeed, a "crap shoot"[29]; if it produces a person well qualified to be president, it is only by luck. Candidates may *claim* that they select running mates who are highly qualified to take over as president, but this claim is seldom true.

Traditionally, vice-presidential candidates have been chosen to give political "balance" to the ticket, to attract voters who might otherwise desert the party or stay home. Democratic presidential candidates sought to give ideological and geographical balance to the ticket. Northern liberal presidential candidates (Adlai Stevenson, John Kennedy) selected southern conservatives (John Sparkman, Estes Kefauver, Lyndon Johnson) as their running mates. Walter Mondale selected New York Congresswoman Geraldine Ferraro in a bold move to exploit the gender gap. Liberal Massachusetts Governor Michael Dukakis returned to the earlier Democratic tradition, choosing to run with conservative Texas Senator Lloyd Bentsen. Bill Clinton sought a different kind of balance: Al Gore's military service in Vietnam and his unimpeachable family life helped offset reservations about Clinton's avoidance of the draft and his past marital troubles. Massachusetts Senator John Kerry was viewed as serious, sober, and reserved, so the choice of the cheerful, enthusiastic, and outgoing North Carolinian John Edwards seemed to balance the ticket in both image and geography.

Republican presidential candidates sought to accommodate either the conservative or moderate wing of their party in their vice-presidential selections. Moderate Eisenhower chose conservative Nixon in 1952. Conservative Ronald Reagan turned to his moderate primary opponent George H. W. Bush in 1980, who in 1988 tapped conservative Dan Quayle. But in 2000 George W. Bush chose to add *experience* to the ticket by choosing Dick Cheney, Secretary of Defense in his father's administration.

POLITICS UP CLOSE

Choosing Veeps in 2008

Vice presidential candidates Sarah Palin and Joe Biden meet to debate during the 2008 campaign.

John McCain was behind in the polls when he surprised political observers with his choice of little-known Alaska Governor Sarah Palin as his vice presidential running mate. Palin was youthful, attractive, folksy, and socially conservative. She captivated Republicans with her life story as a small-town "hockey mom," a mother of five—including a baby with Down syndrome—who first joined the PTA, became Mayor of Wasilla, Alaska, fought the Republican establishment of that state to win the GOP gubernatorial nomination, and then went on to become an extremely popular governor (with over 80

percent approval ratings). McCain hoped that Palin would solidify his base among conservative Republicans and perhaps distract voters from his age. But Palin's inexperience raised questions regarding her qualifications to serve as president.

Barack Obama's selection of Delaware Senator Joe Biden as his running mate balanced the ticket with experience in Washington and foreign-policy expertise. Biden had first won his Senate seat in 1972 as an anti–Vietnam War candidate. He was just 30 years old, the minimum age the Constitution specifies for a member of the Senate. He went on to serve over three decades in the Senate, including prestigious posts as Chairman of the Judiciary Committee and Chairman of the Foreign Relations Committee. He had sought unsuccessfully to be the Democratic presidential nominee himself, even declaring that Obama was not "ready" for the presidency and would need "on-the-job training." Moreover, Biden had voted for the war in Iraq. But his liberal voting record paralleled that of Obama, and his long service in the Senate and his knowledge of foreign affairs provided balance to Obama's relative newness to national politics. Whatever differences Obama and Biden may have had in the past were set aside in order to present a balanced Democratic ticket in 2008.

In 2008, Barack Obama chose Joe Biden, chairman of the Senate Foreign Relations Committee, in an effort to overcome an image of inexperience in foreign affairs. And in a surprise move McCain added excitement to the Republican ticket by selecting Alaska Governor Sarah Palin, social conservative and mother of five children (see *Politics Up Close:* "Choosing Veeps in 2008").

Vice-Presidential Roles Presidents determine what role their vice presidents will play in their administration. Constitutionally, the only role given the vice president is to preside over the Senate and to vote in case of a tie in that body. Presiding over the Senate is so tiresome that vice presidents perform it only on rare ceremonial occasions, but they have occasionally cast important tie-breaking votes. If the president chooses not to give the vice president much responsibility, the vice presidency becomes what its first occupant, John Adams, described as "the most insignificant office that ever the invention of man contrived or his imagination conceived." One of Franklin Roosevelt's three vice presidents, the salty Texan John Nance Garner, put it more pithily, saying that the job "ain't worth a bucket of warm spit" (reporters of that era may have substituted "spit" for Garner's actual wording).

The political functions of vice presidents are more significant than their governmental functions. Vice presidents are obliged to support their president and the administration's policies. But sometimes a president will use the vice president to launch strongly partisan political attacks on opponents while the president remains "above" the political squabbles and hence more "presidential." Richard Nixon served as a partisan "attack dog" for Eisenhower, and then gave

A CONSTITUTIONAL NOTE

How Broad Is the "Executive Power"?

The Constitution states that "The executive Power shall be vested in a President of the United States of America" (Article II). The Constitution also gives the president specific powers; for example "to take care that the laws be faithfully executed"; to appoint and remove executive officials; "to give to the Congress information on the State of the Union and recommend to their Consideration such Measures as he shall judge necessary and expedient"; to veto legislation passed by Congress, subject to override by a two-thirds vote of both houses; to convene special sessions of Congress; to make treaties "with the Advice and Consent of the Senate"; to receive ambassadors; to grant pardons; to appoint federal court and Supreme Court judges, subject to Senate confirmation; and to serve as Commander-in-Chief of the Armed Forces. And the Congress may by law add to the president's powers. But does the Constitution's general grant of "executive power" give the president any powers that are not specified later in the Constitution or given to the president by acts of Congress? Most presidents have asserted a general "executive power," or, as Theodore Roosevelt said, "My belief was that it was not only his right but his duty to do anything that the needs of the nation demanded, unless such action was forbidden by the Constitution or by the laws." But when the Congress has addressed a problem by law, the president is obliged to follow the law, whether he likes it or not.[a] Closely related to the question of executive power is the question of "executive privilege." Can a president withhold information from the Congress or the courts to preserve confidentiality within the executive branch? The Supreme Court has acknowledged a constitutional protection for the "president's need for complete candor and objectivity from advisers" and for "military, diplomatic, or sensitive national security secrets,"[b] But the president cannot withhold information from the courts in a criminal investigation not related to defense or diplomacy, as Richard Nixon found to his dismay in the Watergate affair.

[a]*Youngstown Sheet & Tube Co. v. Sawyer*, 343 U.S. 579 (1952).
[b]*United States v. Nixon*, 418 U.S. 683 (1974).

Spiro Agnew this task in his own administration. The attack role allows the vice president also to help cement political support for the president among highly partisan ideologues. Vice presidents are also useful in campaign fund-raising. Large contributors expect a personal touch; the president cannot be everywhere at once, so the vice president is frequently a guest at political fund-raising events. Presidents also have traditionally sent their vice presidents to attend funerals of world leaders and placed them at the head of governmental commissions.

Vice presidents themselves strive to play a more significant policy-making role, often as senior presidential adviser and confidant. Recent presidents have encouraged the development of the vice presidency along these lines. Walter Mondale, the first modern vice president to perform this function, had an office in the White House next to the president's, had access to all important meetings and policy decisions, and was invited to lunch privately each week with President Carter. Vice President Al Gore was routinely stationed behind President Clinton during major policy pronouncements. Clinton reportedly gave great weight to Gore's views on the environment, on cost savings in government, and on information technology. Gore also spoke out aggressively in defense of Clinton's policies. Thus the senior advisory role is becoming institutionalized over time.

The Waiting Game Politically ambitious vice presidents are obliged to play a torturous waiting game. They can use their time in office to build a network of contacts that can later be tapped for campaign contributions, workers, and support in their own race for the presidency, should they decide to run. But winning the presidency following retirement of their former boss requires a delicate balance. They must show loyalty to the president in order to win the president's endorsement and also to help ensure that the administration in which they participated is judged a success by voters. At the same time, vice presidents must demonstrate that they have independent leadership qualities and a policy agenda of their own to offer voters. This dilemma becomes more acute as their boss's term nears its end.

Historically, only a few sitting vice presidents have won election to the White House: John Adams (1797), Thomas Jefferson (1801), Martin Van Buren (1837), and George H. W. Bush (1988). In addition, four vice presidents won election in their own right after entering the Oval Office as a result of their predecessors' death: Theodore Roosevelt (1901), Calvin Coolidge (1923), Harry Truman (1945), and Lyndon Johnson (1963). Only one nonsitting former vice president has been elected president: Richard Nixon (1968, after losing to Kennedy in 1960). Thus out of the forty-eight men who served the nation as vice president through 2008, only nine were ever elected to higher office.

Summary

▶ **11.1** *Identify the powers and responsibilities of the president.*

As head of the government, the president is expected to set forth policy priorities for the nation, to manage the economy, to mobilize political support for the administration's programs in Congress, to manage the giant federal bureaucracy, and to recruit people for policy-making positions in both the executive and judicial branches of government.

▶ **11.2** *Identify the powers granted to the president by the Constitution.*

Popular expectations of presidential leadership far exceed the formal constitutional powers of the president: chief administrator, chief legislator, chief diplomat, Commander-in-Chief, and chief of state. The vague reference in the Constitution to "executive Power" has been used by presidents to justify actions beyond those specified elsewhere in the Constitution or in laws of Congress.

▶ **11.3** *Assess the sources of the president's political power.*

It is the president's vast political resources that provide the true power base of the presidency. These include the president's reputation for power, personal popularity with the public, access to the media, and party leadership position.

▶ **11.4** *Analyze how presidents' personality and policy positions impact their approval rating.*

Presidential popularity and power are usually the highest at the beginning of the term of office. Presidents are more likely to be successful in Congress during this honeymoon period. Presidents' popularity also rises during crises, especially during international threats and military actions. But prolonged indecision and stalemate erode popular support, as do scandals and economic recessions.

▶ **11.5** *Outline the responsibilities and powers of the president as the nation's chief executive.*

As chief executive, the president oversees the huge federal bureaucracy. Presidential control of the executive branch is exercised through executive orders, appointments and removals, and budgetary recommendations to Congress. But the president's control of the executive branch is heavily circumscribed by Congress, which establishes executive departments and agencies, regulates their activities by law, and determines their budgets each year.

▶ **11.6** *Analyze the factors affecting the success of the president as the chief legislator and lobbyist.*

Presidents are expected not only to initiate programs and policies but also to shepherd them through Congress. Presidential success scores in Congress indicate that presidents are more successful early in their term of office. Presidents who face a Congress controlled by the opposition party are far less successful in winning approval for their programs than presidents whose party holds a majority.

The veto is the president's most powerful weapon in dealing with Congress. The president needs to hold the loyalty of only one more than one-third of either the House or the Senate to sustain a veto. Few vetoes are overridden. The threat of a veto enables the president to bargain in Congress for more acceptable legislation.

▶ **11.7** *Assess the role of the president as a global leader.*

During the long years of the Cold War, the president of the United States was the leader of the "free world." In the post–Cold War world, the president is still the leader of the world's most powerful democracy and is expected to exercise global leadership on behalf of a stable world order.

▶ **11.8** *Trace the expansion of presidential powers as Commander-in-Chief.*

The global power of presidents derives primarily from this presidential role as Commander-in-Chief. Constitutionally, war-making power is divided between Congress and the president, but historically it has been the president who has ordered U.S. military forces into action. In the War Powers Resolution, Congress tried to reassert its war-making power after the Vietnam War, but the act has failed to restrain presidents. Presidents have also used the armed forces in domestic affairs to "take Care that the Laws be faithfully executed."

▶ 11.9 *Characterize the roles and responsibilities of the vice president.*

The principal responsibility of the vice president is to be prepared to assume the responsibilities of the president. However, the selection of the vice president is dominated more by political concerns than by consideration of presidential qualifications. Aside from officially presiding over the U.S. Senate, vice presidents perform whatever roles are assigned them by the president.

Chapter Test

▶ 11.1 *Identify the powers and responsibilities of the president.*

1. The president is expected to be responsible for all of the following *except*
   a. presiding over the Senate in case of a tie vote
   b. administering the federal bureaucracy
   c. expressing the nation's sentiments during a time of crisis
   d. presenting the State of the Union Address each year

2. Which three presidents have been recognized almost universally as "great" leaders?
   a. Washington, Lincoln, and Harding
   b. Lincoln, Jefferson, and Wilson
   c. Franklin Roosevelt, Teddy Roosevelt, and Washington
   d. Franklin Roosevelt, Washington, and Lincoln

3. It would be accurate to say that President George W. Bush
   a. succeeded in reforming social security
   b. failed to reduce taxes
   c. succeeded in reforming education
   d. succeeded in reforming immigration

▶ 11.2 *Identify the powers granted to the president by the Constitution.*

4. The right of the executive branch to withhold confidential communications from the other branches of government is known as
   a. administrative censure
   b. executive privilege
   c. the national security exception
   d. executive classification prerogative

5. The only two presidents to be impeached by the House of Representatives were
   a. Clinton and Nixon
   b. Andrew Johnson and Nixon
   c. Nixon and Lyndon Johnson
   d. Clinton and Andrew Johnson

6. Refusal by the president to spend monies appropriated by Congress is known as
   a. impoundments
   b. legislative deferral
   c. executive rescission
   d. earmarking

▶ 11.3 *Analyze the sources of the president's political power.*

7. The sources of presidential powers include all but which of the following?
   a. access to the media
   b. judicial review
   c. the "Bully Pulpit" and the power to persuade
   d. the president's own popularity

8. The only president to ever resign the office was
   a. Bill Clinton
   b. Lyndon Johnson
   c. Richard Nixon
   d. Andrew Johnson

▶ 11.4 *Analyze how presidents' personality and policy positions impact their approval ratings.*

9. President Obama ran on a platform that supported which of the following?
   a. reducing carbon emissions
   b. providing health insurance for all Americans
   c. ending the war in Iraq "responsibly"
   d. all of the above

▶ 11.5 *Outline the responsibilities and powers of the president as the nation's chief executive.*

10. Formal regulations governing the executive branch operations are known as
    a. presidential directives
    b. executive directives
    c. presidential orders
    d. executive orders

11. It would be accurate to say that presidents
    a. may appoint members of the White House staff without Congressional approval
    b. may appoint cabinet secretaries without Congressional approval
    c. may appoint justices of the Supreme Court without Congressional approval
    d. remove members of the Supreme Court but only with the approval of Congress

▶ 11.6 *Analyze the factors affecting the success of the president as the chief legislator and lobbyist.*

12. The main source of national policy initiatives is the
    a. cabinet
    b. president
    c. Congress
    d. Federal Bureaucracy

13. The person that President Obama primarily relies on to supervise the White House staff is
    a. Vice President Joe Biden
    b. Chief of Staff Joe Biden
    c. Vice President Rahm Emanuel
    d. Chief of Staff Rahm Emanuel

14. Perhaps the most successful initiative of the Obama administration thus far has been
    a. the Mideast Peace Initiative
    b. health care reform
    c. the "No Child Left Behind" education proposals
    d. the Social Security Overhaul Law

▶ 11.7 *Assess the role of the president as a global leader.*

15. The office that is responsible for the overall coordination of the intelligence activities of the United States government is the
    a. Defense Intelligence Agency (DIA)
    b. Central Intelligence Agency (CIA)

c. National Security Agency (NSA)
d. Director of National Intelligence (DNI)

▶ 11.8 *Trace the expansion of presidential powers as Commander-in-Chief.*

16. "At the end of the day" the president's powers in world affairs are primarily dependent on
a. a compliant Congress
b. command of a capable military
c. his status in the United Nations
d. NATO

17. The legislation passed after the Vietnam War, which attempted to limit the war-making powers of the president, was the

a. War Powers Resolution
b. Executive Defense Restrictions Amendment
c. Armed Forces Deployment Resolution
d. Defense Appropriations Act

▶ 11.9 *Characterize the roles and responsibilities of the vice president.*

18. The Constitution stipulates that the vice president is to
a. prepare himself for the presidency
b. represent the government at funerals of dignitaries
c. preside over the Senate
d. preside over the cabinet in the absence of the president

---

mypoliscilab EXERCISES

Apply what you learned in this chapter on MyPoliSciLab.

Read on mypoliscilab.com

eText: Chapter 11

Study and **Review** on **mypoliscilab.com**

Pre-Test

Post-Test

Chapter Exam

Flashcards

Watch on **mypoliscilab.com**

Video: Bush and the Congress

Video: The Government Bails Out Automakers

Explore on **mypoliscilab.com**

Simulation: Presidential Leadership: Which Hat Do You Wear?

Simulation: You Are a President During a Nuclear Power Plant Meltdown

Comparative: Comparing Chief Executives

Timeline: The Executive Order Over Time

Visual Literacy: Presidential Success in Polls and Congress

Key Terms

Suggested Readings

Barber, James David. *The Presidential Character: Predicting Performance in the White House.* 4th ed. New York: Longman, 2009. Barber's original thesis that a president's performance in office is largely a function of active/passive and positive/negative character; includes classifications of twentieth-century presidents through Reagan.

Edwards, George C., and Stephen J. Wayne. *Presidential Leadership.* 8th ed. Belmont, Calif.: Wadsworth, 2010. Comprehensive text covering nomination and election of the president, relations with the public, the media, the bureaucracy, Congress and the courts.

Jacobson, Gary C. *A Divider, Not a Uniter*. New York: Langunton, 2008. Poll data showing that George W. Bush accelerated the polarization of the American people along party lines.

Pfiffner, James P. *The Modern Presidency*. 6th ed. Belmont, CA: Wadsworth, 2011. Text coverage of institutional relationships between president and the public, White House staff, executive branch, Congress, intelligence community, and so on.

Milkus, Stanley, and Michael Nelson. *The American Presidency: Origins and Development, 1776–2007*. 5th ed. Washington, D.C.: CQ Press, 2007. A comprehensive history of the presidency that argues that the institution is best understood by examining its development over time, describes the significant presidential actions in the early days of the Republic that shaped the office, as well as the modern era in which the president has replaced Congress and the political parties as the leading instrument of popular rule.

Nelson, Michael, ed. *The Presidency and the Political System*. 9th ed. Washington, D.C.: CQ Press, 2009. Essays on the presidency up to and including Barack Obama.

Neustadt, Richard E. *Presidential Power*. New York: Wiley, 1960. The classic argument that the president's power is the power to persuade, that the formal constitutional powers of the presidency provide only a framework for the president's use of persuasion, public prestige, reputation for power, and other personal attributes to exercise real power.

Pika, Joseph A., and John Maltese. *The Politics of the Presidency*. 7th ed. Washington, D.C.: CQ Press, 2009. An overview of the institution of the presidency, including George W. Bush as a wartime president.

Schultz, Jeffrey D. *Presidential Scandals*. Washington, D.C.: CQ Press, 1999. An historical survey of scandals in presidential administrations, from George Washington to Bill Clinton.

Suggested Web Sites

American Presidents www.americanpresidents.org
Biographical facts and key events in the lives of all U.S. presidents.

Cabinet www.whitehouse.gov/government/cabinet.html
The White House site provides the names of the current president's cabinet as well as those individuals with "cabinet-rank" status.

Center for the Study of the Presidency
www.thepresidency.org
Studies of the presidency and publication of the scholarly journal *Presidential Studies Quarterly*.

Central Intelligence Agency www.cia.gov
The CIA site provides information about the agency's mission, organization, values, press releases, and congressional testimony along with employment possibilities.

Defense Link www.defenselink.gov
Official site of U.S. Department of Defense, with news and links to Army, Navy, Air Force, and Marine Corps Web sites and other defense agencies and commands.

National Security Council www.whitehouse.gov/nsc
Site provides brief history of NSC plus new releases dealing with national security.

State Department www.state.gov
Official site includes news, travel warnings, international issues, and background notes on countries of the world.

Treaties in Force www.state.gov/www/global/legalaffairs
Complete list of all treaties of the United States in force as of January 1, 2000.

The White House www.whitehouse.gov
This official White House site provides up-to-date information or news about the current president's policies, speeches, appointments, proclamations, and cabinet members.

Chapter Test Answer Key

1. A	**4.** B	**7.** B	**10.** D	**13.** D	**16.** B
2. D	**5.** D	**8.** C	**11.** A	**14.** B	**17.** A
3. C	**6.** A	**9.** D	**12.** B	**15.** D	**18.** C

12

THE BUREAUCRACY

Bureaucratic Politics

66 A wise and frugal government, which shall leave men free to regulate their own pursuits of industry and improvement, and shall not take from the mouth of labor the bread it has earned— this is the sum of good government. **99**　　　Thomas Jefferson

Chapter Outline and Learning Objectives

Bureaucratic Power
▶ 12.1 *Assess the nature, sources, and extent of bureaucratic power.*

The Federal Bureaucracy
▶ 12.2 *Describe the types of agencies in the federal bureaucracy and the extent and purposes of the bureaucracy.*

Bureaucracy and Democracy
▶ 12.3 *Trace changes over time in the size and composition of the bureaucracy and assess the repercussions for democracy.*

Bureaucratic Politics
▶ 12.4 *Explain how the bureaucracy is staffed, to whom it is accountable, and how accountability is affected by politics and bureaucratic culture.*

The Budgetary Process
▶ 12.5 *Outline the budgetary process.*

The Politics of Budgeting
▶ 12.6 *Evaluate the advantages and disadvantages of the current system of budgeting.*

Congressional Constraints on the Bureaucracy
▶ 12.7 *Outline the growth of federal regulation.*

Interest Groups and Bureaucratic Decision Making
▶ 12.8 *Evaluate the cost of federal regulation.*

Judicial Constraints on the Bureaucracy
▶ 12.9 *Summarize the constraints that Congress can place on the bureaucracy.*

✓ *Think* about Politics

1. Do bureaucrats in Washington have too much power?
   YES ⬭ NO ⬭

2. Should the federal bureaucracy be managed by nonpartisan professionals rather than people politically loyal to the president?
   YES ⬭ NO ⬭

3. Should the federal bureaucracy at all levels reflect the gender and minority ratios of the total civilian workforce?
   YES ⬭ NO ⬭

4. Do you believe the bureaucrats in Washington waste a lot of the money we pay in taxes?
   YES ⬭ NO ⬭

5. Do you believe the federal government is spending more money but delivering less service?
   YES ⬭ NO ⬭

6. Do you believe that the overall costs of federal regulatory activity are justified by the benefits?
   YES ⬭ NO ⬭

7. Do you believe bureaucratic regulations of all kinds are hurting America's competitiveness in the global economy?
   YES ⬭ NO ⬭

Power in Washington is not only exercised by the president, Congress, and courts, but also by 2.8 million federal bureaucrats—neither elected nor accountable to ordinary citizens—who determine in large measure who gets what in America.

bureaucracy
Departments, agencies, bureaus, and offices that perform the functions of government.

Bureaucratic Power

▶ 12.1 *Assess the nature, sources, and extent of bureaucratic power.*

Political conflict does not end after a law has been passed by Congress and signed by the president. The arena for conflict merely shifts from Capitol Hill and the White House to the **bureaucracy**—to the myriad departments, agencies, and bureaus of the federal executive branch that implement the law. Despite the popular impression that policy is decided by the president and Congress and merely implemented by the federal bureaucracy, in fact policy is also made by the bureaucracy. Indeed, it is often remarked that "implementation is the continuation of policy making by other means." The Washington bureaucracy is a major base of power in the American system of government—independent of Congress, the president, the courts, and the people. Indeed, controlling the bureaucracy has become a major challenge of democratic government.

The Nature of Bureaucracy   "Bureaucracy" has become a negative term equated with red tape,[1] paper shuffling, duplication of effort, waste and inefficiency, impersonality, senseless regulations, and unresponsiveness to the needs of "real" people. But bureaucracy is really a form of social organization found not only in governments but also in corporations, armies, schools, and many other societal institutions. The German sociologist Max Weber described bureaucracy as a "rational" way for

chain of command
Hierarchical structure of authority in which command flows downward; typical of a bureaucracy.

division of labor
Division of work among many specialized workers in a bureaucracy.

impersonality
Treatment of all persons within a bureaucracy on the basis of "merit" and of all "clients" served by the bureaucracy equally according to rules.

society to organize itself that has the following characteristics: a **chain of command** (hierarchical structure of authority in which command flows downward); a **division of labor** (work divided among many specialized workers in an effort to improve productivity); and **impersonality** (all persons within the bureaucracy treated on "merit" principles, and all "clients" served by the bureaucracy treated equally according to rules; all activities undertaken according to rules; records maintained to assure rules are followed).[2] Thus, according to Weber's definition, General Motors and IBM, the U.S. Marine Corps, the U.S. Department of Education, and all other institutions organized according to these principles are "bureaucracies."

The Growth of Bureaucratic Power

Bureaucratic power has grown with advances in technology and increases in the size and complexity of society. There are a variety of explanations for this growth of power.

- *Needed Expertise and Technological Advances* Congress and the president do not have the time, energy, or expertise to handle the details of policy making. A related explanation is that the increasing complexity and sophistication of technology require technical experts ("technocrats") to actually carry out the intent of Congress and the president. Neither the president nor the 535 members of Congress can look after the myriad details involved in environmental protection, occupational safety, air traffic control, or thousands of other responsibilities of government. So the president and Congress create bureaucracies, appropriate money for them, and authorize them to draw up detailed rules, regulations, and "guidelines" that actually govern the nation. Bureaucratic agencies receive only vague and general directions from the president and Congress. Actual governance is in the hands of the Environmental Protection Agency, the Occupational Safety and Health Administration, the Federal Aviation Administration, and hundreds of similar agencies (see Figure 12.1).

- *Symbolic Politics* But there are also political explanations for the growth of bureaucratic power. Congress and the president often deliberately pass vague and ambiguous laws. These laws allow elected officials to show symbolically their concerns for environmental protection, occupational safety, and so on, yet avoid the controversies surrounding actual application of those lofty principles. Bureaucracies must then give practical meaning to these symbolic measures by developing specific rules and regulations. If the rules and regulations prove unpopular, Congress and the president can blame the bureaucrats and pretend that these unpopular decisions are a product of an "ungovernable" Washington bureaucracy (see *Controversy:* "How Would You Rate These Federal Agencies?").

- *Bureaucratic Explanation* There is also a bureaucratic explanation of the growth in the size and influence of government agencies. Bureaucracy has become its own source of power. Bureaucrats have a personal stake in expanding the size of their own agencies and budgets and adding to their own regulatory authority. They can mobilize their "client" groups (interest groups that directly benefit from the agency's programs, such as environmental groups on behalf of the Environmental Protection Agency, farm groups for the Department of Agriculture, the National Education Association for the Department of Education) in support of larger budgets and expanded authority.

- *Popular Demands* Finally, it has been argued that "big government" is really an expression of democratic sentiments. People want to use the power of government to improve their lives—to regulate and develop the economy, to guarantee civil rights, to develop their communities, and so on. Conservative opponents of government growth are overlooking popular demands.[3]

Think Again

Do bureaucrats in Washington have too much power?

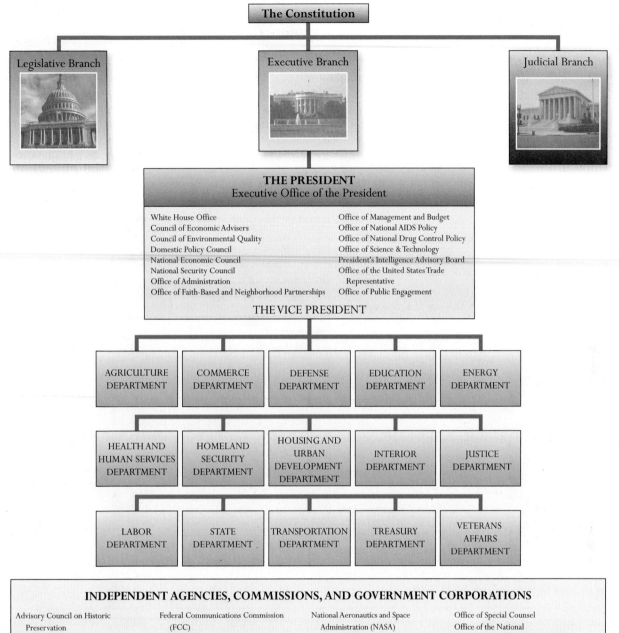

The Constitution

Legislative Branch

Executive Branch

Judicial Branch

THE PRESIDENT
Executive Office of the President

White House Office
Council of Economic Advisers
Council of Environmental Quality
Domestic Policy Council
National Economic Council
National Security Council
Office of Administration
Office of Faith-Based and Neighborhood Partnerships

Office of Management and Budget
Office of National AIDS Policy
Office of National Drug Control Policy
Office of Science & Technology
President's Intelligence Advisory Board
Office of the United States Trade
 Representative
Office of Public Engagement

THE VICE PRESIDENT

AGRICULTURE DEPARTMENT	COMMERCE DEPARTMENT	DEFENSE DEPARTMENT	EDUCATION DEPARTMENT	ENERGY DEPARTMENT
HEALTH AND HUMAN SERVICES DEPARTMENT	HOMELAND SECURITY DEPARTMENT	HOUSING AND URBAN DEVELOPMENT DEPARTMENT	INTERIOR DEPARTMENT	JUSTICE DEPARTMENT
LABOR DEPARTMENT	STATE DEPARTMENT	TRANSPORTATION DEPARTMENT	TREASURY DEPARTMENT	VETERANS AFFAIRS DEPARTMENT

INDEPENDENT AGENCIES, COMMISSIONS, AND GOVERNMENT CORPORATIONS

Advisory Council on Historic Preservation
African Development Foundation
AMTRAK (National Railroad Passenger Corporation)
Central Intelligence Agency (CIA)
Commission on Civil Rights
Commodity Futures Trading Commission
Consumer Product Safety Commission (CPSC)
Corporation for National and Community Service
Defense Nuclear Facilities Safety Board
Election Assistance Commission
Environmental Protection Agency (EPA)
Equal Employment Opportunity Commission (EEOC)
Export-Import Bank of the United States
Farm Credit Administration

Federal Communications Commission (FCC)
Federal Deposit Insurance Corporation (FDIC)
Federal Election Commission (FEC)
Federal Housing Finance Board
Federal Labor Relations Authority
Federal Maritime Commission
Federal Mediation and Conciliation Service
Federal Mine Safety and Health Review Commission
Federal Reserve System
Federal Retirement Thrift Investment Board
Federal Trade Commission (FTC)
General Services Administration (GSA)
Institute of Museum and Library Services
Inter-American Foundation
International Broadcasting Bureau (IBB)
Merit Systems Protection Board

National Aeronautics and Space Administration (NASA)
National Archives and Records Administration (NARA)
National Capital Planning Commission
National Council on Disability
National Credit Union Administration (NCUA)
National Endowment for the Arts
National Endowment for the Humanities
National Labor Relations Board (NLRB)
National Mediation Board
National Science Foundation (NSF)
National Transportation Safety Board
Nuclear Regulatory Commission (NRC)
Occupational Safety and Health Review Commission
Office of Government Ethics
Office of Personnel Management

Office of Special Counsel
Office of the National Counterintelligence Executive
Overseas Private Investment Corporation
Panama Canal Commission
Peace Corps
Pension Benefit Guaranty Corporation
Postal Regulatory Commission
Railroad Retirement Board
Securities and Exchange Commission (SEC)
Selective Service System
Small Business Administration (SBA)
Social Security Administration (SSA)
Tennessee Valley Authority
U.S. Trade and Development Agency
United States Agency for International Development
United States International Trade Commission
United States Postal Service (USPS)

FIGURE 12.1 The Federal Bureaucracy

Although the president has constitutional authority over the operation of the executive branch, Congress creates departments and agencies and appropriates their funds, and Senate approval is needed for presidential appointees to head departments.

CONTROVERSY

How Would You Rate These Federal Agencies?

Americans are familiar with only a few federal agencies. But among the fairly well-known agencies, the Center for Disease Control, the FBI, and the space agency NASA, win majorities in national polls rating them as "excellent" or "good." In contrast, majorities rate the Environmental Protection Agency, the tax collecting Internal Revenue Service, and the Food and Drug Administration as "only fair" or "poor." In past years the Federal Reserve Board was highly rated, but following the financial crisis in 2008, popular regard for the overseer of the nation's banking system plummeted.

Q. How would you rate the job being done by _____? Would you say it is doing an excellent, good, only fair, or poor job?

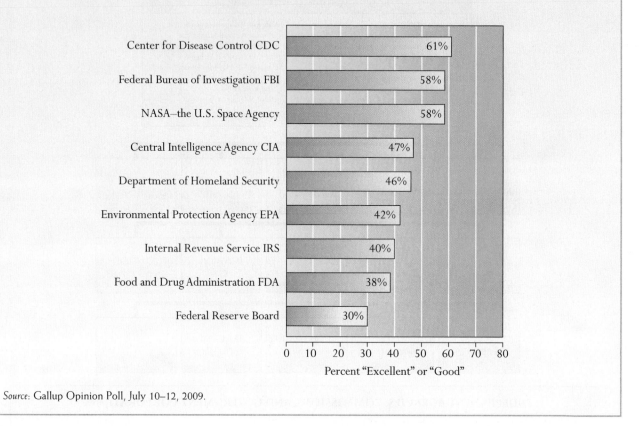

Source: Gallup Opinion Poll, July 10–12, 2009.

Bureaucratic Power: Implementation

Bureaucracies are not *constitutionally* empowered to decide policy questions. But they do so, nevertheless, as they perform their tasks of implementation, regulation, and adjudication.

implementation
Development by the federal bureaucracy of procedures and activities to carry out policies legislated by Congress, it includes regulation as well as adjudication.

Implementation is the development of procedures and activities to carry out policies legislated by Congress. It may involve creating new agencies or bureaus or assigning new responsibilities to old agencies. It often requires bureaucracies to translate laws into operational rules and regulations and usually to allocate resources—money, personnel, offices, supplies—to the new function. All of these tasks involve decisions by bureaucrats, decisions that drive how the law will actually affect society. In some cases, bureaucrats delay the development of regulations based on a new law, assign enforcement responsibility to existing offices with other higher priority tasks, and allocate few people with limited resources to the task. In other cases, bureaucrats act forcefully in making new regulations, insist on strict enforcement, assign responsibilities to newly created aggressive offices with no other assignments, and allocate a great deal of staff time and agency resources to the task. Interested groups have a strong stake in these decisions, and they actively seek to influence the bureaucracy.

Bureaucratic Power: Regulation

Regulation involves the development of formal rules for implementing legislation. The federal bureaucracy publishes about 80,000 pages of rules in the *Federal Register* each year. The Environmental Protection Agency (EPA) is especially active in developing regulations governing the handling of virtually every substance in the air, water, or ground. The rule-making process for federal agencies is prescribed by an Administrative Procedures Act, first passed in 1946 and amended many times. Generally, agencies must:

regulation
Development by the federal bureaucracy of formal rules for implementing legislation.

- Announce in the *Federal Register* that a new regulation is being considered.

- Hold hearings to allow interested groups to present evidence and arguments regarding the proposed regulation.

- Conduct research on the proposed regulation's economic and environmental impacts.

- Solicit "public comments" (usually the arguments of interest groups).

- Consult with higher officials, including the Office of Management and Budget.

- Publish the new regulation in the *Federal Register.*

Regulatory battles are important because formal regulations that appear in the *Federal Register* have the effect of law. Congress can amend or repeal a regulation only by passing new legislation and obtaining the president's signature. Controversial bureaucratic regulations often remain in place because Congress is slow to act, because key committee members block corrective legislation, or because the president refuses to sign bills overturning the regulation.

Bureaucratic Power: Adjudication

Adjudication involves bureaucratic decisions about individual cases. Rule making resembles the legislative process, and adjudication resembles the judicial process. In adjudication, bureaucrats decide whether a person or firm is failing to comply with laws or regulations and, if so, what penalties or corrective actions are to be applied. Regulatory agencies and commissions—for example, the National Labor Relations Board, the Federal Communications Commission, the Equal Employment Opportunity Commission, the Federal Trade Commission, the Securities and Exchange Commission— are heavily engaged in adjudication. Their elaborate procedures and body of previous decisions closely resemble the court system. Losers may appeal to the federal courts, but the record of agency success in the federal courts discourages many appeals.

adjudication
Decision making by the federal bureaucracy as to whether or not an individual or organization has complied with or violated government laws and/or regulations.

Bureaucratic Power: Administrative Discretion

Much of the work of bureaucrats is administrative routine—issuing Social Security checks, printing forms, delivering the mail. Routines are repetitive tasks performed according to established rules and procedures. Yet bureaucrats almost always have some discretion in performing even the most routine tasks. Discretion is greatest when cases do not exactly fit established rules, or when more than one rule might be applied to the same case, resulting in different outcomes. The Internal Revenue Service administers the hundreds of thousands of rules developed to implement

Paper Jam

Jennifer Garbach, left, of Philadelphia, Pennsylvania, and other customers wait in line to mail their parcel packages at the Bustleton branch of the U.S. Post Office in Philadelphia on December 17, 2003.

budget maximization
Bureaucrats' tendencies to expand their agencies' budgets, staff, and authority.

discretionary funds
Budgeted funds not earmarked for specific purposes but available to be spent in accordance with the best judgment of a bureaucrat.

the U.S. Tax Code, but each IRS auditing agent has wide discretion in deciding which rules to apply to a taxpayer's income, deductions, business expenses, and so on. Indeed, identical tax information submitted to different IRS offices almost always results in different estimates of tax liability. But even in more routine tasks, from processing Medicare applications to forwarding mail, individual bureaucrats can be friendly and helpful or hostile and obstructive.[4]

Bureaucratic Power and Budget Maximization   Bureaucrats generally believe strongly in the value of their programs and the importance of their tasks. Senior military officers and civilian officials of the Department of Defense believe in the importance of a strong national defense, and top officials in the Social Security Administration are committed to maintaining the integrity of the retirement system and serving the nation's senior citizens. Beyond these public-spirited motives, bureaucrats, like everyone else, seek higher pay, greater job security, and added power and prestige for themselves.

These public and private motives converge to inspire bureaucrats to seek to expand the powers, functions, and budgets of their departments and agencies. Rarely do bureaucrats request a reduction in authority, the elimination of a program, or a decrease in their agency's budget. Rather, over time, **budget maximization**—expanding the agency's budget, staff, and authority as much as possible—becomes a driving force in government bureaucracies. This is especially true of discretionary funds. **Discretionary funds** are those that bureaucrats have flexibility in deciding how to spend, rather than money committed by law to specific purposes.[5] Thus, bureaucracies continually strive to add new functions, acquire more authority and responsibility, and increase their budgets and personnel. Bureaucratic expansion is just one of the reasons that government grows over time.

The Federal Bureaucracy

▶ 12.2 *Describe the types of agencies in the federal bureaucracy and the extent and purposes of the bureaucracy.*

The federal bureaucracy—officially part of the executive branch of the U.S. government—consists of about 2.8 million civilian employees (plus 1.4 million persons in the armed forces) organized into fifteen cabinet departments, more than sixty independent agencies, and a large Executive Office of the President (see Figure 12.2). The expenditures of *all* governments in the United States—the federal government, the 50 state governments, and some 89,000 local governments—now amount to over *$5 trillion* (roughly one third of the U.S. gross domestic product, or GDP, of $15.0 *trillion*). About $3.8 *trillion* a year (about 25 percent of GDP)—is spent by the *federal* government. Government spending in the United States remains relatively modest compared to that of many nations (see *Compared to What?*: "The Size of Government in Other Nations").

Cabinet Departments   Cabinet departments employ about 60 percent of all federal workers (see Table 12.1). Each department is headed by a secretary

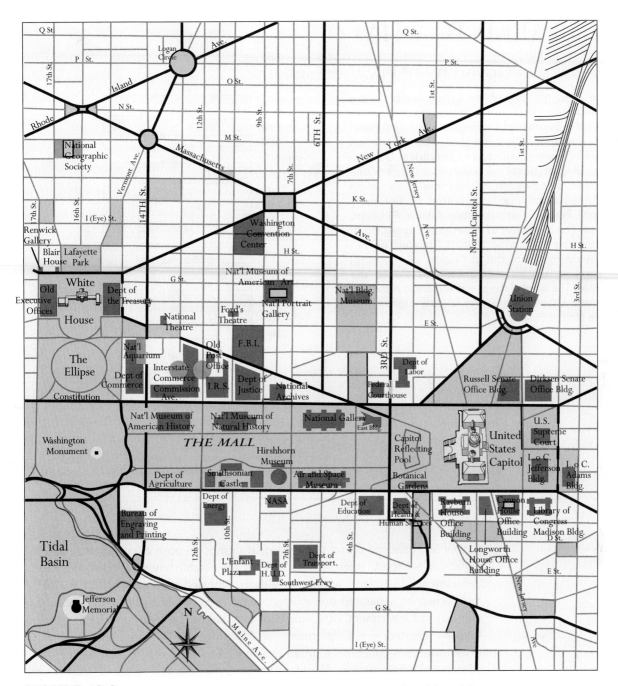

FIGURE 12.2 The Capitol, White House, and Bureaucracy Corridors of Power

This map shows the Capitol, the White House, and the major departments of the federal bureaucracy in Washington, D.C.

(with the exception of the Justice Department, which is headed by the attorney general) who is appointed by the president and must be confirmed by the Senate. Each department is hierarchically organized; each has its own organization chart.

Cabinet status confers great legitimacy on a governmental function and prestige on the secretary, thus strengthening that individual's voice in the government. Therefore the elevation of an executive agency to cabinet level often reflects political considerations as much as or more than national needs. Strong pressures from "client" interest groups (groups principally served by the department),

COMPARED TO WHAT?

The Size of Government in Other Nations

How does the size of the public sector in the United States compare with the size of the public sector in other economically advanced, democratic countries? There is a great deal of variation in the size of government across countries. Government spending accounts for nearly two-thirds of the total output in Sweden. Government spending exceeds one-half of the total output of Denmark, Netherlands, Finland, Germany, Italy, Austria, Belgium, and France. The high level of government spending in these countries primarily reflects greater public-sector involvement in the provision of housing, health care, retirement insurance, and aid to the unemployed. The sizes of the public sectors in Australia, Japan, and Switzerland are only slightly higher than that of the United States.

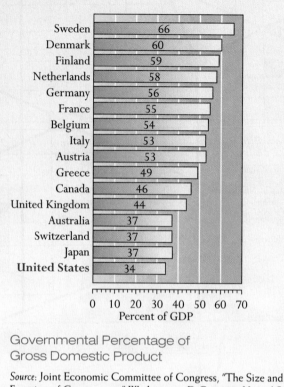

Governmental Percentage of Gross Domestic Product

Source: Joint Economic Committee of Congress, "The Size and Function of Government." Washington, D.C.: 1998. United States updated to 2010.

as well as presidential and congressional desires to pose as defenders and promoters of particular interests, account for the establishment of all of the newer departments. President Woodrow Wilson appealed to the labor movement in 1913 when he separated out a Department of Labor from the earlier business-dominated Department of Commerce and Labor. In 1965, President Lyndon Johnson created the Department of Housing and Urban Development to demonstrate his concern for urban problems. Seeking support from teachers and educational administrators, President Jimmy Carter created a separate Department of Education in 1979 and changed the name of the former Department of Health, Education, and Welfare to the Department of Health and Human Services (perhaps finding the phrase "human services" more politically acceptable than "welfare"). President Ronald Reagan tried, and failed, to "streamline" government by abolishing the Department of Education. But Reagan himself added a cabinet post, elevating the Veterans Administration to the Department of Veterans Affairs in an attempt to ingratiate himself with veterans. President George W. Bush created a new Department of Homeland Security in 2002 in response to the "9/11" terrorist attack on America and the threat of future attacks directly on the soil of the United States.

Cabinet Department Functions
The relative power and prestige of each cabinet-level department is a product not only of its size and budget but also of the importance of its function. By custom, the "pecking order" of departments—and

TABLE 12.1 Who Does What?: Cabinet Departments and Functions

Department and Date Created	Function
State (1789)	Advises the president on the formation and execution of foreign policy; negotiates treaties and agreements with foreign nations; represents the United States in the United Nations and in more than fifty major international organizations and maintains U.S. embassies abroad; issues U.S. passports and, in foreign countries, visas to the United States.
Treasury (1789)	Serves as financial agent for the U.S. government; issues all payments of the U.S. government according to law; manages the debt of the U.S. government by issuing and recovering bonds and paying their interest; collects taxes owed to the U.S. government; collects taxes and enforces laws on alcohol, tobacco, and firearms and on customs duties; manufactures coins and currency.
Defense (1947: formerly the War Department, created in 1789, and the Navy Department, created in 1798)	Provides the military forces needed to deter war and protect the national security interest; includes the Departments of the Army, Navy, and Air Force.
Justice (1789)	Enforces all federal laws, including consumer protection, antitrust, civil rights, drug, and immigration and naturalization; maintains federal prisons.
Interior (1849)	Has responsibility for public lands and natural resources, for American Indian reservations, and for people who live in island territories under U.S. administration; preserves national parks and historical sites.
Agriculture (1889)	Works to improve and maintain farm income and to develop and expand markets abroad for agricultural products; safeguards standards of quality in the food supply through inspection and grading services; administers rural development, credit, and conservation programs; administers food stamp program.
Commerce (1913)	Encourages the nation's international trade, economic growth, and technological advancement; conducts the census; provides social and economic statistics and analyses for business and government; maintains the merchant marine; grants patents and registers trademarks.
Labor (1913)	Oversees working conditions; administers federal labor laws; protects workers' pension rights; sponsors job training programs; keeps track of changes in employment, price, and other national economic indicators.
Health and Human Services (1953 as Health, Education, and Welfare; reorganized with Education as a separate department in 1979)	Administers social welfare programs for the elderly, children, and youths; protects the health of the nation against impure and unsafe foods, drugs, and cosmetics; operates the Centers for Disease Control; funds the Medicare and Medicaid programs.
Housing and Urban Development (1965)	Is responsible for programs concerned with housing needs, fair housing opportunities, and the improvement and development of the nation's communities; administers mortgage insurance programs, rental subsidy programs, and neighborhood rehabilitation and preservation programs.
Transportation (1966)	Is responsible for the nation's highway planning, development, and construction; also urban mass transit, railroads, aviation, and the safety of waterways, ports, highways, and oil and gas pipelines.
Energy (1977)	Is responsible for the research, development, and demonstration of energy technology; marketing of federal electric power; energy conservation; the nuclear weapons program; regulation of energy production and use; and collection and analysis of energy data.
Education (1979)	Administers and coordinates most federal assistance to education.
Veterans Affairs (1989)	Operates programs to benefit veterans and members of their families.
Homeland Security (2002)	Prevents terrorist attacks within the United States, reduces the vulnerability of the nation to terrorism, and minimizes the damage and assists in recovery from terrorist attacks.

Source: The United States Government Manual, Washington, D.C.: Government Printing Office, annual.

Complying with IRS Rules

A woman filing tax forms while referring to the IRS Web site online. The IRS administers the nation's complex tax code and collects revenues from individuals and businesses in order to pay for government programs and services.

therefore the prestige ranking of their secretaries—is determined by their year of origin. Thus the Departments of State, Treasury, Defense (War), and Justice, created by the First Congress in 1789, head the protocol list of departments. Overall, the duties of the fifteen cabinet-level departments of the executive branch cover an enormous range—everything from providing mortgage insurance, to overseeing the armed forces of the United States (see Table 12.1).

Cabinet Appointments The Constitution requires that "Officers of the United States" be confirmed by the Senate. In the past, the Senate rarely rejected a presidential cabinet nomination; the traditional view was that presidents were entitled to pick their own people and even make their own mistakes. In recent years, however, the confirmation process has become more partisan and divisive, with the Senate conducting lengthy investigations and holding public hearings on presidential cabinet nominees. In 1989 the Senate rejected President Bush's nomination of John Tower as secretary of defense in a partisan battle featuring charges that the former Texas senator was a heavy drinker. The intense public scrutiny and potential for partisan attacks, together with financial disclosure and conflict-of-interest laws, may be discouraging some well-qualified people from accepting cabinet posts.

Independent Regulatory Commissions Independent regulatory commissions differ from cabinet departments in their function, organization, and accountability to the president. Their function is to *regulate* a sector of society— transportation, communications, banking, labor relations, and so on (see Table 12.2). These commissions are empowered by Congress both to make and to enforce rules, and they thus function in a legislative and judicial fashion. To symbolize their impartiality, many of these organizations are headed by *commissions*, usually with five to ten members, rather than by a single secretary. Major policy decisions are made by majority vote of the commission. Finally, these agencies are more independent of the president than are cabinet departments. Their governing commissions are appointed by the president and confirmed by the Senate in the same fashion as cabinet secretaries, but their terms are fixed; they cannot be removed by the president.[6] These provisions are designed to insulate regulators from direct partisan or presidential pressures in their decision making.

A few powerful regulatory agencies remain inside cabinet departments. The most notable are the Food and Drug Administration (FDA), which remains in the Department of Health and Human Services and has broad authority to prevent the sale of drugs not deemed by the agency to be both "safe" and "effective"; the Occupational Health and Safety Administration (OSHA) in the Department of Labor, with authority to make rules governing any workplace in America; and the most powerful government agency of all, the Internal Revenue Service in the Treasury Department, with its broad authority to interpret the tax code, maintain records on every American, and investigate and punish alleged violations of the tax code.

Independent Agencies Congress has created a number of independent agencies outside of any cabinet department. Like cabinet departments, these agencies are hierarchically organized with a single head—usually called an "administrator"—who is appointed by the president and confirmed by the Senate. Administrators have no fixed terms of office and can be dismissed by the president; thus they are independent only insofar as they report directly to the president rather than through a cabinet secretary. Politically, this independence ensures that their interests and budgets will not be compromised by other concerns, as may occur in agencies located within departments.

TABLE 12.2 Who Does What?: Major Regulatory Bureaucracies

Commission	Date Created	Primary Functions
Federal Communications Commission (FCC)	1934	Regulates interstate and foreign communications by radio, television, wire, and cable.
Food and Drug Administration (FDA)	1930	Sets standards of safety and efficacy for foods, drugs, and medical devices.
Federal Home Loan Bank	1932	Regulates savings and loan associations that specialize in making home mortgage loans.
Federal Maritime Commission	1961	Regulates the waterborne foreign and domestic offshore commerce of the United States.
Federal Reserve Board (FRB)	1913	Regulates the nation's money supply by making monetary policy, which influences the lending and investing activities of commercial banks and the cost and availability of money and credit.
Federal Trade Commission (FTC)	1914	Regulates business to prohibit unfair methods of competition and unfair or deceptive acts or practices.
National Labor Relations Board (NLRB)	1935	Protects employees' rights to organize; prevents unfair labor practices.
Securities and Exchange Commission (SEC)	1934	Regulates the securities and financial markets (such as the stock market).
Occupational Safety and Health Administration (OSHA)	1970	Issues workplace regulations; investigates, cites, and penalizes for noncompliance.
Consumer Product Safety Commission (CPSC)	1972	Protects the public against product-related deaths, illnesses, and injuries.
Commodity Futures Trading Commission	1974	Regulates trading on the futures exchanges as well as the activities of commodity exchange members, public brokerage houses, commodity salespersons, trading advisers, and pool operators.
Nuclear Regulatory Commission (NRC)	1974	Regulates and licenses the users of nuclear energy.
Federal Energy Regulatory Commission (formerly Federal Power Commission)	1977	Regulates the transportation and sale of natural gas, the transmission and sale of electricity, the licensing of hydroelectric power projects, and the transportation of oil by pipeline.
Equal Employment Opportunity Commission (EEOC)	1964	Investigates and rules on charges of racial, gender, and age discrimination by employers and unions, in all aspects of employment.
Environmental Protection Agency (EPA)	1970	Issues and enforces pollution control standards regarding air, water, solid waste, pesticides, radiation, and toxic substances.
Federal Elections Commission (FEC)	1975	Administers and enforces federal campaign finance laws.

Source: FirstGov, www.firstgov.gov/agencies.

One of the most powerful independent agencies is the Environmental Protection Agency (EPA), which is responsible for implementing federal legislation dealing with clean air, safe drinking water, solid waste disposal, pesticides, radiation, and toxic substances. EPA establishes and enforces comprehensive and complex standards for thousands of substances in the environment. It enjoys the political support of influential environmental interest groups, including the Environmental Defense Fund, Friends of the Earth, National Audubon Society, National

The U.S. Coast Guard at Work

The U.S. Coast Guard Cutter Aspen engaged in oil skimming operations in the Gulf of Mexico in June 2010 as part of a massive clean-up effort following the Deepwater Horizon oil spill.

Wildlife Federation, Natural Resources Defense Council, Sierra Club, and the Wilderness Society.

The "Fed"   The Federal Reserve System is the most independent of all federal government agencies. The function of the "Fed" is to regulate the supply of money and thereby avoid both inflation and recession (see Chapter 16). The Federal Reserve System is independent of either the president or Congress. Its seven-member Board of Governors is appointed for *14-year terms*. Members are appointed by the president, with the consent of the Senate, but they may not be removed from the board except for "cause." No member has ever been removed since the creation of the board in 1913. The chairman of the board serves only a 4-year term, but the chairman's term overlaps that of the president, so that new presidents cannot immediately name their own chair (see *People in Politics*: "Ben Bernanke Managing the Nation's Money").

Government Corporations   Government corporations are created by Congress to undertake independent commercial enterprises. They resemble private corporations in that they typically charge for their services. Like private corporations, too, they are usually governed by a chief executive officer and a board of directors, and they can buy and sell property and incur debts.

Presumably, government corporations perform a service that the private enterprise system has been unable to carry out adequately. The first government corporation was the Tennessee Valley Authority, created by President Franklin Roosevelt during the Depression to build dams and sell electricity at inexpensive rates to impoverished citizens in the mid-South. In 1970 Congress created Amtrak to restore railroad passenger service to the United States. While ridership has increased, competition with government-supported air and highway travel has forced Amtrak to continually seek federal subsidies to maintain operations. The U.S. Post Office had originally been created as a cabinet-level department, but in 1971 it became the U.S. Postal Service, a government corporation with a mandate from Congress to break even. But competition from e-mail and private delivery services, such as UPS and FedEx, has cut into Postal Service revenue and forced it to borrow from the U.S. Treasury to offset deficits.

PEOPLE IN POLITICS

Ben Bernanke—Managing the Nation's Money

Ben Bernanke, formerly a professor of economics at Princeton University, was nominated to serve as Chairman of the Board of Governors of the Federal Reserve System by President George W. Bush and confirmed by the U.S. Senate in 2006. It is Bernanke's job to guide "the Fed" in managing the nation's money supply to avoid both inflation and recession.

Bernanke excelled in public schools in Dillon, South Carolina; he achieved the highest SAT score in the state. He graduated summa cum laude from Harvard University in 1975 and earned his Ph.D. degree in economics from MIT in 1979. He taught at Stanford University and then Princeton University and served as editor of the *American Economic Review*. He wrote textbooks on both micro and macro economics. He served as Chairman of the Council of Economic Advisors before being appointed to head the Fed.

Fed Chairman Ben Bernanke attracts media attention as he prepares for testimony before a congressional Committee.

Bernanke replaced Alan Greenspan who had served under four presidents—Reagan; Bush, Sr.; Clinton; and Bush, Jr. During Greenspan's years inflation averaged only a modest 3% per year and unemployment averaged only 5.5% (This compares with an inflation rate of 6.5% and an unemployment rate of 6.8% in the 18 years prior to Greenspan assuming the post.) But Greenspan was later criticized for having allowed the mortgage industry to make too many substandard housing loans, resulting in an excess of foreclosures and losses for lending banks. Nonetheless upon taking office, Bernanke promptly announced his intention to "maintain continuity" with Greenspan's policies.

Bernanke, together with Treasury Secretary Henry Paulson, developed the $700 billion Wall Street bailout plan hurriedly passed by Congress in 2008. Bernanke testified that the bailout was essential in avoiding a deep recession.

President Barack Obama announced in 2009 that he would reappoint Bernanke to a second term as Fed Chairman. The president credited him with helping to prevent another Great Depression. Bernanke was confirmed by the Senate but only by the narrowest margin (70–30) of any previous Fed chairman.

Contractors and Consultants How has the federal government grown enormously in power and size, yet kept its number of employees at roughly the same level in recent years? The answer is found in the spectacular growth of private firms that live off federal contracting and consulting fees. Nearly one-fifth of all federal government spending flows through private contractors: for supplies, equipment, services, leases, and research and development. An army of scientists, economists, education specialists, management consultants, transportation experts, social scientists, and others are scattered across the country in universities, think tanks, consulting firms, and laboratories. Many are concentrated in the "beltway bandit" firms surrounding Washington, D.C.

The federal grant and contracting system is enormously complex; an estimated 150,000 federal contracting offices in nearly 500 agencies oversee thousands of outside contractors and consultants.[7] Although advertised bidding is sometimes required by law, most contracts and grants are awarded without competition through negotiation with favored firms or "sole source contracts" with organizations believed by bureaucrats to be uniquely qualified. Even when federal agencies issue public requests for proposals (RFPs), often a favored contractor has been alerted and advised by bureaucrats within the agency about how to win the award.

Spoiled Rotten?

During the administration of Andrew Jackson, the spoils system was perhaps more overt than at any other time in the history of the U.S. federal government. Jackson claimed he was trying to involve more of the "common folk" in the government, but his selection of advisers on the basis of personal friendship rather than qualifications sometimes caused him difficulties.

spoils system

Selection of employees for government agencies on the basis of party loyalty, electoral support, and political influence.

merit system

Selection of employees for government agencies on the basis of competence, with no consideration of an individual's political stance and/or power.

Bureaucracy and Democracy

▶ 12.3 *Trace changes over time in the size and composition of the bureaucracy and assess the repercussions for democracy.*

Traditionally, conflict over government employment centered on the question of partisanship versus competence. Should the federal bureaucracy be staffed by people politically loyal to the president, the president's party, or key members of Congress? Or should it be staffed by nonpartisan people selected on the basis of merit and protected from "political" influence?

The Spoils System   Historically, government employment was allocated by the **spoils system**—selecting employees on the basis of party loyalty, electoral support, and political influence. Or, as Senator William Marcy said in 1832, "They see nothing wrong in the rule that to the victors belong the spoils of the enemy."[8] The spoils system is most closely associated with President Andrew Jackson, who viewed it as a popular reform of the earlier tendency to appoint officials on the basis of kinship and class standing. Jackson sought to bring into government many of the common people who had supported him. Later in the nineteenth century, the bartering and sale of government jobs became so scandalous and time-consuming that presidents complained bitterly about the task. When President James Garfield was shot and killed in 1881 by a disgruntled job seeker, the stage was set for reform.

The Merit System   The **merit system**—government employment based on competence, neutrality, and protection from partisanship—was introduced in the Pendleton Act of 1883. The act created the Civil Service Commission to establish a system for selecting government personnel based on merit, as determined by competitive examinations. In the beginning, "civil service" coverage included only about 10 percent of total federal employees. Over the years, however, more and more positions were placed under civil service, primarily at the behest of presidents who sought to "freeze in" their political appointees. By 1978 more than 90 percent of federal employees were covered by civil service or other merit systems.

The civil service system established a uniform General Schedule (GS) of job grades from GS 1 (lowest) to GS 15 (highest), with an Executive Schedule added later for top managers and pay ranges based on an individual's time in the grade. Each grade has specific educational requirements and examinations. College graduates generally begin at GS 5 or above; GS 9 through GS 12 are technical and supervisory positions; and GS 13, 14, and 15 are midlevel management and highly specialized positions. The Executive Schedule (the "supergrades") are reserved for positions of greatest responsibility. (In 2010 annual pay ranged from roughly $30,000 to $48,000 for Grades 5–8, up to $70,000 to $127,000 for Grades 13–15, and $197,000 for some Executive Schedule positions.)

About two-thirds of all federal civilian jobs come under the General Schedule system, with its written examinations and/or training, experience, and educational requirements. Most of the other one-third of federal civilian employees are part of the "excepted services"; they are employed by various agencies that have their own separate merit systems, such as the Federal Bureau of Investigation, the Central Intelligence Agency, the U.S. Postal Service, and the State Department Foreign Service. The military also has its own system of recruitment, promotion, and pay.

Political Involvement Congress passed the Hatch Act in 1939, a law that prohibited federal employees from engaging in partisan political activity, including running for public office, soliciting campaign funds, or campaigning for or against a party or candidate. It also protected federal merit system employees from dismissal for partisan reasons. But over the years many federal employees came to believe that the Hatch Act infringed on their rights as citizens. In 1993, a Democratic-controlled Congress repealed major portions of the Hatch Act, allowing civil servants to hold party positions and involve themselves in political fund-raising and campaigning. They still may not be candidates for public office in partisan elections, or solicit contributions from subordinate employees or people who do business with—or have cases before—their agencies.

Rejected Job-Seeker Gets Vengeance
The assassination of President James A. Garfield on June 2, 1881. He lived another two and a half months, dying on September 19, 1881.

The Problem of Responsiveness The civil service system, like most other "reforms," eventually created problems at least as troubling as those in the system it replaced. First of all, there is the problem of a *lack of responsiveness* to presidential direction. Civil servants, secure in their protected jobs, can be less than cooperative toward their presidentially appointed department or agency heads. They can slow or obstruct policy changes with which they personally disagree. Each bureau and agency develops its own "culture," usually in strong support of the governmental function or client group served by the organization. Changing the culture of an agency is extremely difficult, especially when a presidential administration is committed to reducing its resources, functions, or services. Bureaucrats' powers of policy obstruction are formidable: They can help mobilize interest-group support against the president's policy; they can "leak" damaging information to sympathizers in Congress or the media to undermine the president's policy; they can delay and/or "sabotage" policies with which they disagree.

Think Again

Should the federal bureaucracy be managed by nonpartisan professionals rather than people politically loyal to the president?

The Problem of Productivity Perhaps the most troublesome problem in the federal bureaucracy has involved *productivity*—notably the inability to improve job performance because of the difficulties in rewarding or punishing civil servants. "Merit" salary rewards have generally proven ineffective in rewarding the performance of federal employees. More than 99 percent of federal workers regularly receive annual "merit" pay increases. Moreover, over time, federal employees have secured higher grade classifications and hence higher pay for most of the job positions in the General Schedule. This "inflation" in GS grades, combined with regular increases in salary and benefits, has resulted in many federal employees enjoying higher pay and benefits than employees in the private sector performing similar jobs.

At the same time, very poor performance often goes largely unpunished. Once hired and retained through a brief probationary period, a federal civil servant cannot be dismissed except for "cause." Severe obstacles to firing a civil servant result in a rate of dismissal of about one-tenth of 1 percent of all federal employees (see Table 12.3). It is doubtful that only such a tiny fraction are performing unsatisfactorily. A federal executive confronting a poorly performing or nonperforming employee must be prepared to spend more than a year in extended proceedings to secure a dismissal. Often costly substitute strategies are devised to work around or inspire the resignation of unsatisfactory federal

TABLE 12.3 Firing a Bureaucrat: What Is Required to Dismiss a Federal Employee

Very few federal civil servants are ever dismissed from their jobs.
• Written notice at least 30 days in advance of a hearing to determine incompetence or misconduct.
• A statement of cause, indicating specific dates, places, and actions cited as incompetent or improper.
• The right to a hearing and decision by an impartial official, with the burden of proof falling on the agency that wishes to fire the employee.
• The right to have an attorney and to present witnesses in the employee's favor at the hearing.
• The right to appeal any adverse action to the Merit Systems Protection Board.
• The right to appeal any adverse action by the board to the U.S. Court of Appeals.
• The right to remain on the job and be paid until all appeals are exhausted.

employees—assigning them meaningless or boring tasks, denying them promotions, transferring them to distant or undesirable locations, removing secretaries or other supporting resources, and the like.

President Jimmy Carter at his desk in the Oval Office.

Civil Service Reform Presidents routinely try to remedy some of the problems in the system. The Civil Service Reform Act of 1978, initiated by President Jimmy Carter, replaced the Civil Service Commission with the Office of Personnel Management (OPM) and made OPM responsible for recruiting, examining, training, and promoting federal employees. Unlike the Civil Service Commission, OPM is headed by a single director responsible to the president. The act also sought to (1) streamline procedures through which individuals could be disciplined for poor performance; (2) establish merit pay for middle-level managers; and (3) create a Senior Executive Service (SES) composed of about 8,000 top people designated for higher Executive Schedule grades and salaries who also might be given salary bonuses, transferred among agencies, or demoted, based on performance.

But like many other reforms, this act failed to resolve the major problems— the responsiveness and productivity of the bureaucracy. No senior executives were fired, demoted, or involuntarily transferred. The bonus program proved difficult to implement: There are few recognized standards for judging meritorious work in public service, and bonuses often reflect favoritism as much as merit. Because the act created a separate Merit Systems Protection Board to hear appeals by federal employees from dismissals, suspensions, and demotions, rates of dismissal for all grades have not changed substantially from earlier days.

Bureaucracy and Representation In addition to the questions of responsiveness and productivity, there is also the question of the representativeness of the federal bureaucracy. About 17 percent of the total federal civilian workforce is African American, and 7.5 percent is Hispanic. However, a close look at *top* bureaucratic positions reveals far less diversity. As Table 12.4 shows, only 6.4 percent of federal "executive" positions (levels GS 16–18) are filled by African Americans, and only 3.7 percent by Hispanics. Thus the federal bureaucracy is *un*representative of the general population in its top executive positions.

Think Again

Should the federal bureaucracy at all levels reflect the gender and minority ratios of the total civilian workforce?

TABLE 12.4 Diversity in the Bureaucracy: Minorities in Federal Employment

Minorities are not well-represented at the higher levels of the federal bureaucracy.			
	Percentage White, Non-Hispanic	Percentage African American	Percentage Hispanic
Overall	67.9%	17.2%	7.5%
By pay grade			
GS 1	52.9	25.8	10.2
GS 2	55.8	25.3	10.5
GS 3	55.6	22.1	9.4
GS 4	57.4	24.3	8.6
GS 5	55.3	26.7	9.1
GS 6	58.0	26.3	8.0
GS 7	61.8	22.5	8.9
GS 8	57.4	26.7	10.7
GS 9	65.9	19.5	7.9
GS 10	69.6	18.1	5.8
GS 11	68.0	14.7	10.6
GS 12	72.2	14.8	6.3
GS 13	75.6	12.7	5.2
GS 14	78.0	11.4	4.3
GS 15	81.2	7.1	3.8
Executive	85.2	6.4	3.7
U.S. Population	66.0	13.2	16.0

Note: Table excludes Native Americans, Alaska Natives, and Asian and Pacific Islanders.
Source: Office of Personnel Management. Demographic Profile of the Federal Workforce, 2006. www.opm.gov.

Bureaucratic Politics

▶ 12.4 *Explain how the bureaucracy is staffed, to whom it is accountable, and how accountability is affected by politics and bureaucratic culture.*

To whom is the federal bureaucracy really accountable? The president, Congress, or itself? Article II, Section 2, of the Constitution places the president at the head of the executive branch of government, with the power to "appoint Ambassadors, other public Ministers and Consuls, Judges of the Supreme Court, and all other Officers of the United States . . . which shall be established by Law." Appointment of these officials requires "the Advice and Consent of the Senate"—that is, a majority vote in the Senate. The Constitution also states that "the Congress may by Law vest the Appointment of such inferior Officers, as they think proper, in the President alone." If the bureaucracy is to be made accountable to the president, we would expect the president to directly appoint *policy-making* executive officers. But it is difficult to determine exactly how many positions are truly "policy making."

Presidential "Plums" The president retains direct control over about 3,000 federal jobs. Many of these jobs are considered policy-making positions. They include presidential appointments authorized by law—cabinet and subcabinet officers, judges, U.S. marshals, U.S. attorneys, ambassadors, and members of various boards and commissions. The president also appoints a large number of "Schedule C" jobs throughout the bureaucracy, described as "confidential or policy-determining" in character. Each new administration goes through many months of high-powered lobbying and scrambling to fill these posts. Applicants with congressional sponsors, friends in the White House, or a record of loyal campaign work for the president compete for these "plums." Political loyalty must be weighed against administrative competence.[9]

Rooms at the Top

The federal bureaucracy has "thickened" at the top, even as total federal employment has declined. Over time, departments and agencies have added layers of administrators, variously titled "deputy secretary," "undersecretary," "assistant secretary," "deputy assistant secretary," and so on. Cabinet departments have become top-heavy with administrators, and the same multiplication of layers of executive management has occurred in independent agencies as well.[10]

Whistle-Blowers

The question of bureaucratic responsiveness is complicated by the struggle between the president and Congress to control the bureaucracy. Congress expects federal agencies and employees to respond fully and promptly to its inquiries and to report candidly on policies, procedures, and expenditures. **Whistle-blowers** are federal employees (or employees of a firm contracting with the government) who report government waste, mismanagement, or fraud to the media or to congressional committees or who "go public" with their policy disputes with their superiors. Congress generally encourages whistle-blowing as a means of getting information and controlling the bureaucracy, but the president and agency heads whose policies are under attack are often less kindly disposed toward whistle-blowers.[11] In 1989 Congress passed the Whistleblower Protection Act, which established an independent agency to guarantee whistle-blowers protection against unjust dismissal, transfer, or demotion.

whistle-blowers
Employees who expose waste, fraud or mismanagement in government or government contracting.

Agency Cultures

Over time, every bureaucracy tends to develop its own "culture"—beliefs about the values of the organization's programs and goals and close associations with the agency's client groups and political supporters. Many government agencies are dominated by people who have been in government service most of their lives, and most of these people have worked in the same functional field most of their lives. They believe their work is important, and they resist efforts by either the president or Congress to reduce the activities, size, or budget of their agency. Career bureaucrats tend to support enlargement of the public sector—to enhance education, welfare, housing, environmental and consumer protection, and so on. Bureaucrats not only share a belief in the need for government expansion but also stand to benefit directly from increased authority, staffing, and funding as government takes on new and enlarged responsibilities. (See *Controversy*: "Are Federal Employees Paid Too Much?")

"Reinventing" Government

Reformers lament "the bankruptcy of bureaucracy"—the waste, inefficiency, impersonality, and unresponsiveness of large government organizations. They decry "the routine tendency to protect turf, to resist change, to build empires, to enlarge one's sphere of control, to protect projects and programs regardless of whether or not they are any longer needed."[12] Many bureaucratic reform efforts have foundered, from Hoover Commission studies in the Truman and Eisenhower years to the Grace Commission work in the Reagan administration. Clinton assigned a "reinventing government" task to Vice President

CONTROVERSY

Are Federal Employees Paid Too Much?

Federal employees earn higher average salaries than private-sector workers in similar jobs. Overall, federal workers earned an average salary of $67,691 in 2008 for occupations that are found in both government and the private sector. The average pay for the same mix of jobs in the private sector was $60,048. Moreover, the salary figures did not include the value of health, pension, and other benefits, which averaged $40,785 per federal employee versus $9,882 per private worker.[a]

However, salaries at the top of the federal government—department secretaries, agency and bureau heads—rarely match the top salaries in business firms, some of which have payouts of $1 million or more. And the private sector was found to pay higher-than-government salaries for a select group of high-skilled occupations, including lawyers. Many federal occupations—for example, air traffic controllers, tax collectors, FBI agents—have no direct equivalent in the private sector.

[a]Data from U.S. Bureau of Economic Analysis as reported in *USA TODAY*, March 4, 2010.

Al Gore. Gore produced a report designed to put the "customer" (U.S. citizen) first, to "empower" government employees to get results, to cut red tape, to introduce competition and a market orientation wherever possible, and to decentralize government decision making.[13] Very little of the Gore agenda was accomplished.

Outsourcing   The federal government is increasingly **outsourcing** its work—contracting to private companies for work formerly done by U.S. employees. As various departments across the government—from the Department of Defense to the National Park Service—have turned projects over to private businesses, the number of federal jobs has also declined, from 3.1 million in 1992 to 2.8 million in 2010. Among the advantages of outsourcing: private firms bid competitively for contracts, likely resulting in lower costs for the U.S. government—and therefore the American taxpayer. In addition, the private sector has fewer rules and regulations in comparison with operations within the departments and agencies of the federal government. Businesses may be able to undertake and complete projects faster and more efficiently than can governmental organizations. But outsourcing has its disadvantages—in many ways simply the reverse of its advantages. The low-cost bidder may be a foreign-owned company. Should the U.S. government be concerned about which companies get its contracts, and where the employees of those companies live? Also, the private sector may be less accountable than the public sector. Work being done by for-profit companies may cut corners and be less reliable than that being done by the government itself.

outsourcing
Government contracting with private firms to perform public services.

Presidential Initiative   Presidents can create some new agencies by executive order. Often Congress gives presidents the authority to reorganize agencies by legislation. But presidents have also acted on their own to create new agencies. Indeed, one study concludes that presidents have created about 40 percent of all new agencies[14]—perhaps the most famous was President Kennedy's Peace Corps. Of course, Congress has the last word, inasmuch as the continuation of a presidentially created agency requires funding and Congress controls the purse strings. It can end an agency's existence by cutting off its funds.

Seeing Red

Copies of the Fiscal 2011 *Budget of the U.S. Government,* submitted by the Office of Management and Budget in 2010. The budget called for $3.8 trillion in outlays and a deficit of $1.3 trillion.

Think Again

Do you believe the bureaucrats in Washington waste a lot of the money we pay in taxes?

fiscal year

Yearly government accounting period, not necessarily the same as the calendar year. The federal government's fiscal year begins October 1 and ends September 30.

The Budgetary Process

▶ 12.5 *Outline the budgetary process.*

The federal government's annual budget battles are the heart of the political process. Budget battles decide who gets what and who pays the cost of government. The budget is the single most important policy statement of any government.

The president is responsible for submitting the annual *Budget of the United States Government*—with estimates of revenues and recommendations for expenditures—for consideration, amendment, and approval by the Congress. But the president's budget reflects the outcome of earlier bureaucratic battles over who gets what. Despite highly publicized wrangling between the president and Congress each year—and occasional declarations that the president's budget is "DOA" (dead on arrival)—final congressional appropriations rarely deviate by more than 2 or 3 percent from the original presidential budget. Thus the president and the Office of Management and Budget in the Executive Office of the President have real budgetary power.

The Office of Management and Budget The Office of Management and Budget (OMB) has the key responsibility for budget preparation. In addition to this major task, OMB has related responsibilities for improving the organization and management of the executive agencies, for coordinating the extensive statistical services of the federal government, and for analyzing and reviewing proposed legislation.[15]

Preparation of the budget begins when OMB, after preliminary consultations with the executive agencies and in accord with presidential policy, develops targets or ceilings within which the agencies are encouraged to build their requests (see Figure 12.3). Budget materials and instructions then go to the agencies, with the request that the forms be completed and returned to OMB. This request is followed by about 3 months of arduous work by agency budget officers, department heads, and the "grass-roots" bureaucracy in Washington, D.C., and out in the field. Budget officials at the bureau and departmental levels check requests from the smaller units, compare them with previous years' estimates, hold conferences, and make adjustments. The heads of agencies are expected to submit their completed requests to OMB by July or August. Although these requests usually remain within target levels, occasionally they include some "overceiling" items (requests above the suggested ceilings). With the requests of the spending agencies at hand, OMB begins its own budget review, including hearings at which top agency officials support their requests as convincingly as possible. Frequently OMB must say "no," that is, reduce agency requests. On rare occasions, dissatisfied agencies may ask the budget director to take their cases to the president.

The President's Budget In December, the president and the OMB director devote much time to the key document, *The Budget of the United States Government,* which by now is approaching its final stages of assembly. Each budget is named for the **fiscal year** in which it *ends.* The federal fiscal year begins on October 1 and ends the following September 30. (Thus *The Budget of the United States Government Fiscal Year* 2012 begins October 1, 2011, and ends September 30, 2012.) Although the completed document includes a revenue plan with general estimates for taxes and other income, it is primarily an expenditure budget. (Revenue and tax policy staff work centers in the Treasury Department, not in the Office of Management and Budget.) In late January, the president presents Congress with *The Budget of the United States Government* for the fiscal year beginning October 1.

	WHO	WHAT	WHEN
Presidential budget making	President and OMB	OMB presents long-range forecasts for revenues and expenditures to the president. President and OMB develop general guidelines for all federal agencies. Agencies are sent guidelines and forms for their budget requests.	January February March
	Executive agencies	Agencies prepare and submit budget requests to OMB.	April May June July
	OMB and agencies	OMB reviews agency requests and holds hearings with agency officials.	August September October
	OMB and president	OMB presents revised budget to president. President and OMB write budget message for Congress.	November December January
	President	President presents budget for the next fiscal year to Congress.	February
Congressional budget process	CBO and congressional committees	CBO reviews taxing and spending proposals and reports to House and Senate budget committees.	February– April
	Congress; House and Senate budget committees	Committees present first concurrent resolution, which sets overall total for budget outlays in major categories. Full House and Senate vote on resolution. Committees are instructed to stay within Budget Committee's resolution.	May June
	Congress; House and Senate appropriations committees and budget committees	Appropriations committees and subcommittees draw up detailed appropriations bills and submit them to budget committees for second concurrent resolution. The full House and Senate vote on "reconciliations" and second (firm) concurrent resolution.	July August September
	Congress and president	House and Senate pass various appropriations bills (nine to sixteen bills, by major functional category, such as "defense"). Each is sent to president for signature. (If successfully vetoed, a bill is revised and resubmitted to the president.)	September October
Executive budget implementation	Congress and president	Fiscal year for all federal agencies begins October 1. If no appropriations bill for an agency has been passed by Congress and signed by the president, Congress must pass and the president sign a continuing resolution to allow the agency to spend at last year's level until a new appropriations bill is passed. If no continuing resolution is passed, the agency must officially cease spending government funds and must officially shut down.	After October 1

FIGURE 12.3 How It Works: The Budget Process

Development, presentation, and approval of the federal budget for any fiscal year takes almost 2 full years. The executive branch spends more than a year on the process before Congress even begins its review and revision of the president's proposals. The problems of implementing the budgeted programs then fall to the federal bureaucracy.

After the budget is in legislative hands, the president may recommend further alterations as needs dictate.

budget resolution
Congressional bill setting forth target budget figures for appropriations to various government departments and agencies.

House and Senate Budget Committees The Constitution gives Congress the authority to decide how the government should spend its money: "No money shall be drawn from the Treasury, but in Consequence of Appropriations made by Law" (Article I, Section 9). The president's budget is sent initially to the House and Senate Budget Committees, which rely on their own bureaucracy, the Congressional Budget Office (CBO), to review the president's budget. Based on the CBO's assessment, these committees draft a first **budget resolution** (due May 15) setting forth target goals to guide congressional committees regarding specific appropriations and revenue measures. If proposed spending exceeds the targets in the budget resolution, the resolution comes back to the floor in a reconciliation measure. A second budget resolution (due September 15) sets binding budget figures for committees and subcommittees considering appropriations. In practice, however, these two budget resolutions are often folded into a single measure because Congress does not want to argue the same issues twice.

Congressional Appropriations Committees Congressional approval of each year's spending is usually divided into thirteen separate appropriations bills (acts), each covering separate broad categories of spending (for example, defense, labor, human services and education, commerce, justice). These appropriations bills are drawn up by the House and Senate Appropriations Committees and their specialized subcommittees, which function as overseers of agencies included in their appropriations bills. Committee work in the House of Representatives is usually more thorough than it is in the Senate; the committee in the Senate tends to be a "court of appeal" for agencies opposed to House action. Each committee, moreover, has about ten largely independent subcommittees, each reviewing the requests of a particular agency or a group of related functions. Specific appropriations bills are taken up by the subcommittees in hearings. Departmental officers answer questions on the conduct of their programs and defend their requests for the next fiscal year; lobbyists and other witnesses testify. Although committees and subcommittees have broad discretion in allocating funds to the agencies they monitor, they must stay within overall totals set forth in the second budget resolution adopted by Congress.

authorization
Act of Congress that establishes a government program and defines the amount of money it may spend.

appropriations act
Congressional bill that provides money for programs authorized by Congress.

obligational authority
Feature of some appropriations acts by which an agency is empowered to enter into contracts that will require the government to make payments beyond the fiscal year in question.

Appropriations Acts In examining the interactions between Congress and the federal bureaucracy over spending, it is important to distinguish between appropriations and authorization. An **authorization** is an act of Congress that establishes a government program and defines the amount of money it may spend. Authorizations may be for one or several years. However, an authorization does not actually provide the money that has been authorized; only an **appropriations act** can do that. In fact, appropriations acts, which are usually for a single fiscal year, are almost always *less* than authorizations; deciding how much less is the real function of the Appropriations Committees and subcommittees. (By its own rules, Congress cannot appropriate money for programs it has not already authorized.) Appropriations acts include both obligational authority and outlays.

outlays
Actual dollar amounts to be spent by the federal government in a fiscal year.

   Obligational authority permits a government agency to enter into contracts that will require the government to make payments beyond the fiscal years in question. **Outlays** must be spent in the fiscal year for which they are appropriated.

Continuing Resolutions and "Shutdowns"   All appropriations acts *should* be passed by both houses and signed by the president into law before October 1, the date of the start of the fiscal year. However, it is rare for Congress to meet this deadline, so the government usually finds itself beginning a new fiscal year without a budget. Constitutionally, any U.S. government agency for which Congress does not pass an appropriations act may not draw money from the Treasury and thus is obliged to shut down. To get around this problem, Congress usually adopts a **continuing resolution** that authorizes government agencies to keep spending money for a specified period at the same level as in the previous fiscal year.

A continuing resolution is supposed to grant additional time for Congress to pass, and the president to sign, appropriations acts. But occasionally this process has broken down in the heat of political combat over the budget: the time period specified in a continuing resolution has expired without agreement on appropriations acts or even on a new continuing resolution. Shutdowns occurred during the bitter battle between President Bill Clinton and the Republican-controlled Congress over the fiscal year 1996 budget. In theory, the absence of either appropriations acts or a continuing resolution should cause the entire federal government to "shut down," that is, to cease all operations and expenditures for lack of funds. But in practice, such shutdowns have been only partial, affecting only "nonessential" government employees and causing relatively little disruption.

The Politics of Budgeting

▶ 12.6 *Evaluate the advantages and disadvantages of the current system of budgeting.*

Budgeting is very political. Being a good "bureaucratic politician" involves (1) cultivating a good base of support for requests among the public at large and among interests served by the agency; (2) developing attention, enthusiasm, and support for one's program among top political figures and congressional leaders; (3) winning favorable coverage of agency activities in the media; and (4) following strategies that exploit opportunities.

Budgeting Is "Incremental"   The most important factor determining the size and content of the budget each year is last year's budget. Decision makers generally use last year's expenditures as a *base*; active consideration of budget proposals generally focuses on new items and requested increases over last year's base. The budget of an agency is almost never reviewed as a whole. Agencies are seldom required to defend or explain budget requests that do *not* exceed current appropriations; but requested increases *do* require explanation and are most subject to reduction by OMB or Congress.

The result of **incremental budgeting** is that many programs, services, and expenditures continue long after there is any real justification for them. When new needs, services, and functions arise, they do not displace older ones but rather are *added* to the budget. Budget decisions are made incrementally because policy makers do not have the time, energy, or information to review every dollar of every budget request every year. Nor do policy makers wish to refight every political battle over existing programs every year. So they generally accept last year's base spending level as legitimate and focus attention on proposed increases for each program.

Reformers have proposed "sunset" laws requiring bureaucrats to justify their programs every 5 to 7 years or else the programs go out of existence, as well as **zero-based budgeting** that would force agencies to justify every penny requested—not

---

continuing resolution
Congressional bill that authorizes government agencies to keep spending money for a specified period at the same level as in the previous fiscal year; passed when Congress is unable to enact final appropriations measures by October 1.

incremental budgeting
Method of budgeting that focuses on requested increases in funding for existing programs, accepting as legitimate their previous year's expenditures.

zero-based budgeting
Method of budgeting that demands justification for the entire budget request of an agency, not just its requested increase in funding.

WHAT DO YOU THINK?

How Much Money Does the Government Waste?

Americans are markedly cynical about the amount of waste in government spending. On average, Americans believe that 50 cents of every tax dollar that goes to the federal government in Washington are wasted. This figure is higher than in previous years (when the mean number of cents believed to be wasted ranged from 38 to 45), perhaps as a result of the increased spending in the Obama administration. State and local government are perceived to be somewhat less wasteful than the government in Washington.

Q. Of every tax dollar that goes to [the federal government, your state government, your local government] how many cents of each dollar would you say are wasted?

Mean number of cents of each dollar wasted

	1982	2003	2009
Federal government	45¢	46¢	50¢
State government	38	38	42
Local government	34	36	37

But it is difficult to determine how much money the government actually wastes. What is "waste" to one person may be a necessary and vital government function to another.

The General Accountability Office (GAO) of the U.S. Congress has the authority to audit the operations and finances of federal agencies. The GAO has often found fraud and mismanagement of government operations that come to 10 percent or more of the spending of the agencies that it has reviewed. This suggests the possibility that $380 billion of the federal government's $3.8 trillion budget is being wasted. Independent government commissions that studied federal government operations, such as the Grace Commission during the Reagan administration in the 1980s, put an even higher figure on government waste: more than 20 percent of government spending.

Despite frequent pledges by presidents and Congress to end waste and inefficiency in the federal government, it has proven difficult if not impossible to do so. Many programs that have been identified as having a great deal of waste and fraud are also politically very popular. Medicare, for example—which has been found to pay for unnecessary tests and procedures, for needless medical equipment, and for overpriced drugs—is a very popular program. Promises to eliminate waste in Medicare usually stir concerns, especially among senior citizens. Economic stimulus bills (see Chapter 16) regularly include many wasteful projects, but these same projects meet Congress members' demands for pork-barrel projects that bring contracts and jobs to their districts around the country.

Sources: Gallup poll, September 15, 2009. www.gallup.com; General Accountability Office, *Federal Evaluation Issues*. Washington, D.C.: 1989; *President's Private Sector Survey on Cost Control* (Grace Commission). Washington, D.C.: Government Printing Office, 1984.

just requested increases. In theory, sunset laws and zero-based budgeting would regularly prune unnecessary government programs, agencies, and expenditures and thus limit the growth of government and waste in government (see *What Do You Think?*: "How Much Money Does the Government Waste?"). But in reality, sunset laws and zero-based budgeting require so much effort in justifying already accepted programs that executive agencies and legislative committees grow tired of the effort and return to incrementalism.

The "incremental" nature of budgetary politics helps reduce political conflicts and maintain stability in governmental programs. As bruising as budgetary battles are today, they would be much worse if the president or Congress undertook to review the value of *all* existing expenditures and programs each year. Comprehensive budgetary review would "overload the system" with political conflict by refighting every policy battle every year.

Budgeting Is Nonprogrammatic Budgeting is *nonprogrammatic* in that an agency budget typically lists expenditures under ambiguous phrases: "personnel services," "contractual services," "travel," "supplies," "equipment." It is difficult to tell from such a listing exactly what programs the agency is spending its money on.

A CONFLICTING VIEW

Bureaucratic Regulations Are Suffocating America

Today, bureaucratic regulations of all kinds—environmental controls, workplace safety rules, municipal building codes, government contracting guidelines—have become so numerous, detailed, and complex that they are stifling initiative, curtailing economic growth, wasting billions of dollars, and breeding popular contempt for law and government.

Consider, for example, the Environmental Protection Agency's rules and regulations, now *thirty-two volumes* of fine print. Under one set of rules, before any land on which "toxic" waste was once used can be reused by anyone for any purpose, it must be cleaned to near perfect purity. The dirt must be made cleaner than soil that has never been used for anything. The result is that most new businesses choose to locate on virgin land rather than incur the enormous expense of cleaning dirt, and a great deal of land previously used by industry sits vacant while new land is developed.

These and similar examples of "the death of common sense" in bureaucratic regulations are set forth by critic Philip K. Howard, who argues, "We have constructed a system of regulatory law that basically outlaws common sense."[a]

The explosive growth in federal regulations in the last two decades has added heavy costs to the American economy. The costs of regulations do not appear in the federal budget: rather, they are paid for by businesses, employees, and consumers. Indeed, politicians prefer a regulatory approach to the environment,

health, and safety precisely because it forces costs on the private sector—costs that are largely invisible to voters and taxpayers. Yet as the costs of regulation multiply for American businesses, the prices of their products rise in world markets.

How large is the regulatory bill? Proponents of a regulatory activity usually object to estimating its cost. Politicians who wish to develop an image as protectors of the environment, of consumers, of the disabled, and so on, do not want to call attention to the costs of their legislation. Only recently has the Office of Management and Budget (OMB) even attempted to estimate the costs of federal regulatory activity. Overall, regulatory activity costs Americans between $300 billion (OMB estimate) and $1 trillion a year (estimate by Center for Competitive Enterprise Institute), an amount equal to over one-quarter of the total federal budget.

Regulation also places a heavy burden on innovations and productivity. The costs and delays in winning permission for a new product tend to discourage invention and to drive up prices. For example, new drugs are difficult to introduce in the United States because the Food and Drug Administration (FDA) typically requires up to 10 years of testing. Western European nations are many years ahead in their number of life-saving drugs available; they speak of the "drug lag" in the United States. Critics charge that if aspirin were proposed for marketing today, it would not be approved by the FDA.

[a]Philip K. Howard, *The Death of Common Sense: How Law Is Suffocating America.* New York: Random House, 1995, pp. 10–11.

Such a budget obscures policy decisions by hiding programs behind meaningless phrases. Even if these categories are broken down into line items (for example, under "personnel services," the line-item budget might say, "John Doaks, Assistant Administrator, $85,000"), it is still next to impossible to identify the costs of various programs.

For many years, reformers have called for budgeting by programs. **Program budgeting** would require agencies to present budgetary requests in terms of the end products they will produce or at least to allocate each expense to a specific program. However, bureaucrats are often unenthusiastic about program budgeting; it certainly adds to the time and energy devoted to budgeting, and many agencies are reluctant to describe precisely what it is they do and how much it really costs to do it. Moreover, some political functions are best served by *non*program budgeting. Agreement comes more easily when the items in dispute can be treated in dollars instead of programmatic differences. Congressional appropriations committees can focus on increases or decreases in overall dollar amounts for agencies rather than battle over even more contentious questions of which individual programs are worthy of support.

program budgeting
Identifying items in a budget according to the functions and programs they are to be spent on.

Obama's Economic Team

Budget Director Peter Orszag, Treasury Secretary Timothy Geithner, and Council of Economic Chair Christina Romer testify before the House Appropriations Committee, March 2010. Later that year Orszag and Romer left the administration.

Congressional Constraints on the Bureaucracy

▶ **12.7** *Outline the growth of federal regulation.*

Bureaucracies are unelected hierarchical organizations, yet they must function within democratic government. To wed bureaucracy to democracy, ways must be found to ensure that bureaucracy is responsible to the people. Controlling the bureaucracy is a central concern of democratic government. The federal bureaucracy is responsible to all three branches of government—the president, the Congress, and the courts. Although the president is the nominal head of the executive agencies, Congress—through its power to create or eliminate and fund or fail to fund these agencies—exerts its full share of control. Most of the structure of the executive branch of government (see Figure 12.1) is determined by laws of Congress. Congress has the constitutional power to create or abolish executive departments and independent agencies, or to transfer their functions, as it wishes. Congress can by law expand or contract the discretionary authority of bureaucrats. It can grant broad authority to agencies in vaguely written language, thereby adding to the power of bureaucracies, which can then determine themselves how to define and implement their own authority. In contrast, narrow and detailed laws place constraints on the bureaucracy.

In addition to specific constraints on particular agencies, Congress has placed a number of general constraints on the entire federal bureaucracy. Among the more important laws governing bureaucratic behavior are the following:

- *Administrative Procedures Act (1946):* Requires that agencies considering a new rule or policy give public notice in the *Federal Register,* solicit comments, and hold public hearings before adopting the new measures.

- *Freedom of Information Act (1966):* Requires agencies to allow citizens (and the media) to inspect all public records, with some exceptions for intelligence, current criminal investigations, and personnel actions (see *Politics Up Close:* "How to Use the Freedom of Information Act").

- *Privacy Act (1974):* Requires agencies to keep confidential the personal records of individuals, notably their Social Security files and income tax records.

Senate Confirmation of Appointments The U.S. Senate's power to confirm presidential appointments gives it some added influence over the bureaucracy.[16] It is true that once nominated and confirmed, cabinet secretaries and regulatory commission members can defy the Congress; only the president can remove them from office. Senators usually try to impress their own views on presidential appointees seeking confirmation, however. Senate committees holding confirmation hearings often subject appointees to lengthy lectures on how the members believe their departments or agencies should be run. In extreme cases, when presidential appointees do not sufficiently reflect the views of Senate leaders, their confirmation can be held up indefinitely or, in very rare cases, defeated in a floor vote on confirmation.

POLITICS UP CLOSE

How to Use the Freedom of Information Act

The Freedom of Information Act (FOIA) of 1966 requires agencies of the federal government to provide any member of the public records of the agencies. As amended by the Privacy Act of 1974, individuals can obtain their personal records held by government agencies and are given the right to correct information that is inaccurate. The FOIA does not apply to Congress, the federal courts, state and local government agencies (unless a state has a similar law), military plans and weapons, law enforcement investigations, records of financial institutions, or records which would invade the privacy of others. An agency must respond within 10 days to an FOIA request, but it may charge fees for the costs of searching for the documents and duplicating them.

A good request must "reasonably describe" the records that are being sought; it must be specific enough that an agency employee will be able to locate the records within a reasonable amount of time. A good FOIA request letter includes:

Attention: Freedom of Information/Privacy Request
Name and Address of Agency

This is a request under the Freedom of Information Act, 5 U.S.C. Sec.552

I request a copy of the following documents be provided for me.

_____

_____

I am aware that if my request is denied I am entitled to know the grounds for this denial and make an administrative appeal.

I am willing to pay fees for this request up to a maximum of $___. If you estimate that fees will exceed this limit, please inform me first.

Thank you for your prompt attention.

Signature

Address

Congressional Oversight Congressional oversight of the federal bureaucracy is a continuing activity. Congress justifies its oversight activities on the grounds that its lawmaking powers require it to determine whether the purposes of the laws it passed are being carried out. Congress has a legitimate interest in communicating legislative *intent* to bureaucrats charged with the responsibility for implementing laws of Congress. But often oversight activities are undertaken to influence bureaucratic decision making. Members of Congress may seek to secure favorable treatment for friends and constituents, try to lay the political groundwork for increases or decreases in agency appropriations, or simply strive to enhance their own power or the power of their committees or subcommittees over the bureaucracy.

Oversight is lodged primarily in congressional committees and subcommittees (see "In Committee" in Chapter 10) whose jurisdictions generally parallel those of executive departments and agencies. However, all too frequently, agencies are required to respond to multiple committee inquiries in both the House and the Senate.

Congressional Appropriations The congressional power to grant or to withhold the budget requests of bureaucracies and the president is perhaps Congress's most potent weapon in controlling the bureaucracy. Spending authorizations for executive agencies are determined by standing committees with

Congressional Oversight of the Military
Undersecretary of Defense for Intelligence, Stephen Cambone, flanked by generals, is called to testify before the Senate Arms Forces Committee regarding treatment of detainees at Abu Ghraib prison.

jurisdiction in various policy areas, such as armed services, judiciary, education, and labor (see Table 10.2 in Chapter 10), and appropriations are determined by the House and Senate Appropriations Committees and, more specifically, their subcommittees with particular jurisdictions. These committees and subcommittees exercise great power over executive agencies. The Defense Department, for example, must seek *authorizations* for new weapons systems from the House and Senate Armed Services Committees and *appropriations* to actually purchase these weapons from the House and Senate Appropriations Committees, especially their Defense Appropriations subcommittees.

Congressional Investigation Congressional investigations offer yet another tool for congressional oversight of the bureaucracy. Historically, congressional investigations have focused on scandal and wrongdoing in the executive branch (see "Oversight of the Bureaucracy" in Chapter 10). Occasionally, investigations even produce corrective legislation, although they more frequently produce changes in agency personnel, procedures, or policies. Investigations are more likely to follow media reports of waste, fraud, or scandal than to uncover previously unknown problems. In other words, investigations perform a political function for Congress—assuring voters that the Congress is taking action against bureaucratic abuses. Studies of routine bureaucratic performance are likely to be undertaken by the Government Accountability Office (GAO), an arm of Congress and frequent critic of executive agencies. GAO may undertake studies of the operations of executive agencies on its own initiative but more often responds to requests for studies by specific members of Congress.

casework
Services performed by legislators and their staffs on behalf of individual constituents.

Casework Perhaps the most frequent congressional oversight activities are calls, letters, and visits to the agencies by individual members of Congress seeking to influence particular actions on behalf of themselves or their constituents. A great deal of congressional **casework** involves intervening with executive agencies on behalf of constituents[17] (see Chapter 10). Executive departments and agencies generally try to deal with congressional requests and inquiries as favorably and rapidly as the law allows. Pressure from a congressional office will lead bureaucrats to speed up an application, correct an error, send information, review a case, or reinterpret a regulation to favor a client with congressional contacts. But bureaucrats become very uncomfortable when asked to violate established regulations on behalf of a favored person or firm. The line between serving constituents and unethical or illegal attempts to influence government agencies is sometimes very difficult to discern.

ATF Canine Enforcement
An agent of the federal Bureau of Alcohol, Tobacco, and Firearms shows how dogs can detect bomb-making compounds.

Interest Groups and Bureaucratic Decision Making

▶ 12.8 *Evaluate the cost of federal regulation.*

Interest groups understand that great power is lodged in the bureaucracy. Indeed, interest groups exercise an even closer oversight of bureaucracy than do the president, Congress, and courts, largely because their interests are directly affected by day-to-day bureaucratic decisions. Interest groups focus their attention on the particular departments and agencies that serve or regulate their own members or that function in their chosen policy field. For example, the American Farm Bureau Federation monitors the actions of the Department of Agriculture; environmental lobbies—such as the National Wildlife Federation, the Sierra Club, and the Environmental Defense Fund—watch over the Environmental Protection Agency as well as the National Park Service and U.S. Forest Service. The American Legion, Veterans of Foreign Wars, and Vietnam Veterans "oversee" the Department of Veterans Affairs. Thus specific groups come to have a proprietary interest in "their" specific departments and agencies. Departments and agencies understand that their "client" groups have a continuing interest in their activities.

Many bureaucracies owe their very existence to strong interest groups that successfully lobbied Congress to create them. The Environmental Protection Agency owes its existence to the environmental groups, just as the Equal Employment Opportunity Commission owes its existence to civil rights groups. Thus many bureaucracies nourish interest groups' support to aid in expanding their authority and increasing their budgets (see "Iron Triangles" in Chapter 9).

Interest groups can lobby bureaucracies directly by responding to notices of proposed regulations, testifying at public hearings, and providing information and commentary. Or interest groups can lobby Congress either in support of bureaucratic activity or to reverse a bureaucratic decision. Interest groups may also seek to "build fires" under bureaucrats by holding press conferences, undertaking advertising campaigns, and soliciting media support for agency actions. Or interest groups may even seek to influence bureaucracies through appeals to the federal courts.

Judicial Constraints on the Bureaucracy

▶ 12.9 *Summarize the constraints that Congress can place on the bureaucracy.*

Judicial oversight is another source of restraint on the bureaucracy. Bureaucratic decisions are subject to review by the federal courts. Federal courts can even issue *injunctions* (orders) to an executive agency *before* it issues or enforces a regulation or undertakes a particular action. Thus the judiciary poses a check on bureaucratic power.

Judicial Standards for Bureaucratic Behavior   Historically, the courts have stepped in when agency actions have violated laws passed by Congress, when agencies have exceeded the authority granted them under the laws, when the agency actions have been adjudged "arbitrary and unreasonable," and when agencies have failed in their legal duties under the law. The courts have also restrained the bureaucracy on procedural grounds—ensuring proper notice, fair hearings, rights of appeal, and so on. In short, appeals to the courts must cite failures of agencies to abide by substantive or procedural laws.

Judicial oversight tends to focus on (1) whether or not agencies are acting beyond the authority granted them by Congress; and (2) whether or not they are abiding by rules of procedural fairness. It is important to realize that the courts do not usually involve themselves in the *policy* decisions of bureaucracies. If policy decisions are made in accordance with the legal authority granted agencies by Congress, and if they are made with procedural fairness, the courts generally do not intervene.

Bureaucrats' Success in Court   Bureaucracies have been very successful in defending their actions in federal courts.[18] Individual citizens and interest groups seeking to restrain or reverse the actions or decisions of executive agencies have

A CONSTITUTIONAL NOTE

Congress and the Budget

The Constitution places "the power of the purse" firmly in the hands of Congress: "No money shall be drawn from the Treasury, but in Consequence of Appropriations made by Law" (Article I, Section 9). The Congress has multiple means of controlling the bureaucracy. It can create, eliminate, or reorganize agencies, and it can alter their functions and rules of operation as it sees fit. And the Senate can confirm or withhold confirmation of presidential appointments. In the exercise of these powers Congress can hold hearings, conduct investigations, and interrogate executive officials. But the power over appropriations for departments and agencies remains the most important instrument of congressional control over the bureaucracy. The president, of course, is head of the executive branch and the Constitution charges him to "take care that the laws be faithfully executed" (Article II, Section 3). Prior to 1921, executive departments and agencies submitted their budgets directly to the Congress with very little presidential input or control. But the Budget and Accounting Act of that year established a Bureau of the Budget, which later was placed in the White House directly under the president. The act required all executive agencies to submit their budgets to the Bureau of the Budget, now called the Office of Management and Budget (OMB), and to the president. The president and OMB draw up *The Budget of the United States Government* each year for submission to Congress. The Budget Committees of the House and Senate by resolution set overall totals for budget outlays in major categories. These committees are under no obligation to follow the president's budget recommendations. Later, the Appropriations Committees and subcommittees of each house write up specific appropriations bills. If it wishes, Congress can ignore items in the president's budget and appropriate whatever funds to whatever agencies it chooses. The Appropriations Committees of the House and Senate jealously guard Congress's "power of the purse."

been largely *unsuccessful*. What accounts for this success? Bureaucracies have established elaborate administrative processes to protect their decisions from challenge on procedural grounds. Regulatory agencies have armies of attorneys, paid for out of tax monies, who specialize in these narrow fields of law. It is very expensive for individual citizens to challenge agency actions. Corporations and interest groups must weigh the costs of litigation against the costs of compliance before undertaking a legal challenge of the bureaucracy. Excessive delays in court proceedings, sometimes extending to several years, add to the time and expense of challenging bureaucratic decisions.

Summary

▶ **12.1** *Assess the nature, sources, and extent of bureaucratic power.*

Bureaucratic power has grown with increases in the size of government, advances in technology, and the greater complexity of modern society. Congress and the president do not have the time, resources, or expertise to decide the details of policy across the wide range of social and economic activity in the nation. Bureaucracies must draw up the detailed rules and regulations that actually govern the nation. Often laws are passed for their symbolic value; bureaucrats must give practical meaning to these laws. And the bureaucracy itself is now sufficiently powerful to get laws passed adding to its authority, size, and budget.

Policy implementation is the development of procedures and activities and the allocation of money, personnel, and other resources to carry out the tasks mandated by law. Implementation includes regulation—the making of detailed rules based on the law—as well as adjudication—the application of laws and regulations to specific cases. Bureaucratic power increases with increases in administrative discretion.

▶ **12.2** *Describe the types of agencies in the federal bureaucracy and the extent and purposes of the bureaucracy.*

The federal bureaucracy consists of 2.8 million civilian employees in fifteen cabinet departments and more than sixty independent agencies, as well as a large Executive Office of the President. Federal employment is not growing, but federal spending is growing rapidly.

Today, federal spending amounts to 25 percent of GDP, and federal, state, and local government spending combined amounts to 35 percent of GDP.

▶ 12.3 *Trace changes over time in the size and composition of the bureaucracy and assess the repercussions for democracy.*

Bureaucracies usually seek to expand their own powers, functions, and budgets. Most bureaucrats believe strongly in the value of their own programs and the importance of their tasks. And bureaucrats, like everyone else, seek added power, pay, and prestige. Bureaucratic expansion contributes to the growth of government.

Historically, political conflict over government employment centered on the question of partisanship versus competence. Over time, the "merit system" replaced the "spoils system" in federal employment, but the civil service system raised problems of responsiveness and productivity in the bureaucracy. Civil service reform efforts have not really resolved these problems.

▶ 12.4 *Explain how the bureaucracy is staffed, to whom it is accountable, and how accountability is affected by politics and bureaucratic culture.*

The president's control of the bureaucracy rests principally on the powers to appoint and remove policy-making officials, to recommend increases and decreases in agency budgets, and to recommend changes in agency structure and function.

But the bureaucracy has developed various means to insulate itself from presidential influence. Bureaucrats have many ways to delay and obstruct policy decisions with which they may disagree. Whistle-blowers may inform Congress or the media of waste, mismanagement, or fraud. A network of friends and professional associates among bureaucrats, congressional staffs, and client groups helps create a "culture" within each agency and department. The bureaucratic culture is highly resistant to change.

▶ 12.5 *Outline the budgetary process.*

Budget battles over who gets what begin in the bureaucracy as departments and agencies send their budget requests forward to the president's Office of Management and Budget. OMB usually reduces agency requests in line with the president's priorities. The president submits spending recommendations to Congress early each year in *The Budget*

of the United States Government. Congress is supposed to pass its appropriations acts prior to the beginning of the fiscal year, October 1, but frequently falls behind schedule.

▶ 12.6 *Evaluate the advantages and disadvantages of the current system of budgeting.*

Most budgeting is incremental, in that last year's agency expenditures are usually accepted as a base and attention is focused on proposed increases. Incrementalism saves time and effort and reduces political conflict by not requiring agencies to justify every dollar spent, only proposed increases each year. Nonprogrammatic budgeting also helps reduce conflict over the value of particular programs. The result, however, is that many established programs continue long after the need for them has disappeared.

▶ 12.7 *Outline the growth of federal regulation.*

Congress can exercise control over the bureaucracy in a variety of ways: by creating, abolishing, or reorganizing departments and agencies; by altering their authority and functions; by requiring bureaucrats to testify before congressional committees; by undertaking investigations and studies through the Government Accountability Office; by intervening directly on behalf of constituents; by instructing presidential nominees in Senate confirmation hearings and occasionally delaying or defeating nominations; and especially by withholding or threatening to withhold agency appropriations or by writing very specific provisions into appropriations acts.

▶ 12.8 *Evaluate the cost of federal regulation.*

Interest groups also influence bureaucratic decision making directly by testifying at public hearings and providing information and commentary, and indirectly by contacting the media, lobbying Congress, and initiating lawsuits.

▶ 12.9 *Summarize the constraints that Congress can place on the bureaucracy.*

Judicial control of the bureaucracy is usually limited to determining whether agencies have exceeded the authority granted them by law or have abided by the rules of procedural fairness. Federal bureaucracies have a strong record of success in defending themselves in court.

Chapter Test

▶ 12.1 *Assess the nature, sources, and extent of bureaucratic power.*

1. Bureaucratic power stems from the power to
   a. develop formal rules
   b. adjudicate individual cases
   c. use administrative discretion
   d. all of the above

2. The development of formal rules for the implementation of legislation is called
   a. adjudication
   b. regulation
   c. the legislative process
   d. the administrative process

▶ **12.2** *Describe the types of agencies in the federal bureaucracy and the extent and purposes of the bureaucracy.*

3. It would be accurate to say that the
   a. federal bureaucracy consists of about 2.8 million civilian employees
   b. the federal government spends about 50 percent of the nation's GDP
   c. the senior and most important cabinet office is the Department of the Interior
   d. all of the above

4. Which of the following is not considered to be a major regulatory agency?
   a. Federal Trade Commission
   b. National Aeronautics and Space Administration
   c. Federal Communication Commission
   d. Food and Drug Administration

▶ **12.3** *Trace changes over time in the size and composition of the bureaucracy and assess the repercussions for democracy.*

5. Historically, government employment was based on party loyalty, political support, and friendship. This was known as
   a. the compadre system
   b. the spoils system
   c. the patronage system
   d. the merit system

6. The _____ prohibits federal employees from engaging in partisan political activities.
   a. Hatch Act
   b. Civil Service Reform Act
   c. Partisan Reform Act
   d. Pendleton Act

▶ **12.4** *Explain how the bureaucracy is staffed, to whom it is accountable, and how accountability is affected by politics and bureaucratic culture.*

7. Government contracting with private firms to perform public services is known as
   a. privatization
   b. private-public partnerships
   c. socialism
   d. outsourcing

▶ **12.5** *Outline the budgetary process.*

8. The most important policy statement of any government is its
   a. annual budget
   b. State of the Union Address
   c. National Policy Evaluation Report
   d. Governmental Mission Statement

9. The agency that has the principal responsibility for preparation of the budget is the
   a. Treasury Department
   b. Office of Management and Budget
   c. Congressional Budget Office
   d. Federal Reserve

10. Legislation that provides money for programs authorized by Congress is an
    a. outlay
    b. authorization

c. appropriation act
d. obligation authority

▶ **12.6** *Evaluate the advantages and disadvantages of the current system of budgeting.*

11. A method of budgeting that tries to review the entire budget of an agency (not just the requested changes) is
    a. management by objective budgeting
    b. incremental budgeting
    c. zero-based budgeting
    d. nonprogrammatic budgeting

12. Recent polls by the Gallup Organization show that Americans believe that about _____ percent of their tax dollars are wasted by the governmental bureaucracy.
    a. 50
    b. 40
    c. 60
    d. 30

13. Identifying items in a budget according to the functions and programs that are to be spent on is
    a. nonprogrammatic budgeting
    b. zero-based budgeting
    c. program budgeting
    d. incremental budgeting

▶ **12.7** *Outline the growth of federal regulation.*

14. The agency that is responsible for conducting studies of the federal bureaucratic performance is the
    a. Office of Management and Budget
    b. Congressional Budget Office
    c. General Accountability Office
    d. Office of the Comptroller

15. Services performed by legislators and their staffs on behalf of individual constituents are known as
    a. client services
    b. casework
    c. constituency outreach
    d. homework

▶ **12.8** *Evaluate the cost of federal regulation.*

16. The American Farm Bureau would probably want to pay most of its attention to the activities of which of the following governmental agencies?
    a. Environmental Protection Agency (EPA)
    b. Agriculture Department
    c. Judiciary Department
    d. Interior Department

17. In an effort to influence the bureaucracy, interest groups may
    a. hold press conferences
    b. lobby the bureaucracy directly
    c. testify at public hearings
    d. all of the above

▶ **12.9** *Summarize the constraints that Congress can place on the bureaucracy.*

18. The courts become involved in agency actions when they
    a. violate congressional legislation
    b. have exceeded the authority granted to them
    c. have engaged in activities that have been determined to be arbitrary
    d. all of the above

mypoliscilab EXERCISES

Apply what you learned in this chapter on MyPoliSciLab.

Read on mypoliscilab.com

eText: Chapter 12

Study and Review on mypoliscilab.com

Pre-Test

Post-Test

Chapter Exam

Flashcards

Watch on mypoliscilab.com

Video: The CDC and the Swine Flu

Video: Making Environmental Policy

Video: Internal Problems at the FDA

Explore on mypoliscilab.com

Simulation: You Are the President of MEDICORP

Simulation: You Are the Head of FEMA

Simulation: You Are Deputy Director of the Census Bureau

Simulation: You Are a Federal Administrator

Comparative: Comparing Bureaucracies

Timeline: The Evolution of the Federal Bureaucracy

Visual Literacy: The Changing Face of the Federal Bureaucracy

Key Terms

bureaucracy 425
chain of command 426
division of labor 426
impersonality 426
implementation 428
regulation 429

adjudication 429
budget maximization 430
discretionary funds 430
spoils system 438
merit system 438
whistle-blowers 442

outsourcing 443
fiscal year 444
budget resolution 446
authorization 446
appropriations act 446
obligational
    authority 446

outlays 446
continuing resolution 447
incremental budgeting 447
zero-based budgeting 447
program budgeting 449
casework 452

Suggested Readings

Gormley, William T., and Steven J. Balla. *Bureaucracy and Democracy: Accountability and Performance.* 2nd ed. Washington, D.C.: CQ Press, 2007. Administrative theory and approaches to bureaucratic relationship in a democracy.

Henry, Nicholas. *Public Administration and Public Affairs.* 11th ed. New York: Longman, 2010. Authoritative introductory textbook on public organizations (bureaucracies), public management, and policy implementation.

Howard, Philip K. *The Death of Common Sense: How Law Is Suffocating America.* New York: Random House, 1995. Outrageous stories of bureaucratic senselessness coupled with a plea to allow bureaucrats flexibility in achieving the purposes of laws and holding them accountable for outcomes.

Kettl, Donald F., and James W. Fesler. *The Politics of the Administrative Process.* 4th ed. Washington, D.C.: CQ Press, 2008. Introduction to bureaucracy and public administration, including a case appendix with illustrations complementing each chapter.

Kerwin, Cornelius M. *Rulemaking: How Government Agencies Write Law and Make Policy.* 4th ed. Washington, D.C.: CQ Press, 2010. Argues that rulemaking actually defines the laws of Congress and describes the political activity surrounding rulemaking.

Neiman, Max. *Defending Government: Why Big Government Works.* New York: Longman, 2000. A spirited defense of big government as a product of people's desire to improve their lives.

Osborne, David, and Ted Gaebler. *Reinventing Government.* New York: Addison-Wesley, 1992. The respected manual of the "reinventing government" movement, with recommendations to overcome the routine tendencies of bureaucracies and inject "the entrepreneurial spirit" into them.

Schick, Allen. *The Federal Budget: Politics, Policy, Process.* 3rd ed. Washington, D.C.: Brookings Institution, 2007. A comprehensive explanation of the federal budgetary process.

Smith, Robert W., and Thomas D. Lynch. *Public Budgeting in America.* 5th ed. New York: Longman, 2004. Standard text describing public budget processes, behaviors, and administration.

Wildavsky, Aaron, and Naomi Caiden. *New Politics of the Budgetary Process.* 5th ed. New York: Longman, 2004. An updated version of Wildavsky's classic book on how budgetary decisions are really made.

Wilson, James Q. *Bureaucracy: What Government Agencies Do and Why They Do It.* New York: Basic Books, 1989. In the author's words, "an effort to depict the essential features of bureaucratic life in the government agencies of the United States." Examining what really motivates middle-level public servants, Wilson argues that congressional attempts to "micromanage" government activities hamper the ability of bureaucrats to do their jobs.

Suggested Web Sites

American Society for Public Administration
www.apsanet.org
Organization of scholars and practitioners in public administration. Site includes information on careers, job listings, and so on.

Amtrak www.amtrak.com
The Amtrak Web site provides valuable information about trip planning, reservations, train schedules, and train fares.

Center for Public Integrity www.publicintegrity.org
Reform organization committed to "exposing" corruption, mismanagement, and waste in government.

Code of Federal Regulations www.cfr.law.cornell.edu
All fifty titles of federal regulations can be found at the Cornell Law School site.

Fed World www.fedworld.gov
Run by the U.S. Commerce Department, this site contains information about federal/state–local agency links, government jobs, IRS forms, Supreme Court decisions, and the vast array of governmental services.

Federal Reserve System www.federalreserve.gov
This Federal Reserve System site covers general information about "Fed" operations, including monetary policy, reserve bank services, international banking, and supervisory and regulatory functions.

First Gov www.firstgov.gov
Official Web portal to all federal departments and agencies, information on government benefits, agency links, and so forth.

Food and Drug Administration www.fda.gov
The Food and Drug Administration site is a reflection of the agency's mission "to promote and protect the public health by helping safe and effective products reach the market in a timely way."

Internal Revenue Service www.irs.gov
The tax-collecting IRS is potentially the most powerful of all government agencies, with financial records on every tax-paying American.

Occupational Safety and Health Administration
www.osha.gov
This site covers new information directly related to OSHA's mission "to ensure safe and healthful workplaces in America."

Office of Management and Budget (OMB) www.omb.gov
The OMB site includes all budget documents and information on regulatory oversight.

USA Jobs www.usajobs.gov
This site is the official source for federal employment information.

Chapter Test Answer Key

1. D	4. B	7. D	10. C	13. C	16. B
2. B	5. B	8. A	11. C	14. C	17. D
3. A	6. A	9. B	12. A	15. B	18. D

13 COURTS
Judicial Politics

❝ There is hardly a political question in the United States which does not sooner or later turn into a judicial one. ❞

Alexis de Tocqueville

Chapter Outline and Learning Objectives

Judicial Power
▶ 13.1 *Assess the basis for and use of judicial power.*

Activism Versus Self-Restraint
▶ 13.2 *Compare and contrast the philosophies of judicial activism and judicial restraint.*

Structure and Jurisdiction of Federal Courts
▶ 13.3 *Outline the structure and jurisdiction of the federal courts.*

The Special Rules of Judicial Decision Making
▶ 13.4 *Characterize the "special rules" of judicial decision making.*

The Politics of Selecting Judges
▶ 13.5 *Assess the role of politics in the judicial selection process.*

Who Is Selected?
▶ 13.6 *Identify factors involved in the judicial selection process.*

Supreme Court Decision Making
▶ 13.7 *Outline the decision-making process of the Supreme Court and areas in which the Court has been active.*

Politics and the Supreme Court
▶ 13.8 *Assess the role of politics and ideology in Supreme Court decision making.*

Checking Court Power
▶ 13.9 *Evaluate checks on Supreme Court power.*

☑ *Think* About politics

1. Have the federal courts grown too powerful?
   YES ⬭ NO ⬭

2. Is it really democratic to allow federal court judges, who are appointed, not elected, and who serve for life, to overturn laws of an elected Congress and president?
   YES ⬭ NO ⬭

3. Should the Constitution be interpreted in terms of the original intentions of the Founders rather than the morality of society today?
   YES ⬭ NO ⬭

4. Are the costs of lawsuits in America becoming too burdensome on the economy?
   YES ⬭ NO ⬭

5. Should presidents appoint only judges who agree with their judicial philosophy?
   YES ⬭ NO ⬭

6. Should the Senate confirm Supreme Court appointees who oppose abortion?
   YES ⬭ NO ⬭

7. Should the Supreme Court overturn the law of Congress that prohibits federal funding of abortions for poor women?
   YES ⬭ NO ⬭

8. Is there a need to appoint special prosecutors to investigate presidents and other high officials?
   YES ⬭ NO ⬭

Do the Supreme Court and the federal judiciary in fact have the real power to shape public policies in the United States?

Judicial Power

▶ 13.1 *Assess the basis for and use of judicial power.*

"There is hardly a political question in the United States which does not sooner or later turn into a judicial one."[1] This observation, made in 1835 by French diplomat and traveler Alexis de Tocqueville, is even more accurate today. It is the Supreme Court and the federal judiciary, rather than the president or Congress, that has taken the lead in deciding many of the most heated issues of American politics. It has undertaken to:

- Eliminate racial segregation and decide about affirmative action.

- Ensure separation of church and state and decide about prayer in public schools.

- Determine the personal liberties of women and decide about abortion.

- Define the limits of free speech and free press and decide about obscenity, censorship, and pornography.

- Ensure equality of representation and require legislative districts to be equal in population.

- Define the rights of criminal defendants, prevent unlawful searches, limit the questioning of suspects, and prevent physical or mental intimidation of suspects.

- Protect private homosexual acts between consenting adults from criminal prosecution.

- Decide the life-or-death issue of capital punishment.

Think Again

Have the federal courts grown too powerful?

Courts are "political" institutions. Like Congress, the president, and the bureaucracy, courts decide who gets what in American society. Judges do not merely "apply" the law to specific cases. Years ago, former Supreme Court Justice Felix Frankfurter explained why this mechanistic theory of judicial objectivity fails to describe court decision making.

> The meaning of "due process" and the content of terms like "liberty" are not revealed by the Constitution. It is the Justices who make the meaning. They read into the neutral language of the Constitution their own economic and social views. . . . Let us face the fact that five Justices of the Supreme Court are the molders of policy rather than the impersonal vehicles of revealed truth.[2]

Constitutional Power of the Courts   The Constitution grants "the judicial Power of the United States" to the Supreme Court and other "inferior Courts" that Congress may establish. The Constitution guarantees that the Supreme Court and federal judiciary will be politically independent: judges are appointed, not elected, and hold their appointments for life (barring commission of any impeachable offenses). It also guarantees that their salaries will not be reduced during their time in office. The Constitution goes on to list the kinds of cases and controversies that the federal courts may decide. Federal judicial power extends to any case arising under the Constitution and federal laws and treaties, to cases in which officials of the federal government or of foreign governments are a party, and to cases between states or between citizens of different states.

Interpreting the Constitution: Judicial Review   The Constitution is the "supreme Law of the Land" (Article VI). Judicial power is the power to decide cases and controversies and, in doing so, to decide what the Constitution and laws of Congress really mean. This authority—together with the guaranteed independence of judges—places great power in the Supreme Court and the federal judiciary. Indeed, because the Constitution takes precedence over laws of Congress as well as state constitutions and laws, it is the Supreme Court that ultimately decides whether Congress, the president, the states, and their local governments have acted constitutionally.

judicial review
Power of the courts, especially the Supreme Court, to declare laws of Congress, laws of the states, and actions of the president unconstitutional and invalid.

The power of **judicial review** is the power to invalidate laws of Congress or of the states that conflict with the U.S. Constitution. Judicial review is not specifically mentioned in the Constitution but has long been inferred from it. Even before the states had approved the Constitution, Alexander Hamilton wrote in 1787 that "limited government . . . can be preserved in practice no other way than through the medium of courts of justice, whose duty it is to declare all acts contrary to the manifest tenor of the Constitution void."[3] But it was the historic decision of *Marbury v. Madison* (1803)[4] that officially established judicial review as the most important judicial check on congressional power (see *Politics Up Close:* "John Marshall and Early Supreme Court Politics"). Writing for the majority, Chief Justice Marshall constructed a classic statement in judicial reasoning as he proceeded step by step to infer judicial review from the Constitution's Supremacy (Article VI) and Judicial Power (Article III, Section 1) clauses:

- The Constitution is the supreme law of the land, binding on all branches of government: legislative, executive, and judicial.

- The Constitution deliberately establishes a government with limited powers.

- Consequently, "an act of the legislature repugnant to the Constitution is void." If this were not true, the government would be unchecked and the Constitution would be an absurdity.

POLITICS UP CLOSE

John Marshall and Early Supreme Court Politics

John Marshall was a dedicated Federalist. A prominent Virginia lawyer, he was elected a delegate to Virginia's Constitution-ratifying convention, where he was instrumental in winning his state's approval of the document in 1788. Later Marshall served as secretary of state in the administration of John Adams (1797–1801), where he came into conflict with Adams's vice president, Thomas Jefferson.

In the election of 1800, Jefferson's Democratic-Republicans crushed Adams's Federalist Party. But Adams, taking advantage of the fact that his term of office would not expire until the following March,[a] sought to pack the federal judiciary with Federalists. The lame duck Federalist majority in the Senate confirmed the appointments, and John Marshall was sworn in as Chief Justice of the Supreme Court on February 4, 1801. Many of these "midnight appointments" came at the very last hours of Adams's term of office.

At that time, a specified task of the secretary of state was to deliver judicial commissions to new judges. When Marshall left his position as secretary of state to become Chief Justice, several of these commissions were still undelivered. Jefferson and the Democratic-Republicans were enraged over this last-minute Federalist chicanery, so when Jefferson assumed office in March, he ordered his new secretary of state, James Madison, not to deliver the remaining commissions. William Marbury, one of the disappointed Federalist appointees, brought a lawsuit to the Supreme Court, asking it to issue a writ of mandamus ("we command") to James Madison, ordering him to do his duty and deliver the valid commission.

The Judiciary Act of 1789, which established the federal court system, had included a provision granting original jurisdiction to the Supreme Court to issue writs of mandamus. The case, therefore, came directly to new Chief Justice John Marshall, who had failed to deliver the commission in the first place. (Today, we expect justices who are personally involved in a case to "recuse" themselves—that is, not to participate in that case, allowing the other justices to make the decision—but Marshall's actions were typical of his time.)

John Marshall realized that if he issued a direct order to Madison to deliver the commission, Madison would probably ignore it. The Court had no way to enforce such an order, and Madison had the support of President Jefferson. Issuing the writ would create a constitutional crisis in which the Supreme Court would most likely lose power. But if the Court failed to pronounce Madison's actions unlawful, it would lose legitimacy.

Marshall resolved his political dilemma with a brilliant judicial ploy. Writing for the majority in *Marbury v. Madison*, he announced that Madison was wrong to withhold the commission but that the Supreme Court could not issue a writ of mandamus because Section 13 of the Judiciary Act of 1789, which gave the Court *original* jurisdiction in the case, was unconstitutional. Giving the Supreme Court *original* jurisdiction conflicted with Article III, Section 2, of the Constitution, which gives the Supreme Court original jurisdiction only in cases affecting "Ambassadors, other public Ministers and Consuls, and those in which a State shall be a Party." "In all other Cases," the Constitution states that the Court shall have appellate jurisdiction. Thus Section 13 of the Judiciary Act was unconstitutional.

By declaring part of an act of Congress unconstitutional, Marshall accomplished multiple political objectives. He avoided a showdown with the executive branch that would undoubtedly have weakened the Court. He left Jefferson and Madison with no Court order to disobey. At the same time, Marshall forced Jefferson and the Democratic-Republicans to acknowledge the Supreme Court's power of judicial review—the power to declare an act of Congress unconstitutional. (To do otherwise would have meant acknowledging Marbury's claim.) Thus Marshall sacrificed Marbury's commission to a greater political goal, enhancing the Supreme Court's power.

[a]Not until the adoption of the 20th Amendment in 1933 was the president's inauguration moved up to January.

- Under the judicial power, "It is emphatically the province and duty of each of the judicial departments to say what the law is."

- "So if a law be in opposition to the Constitution . . . the court must determine which of these conflicting rules governs the case. This is the very essence of judicial duty."

Landmark Case

Linda Brown (foreground) in her classroom in Topeka, taken at about the time of the *Brown v. Board of Education* decision. Brown was refused admittance to a white elementary school, and her family was one of the plaintiffs in the case.

- "If, then, the courts are to regard the Constitution, and the Constitution is superior to any ordinary act of the legislature, the Constitution, and not such ordinary act, must govern the case to which they both apply."

- Hence, if a law is repugnant to the Constitution, the judges are duty bound to declare that law void in order to uphold the supremacy of the Constitution.

Judicial Review of State Laws   The power of the federal courts to invalidate *state* laws and constitutions that conflict with federal laws or the federal Constitution is easily defended. Article VI states that the Constitution and federal laws and treaties are the supreme law of the land, "any Thing in the Constitution or Laws of any State to the Contrary notwithstanding." Indeed, the Constitution specifically obligates state judges to be "bound" by the Constitution and federal laws and to give these documents precedence over state constitutions and laws in rendering decisions. Federal court power over state decisions is probably essential to maintaining national unity: fifty different state interpretations of the meaning of the Constitution or of the laws and treaties of Congress would create unimaginable confusion. Thus the power of federal judicial review over state constitutions, laws, and court decisions is seldom questioned.

The Supreme Court has used its power of judicial review more frequently to invalidate state laws than laws of Congress. Some of these decisions had impact far beyond the individual states on trial. For example, the historic 1954 decision in *Brown v. Board of Education of Topeka*, declaring segregation of the races in public schools to be unconstitutional, struck down the laws of twenty-one states[5] (see Chapter 12). The 1973 *Roe v. Wade* decision, establishing the constitutional right to abortion, struck down anti-abortion laws in more than forty states.[6] In 2003 the Court again struck down the laws of more than forty states by holding that private homosexual acts by consenting adults were protected by the Constitution.[7]

Judicial Review of Laws of Congress   Judicial review is potentially the most powerful weapon in the hands of the Supreme Court. It enables the Court to assert its power over the Congress, the president, and the states and to substitute its own judgment for that of other branches of the federal government and the states. However, the Supreme Court has been fairly restrained in its use of judicial review to void acts of Congress. Prior to the Civil War, the Supreme Court invalidated very few laws of any kind. Since that time, however, the general trend has been for the U.S. Supreme Court to strike down more *state* laws as unconstitutional. In contrast, the Court has been relatively restrained in its rejection of *federal* laws; over two centuries the Court has struck down fewer than 150 of the more than 60,000 laws passed by Congress.

Nevertheless, some of the laws overturned by the Supreme Court have been very important. In *Buckley v. Valeo* (1976)[8] the Court struck down provisions of the Federal Election Campaign Act that had limited the amount individuals could spend to finance their own campaigns or express their own independent political views. In *United States v. Morrison* (2000), the Supreme Court struck down Congress's Violence Against Women Act[9] as an unconstitutional expansion of the interstate commerce power and an invasion of powers reserved to the states (see *Controversy:* "Should Violence Against Women Be a Federal Crime?" in Chapter 4). Overall, however, the Supreme Court's use of judicial review against the Congress has been restrained.

Judicial Review of Presidential Actions   The Supreme Court has only rarely challenged presidential power. The Court has overturned presidential policies both on the grounds that they conflicted with laws of Congress and on the grounds that they conflicted with the Constitution. In *Ex parte Milligan* (1866),[10] for example, the Court held (somewhat belatedly) that President Abraham Lincoln could not suspend the writ of habeas corpus in rebellious states during the Civil War. In *Youngstown Sheet & Tube Co. v. Sawyer*, in 1952,[11] it declared President Harry Truman's seizure of the nation's steel mills during the Korean War to be illegal. In 1974, it ordered President Richard Nixon to turn over taped White House conversations to the special Watergate prosecutor, leading to Nixon's forced resignation.[12] And in 1997, the Court held that President Bill Clinton was obliged to respond to a civil suit even while serving in the White House.[13]

Interpreting Federal Laws   The power of the Supreme Court and the federal judiciary does not rest on judicial review alone. The courts also make policy in their interpretation of **statutory laws**—the laws of Congress. Frequently, Congress decides that an issue is too contentious to resolve. Members of Congress cannot themselves agree on specific language, so they write, sometimes deliberately, vague, symbolic language into the law—words and phrases like "fairness," "equitableness," "good faith," "good cause," and "reasonableness"—effectively shifting policy making to the courts by giving courts the power to read meaning into these terms.

statutory laws
Laws made by act of Congress or the state legislatures, as opposed to constitutional law.

Activism Versus Self-Restraint

▶ **13.2** *Compare and contrast the philosophies of judicial activism and judicial restraint.*

Supreme Court Justice Felix Frankfurter once wrote: "The only check upon our own exercise of power is our own sense of self-restraint. For the removal of unwise laws from the statute books, appeal lies not to the courts but to the ballot and to the processes of democratic government."[14]

☑ *Think* Again

Is it really democratic to allow federal court judges, who are appointed, not elected, and who serve for life, to overturn laws of an elected Congress and president? All of these officials, upon taking office, swear to uphold the Constitution.

Judicial Self-Restraint   The idea behind **judicial self-restraint** is that judges should not read their own philosophies into the Constitution and should avoid direct confrontations with Congress, the president, and the states whenever possible. The argument for judicial self-restraint is that federal judges are not elected by the people and therefore should not substitute their own views for the views of elected representatives. The courts should defer to the judgments of the other branches of government unless there is a clear violation of constitutional principle. The benefit of the doubt should be given to actions taken by elected officials. Courts should only impose remedies that are narrowly tailored to correct specific legal wrongs. As Justice Sandra Day O'Connor argued in her Senate confirmation hearings, "The courts should interpret the laws, not make them . . . I do not believe it is a function of the Court to step in because times have changed or social mores have changed."[15]

judicial self-restraint
Self-imposed limitation on judicial power by judges deferring to the policy judgments of elected branches of government.

Wisdom Versus Constitutionality   A law may be unwise, unjust, or even stupid and yet still be constitutional. One should not equate the wisdom of a law with its constitutionality, and the Court should decide only the constitutionality and not the wisdom of a law. Justice Oliver Wendell Holmes once lectured a younger colleague, 61-year-old Justice Harlan Stone, on this point:

> Young man, about 75 years ago I learned that I was not God. And so, when the people . . . want to do something I can't find anything in the Constitution expressly forbidding them to do, I say, whether I like it or not, "Goddamn it, let 'em do it."[16]

Senate Confirmation Testimony

Supreme Court Chief Justice nominee John Roberts answers questions on September 13, 2005, during his second day of hearings before the Senate Judiciary Committee.

original intent
Judicial philosophy under which judges attempt to apply the values of the Founders to current issues.

judicial activism
Making of new law through judicial interpretations of the Constitution.

stare decisis
Judicial precept that the issue has already been decided in earlier cases and the earlier decision need only be applied in the specific case before the bench; the rule in most cases, it comes from the Latin for "the decision stands."

precedent
Legal principle that previous decisions should determine the outcome of current cases; the basis for stability in law.

However, the actual role of the Supreme Court in the nation's power struggles suggests that the Court indeed often equates wisdom with constitutionality. People frequently cite broad phrases in the 5th and 14th Amendments establishing constitutional standards of "due process of law" and "equal protection of the laws" when attacking laws they believe are unfair, unwise, or unjust. Most Americans have come to believe that unwise laws must be unconstitutional. If so, then the courts must be the final arbiters of fairness, wisdom, and justice.

Original Intent   Should the Constitution be interpreted in terms of the intentions of the Founders or according to the morality of society today? Most jurists agree the Constitution is a living document, that it must be interpreted by each generation in the light of current conditions, and to do otherwise would soon render the document obsolete. But in interpreting the document, whose values should prevail—the values of the judges or the values of the Founders? The doctrine of **original intent** takes the values of the Founders as expressed in the text of the Constitution and attempts to apply these values to current conditions. Defenders of original intent argue that the words in the document must be given their historical meaning and that meaning must restrain the courts as well as the legislative and executive branches of government. That is, the Supreme Court should not set aside laws made by elected representatives unless they conflict with the original intent of the Founders. Judges who set aside laws that do not accord with their personal views of today's moral standards are simply substituting their own morality for that of elected bodies. Such decisions lack democratic legitimacy because there is no reason why judges' moral views should prevail over those of elected representatives.

Judicial Activism   However, the doctrine of original intent carries little weight with proponents of judicial activism. The idea behind **judicial activism** is that the Constitution is a living document whose strength lies in its flexibility, and judges should shape constitutional meaning to fit the needs of contemporary society. The argument for judicial activism is that viewing the Constitution as a broad and flexible document saves the nation from having to pass dozens of new constitutional amendments to accommodate changes in society. Instead, the courts need to give contemporary interpretations to constitutional phrases, particularly general phrases such as "due process of law" (5th Amendment), "equal protection of the laws" (14th Amendment), "establishment of religion" (1st Amendment), and "cruel and unusual punishment" (8th Amendment). Courts have the responsibility to review the actions of other branches of government vigorously, to strike down unconstitutional acts, and to impose far-reaching remedies for legal wrongs whenever necessary.

Stare Decisis   Conflicts between judicial activism and judicial self-restraint are underscored by questions of whether to let past decisions stand or to find constitutional support for overturning them. The principle of **stare decisis**, which means the issue has already been decided in earlier cases, is a fundamental notion in law. Reliance on **precedent** gives stability to the law; if every decision were new law, then no one would know what the law is from day to day. Yet the Supreme Court has discarded precedent in many of its most important decisions: *Brown v. Board of Education* (1954), which struck down laws segregating the races; *Baker v. Carr* (1962), which guaranteed equal representation in legislatures; *Roe v. Wade* (1973), which made abortion a constitutional right; and many other classic cases.[17] Former Justice William O. Douglas, a defender of judicial activism, justified disregard of precedent as follows:

> The decisions of yesterday or of the last century are only the starting points. . . . A judge looking at a constitutional decision may have compulsions to revere the past history and accept what was once written. But he remembers above all else that it is the Constitution which he swore to support and defend, not the gloss which his predecessors may have put on it. So he comes to formulate his own laws, rejecting some earlier ones as false and embracing others. He cannot do otherwise unless he lets men long dead and unaware of the problems of the age in which he lives do his thinking for him.[18]

Rules of Restraint   Even an activist Supreme Court adheres to some general rules of judicial self-restraint, however, including the following:

- The Court will pass on the constitutionality of legislation only in an actual case; it will not advise the president or Congress on constitutional questions.

- The Court will not anticipate a question on constitutional law; it does not decide hypothetical cases.

- The Court will not formulate a rule of constitutional law broader than that required by the precise facts to which it must be applied.

- The Court will not decide on a constitutional question if some other ground exists on which it may dispose of the case.

- The Court will not decide on the validity of a law if the complainants fail to show that they have been injured by the law.

- When doubt exists about the constitutionality of a law, the Court will try to interpret the law so as to give it a constitutional meaning and avoid the necessity of declaring it unconstitutional.

- Complainants must have exhausted all remedies available in lower federal courts or state courts before the Supreme Court will accept review.

- The Court will invalidate a law only when a constitutional issue is crucial to the case and is substantial, not trivial.

- Occasionally, the Court defers to Congress and the president, classifies an issue as a political question, and refuses to decide it. The Court has generally stayed out of foreign and military policy areas.

- If the Court holds a law unconstitutional, it will confine its decision to the particular section of the law that is unconstitutional; the rest of the statute stays intact.

Structure and Jurisdiction of Federal Courts

▶ 13.3 *Outline the structure and jurisdiction of the federal courts.*

The federal court system consists of three levels of courts—the Supreme Court, the Courts of Appeals, and the district courts—together with various special courts (see Figure 13.1). Only the Supreme Court is established by the Constitution, although the number of justices is determined by Congress. Article III authorizes Congress to establish such "inferior Courts" as it deems appropriate. Congress has designed a hierarchical system with a U.S. Court of Appeals divided into twelve regional circuit courts, a federal circuit, and ninety-four district courts

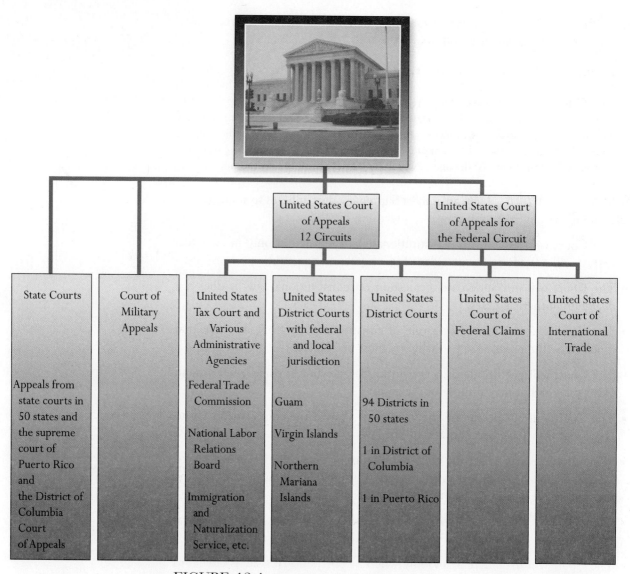

FIGURE 13.1 Structure of Federal Courts

The federal court system of the United States is divided into three levels: the courts of original jurisdiction (state courts, military courts, tax courts, district courts, claims courts, and international trade courts), U.S. Courts of Appeals (which hear appeals from all lower courts except state and military panels), and the U.S. Supreme Court, which can hear appeals from all sources.

jurisdiction
Power of a court to hear a case in question.

original jurisdiction
Refers to a particular court's power to serve as the place where a given case is initially argued and decided.

appellate jurisdiction
Particular court's power to review a decision or action of a lower court.

in the fifty states and one each in Puerto Rico, the U.S. Virgin Islands, Guam, the Northern Marianas, and the District of Columbia. Table 13.1 describes their **jurisdiction** and distinguishes between **original jurisdiction**—where cases are begun, argued, and initially decided—and **appellate jurisdiction**—where cases begun in lower courts are argued and decided on **appeal**.

The Supreme Court is the "court of last resort" in the United States, but it hears only a very small number of cases each year. In a handful of cases, the Supreme Court has original jurisdiction; these concern primarily disputes between states (or states and residents of other states), disputes between a state and the federal government, and disputes involving foreign dignitaries. However, most Supreme Court cases are appellate decisions involving cases from state supreme courts or cases tried first in a U.S. district court.

TABLE 13.1 Who Decides What?: Jurisdiction of Federal Courts

Supreme Court of the United States	United States Courts of Appeals (Circuit Courts)	United States District Courts
Appellate jurisdiction (cases begin in a lower court); hears appeals, at its own discretion, from: 1. Lower federal courts 2. Highest state courts Original jurisdiction (cases begin in the Supreme Court) over cases involving: 1. Two or more states 2. The United States and a state 3. Foreign ambassadors and other diplomats 4. A state and a citizen of a different state (if begun by the state)	No original jurisdiction; hear only appeals from: 1. Federal district courts 2. U.S. regulatory commissions 3. Certain other federal courts	Original jurisdiction over cases involving: 1. Constitution of the United States 2. Federal laws, including federal crimes 3. Civil suits under the federal law 4. Civil suits between citizens of states where the amount exceeds $75,000 5. Admiralty and maritime cases 6. Bankruptcy cases 7. Review of actions of certain federal administrative agencies 8. Other matters assigned to them by Congress

District Courts District courts are the original jurisdiction trial courts of the federal system. Each state has at least one district court, and larger states have more (New York, for example, has four). There are about eight hundred federal district judges, each appointed for life by the president and confirmed by the Senate. The president also appoints a U.S. marshal for each district to carry out orders of the court and maintain order in the courtroom. District courts hear criminal cases prosecuted by the Department of Justice as well as civil cases. As trial courts, the district courts make use of both **grand juries** (called to hear evidence and, if warranted, to indict a defendant by bringing formal criminal charges) and **petit** (regular) **juries** (which determine guilt or innocence). District courts may hear 270,000 civil cases in a year and 70,000 criminal cases.

Courts of Appeals Federal **circuit courts** (see Figure 13.2 Geography of the Federal Court System) are appellate courts. They do not hold trials or accept new evidence but consider only the records of the trial courts and oral or written arguments (**briefs**) submitted by attorneys. Federal law guarantees everyone the right to appeal, so the Courts of Appeal have little discretion in this regard. Appellate judges themselves estimate that more than 80 percent of all appeals are frivolous—that is, without any real basis. There are more than a hundred circuit judges, each appointed for life by the president subject to confirmation by the Senate. Normally, these judges serve together on a panel to hear appeals. More than 90 percent of the cases decided by the Court of Appeals end at this level. Further appeal to the Supreme Court is not automatic; it must be approved by the Supreme Court itself. Because the Supreme Court hears very few cases, in most cases the decision of the circuit court becomes law.

Supreme Court The Supreme Court of the United States is the final interpreter of all matters involving the Constitution and federal laws and treaties, whether the case began in a federal district court or in a state court. Appeals to the U.S. Supreme Court may come from a state court of last resort (usually a

appeal
In general, requests that a higher court review cases decided at a lower level. In the Supreme Court, certain cases are designated as appeals under federal law; formally, these must be heard by the Court.

district courts
Original jurisdiction trial courts of the federal system.

grand juries
Juries called to hear evidence and decide whether defendants should be indicted and tried.

petit (regular) **juries**
Juries called to determine guilt or innocence.

circuit courts
The twelve appellate courts that make up the middle level of the federal court system.

briefs
Documents submitted by an attorney to a court, setting out the facts of the case and the legal arguments in support of the party represented by the attorney.

FIGURE 13.2

Geography of the Federal Court System

For administrative convenience, the U.S. District Courts are organized into twelve circuits (regions), plus the Federal Circuit (Washington, D.C.). Within each region, circuit court judges form panels to hear appeals from district courts. U.S. Circuit Courts of Appeals are numbered. U.S. District Courts are named for geographical regions of the states (East, West, North, South, Middle), for example, U.S. District Court for Northern California.

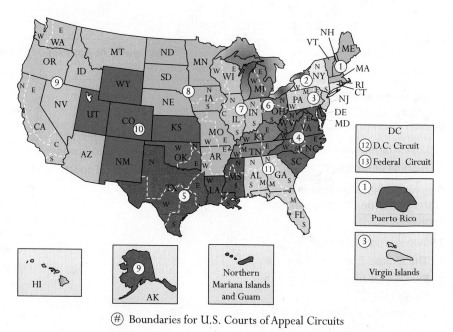

#⃝ Boundaries for U.S. Courts of Appeal Circuits
●⃝ Boundaries for U.S. District Courts

state's supreme court) or from lower federal courts. The Supreme Court determines whether to accept an appeal and consider a case. It may do so when there is a "substantial federal question" presented in a case or when there are "special and important reasons," or it may reject a case—with or without explaining why.

In the early days of the Republic, the size of the Supreme Court fluctuated, but since 1869 the membership has remained at nine: the Chief Justice and eight associate justices. The Supreme Court is in session each year from October through June, hearing oral arguments, accepting written briefs, conferring, and rendering opinions.

Appeals from State Courts   Each of the fifty states maintains its own courts. The federal courts are not necessarily superior to those courts; state and federal courts operate independently. State courts have original jurisdiction in most criminal and civil cases. Because the U.S. Supreme Court has appellate jurisdiction over state supreme courts as well as over lower federal courts, the Supreme Court oversees the nation's entire judicial system, but the great bulk of cases begin and end in the state court systems. The federal courts do not interfere once a case has been started in a state court except in very rare circumstances. And Congress has stipulated that legal disputes between citizens of different states must involve $75,000 or more to be heard in federal courts. Moreover, parties to cases in state courts must "exhaust their remedies"—that is, appeal their case all the way through the state court system—before the federal courts will hear an appeal. Appeals from state supreme courts go directly to the U.S. Supreme Court and not to a federal district or circuit court. Such appeals are usually made on the grounds that a "federal question" is involved in the case—that is, a question has arisen regarding the application of the Constitution or a federal law.

Federal Cases   Some 10 million civil and criminal cases are begun in the nation's courts each year (see *A Conflicting View*: "America Is Drowning Itself in a Sea of Lawsuits"). About 267,000 (less than 3 percent) of the cases are begun in

A CONFLICTING VIEW

America Is Drowning Itself in a Sea of Lawsuits

America is threatening to drown itself in a sea of lawsuits. Civil suits in the nation's courts exceed *10 million* per year. There are more than 805,000 lawyers in the United States (compared to about 650,000 physicians). These lawyers are in business, and their business is litigation. Generating business means generating lawsuits. And just as businesses search for new products, lawyers search for new legal principles on which to bring lawsuits. They seek to expand legal liability for civil actions—that is, to expand the definition of civil wrongdoings, or torts.

Unquestionably, the threat of lawsuits is an important safeguard for society, compelling individuals, corporations, and government agencies to behave responsibly toward others. Because victims require compensation for *actual* damages incurred by the wrongdoing of others, liability laws protect all of us.

But we need to consider the social costs of frivolous lawsuits, especially those brought without any merit but initiated in the hope that individuals or firms will offer a settlement just to avoid the expenses of defending themselves. Legal expenses and excessive jury awards leveled against corporations increase insurance premiums for businesses and service providers. The Insurance Information Institute estimates that the overall cost of civil litigation in America is many times more than that of other industrial nations, perhaps amounting to over 2 percent of our nation's GDP. For example, the risk of lawsuits forces physicians to practice "defensive medicine," ordering expensive tests, multiple consultations with specialists, and expensive procedures, not because they are adjudged medically necessary, but rather to protect themselves from the possibility of a lawsuit.

Insurance premiums have risen sharply for physicians seeking malpractice insurance, as have premiums for recreation facilities, nurseries and day-care centers, motels, and restaurants.

Reforming the nation's liability laws presents major challenges to the political system. The reform movement can count on support from some normally powerful interest groups—insurance companies, manufacturers, drug companies, hospitals, and physicians. But legal reform is an anathema to the legal profession itself, notably the powerful American Association for Justice (formerly the Association of Trial Lawyers). And lawyers compose the single largest occupational background of Congress members—indeed, of politicians generally.

the federal courts. About 8,000 are appealed to the Supreme Court each year, but only about 125 of them are openly argued and decided by signed opinions. The Constitution "reserves" general police powers to the states. That is, civil disputes and most crimes—murder, robbery, assault, and rape—are normally state offenses rather than federal crimes and thus are tried in state and local courts.

Federal court caseloads have risen over the years (see Figure 13.3), in part because more civil disputes are being brought to federal courts. In addition, the U.S. Justice Department is prosecuting more criminal cases as federal law enforcement agencies—such as the Federal Bureau of Investigation (FBI), Drug Enforcement Administration (DEA), Internal Revenue Service (IRS), and Bureau of Alcohol, Tobacco, Firearms, and Explosives (ATF)—have stepped up their investigations. Most of this recent increase is attributable to enforcement of federal drug laws.

Traditionally, federal crimes were offenses directed against the U.S. government, its property, or its employees or were offenses involving the crossing of state lines. Over the years, however, Congress has greatly expanded the list of federal crimes so that federal and state criminal court jurisdictions often overlap, as they do, for example, in most drug violations.

FIGURE 13.3

Overworked?: Caseloads
in Federal Courts

Caseloads in the federal
courts place a heavy burden
on prosecutors and judges.
Increases in civil suits in the
federal courts are the result
of more plaintiffs insisting on
taking their cases to the
federal level both originally
and on appeal. Increases in
criminal cases are the result
of Congress's decision to
make more crimes—
especially drug-related
crimes—federal offenses and
to pursue such criminals
more vigorously.

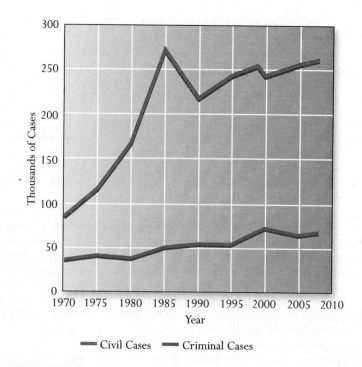

The Special Rules of Judicial Decision Making

▶ 13.4 *Characterize the "special rules" of judicial decision making.*

Courts are political institutions that resolve conflict and decide about public policy. But unlike Congress, the presidency, and the bureaucracy, the courts employ highly specialized rules in going about their work.

Cases and Controversies   Courts do not initiate policy but rather wait until a case or controversy is brought to them for resolution. A case must involve two disputing parties, one of which must have incurred some real damage as a result of the action or inaction of the other. They do *not* issue policy declarations or decide hypothetical cases. Rather, the courts wait until disputing parties bring a case to them that requires them to interpret the meaning of a law or determine its constitutionality in order to resolve the case. Only then do courts render opinions.

The vast majority of cases do *not* involve important policy issues. Courts determine the guilt or innocence of criminal defendants. Courts enforce contracts and award damages to victims of negligence in **civil cases**. And courts render these decisions on the basis of established law. Only occasionally do courts make significant policy decisions.

civil cases
Noncriminal court
proceedings in which a
plaintiff sues a defendant for
damages in payment for harm
inflicted.

adversarial system
Method of decision making in
which an impartial judge or
jury or decision maker hears
arguments and reviews
evidence presented by
opposite sides.

standing
Requirement that the party
who files a lawsuit have a legal
stake in the outcome.

Adversarial Proceedings   Underlying judicial decision making is the assumption that the best way to decide an issue is to allow two disputing parties to present arguments on each side. Judges in the United States do not investigate cases, question witnesses, or develop arguments themselves (as they do in some European countries). This **adversarial system** depends on quality of argument on each side, which means it often depends on the capabilities of attorneys. There is no guarantee that the adversarial process will produce the best policy outcomes.

Standing   To bring an issue into court as a case, individuals or firms or interest groups must have **standing**; that is, they must be directly harmed by a law or action. People cannot "go to court" simply because they do not like what the government is doing. Merely being taxpayers does not entitle people to claim that they are damaged by government actions.[19] Individuals or firms automatically have standing when they are prosecuted by the government for violation of laws or regulations. Thus one way to gain standing in order to challenge the legality of a regulation or the constitutionality of a law is to violate the regulation or law and invite the government to prosecute.

To sue the government, plaintiffs must show they have suffered financial damages, loss of property, or physical or emotional harm as a direct result of the government's action. (The party initiating a suit and claiming damages is the **plaintiff**; the party against whom a suit is brought is the **defendant**.) The ancient legal doctrine of **sovereign immunity** means that one cannot sue the government without the government's consent. But by law, the U.S. government allows itself to be sued in a wide variety of contract and negligence cases. A citizen can also personally sue to force government officials to carry out acts that they are required by law to perform or for acting contrary to law. The government does not allow suits for damages as a result of military actions.

Class Action Suits

Class action suits are cases brought into court by individuals on behalf not only of themselves but also of all other persons "similarly situated." That is, the party bringing the case is acting on behalf of a "class" of people who have suffered the same damages from the same actions of the defendant. One of the most famous and far-reaching class action suits was *Brown v. Board of Education of Topeka* (1954). The plaintiff, Linda Brown of Topeka, Kansas, sued her local board of education on behalf of herself and all other black pupils who were forced to attend segregated schools, charging that such schools violated the Equal Protection Clause of the 14th Amendment. When she won the case, the Court's ruling affected not only Linda Brown and the segregated public schools in Topeka but also all other black pupils similarly situated across the nation (see Chapter 12).

Class action suits have grown in popularity. These suits have enabled attorneys and interest groups to bring multimillion-dollar suits against corporations and governments for damages to large numbers of people, even when none of them has individually suffered sufficient harm to merit bringing a case to court. For example, an individual overcharged by an electric utility would not want to incur the expense of suing for the return of a few dollars. But if attorneys sue the utility on behalf of a large number of customers similarly overcharged, the result may be a multimillion-dollar settlement from which the attorneys can deduct their hefty fees.

Legal Fees

Going to court requires financial resources. Criminal defendants are guaranteed an attorney, without charge if they are poor, by the 6th Amendment's guarantee of "Assistance of Counsel".[20] However, persons who wish to bring a *civil* suit against individuals, corporations, or governments must still arrange for the payment of legal fees. The most common arrangement is the **contingency fee**, in which plaintiffs agree to pay expenses and share one-third or more of the money damages with their lawyers if the case is won. If the case is lost, neither plaintiffs nor their lawyers receive anything for their labors. Lawyers do not usually participate in such arrangements unless the prospects for winning the case are good and the promised monetary reward is substantial. Civil suits against the government have increased since Congress enacted a law requiring governments to pay the attorneys' fees of citizens who successfully bring suit against public officials for violation of their constitutional rights.

plaintiff
Individual or party who initiates a lawsuit or complaint.

defendant
Party against whom a criminal or civil suit is brought.

sovereign immunity
Legal doctrine that individuals can sue the government only with the government's consent.

class action suits
Cases initiated by parties acting on behalf of themselves and all others similarly situated.

Think Again

Are the costs of lawsuits in America becoming too burdensome on the economy?

contingency fee
Fee paid to attorneys to represent the plaintiff in a civil suit and receive in compensation an agreed-upon percentage of damages awarded (if any).

Justice in Black Robes
The Supreme Court of the United States is the final interpreter of the Constitution and federal laws and treaties.

remedies and relief
Orders of a court to correct a wrong, including a violation of the Constitution.

Remedies and Relief   Judicial power has vastly expanded through court determination of **remedies and relief**. These are the orders of a court following a decision that are designed to correct a wrong. In most cases, judges simply fine or sentence criminal defendants to jail or order losing defendants in civil suits to pay monetary damages to the winning plaintiffs. In recent years, however, federal district court judges have issued sweeping orders to governments to correct constitutional violations. For example, a federal district judge took over operation of the Boston public schools for more than 10 years to remedy *de facto* (an existing, although not necessarily deliberate, pattern of) racial segregation. A federal district judge ordered the city of Yonkers, New York, to build public housing in white neighborhoods. A federal district judge took over the operation of the Alabama prison system to ensure proper prisoner treatment. A federal district judge ordered the Kansas City, Missouri, school board to increase taxes to pay for his desegregation plan.[21]

independent counsel, or ("special prosecutor")
A prosecutor appointed by a federal court to pursue charges against a president or other high official. This position was allowed to lapse by Congress in 1999 after many controversial investigations by these prosecutors.

Independent Counsels?   The Ethics in Government Act of 1978 (passed in the wake of the Watergate scandal) granted federal courts the power, upon request of the attorney general, to appoint an **independent counsel**, or "**special prosecutor**," to investigate and prosecute violations of federal law by the president and other high officials. This act was challenged in the U.S. Supreme Court as a transferral of executive power ("to take care that the laws be faithfully executed"—Article II) to the judicial branch of government in violation of the separation of powers in the U.S. Constitution. But the Court upheld the law, noting that the attorney general, an executive branch official appointed by the president, had to request the judiciary to appoint the independent counsel.[22]

Whatever the original intent of the act, special prosecutors were often accused of *bringing politics into the criminal justice system.* Indeed, special prosecutor Kenneth Starr's dogged pursuit of Bill and Hillary Clinton (in "Whitewater" real estate deals and later the Monica Lewinsky sex scandal) was deemed a "witch hunt" by friends of the president. The First Lady linked Starr to "a vast right-wing conspiracy" trying to reverse the outcome of two presidential elections.

Congress allowed the independent counsel law to lapse in 1999. Democrats, infuriated by Starr's investigations, joined Republicans, who had earlier complained when Reagan and Bush administration officials were the targets of prosecution, in killing the act. Getting rid of the law, said its opponents, will help to "decriminalize" politics in Washington.

The Politics of Selecting Judges

▶ 13.5 *Assess the role of politics in the judicial selection process.*

The Constitution specifies that all federal judges, including justices of the Supreme Court, shall be appointed by the president and confirmed by a majority vote of the Senate. Judicial recruitment is a political process: presidents almost always appoint members of their own party to the federal courts. More than 80 percent of federal judges have held some political office prior to their appointment to the court. More important, political philosophy now plays a major role in the selection of judges. Thus the appointment of federal judges has increasingly become an arena for conflict between presidents and their political opponents in the Senate.

The Politics of Presidential Selection   Presidents have a strong motivation to select judges who share their political philosophy. Judicial appointments are made for life. The Constitution stipulates that federal judges "shall hold their Offices during good Behaviour." A president cannot remove a judge for any reason, and Congress cannot impeach judges just because it dislikes their decisions.

This independence of the judiciary has often frustrated presidents and Congresses. Presidents who have appointed people they thought were liberals or conservatives to the Supreme Court have been surprised sometimes by the decisions of their appointees. An estimated one-quarter of the justices of the Supreme Court have deviated from the political expectations of the presidents who appointed them.[23]

It is important to recognize that presidents' use of political criteria in selecting judges has a democratic influence on the courts. Presidents can campaign on the pledge to make the courts more liberal or conservative through their appointive powers, and voters are free to cast their ballots on the basis of this pledge.

Political Litmus Test   Traditionally, presidents and senators have tried to discern where a Supreme Court candidate fits on the continuum of liberal activism versus conservative self-restraint. Democratic presidents and senators usually prefer liberal judges who express an activist philosophy. Republican presidents usually prefer conservative judges who express a philosophy of judicial self-restraint. Until very recently, both the president and the Senate denied using any political "litmus test" in judicial recruitment. A **litmus test** generally refers to recruitment based on a nominee's stand on a single issue. Since the Supreme Court ruling on *Roe v. Wade* (1973), however, the single issue of abortion has come to dominate the politics of judicial recruitment.

The Politics of Senate Confirmation   All presidential nominations for the federal judiciary, including the Supreme Court, are sent to the Senate for confirmation. The Senate refers them to its powerful Judiciary Committee, which holds hearings, votes on the nomination, and then reports to the full Senate, where floor debate may precede the final confirmation vote.

The Senate's involvement in federal district judgeships traditionally centered on the practice of **senatorial courtesy**. If senators from the president's party from the same state for which an appointment was being considered disapproved of a

✔ *Think*
Again

Should presidents appoint only judges who agree with their judicial philosophy?

litmus test
In political terms, a person's stand on a key issue that determines whether he or she will be appointed to public office or supported in electoral campaigns.

senatorial courtesy
Custom of the U.S. Senate with regard to presidential nominations to the judiciary to defer to the judgment of senators from the president's party from the same state as the nominee.

WHAT DO YOU THINK?

Should Supreme Court Nominees Reveal Their Views on Key Cases Before the Senate Votes to Confirm Them?

U.S. Senators on the Judiciary Committee, questioning presidents' Supreme Court nominees, have traditionally been frustrated by the refusal of nominees to comment on issues that are likely to come before the court in future cases. The nominees have argued that giving specific opinions may impinge upon their judicial impartiality when faced with specific cases. A true judicial approach requires that they examine specific facts in a case, listen to the arguments on both sides, and confer with their colleagues on the Court before rendering an opinion. They should not approach cases with preconceived opinions. Thus, when asked if he supported *Roe v. Wade*, John Roberts simply stated that the case was now precedent in constitutional law and entitled to "due respect." "I should stay away from issues that may come before the court again."

But Democratic Sen. Joseph R. Biden, Jr., insisted that Roberts could at least discuss his views about abortion and the right of privacy, as well as other general legal views. "Without any knowledge of your understanding of the law, because you will not share it with us, we are rolling the dice with you, judge."

In her Senate testimony in 2009, Justice Sonia Sotomayor followed the precedent of other nominees to the Supreme Court in declining to take positions on issues that were likely to come before the Court. However, her long record as a federal district judge and later a judge on the Court of Appeals clearly indicated her activist judicial philosophy. As an Appeals Court judge she had ruled against the New Haven Connecticut firefighters who had been denied promotion because African Americans had not performed well on a promotion exam. The Supreme Court later overruled her in a close 5 to 4 decision. So the Democratic-controlled Senate had good reason to believe that she would join the liberal bloc on the Court.

Polls reveal that the general public wants to know the Supreme Court nominee's views on important issues.

Q. When the Senate votes on a nominee for the U.S. Supreme Court should it consider only that person's legal qualifications and background, or, along with legal background, should the Senate also consider how that nominee might vote on major issues the Supreme Court decides?

Legal background only	Issues too	Unsure
36%	51%	10%

Sources: Congressional Quarterly Weekly Report, September 19, 2005, p. 2497; New York Times, September 14, 2005.

nominee, their Senate colleagues would defeat the nomination. But if the president and senators from that party agreed on the nomination, the full Senate, even if controlled by the opposition, customarily confirmed the nomination. During the Reagan-Bush years, however, partisan divisions between these Republican presidents and Senate Democrats eroded the tradition of senatorial courtesy.

Supreme Court nominations have always received close political scrutiny in the Senate. (See *What Do You Think?*: "Should Supreme Court Nominees Reveal Their Views on Key Cases Before the Senate Votes to Confirm Them?") Over the last two centuries, the Senate has rejected or refused to confirm about 20 percent of presidential nominees to the high court (see Table 13.2). In the past, most senators believed that presidents deserved to appoint their own judges; the opposition party would get its own opportunity to appoint judges when it won the presidency. Only if the Senate found some personal disqualification in a nominee's background (for example, financial scandal, evidence of racial or religious bias, judicial incompetence) would a nominee likely be rejected. But publicity and partisanship over confirmation of Supreme Court nominees have increased markedly in recent years.[24]

Filibustering Court Nominees
The Constitution requires only a majority vote of the Senate to "advise and consent" to a presidential nominee for a federal court judgeship, including a seat on the Supreme Court. However, recent partisan battles over nominees have centered on the Senate's filibuster rule and the sixty votes

TABLE 13.2   Senate Confirmation Votes on Supreme Court Nominations since 1950

Nominee	President	Year	Vote
Earl Warren	Eisenhower	1954	NRV[a]
John Marshall Harlan	Eisenhower	1955	71–11
William J. Brennan	Eisenhower	1957	NRV
Charles Whittaker	Eisenhower	1957	NRV
Potter Stewart	Eisenhower	1959	70–17
Byron White	Kennedy	1962	NRV
Arthur Goldberg	Kennedy	1962	NRV
Abe Fortas	Johnson	1965	NRV
Thurgood Marshall	Johnson	1967	69–11
Abe Fortas[b]	Johnson	1968	Withdrawn[c]
Homer Thornberry	Johnson	1968	No action
Warren Burger	Nixon	1969	74–3
Clement Haynsworth	Nixon	1969	Defeated 45–55
G. Harrold Carswell	Nixon	1970	Defeated 45–51
Harry Blackmun	Nixon	1970	94–0
Lewis Powell	Nixon	1971	89–1
William Rehnquist	Nixon	1971	68–26
John Paul Stevens	Ford	1975	98–0
Sandra Day O'Connor	Reagan	1981	99–0
William Rehnquist[b]	Reagan	1986	65–33
Antonin Scalia	Reagan	1986	98–0
Robert Bork	Reagan	1987	Defeated 42–58
Douglas Ginsburg	Reagan	1987	Withdrawn
Anthony Kennedy	Reagan	1988	97–0
David Souter	Bush, Sr.	1990	90–9
Clarence Thomas	Bush, Sr.	1991	52–48
Ruth Bader Ginsburg	Clinton	1993	96–3
Stephen G. Breyer	Clinton	1994	87–9
John G. Roberts, Jr.	Bush, Jr.	2005	78–22
Harriet Miers	Bush, Jr.	2005	Withdrawn
Samuel Alito, Jr.	Bush, Jr.	2005	58–42
Sonia Sotomayor	Obama	2009	68–31
Elena Kagan	Obama	2010	63–37

[a]No recorded vote.
[b]Elevation to Chief Justice.
[c]Nomination withdrawn after Senate vote failed to end filibuster against nomination; vote was 45 to 43 to end filibuster.
Source: Congressional Quarterly's Guide to the U.S. Supreme Court, 4th ed. (Washington, D.C.: CQ Press, 2004); updated by the author.

required for cloture to end a filibuster.[25] President George W. Bush suffered several key defeats of judicial nominees for seats on the U.S. Court of Appeals by failing to get sixty votes to end filibusters over these nominations. All of his nominations were qualified from a judicial point of view, but all were considered too conservative by leading Democrats in the Senate. Republicans threatened to try to end the filibuster rule for judicial nominations. They argued that the Constitution itself specifies a "majority vote of the Senate," not a three-fifths vote for confirmation. But ending the filibuster rule, even for only judicial nominations, would challenge a sacred tradition of the Senate. (Some senators referred to it as the "nuclear option.") A shaky compromise was reached in 2005 when some previously rejected Republican appellate court nominees were confirmed, and Democrats in the Senate promised to use the filibuster only in extraordinary cases. The Democrats chose *not* to filibuster the Supreme Court nominations of John Roberts or Samuel Alito, and Republicans did not filibuster the nomination of Sonia Sotomayor or Elena Kagan.

Who Is Selected?

▶ 13.6 *Identify factors involved in the judicial selection process.*

What background and experiences are brought to the Supreme Court? Despite often holding very different views on the laws, the Constitution, and their interpretation, the justices of the U.S. Supreme Court tend to share a common background of education at the nation's most prestigious law schools and prior judicial experience.

Law Degrees   There is no constitutional requirement that Supreme Court justices be attorneys, but every person who has ever served on the High Court has been trained in law. Moreover, most of the justices have attended one or another of the nation's most prestigious law schools (see Table 13.3).

Judicial Experience   Historically, most Supreme Court justices have been federal or state court judges. All of the justices sitting today have come from the U.S. Court of Appeals. Many justices have served some time as U.S. attorneys in the Department of Justice early in their legal careers. Relatively few have held elected political office, but one chief justice—William Howard Taft—previously held the nation's highest elected post, the presidency.

TABLE 13.3   The Supreme Court: Background of the Justices

Justice	Age at Appointment	President Who Appointed	Law School	Position at Time of Appointment	Years as a Judge Before Appointment
Antonin Scalia	50	Reagan (1986)	Harvard	U.S. Court of Appeals	4
Anthony M. Kennedy	51	Reagan (1988)	Harvard	U.S. Court of Appeals	12
Clarence Thomas	43	Bush, Sr. (1991)	Yale	U.S. Court of Appeals	2
Ruth Bader Ginsburg	60	Clinton (1993)	Columbia	U.S. Court of Appeals	13
Stephen G. Breyer	56	Clinton (1994)	Harvard	U.S. Court of Appeals	14
John G. Roberts, Jr., Chief Justice	50	Bush, Jr. (2005)	Harvard	U.S. Court of Appeals	2
Samuel A. Alito, Jr.	55	Bush, Jr. (2005)	Yale	U.S. Court of Appeals	15
Sonia Sotomayor	55	Obama (2009)	Yale	U.S. Court of Appeals	17
Elena Kagan	50	Obama (2010)	Harvard	Solicitor General	0

Age   Most justices have been in their 50s when appointed to the Court. Presumably this is the age at which people acquire the necessary prominence and experience to bring themselves to the attention of the White House and Justice Department as potential candidates. At the same time, presidents seek to make a lasting imprint on the Court, and candidates in their fifties can be expected to serve on the Court for many more years than older candidates with the same credentials.

Race and Gender   No African American had ever served on the Supreme Court until President Lyndon Johnson's appointment of Thurgood Marshall in 1967. A Howard University Law School graduate, Marshall had served as counsel for the National Association for the Advancement of Colored People Legal Defense Fund and had personally argued the historic *Brown v. Board of Education* case before the Supreme Court in 1954. He served as solicitor general of the United States under President Lyndon Johnson before his elevation to the High Court. Upon Marshall's retirement in 1991, President George H. W. Bush sought to retain minority representation on the Supreme Court, yet at the same time to reinforce conservative judicial views, with his selection of Clarence Thomas.

No woman had served on the Supreme Court prior to the appointment of Sandra Day O'Connor by President Ronald Reagan in 1981. O'Connor was Reagan's first Supreme Court appointment. Although a relatively unknown Arizona state court judge, she had the powerful support of Arizona Republican Senator Barry Goldwater and Stanford classmate Justice William Rehnquist. The second woman to serve on the High Court, Ruth Bader Ginsburg, had served as an attorney for the American Civil Liberties Union while teaching at Columbia Law School and had argued and won several important gender discrimination cases. President Jimmy Carter appointed her in 1980 to the U.S. Court of Appeals; President Bill Clinton elevated her to the Supreme Court in 1993.

Sonia Sotomayor is the third woman and the first Hispanic to serve on the Supreme Court. In her early years, she had been active on behalf of the Puerto Rican Legal Defense and Education Fund. She had compiled a lengthy judicial record on the federal district court and the Court of Appeals and her activist judicial philosophy was well known. She heard appeals in more than 3,000 cases and wrote 380 opinions. She brings more judicial experience to the Supreme Court than any justice in modern times. (See *People in Politics*: "Sonia Sotomayor, A Latina on the Supreme Court.")

In contrast, Elena Kagan comes to the Supreme Court with no judicial experience at all. She is a Princeton graduate, an Oxford scholar, and a magna cum laude graduate of Harvard Law School. Following graduation in 1986 and 2 years of private practice, she joined the faculty of the University of Chicago Law School. Later she went on to serve in the Clinton White House as a legal counselor. She returned to Harvard Law School in 1999, and in 2003 she became Dean. She was pulled back into government service in 2009 as President Barack Obama's Solicitor General.

Supreme Court Decision Making

▶ 13.7 *Outline the decision-making process of the Supreme Court and areas in which the Court has been active.*

The Supreme Court sets its own agenda: it decides what it wants to decide. Of the more than 8,000 requests for hearings that come to its docket each year, the Court issues opinions on only about 125 cases. Another 150 or so cases are decided

PEOPLE IN POLITICS

Sonia Sotomayor, A Latina on the Supreme Court

In nominating her to the U.S. Supreme Court, President Barack Obama proclaimed: "Judge Sonia Sotomayor has lived the American dream." She grew up in a public housing project in the South Bronx, after her family moved to New York from Puerto Rico during World War II. Her father, a factory worker, died when she was 9 years old. Her mother, a nurse, raised her and her younger brother, who is now a physician in Syracuse, New York. Young Sonia was diagnosed with diabetes as a child and began taking daily insulin injections. She excelled in school and graduated as valedictorian at the academically rigorous Cardinal Spellman High School. She was rewarded with a full scholarship to Princeton University.

At Princeton she continued to excel, graduating Phi Beta Kappa in 1976. She also engaged in political activism at Princeton, charging that the University had failed to provide courses in Puerto Rican history and politics or to actively recruit Latino faculty. She attended Yale Law School, again on a full scholarship, and she served as editor of the *Yale Law Journal*. She graduated from law school in 1979 and was admitted to the New York Bar in 1980.

She began her legal career as an assistant district attorney in New York. She was married in 1976 and divorced in 1983; she has no children. After five years as a prosecutor she entered private practice. She served on the Board of Directors of the Puerto Rican Legal Defense and Education Fund. She began her long career as a federal judge following her nomination to the U.S. District Court for the Southern District of New York by Republican President George H. W. Bush in 1991. She was nominated in 1997 by Democratic President Bill Clinton to serve on the Court of Appeals for the Second Circuit. Republican Senators expressed concern at that time about her liberal leanings, so her confirmation was temporarily held up. She was, however, confirmed in 1998 on a 67–29 Senate vote.

In hearings before the Senate Judiciary Committee, she was questioned about this statement she made at a Berkeley Law School lecture in 2001: "I would hope that a wise Latina woman with the richness of her experience would more often than not reach a better conclusion than a white male who hasn't lived that life." In addressing the Senate question, she testified that a judge must always follow the law regardless of personal background (in effect contradicting her earlier controversial statement). Her long judicial record suggests that she will be a strong contributing member to the liberal bloc on the High Court. But inasmuch as the justice she replaced, David Souter, was himself a reliable member of that same bloc, it is not likely that Sotomayor will change the ideological balance of the Court.

---

writ of certiorari
Writ issued by the Supreme Court, at its discretion, to order a lower court to prepare the record of a case and send it to the Supreme Court for review. Most cases come to the Court as petitions for writs of certiorari.

summarily (without opinion) by a Court order either affirming or reversing the lower court decision. The Supreme Court refuses to rule at all on the vast majority of cases that are submitted to it. Thus the rhetorical threat to "take this all the way to the Supreme Court" is usually an empty one. It is important, however, to realize that a refusal to rule also creates law by allowing the decision of the lower court to stand. That is why the U.S. Circuit Courts of Appeals are powerful bodies.

Setting the Agenda: Granting Certiorari   Most cases reach the Supreme Court when a party in a case appeals to the Court to issue a **writ of certiorari** (literally to "make more certain"), a decision by the Court to require a lower federal or state court to turn over its records on a case.[26] To "grant certiorari"—that is, to decide to hear arguments in a case and render a decision—the Supreme Court relies on its **rule of four**: four justices must agree to do so. Deciding which cases to hear takes up a great deal of the Court's time.

What criteria does the Supreme Court use in choosing its policy agenda—that is, in choosing the cases it wishes to decide? The Court rarely explains why it accepts or rejects cases, but there are some general patterns. First, the Court accepts cases involving issues that the justices are interested in. The justices are clearly interested in the area of 1st Amendment freedoms—speech, press, and religion. Members of the Court are also interested in civil rights issues under the Equal Protection Clause of the 14th Amendment and the civil rights laws and in overseeing the criminal justice system and defining the Due Process Clauses of the 5th and 14th Amendments.

In addition, the Court seems to feel an obligation to accept cases involving questions that have been decided differently by different Circuit Courts of Appeals. The Supreme Court generally tries to see to it that "the law" does not differ from one circuit to another. Likewise, the Supreme Court usually acts when lower courts have made decisions clearly at odds with Supreme Court interpretations in order to maintain control of the federal judiciary. Finally, the Supreme Court is more likely to accept a case in which the U.S. government is a party and requests a review, especially when an issue appears to be one of overriding importance to the government. In fact, the U.S. government is a party in almost half of the cases decided by the Supreme Court.

Hearing Arguments   Once the Supreme Court places a case on its decision calendar, attorneys for both sides submit written briefs on the issues. The Supreme Court may also allow interest groups to submit **amicus curiae** (literally, "friend of the court") briefs. This process allows interest groups direct access to the Supreme Court. In the affirmative action case of *University of California Regents v. Bakke* (1978)[27] the Court accepted 59 *amicus curiae* briefs representing more than 100 interest groups. The U.S. government frequently submits amicus curiae arguments in cases in which it is not a party. The **solicitor general** of the United States is responsible for presenting the government's arguments both in cases in which the government is a party and in cases in which the government is merely an amicus curiae.

Oral arguments before the Supreme Court are a time-honored ritual of American government. They take place in the marble "temple"—the Supreme Court building across the street from the U.S. Capitol in Washington, D.C. The justices, clad in their black robes, sit behind a high "bench" and peer down at the attorneys presenting their arguments. Arguing a case before the Supreme Court is said to be an intimidating experience. Each side is usually limited to either a half-hour or an hour of argument, but justices frequently interrupt with their own pointed questioning. Court watchers sometimes try to predict the Court's decision from the tenor of the questioning. Oral argument is the most public phase of Supreme Court decision making, but no one really knows whether these arguments ever change the justices' minds.

In Conference   The actual decisions are made in private conferences among the justices. These conferences usually take place on Wednesdays and Fridays and cover the cases argued orally during the same week. The Chief Justice presides, and only justices (no law clerks) are present. It is customary for the Chief Justice to speak first on the issues, followed by each associate justice in order of seniority. A majority must decide which party wins or loses and whether a lower court's decision is to be affirmed or reversed.

rule of four
At least four justices must agree to hear an appeal (writ of certiorari) from a lower court in order to get a case before the Supreme Court.

amicus curiae
Literally, "friend of the court"; a person, private group or institution, or government agency that is not a party to a case but participates in the case (usually through submission of a brief) at the invitation of the court or on its own initiative.

solicitor general
Attorney in the Department of Justice who represents the U.S. government before the Supreme Court and any other courts.

majority opinion
Opinion in a case that is
subscribed to by a majority of
the judges who participated in
the decision.

concurring opinion
Opinion by a member of a
court that agrees with the
result reached by the court in
the case but disagrees with or
departs from the court's
rationale for the decision.

dissenting opinion
Opinion by a member of a
court that disagrees with the
result reached by the court in
the case.

Writing Opinions   The *written* opinion determines the actual outcome of
the case (votes in conference are not binding). When the decision is unanimous, the
Chief Justice traditionally writes the opinion. In the case of a split decision,
the Chief Justice may take on the task of writing the **majority opinion** or assign it
to another justice in the majority. If the Chief Justice is in the minority, the senior
justice in the majority makes the assignment. Writing the opinion of the Court is
the central task in Supreme Court policy making. Broadly written opinions may
effect sweeping policy changes; narrowly written opinions may decide a particular
case but have very little policy impact. The reasons cited for the decision become
binding law, to be applied by lower courts in future cases. Yet despite the crucial
role of opinion writing in Court policy making, most opinions are actually written
by law clerks who are only recent graduates of the nation's prestigious law schools.
The justices themselves read, edit, correct, and sometimes rewrite drafts prepared
by clerks, but clerks may have a strong influence over the position taken by
justices on the issues.

A draft of the opinion is then circulated among members of the majority. Any
majority member who disagrees with the reasoning in the opinion, and thus disagrees with the policy that is proposed, may either negotiate changes in the
opinion with others in the majority or write a concurring opinion. A **concurring
opinion** agrees with the decision about which party wins the case but sets forth a
different reason for the decision, proposing, in effect, a different policy position.

Justices in the minority often agree to present a **dissenting opinion**. The dissenting opinion sets forth the views of justices who disagree with both the decision and the majority reasoning. Dissenting opinions do not have the force of
law. They are written both to express opposition to the majority view and to
appeal to a future Court to someday modify or reverse the position of the majority. Occasionally, the Court is unable to agree on a clear policy position on particularly vexing questions. If the majority is strongly divided over the reasoning
behind their decision and as many as four justices dissent altogether from the
decision, lower courts will lack clear guidance and future cases will be decided on
a case-by-case basis, depending on multiple factors occurring in each case (see,
for example, "Affirmative Action in the Courts" in Chapter 15). The absence of a
clear opinion of the Court, supported by a unified majority of the justices, invites
additional cases, keeping the issue on the Court's agenda until such time (if any)
as the Court establishes a clear policy on the issue.

Politics and the Supreme Court

▶ 13.8 *Assess the role of politics and ideology in Supreme Court decision making.*

The political views of Supreme Court justices have an important influence on
Court decisions. Justices are swayed primarily by their own ideological views;
but public opinion, the president's position, and the arguments of interest groups
all contribute to the outcome of cases.

Liberal and Conservative Voting Blocs   Although liberal and conservative voting blocs on the Court are visible over time, on any given case particular
justices may deviate from their perceived ideological position. Many cases do not
present a liberal-conservative dimension. Each case presents a separate set of
facts, and even justices who share a general philosophy may perceive the central
facts of a case differently. Moreover, the liberal-versus-conservative dimension
sometimes clashes with the activist-versus-self-restraint dimension. Although we
generally think of liberals as favoring activism and conservatives, self-restraint,

TABLE 13.4 How They Vote: Liberal and Conservative Blocs on the Supreme Court*

	The Warren Court	The Burger Court	The Rehnquist Court	The Roberts Court
	1968	1975	2004	2010
Liberal	Earl Warren	William O. Douglas	John Paul Stevens	Ruth Bader Ginsburg
	Hugo Black	Thurgood Marshall	Ruth Bader Ginsburg	Stephen G. Breyer
	William O. Douglas	William J. Brennan	Stephen G. Breyer	Sonia Sotomayor
	Thurgood Marshall		David Souter	Elena Kagan
	William J. Brennan			
	Abe Fortas			
Moderate	Potter Stewart	Potter Stewart	Anthony Kennedy	Anthony Kennedy
	Byron White	Byron White	Sandra Day O'Connor	
		Lewis Powell		
		Harry Blackmun		
Conservative	John Marshall Harlan	Warren Burger	William Rehnquist	John Roberts
		William Rehnquist	Antonin Scalia	Samuel Alito
			Clarence Thomas	Antonin Scalia
				Clarence Thomas

*All blocs have been designated by the author.

occasionally those who favor self-restraint are obliged to approve of legislation that violates their personal conservative beliefs because opposing it would substitute their judgment for that of elected officials. So ideological blocs are not always good predictors of voting outcomes on the Court.

Over time, the composition of the Supreme Court has changed, as has the power of its various liberal and conservative voting blocs (see Table 13.4). The liberal bloc, headed by Chief Justice Earl Warren, dominated Court decision making from the mid-1950s through the end of the 1960s. The liberal bloc gradually weakened following President Richard Nixon's appointment of Warren Burger as Chief Justice in 1969, but not all of Nixon's appointees joined the conservative bloc; Justice Harry Blackmun and Justice Lewis Powell frequently joined in voting with the liberal bloc. Among Nixon's appointees, only William Rehnquist consistently adopted conservative positions. President Gerald Ford's only appointee to the Court, John Paul Stevens, began as a moderate and drifted to the liberal bloc. As a result, the Burger Court, although generally not as activist as the Warren Court, still did not reverse any earlier liberal holdings.

President Ronald Reagan, who had campaigned on a pledge to restrain the liberal activism of the Court, tried to appoint conservatives. His first appointee, Sandra Day O'Connor, turned out to be less conservative than expected, especially on women's issues and abortion rights. When Chief Justice Burger retired in 1986, Reagan seized on the opportunity to strengthen the conservative bloc by elevating Rehnquist to Chief Justice. Reagan also appointed Antonin Scalia, another strong conservative, to the Court. Reagan added Anthony Kennedy to the Court in 1988, hoping to give Rehnquist and the conservative bloc the opportunity to form a majority. Had President Reagan succeeded in getting the powerful conservative voice of Robert Bork on the Court, it is possible that many earlier liberal decisions, including *Roe v. Wade*, would have been reversed. But the Senate rejected Bork; David Souter, the man ultimately confirmed, eventually drifted toward the liberal bloc.

Liberals worried that the appointment of conservative Clarence Thomas as a replacement for the liberal Thurgood Marshall would give the conservative bloc a commanding voice in Supreme Court policy making. But no solid

The Swing Vote

Supreme Court Justice Anthony Kennedy appears before a House Appropriations financial services and general government subcommittee on March 13, 2008.

conservative majority emerged. Justices Rehnquist, Scalia, and Thomas were considered the core of the conservative bloc, but they had to win over at least two of the more moderate justices in order to form a majority in a case. President Bill Clinton's appointees, Ruth Bader Ginsburg and Stephen G. Breyer, consistently supported liberal views on the Supreme Court. Liberalism on the Court—as measured by pro-individual rights decisions against the government in civil liberties cases, pro-defendant decisions in criminal cases, and pro-women and minorities decisions in civil rights cases—has declined significantly since the 1960s.[28]

The appointment of John Roberts as Chief Justice, replacing William Rehnquist in 2005, added a strong and learned voice to the conservative bloc (see *People in Politics*: "John Roberts, Chief Justice"). And the appointment of Samuel Alito to the Court, replacing moderate Sandra Day O'Connor, gave the conservative bloc four reliable votes. Sonia Sotomayor, a strong liberal, replaced another liberal, David Souter, in 2009. And liberal Elena Kagan replaced liberal John Paul Stevens in 2010, leaving the four-member liberal bloc unchanged in numerical strength. Anthony Kennedy remains as the swing vote in the clash of liberal and conservative blocs on the High Court.

Public Opinion

"By all arguable evidence of the modern Supreme Court, the Court appears to reflect public opinion about as accurately as other policy makers."[29] And indeed, on the liberal-conservative dimension, it can be argued that Supreme Court decisions have generally followed shifts in American public opinion. However, the Court appears to lag behind public opinion. It is doubtful that the justices read opinion polls; their jobs do not depend on public approval ratings. Rather, it is more likely that the justices, whose nomination and confirmation depended on an elected president and Senate, generally share the views of those who put them on the bench. Thus public opinion affects the Court only indirectly, through the nomination and confirmation process.

Presidential Influence

Even after a president's initial appointment of a Justice to the High Court, a president may exercise some influence over judicial decision making. The Office of the **U.S. Solicitor General** is charged with the responsibility of presenting the government's (the president's) views in cases not only to which the U.S. government is a party, but also in cases in which the president and the Attorney General have a strong interest and present their arguments in amicus curiae briefs. The Solicitor General's Office, in both Democratic and Republican presidential administrations, has compiled an enviable record in Supreme Court cases. When representing federal agencies that are parties to cases, the Solicitors General have won two-thirds of their cases before the Supreme Court over the years. And in cases where the Solicitor General has offered an amicus curiae brief, he has won about three-quarters of the cases. In contrast, the states have won fewer than half of the cases before the Supreme Court in which a state has been a party.

Interest-Group Influence

Interest groups have become a major presence in Supreme Court cases. First of all, interest groups (for example, Planned Parenthood, National Association for the Advancement of Colored People, American Civil Liberties Union) sponsor many cases themselves. They find persons they believe to be directly damaged by a public policy, initiate litigation on their behalf, and provide the attorneys and money to pursue these cases all the way to

U.S. Solicitor General
The U.S. government's chief legal counsel, presenting the government's arguments in cases in which it is a party or in which it has an interest.

PEOPLE IN POLITICS

John Roberts, Chief Justice

As one of the youngest Chief Justices in the history of the Supreme Court, John Roberts has the opportunity to mold the Constitution over the years to come to fit his personal views.

Roberts graduated from a Catholic high school in Indiana first in his class and captain of the football team. After 1 year at Sacred Heart University, he transferred to Harvard where he majored in history and graduated summa cum laude and Phi Beta Kappa in 1976. He went on to Harvard Law School and served as editor of the *Harvard Law Review*. He then clerked for Supreme Court Justice William Rehnquist.

Roberts served in the Reagan administration as a special assistant to the Attorney General and later associate counsel in the White House. He served in the first Bush administration as Deputy Solicitor General and argued some thirty-nine cases for the government before the Supreme Court. President George H. W. Bush nominated him for the U.S. Court of Appeals in 1992, but Congress adjourned without confirming the nomination. During the Clinton years Roberts served as a partner in the Washington law firm of Hogan & Hartson. Then in 2003 he was renominated

to the Court of Appeals by President George W. Bush. Although opposed by New York Senator Charles Schumer and Massachusetts Senator Ted Kennedy, he was confirmed by the U.S. Senate.

President Bush originally nominated Roberts to the U.S. Supreme Court in 2005 to fill the vacancy left by retired Justice Sandra Day O'Connor. But following the death of Chief Justice William H. Rehnquist that year, Bush nominated Roberts for the position of Chief Justice. Joseph Alito was nominated to fill the O'Connor vacancy.

Roberts appeared calm and collected during the highly partisan questioning by the Senate Judiciary Committee. Following the custom of nominees to decline to say how they might vote on specific issues before the High Court, he nonetheless stated that *Roe v. Wade* "is settled law of the land." That was not enough to win over many Democrats, including Senators Schumer and Kennedy. Yet Roberts was confirmed by a Senate vote of 78 senators to 22.

In his decisions on the High Court, Roberts reflects the moderate to conservative views that he expressed in Senate committee hearings. He voted to uphold the ban on partial-birth abortions enacted by the Congress, but gave no indication that he might vote to reverse *Roe v. Wade*.

the Supreme Court. Second of all, it is now a rare case that comes to the Court without multiple amicus curiae briefs filed by interest groups.

How influential are interest groups in Supreme Court decisions? Certainly, interest groups have a significant influence in bringing issues before the Supreme Court through their sponsorship of cases. It is unlikely that the Court would have acted when it did on many key issues from racial segregation in 1954 (*Brown v. Board of Education* sponsored by the NAACP) to abortion in 1992 (*Planned Parenthood v. Casey* sponsored by Planned Parenthood) in the absence of interest-group activity. And interest-group *amicus curiae* briefs are now mentioned (cited) in about two-thirds of the written decisions of the Court. However, these briefs may not have much *independent* effect on decisions, that is, they may not have convinced the justices to decide a case one way or another. Several studies have found that interest-group briefs have had very little effect on Supreme Court decisions.[30]

Checking Court Power

▶ 13.9 *Evaluate checks on Supreme Court power.*

Many people are concerned about the extent to which we now rely on a non-elected judiciary to decide key policy issues rather than depending on a democratically elected president or Congress.

Legitimacy as a Restraint on the Judiciary   Court authority derives from legitimacy rather than force. By that we mean that the courts depend on their authority being seen as rightful, on people perceiving an obligation to abide by court decisions whether they agree with them or not. The courts have no significant force at their direct command. Federal marshals, who carry out the orders of federal courts, number only a few thousand. Courts must rely primarily on the executive branch for enforcement of their decisions.

Today, most Americans believe that Supreme Court decisions are authoritative statements about the Constitution and that people have an obligation to obey these decisions whether they agree with them or not.[31] Thus public opinion constrains other public officials—from the president, to governors, to school superintendents, to law enforcement officials—to obey Supreme Court decisions.[32] Their constituents do not hold them personally responsible for unpopular actions ordered by the Supreme Court or federal judges. On the contrary, their constituents generally expect them to comply with court decisions.

Compliance with Court Policy   Federal and state court judges must apply Supreme Court policies when ruling on cases in their own courts. Occasionally, lower courts express their disagreement with the Supreme Court in an opinion, even when they feel obliged to carry out the High Court's policy. At times, lower federal and state courts try to give a narrow interpretation to a Supreme Court decision with which they disagree. But judges who seek to defy the Supreme Court face the ultimate sanction of reversal on appeal by the losing party. Professional pride usually inspires judges to avoid reversals of their judgments by higher courts even though a long record of reversals is not grounds for impeachment or removal of a federal judge.

Public officials who defy Supreme Court rulings risk lawsuits and court orders mandating compliance. Persons injured by noncompliance are likely to file suit against noncomplying officials, as are interest groups that monitor official compliance with the policies they support. These suits are expensive, time consuming, and potentially embarrassing to government officials and agencies. Once a court order is issued, continued defiance can result in fines and penalties for contempt of court.

The president of the United States is subject to federal court orders. Historically, this notion has been challenged: early presidents believed they were separate and at least co-equal to the courts and that their own determination about the legality or constitutionality of their own acts could not be overturned by the courts. President Andrew Jackson could—and did—say: "John Marshall has made his decision. Now let him enforce it," expressing the view that the president was not obliged to enforce court decisions he disagreed with.[33] But in the course of 200 years, the courts—not the president—have gained in legitimacy as the final authority on the law and the Constitution. Today, a president who openly defied the Supreme Court would lose any claims to legitimacy and would risk impeachment by Congress.

The case of Richard Nixon illustrates the weakness of a modern president who would even consider defying the Supreme Court. When Nixon sought to invoke executive privilege to withhold damaging tapes of White House conversations in the Watergate investigation (see *Politics Up Close*: "Watergate and the Limits of Presidential Power" in Chapter 11), federal district judge John Sirica rejected his claim and ordered that the tapes be turned over to the special prosecutor in the case. In arguments before the Supreme Court, Nixon's lawyers contended that the president would not have to comply with a Supreme Court decision to turn

A CONSTITUTIONAL NOTE

The Power of Judicial Review

Nowhere in the Constitution do we find any mention of the power of "judicial review." It is true that the Constitution's Supremacy Clause (Article VI, Section 2) makes the Constitution and national laws and treaties "the supreme law of the land, anything in the Constitution or laws of any *state* to the contrary notwithstanding." The Founders clearly believed that federal court power over state decisions was essential to maintaining national unity. But at the *national* level, why should an appointed court's interpretation of the Constitution prevail over the views of an elected Congress and an elected president? All are pledged to uphold the Constitution. The answer is that the Founders distrusted popular majorities and elected officials subject to their influence. So the Founders deliberately insulated the courts from popular majorities; by appointing judges for life terms, they sought to ensure their independence. Alexander Hamilton viewed the federal courts as a final bulwark against threats to principle and property. Writing in *The Federalist* in late 1787 he said:

"Limited government . . . can be preserved in practice no other way than through the medium of courts of justice, whose duty it is to declare all acts contrary to the manifest tenor of the Constitution void." But it was not until the case of *Marbury v. Madison* in 1803 that John Marshall first assumed the power of judicial review. He argued persuasively that (1) the Constitution is declared "the supreme law of the land," and national as well as state laws must be congruent with it; (2) Article III gives the Supreme Court the "judicial power," which includes the power to interpret the meaning of laws and, in case of conflict between laws, to decide which law shall prevail; and (3) the courts are sworn to uphold the Constitution, so they must declare void any law that conflicts with the Constitution. Despite the logic of the argument, judicial review—the ability of an *un*elected judiciary, serving for life, to invalidate laws of Congress and actions of the president—would appear to be an undemocratic feature of the Constitution.

over the tapes. Yet when the Court ruled unanimously against him, Nixon felt bound to comply and released tapes that were very damaging to his cause. But Nixon understood that refusal to abide by a Supreme Court decision would most assuredly have resulted in impeachment. Under the circumstances, compliance was the better of two unattractive choices.

Presidential Influence on Court Policy   The president and Congress can exercise some restraint over court power through the checks and balances built into the Constitution. Using the office's powers of appointment, presidents have effectively modified the direction of Supreme Court policy and influenced lower federal courts as well. Certainly presidents must await the death or retirement of Supreme Court justices and federal judges, and presidents are constrained by the need to secure Senate confirmation of their appointees. However, over time presidential influence on the courts can be significant. During their combined 12 years in the White House, Ronald Reagan and his successor George H. W. Bush were able to fill 70 percent of federal district and appellate court judgeships and six of nine Supreme Court positions with their own appointees. As noted earlier, however, their appointees did not always reflect these presidents' philosophies in rendering decisions. Nevertheless, the federal courts tilted in a somewhat more conservative direction. President Bill Clinton's appointments generally strengthened liberal, activist impulses throughout the federal judiciary, and George W. Bush's appointees generally supported a conservative, restrained judiciary. Predictably, President Obama's appointees have reflected a strong, liberal activist philosophy.

Congressional Checks on the Judiciary   The Constitution gives Congress control over the structure and jurisdiction of federal district and appellate courts, but congressional use of this control has been restrained. Only the Supreme Court is established by the Constitution; Article III gives

Congress the power to "ordain and establish . . . inferior" courts. In theory, Congress could try to limit court jurisdiction to hear cases that Congress did not wish it to decide. Congress has used this power to lighten the federal courts' workload; for example, Congress has limited the jurisdiction of federal courts in cases between citizens of different states by requiring that the dispute involve more than $75,000. But Congress has never used this power to change court policy—for example, by removing federal court jurisdiction over school prayer cases or desegregation cases. Indeed, federal courts would probably declare unconstitutional any congressional attempt to limit their power to interpret the Constitution by limiting jurisdiction.

Likewise, although Congress could, in theory, expand membership on the Supreme Court, the custom of a nine-member Supreme Court is now so deeply ingrained in American government that "court packing" is politically unthinkable. Franklin Roosevelt's unsuccessful 1937 attempt to expand the Supreme Court was the last serious assault on the size of its membership.

A more common congressional constraint on the Supreme Court is amending statutory laws to reverse federal court interpretations of these laws that Congress believes are in error. Thus when the Supreme Court decided that civil rights laws did not mandate a cutoff of *all* federal funds to a college upon evidence of discrimination in a single program but only the funds for that program,[34] Congress amended its own laws to require the more sweeping remedy. Although members of Congress frequently berate the Court for what they see as misreading of the laws, all Congress needs to do to reverse a Court interpretation of those laws is to pass amendments to them.

Constitutional amendment is the only means by which the Congress and the states can reverse a Supreme Court interpretation of the Constitution itself. After the Civil War, the 13th Amendment abolishing slavery reversed the Supreme Court's *Dred Scott* decision (1857) that slavery was constitutionally protected. The 16th Amendment (1913) gave Congress the power to impose an income tax, thus reversing the Supreme Court's earlier decision in *Pollock v. Farmer's Loan*[35] holding income taxes unconstitutional (1895). But recent attempts to reverse Supreme Court interpretations of the Constitution by passing constitutional amendments on the issues of prayer in public schools, busing, and abortion have all failed to win congressional approval. The barriers to a constitutional amendment are formidable: a two-thirds vote of both houses of Congress and ratification by three-quarters of the states. Thus, for all practical purposes, the Constitution is what the Supreme Court says it is.

Congress can impeach federal court judges, but only for "cause" (committing crimes), not for their decisions. Although impeachment is frequently cited as a constitutional check on the judiciary, it has no real influence over judicial policy making. Only five federal court judges have ever been impeached by the House, convicted by the Senate, and removed from office, although two others were impeached and another nine resigned to avoid impeachment. In 1989, Federal District Court Judge Alcee Hastings became the first sitting judge in more than 50 years to be impeached, tried, and found guilty by the Congress. He was convicted by the Senate of perjury and conspiracy to obtain a $150,000 bribe; but a federal district court judge later ruled that he should have been tried by the full Senate, not a special committee of the Senate. Hastings declared the ruling a vindication; in 1992 he won a congressional seat in Florida, becoming the first person ever to become a member of the House after being impeached by that same body. Even criminal convictions do not ensure removal from office, although judges have resigned under fire.

Summary

▶ **13.1** *Assess the basis for and use of judicial power.*

The power of judicial review is the power to invalidate laws of Congress or of the states that the federal courts believe conflict with the U.S. Constitution. This power is not specifically mentioned in the Constitution but was derived by Chief Justice John Marshall from the Supremacy Clause and the meaning of judicial power in Article III.

The Supreme Court has been fairly restrained in its use of judicial review with regard to laws of Congress and actions of presidents; it has more frequently overturned state laws. The federal courts also exercise great power in the interpretation of the laws of Congress, especially when statutory language is vague.

▶ **13.2** *Compare and contrast the philosophies of judicial activism and judicial restraint.*

Arguments over judicial power are reflected in the conflicting philosophies of judicial activism and judicial self-restraint. Advocates of judicial restraint argue that judges must not substitute their own views for those of elected representatives and the remedy for unwise laws lies in the legislature, not the courts. Advocates of judicial activism argue that the courts must view the Constitution as a living document and its meaning must fit the needs of a changing society.

▶ **13.3** *Outline the structure and jurisdiction of the federal courts.*

The federal judiciary consists of three levels of courts—the Supreme Court, the U.S. Courts of Appeals, and the U.S. District Courts. The district courts are trial courts that hear both civil and criminal cases. The courts of appeals are appellate courts and do not hold trials but consider only the record of trial courts and the arguments (briefs) of attorneys. More than 90 percent of federal cases end in appeals courts. The Supreme Court can hear appeals from state high courts as well as lower federal courts. The Supreme Court hears only about 200 cases a year.

▶ **13.4** *Characterize the "special rules" of judicial decision making.*

Courts function under general rules of restraint that do not bind the president or Congress. The Supreme Court does not decide hypothetical cases or render advisory opinions. The principle of stare decisis, or reliance on precedent, is not set aside lightly.

▶ **13.5** *Assess the role of politics in the judicial selection process.*

The selection of Supreme Court justices and federal judges is based more on political considerations than legal qualifications. Presidents almost always appoint judges from their own party, and presidents increasingly have sought judges who share their ideological views. However, because of the independence of judges once they are appointed, presidents have sometimes been disappointed in the decisions of their appointees. In addition, Senate approval of nominees has become increasingly politicized, with problems most evident when different parties control the White House and the Senate.

▶ **13.6** *Identify factors involved in the judicial selection process.*

The justices of the U.S. Supreme Court tend to share a common background of education at the nation's most prestigious law schools. Most appointees have experience as federal court judges; Elena Kagan is the first Justice in many years to lack judicial experience. Today, one African American and three women serve on the Supreme Court.

▶ **13.7** *Outline the decision-making process of the Supreme Court and areas in which the Court has been active.*

The Supreme Court sets its own agenda for policy making, usually by granting or withholding certiorari. Generally, four justices must agree to grant certiorari for a case to be decided by the Supreme Court. The Supreme Court has been especially active in policy making in interpreting the meaning of the 14th Amendment's guarantee of "equal protection of the laws," as well as of the civil rights and voting rights acts of Congress. It has also been active in defining the meaning of freedom of press, speech, and religion in the 1st Amendment and "due process of law" in the 5th Amendment. The federal courts are active in overseeing government regulatory activity. But federal courts have generally left the areas of national security and international relations to the president and Congress. In addition, the Court tends to accept cases involving questions decided differently by different courts of appeal, cases in which lower courts have challenged Supreme Court interpretations, and cases in which the U.S. government is a party and it requests review.

▶ **13.8** *Assess the role of politics and ideology in Supreme Court decision making.*

The Supreme Court risked its reputation for political impartiality when it intervened in the 2000 presidential election and issued a decision that in effect gave Florida's twenty-five electoral votes to George W. Bush and by so doing won him a majority in the Electoral College.

Liberal and conservative blocs on the Supreme Court can be discerned over time. Generally, liberals have been judicial activists and conservatives have been restraintists. Today a moderate bloc appears to hold the balance of power.

▶ 13.9 *Evaluate checks on Supreme Court power.*

Court power derives primarily from legitimacy rather than force. Most Americans believe that Supreme Court decisions are authoritative statements about the Constitution and people have an obligation to obey these decisions whether they agree with them or not. Although early presidents thought of themselves as constitutional co-equals with the Supreme Court and not necessarily bound by Court decisions, today it would be politically unthinkable for a president to ignore a court order.

There are very few checks on Supreme Court power. Presidents may try to influence Court policy through judicial nominations, but once judges are confirmed by the Senate they can pursue their own impulses. Congress has never used its power to limit the jurisdiction of federal courts in order to influence judicial decisions.

Only by amending the Constitution can Congress and the states reverse a Supreme Court interpretation of its meaning. Congress can impeach federal judges only for committing crimes, not for their decisions.

Chapter Test

▶ 13.1 *Assess the basis for and use of judicial power.*

1. The power of the Supreme Court to declare a law passed by Congress or one of the states unconstitutional is known as
   a. constitutional evaluation
   b. constitutional review
   c. judicial evaluation
   d. judicial review

▶ 13.2 *Compare and contrast the philosophies of judicial activism and judicial restraint.*

2. The idea that "the courts should interpret the laws . . . not make them . . ." is
   a. consistent with the principles of judicial activism
   b. consistent with the ideas of judicial restraint
   c. not consistent with the doctrine of original intent
   d. contrary to the rule of *stare decisis*

3. The rules of self-restraint that are used by the Court include all of the following *except*
   a. the Court will decide on the constitutionality of legislation only in an actual case
   b. the Court will offer only limited advice to the president on constitutional matters
   c. complainants must have exhausted all remedies available in lower courts
   d. the Court will invalidate a law only when a constitutional issue is crucial to the case

4. The rule of *stare decisis*
   a. greatly expands the decision-making freedom of the Justices
   b. is based on statutory law
   c. is based on following precedent and thus limits the decision-making power of the Justices
   d. rejects common law

▶ 13.3 *Outline the structure and jurisdiction of the federal courts.*

5. The trial courts of original jurisdiction in the federal system are the
   a. Circuit Courts
   b. Commissioners Courts
   c. District Courts
   d. Courts of Federal Claims

6. The number of federal court criminal cases has _____ in recent years mostly because of _____.
   a. declined; decriminalization of marijuana
   b. increased; initiatives against domestic terrorism
   c. remained static; leveling off of the numbers of criminal cases
   d. increased; enforcement of federal drug laws

▶ 13.4 *Characterize the "special rules" of judicial decision making.*

7. The idea of sovereign immunity involves
   a. diplomatic immunity for foreign dignitaries
   b. the idea that the government cannot be sued without its consent
   c. the idea that the sovereign nations back their currencies with hard assets
   d. the old belief that royalty was immune to the laws

8. Orders of a court to correct a wrong, including a violation of the Constitution, are known as _____.
   a. directives
   b. remedies and relief
   c. directives
   d. injunctions

▶ 13.5 *Assess the role of politics in the judicial selection process.*

9. The Constitution requires that all federal judges be appointed by the president and confirmed by _____ in the _____.
   a. a two-thirds vote; House of Representatives
   b. a two-thirds vote; Senate
   c. a majority vote; House of Representatives
   d. a majority vote; Senate

10. The *litmus test* that has come to dominate the recruitment process in judicial selection revolves around the case of
    a. *Brown v. Board of Education*
    b. *Roe v. Wade*
    c. *Marbury v. Madison*
    d. *Regents of the University of California v. Bakke*

▶ 13.6 *Identify factors involved in the judicial selection process.*

11. The Justices share commonalties among one another in that they usually
    a. have law degrees
    b. have a common educational background
    c. went to the nation's most prestigious universities
    d. all of the above

▶ 13.7 *Outline the decision-making process of the Supreme Court and areas in which the Court has been active.*

12. At least _____ Justices must agree to hear a case before they will issue a _____, which is the way most cases reach the Supreme Court.
    a. four; writ of certiorari
    b. five; writ of mandamus
    c. six; writ of certiorari
    d. four; writ of habeas corpus

13. The attorney that represents the United States in cases before the Supreme Court is the
    a. attorney general
    b. U.S. Chief Counsel
    c. solicitor general
    d. Judge Advocate General

▶ 13.8 *Assess the role of politics and ideology in Supreme Court decision making.*

14. The current Chief Justice of the Supreme Court is
    a. Warren Burger
    b. Earl Warren
    c. Samuel Alito
    d. John Roberts

15. The "swing vote" on the court today is considered to be _____ because he/she is often the deciding vote between the conservatives and liberal voting blocs.
    a. Antonin Scalia
    b. John Roberts
    c. Anthony Kennedy
    d. Ruth Bader Ginsburg

▶ 13.9 *Evaluate checks on Supreme Court power.*

16. Restraints on the power of the Supreme Court come from all but which of the following?
    a. the president
    b. the Congress
    c. public opinion
    d. judicial review

17. Many people were upset with the Supreme Court in the case of *Bush v. Gore* because they believed that it brought into question
    a. the states' rights arguments on civil rights
    b. the sanctity of the right to vote
    c. the political impartiality of the Court
    d. the fairness of Gore's environmental advertisements

18. The case of *Marbury v. Madison* is notable because it resulted in the court gaining the power of
    a. judicial oversight
    b. *a priori* review
    c. *ex post facto* oversight
    d. judicial review

---

myp●liscilab EXERCISES

Apply what you learned in this chapter on MyPoliSciLab.

📖●—[Read on mypoliscilab.com

eText: Chapter 13

✓—[Study and Review on mypoliscilab.com

Pre-Test

Post-Test

Chapter Exam

Flashcards

◉—[Watch on mypoliscilab.com

Video: Most Significant Abortion Ruling in 30 Years

Video: Court Rules on Hazelton's Immigration Laws

Video: Prosecuting Corruption

Video: Prosecuting Cyber Crime

✳●—[Explore on mypoliscilab.com

Simulation: You Are a Young Lawyer

Simulation: You Are a Supreme Court Justice Deciding a Free Speech Case

Simulation: You Are a Clerk to Supreme Court Justice Judith Gray

Simulation: You Are the President and Need to Appoint a Supreme Court Justice

Comparative: Comparing Judiciaries

Timeline: Chief Justices of the Supreme Court

Visual Literacy: Case Overload

Key Terms

Suggested Readings

Baum, Lawrence. *The Supreme Court.* 10th ed. Washington, D.C.: CQ Press, 2009. Readable introduction to the Supreme Court as a political institution, covering the selection and confirmation of judges, the nature of the issues decided by courts, the process of judicial decision making, and the impact of Supreme Court decisions.

Bork, Robert H. *Coercing Virtue.* Washington, D.C.: AEI Press, 2003. An argument that judges, rather than legislators, are making and repealing law and deciding cases with partisan and ideological subjectivity.

Carp, Robert A., Ronald Stidham, and Kenneth L. Manning. *Judicial Process in America.* 8th ed. Washington, D.C.: CQ Press, 2010. Comprehensive coverage of the America judicial system at all levels.

Epstein, Lee, and Thomas G. Walker. *Constitutional Law for a Changing America: Institutional Power and Constraints.* 7th ed. Washington, D.C.: CQ Press, 2010. Commentary and selected excerpts from cases dealing with the structure and powers of government.

Johnson, Charles, and Danette Buickman. *Independent Counsel: The Law and the Investigations.* Washington, D.C.: CQ Press, 2001. A comprehensive history of the independent counsel law and the investigations conducted under it since 1978, from Watergate to Whitewater.

McClosky, Robert G. *The American Supreme Court.* 4th ed. Rev. by Sanford Levinson. Chicago: University of Chicago Press. 2005. Classic work on the Supreme Court's role in constructing the Constitution, with updates to latest cases.

Neubauer, David W., and Stephen S. Weinhold. *Judicial Politics: Law, Courts, and Politics in the United States.* 5th ed. Belmont, Calif.: Wadsworth, 2010. Introduction to the judicial process with controversial cases in each chapter.

U.S. Supreme Court decisions are available at most public and university libraries as well as at law libraries in volumes of *United States Reports.* Court opinions are cited by the names of the parties, for example, *Brown v. Board of Education of Topeka,* followed by a reference number such as 347 U.S. 483 (1954). The first number in the citation (347) is the volume number; "U.S." refers to *United States Reports;* the subsequent number is the page on which the decision begins; the year the case was decided is in parentheses.

Suggested Web Sites

American Bar Association (ABA) www.abanet.org
ABA news and views; information for law students.

Find Law for Students http://stu.findlaw.com
Law school information for schools A–Z, state bar information, job listings, law school rankings, and so forth.

Law Info www.lawinfo.com
Web site offering legal documents, legal help guides, attorney references, and so forth.

Southern Poverty Law Center www.splcenter.org
Civil rights law firm opposing death penalty, hate groups, display of religion in public places, and so forth.

Southeastern Legal Foundation www.southeasternlegal.org
Public interest law firm advocating limited government, individual freedom, and the free enterprise system.

Supreme Court Cases www.law.cornell.edu
This Cornell Law School's Legal Information Institute site contains up-to-date information about important

legal decisions rendered by federal and state courts along with an exhaustive online law library available to researchers.

U.S. Courts www.uscourts.gov

The goal of this site is "to function as a clearinghouse for information from and about the Judicial Branch of the U.S. government." The site covers the U.S. Supreme Court, U.S. Courts of Appeals, U.S. District Courts, and U.S. Bankruptcy Courts.

The U.S. Supreme Court www.supremecourtus.gov

Official site provides recent decisions, case dockets, oral arguments, and public information.

Chapter Test Answer Key

1. d	4. c	7. b	10. b	13. c	16. d
2. b	5. c	8. b	11. d	14. d	17. c
3. b	6. d	9. b	12. a	15. c	18. d

14 POLITICS AND PERSONAL LIBERTY

> 66 Those who would give up essential liberty to purchase a little temporary safety deserve neither liberty nor safety. 99
>
> Benjamin Franklin

Chapter Outline and Learning Objectives

Power and Individual Liberty

▶ 14.1 *Outline the founders' views on individual liberty and trace the expansion of the Bill of Rights.*

Freedom of Religion

▶ 14.2 *Differentiate the two aspects of freedom of religion.*

Freedom of Speech

▶ 14.3 *Assess the extent of and limits on freedom of speech.*

Privacy, Abortion, and the Constitution

▶ 14.4 *Identify protections granted under the right to privacy.*

Obscenity and the Law

▶ 14.5 *Trace the evolution of the Supreme Court's view of obscenity.*

Freedom of the Press

▶ 14.6 *Assess the importance of freedom of the press and limitations on this freedom.*

Freedom of Assembly and Petition

▶ 14.7 *Outline the right to assembly and petition and limitations on this right.*

Protecting Property Rights

▶ 14.8 *Describe the protection of property rights and related Court decisions.*

The Right to Bear Arms

▶ 14.9 *Explain the Supreme Court's interpretation of the right to bear arms.*

Rights of Criminal Defendants

▶ 14.10 *Identify the constitutional rights of criminal defendants and assess consequences of their implementation.*

The Death Penalty

▶ 14.11 *Analyze the Court's position on the death penalty.*

Think about Politics

1. Do you think the government has become so large and powerful that it poses a threat to the rights and freedoms of ordinary citizens?

   YES ◯ NO ◯

2. Do you believe that using tax funds to pay tuition at church-affiliated schools violates the separation of church and state?

   YES ◯ NO ◯

3. Do the words "under God" in the Pledge of Allegiance violate the separation of church and state?

   YES ◯ NO ◯

4. Do we have a constitutional right to physician-assisted suicide?

   YES ◯ NO ◯

5. Do law-abiding citizens have a constitutional right to carry a handgun for self-protection?

   YES ◯ NO ◯

6. Should persons captured on a foreign battlefield in the war on terrorism be entitled to constitutional protections?

   YES ◯ NO ◯

7. Is the death penalty a "cruel and unusual" punishment?

   YES ◯ NO ◯

Government power defends your most basic rights to life, liberty, and the pursuit of happiness while at the same time ensuring that all other Americans have the same rights. The Founders guaranteed individual liberty in the earliest days of our nation through the first ten amendments to the Constitution—our Bill of Rights.

Power and Individual Liberty

▶ 14.1 *Outline the founders' views on individual liberty and trace the expansion of the Bill of Rights.*

To the authors of the Declaration of Independence, individual liberty was inherent in the human condition. It was not derived from governments or even from constitutions. Rather, governments and constitutions existed to make individual liberty more secure.

> We hold these truths to be self-evident, that all men are created equal, that they are endowed by their Creator with certain unalienable Rights, that among these are Life, Liberty and the pursuit of Happiness. That to secure these rights, Governments are instituted among Men, deriving their just powers from the consent of the governed.

The authors of the Bill of Rights (the first ten amendments to the Constitution) did *not* believe that they were creating individual rights, but rather that they were recognizing and guaranteeing rights that belonged to individuals by virtue of their humanity.

Authority and Liberty To avoid the brutal life of a lawless society, where the weak are at the mercy of the strong, people form governments and endow them with powers to secure peace and self-preservation. People voluntarily relinquish some of their individual freedom to establish a government that is capable of protecting them from their neighbors as well as from foreign aggressors. This government must be strong enough to maintain its own existence or it cannot defend the rights of its citizens.

But what happens when a government becomes too strong and infringes on the liberties of its citizens? How much liberty must individuals surrender to secure an orderly society? This is the classic dilemma of free government: People must create laws and governments to protect their freedom, but the laws and governments themselves restrict freedom.

Democracy and Personal Liberty

When democracy is defined only as a *decision-making process*—widespread popular participation and rule by majority—it offers little protection for individual liberty. Democracy must also be defined to include *substantive values*—a recognition of the dignity of all individuals and their equality under law. Otherwise, some people, particularly "the weaker party, or an obnoxious individual," would be vulnerable to deprivations of life, liberty, or property simply by decisions of majorities (see "The Paradox of Democracy" in Chapter 1). Indeed, the "great object" of the Constitution, according to James Madison, was to preserve popular government yet at the same time to protect individuals from "unjust" majorities.[1]

The purpose of the Constitution—and especially its Bill of Rights, passed by the First Congress in September 1789—is to limit governmental power over the individual, that is, to place personal liberty beyond the reach of government (see Table 14.1). Each individual's rights to life, liberty, and property, due process of law, and equal protection of the law are not subject to majority vote. Or, as Supreme Court Justice Robert Jackson once declared, "One's right to life, liberty, and property, to free speech, a free press, freedom of worship and assembly, and other fundamental rights may not be submitted to vote: they depend on the outcome of no elections."[2]

Nationalizing the Bill of Rights

The Bill of Rights begins with the words "*Congress* shall make no law . . ." indicating that it was originally intended to limit only the powers of the federal government. The Bill of Rights was added to the Constitution because of fear that the *federal* government might become too powerful and encroach on individual liberty. But what about encroachments by state and local governments and their officials?

The 14th Amendment includes the words "No *State* shall . . ."; its provisions are directed specifically at states. Initially, the U.S. Supreme Court rejected the argument that the 14th Amendment's Privileges or Immunities Clause[3] and the Due Process Clause[4] incorporated the Bill of Rights. But beginning in the 1920s, the Court handed down a long series of decisions that gradually brought about the **incorporation** of almost all of the protections of the Bill of Rights into the "liberty" guaranteed against state actions by the due process clause of the 14th Amendment. In *Gitlow v. New York* (1925), the Court ruled that "freedom of speech and of the press—which are protected by the First Amendment from abridgment by Congress—are among the fundamental personal rights and liberties protected by the due process clause of the 14th Amendment from impairment by the states."[5] Over time, the Court applied the same reasoning in incorporating almost all provisions of the Bill of Rights into the 14th Amendment's Due Process Clause. States and all of their subdivisions—cities, counties, townships, school districts, and so forth—are bound by the Bill of Rights.

incorporation
In constitutional law, the application of almost all of the Bill of Rights to the states and all of their subdivisions through the 14th Amendment.

TABLE 14.1 How Are We Protected?: Rights Under the Constitution

The Bill of Rights	
The first ten amendments to the Constitution of the United States, passed by the First Congress of the United States in September 1789 and ratified by the states in December 1791.	
Amendments	**Protections**
1st Amendment: Religion, Speech, Press, Assembly, Petition	
Congress shall make no law respecting an establishment of religion, or prohibiting the free exercise thereof; or abridging the freedom of speech, or of the press; or the right of the people peaceably to assemble, and to petition the Government for a redress of grievances.	Prohibits government establishment of religion. Protects the free exercise of religion. Protects freedom of speech. Protects freedom of the press. Protects freedom of assembly. Protects the right to petition government "for a redress of grievances."
2nd Amendment: Right to Bear Arms	
A well-regulated Militia, being necessary to the security of a free State, the right of the people to keep and bear Arms, shall not be infringed.	Protects the right of people to bear arms and states to maintain militia (National Guard) units.
3rd Amendment: Quartering of Soldiers	
No Soldier shall, in time of peace, be quartered in any house, without the consent of the Owner, nor in time of war, but in manner to be prescribed by law.	Prohibits forcible quartering of soldiers in private homes in peacetime, or in war without congressional authorization.
4th Amendment: Searches and Seizures	
The right of the people to be secure in their persons, houses, papers, and effects, against unreasonable searches and seizures, shall not be violated, and no Warrants shall issue, but upon probable cause, supported by Oath or affirmation, and particularly describing the place to be searched, and the persons or things to be seized.	Protects against "unreasonable searches and seizures." Requires warrants for searches of homes and other places where there is a reasonable expectation of privacy. Judges may issue search warrants only with "probable cause," and such warrants must be specific regarding the place to be searched and the things to be seized.
5th Amendment: Grand Juries, Double Jeopardy, Self-Incrimination, Due Process, Protection against Government Takings of Property	
No person shall be held to answer for a capital, or otherwise infamous crime, unless on a presentment or indictment of a Grand jury, except in cases arising in the land or naval forces, or in the Militia, when in actual service in time of War or public danger; nor shall any person be subject for the same offence to be twice put in jeopardy of life or limb, nor shall be compelled in any criminal case to be a witness against himself, nor be deprived of life, liberty, or property, without due process of law; nor shall private property be taken for public use, without just compensation.	Requires that, before trial for a serious crime, a person (except military personnel) must be indicted by a grand jury. Prohibits double jeopardy (trial for the same offense a second time after being found innocent). Prohibits the government from forcing any person in a criminal case to be a witness against himself or herself. Prohibits the government from taking life, liberty, or property "without due process of law." Prohibits government from taking private property without paying "just compensation."

(Continued)

TABLE 14.1 How Are We Protected?: Rights Under the Constitution *(continued)*

Amendments	Protections
6th Amendment: Fair Trial	
In all criminal prosecutions, the accused shall enjoy the right to a speedy and public trial, by an impartial jury of the State and district wherein the crime shall have been committed, which district shall have been previously ascertained by law, and to be informed of the nature and cause of the accusation, to be confronted with the witnesses against him, to have compulsory process for obtaining witnesses in his favor, and to have the Assistance of Counsel for his defense.	Requires that the accused in a criminal case be given a speedy and public trial, and thus prohibits prolonged incarceration without trial or secret trials. Requires that trials be by jury and take place in the district where the crime was committed. Requires that the accused be informed of the charges, have the right to confront witnesses, have the right to force supporting witnesses to testify, and have the assistance of counsel.
7th Amendment: Trial by Jury in Civil Cases	
In Suits at common law, where the value in controversy shall exceed twenty dollars, the right of trial by jury shall be preserved, and no fact tried by a jury shall be otherwise re-examined in any Court of the United States, than according to the rules of the common law.	Reserves the right to a jury trial in civil cases. Limits the degree to which factual questions decided by a jury may be reviewed by another court.
8th Amendment: Bail, Fines, and Punishment	
Excessive bail shall not be required, nor excessive fines imposed, nor cruel and unusual punishments inflicted.	Prohibits excessive bail. Prohibits excessive fines. Prohibits cruel and unusual punishment.
9th Amendment: Unspecified Rights Retained by People	
The enumeration in the Constitution, of certain rights, shall not be construed to deny or disparage others retained by the people.	Protection of unspecified rights (including privacy) that are not listed in the Constitution. The Constitution shall not be interpreted to be a complete list of rights retained by the people.
10th Amendment: Rights Reserved to the States	
The powers not delegated to the United States by the Constitution, nor prohibited by it to the States, are reserved to the States respectively, or to the people.	States retain powers that are not granted by the Constitution to the national government or prohibited by it to the states.

Rights in the Text of the Constitution

Several rights were written into the text of the Constitution in 1787 and thus precede in time the adoption of the Bill of Rights.

Article I, Section 9: Habeas Corpus, Bills of Attainder, and Ex Post Facto Laws	
The privilege of the Writ of Habeas Corpus shall not be suspended, unless when in Cases of Rebellion or Invasion the public Safety may require it. No Bill of Attainder or ex post facto Law shall be passed.	Habeas corpus prevents imprisonment without a judge's determination that a person is being lawfully detained. Prohibition of bills of attainder prevents Congress (and states) from deciding people guilty of a crime and imposing punishment without trial. Prohibition of ex post facto laws prevents Congress (and states) from declaring acts to be criminal that were committed before the passage of a law making them so.

(Continued)

(Continued)

13th and 14th Amendments

The Bill of Rights begins with the words "Congress shall make no law . . ." indicating that it initially applied only to the *federal* government. Although states had their own constitutions that guarantee many of the same rights, for more than a century the Bill of Rights did not apply to state and local governments. Following the Civil War, the 13th, 14th, and 15th (voting rights) Amendments were passed, restricting *state* governments and their local subdivisions. But not until many years later did the U.S. Supreme Court, in a long series of decisions, apply the Bill of Rights against the states.

13th Amendment

Neither slavery nor involuntary servitude, except as a punishment for crime whereof the party shall have been duly convicted, shall exist within the United States, or any place subject to their jurisdiction.

Prohibits slavery or involuntary servitude except for punishment by law; applies to both governments and private citizens.

14th Amendment

All persons born or naturalized in the United States, and subject to the jurisdiction thereof, are citizens of the United States and of the State wherein they reside. No State shall make or enforce any law which shall abridge the privileges or immunities of citizens of the United States; nor shall any State deprive any person of life, liberty, or property, without due process of law; nor deny to any person within its jurisdiction the equal protection of the laws.

Protects "privileges and immunities of citizenship."
Prevents deprivation of life, liberty, or property "without due process of law"; this phrase incorporates virtually all of the rights specified in the Bill of Rights.
Prevents denial of "equal protection of the laws" for all persons.

Freedom of Religion

▶ 14.2 *Differentiate the two aspects of freedom of religion.*

Americans are a very religious people. Belief in God and church attendance are more widespread in the United States than in any other advanced industrialized nation. Although many early American colonists came to the new land to escape religious persecution, they frequently established their own government-supported churches and imposed their own religious beliefs on others. Puritanism was the official faith of colonial Massachusetts, and Virginia officially established the Church of England. Only two colonies (Maryland and Rhode Island) provided for full religious freedom. In part to lessen the potential for conflict among the states, the Framers of the Bill of Rights sought to prevent the new national government from establishing an official religion or interfering with religious exercises.[6] The very first words of the 1st Amendment set forth *two* separate prohibitions on government: "Congress shall make no law respecting an *establishment of religion,* or prohibiting the *free exercise* thereof." These two restrictions on government power—the Free Exercise Clause and the Establishment Clause—guarantee separate religious freedoms.

Free Exercise of Religion   The **Free Exercise Clause** prohibits government from restricting religious beliefs or practices. Although the wording of the 1st Amendment appears absolute ("Congress shall make *no* law . . ."), the U.S. Supreme Court has never interpreted the phrase to protect any conduct carried on in the name of religion. In the first major decision involving this clause, the Court ruled in 1879 that polygamy could be outlawed by Congress in Utah Territory even though some Mormons argued that it was part of their religious faith.

Free Exercise Clause
Clause in the 1st Amendment to the Constitution that prohibits government from restricting religious beliefs and practices that do not harm society.

Protecting Religious Practices

The Supreme Court held that the religious beliefs of the Amish outweighed the legitimate interests of the state in education. Amish children could not be required to attend public high school.

Think Again

Do you believe that using tax funds to pay tuition at church-affiliated schools violates the separation of church and state?

The Court distinguished between belief and behavior, saying that "Congress was deprived of all legislative power over mere opinion [by the First Amendment], but was left free to reach actions which were in violation of social duties."[7] The Court also employed the Free Exercise Clause to strike down as unconstitutional an attempt by a state to prohibit private religious schools and force all children to attend public schools.[8] This decision protects the entire structure of private religious schools in the nation.

Later, the Supreme Court elaborated on its distinction between religious belief and religious practice. *Beliefs* are protected absolutely, but with regard to religious *practices*, the Court has generally upheld governmental restrictions when enacted for valid secular purposes.[9] Thus the government can outlaw religious practices that threaten health, safety, or welfare. The Free Exercise Clause does *not* confer the *right* to practice human sacrifice or even the ceremonial use of illegal drugs.[10] Individuals must comply with valid and neutral laws even if these laws restrict religious practices.

But the Supreme Court has continued to face many difficulties in applying its "valid secular test" to specific infringements of religious freedom. When some Amish parents refused to allow their children to attend any school beyond the eighth grade, the state of Wisconsin argued that its universal compulsory school attendance law had a valid purpose: the education of children. The Amish parents argued that high school exposed their children to worldly influences and values contrary to their religious beliefs. The Supreme Court sided with the Amish, deciding that their religious claims outweighed the legitimate interests of the state in education.[11] When a Florida city attempted to outlaw the Santeria (a mix of Catholicism and voodoo) practice of slaughtering animals in religious ceremonies, the Supreme Court held that the city's ordinance was "not neutral" and "targeted" a particular religious ceremony and was therefore unconstitutional.[12]

The Supreme Court has upheld government actions that were challenged as infringements of religious freedom in several key cases. The Court approved an Internal Revenue Service action revoking the tax-exempt status of Bob Jones University because of its rules against interracial dating or marriage among its students. The school argued that its rule was based on religious belief, but the Court held that the government had "an overriding interest in eradicating racial discrimination in education."[13] And the Court upheld an Oregon law that prohibited the possession of peyote (a hallucinogenic drug made from cactus plants) against the claims of a Native American church that its use was a religious sacrament.[14] The Court also upheld an Air Force dress code regulation that prevented orthodox Jews from wearing a yarmulke while in uniform. The Court rejected the argument that the regulation violated the Free Exercise Clause, holding instead that "the mission of the military . . . [including fostering] obedience, unity, commitment and esprit de corps" overrides the individual freedom that would protect civilians from such a government regulation.[15]

Congress Overruled　Congress attempted to expand upon the Free Exercise Clause with its Religious Freedom Restoration Act in 1993. Congress was dissatisfied with the Supreme Court's willingness to approve of restrictions on religious practices, restrictions that were part of a valid and neutral law. So Congress mandated that:

> Government shall not substantially burden a person's exercise of religion even if that burden results from a rule of general applicability . . . [unless the government can show that the burden] is in furtherance of a compelling government interest; and is the least restrictive means of furthering that compelling government interest.

Most religious groups praised the act. It had near unanimous support in the Congress. But the Supreme Court decided that the act was an unconstitutional effort by Congress to usurp the power of the courts to interpret the meaning of the Constitution:

> When the court has interpreted the Constitution, it has acted within the province of the judicial branch which embraces the duty to say what the law is . . . the Act contradicts vital principles necessary to maintain separation of powers and the federal balance.[16]

So it is the Supreme Court and not the Congress that has the final say regarding the meaning of the Free Exercise Clause—indeed, of the Constitution.

No Establishment of Religion
Various meanings have been ascribed to the 1st Amendment's **Establishment Clause**.

- The first meaning—what the writers of the Bill of Rights had in mind—is that it merely prohibits the government from officially recognizing and supporting a national church, like the Church of England in that nation.

- A second meaning is somewhat broader: the government may not prefer one religion over another or demonstrate favoritism toward or discrimination against any particular religion, but it might recognize and encourage religious activities in general.

- The most expansive meaning is that the clause creates "a wall of separation between church and state" that prevents government from endorsing, aiding, sponsoring, or encouraging any or all religious activities.

The phrase "separation of church and state" does *not* appear in the Constitution. It was first used by Thomas Jefferson in a letter to a Baptist Church in 1802 assuring them that the federal government would not establish a national church. The current meaning derives from a 1947 decision by Justice Hugo Black, who, writing for the Supreme Court majority, gave the following definition of the **wall-of-separation doctrine**:

> Neither a state nor the Federal Government can set up a church. Neither can pass laws which aid one religion, aid all religions, or prefer one religion over another. Neither can force nor influence a person to go to or to remain away from church . . . or force him to profess a belief or disbelief in any religion. . . . No tax in any amount, large or small, can be levied to support any religious activities or institutions, whatever they may be called, or whatever form they may adopt to teach or practice religion.[17]

Although the Supreme Court has generally voiced its support for the wall-of-separation doctrine, on several occasions it has permitted cracks to develop in the wall. In allowing public schools to give pupils regular releases from school to attend religious instructions given outside of the school, Justice William O. Douglas wrote that the state and religion need not be "hostile, suspicious or even unfriendly."[18]

Establishment Clause
Clause in the 1st Amendment to the Constitution that is interpreted to require the separation of church and state.

wall-of-separation doctrine
The Supreme Court's interpretation of the No Establishment Clause that laws may not have as their purpose aid to one religion or aid to all religions.

Separation Anxiety

A Menorah-lighting ceremony celebrating Chanukah on public property near the White House. The Supreme Court is divided over whether such public displays violate the Establishment Clause of the 1st Amendment, which is interpreted as requiring the separation of church and state.

Lemon test

To be constitutional, a law must have a secular purpose; its primary effect must neither advance nor inhibit religion; and it must not foster excessive government entanglement with religion.

What Constitutes "Establishment"?   It has proven difficult for the Supreme Court to reconcile this wall-of-separation interpretation of the 1st Amendment with the fact that religion plays an important role in the life of most Americans. Public meetings, including sessions of the Congress, often begin with prayers;[19] coins are inscribed with the words "In God We Trust"; and the armed forces provide chaplains for U.S. soldiers.

The Supreme Court has set forth a three-part **Lemon test** for determining whether a particular law constitutes "establishment" of religion and thus violates the 1st Amendment. To be constitutional, a law affecting religious activity:

- Must have a secular purpose.

- As its primary effect, must neither advance nor inhibit religion.

- Must not foster "an excessive government entanglement with religion."[20]

Using this three-part test, the Supreme Court held that it was unconstitutional for a state to pay the costs of teachers' salaries or instructional materials in parochial schools. The justices argued that this practice would require excessive government controls and surveillance to ensure that funds were used only for secular instruction and thus involved "excessive entanglement between government and religion."

However, the Court has upheld the use of tax funds to provide students attending church-related schools with nonreligious textbooks, lunches, transportation, sign-language interpreting, and special education teachers. And the Court has upheld a state's granting of tax credits to parents whose children attend private schools, including religious schools.[21] The Court has also upheld government grants of money to church-related colleges and universities for secular purposes.[22] The Court has ruled that if public buildings are open to use for secular organizations, they must also be opened to use by religious organizations.[23] And the Court has held that a state institution (the University of Virginia) not only can but must grant student activity fees to religious organizations on the same basis as it grants these fees to secular organizations.[24]

The Supreme Court has upheld tax exemptions for churches on the grounds that "the role of religious organizations as charitable associations, in furthering the secular objectives of the state, has become a fundamental concept in our society."[25] It held that schools must allow after-school meetings on school property by religious groups if such a privilege is extended to nonreligious groups.[26] Deductions on federal income tax returns for church contributions are also constitutional. The Supreme Court allows states to close stores on Sundays and otherwise set aside that day, as long as there is a secular purpose—such as "rest, repose, recreation and tranquility"—in doing so.[27]

But the Court has not always acted to "accommodate" religion. In a controversial case, the Court held that a Christmas nativity scene sitting alone on public property was an official "endorsement" of Christian belief and therefore violated the Establishment Clause. However, if the Christian display was accompanied by a Menorah, a traditional Christmas tree, Santa Claus and reindeer, it would simply be "taking note of the season" and not an unconstitutional endorsement of religion.[28] And in another case, the Supreme Court held that a Louisiana law requiring the teaching of "creationism" along with evolution in the public schools was an unconstitutional establishment of a religious belief.[29]

Critics of the Supreme Court have complained of inconsistencies and contradictions in its consideration of cases involving the Establishment Clause. The Court has made some extremely fine distinctions in considering whether the public display of the Ten Commandments is or is not an establishment of religion. The Court held that a law requiring the posting of the Ten Commandments in every classroom in Kentucky was unconstitutional, but a monument to the Ten Commandments on the grounds of the Texas state capital was merely "an acknowledgment of our nation's heritage."[30]

Prayer in the School

The Supreme Court's most controversial interpretation of the Establishment Clause involved the question of prayer and Bible-reading ceremonies conducted by public schools. The practice of opening the school day with prayer and Bible-reading ceremonies was once widespread in American public schools. To avoid the denominational aspects of these ceremonies, New York State's Board of Regents substituted the following nondenominational prayer, which it required to be said aloud in each class in the presence of a teacher at the beginning of each school day: "Almighty God, we acknowledge our dependence upon Thee, and we beg Thy blessings upon us, our parents, our teachers, and our country." New York argued that this brief prayer did not violate the Establishment Clause, because the prayer was denominationally neutral and because student participation in the prayer was voluntary. However, in *Engel v. Vitale* (1962), the Supreme Court stated that "the constitutional prohibition against laws respecting an establishment of a religion must at least mean in this country it is no part of the business of government to compose official prayers for any group of the American people to recite as part of a religious program carried on by government." The Court pointed out that making prayer voluntary did not free it from the prohibitions of the Establishment Clause, and that clause prevented the *establishment* of a religious ceremony by a government agency regardless of whether the ceremony was voluntary.[31]

One year later, in the case of *Abington Township v. Schempp*, the Court considered the constitutionality of Bible-reading ceremonies in the public schools. Here again, even though the children were not required to participate, the Court found that Bible reading as an opening exercise in the schools was a religious ceremony. The justices went to some trouble in the majority opinion to point out that they were not "throwing the Bible out of the schools." They specifically stated that the *study* of the Bible or of religion, when presented objectively and as part of a secular program of education, did not violate the 1st Amendment; but religious *ceremonies* involving Bible reading or prayer established by a state or school did.[32]

"Voluntary" Prayer

State efforts to encourage "voluntary prayer" in public schools have also been struck down by the Supreme Court as unconstitutional. When the state of Alabama authorized a period of silence for "meditation or voluntary prayer" in public schools, the Court ruled that this action was an "establishment of religion." The Court said the law had no secular purpose, that it conveyed "a message of state endorsement and promotion of prayer," and that its real intent was to encourage prayer in public schools.[33] In a stinging dissenting opinion, Justice William Rehnquist noted that the Supreme Court itself opened its session with a prayer and that both houses of Congress opened every session with prayers led by official chaplains paid by the government. In 1992, the Court held that invocations and benedictions at public high school graduation ceremonies were an unconstitutional establishment of religion.[34] And in 2000 the Court ruled that student-led "invocations" at football games were unconstitutional. A Texas school district that allowed students to use its public address system at football games "to solemnize the event" was violating the Establishment

The Prayer Problem
Although the Supreme Court ruled in 1962 (*Engel v. Vitale*) that even voluntary prayer in public schools was an unconstitutional violation of the separation of church and state under the 1st Amendment, the question of prayer in schools remains a heated one. Indeed, recent court rulings regarding nondenominational prayers at graduation ceremonies and sporting events have, if anything, further confused the issue.

Public Prayer
Prayers on official occasions are common. Here President George W. Bush and Vice President Dick Cheney joined hundreds of White House employees in silent prayer on behalf of the victims of the terrorist attacks of September 11, 2001.

Clause. "The Constitution demands that schools not force on students the difficult choice between whether to attend these games or to risk facing a personally offensive religious ritual."[35] (See *Controversy:* "Are We One Nation 'Under God'"?)

State Vouchers to Attend Religious Schools

Another important issue arising under the Establishment Clause is the granting of educational vouchers to parents to spend at any school they choose, including religious schools. State governments redeem the vouchers submitted by schools by paying specific amounts for each student enrolled. When Ohio initiated a "Scholarship Program" that provided tuition aid to certain students in the Cleveland City School District who could choose to use this aid to attend either public or private or religious schools of their parents' choosing, opponents challenged the program in federal court, arguing that it "advanced a religious mission" in violation of the Establishment Clause. Although parents could use the vouchers to send their children to other public schools or nonreligious private schools, over 90 percent of the students participating in the scholarship program were enrolled in religiously affiliated schools. In 2002, the U.S. Supreme Court held (in a narrow 5–4 decision) that the program did *not* violate the Constitution.[36] The Court reasoned that the program was neutral with respect to religion and provided assistance directly to citizens who, in turn, directed this aid to religious schools wholly as a result of their own independent private choices. The incidental advancement of a religious mission is reasonably attributed to the individual recipients, not the government, "whose role ends with the distribution of benefits."

Freedom of Speech

▶ 14.3 *Assess the extent of and limits on freedom of speech.*

Although the 1st Amendment is absolute in its wording ("Congress shall pass no law . . . abridging the freedom of speech"), the Supreme Court has never been willing to interpret this statement as a protection of *all* speech. What kinds of speech does the 1st Amendment protect from government control, and what kinds of speech may be constitutionally prohibited?

Clear and Present Danger Doctrine

The classic example of speech that can be prohibited was given by Justice Oliver Wendell Holmes in 1919: "The most stringent protection of free speech would not protect a man in falsely shouting 'fire' in a theater and causing a panic."[37] Although Holmes recognized that the government may prevent speech that creates a serious and immediate danger to society, he objected to government attempts to stifle critics of its policies, such as the Espionage Act of 1917 and the Sedition Act of 1918. The Sedition Act prohibited, among other things, speech that was meant to discourage the sale of war bonds and "disloyal" speech about the government, the Constitution, the military forces, or the flag of the United States. In the case of *Gitlow v. New York*, the majority supported the right of the government to curtail any speech that "tended to subvert or imperil the government," but Holmes dissented, arguing that "every idea is an incitement. It offers itself for belief and if believed it is acted on unless some other belief outweighs it."[38] Unless the expression of an idea created a *serious and immediate danger*, Holmes argued that it should be tolerated and combated or defeated only by the expression of better ideas.

Holmes's standard for determining the limits of free expression became known as the **clear and present danger doctrine**. Government should not curtail speech merely because it *might tend* to cause a future danger: "The question in every case

Think Again

Do you believe that using tax funds to pay tuition at church-affiliated schools violates the separation of church and state?

clear and present danger doctrine
Standard used by the courts to determine whether speech may be restricted; only speech that creates a serious and immediate danger to society may be restricted.

CONTROVERSY

Are We One Nation "Under God"?

For over 100 years the Pledge of Allegiance has been recited in public school rooms at the beginning of each day. In 1954, at the height of the Cold War, Congress added the words "under God" after "one nation," to emphasize that the United States acknowledged spiritual values in contrast to "godless communism." President Dwight D. Eisenhower, upon signing the bill, said it would strengthen "those spiritual weapons which forever will be our country's most powerful resource in peace and war."

As early as 1943, the Supreme Court declared that public school pupils could not be *required* to recite the pledge. The opinion was widely praised as an expression of our constitutional freedoms: "If there is any fixed star in our constitutional constellation, it is that no official, high or petty, can prescribe what shall be orthodox in politics, nationalism, religion, or other matters of opinion, or force citizens to confess by word or act their faith therein."[a] Pupils who did not wish to take the pledge were free to stand silent in the classroom while the pledge was being recited.

The Supreme Court was called upon to review the phrase "under God" in 2002 when the father of a public school pupil argued that these words constituted an establishment of religion by an instrument of the government, namely the schools, whether or not his daughter was required to participate in the ceremony. He argued that the pledge with "under God" constituted "a ritual proclaiming that there is a God" and therefore violated the Establishment Clause of the 1st Amendment. The Words "under God" asserted monotheism and possibly offended atheists, the non-religious, and others who did not wish to swear an oath of allegiance to a monotheistic deity.

The U.S. Court of Appeals for the Ninth Circuit (with jurisdiction for California and other West Coast states and arguably the most liberal Circuit Court in the nation) agreed that the words "under God" were not neutral and represented a swearing of allegiance to monotheism. The effect of this appeals court's

opinion was to remove the words "under God" from the Pledge. However, subsequently it was revealed that the father (who was divorced) did not have custody over his daughter, and that the custodial mother did not wish her daughter to bring suit over this issue. The Supreme Court, therefore, dismissed the case on this technicality and avoided the substantive issue of whether or not the words "under God" in the Pledge of Allegiance violated the Establishment Clause.[b] The effect of the Supreme Court's decision was to retain the words.

It can be argued that these words do not refer to any specific religion or deity but simply acknowledge the nation's religious heritage. References to God have long been part of our national identity. Our coins invoke the blessing "In God We Trust," chaplains are provided for the Armed Forces, prayers open the sessions of both chambers of Congress as well as the Supreme Court itself. A strong majority (84 percent) of Americans support the inclusion of the words "under God" in the Pledge of Allegiance.

[a]*West Virginia Board of Education v. Barnette*, 319 U.S. 624 (1943).
[b]*Elk Grove United School District v. Newdow*, 542 U.S. 277 (2004).

is whether the words used are used in such circumstances and are of such a nature as to create a clear and present danger that they will bring about the substantive evils that Congress has a right to prevent."[39] Holmes's argument inspired a long struggle in the courts to strengthen constitutional protections for speech and press.

Although Holmes was the first to use the phrase "clear and present danger," it was Justice Louis D. Brandeis who later developed the doctrine into a valuable constitutional principle that the Supreme Court gradually came to adopt. Brandeis explained that the doctrine involved two elements: (1) the clearness or seriousness

A Threat of Violence

The Supreme Court ruled in 2003 that cross burning was meant to intimidate and was therefore *not* protected as symbolic speech by the 1st Amendment.

preferred position
Refers to the tendency of the courts to give preference to the 1st Amendment rights to speech, press, and assembly when faced with conflicts.

of the expression; and (2) the immediacy of the danger flowing from the speech. With regard to immediacy he wrote,

> No danger flowing from speech can be deemed clear and present, unless the incidence of the evil apprehended is so imminent that it may befall before there is opportunity for full discussion. If there be time to expose through discussion the falsehood and fallacies, to avert the evil by the processes of education, the remedy to be applied is more speech, not enforced silence.

And with regard to seriousness he wrote,

> Moreover, even imminent danger cannot justify resort to prohibition [of speech] . . . unless the evil apprehended is relatively serious. Prohibition of free speech and assembly is a measure so stringent that it would be inappropriate as the means for averting a relatively trivial harm to society. . . . There must be the probability of serious injury to the State.[40]

Preferred Position Doctrine   Over the years, the Supreme Court has given the 1st Amendment freedoms of speech, press, and assembly a special **preferred position** in constitutional law. These freedoms are especially important to the preservation of democracy. If speech, press, or assembly are prohibited by government, the people have no way to correct the government through democratic processes. Thus the burden of proof rests on the *government* to justify any restrictions on speech, writing, or assembly.[41] In other words, any speech or writing is presumed constitutional unless the government proves that a serious and immediate danger would ensue if the speech were allowed.

The Cold War Challenge   Despite the Supreme Court's endorsement of the clear and present danger and preferred position doctrines, in times of perceived national crisis the courts have been willing to permit some government restrictions of speech, press, and assembly. At the outbreak of World War II, just prior to U.S. entry into that world conflict, Congress passed the Smith Act, which stated,

> It shall be unlawful for any person to knowingly or willfully advocate, abet, advise, or teach the duty, necessity, desirability, or propriety of overthrowing or destroying any government in the United States by force or violence, or by the assassination of any officer of any such government.

Congress justified its action in terms of national security, initially as a protection against fascism during World War II, then later as a protection against communism in the early days of the Cold War.

In 1949, the Department of Justice prosecuted Eugene V. Dennis and ten other top leaders of the Communist Party of the United States for violation of the Smith Act. A jury found them guilty of violating the act, and the party leaders were sentenced to jail terms ranging from 1 to 5 years. In 1951, the case of *Dennis v. United States* came to the Supreme Court on appeal. In upholding the conviction of the Communist Party leaders, the Court seemed to abandon Brandeis's idea that "present" meant "before there is opportunity for full discussion."[42] It seemed to substitute clear and *probable* for clear and *present*.

Since that time, however, the Supreme Court has returned to a policy closer to the original clear and present danger doctrine. As the Cold War progressed, Americans grew to view communism as a serious threat to democracy, but not a *present* danger. The overthrow of the American government advocated by communists was not an incitement to *immediate* action. A democracy must not itself

Cold War Scare
Eugene Dennis and four others of the twelve Communists being returned to their jail cells after being convicted in 1949 of advocating the overthrow of the government. From left to right: Benjamin Davis, Jr., Eugene Dennis, Gilbert Green, John Williamson, and Gus Hall.

become authoritarian to protect itself from authoritarianism. In later cases, the Supreme Court held that the mere advocacy of revolution, apart from unlawful action, is protected by the 1st Amendment.[43] It struck down federal laws requiring communist organizations to register with the government,[44] laws requiring individuals to sign "loyalty oaths,"[45] laws prohibiting communists from working in defense plants,[46] and laws stripping passports from Communist Party leaders.[47] In short, once the perceived Cold War crisis began to fade, the Supreme Court reasserted the 1st Amendment rights of individuals and groups.

Symbolic Speech

The 1st Amendment's guarantees of speech, press, and assembly are broadly interpreted to mean **freedom of expression**. Political expression encompasses more than just words. For example, when Mary Beth Tinker and her brothers were suspended for wearing black armbands to high school to protest the Vietnam War, they argued that the wearing of armbands constituted **symbolic speech** protected by the 1st Amendment. The Supreme Court agreed, noting that the school did not prohibit all wearing of symbols but instead singled out this particular expression for disciplinary action.[48]

The Supreme Court continues to wrestle with the question of what kinds of conduct are symbolic speech protected by the 1st Amendment and what kinds of conduct are outside of this protection. Symbolic speech, like speech itself, cannot be banned just because it offends people. "If there is only one bedrock principle underlying the First Amendment, it is that the Government may not prohibit the expression of an idea simply because society finds the idea itself offensive or disagreeable."[49] The Court held that flag burning was "symbolic speech"[50] and therefore protected by the 1st Amendment. In contrast, cross burning was "a form of intimidation and a threat of impending violence"[51] and therefore not protected by the 1st Amendment.

Speech and Public Order

The Supreme Court has wrestled with the question of whether speech can be prohibited when it stirs audiences to public disorder, not because the speaker urges lawless action but because the audience reacts to the speech with hostility. In short, can a speaker be arrested because of the *audience's* disorderly behavior? In an early case, the Supreme Court fashioned a

freedom of expression
Collectively, the 1st Amendment rights to free speech, press, and assembly.

symbolic speech
Actions other than speech itself but protected by the 1st Amendment because they constitute political expression.

Student Protest

A UCLA student protests a tuition hike, November, 2009. The University of California Board of Regents raised tuition and cut spending in an effort to close the state's huge budget deficit.

fighting words doctrine, to the effect that words that "ordinary men know are likely to cause a fight" may be prohibited.[52] But later the Court seemed to realize that this doctrine, if broadly applied, could create a huge constitutional hole in the First Amendment guarantee of free speech. Authorities could curtail speech simply because it met with audience hostility. The Court recognized that "speech is often provocative and challenging. It may . . . have profound unsettling effects. . . . That is why freedom of speech, while not absolute, is nevertheless protected against censorship."[53] The Court has also held that the 1st Amendment protects the use of four-letter words when used to express an idea: "One man's vulgarity may be another's lyric."[54] And the Court has consistently refused to allow government authorities to ban speech *before* it has occurred simply because they believe it *may* create a disturbance.

The Supreme Court has held that reasonable restrictions can be placed on the manner and places of protests. Students may conduct protests on designated places on campus or places which do not interrupt the educational process. Cities can require permits for parades as long as they do not discriminate in the issuance of permits. Authorities cannot selectively ban some protests and parades but not others; authorities cannot regulate the content of signs or speech. The Court upheld a state law that prohibited protests within a 100-foot zone around the entrances to health facilities including abortion clinics.[55]

Campus Speech   Many colleges and universities have undertaken to ban speech that is considered racist, sexist, homophobic, or otherwise "insensitive" to the feelings of women and minorities. Varieties of "speech codes," "hate codes," and sexual harassment regulations that prohibit verbal expressions raise serious constitutional questions, especially at state-supported colleges and universities. The 1st Amendment includes insulting or offensive racist or sexist words or comments in its protection (see *Controversy*: "Political Correctness Versus Free Speech on Campus"). Many of these college and university regulations would not withstand a judicial challenge if students or faculty undertook to oppose them in federal court.

Hate Speech and Hate Crimes   "Hate" speech is usually defined as hostile or prejudicial attitudes expressed toward another person's or group's characteristics, notably sex, race, ethnicity, religion, or sexual orientation. Banning hate speech is now common at colleges and universities, in business employment and sports enterprises, on radio and television, and in the press. But do *government* prohibitions on hate speech violate the 1st Amendment?

Historically, the Supreme Court viewed prohibitions on offensive speech as unconstitutional infringements of 1st Amendment freedoms. "The remedy to be applied is more speech, not enforced silence."[56]

The Supreme Court was called upon to review prohibitions on hate speech in 1992 when the city of St. Paul, Minnesota, enacted an ordinance prohibiting any communication that "arouses anger, alarm, or resentment among others on the basis

CONTROVERSY

Political Correctness Versus Free Speech on Campus

Universities have a very special responsibility to protect freedom of expression. The free and unfettered exchange of views is essential to the advancement of knowledge—the very purpose of universities. For centuries universities have fought to protect academic freedom from pressures arising from the world *outside* of the campus—governments, interest groups, financial contributors—arguing that the university must be a protected enclave for free expression of ideas. But today's threat to academic freedom arises from *within* universities—from efforts by administrations, faculty, and campus groups to suppress ideas, opinions, and language that are not "politically correct" (PC). PC activists seek to suppress opinions and expressions they consider to be racist, sexist, "homophobic," or otherwise "insensitive" to specified groups.[a]

The first amendment protects offensive speech.

Speech Codes

The experience at the University of Michigan with its "Policy on Discrimination and Discriminatory Harassment" illustrates the battles occurring on many campuses over 1st Amendment rights. In 1988 a series of racial incidents on campus prompted the university to officially ban "any behavior verbal or physical" that "stigmatized" an individual "on the basis of race, ethnicity, religion, sex, sexual orientation, creed, national origin, ancestry, age, marital status, handicap, or Vietnam era veteran status" or that created "an intimidating, hostile, or demeaning environment for educational pursuits." A published guide provided examples of banned activity, which included the following:

- A male student makes remarks in class like "women just aren't as good in this field as men."
- Jokes about gay men and lesbians.
- Commenting in a derogatory way about a particular person or group's physical appearance or sexual orientation, or their cultural origins, or religious beliefs.

Free Speech

In 1989 "John Doe," a psychology graduate student studying gender differences in personality traits and mental functions, filed suit in federal court requesting that the University of Michigan policy be declared a violation of the 1st Amendment. (He was permitted by the court to remain anonymous because of fear of retribution.) He was joined in his complaint against the university by the American Civil Liberties Union.

In its decision, the court acknowledged that the university had a legal responsibility to prevent racial or sexual discrimination or harassment. However, it did not have a right to

establish an anti-discrimination policy which had the effect of prohibiting certain speech because it disagreed with ideas or messages sought to be conveyed. . . . Nor could the University proscribe speech simply because it was found to be offensive, even gravely so, by large numbers of people. . . . These principles acquire a special significance in the University setting, where the free and unfettered interplay of competing views is essential to the institution's educational mission. . . . While the Court is sympathetic to the University's obligation to ensure educational opportunities for all of its students, such efforts must not be at the expense of free speech.[b]

It seems ironic that students and faculty now must seek the protection of the federal courts from attempts by universities to limit speech. Traditionally, universities themselves fought to protect academic freedom. Academic freedom included the freedom of faculty and students to express themselves in the classroom, on the campus, and in writing, on controversial and sensitive topics, including race and gender. It was recognized that students often express ideas that are biased or ill informed, immature, or crudely expressed. But students were taught that the remedy for offensive language or off-color remarks or ill-chosen examples was more enlightened speech, not the suppression of speech.

[a]Dinesh D'Souza, *Illiberal Education: The Politics of Race and Sex on Campus* (New York: Vintage Books, 1992).

[b]*John Doe v. University of Michigan*, 721 F. Supp. 852 (1989).

of race, color, creed, religion, or gender." The ordinance defined such expressions as "disorderly conduct" and made them misdemeanors punishable by law. But the Supreme Court, in a unanimous decision, struck down the city's effort to prohibit expressions only because they cause "hurt feelings, offense, or resentment." Speech expressing racial, gender, or religious intolerance is still speech, and it is protected by the 1st Amendment.[57]

However, the Supreme Court is willing to recognize that bias-motivated crimes—crimes intentionally directed at a victim because of his or her race, religion, disability, national origin, or sexual orientation—may be more heavily punished than the same crimes inspired by other motives. The Court held that a criminal defendant's "abstract beliefs, however obnoxious to most people, may not be taken into consideration by a sentencing judge."[58] But a defendant's *motive* for committing a particular criminal act has traditionally been a factor in sentencing, and a defendant's verbal statements can be used to determine motive.

Commercial Speech Do 1st Amendment freedoms of expression apply to commercial advertising? The Supreme Court has frequently asserted that **commercial speech** is protected by the 1st Amendment. The Court held that states cannot outlaw price advertising by pharmacists[59] or advertising for services by attorneys[60] and that cities cannot outlaw posting "For Sale" signs on property, even in the interests of halting white flight and promoting racially integrated neighborhoods. Advertising is the "dissemination of information" and is constitutionally protected.[61]

However, the Court has also been willing to weigh the 1st Amendment rights of commercial advertisers against the public interest served by regulation. In other words, the Court seems to suspend its preferred position doctrine with regard to commercial advertising and to call for a "balancing of interests." Thus the Supreme Court has allowed the Federal Communications Commission to regulate the contents of advertising on radio and television and even to ban advertising for cigarettes. The Federal Trade Commission enforces "truth" in advertising by requiring commercial packages and advertisers to prove all claims for their products.

Libel and Slander Libel and slander have never been protected by the 1st Amendment against subsequent punishment (see "Libel and Slander" in Chapter 6). Once a communication is determined to be libelous or slanderous, it is outside of the protection of the 1st Amendment. The courts have traditionally defined "libel" as a "damaging falsehood." However, if plaintiffs are public officials they must prove that the statements made about them are not only false and damaging but also "made with actual malice"—that is, with knowledge that they are false or with "reckless disregard" of the truth—in order to prove libel.[62]

Privacy, Abortion, and the Constitution

▶ 14.4 *Identify protections granted under the right to privacy.*

A right of "privacy" is not expressly provided for anywhere in the Constitution. But does the word *liberty* in the 1st and 14th Amendments include a constitutional right to privacy?

Finding a Right to Privacy The U.S. Supreme Court found a right of privacy in the Constitution when it struck down a Connecticut law prohibiting the use of contraceptives in 1965. Estelle Griswold had opened a birth control clinic

commercial speech
Advertising communications given only partial protection under the 1st Amendment to the Constitution.

on behalf of the Planned Parenthood League of that state and was distributing contraceptives in violation of the state statute prohibiting their use. She challenged the constitutionality of the statute, even though there is no direct reference to birth control in the Bill of Rights. The Supreme Court upheld Griswold's challenge, finding a right of privacy, according to Justice William O. Douglas, in the "penumbras formed by the emanations from" the 1st, 3rd, 4th, 5th, 9th, and 14th Amendments. "Various guarantees create a zone of privacy. . . . Would we allow the police to search the sacred precincts of marital bedrooms for telltale signs of the use of contraceptives? The very idea is repulsive to the notion of privacy surrounding the marriage relationship." In concurrent opinions, other justices found the right of privacy in the 9th Amendment: "The enumeration in the Constitution of certain rights, shall not be construed to deny or disparage others retained by the people."[63]

Roe v. Wade

The fact that the *Griswold Case* dealt with reproduction gave encouragement to groups advocating abortion rights. In 1969, Norma McCorvey sought an abortion in Texas but was refused by doctors who cited a state law prohibiting abortion except to save a woman's life. McCorvey challenged the Texas law in federal courts on a variety of constitutional grounds, including the right to privacy. McCorvey became "Jane Roe," and the case became one of the most controversial in the Supreme Court's history.[64]

The Supreme Court ruled that the constitutional right of privacy as well as the 14th Amendment's guarantee of "liberty" included a woman's decision to bear or not to bear a child. The Court held that the word "person" in the Constitution did *not* include the unborn child; therefore, the 5th and 14th Amendments' guarantee of "life, liberty, or property" did not protect the "life" of the fetus. The Court also ruled that a state's power to protect the health and safety of the mother could not justify any restriction on abortion in the first 3 months of pregnancy. Between the third and sixth months of pregnancy, a state could set standards for abortion procedures in order to protect the health of women, but a state could not prohibit abortions. Only in the final 3 months could a state prohibit or regulate abortion to protect the unborn.

Rather than end the political controversy over abortion, *Roe v. Wade* set off a conflagration. Congress defeated efforts to pass a constitutional amendment restricting abortion or declaring that life begins at conception. However, when Congress banned the use of federal funds under Medicaid (medical care for the poor) for abortions except to protect the life of a woman, the Supreme Court upheld the ban, holding that there was no constitutional obligation for governments to *pay* for abortions.[65]

Vocal Support for Abortion Rights

Abortion rights supporters sound off outside the Democratic National Convention in Denver in August 2008. The Supreme Court has consistently supported the 1973 decision in *Roe v. Wade* protecting abortion, but it has allowed states to enact restrictions that do not place "an undue burden" on a woman's right to choose.

Reaffirming Roe v. Wade

Abortion has become such a polarizing issue that "pro-choice" and "pro-life" groups are generally unwilling to search out a middle ground. Yet the Supreme Court appears to have chosen a policy of affirming a woman's right to abortion while upholding modest restrictions, as evidenced by the Court's ruling in *Planned Parenthood of Pennsylvania v. Casey* (1992).[66]

In this case, the Supreme Court considered a series of restrictions on abortion enacted by Pennsylvania: Physicians must inform women of risks and alternatives; women must wait 24 hours after requesting an abortion before having one; and the parents of minors must be notified. It struck down a requirement that spouses be notified. Later, the court struck drawn a parental notification law that did not provide an exception for a judge to withhold notification when it would not be in the best interest of the minor.

Justice Sandra Day O'Connor took the lead in forming a moderate, swing bloc on the Court. Her majority opinion strongly reaffirmed the fundamental right of abortion, both on the basis of the 14th Amendment and on the principle of stare decisis. But the majority also upheld states' rights to protect any fetus that reached the point of "viability." The Court went on to establish a new standard for constitutionally evaluating restrictions: they must not impose an "undue burden" on women seeking abortion or place "substantial obstacles" in her path. All of Pennsylvania's restrictions met this standard and were upheld except spousal notification.

"Partial Birth Abortion"   An abortion procedure known as "intact dilation and evacuation" or "partial birth abortion" has been the object of prohibitions by a number of states and by Congress itself. This procedure, which is used in very few abortions, involves partial delivery of the fetus feet first, then vacuuming out the brain and crushing the skull to ease complete removal. A Nebraska law banning the procedure was declared an unconstitutional "undue burden" on a woman's right to abortion by the Supreme Court in 2002; the Nebraska law failed to make an exception to save the life of the mother. In response, Congress passed a ban on partial birth abortions in 2003 and President George W. Bush signed it into law. (Earlier bans passed by Congress had been vetoed by President Bill Clinton.) Congress provided an exception—allowing the method if it is necessary to save a mother's life. The Supreme Court upheld this congressional prohibition on partial birth abortions recognizing that government "has the power to restrict abortions after viability if the law contains exceptions for pregnancies endangering the woman's life or health"[67]

Sexual Conduct   "Liberty gives substantial protection to adult persons in deciding how to conduct their lives in matters pertaining to sex." This Supreme Court ruling in *Lawrence v. Texas* (2003) struck down a state law against homosexual sodomy. The ruling overturned an earlier case in which the Court held that the Constitution granted no "fundamental right to homosexuals to engage in acts of consensual sodomy."[68] Rather, the Supreme Court decided that "The liberty protected by the Constitution allows homosexual persons the right to choose to enter upon relationships in the confines of their homes and their own private lives and still retain their dignity as free persons."[69](See "Politics and Sexual Orientation" in Chapter 15.)

Other Private Activities   How far does the right of privacy extend? The Supreme Court appears to have left this question open to argument. In 1969, the Court held that privacy may be constitutionally protected where there is a "reasonable expectation of privacy," notably in one's own home. The Court overturned a criminal conviction for the "mere private possession of obscene material," that is, the possession and viewing of pornography at home.[70]

A Right to Die?   In most states, for most of the nation's history, it has been a crime to help another person to commit suicide. Michigan's prosecution of

Dr. Jack Kevorkian for publicly participating in physician-assisted suicides launched a nationwide debate on the topic. More important, a group of physicians in Washington, along with their gravely ill patients, filed suit in federal court seeking a declaration that their state's law banning physician-assisted suicide violated the "liberty" guaranteed by the 14th Amendment. They argued that mentally competent, terminally ill patients had the "right to die"; that is, they had a privacy right to request and receive aid in ending their life. They relied on the Supreme Court's previous rulings on abortion, contending that Washington's law placed an undue burden on the exercise of a privacy right. But the U.S. Supreme Court held that there is no *constitutional right* to physician-assisted suicide.[71] The Court implied that if the laws governing the practice are to be changed, they must be changed by legislatures, not by reinterpreting the Constitution.

Patients have a right to refuse treatment, even if by so doing they ensure their own deaths. Life-sustaining procedures can be ended at the request of a family member only if there is "clear and convincing evidence" that the patient would not want these procedures.[72] Most states now recognize "living wills" in which people express their wishes while still of sound mind. The absence of a living will, and disputes within the family over what a comatose patient would wish, can cause prolonged and bitter court fights.

Obscenity and the Law

▶ 14.5 *Trace the evolution of the Supreme Court's view of obscenity.*

Obscene materials of all kinds—words, publications, photos, videotapes, films— are *not* protected by the 1st Amendment. Most states ban the publication, sale, or possession of obscene material, and Congress bans its shipment in the mails. Because obscene material is not protected by the 1st Amendment, it can be banned without even an attempt to prove that it results in antisocial conduct. In other words, it is not necessary to show that obscene material would result in a clear and present danger to society, the test used to decide the legitimacy of *speech*. In order to ban obscene materials, the government need only prove that they are *obscene*.

Defining "obscenity" has confounded legislatures and the courts for years, however. State and federal laws often define pornography and obscenity in such terms as "lewd," "lascivious," "filthy," "indecent," "disgusting"—all equally as vague as "obscene." "Pornography" is simply a synonym for "obscenity." *Soft-core pornography* usually denotes nakedness and sexually suggestive poses; it is less likely to confront legal barriers. *Hard-core pornography* usually denotes explicit sexual activity. After many fruitless efforts by the Supreme Court to come up with a workable definition of "pornography" or "obscenity," a frustrated Justice Potter Stewart wrote the now-famous quote in 1974, "I shall not today attempt further to define [hard-core pornography]. . . . But *I know it when I see it.*"[73]

Slackening Standards: *Roth v. United States*   The Court's first comprehensive effort to define "obscenity" came in *Roth v. United States* (1957). Although the Court upheld Roth's conviction for distributing pornographic magazines through the mails, it defined "obscenity" somewhat narrowly: "Whether to the average person applying contemporary community standards, the dominant theme of the material, taken as a whole, appeals to prurient interests."[74]

Note that the material must be obscene to the *average* person, not to children or particular groups of adults who might be especially offended by pornography. The standard is "contemporary," suggesting that what was once regarded as

Peepland in
New York City

The Supreme Court recognizes "local community standards" in determining what is, or is not, obscene.

obscene might be acceptable today. Later, the *community standard* was clarified to mean the "society at large," not a particular state or local community.[75] The material must be "considered as a whole," meaning that even if a work includes some obscene material, it is still acceptable if its "dominant theme" is something other than "prurient." The Court added that a work must be "utterly without redeeming social or literary merit" in order to be judged obscene.[76] The Court never really said what a "prurient" interest was but reassured everyone that "sex and obscenity are not synonymous."

Tightening Standards: *Miller v. California*   The effect of the Roth decision, and the many and varied attempts by lower courts to apply its slippery standards, tended to limit law enforcement efforts to combat pornography during the 1960s and 1970s. The Supreme Court itself came under ridicule when it was reported that the justices had set up a movie room in the basement of the Supreme Court building to view films that had been brought before them in obscenity cases.[77]

So the Supreme Court tried again, in *Miller v. California* (1973), to give law-enforcement officials some clearer standards in determining obscenity. Although the Court retained the "average person" and "contemporary" standards, it redefined "community" to mean the *local* community rather than the society at large. It also defined "prurient" as "patently offensive" representations or descriptions of "ultimate sex acts, normal or perverted, actual or simulated," as well as "masturbation, excretory functions, and lewd exhibition of the genitals." It rejected the earlier requirement that the work had to be "utterly without redeeming social value" in order to be judged obscene, and it substituted instead "lacks serious literary, artistic, political, or scientific value."[78]

The effect of the Supreme Court's *Miller* standards has been to increase the likelihood of conviction in obscenity-pornography cases. It is easier to prove that a work lacks serious value than to prove that it is utterly without redeeming merit. Moreover, the *local community standard* allows prosecution of adult bookstores and X-rated video stores in some communities, while allowing the same stores to operate in other communities. The Supreme Court has also upheld local ordinances that ban nudity in public places, including bars and lounges. The Court rejected the argument that nude dancing was "expressive" conduct.[79]

Porn on the Internet   New technologies continue to challenge courts in the application of 1st Amendment principles. Currently the Internet, the global computer communication network, allows users to gain access to information worldwide. Thousands of electronic bulletin boards give computer users access to everything from bomb-making instructions and sex conversations to obscene photos and even child pornography. Many commercial access services ban obscene messages and exclude bulletin boards with sexually offensive commentary. Software programs that screen out pornographic Web sites are readily available to consumers. But can *government* try to ban such material from the Internet without violating 1st Amendment freedoms?

Congress tried unsuccessfully to ban "indecent" and "patently-offensive" communications from the Internet in its Communications Decency Act of 1996. Proponents of the law cited the need to protect children from pornography. But in 1997 the Supreme Court held the act unconstitutional: "Notwithstanding the legitimacy and importance of the Congressional goal of protecting children from harmful materials, we agree that the statute abridges freedom of speech protected by the First Amendment." Government cannot limit Internet messages "to only

POLITICS UP CLOSE

Child Pornography

In 1982, the U.S. Supreme Court struck a hard blow against child pornography—the "dissemination of material depicting children engaged in sexual conduct regardless of whether the material is obscene."[a] Such material includes any visual depiction of children performing sexual acts or lewdly exhibiting their genitals. The Court reasoned that films or photographs of sexual exploitation and abuse of children were "intrinsically related" to criminal activity; such material was evidence that a crime has been committed. Thus the test for *child* pornography was much stricter than the standards set for obscene material. It is not necessary to show that the sexual depiction of children is "obscene" (under the *Miller* standards) in order to ban such material; it is only necessary to show that children were used in the production of the material.

But what if the images of children involved in sexual activity are produced by means other than using real children, such as the use of youthful-looking adults or computer-imaging technology? In the Child Pornography Prevention Act of 1996, Congress tried to prohibit "any visual depiction, including any photograph, film, video, picture, or computer or computer-generated image . . . [that] is, or appears to be, of a minor engaging in sexually explicit conduct." Congress did not construct this act to meet the *Miller* standards; it prohibited *any* depictions of sexually explicit activity by children, whether or not they contravened community standards or had serious redeeming value.

But the Supreme Court, in a highly controversial (6–3) decision, held that there was an important distinction between actual and virtual child pornography. Virtual child pornography and adults posing as minors do not directly involve the exploitation or abuse of children. The Court held that the congressional definition of child pornography was overly broad; the mere assertion that such material might encourage pedophiles to seduce children was not sufficient to prohibit it. "The First Amendment requires a more precise restriction."[b]

[a]*New York v. Ferber*, 458 U.S. 747 (1982).
[b]*Ashcroft v. Free Speech Coalition*, 535 U.S. 234 (2002).

what is fit for children." The Supreme Court agreed with the assertion that "as the most participatory form of mass speech yet developed [the Internet] deserves the highest protection from government intrusion."[80] (See also *Politics Up Close: "Child Pornography."*)

Freedom of the Press

▶ 14.6 *Assess the importance of freedom of the press and limitations on this freedom.*

Democracy depends on the free expression of ideas. Authoritarian regimes either monopolize the media or subject them to strict licensing and censorship of their content. The idea of a free and independent press is deeply rooted in the evolution of democratic government.

No-Prior-Restraint Doctrine   Long before the Bill of Rights was written, English law protected newspapers from government restrictions or licensing prior to publication—a practice called **prior restraint**. This protection, however, does not mean that publishers are exempt from *subsequent punishment* for libelous, obscene, or other illegal publications. Prior restraint is more dangerous to free expression because it allows the government to censor the work prior to publication and forces the defendants to *prove* that their material should *not* be censored. In contrast, subsequent punishment requires a trial in which the government must prove that the defendant's published materials are unlawful.

In *Near v. Minnesota* (1931), a muckraking publication that accused local officials of trafficking with gangsters was barred from publishing under a Minnesota law that prohibited the publication of a "malicious, scandalous or defamatory

prior restraint
Government actions to restrict publication of a magazine, newspaper, or books on grounds of libel, obscenity, or other legal violations prior to actual publication of the work.

newspaper." The Supreme Court struck down the law as unconstitutional, affirming the *no-prior-restraint doctrine*. However, a close reading of the majority opinion reveals that the doctrine is not absolute. Chief Justice Charles Evans Hughes noted that prior government censorship might be constitutional "if publication . . . threatened the country's safety in times of war."[81]

Yet the question of whether or not the government can restrain publication of stories that present a serious threat to national security remains unanswered. For example, can the government restrain the press from reporting in advance on the time and place of an impending U.S. military action, thereby warning an enemy and perhaps adding to American casualties? In the most important case on this question, *New York Times v. United States* (1971), the Supreme Court upheld the right of the newspaper to publish secret documents that had been stolen from State Department and Defense Department files. The material covered U.S. policy decisions in Vietnam, and it was published while the war was still being waged. But five separate (concurring) opinions were written by justices in the majority as well as two dissenting opinions. Only two justices argued that government can *never* restrain any publication regardless of the seriousness or immediacy of the harm. Others in the majority cited the government's failure to show proof in this case that publication "would surely result in direct, immediate, and irreparable damage to our nation or its people."[82] Presumably, if the government had produced such proof, the case might have been decided differently. The media interpret the decision as a blanket protection to publish anything they wish regardless of harm to government or society.

Film Censorship

The no-prior-restraint doctrine was developed to protect the print media—books, magazines, newspapers. When the motion picture industry was in its infancy, the Supreme Court held that films were "business, pure and simple" and were not entitled to the protection of the 1st Amendment.[83] But as films grew in importance, the Court gradually extended 1st Amendment freedoms to cover motion pictures.[84] However, the Supreme Court has not given the film industry the same strong no-prior-restraint protection it has given the press. The Court has approved government requirements for prior submission of films to official censors, so long as (1) the burden of proof that the film is obscene rests with the censor; (2) a procedure exists for judicial determination of the issue; and (3) censors are required to act speedily.[85] To avoid government-imposed censorship the motion picture industry adopted its own system of rating films:

G: suitable for all audiences
PG: parental guidance suggested
PG-13: parental guidance strongly suggested for children under 13
R: restricted to those 17 or older unless accompanied by a parent or guardian
NC-17: no one under 17 admitted

Some city governments have sought to restrict showing of NC-17 films, and their restrictions have been upheld by the Courts.[86]

Radio and Television Censorship

The Federal Communications Commission was created in 1934 to allocate broadcast frequencies and to license stations. The exclusive right to use a particular frequency is a "public trust." Thus broadcasters, unlike newspapers and magazines, are licensed by the government and subject to government rules. Although the 1st Amendment protects broadcasters, the Supreme Court has recognized the special obligations that may be imposed on them in exchange for the exclusive right to use a broadcast frequency.

THIS POLICE DRAMA CONTAINS ADULT LANGUAGE AND PARTIAL NUDITY. VIEWER DISCRETION IS ADVISED.

Disclaimers
Television networks hope to avoid government-imposed censorship by offering warnings such as "viewer discretion advised."

"No one has a First Amendment right to a license or to monopolize a radio frequency; to deny a station license because 'the public interest' requires it, is not a denial of free speech."[87] Thus the Court has upheld FCC-imposed "equal time" and "fairness" rules against broadcasters, even while striking down government attempts to impose the same rules on newspapers.[88]

Media Claims for Special Rights   The news media make various claims to special rights arising out of the 1st Amendment's guarantee of a free press. Reporters argue, for example, that they should be able to protect their news sources and are not obliged to give testimony in criminal cases when they have obtained evidence in confidence. However, the only witnesses the Constitution exempts from compulsory testimony are defendants themselves, who enjoy the 5th Amendment's protection against "self-incrimination." The Supreme Court has flatly rejected reporters' claims to a privilege against compulsory testimony. "We cannot seriously entertain the notion that the First Amendment protects a newsman's agreement to conceal the criminal conduct of his source, or evidence thereof, on the theory that it is better to write about a crime than to do something about it."[89]

Despite these rulings, reporters regularly boast of their willingness to go to jail to protect sources, and many have done so. But the media have also pressured the nation's legislatures for protection. Congress has passed the Privacy Protection Act, which sharply limits the ability of law-enforcement officials to search press offices, and many states have passed **shield laws** specifically protecting reporters from giving testimony in criminal cases.

Freedom of Assembly and Petition

▶ **14.7** *Outline the right to assembly and petition and limitations on this right.*

The 1st Amendment guarantees "the right of the people peaceably to assemble, and to petition the government for redress of grievances." The right to organize political parties and interest groups derives from the right of assembly. And freedom of petition protects most lobbying activities.

The Right of Association   Freedom of assembly includes the right to form and join organizations and associations. In an important case during the early civil rights movement, the state of Alabama attempted to harass the National Association for the Advancement of Colored People by requiring it to turn over its membership lists to authorities. The Supreme Court held the state's action to be an unconstitutional infringement of the freedom of association.[90] In the 1960s, the Supreme Court struck down attempts by governments to regulate the Communist Party by requiring membership registration, or penalizing individuals for party membership, or by removing party members from privileges other citizens enjoy.[91]

Freedom of association, like freedom of speech and press, is not absolute. Large national organizations, with no firm ideological views, can be forced to abide by anti-discrimination laws. The Court expressly held that the United States Jaycees and later the Rotary Club could not discriminate on the basis of sex. These large, nonideological, nonreligious, nonpolitical groups are granted less protection than "expressive" groups.[92]

"Expressive" groups, including religious organizations, are free to limit participation to persons who subscribe to their views. Anti-discrimination laws, including those protecting homosexuals, cannot force an organization to accept participation by individuals who do not share its expressed views. In a well-publicized case the Supreme Court held that the right of association protected the organizers of

shield laws
Laws in some states that give reporters the right to refuse to name their sources or to release their notes in court cases; may be overturned by the courts when such refusals jeopardize a fair trial for a defendant.

Protesters Cannot Block Access to Clinics

Escorts from Planned Parenthood, in orange vests, walk past a group of anti-abortion protestors during a prayer vigil outside the clinic in Washington, D.C., on Saturday, January 21, 2006.

Boston's St. Patrick's Day parade from being forced by law to include the "Irish-American Gay, Lesbian and Bisexual Group of Boston."[93] And in another well-publicized case the Supreme Court held that the Boy Scouts are not obliged to accept gays as scouts: "The forced inclusion of an unwanted person in a group infringes the group's freedom of expressive association if the presence of that person affects in a significant way the group's ability to advocate public or private viewpoints."[94]

In another important freedom of association case, the Supreme Court held that California's blanket primary law, a statute that extended participation in party primary elections to all registered voters regardless of their political party affiliation, was unconstitutional.[95] The Court struck down the law holding that it forced political parties to associate with those who do not share their beliefs.

The Supreme Court has also protected the right of students to form organizations. "First Amendment rights . . . are available to teachers and students. It can hardly be argued that either teachers or students shed their constitutional rights at the school house gate."[96] Attempts by a college or university to deny official recognition to a student organization based on its views violates the right of association.

Protests, Parades, and Demonstrations   Freedom of assembly includes the right to peacefully protest, parade, and demonstrate. Authorities may, within reasonable limits, enact restrictions regarding the "time, place, and manner" of an assembly so as to preserve public order, smooth traffic flow, freedom of movement, and even peace and quiet. But these regulations cannot be unevenly applied to groups with different views. Thus authorities may require a permit to parade, but they cannot deny a permit to a group because of the nature of their views or content of their message. For example, the Supreme Court held that city authorities in Skokie, Illinois, acted unconstitutionally in prohibiting the American Nazi Party from holding a march in that city even though it was populated with large numbers of Jewish survivors of the Holocaust.[97]

Right of Assembly?

Protesters block Constitution Avenue and access to federal buildings on September 29, 2007, in Washington, D.C., to protest the war in Iraq. The right of assembly does not protect such activity.

Picketing   Assemblies of people have a high potential for creating a public disturbance. Parades block traffic and litter the streets; loudspeakers assault the ears of local residents and bystanders; picket lines may block the free passage of others. Although the right of assembly is protected by the 1st Amendment, its exercise involves conduct as well as expression, and therefore it is usually subject to greater government regulation than expression alone. The Court has generally upheld reasonable use of public property for assembly, but it has not forced *private* property owners to accommodate speeches or assemblies. Airport terminals, shopping malls, and other open forums, which may or may not be publicly owned, have posed problems for the courts.

Freedom of assembly has been tested by opponents of abortion who picket abortion clinics, hoping to embarrass and dissuade women from entering them. Generally, the courts have allowed limits on these demonstrations to ensure that people can move freely in and out of the clinics. Freedom of assembly does not include the right to block access to public or private buildings. And when abortion opponents demonstrated at the residence of a physician who performed abortions, the Supreme Court upheld a local ordinance barring assemblies in residential neighborhoods.[98] Physically obstructing access to buildings almost always violates state or local laws, as does the threat or use of force by picketers. The Supreme Court made a distinction between a "fixed buffer zone," prohibiting assembly around a building entrance, and a "floating buffer zone" (of 15 feet), prohibiting demonstrators from approaching individuals in public places. The "fixed" zone was held to be a constitutional limit on assembly but the "floating" zone was held to be an unconstitutional limit on free speech.[99] In 1994 Congress passed a federal law guaranteeing access to abortion clinics, arguing that the federal government should act to guarantee a recognized constitutional right.

Protecting Property Rights

▶ 14.8 *Describe the protection of property rights and related Court decisions.*

The 5th Amendment provides specific protection for private property against government confiscation: "nor shall private property be taken for public use without just compensation." This **takings clause** recognizes that occasionally governments—federal, state, or local—may be obliged to take property from private owners for public uses, for example, streets, roads, public buildings, parks and the like. But the Founders wanted to be certain that even these "takings" from private owners would have some constitutional protection. Taking land from private owners who do not wish to sell it to the government is known as **eminent domain**. The 5th Amendment's takings clause guarantees that the taking of private property by the government for public use can only be done with just compensation being paid to the owner. Usually, a city or state tries to purchase land from the owners in a mutually agreed transaction. But if the owners do not wish to sell or do not agree with the government's offered price, the issue is determined by a court in eminent domain proceedings. In these proceedings a city or state must go to court and show that the land is needed for a legitimate public purpose; the court will then establish a fair price (just compensation) based on testimony from the owner, the city or state, and impartial appraisers.

takings clause
The 5th Amendment's prohibition against government taking of private property without just compensation.

eminent domain
The action of a government to take property for public use with just compensation even if the owner does not wish to sell.

Public Use   Takings under eminent domain are valid only when the property is to be put to "public use." But what constitutes a "public use"? Traditionally, public use referred to goods that served the general public, including schools, highways, public buildings, public memorials, and other facilities open to the public generally. Over time, however, the public use clause was given expanded meaning. Eminent domain was used in urban renewal projects to eliminate slums and blighted areas of a city.

But what if the property taken under eminent domain is not a slum or blighted area but rather a residential area not unlike residential areas elsewhere in the city, and the government proposes to give the taken property to private developers to build new residences and offices and facilities for new businesses—"city revitalization"? The city of New London, Connecticut, exercised its eminent domain power by taking a number of residential properties from owners (who did not wish to sell) for the purposes of economic development. The city proposed to

Taking Property

Susette Kelo's house is all that remains of a block in Fort Trumbull neighborhood in New London, Connecticut, in 2005. Kelo lost her fight against the city's claim of eminent domain for the purpose of economic development.

give these properties to private developers for projects that would create new jobs and garner new revenues for the city. The Supreme Court, in reviewing the city's action, acknowledged that "the sovereign may not take the property of A for the sole purpose of transferring it to another private party B, even if A is paid just compensation." The Court seemed to say that if the only beneficiary of the government taking of private property was another private party, it would violate the 5th Amendment's takings clause. But the Court reasoned that economic development was a public purpose, arguing that the definition of "public use" can be "broad and inclusive" and that the legislative body rather than the courts should make the determination of whether a project would generally serve the public interest.[100] The fact that a taking benefited some private parties more than others did not make it unconstitutional.

This Supreme Court decision allowing an eminent domain taking for sale to private developers seemed to undermine the 5th Amendment's takings clause. It caused a stir among politicians, the media, and the general public. Some states have considered more restrictive definitions of "public use" than the Supreme Court's, a legislative action that the Court said it would allow.

Takings   What if the government does not "take" ownership of a property but instead restricts the owner's use of it through regulation? Zoning ordinances, environmental regulations, or building and housing codes may reduce the value of a property to the owner. Should the owner be compensated for the loss of full use?

Courts have recognized that governments can make laws to protect the health, safety, and general welfare of its citizens. Owners of property have never been entitled to any compensation for obeying laws or ordinances with a clear public purpose. Yet it was still argued that some city regulations, especially those designed for beauty and aesthetics, had no relation to public health or safety, but rather they simply enacted somebody's preferences over those of their neighbor. But in 1954 the Supreme Court upheld a very broad interpretation of the police power: "It is within the power of the Legislature to determine that the community should be beautiful as well as healthy, spacious as well as clean, well-balanced as well as carefully patrolled."[101] The Court made it difficult to challenge the constitutionality of local planning and zoning ordinances as a "taking" of private property without compensation even though it reduced the value of property to the owner.

Yet in 1992 the Supreme Court stepped in to hold that a regulation that denies a property owner of *all* economically beneficial use of his land (for example, a state coastal zone management regulation preventing any construction on a beach lot) was a "taking" that requires just compensation to the owner in order to be constitutional.[102] But the court did not address the question of how far governments can go in regulating land use without compensating property owners. Depriving land owners of *all* beneficial uses of their land without compensation is clearly unconstitutional. But what if their use of land is devalued by 50 percent or 25 percent? In recent years both Congress and the federal courts, as well as some states, have undertaken to reconsider "how far" governments can go in depriving property owners of value uses of their land.

The Right to Bear Arms

▶ 14.9 *Explain the Supreme Court's interpretation of the right to bear arms.*

The 2nd Amendment to the U.S. Constitution states: "A well regulated Militia, being necessary to the security of a free State, the right of the people to keep and bear Arms, shall not be infringed."

Bearing Arms The history surrounding the adoption of the 2nd Amendment reveals the concern of colonists with attempts by despotic governments to confiscate the arms of citizens and render them helpless to resist tyranny. James Madison wrote in *The Federalist*, No. 46, that "the advantage of being armed which the Americans possess over the people of almost every other nation, forms a barrier against the enterprise of [tyrannical] ambition."[103] The 2nd Amendment was adopted with little controversy; most state constitutions at the time, like Pennsylvania's, declared that "the people have a right to bear arms for the defense of themselves and the state." Early American political rhetoric was filled with praise for an armed citizenry able to protect its freedoms by force if necessary.

An Individual Right But many constitutional scholars argued over the years that the 2nd Amendment protected only the collective right of the states to form militias—that is, their right to maintain National Guard units. They focused on the qualifying phrase "a well-regulated Militia, being necessary to the security of a free State." But after years of controversy, the Supreme Court finally decided the issue in 2008: "The Second Amendment protects an individual right to possess a firearm unconnected with service in a militia, and to use that arm for traditionally lawful purposes, such as self defense within the home."[104] A District of Columbia law prohibiting the possession of handguns violated "the ancient right of individuals to keep and bear arms for self-defense." But the Court went on to warn that "Like most rights the Second Amendment right is not unlimited" and that reasonable restrictions on guns may be constitutional (see *Controversy*: "Gun Control?").

Rights of Criminal Defendants

▶ 14.10 *Identify the constitutional rights of criminal defendants and assess consequences of their implementation.*

While society needs the protection of the police, it is equally important to protect society from the police. Arbitrary searches and arrests, imprisonment without trial, forced confessions, beatings and torture, secret trials, tainted witnesses, excessive punishments, and other human rights violations are all too common throughout the world. The U.S. Constitution limits the powers of the police and protects the rights of the accused (see Table 14.2).

✔ *Think*
Again

Do law-abiding citizens have a constitutional right to carry a handgun for self-protection?

✔ *Think*
Again

Do you believe that the seizure of property believed by police to be used in drug trafficking, without a judicial hearing or trial, violates civil liberty?

Bear Arms: An Individual Right

The 2nd Amendment's "right to bear arms" was interpreted by the Supreme Court to guarantee an individual's right to own guns (as asserted by these protesters), and not merely as a grant of power to the states to maintain National Guard units.

A CONFLICTING VIEW

Gun Control?

New controls on guns are a common policy demand following highly publicized murders or assassination attempts. The Federal Gun Control Act of 1968 was a response to the assassinations of Senator Robert F. Kennedy and Martin Luther King, Jr., in that year, and efforts to legislate additional restrictions occurred after attempts to assassinate presidents Gerald Ford and Ronald Reagan. Today various federal gun control laws include the following:

- A ban on interstate and mail-order sales of handguns
- Prohibition of the sale of firearms to convicted felons
- A requirement that all firearms *dealers* be licensed by the federal Bureau of Alcohol, Tobacco, Firearms, and Explosives
- Requirements that manufacturers record the serial number of all firearms and that dealers record all sales
- Restrictions of private ownership of automatic weapons and military weapons.

Finally, there is the *Brady Law* requirement for a 5-day waiting period for the purchase of a handgun. (The law was named for James S. Brady, former press secretary to President Ronald Reagan, who was severely wounded in the 1981 attempted assassination of the president.) Handgun dealers must send police agencies a form completed by the buyer; police agencies have 5 days to make certain the purchaser is not a convicted felon.

Gun Laws and Crime

There is no systematic evidence that gun control laws reduce violent crime. If we compare violent crime rates in jurisdictions with very restrictive gun laws (for example, New York, Massachusetts, New Jersey, Illinois, and the District of Columbia, all of which prohibit the possession of unlicensed handguns by citizens) to crime rates in jurisdictions with very loose controls, we find no difference in rates of violent crime that cannot be attributed to social conditions.[a]

The 2nd Amendment

The Supreme Court ruled in 2008 that the 2nd Amendment right to bear arms was an individual right, not merely the collective right of the states to maintain militia (National Guard) units.[b] The Court specifically ruled that a total prohibition on the possession of handguns was unconstitutional and that individuals had a constitutional right to possess arms "for traditionally lawful purposes, such as self defense within the home." (The Court also held that a trigger lock requirement "makes it impossible for citizens to use arms for the core lawful purpose of self defense and is hence unconstitutional.") But the Court went on to indicate that certain reasonable prohibitions on guns were constitutional: prohibitions on carrying concealed weapons, prohibitions on the possession of firearms by felons and the mentally ill, and prohibitions on the carrying of firearms in sensitive places such as schools and government buildings, or laws imposing conditions and qualifications on the commercial sale of arms.

[a]Douglas R. Murray, "Handguns, Gun Control Laws and Firearms Violence," *Social Problems* 23 (June 1975, 26–35); James D. Wright and Peter H. Rossi, *Weapons, Crime and Violence in America*. Washington, D.C.: National Institute of Justice, 1981; Gary Kleck, *Targeting Guns*. New York: Aldine de Gruyter, 1997.

[b]*District of Columbia v. Heller*, June 26, 2008.

TABLE 14.2   Individual Rights in the Criminal Justice Process

Rights	Process
4th Amendment: Protection against Unreasonable Searches and Seizures Warranted searches for sworn "probable cause." Exceptions: consent searches, safety searches, car searches, and searches incident to a valid arrest.	**Investigation by Law-enforcement Officers** Expectation that police act lawfully.
5th Amendment: Protection against Self-incrimination Miranda rules **Habeas Corpus** Police holding a person in custody must bring that person before a judge with cause to believe that a crime was committed and the prisoner committed it.	**Arrest** Arrests based on warrants issued by judges and magistrates. Arrests based on crimes committed in the presence of law enforcement officials. Arrests for "probable cause."
8th Amendment: No Excessive Bail Defendant considered innocent until proven guilty; release on bail and amount of bail depends on seriousness of crime, trustworthiness of defendant, and safety of community.	**Hearing and Bail** Preliminary hearing in which prosecutor presents testimony that a crime was committed and probable cause for charging the accused.
5th Amendment: Grand Jury (Federal) Federal prosecutors (but not necessarily state prosecutors) must convince a grand jury that a reasonable basis exists to believe the defendant committed a crime and he or she should be brought to trial.	**Indictment** Prosecutor, or a grand jury in federal cases, issues formal document naming the accused and specifying the charges.
6th Amendment: Right to Counsel Begins in investigation stage, when officials become "accusatory"; extends throughout criminal justice process. Free counsel for indigent defendants.	**Arraignment** Judge reads indictment to the accused and ensures that the accused understands charges and rights and has counsel. Judge asks defendant to choose a plea: Guilty, *nolo contendere* (no contest), or not guilty. If defendant pleads guilty or no contest, a trial is not necessary and defendant proceeds to sentencing.
6th Amendment: Right to a Speedy and Public Trial Impartial jury. Right to confront witnesses. Right to compel favorable witnesses to testify. **4th Amendment: Exclusionary Rule** Illegally obtained evidence cannot be used against defendant.	**Trial** Impartial judge presides as prosecuting and defense attorneys present witnesses and evidence relevant to guilt or innocence of defendant and make arguments to the jury. Jury deliberates in secret and issues a verdict.
8th Amendment: Protection against Cruel and Unusual Punishments	**Sentencing** If the defendant is found not guilty, the process ends. Defendants who plead guilty or no contest and defendants found guilty by jury are sentenced by fine, imprisonment, or both by the judge. Sentences imposed must be commensurate to the crimes committed.
5th Amendment: Protection against Double Jeopardy Government cannot try a defendant again for the same offense.	**Appeal** Defendants found guilty may appeal to higher courts for reversal of verdict or a new trial based on errors made anywhere in the process.

writ of habeas corpus
Court order directing public officials who are holding a person in custody to bring the prisoner into court and explain the reasons for confinement; the right to habeas corpus is protected by Article I of the Constitution.

The Guarantee of the Writ of Habeas Corpus
One of the oldest and most revered rights in English common law is the right to obtain a **writ of habeas corpus**, which is a court order directing public officials who are holding a person in custody to bring the prisoner into court and explain the reasons for confinement. If a judge finds that the prisoner is being unlawfully detained, or finds insufficient evidence that a crime has been committed or that the prisoner could have committed it, the judge must order the prisoner's release. Thus the writ of habeas corpus is a means to test the legality of any imprisonment (see *What Do You Think?*: "Are Persons Captured on the Battlefields of Afghanistan and Iraq Entitled to the Protections of the U.S. Constitution?").

The writ of habeas corpus was considered so fundamental to the Framers of the Constitution that they included it in the original text of Article I: "The privilege of the Writ of Habeas Corpus shall not be suspended, unless when in Cases of Rebellion or Invasion the public Safety may require it." Despite the qualifying phrase, the Supreme Court has never sanctioned suspension of the writ of habeas corpus even during wartime. President Abraham Lincoln suspended the writ of habeas corpus in several areas during the Civil War, but in the case of *Ex parte Milligan* (1866), the Supreme Court ruled that the president had acted unconstitutionally.[105] (With the war over, however, the Court's decision had no practical effect.) Again, in 1946, the Supreme Court declared that the military had had no right to substitute military courts for ordinary courts in Hawaii during World War II, even though Hawaii was in an active theater of war.[106] State courts cannot issue writs of habeas corpus to federal officials, but federal judges may issue such writs to state officials whenever there is reason to believe that a person is being held in violation of the Constitution or laws of the United States.

The Prohibition of Bills of Attainder and Ex Post Facto Laws
Like the guarantee of habeas corpus, protection against bills of attainder and ex post facto laws was considered so fundamental to individual liberty that it was included in the original text of the Constitution. A **bill of attainder** is a legislative act inflicting punishment without judicial trial. An **ex post facto law** is a retroactive criminal law that works against the accused—for example, a law that makes an act criminal after the act is committed or a law that increases the punishment for a crime and applies it retroactively. Both the federal government and the states are prevented from passing such laws.

bill of attainder
Legislative act inflicting punishment without judicial trial; forbidden under Article I of the Constitution.

ex post facto law
Retroactive criminal law that works against the accused; forbidden under Article I of the Constitution.

The fact that relatively few cases of bills of attainder or ex post facto laws have come to the federal courts does not diminish the importance of these protections. Rather, it testifies to the widespread appreciation of their importance in a free society.

search warrant
Court order permitting law-enforcement officials to search a location in order to seize evidence of a crime; issued only for a specified location, in connection with a specific investigation, and on submission of proof that "probable cause" exists to warrant such a search.

Unreasonable Searches and Seizures
Individuals are protected by the 4th Amendment from "unreasonable searches and seizures" of their private "persons, houses, papers, and effects." The 4th Amendment lays out specific rules for searches and seizures of evidence: "No warrants shall issue, but upon probable cause, supported by Oath or affirmation, and particularly describing the place to be searched, and the persons or things to be seized." Judges cannot issue a **search warrant** just to let police see *if* an individual has committed a crime; there must be "probable cause" for such issuance. The indiscriminate searching of whole neighborhoods or groups of people is unconstitutional and is prevented by the 4th Amendment's requirement that the place to be searched must be specifically described in the warrant. The requirement that the things to be seized must be described in the warrant is meant to prevent "fishing expeditions" into an individual's

WHAT DO YOU THINK?

Are Persons Captured on the Battlefields of Afghanistan and Iraq Entitled to the Protections of the U.S. Constitution?

The United States has held 6,000 or more "enemy combatants" captured on the battlefields of Afghanistan and Iraq for many years. Some are held at the U.S. base in Guantánamo Bay, Cuba.

Prisoners of war have never been entitled to constitutional protection. Prisoners of war are uniformed members of the military forces of a nation. (The U.S. held tens of thousands of German and Japanese prisoners of war during World War II.) They are entitled only to "humane treatment" under the Geneva Accords. They are not released until the war is ended.

"Detainees" from the war on terrorism are not officially prisoners of war, inasmuch as they are not uniformed soldiers of any nation. As military detainees, they were not given lawyers or access to courts or, in many cases, even identified by name.

But in 2004 the Supreme Court held that enemy combatants captured on the battlefield and "imprisoned in territory over which the United States exercises an exclusive jurisdiction and control" are entitled to constitutional rights including habeas corpus—the right to bring their case to U.S. courts. "The fact that petitioners are being held in military custody is immaterial."[a]

In response, President George W. Bush created special military tribunals to hear the cases of the detainees. Initially, Congress was not asked to authorize these tribunals. Rather, the president cited his power as Commander-in-Chief in wartime to do so. But the Supreme Court held in 2006 that without congressional authorization, the president had exceeded his authority in creating the military tribunals.[b]

Following this decision, President Bush asked Congress for legislative authorization to establish "military commissions" to try "any alien unlawful enemy combatant." Congress passed the Military Commissions Act in October 2006, with voting on final passage largely along party lines—Republicans in favor and Democrats opposed. The new Act applied to aliens, not citizens, and only to "unlawful" enemy combatants (in contrast to lawful prisoners of war who are "regular forces of a state"). It specifically

Detention camp at the U.S. Guantánamo Bay Navy Base in Cuba.

prohibited habeas corpus appeals to U.S. courts. Military commissions were to function under their own procedural rules—rules that did not necessarily afford full constitutional protections for defendants.

But in a controversial 5–4 decision the Supreme Court held that detainees at Guantánamo "have the constitutional privilege of habeas corpus"—access to federal courts to challenge their detention as enemy combatants. Congress and the president cannot deny them the fundamental right of habeas corpus. Although the Constitution recognizes that habeas corpus can be suspended "in cases of Rebellion or Invasion," this Suspension Clause does not apply to the prisoners at Guantánamo. "Some of the petitioners had been in custody for six years with no definitive judicial determination as to the legality of their detention. Their access to the writ [of habeas corpus] is a necessity to determine the lawfulness of their status, even if, in the end, they do not obtain the relief they seek."[c] In a stinging dissent Justice Scalia wrote: "Today, for the first time in our Nation's history, the Court confers a constitutional right to habeas corpus on alien enemies detained abroad by military forces in the course of an ongoing war. . . . It will almost certainly cause more Americans to be killed."

[a]*Rasul v. Bush*, 542 U.S. 466 (2004).
[b]*Hamdan v. Rumsfeld*, 548 U.S. 557 (2006).
[c]*Boumediene v. Bush*, June 12, 2008.

home and personal effects on the possibility that some evidence of unknown illegal activity might crop up. The only exception is if police, in the course of a valid search for a specified item, find other items whose very possession is a crime—for example, illicit drugs.

A father runs toward his daughter in front of his house in Kansas City, Missouri, as a police tactical team wearing full protective gear goes in.

But the courts also permit police to undertake various other "reasonable" searches *without* a warrant: searches in connection with a valid arrest; searches to protect the safety of police officers; searches to obtain evidence in the immediate vicinity and in the suspect's control; searches to preserve evidence in danger of being immediately destroyed; and searches with the consent of a suspect. Indeed, most police searches today take place without warrant under one or another of these conditions. The Supreme Court has also allowed automobile searches and searches of open fields without warrants in many cases. The requirement of "probable cause" has been very loosely defined; even a "partially corroborated anonymous informant's tip" qualifies as "probable cause" to make a search, seizure, or arrest.[107] And if the police, while making a warranted search, or otherwise lawfully on the premises, see evidence of a crime "in plain view," they may seize such evidence without further authorization.[108] And the Court recently approved "no-knock searches," reversing a long tradition of requiring police to knock and identify themselves before breaking into a home. However, the Court has held that merely stopping a car for a traffic violation does not give police excuse for a search of the car for drugs.[109]

Wiretapping and Electronic Surveillance

The Supreme Court views wiretapping and electronic surveillance as a search and seizure within the meaning of the 4th Amendment; such law enforcement techniques require "probable cause" and a warrant. The government may not undertake to eavesdrop where a person has "a reasonable expectation of privacy" without first showing probable cause and obtaining a warrant. Congress has also enacted a law prohibiting federal agents from intercepting a wire, oral, or electronic communication without first obtaining a warrant.

FISA and Domestic Surveillance

In the Foreign Intelligence Surveillance Act of 1978 (FISA), Congress created a special FISA court to oversee the collection of electronic intelligence within the United States. It requires all intelligence agencies, including the National Security Agency, which is responsible for the collection of electronic intelligence, to obtain warrants upon a showing that the surveillance is required for investigation of possible attacks upon the nation. The FISA court is secret, and the persons under surveillance are not notified.

Following the 9/11 attack, President Bush authorized the National Security Agency to intercept *international* calls to and from Americans—calls involving known or suspected terrorists—without a FISA warrant. The president claimed

Public Surveillance
Two ceiling-mounted video surveillance cameras keep eyes on subway riders in New York, March, 2010. Video cameras are now nearly universal in public places.

that he had inherent constitutional powers as Commander-in-Chief to gather intelligence during war or armed conflict and that the United States is currently at war with international terrorists. Opponents of warrantless surveillance argue that the president is bound by the FISA Act, which specifically requires court warrants for surveillance within the United States, including international calls.

Congress and the president reached a compromise with the FISA Amendments Act of 2008. This act allows the government to undertake warrantless surveillance of suspected terrorists for 7 days before obtaining a FISA warrant. It allows wiretapping of international calls and intercepts of international e-mails. It removes requirements for detailed descriptions of the information sought in a request for a FISA warrant. It protects telecommunications companies from lawsuits for "past or future cooperation" with the government in electronic surveillance. It denies the president's claim that his war powers supersedes FISA laws.[110]

Drug Testing   "Unreasonable" drug testing violates the 4th Amendment. But the Supreme Court has held that it is reasonable to impose mandatory drug testing on railroad workers, federal law-enforcement agents, and even students participating in athletics.[111] However, when the state of Georgia enacted a law requiring drug testing for candidates for public office, the Court found it to be an "unreasonable" search in violation of the 4th Amendment.[112] Apparently mandatory drug testing in occupations affecting public safety and drug testing in schools to protect children are reasonable, while suspicionless drug testing of the general public is not.

Arrests   The Supreme Court permits *arrests without warrants* (1) when a crime is committed in the presence of an officer; and (2) when an arrest is supported by "probable cause" to believe that a crime has been committed by the person apprehended.[113] However, the Court has held that police may not enter a home to arrest its occupant without either a warrant for the arrest or the consent of the owner.[114]

Indictment   The 5th Amendment requires that an **indictment** be issued by a **grand jury** before a person may be brought to trial on a felony offense. This

indictment
Determination by a grand jury that sufficient evidence exists to warrant trial of an individual on a felony charge; necessary before an individual can be brought to trial.

grand jury
Jury charged only with determining whether sufficient evidence exists to support indictment of an individual on a felony charge; the grand jury's decision to indict does not represent a conviction.

provision was designed as a protection against unreasonable and harassing prosecutions by the government. In principle, the grand jury is supposed to determine whether the evidence submitted to it by government prosecutors is sufficient to place a person on trial. In practice, however, grand juries spend very little time deliberating on the vast majority of cases. Neither defendants nor their attorneys are permitted to testify before grand juries without the prosecution's permission, which is rarely given. Thus the prosecutor controls the information submitted to grand juries and instructs them in their duties. In almost all cases, grand juries accept the prosecution's recommendations with little or no discussion. Thus grand juries, whose hearings are secret, do not provide much of a check on federal prosecutors, and their refusal to indict is very rare.

Self-Incrimination and the Right to Counsel Freedom from self-incrimination had its origin in English common law; it was originally designed to prevent persons from being tortured into confessions of guilt. It is also a logical extension of the notion that individuals should not be forced to contribute to their own prosecution, that the burden of proof rests on the state. The 5th Amendment protects people from both physical and psychological coercion.[115] It protects not only accused persons at their own trial but also witnesses testifying in trials of other persons, civil suits, congressional hearings, and so on. Thus "taking the Fifth" has become a standard phrase in our culture: "I refuse to answer that question on the grounds that it might tend to incriminate me." The protection also means that judges, prosecutors, and juries cannot use the refusal of people to take the stand at their own trial as evidence of guilt. Indeed, a judge or attorney is not even permitted to imply this to a jury, and a judge is obligated to instruct a jury not to infer guilt from a defendant's refusal to testify.

It is important to note that individuals may be forced to testify when they are not themselves the object of a criminal prosecution. Government officials may also extend a **grant of immunity from prosecution** to a witness in order to compel testimony. Under a grant of immunity, the government agrees not to use any of the testimony against the witness; in return, the witness provides information that the government uses to prosecute others who are considered more dangerous or more important than the immune witness. Because such grants ensure that nothing the witnesses say can be used against them, immunized witnesses cannot refuse to answer under the 5th Amendment.

The Supreme Court under Chief Justice Earl Warren greatly strengthened the 5th Amendment protection against self-incrimination and the right to counsel in a series of rulings in the 1960s:

- *Gideon v. Wainwright* (1963): Equal protection under the 14th Amendment requires that free legal counsel be appointed for all indigent defendants in all criminal cases.[116]

- *Escobedo v. Illinois* (1964): Suspects are entitled to confer with counsel as soon as police investigation focuses on them or once "the process shifts from investigatory to accusatory."[117]

- *Miranda v. Arizona* (1966): Before questioning suspects, a police officer must inform them of all their constitutional rights, including the right to counsel (appointed at no cost to the suspect if necessary) and the right to remain silent. Although suspects may knowingly waive these rights, the police cannot question anyone who at any point asks for a lawyer or declines "in any

grant of immunity from prosecution
Grant by the government to an individual of freedom from prosecution on a particular charge in return for testimony by that individual that might otherwise be self-incriminating.

manner" to be questioned. If the police commit an error in these procedures, the accused goes free, regardless of the evidence of guilt.[118]

The Exclusionary Rule

Illegally obtained evidence and confessions may not be used in criminal trials. If police find evidence of a crime in an illegal search or if they elicit statements from suspects without informing them of their rights to remain silent or to have counsel, the evidence or statements produced are not admissible in a trial. This **exclusionary rule** is one of the more controversial procedural rights that the Supreme Court has extended to criminal defendants. The rule is also unique to the United States: in Great Britain evidence obtained illegally may be used against the accused, although the accused may bring charges against the police for damages.

The rule provides *enforcement* for the 4th Amendment guarantee against unreasonable searches and seizures, as well as the 5th Amendment guarantee against compulsory self-incrimination and the guarantee of counsel. Initially applied only in federal cases, in *Mapp v. Ohio* (1961) the Supreme Court extended the exclusionary rule to all criminal cases in the United States.[119] A *good faith exception* is made "when law enforcement officers have acted in objective good faith or their transgressions have been minor."[120] And police are *not* prohibited from tricking a suspect into giving them incriminating evidence.[121] But the exclusionary rule is frequently attacked for the high price it extracts from society—the release of guilty criminals. Why punish society because of the misconduct of police? Why not punish police directly, perhaps with disciplinary measures imposed by courts that discover errors, instead of letting guilty persons go free?

exclusionary rule
Rule of law that evidence found in an illegal search or resulting from an illegally obtained confession may not be admitted at trial.

Bail Requirements

The 8th Amendment says only that *"excessive* bail shall not be required." This clause does not say that pretrial release on **bail** will be available to all. The Supreme Court has held that "in our society liberty is the norm, and detention prior to trial or without trial is the carefully limited exception." Pretrial release on bail can be denied on the basis of the seriousness of the crime (bail is often denied in murder cases), the trustworthiness of the defendant (bail is often denied when the prosecution shows that the defendant is likely to flee before trial), or, in a more controversial exception, when release would threaten "the safety of any other person or the community."[122] If the court does not find any of these exceptions, it must set bail no higher than an amount reasonably calculated to ensure the defendant's later presence at trial.

Most criminal defendants cannot afford the bail money required for pretrial release. They must seek the services of a bail bondsman, who charges a heavy fee for filing the bail money with the court. The bail bondsman receives all of the bail money back when the defendant shows up for trial. But even if the defendant is found innocent, the bail bondsman retains the charge fee. (Thus the system is said to discriminate against poor defendants who cannot afford the bondsman's fee.) The failure of a criminal defendant to appear at his or her trial is itself a crime and subjects the defendant to immediate arrest as well as forfeiture of bail. Most states authorize bail bondsmen to find and arrest persons who have "jumped bail," return them to court, and thereby recover the bail money.

bail
Release of an accused person from custody in exchange for promise to appear at trial, guaranteed by money or property that is forfeited to court if defendant does not appear.

Fair Trial

The original text of the Constitution guaranteed jury trials in criminal cases, and the 6th Amendment went on to correct weaknesses the Framers saw in the English justice system at that time—closed proceedings, trials in absentia (where the defendant is not present), secret witnesses, long delays

Benefiting from the Exclusionary Rule

Dollree Mapp was arrested in 1957, but police seized vital evidence against her during an unwarranted, unconstitutional search. In *Mapp v. Ohio* (1961), the U.S. Supreme Court held that evidence obtained illegally could not be used in a criminal trial.

between arrest and trial, biased juries, and the absence of defense counsel. Specifically, the 6th Amendment guarantees the following:

- The right to a speedy and public trial. ("Speedy" refers to the time between arrest and trial, not the time between the crime itself and trial,[123] but the Supreme Court has declined to set a specific time limit that defines "speedy."[124])

- An impartial jury chosen from the state or district where the crime was committed.

- The right to confront (cross-examine) witnesses against the accused.

- The right of the accused to compel (subpoena) favorable witnesses to appear.

- The right of the accused to be represented by counsel.

Over the years the courts have elaborated on these elements of a fair trial so that today trial proceedings follow a rigidly structured format. First, attorneys make opening statements. The prosecution describes the crime and how it will prove beyond a reasonable doubt that the defendant committed it. The defense attorney argues either that the crime did not occur or that the defendant did not do it. Next, each side, again beginning with the prosecution, calls witnesses who first testify on "direct examination" for their side, then are cross-examined by the opposing attorney. Witnesses may be asked to verify evidence that is introduced as "exhibits." Defendants have a right to be present during their own trials (although an abusive and disruptive defendant may be considered to have waived his or her right to be present and be removed from the courtroom).[125] Prosecution witnesses must appear in the courtroom and submit to cross-examination (although special protection procedures, including videotaped testimony, may be used for children).[126] Prosecutors are obliged to disclose any information that might create a reasonable doubt about the defendant's guilt,[127] but the defendant may not be compelled to disclose incriminating information.

After all of the witnesses offered by both sides have been heard and cross-examined, prosecution and defense give their closing arguments. The burden of proof "beyond a reasonable doubt" rests with the prosecution; the defense does not need to prove that the accused is innocent, only that reasonable doubt exists regarding guilt.

Juries must be "impartial": they must not have prejudged the case or exhibit bias or prejudice or have a personal interest in the outcome. Judges can dismiss jurors for "cause." During jury selection, attorneys for the prosecution and defense are allowed a fixed number of "peremptory" challenges of jurors (although they cannot do so on the basis of race or gender).[128] Jury selection is often regarded by attorneys as the key to the outcome of a case; both sides try to get presumed sympathetic people on the jury. In well-publicized cases, judges may "sequester" a jury (keep them in a hotel away from access to the mass media) in order to maintain impartiality. Judges may exclude press or television to prevent trials from becoming spectacles if they wish.[129] By tradition, English juries have had twelve members; however, the Supreme Court has allowed six-member juries in non-death-penalty cases.[130] Also by tradition, juries should arrive at a unanimous decision. If a jury cannot do so, judges declare a "hung" jury and the prosecutor may schedule a retrial. Only a "not guilty" prevents retrial of a defendant. Traditionally, it was believed that a lack of unanimity raised "reasonable doubt" about the defendant's guilt. But the Supreme Court has permitted nonunanimous verdicts in some cases.[131]

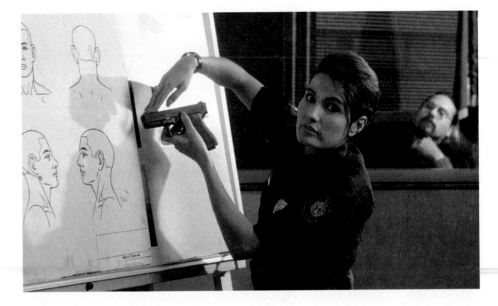

An Austin, Texas, police officer testifies at a criminal trial as the judge looks on. Most criminal cases are resolved through plea bargaining rather than jury trial.

Plea Bargaining   Few criminal cases actually go to trial. More than 90 percent of criminal cases are plea bargained. In **plea bargaining**, the defendant agrees to plead guilty and waives the right to a jury trial in exchange for concessions made by the prosecutor, perhaps the dropping of more serious charges against the defendant or a pledge to seek a reduced sentence or fine. Some critics of plea bargaining view it as another form of leniency in the criminal justice system that reduces its deterrent effects. Other critics view plea bargaining as a violation of the Constitution's protection against self-incrimination and guarantee of a fair jury trial. Prosecutors, they say, threaten defendants with serious charges and stiff penalties in order to force a guilty plea. Still other critics see plea bargaining as an "under-the-table" process that undermines respect for the criminal justice system.

Yet it is vital to the nation's court system that most defendants plead guilty. The court system would quickly break down from overload if any substantial proportion of defendants insisted on jury trials.

plea bargaining
Practice of allowing defendants to plead guilty to lesser crimes than those with which they were originally charged in return for reduced sentences.

Double Jeopardy   The Constitution appears to bar multiple prosecutions for the same offense: "Nor shall any person be subject for the same offense to be twice put in jeopardy of life or limb" (5th Amendment). But very early the Supreme Court held that this clause does not protect an individual from being tried a second time if jurors are deadlocked and cannot reach a verdict in the first trial (a "hung" jury).[132] Moreover, the Supreme Court has held that federal and state governments may separately try a person for the same offense if it violates both federal and state laws.[133] Thus in the well-publicized Rodney King case in 1992, in which police officers were videotaped beating King, a California court found the officers not guilty of assault, but later the U.S. Justice Department won convictions against the officers in a federal court for violating King's civil rights. Finally, a verdict of guilt or innocence in a criminal trial does not preclude a civil trial in which plaintiffs (private citizens) sue for damages inflicted by the accused. Thus O. J. Simpson was found not guilty of murder in a criminal trial but was later found to be responsible for the deaths of two people in a civil trial. Civil courts, of course, can only impose monetary awards; they cannot impose criminal penalties.

Think
Again

Is the death penalty a "cruel and unusual" punishment?

The Death Penalty

▶ *14.11 Analyze the Court's position on the death penalty.*

Perhaps the most heated debate in criminal justice policy today concerns capital punishment. Opponents of the death penalty argue that it violates the prohibition against "cruel and unusual punishments" in the 8th Amendment to the Constitution. They also argue that the death penalty is applied unequally. A large proportion of those executed have been poor, uneducated, and nonwhite. In contrast, many Americans feel that justice demands strong retribution for heinous crimes—a life for a life. A mere jail sentence for a multiple murderer or rapist-murderer seems unjust compared with the damage inflicted on society and the victims. In many cases, a life sentence means less than 10 years in prison under the current early-release and parole policies in many states. Convicted murderers have been set free, and some have killed again (see *Compared To What?:* "The Death Penalty Around the World").

Prohibition Against Unfair Application   Prior to 1971, the death penalty was officially sanctioned by about half of the states. Federal law also retained the death penalty. However, no one had actually suffered the death penalty since 1967 because of numerous legal tangles and direct challenges to the constitutionality of capital punishment.

In *Furman v. Georgia* (1972), the Supreme Court ruled that capital punishment, *as then imposed*, violated the 8th and 14th Amendment prohibitions against cruel and unusual punishment and due process of law. The justices' reasoning in the case was very complex. Only Justices William J. Brennan and Thurgood Marshall declared that capital punishment itself is cruel and unusual. The other justices in the majority felt that death sentences had been applied unfairly; some individuals received the death penalty for crimes for which many others received much lighter sentences. These justices left open the possibility that capital punishment would be constitutional if it was specified for certain kinds of crime and applied uniformly.[134]

After this decision, a majority of states rewrote their death penalty laws to try to ensure fairness and uniformity of application. Generally, these laws mandate the death penalty for murders committed during rape, robbery, hijacking, or kidnapping; murder of prison guards; murder with torture; and multiple murders. They call for two trials to be held—one to determine guilt or innocence and another to determine the penalty. At the second trial, evidence of "aggravating" and "mitigating" factors must be presented; if there are aggravating factors but no mitigating factors, the death penalty may be imposed.

Death Penalty Reinstated   The revised death penalty laws were upheld in a series of cases that came before the Supreme Court in 1976. The Court concluded that "the punishment of death does *not* invariably violate the Constitution." The majority decision noted that the Framers of the Bill of Rights had accepted death as a common penalty for crime. Although acknowledging that the Constitution and its amendments must be interpreted in a dynamic fashion, reflecting changing moral values, the Court's majority noted that most state

Pro–Death Penalty Demonstrators

Demonstrators support the execution of Oklahoma City bomber Timothy McVeigh. He was executed in federal prison in Terre Haute, Indiana, in June, 2001.

COMPARED TO WHAT?

The Death Penalty Around the World

More than half of the world's countries have now abolished the death penalty. Amnesty International, a worldwide organization opposed to the death penalty, reports that fifty-nine countries currently retain the death penalty but only twenty-five of them actually carried out executions in 2008. All European countries have abolished the death penalty. In the Americas only one nation, the United States, continues to employ the death penalty on a regular basis. (Some Caribbean nations, including Trinidad and Tobago, the Bahamas, and Jamaica, continue its use.) Mexico prohibits the death penalty and will not extradite persons facing the death penalty in other countries, including the United States. In 2008, the United Nations General Assembly passed a resolution calling for a general moratorium on executions around the world.

Among the nations with the highest number of executions annually:

China	1,718
Iran	346
Saudi Arabia	102
United States	37
Pakistan	36
Iraq	34
Vietnam	19
Afghanistan	17
North Korea	15
Japan	15

Source: Data from Amnesty International, www.amnesty.org. Figures for 2008; only the United States and Japan are confirmed numbers; others are "at least" estimates.

legislatures have been willing to reenact the death penalty and hundreds of juries have been willing to impose that penalty. Thus "a large proportion of American society continues to regard it as an appropriate and necessary criminal sanction." Moreover, the Court held that the social purposes of retribution and deterrence justify the use of the death penalty; this ultimate sanction is "an expression of society's moral outrage at particularly offensive conduct."[135]

The Court reaffirmed that *Furman v. Georgia* struck down the death penalty only where it was invoked in "an arbitrary and capricious manner." A majority of the justices upheld the death penalty in states where the trial is a two-part proceeding, provided that during the second part the jury is given relevant information and standards for deciding whether to impose the death penalty. The Court approved the consideration of "aggravating and mitigating circumstances." Later the Court held that the jury, not a judge acting alone, must find aggravating circumstances in order to impose the death sentence.[136] The Court also called for automatic review of all death sentences by state supreme courts to ensure that none is imposed under the influence of passion or prejudice, that aggravating factors are supported by the evidence, and that the sentence is not disproportionate to the crime. The court disapproved of state laws making the death

A CONSTITUTIONAL NOTE

The Origins of the Bill of Rights

The Constitution that emerged from the Philadelphia Convention of 1787 did not include a Bill of Rights. This was a particularly glaring omission because the idea of a bill of rights was popular at the time, and most constitutions contain one. The Founders certainly believed in limited government, and they did write a few liberties into the body of the Constitution, including protection against bills of attainder and ex post facto laws, the guarantee of the writ of habeas corpus, a limited definition of treason, and the guarantee of jury trials. But they dismissed the notion of a written Bill of Rights as unnecessary, claiming that the national government, as a government of only enumerated powers, could not exercise any powers not expressly delegated to it. And the power to infringe on free speech or press or otherwise restrain liberty was not among the enumerated powers. It was therefore not necessary to specifically deny the new government the power to interfere with individual liberty. But this logic was unconvincing to Anti-Federalist opponents of the new Constitution; they wanted much firmer written guarantees of liberty in the Constitution. So Federalist supporters of the Constitution made a solemn promise to add a Bill of Rights as amendments to the Constitution in order to help secure votes for its ratification. Thus the fundamental guarantees of liberty in the Bill of Rights were political concessions made to win support for the Constitution itself. True to their word, supporters of the Constitution, including James Madison, secured the congressional passage of twelve amendments in the very first Congress to be convened under the new Constitution. Ten of these amendments—the Bill of Rights—were ratified by the states by 1791.

penalty mandatory in all first-degree murder cases, holding that such laws were "unduly harsh and unworkably rigid." The Court has held that executions of the mentally retarded are "cruel and unusual punishments" prohibited by the 8th Amendment, and that the 8th Amendment prohibits executions of offenders who were under age 18 when their crimes were committed.[137]

Racial Bias   The death penalty has been challenged as a violation of the Equal Protection Clause of the 14th Amendment because of racial bias in the application of the punishment. White murderers are just as likely to receive the death penalty as black murderers. However, some statistics show that if the *victim* is white there is a greater chance that the killer will be sentenced to death than if the victim is black. Nevertheless, the U.S. Supreme Court has ruled that statistical disparity in the race of victims by itself does not bar the use of the death penalty in all cases. There must be evidence of racial bias against a particular defendant in order for the Court to reverse a death sentence.[138]

Summary

Laws and government are required to protect individual liberty. Yet laws and governments themselves restrict liberty. To resolve this dilemma, constitutions seek to limit governmental power over the individual. In the U.S. Constitution, the Bill of Rights is designed to place certain liberties beyond the reach of government.

▶ **14.1** *Outline the founders' views on individual liberty and trace the expansion of the Bill of Rights.*

Initially, the Bill of Rights applied against only the federal government, not state or local governments. But over time, the Bill of Rights was nationalized, as the Supreme Court applied the Due Process Clause of the 14th Amendment to all governments in the United States.

▶ **14.2 Differentiate the two aspects of freedom of religion.**

Freedom of religion encompasses two separate restrictions on government: government must not establish religion or prohibit its free exercise. Although the wording of the 1st Amendment is absolute ("Congress shall make no law . . ."), the Supreme Court has allowed some restrictions on religious practices that threaten health, safety, or welfare.

The Supreme Court's efforts to maintain "a wall of separation" between church and state have proven difficult and controversial. The Court's banning of prayer and religious ceremony in public schools more than 30 years ago remains politically unpopular today.

▶ **14.3 Assess the extent of and limits on freedom of speech.**

The Supreme Court has never adopted the absolutist position that all speech is protected by the 1st Amendment. The Court's clear and present danger doctrine and its preferred position doctrine recognize the importance of free expression in a democracy, yet the Court has permitted some restrictions on expression, especially in times of perceived national crisis.

▶ **14.4 Identify protections granted under the right to privacy.**

The right to privacy encompasses protections for such things as the use of contraceptives, the ability to obtain an abortion, and sexual conduct and other activities performed in one's own home. The Supreme Court has not, however, extended this protection to physician-assisted suicide.

▶ **14.5 Trace the evolution of the Supreme Court's view of obscenity.**

The Supreme Court has placed obscenity outside the protection of the 1st Amendment, but it has encountered considerable difficulty in defining "obscenity."

▶ **14.6 Assess the importance of freedom of the press and limitations on this freedom.**

Freedom of the press prevents government from imposing prior restraint (censorship) on the news media except periodically in wartime, when it has been argued that publication would result in serious harm or loss of life. The Supreme Court has allowed greater government authority over radio and television than over newspapers, on the grounds that radio and television are given exclusive rights to use specific broadcast frequencies.

▶ **14.7 Outline the right to assembly and petition and limitations on this right.**

The 1st Amendment guarantee of the right of assembly and petition protects the organization of political parties and interest groups. It also protects the right of people to peacefully protest, parade, and demonstrate. Governments may, within reasonable limits, restrict these activities for valid reasons but may not apply different restrictions to different groups based on the nature of their views.

▶ **14.8 Describe the protection of property rights and related Court decisions.**

The 5th Amendment provides specific protection for private property against government confiscation "without just compensation." The taking of property from owners who do not wish to sell it is called eminent domain. The Court has allowed the use of eminent domain to serve the public interest, but has also allowed the states to create more restrictive definitions of what constitutes "public use."

▶ **14.9 Explain the Supreme Court's interpretation of the right to bear arms.**

The 2nd Amendment guarantees "the right of the people to keep and bear arms." The Supreme Court has held that this is an individual right, and not just a collective right of the states to maintain National Guard units.

▶ **14.10 Identify the constitutional rights of criminal defendants and assess consequences of their implementation.**

The Constitution includes a number of important procedural guarantees in the criminal justice system: the writ of habeas corpus; prohibitions against bills of attainder and ex post facto laws; protection against unreasonable searches and seizures; protection against self-incrimination; guarantee of legal counsel; protection against excessive bail; guarantee of a fair public and speedy trial by an impartial jury; the right to confront witnesses and to compel favorable witnesses to testify; and protection against cruel or unusual punishment.

Supreme Court's exclusionary rule helps to enforce some of these procedural rights by excluding illegally obtained evidence and self-incriminating statements from criminal trials. In the 1960s, Court interpretations of the 4th and 5th Amendments strengthened the rights of criminal defendants. Police procedures adjusted quickly, and today there is little evidence that procedural rights greatly hamper law enforcement.

Few criminal cases go to trial. Most are plea bargained, with the defendant pleading guilty in exchange for reduced charges and/or a lighter sentence. Although this practice is frequently criticized, without plea bargaining the nation's criminal court system would break down from case overload.

▶ **14.11 Analyze the Court's position on the death penalty.**

The Supreme Court has ruled that the death penalty is not a "cruel and unusual punishment," but the Court has insisted on fairness and uniformity of application.

Chapter Test

▶ **14.1** *Outline the founders' views on individual liberty and trace the expansion of the Bill of Rights.*

1. The founders believed that individual liberty was
   a. derived from the Bill of Rights
   b. inherent in the human condition
   c. conditioned upon the consent of the governed
   d. derived from the legality of governmental authority

2. The purpose of the Bill of Rights was to
   a. guarantee rights by a majority vote of the citizens
   b. limit the powers of the government over individuals
   c. guarantee the powers of government
   d. none of the above

3. The court incorporated the first amendment's protection of freedom of speech and made it applicable to the states in
   a. *Schenck v. U.S.*
   b. *Griswold v. Connecticut*
   c. *Dennis v. U.S.*
   d. *Gitlow v. New York*

▶ **14.2** *Differentiate the two aspects of freedom of religion.*

4. To be constitutional a law dealing with religious beliefs must have
   a. a devoutly held religious basis
   b. as its main intention the advancement of religious activities
   c. the least amount of entanglement possible with the government
   d. reasonable provisions that inhibit religious activities

5. In the ongoing debate about prayer in public schools, it is true that the Supreme Court
   a. will not allow voluntary prayer in schools
   b. will allow a moment of silence
   c. will allow Bible reading in the schools but not prayer
   d. will allow a nondenominational devotional

▶ **14.3** *Assess the extent of and limits on freedom of speech.*

6. Speech that presents society with a "serious and immediate danger" may be curtailed. This is known as the
   a. "preferred position" doctrine
   b. doctrine of original intent
   c. "clear and present danger" doctrine
   d. none of the above

▶ **14.4** *Identify protections granted under the right to privacy.*

7. The right to privacy
   a. is expressly protected by the Constitution
   b. may be deduced from many sources in the Constitution
   c. protects physician-assisted suicide
   d. was first enunciated in *Roe v. Wade*

8. The Supreme Court has held that the right to privacy includes protection in the privacy of your home in regards to
   a. homosexual activity
   b. viewing child pornography on your home computer
   c. the use of legal painkillers
   d. the cultivation of medicinal marijuana plants

▶ **14.5** *Trace the evolution of the Supreme Court's view of obscenity.*

9. The 1st Amendment protects
   a. obscenity
   b. "fighting words"

   c. child pornography
   d. none of the above

10. Using the standards established in *Miller v. California*, the Court
    a. retained the "average person" standard developed in *Roth*
    b. redefined "community" to mean local community standards
    c. defined obscenity as "patently offensive representations"
    d. all of the above

▶ **14.6** *Assess the importance of freedom of the press and limitations on this freedom.*

11. Government actions that restrict publication of a magazine or newspaper before actual publication is
    a. prepublication review
    b. clear and present danger
    c. prior restraint
    d. preemptive censorship

12. The Supreme Court has allowed the banning of child pornography on the grounds that:
    a. it is obscene under community standards
    b. it is evidence of a crime
    c. it is "patently offensive"
    d. it creates a clear and present danger to society

▶ **14.7** *Outline the right to assembly and petition and limitations on this right.*

13. Freedom of assembly includes the right to
    a. protest
    b. demonstrate
    c. join organizations
    d. all of the above

▶ **14.8** *Describe the protection of property rights and related Court decisions.*

14. Property rights are protected by
    a. the property rights clause of the 5th Amendment
    b. the takings clause of the 5th Amendment
    c. the due process clause of the 1st Amendment
    d. the property rights clause of the 1st Amendment

15. The action of a government to take property for public use with just compensation is called _____.
    a. civic taking
    b. eminent domain
    c. public purpose
    d. sovereign immunity

▶ **14.9** *Explain the Supreme Court's interpretation of the right to bear arms.*

16. In 2009, the Supreme Court ruled that:
    a. owning a handgun was an individual right
    b. handgun ownership was not protected by the 2nd Amendment
    c. the 2nd Amendment protected the right of states to maintain National Guards
    d. the "right to bear arms" apply only to the states

▶ 14.10 *Identify the constitutional rights of criminal defendants and assess consequences of their implementation.*

17. All of the following preserve the rights of criminal defendants *except*
   a. guarantee of the writ of habeas corpus
   b. prohibition of ex post facto laws
   c. search warrants required in connection with all valid arrests
   d. consultation with legal counsel

▶ 14.11 *Analyze the Court's position on the death penalty.*

18. The Supreme Court has ruled that capital punishment is
   a. cruel and unusual punishment
   b. violates due process of law
   c. unconstitutional when unfairly applied
   d. regarded as inappropriate by most of American society

---

mypoliscilab EXERCISES

Apply what you learned in this chapter on MyPoliSciLab.

Read on mypoliscilab.com

eText: Chapter 14

Study and **Review** on mypoliscilab.com

Pre-Test

Post-Test

Chapter Exam

Flashcards

Watch on mypoliscilab.com

Video: Funeral Protestors Push the Limits of Free Speech

Video: D.C.'s Right to Bear Arms

Explore on mypoliscilab.com

Simulation: You Are a Police Officer

Simulation: You Are a Supreme Court Justice Deciding a Free Speech Case

Simulation: Balancing Liberty and Security in a Time of War

Comparative: Comparing Civil Liberties

Timeline: Civil Liberties and National Security

Key Terms

incorporation   496
Free Exercise Clause   499
Establishment Clause   501
wall-of-separation doctrine   501
Lemon test   502
clear and present danger doctrine   504

preferred position   506
freedom of expression   507
symbolic speech   507
commercial speech   510
prior restraint   515
shield laws   517
takings clause   519

eminent domain   519
writ of habeas corpus   524
bill of attainder   524
ex post facto law   524
search warrant   524
indictment   527
grand jury   527

grant of immunity from prosecution   528
exclusionary rule   529
bail   529
plea bargaining   531

Suggested Readings

Domino, John C. *Civil Rights and Liberties in the 21st Century.* New York: Longman, 2010. Comprehensive text with landmark rulings on civil liberties.

Epstein, Lee, and Thomas G. Walker. *Constitutional Law for a Changing America: Rights, Liberties and Justice.* 7th ed. Washington, D.C.: CQ Press, 2010. An authoritative text on civil liberties and the rights of the criminally accused.

It describes the political context of Supreme Court decisions and provides key excerpts from the most important decisions.

Garrow, David. *Liberty and Sexuality: The Right to Privacy and the Making of Roe v. Wade.* New York: Macmillan, 1994. Historical account of the background and development of the right to privacy and abortion.

Kobylka, Joseph F. *The Politics of Obscenity*. Westport, Conn.: Greenwood Press, 1991. Comprehensive review of Supreme Court obscenity decisions, arguing that the *Miller* case in 1973 was a turning point away from a more permissive to a more restrictive approach toward sexually oriented material. It examines the litigation strategies of the American Civil Liberties Union and other groups in obscenity cases.

Lewis, Anthony. *Gideon's Trumpet*. New York: Random House, 1964. The classic story of Clarence Gideon and how his handwritten habeas corpus plea made its way to the U.S. Supreme Court, resulting in the guarantee of free legal counsel for poor defendants in felony cases.

Savage, David. *The Supreme Court and Individual Rights*. 4th ed. Washington, D.C.: CQ Press, 2004. An overview of individual rights—freedom of ideas, political participation, due process and criminal rights, equal rights, and personal liberties.

Shiell, Timothy C. *Campus Hate Speech on Trial*. Lawrence, Kans.: University of Kansas Press, 1998. Traditional academic values emphasizing the free exchange of ideas are being sacrificed on campus by anti-hate speech codes.

Sullivan, Harold J. *Civil Rights and Liberties: Provocative Questions and Evolving Answers*. 2nd ed. New York: Longman, 2004. Contemporary issues in civil liberties discussed in a question-and-answer format.

Suggested Web Sites

American Civil Liberties Union (ACLU) www.aclu.org
This American Civil Liberties Union Web site provides ample information about the ACLU as an organization and the issues it deals with.

Americans United for Separation of Church and State www.au.org
Organization advocating elimination of religious activity from public life.

Anti-Defamation League of B'nai B'rith www.adl.org
Organization opposing anti-Semitism and securing justice for the Jewish people.

Brady Campaign www.bradycampaign.org
The nation's leading gun control organization, with facts, legislation, and a "report card" on each state.

Bureau of Alcohol, Tobacco, Firearms, and Explosives www.atf.gov
Federal agency responsible for regulation of alcohol, tobacco, firearms, and explosives; site includes publications on gun crimes.

Bureau of Justice Statistics www.ojp.usdoj.gov/bjs
Federal statistics on jails, prisons, probation, and capital punishment. Click to capital punishment for numbers of executions and persons under sentence of death.

Christian Coalition www.cc.org
Organization dedicated to "take America back" from the "judicial tyranny" that would remove religion from public life.

First Amendment Center www.firstamendmentcenter.org
Vanderbilt University center provides sources of information on 1st Amendment issues.

Internet Freedom www.netfreedom.org
Organization opposed to all forms of censorship and content regulation on the Internet.

National Association of Scholars www.nas.org
Advocacy organization opposing speech codes and other PC violations of individual freedom on campuses.

The National Coalition to Abolish the Death Penalty www.ncadp.org
This site provides information about public policies, institutions, and individuals that collectively work toward the "unconditional rejection of capital punishment."

National Right to Life Committee www.nric.org
Leading anti-abortion organization with information on current legislation and court cases.

Pro-Choice America www.prochoiceamerica.org
Formerly the National Abortion Rights Action League (NARAL), with information on current legislation and court cases.

Right to Keep and Bear Arms www.rkba.org
Organizations advocating self-defense rights with information on legislation, court cases, and related matters.

Chapter Test Answer Key

1. b	**4.** c	**7.** b	**10.** d	**13.** d	**16.** a
2. b	**5.** a	**8.** a	**11.** c	**14.** b	**17.** d
3. d	**6.** c	**9.** d	**12.** b	**15.** b	**18.** c

15 ♚ POLITICS AND CIVIL RIGHTS

> **"** I have a dream that one day this nation will rise up and live out the true meaning of its creed—'We hold these truths to be self-evident, that all men are created equal.' **"**
>
> Martin Luther King, Jr.

40-Year Anniversary of the Assasiation of Dr. Martin Luther King, Jr.

Chapter Outline and Learning Objectives

The Politics of Equality
▶ 15.1 *Assess the role that politics played over the centuries in America's quest for equality.*

Slavery, Segregation, and the Constitution
▶ 15.2 *Analyze how the Constitution was interpreted to first justify and then attack slavery and segregation.*

Equal Protection of the Laws
▶ 15.3 *Differentiate the various meanings of equal protection of the laws.*

The Civil Rights Acts
▶ 15.4 *Outline major civil rights legislation.*

Equality: Opportunity Versus Results
▶ 15.5 *Distinguish between equality of opportunity and equality of results.*

Affirmative Action in the Courts
▶ 15.6 *Trace the Court's evolving attitude toward affirmative action.*

Affirmative Action and "Diversity" in Higher Education
▶ 15.7 *Relate affirmative action to student body diversity.*

Hispanics in America
▶ 15.8 *Characterize the Hispanics in the United States demographically and politically.*

Hispanic Politics
▶ 15.9 *Describe the increasing political role of Hispanics in the United States.*

Native Americans: Trail of Tears
▶ 15.10 *Trace the historical roots of the issues confronting Native Americans.*

The Rights of Disabled Americans
▶ 15.11 *Assess the legal protections offered to disabled Americans.*

Gender Equality and the 14th Amendment
▶ 15.12 *Determine how the 14th Amendment has been interpreted regarding gender equality.*

Gender Equality in the Economy
▶ 15.13 *Assess the relationship between economic opportunities and gender equality.*

Politics and Sexual Orientation
▶ 15.14 *Describe the policy issues arising from sexual orientation.*

✓ *Think* about Politics

1. Should the U.S. Constitution require the government to be color blind with respect to different races in all its laws and actions?
   YES ◯ NO ◯

2. If a city's schools are mostly black and the surrounding suburban schools are mostly white, should busing be used to achieve a better racial balance?
   YES ◯ NO ◯

3. Are differences between blacks and whites in average income mainly a product of discrimination?
   YES ◯ NO ◯

4. Do you generally favor affirmative action programs for women and minorities?
   YES ◯ NO ◯

5. Do you believe racial and sexual preferences in employment and education discriminate against white males?
   YES ◯ NO ◯

6. Do dirty jokes and foul language at work constitute sexual harassment?
   YES ◯ NO ◯

7. Do you think gays and lesbians have a constitutional right to marriage?
   YES ◯ NO ◯

Equality has long been the central issue of American politics. What do we mean by equality? And what, if anything, should government do to achieve it?

The Politics of Equality

▶ 15.1 *Assess the role that politics played over the centuries in America's quest for equality.*

Equality has been the central issue of American politics throughout the history of the nation. It is the issue that sparked the nation's only civil war, and it continues today to be the nation's most vexing political concern.

Conflict begins over the very definition of "equality" (see "Dilemmas of Equality" in Chapter 2). Although Americans agree in the abstract that everyone is equal, they disagree over what they mean by "equality." Traditionally, equality meant "equality of *opportunity*": an equal opportunity to develop individual talents and abilities and to be rewarded for work, initiative, merit, and achievement. Over time, the issue of equality has shifted to "equality of *results*": an equal sharing of income and material rewards.

Hispanic voting increased in the 2008 presidential election. Nevertheless, Hispanic voters made up only 7.4 percent of the total electorate, well below the Hispanic percentage of the general population.

Overall, most Hispanics identify with the Democratic Party. Mexican Americans in the Southwestern states and Puerto Ricans in New York have traditionally supported Democratic candidates, while the strong anti-communist heritage among Cuban Americans has fostered a Republican voting tradition in Florida. Hispanics are generally conservative on social issues (opposing abortion, favoring government vouchers to pay parochial school tuitions) but liberal on economic issues (favoring government provision of health insurance for all, favoring a larger federal government with many services).[34]

The Voting Rights Act of 1965, as later amended and as interpreted by the U.S. Supreme Court, extends voting rights protections to "language minorities," including Hispanics (see "Congressional Apportionment and Redistricting" in Chapter 10). Following redistricting after the 1990 census, Hispanic representation in Congress rose substantially; today there are twenty-three Hispanic members of the House of Representatives—about 5 percent, still well below the percent of the U.S. population which is Hispanic. Hispanics have been elected governors of Arizona, New Mexico, and Florida.

Native Americans: Trail of Tears

▶ 15.10 *Trace the historical roots of the issues confronting Native Americans.*

Christopher Columbus, having erred in his estimate of the circumference of the globe, believed he had arrived in the Indian Ocean when he first came to the Caribbean. He mistook the Arawaks there for people of the East Indies, calling them *Indios*, and this Spanish word passed into English as "Indians"—a word that came to refer to all Native American peoples. But at the time of the first European contacts, these peoples had no common ethnic identity; hundreds of separate cultures and languages were thriving in the Americas. Although estimates vary, most historians believe 7 million to 12 million people lived in the land that is now the United States and Canada; 25 million more lived in Mexico; and as many as 60 million to 70 million in all lived in the Western Hemisphere, a number comparable to Europe's population at the time.

In the centuries that followed, the Native American population of the Western Hemisphere was devastated by warfare, by famine, and, most of all, by epidemic diseases brought from Europe. Overall, the Native population fell by 90 percent, the greatest known human disaster in world history. By 1910 only 210,000 Native Americans lived in the United States. Their population has slowly recovered to the current 2.8 million (less than 1 percent of the U.S. population). Many live on reservations and trust lands, the largest of which is the Navajo and Hopi enclave in the Southwestern United States (see Figure 15.4).

The Trail of Broken Treaties   In the Northwest Ordinance of 1787, Congress, in organizing the western territories of the new nation, declared, "The utmost good faith shall always be observed toward the Indians. Their lands and property shall never be taken from them without their consent." And later, in the Intercourse Act of 1790, Congress declared that public treaties between the United States government and the independent Native nations would be the only legal means of obtaining Indian land.

As president, George Washington forged a treaty with the Creeks: in exchange for land concessions, the United States pledged to protect the boundaries of the

Native American Voices

The American Indian Movement, AIM, has emerged as the leading activist organization supporting Native Americans.

FIGURE 15.4

Native American Peoples

This map shows the locations of the principal Native American reservations in the United States. Tribal governments officially govern these reservations. (Alaska Natives, including Aleuts and Eskimos, live mostly in 200 villages widely scattered across rural Alaska; twelve regional Native American corporations administer property and mineral rights on behalf of Native peoples in that state.)

Creek nation and to allow the Creeks themselves to punish all violators of their laws within these boundaries. This semblance of legality was reflected in hundreds of treaties that followed. (Indeed, in recent years some Native American nations have successfully sued in federal court for reparations and return of lands obtained in violation of the Intercourse Act of 1790 and subsequent treaties.) Yet Native lands were constantly invaded by whites. The resulting Native resistance typically led to wars that ultimately resulted in great loss of life among warriors and their families and the further loss of Native land. The cycle of invasion, resistance, military defeat, and further land concessions continued for 100 years.

"Indian Territories"   Following the purchase of the vast Louisiana Territory in 1803, President Thomas Jefferson sought to "civilize" the Natives by promoting farming in "reservations" that were located west of the Mississippi River. But soon, peoples who had been forced to move from Ohio to Missouri were forced to move again to survive the relentless white expansion. President James Monroe designated as "Indian territory" most of the Great Plains west of the Missouri River. Native peoples increasingly faced three unattractive choices: assimilation, removal, or extinction.

In 1814 the Creeks, encouraged by the British during the War of 1812 to attack American settlements, faced an army of Tennessee volunteer militia led by Andrew Jackson. At the Battle of Horseshoe Bend, Jackson's cannon fire decimated the Creek warriors. In the uneven Treaty of Fort Jackson, the Creeks, Choctaws, and Cherokees were forced to concede millions of acres of land.

By 1830 the "Five Civilized Tribes" of the Southeastern United States (Cherokees, Chickasaws, Choctaws, Creeks, and Seminoles) had ceded most but not all of their lands. When gold was discovered on Cherokee land in northern Georgia in 1829, whites invaded their

A Tragic Ending

A Native American drawing by Amos Bad Heart Bull shows Chief Crazy Horse being assassinated by soldiers at an American post in 1877. Handwritten text on the drawing provides details of the killing.

territory. Congress, at the heeding of the old "Indian fighter" President Andrew Jackson, passed the Removal Act, ordering the forcible relocation of the Natives to Oklahoma Indian Territory. The Cherokees tried to use the whites' law to defend their land, bringing their case to the U.S. Supreme Court. When Chief Justice John Marshall held the Cherokees were a "domestic dependent nation" that could not be forced to give up its land, President Jackson replied scornfully, "John Marshall has made his decision. Now let him enforce it." He sent a 7,000-strong army to pursue Seminoles into the huge Florida Everglades swamp and forced 16,000 Cherokees and other peoples on the infamous "Trail of Tears" march to Oklahoma in 1838.

"Indian Wars"   The "Indian Wars" were fought between the Plains nations and the U.S. Army between 1864 and 1890. Following the Civil War, the federal government began to assign boundaries to each nation and authorized the Bureau of Indian Affairs (BIA) to "assist and protect" Native peoples on their "reservations." But the reservations were repeatedly reduced in size until subsistence by hunting became impossible. Malnutrition and demoralization of the Native peoples were accelerated by the mass slaughter of the buffalo; vast herds, numbering perhaps as many as 70 million, were exterminated over the years. The most storied engagement of the long war occurred at the Little Bighorn River in Montana on June 25, 1876, where Civil War hero General George Armstrong Custer led elements of the U.S. Seventh Cavalry to destruction at the hands of Sioux and Cheyenne warriors led by chiefs Crazy Horse, Sitting Bull, and Gall. But "Custer's last stand" inspired renewed army campaigns against the Plains peoples; the following year, Crazy Horse was forced to surrender. In 1881, destitute Sioux under Chief Sitting Bull returned from exile in Canada to surrender themselves to reservation life. Among the last peoples to hold out were the Apaches, whose famous warrior Geronimo finally surrendered in 1886. Sporadic fighting continued until 1890, when a small malnourished band of Lakota Sioux were wiped out at Wounded Knee Creek.

The Attempted Destruction of Traditional Life   The Dawes Act of 1887 governed federal Native American policy for decades. The thrust of the policy was to break up Native lands, allotting acreage for individual homesteads in order to assimilate Natives into the white agricultural society. Farming was to replace hunting, and traditional Native customs were to be shed for English language and schooling. But this effort to destroy culture never really succeeded. Although Native peoples lost more than half of their 1877 reservation land, few lost their communal ties or accumulated much private property. Life on the reservations was often desperate. Natives suffered the worst poverty of any group in the United States, with high rates of infant mortality, alcoholism, and other diseases. The Federal Bureau of Indian Affairs (BIA), notoriously corrupt and mismanaged, encouraged dependency and regularly interfered with religious affairs and customs.

The New Deal   The New Deal under President Franklin D. Roosevelt came to Native Americans in the form of the Indian Reorganization Act of 1934. This act sought to restore Native tribal structures by recognizing these nations as instruments of the federal government. Landownership was restored, and elected Native tribal councils were recognized as legal governments. Efforts to force assimilation were largely abandoned. The BIA became more sensitive to Native culture and began employing Native Americans in larger numbers. Yet the BIA remained "paternalistic," frequently interfering in tribal "sovereignty."

The American Indian Movement   The civil rights movement of the 1960s inspired a new activism among Native American groups. The American Indian Movement (AIM) was founded in 1968 and attracted national headlines by occupying Alcatraz Island in San Francisco Bay. Violence flared in 1972 when AIM activists took over the site of the Wounded Knee battle and fought with FBI agents. Several Native nations succeeded in federal courts and Congress at winning back lands and/or compensation for lands taken from them in treaty violations.

Native Americans Today   The U.S. Constitution (Article I, Section 8) grants Congress the full power "to regulate Commerce . . . with the Indian Tribes." States are prevented from regulating or taxing Native peoples or extending their courts' jurisdiction over them unless authorized by Congress. The Supreme Court recognizes Native Americans "as members of quasi-sovereign tribal entities"[35] with powers to regulate their own internal affairs, establish their own courts, and enforce their own laws, all subject to congressional supervision. Thus, for example, many Native peoples chose to legalize gambling, including casino gambling, on reservations in states that otherwise prohibited the activity. As citizens, Native Americans have the right to vote in state as well as national elections. Those living off reservations have the same rights and responsibilities as other citizens.

The Bureau of Indian Affairs in the Department of the Interior continues to supervise reservation life, and Native Americans enrolled as members of nations and living on reservations are entitled to certain benefits established by law and treaty. Nevertheless, these peoples remain the poorest and least healthy in the United States, with high incidences of infant mortality, suicide, and alcoholism. Approximately half of all Native Americans live below the poverty line.

The Rights of Disabled Americans

▶ 15.11   *Assess the legal protections offered to disabled Americans.*

Disabled Americans were *not* among the classes of people protected by the landmark Civil Rights Act of 1964. Throughout most of the nation's history, little thought was given to making public or private buildings or facilities accessible to blind, deaf, or mobility-impaired people.[36] Not until the Education of Handicapped Children Act of 1975 did the federal government mandate that the nation's public schools provide free education to handicapped children.

Americans with Disabilities Act   The Americans with Disabilities Act (ADA) of 1990 is a sweeping law that prohibits discrimination against disabled people in private employment, government programs, public accommodations, and telecommunications. The act is vaguely worded in many of its provisions, requiring "reasonable accommodations" for disabled people that do not involve "undue hardship." This means disabled Americans do not have exactly the same standard of protection as minorities or women, who are protected

Enabling the Disabled

The most recent Americans to pressure Congress and the courts for protection of rights long denied them are the nation's disabled citizens. In 1990 disability rights activists succeeded in getting Congress to pass the Americans with Disabilities Act, which mandates the removal of many barriers that have kept handicapped people from working, traveling, and enjoying leisure activities. Nevertheless, many obstacles remain. Here, activists demonstrate in favor of the act.

from discrimination *regardless* of hardship or costs. (It also means that attorneys, consultants, and bureaucrats will make handsome incomes over the years interpreting the meaning of these phrases.) Specifically the ADA includes the following protections:

- *Employment*: Disabled people cannot be denied employment or promotion if, with "reasonable accommodation," they can perform the duties of the job. Reasonable accommodation need not be made if doing so would cause "undue hardship" on the employer.

- *Government programs*: Disabled people cannot be denied access to government programs or benefits. New buses, taxis, and trains must be accessible to disabled persons, including those in wheelchairs.

- *Public accommodations*: Disabled people must enjoy "full and equal" access to hotels, restaurants, stores, schools, parks, museums, auditoriums, and the like. To achieve equal access, owners of existing facilities must alter them "to the maximum extent feasible"; builders of new facilities must ensure that they are readily accessible to disabled persons unless doing so is structurally impossible.

- *Communications*: The Federal Communications Commission is directed to issue regulations that will ensure telecommunications devices for hearing- and speech-impaired people are available "to the extent possible and in the most efficient manner."

Mental and Learning Disabilities The ADA protects the rights of people with learning and psychiatric disabilities, as well as physical disabilities. The U.S. Equal Employment Opportunity Commission has received almost as many complaints about workplace discrimination against the mentally disabled as it has received from people claiming back injuries. But it is far more difficult for employers to determine how to handle a depressed or anxiety-ridden employee than an employee with a visible physical disability. How can employers distinguish uncooperative employees from those with psychiatric disorders?

The American Council on Education reports that following the passage of ADA the percentage of students in colleges and universities claiming a "learning disability" jumped from 3 to 10 percent.[37] A recent decision by the U.S. Department of Education that "attention deficit disorder" is covered by the ADA is expected to result in another significant rise in students claiming disabilities. Colleges and universities are required to provide special accommodations for students with disabilities, including tutors, extra time on examinations, oral rather than written exams, and the like.

Gender Equality and the 14th Amendment

▶ 15.12 *Determine how the 14th Amendment has been interpreted regarding gender equality.*

The historical context of the 14th Amendment implies its intent to guarantee equality for newly freed slaves, but the wording of its Equal Protection Clause applies to "any person." Thus the text of the 14th Amendment could be interpreted to bar any gender differences in the law, in the fashion of the once proposed yet never ratified Equal Rights Amendment. But the Supreme Court has not interpreted the Equal Protection Clause to give the same level of protection to gender equality as to racial equality. Indeed, in 1873 the Supreme Court specifically rejected arguments that

The First Feminists
Elizabeth Cady Stanton addresses a meeting. Stanton, with Lucretia Mott and others, organized one of the defining moments in feminist politics in the United States—the Seneca Falls convention of 1848. Participants at the convention approved a Declaration of Sentiments, modeled on the Declaration of Independence, that demanded legal and political rights for women, including the right to vote.

Think Again

Should gender equality receive the same level of legal protection as racial equality?

this clause applied to women. The Court once upheld a state law banning women from practicing law, arguing that "the natural and proper timidity and delicacy which belongs to the female sex evidently unfits it for many of the occupations of civil life. . . . The paramount destiny and mission of women are to fulfill the noble and benign offices of wife and mother. This is the law of the Creator."[38]

Early Feminist Politics   The earliest active feminist organizations grew out of the pre–Civil War anti-slavery movement. There the first generation of feminists—including Lucretia Mott, Elizabeth Cady Stanton, Lucy Stone, and Susan B. Anthony—learned to organize, hold public meetings, and conduct petition campaigns. After the Civil War, women were successful in changing many state laws that abridged the property rights of married women and otherwise treated them as "chattel" (property) of their husbands. By the early 1900s activists were also successful in winning some protections for women in the workplace, including state laws limiting women's hours of work, working conditions, and physical demands. At the time, these laws were regarded as "progressive."

The most successful feminist efforts of the 1800s centered on protection of women in families. The perceived threats to women's well-being were their husbands' drinking, gambling, and consorting with prostitutes. Women led the Anti-Saloon League, succeeded in outlawing gambling and prostitution in every state except Nevada, and provided the major source of moral support for the 18th Amendment (Prohibition).

In the early twentieth century, the feminist movement concentrated on women's suffrage—the drive to guarantee women the right to vote. The early suffragists employed mass demonstrations, parades, picketing, and occasional disruption and civil disobedience—tactics similar to those of the civil rights movement of the 1960s. The culmination of their efforts was the 1920 passage of the 19th Amendment to the Constitution: "The right of citizens of the United States to vote shall not be denied or abridged by the United States or by any State on account of sex." The suffrage movement gave rise to the League of Women Voters; in addition to women's right to vote, the League has sought protection of women in industry, child welfare laws, and honest election practices.

Judicial Scrutiny of Gender Classifications   In the 1970s, the Supreme Court became responsive to arguments that sex discrimination might violate the Equal Protection Clause of the 14th Amendment. In *Reed v. Reed* (1971), it ruled that sexual classifications in the law "must be reasonable and not arbitrary, and must rest on some ground of difference having fair and substantial relation to . . . important governmental objectives."[39] This is a much more relaxed level of scrutiny than the Supreme Court gives to racial classification in the law.

The Supreme Court continues to wrestle with the question of whether some gender differences can be recognized in law. The question is most evident in laws dealing with sexual activity and reproduction. The Court has upheld statutory rape laws that make it a crime for an adult male to have sexual intercourse with an underage female, regardless of her consent. "We need not to be medical doctors to discern that young men and young women are not similarly situated with respect to the problems and the risks of sexual intercourse. Only women may become pregnant, and they suffer disproportionately the profound physical, emotional and psychological consequences of sexual activity."[40]

Women's participation in military service, particularly combat, raises even more controversial questions regarding permissible gender classifications. The Supreme Court appears to have bowed out of this particular controversy. In

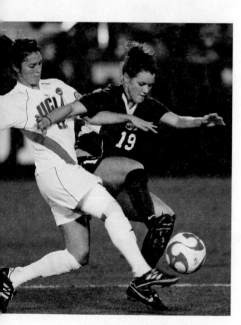

Levelling the Playing Field

Southern California's Megan Ohai, right, battles UCLA's Erin Hardy during the NCAA Women's College Cup national semifinal soccer game on Friday, December 7, 2007, in College Station, Texas.

upholding Congress's draft registration law for men only, the Court ruled that "the constitutional power of Congress to raise and support armies and to make all laws necessary and proper to that end is broad and sweeping."[41] Congress and the Defense Department are responsible for determining assignments for women in the military.

Title IX and Women's Athletics   Perhaps no other gender-related law has had more impact on the nation's colleges and universities than **Title IX**, part of the Education Act Amendments of 1972. Title IX prohibits discrimination against women in college and university athletic programs. But what exactly does this mean? It was not until 1978 that the federal government attempted to set forth regulations concerning intercollegiate athletics. Among the stated goals of these regulations were (1) financial support substantially proportionate to the number of male and female athletes; (2) the provision of opportunities to participate in athletics for men and women substantially proportionate to their enrollments; (3) or, where these conditions were not met, a continuing practice of program expansion for female athletes. Later amendments to Title IX require colleges and universities to report on roster sizes of men's and women's teams and their budgets.

The results of Title IX have been impressive. In 2008, there were more than 170,000 female student athletes, a dramatic increase over the 30,000 when the law was passed in 1972. Women's teams in the National Collegiate Athletic Association doubled from about 4,800 to 9,500.[42] However, while women make up 54 percent of college undergraduate students, the female share of athletes is only 45 percent.

Title IX
A provision in the Federal Education Act forbidding discrimination against women in college athletic programs.

The Equal Rights Amendment   The proposed **Equal Rights Amendment** to the U.S. Constitution, passed by Congress in 1972 but never ratified by the states, was worded very broadly: "Equality of rights under the law shall not be denied or abridged by the United States or any State on account of sex." Had it been ratified by the necessary thirty-eight states, it would have eliminated most, if not all, gender differences in the law. Without the ERA, many important guarantees of equality for women rest on laws of Congress rather than on the Constitution.

Equal Rights Amendment (ERA)
A proposed constitutional amendment, passed by Congress but never ratified by three-quarters of the states, that would have explicitly guaranteed equal rights for women.

Gender Equality in the Economy

▶ 15.13 *Assess the relationship between economic opportunities and gender equality.*

As cultural views of women's roles in society have changed and economic pressures on family budgets have increased, women's participation in the labor force has risen. The gap between women's and men's participation in the nation's workforce is closing over time. With the movement of women into the workforce, feminist political activity has shifted toward economic concerns—gender equality in education, employment, pay, promotion, and credit.

Gender Equality in Civil Rights Laws   Title VII of the Civil Rights Act of 1964 prevents sexual (as well as racial) discrimination in hiring, pay, and promotions. The Equal Employment Opportunity Commission, the federal agency charged with eliminating discrimination in employment, has established guidelines barring stereotyped classifications of "men's jobs" and "women's jobs." The courts have repeatedly struck down state laws and employer practices that differentiate between men and women in hours, pay, retirement age, and so forth.

FIGURE 15.5

The Earnings Gap:
Median Weekly Earnings
of Men and Women

The continuing "earnings gap" between men and women reflects a division in the labor market between traditionally male higher paying occupations and traditionally female lower paying positions.

Note: Figures in parentheses indicate the ratio of women's to men's median weekly earnings.

Source: Bureau of Labor Statistics, www.bls.gov.

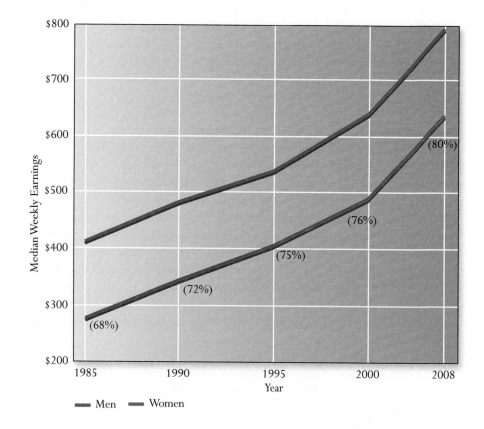

The Federal Equal Credit Opportunity Act of 1974 prohibits sex discrimination in credit transactions. Federal law prevents banks, credit unions, savings and loan associations, retail stores, and credit card companies from denying credit because of sex or marital status. However, these businesses may still deny credit for a poor or nonexistent credit rating, and some women who have always maintained accounts in their husband's name may still face credit problems if they apply in their own name.

The Earnings Gap Despite protections under federal laws, women continue to earn substantially less than men do. Today women, on average, earn about 80 percent of what men do (see Figure 15.5). This earnings gap has been closing very slowly: In 1985 women earned an average 68 percent of men's earnings. The earnings gap is not primarily a product of **direct discrimination;** women in the same job with the same skills, qualifications, experience, and work record are not generally paid less than men. Such direct discrimination has been illegal since the Civil Rights Act of 1964. Rather, the earnings gap is primarily a product of a division in the labor market between traditionally male and female jobs, with lower salaries paid in traditionally female occupations.

direct discrimination
Now illegal practice of differential pay for men versus women even when those individuals have equal qualifications and perform the same job.

The Dual Labor Market and "Comparable Worth" The existence of a "dual" labor market, with male-dominated "blue-collar" jobs distinguishable from female-dominated "pink-collar" jobs, continues to be a major obstacle to economic equality between men and women. These occupational differences result from cultural stereotyping, social conditioning, and training and education—all of which narrow the choices available to women. Although significant progress has been made in reducing occupational sex segregation (see Figure 15.6), many

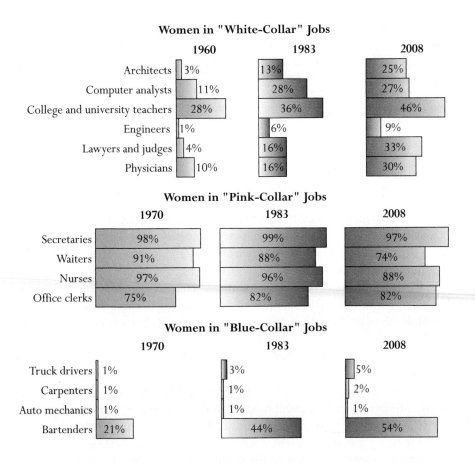

Women in "White-Collar" Jobs

	1960	1983	2008
Architects	3%	13%	25%
Computer analysts	11%	28%	27%
College and university teachers	28%	36%	46%
Engineers	1%	6%	9%
Lawyers and judges	4%	16%	33%
Physicians	10%	16%	30%

Women in "Pink-Collar" Jobs

	1970	1983	2008
Secretaries	98%	99%	97%
Waiters	91%	88%	74%
Nurses	97%	96%	88%
Office clerks	75%	82%	82%

Women in "Blue-Collar" Jobs

	1970	1983	2008
Truck drivers	1%	3%	5%
Carpenters	1%	1%	2%
Auto mechanics	1%	1%	1%
Bartenders	21%	44%	54%

FIGURE 15.6

Where Women Work: Gender Differentiation in the Labor Market

Most of the earnings gap between men and women in the U.S. labor force today is the result of the different job positions held by the two sexes. Although women are increasingly entering "white-collar" occupations long dominated by men, they continue to be disproportionately concentrated in "pink-collar" service positions. "Blue-collar" jobs have been the most resistant to change, remaining a male bastion, although women bartenders now outnumber men.

Sources: Statistical Abstract of the United States, 2009, pp. 384–87.

observers nevertheless doubt that sexually differentiated occupations will be eliminated in the foreseeable future.

As a result of a growing recognition that the wage gap is more a result of occupational differentiation than direct discrimination, some feminist organizations have turned to a new approach—the demand that pay levels in various occupations be determined by **comparable worth** rather than by the labor market. Comparable worth goes beyond paying men and women equally for the same work and calls for paying the same wages for jobs of comparable value to the employer. Advocates of comparable worth argue that governmental agencies or the courts should evaluate traditionally male and female jobs to determine their "worth" to the employer, perhaps by considering responsibilities, effort, knowledge, and skill requirements. Jobs adjudged to be "comparable" would be paid equal wages. Government agencies or the courts would replace the labor market in determining wage rates.

comparable worth
Argument that pay levels for traditionally male and traditionally female jobs should be equalized by paying equally all jobs that are "worth about the same" to an employer.

The "Glass Ceiling"

The barriers to women's advancement to top positions in the corporate and financial worlds are often very subtle, giving rise to the phrase **glass ceiling**. In explaining "why women aren't getting to the top," one observer argues that "at senior management levels competence is assumed. What you're looking for is someone who fits, someone who gets along, someone you trust. Now that's subtle stuff. How does a group of men feel that a woman is going to fit? I think it's very hard." Or, as a woman bank executive says, "The men just don't feel comfortable."[43] Finally, it is important to note that affirmative action efforts by governments—notably the EEOC—are directed primarily at entry-level positions rather than senior management posts.

glass ceiling
"Invisible" barriers to women rising to the highest positions in corporations and the professions.

Sexual Harassment   Sexual harassment on the job is also a violation of Title VII. But it is not always clear what kind of behavior constitutes "sexual harassment." The Supreme Court has defined it as:

> Unwelcome sexual advances, requests for sexual favors, and other verbal or physical conduct of a sexual nature constitute sexual harassment when (1) submission to such conduct is made either explicitly or implicitly a term or condition of an individual's employment; (2) submission to or rejection of such conduct by an individual is used as the basis for employment decisions affecting such individual; or (3) such conduct has the purpose or effect of unreasonably interfering with an individual's work performance or creating an intimidating, hostile, or offensive working environment.[44]

There are no great difficulties in defining sexual harassment when jobs or promotions are conditional on the granting of sexual favors. But several problems arise in defining a "hostile working environment." This phrase may include offensive utterances, sexual innuendoes, dirty jokes, the display of pornographic material, and unwanted proposals for dates. First, it would appear to include speech and hence raise 1st Amendment questions regarding how far speech may be curtailed by law in the workplace. Second, the definition depends more on the subjective feelings of the individual employee about what is "offensive" and "unwanted" than on an objective standard of behavior easily understood by all. Justice Sandra Day O'Connor wrestled with the definition of a "hostile work environment" in *Harris v. Forklift* in 1993. She held that a plaintiff need not show that the utterances caused psychological injury but that a "reasonable person," not just the plaintiff, must perceive the work environment to be hostile or abusive. Presumably a single incident would not constitute harassment; rather, courts should consider "the frequency of the discriminatory conduct," "its severity," and whether it "unreasonably interferes with an employee's work performance."[45]

Politics and Sexual Orientation

▶ 15.14 *Describe the policy issues arising from sexual orientation.*

The political movement on behalf of gay and lesbian rights is often traced back to the 1969 Stonewall riots in New York City, where gays confronted police in an effort to halt harassment. Since that time gays have made considerable strides in winning public acceptance of their lifestyle and in changing public policy. Discrimination based on sexual orientation is not prohibited in *federal* civil rights acts, but over the years many states and cities have enacted laws prohibiting discrimination against homosexuals. Nonetheless, many gay issues remain on the nation's political agenda.

Gay Rights Protest

Protesters march in Los Angeles in opposition to California Proposition 8 (2008) banning same-sex marriage. Voters approved the measure by a 52 to 48 percent margin and the California Supreme Court upheld the vote. But later, federal courts suspended the state constitutional amendment.

Privacy Rights   Historically, "sodomy" was defined as "an act against the laws of human nature" and criminalized in most states. As late as 1986 the U.S. Supreme Court upheld a Georgia law against sodomy holding that "the

Constitution does not confer a fundamental right upon homosexuals to engage in sodomy."[46] But the Supreme Court reversed its position in 2003 in *Lawrence v. Texas*, holding that consenting adults "engaged in sexual practices common to a homosexual lifestyle . . . are entitled to respect for their private lives. . . . Their right to liberty under the Due Process Clause gives them the full right to engage in their conduct without intervention of the government."[47] The Court noted that since its earlier decision, most of the states had repealed their laws against sodomy. *Lawrence v. Texas* is a landmark decision that is likely to affect every type of case involving sexual orientation, including employment, marriage, child custody, and adoption.

However, the Court has refused to interfere with private or religious organizations that ban avowed homosexuals. In *Boy Scouts of America v. Dale* (2000) the Court upheld a Boy Scout prohibition against homosexuals becoming scout leaders.[48] It also upheld the decision by the organizers of New York's annual St. Patrick's Day Parade to exclude a gay and lesbian marching contingent.

"Don't Ask, Don't Tell"   Upon taking office in 1993, President Bill Clinton announced his intention to overturn the military's existing ban on gays serving in the military. Gay rights groups had donated heavily to the Clinton campaign, ranking them—along with the Jewish community, the entertainment industry, and environmentalists—as the Democratic Party's biggest contributors. But military professionals at the time strongly objected to this move, and veterans groups including the American Legion and the Veterans of Foreign Wars criticized the plan. Clinton was obliged to compromise the issue and the policy of "Don't Ask, Don't Tell" emerged. The policy was that the military would no longer inquire into the sexual orientation of service personnel or recruits as long as they do not make their orientation public. Gays and lesbians are still subject to dismissal from the armed forces if they "come out of the closet" or are caught in homosexual acts. President Obama has pledged to end "Don't Ask, Don't Tell" and to allow gays and lesbians to serve openly in the military. Some federal courts have held that the policy violates the rights of homosexuals to equal protection of the law under the 14th Amendment.

Same-Sex Marriage   Vermont decided in 2000 to sanction "civil unions" between same-sex couples. Several other states followed, granting same-sex couples the benefits, protections, and responsibilities that are granted to married couples. In 2003 the Massachusetts Supreme Court ruled that same-sex couples had a right to *marriage* under the Massachusetts state constitution. But most states prohibit same-sex marriage. Many of these prohibitions have come about recently as a result of popular initiative and referendum in the states.[49]

Defense of Marriage Act   Anticipating that some states might pass laws allowing same-sex marriage, or that some state courts might rule that such marriages were constitutionally protected in their states, Congress passed a Defense of Marriage Act in 1996. This Act declared that marriage is between a man and a woman and that "no state . . . shall be required to give effect to any public act, record, or judicial proceeding of any other state respecting a relationship between persons of the same sex that is treated as a marriage." This provision is designed to circumvent the Full Faith and Credit Clause of Article IV U.S. Constitution that requires each state to recognize the "public acts, records, and judicial proceedings of every other state." (Article IV does however include a provision that Congress may "prescribe the manner in which such acts, records, and proceedings shall be proved, and the effect thereof.") The gay rights movement is bitterly opposed to the Defense of Marriage Act, and President Barack Obama has indicated his intention to have Congress overturn it.

AIDS   The gay rights movement was threatened in the early 1980s by the spread of the HIV virus and the deadly disease, acquired immune deficiency syndrome, or AIDS. Gay men were identified as one of the high-risk groups in the United States. The medical consensus was that the disease is spread through a sexual activity especially prevalent among male homosexuals, as well as through the sharing of contaminated needles among intravenous drug users and through blood transfusions. Casual contact (touching, kissing, using common utensils, etc.) does not transmit the disease. But the gay rights movement was successful in its campaign to convince Americans that "anyone could get AIDS," and over time it won the sympathy and support of the American public. Funding for AIDS research rose dramatically. The Center for Disease Control (CDC) gave priority to the search for antidotes to the virus, and at the same time, instituted a public education effort aimed at changing sexual behavior. Gay organizations across the nation distributed material describing safe sex practices. Over time, deaths from AIDS declined and the feared epidemic was held in check.

State Laws   Much of the conflict over gay rights occurs at the state level—in referenda, legislative enactments, and court decisions—yielding a complex mosaic of laws involving sexual orientation throughout the nation. Among the issues confronting the states:

- *Adoption.* Should gay and lesbian couples be allowed to adopt children?

- *Hate Crimes.* Should hate crime laws also protect homosexuals?

- *Health.* Should health insurance companies be required to extend benefits to homosexual spouses?

- *Employment.* Should laws against job discrimination be extended to protect homosexuals?

- *Housing.* Should laws against discrimination in housing be extended to protect homosexuals?

- *Marriage.* Should gay and lesbian couples be allowed to marry?

- *Civil Unions.* Should gay and lesbian couples be allowed to legally form civil unions giving them many of the rights of married couples?

State laws differ on each of these issues, although recent changes have generally benefited gays and lesbians.[50]

Gay Politics   The gay movement includes a loose coalition of groups, including Lesbian Gay Bisexual and Transgender Centers (LGBT); National Gay and Lesbian Task Force; Queer Nation; AIDS Coalition to Unleash Power (ACT-UP); and the Gay Lesbian Alliance against Discrimination (GLAAD). Many of these groups have affiliates in colleges, universities, and communities across the country.

The goals of the movement have evolved over the years from initially seeking protection against government restrictions on private behavior; to later seeking government protection of gays and lesbians from discrimination; to still later seeking societal approval of homosexuality as a morally equivalent alternative lifestyle.[51] Over time public opinion has become much more supportive of gay and lesbian goals.

A CONSTITUTIONAL NOTE

The 14th Amendment

The Constitution of 1787 not only recognized slavery by counting slaves as three-fifths of a person for apportionment of representatives and direct taxes (Article I, Section 2) but also protected slavery by requiring states to return escaped slaves to their owners (Article IV, Section 2). (The Founders appear to have been embarrassed by the word *slave* and employed the euphemism "person held to service or labor.") Following the Civil War the 13th Amendment prohibited slavery and the 15th Amendment prohibited states from denying the right to vote on account of race, color, or previous condition of servitude. But it was the 14th Amendment that eventually became the basis of the civil rights movement in America and the source of the most important guarantees of equality:

> No State shall make or enforce any law which shall abridge the privileges or immunities of citizens of the United States; nor shall any state deprive any person of life, liberty, or property, without due process of law; nor deny to any person within its jurisdiction the equal protection of the laws.

What are the meanings of words such as "liberty," "due process of law," and "equal protection of the laws"? Constitutionally, the history of the civil rights movement centers around definitions of these terms, as does the history of the women's movement.

Summary

▶ 15.1 Assess the role that politics played over the centuries in America's quest for equality.

The original Constitution of 1787 recognized and protected slavery. Not until after the Civil War did the 13th Amendment (1865) abolish slavery. But the 14th Amendment's guarantee of "equal protection of the laws" and the 15th Amendment's guarantee of voting rights were largely ignored in Southern states after the federal government's Reconstruction efforts ended. Segregation was held constitutional by the U.S. Supreme Court in its "separate but equal" decision in *Plessy v. Ferguson* in 1896.

▶ 15.2 Analyze how the Constitution was interpreted to first justify and then attack slavery and segregation.

The NAACP led the long legal battle in the federal courts to have segregation declared unconstitutional as a violation of the Equal Protection Clause of the 14th Amendment. Under the leadership of Thurgood Marshall, a major victory was achieved in the case of *Brown v. Board of Education of Topeka* in 1954.

▶ 15.3 Differentiate the various meanings of equal protection of the laws.

The struggle over school desegregation continues even today. Federal courts are more likely to issue desegregation orders (including orders to bus pupils to achieve racial balance in schools) in school districts where present or past actions by government officials contributed to racial imbalances. Courts are less likely to order desegregation where racial imbalances are a product of residential patterns.

▶ 15.4 Outline major civil rights legislation.

The courts could eliminate *governmental* discrimination by enforcing the 14th Amendment of the Constitution; but only Congress could end private discrimination through legislation. Martin Luther King, Jr.'s, campaign of nonviolent direct action helped bring remaining racial injustices to the attention of Congress. Key legislation includes the Civil Rights Act of 1964, which bans discrimination in public accommodations, government-funded programs, and private employment; the Voting Rights Act of 1965, which authorizes strong federal action to protect voting rights; and the Civil Rights Act of 1968, which outlaws discrimination in housing.

▶ 15.5 Distinguish between equality of opportunity and equality of results.

Today, racial politics center around continuing inequalities between blacks and whites in the areas of income, jobs, housing, health, education, and other conditions of life. Should the government concentrate on "equality of opportunity" and apply "color-blind" standards to both blacks and whites? Or should government take "affirmative action" to assist blacks and other minorities to overcome the results of past unequal treatment?

▶ 15.6 Trace the Court's evolving attitude toward affirmative action.

Generally the Supreme Court is likely to approve of affirmative action programs when these programs have been adopted in response to a past proven history of discrimination, when they are narrowly tailored so as not to adversely affect the rights of individuals, when they do not absolutely bar whites from participating, and when they serve clearly identified, compelling, and legitimate government objectives.

▶ **15.7** *Relate affirmative action to student body diversity.*

Even though there is scant definitive evidence to support the claim that diversity on college campuses improves learning, universities have approved affirmative action programs that take race into consideration when deciding who to admit as a student and who to hire as a professor. The Court has held that the use of racial classifications in the acceptance process would be given "strict scrutiny," but the Justices have not been able to enunciate a clear constitutional principle regarding affirmative action.

▶ **15.8** *Characterize the Hispanics in the United States demographically and politically.*

Economic conditions in Mexico and other Spanish-speaking nations of the Western Hemisphere continue to fuel large-scale immigration, both legal and illegal, into the United States.

▶ **15.9** *Describe the increasing political role of Hispanics in the United States.*

The political power of Mexican Americans, the nation's largest Hispanic group, does not yet match their population percentage. Their voter turnout remains lower than that of other ethnic groups in the United States.

▶ **15.10** *Trace the historical roots of the issues confronting Native Americans.*

Since the arrival of the first Europeans on this continent, Native American peoples have experienced cycles of invasion, resistance, military defeat, and land concessions. Today Native American peoples collectively remain the poorest and least healthy of the nation's ethnic groups.

▶ **15.11** *Assess the legal protections offered to disabled Americans.*

The most recent major civil rights legislation is the Americans with Disabilities Act of 1990, which prohibits discrimination against disabled persons in private employment, government programs, public accommodations, and communications.

▶ **15.12** *Determine how the 14th Amendment has been interpreted regarding gender equality.*

The Equal Protection Clause of the 14th Amendment applies to "any person," but traditionally the Supreme Court has recognized gender differences in laws. Nevertheless, in recent years the Court has struck down gender differences where they are unreasonable or arbitrary and unrelated to legitimate government objectives.

▶ **15.13** *Assess the relationship between economic opportunities and gender equality.*

Gender discrimination in employment has been illegal since the passage of the Civil Rights Act of 1964. Nevertheless, differences in average earnings of men and women persist, although these differences have narrowed somewhat over time. The earnings gap appears to be mainly a product of lower pay in occupations traditionally dominated by women and higher pay in traditionally male occupations. Although neither Congress nor the courts have mandated wages based on comparable worth of traditional men's and women's jobs in private employment, many governmental agencies and some private employers have undertaken to review wage rates to eliminate gender differences.

The Equal Protection Clause does not bar government from treating persons in various income classes differently. However, governments must treat every individual in a class equally, and the classifications must not be "arbitrary" or "unreasonable." The poor cannot demand benefits or services as a matter of constitutional rights; but once government establishes a social welfare program by law, it must provide equal access to all persons "similarly situated."

▶ **15.14** *Describe the policy issues arising from sexual orientation.*

The Supreme Court has held that consenting adults engaging in practices common to a homosexual lifestyle are entitled to the rights of privacy. Various other gay rights issues remain unsettled, including "Don't Ask, Don't Tell" military service policy, and laws surrounding same-sex marriage, adoption, employment, and housing discrimination.

Chapter Test

▶ **15.1** *Assess the role that politics played over the centuries in America's quest for equality.*

1. Perhaps the main debate in America today about equality centers around
   a. equality of opportunity versus equality before the law
   b. equality before the law versus equal access to health care
   c. equality of results versus equal opportunity
   d. genetic equality versus legal equality

▶ **15.2** *Analyze how the Constitution was interpreted to first justify and then attack slavery and segregation.*

2. A major decision by the Supreme Court in the nineteenth century held that slavery was constitutional and that escaped

slaves who made it to a free state should be returned to their owners; this was decided in
a. *Scott v. Sanford*
b. *Plessy v. Ferguson*
c. *Maryland v. Pennsylvania*
d. *Kentucky v. Ohio*

3. The Compromise of 1877 resulted in
a. the reconstruction of the South
b. the beginning of the abolitionist movement
c. the three-fifths solution
d. the occupying union forces leaving the South

4. It would be accurate to maintain that
a. Jim Crow laws were intended to facilitate integration
b. Jim Crow laws led to the three-fifths compromise
c. the separate but equal doctrine resulted in a segregated society in the South
d. with the end of slavery, the federal District of Columbia became an integrated society

▶ **15.3** *Differentiate the various meanings of equal protection of the laws.*

5. The nineteenth century African American who advocated accommodation with segregation was
a. Oscar de la Priest
b. W. E. B. Du Bois
c. Booker T. Washington
d. Stokley Carmichael

6. Racial imbalances that are not caused by governmental action but by residential patterns
a. are "restrictive covenants"
b. are unconstitutional
c. are evidence of "de facto segregation"
d. have resulted in most of the affirmative action programs

▶ **15.4** *Outline major civil rights legislation.*

7. Perhaps the most practical day-to-day result of the Civil Rights Act of 1964 was the
a. desegregation of hotels and restaurants
b. desegregation of public schools
c. desegregation of private clubs
d. end to the prohibition of interracial marriages

8. A method that Martin Luther King, Jr., advocated using for the elimination of discrimination was
a. the development of an Afro-centric culture
b. establishing a separate republic for African Americans in parts of Mississippi and Louisiana
c. nonviolent direct action
d. the development of "black power"

▶ **15.5** *Distinguish between equality of opportunity and equality of results.*

9. It would be accurate to say that income disparity between blacks and whites has
a. increased in recent years
b. decreased in recent years
c. remained about the same
d. has largely been eliminated

10. Eliminating all government recognition of race is consistent with
a. affirmative action
b. set-asides
c. the color-blind standard
d. the use of racial quotas

▶ **15.6** *Trace the Court's evolving attitude toward affirmative action.*

11. In the case of the *University of California Board of Regents v. Bakke* the Supreme Court held that an admissions program
a. with racial quotas was constitutional
b. which took race into consideration was constitutional
c. with set-asides was constitutional
d. which did not take race into consideration violated the 14th Amendment

▶ **15.7** *Relate affirmative action to student body diversity.*

12. In the attempt to bring diversity to U.S. campuses, attempts have been made to give preferential treatment to which of the following groups?
a. Hispanics
b. African Americans
c. Native Americans
d. all of the above

▶ **15.8** *Characterize the Hispanics in the United States demographically and politically.*

13. Today the largest minority group in America is
a. African Americans
b. Hispanic Americans
c. Asian Americans
d. Multiracial Americans

▶ **15.9** *Describe the increasing political role of Hispanics in the United States.*

14. The Hispanic population in America is found primarily in
a. New York and Chicago
b. Florida and Georgia
c. the Southwestern United States
d. the Pacific Rim

▶ **15.10** *Trace the historical roots of the issues confronting Native Americans.*

15. The "Trail of Tears" speaks to
a. the battle at Wounded Knee
b. the end of the "free peoples"
c. the removal of Native peoples from Florida to Oklahoma
d. Custer's brutality toward the Native peoples at Little Bighorn

▶ **15.11** *Assess the legal protections offered to disabled Americans.*

16. The landmark legislation that protects disabled Americans is the
a. Disabled Accommodations Act
b. Handicapped Recovery Act
c. Americans with Disabilities Act
d. Handicapped Employment Act

▶ **15.12** *Determine how the 14th Amendment has been interpreted regarding gender equality.*

17. Some of the early concerns of the first feminists revolved around
a. property rights
b. women's suffrage
c. concerns about their husbands' drinking
d. all of the above

▶ 15.13 *Assess the relationship between economic opportunities and gender equality.*

18. Women have made the least amount of progress in professional advancement in
    a. law
    b. medicine
    c. engineering
    d. education

▶ 15.14 *Describe the policy issues arising from sexual orientation.*

19. The gay rights movement has taken strong positions on which of the following issues
    a. Don't Ask, Don't Tell
    b. same-sex marriage
    c. job discrimination
    d. all of the above

---

myp⬤liscilab EXERCISES

Apply what you learned in this chapter on MyPoliSciLab.

📖—[**Read** on **mypoliscilab.com**

   eText: Chapter 15

✓—[**Study** and **Review** on **mypoliscilab.com**

   Pre-Test

   Post-Test

   Chapter Exam

   Flashcards

👁—[**Watch** on **mypoliscilab.com**

   Video: Should Don't Ask Don't Tell Go Away?

   Video: Supreme Court: No Race-Based Admissions

   Video: Chicago Worker Protest

✳—[**Explore** on **mypoliscilab.com**

   Simulation: You are the Mayor and Need to Make Civil Rights Decisions

   Comparative: Comparing Civil Rights

   Timeline: The Struggle for Equal Protection

   Timeline: The Civil Rights Movement

   Timeline: The Mexican-American Civil Rights Movement

   Timeline: Women's Struggle for Equality

Key Terms

abolition movement   544
Emancipation
    Proclamation   544
Reconstruction   544
Jim Crow   545
separate but equal   545

de facto segregation
    550
nonviolent direct
    action   551
affirmative action   554
quota   555

Bakke case   557
set-aside program
    559
strict scrutiny   559
diversity   559
Title IX   573

Equal Rights Amendment
    (ERA)   573
direct discrimination
    574
comparable worth   575
glass ceiling   575

Suggested Readings

Bowen, William G., and Derek Curtis Bok. *The Shape of the River*. Princeton, N.J.: Princeton University Press, 1999. An argument by two university presidents that preferential treatment of minorities in admissions to prestigious universities has led to the subsequent success in life by the beneficiaries of the preferences.

Conway, M. Margaret, Gertrude A. Steurnagel, and David W. Ahern. *Women and Political Participation*. 3rd ed. Washington, D.C.: CQ Press, 2004. A wide-ranging review of changes in American political culture brought about by women's increasing political clout. Continuing gender differences in representation are explored.

Fox-Genovese, Elizabeth. *Feminism Is Not the Story of My Life*. New York: Doubleday, 1995. Critique of radical feminism for failing to understand the central importance of marriage and motherhood in women's lives, and a discussion of how public policy could ease the clashing demands of work and family on women.

Garcia, F. Chris, and Gabriel Sanchez. *Hispanics and the U.S. Political System: Moving Into the Mainstream*. New York:

Longman, 2007. A description of the growing influence of Hispanics both as voters and politicians.

Harrison, Brigid C. *Women in American Politics*. Belmont, Calif.: Wadsworth, 2003. Comprehensive text on role of women in interest groups, parties, elections, Congress, the executive branch, and the judiciary.

Hero, Rodney E. *Latinos and the U.S. Political System*. Philadelphia: Temple University Press, 1992. General history of political participation of major Latino groups, arguing that different cultural behaviors limit their ability to participate in the interest-group system and policy-making process as currently structured.

LeMay, Michael. *Perennial Struggle: Race, Ethnicity and Minority Group Relations in the United States*, 3rd ed. New York: Longman,

2009. A description and assessment of minority group strategies—accommodation, separatism, radicalism—in coping with their political and economic status.

Thernstrom, Stephen, and Abigail Thernstrom. *America in Black and White*. New York: Simon & Schuster, 1997. Information-rich analysis tracing social and economic progress of African Americans and arguing that gains in education and employment were greater *before* the introduction of affirmative action programs.

Walton, Hanes, and Robert C. Smith. *American Politics and the African-American Quest for Freedom*. 5th ed. New York: Longman, 2010. Comprehensive text arguing the profound influence that African Americans have on American politics.

Suggested Web Sites

ADA Home Page www.usdoj.gov/crt/ada
Federal agency site with guide to disability rights laws.

American Council on Education www.acenet.edu
Information on a wide range of educational issues, including diversity, testing, admissions, and so forth.

American Indian Movement www.aimovement.org
Advocacy organization for Native Americans, with news and views on treaties and treaty violations.

Brown Matters www.brownmatters.org
Chronology of *Brown v. Board of Education*, 1957.

Bureau of Indian Affairs www.doi.gov/bureau-Indian-affairs
Government agency with responsibility for administration of 562 federally recognized tribal governments in the United States.

Center for Individual Rights www.cir-usa.org
Advocacy organization opposing racial preferences.

Equal Employment Opportunity Commission (EEOC) www.eeoc.gov
Federal EEOC site with information on what constitutes discrimination by age, disability, race, ethnicity, religion, gender; how to file a charge; and guidance for employers.

Feminist.Com www.feminist.com
Web site promoting women's business development, with information and advice.

FIRE: Foundation for Equal Rights in Education www.thefire.org
Advocacy organization defending individual rights on campus and opposing racial preferences.

The King Center http://thekingcenter.com
Biography of M. L. K., Jr., together with news and information from Atlanta King Center.

La Raza www.nclr.org
National Council of La Raza. Issue positions, programs, news, dedicated to improving life experiences of Hispanic Americans.

Mexican American Legal Defense League www.maldef.org
Advocacy and litigation on behalf of Latinos, with information on cases dealing with immigration rights.

NAACP Legal Defense Fund www.naacpldf.org
Founded in 1940 by Thurgood Marshall to provide legal assistance to poor African Americans. Originally affiliated with the NAACP; now a separate organization.

National Organization for Women (NOW) www.now.org
Advocacy organization for feminist activists working to protect abortion rights, end discrimination against women, and "eradicate racism, sexism, and homophobia."

Pew Hispanic Center www.pewhispanic.org
Research and surveys on the U.S. Hispanic population.

U.S. Commission on Civil Rights www.usccr.gov
National clearinghouse on information regarding discrimination because of race, color, religion, sex, age, disability, or national origin. Publishes reports, findings, and recommendations.

U.S. Department of Justice, Civil Rights Division www.usdoj.gov/crt
Responsible for enforcement of U.S. civil rights laws. Site includes information on cases.

Chapter Test Answer Key

1. c
2. a
3. d
4. c
5. d
6. c
7. a
8. c
9. c
10. c
11. b
12. d
13. c
14. c
15. c
16. c
17. d
18. c
19. d

16 POLITICS AND THE ECONOMY

> **"** It's the economy, stupid! **"**
>
> James Carville

Outline and Learning Objectives

Politics and Economics
▶ 16.1 *Relate politics and economics as systems.*

Economic Decision Making
▶ 16.2 *Outline the role that fiscal and monetary policy play in economic decision making.*

Measuring the Performance of the American Economy
▶ 16.3 *Identify the different ways of assessing the strength of the economy.*

Government Spending, Deficits, and Debt
▶ 16.4 *Determine the relationships between government spending, deficits, and the national debt.*

The Tax Burden
▶ 16.5 *Analyze the various kinds of taxes and how they distribute the tax burden.*

Tax Politics
▶ 16.6 *Trace changes in tax policies under different administrations in recent decades.*

Think about Politics

1. Do you believe government efforts to manage the economy usually make things better or worse?

    BETTER ◯ **WORSE** ◯

2. Do you believe the government should spend more during recessions to ease economic hardship even if it means larger government deficits?

    YES ◯ **NO** ◯

3. Which is more important: holding down the size of government or providing needed services?

    HOLDING DOWN THE SIZE OF GOVERNMENT ◯
    PROVIDING NEEDED SERVICES ◯

4. Do you think the federal government should increase spending on Social Security and Medicare for the elderly?

    YES ◯ **NO** ◯

5. Do you believe all wage earners should pay the same percentage of income in taxes (a flat tax)?

    YES ◯ **NO** ◯

6. Do you believe the federal government should use the tax laws to equalize income?

    YES ◯ **NO** ◯

What is the proper relationship between government and the economy? How much influence should the government exercise over the production and distribution of goods and services in this country?

Politics and Economics

▶ 16.1 *Relate politics and economics as systems.*

Earlier, we observed that one of America's foremost political scientists, Harold Lasswell, defined "politics" as "who gets what, when, and how." One of America's foremost economists, Paul Samuelson, defined "economics" as "deciding what shall be produced, how, and for whom."[1] The similarity between these definitions is based on the fact that both the political system and the economic system provide society with means for deciding about the production and distribution of goods and services. The political system involves *collective* decisions—choices made by communities, states, or nations—and relies on government coercion through laws, regulations, taxes, and so on to implement them. A free-market economic system involves *individual* decisions—choices made by millions of workers and consumers and thousands of firms—and relies on *voluntary exchange* through buying, selling, borrowing, contracting, and trading to implement them. Both politics and markets function to transform popular demands into goods and services, to allocate costs, and to distribute goods and services.

One of the key questions in any society is how much to rely on government versus the marketplace to provide goods and services. This question of the proper relationship between governments and markets—that is, between politics and economics—is the subject of political economy. The United States is primarily a free-market economy, but the federal government increasingly influences economic activity (see *Politics up Close*: "How Washington Dealt with the Financial Crisis").

585

POLITICS UP CLOSE

How Washington Dealt with the Financial Crisis

Wall Street bankers—current and former officers of Goldman Sachs—testify at a Senate investigation regarding the financial crisis and charges of securities fraud against their firm.

For years, Americans lived on easy credit. Families ran up credit card debt and borrowed heavily for cars, tuition, and especially mortgages. Mortgage lenders approved loans for borrowers without fully examining their ability to pay. Federally chartered corporations, Fannie Mae and Freddie Mac, encouraged mortgage loans to low-income and minority home buyers. Some mortgages were "predatory" with initial low payments followed by steep upward adjustable rates. To make matters worse, banks and financial institutions bundled "subprime" mortgages together and sold them as "derivatives." Risk was largely ignored. Banks, insurers, and lenders all assumed that housing prices would inevitably rise.

But eventually the bubble burst. Housing prices fell dramatically. Homeowners found themselves holding "upside-down" mortgages—mortgages that exceeded the value of their homes. Many were unable or unwilling to meet their mortgage payments. Foreclosures and delinquencies spiraled upward. Investors who held mortgage-backed securities began to incur heavy losses. Investment banks and mortgage insurers including Fannie Mae and Freddie Mac found themselves in serious financial trouble. The stock market plummeted.

Wall Street Bailout   In 2008, the credit crunch ballooned into Wall Street's biggest crisis since the Great Depression. Hundreds of billions of dollars in mortgage related investments went bad, and the nation's leading investment banks and insurance companies sought the assistance of the Treasury Department and the Federal Reserve System. As the hemorrhaging continued, it was soon clear that the nation was in danger of tumbling into a deep recession. In September, President Bush sent the Secretary of the Treasury, accompanied by the Federal Reserve Chairman, to Congress to plead for a massive $700 billion bailout of banks, insurance companies, and investment firms that held mortgage-backed "illiquid assets." They argued that a full-blown depression might result if the federal government failed to intervene in financial markets. House and Senate Democratic and Republican leaders, and even the presidential candidates—Barack Obama and John McCain—all supported the bill. But polls show that most Americans opposed a "Wall Street bailout." Congress members were being asked by their leaders to ignore the folks back home. After an initial House "No" vote that stunned Washington, Congress was eventually

Economic Decision Making

▶ 16.2 *Outline the role that fiscal and monetary policy play in economic decision making.*

fiscal policy
Economic policies involving taxing, spending, and deficit levels of the national government.

Economic decision making involves both fiscal and monetary policy. **Fiscal policy** refers to the taxing, spending, and borrowing activities of the national government. Fiscal policy making takes place within the same system of separated powers and checks and balances that governs other areas of federal policy making (see "Separation of Powers and Checks and Balances" in Chapter 3), with both the Congress and the president sharing responsibility.

monetary policy
Economic policies involving the money supply, interest rates, and banking activity.

Monetary policy refers to decisions regarding the supply of money in the economy, including private borrowing, interest rates, and banking activity. Monetary policy is a principal responsibility of the powerful and independent Federal Reserve Board. Congress established the Federal Reserve Board in 1913 and its power rests

persuaded to approve the Emergency Economic Stabilization Act of 2008.

Treasury's TARP The Treasury Department was given unprecedented power to bail out the nation's financial institutions. The program was named the Troubled Asset Relief Program (TARP). The nation's leading banks, insurance companies, and financial institutions were given TARP funds. In exchange, these institutions were expected to modify home mortgages that were in danger of default, to help mortgage borrowers to refinance their loans at lower interest rates, and to loosen credit in an effort to jumpstart the economy. But most of all the TARP funds ensured the continued stability of the nation's financial system.

Fed Response In addition to the TARP bailouts, the Federal Reserve Board made a dramatic decision to pump over $1.5 trillion into the nation's financial system in order to unlock mortgage, credit card, college, and auto lending. The Fed lowered its own discount rate (the rate it charges member banks to borrow money from the System) to near zero, to encourage banks to make loans. But low-interest rates and easy credit cannot guarantee that banks will lend money or that businesses and individuals will borrow money. As recession deepened in early 2009, President Barack Obama and Congress sought to provide additional economic stimulus.

The Economic Stimulus Package A massive economic stimulus package, officially the American Recovery and Reinvestment Act of 2009, became the centerpiece of President Barack Obama's early policy agenda. Its combination of spending increases and tax cuts totaled $757 billion—the largest single fiscal policy measure in American history. It was written in record time by a Democratic-controlled Congress; House Republicans were unanimous in opposition, and only three Republican senators supported the bill. The stimulus package consisted of roughly two-thirds spending and one-third tax rebates. Democrats in the Congress used the package to increase spending in a wide variety of domestic programs—in education, Medicaid, unemployment compensation, food stamps, health technology, child tax credits, disability payments, higher education grants, renewable energy subsidies, and rail and transit transportation—as well as traditional spending for highways and bridges. Republicans complained that much of the spending had little to do with stimulating the economy but rather increased government involvement in liberal policy areas favored by Democrats. Republicans argued that tax cuts should be the principal approach to stimulating the economy.

GM Bankruptcy General Motors is an American institution, the biggest of the big three domestic automobile manufacturers—GM, Chrysler, and Ford. GM and Chrysler sought federal bankruptcy protection in 2009; Ford managed to stay afloat by itself. Even before declaring bankruptcy, General Motors had received billions of federal dollars in loans and loan guarantees. Federal involvement forced out GM's chief executive officer. In bankruptcy, the federal government took majority ownership of GM. President Obama declared that the federal government had no interest in the day-to-day operations of GM. Yet the White House issued guidelines for limiting the salaries of top executives of GM and other institutions receiving TARP funds.

on congressional legislation. Congress could, if it wished, reduce its power or even abolish the Fed. But no serious effort has ever been undertaken to do so.

Financial Overhaul In an effort to prevent a repeat of the financial crisis, Congress passed a sweeping overhaul of the nation's financial regulations in 2010. Included in the overhaul: new regulations to restrict derivatives; stricter capital requirements for banks; new powers to seize financial institutions on the brink of bankruptcy; a new council of regulators to monitor the fiscal system for major risks; and a new consumer protection agency to monitor consumer credit. The Federal Reserve retained its powers over monetary policy. But critics blasted the bill for failing to reform Freddie Mac and Fannie Mae, the federal corporations that were partly responsible for the crisis.

Congress, the President, and Fiscal Policy The Constitution of the United States places all taxing, borrowing, and spending powers in the hands of Congress. Article I grants Congress the "Power to lay and collect Taxes, Duties, Imposts and Excises, to pay the Debts and provide for the common Defence and general Welfare of the United States," and "to borrow Money on the Credit of the United States." It also declares that "No Money shall be drawn from the Treasury, but in Consequence of Appropriations made by Law." For nearly 150 years the power to spend was interpreted in a limited fashion: Congress could only spend money to perform powers specifically enumerated in Article I, Section 8, of the Constitution. But the Supreme Court has since ruled that the phrase "to pay the Debts and provide for the common Defence and general Welfare" may be broadly interpreted to authorize congressional spending for any purpose that serves the general welfare. Thus today there are no constitutional limits on Congress's spending power. Congress's borrowing power has always been unlimited constitutionally; *there is no constitutional requirement for a balanced budget.*

The Constitution gives the president no formal powers over taxing and spending or borrowing, stating only that the president shall ". . . recommend to [Congress's] Consideration such Measures as he shall judge necessary and expedient" (Article II, Section 3). From this meager constitutional grant of power, however, presidents have gradually acquired leadership over national economic policy. The principal instrument of executive economic policy making is the Budget of the United States Government, which the president submits annually to Congress. The budget sets forth the president's recommendations for spending for the forthcoming fiscal year; revenue estimates, based on existing taxes or recommendations for new or increased tax levels; and estimates of projected deficits and the need for borrowing when, as has usually been the case of late, spending recommendations exceed revenue estimates.

The Fed and Monetary Policy

Most economically advanced democracies have central banks whose principal responsibility is to regulate the supply of money, both currency in circulation and bank deposits. And most of these democracies have found it best to remove this responsibility from the direct control of elected politicians. Politicians everywhere are sorely tempted to inflate the supply of money in order to fund projects and programs with newly created money instead of new taxes. Nations pay for this approach with a general rise in prices and a reduction in goods and services available to private firms and individuals—inflation. Indeed, nations whose control of the money supply has fallen

Defending Deficits

Treasury Secretary Timothy Geithner testifies before the House Ways and Means Committee regarding President Obama's federal budget for fiscal 2011.

victim to irresponsible governments have experienced inflation rates of 500 to 1,000 percent per year, which is to say that their money became worthless.

The Federal Reserve System of the United States is largely independent of either the president or Congress. Its independent status is a result not only of law but also of its structure. It is run by a seven-member board of governors who are appointed by the president, with the consent of the Senate, for *14-year* terms. Members may not be removed from the board except for "cause"; no member has ever been removed since the creation of the board in 1913. The board's chair serves only a 4-year term, but the chair's term overlaps that of the president, so that new presidents cannot immediately name their own chair.

The task of the **Federal Reserve Board (the Fed)** is to regulate the money supply and by so doing to help avoid both inflation and recession. The Fed oversees the operation of the nation's twelve Federal Reserve Banks, which actually issue the nation's currency, called "Federal Reserve Notes." The Federal Reserve Banks are bankers' banks; they do not directly serve private citizens or firms. They hold the deposits, or "reserves," of banks; lend money to banks at "discount rates" that the Fed determines; buy and sell U.S. Government Treasury bonds; and assure regulatory compliance by private banks and protection of depositors against fraud. The Fed determines the reserve requirements of banks and otherwise monitors the health of the banking industry. The Fed also plays an important role in clearing checks throughout the banking system.

The Fed's influence over the economy is mainly through monetary policy—increasing or decreasing the supply of money and hence largely determining interest rates. When **inflation** threatens, the Fed typically acts to limit ("tighten") the supply of money and raise interest rates by (1) raising the reserve requirement of banks and thereby reducing the amount of money they have to loan out; or (2) raising the discount rate and thereby the cost of borrowing by banks; or (3) selling off government bonds to banks and others in "open market operations," thereby reducing the funds banks can lend to individuals and businesses. When **recession** threatens, the Fed typically acts to expand ("ease") the money supply and lower interest rates by taking the opposite of each action just described.

Although it is the Fed that makes monetary policy, voters typically hold the president responsible for recessions. Hence presidents frequently try to persuade ("jawbone") the independent Fed into lowering interest rates, especially in an election year, believing a temporary stimulus to help win the election is worth whatever inflationary effects it might create after the election.

Federal Reserve Board (the Fed)
Independent agency of the executive branch of the federal government charged with overseeing the nation's monetary policy.

inflation
Rise in the general level of prices; not just the prices of some products.

recession
Decline in the general level of economic activity.

Measuring the Performance of the American Economy

▶ 16.3 *Identify the different ways of assessing the strength of the economy.*

Underlying the power of nations and the well-being of their citizens is the strength of their economy—their total productive capacity. The United States produces over $14 *trillion* worth of goods and services in a single year for its 310 million people—more than $45,000 worth of output for every person.

Economic Growth   **Gross domestic product (GDP)** is a widely used measure of the performance of the economy.[2] GDP is a nation's total production of goods and services for a single year valued in terms of market prices. It is the sum of all the goods and services that people have been willing to pay for, from wheat production to bake sales, from machine tools to maid service, from aircraft

gross domestic product (GDP)
Measure of economic performance in terms of the nation's total production of goods and services for a single year, valued in terms of market prices.

POLITICS UP CLOSE

"It's the Economy, Stupid"

The pointed political advice, "It's the economy, stupid," is generally attributed to James Carville, campaign consultant to Democrat Bill Clinton during the 1992 presidential race against incumbent Republican George H. W. Bush. The perceived performance of the economy during the election year is an excellent predictor of presidential voting outcomes. When the economy is prosperous, voters reward the incumbent presidential party. When the economy sours, they vote the incumbent party out of the White House.

Indeed, the percentage vote for the incumbent party's candidate can be predicted reasonably well from responses to the survey question, whether business conditions have improved or gotten worse over the previous year. When a majority of people surveyed in presidential elections from 1980 through 2008 said the economy had gotten "worse," the candidate of the party occupying the White House lost. When a majority of people said the economy was "the same" or "better" than the previous year, the candidate of the incumbent party won the election. The only exception was the presidential election of 2000 where the candidate of the incumbent Democratic Party, Al Gore, lost to the Republican challenger, George W. Bush, despite a strong economy. According to the economic voter theses, Al Gore "should" have won and won easily, not just barely won the popular vote (and lost in the electoral college).

Interestingly, it is not the voters' *own* personal economic well-being that affects their vote but rather the voters' perception of *general* economic conditions. People may report that their own financial situation is good, but vote against the incumbent party when they perceive the general economy as poor. Media attention to the economy during the campaign signals voters about the state of the economy, and increased media attention focuses voters attention on the economy.

It is during the election year, especially as the campaign evolves, that voters turn their attention to the economy. The incumbent party's candidate poll numbers during the campaign often reflect media reports of the state of the economy—falling with reports of economic distress. In the 2008 presidential campaign, the economic meltdown of mid-September led an already pessimistic public to get even more negative in its evaluation of the economy. Republican John McCain's slim chances were demolished by the financial crises. Democrat Barack Obama won the election with 53 percent of the vote, although this outcome was somewhat less than predicted by the economic thesis.

See Robert S. Erickson, "The American Voter and the Economy, 2008"; Thomas M. Holbrook, "Economic Considerations and the 2008 Presidential Election"; and Michael S. Lewis-Beck and Richard Nadeau, "Obama and the Economy 2008," in *P.S. Political Science and Politics* 42 (July 2009): 467–84.

manufacturing to bus rides, from automobiles to chewing gum. GDP counts only final purchases of goods and services (that is, it ignores the purchase of steel by car makers until it is sold as a car) to avoid double counting in the production process. GDP also excludes financial transactions (such as the sale of bonds and stocks) and income transfers (such as Social Security, welfare, and pension payments) that do not add to the production of goods and services. Although GDP is expressed in current dollar prices, it is often recalculated in constant dollar terms to reflect real values over time, adjusting for the effect of inflation. GDP estimates are prepared each quarter by the U.S. Department of Commerce; these figures are widely reported and closely watched by the business and financial community.

Growth in real (constant dollar) GDP measures the performance of the overall economy. Economic recessions and recoveries are measured as fluctuations or swings in the growth of GDP. For example, a recession is usually defined as negative GDP growth in two or more consecutive quarters. Historical data reveal that periods of economic growth have traditionally been followed by periods of contraction, giving rise to the notion of **economic cycles** (see Figure 16.1).

Unemployment From a political standpoint, the **unemployment rate** may be the most important measure of the economy's performance (see *Politics up Close:*

economic cycles
Fluctuations in real GDP growth followed by contraction.

unemployment rate
Percentage of the civilian labor force who are not working but who are looking for work or waiting to return to or to begin a job.

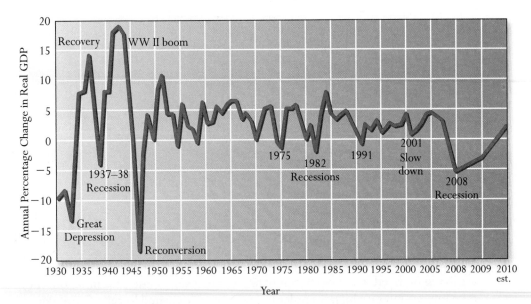

FIGURE 16.1 Growth Cycles: Economic Growth in America

Periods of economic growth are reflected here as increases in the annual percent change in the GDP. Recessions are shown as negative (below zero) GDP growth. The recession that began in 2008 is the worst in over 50 years.

Source: Data from Bureau of Economic Analysis, 2010. www.bea.gov.

"It's the Economy, Stupid"). The unemployment rate is the percentage of the civilian labor force who are looking for work or waiting to return to or begin a job. Unemployment is different from not working; people who have retired or who attend school and people who do not work because of sickness, disability, or unwillingness are not considered part of the labor force and so are not counted as unemployed. People who are so discouraged about finding a job that they have quit looking for work are also not counted in the official unemployment rate. The unemployed do include people who have been terminated from their last job or temporarily laid off from work, as well as people who voluntarily quit and those who have recently entered or reentered the labor force and are now seeking employment.

The unemployment rate is measured each month by the U.S. Department of Labor. It does so by contacting a random sample of more than 50,000 households in many locations throughout the country. Trained interviewers ask a variety of questions to determine how many (if any) members of the household are either working or have a job but did not work at it because of sickness, vacation, strike, or personal reasons (employed); or whether they have no job but are available for work and actively seeking a job (unemployed). The unemployment rate fluctuates with the business cycle, reflecting recessions and recoveries (see Figure 16.2). Generally, unemployment lags behind GDP growth, going down only after the recovery has begun. Following years of economic growth in the 1990s, the nation's unemployment rate fell to near record lows, below 5 percent. But the economic recession beginning in 2008 pushed unemployment above 10 percent again (see Figure 16.2).

Inflation   Inflation erodes the value of the dollar because higher prices mean that the same dollars can now purchase fewer goods and services. Thus inflation erodes the value of savings, reduces the incentive to save, and hurts people who

FIGURE 16.2

Unemployment and
Inflation in America

**The nation suffered higher
unemployment rates during
the relatively mild recessions
of 1975 and 1982. But
unemployment rose to over
10 percent in 2009, the worst
job market in many decades.**

Source: Data from Bureau of Labor
Statistics, 2010. www.bls.gov.

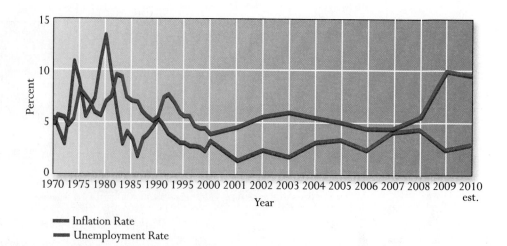

■■■ Inflation Rate
■■■ Unemployment Rate

are living on fixed incomes. When banks and investors anticipate inflation, they
raise interest rates on loans in order to cover the anticipated lower value of repayment dollars. Higher interest rates, in turn, make it more difficult for new or
expanding businesses to borrow money, for home buyers to acquire mortgages,
and for consumers to make purchases on credit. Thus inflation and high interest
rates slow economic growth.

Recession   Economists define a recession as two or more quarters of negative
economic growth, that is, declines in the gross domestic product. (In politics, a
recession is often proclaimed when the economy only slows its growth rate or
when unemployment rises.) Recessions also entail a rise in unemployment and
declines in consumer spending and capital investment. In some recessions, prices
decline as well—"deflation." During the Great Depression of the 1930s the
GDP fell by over 33 percent and the unemployment rate spiraled upward to a
peak of 25 percent. The unemployment rate remained above 10 percent for nearly
10 years, from 1930 to 1940.

Government Spending, Deficits, and Debt

▶ 16.4 *Determine the relationships between government spending, deficits, and the
national debt.*

The expenditures of all governments in the United States—federal, state, and
local governments combined—today amount to over 35 percent of GDP. The
federal government itself spends more than $3.8 trillion each year—about
25 percent of GDP.

"Mandatory" Spending   Much of the growth of federal government
spending over the years is attributed to **mandatory spending** items in the federal
budget. These "uncontrollables" are budget items committed to by past policies
of Congress that are not easily changed in annual budget making. Sources of
mandatory spending include the following:

mandatory spending
Spending for program
commitments made by past
congresses.

entitlement programs
Social welfare programs that
provide classes of people with
legally enforceable rights to
benefits.

• *Entitlement programs:* Federal programs that provide classes of people with a
  legally enforceable right to benefits are called **entitlement programs**. Entitlement programs account for more than half of all federal spending, including
  Social Security, Medicare and Medicaid, food stamps, federal employees'
  retirement pensions, and veterans' benefits (see Figure 16.3). These entitlements
  are benefits that past Congresses have pledged the federal government to pay.

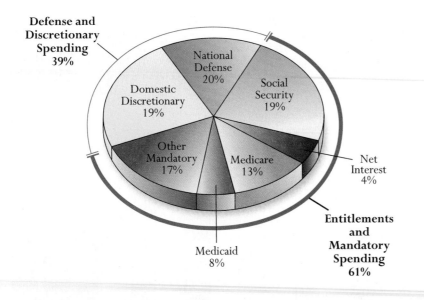

Defense and Discretionary Spending 39%

Domestic Discretionary 19%

National Defense 20%

Social Security 19%

Other Mandatory 17%

Medicare 13%

Net Interest 4%

Medicaid 8%

Entitlements and Mandatory Spending 61%

FIGURE 16.3

Who Gets What?: Federal Budget Shares

Mandatory spending—spending commitments in existing laws, notably Social Security, Medicare, Medicaid, and other entitlements, plus interest on the national debt—accounts for over 60 percent of the federal budget. Discretionary spending, including defense, accounts for only about 40 percent of the budget.

Source: Budget of the United States Government, 2010.

Entitlements are not really uncontrollable. Congress can always amend the basic laws that established them, but doing so is politically difficult and might be regarded as abandonment of a public trust. As more people become "entitled" to government benefits—for example, as more people reach retirement ages and claim Social Security benefits, federal spending increases.

- *Indexing of benefits:* Another reason that spending increases each year is that Congress has authorized automatic increases in benefits to match inflation. Benefits under such programs as Social Security are tied to the Consumer Price Index. This **indexing** pushes up the cost of entitlement programs each year.

- *Increasing costs of in-kind benefits:* Rises in the cost of major **in-kind (noncash) benefits**, particularly the medical costs of Medicaid and Medicare, also guarantee growth in federal spending. These in-kind benefit programs have risen faster in cost than cash benefit programs.

- *Interest on the national debt:* The federal government has a long history of deficit spending. As these annual deficits accumulate, the total national debt increases. Interest payments on the national debt rise accordingly.

"Discretionary" Spending   Washington policymakers consider spending that is not previously mandated by law to be **discretionary**. Almost 40 percent of the federal budget is officially designated as discretionary, but this includes spending for national defense. Nondefense discretionary spending is less than 20 percent of the budget. It includes everything from national parks to federal prisons, from highways to air travel.

Exploding Deficits   The Obama policy agenda calls for massive new government spending and huge federal **deficits**. For many years, federal government spending rose more or less incrementally (see Figure 16.4). But in 2009 federal spending rose by almost $1 trillion from the previous year, the largest single year-to-year increase in history. Federal spending also rose to almost 28 percent of the GDP. That same year federal revenues declined; the extra spending was financed through a $1.7 trillion deficit, the largest annual deficit in history (see Figure 16.5). The bulk of these increases in spending and deficit levels can be attributed to the nation's fiscal crisis and government efforts designed to

indexing
Tying of benefit levels in social welfare programs to the general price level.

in-kind (noncash) benefits
Benefits of a social welfare program that are not cash payments, including free medical care, subsidized housing, and food stamps.

discretionary spending
Spending for programs not previously mandated by law.

deficits
Imbalances in the annual federal budget in which spending exceeds revenues.

FIGURE 16.4

Massive Government
Spending

**Obama's budgets have called
for nearly $4 trillion in
government spending each
year ($3.8 in 2011).**

*Source: Budget of the United States
Government, 2011.*

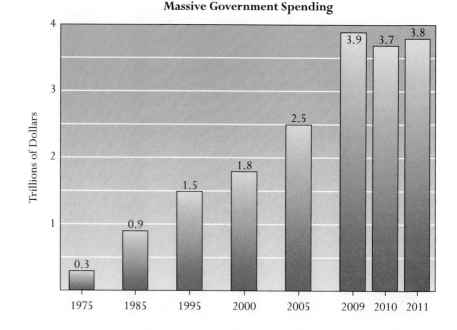

Massive Government Spending

offset recession. But high levels of deficits and federal spending are projected to continue even after 2011.

national debt
Total debt accumulated by the national government over the years.

The Debt Burden   The accumulated annual federal deficits—that is, expenditures exceeding revenues each year—add up to the nation's **national debt**. This debt in 2010 was over $10 trillion ($30,000 for every man, woman, and child in the nation). In only 4 of the last 40 years (1998–2001), has the federal government *not* incurred a deficit. Under current policies the national debt is projected to expand by over $1 trillion each year!

The national debt is owed mostly to U.S. banks and financial institutions and private citizens who buy Treasury bonds. But an increasing share of the debt is owed to foreign banks and governments, including China. As old debt comes due, the U.S. Treasury Department sells new bonds to pay off the old; that is, it continues to "roll over" or "float" the debt.

The ability to float such a huge debt depends on confidence in the U.S. government—confidence that it will continue to pay interest on its debt, that it will pay off the principle of bonds when they come due, and that the value of the bonds will not decline over time because of inflation. As long as banks, governments, and individuals are willing to buy U.S. Treasury bonds, the national debt can be financed forward.

Interest Burden for Future Generations   Interest payments on the national debt comes from current taxes. These payments divert money away from *all* other government programs. Even if the federal government manages to balance future budgets, interest payments will remain obligations of the children and grandchildren of the current generation of policymakers and taxpayers. In effect, policymakers today are shifting the burden of government to future generations.

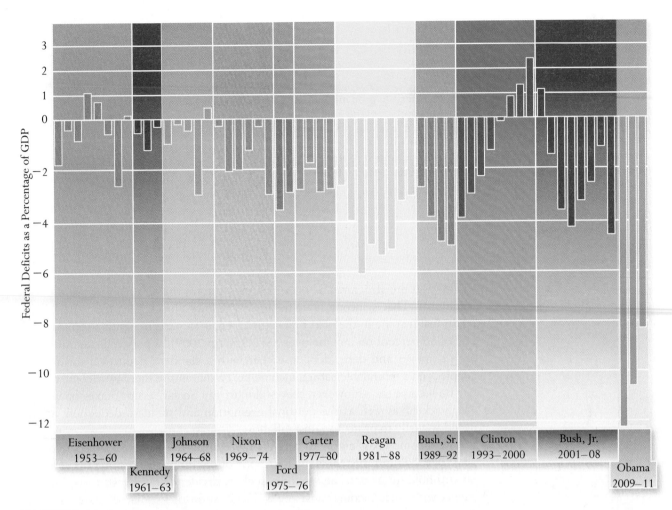

FIGURE 16.5 Federal Deficits Through the Years

This figure shows annual federal deficits as percentages of the GDP. In only 4 of the last 40 years (1998–2001) has the federal government not incurred a deficit. Deficits in the Obama administration have ballooned to levels unprecedented since World War II.

Source: Budget of the United States Government, 2011.

The Tax Burden

▶ 16.5 *Analyze the various kinds of taxes and how they distribute the tax burden.*

The tax burden in the United States is modest compared to burdens in other advanced democracies (see *Compared to What?: "Tax Burdens in Advanced Democracies"*). Federal revenues are derived mainly from (1) individual income taxes, (2) corporate income taxes, (3) Social Security payroll taxes, (4) estate and gift taxes, and (5) excise taxes and custom duties.

Individual Income Taxes   The **individual income tax** is the federal government's largest source of revenue (see Figure 16.6). Following tax cuts enacted by Congress in 2001 and 2003, individual income was taxed at six rates: 10, 15, 25, 28, 33, and 35 percent. These rates were set to expire in 2011, and rates were to revert to earlier higher levels, including a top rate of 39.6 percent.

✓ *Think*
Again

Do you believe all wage earners should pay the same percentage of income in taxes (a flat tax)?

individual income tax
Taxes on individuals' wages and other earned income, the primary source of revenue for the U.S. federal government.

FIGURE 16.6

Where the Money Comes From: Sources of Federal Income

Individual income taxes make up the largest portion of the federal government's revenues (45 percent). The government also relies heavily on the second largest source of its revenues, Social Security taxes.

Source: Budget of the United States Government, 2011.

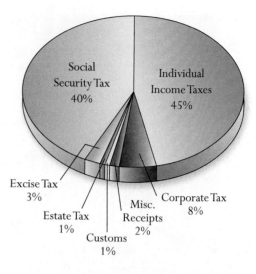

Tax rates are structured as marginal rates, a term that economists use to mean "additional." That is, income up to the top of the lowest bracket is taxed at 10 percent; additional income in the next bracket is taxed at 15 percent, up to a top marginal rate of 35 percent on income over $372,950 (in 2009). A personal exemption for each taxpayer and dependent, together with a standard deduction for married couples and a refundable earned income tax credit, ensure that low income earners pay no income tax. (However, they still must pay Social Security taxes on wages.) Tax brackets, as well as the personal exemption and standard deduction, are indexed annually to protect against inflation.

The income tax is automatically deducted from the paychecks of employees. This "withholding" system is the backbone of the individual income tax. There is no withholding of nonwage income such as dividends on investments, but taxpayers with such income must file a "Declaration of Estimated Taxes" and pay this estimate in quarterly installments. Before April 15 of each year, all income-earning Americans must report their taxable income for the previous year to the Internal Revenue Service on its 1040 Form.

Americans are usually surprised to learn that half of all personal income is not taxed. To understand why, we must know how the tax laws distinguish between *adjusted gross income* (an individual's total money income minus expenses incurred in earning that income) and *taxable income* (that part of adjusted gross income subject to taxation). Federal tax rates apply only to *taxable* income.

tax expenditures
Revenues lost to the federal government because of exemptions, exclusions, deductions, and special-treatment provisions in tax laws.

Tax expenditures are tax revenues lost to the federal government because of exemptions, exclusions, deductions, and special treatments in tax laws. Federal government revenues from individual and business income taxes would be substantially higher were it not for special provisions in tax laws that enable taxpayers to avoid paying taxes on often substantial sums of income. Although each of these "loopholes" supposedly has a larger social goal behind it (for example, the deductibility of mortgage interest is supposed to stimulate the purchase and construction of homes, keeping up the value of those assets for current homeowners and keeping the construction industry employed), critics charge that many cost far more than they are worth to society. These are the major tax expenditures in federal tax law:

• Personal exemptions for taxpayer, spouse, and children

• Deductibility of mortgage interest on homes

• Deductibility of property taxes on first and second homes

• Deferral of capital gains on home sales

COMPARED TO WHAT?

Tax Burdens in Advanced Democracies

Americans complain a lot about taxes. But from a global perspective, overall tax burdens in the United States are relatively low (see figure). Tax revenues in the United States amount to about 29 percent of the gross domestic product (GDP). U.S. taxes are well below the burdens imposed in Sweden, Denmark, and other nations with highly developed welfare systems.

Top marginal tax rates in many nations were reduced during the 1980s and 1990s. For example, the top rate in Great Britain was lowered from 60 to 40 percent, in Japan from 70 to 30 percent, and in Sweden from 80 to 55 percent. Both in the United States and abroad, the notion that excessively high tax rates discourage work, savings, and investment, as well as slow economic growth, won acceptance (although how high is "excessive" is obviously open to different interpretations). Moreover, in a global economy, with increased mobility of individuals and firms, pressures push nations to keep their top tax rates within reasonable limits. Corporations can shift their assets to low-tax jurisdictions, and high personal income tax rates can even threaten a "brain drain" of talented individuals.

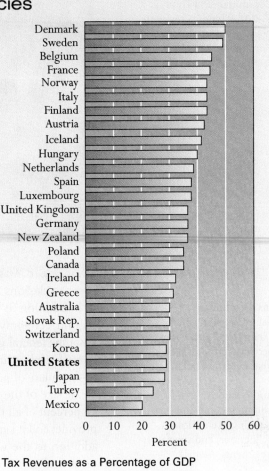

Tax Revenues as a Percentage of GDP

Source: OECD Factbook, 2009, www.oecd.org.

- Deductibility of charitable contributions
- Credit for child-care expenses
- Tax-free deposits for educational savings accounts
- Exclusion of employer contributions to pension plans and medical insurance
- Partial exclusion of Social Security benefits
- Exclusion of interest on public-purpose state and local bonds
- Deductibility of state and local income taxes
- Accelerated depreciation of machinery, equipment, and structures
- Deductible contributions to IRAs and 401(K) retirement plans, and accrued interest and profits in these plans. (But taxes must be paid when cash is taken from these plans.)

There is a continual struggle between proponents of special tax exemptions to achieve social goals and those who believe the tax laws should be simplified and social goals met by direct government expenditures. Much of the political

Debating Taxes
The ranking Republican on the House Ways and Means Committee, Bill Thomas (R-CA), attends a meeting of the House Republican Policy Committee. The Ways and Means Committee exercises jurisdiction over tax matters in the House of Representatives.

tax avoidance
Taking advantage of exemptions, exclusions, deductions, and special treatments in tax laws (legal).

tax evasion
Hiding income and/or falsely claiming exemptions, deductions, and special treatments (illegal).

infighting in Washington involves the efforts of interest groups to obtain exemptions, exclusions, deductions, and special treatments in tax laws.[3]

In addition to these multiple means of **tax avoidance** (legal means), an "underground economy" that facilitates **tax evasion** (illegal means of dodging taxes) costs the federal government many billions of dollars. The federal Internal Revenue Service itself estimates that it is losing about $300 billion per year in revenue due to the failure of people to report income and pay taxes on it. Independent estimates of the size of the underground economy are much higher, perhaps $500 billion, or 15 percent of all taxes due.[4] Many citizens receive cash for goods and services they provide, and it simply does not occur to them to report these amounts as income in addition to the wage statements they receive from their employer. Many others receive all or most of their income from cash transactions; they have a strong incentive to underreport their income. And, of course, illegal criminal transactions such as drug dealing are seldom reported on personal income tax forms. As tax rates rise, hiding income becomes more profitable.

Corporate Income Taxes

The corporate income tax provides only about 8 percent of the federal government's total revenue. The tax is set at 35 percent of net corporate income profits. However, corporations find many ways of reducing their taxable income—often to zero. The result is that many very large corporations pay little in taxes. Religious, charitable, and educational organizations, as well as labor unions, are exempt from corporate income taxes except for income they may derive from "unrelated business activity."

Who really bears the burden of the corporate income tax? Economists differ over whether the corporate income tax is "shifted" to consumers or whether corporations and their stockholders bear its burden. The evidence on the **incidence**—that is, who actually bears the burden—of this tax is inconclusive.[5]

incidence
Actual bearer of a tax burden.

Social Security Taxes

The second largest source of federal revenue is the Social Security tax. It is withheld from paychecks as the "FICA" deduction, an acronym that helps hide the true costs of Social Security and Medicare from wage earners. To keep up with the rising number of beneficiaries and the higher levels of benefits voted for by Congress, including generous automatic cost-of-living increases each year, the Social Security taxes rose to 15.3 percent.

(The Social Security tax is 12.4 percent and the Medicare tax is 2.9 percent; all wage income is subject to the Medicare tax, but wage income above a certain level, $106,800 in 2010, is not subject to the Social Security tax.)

Taxes collected under FICA are earmarked (by Social Security number) for the account of each taxpayer. Workers thus feel they are receiving benefits as a right rather than as a gift of the government. However, less than 15 percent of the benefits being paid to current recipients of Social Security can be attributed to their prior contributions. Current taxpayers are paying more than 85 percent of the benefits received by current retirees.

Today a majority of taxpayers pay more in Social Security taxes than income taxes. Indeed, combined employer and employee Social Security taxes now amount to over $15,600 for each worker at the top of the wage base. If we assume that the employer's share of the tax actually comes out of wages that would otherwise be paid to the employee, then more than 75 percent of all taxpayers pay more in Social Security taxes than in income taxes.

Estate and Gift Taxes   Taxation of property left to heirs is one of the oldest forms of taxation in the world. Federal estate taxes levy a tax rate that rises to 55 percent. Estates worth less than $3.5 million are exempt. Because taxes at death otherwise could be avoided by simply giving estates to heirs while the giver is still alive, a federal gift tax is also levied on anyone who gives gifts in excess of $13,000 annually. Gifts to spouses and charitable contributions are exempt.

Excise Taxes and Custom Duties   Federal excise taxes on the consumption of liquor, tobacco, gasoline, telephones, air travel, and other so-called luxury items, together with customs taxes on imports, provide about 4 percent of total federal revenues.

Tax Politics

▶ 16.6 *Trace changes in tax policies under different administrations in recent decades.*

The politics of taxation centers around the question of who actually bears the heaviest burden of a tax—especially which income groups must devote the largest proportion of their income to taxes. **Progressive taxation** requires high-income groups to pay a larger percentage of their incomes in taxes than low-income groups. **Regressive taxation** takes a larger share of the income of low-income groups. **Proportional (flat) taxation** requires all income groups to pay the same percentage of their income in taxes. Note that the *percentage of income* paid in taxes is the determining factor. Most taxes take more money from the rich than the poor, but a progressive or regressive tax is distinguished by the percentages of income taken from various income groups.

The Argument for Progressivity   Progressive taxation is generally defended on the principle of ability to pay; the assumption is that high-income groups can afford to pay a larger *percentage* of their incomes in taxes at no more of a sacrifice than that required of lower-income groups to devote a smaller proportion of their income to taxation. This assumption is based on what economists call *marginal utility theory* as it applies to money; each additional dollar of income is slightly less valuable to an individual than preceding dollars. For example, a $5,000 increase in the income of an individual already earning $100,000 is much less valuable than a $5,000 increase to an individual earning only $10,000 or to an individual with no income at all.

progressive taxation
System of taxation in which higher-income groups pay a larger percentage of their incomes in taxes than do lower-income groups.

regressive taxation
System of taxation in which lower-income groups pay a larger percentage of their incomes in taxes than do higher-income groups.

proportional (flat) taxation
System of taxation in which all income groups pay the same percentage of their income in taxes.

FIGURE 16.7

Top Personal Income Tax Rates, by President

The top marginal personal income tax rate fell dramatically during the Reagan administration, then began to creep upward again under Presidents Bush and Clinton. George W. Bush lowered the top rate in 2001 and again in 2003, but these tax cuts were scheduled to expire in 2011, bringing the top marginal rate back to 39.6 percent.

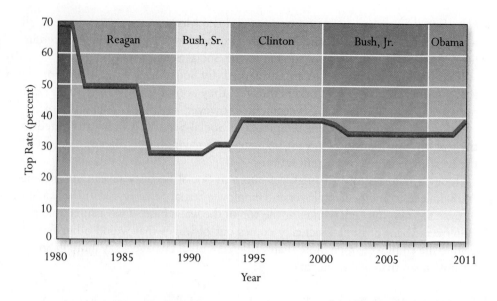

Hence, it is argued that added dollars of income can be taxed at higher rates without violating equitable principles.

The Argument for Proportionality

Opponents of progressive taxation generally assert that equity can only be achieved by taxing everyone at the same percentage of their income, regardless of the size of their income. Progressivity penalizes initiative, enterprise, and the risk taking necessary to create new products and businesses. It also reduces incentives to expand and develop the nation's economy. Highly progressive taxes curtail growth and make everyone poorer (see *A Conflicting View*: "We Should Enact a Flat Tax").

Reagan's Reductions in Progressivity

The most dramatic change in federal tax laws occurred during the Reagan years (see Figure 16.7). The top marginal tax rate fell from 70 percent when President Reagan took office to 28 percent following enactment of tax reform in 1986. The Tax Reform Act of 1986 also reduced fourteen rate brackets to only two rate brackets, 15 and 28 percent.

"Read My Lips"

At the Republican national convention in 1988, presidential nominee George H. W. Bush made a firm pledge to American voters that he would veto any tax increases passed by the Democratic-controlled Congress: "Read my lips! No new taxes." Yet in a 1990 budget summit with Democratic congressional leaders, President Bush agreed to add a top marginal rate of 31 percent to the personal income tax. Breaking his solemn pledge on taxes contributed heavily to Bush's defeat in the 1992 presidential election.

"Soak the Rich"

Proposals to "soak the rich" are always politically very popular. President Clinton pushed Congress to raise the top marginal tax rates to 39.6 percent for families earning $250,000.

Bush Tax Cuts

George W. Bush came into office vowing *not* to make the same mistake as his father, raising tax rates in an effort to compromise with the Democrats. On the contrary, Bush was strongly committed to lowering taxes. He argued that tax cuts would revive the economy. He believed that federal deficits were the result of slow economic growth; tax reductions might temporarily add to deficits,

A CONFLICTING VIEW

We Should Enact a Flat Tax

More than a hundred years ago, Supreme Court Justice Stephen J. Field, in striking down as unconstitutional a progressive income tax enacted by Congress, predicted that such a tax would lead to class wars: "Our political contests will become a war of the poor against the rich, a war constantly growing in intensity and bitterness."[a] But populist sentiment in the early twentieth century—the anger of Midwestern farmers toward Eastern rail tycoons and the beliefs of impoverished Southerners that they would never have incomes high enough to pay an income tax—helped secure the passage of the 16th Amendment to the U.S. Constitution. The federal income tax passed by Congress in 1914 had a top rate of 7 percent; less than 1 percent of the population had incomes high enough to be taxed. Today the top rate is 35 percent (actually over 42 percent when mandated phaseouts of deductions are calculated); about half of the population pays income taxes.

The current income tax progressively penalizes all the behaviors that produce higher incomes—work, savings, investment, and initiative. And whenever incomes are taxed at different rates, people will figure out ways to take advantage of the differential. They will hire lawyers, accountants, and lobbyists to find or create exemptions, exclusions, deductions, and preferential treatments for their own sources of income. The tax laws will become increasingly lengthy and complex. Today about half of all personal income is excluded from federal income taxation.

The Internal Revenue Service (IRS) is the most intrusive of all government agencies, overseeing the finances of every tax-paying citizen and corporation in America. It maintains personal records on more than 100 million Americans and requires them to submit more than a billion forms each year. It may levy fines and penalties and collect taxes on its own initiative; in disputes with the IRS, the burden of proof falls on the taxpayer, not the agency. Its 110,000 employees spend $8 billion per year reviewing tax returns, investigating taxpayers, and collecting revenue. Americans pay an additional $30 billion for the services of tax accountants and preparers, and they waste some $200 billion in hours of record keeping and computing their taxes.

We should replace the current federal income tax system with a simple flat tax that could be calculated on a postcard. The elimination of all exemptions, exclusions, deductions, and special treatments, and the replacement of current progressive tax rates with a flat 19 percent tax on all forms of income, even excluding family incomes under $25,000, would produce just as much revenue as the current complicated system. It would sweep away the nation's army of tax accountants and lawyers and lobbyists and increase national productivity by relieving taxpayers of millions of hours of record keeping and tax preparation. A flat tax could be filed on a postcard form (see below). Removing progressive rates would create incentives to work, save, and invest in America. It would lead to more rapid economic growth and improve efficiency by directing investments to their most productive uses rather than to tax avoidance. It would eliminate current incentives to underreport income, overstate exemptions, and avoid and evade taxation. Finally, by exempting a generous personal and family allowance, the flat tax would be made fair.

Form 1	Individual Wage Tax	2000
Your first name and initial (if joint return, also give spouse's name and initial) Last name		Your social security number
Home address (number and street including apartment number or rural route)		Spouse's social security number
City, town, or post office, state, and ZIP code		Your occupation
		Spouse's occupation

1 Wages and salary	1	
2 Pension and retirement benefits	2	
3 Total compensation (*line 1 plus line 2*)	3	
4 Personal allowance		
(a) 0–$16,500 for married filing jointly	4a	
(b) 0–$9,500 for single	4b	
(c) 0–$14,000 for single head of household	4c	
5 Number of dependents, not including spouse	5	
6 Personal allowances for dependents (*line 5 multiplied by $4,500*)	6	
7 Total personal allowances (*line 4 plus line 6*)	7	
8 Taxable compensation (*line 3 less line 7, if positive; otherwise zero*)	8	
9 Tax (*19% of line 8*)	9	
10 Tax withheld by employer	10	
11 Tax due (*line 9 less line 10, if positive*)	11	
12 Refund due (*line 10 less line 9, if positive*)	12	

[a]*Pollock v. Farmer's Loan*, 158 U.S. 601 (1895).

but eventually the economic growth inspired by lower taxes would increase government revenues and eliminate deficits.[6]

Bush moved the Republican-controlled Congress to lower the top marginal rate to 35 percent, and restructure rates through six brackets—10, 15, 25, 28, 33,

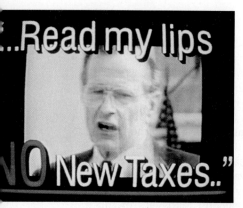

Broken Promise

George Bush's pledge "Read my lips, no new taxes" helped him to victory in 1988. But breaking the pledge in 1990 contributed heavily to his defeat in 1992.

and 35 percent (see Table 16.1). And the Bush 2003 tax package also contained a variety of new credits and special treatments:

Dividends: Corporate stock dividends are to be taxed at a low 15 percent rather than at the same rate as earned income. Bush and the Republicans in Congress initially proposed eliminating all taxes on dividends. They argued that corporations already paid taxes on corporate profits, and inasmuch as dividends come out of profits, taxing them as personal income amounted to "double taxation." They also recognized that nearly one-half of all American families now own stock or mutual funds, and they hoped that this new tax break would be politically popular. The 15 percent tax rate on dividends is less than half of the top marginal rate of 35 percent on earned income.

Marriage penalty: For married couples the new law made the standard personal deduction twice that of a single person. This change corrected a flaw in the tax law that had long plagued married persons filing joint returns.

Child tax credit: The per child tax credit was raised to $1,000 (from $600). This was a politically popular change supported by many Democrats as well as Republicans.

Capital gains: Finally, the Bush tax package chipped away again at the tax on capital gains—profits from the sale of investments held at least 1 year. The capital gains tax was reduced from 20 to 15 percent, a rate less than half of the top marginal rate on earned income of 35 percent.

The Bush tax cuts were scheduled to expire in 2011. Democrats in Congress have expressed their opposition to these cuts, arguing that they primarily benefited the rich. Republicans countered that allowing these cuts to expire is actually a tax increase, and a tax increase will slow economic growth and threaten continuing recession.

Redistributing Income

Barack Obama campaigned on a promise to lower taxes on the middle class, which he defined as 95 percent of taxpayers. He also pledged to raise taxes on upper-income Americans, which he defined as families earning $250,000 a year or more. This combination of changes in taxation would make the Tax Code more progressive, in effect redistributing income among Americans.

Tax "Cuts"

President Obama's economic stimulus package, officially the American Recovery and Reinvestment Act of 2009, included a version of his campaign promise of a middle-class tax cut. The tax cuts in the package, labeled "Making Work Pay," were actually payments of $400 to individuals with incomes under $75,000, and payments of $800 to couples with incomes under $150,000. These payments were made to anyone who paid Social Security taxes. It was not necessary

TABLE 16.1 Progressive Taxation: Marginal Individual Income Tax Rates, by Income Bracket

President George W. Bush succeeded in getting a Republican-controlled Congress to reduce the tax rate in 2001 and 2003, but these reductions were scheduled to expire in 2011.

	Before 2001	2001–2003	2003–2010	2011
Lowest	15%	10%	10%	15%
to	28	15	15	28
Highest	31	27	25	31
Income	36	30	28	36
Brackets	39.6	35	33	39.6
		38.6	35	

POLITICS UP CLOSE

Who Pays the Income Tax?

The federal income tax is highly progressive. Progressive rates, together with the personal and standard deductions for families and the earned income tax credit for low-income earners, combined to remove most of the income tax burden on middle- and low-income Americans. Indeed, the lower half of the nation's taxpayers pay less than 4 percent of total income taxes paid to the federal government (see figure).

The top 50 percent of income earners pay virtually all of the nation's personal income tax. Indeed, the top 10 percent of income earners pay about 68 percent of all of the income taxes collected by the federal government, and the top 1 percent pay over a third of all income taxes.

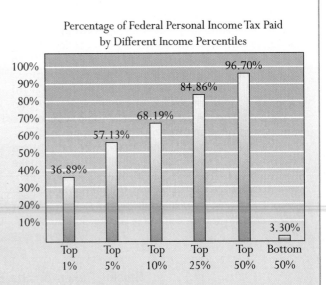

Percentage of Federal Personal Income Tax Paid by Different Income Percentiles

Top 1%: 36.89%
Top 5%: 57.13%
Top 10%: 68.19%
Top 25%: 84.86%
Top 50%: 96.70%
Bottom 50%: 3.30%

Source: Joint Economic Committee, U.S. Congress, April 2007.

to have paid any income taxes in order to receive these tax cuts. Critics labeled these payments "welfare checks."

The stimulus package was initially presented to Congress as an emergency measure requiring quick passage in order to deal with a deepening recession. But President Obama had recommended many of its provisions to Congress as permanent measures in his very first budget message. Making Work Pay tax payments were repackaged as "the first stage" of Obama's middle-class tax cut promise, made during his presidential campaign. These payments are designed to partly offset the Social Security payroll tax (FICA).

Tax Relief or Redistribution?
Obama won tax relief for the "middle class" by making tax payments to couples with incomes under $150,000. But he pushed to raise the top marginal tax rate from 35% to 39.6% for couples with incomes over $250,000.

A CONSTITUTIONAL NOTE

The Constitution and Private Property

The protection of private property was one of the principal motives in convening the Constitutional Convention of 1787. Among the powers set forth in Article I, Section 8, are the "power to lay and collect taxes, duties, imposts, and excises"; "to borrow money"; "to regulate commerce with foreign nations and among the several states and with the Indian Tribes"; "to establish . . . uniform rules of bankruptcy"; "to coin money, regulate the value thereof"; "to provide for the punishment of counterfeiting." And among the powers specifically denied to the states in Section 10 are the powers to "coin money; emit Bills of Credit; make any Thing but Gold and Silver Coin a Tender in Payment of Debts; pass any . . . Law impairing the Obligation of Contracts. . . ." In addition, the Constitution of 1787 created what we call today a *common market* or

free trade area among the states: "No state shall . . . lay any Imports or Duties on Imports or Exports. . . ." This prevents states taxing goods or services moving across state lines or from taxing foreign commerce. In short, the Constitution places power over the economy in the hands of the national government and prevents the states from interfering with commerce. However, for well over a century the Supreme Court interpreted the Interstate Commerce Clause narrowly to include only the regulation of goods and services that actually moved across state lines. It was not until 1937 that the Court, in the important case of *National Labor Relations Board v. Jones and Loughlin Steel Co.*, extended the commerce power to include production and manufacturing that occurred *within* a state but nonetheless affected interstate commerce.

Raising Taxes on the Rich. Republicans argued that allowing the Bush tax cuts to expire in 2011 amounts to a tax increase. But Democrats and President Obama argued that the expiration of these cuts would simply return taxes to their previous levels—raising the top marginal tax rate from 35 to 39.6 percent. President Obama also recommended a phaseout of deductions, including charitable contributions and mortgage payments, for families making over $250,000. Congress appeared less enthusiastic about the phaseout of these deductions.

Income Redistribution. The combination of these changes in the Tax Code—tax payments to lower- and middle-income families and an increase in the top marginal tax rate—has the effect of redistributing after-tax income among Americans. Critics charge that redistribution income is socialism, which penalizes work, initiative, and talent. Americans generally believe in tax progressivity—higher-income people can afford to be taxed at larger percentages of their added incomes than lower-income people. But deliberate attempts by government to use the Tax Code to equalize income represents a new direction in tax policy.

Summary

▶ **16.1** *Relate politics and economics as systems.*

The similarity of the definition of *economics* ("deciding what shall be produced, how and for whom") and *politics* ("deciding who gets what, when and how") reflects the fact that both systems provide society with a means for deciding about the production and distribution of goods and services.

▶ **16.2** *Outline the role that fiscal and monetary policy play in economic decision making.*

Fiscal policy—decisions about government taxing, spending, and deficits or surpluses—is decided in the president's budget

recommendations and in the appropriations acts passed by Congress. Monetary policy is largely decided by the independent Federal Reserve Board.

▶ **16.3** *Identify the different ways of assessing the strength of the economy.*

The performance of the economy can be measured by GDP growth and the unemployment and inflation rates. Politically the unemployment rate may be the most important of these measures of economic performance.

▶ 16.4 *Determine the relationships between government spending, deficits, and the national debt.*

Annual federal budget deficits over the years have led to a national debt of more than $10 trillion, an amount equal to $30,000 for every person in the country. Deficits in the Obama administration are projected to add $1 trillion more to the national debt each year for the foreseeable future.

▶ 16.5 *Analyze the various kinds of taxes and how they distribute the tax burden.*

Tax politics centers on the question of who actually bears the burden of a tax. The individual income tax, the largest source of federal government revenue, is progressive, with higher rates levied at higher-income levels. Progressive taxation is defended on the ability-to-pay principle. But half of all personal income, and a great deal of corporate income, is untaxed, owing to a wide variety of exemptions, exclusions, deductions, and special treatments on tax laws. These provisions are defended in Washington by a powerful array of interest groups.

▶ 16.6 *Trace changes in tax policies under different administrations in recent decades.*

The Reagan administration reduced top-income tax rates from 70 to 28 percent, believing high rates discouraged work, savings, and investment, and thereby curtailed economic growth. But George H. W. Bush agreed to an increase in the top rate to 31 percent. Bill Clinton pushed Congress to raise the top rates to 39.6 percent. George W. Bush succeeded in getting two tax cut bills through Congress in 2001 and 2003. The bills lowered the top marginal income tax rate to 35 percent and lowered the capital gain rate to 15 percent.

Barack Obama pledged not to raise taxes on families earning less than $250,000. In his stimulus package he granted tax rebates of $800 to low- and middle-income families. But the expiration of the Bush tax cuts in 2011 raises the top marginal rate again to 39.6 percent. The combination of tax rebates for low- and middle-income earners and tax increases for high-income earners makes the Tax Code even more progressive—in effect, redistributing income.

Chapter Test

▶ 16.1 *Relate politics and economics as systems.*

1. It would be accurate to say that the political system involves _____ decision making and that the economic system involves _____ decision making.
   a. individual; individual
   b. collective; collective
   c. collective; individual
   d. individual; collective

2. The study of the proper relationship between markets and governments is the study of
   a. political theory
   b. formal economic theory
   c. political economy
   d. public administration

3. The federal government's response to the financial crisis that began in 2008 included
   a. Wall Street bailout
   b. TARP
   c. stimulus package
   d. all of the above

▶ 16.2 *Outline the role that fiscal and monetary policy play in economic decision making.*

4. Decisions about taxing, spending, and borrowing at the national level are known as
   a. fiscal policy
   b. Keynesian policy
   c. monetary policy
   d. reserve policy

5. The principal responsibility for monetary policy rests with
   a. the Federal Reserve Board
   b. the president and Congress
   c. Wall Street bankers and the private sector
   d. the Treasury Department

6. The Federal Reserve would probably react to a decline in the general level of prices—not just the prices of some select products—by _____ interest rates.
   a. raising
   b. lowering
   c. maintaining
   d. eliminating

▶ 16.3 *Identify the different ways of assessing the strength of the economy.*

7. Measures of the performance of the nation's economy include
   a. unemployment rate
   b. gross national product
   c. inflation rate
   d. all of the above

8. From a political point of view, the most important measurement of a nation's economy might well be
   a. per-capita income
   b. unemployment rates
   c. interest rates
   d. national debt growth rates

9. In recent presidential elections, when a majority of people say the economy has gotten worse
   a. the incumbent party's candidate lost
   b. the Republican candidate lost
   c. the incumbent party's candidate won
   d. the Democratic candidate won

10. A general decline in prices is referred to as
    a. inflation
    b. recession
    c. deflation
    d. an economic cycle

▶ **16.4** *Determine the relationships between government spending, deficits, and the national debt.*

11. Spending for program commitments made by previous Congresses is
    a. discretionary spending
    b. mandatory spending
    c. entitlement spending
    d. guaranteed spending

12. So much of the U.S. budget is mandated for entitlements that total discretionary funding accounts for approximately _____ percent of the budget.
    a. 20
    b. 30
    c. 40
    d. 50

▶ **16.5** *Analyze the various kinds of taxes and how they distribute the tax burden.*

13. The federal government's largest source of funds is from
    a. the sale of U.S. bonds
    b. corporate taxes
    c. Social Security taxes
    d. individual income taxes

14. Revenues are lost to the federal government because of _____ in the tax laws.
    a. exemptions
    b. deductions
    c. special treatments
    d. all of the above

15. More people pay this tax than any other federal tax
    a. estate tax
    b. Social Security tax
    c. individual income tax
    d. excise tax

▶ **16.6** *Trace changes in tax policies under different administrations in recent decades.*

16. The federal income tax is a
    a. progressive tax
    b. proportional tax
    c. flat tax
    d. regressive tax

17. A tax that takes a smaller share of the income of high-income tax payers is a
    a. progressive tax
    b. proportional tax
    c. flat tax
    d. regressive tax

---

mypⒶliscilab EXERCISES

Apply what you learned in this chapter on MyPoliSciLab.

☐—Read on **mypoliscilab.com**

   eText: Chapter 16

✓—Study and Review on **mypoliscilab.com**

   Pre-Test

   Post-Test

   Chapter Exam

   Flashcards

◉—Watch on **mypoliscilab.com**

   Video: Economic Policy Debate at the G20

   Video: Fed Approves Mortgage Crackdown

   Video: Recession Hits Indiana

   Video: The Stimulus Breakdown

✳—Explore on **mypoliscilab.com**

   Simulation: Making Economic Policy

   Simulation: You Are the President and Need to Get a Tax Cut Passed

   Comparative: Comparing Economic Policy

   Timeline: Growth of the Budget and Federal Spending

   Visual Literacy: Evaluating Federal Spending and Economic Policy

   Visual Literacy: Where the Money Goes

Key Terms

fiscal policy 586	inflation 589	economic cycles 590	indexing 593
monetary policy 586	recession 589	unemployment rate 590	in-kind (noncash) benefits 593
Federal Reserve Board (the Fed) 589	gross domestic product (GDP) 589	mandatory spending 592	
		entitlement programs 592	discretionary spending 593

Suggested Readings

Balaam, David N., and Michael Veseth. *Introduction to International Political Economy.* 4th ed. New York: Longman, 2008. Comprehensive intro to global politics and economics.

Green, Mark, and Michele Jolin, eds. *Change for America.* New York: Basic Books, 2009. A comprehensive policy agenda— "progressive blueprint"—for the Obama administration.

Jacobs, Laurence R., and Theda S. Skocpol, eds. *Inequality and American Democracy.* New York: Russell Sage Foundation, 2005. A series of essays describing increasing inequality in America and its political and social consequences.

Rothgeb, John M., Jr. *U.S. Trade Policy.* Washington, D.C.: CQ Press, 2001. Concise text on international trade, including history of GATT, WTO, and NAFTA.

Sowell, Thomas. *Basic Economics: A Citizen's Guide to the Economy.* New York: Basic Books, 2003. Introduction to economics with an emphasis on public policy. No jargon or equations.

Steger, Manfred B. *Globalism.* Boston: Rowman & Littlefield, 2002. The politics of pro- and anti-globalist groups, with a sharp critique of the ideology of globalism.

Wolff, Edward N. *Top Heavy* (updated edition). New York: Century Foundation, 2002. The study of the increasing inequality of wealth in United States and an argument for taxing financial wealth (bank accounts, stocks, bonds, property, houses, cars, and so on) as well as income.

Suggested Web Sites

Bureau of Economic Analysis www.bea.gov
Source of official economic statistics, listed A–Z.

Bureau of Labor Statistics www.bls.gov
The U.S. Department of Labor's Bureau of Labor Statistics site contains monthly information about the nation's employment rate plus a wealth of supporting data.

Center on Budget and Policy Priorities www.cbpp.org
Data on budget items, projected costs of federal programs, and so on.

Concord Coalition www.concordcoalition.org
Nonpartisan advocacy organization promoting fiscal responsibility and balanced federal budget.

Council of Economic Advisors (CEA)
www.whitehouse.gov/cea
Official CEA site, with latest Economic Report of the President and timely economic indicators.

Federal Reserve System www.federalreserve.gov
Official site of the Fed, with data on money supply, interest rates, and banking regulation.

Internal Revenue Service (IRS) www.irs.gov
Official IRS site, with downloadable tax forms, information on tax laws, and tax statistics.

National Taxpayers Union www.ntu.org
Advocacy organization for taxpayers "to keep what they have earned," with policy papers and data on tax burdens.

Tax Foundation Advocacy www.taxfoundation.org
Organization devoted to making the public "tax conscious," with information, "fiscal facts," and "tax freedom day."

World Trade Organization (WTO) www.wto.org
Official WTO site, with trade agreements, including General Agreement on Tariffs and Trade (GATT).

Chapter Test Answer Key

1. B	5. C	9. D	13. B	17. A	21. C
2. D	6. D	10. C	14. E	18. C	22. D
3. B	7. C	11. D	15. A	19. D	23. A
4. A	8. B	12. D	16. B	20. A	24. D

17 POLITICS AND SOCIAL WELFARE

❝ When I was young poverty was so common that we didn't know it had a name. ❞

Lyndon B. Johnson

Chapter Outline and Learning Objectives

Power and Social Welfare

▶ 17.1 *Assess the importance of social welfare policy.*

Poverty in the United States

▶ 17.2 *Characterize the extent of poverty in the United States and identify correlates.*

Social Welfare Policy

▶ 17.3 *Outline major social welfare programs in the United States.*

Senior Power

▶ 17.4 *Explain reasons for and consequences of the political strength of older Americans.*

Politics and Welfare Reform

▶ 17.5 *Analyze the role of politics in welfare reform.*

Health Care in America

▶ 17.6 *Compare and contrast the United States and other nations on health care expenditures and measures of health care.*

Health Care Transformation

▶ 17.7 *Assess the role of politics in the efforts to bring about health care reform.*

Think about Politics

1. Do you think government welfare programs perpetuate poverty?
   YES ⬭ NO ⬭

2. Should all retirees receive Social Security benefits regardless of their personal wealth or income?
   YES ⬭ NO ⬭

3. Do you believe the Social Security system will still be solvent when you retire?
   YES ⬭ NO ⬭

4. Should individuals be allowed to invest part of their Social Security taxes in private investments (stocks or bonds)?
   YES ⬭ NO ⬭

5. Should the government pay for nursing home care without forcing beneficiaries to use up all their savings and income?
   YES ⬭ NO ⬭

6. Should the states rather than the federal government decide about welfare policy?
   YES ⬭ NO ⬭

7. Should there be a time limit on how long a person can receive welfare payments?
   YES ⬭ NO ⬭

8. Should government provide health care insurance for all Americans?
   YES ⬭ NO ⬭

Through its social welfare policies, the federal government has the power to redistribute income among people. But most government payments to individuals do not go to poor people but rather to senior citizens whose voting power heavily influences elected officials.

Power and Social Welfare

▶ 17.1 *Assess the importance of social welfare policy.*

Social welfare policy largely determines who gets what from government—who benefits from government spending on its citizens and how much they get. This vast power has made the federal government a major *redistributor* of income from one group to another—from the working population to retirees, from the employed to the unemployed, from taxpayers to poor people. Direct payments to individuals—Social Security, welfare, pension, and other **transfer payments**—now account for about 60 percent of all federal government outlays.

When most Americans think of social welfare programs, they think of poor people. An estimated 35 million to 40 million people in the United States (11 to 15 percent of the population, or roughly one in eight Americans) have incomes below the official **poverty line**—that is, their annual cash income falls below what is required to maintain a decent standard of living (see Figure 17.1).

But poor people are *not* the principal beneficiaries of social welfare spending. Most social welfare spending, including the largest programs—Social Security and Medicare—goes to the *non*-poor (see Figure 17.2). Less than one-third of federal social welfare spending is **means-tested spending**—that is, distributed on the basis of the recipient's income. The middle classes, not the poor, are the major beneficiaries of the nation's social welfare system.

Poverty in the United States

▶ 17.2 *Characterize the extent of poverty in the United States and identify correlates.*

How much poverty really exists in the United States? It depends on how you define the term "poverty." The official definition used by the federal government focuses on the cash income needed to maintain a "decent standard of living." The official poverty line is only a little more than

FIGURE 17.1

America's Poor: The
Rate and Number

**Roughly one in eight
Americans lives below the
official poverty level. Poverty
rises during recessions.**

Source: www.census.gov/hhes/
poverty00/pov00.html.

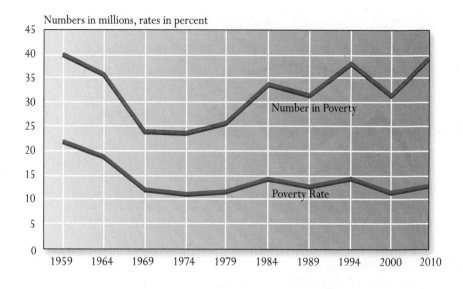

Numbers in millions, rates in percent

(Chart showing "Number in Poverty" and "Poverty Rate" from 1959 to 2010)

---

transfer payments
Direct payments (either in cash
or in goods and/or services) by
governments to individuals as
part of a social welfare program,
not as a result of any service or
contribution rendered by the
individual.

poverty line
Official standard regarding
what level of annual cash
income is sufficient to maintain
a "decent standard of living";
those with incomes below this
level are eligible for most
public assistance programs.

means-tested spending
Spending for benefits that is
distributed on the basis of the
recipient's income.

underclass
People who have remained
poor and dependent on
welfare over a prolonged
period of time.

one-third of the median income of all American families. It takes into account the effects of inflation, rising each year with the rate of inflation.

Temporary Poverty   Poor people are often envisioned as a permanent "underclass" living most of their lives in poverty. But most poverty is not long term. Tracing poor families over time presents a different picture of the nature of poverty from the "snapshot" view taken in any 1 year. For example, over the last decade 11 to 15 percent of the nation's population has been officially classified as poor in any 1 year. However, only *some* poverty is persistent: about 6 to 8 percent of the population remains in poverty for more than 5 years. Thus about half of the people who are counted as poor are experiencing poverty for only a short period of time. For these temporary poor, welfare is a "safety net" that helps them through hard times.

Persistent Poverty   But about half of the people on welfare rolls at any one time are *persistently poor*, that is, likely to remain on welfare for 5 or more years. For these people, welfare is a more permanent part of their lives.

Because they place a disproportionate burden on welfare resources, persistently poor people pose serious questions for social scientists and policymakers. Prolonged poverty and welfare dependency create an **underclass** that suffers from many social ills—teen pregnancy, family instability, drugs, crime, alienation, apathy, and irresponsibility.[1] Government educational, training, and jobs programs, as well as many other social service efforts, fail to benefit many of these people.

Family Structure   Poverty and welfare dependency are much more frequent among female-headed households with no husband present than among husband–wife households (see *Politics Up Close:* "Who Are the Poor?"). Traditionally, "illegitimacy" was held in check by powerful religious and social structures. But these structures weakened over time and the availability of welfare cash benefits, food stamps, medical care, and government housing removed much of the economic hardship once associated with unwed motherhood. Indeed, it was sometimes argued that government welfare programs, however well meaning, ended up perpetuating poverty and social dependency. This argument inspired welfare reform in 1996 (see "Politics and Welfare Reform" later in this chapter).

POLITICS UP CLOSE

Who Are the Poor?

Poverty occurs in many kinds of families and in all races and ethnic groups. However, some groups experience poverty (low income) in greater proportions than the national average (see figure).

Poverty is most common among families headed by women. The incidence of poverty among these families is five times greater than that for married couples. These women and their children constitute over two-thirds of all of the persons living in poverty in the United States. About one of every five children in the United States lives in poverty. These figures describe what has been labeled the "feminization of poverty" in the United States. Clearly, poverty is closely related to family structure. The disintegration of the traditional husband–wife family is the single most influential factor contributing to poverty today.

Blacks also experience poverty in much greater proportions than whites. Over the years, the poverty rate among blacks in the United States has been almost three times higher than the poverty rate among whites. Poverty among Hispanics is also significantly greater than among whites.

In contrast, elderly people in America experience less poverty than the nonaged. The aged are not poor, despite the popularity of the phrase "the poor and the aged." The percentage of persons over 65 years of age

Percentage Living Below the Poverty Level

Total population	13.2%
Husband–wife families	5.5%
Families w/female heads	28.7%
Whites (Non-Hispanic)	8.6%
African Americans	24.7%
Hispanics	23.2%
Over age 65	9.7%
Under age 18	19.0%

with low incomes is *below* the national average. Moreover, elderly people are much wealthier in terms of assets and have fewer expenses than the nonaged. They are more likely than younger people to own homes with paid-up mortgages. Medicare pays a large portion of their medical expenses. With fewer expenses, elderly people, even with relatively smaller cash incomes, experience poverty differently from the way a young mother with children experiences it. Continuing increases in Social Security benefits over the years are largely responsible for this singular "victory" in the war against poverty.

Source: U.S. Bureau of the Census, 2009.

The "Truly Disadvantaged"   The nation's largest cities have become the principal location of many of the social problems confronting our society—poverty, homelessness, racial tension, drug abuse, delinquency, and crime. These problems are all made worse by their concentration in large cities.

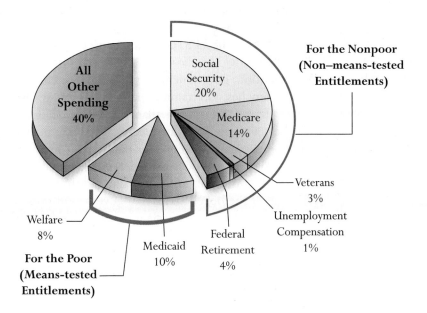

FIGURE 17.2

Who's Entitled?

Social welfare entitlement programs take up over 60 percent of the federal government's budget. But most of these payments go to the nonpoor.

Source: Budget of the United States Government, 2010.

Homeless in America
Some "street people" are unable to benefit from social welfare programs due to alcoholism, drug abuse, mental illness, or other disabilities that cause them to fall through the social welfare safety net.

Why has the inner city become the locus of social problems? Some observers argue that changes in the labor market from industrial goods–producing jobs to professional, financial, and technical service–producing jobs have increasingly divided the labor market into low-wage and high-wage sectors.[2] The decline in manufacturing jobs, together with a shift in remaining manufacturing jobs and commercial (sales) jobs to the suburbs, has left inner-city residents with fewer and lower paying job opportunities. The rise in joblessness in the inner cities has in turn increased the concentration of poor people, added to the number of poor single-parent families, and increased welfare dependency.

Social Welfare Policy

▶ **17.3** *Outline major social welfare programs in the United States.*

Public welfare has been a recognized responsibility of government in English-speaking countries for many centuries. As far back as the Poor Relief Act of 1601, the English Parliament provided workhouses for the "able-bodied poor" (the unemployed) and poorhouses for widows and orphans, elderly and handicapped people.[3] Today, nearly one-third of the U.S. population receives some form of government benefits: Social Security, Medicare or Medicaid, disability insurance, unemployment compensation, government employee retirement, veterans' benefits, food stamps, school lunches, job training, public housing, or cash public assistance payments (see Table 17.1). More than half of all families in the United States include at least one person who receives a government check. Thus the "welfare state" now encompasses a very large part of our society.

social insurance programs
Social welfare programs to which beneficiaries have made contributions so that they are entitled to benefits regardless of their personal wealth.

public assistance programs
Those social welfare programs for which no contributions are required and only those defined as low-income are eligible; includes food stamps, Medicaid, and Family Assistance.

The major social welfare programs can be classified as either **social insurance** or **public assistance**. This distinction is an important one that has on occasion become a major political issue. If the beneficiaries of a government program are required to have made contributions to it before claiming any of its benefits, and if they are entitled to the benefits regardless of their personal wealth—as in Social Security and Medicare—then the program is said to be financed on the social insurance principle. If the program is financed out of general tax revenues and if recipients are required to show that they are poor before claiming its benefits—as

COMPARED TO WHAT?

World Opinion About Obama's International Policies

World opinion generally approves of President Barack Obama's international policy statements. His pledge to make U.S. policies more multilateral—that is, to take into consideration the opinions and interests of other countries in making foreign-policy decisions—is especially popular.

Closing the military prison at Guantánamo and withdrawing U.S. troops from Iraq wins majority support in almost all countries, including the Muslim countries. Only in the United States is opinion closely divided on the closing of Guantánamo's prison.

But sending more troops to Afghanistan does *not* enjoy global support. Majorities in most countries oppose added troop deployments. This opposition includes the publics of several NATO countries that have contributed forces to the effort in Afghanistan, including Britain, Germany, and Canada. Opinion in Muslim countries is decidedly opposed to adding U.S. troops in Afghanistan. Only in Israel does this decision win majority support.

	Obama will be multilateral Yes	Closing Guantánamo Approve	More troops to Afghanistan Approve
United States	85%	45%	54%
Canada	65	70	42
Britain	60	72	41
France	60	82	37
Germany	69	84	32
Spain	47	82	41
Poland	47	57	28
Russia	43	48	13
Turkey	22	51	16
Egypt	31	66	19
Jordan	20	73	11
Lebanon	24	91	20
Palestine	31	93	12
Israel	56	50	54
China	46	68	17
India	66	38	38
Indonesia	62	66	20
Japan	43	61	28
Pakistan	17	33	16
S. Korea	49	63	28
Argentina	41	61	12
Brazil	74	60	27
Mexico	47	45	22
Kenya	77	64	53
Nigeria	66	67	49

Source: Pew Research Center, *Global Attitudes Report* (2009), www.pewglobal.org.

Al Qaeda was responsible for a portion of the violence including the more spectacular suicide attacks, truck bombs, and attacks on religious and political targets. The insurgency raised the flag of "Jihad" and brought in thousands of Islamic radical foreign fighters. The Shiites organized their own militia, the strongest being the Mahdi Army with as many as 60,000 fighters led by Moqtada al-Sadr. Large areas of Iraq came under the control of one or another of these insurgent groups.

American military forces suffered a gruesome toll in lives and limbs. By 2010 over 4,000 American troops had been killed, many from "improvised explosive devices." U.S. Army and Marine forces approached the "breaking point." Nearly every Army and Marine combat unit, and several National Guard and Reserve units, were rotated into Iraq more than once. The strain on U.S. forces worldwide became clearly evident, with both personnel and equipment wearing down.

The "Surge"

The sweeping Democratic victory in the congressional elections of 2006 was widely attributed to popular disaffection with the war in Iraq. Democrats gained control of both the House and the Senate. Many of their supporters expected them to end the war by cutting off funds for the prosecution of the war. At a minimum, opponents of the war wanted Congress to set a timetable for the reduction of U.S. troops in Iraq. But when staring directly at the prospect of cutting off funds for troops in the field, Congress blinked. Resolutions to end the war or to force U.S. troop reductions failed.

Instead, President Bush announced a "surge" in troop strength designed to improve security in Iraq and allow the Iraqi government to reach "benchmarks" in resolving civil strife. The "surge" involved increasing U.S. troop levels in Iraq from roughly 138,000 to 160,000. In January 2007, the president appointed a new commander for Iraq, General David Petraeus. Petraeus was unanimously confirmed by the Senate, but Congress stipulated that in September 2007, the general was to report on progress in Iraq.

Petraeus reported to Congress that the "surge" was working, that progress was being made in stabilizing Iraq and in training Iraqi forces, that U.S. troop levels could be reduced to presurge levels, but that some U.S. forces may be needed in Iraq for 10 years or more. He argued that a timetable for troop reductions would be counterproductive.

Loss of Public Support

Yet it is clear that the American public no longer supports the war and wants U.S. troops withdrawn from Iraq as soon as possible. There is frustration over the failure of the Iraqi government to make progress in resolving sectarian differences. The United States should not be involved in a civil war. U.S. military presence in Iraq is encouraging the growth of Al Qaeda. International opinion strongly opposes the continuation of U.S. military occupation of Iraq. Years after the start of the war, violence continues and there is no end in sight. The U.S. military has been weakened overall by the stresses placed upon it by the fighting in Iraq.

Shortly after the war in Iraq began, most Americans thought Iraq was worth going to war over. Indeed, this opinion climbed to 76 percent immediately following the capture of Baghdad. But as American casualties mounted and no end to the fighting appeared in sight, mass opinion in support of the war declined rapidly. By late 2004 the majority of Americans believed it was "not worth going to war" over Iraq (see Figure 18.3).

Withdrawal of Combat Forces

In the presidential campaign of 2008, Barack Obama pledged to end the war in Iraq "responsibly." He warned against "an occupation of undetermined length, with undetermined costs and undetermined consequences." Upon taking office in January 2009, Obama ordered the U.S. military to plan for a phased withdrawal of American combat forces from Iraq. The U.S. military was ordered to "redeploy" combat brigades at a pace of one to two per month over a 16-month period, ending in the summer of 2010. A "residual force" is to remain in Iraq—to conduct targeted counterterrorism missions against Al Qaeda and to protect American diplomatic and civilian personnel.

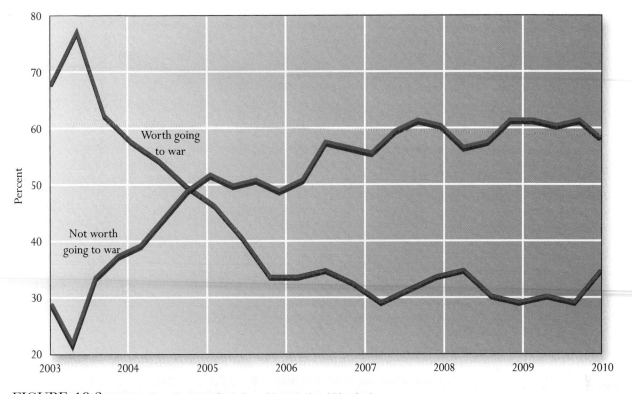

FIGURE 18.3 Changing Public Opinion About the War in Iraq

Support for the war in Iraq among the American people declined over time.

Source: Various polls as reported in The Polling Report, www.pollingreport.com

This residual force will continue to train and support Iraqi security forces "as long as Iraqi leaders move toward political reconciliation and away from sectarianism."[6]

The thrust of U.S. policy in Iraq is to shift from military to diplomatic efforts. The phased withdrawal itself is expected to encourage Iraqis to provide for their own security and to work toward real political reconciliation among the factions. The political tasks expected of the Iraqis included compromises on oil revenue sharing, equitable provision of services, continued reform of security forces, and the elimination of corruption in government.

The War in Afghanistan

▶ 18.6 *Explain the war in Afghanistan and assess its progress.*

While campaigning for the presidency in 2008, Barack Obama drew a sharp distinction between the war in Iraq and the war in Afghanistan. Iraq, he claimed, had diverted America's attention away from the greater dangers posed by Al Qaeda and the Taliban forces in Afghanistan. It was Al Qaeda that was responsible for the September 11, 2001, attacks on the New York World Trade Center and the Pentagon, and it was the Taliban regime in Afghanistan that provided Al Qaeda with safe haven. Evidence was mounting of a resurgence of Al Qaeda

FIGURE 18.4
Battling in Rough Terrain

Afghanistan presents difficult terrain for U.S. counter-insurgency operations. The Taliban and Al Qaeda are largely concentrated in the mountainous areas along the Pakistan border.

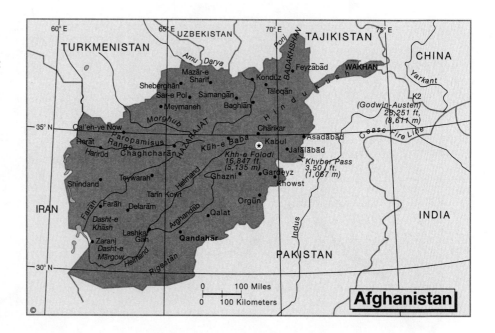

and its Taliban allies in the southern and eastern mountainous areas of Afghanistan and across the border in neighboring Pakistan (see Figure 18.4).

Shortly after entering the White House, President Barack Obama ordered a strategic review of the situation in Afghanistan and Pakistan. The review concluded that the situation was "increasingly perilous" with Al Qaeda and the Taliban controlling large areas in both Afghanistan and Pakistan. Additional combat brigades were ordered to the region as well as thousands of trainees for Afghanistan's army and police forces. The U.S. and NATO commander in Afghanistan, requested additional troops to conduct counterinsurgency operations. President Obama ordered a second review (causing critics to complain of "dithering"). The president eventually granted the general's request, increasing U.S. troop levels.

Counterinsurgency Operations   The announced goal of U.S. policy is to "disrupt, dismantle, and defeat" Al Qaeda in both Afghanistan and Pakistan. Economic and military aid to Pakistan is to be contingent upon that country's commitment to its own security and its willingness to "confront violent extremists." Afghanistan will offer a test of the U.S. military's concept of asymmetrical (counterinsurgency) warfare—"clear, hold, and build."

Afghanistan has a long history of successfully resisting foreign invaders, including the British and the Russians. If Afghans come to see the U.S. as a foreign invader, the prospects for success in that country will be dim indeed.

U.S. policy envisions the eventual transfer of security responsibility to the Afghan army and police forces. These forces are to be expanded and trained by U.S. and NATO personnel. President Obama expressed the hope that U.S. forces could begin withdrawing from Afghanistan in late 2011. But to date the Afghan army has failed to develop the capacity to confront Taliban and Al Qaeda forces. Corruption, inefficiency, and a lack of discipline remain chronic problems in the Afghan army. And the central government in Kabul, headed by Hamid Karzai, is itself corrupt and lacking legitimacy with its own people.

Limited Objectives   U.S. policy recognizes that Afghanistan's 25 million people are divided along tribal and ethnic lines. The central government in Kabul

A CONSTITUTIONAL NOTE

Congress Versus the Commander-in-Chief

The Constitution of 1787 divided war-making powers between the Congress and the president. Article I, Section 8, states that "Congress shall have Power . . . to provide for the common Defense . . . to declare War . . . to raise and support Armies . . . to provide and maintain a Navy . . . to make Rules for the Government and Regulation of the land and naval forces." However, Article II, Section 2, states that "the President shall be the Commander-in-Chief of the Army and Navy of the United States." But today wars are not "declared"; instead they begin with military action, and the president is responsible for the actions of the Armed Forces of the United States. Presidents have sent U.S. troops beyond the borders of the United States in military actions on more than 200 occasions. In contrast, Congress has formally declared war only 5 times: the War of 1812, the Mexican War in 1846, the Spanish-American War in 1898, World War I in 1917, and World War II in 1941. Congress did *not* declare war in the Korean War (1950–53), the Vietnam War (1965–73), the Persian Gulf War (1991), or the wars in Afghanistan (2002–) or Iraq (2003–). While presidents asked for the support of Congress in these wars, no formal declarations of war were ever made. The Supreme Court has consistently refused to hear cases involving the war powers of the president and Congress.

exercises little control over a country the size of Texas. U.S. strategy appears to be to win over local tribes and leaders, including those Taliban forces that are not allied to Al Qaeda. The objective of U.S. policy is not necessarily to bring Western-style democracy to Afghanistan, but rather to ensure that the country does not become a safe haven for Al Qaeda and its terrorist allies.

Public Opinion   The American people appear to be divided over the wisdom of continuing military operations in Afghanistan. Majorities oppose the war itself and oppose increasing American troop levels. However, majorities also say that they approve of the way President Obama is handling "the situation in Afghanistan."

Summary

▶ **18.1** *Characterize the goals and means of international politics.*

There is no world government capable of legislating and enforcing rules of international politics. But various efforts to stabilize relations among nations have been attempted, including the balance-of-power system of alliances in the eighteenth and nineteenth centuries, the collective security arrangements of the League of Nations and the United Nations in the twentieth century, and the regional security approach of the North Atlantic Treaty Organization.

▶ **18.2** *Outline major events of the Cold War and assess its legacy.*

The United Nations was largely ineffective during the Cold War, the confrontation between the Western democracies led by the United States and communist bloc nations led by the Soviet Union. During these years, the Western nations relied principally on the strength of the North Atlantic Treaty Organization (NATO) to deter war in Europe.

For nearly 50 years, the Cold War largely directed U.S. foreign and defense policy. The United States sought to contain Soviet military expansionism and world communist revolutionary forces in all parts of the globe. U.S. involvement in the Korean and Vietnam wars grew out of this containment policy.

The end of the Cold War followed the ouster of communist governments in Eastern Europe in 1989, the unification of Germany in 1990, the collapse of the Warsaw Pact communist military alliance in 1991, and the dissolution of the Soviet Union in 1991. Russia has inherited most of the nuclear weapons and military forces of the former Soviet Union as well as its seat on the UN Security Council.

▶ **18.3** *Trace the evolution of the nuclear weapons policies of the United States.*

During the Cold War years, U.S. and Soviet military forces never engaged in direct combat against each other, although many "proxy" conflicts took place throughout the world. The most serious threat of nuclear war occurred during the Cuban Missile Crisis in 1962.

To maintain nuclear peace, the United States relied primarily on the policy of deterrence—dissuading the Soviets from launching a nuclear attack by maintaining survivable second-strike forces capable of inflicting unacceptable levels of destruction in a retaliatory attack.

In 1970, President Richard Nixon and National Security Adviser Henry Kissinger began negotiations with the Soviet Union with a view to limiting the nuclear arms race. These Strategic Arms Limitation Talks produced the SALT I agreement in 1972, and later, under President Jimmy Carter, the SALT II agreement in 1979. Both agreements set limits on future strategic weapons development but failed to reduce existing weapons stockpiles.

President Ronald Reagan renamed the negotiations START, emphasizing the goal of reductions in weapons rather than limitations, and stressing equality and verification. The START I (1991) and START II (1993) treaties called for reducing nuclear arsenals by two-thirds from Cold War levels.

The New START Treaty negotiated in 2010 calls for further reductions in nuclear warheads. New START is a formal treaty requiring Senate ratification.

▶ **18.4** *Analyze the nature of terrorism and the U.S. response to terrorism.*

Following the Vietnam War, many military leaders argued that U.S. forces should be used only to protect vital American interests, only in support of clearly defined military objectives, only with sufficient strength to ensure decisive victory with the fewest possible casualties, only with the support of the American people and Congress, and only as a last resort.

Recent presidents, however, have used military forces to carry out a variety of missions in addition to conventional war, including peacekeeping, antiterrorist, and humanitarian activities. They have argued that the risks were worth taking in light of the importance of the goals.

▶ **18.5** *Explain the war in Iraq and assess its progress.*

Following the Gulf War, Iraq violated a dozen or more UN resolutions calling on them to destroy chemical and biological weapons and to open their weapons sites for inspection. Saddam Hussein's refusal led to Operation Iraqi Freedom in 1991. Saddam Hussein was apprehended and regime change was accomplished; but the occupation of Iraq was, at least initially, poorly executed. President Obama ran for office promising to end the war in Iraq in a "responsible" manner.

▶ **18.6** *Explain the war in Afghanistan and assess its progress.*

The military phase of America's War on Terrorism began October 7, 2001, when U.S. aircraft began attacks on Al Qaeda bases in Afghanistan and U.S. special forces organized and led Afghan fighters to oust the Taliban regime that had harbored the terrorists. Later, a resurgence of Taliban and Al Qaeda forces caused President Obama to increase U.S. troop strength in Afghanistan.

Military doctrine is increasingly focused on counterinsurgency—confronting irregular forces engaging in tactics such as ambushes, hidden explosives, and suicide bombings.

Chapter Test

▶ **18.1** *Characterize the goals and means of international politics.*

1. In international politics all nations seek the goal of
   a. power
   b. social justice
   c. order and the rule of law
   d. freedom and democracy

2. The idea of collective security was *first* used by the
   a. North Atlantic Treaty Organization (NATO)
   b. League of Nations
   c. North American Free Trade Agreement (NAFTA)
   d. United Nations

3. It would be accurate to say that in the UN General Assembly
   a. voting power is based on a country's population
   b. voting power is based on a country's gross-domestic product
   c. each nation has one vote regardless of population or gross-domestic product
   d. only the "superpowers" have a veto in the UN's General Assembly

4. The notion of regional security is incorporated into the
   a. United Nations
   b. North Atlantic Treaty Organization (NATO)
   c. League of Nations
   d. Security Council

▶ 18.2 *Outline major events of the Cold War and assess its legacy.*

5. During the Cold War the policy of preventing the USSR from expanding its influence was known as
   a. the Marshall Plan
   b. containment
   c. the Truman Doctrine
   d. the NATO

6. The most serious threat of a nuclear holocaust during the Cold War was probably during
   a. the Korean War
   b. the Vietnam War
   c. the fall of the Berlin wall
   d. the Cuban Missile Crisis

7. American military involvement in Vietnam ended with the
   a. Paris Peace Accord in 1973
   b. UN Korea Peace Resolution in 1975
   c. Reagan defense buildup in 1985
   d. collapse of the Soviet Union in 1989

8. The current (2010) president of Russia is
   a. Vladimir Putin
   b. Dmitry Medvedev
   c. Boris Yeltsin
   d. Nikita Khrushchev

▶ 18.3 *Trace the evolution of the nuclear weapons policies of the United States.*

9. President Obama's policies regarding the ballistic missile-defense system (BMD) have resulted in the United States
   a. canceling deployment of BMD sites in Poland
   b. canceling the deployment of the sea-based missile defense system
   c. accelerating the deployment of BMD sites in the Czech Republic
   d. ending research on BMD systems

10. The first treaty that actually resulted in a reduction of strategic nuclear weapons was the
    a. Strategic Arms Limitations Treaty II (SALT II)
    b. Strategic Arms Reductions Treaty I (START I)
    c. New START Treaty
    d. Strategic Arms Limitations Treaty I (SALT I)

11. The Powell Doctrine, advanced by General Colin Powell recommended the use of military force
    a. only in support of U.S. vital interests
    b. to demonstrate U.S. support for democratic governments
    c. to assist in humanitarian aid
    d. all of the above

▶ 18.4 *Analyze the nature of terrorism and the U.S. response to terrorism.*

12. Terrorism is a political act which is distinguished by its willingness to
    a. use weapons of mass destruction
    b. achieve publicity of alleged wrongs

c. consciously target civilians
d. use suicide "martyrs"

13. The military phase of the War on Terrorism began with
    a. Operation Enduring Freedom in Iraq
    b. Operation Enduring Freedom in Afghanistan
    c. Operation Desert Storm in Iraq
    d. Operation Shock and Awe in Afghanistan

▶ 18.5 *Explain the war in Iraq and assess its progress.*

14. President George W. Bush stated the purposes of Operation Iraqi Freedom as
    a. regime change in Bagdad
    b. eliminate Iraq's weapons of mass destruction
    c. insure that Iraq would not harbor terrorists
    d. all of the above

15. It is true that, in general, world public opinion has
    a. opposed Obama's plan to close the Guantánamo prison
    b. supported Obama's decision to increase troop levels in Afghanistan
    c. supported Obama's pledge to become more multilateral
    d. all of the above

16. Public opinion polling on the war in Iraq revealed that it
    a. was never very popular
    b. was supported (at least initially) by three-quarters of the public
    c. never attained the support of 50 percent of the people
    d. has held the support of over 50 percent of the public since 2005

▶ 18.6 *Explain the war in Afghanistan and assess its progress.*

17. The U.S. military's concept of asymmetrical counterinsurgency warfare involves
    a. the use of "overwhelming military force"
    b. extensive reliance on chemical neutralizing agents
    c. the doctrine of "clear, hold, and build"
    d. the use of bombers as in Operation Rolling Thunder

18. The main objective of U.S. policy in Afghanistan is to
    a. bring democracy to Kabul
    b. send the Taliban back to Pakistan
    c. ensure that the country is not used as a safe haven by terrorists
    d. advance the status of women

PEARSON mypoliscilab EXERCISES

Apply what you learned in this chapter on MyPoliSciLab.

Read on mypoliscilab.com

eText: Chapter 18

Study and Review on mypoliscilab.com

Pre-Test

Post-Test

Chapter Exam

Flashcards

Watch on mypoliscilab.com

Video: Sanctions on Iran

Video: NYC's Subway Surveillance System

Video: Three Vivid Years—But Progress?

Explore on mypoliscilab.com

Simulation: You Are the Newly Appointed Ambassador to the Country of Dalmatia

Simulation: You Are the President of the United States

Simulation: You Are President John F. Kennedy

Comparative: Comparing Foreign and Security Policy

Timeline: The Evolution of Foreign Policy

Visual Literacy: Evaluating Defense Spending

Key Terms

collective security   631
Soviet Union   632
superpowers   632
regional security   633
North Atlantic Treaty
   Organization
   (NATO)   633

Cold War   635
Truman Doctrine   635
containment   635
Marshall Plan   635
Korean War   636
Cuban Missile
   Crisis   636

Vietnam War   636
deterrence   639
second-strike
   capability   639
SALT I   639
ABM Treaty   639
SALT II   640

START I   640
START II   640
ballistic missile defense
   (BMD)   640
terrorism   641
preemptive attacks   646

Suggested Readings

Banks, William C., Renee deNevers, and Mitchel B. Wallerstein. *Combatting Terrorism Strategies and Approaches*. Washington, D.C.: CQ Press, 2007. Comprehensive description of a variety of counterterrorism strategies, including law enforcement, diplomacy, and military action.

Clausewitz, Karl von. *On War*. Edited and translated by Michael Howard and Peter Paret. Princeton, N.J.: Princeton University Press, 1984. The classic theory of war and military operations, emphasizing their political character; first published in 1832.

Hastedt, Glenn P. *American Foreign Policy: Past, Present, Future*. 8th ed. New York: Longman, 2011. A foreign policy text that deals with national security issues within the broader context of foreign policy.

International Institute for Strategic Studies. *The Military Balance*. London: International Institute for Strategic Studies, published annually. Careful description of the military forces of more than 160 countries; this book is considered the most authoritative public information available.

Hook, Stephen W., and John Spanier. *American Foreign Policy Since World War II*. 18th ed. Washington, D.C.: CQ Press; 2009. Updated version of classic text on American foreign policy, concluding with "A World of Trouble."

Magstadt, Thomas M. *An Empire If You Can Keep It: Power and Principle in American Foreign Policy*. Washington, D.C.: CQ Press, 2004. Comprehensive text on American foreign policy, describing its history, the Cold War, the Gulf War, September 11, and the War on Terrorism.

Nacos, Brigitte L. *Terrorism and Counterterrorism*. 2nd ed. New York: Longman, 2008. Terrorism's causes, actors, and strategies as well as counterterrorism responses.

Snow, Donald M. *National Security for a New Era*. 4th ed. New York: Longman, 2011. Comprehensive text examining United States national security issues following the end of the Cold War and following 9/11.

Summers, Harry G., Jr. *On Strategy II: A Critical Analysis of the Gulf War*. New York: Dell, 1992. Analysis of the Gulf War based on Clausewitz's classic principles of war. The strategic decisions leading to victory in the Gulf contrast markedly with the decisions in Vietnam that led to defeat, a topic covered in Summers's groundbreaking first book, *On Strategy: A Critical Analysis of the Vietnam War* (New York: Dell, 1984).

Suggested Web Sites

American Security Council www.ascusa.org
Organization providing summary information on national security threats.

CIA-Terrorism www.cia.gov/terrorism
Reports, news, and facts regarding terrorism.

CIA World Factbook www.cia.gov/publications/factbook
Nations listed A–Z with geography, people, economy, government, military, and so on.

Cuban Crisis www.cubacrisis.net
The October 1962 nuclear missile crisis described day to day, with photos.

Defenselink Terrorism www.defenselink.mil/terrorism
Official Defense Department site link to information on terrorism.

Korean War Project Organization www.koreanwar.org
Dedicated to the memory of sacrifices of Americans in Korea, with links to battles, units, and memorials.

NATO www.nato.int
The official "North Atlantic Treaty Organization" site contains basic facts about the alliance, current NATO news and issues, and important NATO policies.

Russia EIN News www.einnews.com/russia
Business, cultural, political, and scientific news from Russia.

State Department www.state.gov
This U.S. Department of State Web site contains background notes on the countries and regions of the world.

Terrorism Research Center www.terrorism.com
The "Terrorism Research Center" Web site is dedicated to "informing the public of the phenomena of terrorism and information warfare." It contains news, analytical essays on terrorist issues, and many links to other terrorism materials and research sources.

United Nations www.un.org
This United Nations site contains basic information about the world body's mission, member states, issues of concern, institutions, and accomplishments.

Chapter Test Answer Key

1. A	4. B	7. A	10. C	13. B	16. B
2. B	5. B	8. B	11. A	14. D	17. C
3. C	6. D	9. A	12. C	15. C	18. C

APPENDIX

The Declaration of Independence

Drafted mainly by Thomas Jefferson, this document, adopted by the Second Continental Congress and signed by John Hancock and fifty-five others, outlined the rights of man and the rights to rebellion and self-government. It declared the independence of the colonies from Great Britain, justified rebellion, and listed the grievances against George III and his government. What is memorable about this famous document is not only that it declared the birth of a new nation, but that it set forth with eloquence our basic philosophy of liberty and representative democracy.

IN CONGRESS, JULY 4, 1776 (The unanimous Declaration of the Thirteen United States of America)

PREAMBLE

When, in the course of human events, it becomes necessary for one people to dissolve the political bands which have connected them with another, and to assume, among the powers of the earth, the separate and equal station to which the laws of nature and of nature's God entitle them, a decent respect to the opinions of mankind requires that they should declare the causes which impel them to the separation.

New Principles of Government

We hold these truths to be self-evident; that all men are created equal, that they are endowed by their Creator with certain unalienable rights, that among these are life, liberty, and the pursuit of happiness.

That, to secure these rights, governments are instituted among men, deriving their just powers from the consent of the governed.

That whenever any form of government becomes destructive of these ends, it is the right of the people to alter or to abolish it, and to institute new government, laying its foundation on such principles, and organizing its powers in such form, as to them shall seem most likely to effect their safety and happiness. Prudence, indeed will dictate that governments long established should not be changed for light and transient causes; and accordingly all experience hath shown that mankind are more disposed to suffer while evils are sufferable, than to right themselves by abolishing the forms to which they are accustomed. But when a long train of abuses and usurpations, pursuing invariably the same object, evinces a design to reduce them under absolute despotism, it is their right, it is their duty, to throw off such government, and to provide new guards for their future security.

Reasons for Separation

Such has been the patient sufferance of these colonies; and such is now the necessity which constrains them to alter their former systems of government. The history of the present king of Great Britain is a history of repeated injuries and usurpations, all having in direct object the establishment of an absolute tyranny over these states. To prove this, let facts be submitted to a candid world.

He has refused his assent to laws, the most wholesome and necessary for the public good.

He has forbidden his governors to pass laws of immediate and pressing importance unless suspended in their operation till his assent should be obtained; and when so suspended, he has utterly neglected to attend to them.

He has refused to pass other laws for the accommodation of large districts of people, unless those people would relinquish the right of representation in the legislature, a right inestimable to them, and formidable to tyrants only.

He has called together legislative bodies at places unusual, uncomfortable, and distant for the depository of their public records, for the sole purpose of fatiguing them into compliance with his measures.

He has dissolved representative houses repeatedly, for opposing, with manly firmness, his invasions on the rights of people.

He has refused, for a long time after such dissolutions, to cause others to be elected; whereby the legislative powers incapable of annihilation, have returned to the people at large for their exercise; the state remaining, in the mean-time, exposed to all the dangers of invasion from without and convulsions within.

He has endeavored to prevent the population of these states; for that purpose obstructing the laws of naturalization of foreigners, refusing to pass others to encourage their migration hither, and raising the conditions of new appropriations of lands.

He has obstructed the administration of justice, by refusing his assent to laws for establishing judiciary powers.

He has made judges dependent on his will alone for the tenure of their offices, and the amount and payment of their salaries.

He has erected a multitude of new offices, and sent hither swarms of officers to harass our people and eat out their substance.

He has kept among us, in times of peace, standing armies, without the consent of our legislature.

He has affected to render the military independent of, and superior to, the civil power.

He has combined with others to subject us to jurisdiction foreign to our constitution and unacknowledged by our laws, giving his assent to their acts of pretended legislation:

For quartering large bodies of armed troops among us;

For protecting them, by a mock trial, from punishment for any murders which they should commit on the inhabitants of these states;

A

For cutting off our trade with all parts of the world;

For imposing taxes on us without our consent;

For depriving us, in many cases, of the benefits of trial by jury;

For transporting us beyond seas, to be tried for pretended offenses;

For abolishing the free system of English laws in a neighboring province, establishing therein an arbitrary government, and enlarging its boundaries, so as to render it at once an example and fit instrument for introducing the same absolute rule into these colonies;

For taking away our charters, abolishing our most valuable laws, and altering, fundamentally, the forms of our governments;

For suspending our own legislatures, and declaring themselves invented with power to legislate for us in all cases whatsoever.

He has abdicated government here, by declaring us out of his protection and waging war against us.

He has plundered our seas, ravaged our coasts, burned our towns, and destroyed the lives of our people.

He is at this time transporting large armies of foreign mercenaries to complete the works of death, desolation, and tyranny already begun with circumstances of cruelty and perfidy scarcely paralleled in the most barbarous ages and totally unworthy of the head of a civilized nation.

He has constrained our fellow-citizens, taken captive on the high seas, to bear arms against their country, to become the executioners of their friends and brethren, or to fall themselves by their hands.

He has excited domestic insurrections among us, and has endeavored to bring on the inhabitants of our frontiers the merciless Indian savages, whose known rule of warfare is an undistinguished destruction of all ages, sexes, and conditions.

In every stage of these oppressions we have petitioned for redress in the most humble terms; our repeated petitions have been answered only by repeated injury. A prince whose character is thus marked by every act which may define a tyrant is unfit to be the ruler of a free people.

Nor have we been wanting in attention to our British brethren. We have warned them, from time to time, of attempts by their legislature to extend an unwarrantable jurisdiction over us. We have reminded them of the circumstances of our emigration and settlement here. We have appealed to their native justice and magnanimity; and we have conjured them, by the ties of our common kindred, to disavow these usurpations, which would inevitably interrupt our connections and correspondence. They, too, have been deaf to the voice of justice and of consanguinity. We must, therefore, acquiesce in the necessity which denounces our separation, and hold them, as we hold the rest of mankind, enemies in war, in peace, friends.

We, therefore, the representatives of the United States of America, in General Congress assembled, appealing to the Supreme Judge of the world for the rectitude of our intentions, do, in the name and by authority of the good people of these colonies, solemnly publish and declare, that these united colonies are, and of right ought to be, free and independent states; that they are absolved from all allegiance to the British crown, and that all political connection between them and the state of Great Britain is, and ought to be, totally dissolved; and that, as free and independent states, they have full power to levy war, conclude peace, contract alliances, establish commerce, and do all other acts and things which independent states may of a right do. And, for the support of this declaration, with a firm reliance on the protection of Divine Providence, we mutually pledge to each other our lives, our fortunes, and our sacred honor.

The Federalist

The Federalist is a collection of eighty-five essays originally published in 1787–88 in support of the new U.S. Constitution. The papers were published in serial fashion in New York newspapers. (Today we might call them "op ed pieces.") The authors used the pseudonym "Publius." Alexander Hamilton, later Secretary of the Treasury under President George Washington, organized the effort and authored most of the papers. John Jay, later to become Chief Justice of the United States Supreme Court, authored a few. But perhaps the most important of these essays, No. 10 and No. 51, were authored by James Madison, the fourth president of the United States and often considered the "Father of the Constitution."

The Federalist, No. 10, James Madison

The Federalist, No. 10, is considered a classic in political philosophy, explaining the nature and sources of "faction" (political conflict) and how a republican government can be constructed to control its effects.

To the People of the State of New York: Among the numerous advantages promised by a well-constructed union, none deserves to be more accurately developed than its tendency to break and control the violence of faction. The friend of popular governments, never finds himself so much alarmed for their character and fate, as when he contemplates their propensity to this dangerous vice. He will not fail, therefore, to set a due value on any plan which, without violating the principles to which he is attached, provides a proper cure for it. The instability, in justice, and confusion introduced into the public councils, have, in truth, been the mortal diseases under which popular governments have everywhere perished; as they continue to be the favourite and fruitful topics from which the adversaries to liberty derive their most specious declamations. The valuable improvements made by the American constitutions on the popular models, both ancient and modern, cannot certainly be too much admired; but it would be an unwarrantable partiality, to contend that they have as effectually obviated the danger on this side, as was wished and expected.

Madison first acknowledges that there are dangers inherent in "popular governments," that they are subject to "mortal diseases," including instability, injustice, and confusion. And he acknowledges that "complaints are everywhere heard" even from "virtuous citizens . . . that our governments are too unstable; that the public good is disregarded in conflicts of rival parties." He is especially concerned about injustices perpetrated by "an interested and overbearing majority."

Complaints are everywhere heard from our most considerate and virtuous citizens, equally the friends of public and private faith, and of public and personal liberty, that our governments are too unstable; that the public good is disregarded in the conflicts of rival parties; and that measures are too often decided, not according to the rules of justice, and the rights of the minor party, but by the superior force of an interested and overbearing majority. However anxiously we may wish that these complaints had no foundation, the evidence of known facts will not permit us to deny that they are in some degree true. It will be found, indeed, on a candid review of our situation, that some of the distresses under which we labour have been erroneously charged on the operation of our governments; but it will be found, at the same time, that other causes will not alone account for many of our heaviest misfortunes; and, particularly, for that prevailing and increasing distrust of public engagements, and alarm for private rights, which are echoed from one end of the continent to the other. These must be chiefly, if not wholly, effects of the unsteadiness and injustice, with which a factious spirit has tainted our public administrations.

Madison defines "faction" as either a majority or minority who

are united by some impulse of passion or of interest adverse to the rights of other citizens or to the permanent interest of the community. He then identifies two methods of controlling the "mischiefs of faction," the first by removing its causes and the second by controlling its effects. One way to remove its causes is to destroy liberty, but of course this remedy is "worse than the disease." Another way to eliminate faction is to force everyone to have the same opinions and passions. (In this warning Madison seems to foresee the efforts at thought control by totalitarian governments of the twentieth century.) But "diversity in the faculties of men, from which the rights of property originate" must be protected by government; efforts to eliminate differences among people is both impractical and unwise.

By a faction, I understand a number of citizens, whether amounting to a majority or minority of the whole, who are united and actuated by some common impulse of passion, or of interest, adverse to the rights of other citizens, or to the permanent and aggregate interests of the community.

There are two methods of curing the mischiefs of faction: the one, by removing its causes; the other, by controlling its effects.

There are again two methods of removing the causes of faction: the one, by destroying the liberty which is essential to its existence; the other, by giving to every citizen the same opinions, the same passions, and the same interests.

It could never be more truly said, than of the first remedy, that it was worse than the disease. Liberty is to faction what air is to fire, an aliment without which it instantly expires. But it could not be a less folly to abolish liberty, which is essential to political life, because it nourishes faction, than it would be to wish the annihilation of air, which is essential to animal life, because it imparts to fire its destructive agency.

The second expedient is as impracticable, as the first would be unwise. As long as the reason of man continues fallible, and he is at liberty to exercise it, different opinions will be formed. As long as the connection subsists between his reason and his self-love, his opinions and his passions will have a reciprocal influence on each other; and the former will be objects to which the latter will attach themselves. The diversity in the faculties of men, from

which the rights of property originate, is not less an insuperable obstacle to an uniformity of interests. The protection of these faculties is the first object of government. From the protection of different and unequal faculties of acquiring property, the possession of different degrees and kinds of property immediately results; and from the influence of these on the sentiments and views of the respective proprietors, ensues a division of the society into different interests and parties.

Madison identifies many of the sources of faction, including religion, government, and attachment to different leaders. Indeed, even "the most frivolous and fanciful distinctions have been sufficient to kindle their unfriendly passions and excite their most violent conflicts. But the most common and durable source of factions, has been the various and unequal distribution of property." Differences between those who have and those who do not have property, differences between creditors and debtors, differences between landed interests, manufacturing interests, mercantile interests, and moneyed interests, all divide people into different classes "actuated by different sentiments and views."

The latent causes of faction are thus sown in the nature of man; and we see them everywhere brought into different degrees of activity, according to the different circumstances of civil society. A zeal for different opinions concerning religion, concerning government, and many other points, as well of speculation as of practice; an attachment to different leaders ambitiously contending for preeminence and power; or to persons of other descriptions whose fortunes have been interesting to the human passions, have, in turn, divided mankind into parties, inflamed them with mutual animosity, and rendered them much more disposed to vex and oppress each other, than to cooperate for their common good. So strong is this propensity of mankind, to fall into mutual animosities, that where no substantial occasion presents itself, the most frivolous and fanciful distinctions have been sufficient to kindle their unfriendly passions and excite their most violent conflicts. But the most common and durable source of factions, has been the various and unequal distribution of property. Those who hold, and those who are without property, have ever formed distinct interests in society. Those who are creditors, and those who are debtors, fall under a like discrimination. A landed interest, a manufacturing interest, a mercantile interest, a moneyed interest, with many lesser interests, grow up of necessity in civilized nations, and divide them into different classes, actuated by different sentiments and views. The regulation of these various and interfering interests forms the principal task of modern legislation, and involves the spirit of the party and faction in the necessary and ordinary operations of the government.

Legislators are themselves advocates and parties to the causes they must decide on. Issues such as payment of debts, restrictions on foreign goods, the apportionment of taxes, all must be decided by legislators who themselves have direct interest in the outcome. "It is vain to say, that enlightened statesmen will be able to adjust these clashing interests, and render them all subservient to the public good. Enlightened statesmen will not always be at the helm."

No man is allowed to be a judge in his own cause; because his interest will certainly bias his judgment, and, not improbably, corrupt his integrity. With equal, nay, with greater reason, a body of men are unfit to be both judges and parties at the same time; yet what are many of the most important acts of legislation, but so many judicial determinations, not indeed concerning the right of single persons, but concerning the rights of large bodies of citizens? And what are the different classes of legislators, but advocates and parties to the causes which they determine? Is a law proposed concerning private debts? It is a question to which the creditors are parties on one side, and the debtors on the other. Justice ought to hold the balance between them. Yet the parties are, and must be, themselves the judges; and the most numerous party, or, in other words, the most powerful faction, must be expected to prevail. Shall domestic manufacturers be encouraged, and in what degree, by restrictions on foreign manufacturers are questions which would be differently decided by the landed and the manufacturing classes; and probably by neither with a sole regard to justice and the public good. The apportionment of taxes, on the various descriptions of property, is an act which seems to require the most exact impartiality; yet there is, perhaps, no legislative act, in which greater opportunity and temptation are given to a predominant party to trample on the rules of justice. Every shilling, with which they

overburden the inferior number, is a shilling saved to their own pockets.

It is in vain to say, that enlightened statesmen will be able to adjust these clashing interests, and render them all subservient to the public good. Enlightened statesmen will not always be at the helm; nor, in many cases, can such an adjustment be made at all, without taking into view indirect and remote considerations, which will rarely prevail over the immediate interest which one party may find in disregarding the rights of another, or the good of the whole.

If faction cannot be removed from politics, then its effects must be controlled. Madison argues that minority factions can be controlled "by the republican principle, which enables the majority to defeat its sinister views, by regular vote." Minority factions may be able to "clog the administration" or "convulse the society" but ultimately they can be defeated by majority sentiments. But the greater problem is posed by majority factions, especially in popular government. The "great object" of popular government must be "to secure the public good, and private rights, against the danger of such a faction, and at the same time to preserve the spirit and the form of popular government."

The inference to which we are brought is, that the *causes* of faction cannot be removed; and that relief is only to be sought in the means of controlling its *effects*.

If a faction consists of less than a majority, relief is supplied by the republican principle, which enables the majority to defeat its sinister views, by regular vote. It may clog the administration, it may convulse the society; but it will be unable to execute and mask its violence under the forms of the Constitution. When a majority is included in a faction, the form of popular government, on the other hand, enables it to sacrifice to its ruling passion or interest, both the public good and the rights of other citizens. To secure the public good, and private rights, against the danger of such a faction, and at the same time to preserve the spirit and the form of popular government, is then the great object to which our inquiries are directed. Let me add, that it is the great desideratum, by which alone this form of government can be rescued from the opprobrium under which it has so long laboured, and be recommended to the esteem and adoption of mankind.

Madison's solution to controlling the effects of a majority faction is

the extensive republic. He first differentiates between a democracy and a republic. In a republic, decision making is delegated to a small number of citizens elected by the rest. In a pure democracy, citizens themselves assemble and administer the government. In such a democracy "there is nothing to check the inducements to sacrifice the weaker party, or an obnoxious individual." Pure democracies "have ever been spectacles of turbulence and contention; have ever been found incompatible with personal security, or the rights of property; and have in general been as short in their lives, as they have been violent in their deaths."

By what means is this object attainable? Evidently by one of two only. Either the existence of the same passion or interest in a majority, at the same time, must be prevented; or the majority, having such coexistent passion or interest, must be rendered, by their number and local situation, unable to concert and carry into effect schemes of oppression. If the impulse and the opportunity be suffered to coincide, we well know that neither moral nor religious motives can be relied on as an adequate control. They are not found to be such on the injustice and violence of individuals, and lose their efficacy in proportion to the number combined together; that is, in proportion as their efficacy becomes needful.

From this view of the subject, it may be concluded, that a pure democracy, by which I mean a society consisting of a small number of citizens, who assemble and administer the government in person, can admit of no cure for the mischiefs of faction. A common passion or interest will, in almost every case, be felt by a majority of the whole; a communication and concert, results from the form of government itself; and there is nothing to check the inducements to sacrifice the weaker party, or an obnoxious individual. Hence, it is, that such democracies have ever been spectacles of turbulence and contention; have ever been found incompatible with personal security, or the rights of property; and have in general been as short in their lives, as they have been violent in their deaths. Theoretic politicians, who have patronized this species of government, have erroneously supposed, that by reducing mankind to a perfect equality in their political rights, they would, at the same time, be perfectly equalized and assimilated in their possessions, their opinions, and their passions.

A republic, by which I mean a government in which the scheme of representation takes place, opens a different prospect, and promises the cure for which we are seeking. Let us examine the points in which it varies from pure democracy, and we shall comprehend both the nature of the cure and the efficacy which it must derive from the union.

In a republic, majority views must be passed through the medium of a chosen body of citizens who Madison believes are least likely to sacrifice the true interest of their country to temporary or partial considerations. "The public voice, pronounced by the representatives of the people, will be more consonant to the public good, than if pronounced by the people themselves." Clearly, Madison does not trust direct democracy.

The two great points of difference, between a democracy and a republic, are, first, the delegation of the government, in the latter, to a small number of citizens, elected by the rest; secondly, the greater number of citizens, and greater sphere of country, over which the latter may be extended.

The effect of the first difference is, on the one hand, to refine and enlarge the public views, by passing them through the medium of a chosen body of citizens, whose wisdom may best discern the true interest of their country, and whose patriotism and love of justice, will be least likely to sacrifice it to temporary or partial considerations. Under such a regulation, it may well happen, that the public voice, pronounced by the representatives of the people, will be more consonant to the public good, than if pronounced by the people themselves, convened for the purpose. On the other hand the effect may be inverted. Men of factious tempers, of local prejudices, or of sinister designs, may by intrigue, by corruption, or by other means, first obtain the suffrages, and then betray the interest of the people. The question resulting is, whether small or extensive republics are most favourable to the election of proper guardians of the public weal; and it is clearly decided in favour of the latter by two obvious considerations.

The larger the republic, the easier it is to "guard against the cabals of a few." Each representative will be chosen by a greater number of citizens in the large republic. Moreover, in a large republic it will be more difficult for a majority faction to emerge: "Extend the sphere, and you take in a greater variety of parties and interests; you make it less probable that a majority of the whole will have a common motive to invade the rights of other citizens; or if such a common motive exists, it will be more difficult for all who feel it to discover their own strength, and to act in unison with each other."

In the first place, it is to be remarked that, however small the republic may be, the representatives must be raised to a certain number, in order to guard against the cabals of a few; and that however large it may be, they must be limited to a certain number, in order to guard against the confusion of a multitude. Hence, the number of representatives in the two cases not being in proportion to that of the constituents, and being proportionally greatest in the small republic, it follows, that if the proportion of fit characters be not less in the large than in the small republic, the former will present a greater option, and consequently a greater probability of a fit choice.

In the next place, as each representative will be chosen by a greater number of citizens in the large than in the small republic, it will be more difficult for unworthy candidates to practice with success the vicious arts, by which elections are too often carried; and the suffrages of the people being more free, will be more likely to centre in men who possess the most attractive merit, and the most diffusive and established characters.

It must be confessed, that in this, as in most other cases, there is a mean, on both sides of which inconveniences will be found to lie. By enlarging too much the number of electors, you render the representatives too little acquainted with all their local circumstances and lesser interests; as by reducing it too much, you render him unduly attached to these, and too little fit to comprehend and pursue great and national objects. The federal constitution forms a happy combination in this respect; the great and aggregate interests being referred to the national, the local and particular to the state legislatures.

The other point of difference is, the greater number of citizens, and extent of territory, which may be brought within the compass of republican, than of democratic government; and it is this circumstance principally which renders factious combinations less to be dreaded in the former, than in the latter. The smaller the society, the fewer probably will be the distinct parties and interests composing it; the fewer the distinct parties and interests, the more frequently will a majority be found of the same party; and the smaller the number of individuals composing a majority, and the smaller the compass within which they are placed, the more easily will they concert and execute their plans of oppression. Extend the sphere, and you take in a greater variety of parties and interests; you make it less probable that a majority of the whole will have a common motive to invade the rights of other citizens; or if such a common motive exists, it will be more difficult for all who feel it to discover their own strength, and to act in unison with each other. Besides other impediments, it may be remarked, that where there is a consciousness of unjust or dishonourable purposes, communication is always checked by distrust, in proportion to the number whose concurrence is necessary.

Modern pluralism cites this argument as a precourser to its own theory about the preservation of democratic values through competition among multiple groups in society. Pluralists believe that Madison was recommending a large republic in order to dilute the influence of any particular interest and ensure that public policy would represent some equilibrium among competing interests in society.

Hence, it clearly appears, that the same advantage, which a republic has over a democracy, in controlling the effects of faction, is enjoyed by a large over a small republic—is enjoyed by the union over the states composing it. Does this advantage consist in the substitution of representatives, whose enlightened views and virtuous sentiments render them superior to local prejudices, and to schemes of injustice? It will not be denied that the representation of the union will be most likely to possess these requisite endowments. Does it consist in the greater security afforded by a greater variety of parties, against the event of any one party being able to outnumber and oppress the rest? In an equal degree does the increased variety of parties, comprised within the union, increase the security? Does it, in fine, consist in the greater obstacles opposed to the concert and accomplishment of the secret wishes of an unjust and interested majority? Here, again, the extent of the union gives it the most palpable advantage.

The influence of factious leaders may kindle a flame within their particular states, but will be unable to spread a general conflagration through the other states; a religious sect may degenerate into a political faction in a part of the confederacy; but the variety of sects dispersed over the entire face of it, must secure the national councils against any danger from that source; a rage for paper money, for an abolition of debts, for an equal division of property, or for any other improper or wicked project, will be less apt to pervade the whole body of the union than a particular member of it; in the same proportion as such a malady is more likely to taint a particular county or district, than an entire state.

In the extent and proper structure of the union, therefore, we behold a republican remedy for the diseases most incident to republican government. And according to the degree of pleasure and pride we feel in being republicans, ought to be our zeal in cherishing the spirit, and supporting the character of federalists.

The Federalist, No. 51, James Madison

The Federalist, No. 51, is an explanation and justification of the governing arrangements set forth in the new Constitution of 1787. Toward the end of the essay, Madison describes the new government as a "compound republic" where "the power surrendered by the people is first divided between two distinct governments, and then the portion allotted to each subdivided among distinct and separate departments." That is to say, the first division of power is between the states and the federal government, and then the federal government and the states divide power between legislature, executive, and judicial branches. "Hence a double security arises to the rights of the people. The different governments will control each other, at the same time that each will be controlled by itself." Thus, *Federalist*, No. 51, explains and defends both federalism and the separation of powers with its checks and balances.

To what expedient, then, shall we finally resort, for maintaining in practice the necessary partition of power among the several departments as laid down in the Constitution? The only answer that can be given is that as all these exterior provisions are found to be inadequate the defect must be supplied, by so contriving the interior structure of the government as that its several constituent parts may, by their mutual relations, be the means of keeping each other in their proper places. Without presuming to undertake a full development of this important idea I will hazard a few general observations which may perhaps place it in a clearer light, and enable us to form a more correct judgment of the principles and structure of the government planned by the convention.

Madison begins his argument by contending that distributing power among the legislative executive and judicial branches "which to a certain extent is admitted on all hands to be essential to the preservation of liberty." Thus separating legislative, executive, and judicial powers is the first step in Madison's plan to preserve liberty.

In order to lay a due foundation for that separate and distinct exercise of the different powers of government, which to a certain extent is admitted on all hands to be essential to the preservation of liberty, it is evident that each department should have a will of its own; and consequently should be so constituted that the members of each should have as little agency as possible in the appointment of the members of the others. Were this principle rigorously adhered to, it would require that all the appointments for the supreme executive, legislative, and judiciary magistracies should be drawn from the same fountain of authority, the people, through channels having no communication whatever with one another. Perhaps such a plan of constructing the several departments would be less difficult in practice than it may in contemplation appear. Some difficulties, however, and some additional expense would attend the execution of it. Some deviations, therefore, from the principle must be admitted. In the constitution of the judiciary department in particular, it might be inexpedient to insist rigorously on the principle: first, because peculiar qualifications being essential in the members, the primary consideration ought to be to select that mode of choice which best secures these qualifications; second, because the permanent tenure by which the appointments are held in that department must soon destroy all sense of dependence on the authority conferring them.

It is equally evident that the members of each department should be as little dependent as possible on those of the others for the emoluments annexed to their offices. Were the executive magistrate, or the judges, not independent of the legislature in this particular, their independence in every other would be merely nominal.

But perhaps, more important, Madison argues that each branch must be provided with the "necessary constitutional means and personal motives to resist encroachment of the others." Thus begins Madison's arguments on behalf of a system of checks and balances between and among the branches of government. "Ambition must be made to counteract ambition." Constitutional arrangements must ensure that officials are supplied with "opposite and rival interests." And in a famous quotation Madison observes: "In framing a government which is to be administered by men over men, the great difficulty lies in this: you must first enable the government to control the governed; and in the next place oblige it to control itself." Madison does not believe that popular government—"a dependence on the people"—is enough by itself to preserve individual liberty and that additional "auxiliary precautions" are also necessary. These auxiliary precautions include federalism and separation of powers and checks and balances.

But the great security against a gradual concentration of the several powers in the same department consists in giving to those who administer each department the necessary constitutional means and personal motives to resist encroachments of the others. The provision for defense must in this, as in all other cases, be made commensurate to the danger of attack. Ambition must be made to counteract ambition. The interest of the man must be connected with the constitutional rights of the place. It may be a reflection on human nature that such devices should be necessary to control the abuses of government. But what is government itself but the greatest of all reflections on human nature? If men were angels, no government would be necessary. If angels were to govern men, neither external nor internal controls on government would be necessary. In framing a government which is to be administered by men over men, the great difficulty lies in this: you must first enable the government to control the governed; and in the next place oblige it to control itself. A dependence on the people is, no doubt, the primary control on the government; but experience has taught mankind the necessity of auxiliary precautions.

This policy of supplying, by opposite and rival interests, the defect of better motives, might be traced through the whole system of human affairs, private as well as public. We see it particularly displayed in all the subordinate distributions of power, where the constant aim is to divide and arrange the several offices in such a manner as that each may be a check on the other—that the private interest of every individual may be a sentinel over the public rights. These inventions of prudence cannot be less requisite in the distribution of the supreme powers of the State.

In a republican government Madison believes the legislative branch should predominate. But the remedy to "dangerous encroachment" by the legislature is for that branch itself to be divided into two bodies, the Senate and a House of Representatives, both with separate "modes of elections and different principles of action."

But it is not possible to give to each department an equal power of self-defense. In republican government, the legislative authority necessarily predominates. The remedy for this inconveniency is to divide the legislature into different branches; and to render them, by modes of election and different principles of action, as little con-

nected with each other as the nature of their common functions and their common dependence on the society will admit. It may even be necessary to guard against dangerous encroachments by still further precautions. As the weight of the legislative authority requires that it should be thus divided, the weakness of the executive may require, on the other hand, that it should be fortified. An absolute negative on the legislature appears, at first view, to be the natural defense with which the executive magistrate should be armed. But perhaps it would be neither altogether safe nor alone sufficient. On ordinary occasions it might not be exerted with the requisite firmness, and on extraordinary occasions it might be perfidiously abused. May not this defect of an absolute negative be supplied by some qualified connection between this weaker department and the weaker branch of the stronger department, by which the latter may be led to support the constitutional rights of the former, without being too much detached from the rights of its own department?

If the principles on which these observations are founded be just, as I persuade myself they are, and they be applied as a criterion to the several State constitutions, and to the federal Constitution, it will be found that if the latter does not perfectly correspond with them, the former are infinitely less able to bear such a test.

Madison summarizes his arguments in the final two paragraphs. First, there is the argument for the "compound republic" where power is divided between the federal and state governments, and then within each of these governments power is separated into legislative, executive, and judicial branches. "The different governments will control each other, at the same time that each will be controlled by itself." Finally Madison echoes the argument made earlier in *Federalist*, No. 10, on behalf of a republican government extending over a large community: "the society itself will be broken into so many parts, interests and classes of citizens, that the rights of individuals, or of the minority, will be in little danger from interested combinations of the majority." The sheer number of interests will act as a protection against domination of any single interest. This argument supports the creation of the national government—"the extended republic of the United States." Freedom is to be protected by competition among multiple interests: "among the great variety of interests, parties, and sects which it embraces, a coalition of a majority of the whole society could seldom take place on any other principles than those of justice and the general good."

There are, moreover, two considerations particularly applicable to the federal system of America, which place that system in a very interesting point of view.

First. In a single republic, all the power surrendered by the people is submitted to the administration of a single government; and the usurpations are guarded against by a division of the government into distinct and separate departments. In the compound republic of America, the power surrendered by the people is first divided between two distinct governments, and then the portion allotted to each subdivided among distinct and separate departments. Hence a double security arises to the rights of the people. The different governments will control each other, at the same time that each will be controlled by itself.

Second. It is of great importance in a republic not only to guard the society against the oppression of its rulers, but to guard one part of the society against the injustice of the other part. Different interests necessarily exist in different classes of citizens. If a majority be united by a common interest, the rights of the minority will be insecure. There are but two methods of providing against this evil: the one by creating a will in the community independent of the majority—that is, of the society itself; the other, by comprehending in the society so many separate descriptions of citizens as will render an unjust combination of a majority of the whole very improbable, if not impracticable. The first method prevails in all governments possessing an hereditary or self-appointed authority. This, at best, is but a precarious security; because a power independent of the society may as well espouse the unjust views of the major as the rightful interests of the minor party, and may possibly be turned against both parties. The second method will be exemplified in the federal republic of the United States. Whilst all authority in it will be derived from and dependent on the society, the society itself will be broken into so many parts, interests and classes of citizens, that the rights of individuals, or of the minority, will be in little danger from interested combinations of the majority. In a free government the security for civil rights must be the same as that for religious rights. It consists in the one case in the multiplicity of interests, and in the other in the multiplicity of sects. The degree of security in both cases will depend on the number of interests and sects; and this may be presumed to depend on the extent of country and number of people comprehended under the same government. This view of the subject must particularly recommend a proper federal system to all the sincere and considerate friends of republican government, since it shows that in exact proportion as the territory of the Union may be formed into more circumscribed Confederacies, or States, oppressive combinations of a majority will be facilitated; the best security, under the republican forms, for the rights of every class of citizen, will be diminished; and consequently the stability and independence of some member of the government, the only other security, must be proportionally increased. Justice is the end of government. It is the end of civil society. It ever has been and ever will be pursued until it be obtained, or until liberty be lost in the pursuit. In a society under the forms of which the stronger faction can readily unite and oppress the weaker, anarchy may as truly be said to reign as in a state of nature, where the weaker individual is not secured against the violence of the stronger; and as, in the latter state, even the stronger individuals are prompted, by the uncertainty of their condition, to submit to a government which may protect the weak as well as themselves; so, in the former state, will the more powerful factions or parties be gradually induced, by a like motive, to wish for a government which will protect all parties, the weaker as well as the more powerful. It can be little doubted that if the State of Rhode Island was separated from the Confederacy and left to itself, the insecurity of rights under the popular form of government within such narrow limits would be displayed by such reiterated oppressions of factious majorities that some power altogether independent of the people would soon be called for by the voice of the very factions whose misrule had proved the necessity of it. In the extended republic of the United States, and among the great variety of interests, parties, and sects which it embraces, a coalition of a majority of the whole society could seldom take place on any other principles than those of justice and the general good; whilst there being thus less danger to a minor from the will of a major party, there must be less pretext, also, to provide for the security of the former, by introducing into the government a will not dependent on the latter, or, in other words, a will independent of the society itself. It is no less certain that it is important, notwithstanding the contrary opinions which have been entertained that the larger the society, provided it lie within a practicable sphere, the more duly capable it will be of self-government. And happily for the *republican cause*, the practicable sphere may be carried to a very great extent by a judicious modification and mixture of the *federal principle*.

PRESIDENTS AND VICE PRESIDENTS

1. George Washington (1789)
   John Adams (1789)

2. John Adams (1797)
   Thomas Jefferson (1797)

3. Thomas Jefferson (1801)
   Aaron Burr (1801)
   George Clinton (1805)

4. James Madison (1809)
   George Clinton (1809)
   Elbridge Gerry (1813)

5. James Monroe (1817)
   Daniel D. Tompkins (1817)

6. John Quincy Adams (1825)
   John C. Calhoun (1825)

7. Andrew Jackson (1829)
   John C. Calhoun (1829)
   Martin Van Buren (1833)

8. Martin Van Buren (1837)
   Richard M. Johnson (1837)

9. William H. Harrison (1841)
   John Tyler (1841)

10. John Tyler (1841)

11. James K. Polk (1845)
    George M. Dallas (1845)

12. Zachary Taylor (1849)
    Millard Fillmore (1849)

13. Millard Fillmore (1850)

14. Franklin Pierce (1853)
    William R. King (1853)

15. James Buchanan (1857)
    John C. Breckinridge (1857)

16. Abraham Lincoln (1861)
    Hannibal Hamlin (1861)
    Andrew Johnson (1865)

17. Andrew Johnson (1865)

18. Ulysses S. Grant (1869)
    Schuyler Colfax (1869)
    Henry Wilson (1873)

19. Rutherford B. Hayes (1877)
    William A. Wheeler (1877)

20. James A. Garfield (1881)
    Chester A. Arthur (1881)

21. Chester A. Arthur (1881)

22. Grover Cleveland (1885)
    T. A. Hendricks (1885)

23. Benjamin Harrison (1889)
    Levi P. Morton (1889)

24. Grover Cleveland (1893)
    Adlai E. Stevenson (1893)

25. William McKinley (1897)
    Garret A. Hobart (1897)
    Theodore Roosevelt (1901)

26. Theodore Roosevelt (1901)
    Charles Fairbanks (1905)

27. William H. Taft (1909)
    James S. Sherman (1909)

28. Woodrow Wilson (1913)
    Thomas R. Marshall (1913)

29. Warren G. Harding (1921)
    Calvin Coolidge (1921)

30. Calvin Coolidge (1923)
    Charles G. Dawes (1925)

31. Herbert C. Hoover (1929)
    Charles Curtis (1929)

32. Franklin D. Roosevelt (1933)
    John Nance Garner (1933)
    Henry A. Wallace (1941)
    Harry S Truman (1945)

33. Harry S Truman (1945)
    Alben W. Barkley (1949)

34. Dwight D. Eisenhower (1953)
    Richard M. Nixon (1953)

35. John F. Kennedy (1961)
    Lyndon B. Johnson (1961)

36. Lyndon B. Johnson (1963)
    Hubert H. Humphrey (1965)

37. Richard M. Nixon (1969)
    Spiro T. Agnew (1969)
    Gerald R. Ford (1973)

38. Gerald R. Ford (1974)
    Nelson A. Rockefeller (1974)

39. James E. Carter Jr. (1977)
    Walter F. Mondale (1977)

40. Ronald W. Reagan (1981)
    George H. W. Bush (1981)

41. George H. W. Bush (1989)
    James D. Quayle III (1989)

42. William J. B. Clinton (1993)
    Albert Gore (1993)

43. George W. Bush (2001)
    Richard Cheney (2001)

44. Barack H. Obama (2009)
    Joseph R. Biden (2009)

GLOSSARY

ABM Treaty Treaty in 1972 between the U.S. and the Soviet Union in which each side agreed not to build or deploy antiballistic missiles.

abolition movement Social movement before the Civil War whose goal was to abolish slavery throughout the United States.

access Meeting and talking with decision makers, a prerequisite to direct persuasion.

adjudication Decision making by the federal bureaucracy as to whether or not an individual or organization has complied with or violated government laws and/or regulation.

adversarial system Method of decision making in which an impartial judge or jury or decision maker hears arguments and reviews evidence presented by opposite sides.

advice and consent The constitutional power of the U.S. Senate to reject or ratify (by a two-thirds vote) treaties made by the president.

affirmative action Any program, whether enacted by a government or by a private organization, whose goal is to overcome the results of past unequal treatment of minorities and/or women by giving members of these groups preferential treatment in admissions, hiring, promotions, or other aspects of life.

affirmative racial gerrymandering Drawing district boundary lines to maximize minority representation.

agenda setting Deciding what will be decided; defining the problems and issues to be addressed by decision makers.

agriculture commissioner The elected official responsible for administering laws and programs that benefit agriculture.

aliens Persons residing in a nation who are not citizens.

amendment Formal change in a bill, law, or constitution.

amicus curiae Literally, "friend of the court"; a person, private group or institution, or government agency that is not a party to a case but participates in the case (usually through submission of a brief) at the invitation of the court or on its own initiative.

amnesty Government forgiveness of a crime, usually granted to a group of people.

Annapolis Convention A 1786 meeting at Annapolis, Maryland, to discuss interstate commerce, that recommended a larger convention—the Constitutional Convention of 1787.

Anti-Federalists Those who opposed the ratification of the U.S. Constitution and the creation of a strong national government.

appeal In general, requests that a higher court review cases decided at a lower level. In the Supreme Court, certain cases are designated as appeals under federal law; formally, these must be heard by the Court.

appellate jurisdiction Particular court's power to review a decision or action of a lower court.

apportionment The allocation of legislative seats to jurisdictions based on population. Seats in the U.S. House of Representatives are apportioned to the states on the basis of their population after every 10 year census.

appropriations act Congressional bill that provides money for programs authorized by Congress.

attorney general The state's chief legal officer, who represents Texas in lawsuits and is responsible for enforcing the state's antitrust, consumer protection, and other civil laws.

authoritarianism Monopoly of political power by an individual or small group that otherwise allows people to go about their private lives as they wish.

authorization Act of Congress that establishes a government program and defines the amount of money it may spend.

backdoor spending Spending by agencies of the federal government whose operations are not included in the federal budget.

bail Release of an accused person from custody in exchange for promise to appear at trial, guaranteed by money or property that is forfeited to court if defendant does not appear.

***Bakke* case** U.S. Supreme Court case challenging affirmative action.

balanced budget Government budget in which expenditures and revenues are equal, so that no deficit or surplus exists.

ballistic missile defense (BMD) Weapons systems capable of detecting, intercepting, and destroying missiles in flight.

beliefs Shared ideas about what is true.

bicameral Any legislative body that consists of two separate chambers or houses; in the United States, the Senate represents 50 statewide voter constituencies, and the House of Representatives represents voters in 435 separate districts.

big-state strategy Presidential political campaign strategy in which a candidate focuses on winning primaries in large states because of their high delegate counts.

bill of attainder Legislative act inflicting punishment without judicial trial; forbidden under Article I of the Constitution.

Bill of Rights Written guarantees of basic individual liberties; the first ten amendments to the U.S. Constitution.

bipartisanship Agreement by members of both the Democratic and the Republican parties.

block grant A federal grant to state or local governments for a general governmental function, allowing greater flexibility in the use of the money.

bribery Giving or offering anything of value in an effort to influence government officials in the performance of their duties.

briefs Documents submitted by an attorney to a court, setting out the facts of the case and the legal arguments in support of the party represented by the attorney.

budget maximization Bureaucrats' tendencies to expand their agencies' budgets, staff, and authority.

budget resolution Congressional bill setting forth target budget figures for appropriations to various government departments and agencies.

bureaucracy Departments, agencies, bureaus, and offices that perform the functions of government.

cabinet The heads (secretaries) of the executive departments together with other top officials accorded cabinet rank by the president; only occasionally does it meet as a body to advise and support the president.

campaign strategy Plan for a political campaign, usually including a theme, an attempt to define the opponent or the issues, and an effort to coordinate images and messages in news broadcasts and paid advertising.

capital gains Profits from buying and selling property including stocks, bonds, and real estate.

capitalism Economic system asserting the individual's right to own private property and to buy, sell, rent, and trade that property in a free market.

capture theory of regulation Theory describing how some regulated industries come to benefit from government regulation and how some regulatory commissions come to represent the industries they are supposed to regulate rather than representing "the people."

careerism In politics, a reference to people who started young working in politics, running for and holding public office, and made politics their career.

casework Services performed by legislators or their staff on behalf of individual constituents.

categorical grant A federal grant to a state or local government for a specific purpose or project; it may be allocated by a formula or by project.

caucus Nominating process in which party leaders select the party's nominee.

censure Public reprimand for wrongdoing, given to a member standing in the chamber before Congress.

centralized federalism Model of federalism in which the national government assumes primary responsibility for determining national goals in all major policy areas and directs state and local government activity through conditions attached to money grants.

chain of command Hierarchical structure of authority in which command flows downward; typical of a bureaucracy.

challengers In politics, a reference to people running against incumbent officeholders.

checks and balances Constitutional provisions giving each branch of the national government certain checks over the actions of other branches.

circuit courts The twelve appellate courts that make up the middle level of the federal court system.

civil cases Noncriminal court proceedings in which a plaintiff sues a defendant for damages in payment for harm inflicted.

civil disobedience Form of public protest involving the breaking of laws believed to be unjust.

class action suits Cases initiated by parties acting on behalf of themselves and all others similarly situated.

class conflict Conflict between upper and lower social classes over wealth and power.

class consciousness Awareness of one's class position and a feeling of political solidarity with others within the same class in opposition to other classes.

classical liberalism Political philosophy asserting the worth and dignity of the individual and emphasizing the rational ability of human beings to determine their own destinies.

clear and present danger doctrine Standard used by the courts to determine whether speech may be restricted; only speech that creates a serious and immediate danger to society may be restricted.

closed primaries Primary elections in which voters must declare (or have previously declared) their party affiliation and can cast a ballot only in their own party's primary election.

closed rule Rule that forbids adding any amendments to a bill under consideration by the House.

cloture Vote to end debate—that is, to end a filibuster—which requires a three-fifths vote of the entire membership of the Senate.

coalition A joining together of interest groups (or individuals) to achieve a common goal.

COLAs Annual cost-of-living adjustments mandated by law in Social Security and other welfare benefits.

Cold War Political, military, and ideological struggle between the United States and the Soviet Union following the end of World War II and ending with the collapse of the Soviet Union's communist government in 1991.

collective security Attempt to bring order to international relations by all nations joining together to guarantee each other's "territorial integrity" and "independence" against "external aggression."

commercial speech Advertising communications given only partial protection under the 1st Amendment to the Constitution.

common market Unified trade area in which all goods and services can be sold or exchanged free from customs or tariffs.

communism System of government in which a single totalitarian party controls all means of production and distribution of goods and services.

comparable worth Argument that pay levels for traditionally male and traditionally female jobs should be equalized by paying equally all jobs that are "worth about the same" to an employer.

comptroller The state's primary tax administrator, accounting officer, and revenue estimator.

concurrent powers Powers exercised by both the national government and state governments in the American federal system.

concurring opinion Opinion by a member of a court that agrees with the result reached by the court in the case but disagrees with or departs from the court's rationale for the decision.

confederation Constitutional arrangement whereby the national government is created by and relies on subnational governments for its authority.

conference committee Meeting between representatives of the House and Senate to reconcile differences over provisions of a bill passed by both houses.

confirmation The constitutionally required consent of the Senate to appointments of high-level executive officials by the president and appointments of federal judges.

congressional hearings Congressional committee sessions in which members listen to witnesses who provide information and opinions on matters of interest to the committee, including pending legislation.

congressional investigation Congressional committee hearings on alleged misdeeds or scandals.

congressional session Each Congress elected in November of even-numbered years meets the following January 3 and remains in session for 2 years. Since the first Congress to meet under the Constitution in 1789, Congresses have been numbered by session (for example, 107th Congress 2001–2003, 108th Congress 2003–2005, 109th Congress 2005–2007).

Connecticut Compromise A constitutional plan that merged elements of a Virginia plan and a New Jersey plan into the present arrangement of the U.S. Congress: one house in which each state has an equal number of votes (the Senate) and one house in which states' votes are based on population (the House of Representatives).

conservatism Belief in the value of free markets, limited government, and individual self-reliance in economic affairs, combined with a belief in the value of tradition, law, and morality in social affairs.

constituency The votes in a legislator's home district.

constitutional county court County court created by the Texas Constitution, presided over by the county judge.

constitutional government Government limited by rule of law in its power over the liberties of individuals.

constitutionalism A government of laws, not people, operating on the principle that governmental power must be limited and government officials should be restrained in their exercise of power over individuals.

containment Policy of preventing an enemy from expanding its boundaries and/or influence, specifically the U.S. foreign policy vis-à-vis the Soviet Union during the Cold War.

contempt In law, willful disobedience to, or open disrespect of, a court or congressional body.

contingency fees Fees paid to attorneys to represent the plaintiff in a civil suit and receive in compensation an agreed-upon percentage of damages awarded (if any).

continuing resolution Congressional bill that authorizes government agencies to keep spending money for a specified period at the same level as in the previous fiscal year; passed when Congress is unable to enact final appropriations measures by October 1.

convention Nominating process in which delegates from local party organizations select the party's nominees.

cooperative federalism Model of federalism in which national, state, and local governments work together exercising common policy responsibilities.

covert action Secret intelligence activity outside U.S. borders undertaken with specific authorization by the president; acknowledgment of U.S. sponsorship would defeat or compromise its purpose.

Cuban Missile Crisis The 1962 confrontation between the Soviet Union and the U.S. over Soviet placement of nuclear missiles in Cuba.

de facto segregation Racial imbalances not directly caused by official actions but rather by residential patterns.

dealignment Declining attractiveness of the parties to the voters, a reluctance to identify strongly with a party, and a decrease in reliance on party affiliation in voter choice.

deductibles Initial charges in insurance plans, paid by beneficiaries.

defendants Parties against whom a criminal or civil suit is brought.

deferrals Items on which a president wishes to postpone spending.

deficit Imbalance in the annual federal budget in which spending exceeds revenues.

delegated, or enumerated, powers Powers specifically mentioned in the Constitution as belonging to the national government.

delegates Accredited voting members of a party's national presidential nominating convention.

democracy Governing system in which the people govern themselves, from the Greek term meaning "rule by the many."

democratic ideals Individual dignity, equality before the law, widespread participation in public decisions, and public decisions by majority rule, with one person having one vote.

Democratic Leadership Council Organization of party leaders who sought to create a "new" Democratic Party to appeal to middle-class, moderate voters.

Democratic Party One of the main parties in American politics; it traces its origins to Thomas Jefferson's Democratic-Republican Party, acquiring its current name under Andrew Jackson in 1828.

dependency ratio In the Social Security system, the number of recipients as a percentage of the number of contributing workers.

deregulation Lifting of government rules and bureaucratic supervision from business and professional activity.

deterrence U.S. approach to deterring any nuclear attack from the Soviet Union by maintaining a second-strike capability.

devolution Passing down of responsibilities from the national government to the states.

Dillon rule Principle holding that local governments are creations of state government and that their powers and responsibilities are defined by the state.

diplomatic recognition Power of the president to grant "legitimacy" to or withhold it from a government of another nation (to declare or refuse to declare it "rightful").

direct democracy Decisions are made directly by the people usually by popular initiative and referendum voting, as opposed to decisions made by elected representatives.

direct discrimination Now-illegal practice of differential pay for men versus women even when those individuals have equal qualifications and perform the same job.

direct primary election Selection of candidates for government office through direct election by the voters of a political party.

discharge petition Petition signed by at least 218 House members to force a vote on a bill within a committee that opposes it.

discretionary funds Budgeted funds not earmarked for specific purposes but available to be spent in accordance with the best judgment of a bureaucrat.

discretionary spending Spending for programs not previously mandated by law.

dissenting opinion Opinion by a member of a court that disagrees with the result reached by the court in the case.

district court Primary trial court in Texas. It has jurisdiction over criminal felony cases and civil disputes.

diversity Term in higher education that refers to racial and ethnic representation among students and faculty.

divided party government One party controls the presidency while the other party controls one or both houses of Congress.

division of labor Division of work among many specialized workers in a bureaucracy.

drafting a bill Actual writing of a bill in legal language.

dual federalism Early concept of federalism in which national and state powers were clearly distinguished and functionally separate.

Earned Income Tax Credit (EITC) Tax refunds in excess of tax payments for low-income workers.

economic cycles Fluctuations in real GDP growth followed by contraction.

Electoral College The 538 presidential electors apportioned among the states according to their congressional representation (plus 3 for the District of Columbia) whose votes officially elect the president and vice president of the United States.

elitism Political system in which power is concentrated in the hands of a relatively small group of individuals or institutions.

Emancipation Proclamation Lincoln's 1862 Civil War declaration that all slaves residing in rebel states were free. It did not abolish all slavery; that would be done by the 13th Amendment.

eminent domain The action of a government to take property for public use with just compensation even if the owner does not wish to sell.

end of history The collapse of communism and the worldwide movement toward free markets and political democracy.

Enlightenment, The Also known as the "Age of Reason," was a philosophical movement in 18th century Western thought based upon a belief in reason and the capacities of individuals, a faith in a scientific approach to knowledge, and a confidence in human progress.

entitlement programs Social welfare programs that provide classes of people with legally enforceable rights to benefits.

entitlements Any social welfare program for which there are eligibility requirements, whether financial or contributory.

enumerated powers Powers specifically mentioned in the Constitution as belonging to the national government.

Equal Rights Amendment (ERA) Proposed amendment to the Constitution guaranteeing that equal rights under the law shall not be denied or abridged on account of sex. Passed by Congress in 1972, the amendment failed to win ratification by three of the necessary three-fourths of the states.

equality of opportunity Elimination of artificial barriers to success in life and the opportunity for everyone to strive for success.

equality of results Equal sharing of income and material goods regardless of one's efforts in life.

equal-time rule Federal Communications Commission (FCC) requirement that broadcasters who sell time to any political candidate must make equal time available to opposing candidates at the same price.

"the Establishment" In the days of one-party Democratic politics in Texas, the Establishment was a loosely knit coalition of Anglo business and oil company executives, bankers, and lawyers who controlled state policy making through the dominant conservative wing of the Democratic Party.

ex post facto law Retroactive criminal law that works against the accused; forbidden under Article I of the Constitution.

exclusionary rule Rule of law that evidence found in an illegal search or resulting from an illegally obtained confession may not be admitted at trial.

executive agreement Agreement with another nation signed by the president of the United States but less formal (and hence potentially less binding) than a treaty because it does not require Senate confirmation.

executive order Formal regulation governing executive branch operations issued by the president.

executive privilege Right of a president to withhold from other branches of government confidential communications within the executive branch; although posited by presidents, it has been upheld by the Supreme Court only in limited situations.

externalities Costs imposed on people who are not direct participants in an activity.

extradition A process by which a person in one state is returned to another state to face criminal charges.

Fair Deal Policies of President Harry Truman extending Roosevelt's New Deal and maintaining the Democratic Party's voter coalition.

Family Assistance Public assistance program that provides monies to the states for their use in helping needy families with children.

fascism Political ideology in which the state and/or race is assumed to be supreme over individuals.

Federal Election Commission (FEC) Agency charged with enforcing federal election laws and disbursing public presidential campaign funds.

Federal Reserve Board (the Fed) Independent agency of the executive branch of the federal government charged with overseeing the nation's monetary policy.

federalism A constitutional arrangement whereby power is divided between national and subnational governments, each of which enforces its own laws directly on its citizens and neither of which can alter the arrangement without the consent of the other.

Federalists Those who supported the U.S. Constitution during the ratification process and who later formed a political party in support of John Adams's presidential candidacy.

"feeding frenzy" Intense media coverage of a scandal or event that blocks out most other news.

felonies Serious criminal offenses that can be punished by imprisonment and/or a fine.

filibuster Delaying tactic by a senator or group of senators, using the Senate's unlimited debate rule to prevent a vote on a bill.

first reading Introduction of a bill in the House or the Senate and its referral to a committee by the presiding officer.

fiscal policy Economic policies involving taxing, spending, and deficit levels of the national government.

fiscal year Yearly government accounting period, not necessarily the same as the calendar year. The federal government's fiscal year begins October 1 and ends September 30.

focus group In a political context, a small number of people brought together in a comfortable setting to discuss and respond to themes and issues, allowing campaign managers to develop and analyze strategies.

Food Stamp Program Public assistance program that provides low-income households with coupons redeemable for enough food to provide a minimal nutritious diet.

franking privilege Free use of the U.S. mails granted to members of Congress to promote communication with constituents.

Free Exercise Clause Clause in the 1st Amendment to the Constitution that prohibits government from restricting religious beliefs and practices.

free market Free competition for voluntary exchange among individuals, firms, and corporations.

free-riders People who do not belong to an organization or pay dues, yet nevertheless benefit from its activities.

free trade A policy of reducing or eliminating tariffs and quotas on imports to stimulate international trade.

freedom of expression Collectively, the 1st Amendment rights to free speech, press, and assembly.

front-end strategy Presidential political campaign strategy in which a candidate focuses on winning early primaries to build momentum.

front loading The scheduling of presidential primary elections early in the year.

gender gap Aggregate differences in political opinions of men and women.

general election Election to choose among candidates nominated by parties and/or independent candidates who gained access to the ballot by petition.

generation gap Differences in politics and public opinion among age groups.

generational effects Historical events that affect the views of those who lived through them.

gerrymandering Drawing district boundary lines for political advantage.

glass ceiling "Invisible" barriers to women rising to the highest positions in corporations and the professions.

GOP "Grand Old Party"—popular label for the Republican Party.

government Organization extending to the whole society that can legitimately use force to carry out its decisions.

government bonds Certificates of indebtedness that pay interest and promise repayment on a future date.

grand jury Jury charged only with determining whether sufficient evidence exists to support indictment of an individual on a felony charge; the grand jury's decision to indict does not represent a conviction.

Grange Organization formed in the late nineteenth century to improve the lot of farmers. The Grange influenced provisions in the Texas Constitution of 1876 limiting taxes and government spending and restricting big business, including banks and railroads.

grant of immunity from prosecution Grant by the government to an individual of freedom from prosecution on a particular charge in return for testimony by that individual that might otherwise be self-incriminating.

grants-in-aid Payments of funds from the national government to state or local governments or from a state government to local governments for specific purposes.

grassroots lobbying Attempts to influence government decision making by inspiring constituents to contact their representatives.

Great Society Policies of President Lyndon Johnson that promised to solve the nation's social and economic problems through government intervention.

gridlock Political stalemate between the executive and legislative branches arising when one branch is controlled by one major political party and the other branch by the other party.

gross domestic product (GDP) Measure of economic performance in terms of the nation's total production of goods and services for a single year, valued in terms of market prices.

halo effect Tendency of survey respondents to provide socially acceptable answers to questions.

health maintenance organizations (HMOs) Health care provider groups that provide a stipulated list of services to patients for a fixed fee that is usually substantially lower than such care would otherwise cost.

home rule Power of local government to pass laws affecting local affairs, so long as those laws do not conflict with state or federal laws.

home style Activities of Congress members specifically directed at their home constituencies.

honeymoon period Early months of a president's term in which his popularity with the public and influence with the Congress are generally high.

horse-race coverage Media coverage of electoral campaigns that concentrates on who is ahead and who is behind, and neglects the issues at stake.

ideological organizations Interest groups that pursue ideologically based (liberal or conservative) agendas.

ideological party Third party that exists to promote an ideology rather than to win elections.

ideology Consistent and integrated system of ideas, values, and beliefs.

immigration policy Regulating the entry of noncitizens into the country.

impeachment Formal charges of wrongdoing brought against a government official, resulting in a trial and, upon conviction, removal from office.

impersonality Treatment of all persons within a bureaucracy on the basis of "merit" and of all "clients" served by the bureaucracy equally according to rules.

implementation Development by the federal bureaucracy of procedures and activities to carry out policies legislated by Congress; it includes regulation as well as adjudication.

implied powers Powers not mentioned specifically in the Constitution as belonging to Congress but inferred as necessary and proper for carrying out the enumerated powers.

impoundment Refusal by a president to spend monies appropriated by Congress; outlawed except with congressional consent by the Budget and Impoundment Control Act of 1974.

inalienable rights The rights of all people derived from natural law and not bestowed by governments, including the rights to life, liberty, and property.

incidence Actual bearer of a tax burden.

income transfers Government transfers of income from taxpayers to persons regarded as deserving.

incorporation In constitutional law, the application of almost all of the Bill of Rights to the states and all of their subdivision through the 14th Amendment.

incremental budgeting Method of budgeting that focuses on requested increases in funding for existing programs, accepting as legitimate their previous year's expenditures.

incumbent Candidate currently in office seeking reelection.

incumbent gerrymandering Drawing legislative district boundaries to advantage incumbent legislators.

independent counsel ("special prosecutor") A prosecutor appointed by a federal court to pursue charges against a president or other high official.

This position was allowed to lapse by Congress in 1999 after many controversial investigations by these prosecutors.

indexing Tying of benefit levels in social welfare programs to the general price level.

indictment Determination by a grand jury that sufficient evidence exists to warrant trial of an individual on a felony charge; necessary before an individual can be brought to trial.

individual income tax Taxes on individuals' wages and other earned income, the primary source of revenue for the U.S. federal government.

inflation Rise in the general level of prices, not just the prices of some products.

information overload Situation in which individuals are subjected to so many communications that they cannot make sense of them.

initiative Allows a specified number or percentage of voters by use of a petition to place a state constitutional amendment or a state law on the ballot for adoption or rejection by the state electorate.

in-kind (noncash) benefits Benefits of a social welfare program that are not cash payments, including free medical care, subsidized housing, and food stamps.

interest group Organization seeking to influence government policy.

interest-group entrepreneurs Leaders who create organizations and market memberships.

intergovernmental relations Network of political, financial, and administrative relationships between units of the federal government and those of state and local governments.

international trade The buying and selling of goods and services between individuals or firms located in different countries.

iron triangles Mutually supportive relationships among interest groups, government agencies, and legislative committees with jurisdiction over a specific policy area.

issue ads Ads that advocate policy positions rather than explicitly supporting or opposing particular candidates.

Jim Crow Second-class-citizen status conferred on blacks by Southern segregation laws; derived from a nineteenth-century song-and-dance act (usually performed by a white man in blackface) that stereotyped blacks.

judicial activism Making of new law through judicial interpretations of the Constitution.

judicial review Power of the courts, especially the Supreme Court, to declare laws of Congress, laws of the states, and actions of the president unconstitutional and invalid.

judicial self-restraint Self-imposed limitation on judicial power by judges deferring to the policy judgments of elected branches of government.

jurisdiction Power of a court to hear a case in question.

Korean War Communist North Korea invaded non-Communist South Korea in June, 1950, causing President Harry S Truman to intervene militarily, with U.N. support. General Douglas MacArthur defeated the North Koreans, but with China's entry into the war, a stalemate resulted. An armistice was signed in 1953, with Korea divided along nearly original lines.

laboratories of democracy A reference to the ability of states to experiment and innovate in public policy.

land commissioner The elected official who manages the state's public lands and administers the Veterans Land Program, which provides low-interest loans to veterans for the purchase of land and houses.

left A reference to the liberal, progressive, and/or socialist side of the political spectrum.

legal equality Belief that the law should apply equally to all persons.

Legislative Budget Board The panel that makes budgetary recommendations to the full legislature. It is chaired by the lieutenant governor and includes the speaker of the House and eight other key lawmakers.

legitimacy Widespread acceptance of something as necessary, rightful, and legally binding.

Lemon test To be constitutional, a law must have a secular purpose; its primary effect must neither advance nor inhibit religion; and it must not foster excessive government entanglement with religion.

Leninism The theories of Vladimir Lenin, among them that advanced capitalist countries turned toward war and colonialism to make their own workers relatively prosperous.

libel Writings that are false and malicious and are intended to damage an individual.

liberalism Belief in the value of strong government to provide economic security and protection for civil rights, combined with a belief in personal freedom from government intervention in social conduct.

libertarian Opposing government intervention in both economic and social affairs, and favoring minimal government in all sectors of society.

life-cycle effects Changes in life circumstances associated with age that affect one's views.

limited government Principle that government power over the individual is limited, that there are some personal liberties that even a majority cannot regulate, and that government itself is restrained by law.

line-item veto Power of the chief executive to reject some portions of a bill without rejecting all of it.

literacy test Examination of a person's ability to read and write as a prerequisite to voter registration, outlawed by Voting Rights Act (1965) as discriminatory.

litigation Legal dispute brought before a court.

litmus test In political terms, a person's stand on a key issue that determines whether he or she will be appointed to public office or supported in electoral campaigns.

lobbying Activities directed at government officials with the hope of influencing their decisions.

lobbyist Person working to influence government policies and actions.

logrolling Bargaining for agreement among legislators to support each other's favorite bills, especially projects that primarily benefit individual members and their constituents.

machine Tightly disciplined party organization, headed by a boss, that relies on material rewards—including patronage jobs—to control politics.

majoritarianism Tendency of democratic governments to allow the faint preferences of the majority to prevail over the intense feelings of minorities.

majority Election by more than 50 percent of all votes cast in the contest.

majority leader In the House, the majority-party leader and second in command to the Speaker; in the Senate, the leader of the majority party.

majority opinion Opinion in a case that is subscribed to by a majority of the judges who participated in the decision.

malapportionment Unequal numbers of people in legislative districts resulting in inequality of voter representation.

managed care Programs designed to keep health care costs down by the establishment of strict guidelines regarding when and what diagnostic and therapeutic procedures should be administered to patients under various circumstances.

mandate Perception of popular support for a program or policy based on the margin of electoral victory won by a candidate who proposed it during a campaign; direct federal orders to state and local governments requiring them to perform a service or to obey federal laws in the performance of their functions.

mandatory spending Spending for program committments made by past congresses.

markup Line-by-line revision of a bill in committee by editing each phrase and word.

Marshall Plan U.S. program to rebuild the nations of Western Europe in the aftermath of World War II in order to render them less susceptible to communist influence and takeover.

Marxism The theories of Karl Marx, among them that capitalists oppress workers and that worldwide revolution and the emergence of a classless society are inevitable.

mass media All means of communication with the general public, including television, newspapers, magazines, radio, books, recordings, motion pictures, and the Internet.

means-tested spending Spending for benefits that is distributed on the basis of the recipient's income.

Medicaid Public assistance program that provides health care to the poor.

Medicare Social insurance program that provides health care insurance to elderly and disabled people.

merit selection Proposal under which the governor would appoint state judges from lists of potential nominees recommended by committees of experts. Appointed judges would have to run later in retention elections to keep their seats but would not have opponents on the ballot. Voters would simply decide whether a judge should remain in office or be replaced by another gubernatorial appointee.

merit system Selection of employees for government agencies on the basis of competence, with no consideration of an individual's political stance and/or power.

minority leader In both the House and Senate, the leader of the opposition party.

Miranda warning Requirement that persons arrested be informed of their rights immediately after arrest.

mobilize In politics, to activate supporters to work for candidates and turn out on Election Day.

monetary policy Economic policies involving the money supply, interest rates, and banking activity.

"Motor Voter Act" Federal mandate that states offer voter registration at driver's licensing and welfare offices.

muckraking Journalistic exposés of corruption, wrongdoing, or mismanagement in government, business, and other institutions of society.

name recognition Public awareness of a candidate—whether they even know his or her name.

national debt Total debt accumulated by the national government over the years.

national health insurance Government-provided insurance to all citizens paid from tax revenues.

National Security Council (NSC) "Inner cabinet" that advises the president and coordinates foreign, defense, and intelligence activities.

National Supremacy Clause Clause in Article VI of the U.S. Constitution declaring the constitution and laws of the national government "the supreme law of the land" superior to the constitutions and laws of the states.

nationalism Belief that shared cultural, historical, linguistic, and social characteristics of a people justify the creation of a government encompassing all of them, the resulting nation-state should be independent and legally equal to all other nation-states.

natural law The law that would govern humans in a state of nature before governments existed.

Necessary and Proper Clause Clause in Article I, Section 8, of the U.S. Constitution granting Congress the power to enact all laws that are "necessary and proper" for carrying out those responsibilities specifically delegated to it. Also referred to as the Implied Powers Clause.

negative campaigning Speeches, commercials, or advertising attacking a political opponent during a campaign.

New Deal Policies of President Franklin D. Roosevelt during the Depression of the 1930s that helped form a Democratic Party coalition of urban working-class, ethnic, Catholic, Jewish, poor, and Southern voters.

new federalism Attempts to return power and responsibility to the states and reduce the role of the national government in domestic affairs.

newsmaking Deciding what events, topics, presentations, and issues will be given coverage in the news.

No Establishment Clause Clause in the 1st Amendment to the Constitution that is interpreted to require the separation of church and state.

nomination Political party's selection of its candidate for a public office.

nominee Political party's entry in a general election race.

nonpartisan elections Elections in which candidates do not officially indicate their party affiliation; often used for city, county, school board, and judicial elections.

nonviolent direct action Strategy used by civil rights leaders such as Martin Luther King, Jr., in which protesters break "unjust" laws openly but in a "loving" fashion in order to bring the injustices of such laws to public attention.

North Atlantic Treaty Organization (NATO) Mutual-security agreement and joint military command uniting the nations of Western Europe, initially formed to resist Soviet expansionism.

obligational authority Feature of some appropriations acts by which an agency is empowered to enter into contracts that will require the government to make payments beyond the fiscal year in question.

open primaries Primary elections in which a voter may cast a ballot in either party's primary election.

open rule Rule that permits unlimited amendments to a bill under consideration by the House.

open seat Seat in a legislature for which no incumbent is running for reelection.

ordinances Local laws enacted by a city council.

organizational sclerosis Society encrusted with so many special benefits to interest groups that everyone's standard of living is lowered.

original intent Judicial philosophy under which judges attempt to apply the values of the Founders to current issues.

original jurisdiction Refers to a particular court's power to serve as the place where a given case is initially argued and decided.

outlays Actual dollar amounts to be spent by the federal government in a fiscal year.

outsourcing Government contracting with private firms to perform public services.

override Voting in Congress to enact legislation vetoed by the president; requires a two-thirds vote in both the House and Senate.

oversight Congressional monitoring of the activities of executive branch agencies to determine if the laws are being faithfully executed.

packing Redistricting in which partisan voters are concentrated in a single district, "wasting" their majority vote and allowing the opposition to win by modest majorities in other districts.

paradox of democracy Potential for conflict between individual freedom and majority rule.

parliamentary government A government in which power is concentrated in the legislature, which chooses from among its members a prime minister and cabinet.

partial preemption Federal government's assumption of some regulatory powers in a particular field, with the stipulation that a state law on the same subject as a federal law is valid if it does not conflict with the federal law in the same area.

party identification Self-described identification with a political party, usually in response to the question, "Generally speaking, how would you identify yourself: as a Republican, Democrat, Independent, or something else?"

party organization National and state party officials and workers, committee members, convention delegates, and others active in the party.

party-in-the-electorate Voters who identify themselves with a party.

party-in-the-government Public officials who were nominated by their party and who identify themselves in office with their party.

party polarization The tendency of the Democratic Party to take more liberal positions and the Republican Party to take more conservative positions on key issues.

party unity Percentage of Democrats and Republicans who stick with their party on party votes.

party vote Majority of Democrats voting in opposition to a majority of Republicans.

passport Evidence of U.S. citizenship, allowing people to travel abroad and reenter the United States.

patronage Appointment to public office based on party loyalty.

perjury Lying while under oath and sworn to tell the truth.

petit (regular) jury Panel of citizens that hears evidence in a civil lawsuit or a criminal prosecution and decides the outcome by issuing a verdict.

plaintiffs Parties initiating suits and claiming damages. In criminal cases, the state acts as plaintiff on behalf of an injured society and requests fines and/or imprisonment as damages. In civil suits, the plaintiff is the injured party and seeks monetary damages.

platform Statement of principles adopted by a political party at its national convention (specific portions of the platform are known as planks); a platform is not binding on the party's candidates.

plea bargaining Practice of allowing defendants to plead guilty to lesser crimes than those with which they were originally charged in return for reduced sentences.

plural executive A fragmented system of authority under which most statewide executive officeholders are elected independently of the governor.

pluralism Theory that democracy can be achieved through competition among multiple organized groups and that individuals can participate in politics through group memberships and elections.

plurality Election by at least one vote more than any other candidate in the race.

pocket veto Effective veto of a bill when Congress adjourns within 10 days of passing it and the president fails to sign it.

political action committees (PACs) Organizations that solicit and receive campaign contributions from corporations, unions, trade associations, and ideological and issue-oriented groups, and their members, then distribute these funds to political candidates.

political alienation Belief that politics is irrelevant to one's life and that one cannot personally affect public affairs.

political culture Widely shared views about who should govern, for what ends, and by what means.

political equality Belief that the law should apply equally to all and that every person's vote counts equally.

political organizations Parties and interest groups that function as intermediaries between individuals and government.

political parties Organizations that seek to achieve power by winning public office.

political science The study of politics: who governs, for what ends, and by what means.

political patronage The hiring of government employees on the basis of personal friendships or favors rather than ability or merit.

politically correct (PC) Repression of attitudes, speech, and writings that are deemed racist, sexist, homophobic (anti-homosexual), or otherwise "insensitive."

politics Deciding who gets what, when, and how.

poll taxes Taxes imposed as a prerequisite to voting; prohibited by the 24th Amendment.

pork barreling Legislation designed to make government benefits, including jobs and projects used as political patronage, flow to a particular district or state.

poverty line Official standard regarding what level of annual cash income is sufficient to maintain a "decent standard of living"; those with incomes below this level are eligible for most public assistance programs.

power of the purse Congress's exclusive, constitutional power to authorize expenditures by all agencies of the federal government.

precedent Legal principle that previous decisions should determine the outcome of current cases; the basis for stability in law.

precinct Subdivision of a city, county, or ward for election purposes.

precinct convention Meeting held by a political party in each precinct on the same day as the party primary. In presidential election years, the precinct conventions and the primaries are the first steps in the selection of delegates to the major parties' national nominating conventions.

preemption Total or partial federal assumption of power in a particular field, restricting the authority of the states.

preemptive attacks The initiation of military action by the United States to prevent terrorists or rogue nations from inflicting heavy damage on the United States.

preferred position Refers to the tendency of the courts to give preference to the 1st Amendment rights to speech, press, and assembly when faced with conflicts.

preferred provider organizations (PPOs) Groups of hospitals and physicians who have joined together to offer their services to private insurers at a discount.

presidential primaries Primary elections in the states in which voters in each party can choose a presidential candidate for its party's nomination. Outcomes help determine the distribution of pledged delegates to each party's national nominating convention.

primary elections Elections to choose party nominees for public office; may be open or closed.

prior restraint Government actions to restrict publication of a magazine, newspaper, or books on grounds of libel, obscenity, or other legal violations prior to actual publication of the work.

probation Procedure under which a convicted criminal is not sent to prison if she or he meets certain conditions, such as restrictions on travel and associates.

professionalism In politics, a reference to the increasing number of officeholders for whom politics is a full-time occupation.

program budgeting Identifying items in a budget according to the functions and programs they are to be spent on.

progressive taxation System of taxation in which higher-income groups pay a larger percentage of their incomes in taxes than do lower-income groups.

proportional (flat) taxation System of taxation in which all income groups pay the same percentage of their income in taxes.

proportional representation Electoral system that allocates seats in a legislature based on the proportion of votes each party receives in a national election.

protectionism A policy of high tariffs and quotas on imports to protect domestic industries.

protest party Third party that arises in response to issues of popular concern which have not been addressed by the major parties.

protests Public marches or demonstrations designed to call attention to an issue and motivate others to apply pressure on public officials.

public assistance programs Those social welfare programs for which no contributions are required and only those living in poverty (by official standards) are eligible; includes food stamps, Medicaid, and Family Assistance.

public goods Goods and services that cannot readily be provided by markets, either because they are too expensive for a single individual to buy or because if one person bought them, everyone else would use them without paying.

public-interest groups Interest groups that claim to represent broad classes of people or the public as a whole.

public opinion Aggregate of preferences and opinions of individuals on significant issues.

public relations Building and maintaining goodwill with the general public.

quota Provision of some affirmative action programs in which specific numbers or percentages of positions are open only to minorities and/or women.

radicalism Advocacy of immediate and drastic changes in society, including the complete restructuring of institutions, values, and beliefs. Radicals may exist on either the extreme left or extreme right.

raiding Organized efforts by one party to get its members to cross over in a primary and defeat an attractive candidate in the opposition party's primary.

Railroad Commission A three-member, elected body that regulates oil and natural gas production and lignite mining in Texas.

ranking minority member The minority-party committee member with the most seniority.

ratification Power of a legislature to approve or reject decisions made by other bodies. State legislators or state conventions must ratify constitutional amendments submitted by Congress. The U.S. Senate must ratify treaties made by the president.

reading Bills are required to go through three readings in both houses of the legislature. The first reading occurs with the introduction of a bill in the House or the Senate and its referral to a committee by the presiding officer. The second reading is the initial debate by the full House or Senate on a bill that has been approved by a committee. The third occurs with the final presentation of a bill before the full House or Senate.

Reagan Coalition Combination of economic and social conservatives, religious fundamentalists, and defense-minded anti-communists who rallied behind Republican President Ronald Reagan.

realignment Major shift in political party support or identification that usually occurs around a critical election. In Texas, realignment took place as a gradual transformation from a one-party system dominated by Democrats to a two-party system in which Republicans became competitive in elections.

recession Decline in the general level of economic activity.

Reconstruction The post–Civil War period when the Southern states were occupied by federal troops and newly freed African Americans occupied many political offices and exercised civil rights.

redistricting Drawing of legislative district boundary lines following each 10-year census.

referenda Proposed laws or constitutional amendments submitted to the voters for their direct approval or rejection, found in state constitutions but not in the U.S. Constitution.

regional security Attempt to bring order to international relations during the Cold War by creating regional alliances between a superpower and nations of a particular region.

registration Requirement that prospective voters establish their identity and place of residence prior to an election in order to be eligible to vote.

regressive taxation System of taxation in which lower-income groups pay a larger percentage of their incomes in taxes than do higher-income groups.

regulation Development by the federal bureaucracy of formal rules for implementing legislation.

remedies and reliefs Orders of a court to correct a wrong, including a violation of the Constitution.

representational federalism Assertion that no constitutional division of powers exists between the nation and the states but the states retain their constitutional role merely by selecting the president and members of Congress.

representative democracy Governing system in which public decision making is delegated to representatives of the people chosen by popular vote in free, open, and periodic elections.

Republican Party One of the two main parties in American politics, it traces its origins to the antislavery and nationalist forces that united in the 1850s and nominated Abraham Lincoln for president in 1860.

republicanism Government by representatives of the people rather than directly by the people themselves.

rescissions Items on which a president wishes to cancel spending.

reserved powers Powers not granted to the national government or specifically denied to the states in the Constitution that are recognized by the 10th Amendment as belonging to the state governments. This guarantee, known as the Reserved Powers Clause, embodies the principle of American federalism.

responsible party model System in which competitive parties adopt a platform of principles, recruiting candidates and directing campaigns based on the platform, and holding their elected officials responsible for enacting it.

restricted rule Rule that allows specified amendments to be added to a bill under consideration by the House.

retail politics Direct candidate contact with individual voters.

retrospective voting Voting for or against a candidate or party on the basis of past performance in office.

revolving doors The movement of individuals from government positions to jobs in the private sector, using the experience, knowledge, and contacts they acquired in government employment.

rider Amendment to a bill that is not germane to the bill's purposes.

right A reference to the conservative, traditional, anti-communist side of the political spectrum.

roll-call vote Vote of the full House or Senate on which all members' individual votes are recorded and made public.

rule Stipulation attached to a bill in the House of Representatives that governs its consideration on the floor, including when and for how long it can be debated and how many (if any) amendments may be appended to it.

rule of four At least four justices must agree to hear an appeal (writ of certiorari) from a lower court in order to get a case before the Supreme Court.

runoff primary Additional primary held between the top two vote-getters in a primary where no candidate has received a majority of the vote.

safe seat Legislative district in which the incumbent regularly wins by a large margin of the vote.

salient issues Issues about which most people have an opinion.

SALT I First arms limitation treaty between the United States and the Soviet Union, signed in 1972, limiting the total number of offensive nuclear missiles; it included the ABM Treaty that reflected the theory that the population centers of both nations should be left undefended.

SALT II Lengthy and complicated treaty between the United States and the Soviet Union, agreed to in 1979 but never ratified by the U.S. Senate, that set limits on all types of strategic nuclear launch vehicles.

school superintendent Top administrator of a school district. He or she is hired by the elected school board to direct the district's daily operations.

search warrant Court order permitting law-enforcement officials to search a location in order to seize evidence of a crime; issued only for a specified location, in connection with a specific investigation, and on submission of proof that "probable cause" exists to warrant such a search.

second reading Initial debate by the full House or Senate on a bill that has been approved by a committee.

second-strike capability Ability of a nation's forces to survive a surprise nuclear attack by the enemy and then to retaliate effectively.

secretary of state The official who administers state election laws, grants charters to corporations, and processes the extradition of prisoners to other states. This officeholder is appointed by the governor.

secular In politics, a reference to opposition to religious practices and symbols in public life.

selective perception Mentally screening out information or opinions with which one disagrees.

senatorial courtesy Custom of the U.S. Senate with regard to presidential nominations to the judiciary to defer to the judgment of senators from the president's party from the same state as the nominee.

seniority system Custom whereby the member of Congress who has served the longest on the majority side of a committee becomes its chair and the member who has served the longest on the minority side becomes its ranking member.

separate but equal Ruling of the Supreme Court in the case of *Plessy v. Ferguson* (1896) to the effect that segregated facilities were legal as long as the facilities were equal.

separation of powers Constitutional division of powers among the three branches of the national government—legislative, executive, and judicial.

set-aside program Program in which a specified number or percentage of contracts must go to designated minorities.

Shays's Rebellion An armed revolt in 1786, led by a Revolutionary War officer Daniel Shays, protesting the discontent of small farmers over debts and taxes, and raising concerns about the ability of the U.S. government under the Articles of Confederation to maintain internal order.

shield laws Laws in some states that give reporters the right to refuse to name their sources or to release their notes in court cases; may be overturned by the courts when such refusals jeopardize a fair trial for a defendant.

single-issue groups Organizations formed to support or oppose government action on a specific issue.

single-issue party Third party formed around one particular cause.

slander Oral statements that are false and malicious and are intended to damage an individual.

social contract The idea the government originates from an implied contract among people who agree to obey laws in exchange for the protection of their natural rights.

social insurance programs Social welfare programs to which beneficiaries have made contributions so that they are entitled to benefits regardless of their personal wealth.

social mobility Extent to which people move upward or downward in income and status over a lifetime or generations.

Social Security Social insurance program composed of the Old Age and Survivors Insurance program, which pays benefits to retired workers who have paid into the program and their dependents and survivors, and the Disability Insurance program, which pays benefits to disabled workers and their families.

socialism System of government involving collective or government ownership of economic enterprise, with the goal being equality of results, not merely equality of opportunity.

socialization The learning of a culture and its values.

soft money Campaign contributions, not subject to regulated limits, given to a party for activities such as party building or voter registration, but not directly for campaigns. Soft-money contributions to national parties were banned in 2002.

soft news News featured in talk shows, late-night comedy and TV news magazines—reaches more people than regular news broadcasts.

solicitor general Attorney in the Department of Justice who represents the U.S. government before the Supreme Court and any other courts.

sound bites Concise and catchy phrases that attract media coverage.

sovereign immunity Legal doctrine that individuals can sue the government only with the government's consent.

Soviet Union The Union of Soviet Socialist Republics (USSR) consisting of Russia and its bordering lands and ruled by the communist regime in Moscow, officially dissolved in 1991.

speaker Presiding officer of the House of Representatives.

Speaker of the House Presiding officer of the House of Representatives.

special, or select, committees Special panels appointed to study major policy issues.

special session Legislative session that can be called at any time by the governor. This session is limited to 30 days and to issues or subjects designated by the governor.

spin doctor Practitioner of the art of spin control, or manipulation of media reporting to favor one's own candidate.

splinter party Third party formed by a dissatisfied faction of a major party.

splintering Redistricting in which a strong minority is divided up and diluted to prevent it from electing a representative.

spoils system Selection of employees for government agencies on the basis of party loyalty, electoral support, and political influence.

staggered terms Terms that begin on different dates, a requirement for members of state boards and commissions appointed by the governor.

standard partial preemption Form of partial preemption in which the states are permitted to regulate activities already regulated by the federal government if the state regulatory standards are at least as stringent as the federal government's.

standing Requirement that the party who files a lawsuit have a legal stake in the outcome.

standing committee Permanent committee of the House or Senate that deals with matters within a specified subject area.

stare decisis Judicial precept that the issue has already been decided in earlier cases and the earlier decision need only be applied in the specific case before the bench; the rule in most cases, it comes from the Latin for "the decision stands."

START I First treaty between the United States and the Soviet Union that actually reduced the strategic nuclear arms of the superpowers, signed in 1991.

START II A treaty between the United States and Russia eliminating all multiwarhead land missiles and reducing nuclear weapons stockpiles; signed in 2003.

State Board of Education An elected panel that oversees some facets of public education in Texas.

statutory laws Laws made by act of Congress or the state legislatures, as opposed to constitutional law.

strict scrutiny Supreme Court holding that race-based actions by government can be done only to remedy past discrimination or to further a "compelling" interest and must be "narrowly tailored" to minimize effects on the rights of others.

subcommittees Specialized committees within standing committees; subcommittee recommendations must be approved by the full standing committee before submission to the floor.

subcultures Variations on the prevailing values and beliefs in a society.

subpoenas Court orders requiring people to testify in court or before grand juries or to produce certain documents.

suffrage Legal right to vote.

Sullivan rule Court guideline that false and malicious statements regarding public officials are protected by the 1st Amendment unless it can be proven they were known to be false at the time they were made or were made with "reckless disregard" for their truth or falsehood.

superdelegates Delegates to the Democratic Party national convention selected because of their position in the government or the party and not pledged to any candidate.

superpowers Refers to the United States and the Soviet Union after World War II, when these two nations dominated international politics.

Supplemental Security Income (SSI) Public assistance program that provides monthly cash payments to the needy elderly (65 or older), blind, and disabled.

survey research Gathering of information about public opinion by questioning a representative sample of the population.

sunset The process under which most state agencies have to be periodically reviewed and recreated by the legislature or go out of business.

swing states States that are not considered to be firmly in the Democratic or Republican column.

symbolic speech Actions other than speech itself but protected by the 1st Amendment because they constitute political expression.

takings clause The 5th Amendment's prohibition against government taking of private property without just compensation.

tariff Tax imposed on imported products (also called a customs duty).

tax avoidance Taking advantage of exemptions, exclusions, deductions, and special treatments in tax laws (legal).

tax evasion Hiding income and/or falsely claiming exemptions, deductions, and special treatments (illegal).

tax expenditures Revenues lost to the federal government because of exemptions, exclusions, deductions, and special-treatment provisions in tax laws.

taxes Compulsory payments to the government.

television malaise Generalized feelings of distrust, cynicism, and powerlessness stemming from television's emphasis on the negative aspects of American life.

Temporary Assistance to Needy Families Welfare reform program replacing federal cash entitlement with grants to the states for welfare recipients.

terrorism Title 22 of the U.S. Code, Section 2656 (d): "The term 'terrorism' means premeditated, politically motivated violence perpetrated against noncombatant targets by subnational groups or clandestine agents, usually intended to influence an audience."

term limits Limitations on the number of terms that an elected official can serve in office. The Constitution (Amendment XXII) limits the president to two terms. There are no limits on the terms of senators or representatives.

third party Political party that challenges the two major parties in an election.

third reading Final presentation of a bill before the full house or senate.

Three-Fifths Compromise A compromise in the Constitutional Convention of 1787 between free and slave states in which slaves would be counted as three-fifths of a person for both taxation and representation.

ticket splitter Person who votes for candidates of different parties for different offices in a general election.

Title IX A provision in the Federal Education Act forbidding discrimination against women in college athletic programs.

total preemption Federal government's assumption of all regulatory powers in a particular field.

totalitarianism Rule by an elite that exercises unlimited power over individuals in all aspects of life.

trade associations Interest groups composed of businesses in specific industries.

transfer payments Direct payments (either in cash or in goods and/or services) by governments to individuals as part of a social welfare program, not as a result of any service or contribution rendered by the individual.

Truman Doctrine U.S. foreign policy, first articulated by President Harry S Truman, that pledged the United States to "support free peoples who are resisting attempted subjugation by armed minorities or by outside pressures."

trustees Legislators who feel obligated to use their own best judgment in decision making.

turnout Number of voters who actually cast ballots in an election, as a percentage of people eligible to register and vote.

turnover Replacement of members of Congress by retirement or resignation, by reapportionment, or (more rarely) by electoral defeat, usually expressed as a percentage of members newly elected.

two-thirds rule Procedure under which the Texas Senate has traditionally operated that requires approval of at least two-thirds of senators before a bill can be debated on the Senate floor. It allows a minority of senators to block controversial legislation.

unanimous consent agreement Negotiated by the majority and minority leaders of the Senate, it specifies when a bill will be taken up on the floor, what amendments will be considered, and when a vote will be taken.

underclass People who have remained poor and dependent on welfare over a prolonged period of time.

unemployment compensation Social insurance program that temporarily replaces part of the wages of workers who have lost their jobs.

unemployment rate Percentage of the civilian labor force who are not working but who are looking for work or waiting to return to or to begin a job.

unfunded mandates Mandates that impose costs on state and local governments (and private industry) without reimbursement from the federal government.

unitary system Constitutional arrangement whereby authority rests with the national government, subnational governments have only those powers given to them by the national government.

U.S. Solicitor General The U.S. government's chief legal council, presenting the government's arguments in cases in which it is a party or in which it has an interest.

values Shared ideas about what is good and desirable.

veto Rejection of a legislative act by the executive branch; in the U.S. federal government, overriding of a veto requires a two-thirds majority in both houses of Congress.

Vietnam War War between non-Communist South Vietnam and Communist North Vietnam from 1956 to 1975, with increasing U.S. involvement, ending with U.S. withdrawal in 1973 and Communist victory in 1975. The war became unpopular in the U.S. after 1968 and caused President Johnson not to run for a second term. More than 58,000 Americans died in the war.

visa A document or stamp on a passport allowing a person to visit a foreign country.

Voting Rights Act Federal law designed to protect the voting rights of minorities by requiring the Justice Department's approval of changes in political districts and certain other electoral procedures. The 1965 act, as amended, has eliminated most of the restrictive practices that limited minority political participation.

wall-of-separation doctrine The Supreme Court's interpretation of the No Establishment Clause that laws may not have as their purpose aid to one religion or aid to all religions.

War Powers Resolution Bill passed in 1973 to limit presidential war-making powers; it restricts when, why, and for how long a president can commit U.S. forces and requires notification of and, in many cases, approval by Congress.

ward Division of a city for electoral or administrative purposes or as a unit for organizing political parties.

Watergate The scandal that led to the forced resignation of President Richard M. Nixon. Adding "gate" as a suffix to any alleged corruption in government suggests an analogy to the Watergate scandal.

Whig Party Formed in 1836 to oppose Andrew Jackson's policies; elected President Harrison in 1840 and Taylor in 1848 but disintegrated over the issue of slavery.

whips In both the House and Senate, the principal assistants to the party leaders and next in command to those leaders.

whistle-blower Employee of the federal government or of a firm supplying the government who reports waste, mismanagement, and/or fraud by a government agency or contractor.

White House press corps Reporters from both print and broadcast media assigned to regularly cover the president.

white primary Democratic Party primary elections in many Southern counties in the early part of the twentieth century that excluded black people from voting.

writ of certiorari Writ issued by the Supreme Court, at its discretion, to order a lower court to prepare the record of a case and send it to the Supreme Court for review. Most cases come to the Court as petitions for writs of certiorari.

writ of habeas corpus Court order directing public officials who are holding a person in custody to bring the prisoner into court and explain the reasons for confinement; the right to habeas corpus is protected by Article I of the Constitution.

zero-based budgeting Method of budgeting that demands justification for the entire budget request of an agency, not just its requested increase in funding.

NOTES

Chapter 1

1. Harold Lasswell, *Politics: Who Gets What, When, and How* (New York: McGraw-Hill, 1936).
2. For an update on the continuing discussion of whether political science is a "science", see Jon R. Bond, "The Scientification of the Study of Politics," *Journal of Politics* 69 (November 2007): 897–907.
3. For a discussion of various aspects of legitimacy and its measurement in public opinion polls, see M. Stephen Weatherford, "Measuring Political Legitimacy," *American Political Science Review* 86 (March 1992): 140–55.
4. Thomas Hobbes, *Leviathan* (1651).
5. John Locke, *Treatise on Government* (1688).
6. See Barbara S. Gamble, "Putting Civil Rights to a Popular Vote," *American Journal of Political Science* 41 (January 1997): 245–69. For an essay on the "paradox" of democracy, see Bonnie Honig, "Between Decision and Deliberation: Political Paradox in Democratic Theory," *American Political Science Review* 101 (February 2007): 1–25.
7. James Madison, Alexander Hamilton, and John Jay, *The Federalist Papers* (New York: Mentor Books, 1961), No. 10, p. 81. Madison's *Federalist Papers*, No. 10 and No. 51, are reprinted in the Appendix.
8. E. E. Schattschneider, *Two Hundred Million Americans in Search of a Government* (New York: Holt, Rinehart & Winston, 1969), p. 63.
9. Harold Lasswell and Daniel Lerner, *The Comparative Study of Elites* (Stanford, Calif.: Stanford University Press, 1952), p. 7.
10. C. Wright Mills's classic study, *The Power Elite* (New York: Oxford University Press, 1956), is widely cited by Marxist critics of American democracy, but it can be read profitably by anyone concerned with the effects of large bureaucracies—corporate, governmental, or military—on democratic government.
11. In *Who Rules America?* (New York: Prentice Hall, 1967) and its sequel, *Who Rules America Now?* (New York: Prentice Hall, 1983), sociologist G. William Domhoff argues that America is ruled by an "upper class" who attend the same prestigious private schools, intermarry among themselves, and join the same exclusive clubs. In *Who's Running America?* (New York: Prentice Hall, 1976) and *Who's Running America? The Bush Restoration* (New York: Prentice Hall, 2002), political scientist Thomas R. Dye documents the concentration of power and the control of assets in the hands of officers and directors of the nation's largest corporations, banks, law firms, networks, foundations, and so forth. Dye argues, however, that most of these "institutional elites" were not born into the upper class but instead climbed the ladder to success.
12. Yale political scientist Robert A. Dahl is an important contributor to the development of pluralist theory, beginning with his *Preface to Democratic Theory* (Chicago: University of Chicago Press, 1956). He often refers to a pluralist system as a *polyarchy*—literally, a system with many centers of power. See his *Polyarchy* (New Haven, Conn.: Yale University Press, 1971), and for a revised defense of pluralism, see his *Democracy and Its Critics* (New Haven, Conn.: Yale University Press, 1989).

Chapter 2

1. Gunnar Myrdal, *An American Dilemma* (New York: Harper, 1944).
2. See Martin Luther King, Jr., "Letter from Birmingham City Jail," April 16, 1963.
3. For a discussion of the sources and consequences of intolerance in the general public, see James L. Gibson, "The Political Consequences of Intolerance: Cultural Conformity and Political Freedom," *American Political Science Review* 86 (June 1992): 338–52.
4. Alexis deTocqueville, *Democracy in America*, orig. 1835 (New York: Penguin Classic Books, 2003). See also Aurelian Craiutu and Jeremy Jennings, "The Third Democracy: Tocqueville's Views of America After 1840," *American Journal of Political Science* 98 (August 2004): 391–404.
5. Quoted in *The Ideas of Equality*, ed. George Abernathy (Richmond, Va.: John Knox Press, 1959), p. 185; also in Herbert McClosky and John Zaller, *The American Ethos: Public Attitudes toward Capitalism and Democracy* (Cambridge, Mass.: Harvard University Press, 1984), p. 72. For a more recent discussion of the American identity see Deborah J. Schildkraut, "Defining American Identity in the Twenty-First Century," *Journal of Politics* 69 (August 2007): 597–615.
6. Quoted in Richard Hofstadter, *The American Political Tradition* (New York: Knopf, 1948), p. 45. Historian Hofstadter describes the thinking of American political leaders from Jefferson and the Founders to Franklin D. Roosevelt.
7. See also Leslie McCall and Lane Kenworthy, "Americans' Social Policy Preferences in an Era of Rising Inequality," *Perspectives on Politics* Vol. 7 (September, 2009), 459–84.
8. For a discussion of how people balance the values of individualism and opposition to big government with humanitarianism and the desire to help others, see Stanley Feldman and John Zaller, "The Political Culture of Ambivalence: Ideological Responses to the Welfare State," *American Journal of Political Science* 36 (February 1992): 268–307.
9. Lawrence R. Jacobs and Theda Skocpol, eds., *Inequality and American Democracy* (New York: Russell Sage Foundation, 2005).
10. Greg J. Duncan, *Years of Poverty, Years of Plenty* (Ann Arbor: University of Michigan Press, 1984); Isabel Sawhill, *Income Mobility in the United States* (Washington, D.C.: Urban Institute, 1996). More recent data on income mobility (2004 to 2007) is reported at www.sipp.census.gov. See also U.S. Bureau of the Census, *Income, Poverty and Health Insurance Coverage* (Washington, D.C.: U.S. Government Printing Office, 2009).
11. *Sale v. Haitian Centers Council*, 125 L. Ed. 2d 128 (1993).
12. Poll figures in this section are derived from the Pew Research Center for the People and the Press, "Religion and American Life," August 24, 2004. www.people-press.org
13. *Congressional Quarterly*, March 7, 2005.
14. See Robert S. Erikson and Kent L. Tedin, *American Public Opinion*. 7th ed. (New York: Pearson, 2007), chap. 3.
15. Francis Fukuyama, *The End of History and the Last Man* (New York: Free Press, 1992).
16. Samuel P. Huntington, *The Clash of Civilizations and the Remaking of World Order* (New York: Simon & Schuster, 1996).
17. Herbert Marcuse, *One-Dimensional Man* (Boston: Beacon Press, 1964).
18. Allan Bloom, *The Closing of the American Mind* (New York: Simon & Schuster, 1987), p. 15.

Chapter 3

1. In *Federalist Papers*, No. 53, James Madison distinguishes a "constitution" from a law: a constitution is "established by the people and unalterable by the government, and a law established by the government and alterable by the government."
2. Another important decision on opening day of the Constitutional Convention was to keep the proceedings secret. James Madison made his own notes on the convention proceedings, and they were published many years later. See Max Ferrand, ed., *The Records of the Federal Convention of 1787* (New Haven, Conn.: Yale University Press, 1911).
3. See Edward Millican, *One United People: The Federalist Papers and the National Idea* (Lexington. University Press of Kentucky, 1990).
4. See David Brian Robertson, "Madison's Opponents and Constitutional Design," *American Political Science Review* 99 (May 2005): 225–43.
5. Charles A. Beard, *An Economic Interpretation of the Constitution* (New York: Macmillan, 1913).
6. Robert E. Brown, *Charles Beard and the Constitution* (Princeton, N.J.: Princeton University Press, 1956).
7. James Madison, *Federalist Papers*, No. 51, reprinted in the Appendix.
8. Ibid.
9. Alexander Hamilton, *Federalist Papers*, No. 78.

Chapter 4

1. The states are listed in the order in which their legislatures voted to secede. While occupied by Confederate troops, secessionist legislators in Missouri and Kentucky also voted to secede, but Unionist representatives from these states remained in Congress.
2. *Texas v. White*, 7 Wallace 700 (1869).
3. James Madison, *Federalist Papers*, No. 51, reprinted in the Appendix.
4. Ibid.
5. The arguments for "competitive federalism" are developed at length in Thomas R. Dye, *American Federalism: Competition Among Governments* (Lexington, Mass.: Lexington Books, 1990).
6. David Osborne, *Laboratories of Democracy* (Cambridge, Mass.: Harvard Business School, 1988).
7. Morton Grodzins, *The American System* (Chicago: Rand McNally, 1966), pp. 8–9.
8. Ibid., p. 265.
9. Charles Press, *State and Community Governments in the Federal System* (New York: Wiley, 1979), p. 78.
10. *Garcia v. San Antonio Metropolitan Transit Authority*, 469 U.S. 528 (1985).
11. See Michael S. Greve, *Real Federalism: Why It Matters, How It Could Happen* (Washington, D.C.: AEI Press, 1999).
12. *U.S. v. Lopez*, 514 U.S. 549 (1995).
13. *Seminole Tribe of Florida v. Florida*, 517 U.S. 44 (1996).
14. *Alden v. Maine*, 67 U.S.L.W. 1401 (1999).
15. *Printz v. U.S.*, 521 U.S. 890 (1997).
16. *U.S. v. Morrison*, 529 U.S. 598 (2000).
17. *Federal-State-Local Relations: Federal Grants in Aid*, House Committee on Government Operations, 85th Cong., 2d sess., p. 7.
18. Craig Volden, "Intergovernmental Political Competition in American Federalism," *American Journal of Political Science* 49 (April 2005): 327–42.

Chapter 5

1. See James A. Stimson, Michael B. MacKuen, and Robert S. Erikson, "Dynamic Representation," *American Political Science Review* 89 (September 1995): 543–61.
2. Robert S. Erikson and Kent L. Tedin, *American Public Opinion*, 7th ed. (New York: Longman, 2007).
3. Ibid., p. 35.
4. Sandra K. Schwartz, "Preschoolers and Politics," in *New Directions in Political Socialization*, eds. David C. Schwartz and Sandra K. Schwartz (New York: Free Press, 1975), p. 242.
5. See M. Kent Jennings, Laura Stoker, and Jake Bowers, "Politics Across Generations: Family Transmission Reexamined," *Journal of Politics* 71 (July 2009): 782–99.
6. John R. Alford, Carolyn L. Funk, and John R. Hibbing, "Are Political Orientations Genetically Transmitted?" *American Political Science Review* 99 (May 2005): 153–67; James H. Fowler and Christopher T. Dawes, "Two Genes Predict Voter Turnout," *Journal of Politics* 70 (July 2008), 579–94.
7. Robert D. Hess and Judith V. Torney, *The Development of Political Attitudes in Children* (Chicago: Aldine, 1977), p. 42.
8. Cindy D. Kam and Carl L. Palmer, "Reconsidering the Effects of Education on Political Participation," *Journal of Politics* 70 (July 2008), 612–31.
9. Geoffrey C. Longman, "Religion and Political Behavior in the United States," *Public Opinion Quarterly* 61 (Summer 1997): 288–316.
10. See John C. Green, "The Christian Right in the 1994 Elections," *P.S.: Political Science and Politics* 28 (March 1995): 5–23.
11. See also Richard R. Lau and David P. Redlawsk, "Older but Wiser: Effects of Age on Political Cognition," *Journal of Politics* 70 (January 2008): 168–85.
12. Janet M. Box-Steffensmeier, Suzanna De Boef, and Tse-Min Lin, "The Dynamics of the Partisan Gender Gap," *American Political Science Review* 98 (August 2004): 515–28.
13. Jon Horwitz and Mark Peffley, "Explaining the Great Racial Divide: Perceptions of Fairness in the U.S. Criminal Justice System," *Journal of Politics* 67 (August 2005): 768–83.
14. See Marissa A. Abrajano, R. Michael Alvarez, and Jonathan Nagler, "The Hispanic Vote in the 2004 Presidential Election," *Journal of Politics* 70 (April, 2008): 368–82; Marco Battaglini, Rebecca Morton, and Thomas Palfrey, "Si Se Puede! Latino Candidates and the Mobilization of Latino Voters," *American Political Science Review* 101 (August 2007): 409–24. See also F. Chris Garcia and Gabriel Sanchez, *Hispanics and the U.S. Political System: Moving into the Mainstream* (New York, Longman, 2008).
15. V. O. Key, Jr., *Public Opinion and American Democracy* (New York: Knopf, 1967), p. 536.
16. *Smith v. Allwright*, 321 U.S. 649 (1944).
17. *Harper v. Virginia State Board of Elections*, 383 U.S. 663 (1966).
18. Staci L. Rhine, "Registration Reform and Turnout," *American Politics Quarterly* 23 (October 1995): 409–26; Stephen Knack, "Does 'Motor Voter' Work?" *Journal of Politics* 57 (August 1995): 796–811; Michael D. Martinez and David B. Hill, "Did Motor Voter Work?" *American Politics Quarterly* 27 (February 1997): 296–315.
19. Richard G. Niemi and Paul S. Herrnson, "Beyond the Butterfly: The Complexity of U.S. Ballots," *Perspectives on Politics* 1 (June, 2003): 317–26.
20. See R. Michael Alvarez, Thad E. Hall, Morgan H. Llewellyn, "Are Americans Confident Their Ballots Are Counted" *Journal of Politics* vol. 70 (July 2008) 754–66.
21. *Crawford v. Marion County Election Board* April 28, 2008.
22. *General Social Survey, 1998* (Chicago: National Opinion Research Center, 1999).
23. Sidney Verba, Kay Scholzman, Henry Brady, and Norman Nie, "Citizen Activity: Who Participates? What Do They Say?" *American Political Science Review* 87 (June 1993): 303–18.
24. John Stuart Mill, *Considerations on Representative Government* (Chicago: Regnery, Gateway, 1962; original publication 1859), p. 144.
25. Ibid., p. 130.
26. Quotation from Austin Ranney in "Non-Voting Is Not a Social Disease," *Public Opinion* 6 (November/December 1983): 18.
27. Martin Luther King, Jr., "Letter from Birmingham City Jail," April 16, 1963.

Chapter 6

1. For an overview of the mass media in American politics, see Doris A. Graber, *Mass Media and American Politics*, 8th ed. (Washington, D.C.: CQ Press, 2009).
2. Pew Research Center for People and the Press. http://people-press.org June, 2000.
3. See Lance Bennett, *News: The Politics of Illusion*, 5th ed. (New York: Longman, 2007).
4. E. E. Schattschneider, *The Semisovereign People* (New York: Holt, Rinehart & Winston, 1961), p. 68.
5. William A. Henry, "News as Entertainment," in *What's News*, ed. Elie Abel (San Francisco: Institute for Contemporary Studies, 1981), p. 133.
6. Shanto Iyengar, *Is Anyone Responsible? How Television Frames Political Issues* (Chicago: University of Chicago Press, 1991).
7. Graber, *Mass Media*, p. 35.
8. Matthew A. Baum, "Sex, Lies, and War: How Soft News Brings Foreign Policy to the Inattentive Public," *American Political Science Review* 96 (March 2002): 91–109.
9. Larry Sabato, Mark Stencel, and S. Robert Lichter, *Peep Show? Media Politics in an Age of Scandal* (Lanham, Md.: Rowman & Littlefield, 2001).
10. Ben J. Wattenberg, *The Good News Is the Bad News Is Wrong* (New York: Simon & Schuster, 1984).
11. Ted Smith, "The Watchdog's Bite," *American Enterprise* 2 (January/February 1990): 66.
12. Larry Sabato, *Feeding Frenzy: How Attack Journalism Has Transformed American Politics* (New York: Free Press, 1991).
13. Graber, *Mass Media*, p. 946.
14. S. Robert Lichter, Stanley Rothman, and Linda S. Lichter, *The Media Elite* (Bethesda, Md.: Adler and Adler, 1986).
15. David Prindle, "Hollywood Liberalism" *Social Science Quarterly* 71 (March 1993): 121.
16. David C. Barker, "Rushed Decisions: Political Talk Radio and Vote Choice," *Journal of Politics* 61 (May 1999): 527–39.
17. Diana C. Mutz and Byron Reeves, "The New Videomalaise: Effects of Televised Incivility on Political Trust," *American Political Science Review* 99 (February 2005): 1–15.
18. Marcus Prior, "News Versus Entertainment; How Increasing Media Choice Widens Gaps in Political Knowledge and Turnout," *American Journal of Political Science* 49 (July 2005): 577–92.

19. Shanto Iyengar, et al., "Selective Exposure to Campaign Communication" *Journal of Politics* 70 (January 2008): 186–200.

20. Julianne F. Flowers, Audrey A. Haynes, and Michael H. Crespin, "The Media, the Campaign, and the Message," *American Journal of Political Science* 47 (April 2003): 259–73.

21. See also Martin Gilens, Lynn Vavreck, and Martin Cohen, "The Mass Media and the Public's Assessment of Presidential Candidates, 1952–2000." *Journal of Politics* 69 (November 2007): 1160–75.

22. See David S. Castle, "Media Coverage of Presidential Primaries," *American Politics Quarterly* 19 (January 1991): 13–42; Christine

F. Ridout, "The Role of Media Coverage of Iowa and New Hampshire," *American Politics Quarterly* 19 (January 1991): 43–58.

23. *New York Times v. U.S.*, 376 U.S. 713 (1971).

24. *New York Times v. Sullivan*, 376 U.S. 254 (1964).

25. See Arthur Lupia and Tasha S. Philpot "Views from Inside the Net," *Journal of Politics* 67 (November 2005): 1122–42.

26. *Reno v. American Civil Liberties Union* 117 S.Ct. 2329 (1997).

27. Bernard Cohen, *The Press and Foreign Policy* (Princeton, N.J.: Princeton University Press, 1963), p. 16.

28. Austin Ranney, *Channels of Power* (New York: Basic Books, 1983), p. 81.

29. Benjamin J. Page, Robert Y. Shapiro, and Glen R. Dempsey, "What Moves Public Opinion," *American Political Science Review* 81 (March 1987): 23–43.

30. National Institute of Mental Health, *Television and Behavior* (Washington, D.C.: Government Printing Office, 1982).

31. Brandon Centerwall, "Exposure to Television as a Risk Factor for Violence," *American Journal of Epidemiology* 129 (April 1989): 643–52.

Chapter 7

1. Gaetano Mosca, *The Ruling Class* (New York: McGraw-Hill, 1939), p. 51.

2. James Madison, *Federalist Papers*, No. 10, reprinted in the Appendix.

3. George Washington, Farewell Address, September 17, 1796, in *Documents on American History*, 10th ed., eds. Henry Steele Commager and Milton Cantor (Upper Saddle River, N.J.: Prentice Hall, 1988), 1: 172.

4. Colleen A. Sheehan "The Battle over Republicanism and the Role of Public Opinion," *American Political Science Review* 98 (August 2004), 405–24.

5. Samuel Merrill III, Bernard Grofman, and Thomas L. Brunell, "Cycles in American Electoral Politics, 1854–2006," *American Political Science Review* 102 (February 2008): 1–18.

6. E. E. Schattschneider, *Party Government* (New York: Holt, Rinehart & Winston, 1942), p. 1.

7. Geofrey C. Layman and Thomas M. Carsey, "Party Polarization and Conflict Extension in the American Electorate," *American Journal of Political Science* 46 (October 2002): 786–802.

8. See Thomas R. Dye and Susan MacManus, *Politics in States and Communities*, 13th ed. (Upper Saddle River, N.J.: Prentice Hall, 2008).

9. Parties may be increasing their influence in elections due to the growth of party committees in the financing of political campaigns. See Paul S. Herrnson, "The Roles of Party Organization, Party-Centered Committees, and Party Allies in Elections," *Journal of Politics* 71 (October, 2009): 1207–24.

10. Conventions continue to play a modest role in nominations in some states:

• Colorado: Parties may hold a preprimary convention to designate a candidate to be listed first on the primary ballot. All candidates receiving at least 30 percent of the delegate vote will be listed on the primary ballot.

• Connecticut: Party conventions are held to endorse candidates. If no one challenges the endorsed candidate, no primary election is held. If a challenger receives 20 percent of the delegate vote, a primary election will be held to determine the party's nominee in the general election.

• New York: Party conventions choose the party's "designated" candidate in primary elections. Anyone receiving 25 percent of the delegates also appears on the ballot.

• Utah: Party conventions select party's nominees.

• Illinois, Indiana, Michigan, and South Carolina: Party conventions nominate candidates for some minor state offices.

11. For an argument that primary elections force parties to be more responsive to voters, see John G. Geer and Mark E. Shere, "Party Competition and the Prisoner's Dilemma: An Argument for the Direct Primary," *Journal of Politics* 54 (August 1992): 365–74.

12. For an up-to-date listing of state primaries and relevant information about them, see *The Book of the States*, published biannually by the Council of State Governments, Lexington, Kentucky.

13. The U.S. Supreme Court declared that the "blanket primary" violated the First Amendment freedom of association right of political parties to choose their own candidates. California had adopted a primary

system that gave all voters, regardless of party affiliation, ballots that included the names of *all* candidates in *both* parties. Candidates of each party who received the most votes were to become the nominees of those parties and move on to face each other in the general election. But the Supreme Court held that the blanket primary violated the First Amendment right of association *California Democratic Party v. Jones*, 530 U.S. 567 (2000).

14. Congressional Quarterly, *National Party Conventions 1811–1996* (Washington, D.C.: CQ Press, 1997).

15. For evidence that the national party conventions raise the poll standings of their presidential nominees, see James E. Campbell, Lynna L. Cherry, and Kenneth A. Wink, "The Convention Bump," *American Politics Quarterly* 20 (July 1992): 287–307.

16. See John A. Clark, John M. Bruce, John H. Kessel, and William G. Jacoby, "I'd Rather Switch Than Fight: Lifelong Democrats and Converts to Republicanism among Campaign Activists," *American Journal of Political Science* 35 (August 1991): 577–97.

17. For a scholarly debate over realignment, see Byron E. Schafer, ed., *The End of Realignment: Interpreting American Election Eras* (Madison: University of Wisconsin Press, 1991).

18. Shigeo Hirano and James M. Snyder, Jr., "The Decline of Third-Party Voting in the United States," *Journal of Politics* 69 (February, 2007): 1–16.

19. Gary Miller and Norman Schofield, "Activists and Partisan Realignment in the United States," *American Political Science Review* 97 (May 2003): 245–60.

Chapter 8

1. Gerald Pomper, *Elections in America* (New York: Dodd, Mead, 1968).

2. Morris P. Fiorina, *Retrospective Voting in American National Elections* (New Haven, Conn.: Yale University Press, 1981).

3. Quoted in *Congressional Quarterly Almanac*, 1965 (Washington, D.C.: Congressional Quarterly, Inc., 1966), p. 267.

4. Alan Ehrenhalt, *The United States of Ambition: Politicians, Power and the Pursuit of Office* (New York: Random House, 1991), p. 22.

5. See Jamie L. Carson, "Strategy, Selection and Candidate Competition in U.S. House

and Senate Elections", *Journal of Politics* 67 (February 2005): 1–26.

6. Alan I. Abramowitz, "Incumbency, Campaign Spending, and the Decline of Competition in U.S. House Elections," *Journal of Politics* 53 (February 1991): 55–70.

7. Michael Tomz and Robert P. Van Houweling, "The Electoral Implications of Candidate Ambiguity," *American Political Science Review* 103 (February 2009): 83–94.

8. Herbert Alexander, as quoted in Richard R. Lau et al., "The Effects of Negative Political

Advertisements," *American Political Science Review* 93 (December 1999): 851–75.

9. Lee Sigelman and Emmett H. Buell, Jr., "You Take the High Road and I'll Take the Low Road? The Interplay of Attack Strategies and Tactics in Presidential Campaigns," *The Journal of Politics* 46 (May 2003): 518–31; Richard R. Lau and Gerald M. Pomper, "Effectiveness of Negative Campaigning in U.S. Senate Elections," *American Journal of Political Science* 46 (January 2002): 47–66; Daniel Stevens, et al., "What's Good for the Goose is Bad for the Gander: Negative

Chapter 8 *continued*

Political Advertising, Partisanship and Turnout," *Journal of Politics* 70 (April 2008): 527–41.

10. Ted Brader, "Striking a Responsive Chord: How Political Ads Motivate and Persuade Voters by Appealing to Emotions," *American Journal of Political Science* 49 (April 2005): 388–405.

11. Paul Friedman, Michael Franz, and Kenneth Goldstein, "Campaign Advertising and Democratic Citizenship," *American Journal of Political Science* 48 (October 2004): 723–41. But see also Jonathan S. Krasno and Donald P. Green, "Do Televised Presidential Ads Increase Voter Turnout?" *Journal of Politics* 70 (January, 2008): 245–61.

12. Thomas M. Holbrook and Scott D. McClung, "The Mobilization of Core Supporters," *American Journal of Political Science,* 49 (October 2005): 689–703.

13. Center for Responsive Politics, *The Big Picture: The Money Behind the 2000 Elections* (Washington, D.C., 2001).

14. In the important U.S. Supreme Court decision in *Buckley v. Valeo* in 1976, James L. Buckley, former U.S. senator from New York, and his brother, William F. Buckley, the wellknown conservative commentator, argued successfully that the laws limiting an individual's right to participate in political campaigns—financially or otherwise—violated First Amendment freedoms. Specifically, the U.S. Supreme Court held that no government could limit individuals' rights to spend money or publish or broadcast their own views on issues or elections. Candidates can spend as much of their own money as they wish on their own campaigns. Private individuals can spend as much as they wish to circulate their own views on an election, although their contributions to candidates and parties can still be limited. The Court, however, permitted governmental limitations on parties and campaign organizations and allowed the use of federal funds for financing campaigns. *Buckley v. Valeo,* 424 U.S. 1 (1976).

15. Sanford C. Gordon and Catherine Hafer, "Flexing Muscles: Corporate Political Expenditures As Signals to the Bureaucracy," *American Political Science Review* 99 (May 2005): 245–61.

16. *Buckley v. Valeo,* 424 U.S. 1 (1976).

17. *FEC v. Colorado Republican Committee,* 533 U.S. 431 (2001).

18. *McConnell v. FEC,* 540 U.S. 93 (2003).

19. Quotations from *Citizens United v. FEC,* January 21, 2010.

20. Lynn Vavreck, Constantine J. Spiliotes and Linda L. Fowler, "The Effects of Retail Politics in the New Hampshire Primary," *American Journal of Political Science* 46 (July 2002): 595–610.

21. Matthew A. Baum, "Talking the Vote: Why Presidential Candidates Hit the Talk Show Circuit," *American Journal of Political Science* 49 (April 2005): 213–34.

22. University-based political scientists rely heavily on a series of National Election Studies, originated at the Survey Research Center at the University of Michigan, which have surveyed the voting-age population in every presidential election and most congressional elections since 1952.

23. For an updated summary of the extensive literature on voting behavior, see Michael S. Lewis-Beck, William G. Jakoby, Helmut Norpoth, and Herbert F. Weiberg, *The American Voter Revisited* (Ann Arbor, Mich., University of Michigan Press, 2008).

24. See Martin P. Wattenberg, *The Rise of Candidate-Centered Politics* (Cambridge, Mass.: Harvard University Press, 1991).

25. Responsibility for the economy, however, is also affected by the voters' partisanship, ideology and views about whether the president or Congress is chiefly responsible. See Joseph J. Rudolph, "Who's Responsible for the Economy?," *American Journal of Political Science* 47 (October 2003): 698–713.

26. For an argument that voters look ahead to the economic future and reward or punish the president based on rational expectations, see Michael B. MacKuen, Robert S. Erickson, and James A. Stimson, "Peasants or Bankers? The American Electorate and the U.S. Economy," *American Political Science Review* 86 (September 1992): 680–95.

27. Sunshine Hillygus and Todd G. Shields, *The Persuadable Voter* (Princeton, N.J.: Princeton University Press, 2008).

Chapter 9

1. Political scientist David Truman's classic definition of an interest group: "any group that is based on one or more shared attitudes and makes certain demands upon other groups or organizations in society." See *The Governmental Process* (New York: Knopf, 1971), p. 33.

2. James Madison, *Federalist Papers,* No. 10, reprinted in the Appendix.

3. Gale Research Company, *Encyclopedia of Associations* (Detroit: Gale Research, 2004).

4. Frank R. Baumgartner and Beth L. Leech, "Interest Niches and Policy Bandwagons: Patterns of Interest Group Involvement in National Politics," *The Journal of Politics* 63 (November 2001): 1191–1213.

5. Jeffrey M. Berry, *The New Liberalism: The Rising Power of Citizen Groups* (Washington, D.C.: Brookings Institution Press, 1999).

6. Kay Lehmann Scholzman, "What Accent the Heavenly Chorus? Political Equality and the American Pressure System," *Journal of Politics* 46 (November 1984): 1006–32; see also Jeffrey M. Berry, Kent E. Portney, and Ken Thomson, *The Case for Participatory Democracy* (Washington, D.C.: Brookings Institution Press, 1994).

7. Center for Responsive Politics, *www .opensecrets.org* (2009).

8. Leonard Silk and Mark Silk. *The American Establishment* (New York: Basic Books, 1980), p. 160.

9. Mark Green and Michelle Jolin (eds.), *Change for America* (New York: Basic Books, 2009).

10. Jeffrey M. Berry, *The New Liberalism* (Washington, D.C.: Brookings Institution Press, 1999).

11. Quotation from Roger Kersh, "Corporate Lobbyists as Political Actors," in *Interest Group Politics,* 6th ed., ed. Allan J. Cigler and Burdett A. Loomis (Washington, D.C.: CQ Press, 2002).

12. For evidence that vote buying on congressional roll calls is rare, see Janet M. Grenzke, "Shopping in the Congressional Supermarket: The Currency Is Complex," *American Journal of Political Science* 33 (February 1989): 1–24. But for evidence that committee participation by members of Congress is influenced by political action committee money, see Richard L. Hall and Frank W. Wayman, "Buying Time: Moneyed Interests and the Mobilization of Bias in Congressional Committees," *American Political Science Review* 84 (September 1990): 797–819.

13. Robert H. Salisbury, "Who You Know versus What You Know: The Use of Government Experience by Washington Lobbyists," *American Journal of Political Science* 33 (February 1989): 175–95.

14. *Brown v. Board of Education of Topeka,* 349 U.S. 294 (1955).

Chapter 10

1. James Madison, *Federalist Papers,* No. 10, reprinted in the Appendix.

2. Quoted in Jay M. Schafritz, *The Harper Collins Dictionary of American Government and Politics* (New York: HarperCollins, 1992), p. 56.

3. See David Auerswald and Forrest Maltzman, "Policymaking through Advice and Consent: Treaty Consideration by the United States Senate," *Journal of Politics* 65 (November 2003): 1097–1110.

4. *McGrain v. Doughtery,* 273 U.S. 13J (1927).

5. *Baker v. Carr,* 369 U.S. 186 (1962), *Wesberry v. Sanders,* 370 U.S. 1 (1964).

6. *Gray v. Sanders,* 322 U.S. 368 (1963).

7. *Department of Commerce v. U.S. House of Representatives,* 525 U.S. 316 (1999).

8. *Gaffney v. Cummings,* 412 U.S. 763 (1973).

9. *Davis v. Bandemer* 478 U.S. 109 (1986).

10. *Vieth v. Jubelirer* 241 F. Supp. 2d 478 (2004).

11. *League of United Latin American Citizens v. Perry,* June 28, 2006.

12. Scott W. Desposato and John R. Petrocik, "The Variable Incumbency Advantage: New Voters, Redistricting, and Personal Vote,"

American Journal of Political Science 47 (January 2003): 18–32; John N. Friedman and Richard T. Holden, "The Rising Incumbent Reelection Rate: What's Gerrymandering Got to Do With It?" *Journal of Politics* 71 (April 2009): 593–611.

13. *Thornburg v. Gingles*, 478 U.S. 30 (1986).

14. *Shaw v. Reno*, 125 I. Ed. 2d 511 (1993).

15. *Miller v. Johnson*, 115 S. Ct. 2475 (1995).

16. See Roger H. Davidson and Walter J. Oleszek, *Congress and Its Members*, 9th ed. (Washington, D.C.: CQ Press, 2004).

17. David Lublin, *The Paradox of Representation: Racial Gerrymandering and Minority Interests in Congress* (Princeton, N.J.: Princeton University Press, 1997). See also David Lublin and D. Stephen Voss, "The Missing Middle," *Journal of Politics* 65 (February 2003). 227–37.

18. *Georgia v. Ashcroft*, 539 U.S. 461 (2003).

19. For an in-depth analysis of who decides to run for Congress and who does not, see Linda L. Fowler and Robert D. McClure, *Political Ambition: Who Decides to Run for Congress* (New Haven, Conn.: Yale University Press, 1990).

20. See Michael K. Moore and John R. Hibbing, "Situational Dissatisfaction in Congress: Explaining Voluntary Departures," *Journal of Politics* 60 (November 1998): 1088–1107.

21. *U.S. Term Limits v. Thornton*, 115 S.C. 1842, (1995).

22. See Gary Jacobson, *The Politics of Congressional Elections*, 5th ed. (New York: HarperCollins, 2000).

23. See David Epstein and Peter Zemsky, "Money Talks: Deterring Quality Challengers in Congressional Elections," *American Political Science Review* 89 (June 1995): 295–322.

24. See Thomas E. Mann and Raymond Wolfinger, "Candidates and Parties in Congressional Elections," *American Political Science Review* 84 (September 1990): 545–64.

25. See Mary T. Hanna, "Political Science Caught Flat-Footed by Midterm Elections," *Chronicle of Higher Education*, November 30, 1994, pp. B1–2.

26. See Richard Fenno, *Going Home: Black Representatives and Their Constituents* (Chicago: University of Chicago Press, 2003).

27. Paul S. Herrnson, J. Celeste Lay, and Atiya Kai Stokes, "Women Running 'As Women,'" *Journal of Politics* 65 (February 2003): 244–55; see also Jennifer Lawless and Kathryn Pearson, "The Primary Reason for Women's Underrepresentation? Reevaluating the Conventional Wisdom," *Journal of Politics* 70 (January 2008): 67–82.

28. See Glen S. Krutz, "Issues and Institutions: 'Winnowing' in the U.S. Congress," *American Journal of Political Science* 49 (April 2005): 313–26.

29. U.S. House of Representatives, Commission on Administrative Review, *Administrative Reorganization and Legislative Management*, 95th Cong., 1st sess, H. Doc. 95–232, pp. 17–19.

30. Richard F. Fenno, *Home Style* (Boston: Little, Brown, 1978).

31. Roger H. Davidson and Walter J. Oleszek, *Congress and Its Members* (Washington, D.C.: CQ Press, 2000).

32. Glenn R. Parker, *Characteristics of Congress* (Upper Saddle River, N.J.: Prentice Hall, 1989), p. 30.

33. Richard F. Fenno, *The Making of a Senator: Dan Quayle* (Washington, D.C.: CQ Press, 1989), p. 119. Also cited in Davidson and Oleszek, *Congress and Its Members*, 9th ed., p. 120.

34. Davidson and Oleszek, *Congress and Its Members*, 9th ed., p. 129.

35. Gary W. Cox and Eric Magar, "How Much Is Majority Status in the U.S. Congress Worth?" *American Political Science Review* 93 (June 1999): 299–310.

36. See Roger H. Davidson, Walter J. Oleszek, and Frances E. Lee, *Congress and Its Members* 11th ed. (Washington D.C.: CQ Press, 2008).

37. John R. Hibbing, *Congressional Careers* (Chapel Hill: University of North Carolina Press, 1991).

38. See Charles Stewart and Tim Groseclose, "The Value of Committee Seats in the United States Senate," *American Journal of Political Science* 43 (July 1999): 963–73; see also Kevin M. Esterling, "Buying Expertise: Campaign Contributions and Attention to Policy Analysis in Congressional Committees," *American Political Science Review* 101 (February 2007): 93–110.

39. See John W. Patty, "The House Discharge Procedure and Majoritarian Politics," *Journal of Politics* 69 (August 2007): 678–88.

40. Nathan W. Monroe and Gregory Robinson, "Do Restrictive Rules Produce Nonmedian Outcomes," *Journal of Politics* 70 (January 2008): 217–31.

41. Larry Markinson, *The Cash Constituents of Congress* (Washington, D.C.: CQ Press, 1992).

42. Andrew Rehfield, "Representation Rethought: On Trustees, Delegates, and Gyroscopes in the Study of Representation and Democracy," *American Political Science Review* 101 (May 2009): 214–26.

43. Donald Matthews, *U.S. Senators and Their World* (New York: Vintage Books, 1960).

44. David Rohde, Norman J. Ornstein, and Robert L. Peabody, "Political Change and Legislative Norms," in *Studies of Congress*, ed. Glenn R. Parker (Washington, D.C.: CQ Press, 1985), p. 175.

45. See John R. Hibbing, "Contours of the Modern Congressional Career," *American Political Science Review* 85 (June 1991): 405–28.

46. Richard Fenno, *Power of the Purse* (Boston: Little, Brown, 1965), p. 620.

47. See David R. Mayhew, *Divided We Govern* (New Haven, Conn.: Yale University Press, 1991); Sarah A. Binder, "The Dynamics of Legislative Gridlock," *American Political Science Review* 93 (September 1999): 519–33.

48. *Congressional Quarterly Weekly Report*, November 23, 1991, p. 3437.

Chapter 11

1. See Michael Less Benedict, *The Impeachment and Trial of Andrew Johnson* (New York: Norton, 1973).

2. William Howard Taft, *Our Chief Magistrate and His Powers* (New York: Columbia University Press, 1938), p. 138, reprinted in *The Presidency*, ed. John P. Roche (New York: Harcourt Brace Jovanovich, 1964), p. 23.

3. Quoted in Arthur B. Tourtellot, *Presidents on the Presidency* (New York: Doubleday, 1964), pp. 55–56.

4. *Youngstown Sheet & Tube Co. v. Sawyer*, 343 U.S. 579 (1952).

5. *United States v. Nixon*, 418 U.S. 683 (1974).

6. *Nixon v. Fitzgerald*, 457 U.S. 731 (1982).

7. *Clinton v. Jones*, 520 U.S. 681 (1997).

8. Quoted in Richard Neustadt, *Presidential Power* (New York: Wiley, 1960), p. 9.

9. See Paul Brace and Barbara Hinckley, "The Structure of Presidential Approval," *Journal of Politics* 53 (November 1991): 993–1017.

10. See Suzanne L. Pancer, "Toward an Understanding of 'Rally' Effect," *Public Opinion Quarterly* 59 (September 1995): 526–46; Wave J. Aetherington and Michael Nelson: "Anatomy of a Rally Effect," *P.S. Political Science and Politics* 36 (January 2003): 37–42.

11. John Mueller, *War, Presidents, and Public Opinion* (New York: Wiley, 1973).

12. See George C. Edwards and B. Dan Wood, "Who Influences Whom," *American Political Science Review* 93 (June 1999): 327–44.

13. Garry Young and William B. Perkins, "Presidential Rhetoric, the Public Agenda, and the End of Presidential Television's 'Golden Age,'" *Journal of Politics* 67 (November 2005): 1190–1205.

14. Michael Bailey, Lee Sigelman, and Clyde Wilcox, "Presidential Persuasion on Social Issues," *Political Research Quarterly* 56 (March 2003): 49–58.

15. George C. Edwards and Stephen J. Wayne, *Presidential Leadership*, 6th ed. (Belmont, Calif.: Wadsworth, 2003), p. 118.

16. Lawrence R. Jacobs and Robert Y. Schapiro, *Politicians Don't Pander* (Chicago: University of Chicago Press, 2000).

17. Brandice Canes-Wrone and Kenneth W. Shotts, "The Conditional Nature of Presidential Responsiveness to Public Opinion," *American Journal of Political Science* 48 (October 2004): 690–706.

18. *Youngstown Sheet & Tube Co. v. Sawyer*, 343 U.S. 579 (1952).

19. Kenneth R. Mayer, "Executive Orders and Presidential Power," *Journal of Politics* 61 (May 1999): 445–66; Christopher J. Deering and Forrest Maltzman, "The Politics of Executive Orders," *Political Research Quarterly* 52 (December 1999): 767–83.

20. See also Jeffrey E. Cohen, *The Politics of the U.S. Cabinet* (Pittsburgh: University of Pittsburgh Press, 1988).

21. John Kingdon, *Agenda, Alternatives, and Public Policies* (Boston: Little, Brown, 1984), p. 25.

22. Mathew N. Beckmann, "The President's Playbook: White House Strategies for Lobbying Congress," *Journal of Politics* 70 (April 2008): 407–19.

23. See Daniel E. Ingberman and Dennis A. Yao, "Presidential Commitment and the Veto," *American Journal of Political Science* 35 (May 1991): 357–89; and Samuel B. Hoff, "Saying No," *American Politics Quarterly* 19 (July 1991): 310–23.

24. *Clinton v. City of New York*, 524 U.S. 417 (1998).

25. Brandice Canes-Wrone, William C. Howell, David E. Lewis, "Toward a Broader Understanding of Presidential Power," *Journal of Politics* 70 (January 2008): 1–16.

Chapter 11 *continued*

26. G.J.A. O'Toole, *Honorable Treachery: A History of U.S. Intelligence from the American Revolution to the CIA* (New York: Atlantic Monthly Press, 1991).

27. National Commission on Terrorist Attacks upon the United States, *The 9/11 Commission Report*. New York: W.W. Norton, 2004.

28. *Mora v. McNamara*, 389 U.S. 934 (1964); *Massachusetts v. Laird*, 400 U.S. 886 (1970). The Court specifically refused to intervene in the conduct of the Vietnam War by presidents Johnson and Nixon.

29. Jules Witcover, *Crap Shoot: Rolling the Dice on the Vice Presidency* (New York: Crow Publishing, 1992).

Chapter 12

1. "Red tape" derives its meaning from the use of reddish tape by seventeenth-century English courts to bind legal documents. Unwrapping court orders entangled one in "red tape." See Herbert Kaufman, *Red Tape: Its Uses and Abuses* (Washington, D.C.: Brookings Institution, 1977).

2. H. H. Gerth and C. Wright Mills, *From Max Weber* (New York: Oxford Press, 1958).

3. Max Neiman, *Defending Government: Why Big Government Works* (Upper Saddle River, N.J.: Prentice Hall, 2000).

4. James Q. Wilson, *Bureaucracy: What Government Agencies Do and Why They Do It* (New York: Basic Books, 1989).

5. William Niskanen, *Bureaucracy and Representative Government* (Chicago: Aldine, 1971).

6. The constitutional question of whether Congress can establish an executive branch commission and protect its members from dismissal by the president was settled in *Humphrey's Executor v. United States* (1935). Franklin Roosevelt fired Humphrey from the Federal Trade Commission despite a fixed term set by Congress. Humphrey died shortly afterward, and when the executors of his estate sued for his back pay, the Supreme Court ruled that his firing was illegal.

7. See Nicholas Henry, *Public Administration and Public Affairs*, 11th ed. (New York: Longman, 2010), Chapter 11.

8. Quoted in U.S. Civil Service Commission, *Biography of an Ideal: A History of the Civil Service System* (Washington, D.C.: Government Printing Office, 1973), p. 16.

9. See John D. Huber and Nalan McCarty, "Bureaucratic Capacity, Delegation, and Political Reform," *American Political Science Review* 98 (August 2004): 481–94.

10. Paul C. Light, *Thickening Government: Federal Hierarchy and the Diffusion of Accountability* (Washington, D.C.: Brookings Institution, 1995).

11. Michael M. Ting, "Whistleblowing," *American Political Science Review* 102 (May 2008): 249–60.

12. David Osborne and Ted Gaebler, *Reinventing Government* (New York: Addison-Wesley, 1992).

13. Al Gore, *Creating a Government That Works Better and Costs Less* (Washington, D.C.: Government Printing Office, 1993).

14. William G. Howell and David E. Lewis, "Agencies by Presidential Design," *Journal of Politics* 64 (November 2002): 1098–1114.

15. OMB also forecasts economic activity, government spending and debt; see George A. Krause and J. Kevin Corder, "Explaining Bureaucratic Optimism," *American Political Science Review* 101 (February 2007): 129–42.

16. For research suggesting that the appointive power is a more important instrument of political control of the bureaucracy than budgets or legislation, see B. Dan Wood and Richard W. Waterman, "The Dynamics of Political Control of the Bureaucracy," *American Political Science Review* 83 (September 1991): 801–28.

17. Evidence of the effectiveness of interventions by members of Congress in local offices of federal agencies is provided by John T. Scholz, Jim Twombly, and Barbara Headrick, "Street-Level Political Controls over Federal Bureaucracy," *American Political Science Review* 85 (September 1991): 829–50.

18. Bradley Cannon and Michael Giles, "Recurring Litigants: Federal Agencies before the Supreme Court," *Western Political Quarterly* 15 (September 1972): 183–91; Reginald S. Sheehan, "Federal Agencies and the Supreme Court," *American Politics Quarterly* 20 (October 1992): 478–500.

Chapter 13

1. Alexis de Tocqueville, *Democracy in America* (1835; New York: Mentor Books, 1956), p. 75.

2. Felix Frankfurter, "The Supreme Court and the Public," *Forum* 83 (June 1930): 332.

3. Alexander Hamilton, *Federalist Papers*, No. 78 (New York: Modern Library, 1937), p. 505.

4. *Marbury v. Madison*, 1 Cranch 137 (1803).

5. *Brown v. Board of Education of Topeka*, 347 U.S. 483 (1954).

6. *Roe v. Wade*, 410 U.S. 113 (1973).

7. *Lawrence v. Texas*, 539 U.S. 558(2003).

8. *Buckley v. Valeo*, 424 U.S. 1 (1976).

9. *U.S. v. Morrison*, 529 U.S. 598 (2000).

10. *Ex parte Milligan*, 4 Wallace 2 (1866).

11. *Youngstown Sheet & Tube Co. v. Sawyer*, 343 U.S. 579 (1952).

12. *United States v. Nixon*, 418 U.S. 683 (1974).

13. *Clinton v. Jones*, 520 U.S. 681 (1997).

14. *West Virginia Board of Education v. Barnette*, 319 U.S. 624 (1943).

15. Quoted in Henry J. Abraham, *Justices and Presidents*, 3rd ed. (New York: Oxford University Press, 1992), p. 7.

16. Quoted in Charles P. Curtis, *Lions under the Throne* (Boston: Houghton Mifflin, 1947), p. 281.

17. See Michael A. Bailey and Forrest Maltzman. "Does Legal Doctrine Matter? Unpacking Law and Policy Preferences on the U.S. Supreme Court," *American Political Science Review* 102 (August 2008): 369–77.

18. William O. Douglas, "Stare Decisis," *Record*, April 1947, cited in Henry J. Abraham, *The Judicial Process* (New York: Oxford University Press, 1968), p. 58.

19. *Flast v. Cohen*, 392 U.S. 83 (1968).

20. *Gideon v. Wainwright*, 372 U.S. 335 (1963).

21. *Missouri v. Jenkins*, 110 S.C. 1651 (1990).

22. *Morrison v. Olson*, 487 U.S. 654 (1988).

23. Robert Scigliano, *The Supreme Court and the Presidency* (New York: Free Press, 1971), pp. 147–48.

24. See Bryon J. Moraski and Charles R. Shipan, "The Politics of Supreme Court Nominations," *American Journal of Political Science* 43 (October 1999): 1069–95.

25. See Charles R. Shipan and Megan L. Shannon, "Delaying Justices, *American Journal of Political Science* 47 (October 2003): 654–68; Sarah A. Binder and Forrest Maltzman, "Senatorial Delay in Confirming Federal Judges," *American Journal of Political Science* 46 (January 2002): 190–99; David W. Rohde and Kenneth A. Shepsle, "Advising and Consenting in the 60-Vote Senate: Strategic Appointments to the Supreme Court," *Journal of Politics* 69 (August 2007): 664–77.

26. At one time the U.S. Supreme Court was legally required to accept certain "writs of appeal," but today very few cases come to the Court in this fashion.

27. *University of California Regents v. Bakke*, 438 U.S. 265 (1978).

28. See Lee Epstein et al., *The Supreme Court Compendium*, 3rd ed. (Washington, D.C.: CQ Press, 2002).

29. Thomas Marshall, *Public Opinion and the Supreme Court* (New York: Unwin Hyman, 1989), p. 97; see also Michael W. Giles, Bethany Blackstone, and Richard L. Vining, Jr., "The Supreme Court in American Democracy: Unraveling the Linkages Between Public Opinion and Judicial Decision Making," *Journal of Politics* 70 (April 2008): 293–306.

30. Lee Epstein and C. K. Rowland, "Debunking the Myth of Interest Group Invincibility," *American Political Science Review* 85 (1991): 205–17.

31. James L. Gibson et al., "Measuring Attitudes toward the United States Supreme Court," *American Journal of Political Science* 47 (April 2003): 354–67; Stephen P. Nicholson and Robert H. Howard, "Framing Support for the Supreme Court in the Aftermath of *Bush v. Gore*," *Journal of Politics* 65 (August 2003): 676–95.

32. James R. Zink, James F. Spriggs II, and John T. Scott, "Courting the Public: The Influence of Decision Attributes on Individuals' Views of Court Opinions," *Journal of Politics*, 71 (July 2009): 909–25.

33. President Andrew Jackson's comments came in response to the Court's ruling in the case of *Cherokee Nation v. Georgia* (1831) and *Worcester v. Georgia* (1832), which forbade the federal or state governments from seizing Native American lands and forcing the people to move. Refusal by Jackson, an old "Indian fighter," to enforce the Court's decisions resulted in the infamous "Trail of Tears," the forced march of the Georgia Cherokees that left one-quarter of them dead along the path west.

34. *Grove City College v. Bell*, 465 U.S. 555 (1984).

35. *Pollock v. Farmer's Loan*, 158 U.S. 601 (1895).

Chapter 14

1. James Madison, *Federalist Papers*, No. 10, reprinted in the Appendix.

2. *West Virginia Board of Education v. Barnette*, 319 U.S. 624 (1943).

3. *Slaughter-House Cases*, 16 Wallace 36 (1873).

4. *Hurtado v. California*, 110 U.S. 516 (1884).

5. *Gitlow v. New York*, 268 U.S. 652 (1925).

6. For an argument that Madison and some other Framers not only were concerned with lessening religious conflict but also were hostile to religion generally, see Thomas Lindsay, "James Madison on Religion and Politics," *American Political Science Review* 85 (December 1991): 1051–65.

7. *Reynolds v. United States*, 98 U.S. 145 (1879).

8. *Pierce v. Society of Sisters*, 268 U.S. 510 (1925).

9. *Cantwell v. Connecticut*, 310 U.S. 296 (1940).

10. *Employment Division v. Smith*, 494 U.S. 872 (1990).

11. *Wisconsin v. Yoder*, 406 U.S. 295 (1972).

12. *Church of Lukumi Babalu Aye v. City of Hialeah*, 508 U.S. 520 (1993).

13. *Bob Jones University v. United States*, 461 U.S. 574 (1983).

14. *Employment Division of Oregon v. Smith*, 494 U.S. 872 (1990).

15. *Goldman v. Weinberger*, 475 U.S. 503 (1986).

16. *City of Borne v. Flores*, 521 U.S. 507 (1997).

17. *Everson v. Board of Education*, 330 U.S. 1, 15, 16 (1947).

18. *Zorach v. Clausen*, 343 U.S. 306 (1952).

19. Opening public meetings with prayer was ruled constitutional as "a tolerable acknowledgment of beliefs widely held among the people of this country." *Marsh v. Chambers*, 463 U.S. 783 (1983).

20. *Lemon v. Kurtzman*, 403 U.S. 602 (1971).

21. *Muehler v. Adams*, 463 U.S. 388 (1983).

22. *Tilton v. Richardson*, 403 U.S. 672 (1971).

23. *Lambs Chapel v. Center Moriches Union Free School District*, 508 U.S. 384 (1993).

24. *Rosenberger v. University of Virginia*, 515 U.S. 819 (1995).

25. *Walz v. Tax Commission*, 397 U.S. 664 (1970).

26. *Board of Education v. Mergens*, 497 U.S. 111 (1990).

27. *McGowan v. Maryland*, 366 U.S. 429 (1961), and *Braunfeld v. Brown*, 366 U.S. 599 (1961).

28. *County of Allegheny v. ACLU*, 492 U.S. 573 (1989).

29. *Edwards v. Aguillard*, 482 U.S. 578 (1987).

30. *VanOrden v. Perry*, 545 U.S. 677 (2005).

31. *Engel v. Vitale*, 370 U.S. 421 (1962).

32. *Abington School District v. Schempp*, 374 U.S. 203 (1963).

33. *Wallace v. Jaffree*, 472 U.S. 38 (1985).

34. *Lee v. Weisman*, 505 U.S. 577 (1992).

35. *Santa Fe Independent School District v. Doe*, 120 S.Ct. 2266 (2000).

36. *Zelman v. Simmons-Harris*, June 27, 2002.

37. *Schenck v. United States*, 249 U.S. 47 (1919).

38. *Gitlow v. New York*, 268 U.S. 652 (1925).

39. *Schenck v. United States*, 249 U.S. 47, 52 (1919).

40. *Whitney v. California*, 274 U.S. 357, 377 (1927), concurring opinion.

41. *Thomas v. Collins*, 323 U.S. 516 (1945).

42. *Dennis v. United States*, 341 U.S. 494 (1951).

43. *Yates v. United States*, 354 U.S. 298 (1957).

44. *Albertson v. Subversive Activities Control Board*, 382 U.S. 70 (1965).

45. *Whitehill v. Elkins*, 389 U.S. 54 (1967).

46. *United States v. Robel*, 389 U.S. 258 (1967).

47. *Aptheker v. Secretary of State*, 378 U.S. 500 (1964).

48. *Tinker v. Des Moines Independent Community School District*, 393 U.S. 503 (1969).

49. *Texas v. Johnson*, 491 U.S. 397 (1989).

50. *Texas v. Johnson*, 491 U.S. 397 (1989).

51. *Virginia v. Black*, 538 U.S. 343 (2003).

52. *Chaplinsky v. New Hampshire*, 315 U.S. 568 (1942).

53. *Terminiello v. Chicago*, 337 U.S. 1 (1949).

54. *Cohen v. California*, 403 U.S. 15 (1971).

55. *Hill v. Colorado*, 530 U.S. 703 (2000).

56. Justice Louis D. Brandeis opinion in *Whitney v. California*, 274 U.S. 357 (1927).

57. *R. A. V. v. City of St. Paul, Minnesota*, 505 U.S. 377 (1992).

58. *Wisconsin v. Mitchell*, 508 U.S. 476 (1993).

59. *Virginia State Board of Pharmacy v. Virginia Consumer Council, Inc.*, 425 U.S. 748 (1976).

60. *Bates v. Arizona State Bar*, 433 U.S. 350 (1977).

61. *Linmark Associates, Inc. v. Township of Willingboro*, 431 U.S. 85 (1977).

62. *New York Times v. Sullivan*, 376 U.S. 254 (1964).

63. *Griswold v. Connecticut*, 381 U.S. 479 (1965).

64. *Roe v. Wade*, 410 U.S. 113 (1973).

65. *Harris v. McRae*, 448 U.S. 297 (1980).

66. *Planned Parenthood v. Casey*, 510 U.S. 110 (1992).

67. *Gonzales v. Carhart*, April 18, 2007.

68. *Bowers v. Hardwick*, 478 U.S. 186 (1986).

69. *Lawrence v. Texas*, 539 U.S. 558 (2003).

70. *Stanley v. Georgia*, 394 U.S. 557 (1969).

71. *Washington v. Glucksberg*, 117 S.Ct. 2258 (1997).

72. *Cruzan v. Missouri Department of Health*, 497 U.S. 261 (1990).

73. *Gertz v. Robert Welch, Inc.*, 418 U.S. 323 (1974).

74. *Roth v. United States*, 354 U.S. 476 (1957).

75. *Jacobellis v. Ohio*, 378 U.S. 184 (1964).

76. *Jacobellis v. Ohio*, 378 U.S. 184 (1964).

77. Bob Woodward and Scott Armstrong, *The Brethren* (New York: Avon, 1979), p. 233.

78. *Miller v. California*, 5413 U.S. 15 (1973).

79. *Barnes v. Glenn Theatre*, 501 U.S. 560 (1991).

80. *Reno v. American Civil Liberties Union*, 117 S.Ct. 2329 (1997).

81. *Near v. Minnesota*, 283 U.S. 697 (1931).

82. *New York Times v. United States*, 403 U.S. 713 (1971).

83. *Mutual Film Corp. v. Industrial Commission*, 236 U.S. 230 (1915).

84. *Times Film Corporation v. Chicago*, 365 U.S. 43 (1961).

85. *Freedman v. Maryland*, 380 U.S. 51 (1965).

86. *Young v. American Mini Theaters, Inc.*, 427 U.S. 50 (1976).

87. *Red Lion Broadcasting Co. v. Federal Communications Commission*, 395 U.S. 367 (1969).

88. *Miami Herald Publishing Co. v. Tornillo*, 418 U.S. 241 (1974).

89. *Branzburg v. Hayes*, 408 U.S. 665 (1972).

90. *NAACP v. Alabama ex rel. Patterson*, 357 U.S. 449 (1958).

91. *Aptheker v. Secretary of State*, 378 U.S. 500 (1964).

92. *Roberts v. United States Jaycees*, 468 U.S. 609 (1984).

93. *Hurley v. Irish-American Gay Lesbian and Bisexual Group of Boston*, 515 U.S. 557 (1995).

94. *Bay Scouts of America v. Dale*, 530 U.S. 640 (2000).

95. *California Democratic Party v. Jones*, 530 U.S. 567 (2000).

96. *Healy v. James*, 408 U.S. 169 (1972).

97. *National Socialist Party of America v. Skokie*, 432 U.S. 43 (1977).

98. *Frisby v. Schultz*, 487 U.S. 474 (1988).

99. *Schenck v. Pro Choice Network of Western New York*, 519 U.S. 357 (1997).

100. *Kelo v. New London*, 545 U.S. 469 (2005).

101. *Village of Euclid v. Amber Realty*, 272 U.S. 365 (1954).

102. *Lucas v. South Carolina Coastal Council*, 112 Sup. Ct. 2886 (1992).

103. James Madison, *Federalist Papers*, No. 46.

104. *District of Columbia v. Heller*, 554 U.S. 126 (2008).

105. *Ex parte Milligan*, 4 Wallace 2 (1866).

106. *Duncan v. Kahanamosby*, 327 U.S. 304 (1946).

107. *Illinois v. Gates*, 462 U.S. 213 (1983).

108. *Arizona v. Hicks*, 480 U.S. 321 (1987).

109. *Knowles v. Iowa*, 525 U.S. 113 (1998).

110. *Youngstown Sheet & Tube Co. v. Sawyer*, 343 U.S. 579 (1952).

111. *Veronia School District v. Acton*, 515 U.S. 646 (1995).

112. *Chandler v. Miller*, 520 U.S. 305 (1997).

113. *United States v. Watson*, 423 U.S. 411 (1976).

114. *Payton v. New York*, 445 U.S. 573 (1980).

115. *Spano v. New York*, 360 U.S. 315 (1959).

116. *Gideon v. Wainwright*, 372 U.S. 335 (1963).

117. *Escobedo v. Illinois*, 378 U.S. 478 (1964).

118. *Miranda v. Arizona*, 384 U.S. 436 (1966).

119. *Mapp v. Ohio*, 367 U.S. 643 (1961).

120. *United States v. Leon*, 468 U.S. 897 (1984).

121. *Illinois v. Perkins*, 497 U.S. 177 (1990).

122. *United States v. Salerno*, 481 U.S. 739 (1987).

123. *U.S. v. Marion*, 404 U.S. 307 (1971).

124. *Barker v. Wingo*, 407 U.S. 514 (1972).

125. *Illinois v. Allen*, 397 U.S. 337 (1970).

126. *Maryland v. Craig*, 497 U.S. 1 (1990).

127. *Brady v. Maryland*, 373 U.S. 83 (1963).

128. *Batson v. Kentucky*, 476 U.S. 79 (1986).

129. *Sheppard v. Maxwell*, 384 U.S. 333 (1966).

130. *Williams v. Florida*, 399 U.S. 78 (1970).

Chapter 14 continued

131. *Johnson v. Louisiana*, 406 U.S. 356 (1970); *Apodaca v. Oregon*, 406 U.S. 404 (1972).
132. *U.S. v. Perez*, 9 Wheat 579 (1824).
133. *Heath v. Alabama*, 474 U.S. 82 (1985).
134. *Furman v. Georgia*, 408 U.S. 238 (1972).
135. *Gregg v. Georgia*, 428 U.S. 153 (1976); *Proffitt v. Florida*, 428 U.S. 242 (1976); *Jurek v. Texas*, 428 U.S. 262 (1976).
136. *Ring v. Arizona*, 536 U.S. 550 (2002).
137. *Atkins v. Virginia*, 536 U.S. 304 (2002).
138. *Roper v. Simmons*, 543 U.S. 551 (2005).

Chapter 15

1. *Dred Scott v. Sandford*, 60 U.S. 393 (1857).
2. See C. Vann Woodward, *Reunion and Reaction* (Boston: Little, Brown, 1951), and Woodward, *The Strange Career of Jim Crow* (New York: Oxford University Press, 1957).
3. *Civil Rights Cases*, 100 U.S. 3 (1883).
4. *Plessy v. Ferguson*, 163 U.S. 537 (1896).
5. *Sweatt v. Painter*, 339 U.S. 629 (1950).
6. *Brown v. Board of Education of Topeka*, 347 U.S. 483 (1954).
7. Kenneth Clark, *Dark Ghetto* (New York: Harper & Row, 1965), p. 75.
8. The Supreme Court ruled that Congress was bound to respect the Equal Protection Clause of the 14th Amendment even though the amendment is directed at states, because equal protection is a liberty guaranteed by the 5th Amendment. *Bolling v. Sharpe*, 347 U.S. 497 (1954).
9. *Brown v. Board of Education of Topeka (II)*, 349 U.S. 294 (1955).
10. *Alexander v. Holmes Board of Education*, 396 U.S. 19 (1969).
11. *Swann v. Charlotte-Mecklenburg County Board of Education*, 402 U.S. (1971).
12. *Milliken v. Bradley*, 418 U.S. 717 (1974).
13. *Board of Education v. Dowell*, 498 U.S. 550 (1991).
14. *Parents Involved in Community Schools v. Seattle School District*, June 28, 2007.
15. *University of California Regents v. Bakke*, 438 U.S. 265 (1978).
16. Bakke's overall grade point average was 3.46, and the average for special admissions students was 2.62. Bakke's MCAT scores were verbal, 96; quantitative, 94; science, 97; general information, 72. The average MCAT scores for special admissions students were verbal, 34; quantitative, 30; science, 37; general information, 18.
17. *United Steelworkers of America v. Weber*, 443 U.S. 193 (1979).
18. *United States v. Paradise*, 480 U.S. 149 (1987).
19. *Firefighters Local Union 1784 v. Stotts*, 467 U.S. 561 (1984).
20. *City of Richmond v. Crosen Co.*, 488 U.S. 469 (1989).
21. *Adarand Construction v. Pena*, 132 L. Ed., 2d 158 (1995).
22. *Parents Involved in Community Schools v. Seattle School District*, June 28, 2007.
23. *Hopwood v. Texas*, 513 U.S. 1033 (1996).
24. *Grutter v. Bollinger* 539 U.S. 306 (2003).
25. *Gratz v. Bollinger* 539 U.S. 244 (2003).
26. U.S. Department of Education, Office of Civil Rights, "Race-neutral Alternatives in Postsecondary Education," March 2003.
27. State of California, Proposition 209 "Prohibition Against Discrimination or Preferential Treatment by State and Other Public Entities," http://vote96.ss.ca.gov.
28. *Coalition for Economic Equity v. Pete Wilson*, Ninth Circuit Court of Appeals, April 1997.
29. Rodolfo O. de la Garza et al., *Latino Voices: Mexican, Puerto Rican, and Cuban Perspectives on American Politics* (Boulder, Colo.: Westview Press, 1992).
30. See F. Luis Garcia, *Latinos in the Political System* (Notre Dame, Ind.: Notre Dame University Press, 1988). John D. Griffin and Brian Newman, "The Unequal Representation of Latinos and Whites," *Journal of Politics* 69 (November, 2007), 1032–46; Matt A. Barreto, "Si Se Puede! Latino Candidates and the Mobilization of Latino Voters," *American Political Science Review*, 101 (August, 2007): 425–38.
31. Linda Chavez, "Tequila Sunrise: The Slow but Steady Progress of Hispanic Immigrants," *Policy Review* (Spring 1989): 64–67.
32. Peter Mathiessen, *Sal Si Puedes: Cesar Chavez and the New American Revolution* (New York: Random House, 1969).
33. *Plyer v. Doe*, 457 U.S. 202 (1982).
34. See Marisa A. Abrajano, R. Michael Alvarez, Jonathan Nagler, "The Hispanic Vote in the 2004 Presidential Election," *Journal of Politics* 70 (April 2008): 368–82.
35. *Morton v. Mancari*, 417 U.S. 535 (1974).
36. See Joseph P. Shapiro, *No Pity: People with Disabilities Forging a New Civil Rights Movement* (New York: Times Books/ Random House, 1993).
37. *The Chronicle of Higher Education*, December 8, 2000.
38. *Bradwell v. Illinois*, 16 Wall 130 (1873).
39. *Reed v. Reed*, 404 U.S. 71 (1971).
40. *Michael M. v. Superior Court of Sonoma County*, 450 U.S. 464 (1981).
41. *Statistical Abstract of the United States*, 2007, p. 379.
42. NCAA, *Participation Study*, www.ncaa.org.
43. Susan Fraker, "Why Women Aren't Getting to the Top," *Fortune*, April 16, 1984, pp. 40–45.
44. *Mentor Savings Bank v. Vinson*, 477 U.S. 57 (1986).
45. *Harris v. Forklift Systems*, 510 U.S. 17 (1993).
46. *Bowers v. Hardwick*, 478 U.S. 186 (1986).
47. *Lawrence v. Texas*, 539 U.S. 558 (2003).
48. *Boy Scouts of America v. Dale*, 530 U.S. 640 (2000).
49. See Thomas B. Dye and Susan MacManus, *Politics in States and Communities*. 13th ed. (New York: Pearson, 2009), pp. 58, 545.
50. See Jeffery R. Lax and Justin H. Phillips, "Gay Rights in the States: Public Opinion and Policy Responsiveness," *American Political Science Review* 103 (August, 2009), pp. 367–86.
51. See Margaret Ellis, "Gay Rights: Lifestyle or Immorality," in Raymond Talalovich and Byron Daynes, eds. *Moral Controversies in American Politics*. 3rd ed. (Armonk. NY: M. E. Sharpe, 2005).

Chapter 16

1. Paul Samuelson, *Economics*, 12th ed. (New York: McGraw-Hill, 1985), p. 5.
2. GDP differs very little from gross national product, GNP, which is often used to compare the performance of national economies.
3. For a revealing case study of interest-group efforts to maintain tax breaks during the struggle over the Tax Reform Act of 1986, see Jeffrey H. Birnbaum and Alan S. Murray, *Showdown at Gucci Gulch* (New York: Random House, 1986).
4. "The Underground Economy," National Center for Policy Analysis, 1998.
5. Joseph A. Pechman, *Federal Tax Policy*. 5th ed. (Washington, D.C.: Brookings Institution, 1987).
6. See Peter R. Orszag, *Taxing the Future* (Washington D.C.: Brookings Institute, 2006).

Chapter 17

1. Christopher Jenks and Paul E. Peterson, eds., *The Urban Underclass* (Washington, D.C.: Brookings Institution, 1991). See also William A. Kelso, *Poverty and the Underclass* (New York: New York University Press, 1994).
2. See William Julius Wilson, *The Truly Disadvantaged* (Chicago: University of Chicago Press, 1987).
3. See Michael B. Katz, *In the Shadow of the Poorhouse* (New York: Basic Books, 1996).
4. See Charles Murray, *Losing Ground* (New York: Basic Books, 1984).
5. *Statistical Abstract of the United States*, 2009, p. 67.
6. See Joe Soss and Stanford F. Schram. "A Public Transformed? Welfare Reform as Policy Feedback," *American Political Science Review* 101 (February 2002): 111–22.
7. Office of Management and Budget, *Budget of the United States Government*, 2010, p. 28.

Regional Cooking

The Europeans, following their long association with cocoa as a drink, soon discovered the delights of chocolate and set about using it to create some of the most delicious classic dessert recipes—rich, creamy, and incredibly good to eat.

In Austria, tortes are very popular, particularly Anna Sacher's delectable Sachertorte, which dates from 1883. The French offer a melting roulade, a light-as-air mixture that is cooked in a long rectangle, then rolled around a filling—there is plenty of scope for variations on this basic recipe. Also from France comes Chocolate Mousse, a melt-in-your-mouth dessert based on chocolate and eggs, to which can be added heavy cream, brandy, rum—or even Champagne.

The Italians really know how to impress with their chocolate desserts. Chocolate Zabaglione, laced with Marsala, is whisked over hot water until thick, and served immediately—so it needs patient guests and a confident cook! Tiramisu is based on a smooth and versatile cream cheese, mascarpone, which is layered with coffee-drenched sponge and chunks of chocolate. And the Italians are, of course, wonderful at making ice cream—the combination of chocolate and mint is a classic favorite. For special occasions, two Tuscan specialties are Panforte di Siena—a rich, cocoa-flavored mixture of dried fruit, nuts, and honey—and Florentines—thin, crispy cookies topped with chocolate.

From Germany comes the Black Forest Gâteau, a chocolate cake soaked in liqueur and filled with whipped cream and cherries. Adapted into a trifle, this makes a very special dessert.

It may seem a strange and newly fashionable idea to combine the creamy sweetness of chocolate with the hot and fiery chile, but in fact chile was one of the flavorings used in the original cocoa drink, Xocotlatl, and the combination is still used in Mexican cooking today. That chocolate and chile have an affinity is evident in one of the most popular Mexican dishes, Mole Poblano, a blend of toasted fresh chiles, onions, garlic, tomatoes, spices, nuts, raisins—and chocolate, which is even used to garnish the dish. Chocolate also adds flavor and richness to Mexican Beef Stew.

More conventionally, chocolate is used in desserts such as Empanadas, little parcels of banana and chocolate in phyllo pastry, and chocolate meringues, delicious served with strawberries and chocolate-flavored cream. The Mexicans also make a modern version of the original cocoa drink, which is spiced with cinnamon and thickened with tortilla flour.

In North America, where home-baked cookies and traybakes are such a feature of everyday life and social occasions, chocolate is a very popular ingredient. From here come such tempting treats as the moist, chewy, Chocolate Brownie, Crispy Chocolate Bites, and Rocky Road Bites, which often find their way into ice cream. Some recipes reflect the area in which a recipe originated—one that particularly catches the attention is Mississippi Mud Pie, definitely not a dish for the faint-hearted! And Devil's Food Cake, with its sumptuous chocolate frosting, is just as the name suggests—positively wicked!

How to Use Chocolate

Chocolate is delicious whether cooked or uncooked. It comes in many forms, of course, and here is a selection of some of the most popular ones, which can all be used in a wide variety of mouthwatering recipes.

Semisweet Chocolate

Semisweet chocolate that contains around 50% cocoa solids is ideal for most everyday cooking purposes. For special recipes, choose a luxury or bittersweet chocolate with a cocoa solid content of 70–75% for a richer, more intense flavor.

White Chocolate

For color contrast, especially for cake decoration, white chocolate is unbeatable. However, white chocolate has a lower content of cocoa butter and cocoa solids, so choose a luxury cooking variety and take care not to overheat it when melting it.

Chocolate Chips

Available in semisweet, milk, or white chocolate, these chips are useful for baking and decoration. They are especially good in cookies, as well as candies and a whole range of delicious confections.

Milk Chocolate

This variety has a milder, creamier flavor. It is also useful for decorations. Care must be taken when melting it, however, because milk chocolate is more sensitive to heat than semisweet chocolate is.

Unsweetened Cocoa

Unsweetened cocoa tastes bitter, and gives a good, strong chocolate flavor in cooking. It is mostly used in cakes.

Chocolate-Flavored Cake Covering

This product has an inferior flavor, but it is very useful for making decorations because of its high fat content. As a compromise, you could add a few squares to a good-quality chocolate.

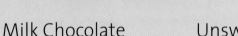

COOK'S TIP

Most chocolate, including unsweetened cocoa , can be stored for up to a year if it is kept in a cool, dry place away from direct heat or sunlight.

Preparing Chocolate

To melt chocolate on a stove:

1 Break the chocolate into small, equal-size pieces and put it into a heatproof bowl.

2 Place the bowl over a pan of hot but not boiling water, making sure the base of the bowl does not come into contact with the water.

3 Once the chocolate starts to melt, stir gently until smooth, then remove from the heat.

Note: Do not melt chocolate over direct heat (unless melting with other ingredients—in this case, keep the heat very low).

To melt chocolate in a microwave oven:

1 Break chocolate into small pieces and place them in a microwave-proof bowl.

2 Put the bowl in the microwave oven and melt. As a guide, melt 4½ oz/125 g semisweet chocolate on High for 2 minutes, and white or milk chocolate on Medium for 2–3 minutes.

Note: As microwave oven temperatures and settings vary, you should consult the manufacturer's instructions first.

3 Stir the chocolate, let stand for a few minutes, then stir well again. If necessary, return the bowl to the microwave for 30 seconds more.

Chocolate Decorations

Decorations add a special touch to a cake or dessert. They can be interleaved with nonstick baking parchment and stored in airtight containers. Semisweet chocolate will keep for 4 weeks, and milk or white chocolate for 2 weeks.

Caraque

1 Spread the melted chocolate over a clean acrylic cutting board and let it set.

2 When the chocolate has set, hold the board firmly, position a large, smooth-bladed knife on the chocolate, and pull the blade toward you at an angle of 45°, scraping along the chocolate to form the caraque. You should end up with irregularly shaped long curls (see below).

3 Using the knife blade, lift the caraque off the board.

Quick Curls

1 For quick curls, choose a thick bar of chocolate, and keep it at room temperature.

2 Using a sharp, swivel-bladed vegetable peeler, scrape lightly along the chocolate to form fine curls, or more firmly to form thicker curls.

Leaves

1 Use freshly picked leaves with well-defined veins that are clean, dry, and pliable. Holding a leaf by its stem, paint a smooth layer of melted chocolate onto the underside with a small paintbrush or pastry brush.

2 Repeat with the remaining leaves, then place them, chocolate side up, on a baking sheet lined with silicone paper.

3 Chill for at least an hour until set. When set, carefully peel each leaf away from its chocolate coating.

How to Use This Book

Each recipe contains a wealth of useful information, including preparation and cooking times, and level of difficulty. All of this information is explained in detail below.

A full-color photograph of the finished dish.

The ingredients for each recipe are listed in the order that they are used.

The method is clearly explained with step-by-step instructions that are easy to follow.

Cook's tips provide useful information regarding ingredients or hints on cooking techniques.

The number of stars represents the difficulty of each recipe, ranging from very easy (1 star) to challenging (4 stars).

This amount of time represents the preparation of ingredients, including cooling, chilling, and soaking times.

This represents the cooking time.

Cakes, Gâteaux, *and* Loaves

It is hard to resist the pleasure of a sumptuous piece of chocolate cake and no chocolate book would be complete without a selection of cakes, gâteaux, and loaves—there are plenty to choose from in this chapter. The more experimental among you can vary the fillings or decorations according to what takes your fancy. Alternatively, follow our easy step-by-step instructions and look at our glossy pictures to guide you to perfect results.

The gâteaux in this book are a feast for the eyes, and so are the delicious cakes, many of which can be made with surprising ease. The loaves are the perfect indulgence for snacktimes and can be made with very little effort. So next time you feel like a mouthwatering slice of something, these recipes are sure to be a success.

This is a good family cake that keeps well. Baked in a shallow rectangular cake pan, the squares are ideal for serving with a morning cup of coffee.

Chocolate Tray Bake

SERVES 15

3 cups self-rising flour, sifted
3 tbsp unsweetened cocoa, sifted
1 cup superfine sugar
1 cup soft margarine
4 eggs, beaten
4 tbsp milk
$\frac{1}{3}$ cup milk chocolate chips
$\frac{1}{3}$ cup semisweet chocolate chips
$\frac{1}{3}$ cup white chocolate chips
confectioners' sugar, to dust

1 Grease a 13 x 9 x 2-inch/33 x 23 x 5-cm cake pan.

2 Place all of the ingredients except for the chocolate chips and confectioners' sugar in a large mixing bowl and beat together until smooth.

3 Beat in the milk, semisweet, and white chocolate chips.

4 Spoon the batter into the prepared cake pan and level the top. Bake in a preheated oven, 350°F/180°C, for 30–40 minutes, until risen and springy to the touch. Let cool in the pan.

5 Once cool, dust with confectioners' sugar. Cut into squares to serve.

very easy
10 mins
30–40 mins

🖐 COOK'S TIP

For an attractive finish, cut thin strips of paper and lay in a criss-cross pattern on top of the cake. Dust lightly with confectioners' sugar, then carefully remove the paper strips.

Decorated with thick yogurt and canned pineapple, this is a lowfat cake, but it is by no means lacking in flavor.

Chocolate *and* Pineapple Cake

1 Lightly grease an 8-inch/20-cm square cake pan.

2 Place the lowfat spread, superfine sugar, flour, unsweetened cocoa, baking powder, and eggs in a large mixing bowl. Beat with a wooden spoon or electric hand whisk until smooth.

3 Pour the cake batter into the prepared pan and level the surface. Bake in a preheated oven, 375°F/190°C, for 20–25 minutes or until springy to the touch. Let the cake cool slightly in the pan before carefully transferring to a wire rack to cool completely.

4 Drain the pineapple, chop the pineapple pieces, and drain again. Reserve a little pineapple for decoration, then stir the rest of the pineapple into the yogurt, and sweeten to taste with confectioners' sugar.

5 Spread the pineapple and yogurt mixture over the cake and decorate with the reserved pineapple pieces. Sprinkle with the grated chocolate.

SERVES 9

⅔ cup lowfat spread
½ cup superfine sugar
¾ cup self-rising flour, sifted
3 tbsp unsweetened cocoa, sifted
1½ tsp baking powder
2 eggs
8 oz/225 g canned pineapple pieces in natural juice
½ cup lowfat thick plain yogurt
about 1 tbsp confectioners' sugar
grated chocolate, to decorate

🍳 **COOK'S TIP**

Store the cake, undecorated, in an airtight container for up to 3 days. Once decorated, refrigerate and use within 2 days.

⭐⭐   easy

🕐   40 mins

🕐   20–25 mins

An all-time favorite combination of flavors makes this cake ideal for a treat. Omit the frosting, if preferred, and sprinkle with confectioners' sugar.

Chocolate *and* Orange Cake

SERVES 8

¾ cup superfine sugar
¾ cup butter or block margarine
3 eggs, beaten
1½ cups self-rising flour, sifted
2 tbsp unsweetened cocoa, sifted
2 tbsp milk
3 tbsp orange juice
grated rind of ½ orange

frosting
1½ cups confectioners' sugar
2 tbsp orange juice

1 Lightly grease an 8-inch/20-cm deep round cake pan.

2 Beat together the sugar and butter or margarine in a bowl until light and fluffy. Gradually add the eggs, beating well after each addition. Carefully fold in the flour.

3 Divide the batter in half. Add the cocoa and milk to one half, stirring until well combined. Flavor the other half with the orange juice and rind.

4 Place spoonfuls of each batter into the prepared pan and swirl together with a skewer to create a marbled effect. Bake in a preheated oven, 375°F/190°C, for 25 minutes or until the cake is springy to the touch.

5 Let the cake cool in the pan for a few minutes before transferring to a wire rack to cool completely.

6 To make the frosting, sift the confectioners' sugar into a mixing bowl and mix in enough of the orange juice to form a smooth frosting. Spread the frosting over the top of the cake, decorate with feather frosting (see Cook's Tip), and let set.

COOK'S TIP

For feather frosting, pipe parallel lines of chocolate frosting or melted chocolate across the cake. Draw a toothpick across the lines at a right angle, alternating the direction of your pull.

easy
1 hr
25 mins

This easy to make family cake is ideal for an everyday treat. Keep the decoration simple—you could use a store-bought frosting or filling, if preferred.

Family Chocolate Cake

1 Lightly grease two 7-inch/18-cm shallow cake pans.

2 Place all of the ingredients for the cake in a large mixing bowl and beat with a wooden spoon or electric hand whisk to form a smooth batter.

3 Divide the batter among the prepared pans and level the tops. Bake in a preheated oven, 375°F/190°C, for 20 minutes or until springy to the touch. Cool for a few minutes in the pans before carefully transferring to a wire rack to cool completely.

4 To make the filling, beat the confectioners' sugar and butter together in a bowl until light and fluffy. Melt the cooking chocolate and beat half into the mixture. Use the filling to sandwich the 2 cakes together.

5 Spread the remaining melted cooking chocolate over the top of the cake. Pipe circles of contrasting melted milk or white chocolate and feather into the cooking chocolate with a toothpick, if desired (see Cook's Tip on page 22). Let the frosting set before serving.

SERVES 8

½ cup soft margarine
½ cup superfine sugar
2 eggs
1 tbsp light corn syrup
1 cup self-rising flour, sifted
2 tbsp unsweetened cocoa, sifted

filling and topping
4 tbsp confectioners' sugar, sifted
2 tbsp butter
3½ oz/100 g white or milk
   cooking chocolate
a little milk or white chocolate,
   melted (optional)

COOK'S TIP

This cake is at its best when freshly baked.

easy

1 hr

20 mins

An old-fashioned favorite, this cake will keep well if stored in an airtight container or wrapped in foil in a cool place.

Chocolate *and* Vanilla Loaf

SERVES 10

¾ cup superfine sugar
¾ cup soft margarine
½ tsp vanilla extract
3 eggs
2 cups self-rising flour, sifted
1¾ oz/50 g semisweet chocolate, melted
confectioners' sugar, to dust

1 Lightly grease a 1-lb/450-g loaf pan.

2 Beat together the sugar and soft margarine in a bowl until light and fluffy.

3 Beat in the vanilla extract. Gradually add the eggs, beating well after each addition. Carefully fold in the self-rising flour.

4 Divide the batter in half. Stir the semisweet chocolate into one half of the batter until well combined.

5 Place the vanilla mixture in the pan and level the top. Spread the chocolate batter over the vanilla layer.

6 Bake the loaf in a preheated oven, 375°F/ 190°C, for 30 minutes or until springy to the touch.

7 Let the loaf cool in the pan for a few minutes before transferring to a wire rack to cool completely.

8 Serve the loaf dusted with confectioners' sugar.

🍲 COOK'S TIP

Freeze the loaf undecorated for up to 2 months. Thaw at room temperature.

very easy

50 mins

30 mins

What better in the afternoon than to sit down with a cup of coffee and a slice of fruit bread, and when it's made of chocolate it's even better.

Chocolate Tea Bread

1 Lightly grease a 2-lb/900-g loaf pan and line the base of the pan with baking parchment.

2 Cream together the butter and sugar in a bowl until light and fluffy.

3 Gradually add the eggs, beating well after each addition. If the batter begins to curdle, beat in 1–2 tablespoons of the flour.

4 Stir in the chocolate chips, raisins, walnuts, and orange rind. Fold in the flour. Spoon the batter into the prepared loaf pan and then make a slight dip in the center of the top with the back of a spoon.

5 Bake in a preheated oven, 325°F/ 170°C, for 1 hour or until a fine skewer inserted into the center of the loaf comes out clean.

6 Let the loaf cool in the pan for 5 minutes before carefully turning out onto a wire rack to cool completely.

SERVES 4

¾ cup butter, softened
⅔ cup light brown sugar
4 eggs, beaten lightly
2 cups self-rising flour, sifted
8 oz/225 g semisweet chocolate chips
½ cup raisins
½ cup chopped walnuts
finely grated rind of 1 orange

 COOK'S TIP

Use white or milk chocolate chips instead of semisweet chocolate chips, or a mixture of all three, if desired. Dried cranberries instead of the raisins also work well in this recipe.

✪✪✪ moderate
🕐 45 mins
🕐 1 hr

Chocolate cake and a creamy coffee-flavored filling are combined in this delicious mocha cake.

Mocha Layer Cake

SERVES 8

1¾ cups self-rising flour
¼ tsp baking powder
4 tbsp unsweetened cocoa
½ cup superfine sugar
2 eggs
2 tbsp light corn syrup
⅔ cup sunflower oil
⅔ cup milk

filling
1 tsp instant coffee powder
1 tbsp boiling water
1¼ cups heavy cream
2 tbsp confectioners' sugar

to decorate
1¾ oz/50 g Quick Chocolate Curls (see page 15) or grated chocolate
chocolate Caraque (see page 15)
confectioners' sugar, to dust

1 Lightly grease three 7-inch/18-cm cake pans.

2 Sift the flour, baking powder, and cocoa into a large mixing bowl. Stir in the sugar. Make a well in the center and put in the eggs, syrup, oil, and milk. Beat the liquids with a wooden spoon, gradually mixing in the dry ingredients to make a smooth batter. Divide the mixture among the prepared pans.

3 Bake in a preheated oven, 350°F/ 180°C, for 35–45 minutes or until springy to the touch. Let cool in the pans for 5 minutes, then turn out onto wire racks to cool completely.

4 Dissolve the instant coffee in the boiling water and place in a bowl with the cream and confectioners' sugar. Whip until the cream is just holding its shape. Use half of the cream to sandwich the 3 cakes together.

5 Transfer to a serving plate. Spread the remaining cream over the top and sides of the cake. Lightly press the chocolate curls or grated chocolate into the cream around the edge of the cake. Lay the caraque over the top. Cut a few thin strips of baking parchment and place on top of the caraque. Dust lightly with confectioners' sugar, then carefully remove the paper. Chill until ready to serve.

moderate
50 mins
35–45 mins

Thin layers of delicious light chocolate cake are sandwiched together with a rich chocolate frosting.

Rich Chocolate Layer Cake

1 Grease a deep 9-inch/23-cm square cake pan and line the base of the pan with baking parchment.

2 Whisk the eggs and superfine sugar in a mixing bowl with an electric whisk for about 10 minutes or until the mixture is very thick. Lift the whisk up and let the mixture drizzle back—it will leave a trail for a few seconds when thick enough.

3 Sift the flour and cocoa together and fold half into the cake batter. Drizzle over the melted butter and fold in with the rest of the flour and cocoa. Pour into the prepared pan and bake in a preheated oven, 350°F/180°C, for 30–35 minutes or until springy to the touch. Let the cake cool slightly, then remove from the pan, and cool completely on a wire rack.

4 Melt the chocolate and butter together, then remove from the heat. Stir in the confectioners' sugar, let cool, then beat until thick enough to spread.

5 Halve the cooled cake lengthwise and cut each half into 3 layers. Sandwich the layers together with three-fourths of the chocolate filling. Spread the remainder over the cake and mark a wavy pattern on the top. Press the almonds onto the sides. Decorate with chocolate curls or grated chocolate.

SERVES 10

7 eggs
scant 1 cup superfine sugar
1¼ cups all-purpose flour
½ cup unsweetened cocoa
4 tbsp butter, melted

filling
7 oz/200 g semisweet chocolate
½ cup butter
¼ cup confectioners' sugar

to decorate
¾ cup lightly crushed, toasted sliced almonds
Quick Chocolate Curls (see page 15) or grated chocolate

COOK'S TIP

When folding in dry ingredients, use a metal spoon and turn it in a gentle figure-eight movement until they are incorporated.

 moderate
1 hr 5 mins
30–35 mins

This is a classic recipe, consisting of a rich melt-in-your-mouth chocolate cake with a wonderful citrus-flavored frosting.

Devil's Food Cake

SERVES 6

2¼ cups self-rising flour
1 tsp baking soda
1 cup butter
2⅔ cups dark brown sugar
1 tsp vanilla extract
3 eggs
3½ oz/100 g semisweet chocolate, melted
½ cup buttermilk
1 cup boiling water
candied orange rind, to decorate

frosting
1¼ cups superfine sugar
2 egg whites
1 tbsp lemon juice
3 tbsp orange juice

1 Lightly grease 2 shallow 8-inch/20-cm round cake pans and line the bases. Sift the flour and baking soda together.

2 Beat the butter and sugar in a bowl until pale and fluffy. Beat in the vanilla extract and the eggs one at a time, beating well after each addition. Add a little flour if the mixture begins to curdle.

3 Fold the melted chocolate into the batter until well blended. Gradually fold in the flour, then stir in the buttermilk and boiling water.

4 Divide the batter among the pans and level the tops. Bake in a preheated oven, 375°F/190°C, for 30 minutes, until springy to the touch. Let the cake cool in the pan for 5 minutes, then transfer to a wire rack to cool completely.

5 Place the frosting ingredients in a large bowl set over a pan of gently simmering water. Whisk, preferably with an electric beater, until thickened and forming soft peaks. Remove from the heat and whisk until the mixture is cool.

6 Sandwich the 2 cakes together with a little of the frosting, then spread the remainder over the to and sides of the cake, swirling it as you do so. Decorate with the candied orange rind.

moderate

1 hr

30 mins

What could be nicer than passion cake with added chocolate? Rich and moist, this cake is fabulous with afternoon tea or coffee.

Chocolate Passion Cake

1 Lightly grease and line the base of a deep 8-inch/20-cm round cake pan.

2 Place the eggs and superfine sugar in a large mixing bowl set over a pan of simmering water and whisk until very thick. Lift the whisk up and let the mixture drizzle—it will leave a trail for a few seconds when thick enough.

3 Remove the bowl from the heat. Sift the flour and unsweetened cocoa into the bowl and carefully fold in. Fold in the grated carrots, walnuts, and oil until they are just combined.

4 Pour the batter into the prepared pan and bake in a preheated oven, 375°F/190°C, for 45 minutes. Let the cake cool slightly, then turn out onto a wire rack to cool completely.

5 Beat together the soft cheese and confectioners' sugar until combined. Beat in the melted chocolate. Split the cake in half and sandwich together again with half of the chocolate mixture. Cover the top of the cake with the remainder of the chocolate mixture, swirling it with a knife. Chill or serve the cake at once.

SERVES 6

5 eggs
²⁄₃ cup superfine sugar
1¼ cups all-purpose flour
¹⁄₃ cup unsweetened cocoa
2 carrots, peeled, grated finely, and squeezed until dry
¹⁄₃ cup chopped walnuts
2 tbsp sunflower oil

filling and topping
12 oz/350 g medium fat soft cheese
1½ cups confectioners' sugar
6 oz/175 g milk or semisweet chocolate, melted

 COOK'S TIP

The undecorated cake can be frozen for up to 2 months. Thaw at room temperature for 3 hours or overnight in the refrigerator.

✪✪✪ moderate
45 mins
45 mins

Adding yogurt to the cake batter gives this baked chocolate cake a deliciously moist texture.

Chocolate Yogurt Cake

SERVES 8

²/₃ cup vegetable oil
²/₃ cup whole milk plain yogurt
1¼ cups light brown sugar
3 eggs, beaten
¾ cup whole-wheat flour
1 cup self-rising flour
2 tbsp unsweetened cocoa
1 tsp baking powder
1 tsp baking soda
1¾ oz/50 g semisweet chocolate, melted

filling and topping

²/₃ cup whole milk plain yogurt
²/₃ cup heavy cream
8 oz/225 g fresh berries, such as strawberries
   or raspberries

1 Grease a deep 9-inch/23-cm round cake pan and line the base of the pan with baking parchment.

2 Place the oil, yogurt, sugar, and beaten eggs in a large mixing bowl and beat together until well combined. Sift the flours, cocoa, baking powder, and baking soda together and beat into the cake batter until well combined. Beat in the melted chocolate.

3 Pour into the prepared pan and bake in a preheated oven, 350°F/180°C, for 45–50 minutes or until a fine skewer inserted into the center comes out clean. Let the cake cool in the pan for 5 minutes, then turn out onto a wire rack to cool completely. When cold, split the cake into 3 layers.

4 To make the filling, place the yogurt and cream in a large mixing bowl and whisk well until the mixture stands in soft peaks.

5 Place one layer of cake on a serving plate and spread with some of the cream. Top with a little of the fruit (slicing larger fruit such as strawberries). Repeat with the next layer. Top with the final layer of cake and spread with the rest of the cream. Arrange more fruit on top. Chill until ready to serve.

COOK'S TIP

When slicing a cake into layers, use a serrated knife in a gentle, sawing motion to avoid breaking up the crumb.

easy
55 mins
45–50 mins

This unusual cake is very popular with children, who love the appearance of the layers when it is sliced.

Chocolate Layer Log

1 Grease and line the sides of two 14-oz/400-g food cans.

2 Beat together the margarine and sugar in a bowl until light and fluffy. Gradually add the eggs, beating well after each addition. Sift together the flour and cocoa powder and fold into the cake batter. Fold in the milk.

3 Divide the batter among the two prepared cans. Stand the cans on a cookie sheet and bake in a preheated oven, 350°F/180°C, for 40 minutes or until springy to the touch. Leave to cool for about 5 minutes in the cans, then turn out, and cool completely on a wire rack.

4 Meanwhile, make the buttercream. Put the chocolate and milk in a pan and heat gently until the chocolate has melted, stirring to combine. Let cool slightly. Beat together the butter and confectioners' sugar until light and fluffy. Beat in the orange liqueur. Gradually beat in the chocolate mixture.

5 To assemble, cut both cakes into ½-inch/1-cm thick slices, then reassemble them by sandwiching the slices together with some of the buttercream.

6 Place the 2 reassembled cakes end to end on a serving plate and spread the remaining buttercream over the top and sides. Decorate with the chocolate curls, then serve the cake cut diagonally into slices.

SERVES 8

½ cup soft margarine
½ cup superfine sugar
2 eggs
¾ cup self-rising flour
¼ cup unsweetened cocoa
2 tbsp milk

buttercream
2¾ oz/75 g white chocolate
2 tbsp milk
⅔ cup butter
¾ cup confectioners' sugar
2 tbsp orange-flavored liqueur
Quick Chocolate Curls (see page 15), to decorate

moderate

55 mins

40 mins

A semisweet chocolate sponge sandwiched together with a light, creamy orange mousse, this spectacular cake is completely irresistible.

Mousse Cake

SERVES 12

¾ cup butter
¾ cup superfine sugar
4 eggs, beaten lightly
1¾ cups self-rising flour
1 tbsp unsweetened cocoa
1¾ oz/50 g semisweet, orange-flavored chocolate, melted

orange mousse
2 eggs, separated
4 tbsp superfine sugar
generous ¾ cup freshly squeezed orange juice
2 tsp gelatin
3 tbsp water
1¼ cups heavy cream
peeled orange slices, to decorate

1 Grease an 8-inch/20-cm springform cake pan and and line the base with baking parchment. Beat the butter and sugar in a bowl until light and fluffy. Gradually add the eggs, beating well after each addition. Sift together the flour and cocoa and fold into the cake batter. Fold in the chocolate.

2 Pour into the prepared pan and level the top. Bake in a preheated oven, 350°F/180°C, for 40 minutes or until springy to the touch. Let the cake cool for 5 minutes in the pan, then turn out, and cool completely on a wire rack.

3 Meanwhile, make the orange mousse. Beat the egg yolks and sugar until light, then whisk in the orange juice. Sprinkle the gelatin over the water in a small bowl and leave to go spongy, then place over a pan of hot water, and stir until the gelatin has dissolved. Stir into the mousse.

4 Whip the cream until holding its shape, reserve a little for decoration, and fold the rest into the mousse. With a clean whisk, whisk the egg whites until standing in soft peaks, then fold in. Let stand in a cool place until starting to set, stirring occasionally.

5 Cut the cold cake into 2 layers. Place one layer of the cake in the pan. Pour in the mousse and press the second cake layer on top. Chill until set. Transfer to a serving dish, pipe cream rosettes on the top, and arrange orange slices overlapping in the center.

moderate

1 hr 15 mins

40 mins

Don't worry if the cake cracks when rolled, this is quite normal. If it doesn't crack, consider yourself a real chocolate wizard in the kitchen!

Chocolate Roulade

1 Line a 15 x 10-inch/38 x 25-cm jelly roll pan with baking parchment. Melt the chocolate in the water, stirring. Let cool slightly.

2 Place the eggs and sugar in a bowl and whisk for 10 minutes or until the mixture is pale and foamy and the whisk leaves a trail when lifted. Whisk in the chocolate in a thin stream. Sift the flour and cocoa together and fold into the mixture. Pour into the pan and level the top.

3 Bake in a preheated oven, 400°F/ 200°C, for 12 minutes. Dust a sheet of baking parchment with a little confectioners' sugar, turn out the roulade onto it and peel off the lining parchment. Roll up the roulade with the fresh parchment inside. Place on a wire rack, cover with a damp dish towel, and let cool completely.

4 Whisk the cream. Unroll the roulade and spread with the cream. Sprinkle over the sliced strawberries and re-roll.

5 Place the roulade on a plate and dust with confectioners' sugar. Serve sliced, decorated with chocolate leaves and strawberries.

SERVES 6

5½ oz/150 g semisweet chocolate
2 tbsp water
6 eggs
¾ cup superfine sugar
¼ cup all-purpose flour
1 tbsp unsweetened cocoa
confectioners' sugar, to dust

filling
1¼ cups heavy cream
generous ½ cup sliced strawberries

to decorate
confectioners' sugar
chocolate Leaves (see page 15)
strawberries

COOK'S TIP

Add chopped preserved ginger to the cream filling instead of strawberries.

moderate
1 hr
12 mins

This wonderful cake originates from Hungary and consists of thin layers of light sponge cake topped with a crunchy caramel layer.

Dobos Torte

SERVES 8

3 eggs
½ cup superfine sugar
1 tsp vanilla extract
¾ cup all-purpose flour, sifted

filling
6 oz/175 g semisweet chocolate
¾ cup butter
2 tbsp milk
3 cups confectioners' sugar

caramel
½ cup granulated sugar
4 tbsp water

1 Draw four 7-inch/18-cm circles on sheets of baking parchment and cut them out. Take 2 cookie sheets and place a circle upside down on each.

2 Beat the eggs and superfine sugar in a large mixing bowl with an electric whisk for 10 minutes or until the mixture is light and foamy and the whisk leaves a trail. Fold in the vanilla extract and flour.

3 Spoon a fourth of the batter onto one of the paper circles and spread out to the size of the circle. Repeat with the other circle. Bake in a preheated oven, 400°F/200°C, for 5–8 minutes or until golden brown. Transfer to wire racks to cool. Repeat with the remaining mixture.

4 To make the filling, melt the chocolate and cool slightly. Beat the butter, milk, and confectioners' sugar until pale and fluffy. Whisk in the chocolate.

5 Place the sugar and water for the caramel in a heavy pan. Heat gently, stirring, to dissolve the sugar. Boil gently until pale golden in color. Remove from the heat. Pour over one cake layer as a topping. Let harden slightly, then mark into 8 portions with an oiled knife.

6 Remove the cakes from the parchment. Trim the edges. Sandwich the layers together with some of the filling, finishing with the caramel-topped cake. Place on a serving plate, spread the sides with the remaining filling mixture, and pipe 8 rosettes around the top.

challenging

40 mins

10–12 mins

This rich melt-in-the mouth cake originates in Austria. Make sure you have a steady hand when writing the name on the top.

Sachertorte

1 Grease a 9-inch/23-cm springform cake pan and line the base. Beat the butter and ⅓ cup of the sugar until pale and fluffy. Add the egg yolks and beat well. Add the chocolate in a thin stream, beating well. Fold in the flour. Whisk the egg whites until they stand in soft peaks. Add the remaining sugar and whisk for 2 minutes by hand, or 45–60 seconds if using an electric whisk, until glossy. Gently fold half into the chocolate mixture, then fold in the remainder.

2 Spoon the batter into the prepared pan and level the top. Bake in a preheated oven, 300°F/150°C, for 1–1¼ hours, until a skewer inserted into the center comes out clean. Cool in the pan for 5 minutes, then transfer to a wire rack to cool completely.

3 To make the frosting, melt the chocolate and beat in the coffee until smooth. Sift the confectioners' sugar into a bowl. Whisk in the melted chocolate mixture to give a thick frosting. Cut the cake into 2 layers. Warm the apricot preserve, spread over one half of the cake and sandwich together. Invert the cake on a wire rack. Spoon the frosting over the cake and spread to coat the top and sides. Let the frosting set for 5 minutes, letting any excess drop through the rack. Transfer to a serving plate and let set for at least 2 hours.

4 To decorate, spoon the melted chocolate into a small pastry bag and pipe the word "Sacher" or "Sachertorte" on the top of the cake. Let it harden before serving the cake.

SERVES 10

⅔ cup sweet butter
⅔ cup superfine sugar
6 eggs, separated
6 oz/175 g semisweet chocolate, melted
1¼ cups all-purpose flour, sifted

frosting and filling
6 oz/175 g semisweet chocolate
5 tbsp strong black coffee
1 cup confectioners' sugar
6 tbsp good apricot preserve
1¾ oz/50 g semisweet chocolate, melted

 challenging
3 hrs 30 mins
1 hr–1 hr 15 mins

Ganache—a divine mixture of chocolate and cream—is used to fill and decorate this rich chocolate cake, making it a chocolate-lover's dream.

Chocolate Ganache Cake

SERVES 10

³/₄ cup butter
³/₄ cup superfine sugar
4 eggs, beaten lightly
1³/₄ cups self-rising flour
1 tbsp unsweetened cocoa
1³/₄ oz/50 g semisweet chocolate, melted

ganache

2 cups heavy cream
13 oz/375 g semisweet chocolate, broken
    into pieces

to finish

7 oz/200 g chocolate-flavored cake covering

1 Lightly grease an 8-inch/20-cm springform cake pan and line the base. Beat the butter and sugar until light and fluffy. Gradually add the eggs, beating well after each addition. Sift together the flour and cocoa. Fold into the cake batter. Fold in the melted chocolate.

2 Pour into the prepared pan and level the top. Bake in a preheated oven, 350°F/180°C, for 40 minutes or until springy to the touch. Let the cake cool for 5 minutes in the pan, then turn out onto a wire rack, and let cool completely. Cut the cold cake into 2 layers.

3 To make the ganache, place the cream in a pan and bring to a boil, stirring. Add the chocolate and stir until melted and combined. Pour into a bowl and whisk for about 5 minutes or until the ganache is fluffy and cool.

4 Reserve one third of the ganache. Use the remaining ganache to sandwich the cake together and spread over the top and sides of the cake.

5 Melt the cake covering and spread it over a large sheet of baking parchment. Let cool until just set. Cut into strips a little wider than the height of the cake. Place the strips around the edge of the cake, overlapping them slightly.

6 Pipe the reserved ganache in tear drops or shells to cover the top of the cake. Chill for 1 hour.

✪✪✪✪ challenging
2 hrs 5 mins
40 mins

This is the traditional French Christmas cake. It consists of a chocolate cake roll filled with and encased in a delicious rich chocolate frosting.

Bûche *de* Noël

1 Grease and line a 12 x 9-inch/ 30 x 23-cm jelly roll pan.

2 Beat the eggs and superfine sugar in a bowl with an electric whisk for 10 minutes, or until the mixture is very light and foamy and the whisk leaves a trail. Sift the flour and cocoa and fold in. Pour into the prepared pan and bake in a preheated oven, 400°F/200°C, for 12 minutes or until springy to the touch. Turn out onto baking parchment sprinkled with superfine sugar. Peel off the lining parchment and trim the edges. Cut a small slit halfway into the cake, ½ inch/1 cm from one of the short ends. Starting at that end, roll up tightly, enclosing the parchment. Place on a wire rack to cool.

3 To make the frosting, break the chocolate into pieces and melt in a heatproof bowl over a pan of hot water. Beat in the egg yolks, whisk in the milk, and cook until the mixture thickens enough to coat the back of a wooden spoon, stirring. Cover with dampened waxed paper and cool. Beat the butter and sugar until pale. Beat in the cooled chocolate custard and the rum, if using.

4 Unroll the cake, spread with one third of the frosting, and roll up. Place on a serving plate. Spread the remaining frosting over the cake and mark with a fork to give the effect of bark. Let the frosting set. Pipe white frosting to form the rings of the log. Sprinkle with confectioners' sugar and decorate with holly leaves.

SERVES 10

cake
4 eggs
½ cup superfine sugar, plus sugar for dusting
⅔ cup self-rising flour
2 tbsp unsweetened cocoa

frosting
5½ oz/150 g semisweet chocolate
2 egg yolks
⅔ cup milk
½ cup butter
4 tbsp confectioners' sugar
2 tbsp rum (optional)

to decorate
a little white royal frosting
confectioners' sugar, to dust
holly leaves

challenging

1 hr

12 mins

Soft chocolate sponge cake topped with a rich chocolate truffle mixture makes a cake that chocoholics will die for.

Chocolate Truffle Cake

SERVES 12

⅓ cup butter
⅓ cup superfine sugar
2 eggs, beaten lightly
⅔ cup self-rising flour
½ tsp baking powder
¼ cup unsweetened cocoa
½ cup ground almonds

truffle topping
12 oz/350 g semisweet chocolate
½ cup butter
1¼ cups heavy cream
1¼ cups plain cake crumbs
3 tbsp dark rum

to decorate
ground cherries
1¾ oz/50 g semisweet chocolate, melted

1 Lightly grease an 8-inch/20-cm round springform pan and line the base. Beat together the butter and sugar until light and fluffy. Gradually add the eggs, beating well after each addition.

2 Sift the flour, baking powder, and unsweetened cocoa together and fold into the mixture along with the ground almonds. Pour the batter into the prepared pan and bake in a preheated oven, 350°F/180°C, for 20–25 minutes or until springy to the touch. Let the cake cool slightly in the pan, then transfer to a wire rack to cool completely. Wash and dry the pan and return the cooled cake to the pan.

3 To make the topping, heat the chocolate, butter, and cream in a heavy pan over low heat and stir until smooth. Cool, then chill for 30 minutes. Beat well with a wooden spoon and chill for 30 minutes more. Beat the mixture again, then add the cake crumbs and rum, beating until well combined. Spoon over the sponge cake and chill for 3 hours.

4 Meanwhile, dip the ground cherries in the melted chocolate until partially covered. Set aside on baking parchment to set. Transfer the cake to a serving plate and decorate with ground cherries.

✪✪✪ moderate
🕐 4 hrs 45 mins
🕐 20–25 mins

A light white sponge cake, topped with a rich, creamy-white chocolate truffle mixture, makes an out-of-this-world treat.

White Truffle Cake

1 Grease an 8-inch/20-cm round springform pan and line the base.

2 Whisk the eggs and superfine sugar in a mixing bowl for 10 minutes, or until the mixture is very light and foamy and the whisk leaves a trail that lasts a few seconds when lifted. Sift the flour and fold in with a metal spoon. Fold in the melted white chocolate. Pour into the pan and bake in a preheated oven, 350°F/ 180°C, for 25 minutes or until springy to the touch. Let cool slightly, then transfer to a wire rack to cool completely. Wash and dry the pan and return the cold cake to it.

3 To make the topping, place the cream in a pan and bring to a boil, stirring to prevent it from sticking to the base of the pan. Cool slightly, then add the white chocolate pieces, and stir until melted and combined. Remove from the heat and stir until almost cool, then stir in the mascarpone. Pour the mixture on top of the cake and chill for 2 hours.

4 Remove the cake from the pan and transfer to a serving plate. Decorate with caraque and dust with cocoa.

SERVES 12

2 eggs
4 tbsp superfine sugar
1/3 cup all-purpose flour
1³/4 oz/50 g white chocolate, melted

truffle topping
1¹/4 cups heavy cream
12 oz/350 g white chocolate, broken into pieces
generous 1 cup mascarpone cheese

to decorate
semisweet, milk, or white chocolate Caraque (see page 15)
unsweetened cocoa, to dust

COOK'S TIP
Strawberries or raspberries would make a delicious alternative topping.

easy

3 hrs 15 mins

25 mins

A vacherin is made of layers of crisp meringue sandwiched together with fruit and cream. It makes a fabulous dessert for special occasions and celebrations.

Raspberry Vacherin

SERVES 10

3 egg whites
¾ cup superfine sugar
1 tsp cornstarch
1 oz/25 g semisweet chocolate, grated

filling
6 oz/175 g semisweet chocolate
2 cups heavy cream, whipped
2 cups fresh raspberries
a little melted chocolate, to decorate

1 Draw 3 rectangles, 4 x 10 inches/ 10 x 25 cm, on sheets of baking parchment and place on 2 cookie sheets.

2 Whisk the egg whites in a mixing bowl until standing in soft peaks, then gradually whisk in half of the sugar, and continue whisking until the mixture is very stiff and glossy. Carefully fold in the rest of the sugar, the cornstarch, and the grated chocolate with a metal spoon or a spatula.

3 Spoon the meringue mixture into a pastry bag fitted with a ½-inch/1-cm plain tip and pipe lines across the rectangles.

4 Bake in a preheated oven, 275°F/140°C, for 1½ hours, changing the positions of the cookie sheets halfway through. Without opening the oven door, turn off the oven and let the meringues cool inside the oven, then peel away the baking parchment.

5 To make the filling, melt the chocolate and spread it over 2 of the meringue layers. Let the chocolate harden.

6 Place 1 chocolate-coated meringue on a serving plate and top with about one third of the cream and raspberries. Carefully place the second chocolate-coated meringue on top and gently spread with half of the remaining cream and raspberries.

7 Place the last meringue on the top and decorate with the remaining cream and raspberries. Drizzle a little melted chocolate over the top and serve.

challenging

1 hr 45 mins

1 hr 30 mins

The addition of nuts and raisins has given this dessert extra texture, making it similar to that of chocolate brownies.

Chocolate Brownie Roulade

1 Grease a 12 x 8-inch/30 x 20-cm jelly roll pan, line with baking parchment, and grease the parchment.

2 Melt the chocolate with the water in a small pan over low heat until the chocolate has just melted. Let cool.

3 In a bowl, whisk the sugar and egg yolks for 2–3 minutes with a hand-held electric whisk until thick and pale. Fold in the cooled chocolate, the raisins, and pecan nuts.

4 In a separate bowl, whisk the egg whites with the salt. Fold one fourth of the egg whites into the chocolate mixture, then fold in the rest of the whites, working lightly and quickly.

5 Transfer the batter to the prepared pan and bake in a preheated oven, 350°F/180°C, for 25 minutes, until risen and just firm to the touch. Let the cake cool slightly, cover with a sheet of nonstick baking parchment and a damp clean dish towel, and then set aside until completely cold.

6 Turn the roulade out onto another piece of baking parchment dusted with confectioners' sugar and peel off the lining parchment.

7 Trim the edges of the roulade and spread with the cream. Starting from a short end, roll the sponge cake away from you, using the parchment to guide you. Transfer to a serving plate and chill until ready to serve. Dust thickly with confectioners' sugar before serving.

SERVES **8**

5 ½ oz/150 g semisweet chocolate, broken into pieces
3 tbsp water
¾ cup superfine sugar
5 eggs, separated
2 tbsp raisins, chopped
2 tbsp chopped pecan nuts
pinch of salt
confectioners' sugar, to dust
1¼ cups heavy cream, whipped lightly

✪✪✪   moderate

1 hr

25 mins

The white chocolate makes this a very rich cake, so it is best to serve it cut into small squares or bars, or sliced thinly.

Chocolate *and* Apricot Squares

SERVES 12

½ cup butter
6 oz/175 g white chocolate, chopped
4 eggs
½ cup superfine sugar
1¾ cups all-purpose flour, sifted
1 tsp baking powder
pinch of salt
scant 1 cup no-soak dried apricots, chopped

1 Lightly grease a 9-inch/23-cm square cake pan and line the base with baking parchment.

2 Melt the butter and chocolate in a heatproof bowl set over a pan of simmering water. Stir frequently with a wooden spoon until the mixture is smooth and glossy. Let the mixture cool slightly.

3 Beat the eggs and superfine sugar into the butter and chocolate mixture until well combined.

4 Fold in the flour, baking powder, salt, and chopped dried apricots, and mix together well.

5 Pour the batter into the pan and bake in a preheated oven, 350°F/ 180°C, for 25–30 minutes. The center of the cake may not be completely firm, but it will set as it cools. Let it cool in the pan.

6 When the cake is completely cold turn it out and slice into squares or bars.

🍴 **COOK'S TIP**

Replace the white chocolate with milk or semisweet chocolate, if you prefer.

⭐⭐   easy
🕐   50 mins
🕐   25–30 mins

Serve this tasty snack plain, with butter or jelly, or Italian style with mascarpone cheese.

Italian Chocolate Chip Bread

1 Oil a cookie sheet. Sift the flour, cocoa, and salt into a bowl. Add the butter and cut it into the flour mixture, then stir in the sugar and yeast.

2 Gradually add the water, stirring well to mix. When the dough becomes too firm to stir with a spoon, gather it together with your hands. Turn it out onto a lightly floured counter and knead thoroughly until smooth and elastic.

3 Knead the chocolate chips into the dough, distributing them evenly throughout. Form into a round loaf, then place on the cookie sheet, cover with oiled plastic wrap, and set aside in a warm place for 1½–2 hours, until doubled in bulk.

4 Remove and discard the plastic wrap and bake the loaf in a preheated oven, 425°F/220°C, for 10 minutes. Lower the temperature to 375°F/190°C and bake for 15 minutes more.

5 Transfer the loaf to a wire rack and brush with melted butter. Cover with a clean dish towel until cooled.

SERVES 4

2 cups all-purpose flour, plus flour for dusting
1 tbsp unsweetened cocoa
pinch of salt
1 tbsp sweet butter, plus ½ tsp extra, melted, for brushing
1 tbsp superfine sugar
1 tsp rapid-rise dry yeast
⅔ cup lukewarm water
⅓ cup semisweet chocolate chips

easy

2 hrs 30 mins

25 mins

The sweetness of the whipped marshmallow frosting complements the mouthwatering flavor of this moist semisweet chocolate sponge cake.

Chocolate Marshmallow Cake

SERVES 6

6 tbsp sweet butter
generous 1 cup superfine sugar
½ tsp vanilla extract
2 eggs, beaten lightly
3 oz/85 g semisweet chocolate, broken into pieces
⅔ cup buttermilk
1¼ cups self-rising flour
½ tsp baking soda
pinch of salt
2 oz/55 g milk chocolate, grated, to decorate

frosting
6 oz/175 g white marshmallows
1 tbsp milk
2 egg whites
2 tbsp superfine sugar

moderate
1 hr 30 mins
50 mins

1 Grease a 3¾-cup ovenproof bowl. Cream the butter, sugar, and vanilla together until pale and fluffy, then gradually beat in the eggs.

2 Melt the semisweet chocolate in a heatproof bowl over a pan of simmering water. When the chocolate has melted, gradually stir in the buttermilk, until well combined. Remove the pan from the heat and cool slightly.

3 Sift the flour, baking soda, and salt into a separate bowl.

4 Alternately add the chocolate mixture and the flour to the batter, a little at a time. Spoon into the ovenproof bowl and smooth the surface.

5 Bake in a preheated oven, 325°F/160°C, for about 50 minutes, until a skewer inserted into the center of the cake comes out clean. Turn out onto a wire rack to cool.

6 Meanwhile, make the frosting. Put the marshmallows and milk in a small pan and heat very gently until the marshmallows have melted. Remove the pan from the heat and set aside to cool.

7 Whisk the egg whites until soft peaks form, then add the sugar, and continue whisking until stiff peaks form. Fold the egg white into the cooled marshmallow mixture and set aside for 10 minutes.

8 When the cake is cool, cover the top and sides with the marshmallow frosting. Top with grated milk chocolate.

Ideal for children to make, this cake does not require an oven and it is prepared very rapidly—but it does need to chill overnight.

No-Bake Refrigerator Cake

1 Line a 1-lb/450-g loaf pan with waxed paper or baking parchment.

2 Put the butter and chocolate in the top of a double boiler or in a heatproof bowl set over a pan of barely simmering water. Stir constantly over low heat until they have melted and the mixture is smooth. Remove from the heat and cool slightly.

3 In a separate bowl, combine the cherries and walnuts. Spoon one-third of the chocolate mixture into the prepared pan, cover with a layer of cookies, and top with half the cherries and walnuts. Make further layers, ending with a layer of chocolate mixture. Cover with plastic wrap and chill in the refrigerator for at least 12 hours. Turn the cake out onto a serving dish and cut into thin slices.

SERVES 8

1 cup sweet butter, diced
8 oz/225 g semisweet chocolate,
    broken into pieces
1/3 cup chopped candied cherries
1/2 cup chopped walnuts
12 rectangular semisweet chocolate cookies

COOK'S TIP

Try replacing the cherries and walnuts with chopped dried apricots and almonds, or raisins and pecan nuts.

easy

12 hrs 20 mins

5–8 mins

This is the ideal snack to eat with a mid-morning cup of coffee. Serve with whipped cream for a special treat.

Swedish Chocolate Cake

SERVES 8

⅓ cup dry white bread crumbs
5 tbsp sweet butter
scant 1 cup superfine sugar
2 eggs, separated
1 tsp vanilla extract
1½ cups all-purpose flour
1 tsp baking powder
½ cup light cream
3 oz/85 g semisweet chocolate, melted

1 Grease a deep 9-inch/23-cm round cake pan. Sprinkle the bread crumbs into the pan and press them onto the base and sides.

2 Cream the butter with the sugar until pale and fluffy. Beat in the egg yolks, one at a time, and add the vanilla.

3 Sift one third of the flour with the baking powder, then beat into the egg mixture. Combine the cream and melted chocolate, then beat one-third of this mixture into the egg mixture. Continue adding the flour and the chocolate mixture alternately, beating well after each addition.

4 Whisk the egg whites in a separate bowl until they form stiff peaks. Fold the egg whites into the batter.

5 Pour into the prepared pan and bake in a preheated oven, 300°F/150°C, for about 50 minutes, until a skewer inserted into the center of the cake comes out clean. Turn the cake out onto a wire rack to cool before serving.

 moderate

🕐 30 mins

🕐 1 hr

🧑‍🍳 **COOK'S TIP**

Try flavoring this cake with the grated rind of half an orange instead of the vanilla extract.

Moist and moreish, this fruity chocolate cake will prove to be a popular after-school snack.

Date *and* Chocolate Cake

1 Grease and flour two 7-inch/18-cm layer pans. Put the chocolate, grenadine, and syrup in the top of a double boiler or in a heatproof bowl set over a pan of barely simmering water. Stir over low heat until the chocolate has melted and the mixture is smooth. Remove from the heat and let cool.

2 Cream the butter and superfine sugar together until pale and fluffy, then gradually beat in the eggs, and then the cooled chocolate mixture.

3 Sift the flour into another bowl and stir in the ground rice. Fold the flour mixture into the creamed mixture.

4 Divide the mixture among the prepared layer pans and smooth the surface. Bake in a preheated oven, 350°F/180°C, for 20–25 minutes, until golden and firm to the touch. Turn out onto a wire rack to cool.

5 To make the filling, put all the ingredients into a pan and stir over low heat for 4–5 minutes, until thoroughly combined. Remove from the heat, let cool, and then use the filling to sandwich the cakes together. Dust the top of the cake with confectioners' sugar to decorate.

SERVES 4

115 g/4 oz semisweet chocolate, broken into pieces
1 tbsp grenadine
1 tbsp light corn syrup
1/2 cup sweet butter
1/4 cup superfine sugar
2 extra large eggs
2/3 cup self-rising flour
2 tbsp ground rice
1 tbsp confectioners' sugar, to decorate

FILLING
2/3 cup chopped dried dates
1 tbsp lemon juice
1 tbsp orange juice
1 tbsp raw brown sugar
1/4 cup blanched almonds, chopped
2 tbsp apricot preserve

⭐⭐⭐ moderate

🕐 25 mins

🕐 40 mins

Hot Desserts

Chocolate is comforting at any time but no more so than when served in a steaming hot dessert. It is hard to think of anything more warming, comforting, and homely than tucking into a hot Steamed Chocolate Fudge Pudding or a Hot Chocolate Soufflé, and children will love the chocolate addition to nursery favorites such as Bread & Butter Pudding. In fact, there are several old favorites that have been given the chocolate treatment, bringing them bang up to date and putting them on the chocolate lover's map.

When you are feeling in need of something a little more sophisticated, try the new-style chocolate Apple Pancake Stacks, or Chocolate Meringue Pie, or Chocolate Zabaglione for a sophisticated, frothy, warm dessert set to get your tastebuds in a whirl! This chapter is packed full of chocolate delights, with different tastes and textures to add warmth to any day.

An old-time British favorite with an up-to-date twist, this dessert makes the perfect end to a special family meal.

Chocolate Queen *of* Puddings

SERVES 4

1¾ oz/ 50 g semisweet chocolate
2 cups chocolate-flavored milk
1¾ cups fresh white or whole-wheat bread crumbs
½ cup superfine sugar
2 eggs, separated
4 tbsp black cherry jelly

1 Break the chocolate into small pieces and place in a pan with the chocolate-flavored milk. Heat gently, stirring until the chocolate melts. Bring almost to a boil, then remove the pan from the heat.

2 Place the bread crumbs in a large mixing bowl with 5 teaspoons of the sugar. Pour over the chocolate milk and mix well. Beat in the egg yolks.

3 Spoon into a 5-cup pie dish and bake in a preheated oven, 350°F/180°C, for 25–30 minutes or until set and firm to the touch.

4 Whisk the egg whites in a large grease-free bowl until standing in soft peaks. Gradually whisk in the remaining superfine sugar and whisk until you have a glossy, thick meringue.

5 Spread the black cherry jelly over the chocolate layer and pile or pipe the meringue on top. Return the dessert to the oven for about 15 minutes or until the meringue is crisp and golden.

⊛ **COOK'S TIP**

If you prefer, add ½ cup dry unsweetened coconut to the bread crumbs and omit the black cherry jelly.

★★★ moderate

🕐 25 mins

🕐 40–45 mins

Eve's Dessert is traditionally made with apples, but here raspberries are added and the dessert is served with a bitter chocolate sauce.

Chocolate Eve's Dessert

1 Place the apple slices and raspberries in a shallow 5-cup ovenproof dish.

2 Place the raspberry jelly and port (if using) in a small pan and heat gently, stirring, until the jelly melts. Pour the mixture over the fruit.

3 Place all of the ingredients for the sponge topping in a large mixing bowl and beat until smooth.

4 Spoon the sponge batter over the fruit and level the top. Bake in a preheated oven, 350°F/180°C, for 40–45 minutes or until the sponge is golden and springy to the touch.

5 To make the sauce, break the chocolate into small pieces and place in a heavy pan with the cream. Heat gently, beating until smooth. Serve the sauce warm with the dessert.

SERVES 4

1⅓ cups fresh or frozen raspberries
2 eating apples, peeled, cored, and sliced thickly
4 tbsp seedless raspberry jelly
2 tbsp port (optional)

sponge topping
4 tbsp soft margarine
4 tbsp superfine sugar
⅔ cup self-rising flour, sifted
1¾ oz/50 g white chocolate, grated
1 egg
2 tbsp milk

bitter chocolate sauce
3 oz/85 g semisweet chocolate
⅔ cup light cream

COOK'S TIP

Use semisweet chocolate in the sponge topping, and apricot halves, covered with peach schnapps and apricot jelly for the fruit layer.

easy

15 mins

40–45 mins

Individually made desserts look professional and are quick to cook. If you do not have small ovenproof bowls, you can use small cups instead.

Mini Chocolate Gingers

SERVES 4

generous ⅓ cup soft margarine
¾ cup self-rising flour, sifted
½ cup superfine sugar
2 eggs
¼ cup unsweetened cocoa, sifted
1 oz/25 g semisweet chocolate
1¾ oz/50 g preserved ginger, plus
    extra to decorate
confectioners' sugar, to dust

chocolate custard
2 egg yolks
1 tbsp superfine sugar
1 tbsp cornstarch
1¼ cups milk
3½ oz/100 g semisweet chocolate,
    broken into pieces

1 Lightly grease 4 small individual molds. Place the margarine, flour, sugar, eggs, and cocoa in a mixing bowl and beat until well combined and smooth. Chop the chocolate and ginger and stir into the mixture.

2 Spoon the batter into the prepared molds and level the tops. The mixture should three-fourths fill the molds. Cover the molds with disks of baking parchment, then cover with pleated sheets of foil. Steam for 45 minutes, until the sponge desserts are cooked and springy to the touch.

3 Meanwhile, make the custard. Beat together the egg yolks, sugar, and cornstarch to form a smooth paste. Heat the milk until boiling and pour over the egg mixture. Return to the pan and cook over very low heat, stirring, until thick. Remove from the heat, add the chocolate and stir until melted.

4 Lift the molds from the steamer. Run a knife around the edges of the molds and turn out onto serving plates. Dust with sugar and drizzle chocolate custard over the top. Decorate with extra preserved ginger. Serve the remaining custard separately.

★★★   moderate

       10 mins

       45 mins

Buttery brioche gives this traditional British dessert a lovely rich flavor, but this recipe also works well with soft-baked batch bread.

Bread *and* Butter Pudding

1 Cut the brioche into thin slices. Lightly butter one side of each slice.

2 Place a layer of brioche, buttered-side down, in the base of a shallow ovenproof dish. Sprinkle a few chocolate chips over the top.

3 Continue layering the brioche and chocolate chips, finishing with a layer of bread on top.

4 Whisk together the egg, egg yolks, and sugar until well combined. Heat the milk in a small pan until it just begins to simmer. Gradually add to the egg mixture, whisking well.

5 Pour the custard over the bread and let stand for 5 minutes. Press the brioche down into the milk.

6 Place the dish in a roasting pan and add boiling water to come halfway up the side of the dish (this is known as a bain-marie). Bake in a preheated oven, 350°F/180°C, for 30 minutes or until the custard has set. Let the dessert cool for about 5 minutes before serving.

SERVES 4

8 oz/225 g brioche
1 tbsp butter
1¾ oz/50 g semisweet chocolate chips
1 egg
2 egg yolks
4 tbsp superfine sugar
scant 2 cups canned light evaporated milk

COOK'S TIP

For a double-chocolate dessert, heat the milk with 1 tablespoon of unsweetened cocoa, stirring until well dissolved, then continue from Step 4.

easy

2 hrs 15 mins

35–40 mins

This fabulous steamed sponge dessert, served with a rich chocolate fudge sauce, is perfect for cold winter days.

Chocolate Fudge Sponge Dessert

SERVES 6

generous ⅓ cup soft margarine
1¼ cups self-rising flour
½ cup light corn syrup
3 eggs
¼ cup unsweetened cocoa

chocolate fudge sauce
3½ oz/100 g semisweet chocolate
½ cup condensed milk
4 tbsp heavy cream

1 Lightly grease a 5-cup mold.

2 Place the ingredients for the sponge dessert in a separate mixing bowl and beat until well combined and smooth.

3 Spoon into the prepared mold and level the top. Cover with a disk of waxed paper and tie a pleated sheet of foil over the bowl. Steam for 1½-2 hours, until the sponge dessert is cooked and springy to the touch.

4 To make the sauce, break the chocolate into small pieces and place in a small pan with the condensed milk. Heat gently, stirring until the chocolate melts.

5 Remove the pan from the heat and stir in the heavy cream.

6 To serve the sponge dessert, turn it out onto a serving plate and pour over a little of the chocolate fudge sauce. Serve the remaining sauce separately.

easy
10 mins
35–40 mins

COOK'S TIP

When covering steamed desserts, tie the foil tightly with a length of string, then make a "handle" with an additional length of string, so that it is easy to lift the mold out of the pan or steamer.

The addition of chocolate to a crumble topping makes it even more of a treat, and is a good way of enticing children to eat a fruit dessert.

Chocolate Fruit Crumble

1 Lightly grease an ovenproof dish with a little butter or margarine.

2 Drain the apricots, reserving 4 tablespoons of the juice. Place the apples and apricots in the prepared ovenproof dish with the reserved apricot juice and toss to mix.

3 Sift the flour into a mixing bowl. Cut the butter into small cubes and rub in with your fingertips until the mixture resembles fine bread crumbs. Stir in the rolled oats, sugar, and chocolate chips.

4 Sprinkle the crumble mixture over the apples and apricots and level the top. Do not press the crumble into the fruit.

5 Bake in a preheated oven, 180°C/350°F, for 40–45 minutes or until the topping is golden. Serve hot or cold.

SERVES 4

14 oz/400 g canned apricots in natural juice
1 lb/450 g cooking apples, peeled and
  sliced thickly
3/4 cup all-purpose flour
6 tbsp butter
2/3 cup rolled oats
4 tbsp superfine sugar
2/3 cup chocolate chips

 COOK'S TIP

Other fruits can be used to make this crumble—fresh pears mixed with fresh or frozen raspberries work well. If you do not use canned fruit, add 4 tablespoons of orange juice to the fresh fruit.

easy

5–10 mins

40–45 mins

In this recipe, the mixture separates out during cooking to produce a cream sponge topping and a delicious chocolate sauce underneath.

Saucy Chocolate Pudding

SERVES 4

1¼ cups milk
2¾ oz/75 g semisweet chocolate, broken into pieces
½ tsp vanilla extract
½ cup superfine sugar
generous ⅓ cup butter
1¼ cups self-rising flour
2 tbsp unsweetened cocoa
confectioners' sugar, to dust

for the sauce
3 tbsp unsweetened cocoa
⅓ cup light brown sugar
1¼ cups boiling water

1 Lightly grease a 3¾ cup-ovenproof dish.

2 Place the milk in a small pan with the chocolate and stir over gentle heat until the chocolate melts. Remove from the heat and let the mixture cool slightly. Stir in the vanilla extract.

3 Beat together the superfine sugar and butter in a bowl until light and fluffy. Sift the flour and cocoa together. Add to the bowl with the chocolate milk and beat until smooth, using an electric whisk if you have one. Pour the batter into the prepared dish.

4 To make the sauce, combine the cocoa and sugar. Add a little of the boiling water and mix to a smooth paste, then stir in the remaining water. Pour the sauce over the batter but do not mix in.

5 Place the dish on a cookie sheet and bake in a preheated oven, 350°F/180°C, for 40 minutes or until dry on top and springy to the touch. Let stand for 5 minutes, then dust with a little confectioners' sugar just before serving.

 COOK'S TIP

For a mocha sauce, add 1 tablespoon instant coffee to the cocoa and sugar in Step 4, before mixing to a paste with the boiling water.

easy

15 mins

45 mins

Crumbly cookie base, rich creamy chocolate filling topped with fluffy meringue—what could be more indulgent than this fabulous dessert?

Chocolate Meringue Pie

1 Place the graham crackers in a plastic bag and crush with a rolling pin. Pour into a mixing bowl. Melt the butter and stir it into the crumbs until well mixed. Press the mixture firmly into the base and up the sides of a 9-inch/23-cm tart pan or dish.

2 To make the filling, beat the egg yolks, superfine sugar, and cornstarch in a large bowl until they form a smooth paste, adding a little of the milk if necessary. Heat the milk until almost boiling, then slowly pour it onto the egg mixture, whisking well.

3 Return the mixture to the pan and cook gently, whisking constantly, until it thickens. Remove from the heat. Whisk in the melted chocolate, then pour it into the pie shell.

4 To make the meringue, whisk the egg whites in a large mixing bowl until standing in soft peaks. Gradually whisk in about two thirds of the sugar until the mixture is stiff and glossy. Fold in the remaining sugar and the vanilla extract.

5 Spread the meringue over the filling, swirling the surface with the back of a spoon to give it an attractive finish. Bake in the center of a preheated oven, 325°F/160°C, for 30 minutes or until the meringue is golden. Serve the pie hot or just warm.

SERVES 6

8 oz/225 g semisweet chocolate graham crackers
4 tbsp butter

filling
3 egg yolks
4 tbsp superfine sugar
4 tbsp cornstarch
2½ cups milk
3½ oz/100 g semisweet chocolate, melted

meringue
2 egg whites
½ cup superfine sugar
¼ tsp vanilla extract

challenging

30 mins

35 mins

Crêpes are given the chocolate treatment here to make a fabulous dinner party dessert. Prepare them ahead of time for trouble-free entertaining.

Chocolate *and* Banana Crêpes

SERVES 4

3 large bananas
6 tbsp orange juice
grated rind of 1 orange
2 tbsp orange- or banana-flavored liqueur

hot chocolate sauce
1 tbsp unsweetened cocoa
2 tsp cornstarch
3 tbsp milk
1½ oz/40 g semisweet chocolate
1 tbsp butter
½ cup light corn syrup
¼ tsp vanilla extract

pancakes
¾ cup all-purpose flour
1 tbsp unsweetened cocoa
1 egg
1 tsp sunflower oil
1¼ cups milk
oil, for frying

1 Peel and slice the bananas and arrange them in a dish with the orange juice and rind and the liqueur.

2 Mix the cocoa and cornstarch in a bowl, then stir in the milk. Break the semisweet chocolate into pieces and place in a pan with the butter and light corn syrup. Heat gently, stirring until well blended. Add the cocoa mixture and bring to a boil over gentle heat, stirring. Simmer for 1 minute, then remove from the heat, and stir in the vanilla extract.

3 To make the crêpes, sift the flour and cocoa into a mixing bowl and make a well in the center. Add the egg and oil. Gradually whisk in the milk to form a smooth batter. Heat a little oil in a heavy skillet and pour off any excess. Pour in a little batter and tilt the pan to coat the base evenly. Cook over medium heat until the underside is browned. Flip the crêpe over and cook the other side. Slide the crêpe out of the skillet and keep warm. Repeat until all the batter has been used.

4 To serve, reheat the chocolate sauce. Fold the crêpes in fourths and fill with the banana slices. Pour over a little chocolate sauce and serve.

✪✪✪✪ challenging

🕐 10 mins

🕐 15 mins

If you cannot wait to get your first chocolate "fix" of the day, serve these pancakes for breakfast. They also make a perfect family dessert.

Apple Pancake Stacks

1 Sift the flour and baking powder into a mixing bowl. Stir in the superfine sugar. Make a well in the center and add the egg and melted butter. Gradually whisk in the milk to form a smooth batter.

2 Peel, core, and grate the apple and stir in with the chocolate chips.

3 Heat a griddle pan or heavy skillet over medium heat and grease it lightly. For each pancake, place about 2 tablespoons of the batter on the griddle or skillet and spread to make a 3-inch/7.5-cm circle.

4 Cook for a few minutes until bubbles appear on the surface of the pancake. Turn over and cook for 1 minute more. Remove from the griddle or skillet and keep warm. Repeat with the remaining batter to make 12 pancakes.

5 To serve, stack 2 or 3 pancakes on an individual serving plate and drizzle with the hot chocolate sauce or maple syrup.

SERVES **4**

2 cups all-purpose flour
1½ tsp baking powder
4 tbsp superfine sugar
1 egg
1 tbsp butter, melted, plus butter
   for greasing
1¼ cups milk
1 eating apple
1¾ oz/50 g semisweet chocolate chips
Glossy Chocolate Sauce (see page 75) or
   maple syrup, to serve

COOK'S TIP

To keep the cooked pancakes warm, pile them on top of each other with waxed paper in between to prevent them from sticking to one another.

moderate

20 mins

45 mins

This is a fun dessert to serve at the end of the meal. Prepare in advance, then just warm through before serving.

Chocolate Fondue

SERVES 4
8 oz/225 g semisweet chocolate
generous ¾ cup heavy cream
2 tbsp brandy

to serve
selection of fruit
white and pink marshmallows
cookies

1 Break the chocolate into small pieces and place in a small pan with the cream. Heat the mixture gently, stirring constantly until the chocolate has melted and blended with the cream.

2 Remove the pan from the heat and stir in the brandy.

3 Pour into a fondue pot or a small flameproof dish and keep warm, preferably over a small burner.

4 Serve with a selection of fruit, marshmallows, and cookies for dipping. The fruit and marshmallows can be spiked on fondue forks, wooden skewers, or ordinary forks, for dipping into the chocolate fondue.

very easy
15 mins
5 mins

COOK'S TIP

To prepare the fruit for dipping, cut larger fruit into bite-size pieces. Fruit that discolors, such as bananas, apples, and pears, should be dipped in a little lemon juice as soon as it is cut.

Served with hot chocolate custard, this wonderful light soufflé is a chocoholic's dream.

Hot Chocolate Soufflé

1 Grease a 5-cup soufflé dish and sprinkle with superfine sugar.

2 Heat the milk with the butter in a pan until almost boiling. Mix the egg yolks, cornstarch, and superfine sugar in a bowl and pour on some of the hot milk, whisking. Return it to the pan and cook gently, stirring constantly until thickened. Break the chocolate into pieces and stir into the mixture until melted. Remove from the heat and stir in the vanilla extract.

3 Whisk the egg whites until standing in soft peaks. Fold half of the egg whites into the chocolate mixture. Fold in the rest with the chocolate chips. Pour into the dish and bake in a preheated oven, 350°F/180°C, for 40–45 minutes, until well risen.

4 Meanwhile, make the custard. Put the cornstarch and sugar in a small bowl and mix to a smooth paste with a little of the milk. Heat the remaining milk until almost boiling. Pour a little of the hot milk onto the cornstarch, mix well, then pour back into the pan. Cook gently, stirring until thickened. Break the chocolate into pieces and add to the custard, stirring until melted.

5 Dust the soufflé with confectioners' sugar and serve immediately with the chocolate custard.

SERVES 4

1¼ cups milk
2 tbsp butter
4 extra large eggs, separated
1 tbsp cornstarch
4 tbsp superfine sugar
3½ oz/100 g semisweet chocolate
½ tsp vanilla extract
⅔ cup semisweet chocolate chips
superfine and confectioners' sugar, to dust

chocolate custard
2 tbsp cornstarch
1 tbsp superfine sugar
2 cups milk
1¾ oz/50 g semisweet chocolate

 challenging
15 mins
40–45 mins

As this recipe uses only a little chocolate, choose one with a minimum of 70 percent cocoa solids for a good flavor.

Chocolate Zabaglione

SERVES 4

4 egg yolks
4 tbsp superfine sugar
1¾ oz/50 g semisweet chocolate
½ cup Marsala wine
unsweetened cocoa, to dust

1 In a large glass mixing bowl and, using an electric whisk, whisk together the egg yolks and superfine sugar until you have a very pale mixture.

2 Grate the chocolate finely and fold into the egg mixture with the Marsala.

3 Place the mixing bowl over a pan of gently simmering water and set the electric whisk on the lowest speed or change to a hand-held balloon whisk. Cook gently, whisking constantly, until the mixture thickens; take care not to overcook or the mixture will curdle.

4 Spoon the hot mixture into warmed individual glass dishes or coffee cups and dust with cocoa. Serve the zabaglione as soon as possible so that it is warm, light, and fluffy.

easy

10 mins

5 mins

COOK'S TIP

Make the dessert just before serving as it will separate if you let it stand. If it begins to curdle, remove it from the heat immediately and place it in a bowl of cold water to stop the cooking and whisk furiously until smooth.

This sponge dessert is very light and is delicious with a chocolate or coffee sauce.

Coffee Sponge Dessert

1 Lightly grease a 2½-cup heatproof bowl. Cream the margarine and sugar until light and fluffy and beat in the eggs.

2 Sift the flour and baking powder onto the mixture and stir in. Stir in the milk and coffee extract, to make a smooth batter.

3 Spoon the mixture into the prepared bowl and cover with a pleated piece of baking parchment and then a pleated piece of foil, securing around the bowl with string. Place in a steamer or large pan and half fill with boiling water. Cover and steam for 1–1¼ hours or until cooked through.

4 To make the sauce, put the milk, soft brown sugar, and cocoa in a pan and heat until the sugar dissolves. Blend the cornstarch with 4 tablespoons of cold water to make a paste and stir into the pan. Bring to a boil, stirring, until thickened. Cook over gentle heat for 1 minute.

5 Turn the dessert out onto a serving plate and spoon the sauce over the top. Serve at once.

SERVES **4**

2 tbsp margarine
2 tbsp soft brown sugar
2 eggs
⅓ cup all-purpose flour
¾ tsp baking powder
6 tbsp milk
1 tsp coffee extract

sauce
1¼ cups milk
1 tbsp soft brown sugar
1 tsp unsweetened cocoa
2 tbsp cornstarch

COOK'S TIP

The sponge dessert is covered with pleated parchment and foil to let it rise. The foil will react with the steam and must therefore not be placed directly against the surface.

⭐⭐⭐   moderate
🕐   10 mins
🕐   1 hr–1 hr 15 mins

This dessert has a hidden surprise when cooked because it separates to give a rich chocolate sauce at the base of the dish.

Baked Fudge Dessert

SERVES 4

4 tbsp margarine
½ cup soft light brown sugar
2 eggs, beaten
1¼ cups milk
⅓ cup chopped walnuts
¼ cup all-purpose flour
2 tbsp unsweetened cocoa
confectioners' sugar and unsweetened cocoa, to dust

1 Lightly grease a 4-cup ovenproof dish.

2 Cream together the margarine and sugar in a large mixing bowl until fluffy. Beat in the eggs. Gradually stir in the milk and add the walnuts.

3 Sift the flour and cocoa into the mixture and fold in gently with a metal spoon, until well mixed.

4 Spoon the batter into the dish and cook in a preheated oven, 350°F/180°C, for 35–40 minutes or until the sponge is cooked.

5 Dust with confectioners' sugar and cocoa and serve.

easy

10 mins

35–45 mins

🍳 **COOK'S TIP**

Add 1–2 tablespoons of brandy or rum to the mixture for a slightly alcoholic dessert, or 1–2 tablespoons of orange juice for a child-friendly version.

These rich individual desserts with a cream sauce always look and taste impressive at the end of a meal.

Sticky Chocolate Sponges

1 Lightly grease 6 individual ¾-cup pudding molds.

2 In a bowl, cream together the butter and sugar until pale and fluffy. Beat in the eggs a little at a time, beating well after each addition.

3 Sift the flour, salt, and cocoa into the creamed mixture, and fold in with a metal spoon. Stir in the chopped chocolate until evenly combined.

4 Divide the mixture between the prepared molds. Cover the molds with circles of baking parchment and then with pleated squares of foil. Press the edges to seal.

5 Place the molds in a roasting pan and pour in boiling water to come halfway up the sides of the molds.

6 Bake in a preheated oven, 350°F/180°C, for 50 minutes or until a skewer inserted into the center of the sponges comes out clean.

7 Meanwhile, make the sauce. Put the cream, sugar, and butter in a pan and bring gradually to a boil, stirring to dissolve the sugar. Simmer gently for 1–2 minutes.

8 To serve, run a knife around the edge of each sponge, then turn out onto serving plates. Serve with the cream sauce.

SERVES 6

½ cup butter, softened
1 cup soft brown sugar
3 eggs, beaten
1 cup self-rising flour
pinch of salt
¼ cup unsweetened cocoa
1 oz/25 g semisweet chocolate, chopped finely
2¾ oz/75 g white chocolate, chopped finely

sauce
⅔ cup heavy cream
½ cup soft brown sugar
2 tbsp butter

moderate

20 mins

1 hr

This chocolate dessert is served with hot fudge sauce, making it the most delicious way to use up bread that is slightly stale.

Chocolate Bread Pudding

SERVES 4

6 thick slices white bread, crusts removed
2 cups milk
¾ cup canned evaporated milk
2 tbsp unsweetened cocoa
2 eggs
2 tbsp molasses sugar
1 tsp vanilla extract
confectioners' sugar, to dust

hot fudge sauce
1 tbsp cornstarch
⅔ cup milk
2 oz/55 g semisweet chocolate, broken into pieces
1 tbsp unsweetened cocoa
2 tbsp light corn syrup
¼ cup butter or margarine
2 tbsp molasses sugar

1 Grease a shallow ovenproof dish. Cut the bread into squares and layer them in the dish.

2 Put the milk, evaporated milk, and cocoa in a pan and heat gently, stirring occasionally, until lukewarm.

3 Whisk together the eggs, sugar, and vanilla extract. Add the warm milk mixture and whisk well.

4 Pour into the prepared dish, making sure that all the bread is completely covered. Cover with plastic wrap and chill in the refrigerator for 1–2 hours.

5 Bake the pudding in a preheated oven, 350°F/180°C, for 35–40 minutes, until set. Remove the pudding from the oven and let stand for 5 minutes.

6 To make the sauce, mix the cornstarch to a smooth paste with a little of the milk, then place in a pan with the rest of the milk and the remaining sauce ingredients. Heat gently, stirring constantly, until smooth.

7 Dust the pudding with confectioners' sugar and serve immediately with the hot fudge sauce.

✪✪✪　　moderate

🕐　　2 hrs 15 mins

🕐　　45 mins

Phyllo pastry makes these empanadas light and crisp on the outside, while the filling melts into a scrumptious hot banana-chocolate goo.

Banana Empanadas

1 Peel and dice the bananas and place in a bowl. Add the sugar and lemon juice and stir well to combine. Stir in the chocolate.

2 Working one at a time, lay a long rectangular sheet of phyllo pastry out in front of you and then brush it with melted butter or oil.

3 Place a couple of teaspoons of the banana and chocolate mixture in one corner of the phyllo pastry, then fold over into a triangle shape to enclose the filling. Continue to fold in a triangular shape until the pastry is completely wrapped around the filling. Make the rest of the empanadas in the same way.

4 Brush the parcels with a little more butter or oil and dust with confectioners' sugar and cinnamon. Place them on a cookie sheet.

5 Bake in a preheated oven, 375°F/190°C, for about 15 minutes or until the empanadas are golden. Remove from the oven and serve immediately—warn people that the filling is very hot.

SERVES 4

2 ripe sweet bananas
1–2 tsp sugar
juice of ½ lemon
6–7 oz/175–200 g semisweet chocolate, broken into small pieces
about 8 sheets of phyllo pastry, halved lengthwise
melted butter or vegetable oil, for brushing
confectioners' sugar and ground cinnamon, to dust

 COOK'S TIP

You could use ready-made puff pie dough instead of phyllo. Roll it out very thinly and cut into squares. Fill, fold into triangles, and seal. Bake at 400°F/200°C until golden.

⭐⭐⭐ moderate
🕐 10 mins
🕐 15 mins

Melt-in-your-mouth, spicy poached pears are enveloped in a wonderfully indulgent chocolate fudge sauce.

Chocolate Fudge Pears

SERVES 4

4 eating pears
1–2 tbsp lemon juice
1¼ cups water
5 tbsp superfine sugar
2-inch/5-cm piece of cinnamon stick
2 cloves
scant 1 cup heavy cream
½ cup milk
scant 1 cup light brown sugar
2 tbsp sweet butter, diced
2 tbsp maple syrup
7 oz/200 g semisweet chocolate,
   broken into pieces

1 Peel the pears using a swivel vegetable peeler. Carefully cut out the cores from underneath, but leave the stalks intact because they look attractive. Brush the pears with the lemon juice to prevent discoloration.

2 Pour the water into a large, heavy pan and add the superfine sugar. Stir over low heat until the sugar has dissolved. Add the pears, cinnamon, and cloves and bring to a boil. (Add a little more water if the pears are not almost covered.) Lower the heat and simmer very gently for 20 minutes.

3 Meanwhile, pour the cream and milk into another heavy pan and add the brown sugar, butter, and maple syrup. Stir over low heat until the sugar has dissolved and the butter has melted. Still stirring, bring to a boil and continue to boil, stirring constantly, for 5 minutes, until thick and smooth. Remove the pan from the heat and stir in the chocolate, a little at a time, waiting until each batch has melted before adding the next. Set aside.

4 Transfer the pears to individual serving plates using a slotted spoon and keep warm. Bring the poaching syrup back to a boil and cook until reduced. Remove and discard the cinnamon and cloves, then stir the syrup into the chocolate sauce. Pour the sauce over the pears and serve immediately.

moderate
10 mins
30–35 mins

Light as air, these delicious little soufflés are the perfect choice for a dinner party dessert.

Individual Soufflés

1 Butter 6 custard pots or individual heatproof bowls and sprinkle with superfine sugar to coat the bases and sides. Tip out any excess. Stand the pots on a cookie sheet.

2 Chop the butter and place it in a heavy pan with the chocolate. Stir over very low heat until melted and smooth. Remove the pan from the heat and cool slightly. Beat in the egg yolks, one at a time, and stir in the orange liqueur. Set aside, stirring occasionally.

3 Gently whisk the egg whites until they are frothy, then sprinkle in the cream of tartar, and whisk rapidly until the mixture forms soft peaks. Add 1 tablespoon of superfine sugar and whisk rapidly again. Add the remaining superfine sugar, one tablespoon at a time, whisking until the whites form stiff, glossy peaks. Gently stir about one-fourth of the whites into the cooled chocolate mixture, then fold the chocolate mixture into the remaining whites using a metal spoon.

4 Divide the mixture among the prepared pots and bake in a preheated oven, 425°F/220°C, for 10 minutes, until risen and set. Dust the soufflés with confectioners' sugar and serve immediately, handing the sauce separately.

SERVES 4

3 tbsp superfine sugar, plus 1 tbsp extra for sprinkling
²⁄₃ cup sweet butter
6 oz/175 g semisweet chocolate, broken into small pieces
4 extra large eggs, separated
2 tbsp orange liqueur
¼ tsp cream of tartar
1 tbsp confectioners' sugar, to dust
1¼ cups French Chocolate Sauce (see page 74), to serve

COOK'S TIP

If you are serving these soufflés at a dinner party, you can prepare up to Step 2 in advance, including the first step of the sauce recipe. The preparation can then be completed and the soufflé baked after the entrée.

✪✪✪✪ challenging

15 mins

10 mins

Serve these sweet soufflé-filled, golden chocolate crêpes with flambéed summer berries for a superb contrast.

Chocolate Crêpes

SERVES 6

⅔ cup all-purpose flour
1 tbsp unsweetened cocoa
1 tsp superfine sugar
2 eggs, beaten lightly
¾ cup milk
2 tsp dark rum
2 tbsp melted sweet butter, plus extra
 for brushing
confectioners' sugar, to dust

filling
5 tbsp heavy cream
8 oz/225 g semisweet chocolate
3 eggs, separated
2 tbsp superfine sugar

berry sauce
2 tbsp butter
4 tbsp superfine sugar
⅔ cup orange juice
2 cups mixed berries, such as raspberries,
 blackberries, and strawberries
3 tbsp white rum

challenging

1 hr 10 mins

1 hr

1 Sift the flour, cocoa, and superfine sugar into a bowl. Make a well in the center, add the eggs, and beat in gradually. Beat in the milk until smooth. Stir in the rum and melted butter. Cover and let stand for 30 minutes.

2 Brush a 7-inch/18-cm crêpe pan with melted butter and set over medium heat Pour 3 tablespoonfuls of the batter into the pan, swirling it to cover the base. Cook for 3 minutes, turning once, then slide onto a plate. Cook another 11 crêpes in the same way. Stack them interleaved with baking parchment.

3 For the filling, put the cream and chocolate in a pan and melt gently, stirring. In a bowl, beat the egg yolks with half the sugar until creamy, beat in the chocolate cream, and let cool. In a separate bowl, whisk the egg whites into soft peaks, add the rest of the sugar, and beat until stiff. Stir a spoonful of the whites into the chocolate mixture, then fold in the remaining egg whites with a metal spoon.

4 Spread each crêpe with 1 tablespoon of the filling, then fold into fourths. Place on the cookie sheet and brush the tops with melted butter. Bake in a preheated oven, 400°F/200°C, for 20 minutes.

5 For the berry sauce, melt the butter in a heavy skillet over low heat, stir in the sugar, and cook until golden. Stir in the orange juice and cook until syrupy. Add the berries and warm through, stirring gently. Add the rum, heat gently for 1 minute, then ignite. Shake the pan until the flames have died down. Transfer the crêpes to serving plates with the sauce and serve.

A warming way to end supper on a wintry evening, this steamed sponge dessert is very easy to make.

Chocolate Sponge *with* Rum Sauce

1 Grease and flour a 5-cup ovenproof bowl. Put the butter, chocolate, sugar, and vanilla in the top of a double boiler or a heatproof bowl set over a pan of barely simmering water. Heat gently until the butter and sugar have melted, then remove from the heat, and cool slightly. Beat in the eggs. Sift in the flour, stir in the milk, and mix well. Pour the mixture into the prepared ovenproof bowl, cover the top with baking parchment and pleated foil and tie with string. Steam the sponge dessert for 1 hour, adding more boiling water if necessary.

2 Meanwhile make the sauce. Blend the cornstarch with a little of the milk, then place in a small pan with the rest of the milk and the sugar, and stir over medium heat. Bring to a boil, stirring constantly, then lower the heat, and simmer until thickened. Remove from the heat and stir in the rum.

3 To serve, remove the sponge dessert from the heat and discard the parchment and foil. Run a round-bladed knife around the side of the bowl, place a serving plate on top of the sponge dessert and, holding them together, invert. Serve immediately, handing the sauce separately.

SERVES 4

4 tbsp sweet butter
2 oz/55 g semisweet chocolate
scant ⅔ cup superfine sugar
¼ tsp vanilla extract
2 eggs, beaten lightly
1¼ cups self-rising flour
5 tbsp milk

rum sauce
1¼ cups milk
2 tbsp cornstarch
2 tbsp superfine sugar
2 tbsp dark rum

COOK'S TIP

You could add 2 tablespoons of rum to the sponge dessert in place of some of the milk, if you like.

⊛⊛ easy

🕐 15 mins

🕐 1 hr

The sharpness of the apple and cranberries contrasts deliciously with the sweetness of the chocolate in this wonderful, fluffy sponge dessert.

Chocolate Cranberry Sponge Dessert

SERVES 4

4 tbsp dark brown sugar, plus 2 tsp extra
   for sprinkling
1 large tart apple
4 tbsp sweet butter
¾ cup cranberries, thawed if frozen
2 eggs, beaten lightly
⅔ cup self-rising flour
3 tbsp unsweetened cocoa

sauce
6 oz/175 g semisweet chocolate,
   broken into pieces
1¾ cups evaporated milk
1 tsp vanilla extract
½ tsp almond extract

1 Grease a 5-cup ovenproof bowl, sprinkle with brown sugar to coat the sides and tip out any excess. Peel, core, and dice the apple and mix with the cranberries. Put the fruit in the prepared ovenproof bowl.

2 Place the butter, brown sugar, and eggs in a large bowl. Sift in the flour and cocoa and beat well until thoroughly mixed. Pour the batter into the ovenproof bowl on top of the fruit, cover the top with baking parchment and foil, and tie with string. Steam for about 1 hour, until risen, adding more boiling water if necessary.

3 Meanwhile, make the sauce. Put the semisweet chocolate and evaporated milk in the top of a double boiler or a heatproof bowl set over a pan of barely simmering water. Stir until the chocolate has melted, then remove from the heat. Whisk in the vanilla and almond extracts and continue to beat until the sauce is thick and smooth.

4 To serve, remove the sponge dessert from the heat. Run a round-bladed knife around the side of the bowl, place a serving plate on top of the sponge dessert, and, holding them together, invert. Serve immediately, handing the sauce separately.

COOK'S TIP

When cranberries are unavailable, you could use blueberries or raspberries.

easy

25 mins

1 hr

This creamy white chocolate sauce adds a touch of luxury and sophistication to the dinner table. Serve with vanilla ice cream or chocolate sponge dessert.

White Chocolate Fudge Sauce

1 Pour the cream into the top of a double boiler or a heatproof bowl set over a pan of barely simmering water. Add the butter and sugar and stir until the mixture is smooth. Remove from the heat.

2 Stir in the chocolate, a few pieces at a time, waiting until each batch has melted before adding the next. Add the brandy and stir the sauce until smooth. Cool to room temperature before serving.

MAKES 1 CUP

²⁄₃ cup heavy cream
4 tbsp sweet butter, diced
3 tbsp superfine sugar
6 oz/175 g white chocolate, broken into pieces
2 tbsp brandy

COOK'S TIP

Semisweet or milk chocolate can also be used in this recipe.

very easy

5 mins, plus 20 mins

10–15 mins

CHOCOLATE

This rich, warm—and alcoholic—sauce is superb with both hot and cold desserts and positively magical with ice cream.

French Chocolate Sauce

MAKES ²⁄₃ CUP

6 tbsp heavy cream
3 oz/85 g semisweet chocolate, broken into small pieces
2 tbsp orange liqueur

1 Bring the cream gently to a boil in a small, heavy pan over low heat. Remove the pan from the heat, add the chocolate, and stir until smooth.

2 Stir in the orange liqueur and serve immediately, or keep the sauce warm in a heatproof bowl over a pan of barely simmering water until required.

🍳 **COOK'S TIP**

Try using different flavors of liqueur, such as mint or coffee.

very easy

5 mins

10–15 mins

This simple sauce is a deliciously rich accompaniment to hot and cold desserts and is suitable for all the family.

Glossy Chocolate Sauce

1 Put the sugar and water into a small, heavy pan set over low heat and stir until the sugar has dissolved. Stir in the chocolate, a few pieces at a time, waiting until each batch has melted before adding the next. Stir in the butter, a few pieces at a time, waiting until each batch has been incorporated before adding the next. Do not let the sauce boil.

2 Stir in the orange juice and remove the pan from the heat. Serve immediately or keep warm until required.

MAKES ²/₃ CUP

½ cup superfine sugar
4 tbsp water
6 oz/175 g semisweet chocolate, broken into pieces
2 tbsp diced sweet butter
2 tbsp orange juice

COOK'S TIP

To freeze the sauce, let it cool, transfer to a freezerproof container, and freeze for up to 3 months. Thaw at room temperature before reheating to serve.

very easy

5 mins

10–15 mins

Cold Desserts

Cool, creamy, sumptuous, indulgent are just a few of the words that spring to mind when you think of cold chocolate desserts. The desserts contained in this chapter are a combination of all of these.

Some of the desserts are surprisingly quick and simple to make, while others are more elaborate. One of the best things about these desserts is they can all be made in advance, sometimes days in advance, making them perfect for entertaining. A quick decoration when necessary is all that is needed on the day. Even the Baked Chocolate Alaska can be assembled in advance and popped into the oven just before serving.

The classic combination of chocolate and mint flavors makes an attractive dessert for special occasions and celebrations.

Chocolate Mint Swirl

SERVES 6

1¼ cups heavy cream
⅔ cup mascarpone cheese
2 tbsp confectioners' sugar
1 tbsp crème de menthe
6 oz/175 g semisweet chocolate, melted
chocolate, to decorate

1 Place the cream in a large mixing bowl and whisk until standing in soft peaks.

2 Fold in the mascarpone cheese and confectioners' sugar, then place about one-third of the mixture in a smaller bowl. Stir the crème de menthe into the smaller bowl. Stir the melted chocolate into the remaining larger bowl.

3 Place alternate spoonfuls of the 2 mixtures in serving glasses, then swirl the mixture together to give a decorative effect. Chill until required.

4 To make the piped chocolate decorations, melt a small amount of chocolate and place in a paper pastry bag.

5 Place a sheet of baking parchment on a board and pipe squiggles, stars, or flower shapes with the melted chocolate. Alternatively, to make curved decorations, pipe decorations onto a long strip of baking parchment, then carefully place the strip over a rolling pin, securing with sticky tape. Let the chocolate set, then carefully remove from the baking parchment.

6 Decorate each dessert with the piped chocolate decorations and serve.

⭐⭐ easy

🕐 45 mins

🕐 5 mins

COOK'S TIP

Pipe the patterns freehand, as described above, or draw patterns on baking parchment first, turn the parchment over, and then pipe the chocolate, following the drawn outline.

Wickedly rich little pots, flavored with a hint of dark rum, are pure indulgence on any occasion!

Chocolate Rum Pots

1 Melt the chocolate and let cool slightly.

2 Whisk the egg yolks with the superfine sugar in a bowl until very pale and fluffy.

3 Drizzle the chocolate into the mixture and fold in together with the rum and the heavy cream.

4 Whisk the egg whites in a grease-free bowl until standing in soft peaks. Fold the egg whites into the chocolate mixture in 2 batches. Divide the mixture among 6 individual dishes and chill for at least 2 hours.

5 To serve, decorate with and marbled chocolate shapes.

SERVES 6

8 oz/225 g semisweet chocolate
4 eggs, separated
1/3 cup superfine sugar
4 tbsp dark rum
4 tbsp heavy cream

to decorate
a little whipped cream
Marbled Chocolate Shapes (see page 108)

COOK'S TIP

Make sure you use a perfectly grease-free bowl and whisk for whisking the egg whites. They will not aerate if any grease is present as the smallest amount breaks down the bubbles in the whites, preventing them from holding air.

easy

2 hrs 20 mins

5 mins

CHOCOLATE

These creamy chocolate- and coffee-flavored desserts make a perfect end to a fine meal.

Mocha Creams

SERVES 4

8 oz/225 g semisweet chocolate
1 tbsp instant coffee powder
1¼ cups boiling water
1 envelope gelatin
3 tbsp cold water
1 tsp vanilla extract
1 tbsp coffee-flavored liqueur (optional)
1¼ cups heavy cream
4 chocolate coffee beans, to decorate
8 amaretti cookies, to serve

1 Break the chocolate into small pieces and place in a pan with the coffee. Add the boiling water and heat gently, stirring until the chocolate melts.

2 Sprinkle the gelatin over the cold water and let it go spongy, then whisk it into the hot chocolate mixture to dissolve it.

3 Stir in the vanilla extract and coffee-flavored liqueur, if using. Let stand in a cool place until just beginning to thicken, whisking from time to time.

4 Whisk the heavy cream until it is standing in soft peaks. Reserve a little for decorating the desserts and fold the remainder into the chocolate mixture. Spoon into serving dishes and let set.

5 Decorate with the reserved cream and coffee beans and serve with the amaretti cookies.

easy

30 mins

5 mins

COOK'S TIP

To add a delicious almond flavor to the dessert, replace the coffee-flavored liqueur with amaretto liqueur.

Three layers of rich mousse give this elegant dessert extra chocolate appeal. It is a little awkward to prepare, but well worth the extra effort.

Layered Chocolate Mousse

1 Line a 1-lb/450-g loaf pan with baking parchment. Separate the eggs, putting each egg white in a separate bowl. Place the egg yolks, cornstarch, and sugar in a large mixing bowl and whisk until well combined. Place the milk in a pan and heat gently, stirring until almost boiling. Pour the milk onto the egg yolks, whisking.

2 Set the bowl over a pan of gently simmering water and cook, stirring, until the mixture thickens enough to thinly coat the back of a wooden spoon.

3 Sprinkle the gelatin over the water in a small heatproof bowl and let it go spongy. Place over a pan of hot water and stir until dissolved. Stir into the hot egg yolk mixture. Let the mixture cool.

4 Whip the cream until just holding its shape. Fold into the egg custard, then divide the mixture into 3. Melt the 3 types of chocolate separately. Fold the semisweet chocolate into one egg custard portion. Whisk one egg white until standing in soft peaks and fold into the semisweet chocolate custard until combined. Pour into the prepared pan and level the top. Chill in the coldest part of the refrigerator until just set. The remaining mixtures should stay at room temperature.

5 Fold the white chocolate into another portion of the egg custard. Whisk another egg white and fold in. Pour on top of the semisweet chocolate layer and chill quickly. Repeat with the remaining milk chocolate and egg white. Chill for at least 2 hours, until set. To serve, carefully turn out onto a serving dish and decorate with chocolate caraque.

SERVES **8**

3 eggs
1 tsp cornstarch
4 tbsp superfine sugar
1¼ cups milk
1 envelope gelatin
3 tbsp water
1¼ cups heavy cream
2¾ oz/75 g semisweet chocolate
2¾ oz/75 g white chocolate
2¾ oz/75 g milk chocolate
chocolate Caraque, to decorate (see page 15)

moderate

3 hrs

10 mins

This classic French dish is part way between a mousse and a parfait. It is usually chilled in a large mold, but here it is made in individual molds.

Chocolate Marquise

SERVES 6

7 oz/200 g semisweet chocolate
generous ⅓ cup butter
3 egg yolks
⅓ cup superfine sugar
1 tsp chocolate extract or 1 tbsp chocolate-
    flavored liqueur
1¼ cups heavy cream

to serve
chocolate-dipped fruits
crème fraîche
unsweetened cocoa, to dust

1 Break the chocolate into pieces. Place the chocolate and butter in a bowl over a pan of gently simmering water and stir until melted and well combined. Remove from the heat and let cool.

2 Place the egg yolks in a mixing bowl with the sugar and whisk until pale and fluffy. Using an electric whisk running on low speed, slowly whisk in the cool chocolate mixture. Stir in the chocolate extract or chocolate-flavored liqueur.

3 Whip the cream until just holding its shape. Fold into the chocolate mixture. Spoon into 6 small custard pots, or individual metal molds. Chill the desserts for at least 2 hours.

4 To serve, turn out the desserts onto individual serving dishes. If you have difficulty turning them out, dip the pots or molds into a bowl of warm water for a few seconds to help the marquise to slip out. Serve with chocolate-dipped fruit and crème fraîche and dust with cocoa.

COOK'S TIP

The slight tartness of the crème fraîche contrasts well with this very rich dessert. Dip the fruit in white chocolate to give a good color contrast.

easy
2hrs 30 mins
5 mins

This iced dessert is somewhere between a chocolate mousse and an ice cream. Serve it with a chocolate sauce or a fruit coulis and fresh fruit.

Iced White Chocolate Terrine

1 Line a 1-lb/450-g loaf pan with foil or plastic wrap, pressing out as many creases as you can.

2 Place the granulated sugar and water in a heavy pan and heat gently, stirring until the sugar has dissolved. Bring to a boil and boil for 1–2 minutes, until syrupy, then remove from the heat.

3 Break the white chocolate into small pieces and stir it into the syrup, continuing to stir until the chocolate has melted and combined with the syrup. Let the mixture cool slightly.

4 Beat the egg yolks into the chocolate mixture. Let cool completely.

5 Lightly whip the cream until just holding its shape and fold it into the chocolate mixture.

6 Whisk the egg whites in a grease-free bowl until they are standing in soft peaks. Fold the whites into the chocolate mixture. Pour into the prepared loaf pan and freeze overnight.

7 To serve, remove the terrine from the freezer about 10–15 minutes before serving. Turn out of the pan and cut into slices to serve.

SERVES 8

2 tbsp granulated sugar
5 tbsp water
10½ oz/300 g white chocolate
3 eggs, separated
1¼ cups heavy cream

to serve
chocolate sauce or fruit coulis
fresh berries

 COOK'S TIP

To make a coulis, place 8 oz/ 225 g soft fruit of your choice in a food processor. Add 1–2 tablespoons confectioners' sugar and blend to a paste. If the fruit contains seeds, push the paste through a strainer to remove them.

moderate
12 hrs 50 mins
55 mins

A banana split in a glass! Choose the best vanilla ice cream you can find, or better still, make your own.

Chocolate Banana Sundae

SERVES 4

glossy chocolate sauce
2 oz/55 g semisweet chocolate
4 tbsp light corn syrup
1 tbsp butter
1 tbsp brandy or rum (optional)

sundae
4 bananas
⅔ cup heavy cream
8–12 scoops good quality vanilla ice cream
¾ cup slivered or chopped almonds, toasted
grated chocolate, to sprinkle
4 fan wafers, to serve

1 To make the chocolate sauce, break the chocolate into small pieces and place in a heatproof bowl with the syrup and butter. Heat over a pan of hot water until melted, stirring until well combined. Remove the bowl from the heat and stir in the brandy or rum, if using.

2 Slice the bananas and whip the cream until just holding its shape. Place a scoop of ice cream in the base of each of 4 tall sundae dishes. Top with slices of banana, some chocolate sauce, a spoonful of cream, and a generous sprinkling of nuts.

3 Repeat the layers, finishing with a good spoonful of cream. Sprinkle with nuts, and a little grated chocolate. Serve with fan wafers.

⭐⭐ easy
🕐 15 mins
🕐 5 mins

COOK'S TIP

For a traditional banana split, halve the bananas lengthwise and place on a plate with two scoops of ice cream between. Top with cream and sprinkle with nuts. Serve with the glossy chocolate sauce poured over the top.

A cool dessert that leaves the cook completely unflustered—you can even assemble it in advance and keep it in the freezer until required.

Baked Chocolate Alaska

1 Lightly grease a 7-inch/18-cm round cake pan and line the base with baking parchment.

2 Whisk the eggs and superfine sugar in a mixing bowl until very thick and pale. Sift the flour and cocoa together and carefully fold in.

3 Pour into the prepared pan and bake in a preheated oven, 425°F/220°C, for 7 minutes or until golden and springy to the touch. Transfer to a wire rack and let cool completely. Leave the oven on.

4 Whisk the egg whites in a grease-free bowl until they are standing in soft peaks. Gradually add the sugar, whisking until thick and glossy.

5 Place the sponge cake on a cookie sheet and pile the ice cream onto the center in a heaping dome.

6 Pipe or spread the meringue over the ice cream, making sure the ice cream is completely enclosed. (At this point the dessert can be frozen, if wished.)

7 Return the cake to the oven for 5 minutes, until the meringue is just golden. Serve immediately.

SERVES 4

2 eggs
4 tbsp superfine sugar
¼ cup all-purpose flour
2 tbsp unsweetened cocoa
4 cups good quality chocolate ice cream

meringue
3 egg whites
⅔ cup superfine sugar

 COOK'S TIP

This dessert is delicious served with a black currant coulis. Cook a few black currants in a little orange juice until soft, blend to a paste, and push through a strainer, then sweeten to taste with a little confectioners' sugar.

✪✪✪ moderate
🕐 50 mins
🕐 12 mins

A rich chocolate ice cream, delicious on its own or served with chocolate sauce. For a special dessert, serve it in these attractive trellis shells.

Rich Chocolate Ice Cream

SERVES 6
1 egg
3 egg yolks
scant ½ cup superfine sugar
1¼ cups milk
9 oz/250 g semisweet chocolate
1¼ cups heavy cream

trellis shells
7 oz/200 g semisweet chocolate

1 Beat together the egg, egg yolks, and superfine sugar in a mixing bowl until well combined. Heat the milk until it is almost boiling.

2 Gradually pour the hot milk onto the eggs, whisking as you do so. Place the bowl over a pan of gently simmering water and cook, stirring, until the mixture thickens sufficiently to thinly coat the back of a wooden spoon.

3 Break the semisweet chocolate into small pieces and add to the hot custard. Stir until the chocolate has melted. Cover with a sheet of dampened baking parchment and let stand until cold.

4 Whip the cream until just holding its shape, then fold into the cold chocolate custard. Transfer to a freezerproof container and freeze for 1–2 hours, until the mixture is frozen 1 inch/2.5 cm from the sides.

5 Scrape the ice cream into a chilled bowl and beat again until smooth. Re-freeze until firm.

6 To make the trellis shells, invert 2 muffin pans and cover 12 alternate mounds with plastic wrap. Melt the chocolate, place it in a paper pastry bag, and snip off the end.

7 Pipe a circle around the base of the mound, then pipe chocolate back and forth over it to form a trellis; carefully pipe a double thickness. Pipe around the base again. Chill until set, then lift from the pan, and remove the plastic wrap. Serve the ice cream in the trellis shells.

moderate

4–5 hrs

12 mins

This white chocolate ice cream is served in a cookie cup. If desired, top with a chocolate sauce for a true chocolate addict's treat.

White Chocolate Ice Cream

1 Place baking parchment on 2 cookie sheets. To make the ice cream, beat the egg, egg yolk, and sugar. Break the chocolate into pieces, place in a bowl with 3 tablespoons of the milk and melt over a pan of hot water. Heat the remaining milk until almost boiling and pour onto the eggs, whisking. Place over a pan of simmering water and cook, stirring, until the mixture thickens enough to coat the back of a wooden spoon. Whisk in the chocolate. Cover with dampened baking parchment and let stand until cold.

2 Whip the cream until just holding its shape and fold into the custard. Transfer to a freezerproof container and freeze the mixture for 1–2 hours, until frozen 1 inch/2.5 cm from the sides. Scrape into a bowl and beat again until smooth. Re-freeze until firm.

3 To make the cups, beat the egg white and sugar together. Beat in the flour and cocoa, then the butter. Place 1 tablespoon of mixture on one cookie sheet and spread out into a 5-inch/13-cm circle. Bake in a preheated oven, 400°F/200°C, for 4–5 minutes. Remove and mold over an upturned cup. Let the cookie cup set, then cool on a wire rack. Repeat to make 6 cookie cups. Serve the ice cream in the cups.

SERVES 6

1 egg
1 egg yolk
3 tbsp superfine sugar
5½ oz/150 g white chocolate
1¼ cups milk
⅔ cup heavy cream

cookie cups
1 egg white
4 tbsp superfine sugar
2 tbsp all-purpose flour, sifted
2 tbsp unsweetened cocoa, sifted
2 tbsp butter, melted

🍳 **COOK'S TIP**

Transfer the ice cream to the refrigerator about 20 minutes before it is required, so that it can soften slightly. However, do not scoop it into the cookie cups until ready to serve.

 moderate

4–5 hrs

15 mins

This chocolate dessert, consisting of a rich chocolate mousse-like filling enclosed in lady-fingers, is a variation of a popular classic.

Chocolate Charlotte

SERVES **8**

about 22 lady-fingers
4 tbsp orange-flavored liqueur
9 oz/250 g semisweet chocolate, melted
⅔ cup heavy cream
4 eggs
⅔ cup superfine sugar

to decorate
⅔ cup whipping cream
2 tbsp superfine sugar
½ tsp vanilla extract
semisweet chocolate Quick Curls
    (see page 15)

1 Line the base of a Charlotte mold or a deep 7-inch/18-cm round cake pan with baking parchment.

2 Place the lady-fingers on a tray and sprinkle with half of the orange-flavored liqueur. Use to line the sides of the mold or pan, trimming if necessary to make a tight fit.

3 Mix the melted chocolate with the heavy cream. Separate the eggs and place the whites in a large grease-free bowl. Beat the egg yolks into the chocolate mixture.

4 Whisk the egg whites until standing in stiff peaks, then gradually add the superfine sugar, whisking until stiff and glossy. Carefully fold the egg whites into the chocolate mixture in 2 batches, taking care not to knock out the air. Pour into the center of the mold. Trim the lady-fingers so that they are level with the chocolate mixture. Chill for at least 5 hours.

5 To decorate, whisk the cream, sugar, and vanilla extract until standing in soft peaks. Turn out the charlotte onto a serving dish. Pipe cream rosettes around the base and decorate with chocolate curls and other decorations of your choice.

moderate

5 hrs 40 mins

5 mins

Semisweet and white chocolate cheesecake fillings are marbled together to give an attractive finish to this rich and decadent dessert.

Marbled Cheesecake

1 Place the toasted oat cereal in a plastic bag and crush with a rolling pin. Pour the crushed cereal into a mixing bowl and stir in the hazelnuts.

2 Melt the butter and chocolate together over low heat and stir into the cereal mixture, stirring until well coated.

3 Using the base of a glass, press the mixture into the base and up the sides of an 8-inch/20-cm springform pan.

4 Beat together the cheese and sugar with a wooden spoon until smooth. Beat in the yogurt. Whip the cream until just holding its shape and fold into the mixture. Sprinkle the gelatin over the water in a heatproof bowl and let it go spongy. Place over a pan of hot water and stir until dissolved. Stir into the mixture.

5 Divide the mixture in half and beat the semisweet chocolate into one half and the white chocolate into the other half.

6 Place alternate spoonfuls of mixture on top of the cereal base. Swirl the filling together with the tip of a knife to give a marbled effect. Level the top with a scraper or a spatula. Chill for at least 2 hours, until set, before serving.

SERVES 10

base
8 oz/225 g toasted oat cereal
½ cup toasted hazelnuts, chopped
4 tbsp butter
1 oz/25 g semisweet chocolate

filling
12 oz/350 g whole milk soft cheese
½ cup superfine sugar
generous ¾ cup thick yogurt
1¼ cups heavy cream
1 envelope gelatin
3 tbsp water
6 oz/175 g semisweet chocolate, melted
6 oz/175 g white chocolate, melted

🍮 COOK'S TIP

If you prefer to use leaf gelatin, you will need about 2½ leaves. Follow the instructions on the envelope for dissolving them.

 moderate

2 hrs 30 mins

5 mins

The exotic combination of banana and coconut goes well with chocolate. Grated fresh coconut gives a better flavor than dry unsweetened coconut.

Banana Coconut Cheesecake

SERVES 10

8 oz/225 g chocolate chip cookies
4 tbsp butter, melted
12 oz/350 g medium-fat soft cheese
$\frac{1}{3}$ cup superfine sugar
$1\frac{3}{4}$ oz/50 g fresh coconut, grated
2 tbsp coconut-flavored liqueur
2 ripe bananas
$4\frac{1}{2}$ oz/125 g semisweet chocolate
1 envelope gelatin
3 tbsp water
$\frac{2}{3}$ cup heavy cream

to decorate
1 banana
lemon juice
a little melted chocolate

1 Place the cookies in a plastic bag and crush with a rolling pin. Tip into a mixing bowl and stir in the melted butter. Firmly press the cookie mixture into the base and up the sides of an 8-inch/20-cm springform pan.

2 Beat together the soft cheese and sugar until well combined, then beat in the grated coconut and coconut-flavored liqueur. Mash the bananas and beat them in. Melt the semisweet chocolate and then beat in to the soft cheese mixture until well combined.

3 Sprinkle the gelatin over the water in a heatproof bowl and let it go spongy. Place over a pan of hot water and stir until dissolved. Stir into the chocolate mixture. Whisk the cream until just holding its shape and stir into the chocolate mixture. Spoon over the pie shell and chill for 2 hours, until set.

4 To serve, carefully transfer to a serving plate. Slice the banana, toss in lemon juice, and arrange around the edge of the cheesecake. Drizzle with melted chocolate and let set.

⭐⭐⭐   moderate
         2 hrs 30 mins
         5 mins

COOK'S TIP

To crack the coconut, pierce 2 of the "eyes" and drain off the liquid. Tap hard around the center with a hammer until it cracks and lever it apart.

A crumbly ginger chocolate shell topped with velvety smooth chocolate brandy cream makes this a blissful cake.

Chocolate Brandy Torte

1 Crush the gingersnaps in a bag with a rolling pin or in a food processor. Melt the chocolate and butter together and pour over the gingersnaps. Mix well, then use to line the base and sides of a 9-inch/23-cm loose-based fluted flan pan or springform pan. Chill while preparing the filling.

2 To make the filling, melt the semisweet chocolate in a heatproof bowl set over a pan of barely simmering water, remove from the heat, and beat in the mascarpone cheese, egg yolks, and brandy.

3 Lightly whip the cream until just holding its shape and gently fold in the chocolate mixture.

4 Whisk the egg whites in a grease-free bowl until standing in soft peaks. Add the superfine sugar, a little at a time, and whisk until thick and glossy. Fold into the chocolate mixture, in 2 batches, until just mixed.

5 Spoon the mixture into the prepared gingersnap shell and chill for at least 2 hours. Carefully transfer to a serving plate. To decorate, whip the cream and pipe swirls onto the torte. Top with the chocolate coffee beans and sprinkle with grated chocolate.

SERVES 12

base
9 oz/250 g gingersnaps
2³/₄ oz/75 g semisweet chocolate
generous ¹/₃ cup butter

filling
8 oz/225 g semisweet chocolate, broken into pieces
generous 1 cup mascarpone cheese
2 eggs, separated
3 tbsp brandy
1¹/₄ cups heavy cream
4 tbsp superfine sugar

to decorate
scant ¹/₂ cup heavy cream
chocolate coffee beans
grated chocolate

COOK'S TIP

If chocolate coffee beans are unavailable, use chocolate-coated raisins or pieces of preserved ginger to decorate.

easy
2 hrs 40 mins
5 mins

Stacks of crisp shortcake are sandwiched with chocolate-flavored cream and fresh raspberries and served with a fresh raspberry coulis.

Chocolate Shortcake Towers

SERVES 6

shortcake
1 cup butter
½ cup light brown sugar
1¾ oz/50 g semisweet chocolate, grated
scant 2½ cups all-purpose flour, sifted,
plus extra for dusting

to finish
2 cups fresh raspberries
2 tbsp confectioners' sugar
1¼ cups heavy cream
3 tbsp milk
3½ oz/100 g white chocolate, melted
confectioners' sugar, to dust

1 Lightly grease a cookie sheet. To make the shortcake, beat together the butter and sugar until light and fluffy. Beat in the semisweet chocolate. Mix in the flour to form a stiff dough.

2 Roll out the dough on a lightly floured counter and stamp out 18 circles with a 3-inch/7.5-cm cookie cutter. Place the circles on the cookie sheet and bake in a preheated oven, 400°F/200°C, for 10 minutes, until crisp and golden. Let cool on the sheet.

3 To make the coulis, set aside generous ½ cup of the raspberries. Blend the remainder in a food processor with the confectioners' sugar, then push through a strainer to remove the seeds. Chill. Set aside 2 teaspoons of the cream. Whip the remainder until just holding its shape. Fold in the milk and the melted chocolate.

4 For each tower, spoon a little coulis onto a serving plate. Drop small dots of the reserved cream into the coulis around the edge of the plate and use a skewer to drag through the cream to make an attractive pattern.

5 Place a shortcake circle on the plate and spoon on a little of the chocolate cream. Top with 2 or 3 raspberries, top with another shortcake, and repeat. Place a third shortcake circle on top. Dust with confectioners' sugar.

✪✪✪ moderate
🕐 30 mins
🕐 10 mins

Combine all the delightful flavors of a Black Forest Gâteau in this new guise—the results are stunning.

Black Forest Trifle

1 Place the slices of chocolate roll in the base of a glass serving bowl.

2 Drain the black cherries, reserving 6 tablespoons of the juice. Place the cherries and the reserved juice on top of the cake. Sprinkle with the kirsch.

3 In a bowl, mix the cornstarch and superfine sugar. Stir in enough of the milk to mix to a smooth paste. Beat in the egg yolks and the whole egg.

4 Heat the remaining milk in a small pan until almost boiling, then gradually pour it onto the egg mixture, whisking well until it is combined.

5 Place the bowl over a pan of hot water and cook over low heat until the custard thickens, stirring. Add the chocolate and stir until melted.

6 Pour the chocolate custard over the cherries and let cool. When cold, spread the cream over the custard, swirling with the back of a spoon. Chill in the refrigerator before decorating.

7 Decorate with chocolate caraque and whole maraschino cherries, if using, before serving.

SERVES **6**

6 thin slices chocolate buttercream roll
1 lb 12 oz/800 g canned black cherries in juice
2 tbsp kirsch
1 tbsp cornstarch
2 tbsp superfine sugar
generous 1¾ cups milk
3 egg yolks
1 egg
2¾ oz/75 g semisweet chocolate
1¼ cups heavy cream, whipped lightly

to decorate
chocolate Caraque (see page 15)
maraschino cherries (optional)

 COOK'S TIP

The Black Forest Gâteau, or Schwarzwälder Kirschtorte, originates from southern Germany, and would have been made with about a cupful of kirsch (cherry liqueur).

✪✪✪ moderate

1 hr 30 mins

10 mins

Any dry sparkling wine made by the traditional method used for Champagne can be used for this elegant dessert.

Champagne Mousse

SERVES 4

sponge
4 eggs
½ cup superfine sugar
⅔ cup self-rising flour
2 tbsp unsweetened cocoa
2 tbsp butter, melted

mousse
1 envelope gelatin
3 tbsp water
1¼ cups Champagne
1¼ cups heavy cream
2 egg whites
⅓ cup superfine sugar

to decorate
2 oz/55 g semisweet chocolate-flavored
    cake covering, melted

 challenging
3 hrs 15 mins
8 mins

1 Line a 15 x 10-inch/38 x 25-cm jelly roll pan with greased baking parchment. Place the eggs and sugar in a bowl and beat, using an electric whisk if you have one, until the mixture is very thick and the whisk leaves a trail when lifted. If using a balloon whisk, stand the bowl over a pan of hot water while whisking. Sift the flour and cocoa together and fold into the egg mixture. Fold in the butter. Pour into the pan and bake in a preheated oven, 400°F/200°C, for 8 minutes or until springy to the touch. Cool for 5 minutes, then turn out onto a wire rack, and let stand until cold. Meanwhile, line four 4-inch/10-cm baking rings with baking parchment. Line the sides with 1-inch/2.5-cm strips of cake and the base with circles.

2 For the mousse, sprinkle the gelatin over the water in a heatproof bowl and let it go spongy. Place the bowl over a pan of hot water and stir until dissolved. Stir in the Champagne.

3 Whip the cream until just holding its shape. Fold in the Champagne mixture. Stand in a cool place until on the point of setting, stirring occasionally. Whisk the egg whites until standing in soft peaks, add the sugar, and whisk until glossy. Fold into the setting mixture. Spoon into the sponge cases, allowing the mixture to go above the sponge. Chill for 2 hours. Pipe the melted cake covering in squiggles on a piece of parchment, let them set, then use them to decorate the mousses.

Hidden in a ring of chocolate sponge cake lies the secret of this freezer cake—a chocolate mint ice cream. You could use orange or coffee ice cream if you prefer.

Chocolate Freezer Cake

1 Lightly grease a 9-inch/23-cm ring pan. Place the eggs and sugar in a large mixing bowl. Using an electric whisk if you have one, whisk the mixture until it is very thick and the whisk leaves a trail. If using a balloon whisk, stand the bowl over a pan of hot water while whisking.

2 Sift the flour and cocoa together and fold into the egg mixture. Pour into the prepared pan and bake in a preheated oven, 350°F/180°C, for 30 minutes or until springy to the touch. Let cool in the pan for a few minutes before turning out onto a wire rack to cool completely.

3 Wash and dry the cake pan and line with a strip of plastic wrap, overhanging slightly. Invert the cake so it is base-side up, and carefully cut off the top 1/2 inch/1 cm in one slice. Set aside.

4 Return the cake to the pan. Using a spoon, scoop out the center of the cake, leaving a shell approximately 1 cm/1/2 inch thick.

5 Remove the ice cream from the freezer and let stand for a few minutes, then beat with a wooden spoon until softened a little. Fill the center of the cake with the ice cream, leveling the top. Replace the top of the cake.

6 Cover with the overhanging plastic wrap and freeze for at least 2 hours.

7 To serve, turn the cake out onto a serving dish and drizzle over some of the chocolate sauce in an attractive pattern, if you wish. Cut the cake into slices and serve with the remaining sauce .

SERVES **8**

4 eggs
3/4 cup superfine sugar
3/4 cup self-rising flour
scant 1/3 cup unsweetened cocoa
2 1/4 cups chocolate and mint ice cream
Glossy Chocolate Sauce (see page 103)

easy

3 hrs

30 mins

An all-time favorite with chocoholics—the "mud" refers to the gooey, rich chocolate layer of the cake.

Mississippi Mud Pie

SERVES 8

2 cups all-purpose flour, plus flour
   for dusting
¼ cup unsweetened cocoa
⅔ cup butter
2 tbsp superfine sugar
about 2 tbsp cold water

filling
¾ cup butter
2⅓ cups dark brown sugar
4 eggs, beaten lightly
4 tbsp unsweetened cocoa, sifted
5½ oz/150 g semisweet chocolate, melted
1¼ cups light cream
1 tsp chocolate extract

to decorate
1¾ cups heavy cream, whipped
chocolate flakes and Quick Chocolate Curls
   (see page 15)

moderate
3 hrs 30 mins
1 hr 10 mins

1 To make the pie dough, sift the flour and cocoa into a mixing bowl. Rub in the butter until the mixture resembles fine bread crumbs. Stir in the sugar and enough cold water to mix to a soft dough. Chill for 15 minutes.

2 Roll out the dough on a lightly floured counter and use to line a deep 9-inch/23-cm loose-based flan pan or ceramic flan dish. Line with foil or baking parchment and baking beans. Bake blind in a preheated oven, 375°F/190°C, for 15 minutes. Remove the beans and foil or parchment and cook for 10 minutes more, until crisp.

3 To make the filling, beat the butter and sugar in a bowl and gradually beat in the eggs with the cocoa. Beat in the melted chocolate with the light cream and the chocolate extract.

4 Pour the mixture into the cooked pie shell and bake at 325°F/170°C for 45 minutes or until the filling is set.

5 Let the mud pie cool completely, then transfer the pie to a serving plate, if preferred. Cover with the whipped cream and chill.

6 Decorate the pie with chocolate flakes and quick chocolate curls.

COOK'S TIP

Ceramic or metal baking beans are available from kitchen stores. Alternatively, you can use dried beans kept specifically for the purpose.

Chocolate profiteroles are a popular choice for dessert. In this recipe they are filled with a delicious banana-flavored cream— the perfect combination!

Banana Cream Profiteroles

1 Lightly grease a cookie sheet and sprinkle with a little water. To make the dough, place the water in a pan. Cut the butter into small pieces and add to the pan. Heat gently until the butter melts, then bring to a rolling boil. Remove the pan from the heat and add the flour in one go, beating well until the mixture leaves the sides of the pan and forms a ball. Let cool slightly, then gradually beat in the eggs to form a smooth, glossy paste. Spoon the paste into a large pastry bag fitted with a ½-inch/1-cm plain tip.

2 Pipe about 18 small balls of the paste onto the cookie sheet, allowing enough room for them to expand during cooking. Bake in a preheated oven, 425°F/220°C, for 15–20 minutes, until crisp and golden. Remove from the oven and make a small slit in each one for the steam to escape. Cool on a wire rack.

3 To make the chocolate sauce, place all the ingredients in a heatproof bowl, set over a pan of simmering water and heat until combined and smooth, stirring constantly.

4 To make the filling, whip the cream until standing in soft peaks. Mash the banana with the sugar and liqueur. Fold into the cream. Place in a pastry bag fitted with a ½-inch/1-cm plain tip and pipe into the profiteroles. Serve with the sauce poured over.

SERVES 4

choux pastry
⅔ cup water
5 tbsp butter
¾ cup strong all-purpose flour, sifted
2 eggs

chocolate sauce
3½ oz/100 g semisweet chocolate, broken into pieces
2 tbsp water
4 tbsp confectioners' sugar
2 tbsp sweet butter

filling
1¼ cups heavy cream
1 banana
2 tbsp confectioners' sugar
2 tbsp banana-flavored liqueur

✪✪✪✪ challenging
45 mins
15–20 mins

This is a modern version of the well-known and very traditional chocolate dessert from Italy.

Tiramisu Layers

SERVES 4

²⁄₃ cup heavy cream
1¾ cups mascarpone cheese
10½ oz/300 g semisweet chocolate, melted
1¾ cups black coffee with ¼ cup superfine sugar, cooled
6 tbsp dark rum or brandy
36 lady-fingers, about 400 g/14 oz
unsweetened cocoa, to dust

1 Whip the cream until it just holds its shape. Stir in the mascarpone and melted chocolate.

2 Mix the sweetened coffee and rum or brandy together in a bowl. Dip the lady-fingers into the mixture briefly so that they absorb the coffee mixture but do not become soggy.

3 Place 3 lady-fingers on each of 4 serving plates.

4 Spoon a layer of the chocolate, mascarpone, and cream mixture over the lady-fingers.

5 Place 3 more lady-fingers on top of the chocolate and mascarpone mixture. Spread another layer of chocolate and mascarpone and place 3 more lady-fingers on top.

6 Chill the tiramisu in the refrigerator for at least 1 hour. Dust with a little cocoa just before serving.

🖐 COOK'S TIP

For a nutty flavor, try adding ⅓ cup toasted, chopped hazelnuts to the chocolate and mascarpone mixture in Step 1.

easy

1 hr 25 mins

5 mins

Another rich chocolate dessert, this loaf is very simple to make and can be served as a coffee-time treat as well.

Rich Chocolate Loaf

1 Line a 1½-lb/675-g loaf pan with a sheet of kitchen foil.

2 Place the semisweet chocolate, butter, condensed milk, and cinnamon in a heavy pan. Heat gently for 3–4 minutes, stirring, until melted and smoothly combined.

3 Stir the almonds, cookies, and apricots into the chocolate mixture until thoroughly coated with chocolate.

4 Pour the mixture into the prepared pan and chill in the refrigerator for about 1 hour or until set.

5 The loaf is very rich, so cut it into thin slices to serve.

MAKES 16 SLICES

5½ oz/150 g semisweet chocolate
6 tbsp sweet butter
scant 1 cup condensed milk
2 tsp cinnamon
scant ¾ cup almonds, chopped roughly
2¾ oz/75 g amaretti cookies, broken
scant ¼ cup no-soak dried apricots, chopped coarsely

🍳 **COOK'S TIP**

This simple but luxurious recipe can be adapted endlessly, according to your taste or what is available in your pantry.

⭐ very easy
🕐 1 hr 20 mins
🕐 5 mins

This is a light and fluffy mousse with a subtle hint of orange. It is wickedly delicious served with a fresh fruit sauce.

Chocolate Mousse

SERVES 8

3½ oz/100 g semisweet chocolate, melted
1¼ cups plain yogurt
⅔ cup lowfat soft cheese
4 tbsp superfine sugar
1 tbsp orange juice
1 tbsp brandy
1½ tsp Gelozone (vegetarian gelatin)
9 tbsp cold water
2 extra large egg whites
coarsely grated semisweet and white
   chocolate and orange rind, to decorate

1 Put the melted chocolate, plain yogurt, soft cheese, superfine sugar, orange juice, and brandy in a food processor and process for 30 seconds. Transfer the mixture to a large bowl.

2 Sprinkle the Gelozone over the water and stir until dissolved.

3 In a pan, bring the Gelozone and water to a boil and boil for 2 minutes. Cool slightly, then stir into the chocolate.

4 Whisk the egg whites until stiff peaks form and fold into the chocolate mixture using a metal spoon.

5 Line a 1 lb 2-oz/500-g loaf pan with plastic wrap. Spoon the mousse into the pan. Chill in the refrigerator for 2 hours, until set. Turn the mousse out onto a serving plate, decorate, and serve.

easy
2 hrs 15 mins
5 mins

COOK'S TIP

For a quick mandarin sauce to serve with the mousse, process a can of mandarin segments in natural juice in a food processor and press through a strainer. Sweeten with 1 tablespoon honey.

This dairy-free cheesecake is easy to prepare and lower in fat than most traditional cheesecakes.

Chocolate Bean Curd Cheesecake

1 Put the flour, ground almonds, and 1 tablespoon of the sugar in a bowl and mix well. Rub the margarine into the mixture and form into a dough.

2 Lightly grease and line the base of a 9-inch/23-cm springform pan. Press the dough into the base of the pan, pushing it right up to the edges.

3 Coarsely chop the bean curd and put in a food processor with the vegetable oil, orange juice, brandy, cocoa, almond extract, and remaining sugar. Process until smooth and creamy. Pour over the dough in the pan and cook in a preheated oven, 325°F/160°C, for 1–1¼ hour, or until set.

4 Let cool in the pan for 5 minutes, then remove from the pan, and chill in the refrigerator. Dust with confectioners' sugar and cocoa. Decorate with ground cherries and serve.

SERVES 12

¾ cup all-purpose flour, sifted
¾ cup ground almonds
1⅓ cups raw brown sugar
⅔ cup margarine
1½ lb/675 g firm bean curd
¾ cup vegetable oil
½ cup orange juice
¾ cup brandy
½ cup unsweetened cocoa
2 tsp almond extract

to decorate
confectioners' sugar
unsweetened cocoa
ground cherries

COOK'S TIP

Ground cherries make an attractive decoration for many desserts. Peel open the papery husks to expose the bright orange fruits.

easy

15 mins

1 hr–1 hr 15 mins

A combination of feather-light chocolate and coffee mousses, swirled together in their serving glasses.

Mocha Swirl Mousse

SERVES 4

1 tbsp coffee and chicory extract
2 tsp unsweetened cocoa, plus extra for dusting
1 tsp lowfat instant cocoa
⅔ cup lowfat crème fraîche, plus 4 tsp to serve
2 tsp powdered gelatin
2 tbsp water
2 extra large egg whites
2 tbsp superfine sugar
4 chocolate coffee beans, to serve

1 Place the coffee and chicory extract in one bowl, and 2 teaspoons cocoa powder and the instant cocoa in another bowl. Divide the crème fraîche between the 2 bowls and mix both well.

2 Sprinkle the gelatin over the water in a heatproof bowl and let it go spongy. Place over a pan of hot water and stir until dissolved. In a grease-free bowl, whisk the egg whites and sugar until stiff and divide this evenly among the 2 mixtures.

3 Divide the dissolved gelatin among the 2 mixtures and, using a large metal spoon, gently fold in until well mixed.

4 Spoon small amounts of the 2 mousses alternately into 4 serving glasses and swirl together gently. Chill for 1 hour or until set.

5 To serve, top each mousse with a teaspoon of crème fraîche, a chocolate coffee bean and a light dusting of cocoa. Serve immediately.

easy
1 hr 15 mins
0 mins

👨‍🍳 COOK'S TIP

For vegetarians, instead of gelatin, use the vegetarian equivalent, Gelozone, available from health-food stores. Be sure to read the instructions on the package first, because it is prepared differently from gelatin.

This famous Tuscan honey and nut cake is a Christmas specialty. In Italy it is sold in pretty boxes, and served in very thin slices.

Panforte di Siena

1 Toast the almonds under the broiler until lightly browned, and place them in a bowl.

2 Toast the hazelnuts until the skins split. Place on a dry dish towel and rub off the skins. Coarsely chop the hazelnuts and add to the almonds with the candied peel.

3 Chop the apricots and pineapple fairly finely, add to the nuts with the orange rind, and mix well.

4 Sift together the flour, cocoa, and cinnamon; mix into the nut mixture.

5 Line an 8-inch/20-cm round cake pan or deep loose-based flan pan with baking parchment.

6 Put the superfine sugar and honey in a pan and heat until the sugar dissolves, then boil gently for about 5 minutes or until the mixture thickens and begins to turn a deeper shade of brown. Quickly add to the chocolate nut mixture and mix together evenly. Turn into the prepared pan and level the top using the back of a damp spoon.

7 Cook in a preheated oven, 300°F/ 150°C, for 1 hour. Remove from the oven and let cool completely in the pan. Take out of the pan and carefully peel off the parchment. Before serving, dredge the cake heavily with sifted confectioners' sugar. Serve in thin slices.

SERVES 12

1 cup split whole almonds
¾ cup hazelnuts
½ cup cut candied peel
¼ cup no-soak dried apricots
¼ cup candied pineapple
grated rind of 1 large orange
½ cup all-purpose flour
2 tbsp unsweetened cocoa
2 tsp ground cinnamon
½ cup superfine sugar
½ cup honey
confectioners' sugar, for dredging

moderate

10 mins

1 hr 15 mins

Rich, creamy gelati, or ice creams, are one of the great Italian culinary contributions to the world. This version is made with fresh mint.

Mint-Chocolate Gelato

SERVES 4

6 extra large eggs
¾ cup superfine sugar
1¼ cups milk
⅔ cup heavy cream
large handful of fresh mint leaves, rinsed and dried
2 drops green food coloring, optional
2 oz/55 g semisweet chocolate, chopped finely

1 Put the eggs and sugar in a heatproof bowl that will sit over a pan with plenty of room underneath. Using an electric mixer, beat the eggs and sugar together until thick and creamy.

2 Put the milk and cream in the pan and bring to a simmer, stirring. Pour onto the eggs, whisking constantly.

3 Rinse the pan and put 1 inch/2.5 cm water in the base. Place the bowl on top, making sure the base does not touch the water. Turn the heat to medium–high and stir the custard over the hot water until it is thick enough to coat the back of the spoon and your finger leaves a mark when you pull it across the spoon.

4 Tear the mint leaves and stir them into the custard. Remove the custard from the heat. Let cool, then cover, and set aside to steep for at least 2 hours, chilling for the last 30 minutes.

5 Strain the mixture through a small nylon strainer to remove the pieces of mint. Stir in the food coloring, if using. Transfer to a freezerproof container and freeze the mixture for 1–2 hours until frozen 1 inch/2.5 cm from the sides.

6 Scrape into a bowl and beat again until smooth. Stir in the chocolate pieces, smooth the top, cover with plastic wrap or foil, and freeze until set. Store the ice cream frozen for up to 3 months. Soften in the refrigerator for 20 minutes before serving.

moderate
5–6 hrs
20 mins

Richly flavored and with a wonderful texture, this homemade ice cream really couldn't be simpler.

Chocolate Marshmallow Ice

1 Put the chocolate and marshmallows in a pan and pour in the milk. Warm over very low heat until the chocolate and marshmallows have melted. Remove from the heat and let cool completely.

2 Whisk the cream until thick, then fold it into the cold chocolate mixture with a metal spoon. Pour into a 1-lb/450-g loaf pan and freeze for at least 2 hours, until firm (it will keep for 1 month in the freezer).

SERVES 4

3 oz/85 g semisweet chocolate, broken into pieces
6 oz/175 g white marshmallows
⅔ cup milk
1¼ cups heavy cream

COOK'S TIP

As a variation, you could make half of the mixture with semisweet chocolate and half with white chocolate and swirl the 2 mixtures together in the pan before freezing.

very easy

2 hrs 40 mins

5–10 mins

This is a truly special sherbet and it is worth buying the best possible quality chocolate for it.

Chocolate Sherbet

SERVES **6**

5 oz/140 g fine bittersweet chocolate, chopped coarsely
5 oz/140 g fine semisweet chocolate, chopped coarsely
scant 2 cups water
1 cup superfine sugar
langues de chats cookies, to serve

1 Put both types of chocolate into a food processor and process briefly until very finely chopped.

2 Pour the water into a heavy pan and add the sugar. Stir over medium heat to dissolve, then bring to a boil. Boil for 2 minutes, without stirring, then remove the pan from the heat.

3 With the motor of the food processor running, pour the hot syrup onto the chocolate. Process until all the chocolate has melted and the mixture is smooth. Scrape down the sides of the food processor, if necessary. Strain the chocolate mixture into a freezerproof container and let cool.

4 When the mixture is cool, place it in the freezer for about 1 hour, until slushy, but beginning to become firm around the edges. Tip the mixture into the food processor and process until smooth. Return to the container and freeze for at least 2 hours until firm.

5 Remove the sherbet from the freezer about 10 minutes before serving and let stand at room temperature to let it soften slightly. Serve in scoops with langues de chats cookies.

easy

3 hrs 10 mins

10 mins

What could be more delicious than creamy, tender rice cooked in a rich chocolate sauce? This dessert is almost like a dense chocolate mousse.

Chocolate Rice Dessert

1 Bring a pan of water to a boil. Sprinkle in the rice and add the salt. Reduce the heat and simmer gently for 15–20 minutes, until the rice is just tender. Drain, rinse, and drain again.

2 Heat the milk and the sugar in a large, heavy pan over medium heat until the sugar dissolves, stirring frequently. Add the chocolate and butter and stir until melted and smooth.

3 Stir in the cooked rice and reduce the heat to low. Cover and simmer, stirring occasionally, for 30 minutes, until the milk is absorbed and the mixture thickened. Stir in the vanilla extract and brandy. Remove from the heat and let cool to room temperature.

4 Whisk the cream until soft peaks form. Stir one heaping spoonful of the cream into the chocolate rice mixture to lighten it, then fold in the remaining cream.

5 Spoon into glass serving dishes, cover, and chill for about 2 hours. If wished, decorate with piped whipped cream and top with chocolate curls.

S E R V E S   8

½ cup long-grain white rice
pinch of salt
2½ cups milk
½ cup granulated sugar
7 oz/200 g bitter or semisweet
    chocolate, chopped
4 tbsp butter, diced
1 tsp vanilla extract
2 tbsp brandy
¾ cup heavy cream
whipped cream, for piping (optional)
Quick Chocolate Curls (see page 15), to
    decorate (optional)

COOK'S TIP

To mold the chocolate rice, soften 1 envelope gelatin in about ¼ cup cold water and heat gently until dissolved. Stir into the chocolate just before folding in the cream. Pour into a rinsed mold, let set, then unmold.

easy
2 hrs 5 mins
1 hr 10 mins

The slight tartness of easy-to-peel satsuma oranges beautifully counterbalances the richness of this delicious and unusual trifle.

Chocolate *and* Orange Trifle

SERVES 6

4 trifle sponges
2 large chocolate coconut
    macaroons, crumbled
4 tbsp sweet sherry
8 satsumas
2 egg yolks
2 tbsp superfine sugar
2 tbsp cornstarch
scant 1 cup milk
generous 1 cup mascarpone cheese
7 oz/200 g semisweet chocolate, melted
1 cup heavy cream

to decorate
marbled chocolate shapes (see Cook's Tip)
10–12 satsuma segments

1 Break up the trifle sponges and place them in a large glass serving dish. Sprinkle the crumbled macaroons on top, then sprinkle with the sherry. Squeeze the juice from two of the satsumas and sprinkle it over the crumbled macaroons. Peel and segment the remaining satsumas and arrange them in the dish.

2 In a large bowl, combine the egg yolks, sugar, and cornstarch to make a smooth paste. Bring the milk to just below boiling point in a small pan. Remove from the heat and pour it into the egg yolk mixture, stirring constantly. Return the custard to a clean pan and cook over low heat, stirring constantly, until thickened and smooth.

3 Return the custard to the bowl, then stir in the mascarpone and melted chocolate until thoroughly combined. Spread the chocolate custard evenly over the trifle and chill in the refrigerator for 1 hour, until set.

4 Whip the cream until thick, then spread it over the top of the trifle. Decorate with marbled chocolate shapes and satsuma segments.

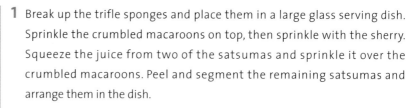

⊛ **COOK'S TIP**

To make marbled chocolate shapes, spread melted semisweet chocolate on a piece of baking parchment and immediately pipe a fine scribble of melted white chocolate over it. Marble with a toothpick. When firm, cut into shapes.

easy

1 hr 25 mins

15–20 mins

Sweet strawberries are teamed with creamy mascarpone cheese and luxurious white chocolate in this mouthwatering cheesecake.

Strawberry Cheesecake

1 Melt the butter in a pan over low heat and stir in the crushed crackers and the nuts. Spoon the mixture into a 9-inch/ 23-cm loose-based cake pan and press evenly over the base with the back of a spoon. Set aside.

2 To make the filling, beat the cheese until smooth, then beat in the eggs and sugar. Cool the chocolate slightly, then stir into the cheese mixture. Finally, stir in the strawberries.

3 Spoon the mixture into the cake pan, spread out evenly, and smooth the surface. Bake in a preheated oven, 300°F/150°C, for 1 hour, until the filling is just firm. Turn off the oven but let the cheesecake cool in the oven until completely cold.

4 Transfer the cheesecake to a serving plate and spread the mascarpone on top. Decorate with chocolate caraque and whole strawberries.

SERVES **8**

base
¼ cup sweet butter
2⅔ cups crushed graham crackers
½ cup chopped walnuts

filling
2 cups mascarpone cheese
2 eggs, beaten
3 tbsp superfine sugar
9 oz/250 g white chocolate, melted
2 cups strawberries, hulled and cut into fourths

topping
¾ cup mascarpone cheese
chocolate Caraque (see page 15)
16 whole strawberries

easy

1 hr, plus 2 hrs

3 hrs

This classic American dessert is packed with deliciously contrasting flavors and textures and is simply irresistible.

Chocolate Pecan Pie

MAKES A 10 INCH/25 CM PIE

pie dough
2½ cups all-purpose flour, plus flour
   for dusting
½ cup unsweetened cocoa
1 cup confectioners' sugar
pinch of salt
scant 1 cup sweet butter at room
   temperature, diced
1 egg yolk

filling
3 cups shelled pecan nuts
6 tbsp sweet butter
generous 1 cup brown sugar
3 eggs
2 tbsp heavy cream
¼ cup all-purpose flour
3 oz/85 g semisweet chocolate, melted
1 tbsp confectioners' sugar, to dust

1 To make the pie dough, sift the flour, cocoa, sugar, and salt into a mixing bowl and make a well in the center. Put the butter and egg yolk in the well and knead together, then gradually mix in the dry ingredients. Knead lightly into a ball. Cover with plastic wrap and chill in the refrigerator for 1 hour.

2 Unwrap the dough and roll it out on a lightly floured counter. Use it to line a 10-inch/25-cm nonstick springform pie pan and prick the shell with a fork. Line the pie shell with baking parchment and fill with baking beans. Bake in a preheated oven, 350°F/180°C, for 15 minutes. Remove from the oven, discard the beans and parchment, and let cool. Leave the oven on.

3 Coarsely chop 2 cups of the pecans. Mix the butter with ⅓ cup of the brown sugar. Beat in the eggs, one at a time, then add the remaining brown sugar and mix well. Stir in the cream, flour, melted chocolate, and chopped pecans.

4 Spoon the filling into the pie shell and smooth the surface. Cut the remaining pecan nuts in half and arrange in concentric circles over the pie.

5 Bake in the preheated oven for 30 minutes, then cover the top of the pie with foil to prevent it from burning, and bake for 25 minutes more. Remove the pie from the oven and let cool slightly before removing from the pan and transferring to a wire rack to cool completely. Dust with confectioners' sugar before serving.

moderate

2 hrs 40 mins

1 hr 15 mins

This is a family favorite—
spiral slices of moist
sponge cake and ice cream
never fail to please.

Chocolate Ice Cream Roll

1 Line a 15 x 10-inch/38 x 25-cm jelly roll pan with waxed paper. Grease the base and dust with flour. Put the eggs and superfine sugar into the top of a double boiler or in a heatproof bowl set over a pan of barely simmering water. Beat over low heat for 5–10 minutes until the mixture is pale and fluffy. Remove from the heat and continue beating for 10 minutes, until the mixture is cool and the whisk leaves a ribbon trail when lifted. Sift the flour and cocoa over the surface and gently fold it in.

2 Pour the mixture into the prepared pan and spread out evenly with a spatula. Bake in a preheated oven, 375°F/190°C, for 15 minutes, until firm to the touch and beginning to shrink from the sides of the pan.

3 Spread out a clean dish towel and cover with a sheet of baking parchment. Lightly dust it with confectioners' sugar. Turn out the cake onto the baking parchment and carefully peel off the lining paper. Trim off any crusty edges. Starting from a short side, pick up the cake and the baking parchment and roll them up together. Wrap the dish towel around the rolled cake and place on a wire rack to cool.

4 Put the frozen ice cream in the refrigerator for 15–20 minutes to soften slightly. Unroll the cake and spread it evenly with the ice cream. Roll it up again without the baking parchment. Wrap in foil and freeze until firm.

5 Transfer the cake to the refrigerator about 20 minutes before serving. Unwrap, place on a serving plate, and dust with confectioners' sugar. Arrange the chocolate curls on top. Serve in slices with the sauce.

SERVES 8

generous ¾ cup all-purpose flour, plus extra for dusting
4 eggs
generous ½ cup superfine sugar
3 tbsp unsweetened cocoa
confectioners' sugar, to dust
2½ cups chocolate ice cream
semisweet chocolate Quick Curls, to decorate (see page 15)
1 cup White Chocolate Fudge Sauce, to serve (see page 73)

⭐⭐⭐   moderate
🕐   1 hr 15 mins
🕐   20–25 mins

This richly flavored tart looks superb and tastes wonderful—a perfect choice for a special occasion dinner party.

Blackberry Chocolate Flan

SERVES 6

2 cups all-purpose flour, plus flour
    for dusting
½ cup unsweetened cocoa
1 cup confectioners' sugar
pinch of salt
scant 1 cup sweet butter, diced
1 egg yolk

filling
1¼ cups heavy cream
⅔ cup blackberry jelly
8 oz/225 g semisweet chocolate,
    broken into pieces
¼ cup diced sweet butter

sauce
4 cups blackberries
1 tbsp lemon juice
2 tbsp superfine sugar
2 tbsp crème de cassis

moderate

2 hrs 30 mins

15 mins

1 First, make the pie dough. Sift the flour, cocoa, confectioners' sugar, and salt into a mixing bowl and make a well in the center. Put the butter and egg yolk in the well and gradually mix in the dry ingredients, using a pie dough blender or two forks. Knead lightly and form into a ball. Cover with plastic wrap and chill in the refrigerator for 1 hour.

2 Roll out the dough on a lightly floured counter. Use it to line a 12 x 4-inch/ 30 x 10-cm rectangular tart pan and prick the pie shell with a fork. Line the shell with baking parchment and fill with baking beans. Bake in a preheated oven, 350°F/180°C, for 15 minutes. Remove from the oven, remove the beans and baking parchment, and set aside to cool.

3 To make the filling, put the cream and jelly into a pan and bring to a boil over low heat. Remove the pan from the heat and stir in the chocolate and butter until melted and smooth. Pour the mixture into the pie shell and set aside to cool.

4 To make the sauce, put 1⅓ cups of the blackberries, the lemon juice, and superfine sugar into a food processor and process until smooth. Transfer to a bowl and stir in the crème de cassis.

5 Remove the tart from the pan and place on a serving plate. Arrange the remaining blackberries on top and brush with a little of the blackberry sauce. Serve the tart and hand the sauce separately.

This famous Italian cream bombe is named *Zuccotto* because its shape resembles a pumpkin, or *zucca*.

Zuccotto

1 In a large bowl, whisk the cream until it is stiff, then fold in the sugar, followed by the hazelnuts, cherries, and chocolate. Cover with plastic wrap and chill in the refrigerator until required.

2 Meanwhile, cut the sponge cakes in half horizontally and then cut the pieces to line the base and sides of a 5-cup bowl. Reserve the remaining sponge cake. Mix together the brandy and amaretto and sprinkle over the sponge cake lining.

3 Remove the cream filling from the refrigerator and spoon it into the lined bowl. Cover the top with the remaining sponge cake, cut to fit. Cover with plastic wrap and chill the bombe in the refrigerator for at least 2 hours.

4 To serve, remove the zuccotto from the refrigerator and run a round-bladed knife around the sides to loosen it. Place a serving plate on top of the bowl and, holding them firmly together, invert. Dust two opposite fourths with confectioners' sugar and the other opposite fourths with cocoa to make alternating sections of color.

SERVES **8**

2½ cups heavy cream
¼ cup confectioners' sugar
½ cup hazelnuts, toasted
8 oz/225 g cherries, halved and pitted
4 oz/115 g semisweet chocolate, chopped finely
2 x 8-inch/20-cm round chocolate sponge cakes
4 tbsp brandy
4 tbsp amaretto liqueur

to decorate
2 tbsp confectioners' sugar, sifted
2 tbsp unsweetened cocoa, sifted

COOK'S TIP

Substitute almonds for the hazelnuts and a mixture of candied cherries and candied peel for the fresh cherries, if you like.

 moderate
2 hrs 30 mins
0 mins

Contrasting flavors, textures, and colors are combined to create this delectable masterpiece.

Chocolate *and* Orange Slices

S E R V E S 8

2 tsp butter, for greasing
1 lb/450 g semisweet chocolate, broken into pieces
3 small, loose-skinned oranges, such as tangerines, mandarins, or satsumas
4 egg yolks
scant 1 cup crème fraîche
2 tbsp raisins
1¼ cups whipped cream, to serve

1 Grease a 1-lb/450-g loaf pan and line it with plastic wrap. Melt 14 oz/400 g of the chocolate and cool slightly.

2 Meanwhile, peel the oranges, removing all traces of pith. Cut the rind into very thin sticks. Beat the egg yolks into the chocolate, one at a time, then add most of the orange rind (reserve the rest for decoration), and the crème fraîche and raisins, and beat until smooth and thoroughly combined. Spoon the mixture into the prepared pan, cover with plastic wrap, and chill in the refrigerator for 3–4 hours, until set.

3 Meanwhile, melt the remaining chocolate. Segment the oranges. Dip each segment into the melted chocolate and spread out on a sheet of baking parchment for about 30 minutes, until set.

4 To serve, remove the pan from the refrigerator and turn out the chocolate mold. Remove the plastic wrap and cut the mold into slices. Place a slice on each of 8 individual serving plates and decorate with the chocolate-coated orange segments and the remaining orange rind. Serve immediately, with whipped cream.

COOK'S TIP

Take care to remove all traces of pith from the orange rind, as it tastes bitter and has a fibrous texture.

moderate
4 hrs 40 mins
10 mins

Don't be alarmed—this Italian dish gets its name from its appearance, and not from its ingredients.

Chocolate Salami

1 Put the chocolate in the top of a double boiler or in a heatproof bowl set over a pan of barely simmering water. Add the liqueur or brandy and 2 tablespoons of the butter. Stir over low heat until melted and smooth. Remove from the heat and cool slightly.

2 Stir in the egg yolks, then stir in the remaining butter, a little at a time, making sure each addition is fully incorporated before adding more. Stir in about three-fourths of the crushed cookies and all the toasted almonds. Cover with plastic wrap and set aside for 45–60 minutes, until beginning to set. Meanwhile, put the remaining crushed cookies in a food processor and process until finely crushed. Transfer them to a bowl and stir in the ground almonds. Set aside.

3 Lightly oil a sheet of baking parchment and turn out the chocolate mixture onto it. Using a spatula, shape the mixture into a salami, measuring about 14 inches/35 cm long. Wrap the salami in the parchment and place in the freezer for 4–6 hours, until set.

4 About 1¼ hours before serving, spread out the ground almond mixture on a sheet of baking parchment. Remove the salami from the freezer and unwrap. Roll it over the ground almond mixture until thoroughly and evenly coated. Cover with plastic wrap, then set aside for 1 hour at room temperature. Cut into slices and serve.

SERVES 10

350 g/12 oz semisweet chocolate, broken into small pieces
4 tbsp amaretto liqueur or brandy
1 cup sweet butter, cut into small pieces
2 egg yolks
24 plain cookies, such as Petit Beurre, crushed coarsely
½ cup toasted slivered almonds, chopped
¼ cup ground almonds

moderate

6 hrs 25 mins

5 mins

A mixture of green and black grapes decorates the creamy chocolate filling in these crisp little phyllo pastry nests.

Phyllo Nests

SERVES 4

1 tbsp sweet butter
6 sheets phyllo pastry, each about
    12 x 6 inches/30 x 15 cm
1½ oz/40 g semisweet chocolate, melted
½ cup ricotta cheese
16 seedless green grapes, halved
24 seedless black grapes, halved

1 Put the butter in a small pan and set over low heat until melted. Remove from the heat. Cut each sheet of phyllo pastry into four, to give 24 rectangles, each measuring about 6 x 3 inches/15 x 7.5 cm, then stack them all on top of each other. Brush 4 shallow muffin pans with melted butter. Line 1 pan with a rectangle of phyllo pastry, brush with melted butter, and place another rectangle on top at an angle to the first, and brush it with melted butter. Continue in this way, lining each pan with 6 rectangles, each brushed with melted butter. Brush the top layers with melted butter.

2 Bake in the preheated oven, 375°F/190°C, for 7–8 minutes, until golden and crisp. Remove from the oven and set aside to cool in the pans.

3 Brush the insides of the pastry shells with about half the melted chocolate. Beat the ricotta in a small bowl until smooth, then beat in the remaining melted chocolate.

4 Divide the chocolate ricotta between the pastry shells and arrange the grapes alternately around the edges. Carefully lift the shells out of the pans and serve immediately.

moderate

45 mins

15–20 mins

This unusual combination of flavors makes a sophisticated and tempting dessert to serve at a dinner party.

Chocolate *and* Pernod Creams

1 Put the chocolate in the top of a double boiler or in a heatproof bowl set over a pan of barely simmering water. Stir over low heat until melted. Remove the pan from the heat and cool slightly.

2 Pour the milk and cream into a pan over low heat and bring to just below boiling point, stirring occasionally. Remove the pan from the heat and then set aside.

3 Beat the sugar and the arrowroot mixture into the melted chocolate. Gradually stir in the hot milk and cream mixture, then stir in the Pernod. Return the double boiler to the heat or set the bowl over a pan of barely simmering water and cook over low heat for 10 minutes, stirring constantly, until thick and smooth. Remove from the heat and let cool.

4 Pour the chocolate and Pernod mixture into 4 individual serving glasses. Cover with plastic wrap and chill in the refrigerator for 2 hours before serving with langues de chats cookies or chocolate-tipped rolled wafers.

SERVES 4

2 oz/55 g semisweet chocolate, broken into pieces
scant 1 cup milk
1¼ cups heavy cream
2 tbsp superfine sugar
1 tbsp arrowroot mixed with 2 tbsp milk
3 tbsp Pernod
langues de chats cookies, or chocolate-tipped rolled wafers, to serve

 COOK'S TIP

Arrowroot is used rather than cornstarch to thicken this delicate dessert as it becomes clear and completely flavorless when cooked.

⭐⭐ easy

🕐 2 hrs 10 mins

🕐 20 mins

These pretty, colorful desserts are deliciously refreshing and would make a good finale to an *al fresco* meal.

White Chocolate Molds

SERVES 8

scant 1 cup heavy cream
3 tbsp crème fraîche
4½ oz/125 g white chocolate, melted
2 eggs, separated
3 tbsp water
1½ tsp gelatin
vegetable oil, for greasing
1 cup sliced strawberries
scant 1 cup raspberries
1¼ cups black currants
5 tbsp superfine sugar
½ cup crème de framboise
12 black currant leave (if available)

1 Pour the cream into a pan and bring to just below boiling point over low heat. Pour into a mixing bowl, then stir in the crème fraîche and the melted chocolate. Let cool slightly, then beat in the egg yolks, one at a time.

2 Pour the water into a small, heatproof bowl and sprinkle the gelatin on the surface. Let stand for 2–3 minutes, until spongy, then set over a pan of barely simmering water until completely dissolved. Stir the gelatin into the chocolate mixture and let stand until nearly set.

3 Brush the inside of 6 timbales, dariole molds, or small cups with oil, and line the bases with baking parchment. Whisk the egg whites until soft peaks form, then fold them into the chocolate mixture. Divide the mixture evenly among the prepared molds and smooth the surface. Cover with plastic wrap and chill in the refrigerator for 2 hours, until set.

4 Put the strawberries, raspberries, and black currants in a bowl and sprinkle with the superfine sugar. Pour in the liqueur and stir gently to mix. Cover with plastic wrap and chill in the refrigerator for 2 hours.

5 To serve, run a round-bladed knife around the sides of the molds and turn out onto individual serving plates. Divide the fruit among the plates and serve immediately, garnished with black currant leaves, if available.

moderate

3 hrs 20 mins

15 mins

Richly flavored molded ice creams make a scrumptious summertime dessert for all the family.

Chocolate *and* Hazelnut Parfait

1 Spread the hazelnuts on a cookie sheet and toast under a broiler preheated to medium, shaking the sheet from time to time, for about 5 minutes, until golden all over. Set aside to cool.

2 Put the toasted hazelnuts in a food processor and process until finely ground.

3 Whisk the cream until it is stiff, then fold in the ground hazelnuts, and set aside. In a large bowl, whisk the egg yolks with 3 tablespoons of the sugar for 10 minutes, until pale and thick.

4 Whisk the egg whites in a separate bowl until soft peaks form. Whisk in the remaining sugar, a little at a time, until the whites are stiff and glossy. Stir the cooled melted chocolate into the egg yolk mixture, then fold in the cream, and then the egg whites. Divide the mixture among 6 freezerproof timbales or molds, cover with plastic wrap, and freeze for at least 8 hours or overnight, until firm.

5 Transfer the parfaits to the refrigerator about 10 minutes before serving to soften slightly. Turn out onto individual serving plates, dust the tops lightly with cocoa, decorate with mint sprigs, and serve with wafers.

SERVES 6

1½ cups blanched hazelnuts
2½ cups heavy cream
3 eggs, separated
2½ cups confectioners' sugar, sifted
6 oz/175 g semisweet chocolate, melted and cooled
1 tbsp sifted unsweetened cocoa, to dust
6 small fresh mint sprigs, to decorate
wafer cookies, to serve

COOK'S TIP
Keep a sharp eye on nuts toasting under the broiler, as they can burn very quickly and easily.

moderate
8 hrs 30 mins
10 mins

Ice cream is always a popular summer dessert—try this rather different recipe for a change.

Chocolate *and* Honey Ice Cream

SERVES 8

2 cups milk
7 oz/200 g semisweet chocolate,
    broken into pieces
4 eggs, separated
scant ½ cup superfine sugar
pinch of salt
2 tbsp honey
12 fresh strawberries, washed and hulled

1 Pour the milk into a pan, add 5½ oz/ 150 g of the chocolate and stir over medium heat for 3–5 minutes, until melted. Remove the pan from the heat and set aside.

2 In a separate bowl, whisk the egg yolks with all but 1 tablespoon of the sugar until pale and thickened. Gradually whisk in the milk mixture, a little at a time. Return the mixture to a clean pan and cook over low heat, whisking constantly, until smooth and thickened. Remove from the heat and set aside to cool completely. Cover with plastic wrap and chill in the refrigerator for 30 minutes.

3 Whisk the egg whites with a pinch of salt until soft peaks form. Gradually whisk in the remaining sugar and continue whisking until stiff and glossy. Remove the chocolate mixture from the refrigerator and stir in the honey, then gently fold in the egg whites.

4 Divide the mixture between 6 individual freezerproof molds and place in the freezer for at least 4 hours, until frozen. Meanwhile, put the remaining chocolate in the top of a double boiler or in a heatproof bowl set over a pan of barely simmering water. Stir over low heat until melted and smooth, then dip the strawberries in the melted chocolate so that they are half-coated. Place on a sheet of baking parchment to set. Transfer the ice cream to the refrigerator for 10 minutes before serving. Turn out onto serving plates and decorate with the chocolate-dipped strawberries.

moderate

5 hrs 30 mins

15 mins

The nutty crust of this delectable pie contrasts with the tempting, creamy chocolate filling.

Chocolate Chiffon Pie

1 Put the Brazil nuts in a food processor and process until finely ground. Add the granulated sugar and melted butter and process briefly to combine. Tip the mixture into a 9-inch/23-cm round pie pan or dish and press it onto the base and sides with a spoon or your fingertips. Bake in a preheated oven, 400°F/200°C, for 8–10 minutes, until light golden brown. Set aside to cool.

2 Pour the milk into the top of a double boiler or into a heatproof bowl and sprinkle the gelatin over the surface. Let it soften for 2 minutes, then place over a pan of barely simmering water. Stir in half the superfine sugar, with the egg yolks and chocolate. Stir constantly over low heat for 4–5 minutes, until the gelatin has dissolved and the chocolate has melted. Remove from the heat and beat until the mixture is smooth and thoroughly blended. Stir in the vanilla extract, cover with plastic wrap, and chill in the refrigerator for 45–60 minutes, until just beginning to set.

3 Whip the cream until it is stiff, then fold all but about 3 tablespoons into the chocolate mixture. Whisk the egg whites in another bowl until soft peaks form. Add 2 teaspoons of the remaining sugar and whisk until stiff peaks form. Fold in the remaining sugar, then fold the egg whites into the chocolate mixture. Pour the filling into the pie dish and chill in the refrigerator for 3 hours, or until set. Decorate the pie with the remaining whipped cream and the chopped nuts before serving.

SERVES 8

5 oz/140 g shelled Brazil nuts
2 tbsp granulated sugar
2 tsp melted butter
1 cup milk
2 tsp gelatin
generous ½ cup superfine sugar
2 eggs, separated
8 oz/225 g semisweet chocolate, chopped coarsely
1 tsp vanilla extract
⅔ cup heavy cream
2 tbsp chopped brazil nuts

moderate
5 hrs 5 mins
15 mins

Small Cakes *and* Cookies

This chapter contains everyday delights for chocolate fans. You are sure to be tempted by our wonderful array of cookies and small cakes. Make any day special with a homemade chocolate cookie to be served with coffee, as a snack, or to accompany a special dessert. Although some take a little longer to make, most are quick and easy to prepare and decoration is often simple, although you can get carried away if you like!

You'll find recipes for old favorites, such as Chocolate Chip Muffins and Chocolate Chip Cookies, Chocolate Cup Cakes and Sticky Chocolate Brownies. There are also some new cookies and small cakes, such as Chocolate Coconut Squares or Chocolate Pretzels. Finally, we have given the chocolate treatment to some traditional recipes—try Chocolate Shortbread or Chocolate Macaroons.

A variation on an old favorite, these scrumptious little cakes will appeal to both children and adults.

Chocolate Cup Cakes

MAKES 18

generous ⅓ cup butter, softened
½ cup superfine sugar
2 eggs, beaten lightly
1¼ cups self-rising flour
2 tbsp milk
⅓ cup semisweet chocolate chips
¼ cup unsweetened cocoa

frosting

5½ oz/150 g lowfat soft cheese
8 oz/225 g white chocolate, melted
and cooled

1 Line an 18-hole shallow muffin pan with individual paper cases.

2 Beat together the butter and sugar until pale and fluffy. Gradually add the eggs, beating well after each addition. Add a little of the flour if the mixture begins to curdle. Add the milk, then fold in the chocolate chips.

3 Sift together the flour and cocoa and fold into the mixture with a metal spoon or spatula. Divide the mixture equally among the paper cases and level the tops.

4 Bake in a preheated oven, 350°F/180°C, for 20 minutes or until well risen and springy to the touch. Let the cakes cool on a wire rack.

5 To make the frosting, beat the soft cheese until softened slightly, then beat in the melted chocolate. Spread a little of the frosting over each cake and chill for 1 hour before serving.

easy
1 hr 15 mins
20 mins

🍫 COOK'S TIP

Add white chocolate chips or chopped pecan nuts to the mixture instead of the semisweet chocolate chips, if you prefer. You can also add the finely grated rind of 1 orange for a chocolate and orange flavor.

A little bit awkward to make but well worth the effort. Indulge in these tasty cakes with coffee, or serve them as a dessert with summer fruits.

Chocolate Rum Babas

1 Lightly oil 4 individual ring pans. Sift the flour and cocoa together into a large warmed mixing bowl. Stir in the yeast, salt, sugar, and grated chocolate. In a separate bowl, beat the eggs together, add the milk and butter, and continue beating until mixed.

2 Make a well in the center of the dry ingredients and pour in the egg mixture, beating to mix to a batter. Beat for 10 minutes, ideally in an electric mixer with a dough hook. Divide the mixture among the pans—it should come halfway up the sides.

3 Place on a cookie sheet and cover with a damp dish towel. Let stand in a warm place until the mixture rises almost to the tops of the pans. Bake in a preheated oven, 400°F/200°C, for 15 minutes.

4 To make the syrup, gently heat all of the ingredients in a small pan. Turn out the babas and place on a rack placed above a tray to catch the syrup. Drizzle the syrup over the babas and let stand for at least 2 hours for the syrup to soak in. Once or twice, spoon up the syrup that has dripped onto the tray and drizzle it over the babas again.

5 Fill the centers of the babas with whipped cream and sprinkle a little cocoa over the top. Serve the babas with fresh fruit, if desired.

SERVES 4

¾ cup strong all-purpose flour
¼ cup unsweetened cocoa
1 envelope rapid-rise dry yeast
pinch of salt
1 tbsp superfine sugar
1½ oz/40 g semisweet chocolate, grated
2 eggs
3 tbsp lukewarm milk
4 tbsp butter, melted

syrup
4 tbsp honey
2 tbsp water
4 tbsp rum

to serve
whipped cream
unsweetened cocoa, to dust
fresh fruit (optional)

★★★★ challenging
3 hrs
15 mins

Children will enjoy making these as an introduction to chocolate cooking, and they keep well if stored in the refrigerator.

No-Bake Chocolate Squares

MAKES 16

9½ oz/275 g semisweet chocolate
¾ cup butter
4 tbsp light corn syrup
2 tbsp dark rum (optional)
6 oz/175 g plain cookies
1 oz/25 g toasted rice cereal
½ cup chopped walnuts or pecan nuts
½ cup candied cherries, chopped coarsely
1 oz/25 g white chocolate, to decorate

1 Place the semisweet chocolate in a large mixing bowl with the butter, syrup, and rum, if using, and set over a pan of gently simmering water until melted, stirring until blended.

2 Break the cookies into small pieces and stir into the chocolate mixture along with the toasted rice cereal, nuts, and cherries.

3 Line a 7-inch/18-cm square cake pan with baking parchment. Pour the mixture into the pan and level the top, pressing down well with the back of a spoon. Chill for 2 hours.

4 To decorate, melt the white chocolate and drizzle it over the top of the cake randomly. Let it set. To serve, carefully turn out of the pan and remove the baking parchment. Cut the cake into 16 squares to serve.

✪ COOK'S TIP

Brandy or an orange-flavored liqueur can be used instead of the rum, if you prefer. Cherry brandy also works well.

very easy

2 hrs 15 mins

5 mins

Everyone loves chocolate brownies and these are so gooey and delicious they are impossible to resist!

Sticky Chocolate Brownies

1 Lightly grease an 8-inch/20-cm shallow square cake pan and line the base with baking parchment.

2 Place the butter, sugars, chocolate, and light corn syrup in a heavy pan and heat gently, stirring until the mixture is well blended and smooth. Remove from the heat and let cool.

3 Beat together the eggs and the chocolate or vanilla extract. Whisk in the cooled chocolate mixture.

4 Sift together the flour, cocoa, and baking powder, and fold carefully into the egg and chocolate mixture using a metal spoon or spatula.

5 Spoon the mixture into the prepared pan and bake in a preheated oven, 350°F/180°C, for 25 minutes, until the top is crisp and the edge of the cake is beginning to shrink away from the pan. The inside of the cake will still be quite stodgy and soft to the touch.

6 Let the cake cool completely in the pan, then cut it into squares to serve.

MAKES 9

generous ⅓ cup sweet butter
¾ cup superfine sugar
½ cup dark brown sugar
4½ oz/125 g semisweet chocolate
1 tbsp light corn syrup
2 eggs
1 tsp chocolate or vanilla extract
¾ cup all-purpose flour
2 tbsp unsweetened cocoa
½ tsp baking powder

COOK'S TIP

This cake can be well wrapped and frozen for up to 2 months. Thaw at room temperature for about 2 hours or overnight in the refrigerator.

easy

1 hr 20 mins

25 mins

Here, a traditional brownie mixture has a tasty cream cheese ribbon running through the center and is topped with a rich chocolate fudge frosting.

Chocolate Fudge Brownies

MAKES 16

7 oz/200 g lowfat soft cheese
½ tsp vanilla extract
generous 1 cup superfine sugar
2 eggs
generous ⅓ cup butter
3 tbsp unsweetened cocoa
¾ cup self-rising flour, sifted
⅓ cup chopped pecan nuts, plus pecan nuts to decorate (optional)

fudge frosting
4 tbsp butter
1 tbsp milk
⅔ cup confectioners' sugar
2 tbsp unsweetened cocoa

easy
1 hr 20 mins
40–45 mins

1 Lightly grease an 8-inch/20-cm shallow square cake pan and line the base with baking parchment.

2 Beat together the cheese, vanilla extract, and 5 teaspoons of superfine sugar until smooth, then set aside.

3 Beat the eggs and remaining superfine sugar together until light and fluffy. Place the butter and cocoa in a small pan and heat gently, stirring until the butter melts and the mixture combines, then stir it into the egg mixture. Fold in the flour and nuts.

4 Pour half of the brownie batter into the pan and level the top. Carefully spread the soft cheese mixture over it, then cover it with the remaining brownie mixture. Bake in a preheated oven, 350°F/180°C, for 40–45 minutes. Cool in the pan.

5 To make the frosting, melt the butter in the milk. Stir in the confectioners' sugar and cocoa. Spread the frosting over the brownies and decorate with pecan nuts, if using. Let the frosting set, then cut into squares to serve.

⊛ COOK'S TIP

Omit the cheese layer if preferred. Use walnuts in place of the pecan nuts.

Muffins are always popular and are so simple to make. You can make mini muffins as fabulous bite-size treats for young children.

Chocolate Chip Muffins

1 Line 12 muffin pans with paper cases.

2 Place the margarine and sugar in a mixing bowl and beat with a wooden spoon until light and fluffy. Beat in the eggs, yogurt, and milk until combined.

3 Sift the flour and baking soda together and add to the mixture with the chocolate chips. Stir until just blended.

4 Spoon the mixture into the paper cases and bake in a preheated oven, 375°F/190°C, for 25 minutes, or until a fine skewer inserted into the center comes out clean. Let the muffins cool in the pan for 5 minutes, then turn them out onto a wire rack to cool completely.

MAKES 12

generous ⅓ cup soft margarine
1 cup superfine sugar
2 extra large eggs
⅔ cup whole milk plain yogurt
5 tbsp milk
2 cups all-purpose flour
1 tsp baking soda
6 oz/175 g semisweet chocolate chips

COOK'S TIP

The mixture can also be used to make 6 large or 24 mini muffins. Bake mini muffins for 10 minutes or until springy to the touch.

easy

45 mins

25 mins

A plain biscuit mixture is transformed into a chocoholic's treat by the simple addition of chocolate chips.

Chocolate Biscuits

MAKES 9

2 cups self-rising flour, sifted, plus flour for dusting
5 tbsp butter
1 tbsp superfine sugar
⅓ cup chocolate chips
about ⅔ cup milk

1 Lightly grease a cookie sheet. Place the flour in a mixing bowl. Cut the butter into small pieces and rub it into the flour with your fingertips until the mixture resembles fine bread crumbs.

2 Stir in the superfine sugar and chocolate chips, then mix in enough of the milk to form a soft dough.

3 On a lightly floured counter, roll out the dough to form a 4 x 6-inch/ 10 x 15-cm rectangle, about 1 inch/2.5 cm thick. Cut the dough into 9 squares. Place the biscuits spaced well apart on the prepared cookie sheet.

4 Brush the biscuits with a little milk and bake in a preheated oven, 425°F/220°C, for 10–12 minutes, until risen and golden.

easy
10 mins
10–12 mins

🍴 COOK'S TIP

To be at their best, rolled biscuits should be served freshly baked and still warm. Split the warm biscuits and spread them with a little chocolate and hazelnut spread or a good spoonful of whipped cream—or both.

These croissants can be a bit time-consuming to make, but the flaky pie dough enclosing a fabulous rich chocolate filling make them worth the effort.

Pain *au* Chocolat

1 Lightly grease a cookie sheet. Sift the flour and salt into a mixing bowl and stir in the yeast. Rub in the fat with your fingertips. Add the egg and enough of the water to make a soft dough. Knead the dough for about 10 minutes, until smooth and elastic.

2 Roll out to form a 15 x 8-inch/38 x 20-cm rectangle. Divide the butter into 3 portions and dot one portion over two thirds of the rectangle, leaving a small border around the edge.

3 Fold the rectangle into 3 by first folding the third part of the dough over and then the other third. Seal the edges of the dough by pressing with a rolling pin. Give the dough a 90-degree turn so the sealed edges are at the top and base. Re-roll and fold (without adding butter), then wrap the dough, and chill for 30 minutes.

4 Repeat Steps 2 and 3 twice, chilling the dough each time. Re-roll and fold twice more without butter. Chill for a final 30 minutes.

5 Roll the dough to an 18 x 12-inch/ 45 x 30-cm rectangle, trim, and halve lengthwise. Cut each half into 6 rectangles and brush with beaten egg. Place a chocolate square at one end of each rectangle and roll up to form a sausage. Press the ends together and place, seam-side down, on the cookie sheet. Cover and let rise for 40 minutes in a warm place. Brush with egg and bake in a preheated oven, 425°F/220°C, for 20–25 minutes, until golden. Cool on a wire rack. Serve warm or cold.

MAKES 12

4 cups strong all-purpose flour
½ tsp salt
1 envelope rapid-rise dry yeast
2 tbsp shortening
1 egg, beaten lightly
1 cup lukewarm water
¾ cup butter, softened
3½ oz/100 g semisweet chocolate, broken into 12 squares
beaten egg, to glaze
confectioners' sugar, to dust

challenging

4 hrs 30 mins

20–25 mins

Pâtisserie cream is the traditional filling for éclairs, but if time is short you can fill them with whipped cream.

Chocolate Eclairs

MAKES 10

dough
²/₃ cup water
5 tbsp butter, cut into small pieces
³/₄ cup strong all-purpose flour, sifted
2 eggs, beaten lightly

patisserie cream
2 eggs, beaten lightly
¹/₄ cup superfine sugar
2 tbsp cornstarch
1¹/₄ cups milk
¹/₄ tsp vanilla extract

frosting
2 tbsp butter
1 tbsp milk
1 tbsp unsweetened cocoa
¹/₂ cup confectioners' sugar
a little white chocolate, melted

1 Lightly grease a cookie sheet. Place the water in a pan, add the butter, and heat gently until the butter melts. Bring to a rolling boil, then remove the pan from the heat, and add the flour in one go. Beat well until the mixture leaves the sides of the pan and forms a ball. Let cool slightly, then gradually beat in the eggs to form a smooth, glossy paste. Spoon into a large pastry bag fitted with a ¹/₂-inch/1-cm plain tip.

2 Sprinkle the cookie sheet with a little water. Pipe éclairs 3 inches/7.5 cm long, spaced well apart. Bake in a preheated oven, 400°F/200°C, for 30–35 minutes or until crisp and golden. Make a small slit in each one to let the steam escape. Cool on a wire rack.

3 Meanwhile, make the pâtisserie cream. Whisk the eggs and sugar until thick and creamy, then whisk in the cornstarch. Heat the milk until almost boiling and pour onto the eggs, whisking. Transfer to the pan and cook over low heat, stirring until thick. Remove the pan from the heat and stir in the vanilla extract. Cover with baking parchment and let cool.

4 To make the frosting, melt the butter with the milk in a pan, remove from the heat, and stir in the cocoa and sugar. Split the éclairs lengthwise and pipe in the pâtisserie cream. Spread the frosting over the top of the éclairs. Drizzle over the white chocolate, swirl in, and let set.

challenging

1 hr

30–35 mins

These melt-in-your-mouth meringues are ideal for a buffet dessert—pile them high in a pyramid for pure, bite-size magic.

Chocolate Meringues

1 Line 2 cookie sheets with baking parchment. Whisk the egg whites until standing in soft peaks, then gradually whisk in half of the sugar. Continue whisking until the mixture is very stiff and glossy.

2 Carefully fold in the remaining sugar, cornstarch, and grated chocolate with a metal spoon or spatula.

3 Spoon the mixture into a pastry bag fitted with a large star or plain tip. Pipe 16 large rosettes or mounds on the lined cookie sheets.

4 Bake in a preheated oven, 275°F/140°C, for about 1 hour, changing the position of the cookie sheets halfway through cooking. Without opening the oven door, turn off the oven and let the meringues cool in the oven. Once they are cold, carefully peel away the baking parchment.

5 Melt the semisweet chocolate and spread it over the base of the meringues. Stand them upside down on a wire rack until the chocolate has set. Whip together the cream, confectioners' sugar, and brandy (if using), until the cream holds its shape. Spoon into a pastry bag and pipe onto half of the meringues. Finish each with a second meringue and serve at once.

MAKES 8

4 egg whites
1 cup superfine sugar
1 tsp cornstarch
1½ oz/40 g semisweet chocolate, grated

to complete
3½ oz/100 g semisweet chocolate
⅔ cup heavy cream
1 tbsp confectioners' sugar
1 tbsp brandy (optional)

🍳 COOK'S TIP

To make mini meringues, use a star-shaped tip and pipe about 24 small rosettes. Bake for about 40 minutes, then let cool in the oven.

⭐⭐   easy
🕐   1 hr 25 mins
🕐   1 hr

These delicious chocolate and hazelnut cookies are very simple to make, yet so effective. For very young children, leave out the chopped nuts.

Chocolate Hazelnut Palmiers

MAKES 26

13 oz/375 g ready-made puff pie dough
8 tbsp chocolate hazelnut spread
½ cup chopped toasted hazelnuts
2 tbsp superfine sugar

1 Lightly grease a cookie sheet. On a lightly floured counter, roll out the puff pie dough to a rectangle about 15 x 9 inches/38 x 23 cm in size.

2 Spread the chocolate hazelnut spread over the pie dough using a spatula, then sprinkle the chopped hazelnuts over the top.

3 Roll up one long side of the pie dough to the center, then roll up the other side so that they meet in the middle. Where the pieces meet, dampen the edges with a little water to join them. Using a sharp knife, cut into thin slices. Place each slice on the prepared cookie sheet and flatten slightly with a spatula. Sprinkle the slices with the superfine sugar.

4 Bake in a preheated oven, 425°F/ 220°C, for about 10–15 minutes, until golden. Transfer to a wire rack to cool.

⊛ **COOK'S TIP**

For an extra chocolate flavor, dip the cooked and cooled palmiers in melted semisweet chocolate to half-cover each cookie.

easy

5 mins

10–15 mins

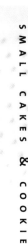
These cookies consist of a chewy coconut layer resting on a crisp chocolate cookie base, cut into squares to serve.

Chocolate Coconut Squares

1 Grease a shallow 8-inch/20-cm square cake pan and line the base.

2 Crush the crackers in a plastic bag with a rolling pin or process them in a food processor. Melt the butter in a pan and stir in the crushed crackers until well combined. Press the mixture into the base of the pan.

3 Beat together the evaporated milk, egg, vanilla, and sugar until smooth. Stir in the flour and dry unsweetened coconut. Pour over the cracker layer and use a spatula to level the top.

4 Bake in a preheated oven, 375°F/190°C, for 30 minutes or until the coconut topping has become firm and just golden.

5 Let cool in the cake pan for about 5 minutes, then cut into squares. Let cool completely in the pan.

6 Carefully remove the squares from the pan and place them on a board. Melt the semisweet chocolate (if using) and drizzle it over the squares to decorate them. Let the chocolate set before serving.

MAKES 9

8 oz/225 g semisweet chocolate graham crackers
⅓ cup butter or margarine
¾ cup canned evaporated milk
1 egg, beaten
1 tsp vanilla extract
2 tbsp superfine sugar
⅓ cup self-rising flour, sifted
1⅓ cups dry unsweetened coconut
1¾ oz/50 g semisweet chocolate (optional)

 COOK'S TIP

Store the squares in an airtight container for up to 4 days. They can be frozen, undecorated, for up to 2 months. Thaw at room temperature.

★★★ moderate
🕐 1 hr 15 mins
🕐 30 mins

A favorite with children, this version of crispy cakes has been given a new twist which is sure to be popular.

Chocolate Crispy Bites

MAKES 16

white layer
4 tbsp butter
1 tbsp light corn syrup
5½ oz/150 g white chocolate, broken into pieces
1¾ oz/50 g toasted rice cereal

semisweet layer
4 tbsp butter
2 tbsp light corn syrup
4½ oz/125 g semisweet chocolate, broken into pieces
2¾ oz/75 g toasted rice cereal

1 Grease an 8-inch/20-cm square cake pan and line with baking parchment.

2 To make the white chocolate layer, melt the butter, light corn syrup, and chocolate in a bowl set over a pan of gently simmering water. Remove from the heat and stir in the rice cereal until it is well combined. Press into the prepared pan and level the surface.

3 To make the semisweet chocolate layer, melt the butter, light corn syrup, and semisweet chocolate in a bowl set over a pan of gently simmering water. Remove from the heat and stir in the rice cereal. Pour the semisweet chocolate over the hardened white chocolate layer, cool, and chill until hardened.

4 Turn out of the cake pan and cut into small squares, using a sharp knife.

easy

45 mins

5–10 mins

These unusual cookie treats are delicious served with coffee. They also make an ideal dessert cookie to serve with ice cream.

Dutch Macaroons

1 Cover 2 cookie sheets with rice paper. Whisk the egg whites in a large mixing bowl until stiff, then fold in the sugar and ground almonds.

2 Place the mixture in a large pastry bag fitted with a ½-inch/1-cm plain tip and pipe bars, about 3 inches/7.5 cm long, allowing space for the mixture to spread during cooking.

3 Bake in a preheated oven, 350°F/180°C, for 15–20 minutes, until golden. Transfer to a wire rack and let cool. Remove the excess rice paper from around the edges.

4 Melt the chocolate and dip the underside of each cookie into the chocolate. Place the macaroons on a sheet of baking parchment and let set.

5 Pipe any remaining chocolate over the top of the cookies (you may need to reheat the chocolate in order to do this.) Let it set before serving.

MAKES 20

rice paper
2 egg whites
1 cup superfine sugar
1²⁄₃ cups ground almonds
8 oz/225 g semisweet chocolate

 COOK'S TIP

Rice paper is edible so you can just break off the excess from around the edge of the cookies. Remove it completely before dipping the macaroons in the chocolate, if you prefer.

easy
40 mins
15–20 mins

It is difficult to say "No" to these wonderfully rich cookies, which consist of a crunchy oat layer, a creamy caramel filling, and a chocolate top.

Chocolate Caramel Squares

MAKES 16

generous ⅓ cup soft margarine
⅓ cup light brown sugar
1 cup all-purpose flour, sifted
½ cup rolled oats

caramel filling
2 tbsp butter
2 tbsp light brown sugar
generous ¾ cup condensed milk

topping
100 g/3½ oz semisweet chocolate
25 g/1 oz white chocolate (optional)

1 Beat together the margarine and brown sugar in a bowl until light and fluffy. Beat in the flour and the rolled oats. Use your fingertips to bring the mixture together, if necessary.

2 Press the oat mixture into the base of a shallow 8-inch/20-cm square cake pan.

3 Bake in a preheated oven, 350°F/180°C, for 25 minutes or until just golden and firm. Cool in the pan.

4 Place the ingredients for the caramel filling in a pan and heat gently, stirring, until the sugar has dissolved and the ingredients combine. gradually bring to a boil over very low heat, then boil very gently for 3–4 minutes, stirring constantly, until thickened.

5 Pour the caramel filling over the oat layer in the pan and let set.

6 Melt the semisweet chocolate and spread it over the caramel. If using the white chocolate, melt it and pipe lines of white chocolate over the semisweet chocolate. Using a toothpick or skewer, feather the white chocolate into the semisweet chocolate. Let set. Cut into squares to serve.

COOK'S TIP

If you wish, you can line the pan with baking parchment so that the cake can be lifted out before cutting into pieces.

★★★ moderate
🕐 40 mins
🕐 25 mins

Turn ordinary oat cookies into something special with the addition of some chocolate chips. Use white rather than semisweet chocolate chips, if you prefer.

Chocolate Chip Oaties

1 Lightly grease a shallow 8-inch/20-cm square cake pan.

2 Place the butter, superfine sugar, and light corn syrup in a pan and cook over low heat, stirring constantly, until the butter and sugar melt and the mixture is well combined.

3 Remove the pan from the heat and stir in the rolled oats until they are well coated. Add the chocolate chips and the golden raisins and mix well to combine. Turn into the prepared pan and press down well.

4 Bake in a preheated oven, 350°F/180°C, for 30 minutes. Cool slightly, then mark into bars. When almost cold, cut into bars or squares and transfer to a wire rack to cool completely.

MAKES 12

½ cup butter
⅓ cup superfine sugar
1 tbsp light corn syrup
4 cups rolled oats
½ cup semisweet chocolate chips
⅓ cup golden raisins

 COOK'S TIP

These cookies will keep in an airtight container for up to 1 week, but they are so delicious they are unlikely to last that long!

easy

40 mins

30 mins

No chocolate cook's repertoire would be complete without a chocolate chip cookie recipe. This recipe can be used to make several variations (see Cook's Tip).

Chocolate Chip Cookies

MAKES 18

1½ cups all-purpose flour, sifted
1 tsp baking powder
½ cup soft margarine
scant ⅔ cup light brown sugar
¼ cup superfine sugar
½ tsp vanilla extract
1 egg
⅔ cup semisweet chocolate chips

1 Place all of the ingredients in a large mixing bowl and beat until they are thoroughly combined.

2 Lightly grease 2 cookie sheets. Place tablespoonfuls of the mixture on the cookie sheets, spacing them well apart to allow adequate room for spreading during cooking.

3 Bake in a preheated oven, 375°F/190°C, for 10–12 minutes or until the cookies are golden brown.

4 Using a spatula, transfer the cookies to a wire rack to cool completely.

very easy
35 mins
10 mins

COOK'S TIP

For Chocolate and Nut Cookies, add ½ cup chopped hazelnuts to the basic mixture. For Double Chocolate Cookies, beat in 1½ oz/40 g melted semisweet chocolate. For White Chocolate Chip Cookies, use white chocolate chips.

This buttery chocolate shortbread is the perfect addition to the cookie jar of any chocolate lover.

Chocolate Shortbread

1 Place all of the ingredients in a large mixing bowl and then beat together until they form a dough. Knead the dough lightly.

2 Lightly grease a cookie sheet. Place the dough on the cookie sheet and roll out to form a 8-inch/2-cm circle.

3 Pinch the edges of the dough with your fingertips to form a decorative edge. Prick the dough all over with a fork and lightly mark into 12 wedges, using a sharp knife.

4 Bake in a preheated oven, 325°F/160°C, for 40 minutes, until firm and golden. Let cool slightly before cutting the shortbread into wedges. Transfer to a wire rack to cool completely.

MAKES 12

1½ cups all-purpose flour, sifted
1 tbsp unsweetened cocoa
4 tbsp superfine sugar
⅔ cup butter, softened
1¾ oz/50 g semisweet chocolate, chopped finely

COOK'S TIP

For round shortbread cookies, roll out the dough to ¾ inch/8 mm thick. Cut out 3-inch/7.5-cm circles. Transfer to a greased cookie sheet and bake until golden. If liked, coat half of each cookie in melted chocolate.

very easy
40 mins
40 mins

These cookies have a fabulously light, melting texture. You can leave them plain, but for real indulgence dip them in melted chocolate.

Viennese Chocolate Fingers

MAKES 18

½ cup sweet butter
6 tbsp confectioners' sugar
1½ cups self-rising flour, sifted
3 tbsp cornstarch
7 oz/200 g semisweet chocolate

1 Lightly grease 2 cookie sheets. Beat the butter and sugar in a mixing bowl until light and fluffy. Gradually beat in the flour and cornstarch.

2 Melt $2^3/_4$ oz/75 g of the semisweet chocolate and beat into the cookie dough.

3 Place in a pastry bag fitted with a large star tip and pipe fingers about 2 inches/5 cm long on the cookie sheets, spaced apart to allow for spreading.

4 Bake in a preheated oven, 375°F/190°C, for 12–15 minutes. Let the fingers cool slightly on the cookie sheets, then transfer with a spatula to a wire rack and let cool completely.

5 Melt the remaining chocolate and dip one end of each cookie in the chocolate, allowing the excess to drip back into the bowl. Place the cookies on a sheet of baking parchment and let the chocolate set before serving.

COOK'S TIP

If the cookie dough is too thick to pipe, beat in a little milk to thin it out.

⭐⭐⭐   moderate
🕐   1 hr
🕐   15 mins

If you thought of pretzels as savories, then think again. These are fun to make and prove that pretzels come in a sweet variety, too.

Chocolate Pretzels

1 Lightly grease a cookie sheet. Beat together the butter and sugar in a mixing bowl until light and fluffy. Beat in the egg.

2 Sift together the flour and cocoa and gradually beat in to form a soft dough. Use your fingers to incorporate the last of the flour and bring the dough together. Chill for 15 minutes.

3 Break small pieces from the dough and roll into thin sausage shapes about 4 inches/10 cm long and ¼ inch/5 mm thick. Twist into pretzel shapes by making a circle, then twisting the ends through each other to form a letter "B." Place on the prepared cookie sheet, slightly spaced apart to allow for spreading during cooking.

4 Bake in a preheated oven, 375°F/190°C, for 8–12 minutes. Let the pretzels cool slightly on the cookie sheet, then carefully transfer them to a wire rack to cool completely.

5 Melt the butter and chocolate in a bowl set over a pan of gently simmering water, stirring to combine. Dip half of each pretzel into the chocolate and allow the excess chocolate to drip back into the bowl. Place the pretzels on a sheet of baking parchment and let set.

6 When set, dust the plain side of each pretzel with confectioners' sugar.

MAKES 30

generous ⅓ cup sweet butter
½ cup superfine sugar
1 egg
2 cups all-purpose flour
¼ cup unsweetened cocoa

to finish
1 tbsp butter
3½ oz/100 g semisweet chocolate
confectioners' sugar, to dust

✪✪✪✪ challenging
🕐 1 hr 30 mins
🕐 8–12 mins

A good everyday cookie, these wheatmeals will keep well in an airtight container for at least a week. Dip them in white, milk, or semisweet chocolate.

Chocolate Wheatmeals

MAKES 20

¹⁄₃ cup butter
²⁄₃ cup raw brown sugar
1 egg
1 oz/25 g wheatgerm
1 cup whole-wheat self-rising flour, sifted
½ cup self-rising flour, sifted
4½ oz/125 g semisweet, milk, or
    white chocolate

1 Lightly grease a cookie sheet. Beat the butter and sugar until fluffy. Add the egg and beat well. Stir in the wheatgerm and flours. Bring the mixture together with your hands.

2 Roll rounded teaspoonfuls of the mixture into balls and place on the prepared cookie sheet, allowing plenty of room for the cookies to spread during cooking.

3 Flatten the cookies slightly with the prongs of a fork. Bake in a preheated oven, 350°F/180°C, for 15–20 minutes, until golden. Let cool on the cookie sheet for a few minutes before transferring to a wire rack to cool completely.

4 Melt the chocolate, then dip each cookie in the chocolate to cover the flat side and come a little way around the edges. Let the excess chocolate drip back into the bowl.

5 Place the cookies on a sheet of baking parchment and let the chocolate set in a cool place before serving.

easy

1 hr

15–20 mins

⊕ **COOK'S TIP**

These cookies can be frozen very successfully. Freeze them at the end of Step 3 for up to 3 months. Thaw and then dip them in melted chocolate.

No Sicilian celebration is complete without cannoli. If you can't find the special molds, use large dried pasta tubes covered with foil, shiny side out.

Cannoli

1 Combine the lemon juice, water, and egg. Put the flour, sugar, spice, and salt in a food processor and quickly process. Add the butter, then, with the motor running, pour the egg mixture through the feeder tube. Process until the mixture just forms a dough.

2 Turn the dough out onto a lightly floured counter and knead lightly. Wrap and chill for at least 1 hour.

3 Meanwhile, make the filling. Beat the ricotta cheese until smooth. Sift in the confectioners' sugar, then beat in the remaining ingredients. Cover and chill until required.

4 Roll out the dough on a floured counter until ¹⁄₁₆ inch/2 mm thick. Using a rule, cut out 3 ½ x 3-inch/ 8.5 x 7.5-cm pieces, re-rolling and cutting the trimmings; the dough should make about 20 pieces.

5 Heat 2 inches/5 cm oil in a pan to 375°F/190°C. Roll a piece of dough around a greased cannoli mold, to just overlap the edge. Seal with egg white, pressing firmly. Repeat with all the molds you have. Fry 2 or 3 molds until the cannoli are golden, crisp, and bubbly.

6 Remove with a slotted spoon and drain on paper towels. Let cool, then carefully slide off the molds. Repeat with the remaining cannoli.

7 Store unfilled in an airtight container for up to 2 days. Pipe in the filling no more than 30 minutes before serving to prevent the cannoli from becoming soggy. Sift confectioners' sugar over the top and serve.

MAKES 20

3 tbsp lemon juice
3 tbsp water
1 extra large egg
1¾ cups all-purpose flour, sifted, plus extra for dusting
1 tbsp superfine sugar
1 tsp ground allspice
pinch of salt
2 tbsp butter, softened
sunflower oil, for deep-frying
1 medium egg white, beaten lightly
confectioners' sugar

filling
3¼ cups ricotta cheese, drained
4 tbsp confectioners' sugar
1 tsp vanilla extract
finely grated rind of 1 large orange
4 tbsp very finely chopped candied fruit
1¾ oz/50 g semisweet chocolate, grated
pinch of ground cinnamon
2 tbsp Marsala wine or orange juice

⭐⭐⭐⭐ challenging
🕐 1 hr 45 mins
🕐 15–20 mins

Pine nuts and orange rind are popular ingredients in Mediterranean dishes—here they add an extra twist of flavor to luscious chocolate tartlets.

Pine Nut Tartlets

SERVES 8

2 oz/55 g semisweet chocolate with at least 70% cocoa solids, broken into pieces
4 tbsp sweet butter
¾ cup plus 2 tbsp superfine sugar
5 tbsp light brown sugar
6 tbsp milk
3½ tbsp light corn syrup
finely grated rind of 2 large oranges
2 tbsp freshly squeezed orange juice
1 tsp vanilla extract
3 extra large eggs, beaten lightly
scant 1 cup pine nuts

tartlet shells
1¾ cups all-purpose flour
pinch of salt
generous ⅓ cup butter
1 cup confectioners' sugar
1 extra large egg
2 extra large egg yolks

1 To make the dough, sift the flour and salt into a bowl. Make a well in the center and add the butter, confectioners' sugar, whole egg, and egg yolks. Using your fingertips, mix the ingredients in the well into a paste.

2 Gradually incorporate the surrounding flour to make a soft dough. Quickly and lightly knead the dough. Shape into a ball, wrap in plastic wrap, and chill for at least 1 hour.

3 Roll the dough into 8 circles, 6 inches/15 cm across. Use to line 8 loose-based 4-inch/10-cm tartlet pans. Line each with baking parchment and fill with baking beans. Chill for 10 minutes.

4 Bake in a preheated oven, 400°F/200°C, for 5 minutes. Remove the parchment and beans and bake for 8 minutes more. Let cool on a wire rack. Reduce the oven temperature to 350°F/180°C.

5 Meanwhile, put the chocolate and butter in a pan and stir over medium heat until blended.

6 Stir in the remaining ingredients. Spoon the filling into the tartlet shells on a cookie sheet. Bake for 25–30 minutes or until the tops puff up and crack and feel set. Cover with baking parchment for the final 5 minutes if the shells are browning too much. Transfer to a wire rack and let cool for at least 15 minutes before unmolding. Serve warm or at room temperature.

moderate

1 hr 40 mins

45 mins

These chunky cookies simply melt in your mouth and the white chocolate gives them a deliciously rich flavor.

White Chocolate Cookies

1 Lightly grease 4 cookie sheets. In a large mixing bowl, cream together the butter and sugar until light and fluffy. Gradually add the beaten egg, beating well after each addition.

2 Sift the flour and salt into the creamed mixture and blend well. Stir in the white chocolate chunks and Brazil nuts.

3 Place heaping teaspoons of the white chocolate mixture on the prepared cookie sheets. Do not put more than 6 teaspoons of the mixture onto each cookie sheet, as the cookies will spread considerably during cooking.

4 Bake in a preheated oven, 375°F/190°C, for 10–12 minutes or until just golden brown. Transfer the cookies to wire racks and let stand until completely cold before serving.

MAKES 24

½ cup butter, softened
¾ cup soft brown sugar
1 egg, beaten
1¾ cups self-rising flour
pinch of salt
4½ oz/125 g white chocolate, chopped coarsely
⅓ cup chopped Brazil nuts

COOK'S TIP

Use semisweet or milk chocolate instead of white chocolate, if you prefer.

easy

40 mins

10–12 mins

Classic gooey macaroons are always a favorite for coffee time. They are made even better by the addition of rich semisweet chocolate.

Chocolate Macaroons

MAKES 18

2 egg whites
pinch of salt
1 cup superfine sugar
1¼ cups ground almonds
2¾ oz/75 g semisweet chocolate, melted and cooled
dry unsweetened coconut, to sprinkle (optional)

1 Grease 2 cookie sheets and line with baking parchment or rice paper.

2 In a mixing bowl, whisk the egg whites with the salt until they form soft peaks. Gradually whisk in the sugar, then fold in the almonds and cooled melted chocolate.

3 Place heaping teaspoons of the mixture spaced well apart on the prepared cookie sheets and spread into circles about 2½ inches/6 cm across. Sprinkle with dry unsweetened coconut, if using.

4 Bake in a preheated oven, 300°F/150°C, for about 25 minutes or until the macaroons are firm.

5 Let cool before carefully lifting from the cookie sheets. Transfer the macaroons to a wire rack and let cool completely before serving.

⭐⭐⭐ moderate

🕐 1 hr

🕐 25 mins

🍳 **COOK'S TIP**

For a traditional finish, top each chocolate macaroon with half a candied cherry before baking.

These luxury cookies will be popular at any time of the year, but they make a particularly wonderful treat at Christmas.

Florentines

1 Line 2 large cookie sheets with baking parchment.

2 Heat the butter and sugar in a small pan until the butter has just melted and the sugar dissolved. Remove the pan from the heat.

3 Stir in the flour and mix well. Stir in the chopped almonds, candied peel, raisins, cherries, and lemon rind. Place teaspoonfuls of the mixture well apart on the cookie sheets.

4 Bake in a preheated oven, 350°F/180°C, for 10 minutes or until they are a light golden color.

5 As soon as the florentines are removed from the oven, press the edges into neat shapes while still on the cookie sheets, using a cookie cutter. Let cool on the cookie sheets until firm, then transfer to a wire rack to cool completely.

6 Spread the melted chocolate over the smooth side of each florentine. As the chocolate begins to set, mark wavy lines in it with a fork. Let the florentines set, chocolate side up.

MAKES 10

4 tbsp butter
$^1/_4$ cup superfine sugar
scant $^1/_4$ cup all-purpose flour, sifted
$^1/_3$ cup almonds, chopped
$^1/_3$ cup chopped candied peel
$^1/_4$ cup raisins, chopped
2 tbsp chopped candied cherries
finely grated rind of $^1/_2$ lemon
$4^1/_2$ oz/125 g semisweet chocolate, melted

 COOK'S TIP

Replace the semisweet chocolate with white chocolate or, for a dramatic effect, cover half of the florentines in semisweet chocolate and half in white.

⊛⊛⊛ moderate

⊘ 50 mins

⊙ 10 mins

These little cakes look wonderful and are well worth the preparation time. The magical combination of flavors is out of this world.

Chestnut Cream Squares

MAKES 30

base layer
6 tbsp sweet butter
4 tbsp confectioners' sugar
3 oz/85 g semisweet chocolate, melted
4 eggs, separated
1/2 cup superfine sugar
2/3 cup all-purpose flour, sifted
5 tbsp Morello cherry jelly
3 tbsp kirsch

dark layer
generous 1/3 cup milk
4 tsp superfine sugar
1/4 tsp vanilla extract
1 egg yolk
1 tbsp cornstarch
generous 2 tbsp confectioners' sugar
3 1/2 oz/100 g semisweet chocolate, melted
1 1/4 cups heavy cream, whipped

white layer
2 1/4 cups heavy cream
1 tbsp confectioners' sugar

chestnut layer
1 1/2 cups canned chestnut paste
4 tsp dark rum
2 tsp superfine sugar
30 cherries, to decorate

★★★★ challenging
🕐 12 hrs 45 mins
🕐 55–60 mins

1 Line a 12 x 10 x 2-inch/30 x 25 x 5-cm rectangular cake pan with baking parchment. For the base layer, mix the butter, confectioners' sugar, and chocolate. Beat in the egg yolks, 1 at a time.

2 Whisk the egg whites until soft peaks form, then whisk in the superfine sugar until stiff and glossy. Fold in the chocolate mixture and the flour. Spoon into the prepared pan and smooth the surface. Bake in a preheated oven, 350°F/180°C, for 30 minutes. Let cool.

3 Bring the jelly to a boil in a small pan, strain, and cool. Turn out the cake. Wash and dry the cake pan and line with baking parchment. Return the cake to the pan. Sprinkle with the kirsch and spread with the jelly.

4 For the dark layer, put the milk, superfine sugar, and vanilla in a pan and bring to a boil. Mix the egg yolk, cornstarch, and 2 tablespoons of the hot milk in a bowl, then add back to the pan of milk. Cook, stirring, for 3–5 minutes, until thickened. Stir in the confectioners' sugar and melted chocolate. Remove from the heat and stir in the cream. Spread in the pan, cover, and freeze for 1 1/2–2 hours.

5 Make the white layer: whisk the cream with the sugar until thick, then spread over the dark layer. Cover and freeze for 8 hours.

6 Remove the cake from the pan. Beat together the chestnut paste, rum, and sugar. Cut the cake into 30 squares, pipe each with a swirl of chestnut mixture and top with a cherry. Chill for 30 minutes before serving.

These crisp Italian biscotti are made with fine cornmeal as well as wheat flour, to give them an interesting texture.

Chocolate Pistachio Cookies

1 Lightly grease a cookie sheet. Put the chocolate and butter in the top of a double boiler or in a heatproof bowl set over a pan of barely simmering water. Stir over low heat until melted and smooth. Remove from the heat and cool slightly.

2 Sift the flour and baking powder into a bowl and mix in the superfine sugar, cornmeal, lemon rind, liqueur, egg, and pistachios. Stir in the chocolate mixture and mix to a soft dough.

3 Lightly dust your hands with flour, divide the dough in half, and shape each piece into an 11-inch/28-cm long cylinder. Transfer the cylinders to the prepared cookie sheet and flatten, with the palm of your hand, to about 2 cm/³/₄ inch thick. Bake in a preheated oven, 325°F/160°C, for about 20 minutes, until firm to the touch.

4 Remove the cookie sheet from the oven and let the cooked pieces cool. When cool, put the cooked pieces on a cutting board and slice them diagonally into thin cookies. Return them to the cookie sheet and bake for 10 minutes more, until crisp. Remove from the oven and transfer to a wire rack to cool. Dust lightly with confectioners' sugar.

MAKES 24

6 oz/175 g semisweet chocolate, broken into pieces
2 tbsp sweet butter
2¹/₂ cups self-rising flour
1¹/₂ tsp baking powder
scant ¹/₂ cup superfine sugar
¹/₂ cup cornmeal
finely grated rind of 1 lemon
2 tsp amaretto liqueur
1 egg, beaten lightly
³/₄ cup coarsely chopped pistachio nuts
2 tbsp confectioners' sugar, to dust

COOK'S TIP

Amaretto liqueur is flavored with apricot kernels and has a flavor strongly reminiscent of almonds. If you prefer, use an orange liqueur.

moderate
55 mins
35 mins

Candies *and* Drinks

There is nothing quite so nice as homemade chocolates and candies—they leave the average box of chocolates in the shade! You'll find recipes in this chapter to suit everybody's taste. Wonderful, rich, melt-in-your-mouth Rum Truffles, Marzipan Cherries, Rocky Road Bites, and rich Chocolate Liqueurs—they're all here. There is even some Easy Chocolate Fudge, so there is no need to fiddle about with candy thermometers.

Looking for something to wash it all down? We have included delightfully cool summer chocolate drinks and, for warmth and comfort on winter nights, hot drinks that will simply put instant hot chocolate to shame. Enjoy!

Young children will love these chewy bites. You can vary the ingredients and use different nuts and dried fruit according to personal taste.

Rocky Road Bites

MAKES 18

4½ oz/125 g milk chocolate
2 oz/55 g mini multi-colored marshmallows
¼ cup chopped walnuts
1 oz/25 g no-soak dried apricots, chopped

1 Line a cookie sheet with baking parchment and set aside.

2 Break the milk chocolate into small pieces and place in a large heatproof bowl. Set the bowl over a pan of barely simmering water and stir until the chocolate has melted.

3 Stir in the marshmallows, walnuts, and apricots, and toss in the melted chocolate until well covered.

4 Place heaping teaspoons of the mixture onto the prepared cookie sheet. Chill in the refrigerator until set.

5 Once set, carefully remove the candies from the baking parchment. They can be placed in paper candy cases to serve, if desired.

very easy

40 mins

5 mins

COOK'S TIP

Light, fluffy marshmallows are available in white or pastel colors. If you cannot find mini marshmallows, use large ones and snip them into smaller pieces with kitchen scissors before mixing them into the melted chocolate in Step 3.

This is the easiest fudge to make—for a really rich flavor, use a good bittersweet chocolate with a high cocoa content, ideally at least 70 percent.

Easy Chocolate Fudge

1 Lightly grease an 8-inch/20-cm square cake pan.

2 Break the chocolate into pieces and place in a large pan with the butter and condensed milk.

3 Heat gently, stirring, until the chocolate and butter melt and the mixture is smooth. Do not let it boil.

4 Remove the pan from the heat. Beat in the vanilla extract, then beat the mixture for a few minutes until thickened. Pour it into the prepared pan and level the top.

5 Chill the mixture in the refrigerator until firm.

6 Tip the fudge out onto a cutting board and cut into squares to serve.

MAKES 25

1 lb 2 oz/500 g bittersweet chocolate
⅓ cup sweet butter
1¾ cups condensed milk
½ tsp vanilla extract

 COOK'S TIP

Store the fudge in an airtight container in a cool, dry place for up to 1 month. Do not freeze.

easy

1 hr 10 mins

5 mins

Chocolate, nuts, and dried fruit—the perfect combination—are all found in this simple-to-make fudge.

Fruit *and* Nut Fudge

MAKES 25

9 oz/250 g semisweet chocolate
2 tbsp butter
4 tbsp evaporated milk
3 cups confectioners' sugar, sifted
½ cup coarsely chopped hazelnuts
⅓ cup golden raisins

1 Lightly grease an 8-inch/20-cm square cake pan.

2 Break the chocolate into small pieces and place it in a heatproof bowl with the butter and evaporated milk. Set the bowl over a pan of gently simmering water and stir until the chocolate and butter have melted and the ingredients are well combined.

3 Remove the bowl from the heat and gradually beat in the confectioners' sugar. Stir the hazelnuts and golden raisins into the mixture. Press the fudge into the prepared pan and level the top. Chill until firm.

4 Tip the fudge out onto a cutting board and cut into squares. Chill in the refrigerator until required.

 COOK'S TIP

Vary the nuts used in this recipe; try making the fudge with almonds, Brazil nuts, walnuts, or pecan nuts.

easy

1 hr 10 mins

5 mins

These cherry and marzipan candies are easy to make. Serve as petits fours at the end of a meal or as an indulgent nibble at any time of day.

Marzipan Cherries

1 Line a cookie sheet with a sheet of baking parchment.

2 Cut the cherries in half and place in a small bowl. Add the rum or brandy and stir to coat. Let the cherries soak for at least 1 hour, stirring occasionally.

3 Divide the marzipan into 24 pieces and roll each piece into a ball. Press half a cherry into the top of each marzipan ball.

4 Break the chocolate into pieces, place in a bowl, and set over a pan of hot water. Stir until all the chocolate has melted.

5 Dip each candy into the melted chocolate using a toothpick, letting the excess drip back into the bowl. Place the coated cherries on the baking parchment and chill until set.

6 If liked, melt a little extra chocolate and drizzle it over the top of the coated cherries. Let set.

MAKES 25

12 candied cherries
2 tbsp rum or brandy
9 oz/250 g marzipan
5½ oz/125 g semisweet chocolate
extra milk, semisweet, or white chocolate, to decorate (optional)

🍴 **COOK'S TIP**

As an alternative, flatten the marzipan and use it to mold around the cherries to cover them, then dip in the chocolate as above.

 moderate

1 hr 30 mins

5 mins

These tasty chocolate cups are filled with a delicious liqueur-flavored filling. Use your favorite liqueur to flavor the cream.

Chocolate Liqueurs

MAKES 40

3½ oz/100 g semisweet chocolate, melted
about 5 candied cherries, halved
about 10 hazelnuts or macadamia nuts
⅔ cup heavy cream
2 tbsp confectioners' sugar
4 tbsp liqueur

to finish
1¾ oz/50 g semisweet chocolate, melted
a little white chocolate, melted
white chocolate Quick Curls (see page 15)
extra nuts and cherries

1 Line a cookie sheet with a sheet of baking parchment. Spoon the melted chocolate into 20 paper candy cases, spreading up the sides with a small spoon or brush. Place upside down on the cookie sheet and let set.

2 Carefully peel away the paper cases. Place a cherry half or a nut in each chocolate cup.

3 To make the filling, place the heavy cream in a mixing bowl and sift the confectioners' sugar on top. Whisk the cream until it is just holding its shape, then whisk in the liqueur.

4 Place the cream in a pastry bag fitted with a ½-inch/1-cm plain tip and pipe a little into each chocolate case. Chill for 20 minutes.

5 To finish, spoon the melted semisweet chocolate over the cream to cover it and pipe the melted white chocolate on top, swirling it into the semisweet chocolate with a toothpick. Let the candies harden. Alternatively, cover the cream with the melted semisweet chocolate and decorate with white chocolate curls before setting. Or place a small piece of nut or cherry on top of the cream, then cover with semisweet chocolate.

🍳 COOK'S TIP

Candy cases can vary in size. Use the smallest you can find for this recipe.

challenging

1 hr

5 mins

A creamy, orange-flavored chocolate filling in white chocolate cups makes a wonderful treat.

Collettes

1 Line a cookie sheet with baking parchment. Spoon the melted white chocolate into 20 paper candy cases, spreading up the sides with a small spoon or brush. Place upside down on the prepared cookie sheet and let set.

2 When set, carefully peel away the paper cases.

3 To make the filling, put the melted orange-flavored chocolate in a mixing bowl with the heavy cream and the confectioners' sugar. Beat until smooth. Chill until the mixture becomes firm enough to pipe, stirring occasionally.

4 Place the filling in a pastry bag fitted with a star tip and pipe a little into each candy case. Chill until required.

MAKES 20

3½ oz/100 g white chocolate, melted

filling
5½ oz/150 g orange-flavored semisweet chocolate, melted
⅔ cup heavy cream
2 tbsp confectioners' sugar

🧑‍🍳 COOK'S TIP

If the paper candy cases do not hold their shape well, use 2 cases to make a double thickness mold. Foil cases are firmer, so use these if you can find them.

 ⭐⭐⭐   moderate
🕐   40 mins
🕐   5 mins

Small tartlet shells are filled with a rich chocolate cream to serve as petits fours. Use individual tartlet pans to make the shells.

Mini Chocolate Tartlets

MAKES 18

1½ cups all-purpose flour, plus flour
   for dusting
⅓ cup butter
1 tbsp superfine sugar
about 1 tbsp water

filling
3½ oz/100 g fullfat soft cheese
2 tbsp superfine sugar
1 medium egg, beaten lightly
1¾ oz/50 g semisweet chocolate, melted

to decorate
½ cup heavy cream
semisweet chocolate Quick Curls
   (see page 15)
unsweetened cocoa, to dust

1 Sift the flour into a mixing bowl. Cut the butter into small pieces and rub in with your fingertips until the mixture resembles fine bread crumbs. Stir in the sugar. Add enough water to mix to a soft dough, then cover with plastic wrap, and chill for 15 minutes.

2 Roll out the dough on a lightly floured counter and use to line 18 mini tartlet pans or mini muffin pans. Prick the tartlet shells with a toothpick.

3 Beat together the full-fat soft cheese and the sugar. Beat in the egg and the melted chocolate Spoon into the tartlet shells and bake in a preheated oven, 375°F/190°C, for 15 minutes, until the dough is crisp and the filling set. Place the pans on a wire rack to cool completely.

4 Chill the tartlets. Whip the cream until it is just holding its shape. Place in a pastry bag fitted with a star tip. Pipe rosettes of cream on top of the tartlets. Decorate with chocolate curls and dust with cocoa.

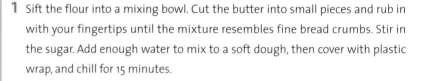

COOK'S TIP

The tartlets can be made up to 3 days ahead. Decorate on the day of serving, preferably no more than 4 hours in advance.

⭐⭐⭐   moderate

1 hr 30 mins

15 mins

These unusual cone-shaped mint-cream chocolates make a change from the more usual cup shape, and are perfect for an after-dinner chocolate.

Mini Chocolate Cones

1 Cut 10 circles, 3 inches/7.5 cm across, out of baking parchment. Cut a straight line from the edge to the center of each circle, then shape into a cone, and secure on the outside with sticky tape.

2 Using a small brush, coat the inside of each cone with the melted chocolate.

3 Brush a second layer of chocolate on the inside of the cones and chill until set. Carefully peel away the parchment.

4 Place the heavy cream, confectioners' sugar, and crème de menthe in a mixing bowl and whip until just holding its shape. Place in a pastry bag fitted with a star tip and pipe the mixture into the chocolate cones.

5 Decorate the cones with chocolate coffee beans (if using) and chill in the refrigerator until required.

MAKES 10

2¾ oz/75 g semisweet chocolate, melted
generous ⅓ cup heavy cream
1 tbsp confectioners' sugar
1 tbsp crème de menthe
chocolate coffee beans, to
    decorate (optional)

COOK'S TIP

The chocolate cones can be made in advance and kept in the refrigerator for up to 1 week. However, you should not fill them more than 2 hours before you are going to serve them.

 challenging

40 mins

5 mins

Truffles are always popular. They make a fabulous gift or, served with coffee, they are a perfect end to a meal.

Rum Truffles

MAKES 20

4½ oz/125 g semisweet chocolate
small pat of butter
2 tbsp rum
½ cup dry unsweetened coconut
scant 2 cups cake crumbs
6 tbsp confectioners' sugar
2 tbsp unsweetened cocoa

1 Break the chocolate into pieces and place in a bowl with the butter. Set the bowl over a pan of gently simmering water. Stir until melted and combined.

2 Remove from the heat and beat in the rum. Stir in the dry unsweetened coconut, cake crumbs, and two-thirds of the confectioners' sugar. Beat until combined. Add a little extra rum if the mixture is stiff.

3 Roll the mixture into small balls and place them on a sheet of baking parchment. Chill until firm.

4 Sift the remaining confectioners' sugar onto a large plate. Sift the cocoa onto another plate. Roll half of the truffles in the confectioners' sugar until coated and roll the remaining truffles in the cocoa.

5 Place the truffles in paper candy cases and chill until required.

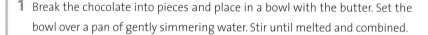

🧑‍🍳 **COOK'S TIP**

Make the truffles with white chocolate and replace the rum with coconut liqueur or milk, if you prefer. Roll them in unsweetened cocoa or dip in melted milk chocolate.

⭐⭐ easy
🕐 45 mins
🕐 5 mins

Marzipan, honey, and semisweet and milk chocolate are combined into little morsels of sheer delight.

Double Chocolate Truffles

1 Line 2 cookie sheets with baking parchment. Beat together the butter and grated marzipan until thoroughly combined and fluffy. Stir in the honey, a little at a time, then stir in the vanilla extract.

2 Place the semisweet chocolate and 7 oz/200 g of the milk chocolate in the top of a double boiler or in a heatproof bowl set over a pan of barely simmering water. Stir over low heat until melted and smooth. Remove from the heat and let cool slightly.

3 Stir the melted chocolate into the marzipan mixture, then spoon the chocolate and marzipan mixture into a pastry bag fitted with a large, round tip, and pipe small balls onto the prepared cookie sheets. Let cool and set.

4 Put the remaining milk chocolate in the top of a double boiler or in a heatproof bowl set over a pan of barely simmering water. Stir over low heat until melted, then remove from the heat. Dip the truffles, 1 at a time, in the melted chocolate to coat them, then texture some of them by gently tapping them with a fork. Place on the cookie sheets to cool and set.

MAKES 60

¾ cup sweet butter
⅔ cup grated marzipan
4 tbsp honey
½ tsp vanilla extract
7 oz/200 g semisweet chocolate, broken into pieces
12 oz/350 g milk chocolate, broken into pieces

challenging

1 hr 25 mins

10 mins

The perfect pick-me-up on a cold winter's night, this delicious drink will get the taste buds tingling.

Chocolate Eggnog

SERVES 4

8 egg yolks
1 cup sugar
4 cups milk
8 oz/225 g semisweet chocolate, grated
⅔ cup dark rum

1 Whisk the egg yolks with the sugar until pale and thickened.

2 Pour the milk into a large pan, add the grated chocolate, and bring to a boil. Remove from the heat and gradually beat in the egg yolk mixture. Stir in the rum and pour into 4 heatproof glasses.

⊛ COOK'S TIP

Eggnog can also be made using brandy or whiskey.

very easy

10 mins

5 mins

Brandy and chocolate have a natural affinity, as this richly flavored drink more than amply demonstrates.

Hot Brandy Chocolate

1 Pour the milk into a pan and bring to a boil, then remove from the heat. Place the chocolate in a small pan and add 2 tablespoons of the hot milk. Stir over low heat until the chocolate has melted. Stir the chocolate mixture back into the hot milk and add the sugar.

2 Stir in the brandy and pour into 4 heatproof glasses. Top each with a swirl of whipped cream and sprinkle with a little sifted cocoa.

SERVES 4

4 cups milk
4 oz/115 g semisweet chocolate, broken into pieces
2 tbsp sugar
5 tbsp brandy

to decorate
6 tbsp whipped cream
4 tsp unsweetened cocoa, sifted

COOK'S TIP

You can vary this recipe by using rum, whiskey, or your favorite liqueur.

very easy

10 mins

7–10 mins

Rich and soothing, a hot chocolate drink in the evening can be just what you need to help ease away the stresses of the day.

Hot Chocolate Drinks

EACH SERVES 2

spicy hot chocolate

2½ cups milk
1 tsp ground allspice
3½ oz/100 g semisweet chocolate
4 cinnamon sticks
generous ⅓ cup heavy cream,
    whipped lightly

chocolate & orange toddy

2¾ oz/75 g orange-flavored
    semisweet chocolate
2½ cups milk
3 tbsp rum
2 tbsp heavy cream
grated nutmeg

1 To make Spicy Hot Chocolate, pour the milk into a small pan. Sprinkle in the ground allspice.

2 Break the semisweet chocolate into squares and add to the milk. Heat the mixture over low heat until the milk is just boiling, stirring constantly to prevent the milk from burning on the base of the pan.

3 Place 2 cinnamon sticks in each of 2 cups and pour in the spicy hot chocolate. Top with the whipped cream and serve.

4 To make Chocolate & Orange Toddy, break the orange-flavored semisweet chocolate into squares and place in a small pan with the milk. Heat the mixture over low heat until just boiling, stirring constantly.

5 Remove the pan from the heat and stir in the rum. Pour into 2 cups.

6 Pour the cream over the back of a spoon or swirl onto the top so that it sits on top of the hot chocolate. Sprinkle with grated nutmeg and serve at once.

✪ very easy
◔ 5 mins each
◷ 5 mins each

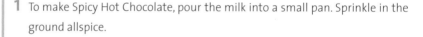

🍳 COOK'S TIP

Using a cinnamon stick as a stirrer will give any hot chocolate drink a sweet, delicate flavor of cinnamon without overpowering the flavor of the chocolate.

These delicious chocolate summer drinks are perfect for making a chocoholic's summer day!

Cold Chocolate Drinks

1 To make the Chocolate Milk Shake, pour half of the milk into a blender.

2 Add the instant cocoa to the blender and 1 scoop of the chocolate ice cream. Blend until frothy and well mixed. Stir in the remaining milk.

3 Place the remaining 2 scoops of chocolate ice cream in 2 serving glasses and carefully pour the chocolate milk over the ice cream.

4 Sprinkle a little cocoa (if using) over the top of each drink and serve.

5 To make the Chocolate Ice Cream Soda, divide the Glossy Chocolate Sauce between 2 glasses. (You can use a ready-made chocolate dessert sauce instead of the Glossy Chocolate Sauce).

6 Add a little club soda to each glass and stir well to combine the sauce and soda . Place a scoop of ice cream in each glass and top off with more of the club soda.

7 Place a spoon of whipped heavy cream on the top, if liked, and sprinkle with a little grated semisweet or milk chocolate.

EACH SERVES 2

chocolate milk shake
2 cups ice cold milk
3 tbsp instant cocoa
3 scoops chocolate ice cream
unsweetened or instant cocoa, to dust (optional)

chocolate ice cream soda
5 tbsp Glossy Chocolate Sauce (see page 75)
club soda
2 scoops of chocolate ice cream
heavy cream, whipped (optional)
semisweet or milk chocolate, grated

COOK'S TIP

Served in a tall glass, a milk shake or an ice cream soda makes a scrumptious snack in a drink. Serve with straws, if wished.

easy
5 mins each
15 mins each

Savories

Chocolate may seem an unusual ingredient to use in savory dishes, but Mexican cooks have long known about its wonderful affinity for chiles and red bell peppers. It can be used to add a marvelous new flavor to dishes that you may have normally cooked in a more traditional way. Chiles, red bell peppers, and chocolate feature in two of the recipes in this section, Mole Poblano and Mexican Beef Stew. For a lighter dish that is also suitable for vegetarians, try the Nut and Chocolate Pasta. Finally, the Veal in Chocolate Sauce is perfect for a dinner party, where the chocolate will add an interesting flavor to this meat stew to surprise and satisfy you and your guests.

This great Mexican celebration dish, ladled out at fiestas, baptisms, and weddings, is known for its combination of fiery chiles and chocolate.

Mole Poblano

SERVES 4

3 mulato chiles
3 mild ancho chiles
5–6 New Mexico or California chiles
1 onion, chopped
5 garlic cloves, chopped
1 lb/450 g ripe tomatoes
2 tortillas, preferably stale, cut into small pieces
pinch of ground cloves
pinch of fennel seeds
pinch each of ground cinnamon, coriander, and cumin
3 tbsp lightly toasted sesame seeds or tahini
3 tbsp sliced or coarsely ground blanched almonds
2 tbsp raisins
1 tbsp peanut butter (optional)
2 cups chicken bouillon
3–4 tbsp grated semisweet chocolate, plus extra for garnishing
2 tbsp mild chili powder
3 tbsp vegetable oil
salt and pepper
about 1 tbsp lime juice

1 Using metal tongs, toast each chile over an open flame for a few seconds until the color darkens. Alternatively, roast the chiles in an ungreased skillet over medium heat, turning constantly, for about 30 seconds.

2 Place the toasted chiles in a bowl or a pan and pour boiling water over to cover. Cover with a lid and set aside to soften for at least 1 hour or overnight. Once or twice lift the lid and rearrange the chiles so that they soak evenly.

3 Remove the softened chiles with a slotted spoon. Discard the stems and seeds and cut the flesh into pieces. Place in a blender.

4 Add the onion, garlic, tomatoes, tortillas, cloves, fennel seeds, cinnamon, coriander, cumin, sesame seeds or tahini, almonds, raisins, and peanut butter if using, then process to combine. With the motor running, add enough stock through the feed tube to make a smooth paste. Stir in the remaining bouillon, chocolate, and chili powder.

5 Heat the oil in a heavy pan until it is smoking, then pour in the mole mixture. It will splatter and pop as it hits the hot oil. Cook for about 10 minutes, stirring occasionally to prevent it from burning.

6 Season to taste with salt, pepper, and lime juice, garnish with grated chocolate, and serve immediately.

moderate

1 hr 20 mins

15 mins

Colorful and richly flavored, this stew is somewhat time-consuming, but well worth the effort.

Mexican Beef Stew

1 Arrange the red bell peppers on a cookie sheet and cook in a preheated oven, 475°F/240°C, for about 20 minutes, until the skins have blackened and are beginning to blister. Using tongs, transfer them to a plastic bag. Tie the top and set aside.

2 Meanwhile, cut a cross in the skin on the base of the tomato. Put it in a bowl, cover with boiling water, and let stand for 1 minute. Remove the tomato from the water, then peel, and seed it. Dice the tomato flesh and put it into a food processor. When the bell peppers are cool enough to handle, peel and seed them, then chop the flesh. Add the bell peppers to the food processor together with the onion, chocolate, garlic, and vinegar. Process the ingredients to a paste.

3 Heat the oil in a flameproof casserole or large pan. Add the steak, in batches if necessary, and cook over medium heat, stirring frequently, until browned all over. Season to taste with salt and pepper. Add the chocolate paste and beef bouillon. Tie the cloves and cinnamon in a small piece of cheesecloth and add to the pan. Bring to a boil, then lower the heat, cover, and simmer for 1–1¼ hours.

4 Add the carrots and potato to the pan, stir well, and simmer for 30 minutes more. Remove and discard the cheesecloth bag. Taste the stew and adjust the seasoning if necessary. Garnish with the fresh cilantro and serve immediately with cooked green vegetables, such as green beans.

SERVES 4

2 red bell peppers
1 beefsteak tomato
1 onion, cut into fourths
2 oz/55 g semisweet chocolate, broken into pieces
2 garlic cloves, chopped coarsely
3 tbsp red wine vinegar
3 tbsp vegetable oil
1 lb 12 oz/800 g lean braising steak, diced
salt and pepper
1½ cups beef bouillon
2 cloves
1-inch/2.5-cm piece of cinnamon stick
2 large carrots, chopped finely
1 large potato, diced
1 tbsp chopped fresh cilantro, to garnish

★★★ moderate
🕐 15 mins
🕐 2 hrs–2 hrs 15 mins

This is a popular entrée in northern Europe, and makes a satisfying vegetarian supper.

Nut *and* Chocolate Pasta

SERVES 4

12 oz/350 g dried ribbon pasta, such as tagliatelle or fettuccine
1 tsp butter, for greasing
2–3 tbsp fresh white bread crumbs
salt

sauce
6 tbsp butter
¾ cup confectioners' sugar
4 eggs, separated
¾ cup ground roasted hazelnuts
3 oz/85 g semisweet chocolate, grated
4 tbsp fresh white bread crumbs
½ tsp ground cinnamon
finely grated rind of ½ lemon

1 Bring a large pan of lightly salted water to a boil. Add the pasta and cook for 6 minutes or according to the instructions on the package, until tender, but still firm to the bite. Drain, rinse under cold running water, and set aside.

2 To make the sauce, beat together the butter, half the sugar, and the egg yolks until frothy.

3 In a separate bowl, whisk the egg whites with the remaining sugar until stiff, then fold them into the butter mixture.

4 In another bowl, mix the hazelnuts, grated chocolate, bread crumbs, cinnamon, and lemon rind, then stir into the egg mixture. Add the pasta and stir gently to mix.

5 Grease an ovenproof dish with butter and sprinkle with bread crumbs. Tap lightly to coat the base and sides, then tip out any excess. Spoon the pasta mixture into the dish and bake in a preheated oven, 400°F/200°C, for 25–30 minutes. Serve immediately, with roasted vine tomatoes (see Cook's Tip), if desired.

COOK'S TIP

To roast vine tomatoes, put 12 small tomatoes in an ovenproof dish, sprinkle with 2 tablespoons olive oil, and season with salt and pepper to taste. Roast in a preheated oven, 400°F/200°C, for 15–20 minutes.

★★★   moderate
        20 mins
        35–40 mins

Chocolate can enrich stews based on a broad range of meats, including game, but it is important to be light-handed or it can become unpleasantly cloying.

Veal *in* Chocolate Sauce

1 Heat 3 tablespoons of the oil in a large, flameproof casserole. Add the veal and cook over medium heat, stirring, until lightly browned. Remove from the casserole and set aside. Add the onion, garlic, carrots, celery, and chiles to the casserole and cook, stirring, for 5 minutes, until the onion is softened.

2 Stir in 1¼ cups of the wine and all of the bouillon, and return the meat to the casserole. Add the thyme, bay leaf, juniper berries, cloves, and cinnamon, and season with salt and pepper. Bring to a boil, stirring, then cook in a preheated oven, 400°F/200°C, for 1 hour. Top up the casserole with more wine from time to time, if necessary.

3 Meanwhile, make a cross in the base of the chestnuts, put them on a cookie sheet, bake in the oven for 20 minutes, then shell them.

4 While the chestnuts are cooking, place the shallots in a small roasting pan and coat them with the remaining oil. Roast in the oven for 15–20 minutes, until golden and tender.

5 Remove the casserole from the oven and lift out the meat with a slotted spoon. Place it in a serving dish, add the chestnuts and shallots, and keep warm. Strain the cooking juices into a clean pan. Discard the contents of the strainer. Set the pan over medium heat, bring to a boil, and cook until slightly reduced. Stir in the chocolate until melted and adjust the seasoning, if necessary. Pour the sauce over the meat, garnish with the parsley and bay leaves if using, and serve.

SERVES **8**

5 tbsp vegetable oil
1½ lb/675 g boneless veal (or pork), cut into 1-inch/2.5-cm cubes
1 onion, chopped
2 garlic cloves, chopped
2 carrots, chopped
2 celery stalks, chopped
2 fresh red chiles, seeded and chopped
1¼–1¾ cups red wine
½ cup beef bouillon
2 tsp chopped fresh thyme
1 bay leaf
4 juniper berries, crushed lightly
2 cloves
1-inch/2.5-cm piece of cinnamon stick
salt and pepper
8 oz/225 g chestnuts
8 shallots, cut into fourths
2 oz/55 g semisweet chocolate, grated

garnish
2 tbsp chopped fresh parsley
2 fresh bay leaves, optional

✪✪✪   moderate
🕒   20 mins
🕐   1 hr 45 mins

Index